AI

DOONESBURY
DELUXE

DOONESBURY BOOKS BY G.B. TRUDEAU

Still a Few Bugs in the System
The President Is a Lot Smarter Than You Think
But This War Had Such Promise
Call Me When You Find America
Guilty, Guilty, Guilty!
"What Do We Have for the Witnesses, Johnnie?"
Dare To Be Great, Ms. Caucus
Wouldn't a Gremlin Have Been More Sensible?
"Speaking of Inalienable Rights, Amy…"
You're Never Too Old for Nuts and Berries
An Especially Tricky People
As the Kid Goes for Broke
Stalking the Perfect Tan
"Any Grooming Hints for Your Fans, Rollie?"
But the Pension Fund Was Just Sitting There
We're Not Out of the Woods Yet
A Tad Overweight, but Violet Eyes to Die For
And That's My Final Offer!
He's Never Heard of You, Either
In Search of Reagan's Brain
Ask for May, Settle for June
Unfortunately, She Was Also Wired for Sound
The Wreck of the "Rusty Nail"
You Give Great Meeting, Sid
Doonesbury: A Musical Comedy
Check Your Egos at the Door
That's *Doctor* Sinatra, You Little Bimbo!
Death of a Party Animal
Downtown Doonesbury
Calling Dr. Whoopee

IN LARGE FORMAT

The Doonesbury Chronicles
Doonesbury's Greatest Hits
The People's Doonesbury
Doonesbury Dossier: The Reagan Years
Doonesbury Deluxe: Selected Glances Askance

DOONESBURY DELUXE

G B Trudeau

SELECTED GLANCES ASKANCE

INTRODUCTION BY STUDS TERKEL

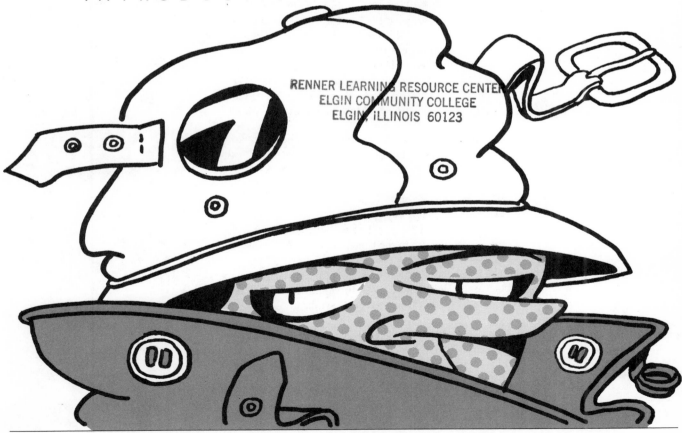

RENNER LEARNING RESOURCE CENTER
ELGIN COMMUNITY COLLEGE
ELGIN, ILLINOIS 60123

HENRY HOLT AND COMPANY / NEW YORK

For GF, with love

Copyright ©1984, 1985, 1986, 1987 by G.B. Trudeau
Introduction copyright ©1987 by Henry Holt and Company, Inc.
All rights reserved, including the right to reproduce this
book or portions thereof in any form.
Published by Henry Holt and Company, Inc.,
521 Fifth Avenue, New York, New York 10175.
Published in Canada by Fitzhenry & Whiteside Limited,
195 Allstate Parkway, Markham, Ontario L3R 4T8.

Library of Congress Catalog Card Number: 87-80724
ISBN Hardbound: 0-8050-0595-1
ISBN Paperback: 0-8050-0596-X

First Edition

Designer: Robert Bull Design
Printed in the United States of America

The cartoons in this book have appeared in newspapers
in the United States and abroad under the auspices of
Universal Press Syndicate.

1 3 5 7 9 10 8 6 4 2

ISBN 0-8050-0595-1 HARDBOUND
ISBN 0-8050-0596-X PAPERBACK

INTRODUCTION
BY
STUDS TERKEL

A funny thing happened to Garry Trudeau on his way to an honorary degree. It was at Grinnell College, 1977.

While the prexy held forth each diploma, dozens of graduates, some in cap and gown, others in blue jeans, stood sober ritual on its head. They danced toward the young cartoonist, shook his hand, and whispered things.

Seated next to him, I was astonished. Yet it seemed so natural, so matter of course. As they offered their regards to Joanie, Mike, Zonker, J.J., and the others of *Doonesbury*'s world, the ceremony took a half hour longer than usual. Nobody seemed to mind.

What makes the remembrance so indelible is the nature of Trudeau's work; it's indubitably political.

During the ensuing ten years, a stillness, for the most part, has descended on the American campus. Causes have become personal rather than communal; the official word accepted rather than questioned. Yet Trudeau's singular popularity among the young and their mellowed antecedents—the dancing graduates of that summery afternoon—is more impressive than ever. Nor has his social commentary ever been more trenchant.

Since the last *Doonesbury* anthology appeared, we've been tuned in to all sorts of strange music: televangelism's mega-million $ Te Deum; the contrabucks scandal; Grenada overcome; the drug-testing Olympics; Rube Goldberg's Star Wars; and Rawhide about to ride off the Oval Office movie set into a Hollywood twilight (if he doesn't forget).

These happenings, among scores of others equally surreal, have added a cockeyed dimension to the roller-coaster personal lives of Trudeau's people. As the baby boomers—say, Joanie and Rick—raise a kid of their own, this new person's first words are "although," "but," "unless," and "and." Orwell couldn't have put it any better.

There you have it: with a line or two, Trudeau makes clear what another might take a doctoral treatise to explain.

A book is yet to be written about our loss of tribal memory, the absence of our sense of history. Still, it may not be necessary. Consider Trudeau's despairing college prof challenging the somnambulism of his class: "The Constitution itself should never have been ratified. It's a dangerous document! All power should rest with the executive! What do you think of that?" The scribbling students awaken: "I didn't know half this stuff." Not a bad cautionary tale during this bicentennial year.

Free, easy, jazzy as a Johnny Mercer lyric; clean and minimal as a Basie piano; Trudeau's work breathes life into the Miesian doctrine: less is more. It is in this understatement that we recognize the hipness in the deadpan innocence of Mike Doonesbury and his circle; and that in the diversity within their sameness, we see the boomers as more than still life portraits. We see in their sometimes antic, sometimes poignant growing up the pursuit of a "goofy" ideal; or, at any rate, something better than what is. Reading *Doonesbury* offers a reed of hope as well as laughter.

PART ONE

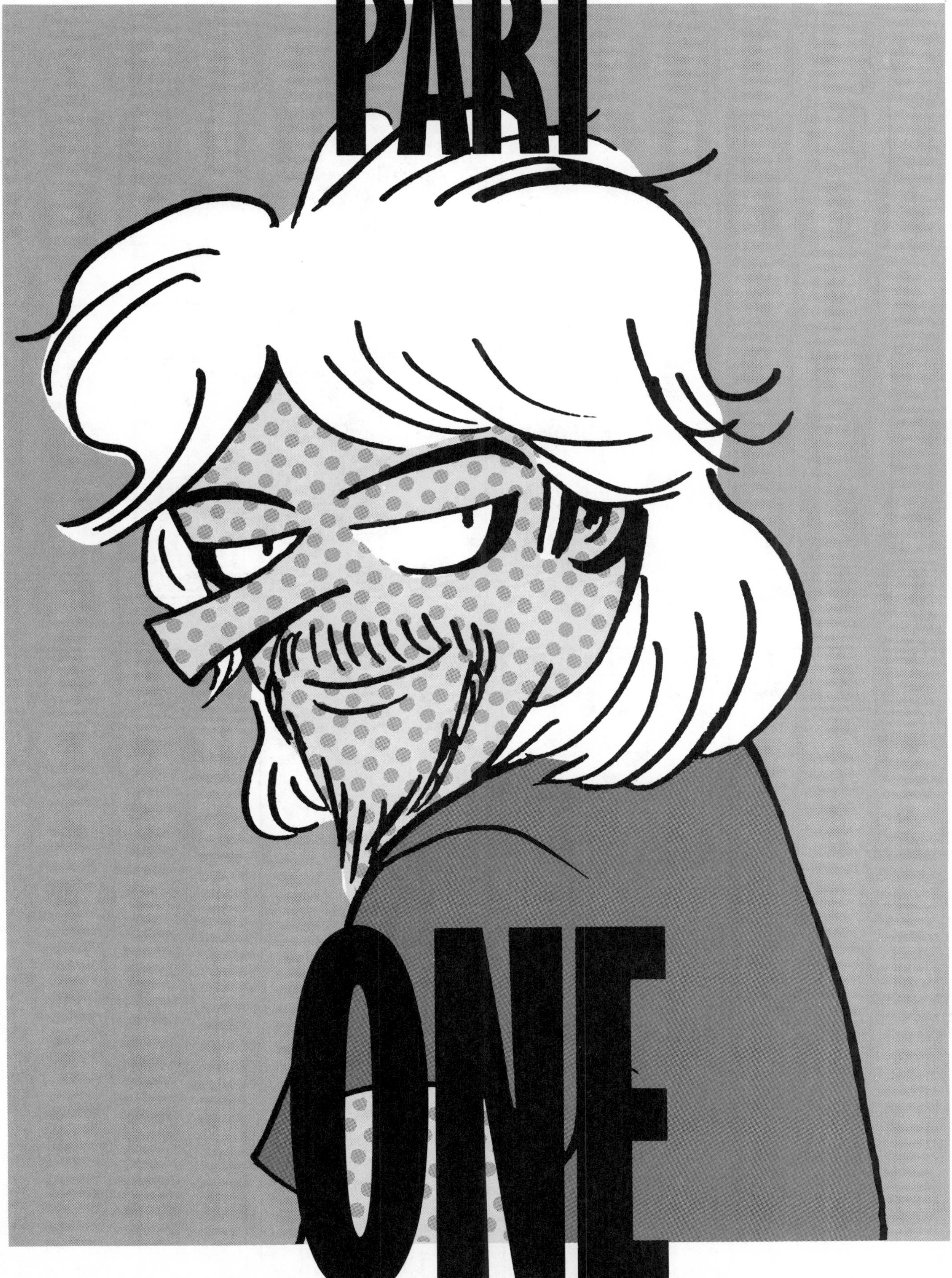

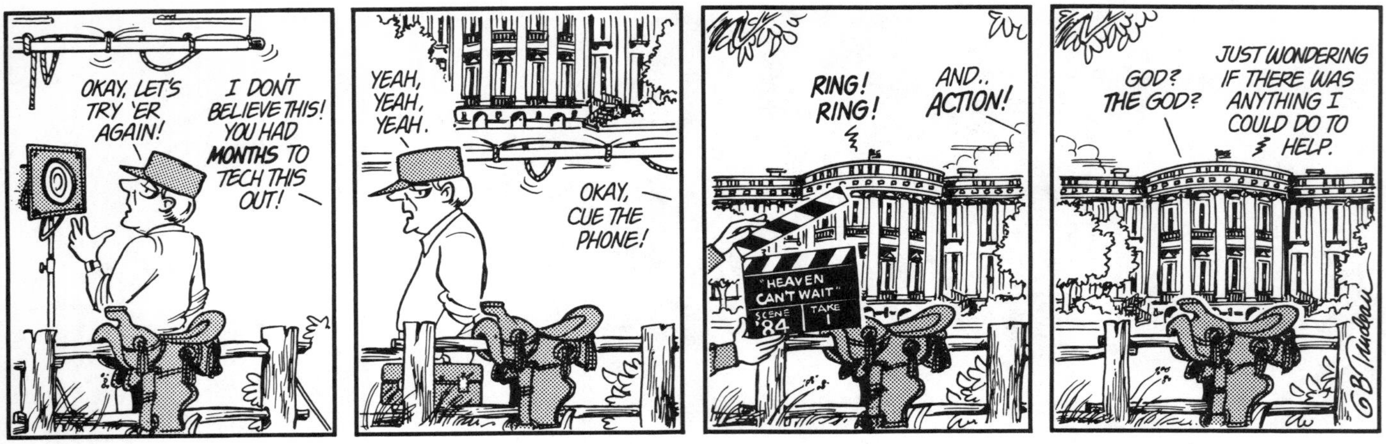
OKAY, LET'S TRY 'ER AGAIN!
I DON'T BELIEVE THIS! YOU HAD **MONTHS** TO TECH THIS OUT!
YEAH, YEAH, YEAH.
OKAY, CUE THE PHONE!
RING! RING!
AND.. **ACTION!**
"HEAVEN CAN'T WAIT"
SCENE '84
TAKE 1
GOD? **THE** GOD?
JUST WONDERING IF THERE WAS ANYTHING I COULD DO TO HELP.
©B Trudeau

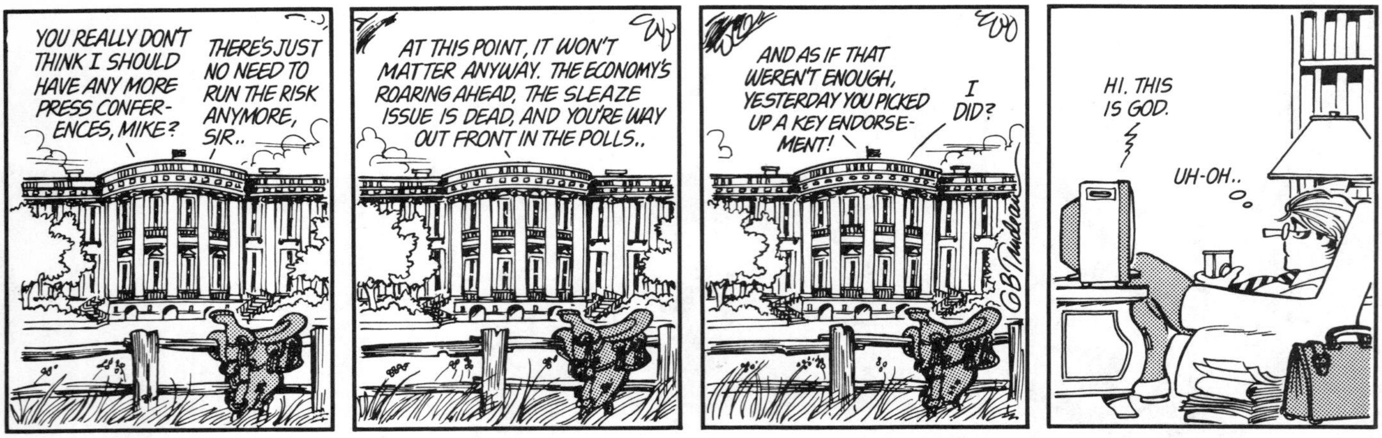
YOU REALLY DON'T THINK I SHOULD HAVE ANY MORE PRESS CONFERENCES, MIKE?
THERE'S JUST NO NEED TO RUN THE RISK ANYMORE, SIR..
AT THIS POINT, IT WON'T MATTER ANYWAY. THE ECONOMY'S ROARING AHEAD, THE SLEAZE ISSUE IS DEAD, AND YOU'RE WAY OUT FRONT IN THE POLLS..
AND AS IF THAT WEREN'T ENOUGH, YESTERDAY YOU PICKED UP A KEY ENDORSEMENT!
I DID?
©B Trudeau
HI. THIS IS GOD.
UH-OH..

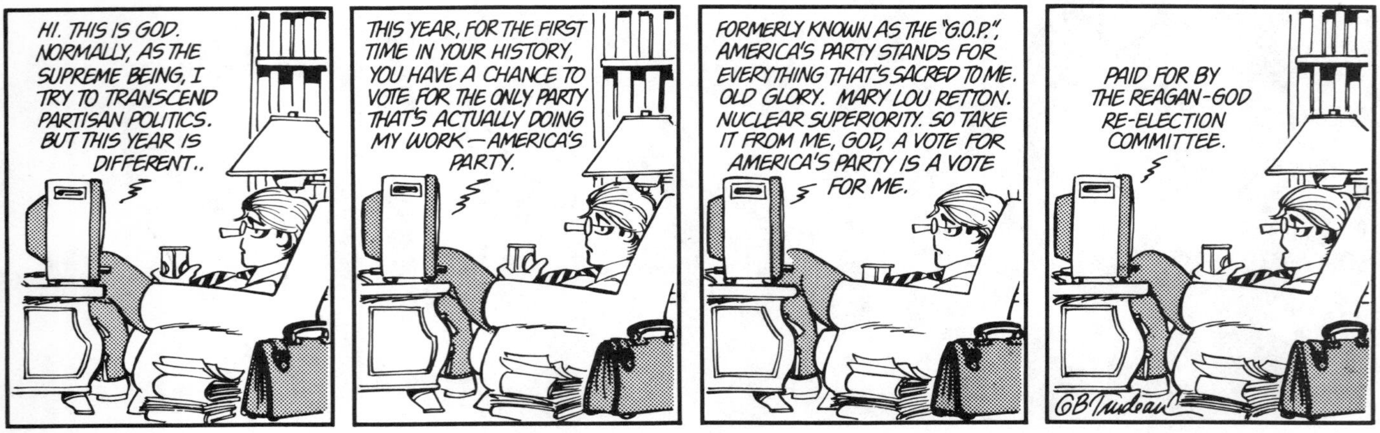
HI. THIS IS GOD. NORMALLY, AS THE SUPREME BEING, I TRY TO TRANSCEND PARTISAN POLITICS. BUT THIS YEAR IS DIFFERENT..
THIS YEAR, FOR THE FIRST TIME IN YOUR HISTORY, YOU HAVE A CHANCE TO VOTE FOR THE ONLY PARTY THAT'S ACTUALLY DOING MY WORK—AMERICA'S PARTY.
FORMERLY KNOWN AS THE "G.O.P.", AMERICA'S PARTY STANDS FOR EVERYTHING THAT'S SACRED TO ME. OLD GLORY. MARY LOU RETTON. NUCLEAR SUPERIORITY. SO TAKE IT FROM ME, GOD, A VOTE FOR AMERICA'S PARTY IS A VOTE FOR ME.
PAID FOR BY THE REAGAN-GOD RE-ELECTION COMMITTEE.
©B Trudeau

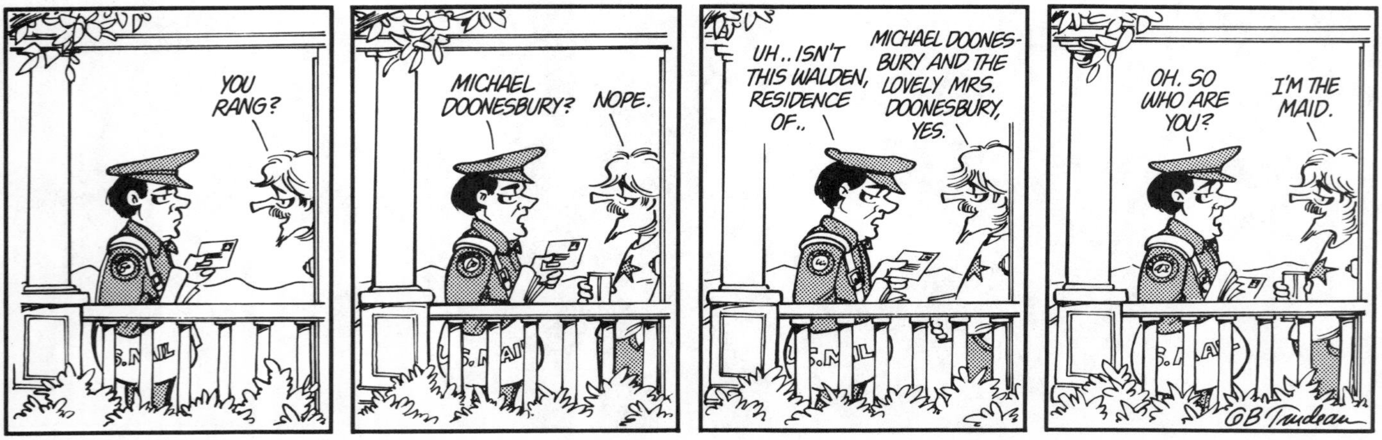
YOU RANG?
MICHAEL DOONESBURY?
NOPE.
UH.. ISN'T THIS WALDEN, RESIDENCE OF..
MICHAEL DOONESBURY AND THE LOVELY MRS. DOONESBURY, YES.
OH. SO WHO ARE YOU?
I'M THE MAID.
©B Trudeau

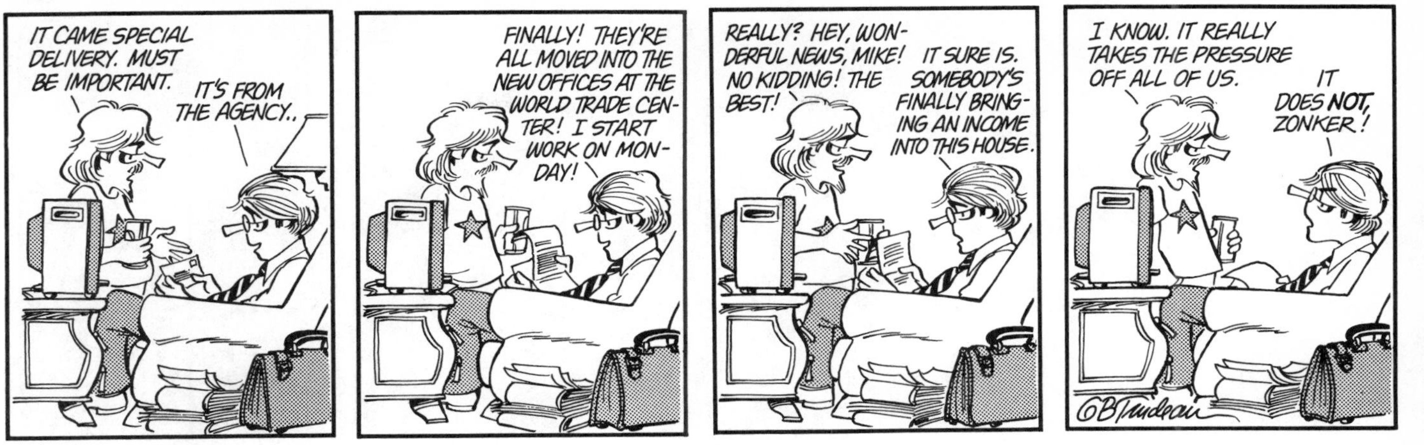
IT CAME SPECIAL DELIVERY. MUST BE IMPORTANT.
IT'S FROM THE AGENCY..
FINALLY! THEY'RE ALL MOVED INTO THE NEW OFFICES AT THE WORLD TRADE CENTER! I START WORK ON MONDAY!
REALLY? HEY, WONDERFUL NEWS, MIKE! NO KIDDING! THE BEST!
IT SURE IS. SOMEBODY'S FINALLY BRINGING AN INCOME INTO THIS HOUSE.
I KNOW. IT REALLY TAKES THE PRESSURE OFF ALL OF US.
IT DOES **NOT,** ZONKER!
GB Trudeau

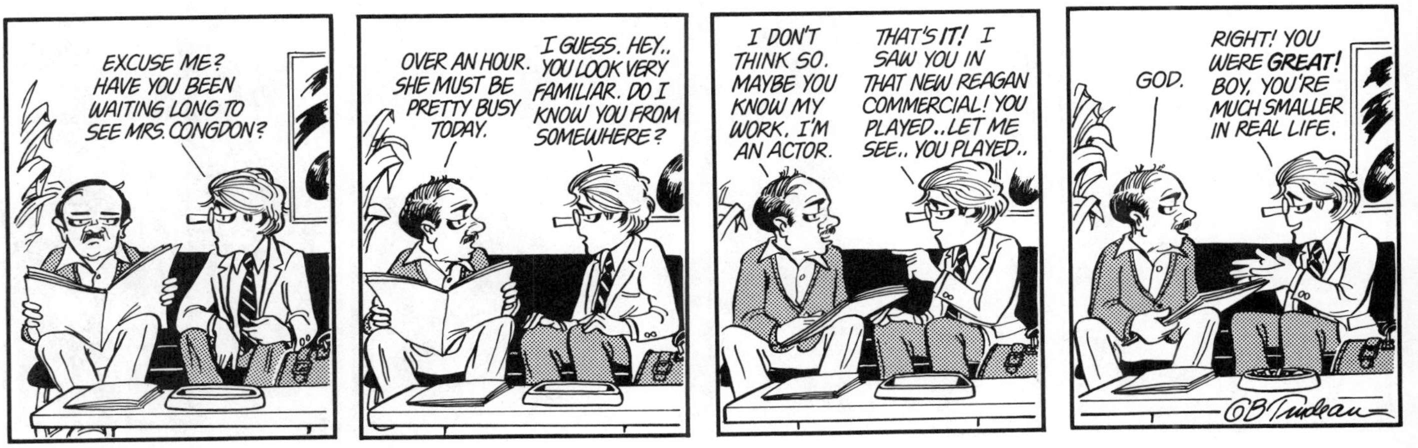
EXCUSE ME? HAVE YOU BEEN WAITING LONG TO SEE MRS. CONGDON?
OVER AN HOUR. SHE MUST BE PRETTY BUSY TODAY.
I GUESS. HEY.. YOU LOOK VERY FAMILIAR. DO I KNOW YOU FROM SOMEWHERE?
I DON'T THINK SO. MAYBE YOU KNOW MY WORK. I'M AN ACTOR.
THAT'S **IT!** I SAW YOU IN THAT NEW REAGAN COMMERCIAL! YOU PLAYED.. LET ME SEE.. YOU PLAYED..
GOD.
RIGHT! YOU WERE **GREAT!** BOY, YOU'RE MUCH SMALLER IN REAL LIFE.
GB Trudeau

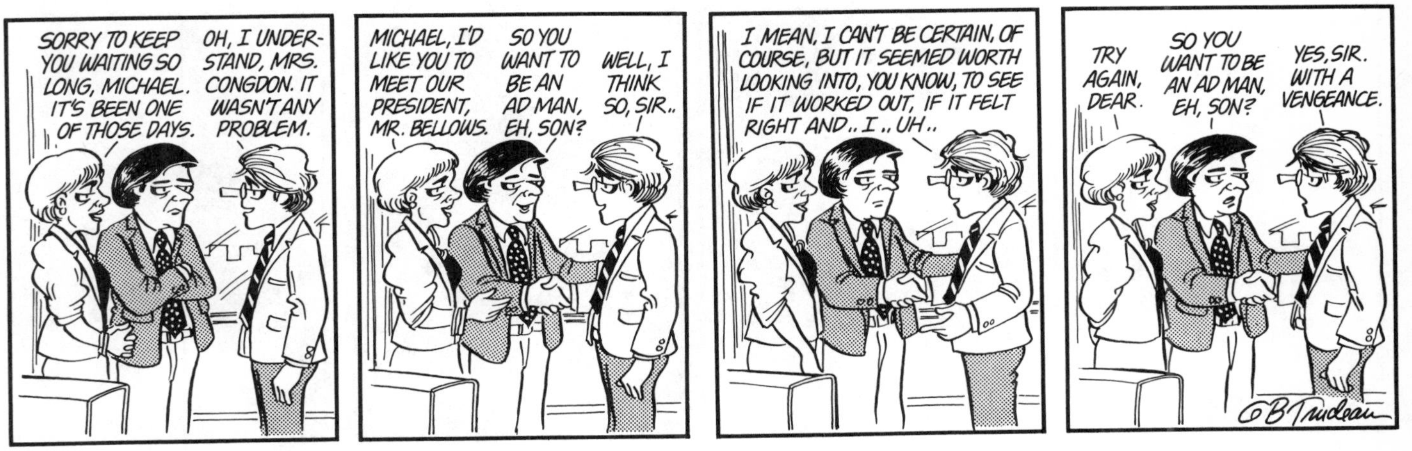
SORRY TO KEEP YOU WAITING SO LONG, MICHAEL. IT'S BEEN ONE OF THOSE DAYS.
OH, I UNDERSTAND, MRS. CONGDON. IT WASN'T ANY PROBLEM.
MICHAEL, I'D LIKE YOU TO MEET OUR PRESIDENT, MR. BELLOWS.
SO YOU WANT TO BE AN AD MAN, EH, SON?
WELL, I THINK SO, SIR..
I MEAN, I CAN'T BE CERTAIN, OF COURSE, BUT IT SEEMED WORTH LOOKING INTO, YOU KNOW, TO SEE IF IT WORKED OUT, IF IT FELT RIGHT AND.. I .. UH ..
TRY AGAIN, DEAR.
SO YOU WANT TO BE AN AD MAN, EH, SON?
YES, SIR. WITH A VENGEANCE.
GB Trudeau

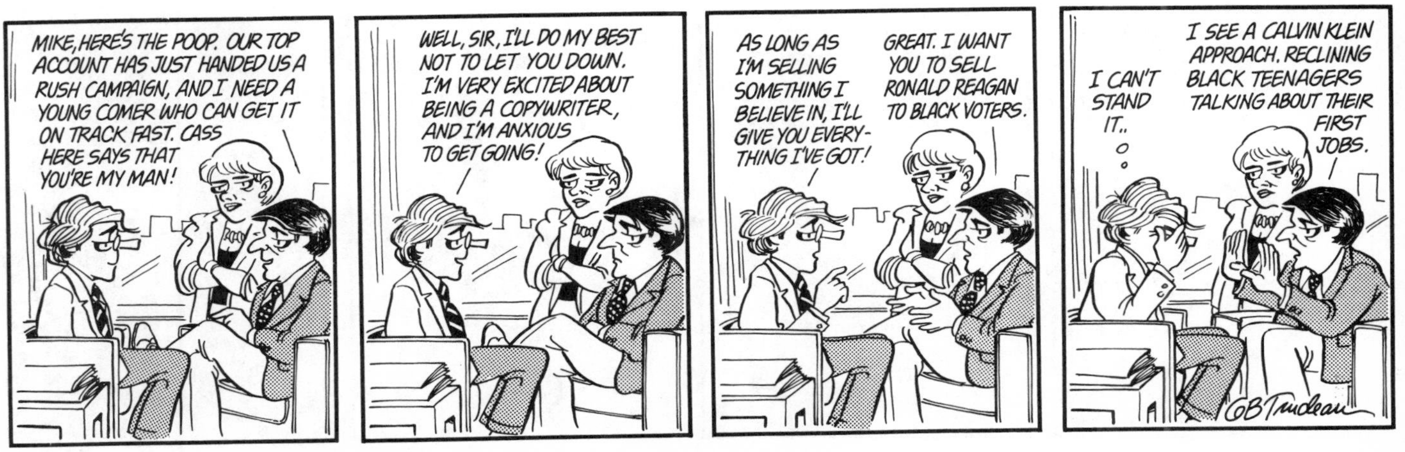
MIKE, HERE'S THE POOP. OUR TOP ACCOUNT HAS JUST HANDED US A RUSH CAMPAIGN, AND I NEED A YOUNG COMER WHO CAN GET IT ON TRACK FAST. CASS HERE SAYS THAT YOU'RE MY MAN!
WELL, SIR, I'LL DO MY BEST NOT TO LET YOU DOWN. I'M VERY EXCITED ABOUT BEING A COPYWRITER, AND I'M ANXIOUS TO GET GOING!
AS LONG AS I'M SELLING SOMETHING I BELIEVE IN, I'LL GIVE YOU EVERYTHING I'VE GOT!
GREAT. I WANT YOU TO SELL RONALD REAGAN TO BLACK VOTERS.
I CAN'T STAND IT..
I SEE A CALVIN KLEIN APPROACH. RECLINING BLACK TEENAGERS TALKING ABOUT THEIR FIRST JOBS.
GB Trudeau

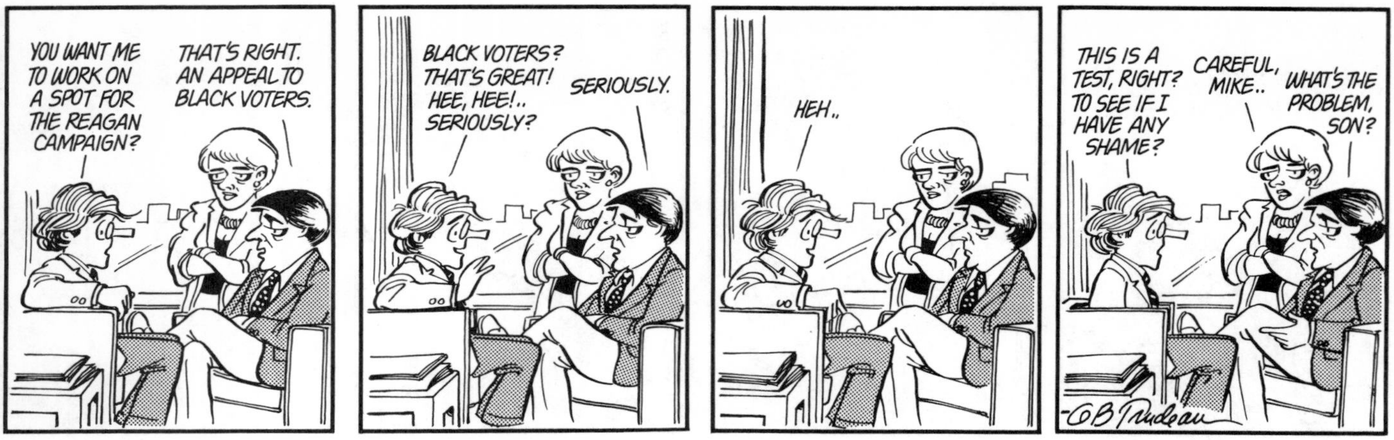
YOU WANT ME TO WORK ON A SPOT FOR THE REAGAN CAMPAIGN?
THAT'S RIGHT. AN APPEAL TO BLACK VOTERS.
BLACK VOTERS? THAT'S GREAT! HEE, HEE!.. SERIOUSLY?
SERIOUSLY.
HEH..
THIS IS A TEST, RIGHT? TO SEE IF I HAVE ANY SHAME?
CAREFUL, MIKE..
WHAT'S THE PROBLEM, SON?
©B Trudeau

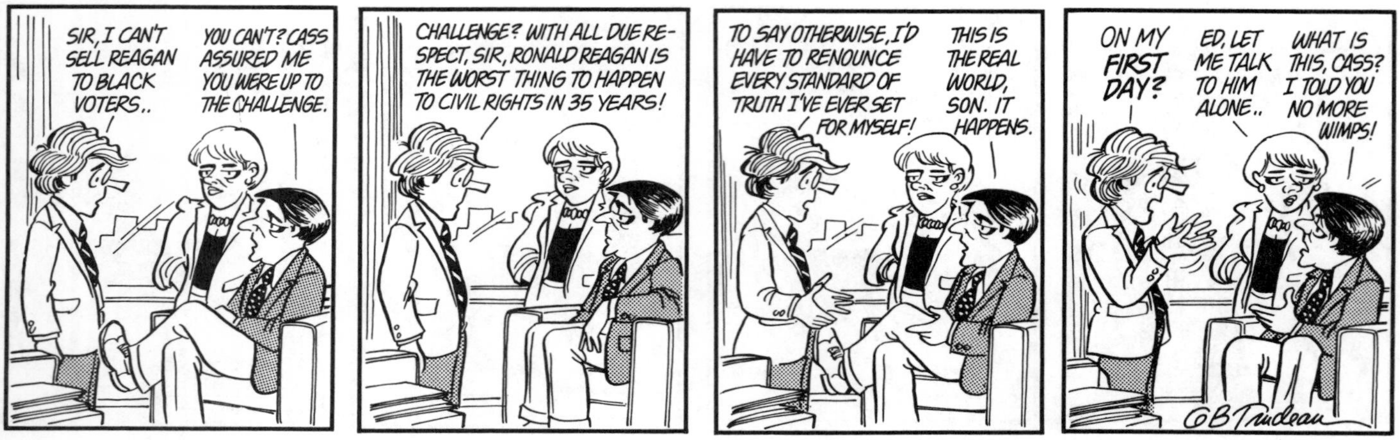
SIR, I CAN'T SELL REAGAN TO BLACK VOTERS..
YOU CAN'T? CASS ASSURED ME YOU WERE UP TO THE CHALLENGE.
CHALLENGE? WITH ALL DUE RESPECT, SIR, RONALD REAGAN IS THE WORST THING TO HAPPEN TO CIVIL RIGHTS IN 35 YEARS!
TO SAY OTHERWISE, I'D HAVE TO RENOUNCE EVERY STANDARD OF TRUTH I'VE EVER SET FOR MYSELF!
THIS IS THE REAL WORLD, SON. IT HAPPENS.
ON MY FIRST DAY?
ED, LET ME TALK TO HIM ALONE..
WHAT IS THIS, CASS? I TOLD YOU NO MORE WIMPS!
©B Trudeau

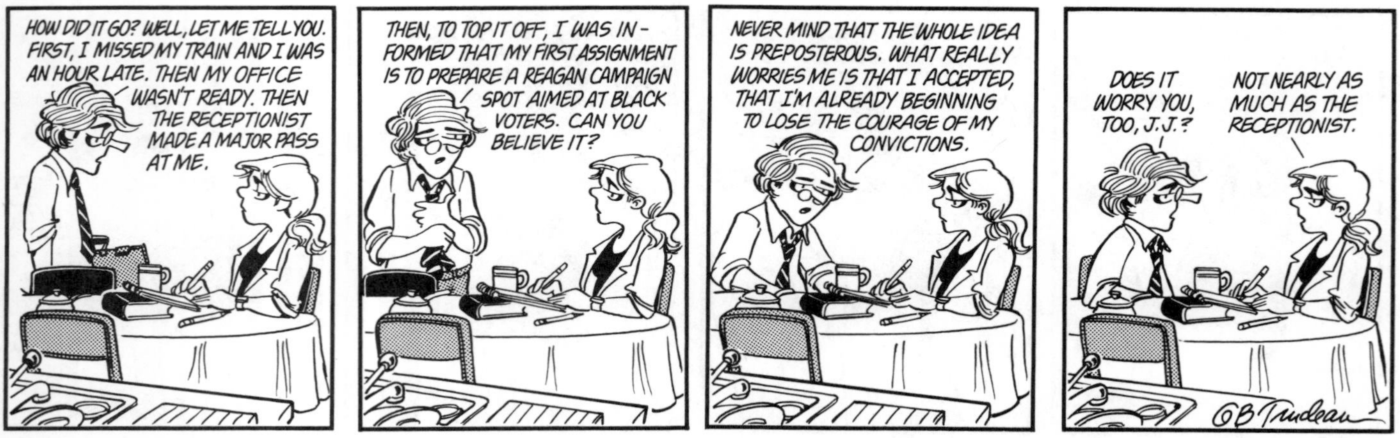
HOW DID IT GO? WELL, LET ME TELL YOU. FIRST, I MISSED MY TRAIN AND I WAS AN HOUR LATE. THEN MY OFFICE WASN'T READY. THEN THE RECEPTIONIST MADE A MAJOR PASS AT ME.
THEN, TO TOP IT OFF, I WAS INFORMED THAT MY FIRST ASSIGNMENT IS TO PREPARE A REAGAN CAMPAIGN SPOT AIMED AT BLACK VOTERS. CAN YOU BELIEVE IT?
NEVER MIND THAT THE WHOLE IDEA IS PREPOSTEROUS. WHAT REALLY WORRIES ME IS THAT I ACCEPTED, THAT I'M ALREADY BEGINNING TO LOSE THE COURAGE OF MY CONVICTIONS.
DOES IT WORRY YOU, TOO, J.J.?
NOT NEARLY AS MUCH AS THE RECEPTIONIST.
©B Trudeau

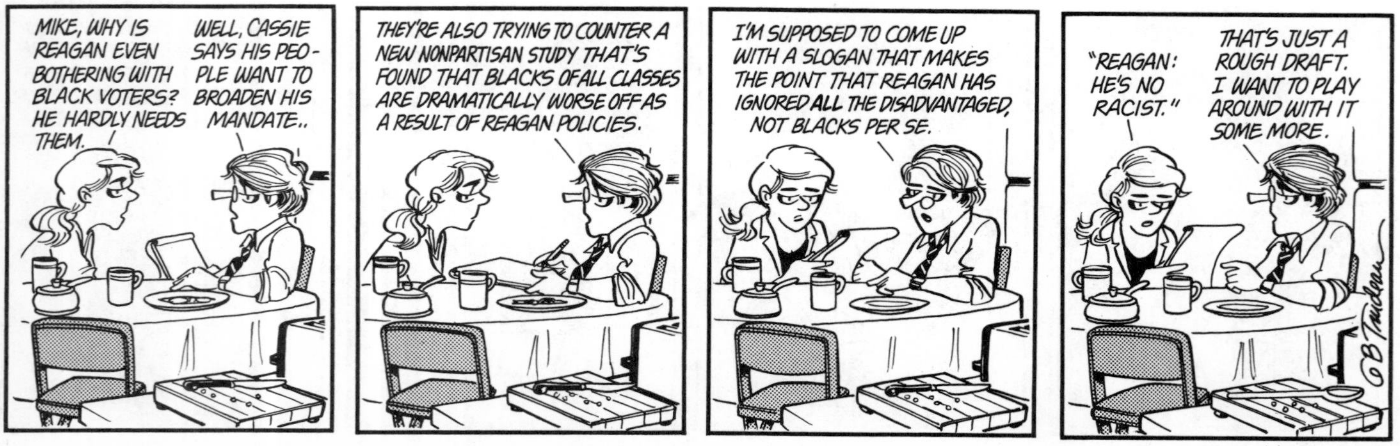
MIKE, WHY IS REAGAN EVEN BOTHERING WITH BLACK VOTERS? HE HARDLY NEEDS THEM.
WELL, CASSIE SAYS HIS PEOPLE WANT TO BROADEN HIS MANDATE..
THEY'RE ALSO TRYING TO COUNTER A NEW NONPARTISAN STUDY THAT'S FOUND THAT BLACKS OF ALL CLASSES ARE DRAMATICALLY WORSE OFF AS A RESULT OF REAGAN POLICIES.
I'M SUPPOSED TO COME UP WITH A SLOGAN THAT MAKES THE POINT THAT REAGAN HAS IGNORED ALL THE DISADVANTAGED, NOT BLACKS PER SE.
"REAGAN: HE'S NO RACIST."
THAT'S JUST A ROUGH DRAFT. I WANT TO PLAY AROUND WITH IT SOME MORE.
©B Trudeau

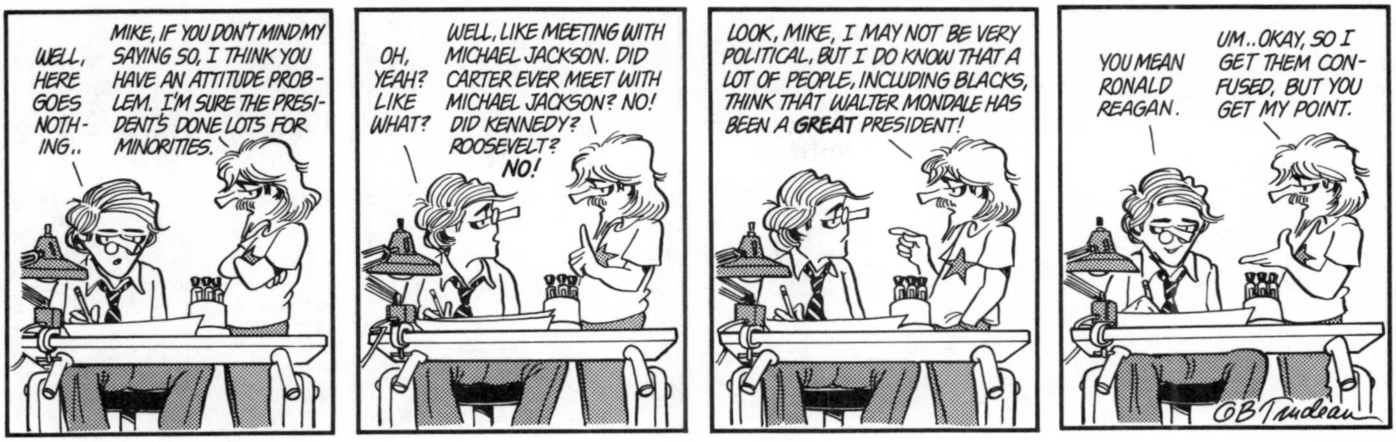
WELL, HERE GOES NOTHING..
MIKE, IF YOU DON'T MIND MY SAYING SO, I THINK YOU HAVE AN ATTITUDE PROBLEM. I'M SURE THE PRESIDENT'S DONE LOTS FOR MINORITIES.
OH, YEAH? LIKE WHAT?
WELL, LIKE MEETING WITH MICHAEL JACKSON. DID CARTER EVER MEET WITH MICHAEL JACKSON? NO! DID KENNEDY? ROOSEVELT? NO!
LOOK, MIKE, I MAY NOT BE VERY POLITICAL, BUT I DO KNOW THAT A LOT OF PEOPLE, INCLUDING BLACKS, THINK THAT WALTER MONDALE HAS BEEN A GREAT PRESIDENT!
YOU MEAN RONALD REAGAN.
UM.. OKAY, SO I GET THEM CONFUSED, BUT YOU GET MY POINT.
©B Trudeau

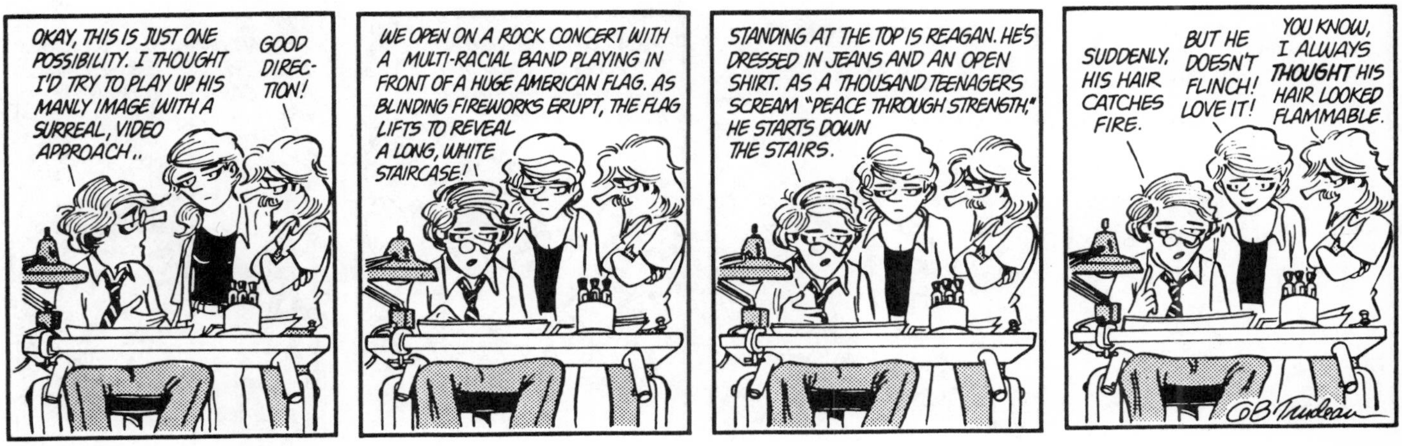
OKAY, THIS IS JUST ONE POSSIBILITY. I THOUGHT I'D TRY TO PLAY UP HIS MANLY IMAGE WITH A SURREAL, VIDEO APPROACH..
GOOD DIRECTION!
WE OPEN ON A ROCK CONCERT WITH A MULTI-RACIAL BAND PLAYING IN FRONT OF A HUGE AMERICAN FLAG. AS BLINDING FIREWORKS ERUPT, THE FLAG LIFTS TO REVEAL A LONG, WHITE STAIRCASE!
STANDING AT THE TOP IS REAGAN. HE'S DRESSED IN JEANS AND AN OPEN SHIRT. AS A THOUSAND TEENAGERS SCREAM "PEACE THROUGH STRENGTH," HE STARTS DOWN THE STAIRS.
SUDDENLY, HIS HAIR CATCHES FIRE.
BUT HE DOESN'T FLINCH! LOVE IT!
YOU KNOW, I ALWAYS THOUGHT HIS HAIR LOOKED FLAMMABLE.
©B Trudeau

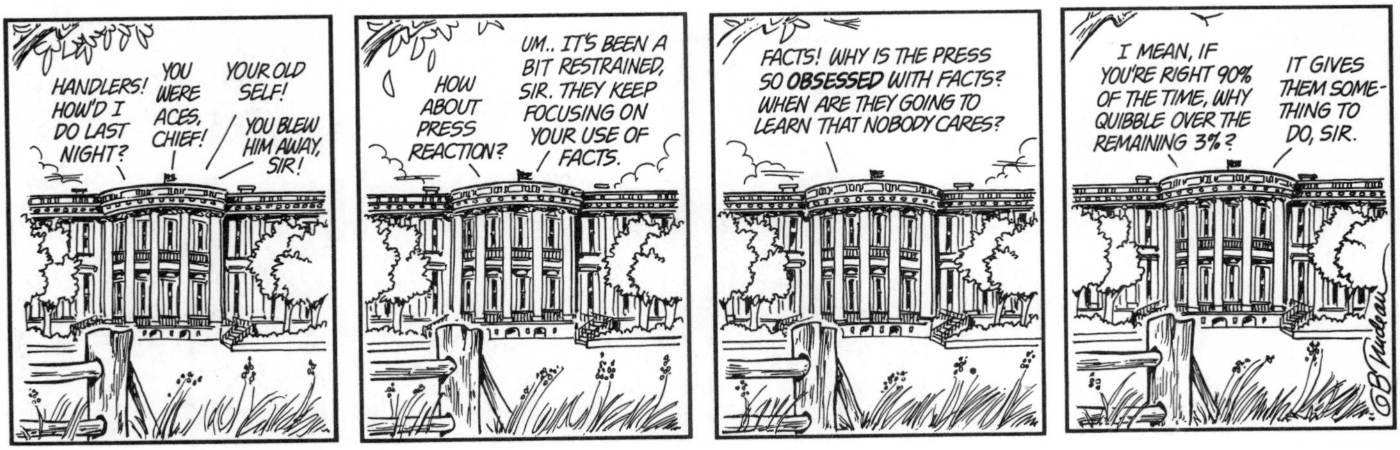
HANDLERS! HOW'D I DO LAST NIGHT?
YOU WERE ACES, CHIEF!
YOUR OLD SELF!
YOU BLEW HIM AWAY, SIR!
HOW ABOUT PRESS REACTION?
UM.. IT'S BEEN A BIT RESTRAINED, SIR. THEY KEEP FOCUSING ON YOUR USE OF FACTS.
FACTS! WHY IS THE PRESS SO OBSESSED WITH FACTS? WHEN ARE THEY GOING TO LEARN THAT NOBODY CARES?
I MEAN, IF YOU'RE RIGHT 90% OF THE TIME, WHY QUIBBLE OVER THE REMAINING 3%?
IT GIVES THEM SOMETHING TO DO, SIR.
©B Trudeau

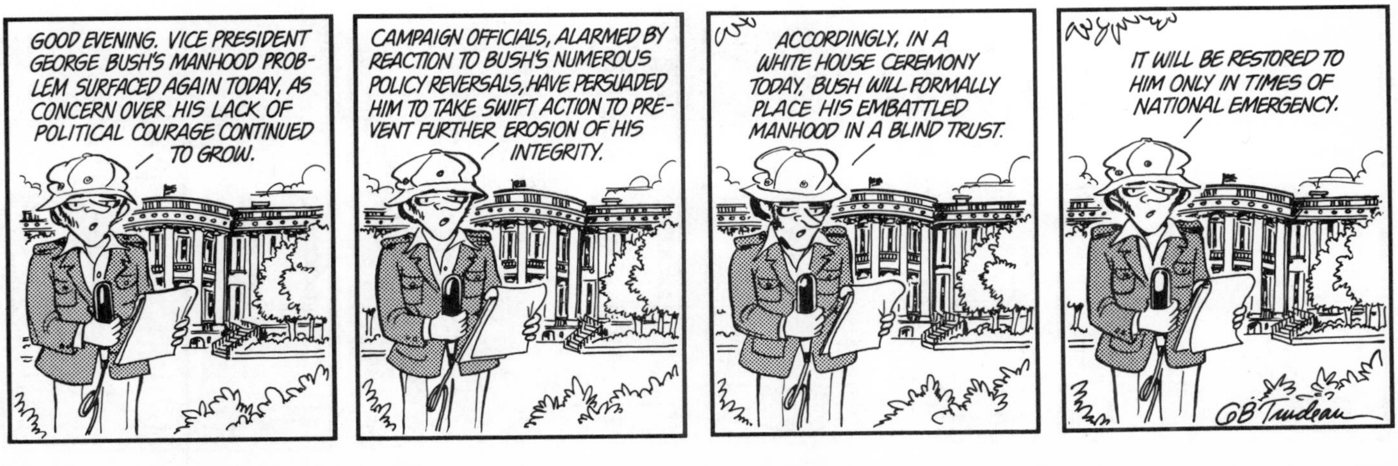
GOOD EVENING. VICE PRESIDENT GEORGE BUSH'S MANHOOD PROBLEM SURFACED AGAIN TODAY, AS CONCERN OVER HIS LACK OF POLITICAL COURAGE CONTINUED TO GROW.
CAMPAIGN OFFICIALS, ALARMED BY REACTION TO BUSH'S NUMEROUS POLICY REVERSALS, HAVE PERSUADED HIM TO TAKE SWIFT ACTION TO PREVENT FURTHER EROSION OF HIS INTEGRITY.
ACCORDINGLY, IN A WHITE HOUSE CEREMONY TODAY, BUSH WILL FORMALLY PLACE HIS EMBATTLED MANHOOD IN A BLIND TRUST.
IT WILL BE RESTORED TO HIM ONLY IN TIMES OF NATIONAL EMERGENCY.
©B Trudeau

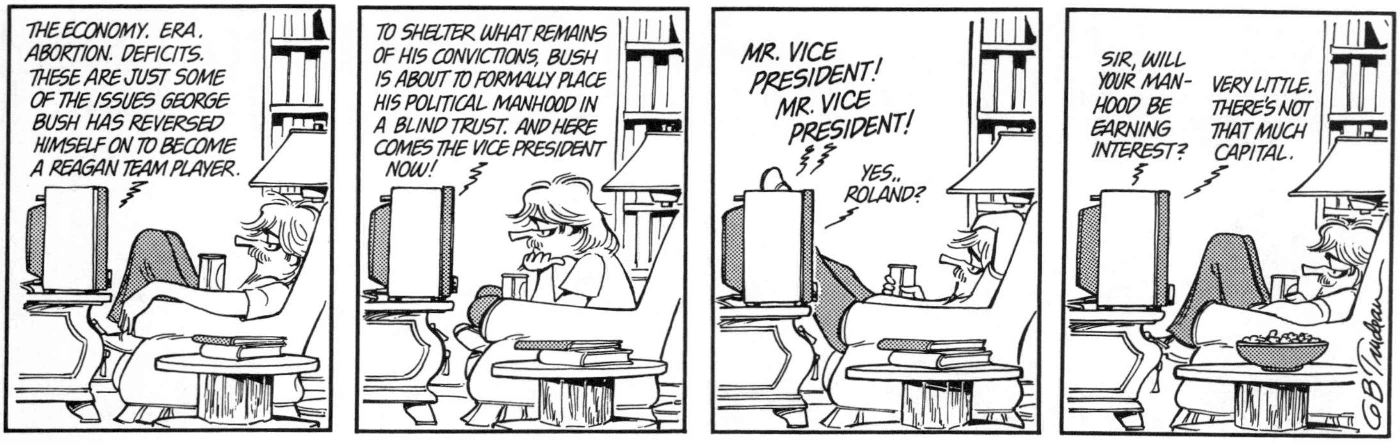
THE ECONOMY. ERA. ABORTION. DEFICITS. THESE ARE JUST SOME OF THE ISSUES GEORGE BUSH HAS REVERSED HIMSELF ON TO BECOME A REAGAN TEAM PLAYER.
TO SHELTER WHAT REMAINS OF HIS CONVICTIONS, BUSH IS ABOUT TO FORMALLY PLACE HIS POLITICAL MANHOOD IN A BLIND TRUST. AND HERE COMES THE VICE PRESIDENT NOW!
MR. VICE PRESIDENT! MR. VICE PRESIDENT!
YES.. ROLAND?
SIR, WILL YOUR MANHOOD BE EARNING INTEREST?
VERY LITTLE. THERE'S NOT THAT MUCH CAPITAL.
G.B. Trudeau

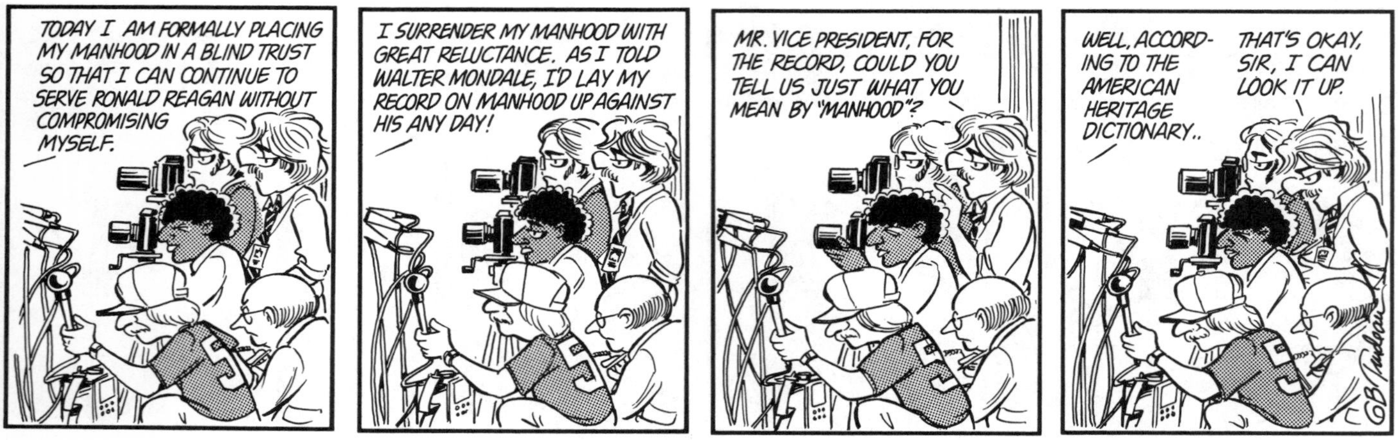
TODAY I AM FORMALLY PLACING MY MANHOOD IN A BLIND TRUST SO THAT I CAN CONTINUE TO SERVE RONALD REAGAN WITHOUT COMPROMISING MYSELF.
I SURRENDER MY MANHOOD WITH GREAT RELUCTANCE. AS I TOLD WALTER MONDALE, I'D LAY MY RECORD ON MANHOOD UP AGAINST HIS ANY DAY!
MR. VICE PRESIDENT, FOR THE RECORD, COULD YOU TELL US JUST WHAT YOU MEAN BY "MANHOOD"?
WELL, ACCORDING TO THE AMERICAN HERITAGE DICTIONARY..
THAT'S OKAY, SIR, I CAN LOOK IT UP.
G.B. Trudeau

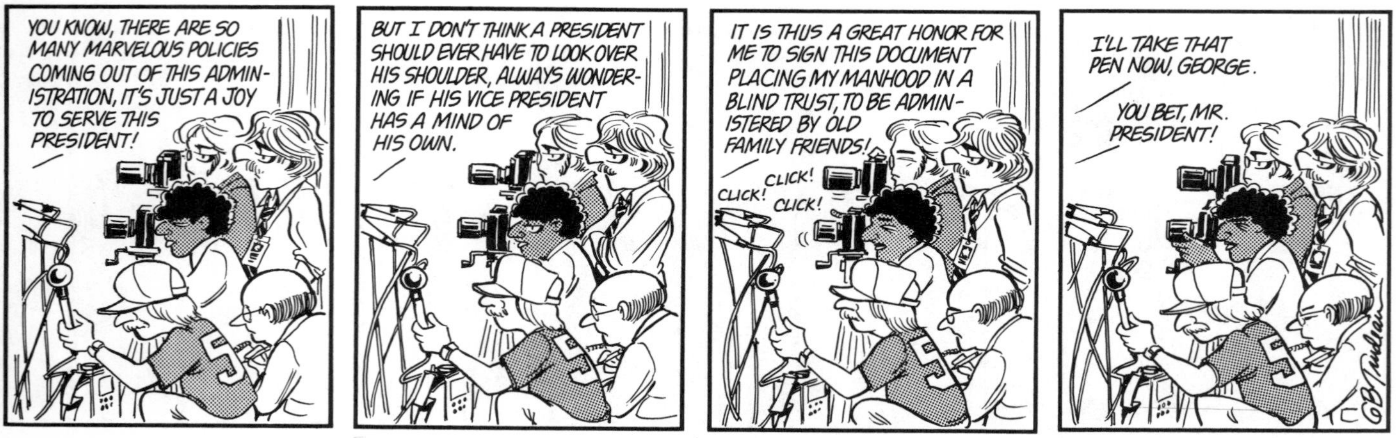
YOU KNOW, THERE ARE SO MANY MARVELOUS POLICIES COMING OUT OF THIS ADMINISTRATION, IT'S JUST A JOY TO SERVE THIS PRESIDENT!
BUT I DON'T THINK A PRESIDENT SHOULD EVER HAVE TO LOOK OVER HIS SHOULDER, ALWAYS WONDERING IF HIS VICE PRESIDENT HAS A MIND OF HIS OWN.
IT IS THUS A GREAT HONOR FOR ME TO SIGN THIS DOCUMENT PLACING MY MANHOOD IN A BLIND TRUST, TO BE ADMINISTERED BY OLD FAMILY FRIENDS!
CLICK! CLICK! CLICK!
I'LL TAKE THAT PEN NOW, GEORGE.
YOU BET, MR. PRESIDENT!
G.B. Trudeau

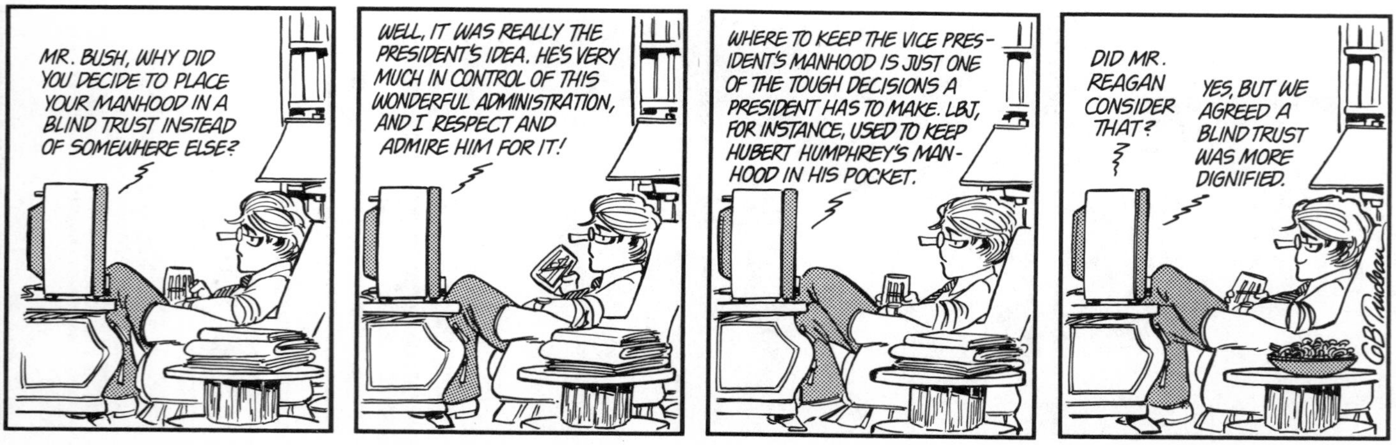
MR. BUSH, WHY DID YOU DECIDE TO PLACE YOUR MANHOOD IN A BLIND TRUST INSTEAD OF SOMEWHERE ELSE?
WELL, IT WAS REALLY THE PRESIDENT'S IDEA. HE'S VERY MUCH IN CONTROL OF THIS WONDERFUL ADMINISTRATION, AND I RESPECT AND ADMIRE HIM FOR IT!
WHERE TO KEEP THE VICE PRESIDENT'S MANHOOD IS JUST ONE OF THE TOUGH DECISIONS A PRESIDENT HAS TO MAKE. LBJ, FOR INSTANCE, USED TO KEEP HUBERT HUMPHREY'S MANHOOD IN HIS POCKET.
DID MR. REAGAN CONSIDER THAT?
YES, BUT WE AGREED A BLIND TRUST WAS MORE DIGNIFIED.
G.B. Trudeau

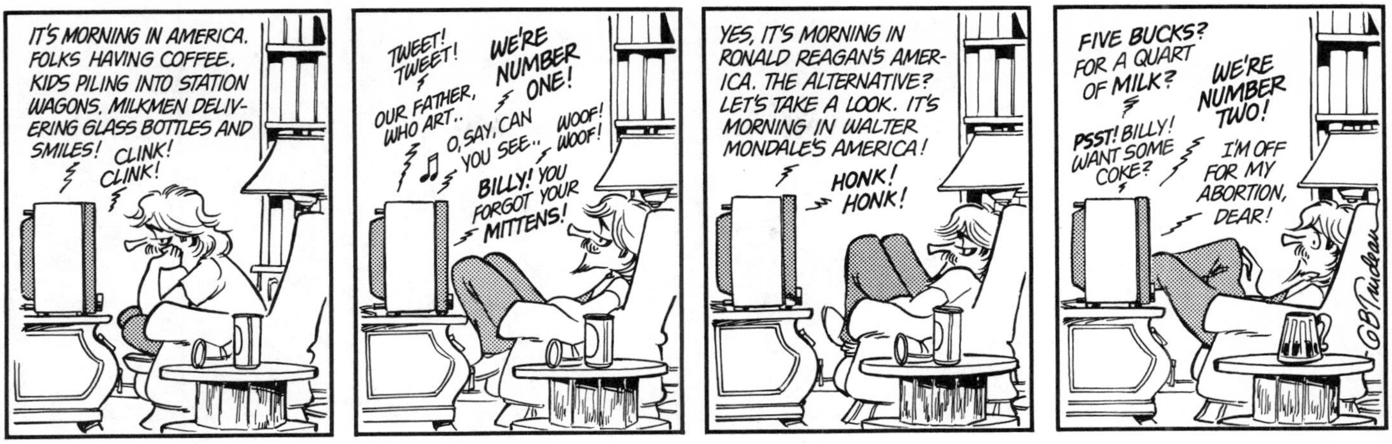
IT'S MORNING IN AMERICA. FOLKS HAVING COFFEE. KIDS PILING INTO STATION WAGONS. MILKMEN DELIVERING GLASS BOTTLES AND SMILES!
CLINK! CLINK!
TWEET! TWEET!
WE'RE NUMBER ONE!
OUR FATHER, WHO ART..
O, SAY, CAN YOU SEE..
WOOF! WOOF!
BILLY! YOU FORGOT YOUR MITTENS!
YES, IT'S MORNING IN RONALD REAGAN'S AMERICA. THE ALTERNATIVE? LET'S TAKE A LOOK. IT'S MORNING IN WALTER MONDALE'S AMERICA!
HONK! HONK!
FIVE BUCKS? FOR A QUART OF MILK?
WE'RE NUMBER TWO!
PSST! BILLY! WANT SOME COKE?
I'M OFF FOR MY ABORTION, DEAR!
GBTrudeau

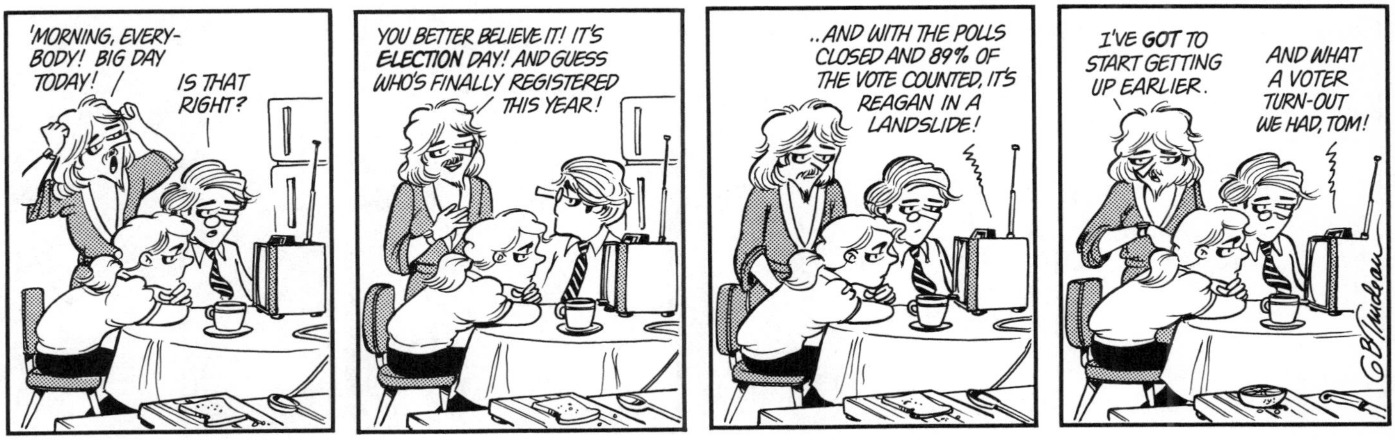
'MORNING, EVERYBODY! BIG DAY TODAY!
IS THAT RIGHT?
YOU BETTER BELIEVE IT! IT'S ELECTION DAY! AND GUESS WHO'S FINALLY REGISTERED THIS YEAR!
..AND WITH THE POLLS CLOSED AND 89% OF THE VOTE COUNTED, IT'S REAGAN IN A LANDSLIDE!
I'VE GOT TO START GETTING UP EARLIER.
AND WHAT A VOTER TURN-OUT WE HAD, TOM!
GBTrudeau

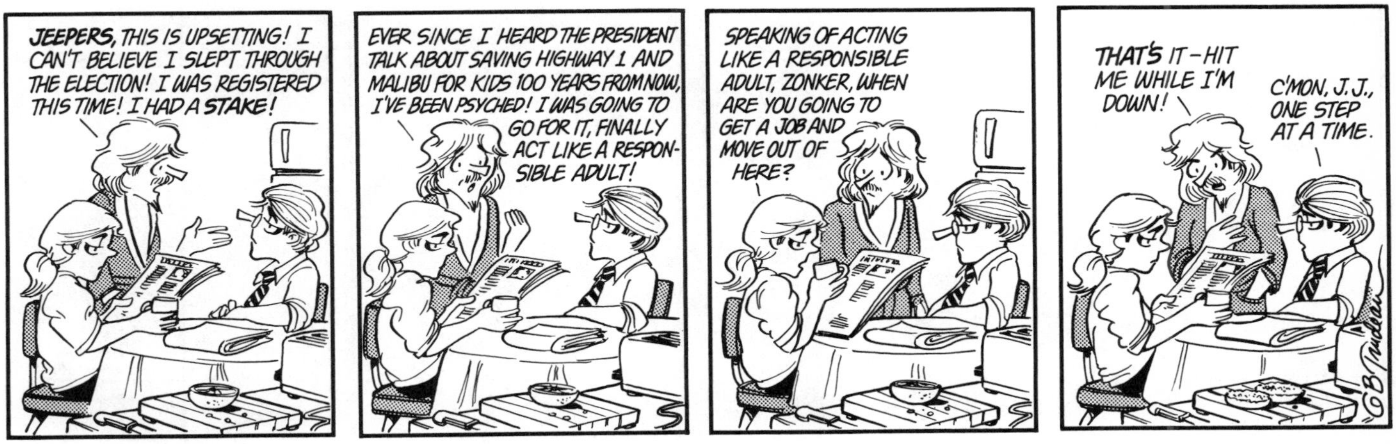
JEEPERS, THIS IS UPSETTING! I CAN'T BELIEVE I SLEPT THROUGH THE ELECTION! I WAS REGISTERED THIS TIME! I HAD A STAKE!
EVER SINCE I HEARD THE PRESIDENT TALK ABOUT SAVING HIGHWAY 1 AND MALIBU FOR KIDS 100 YEARS FROM NOW, I'VE BEEN PSYCHED! I WAS GOING TO GO FOR IT, FINALLY ACT LIKE A RESPONSIBLE ADULT!
SPEAKING OF ACTING LIKE A RESPONSIBLE ADULT, ZONKER, WHEN ARE YOU GOING TO GET A JOB AND MOVE OUT OF HERE?
THAT'S IT–HIT ME WHILE I'M DOWN!
C'MON, J.J., ONE STEP AT A TIME.
GBTrudeau

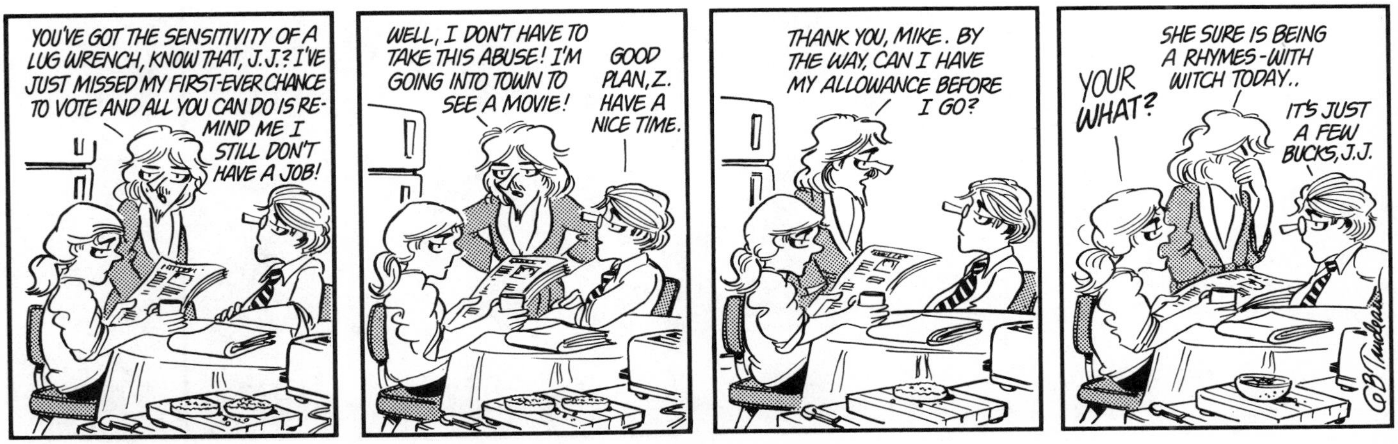
YOU'VE GOT THE SENSITIVITY OF A LUG WRENCH, KNOW THAT, J.J.? I'VE JUST MISSED MY FIRST-EVER CHANCE TO VOTE AND ALL YOU CAN DO IS REMIND ME I STILL DON'T HAVE A JOB!
WELL, I DON'T HAVE TO TAKE THIS ABUSE! I'M GOING INTO TOWN TO SEE A MOVIE!
GOOD PLAN, Z. HAVE A NICE TIME.
THANK YOU, MIKE. BY THE WAY, CAN I HAVE MY ALLOWANCE BEFORE I GO?
YOUR WHAT?
SHE SURE IS BEING A RHYMES-WITH WITCH TODAY..
IT'S JUST A FEW BUCKS, J.J.
GBTrudeau

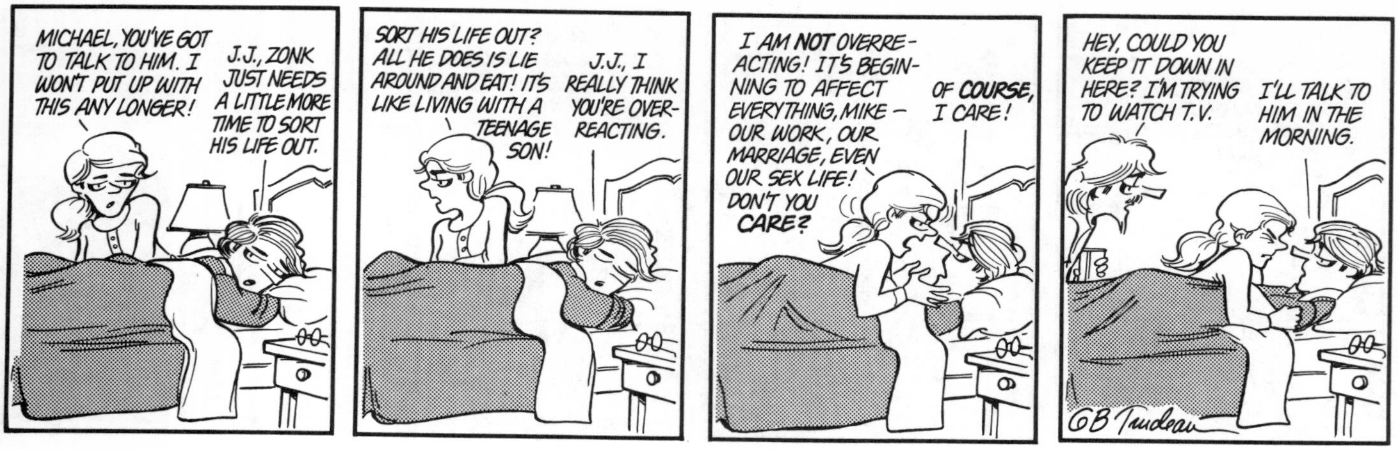
MICHAEL, YOU'VE GOT TO TALK TO HIM. I WON'T PUT UP WITH THIS ANY LONGER!
J.J., ZONK JUST NEEDS A LITTLE MORE TIME TO SORT HIS LIFE OUT.
SORT HIS LIFE OUT? ALL HE DOES IS LIE AROUND AND EAT! IT'S LIKE LIVING WITH A TEENAGE SON!
J.J., I REALLY THINK YOU'RE OVER-REACTING.
I AM NOT OVERRE-ACTING! IT'S BEGIN-NING TO AFFECT EVERYTHING, MIKE – OUR WORK, OUR MARRIAGE, EVEN OUR SEX LIFE! DON'T YOU CARE?
OF COURSE, I CARE!
HEY, COULD YOU KEEP IT DOWN IN HERE? I'M TRYING TO WATCH T.V.
I'LL TALK TO HIM IN THE MORNING.
GB Trudeau

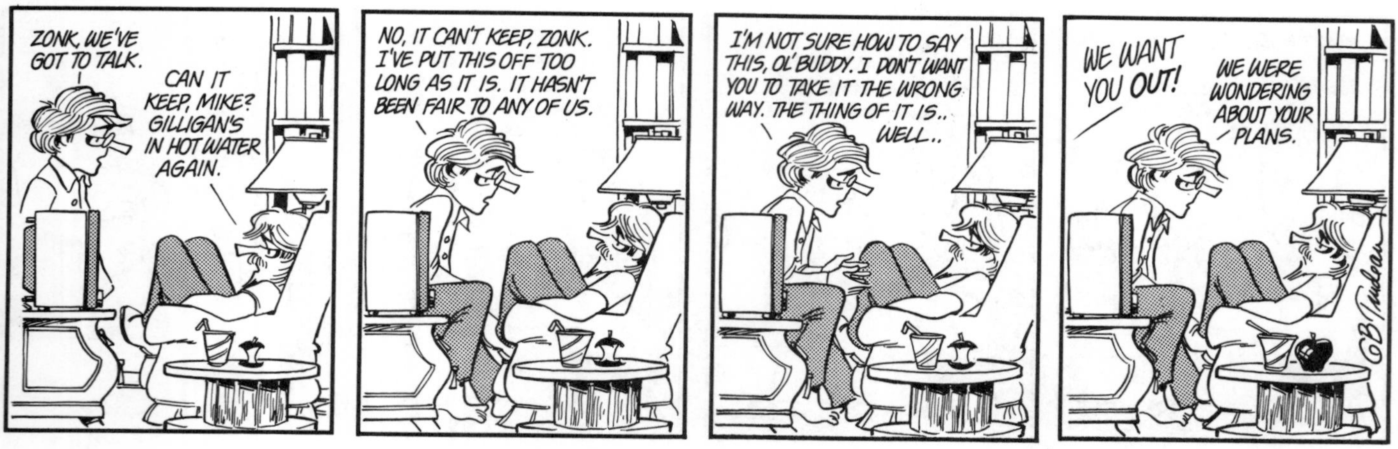
ZONK, WE'VE GOT TO TALK.
CAN IT KEEP, MIKE? GILLIGAN'S IN HOT WATER AGAIN.
NO, IT CAN'T KEEP, ZONK. I'VE PUT THIS OFF TOO LONG AS IT IS. IT HASN'T BEEN FAIR TO ANY OF US.
I'M NOT SURE HOW TO SAY THIS, OL' BUDDY. I DON'T WANT YOU TO TAKE IT THE WRONG WAY. THE THING OF IT IS.. WELL..
WE WANT YOU OUT!
WE WERE WONDERING ABOUT YOUR PLANS.
GB Trudeau

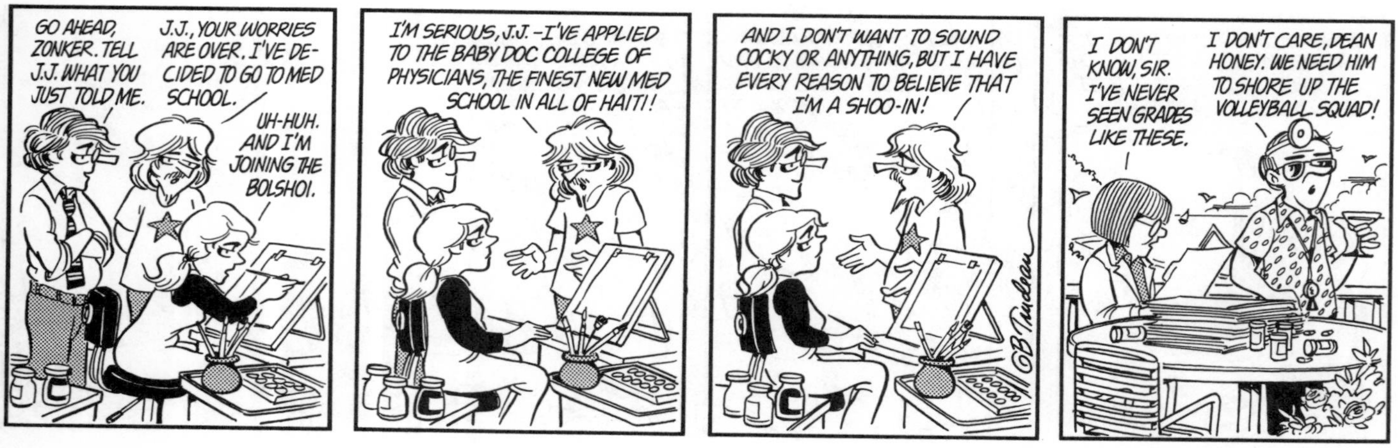
GO AHEAD, ZONKER. TELL J.J. WHAT YOU JUST TOLD ME.
J.J., YOUR WORRIES ARE OVER. I'VE DE-CIDED TO GO TO MED SCHOOL.
UH-HUH. AND I'M JOINING THE BOLSHOI.
I'M SERIOUS, J.J.–I'VE APPLIED TO THE BABY DOC COLLEGE OF PHYSICIANS, THE FINEST NEW MED SCHOOL IN ALL OF HAITI!
AND I DON'T WANT TO SOUND COCKY OR ANYTHING, BUT I HAVE EVERY REASON TO BELIEVE THAT I'M A SHOO-IN!
GB Trudeau
I DON'T KNOW, SIR. I'VE NEVER SEEN GRADES LIKE THESE.
I DON'T CARE, DEAN HONEY. WE NEED HIM TO SHORE UP THE VOLLEYBALL SQUAD!

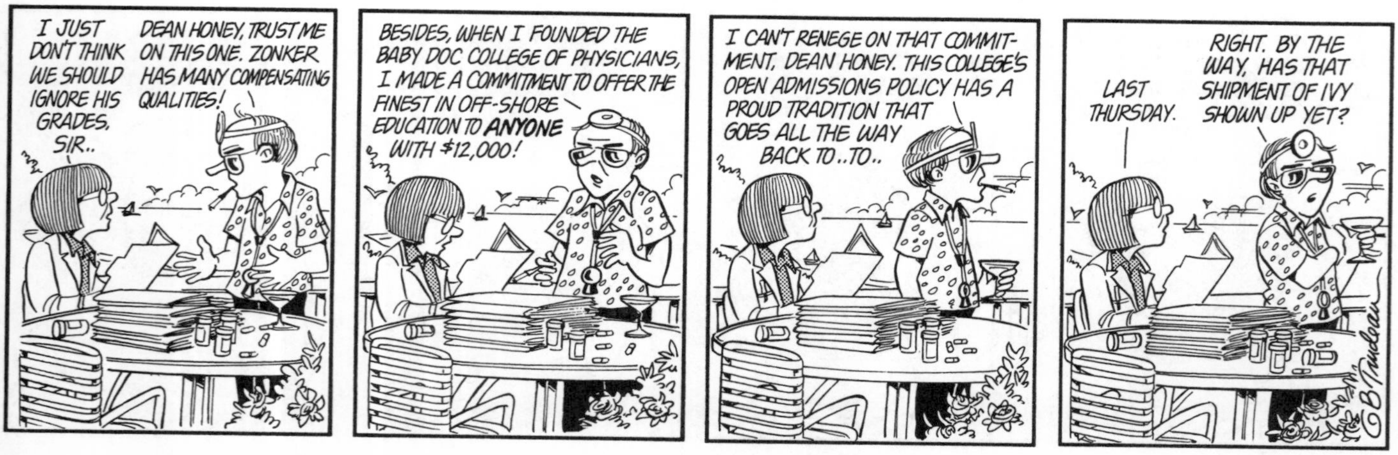
I JUST DON'T THINK WE SHOULD IGNORE HIS GRADES, SIR..
DEAN HONEY, TRUST ME ON THIS ONE. ZONKER HAS MANY COMPENSATING QUALITIES!
BESIDES, WHEN I FOUNDED THE BABY DOC COLLEGE OF PHYSICIANS, I MADE A COMMITMENT TO OFFER THE FINEST IN OFF-SHORE EDUCATION TO ANYONE WITH $12,000!
I CAN'T RENEGE ON THAT COMMIT-MENT, DEAN HONEY. THIS COLLEGE'S OPEN ADMISSIONS POLICY HAS A PROUD TRADITION THAT GOES ALL THE WAY BACK TO..TO..
LAST THURSDAY.
RIGHT. BY THE WAY, HAS THAT SHIPMENT OF IVY SHOWN UP YET?
GB Trudeau

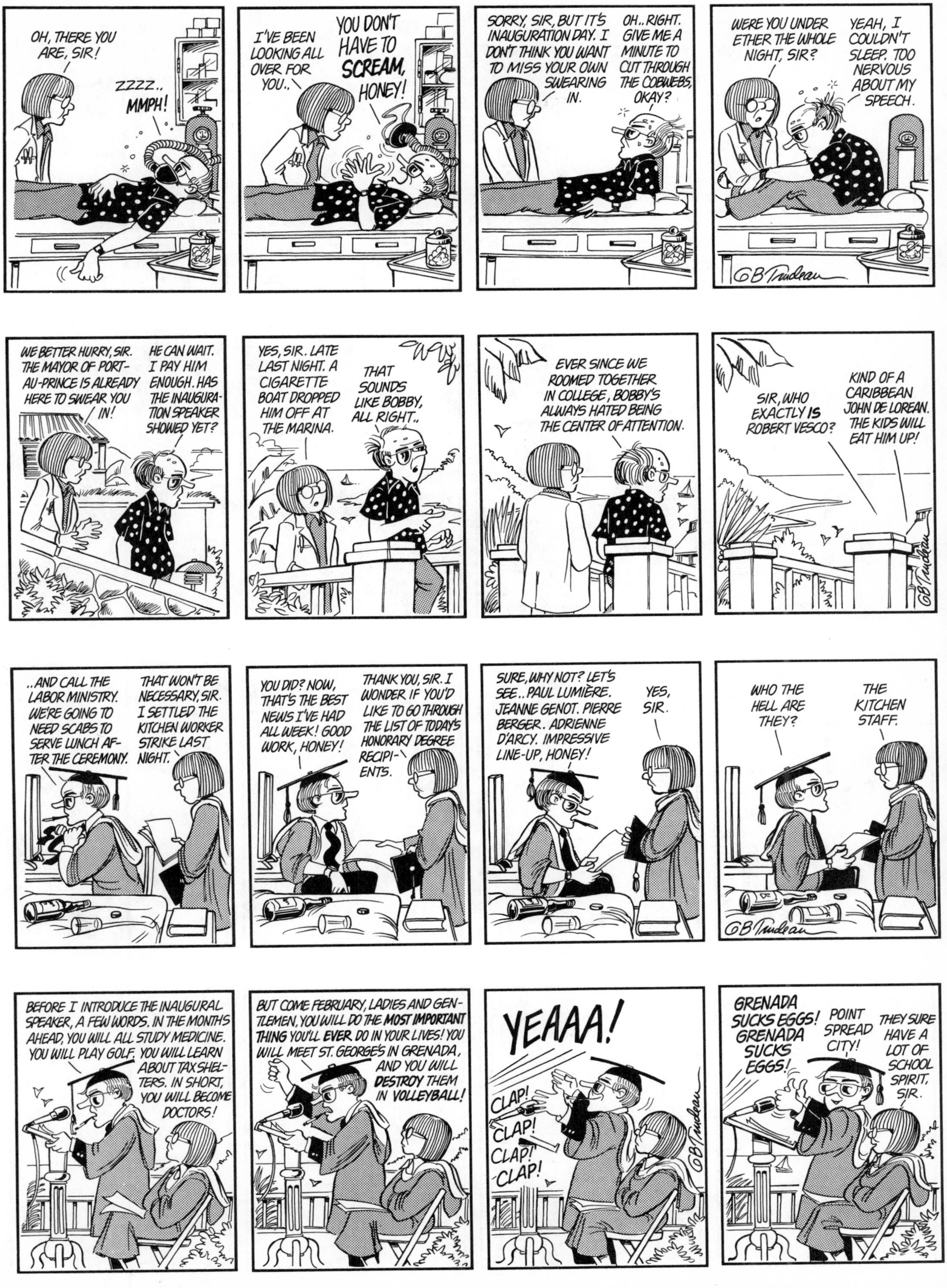
OH, THERE YOU ARE, SIR!
ZZZZ.. MMPH!
I'VE BEEN LOOKING ALL OVER FOR YOU..
YOU DON'T HAVE TO SCREAM, HONEY!
SORRY, SIR, BUT IT'S INAUGURATION DAY. I DON'T THINK YOU WANT TO MISS YOUR OWN SWEARING IN.
OH.. RIGHT. GIVE ME A MINUTE TO CUT THROUGH THE COBWEBS, OKAY?
WERE YOU UNDER ETHER THE WHOLE NIGHT, SIR?
YEAH, I COULDN'T SLEEP. TOO NERVOUS ABOUT MY SPEECH.
GB Trudeau
WE BETTER HURRY, SIR. THE MAYOR OF PORT-AU-PRINCE IS ALREADY HERE TO SWEAR YOU IN!
HE CAN WAIT. I PAY HIM ENOUGH. HAS THE INAUGURATION SPEAKER SHOWED YET?
YES, SIR. LATE LAST NIGHT. A CIGARETTE BOAT DROPPED HIM OFF AT THE MARINA.
THAT SOUNDS LIKE BOBBY, ALL RIGHT..
EVER SINCE WE ROOMED TOGETHER IN COLLEGE, BOBBY'S ALWAYS HATED BEING THE CENTER OF ATTENTION.
SIR, WHO EXACTLY IS ROBERT VESCO?
KIND OF A CARIBBEAN JOHN DE LOREAN. THE KIDS WILL EAT HIM UP!
GB Trudeau
..AND CALL THE LABOR MINISTRY. WE'RE GOING TO NEED SCABS TO SERVE LUNCH AFTER THE CEREMONY.
THAT WON'T BE NECESSARY, SIR. I SETTLED THE KITCHEN WORKER STRIKE LAST NIGHT.
YOU DID? NOW, THAT'S THE BEST NEWS I'VE HAD ALL WEEK! GOOD WORK, HONEY!
THANK YOU, SIR. I WONDER IF YOU'D LIKE TO GO THROUGH THE LIST OF TODAY'S HONORARY DEGREE RECIPIENTS.
SURE, WHY NOT? LET'S SEE.. PAUL LUMIÈRE. JEANNE GENOT. PIERRE BERGER.. ADRIENNE D'ARCY. IMPRESSIVE LINE-UP, HONEY!
YES, SIR.
WHO THE HELL ARE THEY?
THE KITCHEN STAFF.
GB Trudeau
BEFORE I INTRODUCE THE INAUGURAL SPEAKER, A FEW WORDS. IN THE MONTHS AHEAD, YOU WILL ALL STUDY MEDICINE. YOU WILL PLAY GOLF. YOU WILL LEARN ABOUT TAX SHELTERS. IN SHORT, YOU WILL BECOME DOCTORS!
BUT COME FEBRUARY, LADIES AND GENTLEMEN, YOU WILL DO THE MOST IMPORTANT THING YOU'LL EVER DO IN YOUR LIVES! YOU WILL MEET ST. GEORGE'S IN GRENADA, AND YOU WILL DESTROY THEM IN VOLLEYBALL!
YEAAA!
CLAP! CLAP! CLAP! CLAP!
GB Trudeau
GRENADA SUCKS EGGS! GRENADA SUCKS EGGS!
POINT SPREAD CITY!
THEY SURE HAVE A LOT OF SCHOOL SPIRIT, SIR.

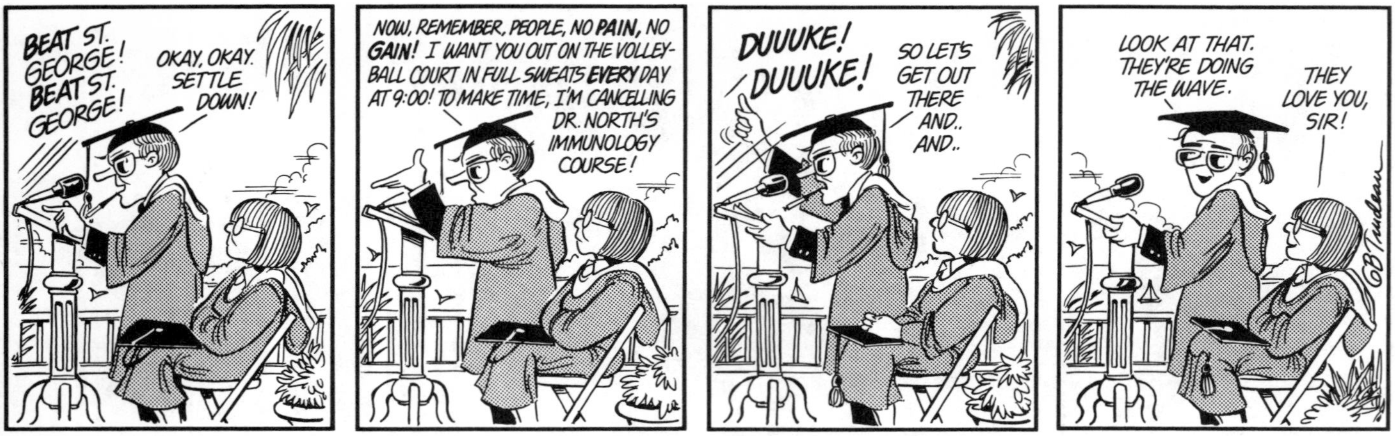
BEAT ST. GEORGE! BEAT ST. GEORGE!
OKAY, OKAY. SETTLE DOWN!
NOW, REMEMBER, PEOPLE, NO PAIN, NO GAIN! I WANT YOU OUT ON THE VOLLEYBALL COURT IN FULL SWEATS EVERY DAY AT 9:00! TO MAKE TIME, I'M CANCELLING DR. NORTH'S IMMUNOLOGY COURSE!
DUUUKE! DUUUKE!
SO LET'S GET OUT THERE AND.. AND..
LOOK AT THAT. THEY'RE DOING THE WAVE.
THEY LOVE YOU, SIR!

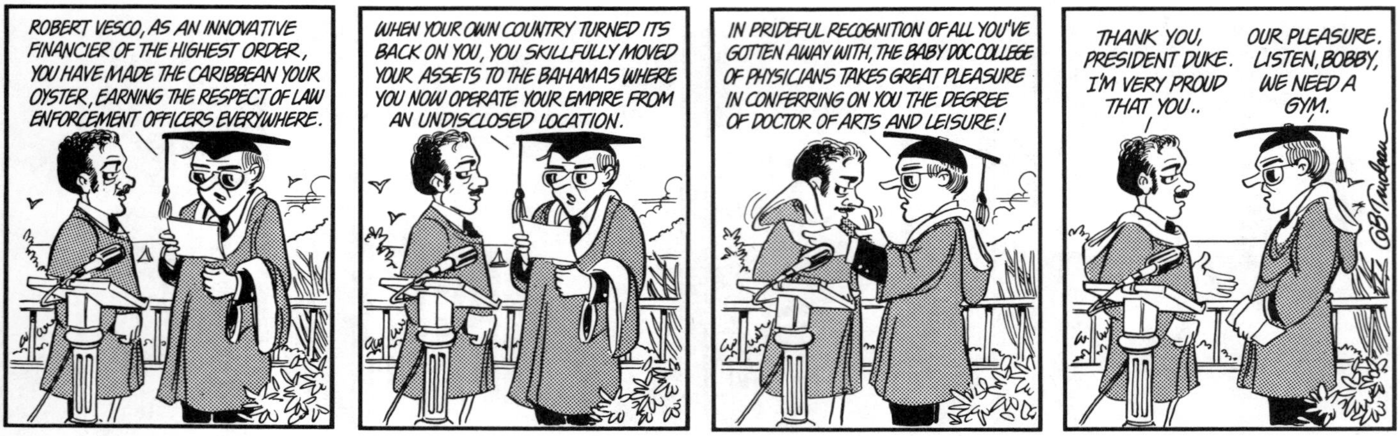
ROBERT VESCO, AS AN INNOVATIVE FINANCIER OF THE HIGHEST ORDER, YOU HAVE MADE THE CARIBBEAN YOUR OYSTER, EARNING THE RESPECT OF LAW ENFORCEMENT OFFICERS EVERYWHERE.
WHEN YOUR OWN COUNTRY TURNED ITS BACK ON YOU, YOU SKILLFULLY MOVED YOUR ASSETS TO THE BAHAMAS WHERE YOU NOW OPERATE YOUR EMPIRE FROM AN UNDISCLOSED LOCATION.
IN PRIDEFUL RECOGNITION OF ALL YOU'VE GOTTEN AWAY WITH, THE BABY DOC COLLEGE OF PHYSICIANS TAKES GREAT PLEASURE IN CONFERRING ON YOU THE DEGREE OF DOCTOR OF ARTS AND LEISURE!
THANK YOU, PRESIDENT DUKE. I'M VERY PROUD THAT YOU..
OUR PLEASURE. LISTEN, BOBBY, WE NEED A GYM.

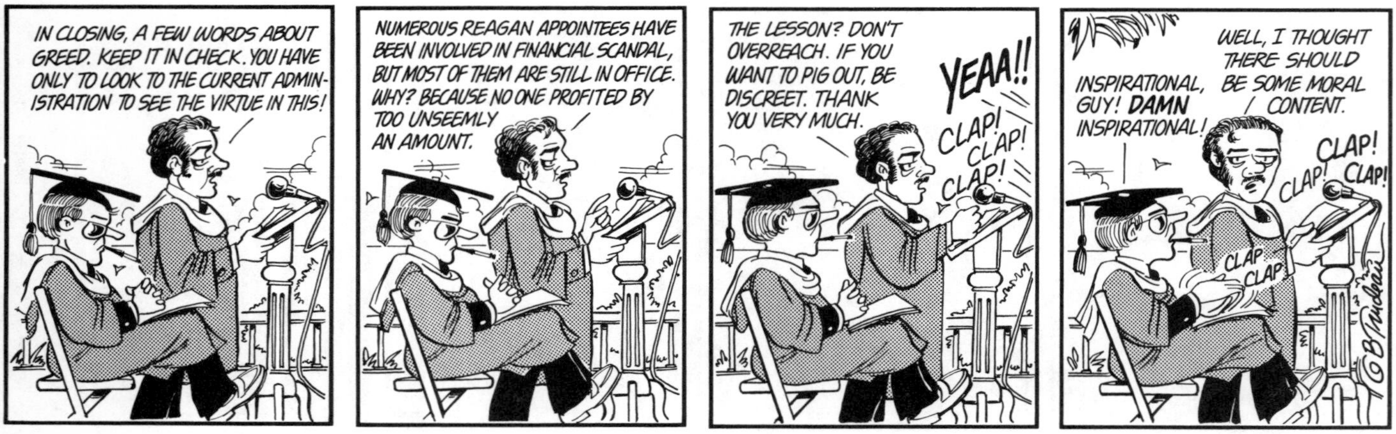
IN CLOSING, A FEW WORDS ABOUT GREED. KEEP IT IN CHECK. YOU HAVE ONLY TO LOOK TO THE CURRENT ADMINISTRATION TO SEE THE VIRTUE IN THIS!
NUMEROUS REAGAN APPOINTEES HAVE BEEN INVOLVED IN FINANCIAL SCANDAL, BUT MOST OF THEM ARE STILL IN OFFICE. WHY? BECAUSE NO ONE PROFITED BY TOO UNSEEMLY AN AMOUNT.
THE LESSON? DON'T OVERREACH. IF YOU WANT TO PIG OUT, BE DISCREET. THANK YOU VERY MUCH.
YEAA!!
CLAP! CLAP! CLAP!
INSPIRATIONAL, GUY! DAMN INSPIRATIONAL!
WELL, I THOUGHT THERE SHOULD BE SOME MORAL CONTENT.
CLAP! CLAP! CLAP!
CLAP CLAP

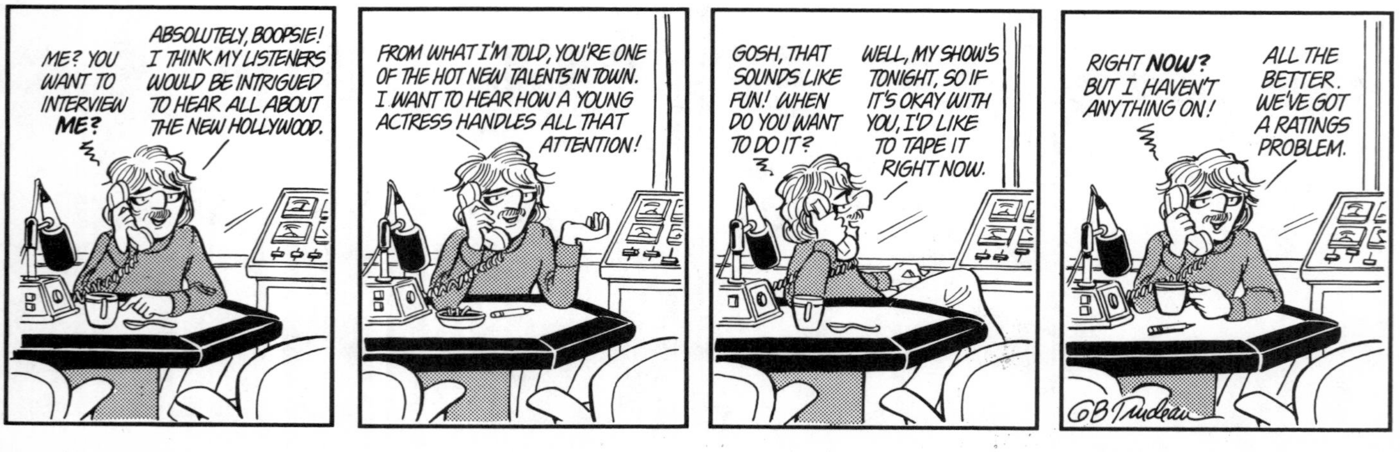
ME? YOU WANT TO INTERVIEW ME?
ABSOLUTELY, BOOPSIE! I THINK MY LISTENERS WOULD BE INTRIGUED TO HEAR ALL ABOUT THE NEW HOLLYWOOD.
FROM WHAT I'M TOLD, YOU'RE ONE OF THE HOT NEW TALENTS IN TOWN. I WANT TO HEAR HOW A YOUNG ACTRESS HANDLES ALL THAT ATTENTION!
GOSH, THAT SOUNDS LIKE FUN! WHEN DO YOU WANT TO DO IT?
WELL, MY SHOW'S TONIGHT, SO IF IT'S OKAY WITH YOU, I'D LIKE TO TAPE IT RIGHT NOW.
RIGHT NOW? BUT I HAVEN'T ANYTHING ON!
ALL THE BETTER. WE'VE GOT A RATINGS PROBLEM.

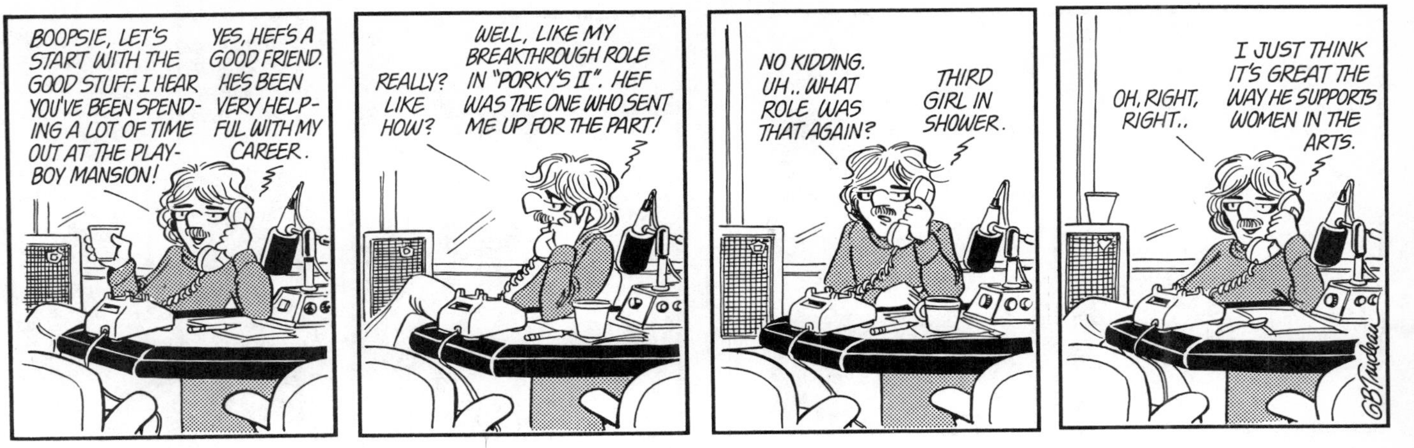
BOOPSIE, LET'S START WITH THE GOOD STUFF. I HEAR YOU'VE BEEN SPENDING A LOT OF TIME OUT AT THE PLAYBOY MANSION!
YES, HEF'S A GOOD FRIEND. HE'S BEEN VERY HELPFUL WITH MY CAREER.
REALLY? LIKE HOW?
WELL, LIKE MY BREAKTHROUGH ROLE IN "PORKY'S II". HEF WAS THE ONE WHO SENT ME UP FOR THE PART!
NO KIDDING. UH.. WHAT ROLE WAS THAT AGAIN?
THIRD GIRL IN SHOWER.
OH, RIGHT, RIGHT..
I JUST THINK IT'S GREAT THE WAY HE SUPPORTS WOMEN IN THE ARTS.

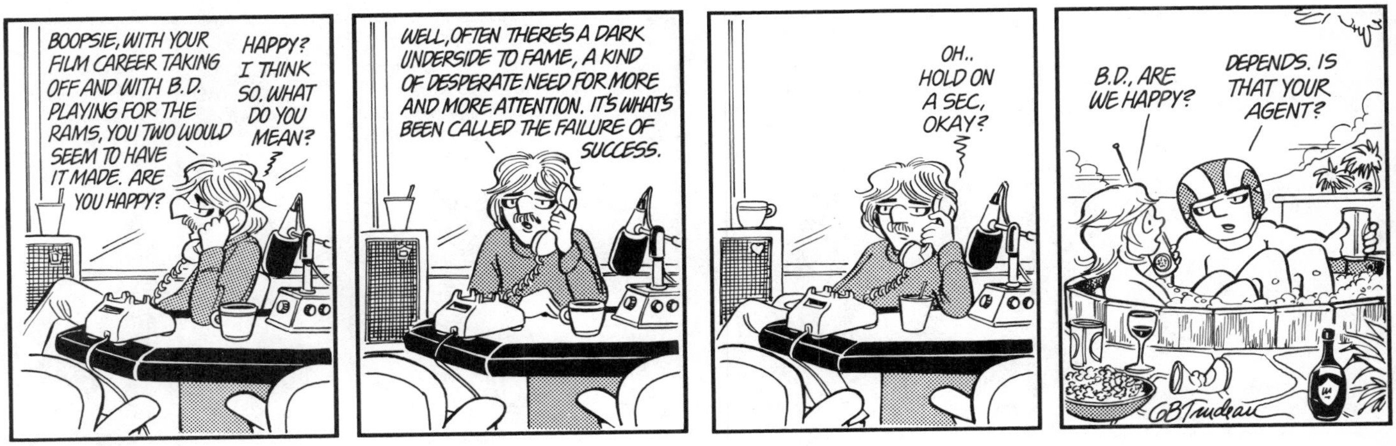
BOOPSIE, WITH YOUR FILM CAREER TAKING OFF AND WITH B.D. PLAYING FOR THE RAMS, YOU TWO WOULD SEEM TO HAVE IT MADE. ARE YOU HAPPY?
HAPPY? I THINK SO. WHAT DO YOU MEAN?
WELL, OFTEN THERE'S A DARK UNDERSIDE TO FAME, A KIND OF DESPERATE NEED FOR MORE AND MORE ATTENTION. IT'S WHAT'S BEEN CALLED THE FAILURE OF SUCCESS.
OH.. HOLD ON A SEC, OKAY?
B.D., ARE WE HAPPY?
DEPENDS. IS THAT YOUR AGENT?

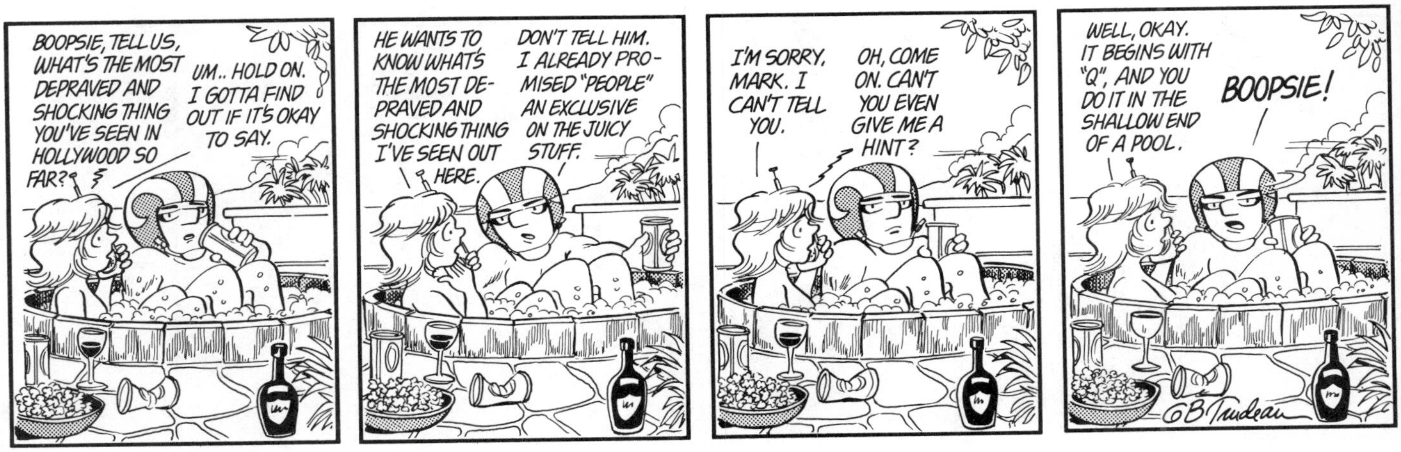
BOOPSIE, TELL US, WHAT'S THE MOST DEPRAVED AND SHOCKING THING YOU'VE SEEN IN HOLLYWOOD SO FAR?
UM.. HOLD ON. I GOTTA FIND OUT IF IT'S OKAY TO SAY.
HE WANTS TO KNOW WHAT'S THE MOST DEPRAVED AND SHOCKING THING I'VE SEEN OUT HERE.
DON'T TELL HIM. I ALREADY PROMISED "PEOPLE" AN EXCLUSIVE ON THE JUICY STUFF.
I'M SORRY, MARK. I CAN'T TELL YOU.
OH, COME ON. CAN'T YOU EVEN GIVE ME A HINT?
WELL, OKAY. IT BEGINS WITH "Q", AND YOU DO IT IN THE SHALLOW END OF A POOL.
BOOPSIE!

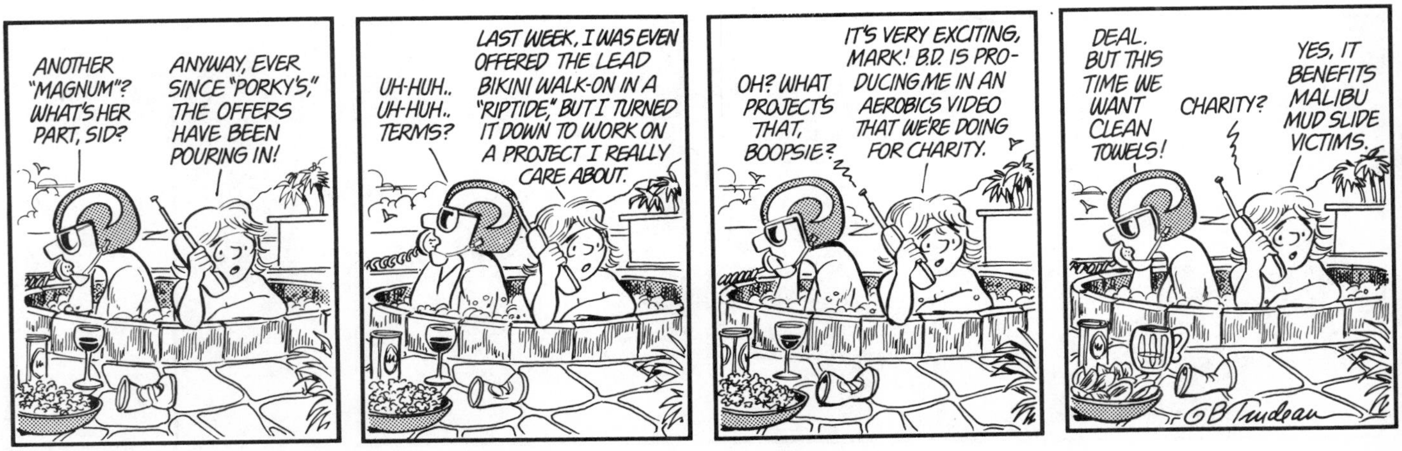
ANOTHER "MAGNUM"? WHAT'S HER PART, SID?
ANYWAY, EVER SINCE "PORKY'S," THE OFFERS HAVE BEEN POURING IN!
UH-HUH.. UH-HUH.. TERMS?
LAST WEEK, I WAS EVEN OFFERED THE LEAD BIKINI WALK-ON IN A "RIPTIDE," BUT I TURNED IT DOWN TO WORK ON A PROJECT I REALLY CARE ABOUT.
OH? WHAT PROJECT'S THAT, BOOPSIE?
IT'S VERY EXCITING, MARK! B.D. IS PRODUCING ME IN AN AEROBICS VIDEO THAT WE'RE DOING FOR CHARITY.
DEAL. BUT THIS TIME WE WANT CLEAN TOWELS!
CHARITY?
YES, IT BENEFITS MALIBU MUD SLIDE VICTIMS.

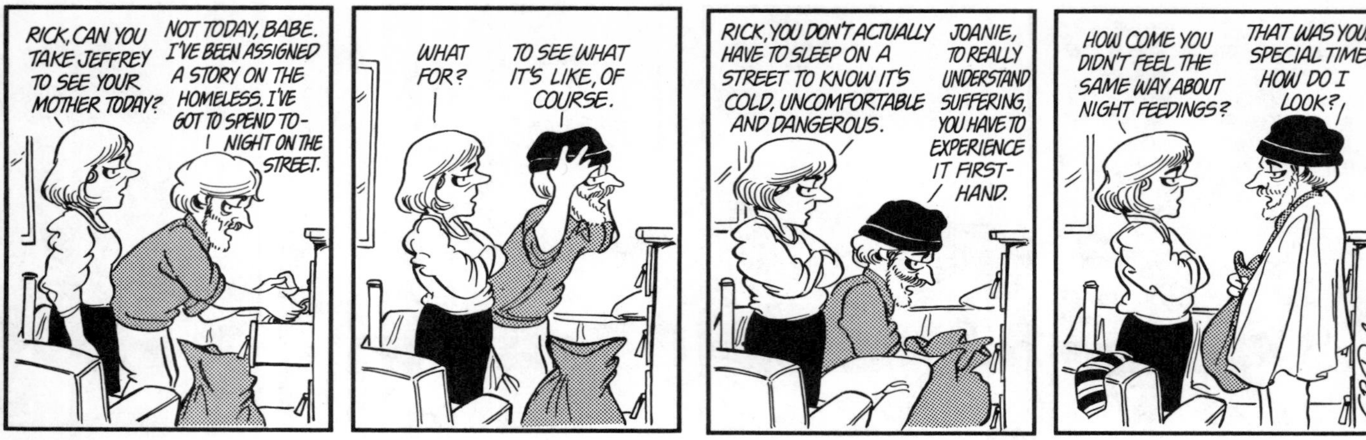
RICK, CAN YOU TAKE JEFFREY TO SEE YOUR MOTHER TODAY?
NOT TODAY, BABE. I'VE BEEN ASSIGNED A STORY ON THE HOMELESS. I'VE GOT TO SPEND TO-NIGHT ON THE STREET.
WHAT FOR?
TO SEE WHAT IT'S LIKE, OF COURSE.
RICK, YOU DON'T ACTUALLY HAVE TO SLEEP ON A STREET TO KNOW IT'S COLD, UNCOMFORTABLE AND DANGEROUS.
JOANIE, TO REALLY UNDERSTAND SUFFERING, YOU HAVE TO EXPERIENCE IT FIRST-HAND.
HOW COME YOU DIDN'T FEEL THE SAME WAY ABOUT NIGHT FEEDINGS?
THAT WAS YOUR SPECIAL TIME. HOW DO I LOOK?
GB Trudeau

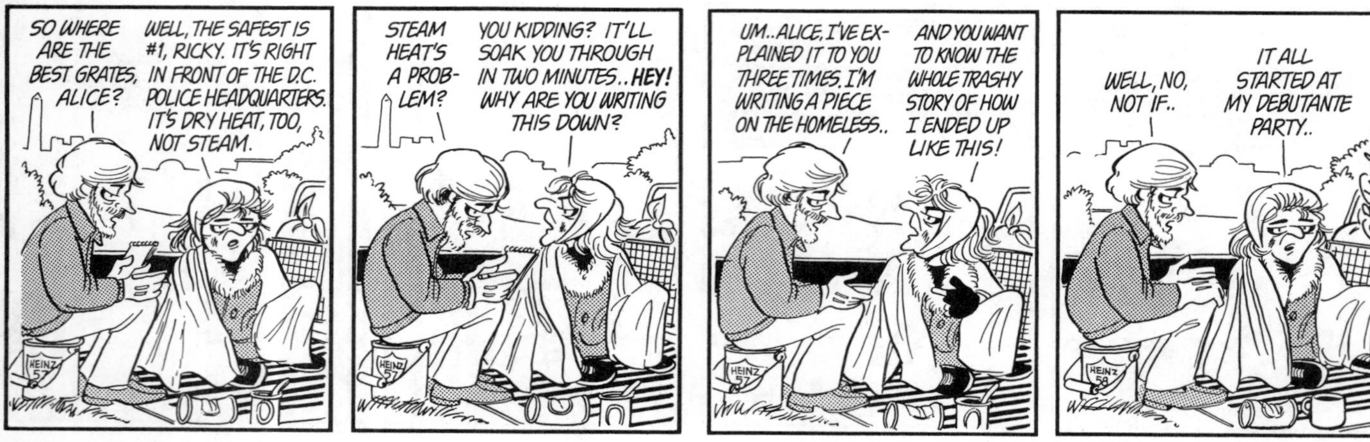
SO WHERE ARE THE BEST GRATES, ALICE?
WELL, THE SAFEST IS #1, RICKY. IT'S RIGHT IN FRONT OF THE D.C. POLICE HEADQUARTERS. IT'S DRY HEAT, TOO, NOT STEAM.
STEAM HEAT'S A PROB-LEM?
YOU KIDDING? IT'LL SOAK YOU THROUGH IN TWO MINUTES.. **HEY!** WHY ARE YOU WRITING THIS DOWN?
UM.. ALICE, I'VE EX-PLAINED IT TO YOU THREE TIMES. I'M WRITING A PIECE ON THE HOMELESS..
AND YOU WANT TO KNOW THE WHOLE TRASHY STORY OF HOW I ENDED UP LIKE THIS!
WELL, NO, NOT IF..
IT ALL STARTED AT MY DEBUTANTE PARTY..
GB Trudeau

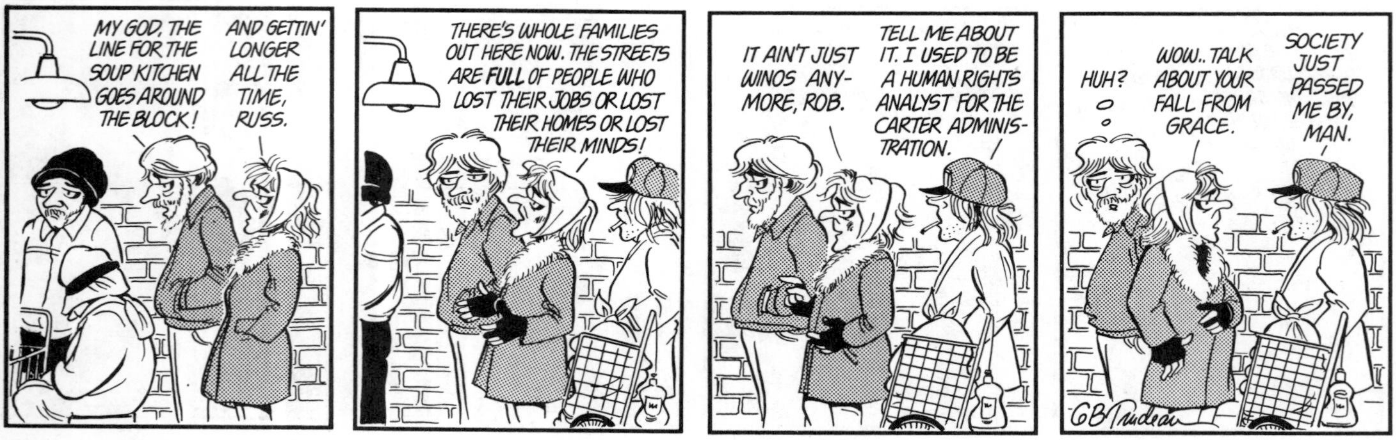
MY GOD, THE LINE FOR THE SOUP KITCHEN GOES AROUND THE BLOCK!
AND GETTIN' LONGER ALL THE TIME, RUSS.
THERE'S WHOLE FAMILIES OUT HERE NOW. THE STREETS ARE **FULL** OF PEOPLE WHO LOST THEIR JOBS OR LOST THEIR HOMES OR LOST THEIR MINDS!
IT AIN'T JUST WINOS ANY-MORE, ROB.
TELL ME ABOUT IT. I USED TO BE A HUMAN RIGHTS ANALYST FOR THE CARTER ADMINIS-TRATION.
HUH?
WOW.. TALK ABOUT YOUR FALL FROM GRACE.
SOCIETY JUST PASSED ME BY, MAN.
GB Trudeau

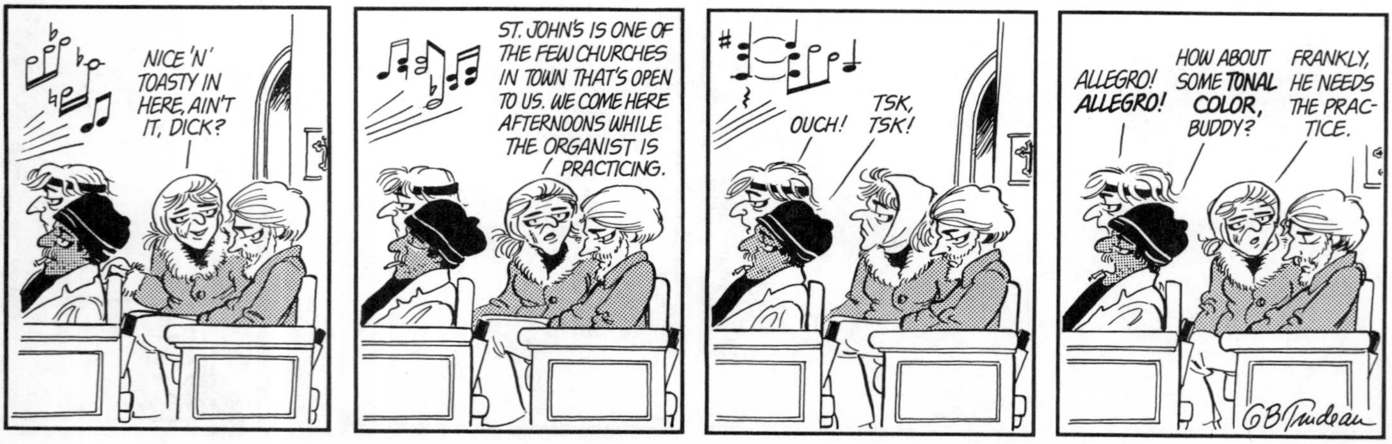
NICE 'N' TOASTY IN HERE, AIN'T IT, DICK?
ST. JOHN'S IS ONE OF THE FEW CHURCHES IN TOWN THAT'S OPEN TO US. WE COME HERE AFTERNOONS WHILE THE ORGANIST IS PRACTICING.
OUCH!
TSK, TSK!
ALLEGRO! **ALLEGRO!**
HOW ABOUT SOME **TONAL COLOR,** BUDDY?
FRANKLY, HE NEEDS THE PRAC-TICE.
GB Trudeau

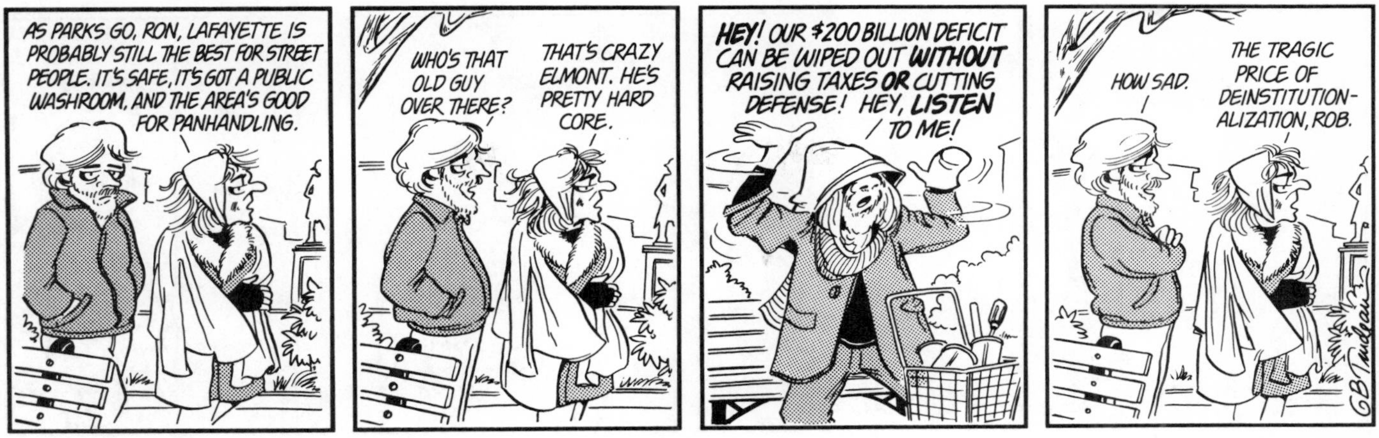
AS PARKS GO, RON, LAFAYETTE IS PROBABLY STILL THE BEST FOR STREET PEOPLE. IT'S SAFE, IT'S GOT A PUBLIC WASHROOM, AND THE AREA'S GOOD FOR PANHANDLING.
WHO'S THAT OLD GUY OVER THERE?
THAT'S CRAZY ELMONT. HE'S PRETTY HARD CORE.
HEY! OUR $200 BILLION DEFICIT CAN BE WIPED OUT WITHOUT RAISING TAXES OR CUTTING DEFENSE! HEY, LISTEN TO ME!
HOW SAD.
THE TRAGIC PRICE OF DEINSTITUTION-ALIZATION, ROB.
GBTrudeau

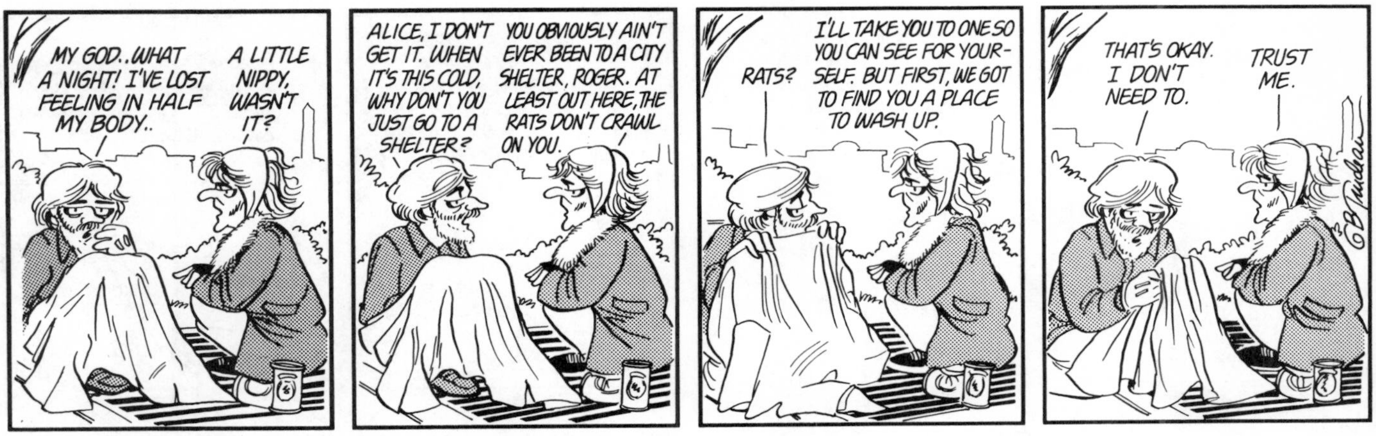
MY GOD.. WHAT A NIGHT! I'VE LOST FEELING IN HALF MY BODY..
A LITTLE NIPPY, WASN'T IT?
ALICE, I DON'T GET IT. WHEN IT'S THIS COLD, WHY DON'T YOU JUST GO TO A SHELTER?
YOU OBVIOUSLY AIN'T EVER BEEN TO A CITY SHELTER, ROGER. AT LEAST OUT HERE, THE RATS DON'T CRAWL ON YOU.
RATS?
I'LL TAKE YOU TO ONE SO YOU CAN SEE FOR YOUR-SELF. BUT FIRST, WE GOT TO FIND YOU A PLACE TO WASH UP.
THAT'S OKAY. I DON'T NEED TO.
TRUST ME.
GBTrudeau

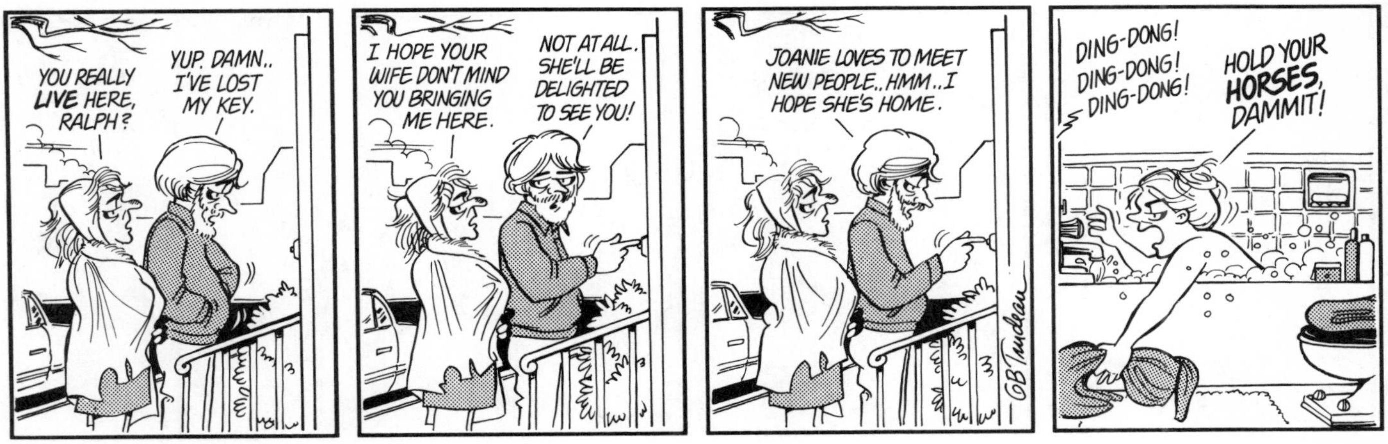
YOU REALLY LIVE HERE, RALPH?
YUP. DAMN.. I'VE LOST MY KEY.
I HOPE YOUR WIFE DON'T MIND YOU BRINGING ME HERE.
NOT AT ALL. SHE'LL BE DELIGHTED TO SEE YOU!
JOANIE LOVES TO MEET NEW PEOPLE.. HMM.. I HOPE SHE'S HOME.
GBTrudeau
DING-DONG! DING-DONG! DING-DONG!
HOLD YOUR HORSES, DAMMIT!

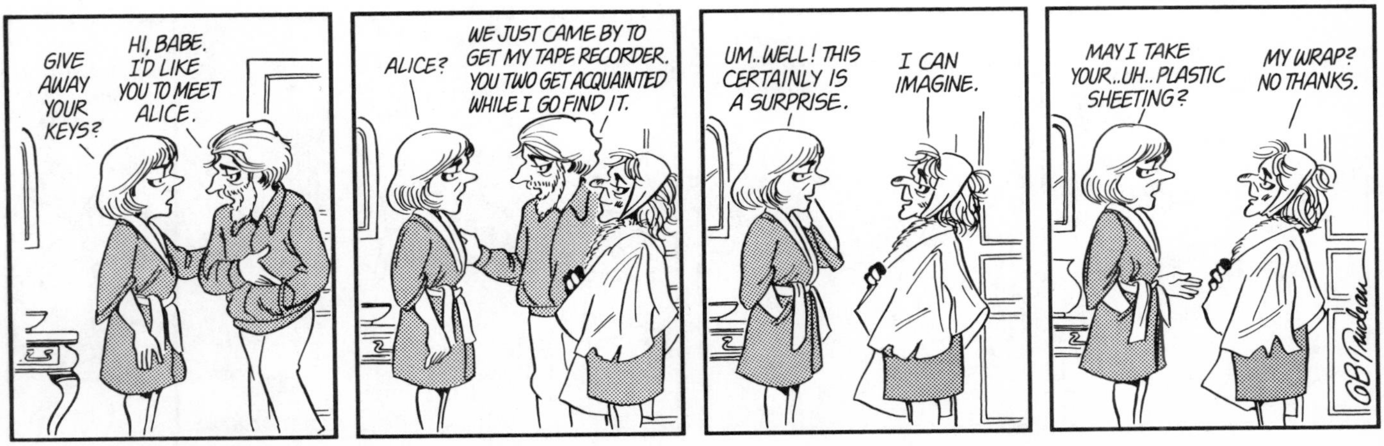
GIVE AWAY YOUR KEYS?
HI, BABE. I'D LIKE YOU TO MEET ALICE.
ALICE?
WE JUST CAME BY TO GET MY TAPE RECORDER. YOU TWO GET ACQUAINTED WHILE I GO FIND IT.
UM.. WELL! THIS CERTAINLY IS A SURPRISE.
I CAN IMAGINE.
MAY I TAKE YOUR.. UH.. PLASTIC SHEETING?
MY WRAP? NO THANKS.
GBTrudeau

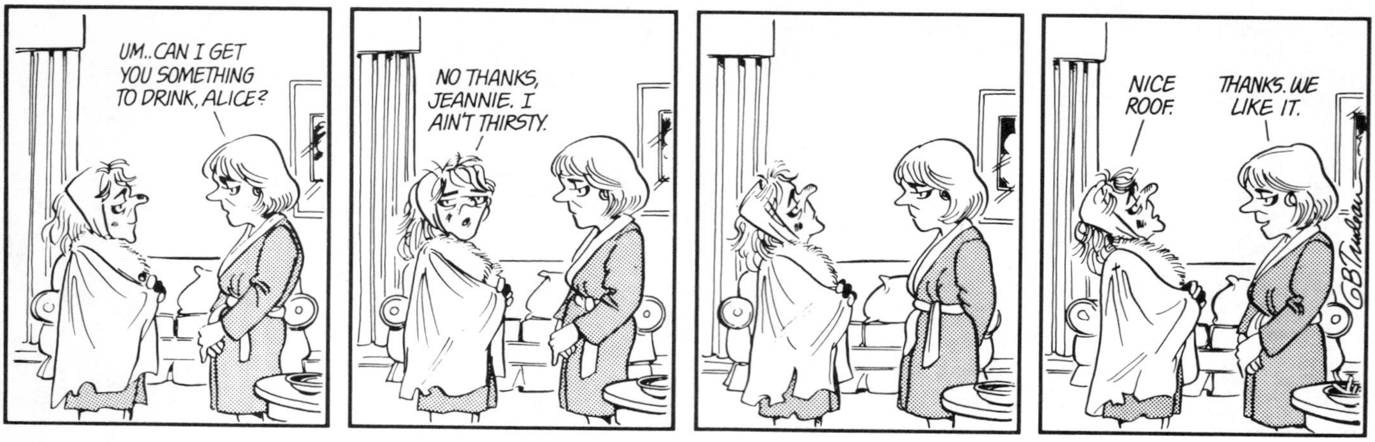
UM..CAN I GET YOU SOMETHING TO DRINK, ALICE?
NO THANKS, JEANNIE. I AIN'T THIRSTY.
NICE ROOF.
THANKS. WE LIKE IT.
©B Trudeau

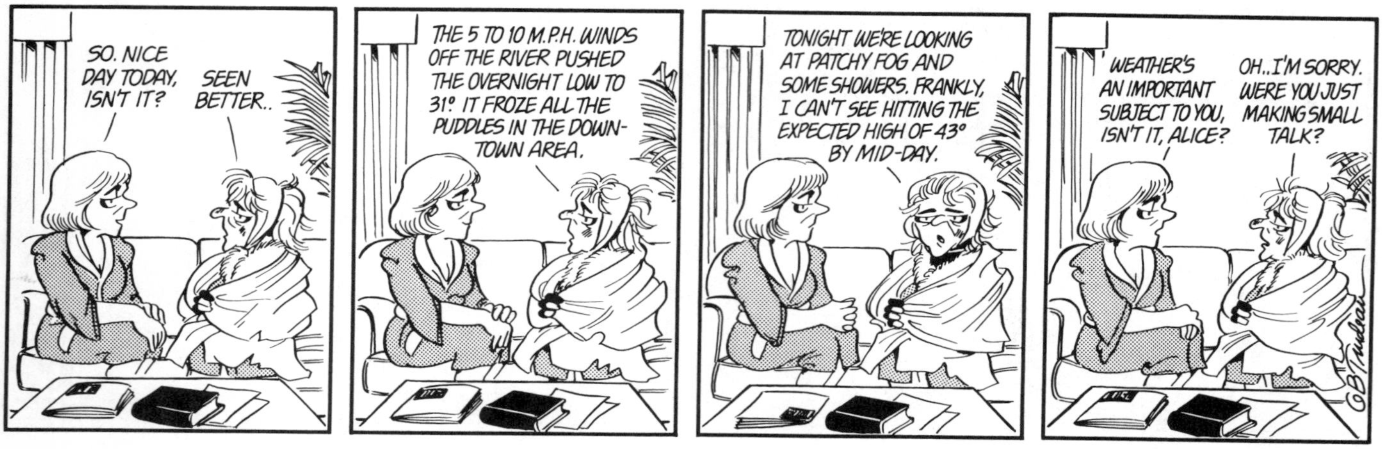
SO. NICE DAY TODAY, ISN'T IT?
SEEN BETTER..
THE 5 TO 10 M.P.H. WINDS OFF THE RIVER PUSHED THE OVERNIGHT LOW TO 31°. IT FROZE ALL THE PUDDLES IN THE DOWN-TOWN AREA.
TONIGHT WE'RE LOOKING AT PATCHY FOG AND SOME SHOWERS. FRANKLY, I CAN'T SEE HITTING THE EXPECTED HIGH OF 43° BY MID-DAY.
WEATHER'S AN IMPORTANT SUBJECT TO YOU, ISN'T IT, ALICE?
OH..I'M SORRY. WERE YOU JUST MAKING SMALL TALK?
©B Trudeau

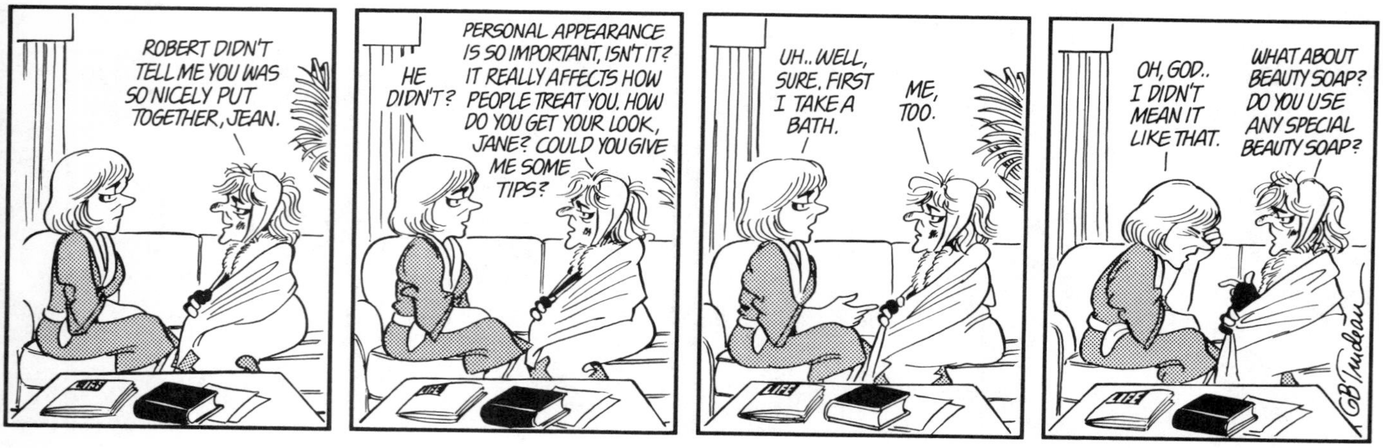
ROBERT DIDN'T TELL ME YOU WAS SO NICELY PUT TOGETHER, JEAN.
HE DIDN'T?
PERSONAL APPEARANCE IS SO IMPORTANT, ISN'T IT? IT REALLY AFFECTS HOW PEOPLE TREAT YOU. HOW DO YOU GET YOUR LOOK, JANE? COULD YOU GIVE ME SOME TIPS?
UH..WELL, SURE. FIRST I TAKE A BATH.
ME, TOO.
OH, GOD.. I DIDN'T MEAN IT LIKE THAT.
WHAT ABOUT BEAUTY SOAP? DO YOU USE ANY SPECIAL BEAUTY SOAP?
©B Trudeau

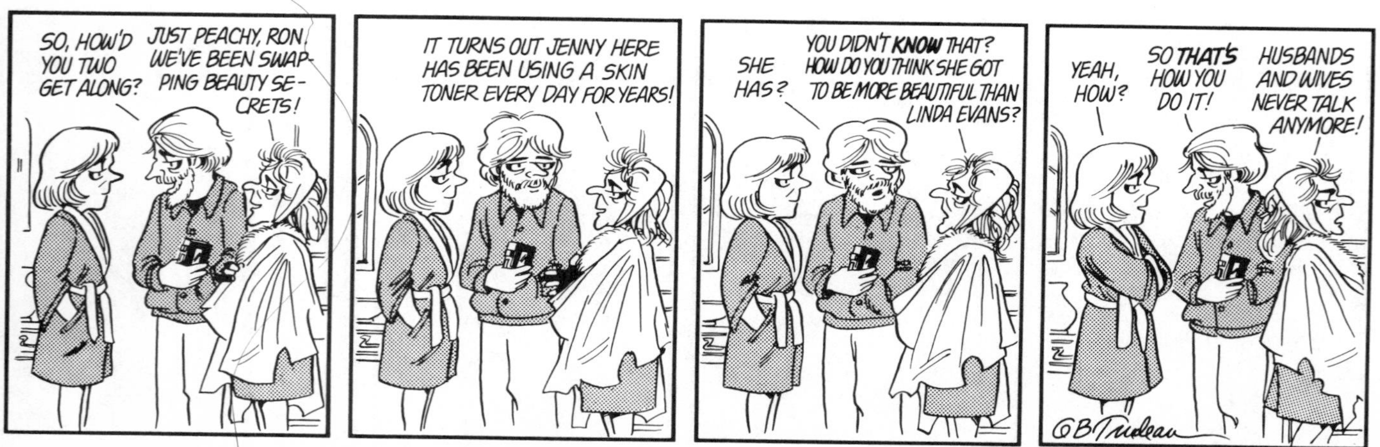
SO, HOW'D YOU TWO GET ALONG?
JUST PEACHY, RON. WE'VE BEEN SWAP-PING BEAUTY SE-CRETS!
IT TURNS OUT JENNY HERE HAS BEEN USING A SKIN TONER EVERY DAY FOR YEARS!
SHE HAS?
YOU DIDN'T **KNOW** THAT? HOW DO YOU THINK SHE GOT TO BE MORE BEAUTIFUL THAN LINDA EVANS?
YEAH, HOW?
SO **THAT'S** HOW YOU DO IT!
HUSBANDS AND WIVES NEVER TALK ANYMORE!
©B Trudeau

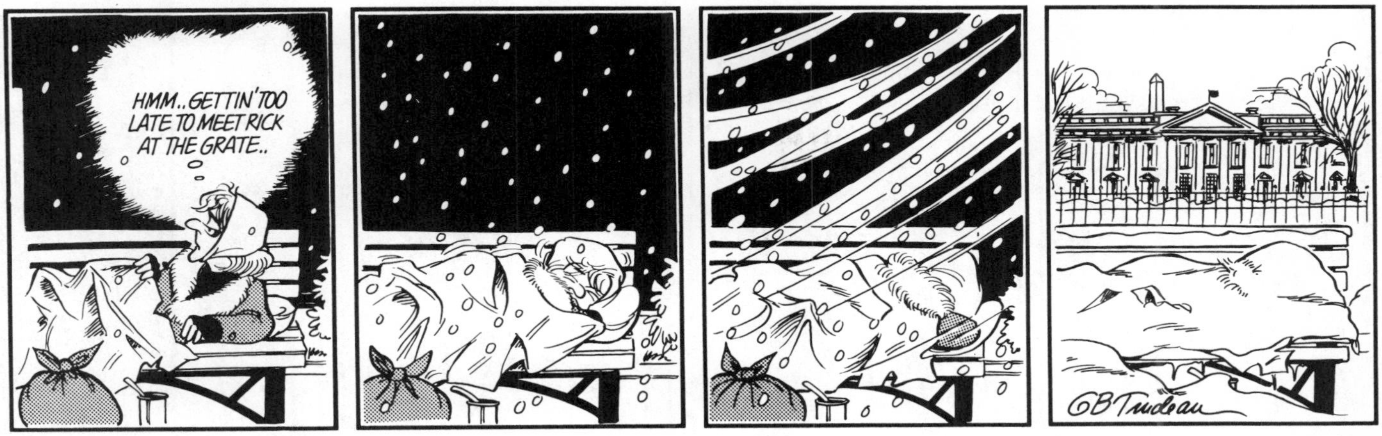
HMM.. GETTIN' TOO LATE TO MEET RICK AT THE GRATE..
GBTrudeau

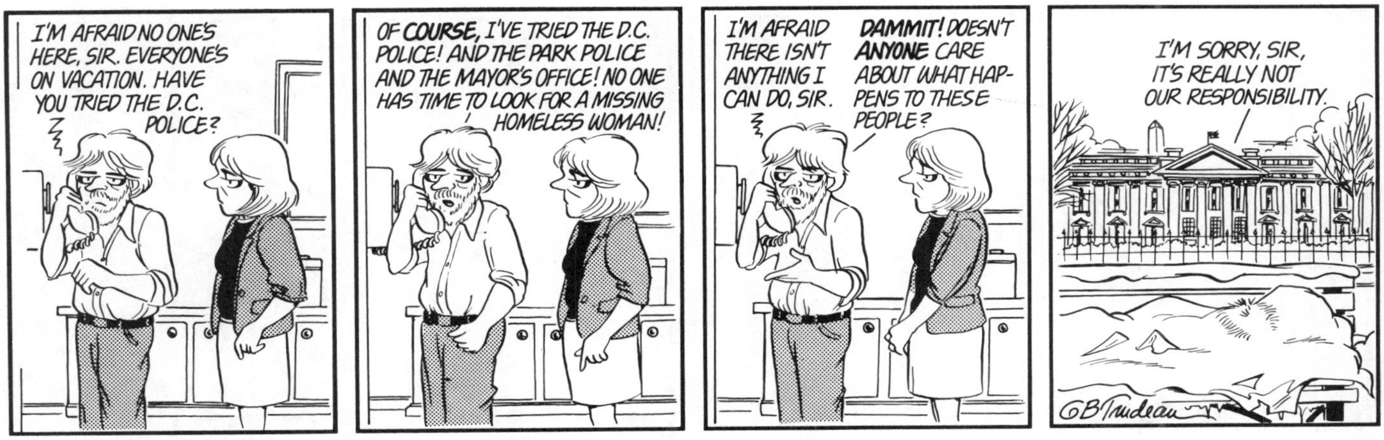
I'M AFRAID NO ONE'S HERE, SIR. EVERYONE'S ON VACATION. HAVE YOU TRIED THE D.C. POLICE?
OF COURSE, I'VE TRIED THE D.C. POLICE! AND THE PARK POLICE AND THE MAYOR'S OFFICE! NO ONE HAS TIME TO LOOK FOR A MISSING HOMELESS WOMAN!
I'M AFRAID THERE ISN'T ANYTHING I CAN DO, SIR.
DAMMIT! DOESN'T ANYONE CARE ABOUT WHAT HAPPENS TO THESE PEOPLE?
I'M SORRY, SIR, IT'S REALLY NOT OUR RESPONSIBILITY.
GBTrudeau

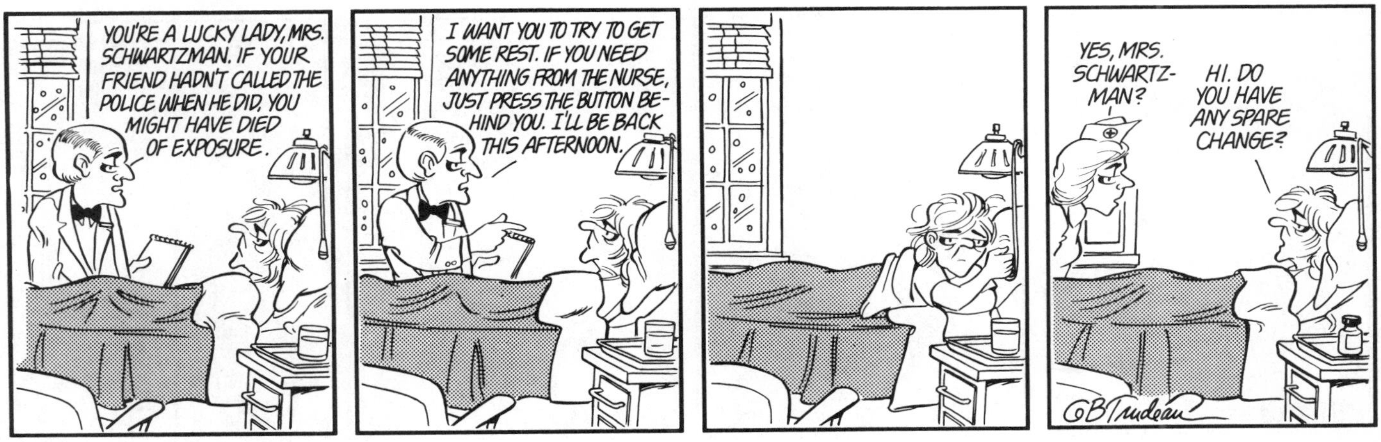
YOU'RE A LUCKY LADY, MRS. SCHWARTZMAN. IF YOUR FRIEND HADN'T CALLED THE POLICE WHEN HE DID, YOU MIGHT HAVE DIED OF EXPOSURE.
I WANT YOU TO TRY TO GET SOME REST. IF YOU NEED ANYTHING FROM THE NURSE, JUST PRESS THE BUTTON BEHIND YOU. I'LL BE BACK THIS AFTERNOON.
YES, MRS. SCHWARTZMAN?
HI. DO YOU HAVE ANY SPARE CHANGE?
GBTrudeau

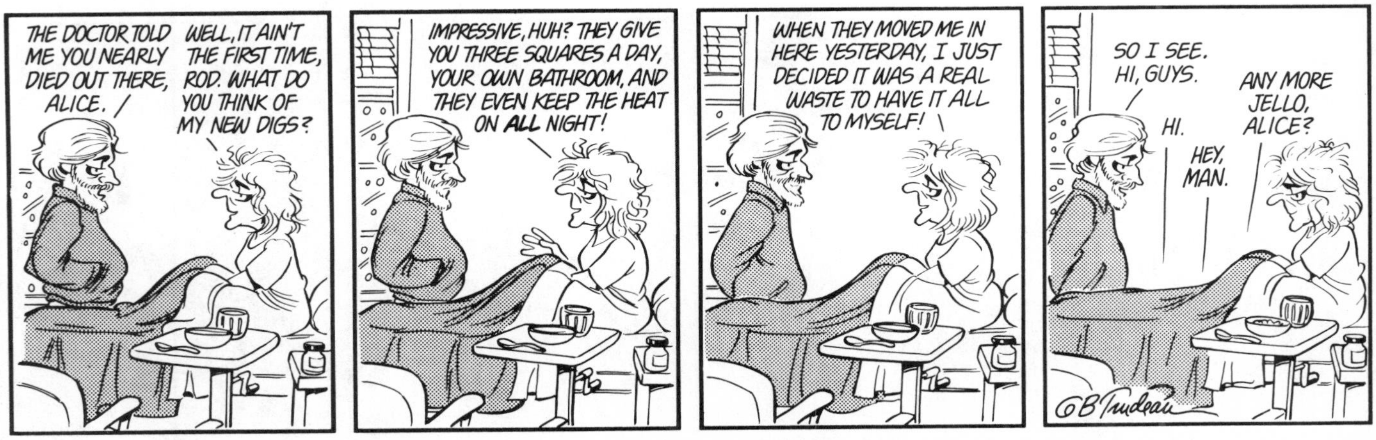
THE DOCTOR TOLD ME YOU NEARLY DIED OUT THERE, ALICE.
WELL, IT AIN'T THE FIRST TIME, ROD. WHAT DO YOU THINK OF MY NEW DIGS?
IMPRESSIVE, HUH? THEY GIVE YOU THREE SQUARES A DAY, YOUR OWN BATHROOM, AND THEY EVEN KEEP THE HEAT ON ALL NIGHT!
WHEN THEY MOVED ME IN HERE YESTERDAY, I JUST DECIDED IT WAS A REAL WASTE TO HAVE IT ALL TO MYSELF!
SO I SEE. HI, GUYS.
HI.
HEY, MAN.
ANY MORE JELLO, ALICE?
GBTrudeau

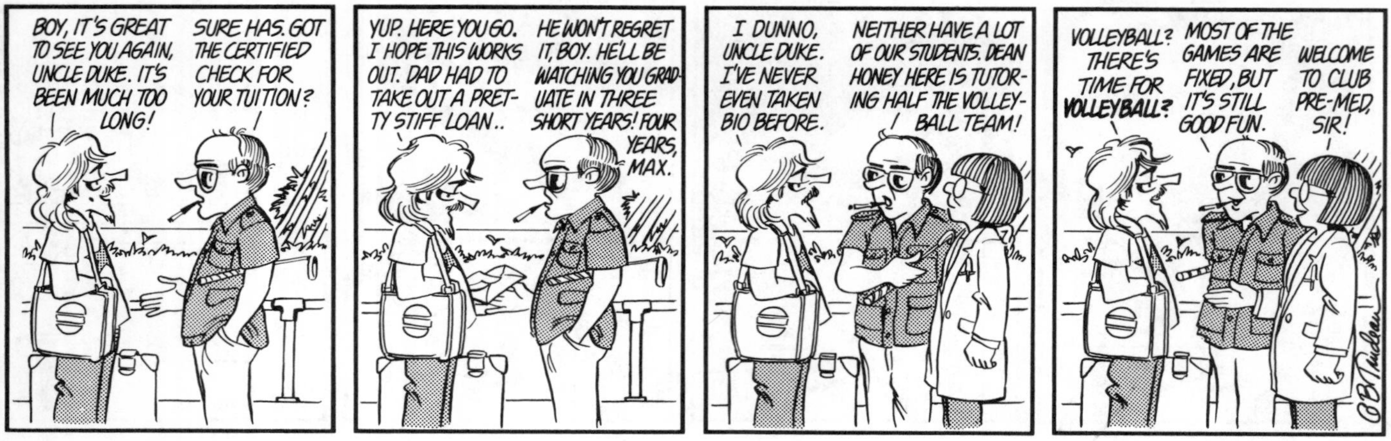
BOY, IT'S GREAT TO SEE YOU AGAIN, UNCLE DUKE. IT'S BEEN MUCH TOO LONG!
SURE HAS. GOT THE CERTIFIED CHECK FOR YOUR TUITION?
YUP. HERE YOU GO. I HOPE THIS WORKS OUT. DAD HAD TO TAKE OUT A PRETTY STIFF LOAN..
HE WON'T REGRET IT, BOY. HE'LL BE WATCHING YOU GRADUATE IN THREE SHORT YEARS! FOUR YEARS, MAX.
I DUNNO, UNCLE DUKE. I'VE NEVER EVEN TAKEN BIO BEFORE.
NEITHER HAVE A LOT OF OUR STUDENTS. DEAN HONEY HERE IS TUTORING HALF THE VOLLEYBALL TEAM!
VOLLEYBALL? THERE'S TIME FOR **VOLLEYBALL?**
MOST OF THE GAMES ARE FIXED, BUT IT'S STILL GOOD FUN.
WELCOME TO CLUB PRE-MED, SIR!

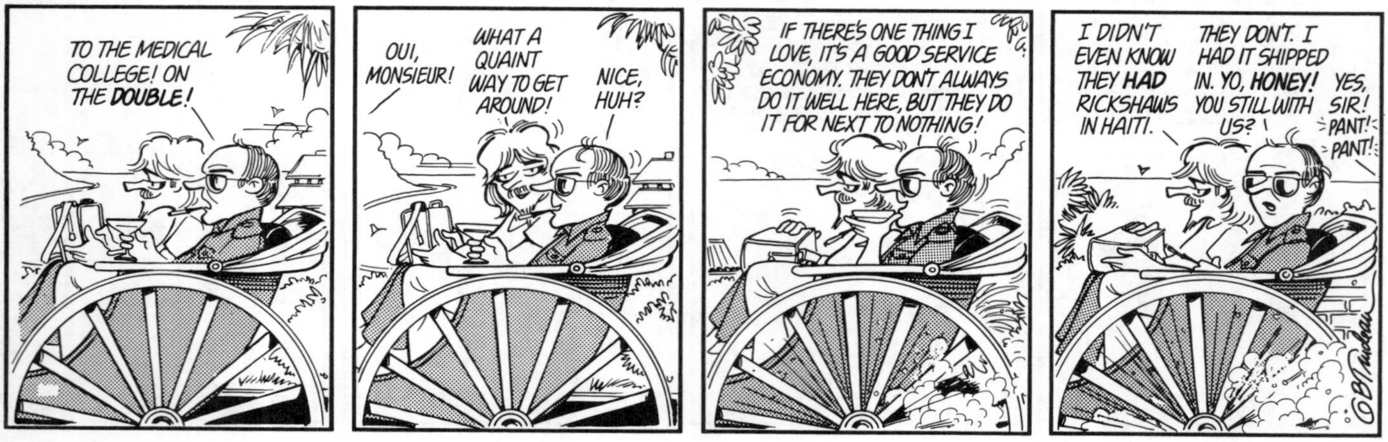
TO THE MEDICAL COLLEGE! ON THE **DOUBLE!**
OUI, MONSIEUR!
WHAT A QUAINT WAY TO GET AROUND!
NICE, HUH?
IF THERE'S ONE THING I LOVE, IT'S A GOOD SERVICE ECONOMY. THEY DON'T ALWAYS DO IT WELL HERE, BUT THEY DO IT FOR NEXT TO NOTHING!
I DIDN'T EVEN KNOW THEY **HAD** RICKSHAWS IN HAITI.
THEY DON'T. I HAD IT SHIPPED IN. YO, **HONEY!** YOU STILL WITH US?
YES, SIR! PANT! PANT!

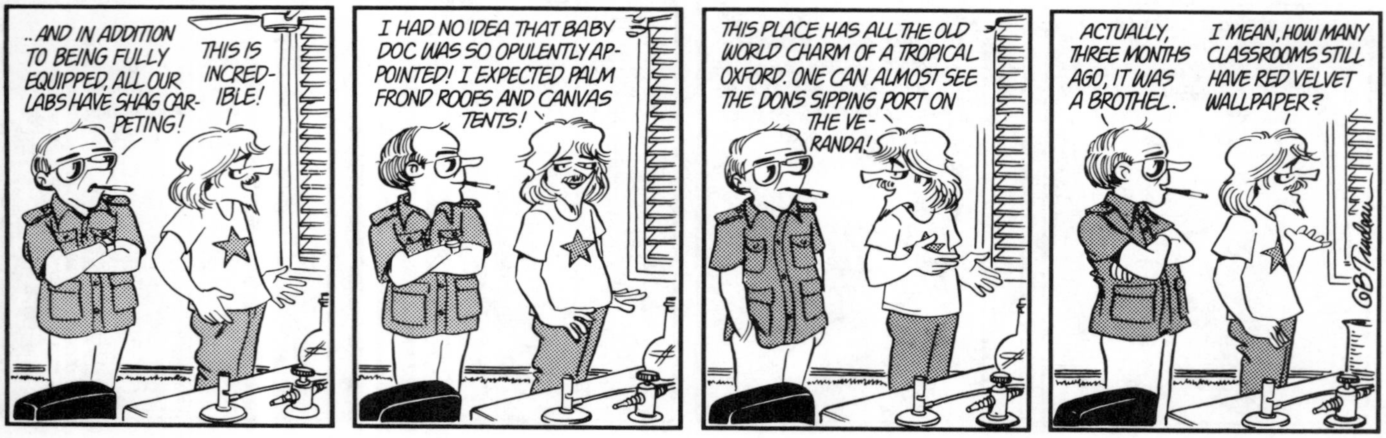
..AND IN ADDITION TO BEING FULLY EQUIPPED, ALL OUR LABS HAVE SHAG CARPETING!
THIS IS INCREDIBLE!
I HAD NO IDEA THAT BABY DOC WAS SO OPULENTLY APPOINTED! I EXPECTED PALM FROND ROOFS AND CANVAS TENTS!
THIS PLACE HAS ALL THE OLD WORLD CHARM OF A TROPICAL OXFORD. ONE CAN ALMOST SEE THE DONS SIPPING PORT ON THE VERANDA!
ACTUALLY, THREE MONTHS AGO, IT WAS A BROTHEL.
I MEAN, HOW MANY CLASSROOMS STILL HAVE RED VELVET WALLPAPER?

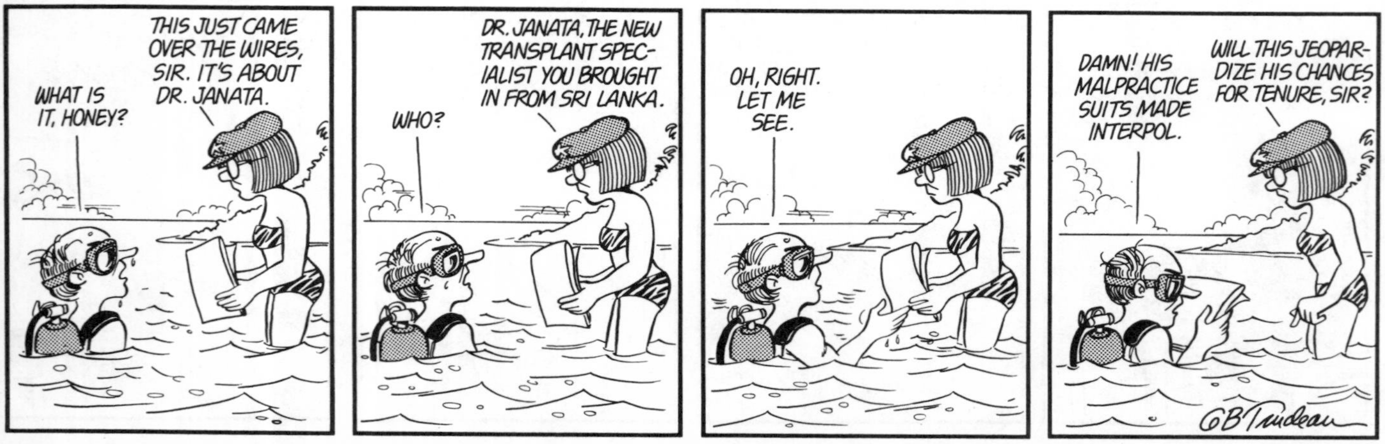
WHAT IS IT, HONEY?
THIS JUST CAME OVER THE WIRES, SIR. IT'S ABOUT DR. JANATA.
WHO?
DR. JANATA, THE NEW TRANSPLANT SPECIALIST YOU BROUGHT IN FROM SRI LANKA.
OH, RIGHT. LET ME SEE.
DAMN! HIS MALPRACTICE SUITS MADE INTERPOL.
WILL THIS JEOPARDIZE HIS CHANCES FOR TENURE, SIR?

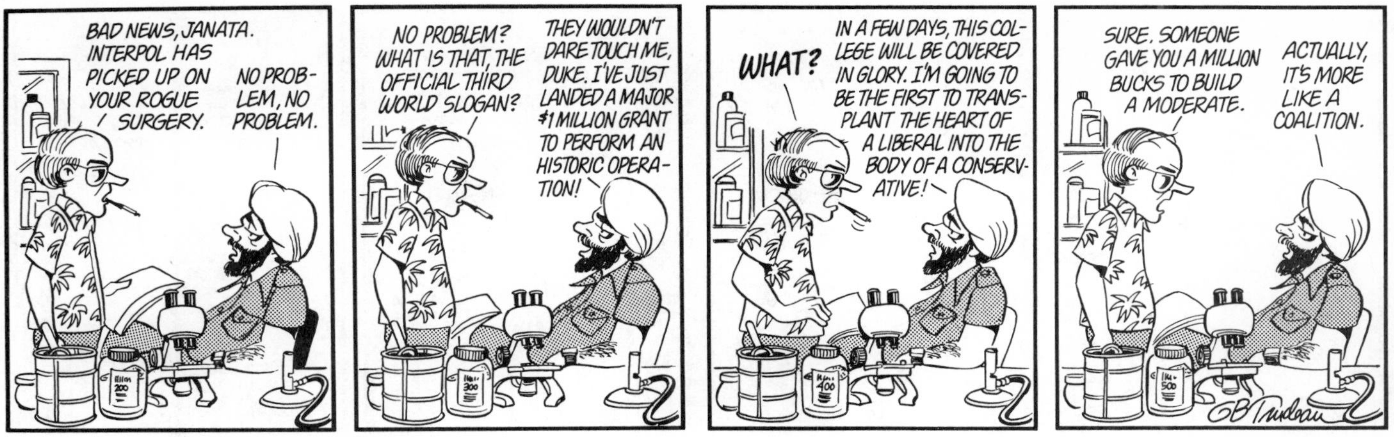
BAD NEWS, JANATA. INTERPOL HAS PICKED UP ON YOUR ROGUE SURGERY.
NO PROBLEM, NO PROBLEM.
NO PROBLEM? WHAT IS THAT, THE OFFICIAL THIRD WORLD SLOGAN?
THEY WOULDN'T DARE TOUCH ME, DUKE. I'VE JUST LANDED A MAJOR $1 MILLION GRANT TO PERFORM AN HISTORIC OPERATION!
WHAT?
IN A FEW DAYS, THIS COLLEGE WILL BE COVERED IN GLORY. I'M GOING TO BE THE FIRST TO TRANSPLANT THE HEART OF A LIBERAL INTO THE BODY OF A CONSERVATIVE!
SURE. SOMEONE GAVE YOU A MILLION BUCKS TO BUILD A MODERATE.
ACTUALLY, IT'S MORE LIKE A COALITION.

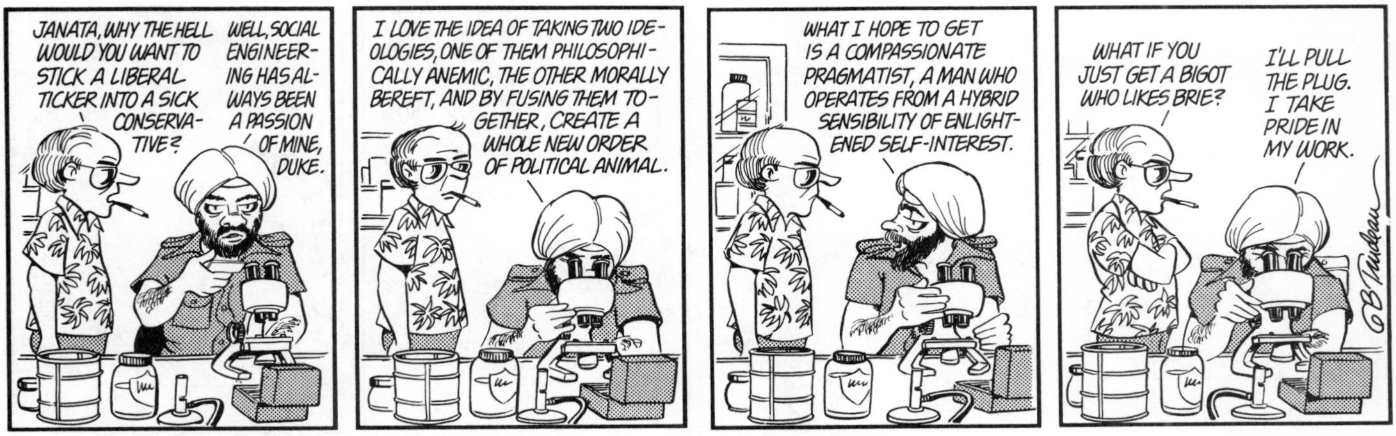
JANATA, WHY THE HELL WOULD YOU WANT TO STICK A LIBERAL TICKER INTO A SICK CONSERVATIVE?
WELL, SOCIAL ENGINEERING HAS ALWAYS BEEN A PASSION OF MINE, DUKE.
I LOVE THE IDEA OF TAKING TWO IDEOLOGIES, ONE OF THEM PHILOSOPHICALLY ANEMIC, THE OTHER MORALLY BEREFT, AND BY FUSING THEM TOGETHER, CREATE A WHOLE NEW ORDER OF POLITICAL ANIMAL.
WHAT I HOPE TO GET IS A COMPASSIONATE PRAGMATIST, A MAN WHO OPERATES FROM A HYBRID SENSIBILITY OF ENLIGHTENED SELF-INTEREST.
WHAT IF YOU JUST GET A BIGOT WHO LIKES BRIE?
I'LL PULL THE PLUG. I TAKE PRIDE IN MY WORK.

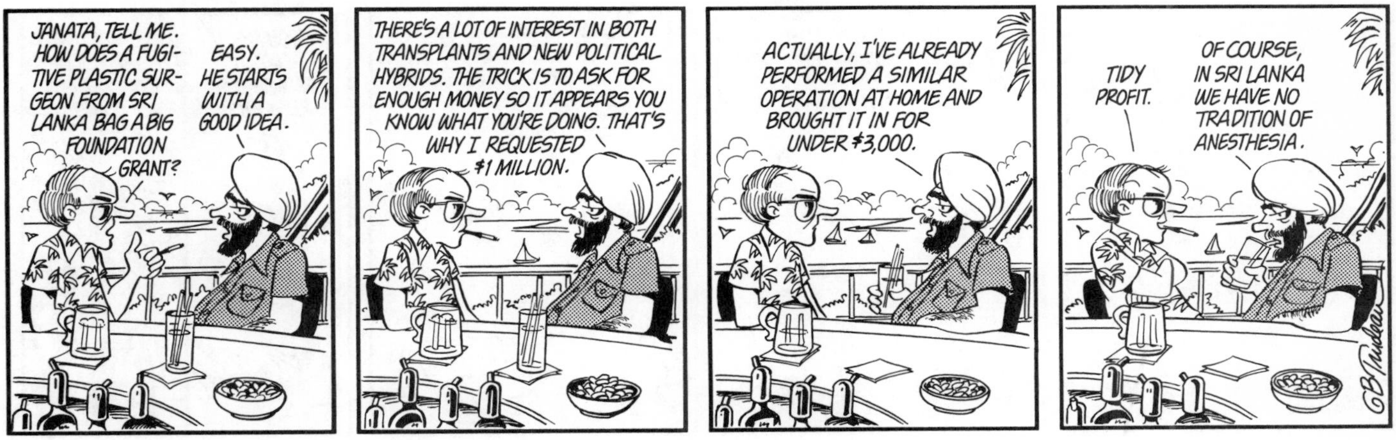
JANATA, TELL ME. HOW DOES A FUGITIVE PLASTIC SURGEON FROM SRI LANKA BAG A BIG FOUNDATION GRANT?
EASY. HE STARTS WITH A GOOD IDEA.
THERE'S A LOT OF INTEREST IN BOTH TRANSPLANTS AND NEW POLITICAL HYBRIDS. THE TRICK IS TO ASK FOR ENOUGH MONEY SO IT APPEARS YOU KNOW WHAT YOU'RE DOING. THAT'S WHY I REQUESTED $1 MILLION.
ACTUALLY, I'VE ALREADY PERFORMED A SIMILAR OPERATION AT HOME AND BROUGHT IT IN FOR UNDER $3,000.
TIDY PROFIT.
OF COURSE, IN SRI LANKA WE HAVE NO TRADITION OF ANESTHESIA.

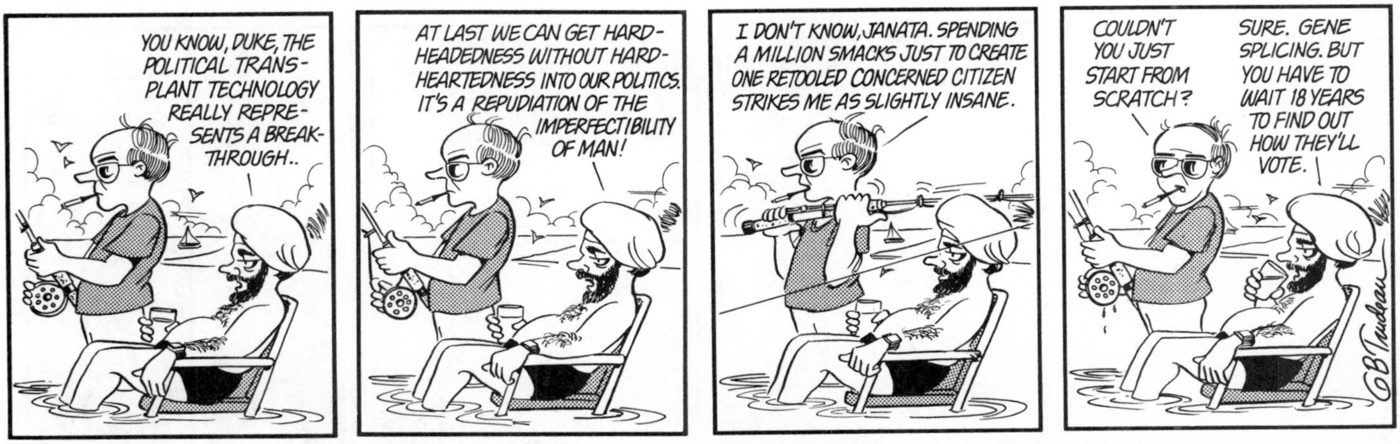
YOU KNOW, DUKE, THE POLITICAL TRANSPLANT TECHNOLOGY REALLY REPRESENTS A BREAKTHROUGH..
AT LAST WE CAN GET HARD-HEADEDNESS WITHOUT HARD-HEARTEDNESS INTO OUR POLITICS. IT'S A REPUDIATION OF THE IMPERFECTIBILITY OF MAN!
I DON'T KNOW, JANATA. SPENDING A MILLION SMACKS JUST TO CREATE ONE RETOOLED CONCERNED CITIZEN STRIKES ME AS SLIGHTLY INSANE.
COULDN'T YOU JUST START FROM SCRATCH?
SURE. GENE SPLICING. BUT YOU HAVE TO WAIT 18 YEARS TO FIND OUT HOW THEY'LL VOTE.

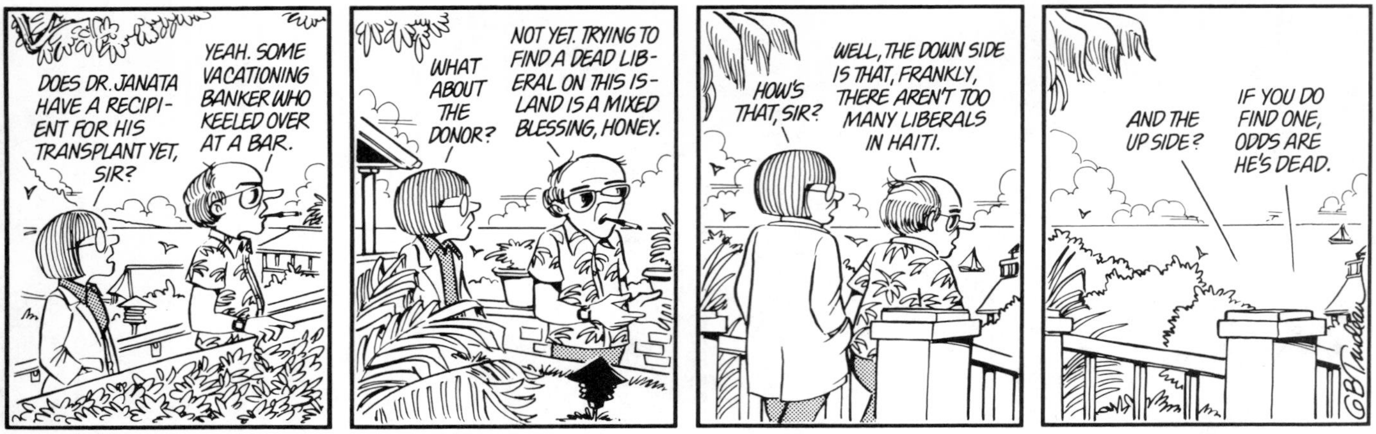
DOES DR. JANATA HAVE A RECIPIENT FOR HIS TRANSPLANT YET, SIR?
YEAH. SOME VACATIONING BANKER WHO KEELED OVER AT A BAR.
WHAT ABOUT THE DONOR?
NOT YET. TRYING TO FIND A DEAD LIBERAL ON THIS ISLAND IS A MIXED BLESSING, HONEY.
HOW'S THAT, SIR?
WELL, THE DOWN SIDE IS THAT, FRANKLY, THERE AREN'T TOO MANY LIBERALS IN HAITI.
AND THE UP SIDE?
IF YOU DO FIND ONE, ODDS ARE HE'S DEAD.

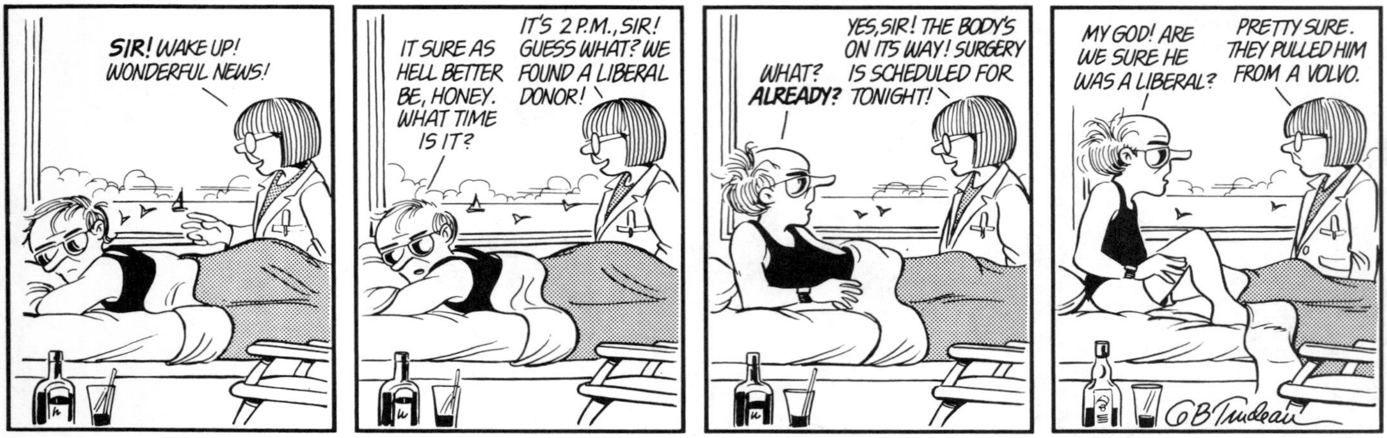
SIR! WAKE UP! WONDERFUL NEWS!
IT SURE AS HELL BETTER BE, HONEY. WHAT TIME IS IT?
IT'S 2 P.M., SIR! GUESS WHAT? WE FOUND A LIBERAL DONOR!
WHAT? ALREADY?
YES, SIR! THE BODY'S ON ITS WAY! SURGERY IS SCHEDULED FOR TONIGHT!
MY GOD! ARE WE SURE HE WAS A LIBERAL?
PRETTY SURE. THEY PULLED HIM FROM A VOLVO.

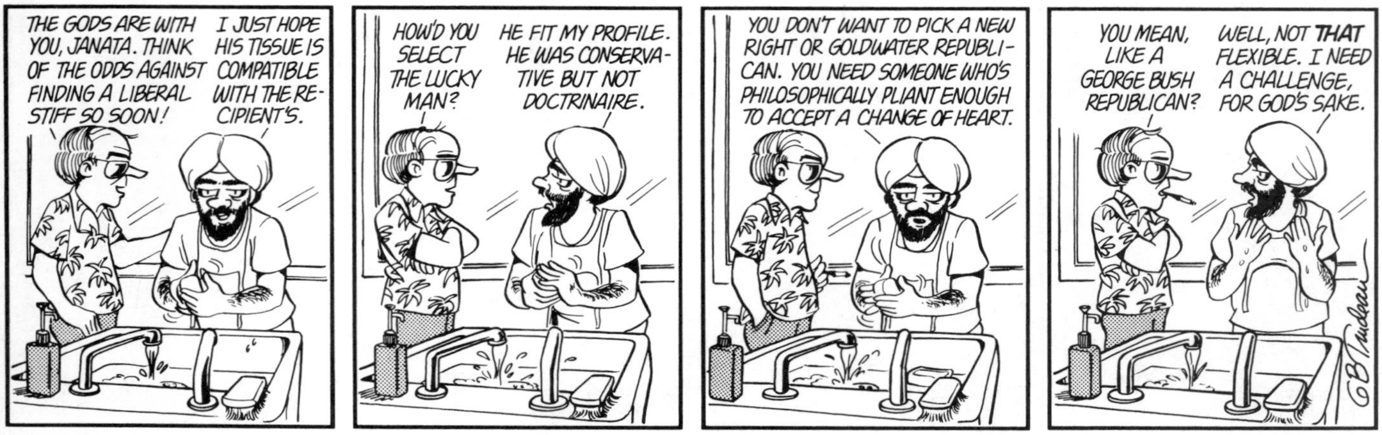
THE GODS ARE WITH YOU, JANATA. THINK OF THE ODDS AGAINST FINDING A LIBERAL STIFF SO SOON!
I JUST HOPE HIS TISSUE IS COMPATIBLE WITH THE RECIPIENT'S.
HOW'D YOU SELECT THE LUCKY MAN?
HE FIT MY PROFILE. HE WAS CONSERVATIVE BUT NOT DOCTRINAIRE.
YOU DON'T WANT TO PICK A NEW RIGHT OR GOLDWATER REPUBLICAN. YOU NEED SOMEONE WHO'S PHILOSOPHICALLY PLIANT ENOUGH TO ACCEPT A CHANGE OF HEART.
YOU MEAN, LIKE A GEORGE BUSH REPUBLICAN?
WELL, NOT THAT FLEXIBLE. I NEED A CHALLENGE, FOR GOD'S SAKE.

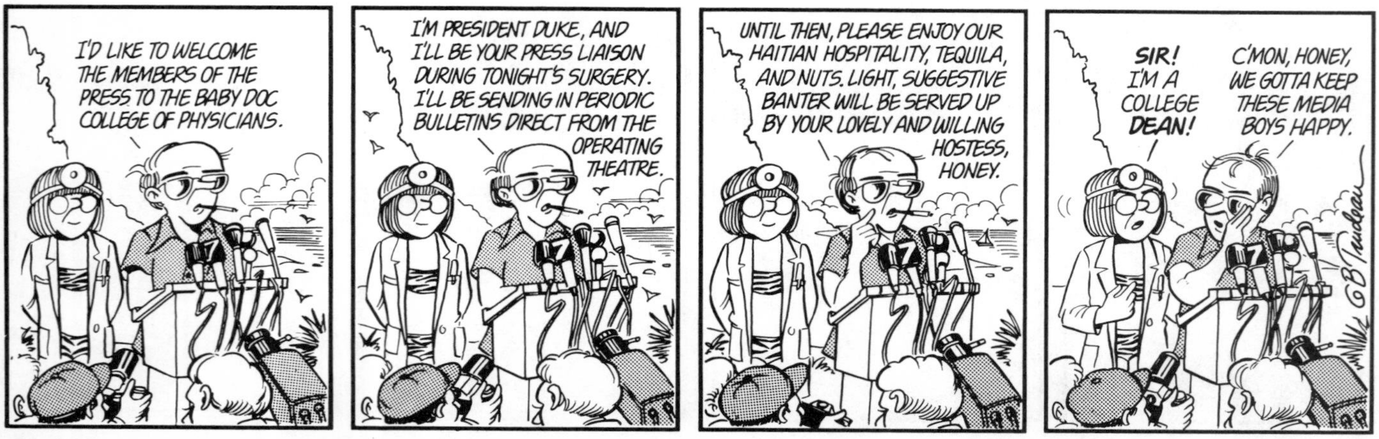
I'D LIKE TO WELCOME THE MEMBERS OF THE PRESS TO THE BABY DOC COLLEGE OF PHYSICIANS.
I'M PRESIDENT DUKE, AND I'LL BE YOUR PRESS LIAISON DURING TONIGHT'S SURGERY. I'LL BE SENDING IN PERIODIC BULLETINS DIRECT FROM THE OPERATING THEATRE.
UNTIL THEN, PLEASE ENJOY OUR HAITIAN HOSPITALITY, TEQUILA, AND NUTS. LIGHT, SUGGESTIVE BANTER WILL BE SERVED UP BY YOUR LOVELY AND WILLING HOSTESS, HONEY.
SIR! I'M A COLLEGE DEAN!
C'MON, HONEY, WE GOTTA KEEP THESE MEDIA BOYS HAPPY.

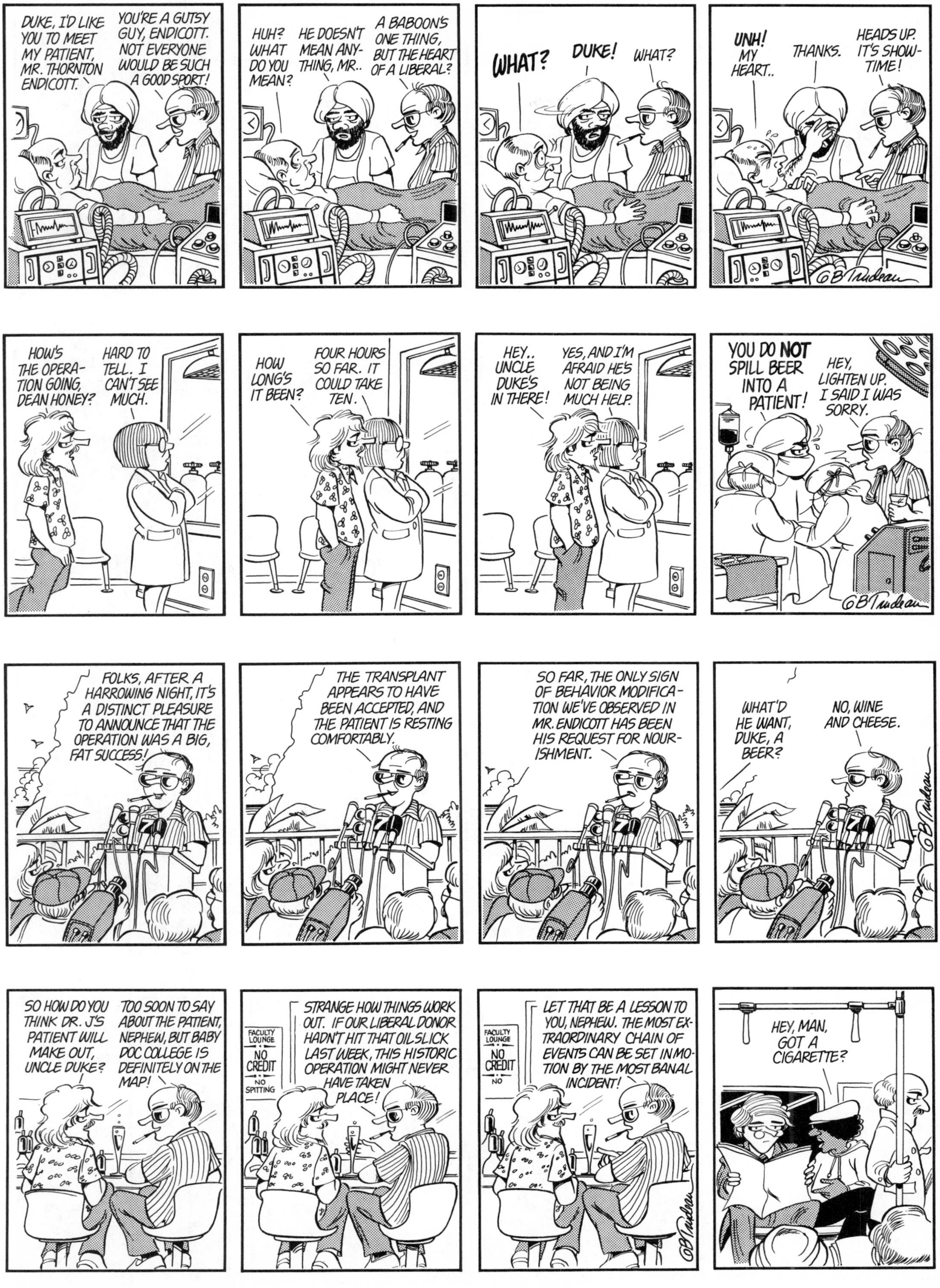
DUKE, I'D LIKE YOU TO MEET MY PATIENT, MR. THORNTON ENDICOTT.
YOU'RE A GUTSY GUY, ENDICOTT. NOT EVERYONE WOULD BE SUCH A GOOD SPORT!
HUH? WHAT DO YOU MEAN?
HE DOESN'T MEAN ANYTHING, MR..
A BABOON'S ONE THING, BUT THE HEART OF A LIBERAL?
WHAT?
DUKE!
WHAT?
UNH! MY HEART..
THANKS.
HEADS UP. IT'S SHOW-TIME!
G.B. Trudeau
HOW'S THE OPERATION GOING, DEAN HONEY?
HARD TO TELL. I CAN'T SEE MUCH.
HOW LONG'S IT BEEN?
FOUR HOURS SO FAR. IT COULD TAKE TEN.
HEY.. UNCLE DUKE'S IN THERE!
YES, AND I'M AFRAID HE'S NOT BEING MUCH HELP.
YOU DO NOT SPILL BEER INTO A PATIENT!
HEY, LIGHTEN UP. I SAID I WAS SORRY.
G.B. Trudeau
FOLKS, AFTER A HARROWING NIGHT, IT'S A DISTINCT PLEASURE TO ANNOUNCE THAT THE OPERATION WAS A BIG, FAT SUCCESS!
THE TRANSPLANT APPEARS TO HAVE BEEN ACCEPTED, AND THE PATIENT IS RESTING COMFORTABLY.
SO FAR, THE ONLY SIGN OF BEHAVIOR MODIFICATION WE'VE OBSERVED IN MR. ENDICOTT HAS BEEN HIS REQUEST FOR NOURISHMENT.
WHAT'D HE WANT, DUKE, A BEER?
NO, WINE AND CHEESE.
G.B. Trudeau
SO HOW DO YOU THINK DR. J'S PATIENT WILL MAKE OUT, UNCLE DUKE?
TOO SOON TO SAY ABOUT THE PATIENT, NEPHEW, BUT BABY DOC COLLEGE IS DEFINITELY ON THE MAP!
FACULTY LOUNGE
NO CREDIT
NO SPITTING
STRANGE HOW THINGS WORK OUT. IF OUR LIBERAL DONOR HADN'T HIT THAT OIL SLICK LAST WEEK, THIS HISTORIC OPERATION MIGHT NEVER HAVE TAKEN PLACE!
LET THAT BE A LESSON TO YOU, NEPHEW. THE MOST EXTRAORDINARY CHAIN OF EVENTS CAN BE SET IN MOTION BY THE MOST BANAL INCIDENT!
G.B. Trudeau
HEY, MAN, GOT A CIGARETTE?

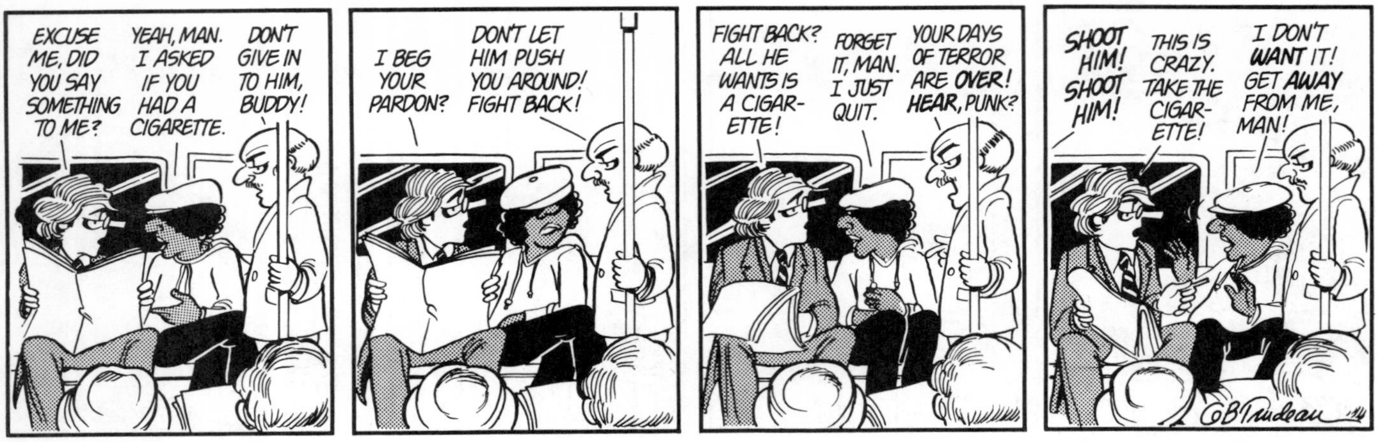
EXCUSE ME, DID YOU SAY SOMETHING TO ME?
YEAH, MAN. I ASKED IF YOU HAD A CIGARETTE.
DON'T GIVE IN TO HIM, BUDDY!
I BEG YOUR PARDON?
DON'T LET HIM PUSH YOU AROUND! FIGHT BACK!
FIGHT BACK? ALL HE WANTS IS A CIGARETTE!
FORGET IT, MAN. I JUST QUIT.
YOUR DAYS OF TERROR ARE OVER! HEAR, PUNK?
SHOOT HIM! SHOOT HIM!
THIS IS CRAZY. TAKE THE CIGARETTE!
I DON'T WANT IT! GET AWAY FROM ME, MAN!
GB Trudeau

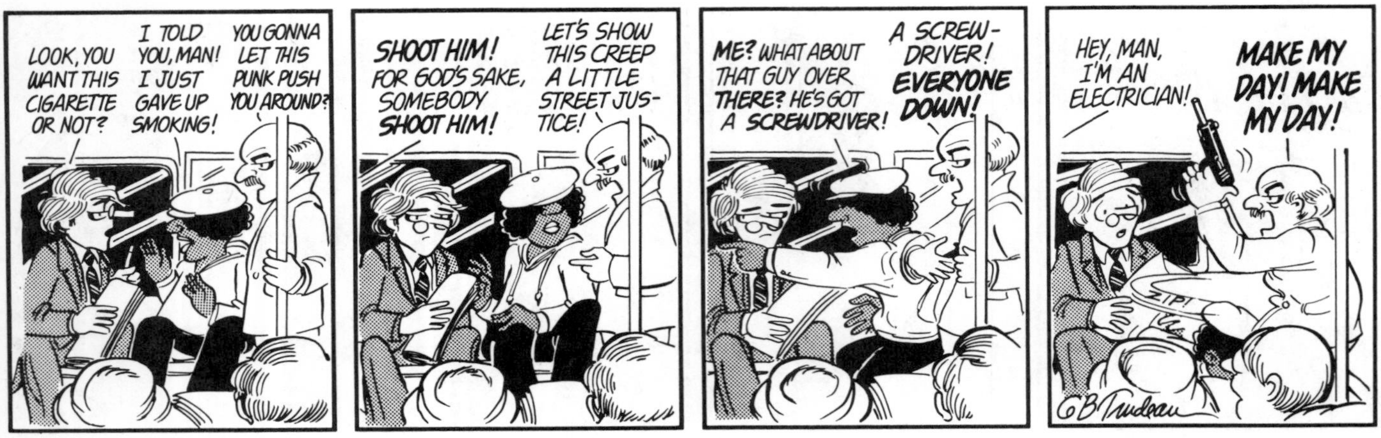
LOOK, YOU WANT THIS CIGARETTE OR NOT?
I TOLD YOU, MAN! I JUST GAVE UP SMOKING!
YOU GONNA LET THIS PUNK PUSH YOU AROUND?
SHOOT HIM! FOR GOD'S SAKE, SOMEBODY SHOOT HIM!
LET'S SHOW THIS CREEP A LITTLE STREET JUSTICE!
ME? WHAT ABOUT THAT GUY OVER THERE? HE'S GOT A SCREWDRIVER!
A SCREWDRIVER! EVERYONE DOWN!
HEY, MAN, I'M AN ELECTRICIAN!
MAKE MY DAY! MAKE MY DAY!
ZIP!
GB Trudeau

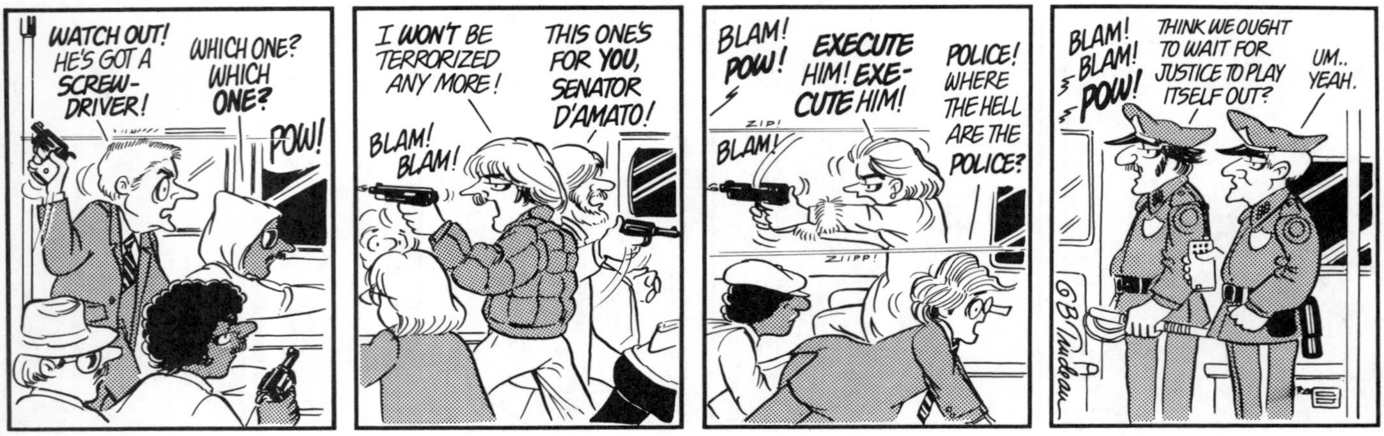
WATCH OUT! HE'S GOT A SCREWDRIVER!
WHICH ONE? WHICH ONE?
POW!
I WON'T BE TERRORIZED ANY MORE!
THIS ONE'S FOR YOU, SENATOR D'AMATO!
BLAM! BLAM!
BLAM! POW!
EXECUTE HIM! EXECUTE HIM!
POLICE! WHERE THE HELL ARE THE POLICE?
ZIP!
BLAM!
ZIPP!
BLAM! BLAM! POW!
THINK WE OUGHT TO WAIT FOR JUSTICE TO PLAY ITSELF OUT?
UM.. YEAH.
GB Trudeau

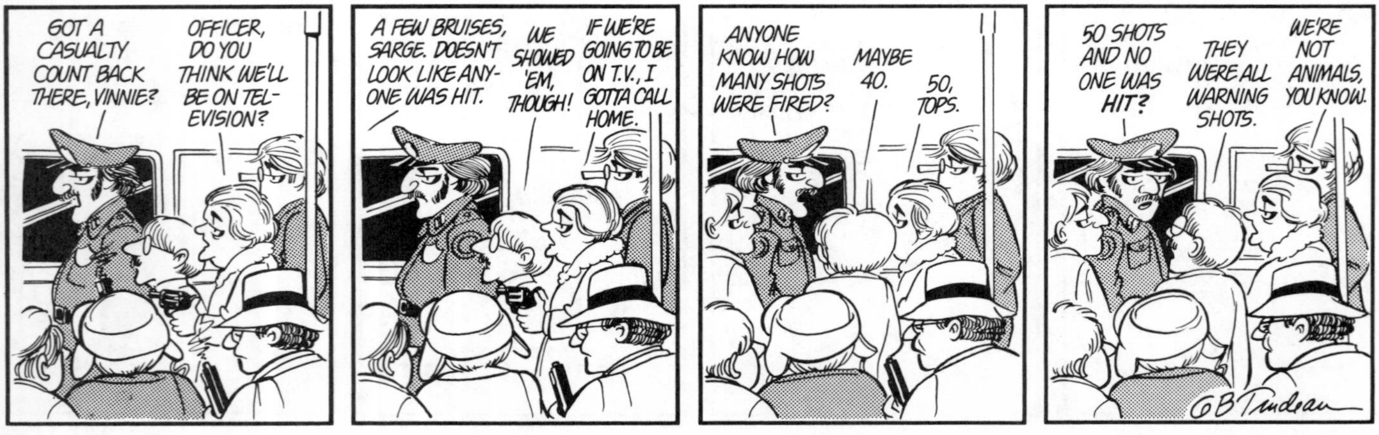
GOT A CASUALTY COUNT BACK THERE, VINNIE?
OFFICER, DO YOU THINK WE'LL BE ON TELEVISION?
A FEW BRUISES, SARGE. DOESN'T LOOK LIKE ANYONE WAS HIT.
WE SHOWED 'EM, THOUGH!
IF WE'RE GOING TO BE ON T.V., I GOTTA CALL HOME.
ANYONE KNOW HOW MANY SHOTS WERE FIRED?
MAYBE 40.
50, TOPS.
50 SHOTS AND NO ONE WAS HIT?
THEY WERE ALL WARNING SHOTS.
WE'RE NOT ANIMALS, YOU KNOW.
GB Trudeau

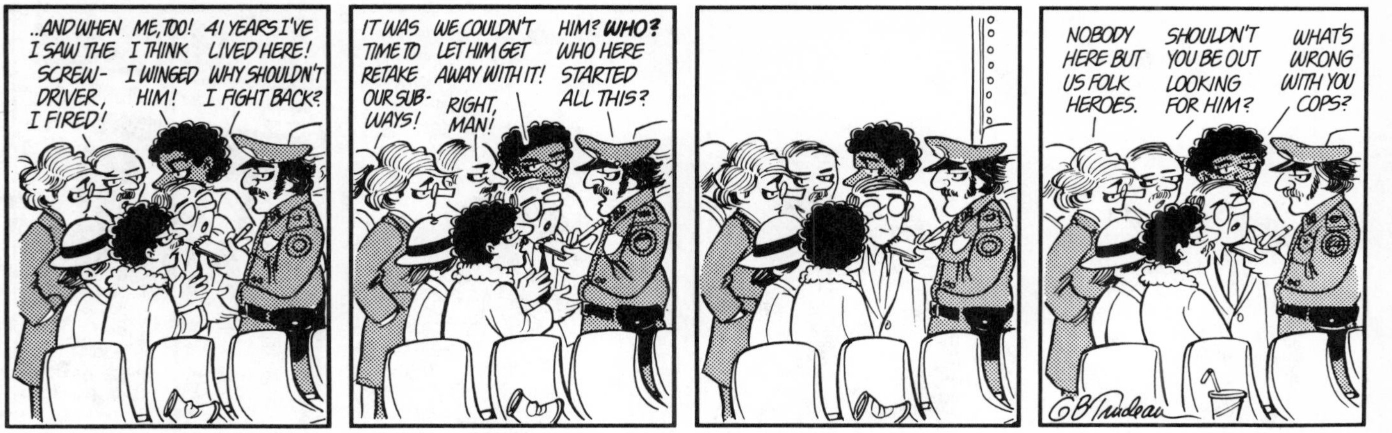
..AND WHEN I SAW THE SCREW-DRIVER, I FIRED!
ME, TOO! I THINK I WINGED HIM!
41 YEARS I'VE LIVED HERE! WHY SHOULDN'T I FIGHT BACK?
IT WAS TIME TO RETAKE OUR SUBWAYS!
WE COULDN'T LET HIM GET AWAY WITH IT!
RIGHT, MAN!
HIM? WHO? WHO HERE STARTED ALL THIS?
NOBODY HERE BUT US FOLK HEROES.
SHOULDN'T YOU BE OUT LOOKING FOR HIM?
WHAT'S WRONG WITH YOU COPS?
GB Trudeau

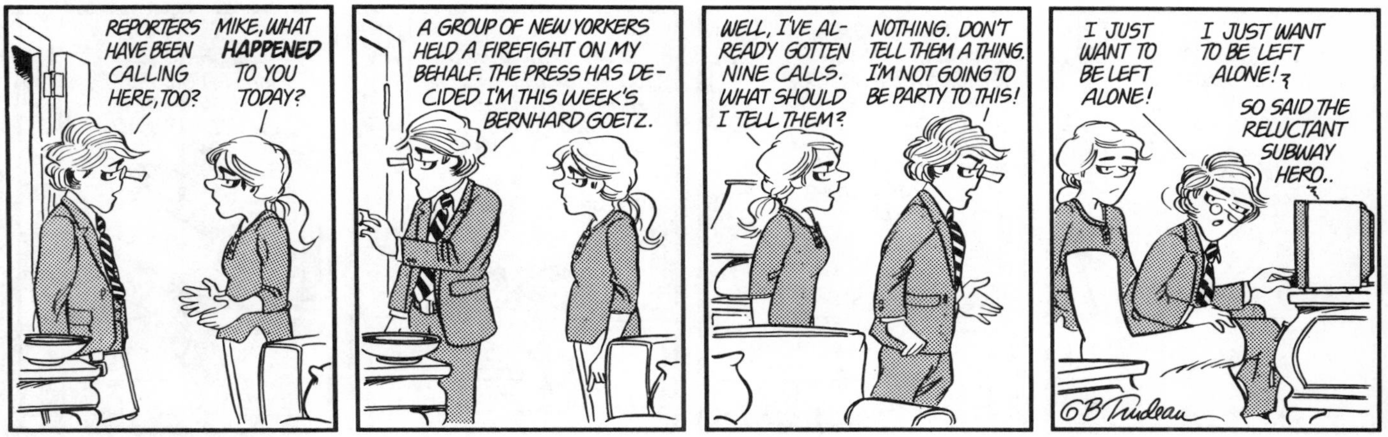
REPORTERS HAVE BEEN CALLING HERE, TOO?
MIKE, WHAT HAPPENED TO YOU TODAY?
A GROUP OF NEW YORKERS HELD A FIREFIGHT ON MY BEHALF. THE PRESS HAS DECIDED I'M THIS WEEK'S BERNHARD GOETZ.
WELL, I'VE ALREADY GOTTEN NINE CALLS. WHAT SHOULD I TELL THEM?
NOTHING. DON'T TELL THEM A THING. I'M NOT GOING TO BE PARTY TO THIS!
I JUST WANT TO BE LEFT ALONE!
I JUST WANT TO BE LEFT ALONE!
SO SAID THE RELUCTANT SUBWAY HERO..
GB Trudeau

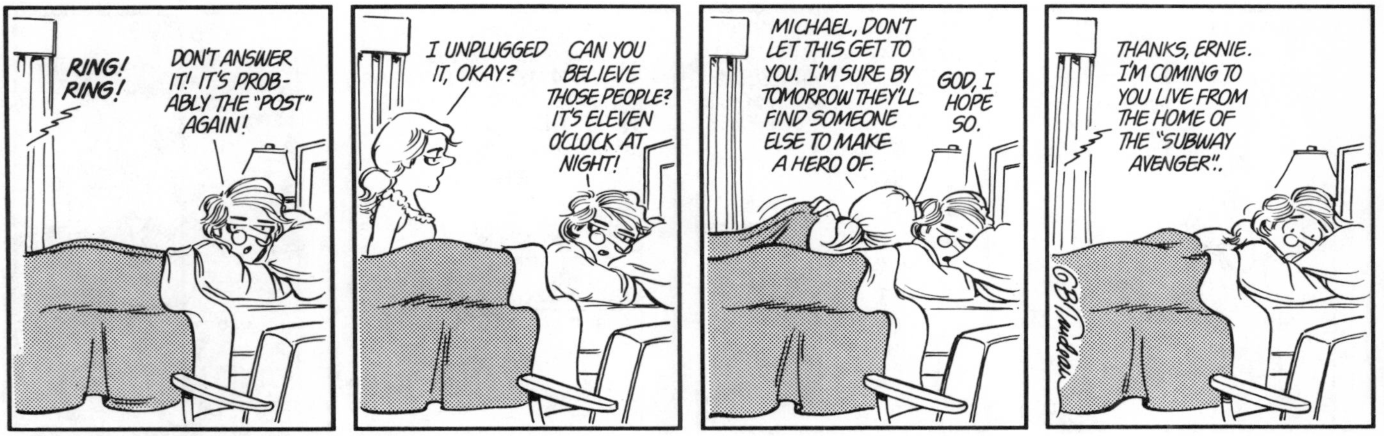
RING! RING!
DON'T ANSWER IT! IT'S PROBABLY THE "POST" AGAIN!
I UNPLUGGED IT, OKAY?
CAN YOU BELIEVE THOSE PEOPLE? IT'S ELEVEN O'CLOCK AT NIGHT!
MICHAEL, DON'T LET THIS GET TO YOU. I'M SURE BY TOMORROW THEY'LL FIND SOMEONE ELSE TO MAKE A HERO OF.
GOD, I HOPE SO.
THANKS, ERNIE. I'M COMING TO YOU LIVE FROM THE HOME OF THE "SUBWAY AVENGER".
GB Trudeau

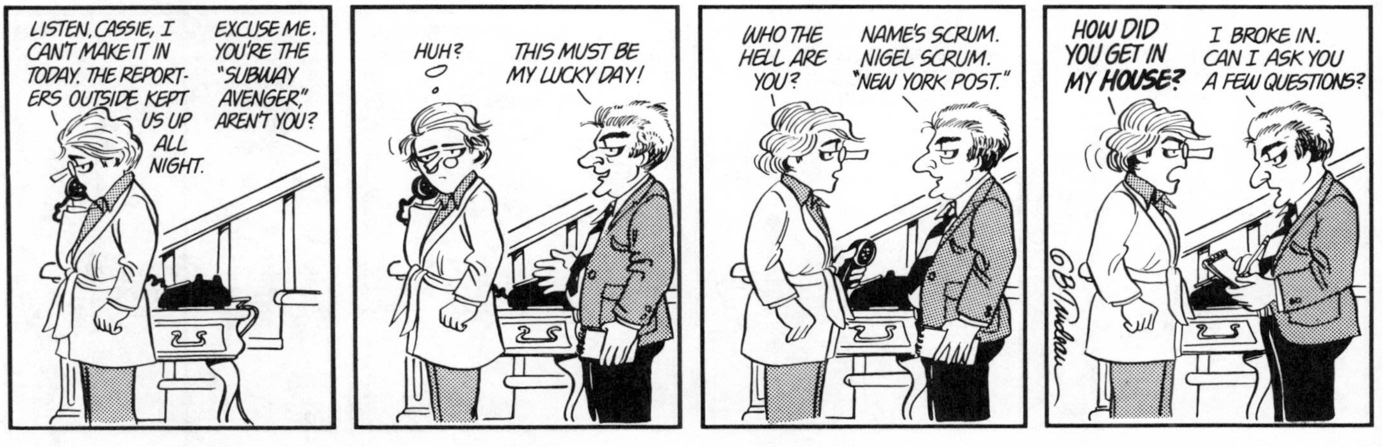
LISTEN, CASSIE, I CAN'T MAKE IT IN TODAY. THE REPORTERS OUTSIDE KEPT US UP ALL NIGHT.
EXCUSE ME. YOU'RE THE "SUBWAY AVENGER," AREN'T YOU?
HUH?
THIS MUST BE MY LUCKY DAY!
WHO THE HELL ARE YOU?
NAME'S SCRUM. NIGEL SCRUM. "NEW YORK POST."
HOW DID YOU GET IN MY HOUSE?
I BROKE IN. CAN I ASK YOU A FEW QUESTIONS?
GB Trudeau

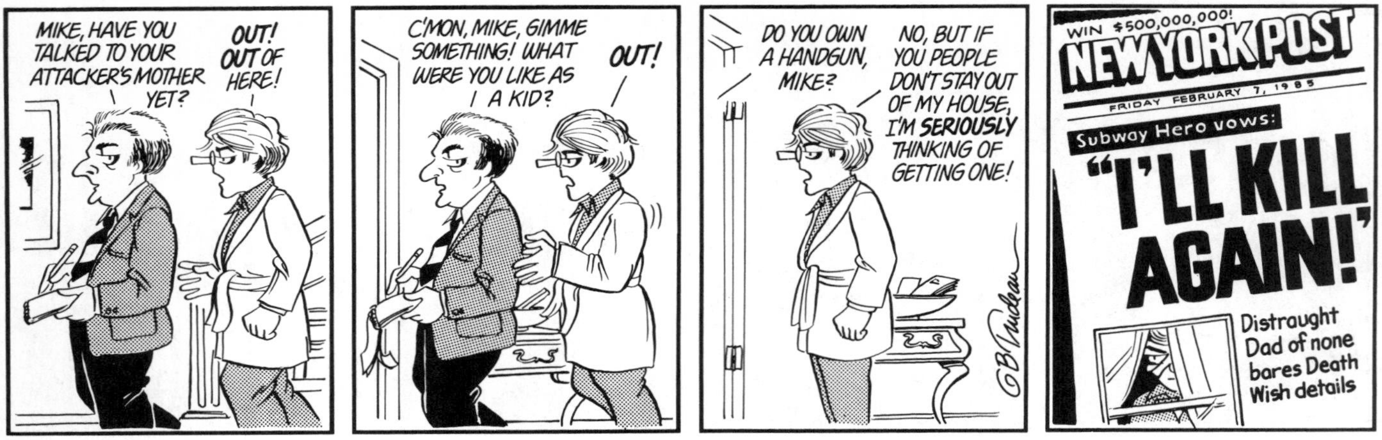
MIKE, HAVE YOU TALKED TO YOUR ATTACKER'S MOTHER YET?
OUT! OUT OF HERE!
C'MON, MIKE, GIMME SOMETHING! WHAT WERE YOU LIKE AS A KID?
OUT!
DO YOU OWN A HANDGUN, MIKE?
NO, BUT IF YOU PEOPLE DON'T STAY OUT OF MY HOUSE, I'M SERIOUSLY THINKING OF GETTING ONE!
©B Trudeau
WIN $500,000,000!
NEW YORK POST
FRIDAY FEBRUARY 7, 1985
Subway Hero vows:
"I'LL KILL AGAIN!"
Distraught Dad of none bares Death Wish details

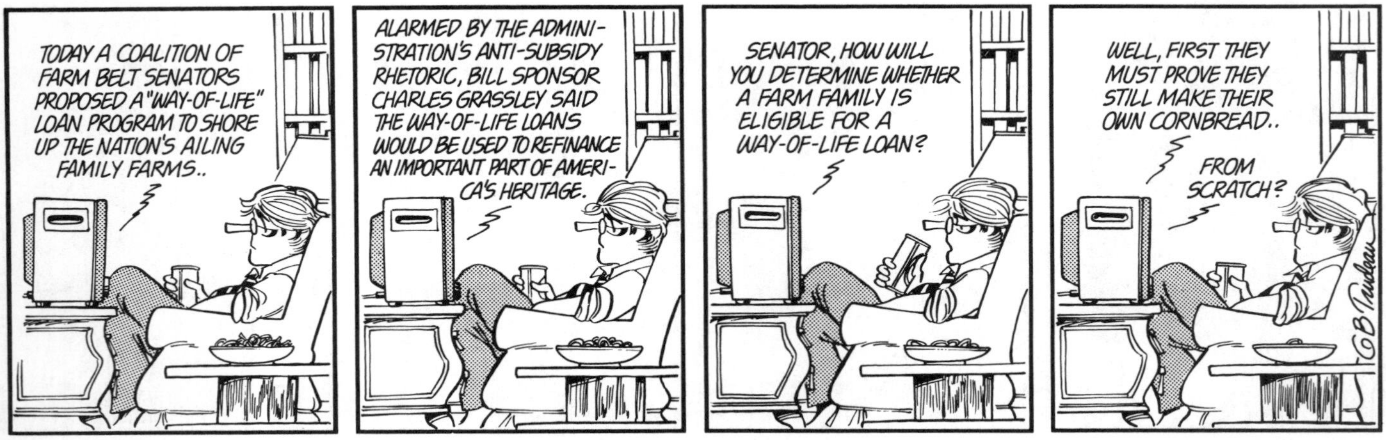
TODAY A COALITION OF FARM BELT SENATORS PROPOSED A "WAY-OF-LIFE" LOAN PROGRAM TO SHORE UP THE NATION'S AILING FAMILY FARMS..
ALARMED BY THE ADMINISTRATION'S ANTI-SUBSIDY RHETORIC, BILL SPONSOR CHARLES GRASSLEY SAID THE WAY-OF-LIFE LOANS WOULD BE USED TO REFINANCE AN IMPORTANT PART OF AMERICA'S HERITAGE.
SENATOR, HOW WILL YOU DETERMINE WHETHER A FARM FAMILY IS ELIGIBLE FOR A WAY-OF-LIFE LOAN?
WELL, FIRST THEY MUST PROVE THEY STILL MAKE THEIR OWN CORNBREAD..
FROM SCRATCH?
©B Trudeau

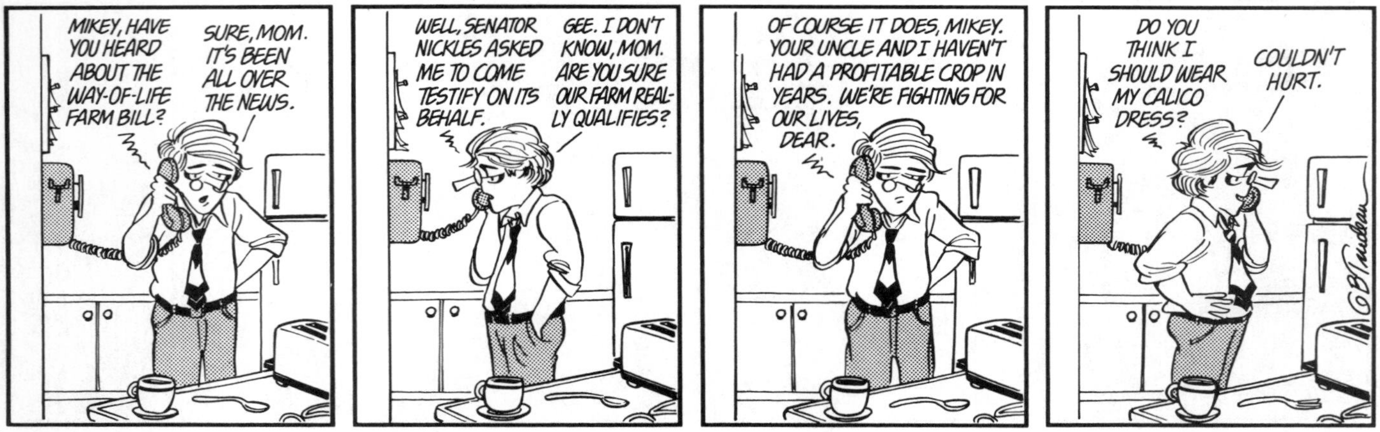
MIKEY, HAVE YOU HEARD ABOUT THE WAY-OF-LIFE FARM BILL?
SURE, MOM. IT'S BEEN ALL OVER THE NEWS.
WELL, SENATOR NICKLES ASKED ME TO COME TESTIFY ON ITS BEHALF.
GEE. I DON'T KNOW, MOM. ARE YOU SURE OUR FARM REALLY QUALIFIES?
OF COURSE IT DOES, MIKEY. YOUR UNCLE AND I HAVEN'T HAD A PROFITABLE CROP IN YEARS. WE'RE FIGHTING FOR OUR LIVES, DEAR.
DO YOU THINK I SHOULD WEAR MY CALICO DRESS?
COULDN'T HURT.
©B Trudeau

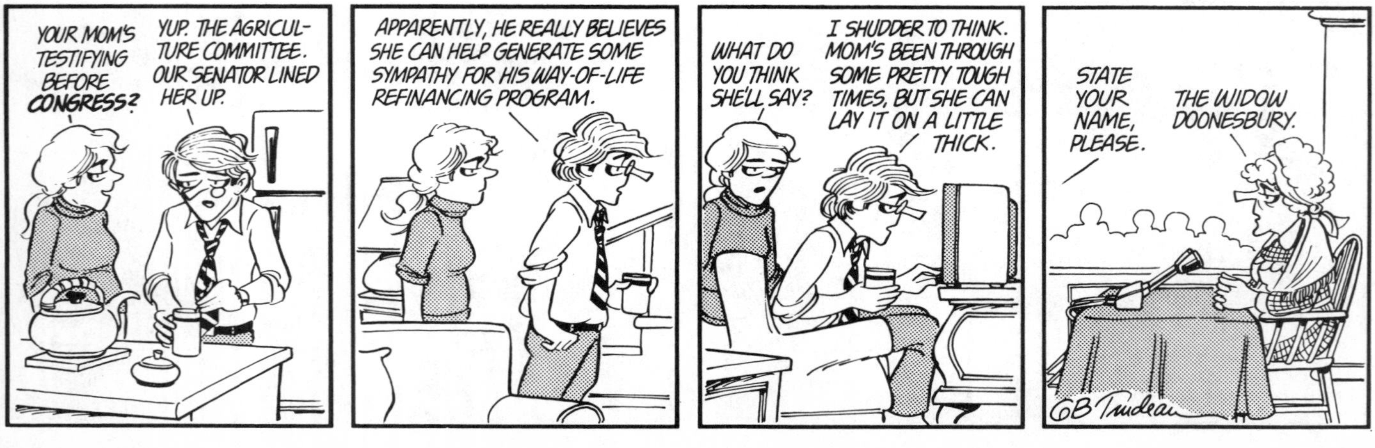
YOUR MOM'S TESTIFYING BEFORE CONGRESS?
YUP. THE AGRICULTURE COMMITTEE. OUR SENATOR LINED HER UP.
APPARENTLY, HE REALLY BELIEVES SHE CAN HELP GENERATE SOME SYMPATHY FOR HIS WAY-OF-LIFE REFINANCING PROGRAM.
WHAT DO YOU THINK SHE'LL SAY?
I SHUDDER TO THINK. MOM'S BEEN THROUGH SOME PRETTY TOUGH TIMES, BUT SHE CAN LAY IT ON A LITTLE THICK.
STATE YOUR NAME, PLEASE.
THE WIDOW DOONESBURY.
©B Trudeau

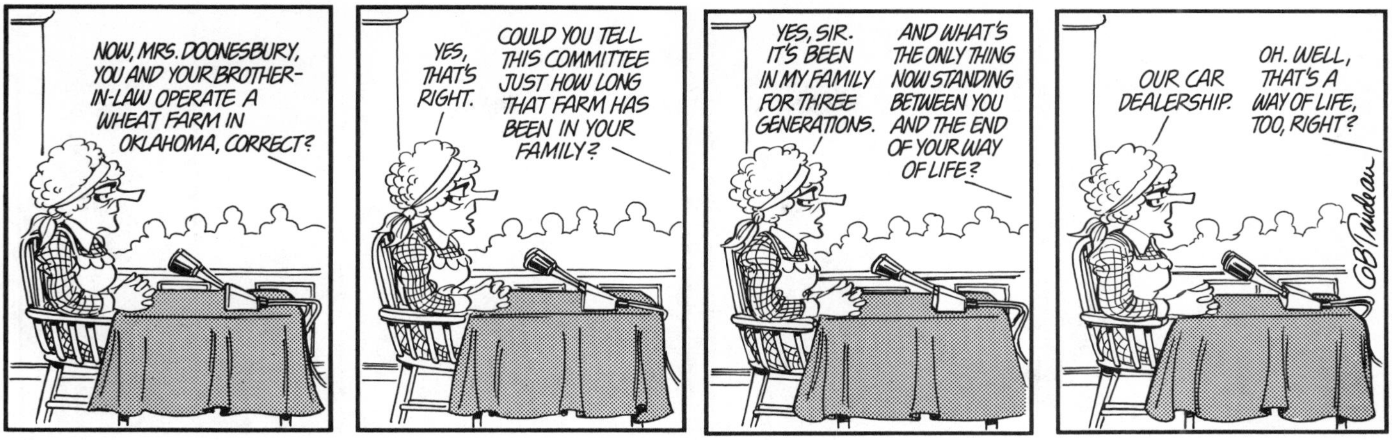
NOW, MRS. DOONESBURY, YOU AND YOUR BROTHER-IN-LAW OPERATE A WHEAT FARM IN OKLAHOMA, CORRECT?
YES, THAT'S RIGHT.
COULD YOU TELL THIS COMMITTEE JUST HOW LONG THAT FARM HAS BEEN IN YOUR FAMILY?
YES, SIR. IT'S BEEN IN MY FAMILY FOR THREE GENERATIONS.
AND WHAT'S THE ONLY THING NOW STANDING BETWEEN YOU AND THE END OF YOUR WAY OF LIFE?
OUR CAR DEALERSHIP.
OH. WELL, THAT'S A WAY OF LIFE, TOO, RIGHT?
GB Trudeau

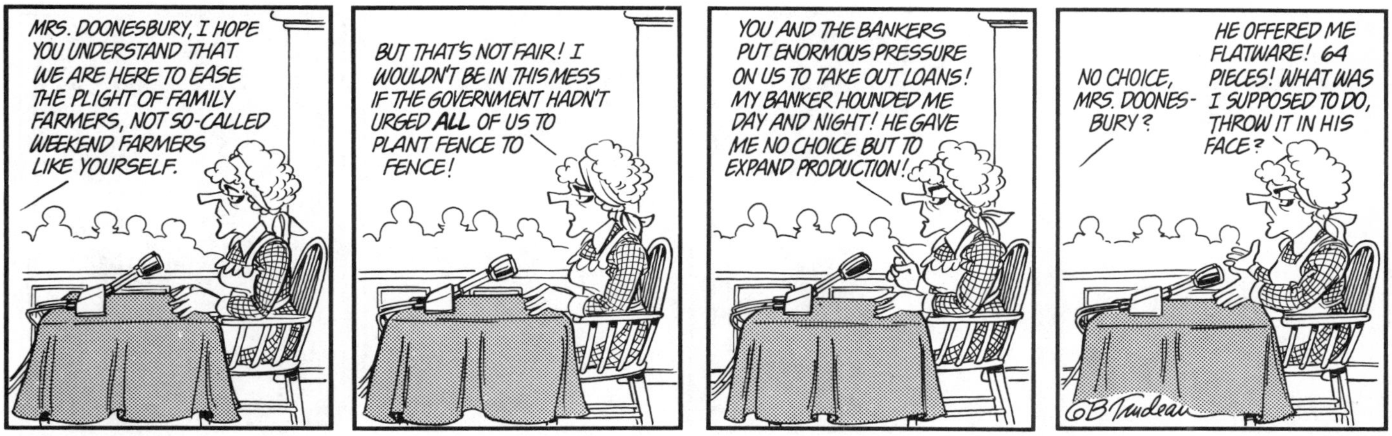
MRS. DOONESBURY, I HOPE YOU UNDERSTAND THAT WE ARE HERE TO EASE THE PLIGHT OF FAMILY FARMERS, NOT SO-CALLED WEEKEND FARMERS LIKE YOURSELF.
BUT THAT'S NOT FAIR! I WOULDN'T BE IN THIS MESS IF THE GOVERNMENT HADN'T URGED **ALL** OF US TO PLANT FENCE TO FENCE!
YOU AND THE BANKERS PUT ENORMOUS PRESSURE ON US TO TAKE OUT LOANS! MY BANKER HOUNDED ME DAY AND NIGHT! HE GAVE ME NO CHOICE BUT TO EXPAND PRODUCTION!
NO CHOICE, MRS. DOONESBURY?
HE OFFERED ME FLATWARE! 64 PIECES! WHAT WAS I SUPPOSED TO DO, THROW IT IN HIS FACE?
GB Trudeau

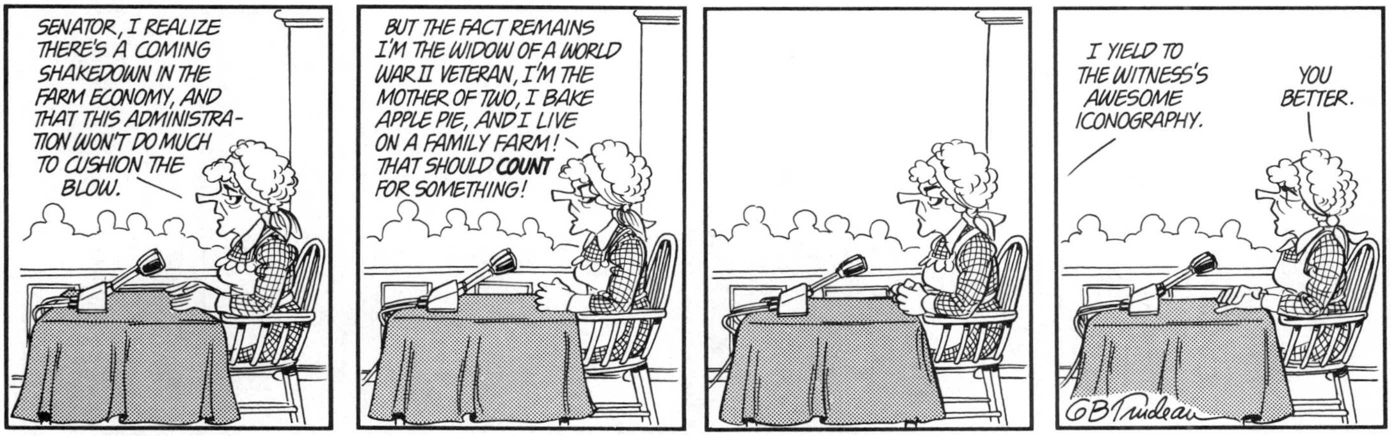
SENATOR, I REALIZE THERE'S A COMING SHAKEDOWN IN THE FARM ECONOMY, AND THAT THIS ADMINISTRATION WON'T DO MUCH TO CUSHION THE BLOW.
BUT THE FACT REMAINS I'M THE WIDOW OF A WORLD WAR II VETERAN, I'M THE MOTHER OF TWO, I BAKE APPLE PIE, AND I LIVE ON A FAMILY FARM! THAT SHOULD **COUNT** FOR SOMETHING!
I YIELD TO THE WITNESS'S AWESOME ICONOGRAPHY.
YOU BETTER.
GB Trudeau

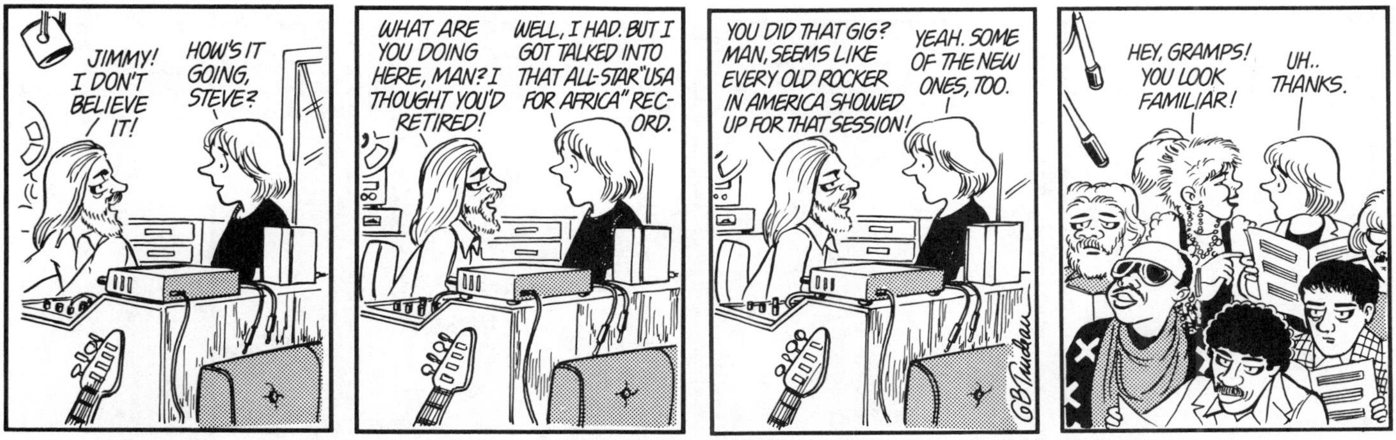
JIMMY! I DON'T BELIEVE IT!
HOW'S IT GOING, STEVE?
WHAT ARE YOU DOING HERE, MAN? I THOUGHT YOU'D RETIRED!
WELL, I HAD. BUT I GOT TALKED INTO THAT ALL-STAR "USA FOR AFRICA" RECORD.
YOU DID THAT GIG? MAN, SEEMS LIKE EVERY OLD ROCKER IN AMERICA SHOWED UP FOR THAT SESSION!
YEAH. SOME OF THE NEW ONES, TOO.
GB Trudeau
HEY, GRAMPS! YOU LOOK FAMILIAR!
UH.. THANKS.

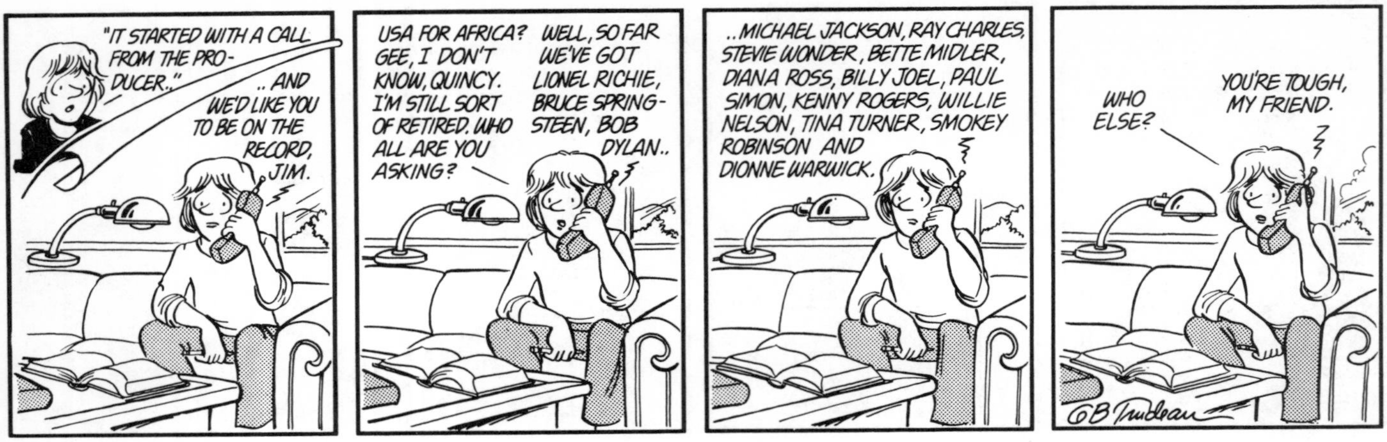
"IT STARTED WITH A CALL FROM THE PRO-DUCER."
.. AND WE'D LIKE YOU TO BE ON THE RECORD, JIM.
USA FOR AFRICA? GEE, I DON'T KNOW, QUINCY. I'M STILL SORT OF RETIRED. WHO ALL ARE YOU ASKING?
WELL, SO FAR WE'VE GOT LIONEL RICHIE, BRUCE SPRING-STEEN, BOB DYLAN..
..MICHAEL JACKSON, RAY CHARLES, STEVIE WONDER, BETTE MIDLER, DIANA ROSS, BILLY JOEL, PAUL SIMON, KENNY ROGERS, WILLIE NELSON, TINA TURNER, SMOKEY ROBINSON AND DIONNE WARWICK.
WHO ELSE?
YOU'RE TOUGH, MY FRIEND.
GB Trudeau

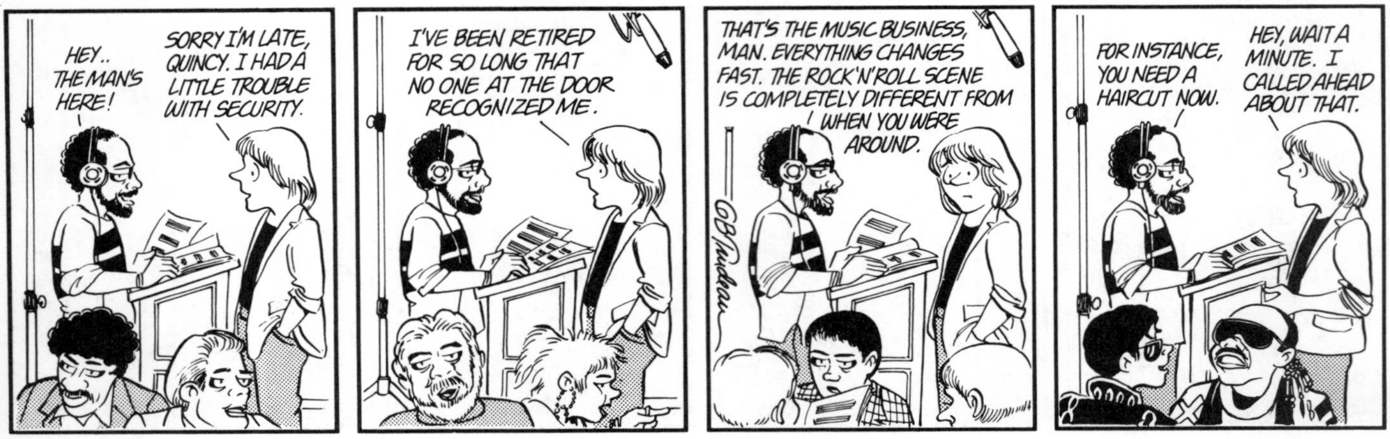
HEY.. THE MAN'S HERE!
SORRY I'M LATE, QUINCY. I HAD A LITTLE TROUBLE WITH SECURITY.
I'VE BEEN RETIRED FOR SO LONG THAT NO ONE AT THE DOOR RECOGNIZED ME.
THAT'S THE MUSIC BUSINESS, MAN. EVERYTHING CHANGES FAST. THE ROCK'N'ROLL SCENE IS COMPLETELY DIFFERENT FROM WHEN YOU WERE AROUND.
GB Trudeau
FOR INSTANCE, YOU NEED A HAIRCUT NOW.
HEY, WAIT A MINUTE. I CALLED AHEAD ABOUT THAT.

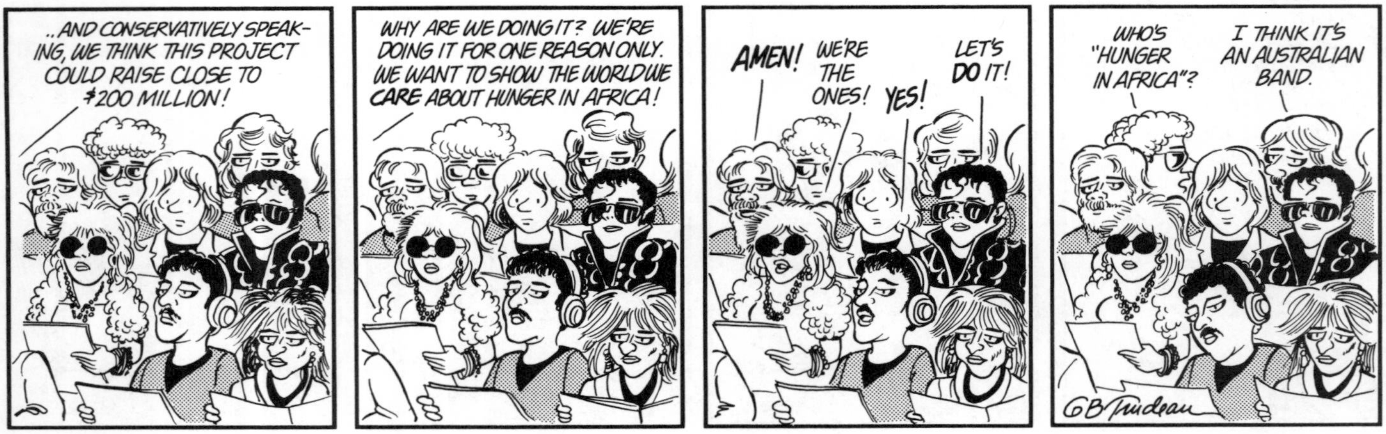
..AND CONSERVATIVELY SPEAK-ING, WE THINK THIS PROJECT COULD RAISE CLOSE TO $200 MILLION!
WHY ARE WE DOING IT? WE'RE DOING IT FOR ONE REASON ONLY. WE WANT TO SHOW THE WORLD WE CARE ABOUT HUNGER IN AFRICA!
AMEN!
WE'RE THE ONES!
YES!
LET'S DO IT!
WHO'S "HUNGER IN AFRICA"?
I THINK IT'S AN AUSTRALIAN BAND.
GB Trudeau

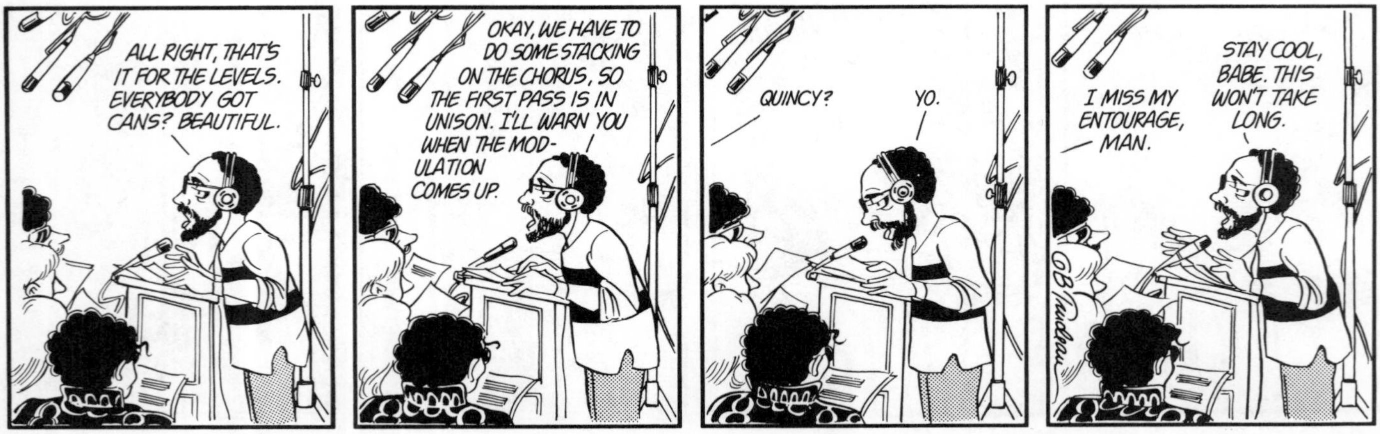
ALL RIGHT, THAT'S IT FOR THE LEVELS. EVERYBODY GOT CANS? BEAUTIFUL.
OKAY, WE HAVE TO DO SOME STACKING ON THE CHORUS, SO THE FIRST PASS IS IN UNISON. I'LL WARN YOU WHEN THE MOD-ULATION COMES UP.
QUINCY?
YO.
I MISS MY ENTOURAGE, MAN.
STAY COOL, BABE. THIS WON'T TAKE LONG.
GB Trudeau

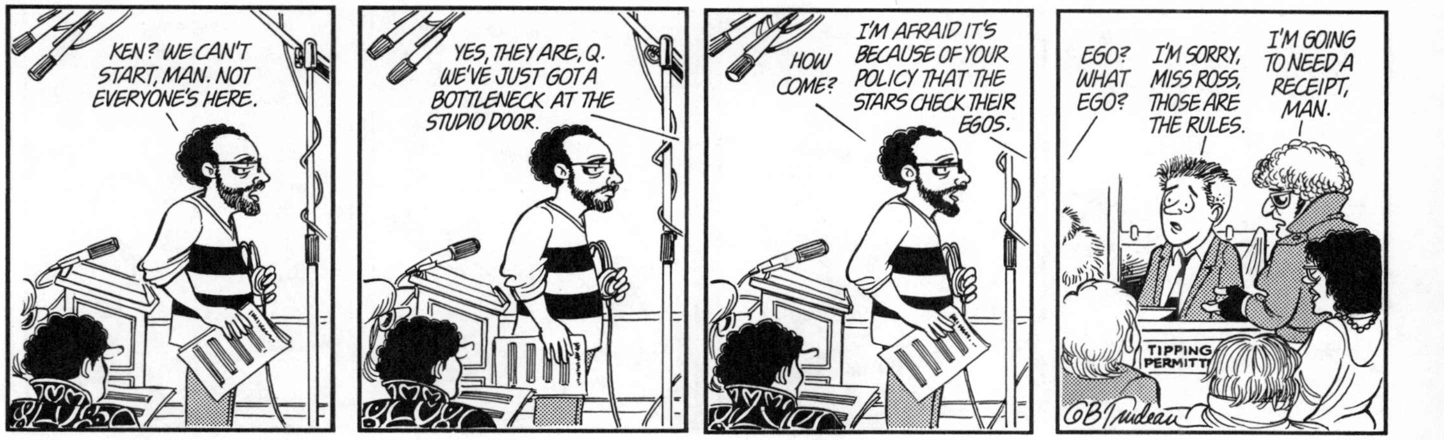
KEN? WE CAN'T START, MAN. NOT EVERYONE'S HERE.
YES, THEY ARE, Q. WE'VE JUST GOT A BOTTLENECK AT THE STUDIO DOOR.
HOW COME?
I'M AFRAID IT'S BECAUSE OF YOUR POLICY THAT THE STARS CHECK THEIR EGOS.
EGO? WHAT EGO?
I'M SORRY, MISS ROSS, THOSE ARE THE RULES.
I'M GOING TO NEED A RECEIPT, MAN.
TIPPING PERMITT

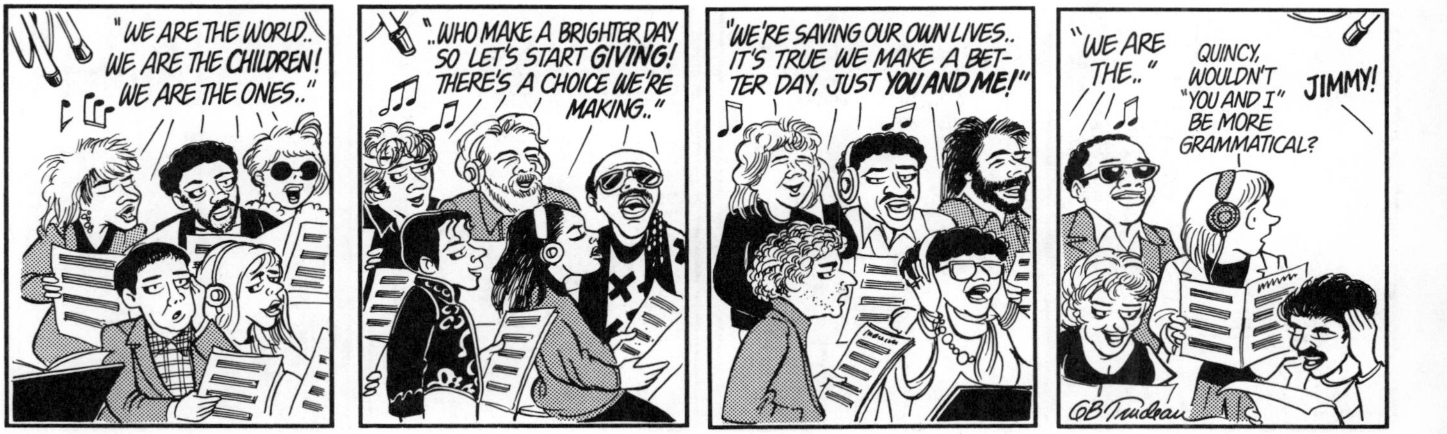
"WE ARE THE WORLD.. WE ARE THE CHILDREN! WE ARE THE ONES.."
"..WHO MAKE A BRIGHTER DAY SO LET'S START GIVING! THERE'S A CHOICE WE'RE MAKING.."
"WE'RE SAVING OUR OWN LIVES.. IT'S TRUE WE MAKE A BETTER DAY, JUST YOU AND ME!"
"WE ARE THE.."
QUINCY, WOULDN'T "YOU AND I" BE MORE GRAMMATICAL?
JIMMY!

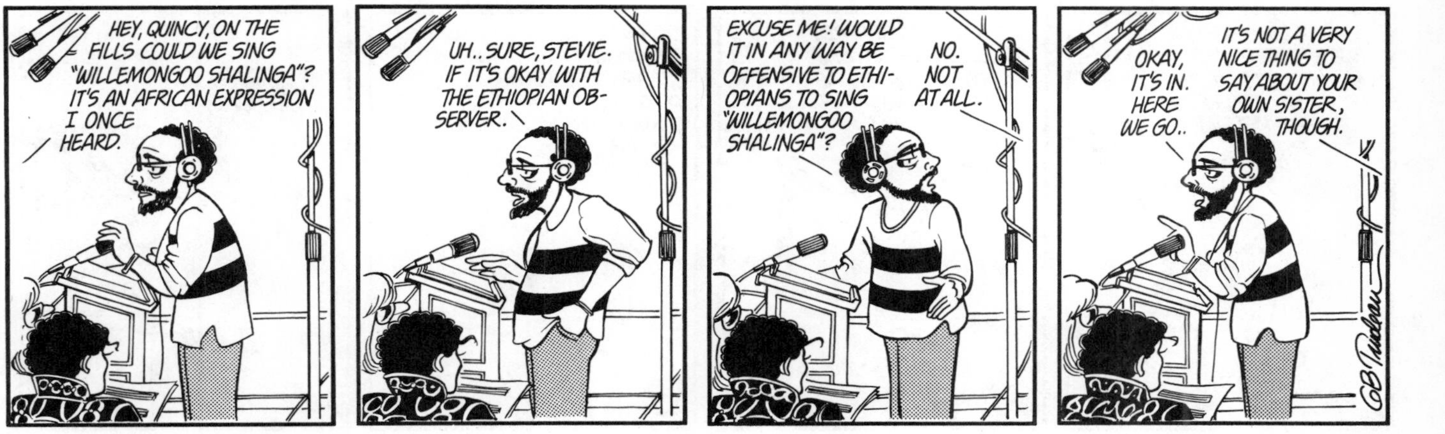
HEY, QUINCY, ON THE FILLS COULD WE SING "WILLEMONGOO SHALINGA"? IT'S AN AFRICAN EXPRESSION I ONCE HEARD.
UH.. SURE, STEVIE. IF IT'S OKAY WITH THE ETHIOPIAN OBSERVER.
EXCUSE ME! WOULD IT IN ANY WAY BE OFFENSIVE TO ETHIOPIANS TO SING "WILLEMONGOO SHALINGA"?
NO. NOT AT ALL.
OKAY, IT'S IN. HERE WE GO..
IT'S NOT A VERY NICE THING TO SAY ABOUT YOUR OWN SISTER, THOUGH.

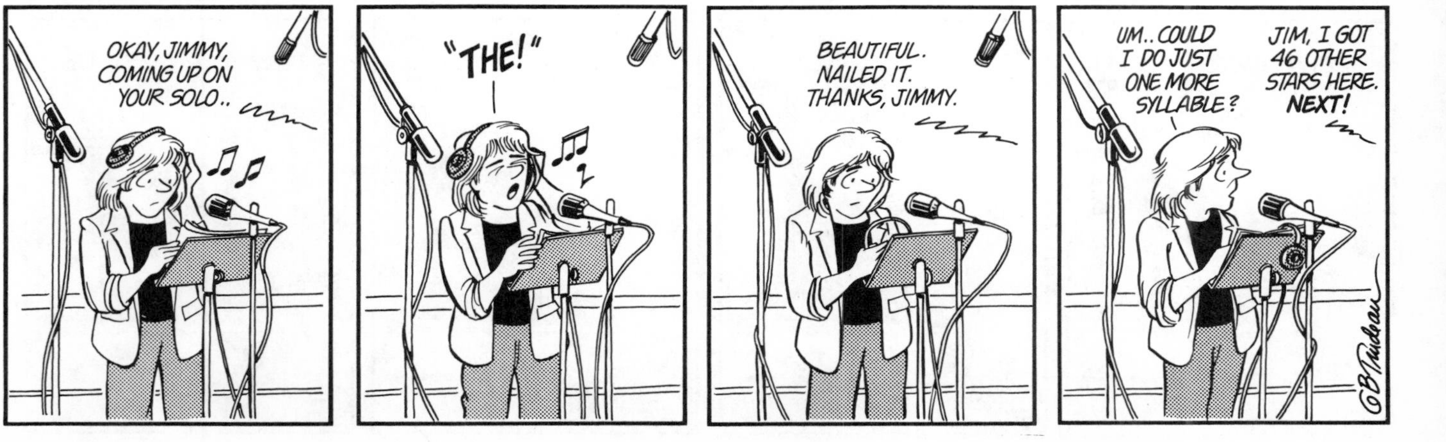
OKAY, JIMMY, COMING UP ON YOUR SOLO..
"THE!"
BEAUTIFUL. NAILED IT. THANKS, JIMMY.
UM.. COULD I DO JUST ONE MORE SYLLABLE?
JIM, I GOT 46 OTHER STARS HERE. NEXT!

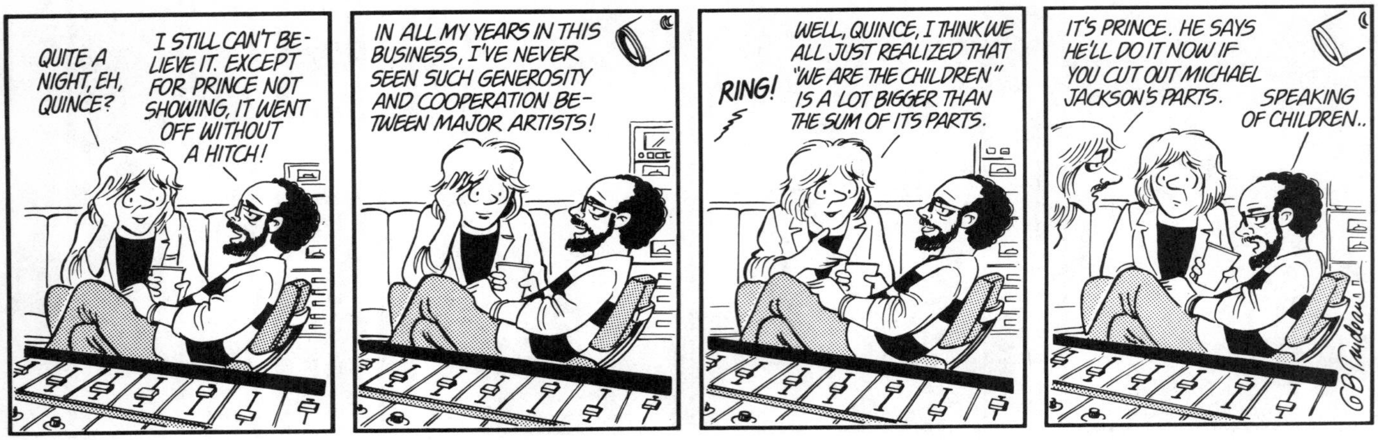
QUITE A NIGHT, EH, QUINCE?
I STILL CAN'T BE-LIEVE IT. EXCEPT FOR PRINCE NOT SHOWING, IT WENT OFF WITHOUT A HITCH!
IN ALL MY YEARS IN THIS BUSINESS, I'VE NEVER SEEN SUCH GENEROSITY AND COOPERATION BE-TWEEN MAJOR ARTISTS!
RING!
WELL, QUINCE, I THINK WE ALL JUST REALIZED THAT "WE ARE THE CHILDREN" IS A LOT BIGGER THAN THE SUM OF ITS PARTS.
IT'S PRINCE. HE SAYS HE'LL DO IT NOW IF YOU CUT OUT MICHAEL JACKSON'S PARTS.
SPEAKING OF CHILDREN..

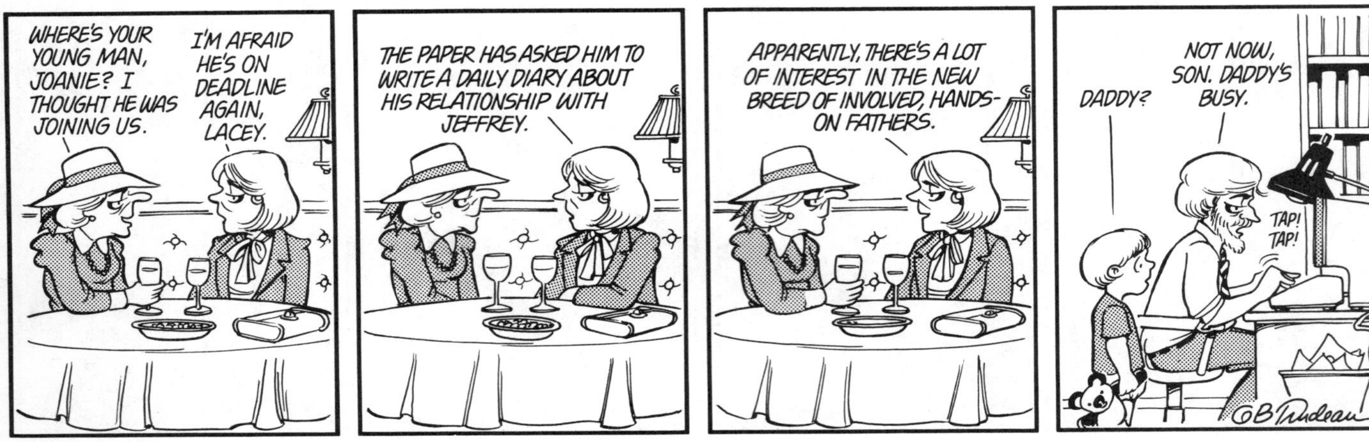
WHERE'S YOUR YOUNG MAN, JOANIE? I THOUGHT HE WAS JOINING US.
I'M AFRAID HE'S ON DEADLINE AGAIN, LACEY.
THE PAPER HAS ASKED HIM TO WRITE A DAILY DIARY ABOUT HIS RELATIONSHIP WITH JEFFREY.
APPARENTLY, THERE'S A LOT OF INTEREST IN THE NEW BREED OF INVOLVED, HANDS-ON FATHERS.
DADDY?
NOT NOW, SON. DADDY'S BUSY.
TAP! TAP!

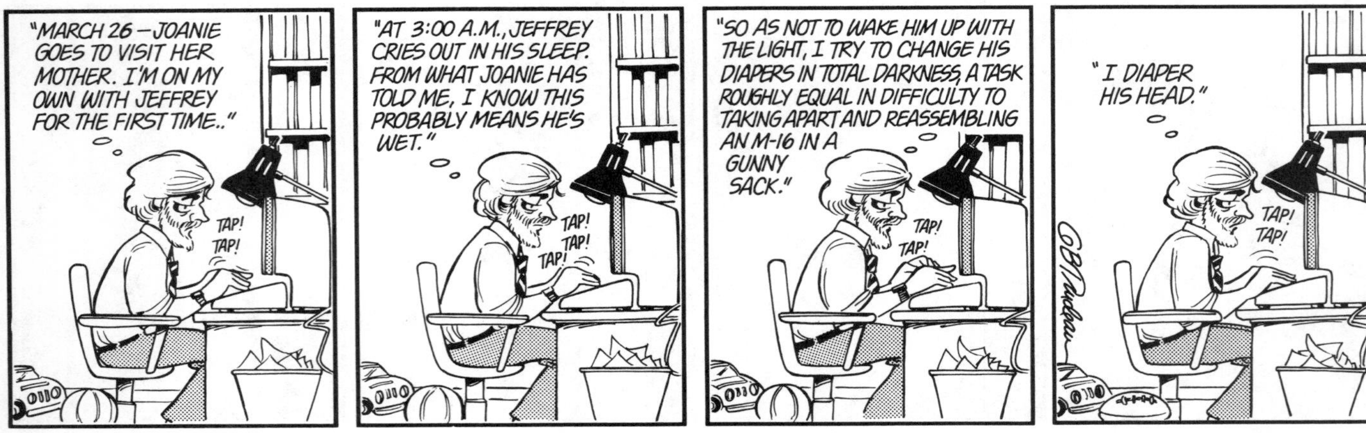
"MARCH 26 — JOANIE GOES TO VISIT HER MOTHER. I'M ON MY OWN WITH JEFFREY FOR THE FIRST TIME.."
TAP! TAP!
"AT 3:00 A.M., JEFFREY CRIES OUT IN HIS SLEEP. FROM WHAT JOANIE HAS TOLD ME, I KNOW THIS PROBABLY MEANS HE'S WET."
TAP! TAP! TAP!
"SO AS NOT TO WAKE HIM UP WITH THE LIGHT, I TRY TO CHANGE HIS DIAPERS IN TOTAL DARKNESS, A TASK ROUGHLY EQUAL IN DIFFICULTY TO TAKING APART AND REASSEMBLING AN M-16 IN A GUNNY SACK."
TAP! TAP!
"I DIAPER HIS HEAD."
TAP! TAP!

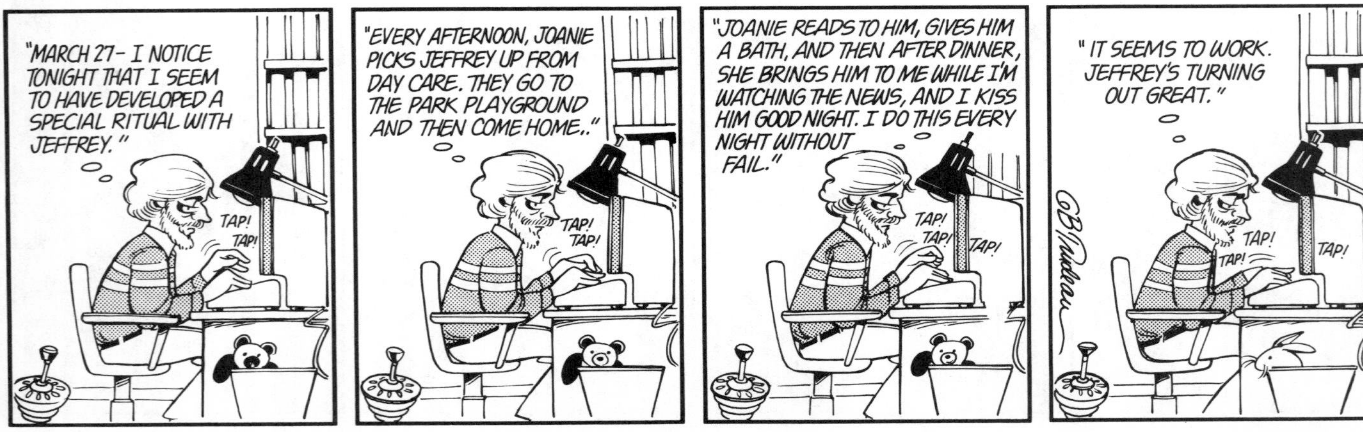
"MARCH 27 – I NOTICE TONIGHT THAT I SEEM TO HAVE DEVELOPED A SPECIAL RITUAL WITH JEFFREY."
TAP! TAP!
"EVERY AFTERNOON, JOANIE PICKS JEFFREY UP FROM DAY CARE. THEY GO TO THE PARK PLAYGROUND AND THEN COME HOME.."
TAP! TAP!
"JOANIE READS TO HIM, GIVES HIM A BATH, AND THEN AFTER DINNER, SHE BRINGS HIM TO ME WHILE I'M WATCHING THE NEWS, AND I KISS HIM GOOD NIGHT. I DO THIS EVERY NIGHT WITHOUT FAIL."
TAP! TAP! TAP!
"IT SEEMS TO WORK. JEFFREY'S TURNING OUT GREAT."
TAP! TAP! TAP!

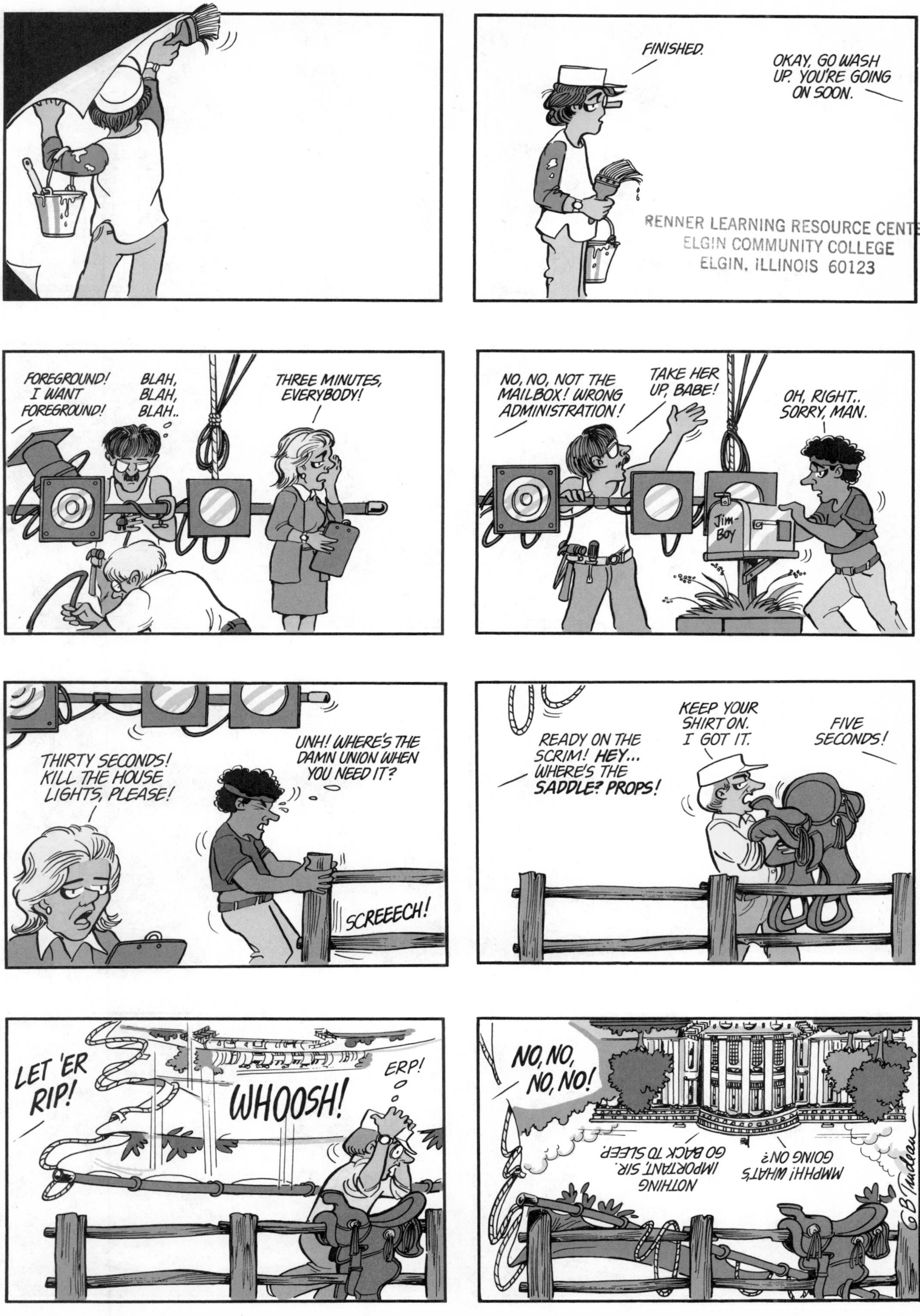
FINISHED.
OKAY, GO WASH UP. YOU'RE GOING ON SOON.
FOREGROUND! I WANT FOREGROUND!
BLAH, BLAH, BLAH..
THREE MINUTES, EVERYBODY!
NO, NO, NOT THE MAILBOX! WRONG ADMINISTRATION!
TAKE HER UP, BABE!
OH, RIGHT.. SORRY, MAN.
JIM-BOY
THIRTY SECONDS! KILL THE HOUSE LIGHTS, PLEASE!
UNH! WHERE'S THE DAMN UNION WHEN YOU NEED IT?
SCREEECH!
READY ON THE SCRIM! HEY... WHERE'S THE SADDLE? PROPS!
KEEP YOUR SHIRT ON. I GOT IT.
FIVE SECONDS!
LET 'ER RIP!
WHOOSH!
ERP!
NO, NO, NO, NO!
MMPHH! WHAT'S GOING ON?
NOTHING IMPORTANT, SIR. GO BACK TO SLEEP.
©GBTrudeau

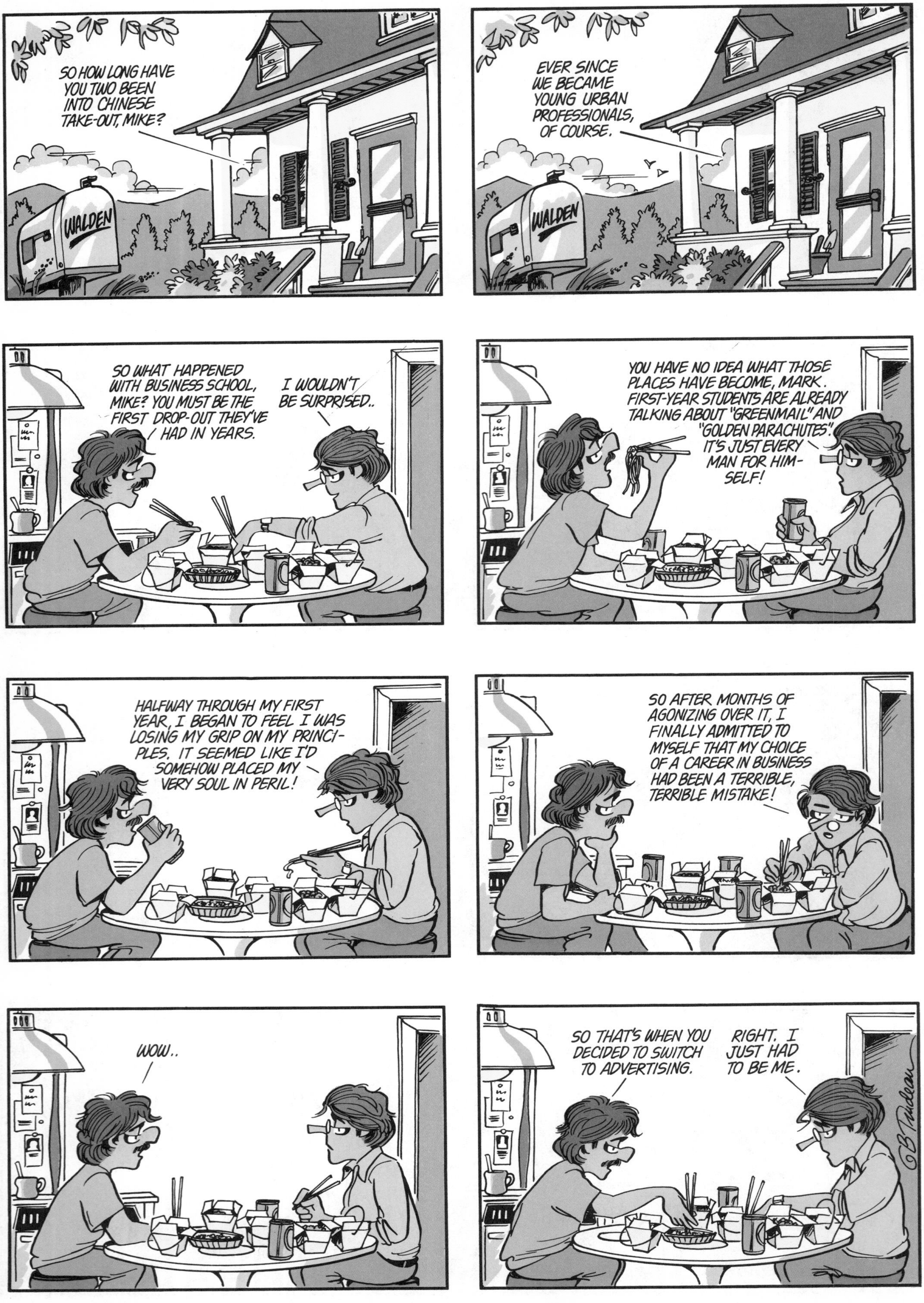
SO HOW LONG HAVE YOU TWO BEEN INTO CHINESE TAKE-OUT, MIKE?
WALDEN
EVER SINCE WE BECAME YOUNG URBAN PROFESSIONALS, OF COURSE.
WALDEN
SO WHAT HAPPENED WITH BUSINESS SCHOOL, MIKE? YOU MUST BE THE FIRST DROP-OUT THEY'VE HAD IN YEARS.
I WOULDN'T BE SURPRISED..
YOU HAVE NO IDEA WHAT THOSE PLACES HAVE BECOME, MARK. FIRST-YEAR STUDENTS ARE ALREADY TALKING ABOUT "GREENMAIL" AND "GOLDEN PARACHUTES". IT'S JUST EVERY MAN FOR HIMSELF!
HALFWAY THROUGH MY FIRST YEAR, I BEGAN TO FEEL I WAS LOSING MY GRIP ON MY PRINCIPLES. IT SEEMED LIKE I'D SOMEHOW PLACED MY VERY SOUL IN PERIL!
SO AFTER MONTHS OF AGONIZING OVER IT, I FINALLY ADMITTED TO MYSELF THAT MY CHOICE OF A CAREER IN BUSINESS HAD BEEN A TERRIBLE, TERRIBLE MISTAKE!
WOW..
SO THAT'S WHEN YOU DECIDED TO SWITCH TO ADVERTISING.
RIGHT. I JUST HAD TO BE ME.
©B Trudeau

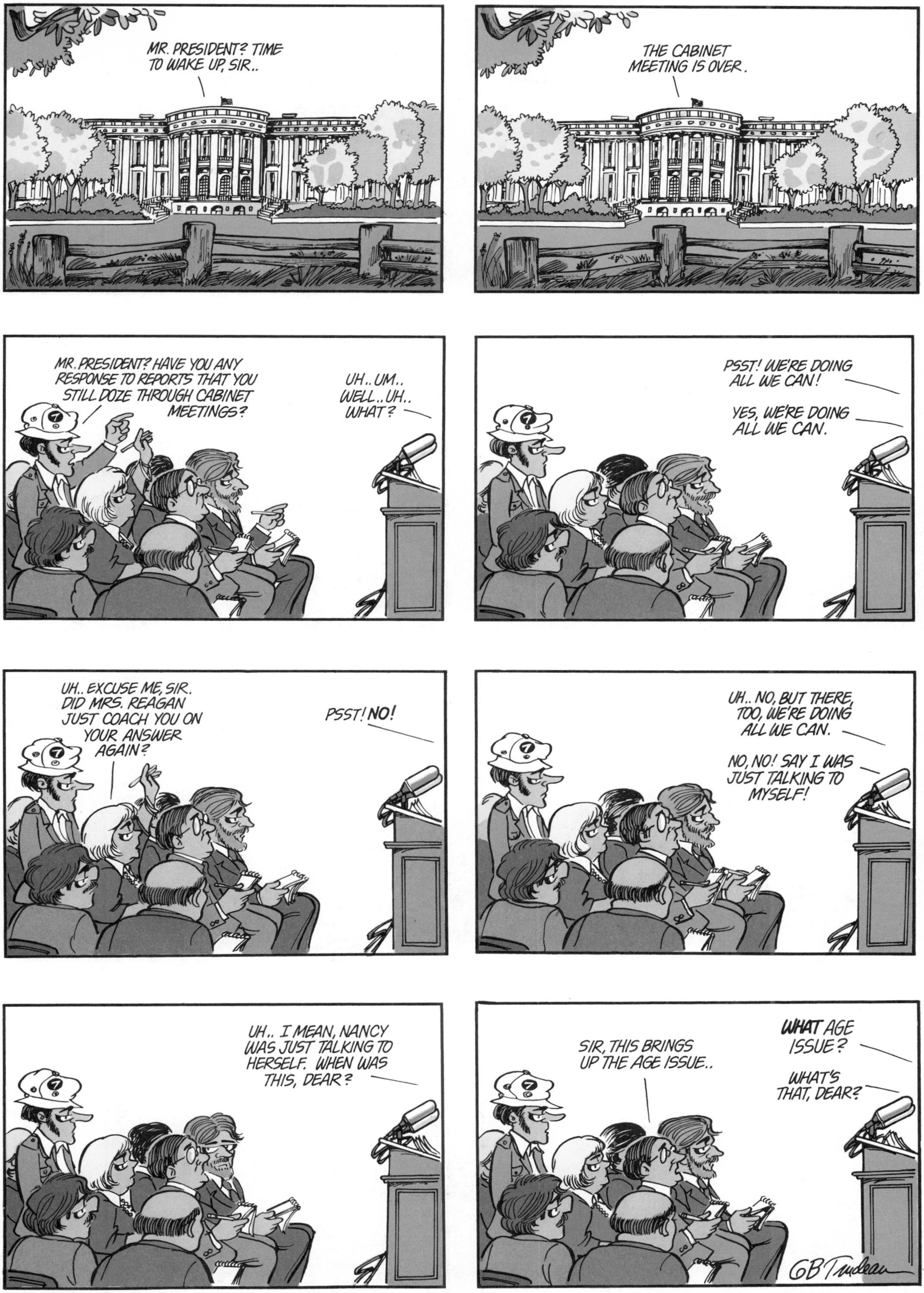
MR. PRESIDENT? TIME TO WAKE UP, SIR..
THE CABINET MEETING IS OVER.
MR. PRESIDENT? HAVE YOU ANY RESPONSE TO REPORTS THAT YOU STILL DOZE THROUGH CABINET MEETINGS?
UH.. UM.. WELL.. UH.. WHAT?
PSST! WE'RE DOING ALL WE CAN!
YES, WE'RE DOING ALL WE CAN.
UH.. EXCUSE ME, SIR.. DID MRS. REAGAN JUST COACH YOU ON YOUR ANSWER AGAIN?
PSST! NO!
UH.. NO, BUT THERE, TOO, WE'RE DOING ALL WE CAN.
NO, NO! SAY I WAS JUST TALKING TO MYSELF!
UH.. I MEAN, NANCY WAS JUST TALKING TO HERSELF. WHEN WAS THIS, DEAR?
SIR, THIS BRINGS UP THE AGE ISSUE..
WHAT AGE ISSUE?
WHAT'S THAT, DEAR?
GB Trudeau

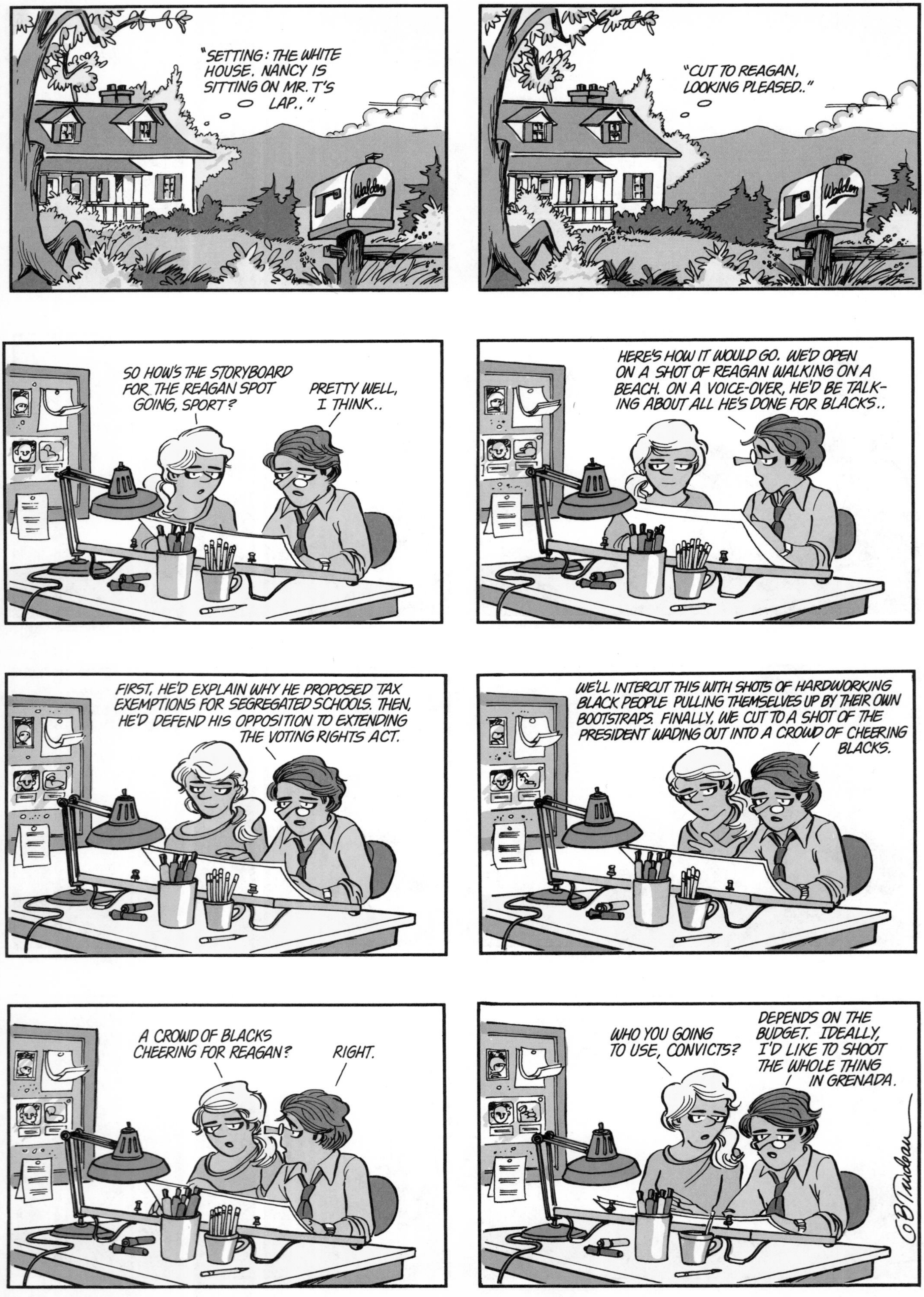
"SETTING: THE WHITE HOUSE. NANCY IS SITTING ON MR. T'S LAP.."
"CUT TO REAGAN, LOOKING PLEASED.."
SO HOW'S THE STORYBOARD FOR THE REAGAN SPOT GOING, SPORT?
PRETTY WELL, I THINK..
HERE'S HOW IT WOULD GO. WE'D OPEN ON A SHOT OF REAGAN WALKING ON A BEACH. ON A VOICE-OVER, HE'D BE TALKING ABOUT ALL HE'S DONE FOR BLACKS..
FIRST, HE'D EXPLAIN WHY HE PROPOSED TAX EXEMPTIONS FOR SEGREGATED SCHOOLS. THEN, HE'D DEFEND HIS OPPOSITION TO EXTENDING THE VOTING RIGHTS ACT.
WE'LL INTERCUT THIS WITH SHOTS OF HARDWORKING BLACK PEOPLE PULLING THEMSELVES UP BY THEIR OWN BOOTSTRAPS. FINALLY, WE CUT TO A SHOT OF THE PRESIDENT WADING OUT INTO A CROWD OF CHEERING BLACKS.
A CROWD OF BLACKS CHEERING FOR REAGAN?
RIGHT.
WHO YOU GOING TO USE, CONVICTS?
DEPENDS ON THE BUDGET. IDEALLY, I'D LIKE TO SHOOT THE WHOLE THING IN GRENADA.
©G.B.Trudeau

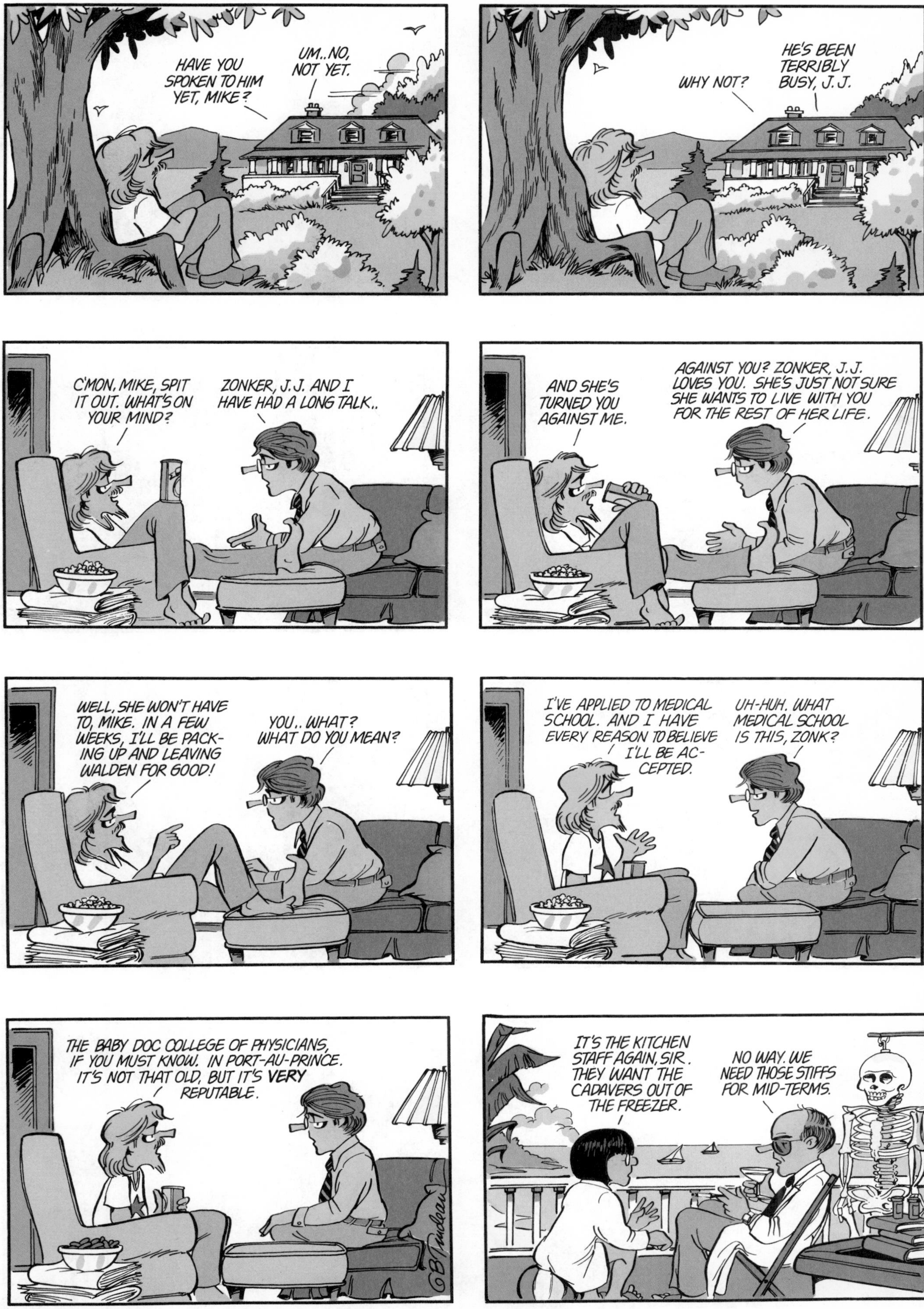

HAVE YOU SPOKEN TO HIM YET, MIKE?
UM.. NO, NOT YET.
WHY NOT?
HE'S BEEN TERRIBLY BUSY, J. J.
C'MON, MIKE, SPIT IT OUT. WHAT'S ON YOUR MIND?
ZONKER, J. J. AND I HAVE HAD A LONG TALK..
AND SHE'S TURNED YOU AGAINST ME.
AGAINST YOU? ZONKER, J. J. LOVES YOU. SHE'S JUST NOT SURE SHE WANTS TO LIVE WITH YOU FOR THE REST OF HER LIFE.
WELL, SHE WON'T HAVE TO, MIKE. IN A FEW WEEKS, I'LL BE PACKING UP AND LEAVING WALDEN FOR GOOD!
YOU.. WHAT? WHAT DO YOU MEAN?
I'VE APPLIED TO MEDICAL SCHOOL. AND I HAVE EVERY REASON TO BELIEVE I'LL BE ACCEPTED.
UH-HUH. WHAT MEDICAL SCHOOL IS THIS, ZONK?
THE BABY DOC COLLEGE OF PHYSICIANS, IF YOU MUST KNOW. IN PORT-AU-PRINCE. IT'S NOT THAT OLD, BUT IT'S **VERY** REPUTABLE.
IT'S THE KITCHEN STAFF AGAIN, SIR. THEY WANT THE CADAVERS OUT OF THE FREEZER.
NO WAY. WE NEED THOSE STIFFS FOR MID-TERMS.

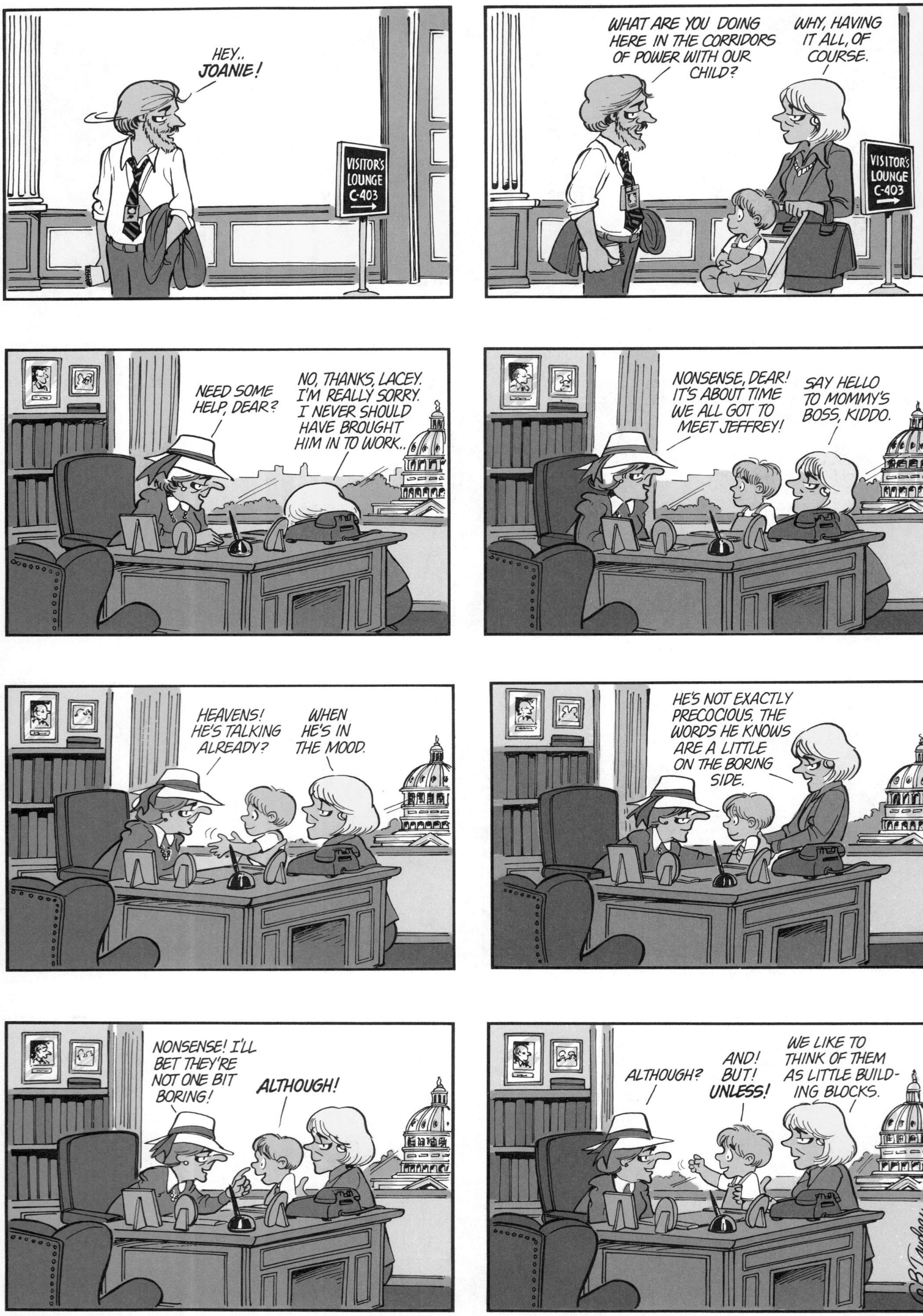
HEY.. JOANIE!
VISITOR'S LOUNGE C-403
WHAT ARE YOU DOING HERE IN THE CORRIDORS OF POWER WITH OUR CHILD?
WHY, HAVING IT ALL, OF COURSE.
VISITOR'S LOUNGE C-403
NEED SOME HELP, DEAR?
NO, THANKS, LACEY. I'M REALLY SORRY. I NEVER SHOULD HAVE BROUGHT HIM IN TO WORK..
NONSENSE, DEAR! IT'S ABOUT TIME WE ALL GOT TO MEET JEFFREY!
SAY HELLO TO MOMMY'S BOSS, KIDDO.
HEAVENS! HE'S TALKING ALREADY?
WHEN HE'S IN THE MOOD.
HE'S NOT EXACTLY PRECOCIOUS. THE WORDS HE KNOWS ARE A LITTLE ON THE BORING SIDE.
NONSENSE! I'LL BET THEY'RE NOT ONE BIT BORING!
ALTHOUGH!
ALTHOUGH?
AND! BUT! UNLESS!
WE LIKE TO THINK OF THEM AS LITTLE BUILDING BLOCKS.

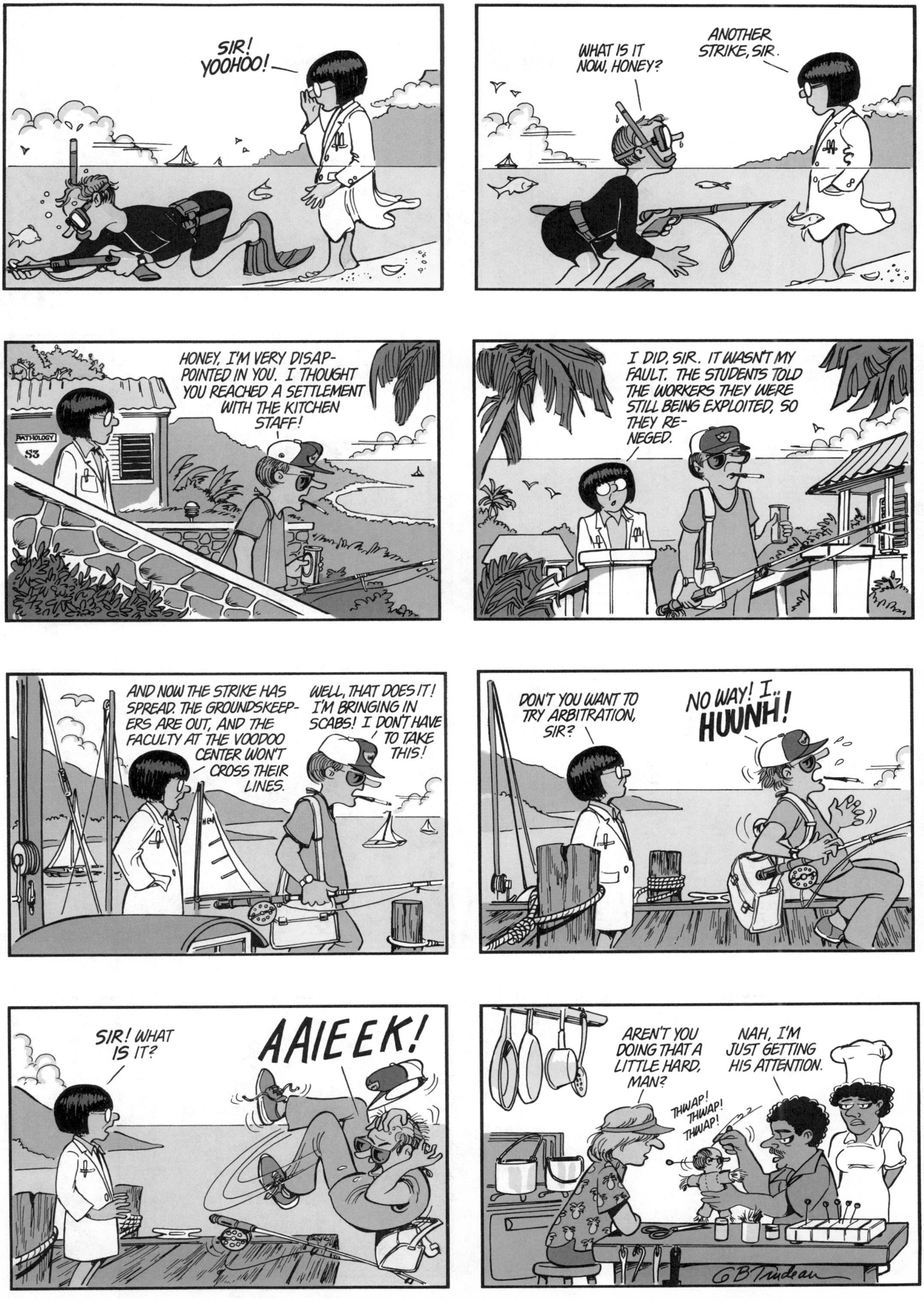
SIR! YOOHOO!
WHAT IS IT NOW, HONEY?
ANOTHER STRIKE, SIR.
HONEY, I'M VERY DISAPPOINTED IN YOU. I THOUGHT YOU REACHED A SETTLEMENT WITH THE KITCHEN STAFF!
PATHOLOGY
I DID, SIR. IT WASN'T MY FAULT. THE STUDENTS TOLD THE WORKERS THEY WERE STILL BEING EXPLOITED, SO THEY RENEGED.
AND NOW THE STRIKE HAS SPREAD. THE GROUNDSKEEPERS ARE OUT, AND THE FACULTY AT THE VOODOO CENTER WON'T CROSS THEIR LINES.
WELL, THAT DOES IT! I'M BRINGING IN SCABS! I DON'T HAVE TO TAKE THIS!
DON'T YOU WANT TO TRY ARBITRATION, SIR?
NO WAY! I.. HUUNH!
SIR! WHAT IS IT?
AAIEEK!
AREN'T YOU DOING THAT A LITTLE HARD, MAN?
NAH, I'M JUST GETTING HIS ATTENTION.
THWAP! THWAP! THWAP!
GBTrudeau

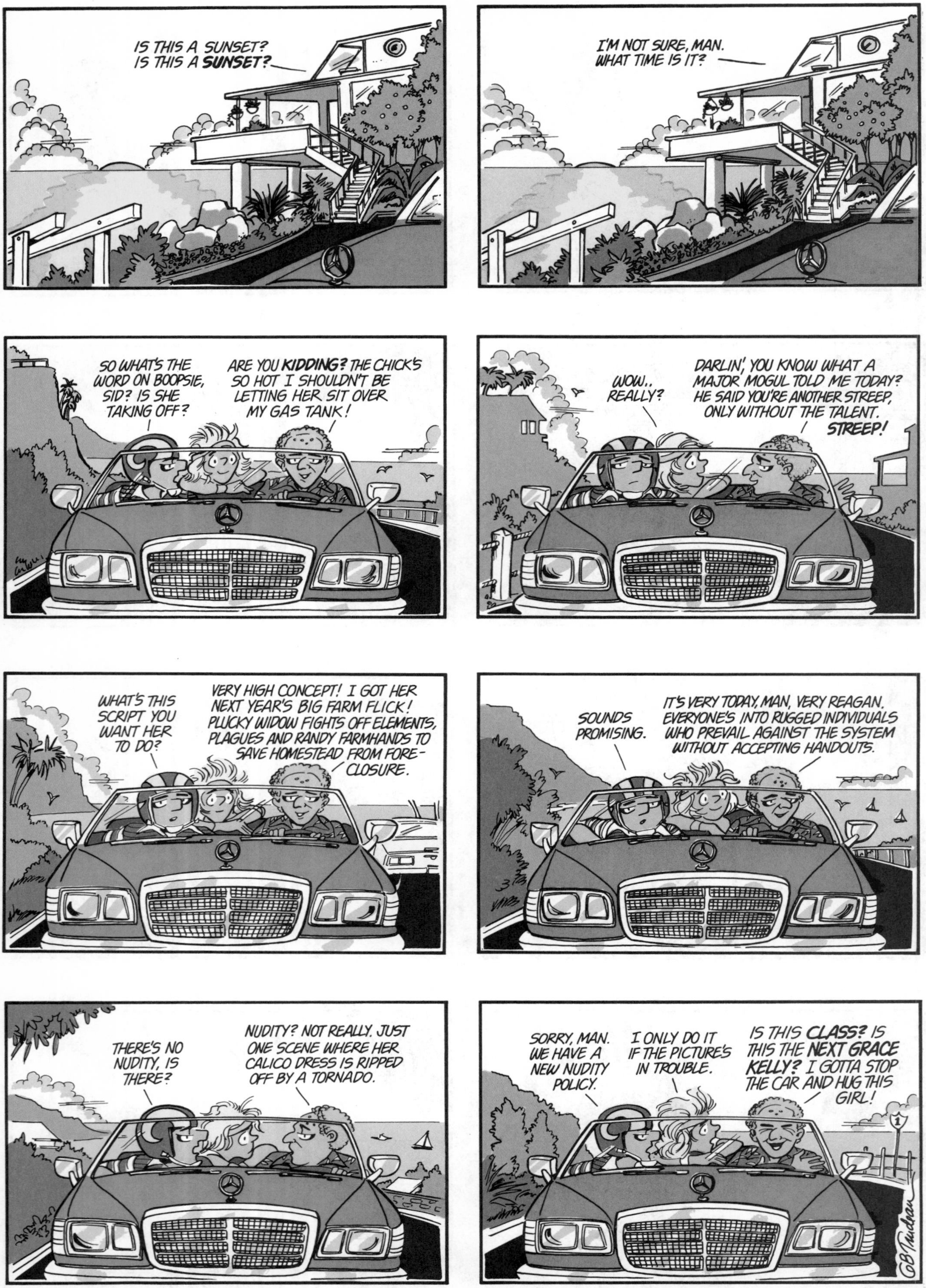
IS THIS A SUNSET? IS THIS A **SUNSET?**
I'M NOT SURE, MAN. WHAT TIME IS IT?
SO WHAT'S THE WORD ON BOOPSIE, SID? IS SHE TAKING OFF?
ARE YOU **KIDDING?** THE CHICK'S SO HOT I SHOULDN'T BE LETTING HER SIT OVER MY GAS TANK!
WOW.. REALLY?
DARLIN', YOU KNOW WHAT A MAJOR MOGUL TOLD ME TODAY? HE SAID YOU'RE ANOTHER STREEP, ONLY WITHOUT THE TALENT. **STREEP!**
WHAT'S THIS SCRIPT YOU WANT HER TO DO?
VERY HIGH CONCEPT! I GOT HER NEXT YEAR'S BIG FARM FLICK! PLUCKY WIDOW FIGHTS OFF ELEMENTS, PLAGUES AND RANDY FARMHANDS TO SAVE HOMESTEAD FROM FORE-CLOSURE.
SOUNDS PROMISING.
IT'S VERY TODAY, MAN, VERY REAGAN. EVERYONE'S INTO RUGGED INDIVIDUALS WHO PREVAIL AGAINST THE SYSTEM WITHOUT ACCEPTING HANDOUTS.
THERE'S NO NUDITY, IS THERE?
NUDITY? NOT REALLY. JUST ONE SCENE WHERE HER CALICO DRESS IS RIPPED OFF BY A TORNADO.
SORRY, MAN. WE HAVE A NEW NUDITY POLICY.
I ONLY DO IT IF THE PICTURE'S IN TROUBLE.
IS THIS **CLASS?** IS THIS THE **NEXT GRACE KELLY?** I GOTTA STOP THE CAR AND HUG THIS GIRL!
GB Trudeau

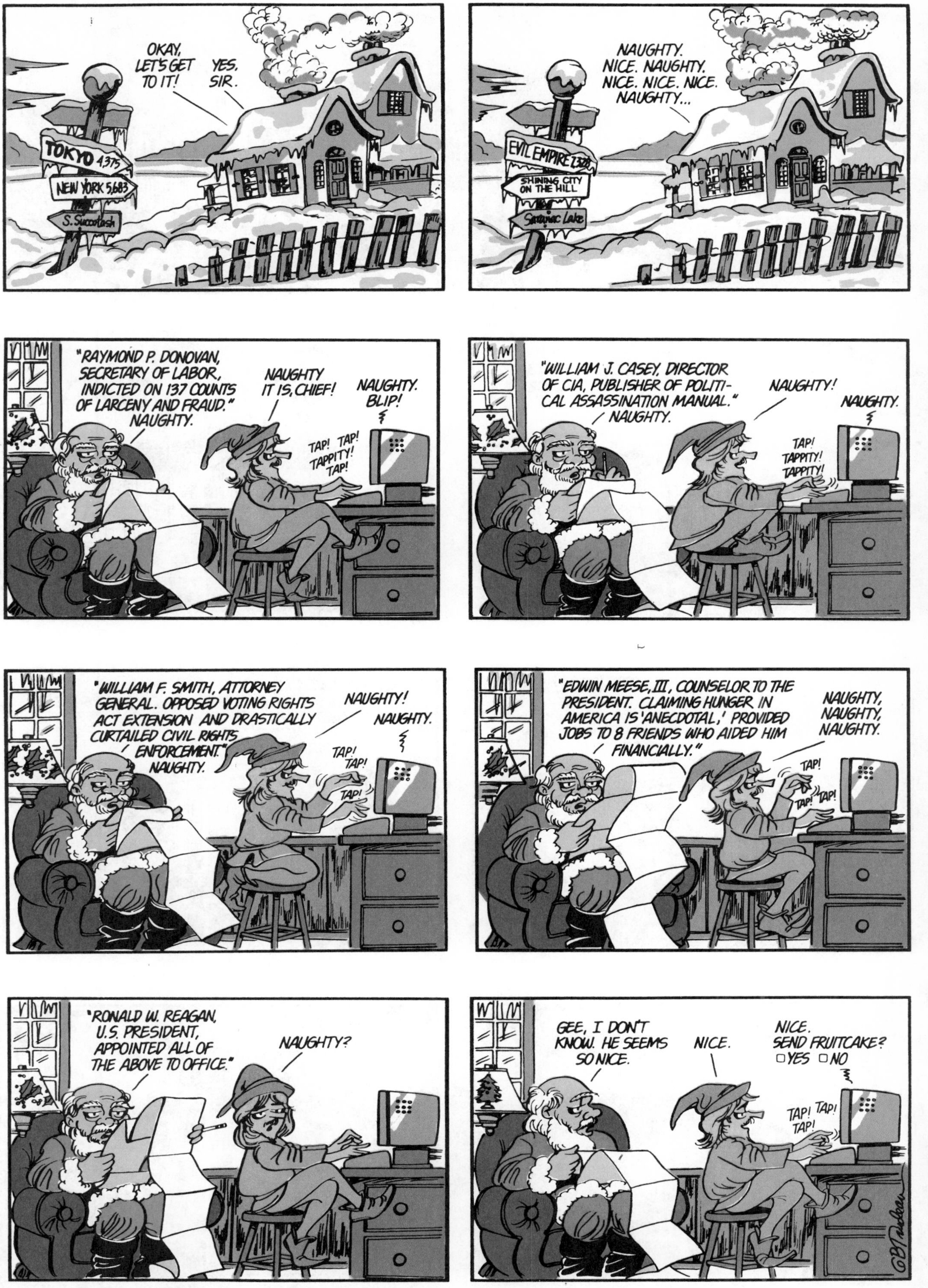
TOKYO 4,375
NEW YORK 5,683
S. Succotash
OKAY, LET'S GET TO IT!
YES, SIR.
EVIL EMPIRE
SHINING CITY ON THE HILL
NAUGHTY. NICE. NAUGHTY. NICE. NICE. NICE. NAUGHTY...
"RAYMOND P. DONOVAN, SECRETARY OF LABOR, INDICTED ON 137 COUNTS OF LARCENY AND FRAUD." NAUGHTY.
NAUGHTY IT IS, CHIEF!
NAUGHTY. BLIP!
TAP! TAP! TAPPITY! TAP!
"WILLIAM J. CASEY, DIRECTOR OF CIA, PUBLISHER OF POLITICAL ASSASSINATION MANUAL." NAUGHTY.
NAUGHTY!
NAUGHTY.
TAP! TAPPITY! TAPPITY!
"WILLIAM F. SMITH, ATTORNEY GENERAL. OPPOSED VOTING RIGHTS ACT EXTENSION AND DRASTICALLY CURTAILED CIVIL RIGHTS ENFORCEMENT." NAUGHTY.
NAUGHTY!
NAUGHTY.
TAP! TAP! TAP!
"EDWIN MEESE, III, COUNSELOR TO THE PRESIDENT. CLAIMING HUNGER IN AMERICA IS 'ANECDOTAL,' PROVIDED JOBS TO 8 FRIENDS WHO AIDED HIM FINANCIALLY."
NAUGHTY, NAUGHTY, NAUGHTY.
TAP! TAP! TAP!
"RONALD W. REAGAN, U.S. PRESIDENT, APPOINTED ALL OF THE ABOVE TO OFFICE."
NAUGHTY?
GEE, I DON'T KNOW. HE SEEMS SO NICE.
NICE.
NICE. SEND FRUITCAKE? □YES □NO
TAP! TAP! TAP!

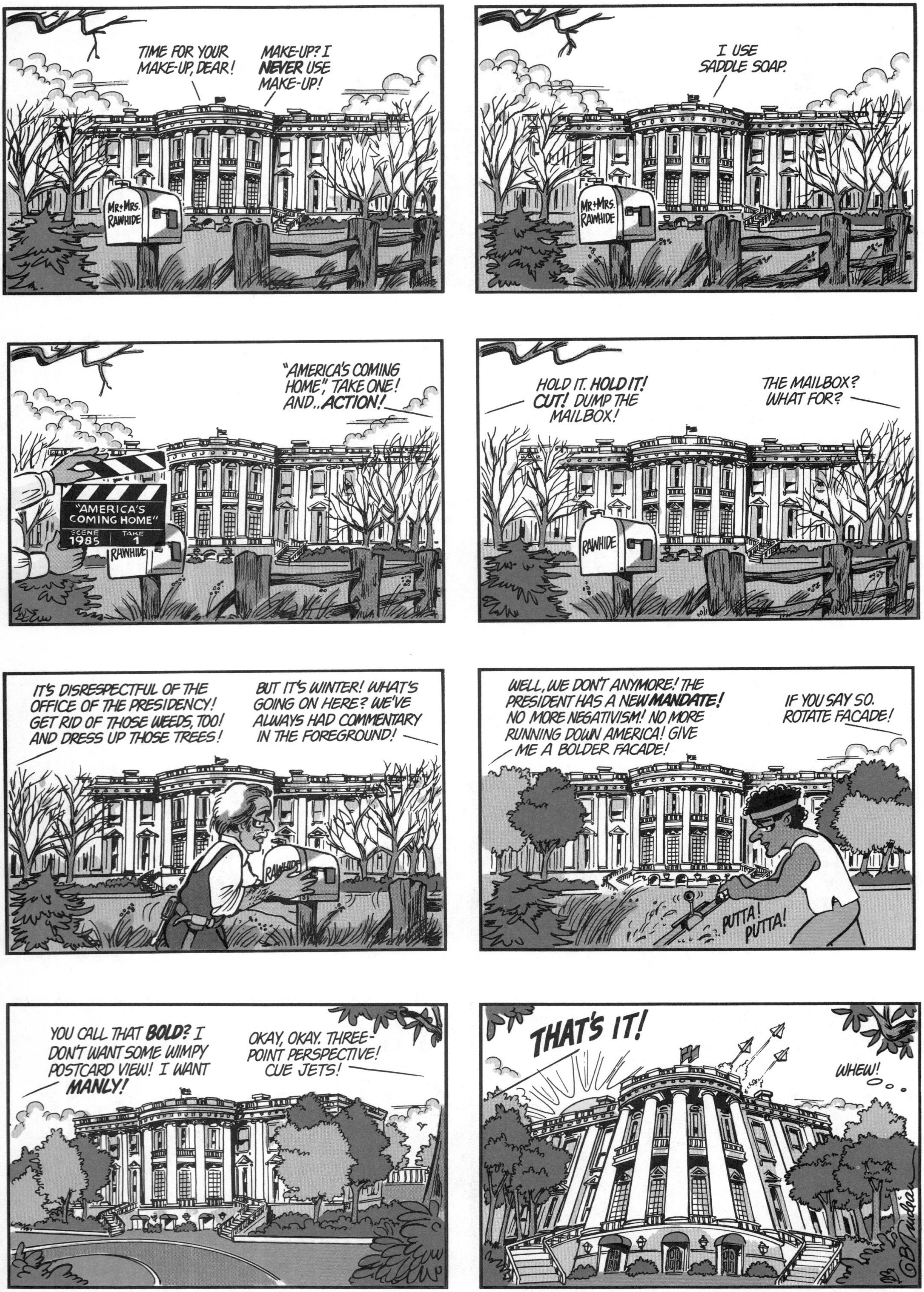
TIME FOR YOUR MAKE-UP, DEAR!
MAKE-UP? I **NEVER** USE MAKE-UP!
MR+MRS. RAWHIDE
I USE SADDLE SOAP.
MR+MRS. RAWHIDE
"AMERICA'S COMING HOME", TAKE ONE! AND.. **ACTION!**
"AMERICA'S COMING HOME" SCENE 1985 TAKE 1
RAWHIDE
HOLD IT. **HOLD IT! CUT!** DUMP THE MAILBOX!
THE MAILBOX? WHAT FOR?
RAWHIDE
IT'S DISRESPECTFUL OF THE OFFICE OF THE PRESIDENCY! GET RID OF THOSE WEEDS, TOO! AND DRESS UP THOSE TREES!
BUT IT'S WINTER! WHAT'S GOING ON HERE? WE'VE ALWAYS HAD COMMENTARY IN THE FOREGROUND!
RAWHIDE
WELL, WE DON'T ANYMORE! THE PRESIDENT HAS A NEW **MANDATE!** NO MORE NEGATIVISM! NO MORE RUNNING DOWN AMERICA! GIVE ME A BOLDER FACADE!
IF YOU SAY SO. ROTATE FACADE!
PUTTA! PUTTA!
YOU CALL THAT **BOLD?** I DON'T WANT SOME WIMPY POSTCARD VIEW! I WANT **MANLY!**
OKAY, OKAY. THREE-POINT PERSPECTIVE! CUE JETS!
THAT'S IT!
WHEW!

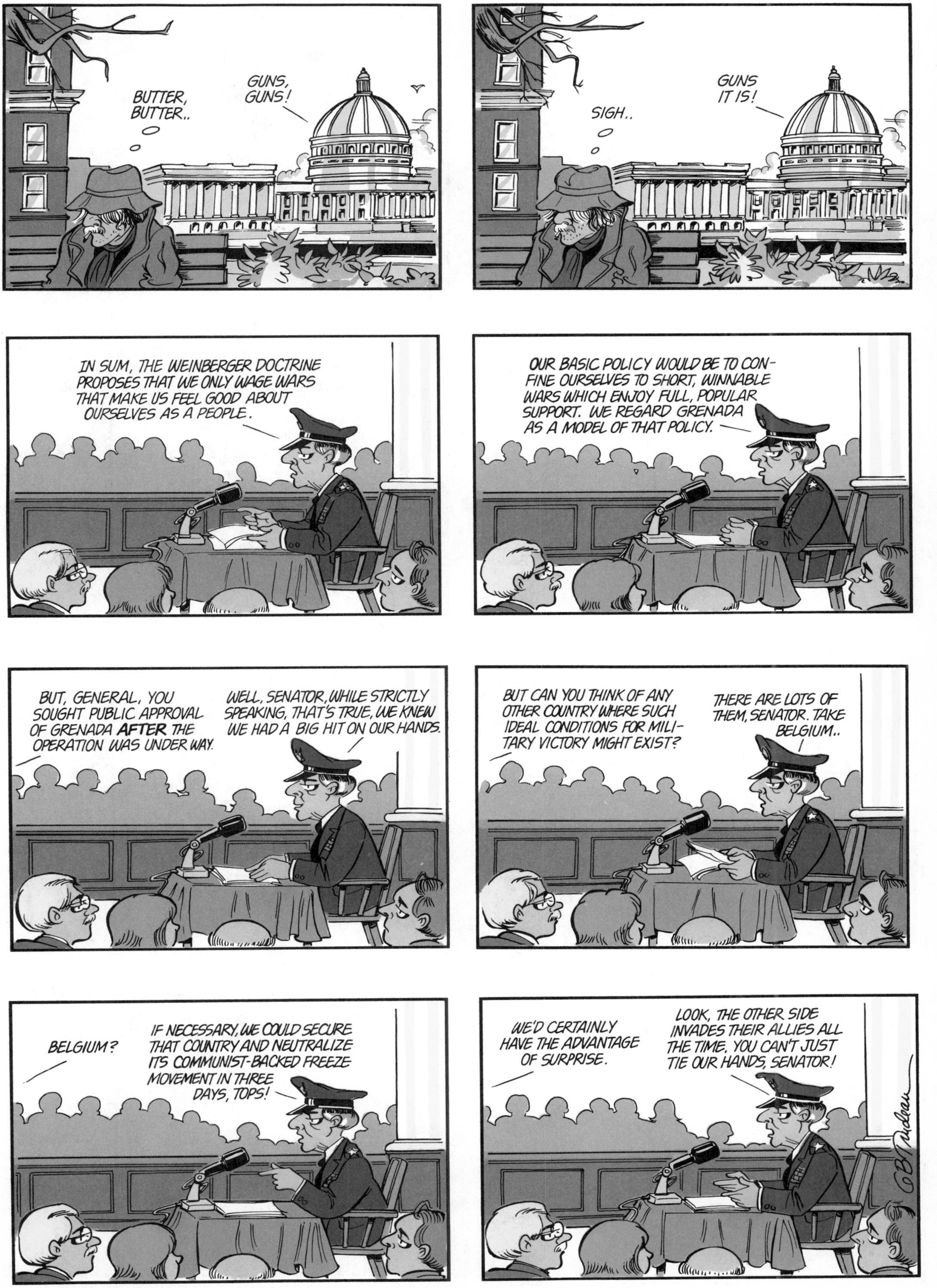
BUTTER, BUTTER..
GUNS, GUNS!
SIGH..
GUNS IT IS!
IN SUM, THE WEINBERGER DOCTRINE PROPOSES THAT WE ONLY WAGE WARS THAT MAKE US FEEL GOOD ABOUT OURSELVES AS A PEOPLE.
OUR BASIC POLICY WOULD BE TO CONFINE OURSELVES TO SHORT, WINNABLE WARS WHICH ENJOY FULL, POPULAR SUPPORT. WE REGARD GRENADA AS A MODEL OF THAT POLICY.
BUT, GENERAL, YOU SOUGHT PUBLIC APPROVAL OF GRENADA **AFTER** THE OPERATION WAS UNDER WAY.
WELL, SENATOR, WHILE STRICTLY SPEAKING, THAT'S TRUE, WE KNEW WE HAD A BIG HIT ON OUR HANDS.
BUT CAN YOU THINK OF ANY OTHER COUNTRY WHERE SUCH IDEAL CONDITIONS FOR MILITARY VICTORY MIGHT EXIST?
THERE ARE LOTS OF THEM, SENATOR. TAKE BELGIUM..
BELGIUM?
IF NECESSARY, WE COULD SECURE THAT COUNTRY AND NEUTRALIZE ITS COMMUNIST-BACKED FREEZE MOVEMENT IN THREE DAYS, TOPS!
WE'D CERTAINLY HAVE THE ADVANTAGE OF SURPRISE.
LOOK, THE OTHER SIDE INVADES THEIR ALLIES ALL THE TIME. YOU CAN'T JUST TIE OUR HANDS, SENATOR!

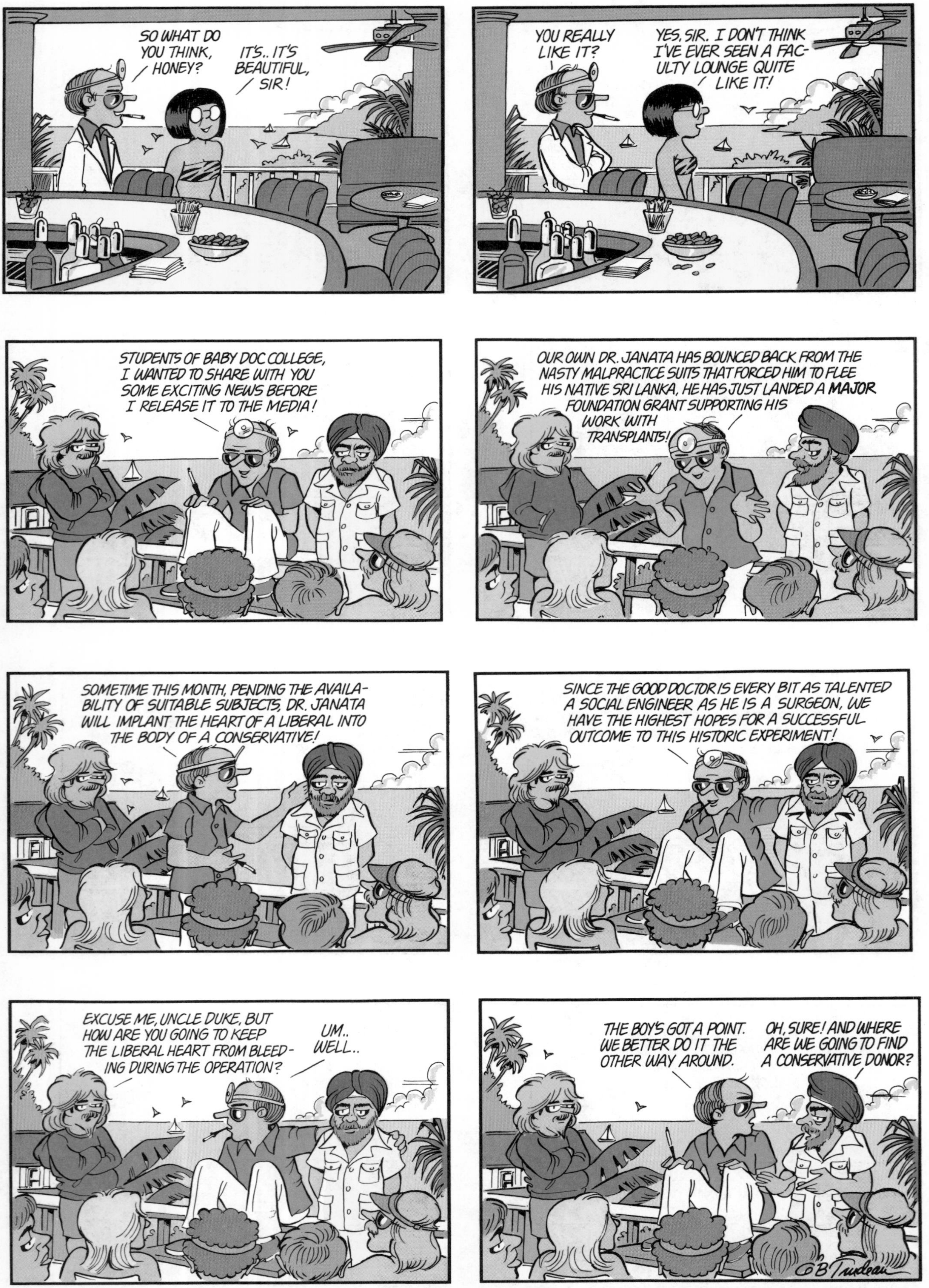

SO WHAT DO YOU THINK, HONEY?
IT'S.. IT'S BEAUTIFUL, SIR!
YOU REALLY LIKE IT?
YES, SIR. I DON'T THINK I'VE EVER SEEN A FACULTY LOUNGE QUITE LIKE IT!
STUDENTS OF BABY DOC COLLEGE, I WANTED TO SHARE WITH YOU SOME EXCITING NEWS BEFORE I RELEASE IT TO THE MEDIA!
OUR OWN DR. JANATA HAS BOUNCED BACK FROM THE NASTY MALPRACTICE SUITS THAT FORCED HIM TO FLEE HIS NATIVE SRI LANKA, HE HAS JUST LANDED A **MAJOR** FOUNDATION GRANT SUPPORTING HIS WORK WITH TRANSPLANTS!
SOMETIME THIS MONTH, PENDING THE AVAILABILITY OF SUITABLE SUBJECTS, DR. JANATA WILL IMPLANT THE HEART OF A LIBERAL INTO THE BODY OF A CONSERVATIVE!
SINCE THE GOOD DOCTOR IS EVERY BIT AS TALENTED A SOCIAL ENGINEER AS HE IS A SURGEON, WE HAVE THE HIGHEST HOPES FOR A SUCCESSFUL OUTCOME TO THIS HISTORIC EXPERIMENT!
EXCUSE ME, UNCLE DUKE, BUT HOW ARE YOU GOING TO KEEP THE LIBERAL HEART FROM BLEEDING DURING THE OPERATION?
UM.. WELL..
THE BOY'S GOT A POINT. WE BETTER DO IT THE OTHER WAY AROUND.
OH, SURE! AND WHERE ARE WE GOING TO FIND A CONSERVATIVE DONOR?
G.B. Trudeau

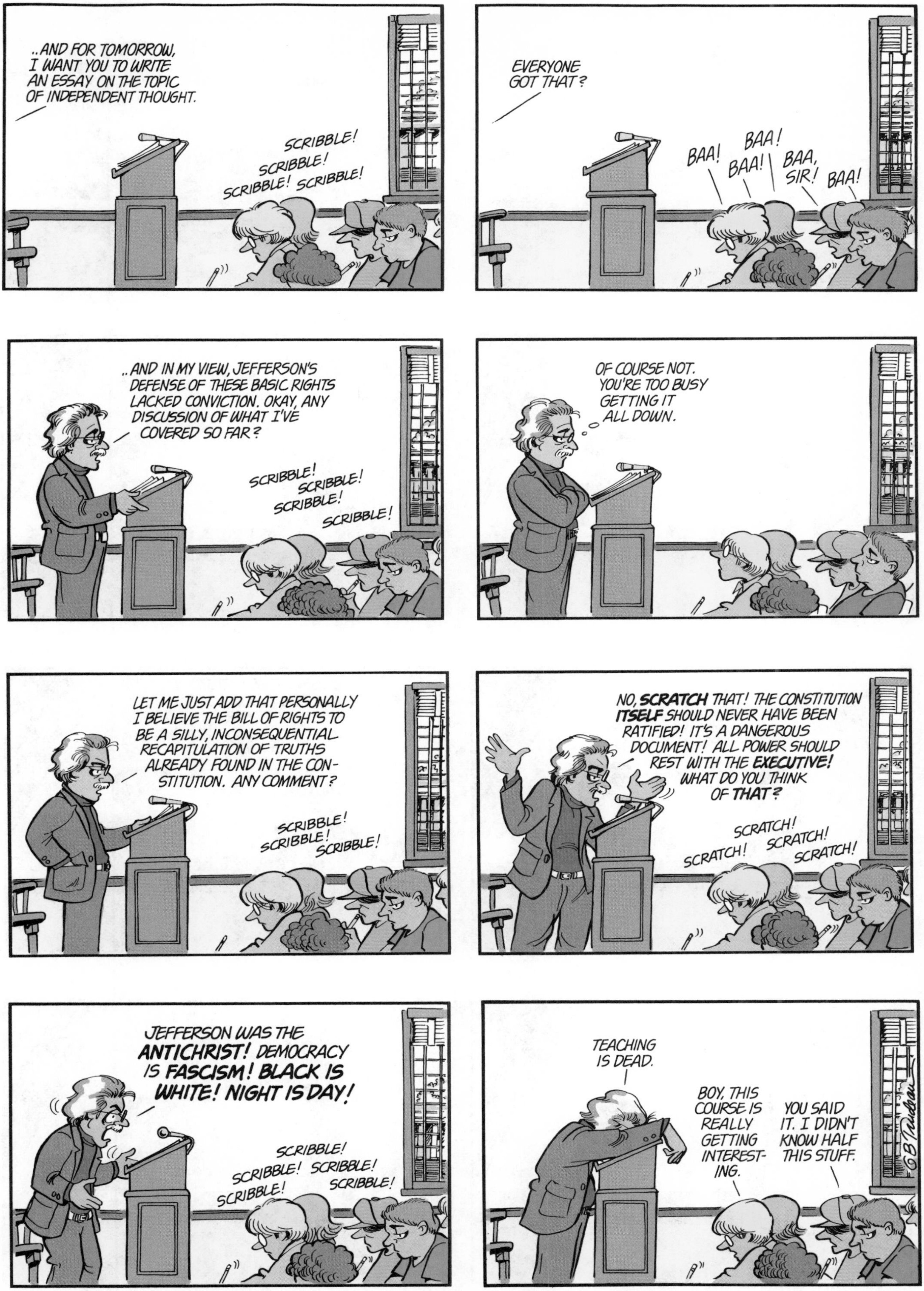
..AND FOR TOMORROW, I WANT YOU TO WRITE AN ESSAY ON THE TOPIC OF INDEPENDENT THOUGHT.
SCRIBBLE! SCRIBBLE! SCRIBBLE! SCRIBBLE!
EVERYONE GOT THAT?
BAA! BAA! BAA! BAA, SIR! BAA!
..AND IN MY VIEW, JEFFERSON'S DEFENSE OF THESE BASIC RIGHTS LACKED CONVICTION. OKAY, ANY DISCUSSION OF WHAT I'VE COVERED SO FAR?
SCRIBBLE! SCRIBBLE! SCRIBBLE! SCRIBBLE!
OF COURSE NOT. YOU'RE TOO BUSY GETTING IT ALL DOWN.
LET ME JUST ADD THAT PERSONALLY I BELIEVE THE BILL OF RIGHTS TO BE A SILLY, INCONSEQUENTIAL RECAPITULATION OF TRUTHS ALREADY FOUND IN THE CON-STITUTION. ANY COMMENT?
SCRIBBLE! SCRIBBLE! SCRIBBLE!
NO, **SCRATCH** THAT! THE CONSTITUTION **ITSELF** SHOULD NEVER HAVE BEEN RATIFIED! IT'S A DANGEROUS DOCUMENT! ALL POWER SHOULD REST WITH THE **EXECUTIVE!** WHAT DO YOU THINK OF **THAT?**
SCRATCH! SCRATCH! SCRATCH! SCRATCH!
JEFFERSON WAS THE **ANTICHRIST!** DEMOCRACY IS **FASCISM! BLACK IS WHITE! NIGHT IS DAY!**
SCRIBBLE! SCRIBBLE! SCRIBBLE! SCRIBBLE! SCRIBBLE!
TEACHING IS DEAD.
BOY, THIS COURSE IS REALLY GETTING INTEREST-ING.
YOU SAID IT. I DIDN'T KNOW HALF THIS STUFF.

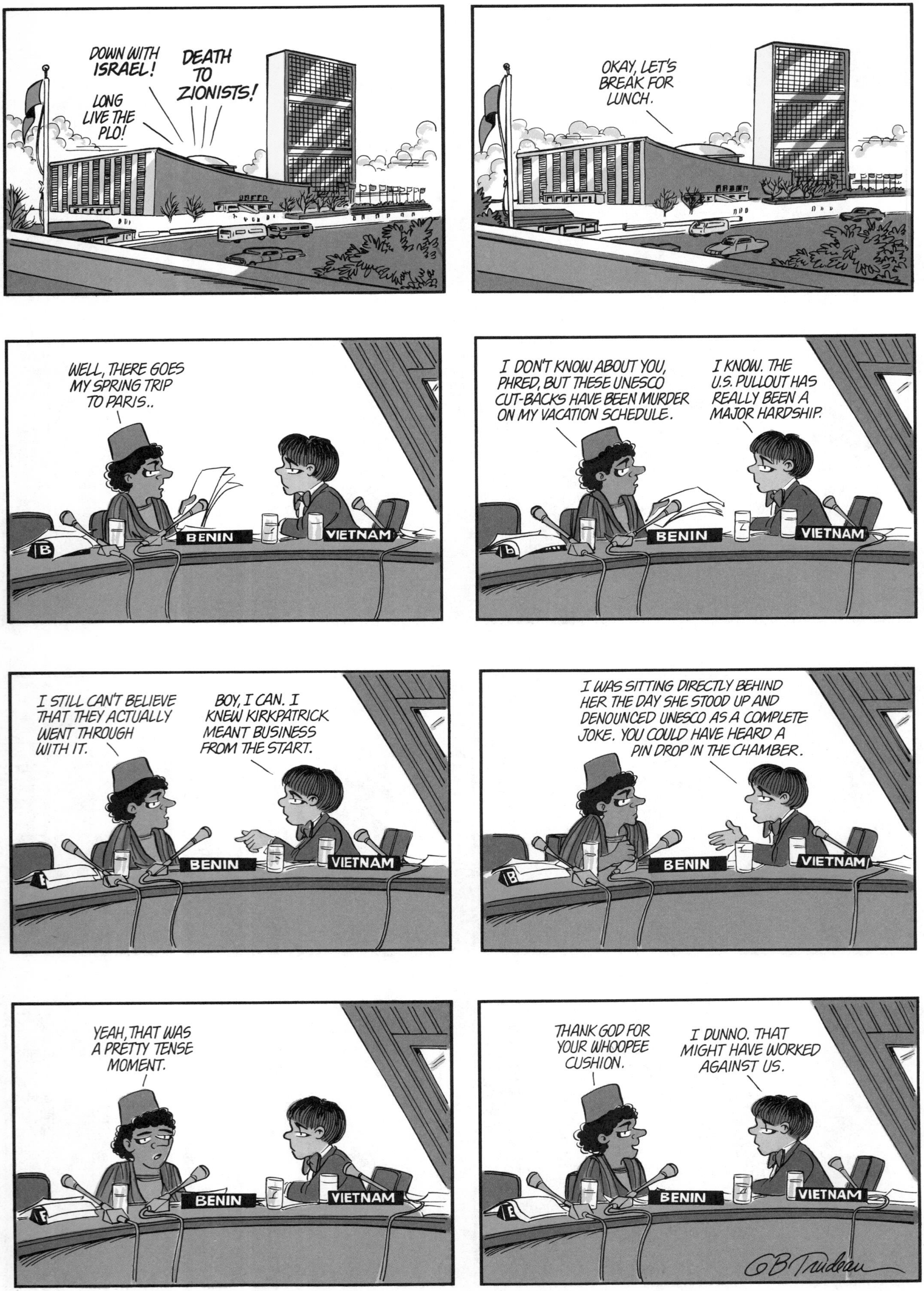
DOWN WITH ISRAEL!
LONG LIVE THE PLO!
DEATH TO ZIONISTS!
OKAY, LET'S BREAK FOR LUNCH.
WELL, THERE GOES MY SPRING TRIP TO PARIS..
BENIN
VIETNAM
I DON'T KNOW ABOUT YOU, PHRED, BUT THESE UNESCO CUT-BACKS HAVE BEEN MURDER ON MY VACATION SCHEDULE.
I KNOW. THE U.S. PULLOUT HAS REALLY BEEN A MAJOR HARDSHIP.
BENIN
VIETNAM
I STILL CAN'T BELIEVE THAT THEY ACTUALLY WENT THROUGH WITH IT.
BOY, I CAN. I KNEW KIRKPATRICK MEANT BUSINESS FROM THE START.
BENIN
VIETNAM
I WAS SITTING DIRECTLY BEHIND HER THE DAY SHE STOOD UP AND DENOUNCED UNESCO AS A COMPLETE JOKE. YOU COULD HAVE HEARD A PIN DROP IN THE CHAMBER.
BENIN
VIETNAM
YEAH, THAT WAS A PRETTY TENSE MOMENT.
BENIN
VIETNAM
THANK GOD FOR YOUR WHOOPEE CUSHION.
I DUNNO. THAT MIGHT HAVE WORKED AGAINST US.
BENIN
VIETNAM
GB Trudeau

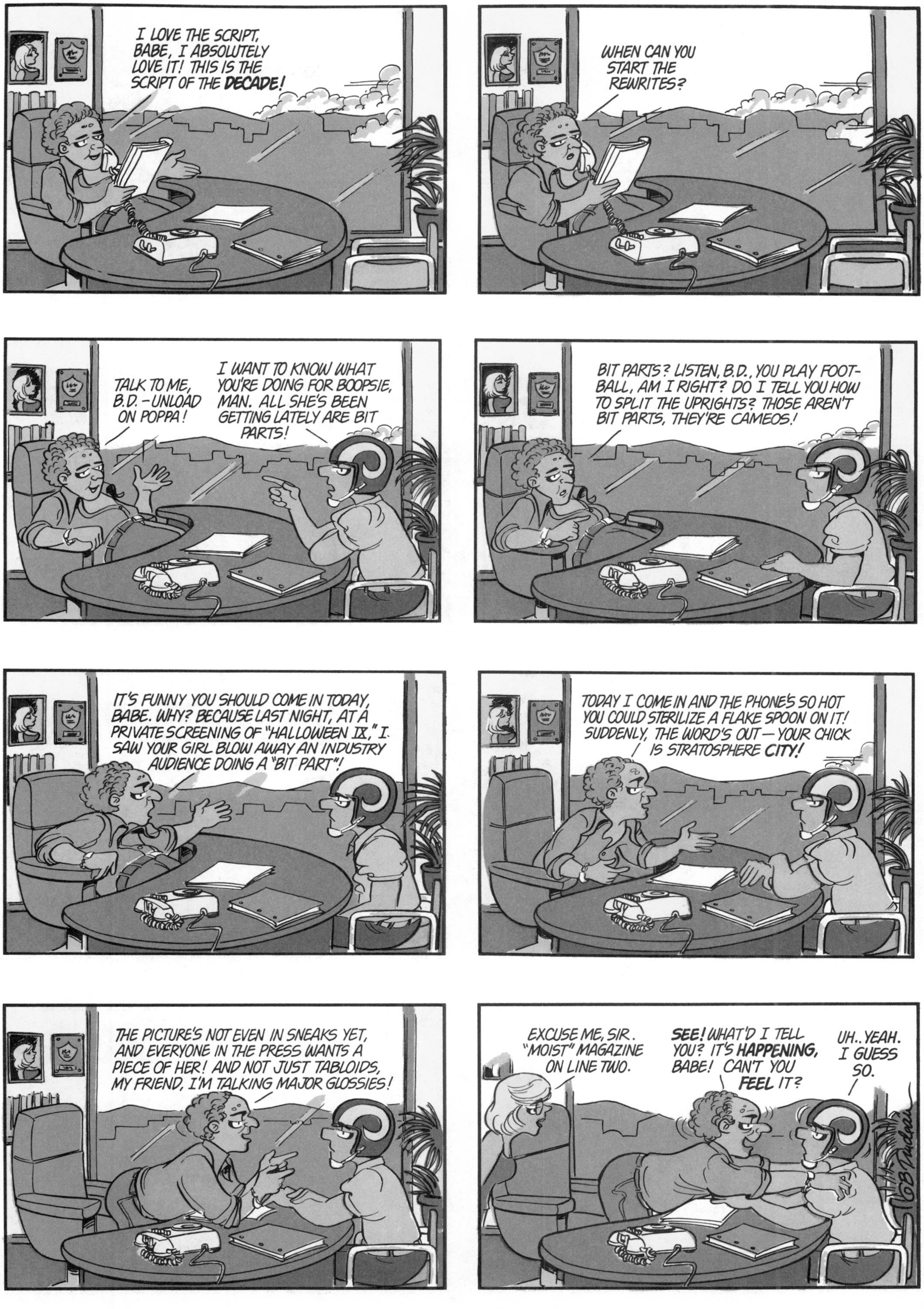

I LOVE THE SCRIPT, BABE, I ABSOLUTELY LOVE IT! THIS IS THE SCRIPT OF THE **DECADE**!
WHEN CAN YOU START THE REWRITES?
TALK TO ME, B.D. – UNLOAD ON POPPA!
I WANT TO KNOW WHAT YOU'RE DOING FOR BOOPSIE, MAN. ALL SHE'S BEEN GETTING LATELY ARE BIT PARTS!
BIT PARTS? LISTEN, B.D., YOU PLAY FOOTBALL, AM I RIGHT? DO I TELL YOU HOW TO SPLIT THE UPRIGHTS? THOSE AREN'T BIT PARTS, THEY'RE CAMEOS!
IT'S FUNNY YOU SHOULD COME IN TODAY, BABE. WHY? BECAUSE LAST NIGHT, AT A PRIVATE SCREENING OF "HALLOWEEN IX," I SAW YOUR GIRL BLOW AWAY AN INDUSTRY AUDIENCE DOING A "BIT PART"!
TODAY I COME IN AND THE PHONE'S SO HOT YOU COULD STERILIZE A FLAKE SPOON ON IT! SUDDENLY, THE WORD'S OUT — YOUR CHICK IS STRATOSPHERE **CITY**!
THE PICTURE'S NOT EVEN IN SNEAKS YET, AND EVERYONE IN THE PRESS WANTS A PIECE OF HER! AND NOT JUST TABLOIDS, MY FRIEND, I'M TALKING MAJOR GLOSSIES!
EXCUSE ME, SIR. "MOIST" MAGAZINE ON LINE TWO.
SEE! WHAT'D I TELL YOU? IT'S **HAPPENING**, BABE! CAN'T YOU **FEEL** IT?
UH.. YEAH. I GUESS SO.

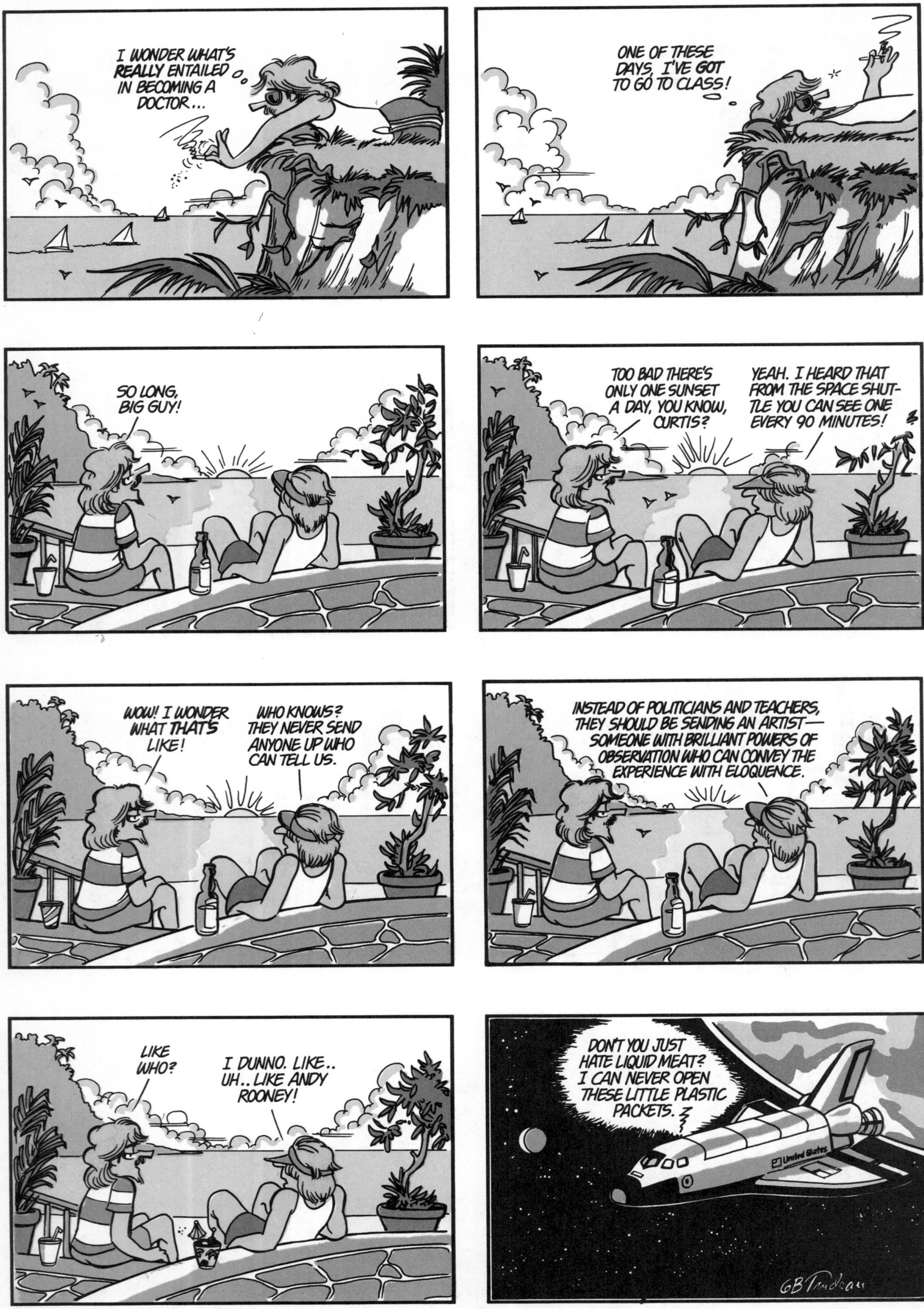
I WONDER WHAT'S REALLY ENTAILED IN BECOMING A DOCTOR...
ONE OF THESE DAYS, I'VE GOT TO GO TO CLASS!
SO LONG, BIG GUY!
TOO BAD THERE'S ONLY ONE SUNSET A DAY, YOU KNOW, CURTIS?
YEAH. I HEARD THAT FROM THE SPACE SHUT-TLE YOU CAN SEE ONE EVERY 90 MINUTES!
WOW! I WONDER WHAT THAT'S LIKE!
WHO KNOWS? THEY NEVER SEND ANYONE UP WHO CAN TELL US.
INSTEAD OF POLITICIANS AND TEACHERS, THEY SHOULD BE SENDING AN ARTIST— SOMEONE WITH BRILLIANT POWERS OF OBSERVATION WHO CAN CONVEY THE EXPERIENCE WITH ELOQUENCE.
LIKE WHO?
I DUNNO. LIKE.. UH.. LIKE ANDY ROONEY!
DON'T YOU JUST HATE LIQUID MEAT? I CAN NEVER OPEN THESE LITTLE PLASTIC PACKETS.
United States
GB Trudeau

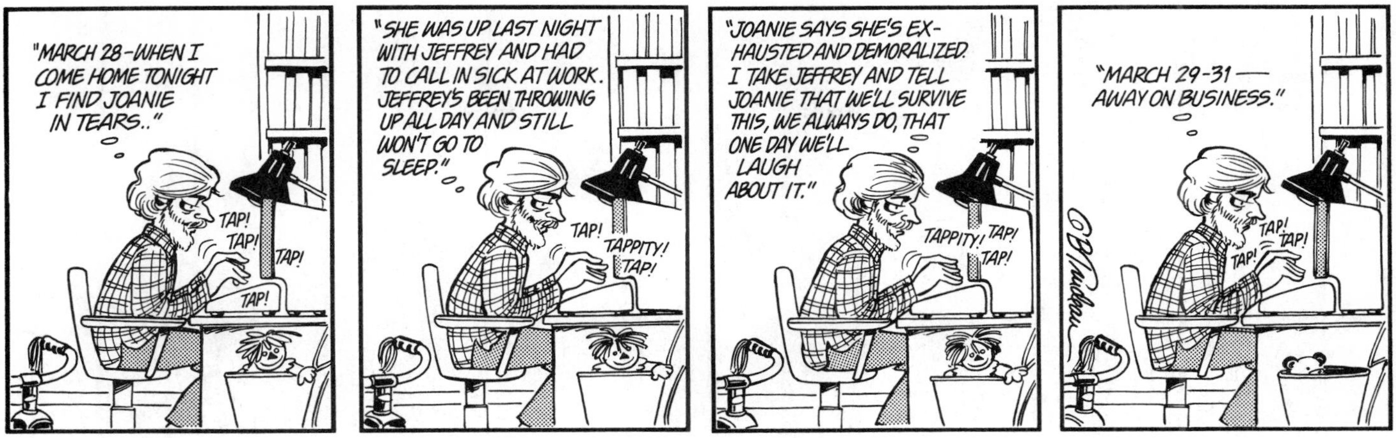
"MARCH 28—WHEN I COME HOME TONIGHT I FIND JOANIE IN TEARS.."
TAP! TAP! TAP! TAP!
"SHE WAS UP LAST NIGHT WITH JEFFREY AND HAD TO CALL IN SICK AT WORK. JEFFREY'S BEEN THROWING UP ALL DAY AND STILL WON'T GO TO SLEEP."
TAP! TAPPITY! TAP!
"JOANIE SAYS SHE'S EXHAUSTED AND DEMORALIZED. I TAKE JEFFREY AND TELL JOANIE THAT WE'LL SURVIVE THIS, WE ALWAYS DO, THAT ONE DAY WE'LL LAUGH ABOUT IT."
TAPPITY! TAP! TAP!
"MARCH 29-31— AWAY ON BUSINESS."
TAP! TAP! TAP!
GB Trudeau

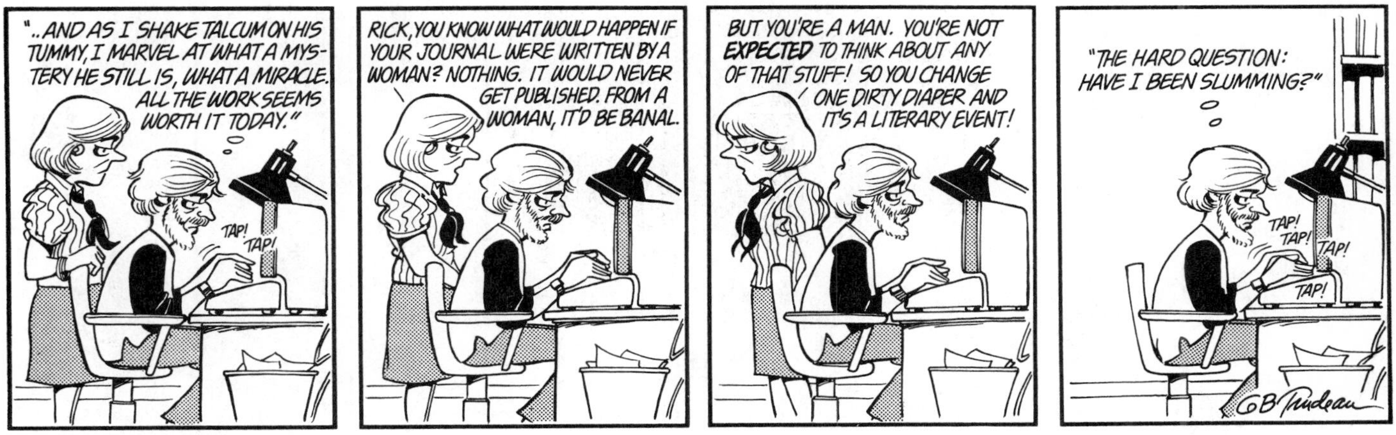
"..AND AS I SHAKE TALCUM ON HIS TUMMY, I MARVEL AT WHAT A MYSTERY HE STILL IS, WHAT A MIRACLE. ALL THE WORK SEEMS WORTH IT TODAY."
TAP! TAP!
RICK, YOU KNOW WHAT WOULD HAPPEN IF YOUR JOURNAL WERE WRITTEN BY A WOMAN? NOTHING. IT WOULD NEVER GET PUBLISHED. FROM A WOMAN, IT'D BE BANAL.
BUT YOU'RE A MAN. YOU'RE NOT **EXPECTED** TO THINK ABOUT ANY OF THAT STUFF! SO YOU CHANGE ONE DIRTY DIAPER AND IT'S A LITERARY EVENT!
"THE HARD QUESTION: HAVE I BEEN SLUMMING?"
TAP! TAP! TAP! TAP!
GB Trudeau

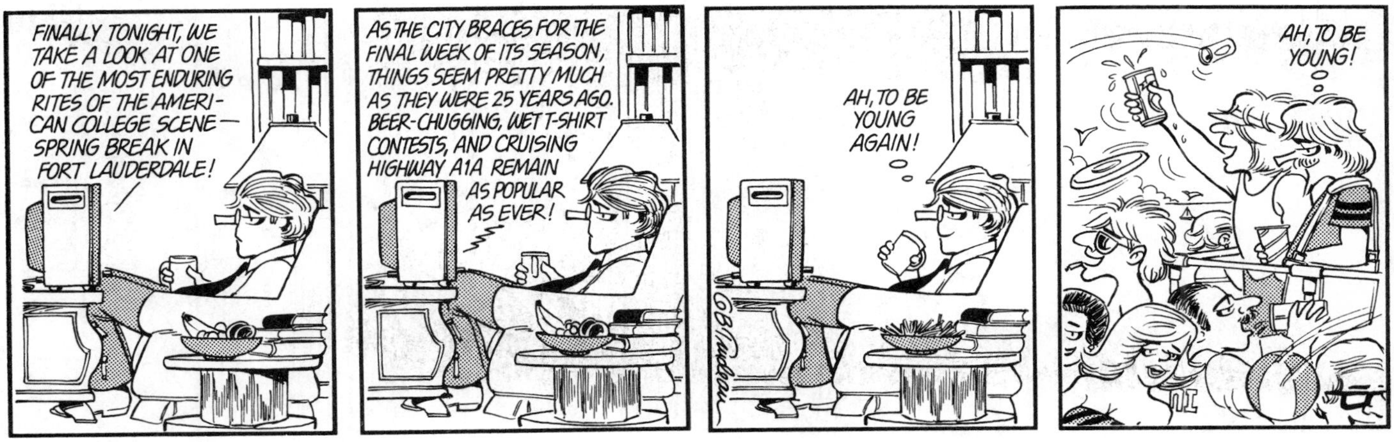
FINALLY TONIGHT, WE TAKE A LOOK AT ONE OF THE MOST ENDURING RITES OF THE AMERICAN COLLEGE SCENE— SPRING BREAK IN FORT LAUDERDALE!
AS THE CITY BRACES FOR THE FINAL WEEK OF ITS SEASON, THINGS SEEM PRETTY MUCH AS THEY WERE 25 YEARS AGO. BEER-CHUGGING, WET T-SHIRT CONTESTS, AND CRUISING HIGHWAY A1A REMAIN AS POPULAR AS EVER!
GB Trudeau
AH, TO BE YOUNG AGAIN!
AH, TO BE YOUNG!

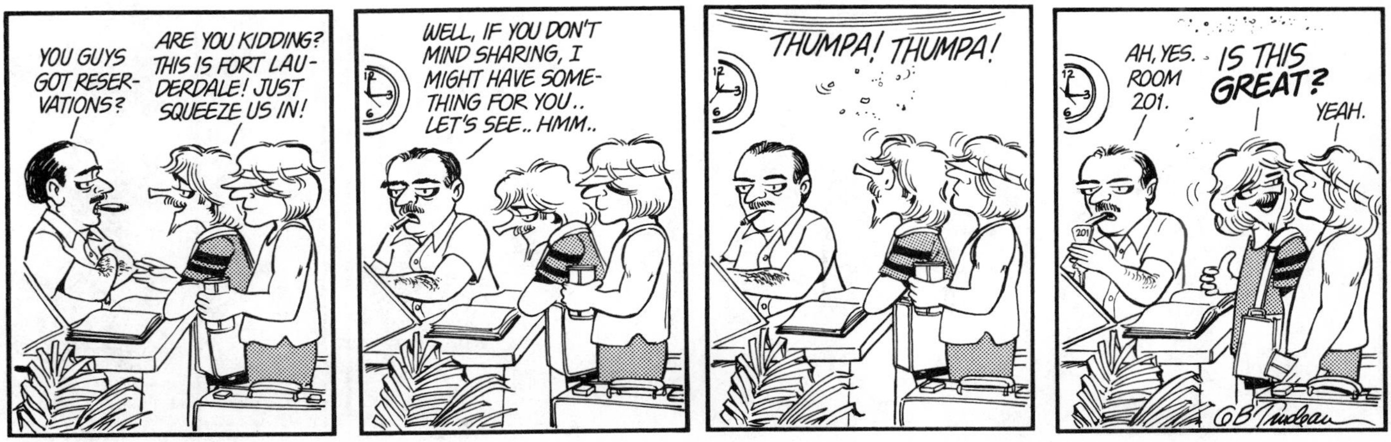
YOU GUYS GOT RESERVATIONS?
ARE YOU KIDDING? THIS IS FORT LAUDERDALE! JUST SQUEEZE US IN!
WELL, IF YOU DON'T MIND SHARING, I MIGHT HAVE SOMETHING FOR YOU.. LET'S SEE.. HMM..
THUMPA! THUMPA!
AH, YES. ROOM 201.
IS THIS **GREAT?**
YEAH.
GB Trudeau

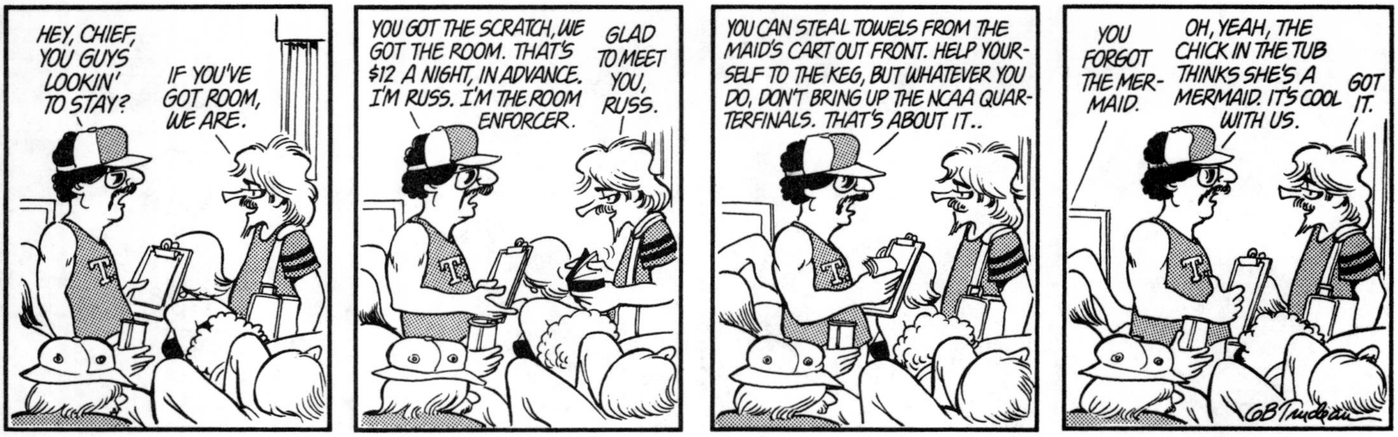
HEY, CHIEF, YOU GUYS LOOKIN' TO STAY?
IF YOU'VE GOT ROOM, WE ARE.
YOU GOT THE SCRATCH, WE GOT THE ROOM. THAT'S $12 A NIGHT, IN ADVANCE. I'M RUSS. I'M THE ROOM ENFORCER.
GLAD TO MEET YOU, RUSS.
YOU CAN STEAL TOWELS FROM THE MAID'S CART OUT FRONT. HELP YOURSELF TO THE KEG, BUT WHATEVER YOU DO, DON'T BRING UP THE NCAA QUARTERFINALS. THAT'S ABOUT IT..
YOU FORGOT THE MERMAID.
OH, YEAH, THE CHICK IN THE TUB THINKS SHE'S A MERMAID. IT'S COOL WITH US.
GOT IT.
GBTrudeau

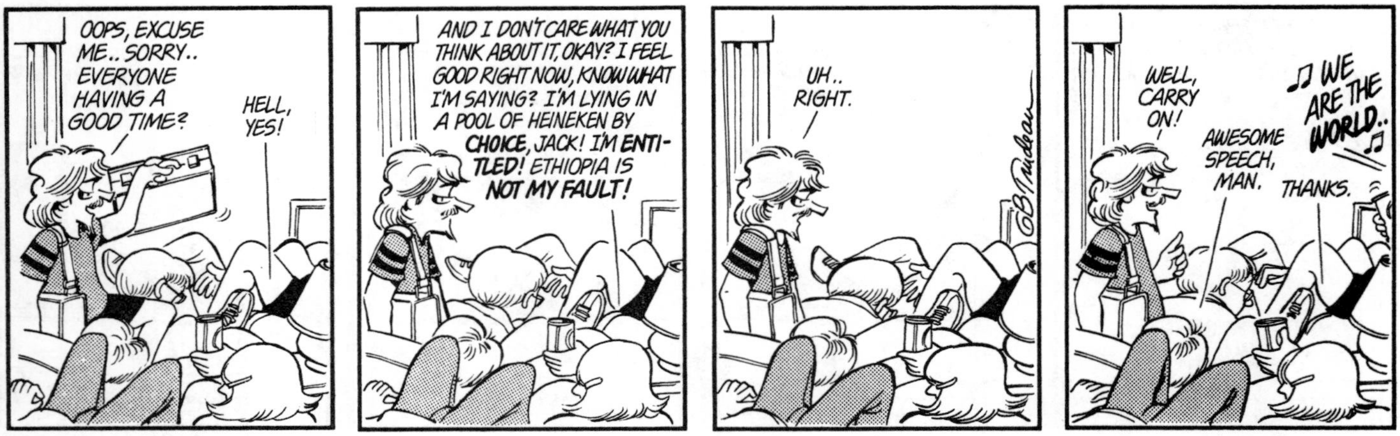
OOPS, EXCUSE ME.. SORRY.. EVERYONE HAVING A GOOD TIME?
HELL, YES!
AND I DON'T CARE WHAT YOU THINK ABOUT IT, OKAY? I FEEL GOOD RIGHT NOW, KNOW WHAT I'M SAYING? I'M LYING IN A POOL OF HEINEKEN BY CHOICE, JACK! I'M ENTITLED! ETHIOPIA IS NOT MY FAULT!
UH.. RIGHT.
GBTrudeau
WELL, CARRY ON!
AWESOME SPEECH, MAN.
THANKS.
♫ WE ARE THE WORLD.. ♫

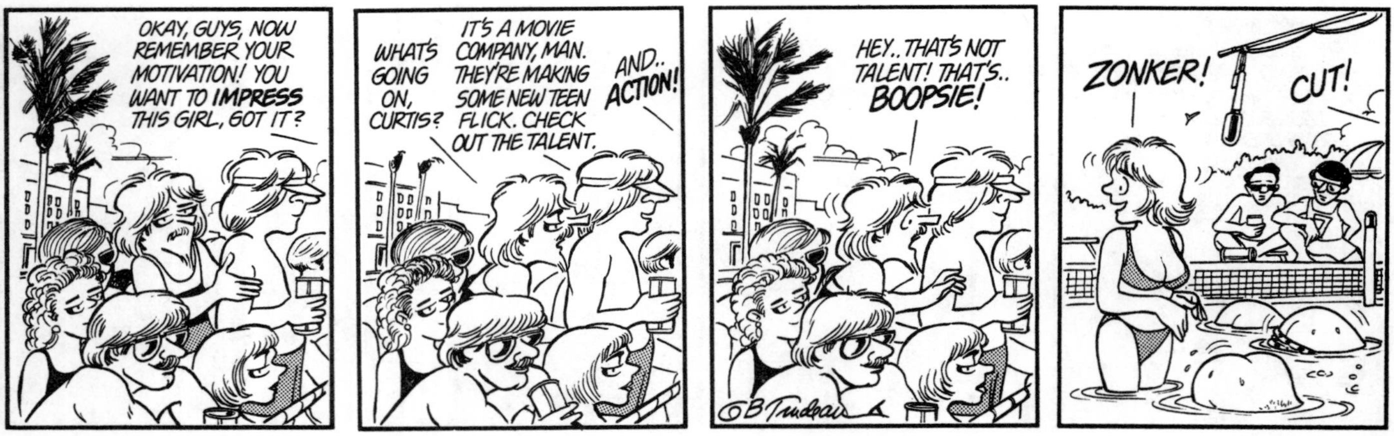
OKAY, GUYS, NOW REMEMBER YOUR MOTIVATION! YOU WANT TO IMPRESS THIS GIRL, GOT IT?
WHAT'S GOING ON, CURTIS?
IT'S A MOVIE COMPANY, MAN. THEY'RE MAKING SOME NEW TEEN FLICK. CHECK OUT THE TALENT.
AND.. ACTION!
HEY.. THAT'S NOT TALENT! THAT'S.. BOOPSIE!
GBTrudeau
ZONKER!
CUT!

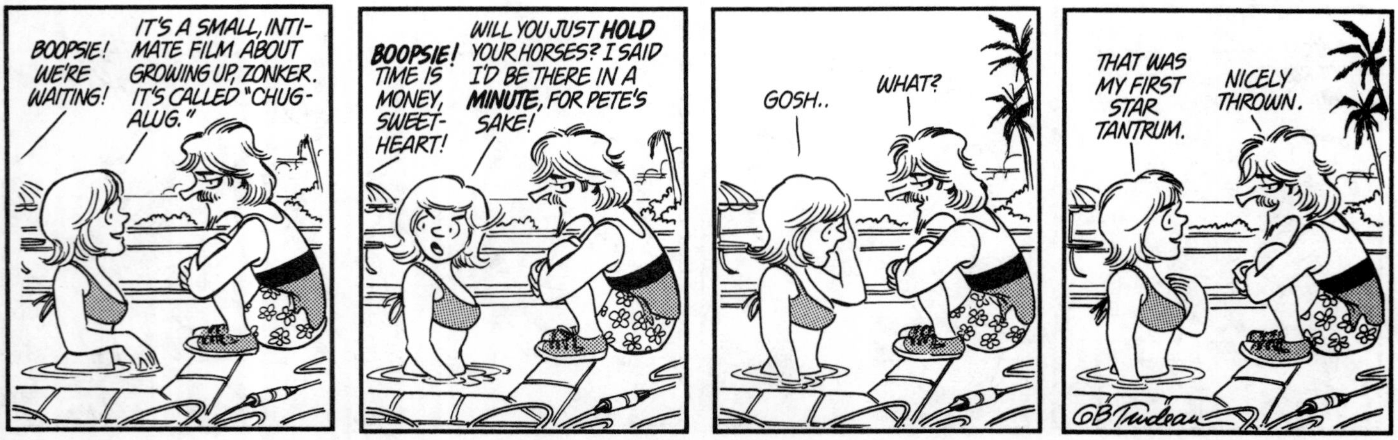
BOOPSIE! WE'RE WAITING!
IT'S A SMALL, INTIMATE FILM ABOUT GROWING UP, ZONKER. IT'S CALLED "CHUGALUG."
BOOPSIE! TIME IS MONEY, SWEETHEART!
WILL YOU JUST HOLD YOUR HORSES? I SAID I'D BE THERE IN A MINUTE, FOR PETE'S SAKE!
GOSH..
WHAT?
THAT WAS MY FIRST STAR TANTRUM.
NICELY THROWN.
GBTrudeau

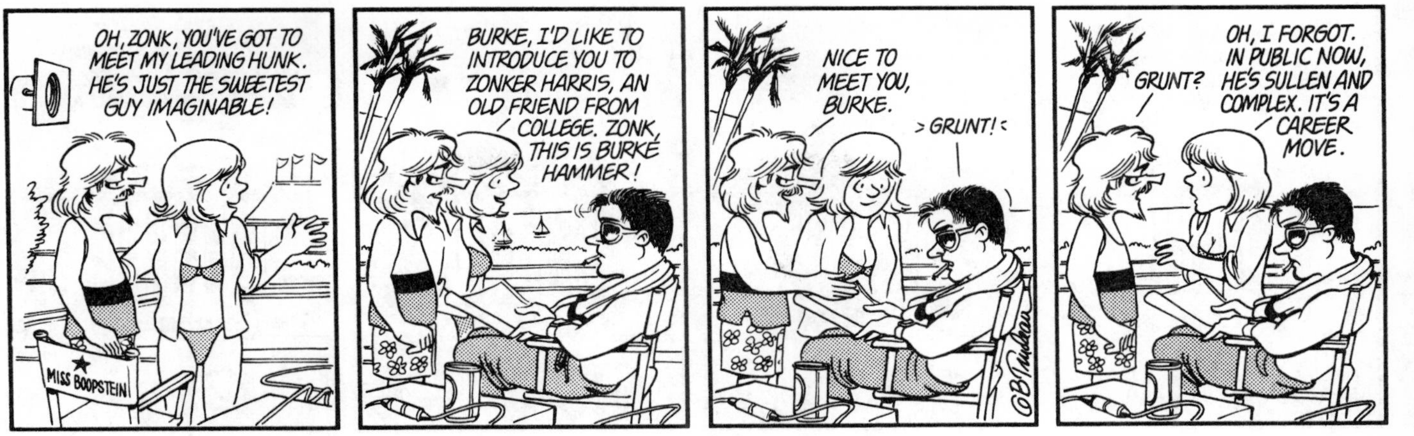
OH, ZONK, YOU'VE GOT TO MEET MY LEADING HUNK. HE'S JUST THE SWEETEST GUY IMAGINABLE!
MISS BOOPSTEIN
BURKE, I'D LIKE TO INTRODUCE YOU TO ZONKER HARRIS, AN OLD FRIEND FROM COLLEGE. ZONK, THIS IS BURKE HAMMER!
NICE TO MEET YOU, BURKE.
>GRUNT!<
GRUNT?
OH, I FORGOT. IN PUBLIC NOW, HE'S SULLEN AND COMPLEX. IT'S A CAREER MOVE.
©B Trudeau

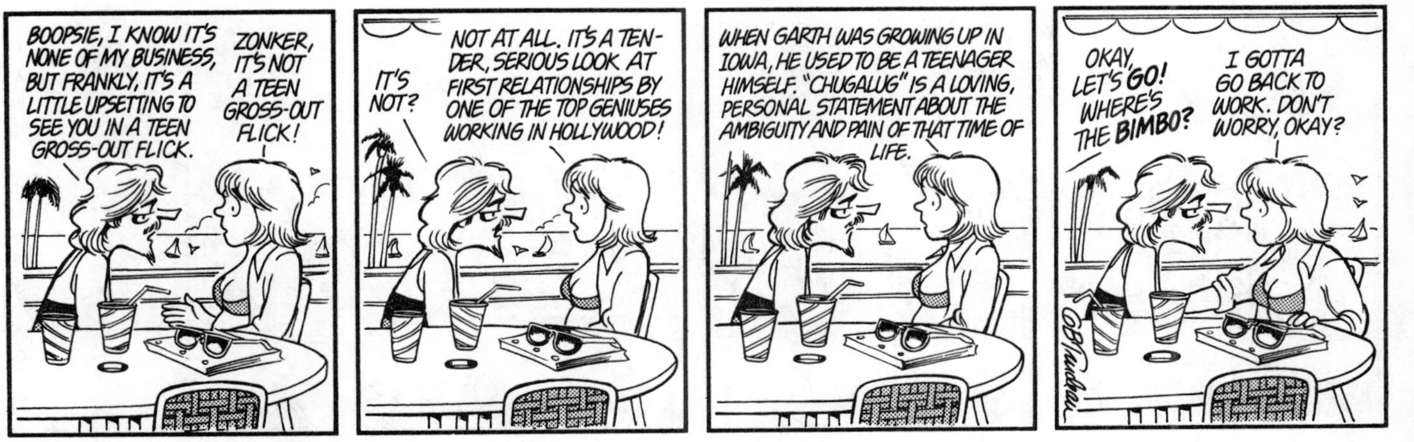
BOOPSIE, I KNOW IT'S NONE OF MY BUSINESS, BUT FRANKLY, IT'S A LITTLE UPSETTING TO SEE YOU IN A TEEN GROSS-OUT FLICK.
ZONKER, IT'S NOT A TEEN GROSS-OUT FLICK!
IT'S NOT?
NOT AT ALL. IT'S A TENDER, SERIOUS LOOK AT FIRST RELATIONSHIPS BY ONE OF THE TOP GENIUSES WORKING IN HOLLYWOOD!
WHEN GARTH WAS GROWING UP IN IOWA, HE USED TO BE A TEENAGER HIMSELF. "CHUGALUG" IS A LOVING, PERSONAL STATEMENT ABOUT THE AMBIGUITY AND PAIN OF THAT TIME OF LIFE.
OKAY, LET'S **GO!** WHERE'S THE **BIMBO?**
I GOTTA GO BACK TO WORK. DON'T WORRY, OKAY?
©B Trudeau

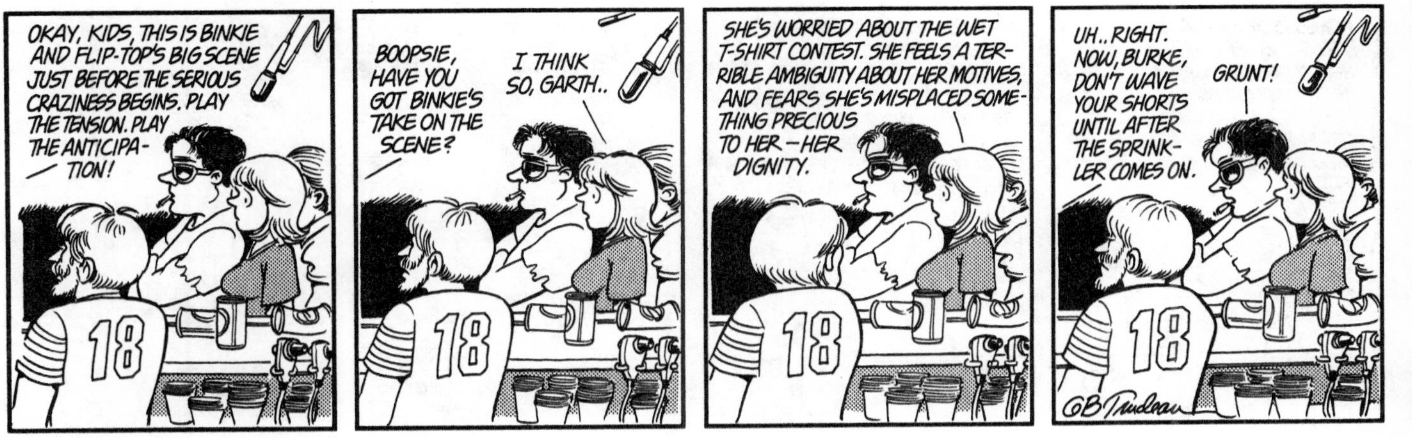
OKAY, KIDS, THIS IS BINKIE AND FLIP-TOP'S BIG SCENE JUST BEFORE THE SERIOUS CRAZINESS BEGINS. PLAY THE TENSION. PLAY THE ANTICIPATION!
18
BOOPSIE, HAVE YOU GOT BINKIE'S TAKE ON THE SCENE?
I THINK SO, GARTH..
18
SHE'S WORRIED ABOUT THE WET T-SHIRT CONTEST. SHE FEELS A TERRIBLE AMBIGUITY ABOUT HER MOTIVES, AND FEARS SHE'S MISPLACED SOMETHING PRECIOUS TO HER — HER DIGNITY.
18
UH.. RIGHT. NOW, BURKE, DON'T WAVE YOUR SHORTS UNTIL AFTER THE SPRINKLER COMES ON.
GRUNT!
18
©B Trudeau

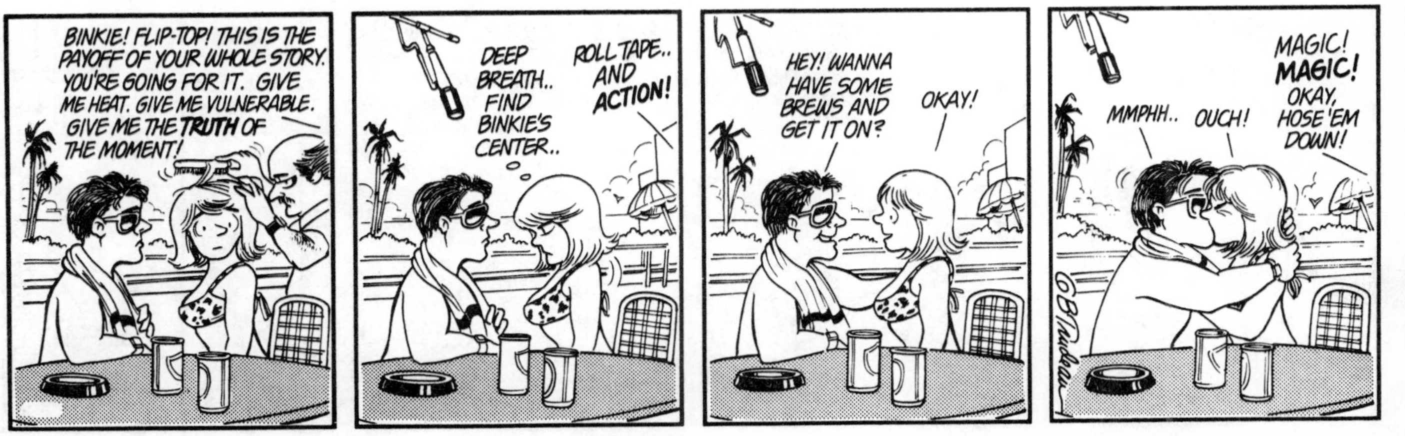
BINKIE! FLIP-TOP! THIS IS THE PAYOFF OF YOUR WHOLE STORY. YOU'RE GOING FOR IT. GIVE ME HEAT. GIVE ME VULNERABLE. GIVE ME THE **TRUTH** OF THE MOMENT!
DEEP BREATH.. FIND BINKIE'S CENTER..
ROLL TAPE.. AND **ACTION!**
HEY! WANNA HAVE SOME BREWS AND GET IT ON?
OKAY!
MMPHH..
OUCH!
MAGIC! **MAGIC!** OKAY, HOSE 'EM DOWN!
©B Trudeau

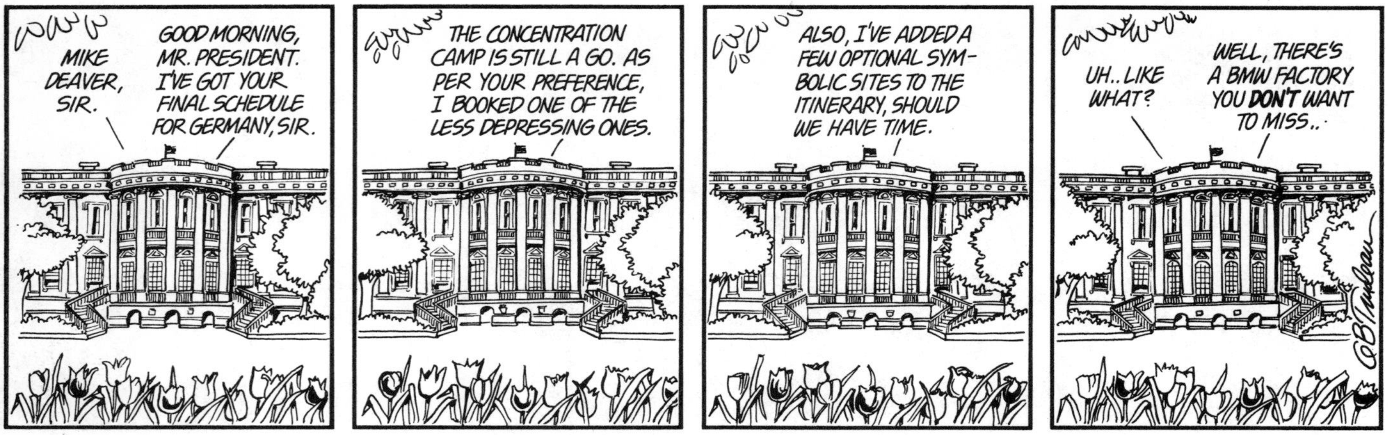
MIKE DEAVER, SIR.
GOOD MORNING, MR. PRESIDENT. I'VE GOT YOUR FINAL SCHEDULE FOR GERMANY, SIR.
THE CONCENTRATION CAMP IS STILL A GO. AS PER YOUR PREFERENCE, I BOOKED ONE OF THE LESS DEPRESSING ONES.
ALSO, I'VE ADDED A FEW OPTIONAL SYM-BOLIC SITES TO THE ITINERARY, SHOULD WE HAVE TIME.
UH.. LIKE WHAT?
WELL, THERE'S A BMW FACTORY YOU DON'T WANT TO MISS..

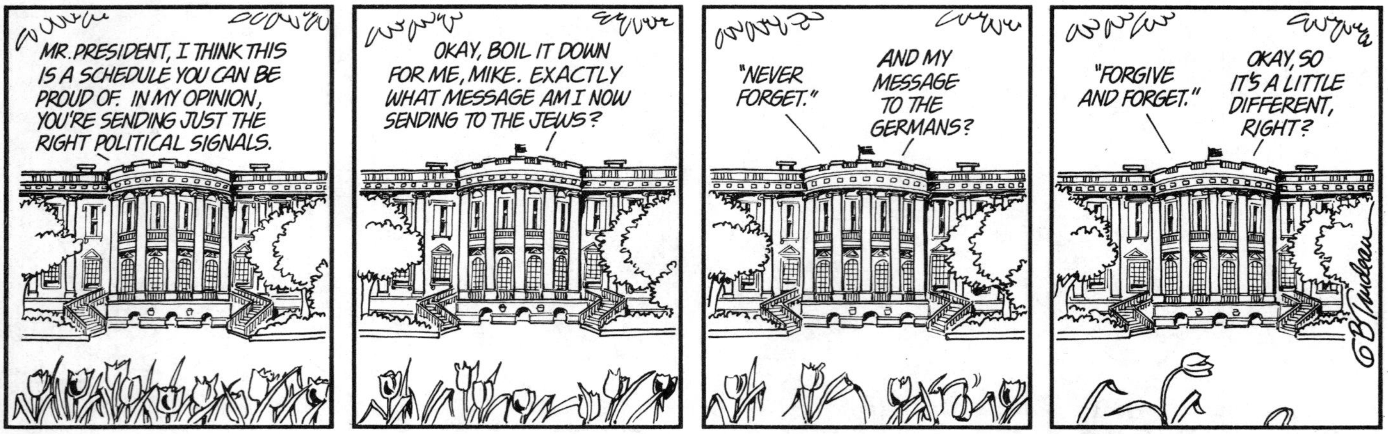
MR. PRESIDENT, I THINK THIS IS A SCHEDULE YOU CAN BE PROUD OF. IN MY OPINION, YOU'RE SENDING JUST THE RIGHT POLITICAL SIGNALS.
OKAY, BOIL IT DOWN FOR ME, MIKE. EXACTLY WHAT MESSAGE AM I NOW SENDING TO THE JEWS?
"NEVER FORGET."
AND MY MESSAGE TO THE GERMANS?
"FORGIVE AND FORGET."
OKAY, SO IT'S A LITTLE DIFFERENT, RIGHT?

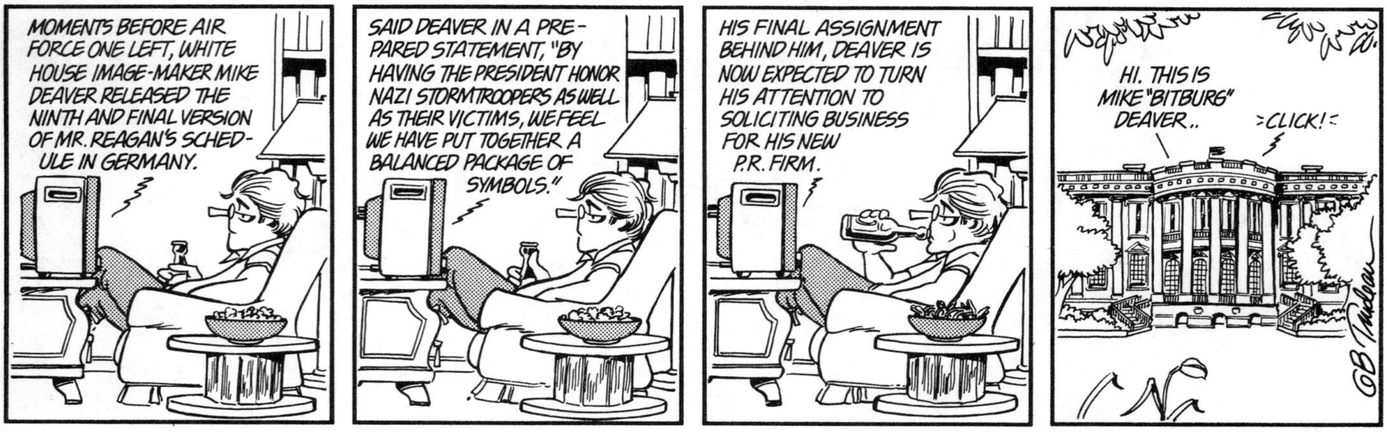
MOMENTS BEFORE AIR FORCE ONE LEFT, WHITE HOUSE IMAGE-MAKER MIKE DEAVER RELEASED THE NINTH AND FINAL VERSION OF MR. REAGAN'S SCHED-ULE IN GERMANY.
SAID DEAVER IN A PRE-PARED STATEMENT, "BY HAVING THE PRESIDENT HONOR NAZI STORMTROOPERS AS WELL AS THEIR VICTIMS, WE FEEL WE HAVE PUT TOGETHER A BALANCED PACKAGE OF SYMBOLS."
HIS FINAL ASSIGNMENT BEHIND HIM, DEAVER IS NOW EXPECTED TO TURN HIS ATTENTION TO SOLICITING BUSINESS FOR HIS NEW P.R. FIRM.
HI. THIS IS MIKE "BITBURG" DEAVER..
CLICK!

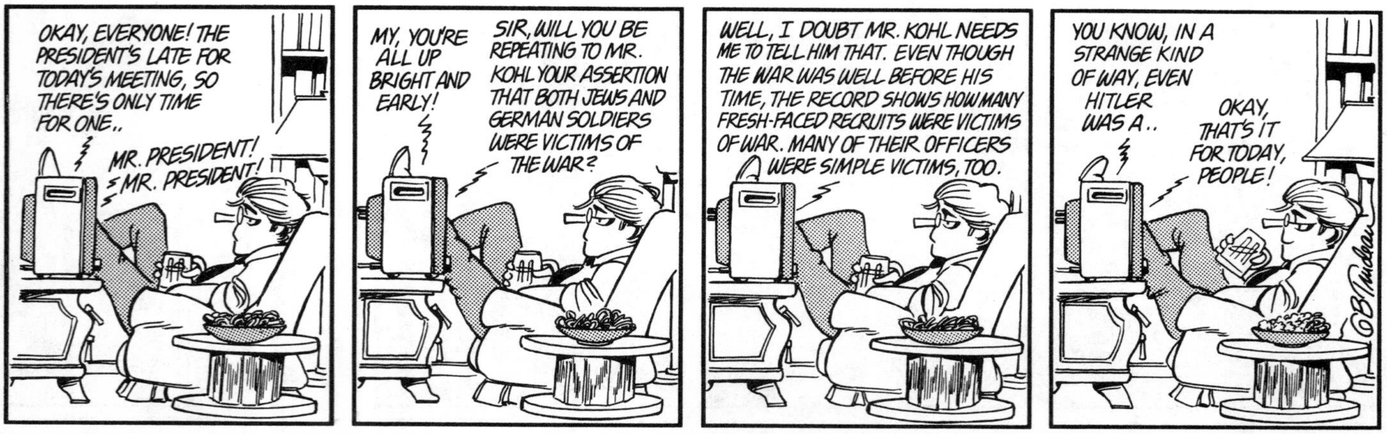
OKAY, EVERYONE! THE PRESIDENT'S LATE FOR TODAY'S MEETING, SO THERE'S ONLY TIME FOR ONE..
MR. PRESIDENT! MR. PRESIDENT!
MY, YOU'RE ALL UP BRIGHT AND EARLY!
SIR, WILL YOU BE REPEATING TO MR. KOHL YOUR ASSERTION THAT BOTH JEWS AND GERMAN SOLDIERS WERE VICTIMS OF THE WAR?
WELL, I DOUBT MR. KOHL NEEDS ME TO TELL HIM THAT. EVEN THOUGH THE WAR WAS WELL BEFORE HIS TIME, THE RECORD SHOWS HOW MANY FRESH-FACED RECRUITS WERE VICTIMS OF WAR. MANY OF THEIR OFFICERS WERE SIMPLE VICTIMS, TOO.
YOU KNOW, IN A STRANGE KIND OF WAY, EVEN HITLER WAS A..
OKAY, THAT'S IT FOR TODAY, PEOPLE!

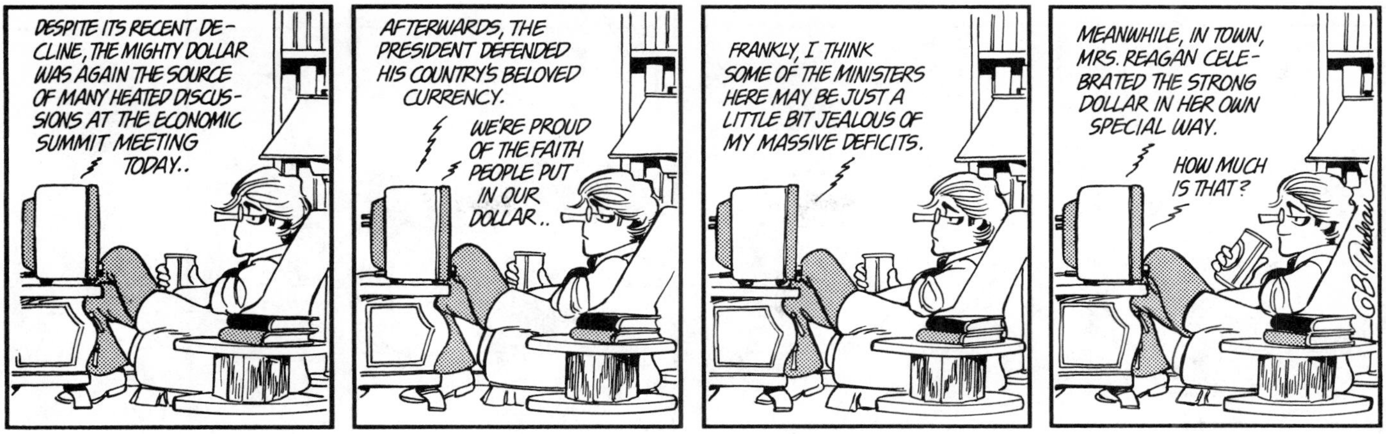
DESPITE ITS RECENT DECLINE, THE MIGHTY DOLLAR WAS AGAIN THE SOURCE OF MANY HEATED DISCUSSIONS AT THE ECONOMIC SUMMIT MEETING TODAY..
AFTERWARDS, THE PRESIDENT DEFENDED HIS COUNTRY'S BELOVED CURRENCY.
WE'RE PROUD OF THE FAITH PEOPLE PUT IN OUR DOLLAR..
FRANKLY, I THINK SOME OF THE MINISTERS HERE MAY BE JUST A LITTLE BIT JEALOUS OF MY MASSIVE DEFICITS.
MEANWHILE, IN TOWN, MRS. REAGAN CELEBRATED THE STRONG DOLLAR IN HER OWN SPECIAL WAY.
HOW MUCH IS THAT?
©BTrudeau

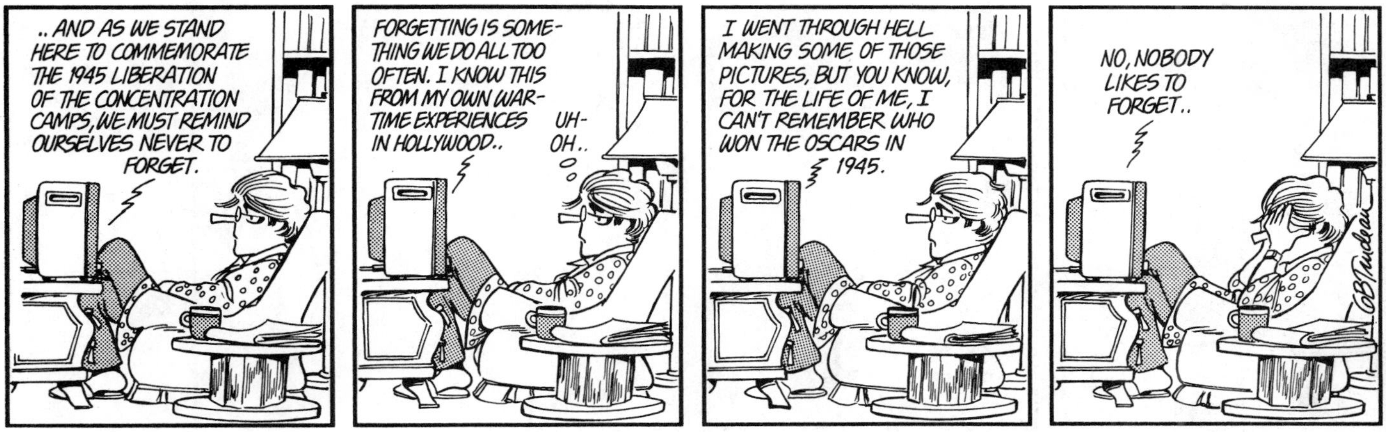
..AND AS WE STAND HERE TO COMMEMORATE THE 1945 LIBERATION OF THE CONCENTRATION CAMPS, WE MUST REMIND OURSELVES NEVER TO FORGET.
FORGETTING IS SOMETHING WE DO ALL TOO OFTEN. I KNOW THIS FROM MY OWN WARTIME EXPERIENCES IN HOLLYWOOD..
UH-OH..
I WENT THROUGH HELL MAKING SOME OF THOSE PICTURES, BUT YOU KNOW, FOR THE LIFE OF ME, I CAN'T REMEMBER WHO WON THE OSCARS IN 1945.
NO, NOBODY LIKES TO FORGET..
©BTrudeau

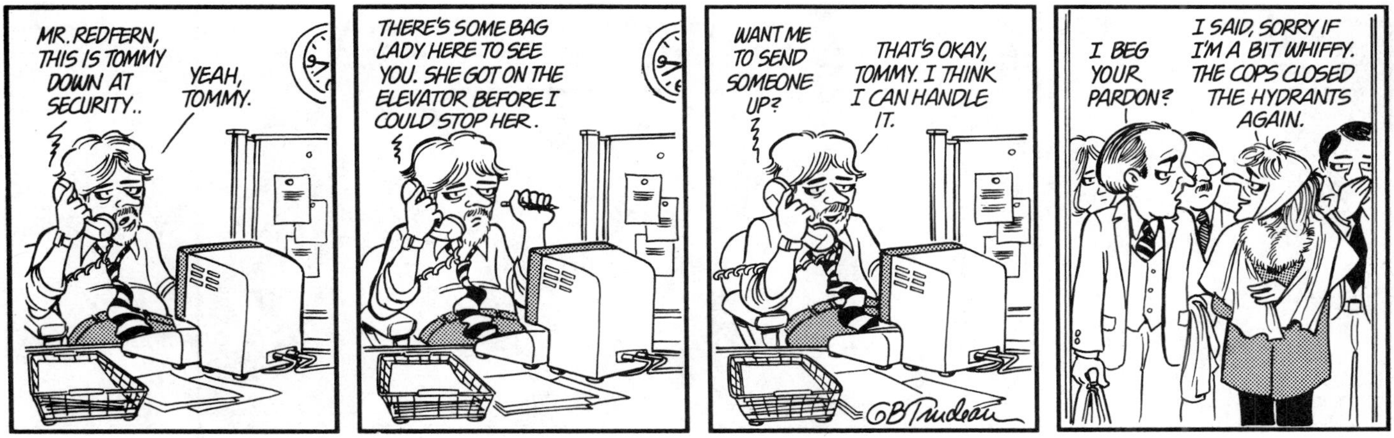
MR. REDFERN, THIS IS TOMMY DOWN AT SECURITY..
YEAH, TOMMY.
THERE'S SOME BAG LADY HERE TO SEE YOU. SHE GOT ON THE ELEVATOR BEFORE I COULD STOP HER.
WANT ME TO SEND SOMEONE UP?
THAT'S OKAY, TOMMY. I THINK I CAN HANDLE IT.
©BTrudeau
I BEG YOUR PARDON?
I SAID, SORRY IF I'M A BIT WHIFFY. THE COPS CLOSED THE HYDRANTS AGAIN.

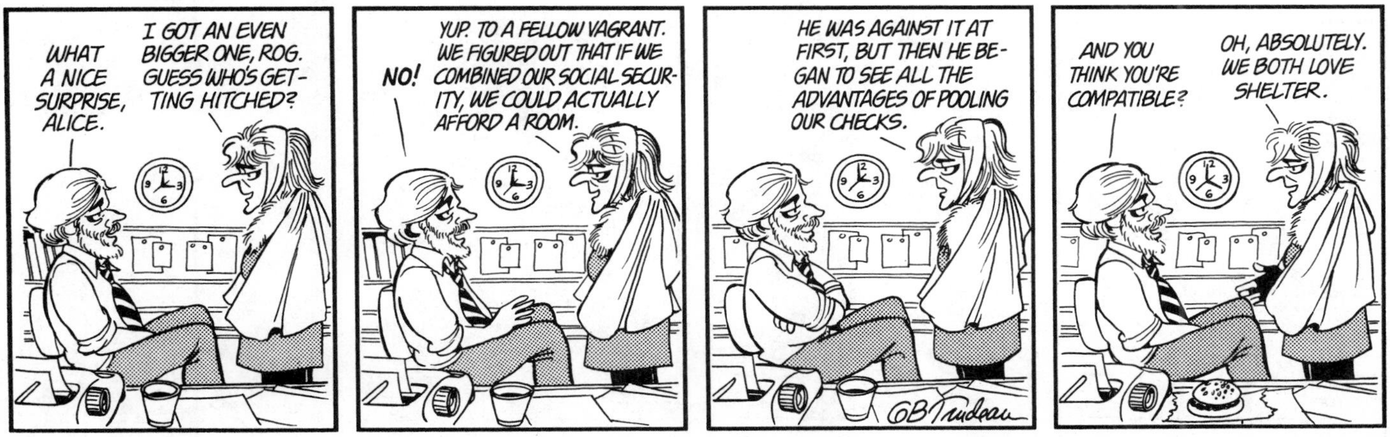
WHAT A NICE SURPRISE, ALICE.
I GOT AN EVEN BIGGER ONE, ROG. GUESS WHO'S GETTING HITCHED?
NO!
YUP. TO A FELLOW VAGRANT. WE FIGURED OUT THAT IF WE COMBINED OUR SOCIAL SECURITY, WE COULD ACTUALLY AFFORD A ROOM.
HE WAS AGAINST IT AT FIRST, BUT THEN HE BEGAN TO SEE ALL THE ADVANTAGES OF POOLING OUR CHECKS.
©BTrudeau
AND YOU THINK YOU'RE COMPATIBLE?
OH, ABSOLUTELY. WE BOTH LOVE SHELTER.

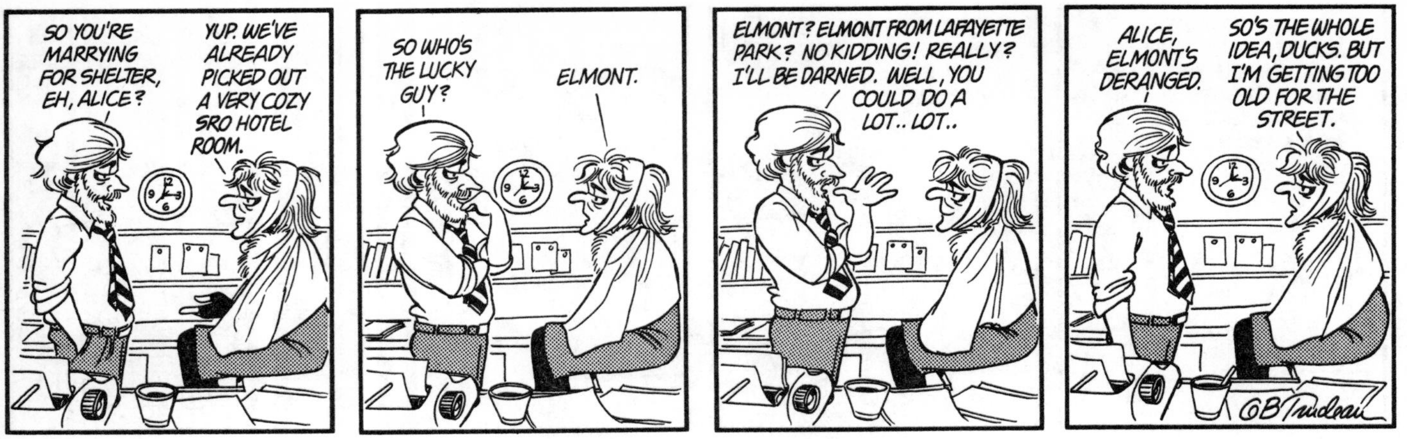
SO YOU'RE MARRYING FOR SHELTER, EH, ALICE?
YUP. WE'VE ALREADY PICKED OUT A VERY COZY SRO HOTEL ROOM.
SO WHO'S THE LUCKY GUY?
ELMONT.
ELMONT? ELMONT FROM LAFAYETTE PARK? NO KIDDING! REALLY? I'LL BE DARNED. WELL, YOU COULD DO A LOT.. LOT..
ALICE, ELMONT'S DERANGED.
SO'S THE WHOLE IDEA, DUCKS. BUT I'M GETTING TOO OLD FOR THE STREET.
©B Trudeau

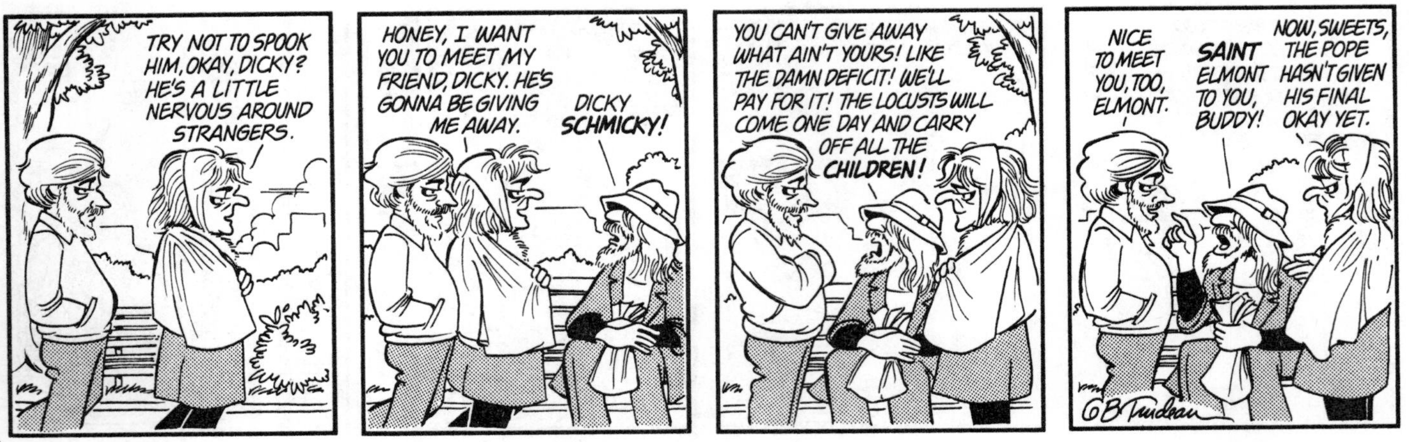
TRY NOT TO SPOOK HIM, OKAY, DICKY? HE'S A LITTLE NERVOUS AROUND STRANGERS.
HONEY, I WANT YOU TO MEET MY FRIEND, DICKY. HE'S GONNA BE GIVING ME AWAY.
DICKY SCHMICKY!
YOU CAN'T GIVE AWAY WHAT AIN'T YOURS! LIKE THE DAMN DEFICIT! WE'LL PAY FOR IT! THE LOCUSTS WILL COME ONE DAY AND CARRY OFF ALL THE CHILDREN!
NICE TO MEET YOU, TOO, ELMONT.
SAINT ELMONT TO YOU, BUDDY!
NOW, SWEETS, THE POPE HASN'T GIVEN HIS FINAL OKAY YET.
©B Trudeau

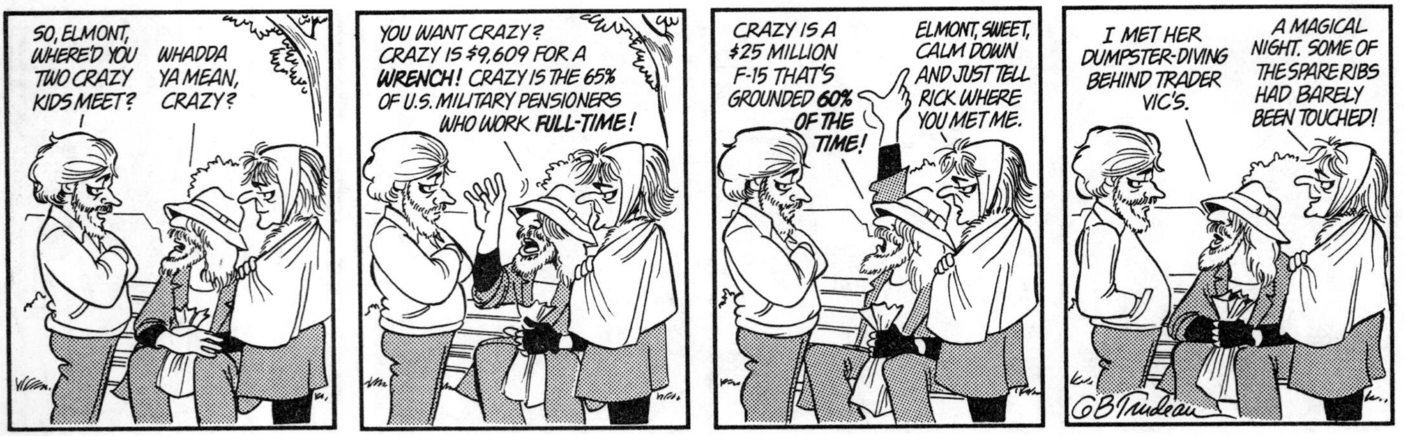
SO, ELMONT, WHERE'D YOU TWO CRAZY KIDS MEET?
WHADDA YA MEAN, CRAZY?
YOU WANT CRAZY? CRAZY IS $9,609 FOR A WRENCH! CRAZY IS THE 65% OF U.S. MILITARY PENSIONERS WHO WORK FULL-TIME!
CRAZY IS A $25 MILLION F-15 THAT'S GROUNDED 60% OF THE TIME!
ELMONT, SWEET, CALM DOWN AND JUST TELL RICK WHERE YOU MET ME.
I MET HER DUMPSTER-DIVING BEHIND TRADER VIC'S.
A MAGICAL NIGHT. SOME OF THE SPARE RIBS HAD BARELY BEEN TOUCHED!
©B Trudeau

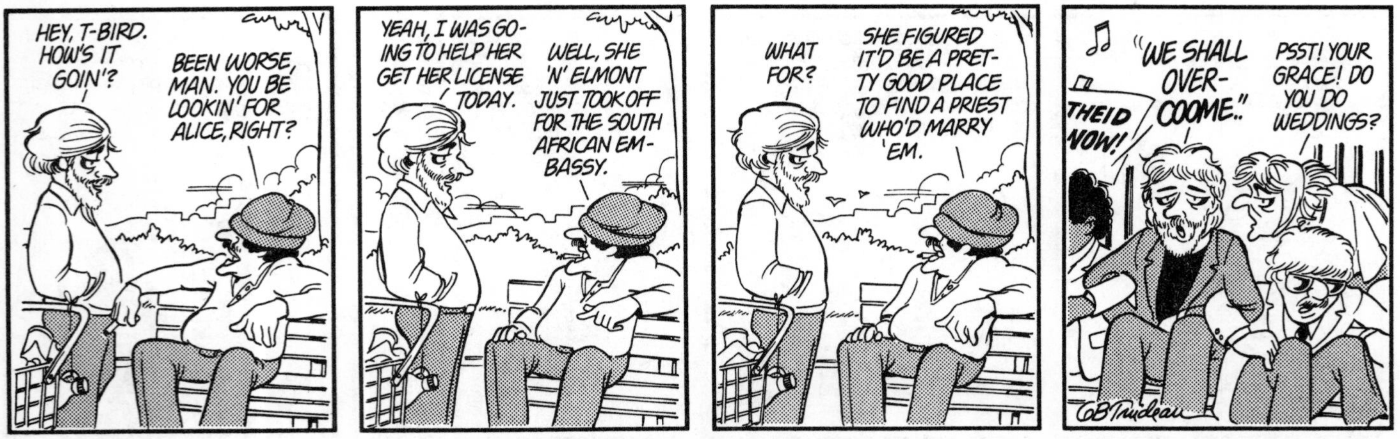
HEY, T-BIRD. HOW'S IT GOIN'?
BEEN WORSE, MAN. YOU BE LOOKIN' FOR ALICE, RIGHT?
YEAH, I WAS GOING TO HELP HER GET HER LICENSE TODAY.
WELL, SHE 'N' ELMONT JUST TOOK OFF FOR THE SOUTH AFRICAN EMBASSY.
WHAT FOR?
SHE FIGURED IT'D BE A PRETTY GOOD PLACE TO FIND A PRIEST WHO'D MARRY 'EM.
THEID NOW!
"WE SHALL OVER-COOME.."
PSST! YOUR GRACE! DO YOU DO WEDDINGS?
©B Trudeau

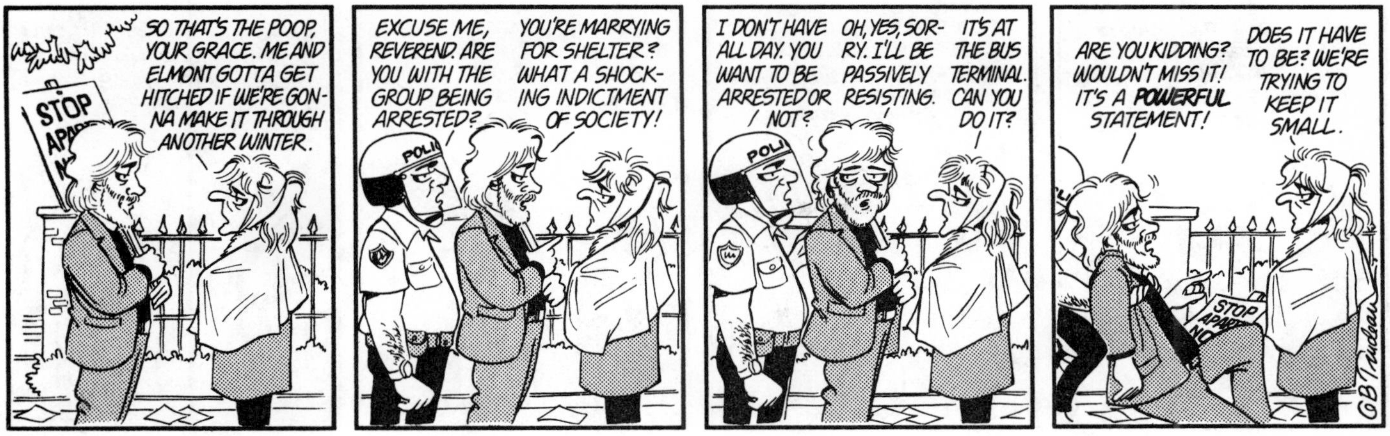
SO THAT'S THE POOP, YOUR GRACE. ME AND ELMONT GOTTA GET HITCHED IF WE'RE GONNA MAKE IT THROUGH ANOTHER WINTER.
EXCUSE ME, REVEREND. ARE YOU WITH THE GROUP BEING ARRESTED?
YOU'RE MARRYING FOR SHELTER? WHAT A SHOCKING INDICTMENT OF SOCIETY!
I DON'T HAVE ALL DAY. YOU WANT TO BE ARRESTED OR NOT?
OH, YES, SORRY. I'LL BE PASSIVELY RESISTING.
IT'S AT THE BUS TERMINAL. CAN YOU DO IT?
ARE YOU KIDDING? WOULDN'T MISS IT! IT'S A **POWERFUL** STATEMENT!
DOES IT HAVE TO BE? WE'RE TRYING TO KEEP IT SMALL.
GBTrudeau

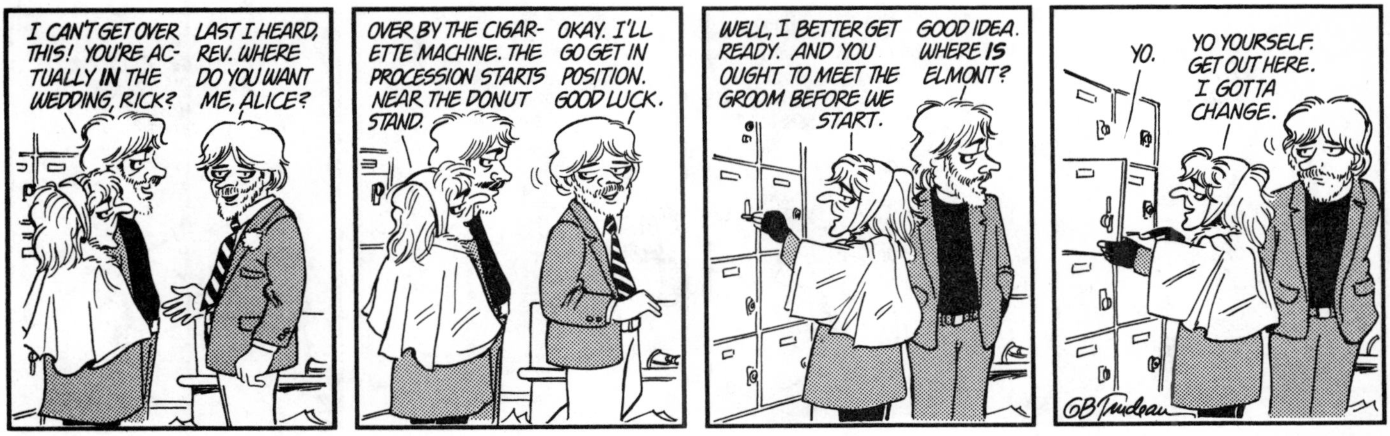
I CAN'T GET OVER THIS! YOU'RE ACTUALLY **IN** THE WEDDING, RICK?
LAST I HEARD, REV. WHERE DO YOU WANT ME, ALICE?
OVER BY THE CIGARETTE MACHINE. THE PROCESSION STARTS NEAR THE DONUT STAND.
OKAY. I'LL GO GET IN POSITION. GOOD LUCK.
WELL, I BETTER GET READY. AND YOU OUGHT TO MEET THE GROOM BEFORE WE START.
GOOD IDEA. WHERE **IS** ELMONT?
YO.
YO YOURSELF. GET OUT HERE. I GOTTA CHANGE.
GBTrudeau

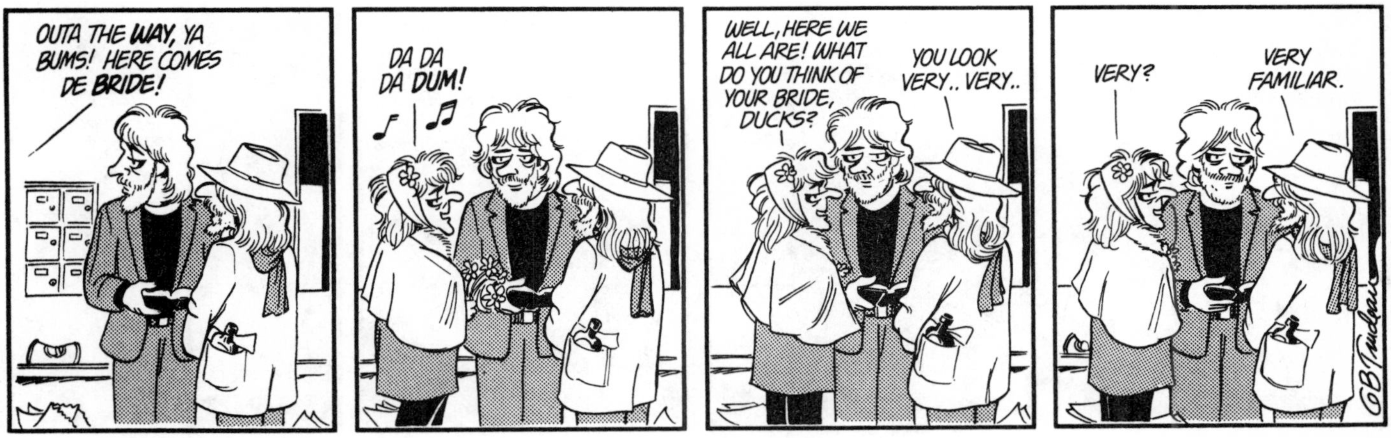
OUTA THE **WAY**, YA BUMS! HERE COMES DE **BRIDE**!
DA DA DA **DUM**!
WELL, HERE WE ALL ARE! WHAT DO YOU THINK OF YOUR BRIDE, DUCKS?
YOU LOOK VERY.. VERY..
VERY?
VERY FAMILIAR.
GBTrudeau

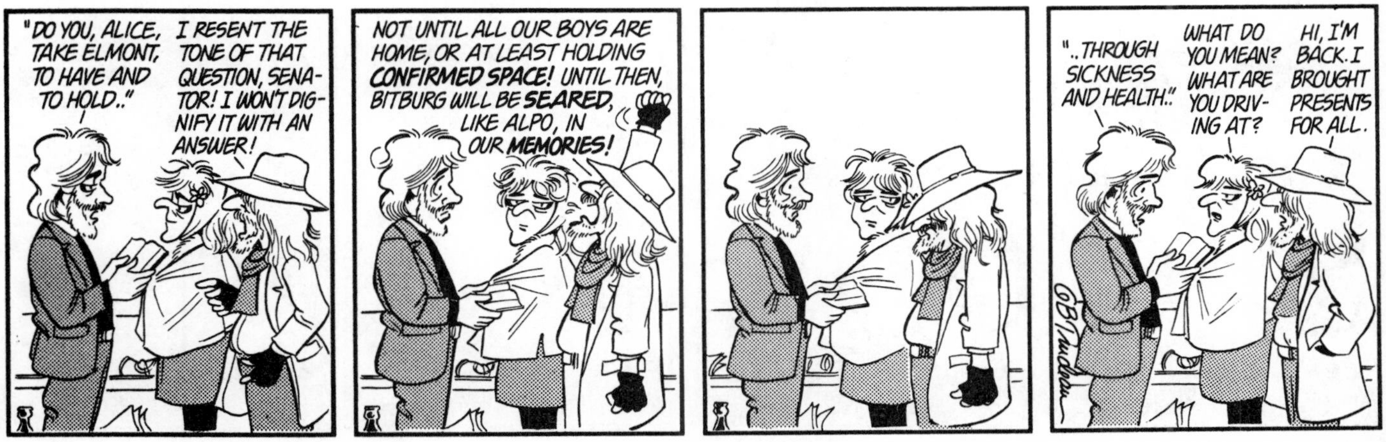
"DO YOU, ALICE, TAKE ELMONT, TO HAVE AND TO HOLD.."
I RESENT THE TONE OF THAT QUESTION, SENATOR! I WON'T DIGNIFY IT WITH AN ANSWER!
NOT UNTIL ALL OUR BOYS ARE HOME, OR AT LEAST HOLDING **CONFIRMED SPACE**! UNTIL THEN, BITBURG WILL BE **SEARED**, LIKE ALPO, IN OUR **MEMORIES**!
"..THROUGH SICKNESS AND HEALTH."
WHAT DO YOU MEAN? WHAT ARE YOU DRIVING AT?
HI, I'M BACK. I BROUGHT PRESENTS FOR ALL.
GBTrudeau

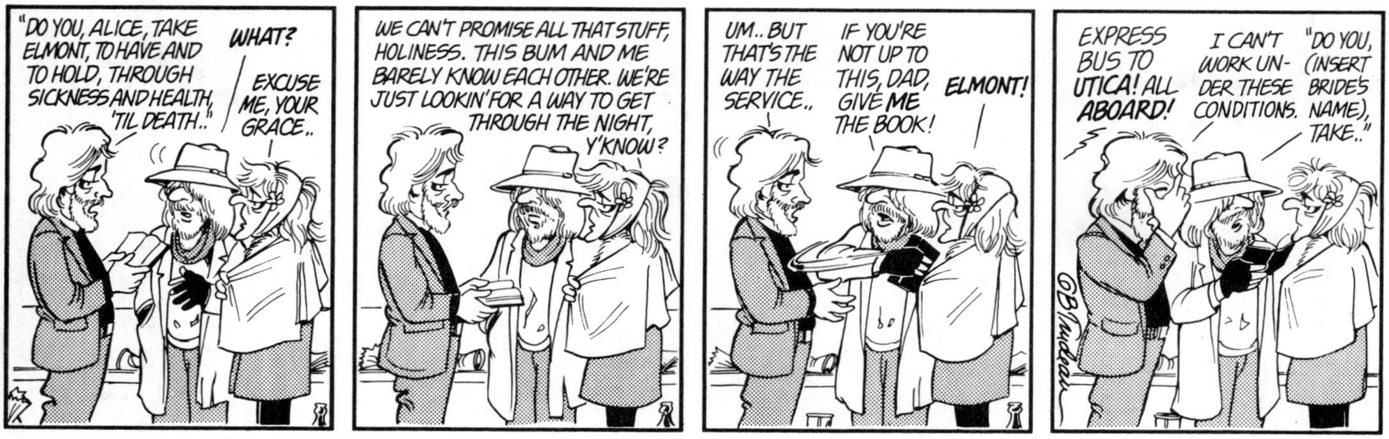
"DO YOU, ALICE, TAKE ELMONT, TO HAVE AND TO HOLD, THROUGH SICKNESS AND HEALTH, 'TIL DEATH.."
WHAT?
EXCUSE ME, YOUR GRACE..
WE CAN'T PROMISE ALL THAT STUFF, HOLINESS. THIS BUM AND ME BARELY KNOW EACH OTHER. WE'RE JUST LOOKIN' FOR A WAY TO GET THROUGH THE NIGHT, Y'KNOW?
UM.. BUT THAT'S THE WAY THE SERVICE..
IF YOU'RE NOT UP TO THIS, DAD, GIVE ME THE BOOK!
ELMONT!
EXPRESS BUS TO UTICA! ALL ABOARD!
I CAN'T WORK UNDER THESE CONDITIONS.
"DO YOU, (INSERT BRIDE'S NAME), TAKE.."

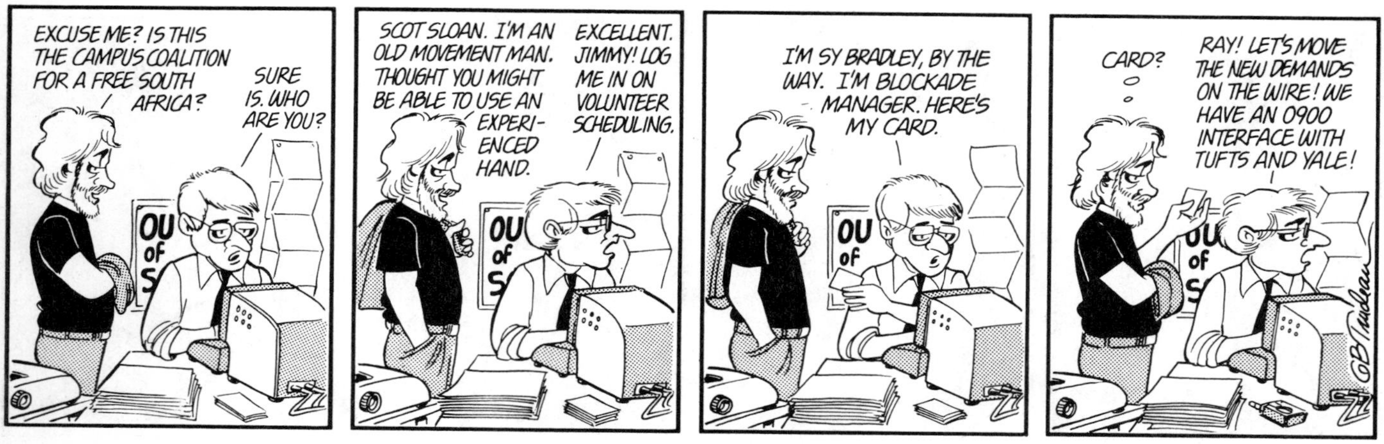
EXCUSE ME? IS THIS THE CAMPUS COALITION FOR A FREE SOUTH AFRICA?
SURE IS. WHO ARE YOU?
SCOT SLOAN. I'M AN OLD MOVEMENT MAN. THOUGHT YOU MIGHT BE ABLE TO USE AN EXPERIENCED HAND.
EXCELLENT. JIMMY! LOG ME IN ON VOLUNTEER SCHEDULING.
I'M SY BRADLEY, BY THE WAY. I'M BLOCKADE MANAGER. HERE'S MY CARD.
CARD?
RAY! LET'S MOVE THE NEW DEMANDS ON THE WIRE! WE HAVE AN 0900 INTERFACE WITH TUFTS AND YALE!

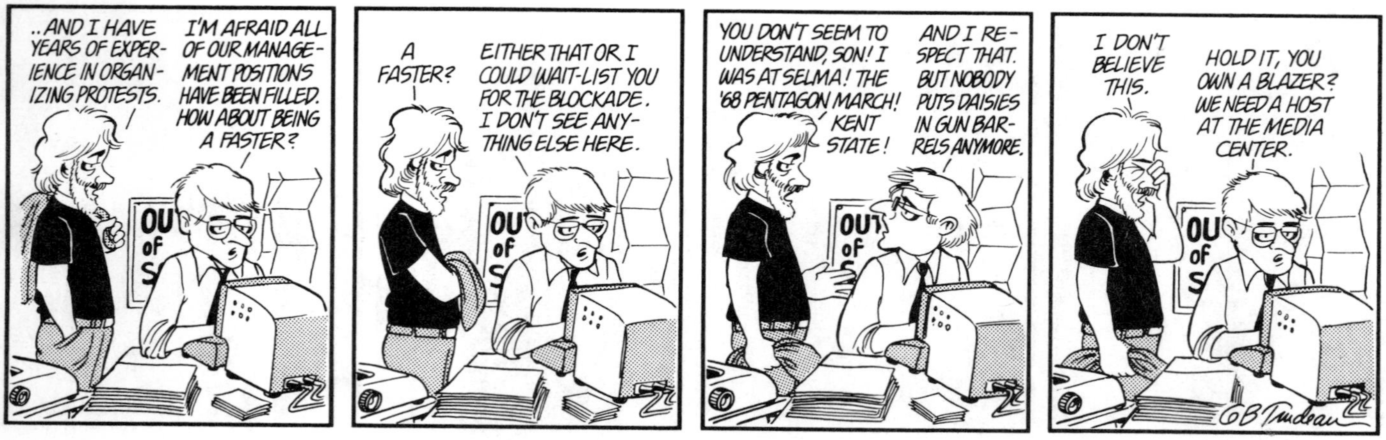
..AND I HAVE YEARS OF EXPERIENCE IN ORGANIZING PROTESTS.
I'M AFRAID ALL OF OUR MANAGEMENT POSITIONS HAVE BEEN FILLED. HOW ABOUT BEING A FASTER?
A FASTER?
EITHER THAT OR I COULD WAIT-LIST YOU FOR THE BLOCKADE. I DON'T SEE ANYTHING ELSE HERE.
YOU DON'T SEEM TO UNDERSTAND, SON! I WAS AT SELMA! THE '68 PENTAGON MARCH! KENT STATE!
AND I RESPECT THAT. BUT NOBODY PUTS DAISIES IN GUN BARRELS ANYMORE.
I DON'T BELIEVE THIS.
HOLD IT, YOU OWN A BLAZER? WE NEED A HOST AT THE MEDIA CENTER.

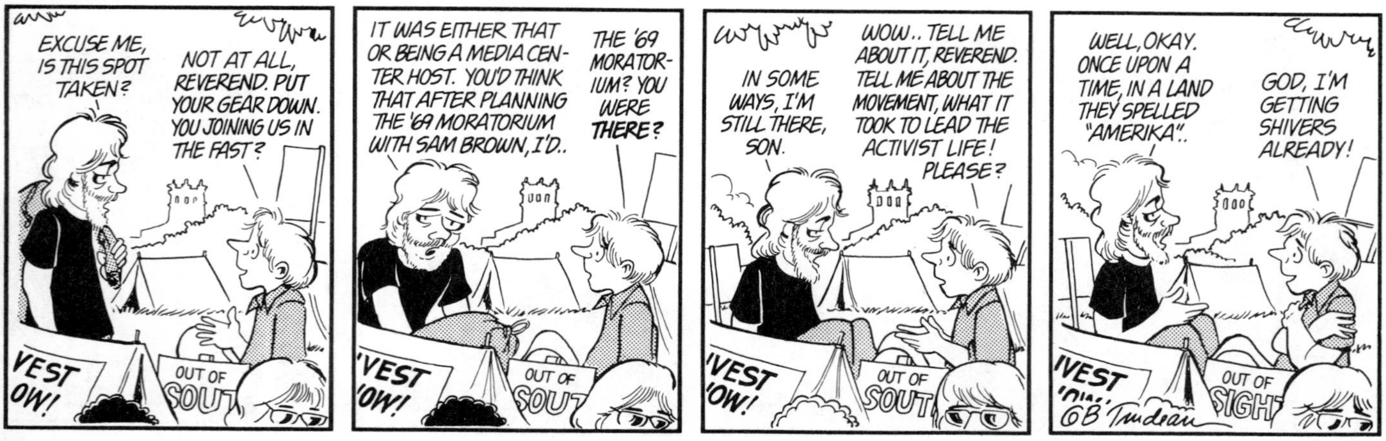
EXCUSE ME, IS THIS SPOT TAKEN?
NOT AT ALL, REVEREND. PUT YOUR GEAR DOWN. YOU JOINING US IN THE FAST?
IT WAS EITHER THAT OR BEING A MEDIA CENTER HOST. YOU'D THINK THAT AFTER PLANNING THE '69 MORATORIUM WITH SAM BROWN, I'D..
THE '69 MORATORIUM? YOU WERE THERE?
IN SOME WAYS, I'M STILL THERE, SON.
WOW.. TELL ME ABOUT IT, REVEREND. TELL ME ABOUT THE MOVEMENT, WHAT IT TOOK TO LEAD THE ACTIVIST LIFE! PLEASE?
WELL, OKAY. ONCE UPON A TIME, IN A LAND THEY SPELLED "AMERIKA"..
GOD, I'M GETTING SHIVERS ALREADY!

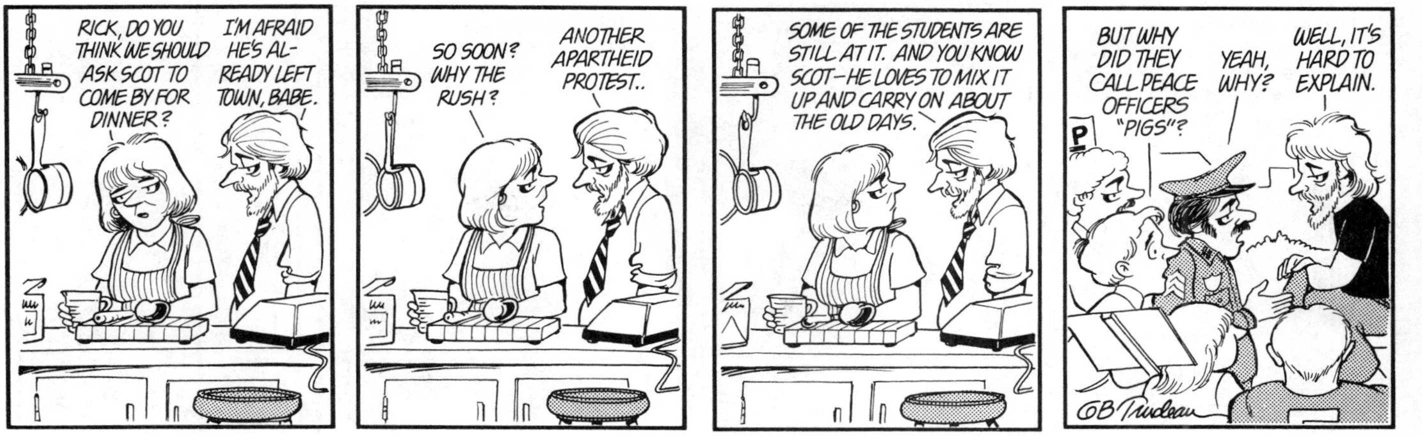
RICK, DO YOU THINK WE SHOULD ASK SCOT TO COME BY FOR DINNER?
I'M AFRAID HE'S ALREADY LEFT TOWN, BABE.
SO SOON? WHY THE RUSH?
ANOTHER APARTHEID PROTEST..
SOME OF THE STUDENTS ARE STILL AT IT. AND YOU KNOW SCOT—HE LOVES TO MIX IT UP AND CARRY ON ABOUT THE OLD DAYS.
BUT WHY DID THEY CALL PEACE OFFICERS "PIGS"?
YEAH, WHY?
WELL, IT'S HARD TO EXPLAIN.
GB Trudeau

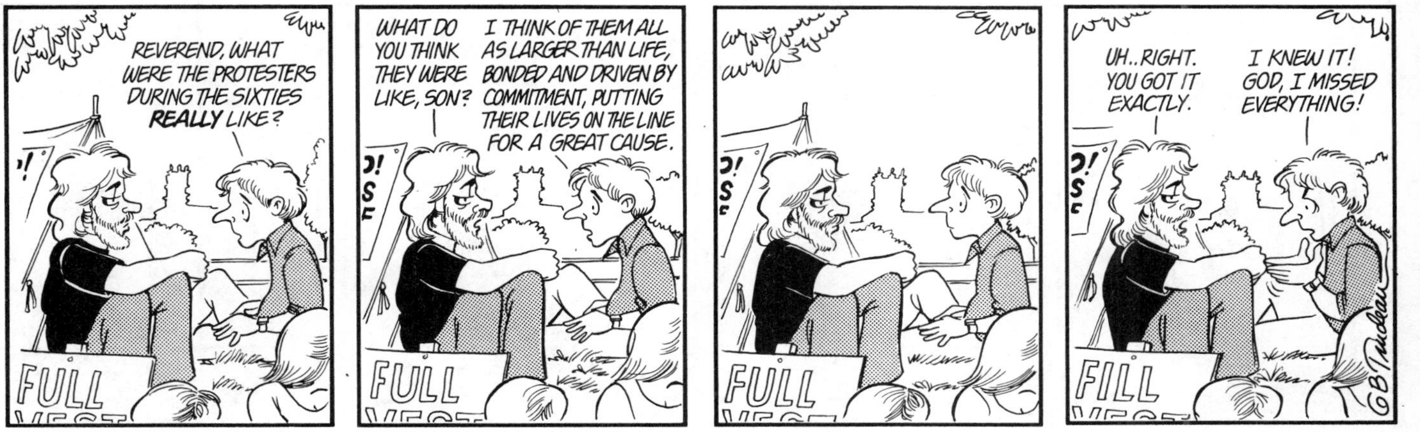
REVEREND, WHAT WERE THE PROTESTERS DURING THE SIXTIES **REALLY** LIKE?
FULL
WHAT DO YOU THINK THEY WERE LIKE, SON?
I THINK OF THEM ALL AS LARGER THAN LIFE, BONDED AND DRIVEN BY COMMITMENT, PUTTING THEIR LIVES ON THE LINE FOR A GREAT CAUSE.
FULL
FULL
UH..RIGHT. YOU GOT IT EXACTLY.
I KNEW IT! GOD, I MISSED EVERYTHING!
FILL
GB Trudeau

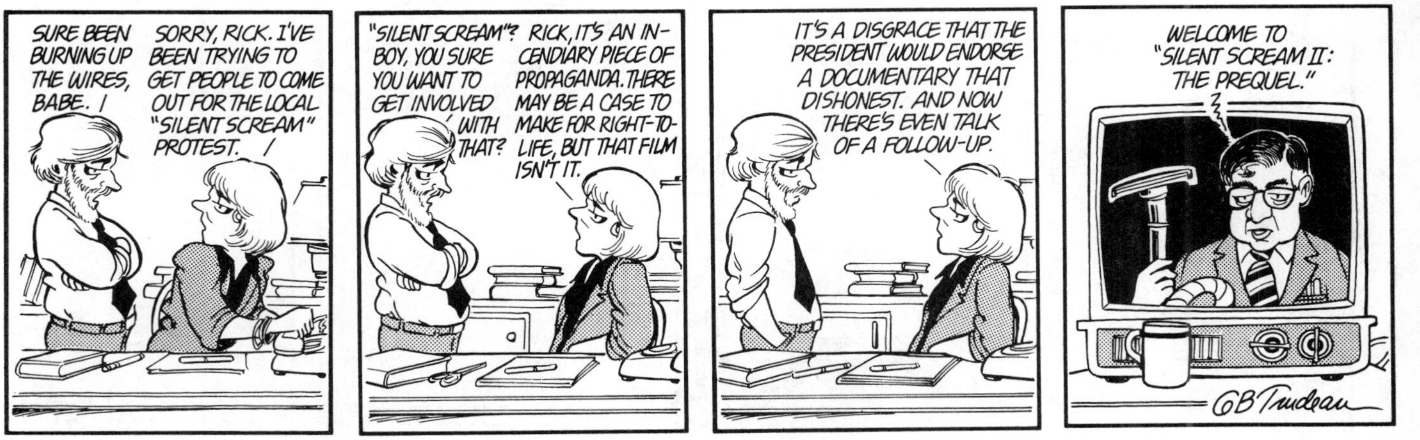
SURE BEEN BURNING UP THE WIRES, BABE.
SORRY, RICK. I'VE BEEN TRYING TO GET PEOPLE TO COME OUT FOR THE LOCAL "SILENT SCREAM" PROTEST.
"SILENT SCREAM"? BOY, YOU SURE YOU WANT TO GET INVOLVED WITH THAT?
RICK, IT'S AN INCENDIARY PIECE OF PROPAGANDA. THERE MAY BE A CASE TO MAKE FOR RIGHT-TO-LIFE, BUT THAT FILM ISN'T IT.
IT'S A DISGRACE THAT THE PRESIDENT WOULD ENDORSE A DOCUMENTARY THAT DISHONEST. AND NOW THERE'S EVEN TALK OF A FOLLOW-UP.
WELCOME TO "SILENT SCREAM II: THE PREQUEL."
GB Trudeau

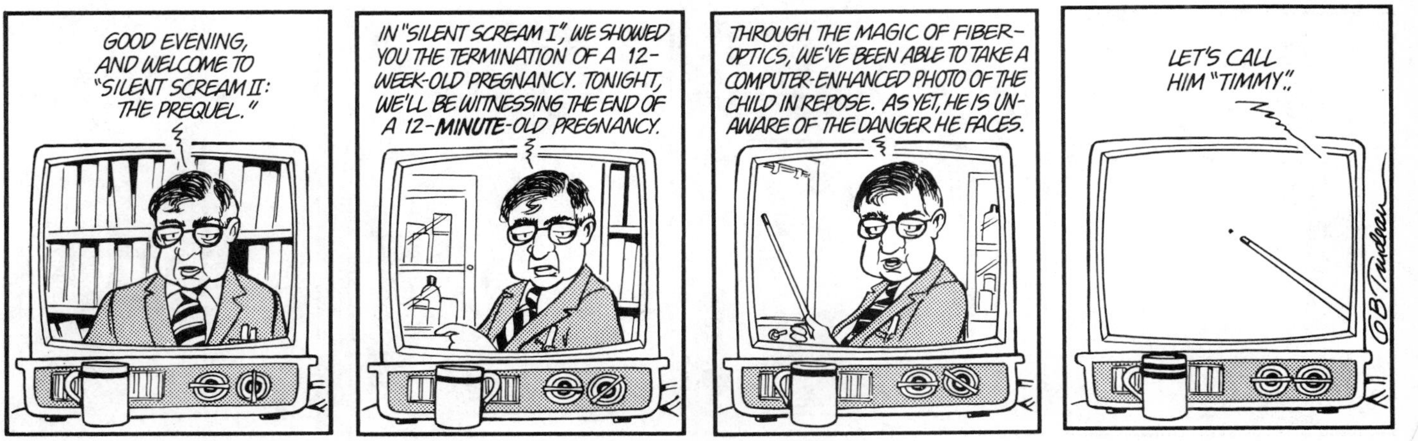
GOOD EVENING, AND WELCOME TO "SILENT SCREAM II: THE PREQUEL."
IN "SILENT SCREAM I," WE SHOWED YOU THE TERMINATION OF A 12-WEEK-OLD PREGNANCY. TONIGHT, WE'LL BE WITNESSING THE END OF A 12-**MINUTE**-OLD PREGNANCY.
THROUGH THE MAGIC OF FIBER-OPTICS, WE'VE BEEN ABLE TO TAKE A COMPUTER-ENHANCED PHOTO OF THE CHILD IN REPOSE. AS YET, HE IS UNAWARE OF THE DANGER HE FACES.
LET'S CALL HIM "TIMMY".
GB Trudeau

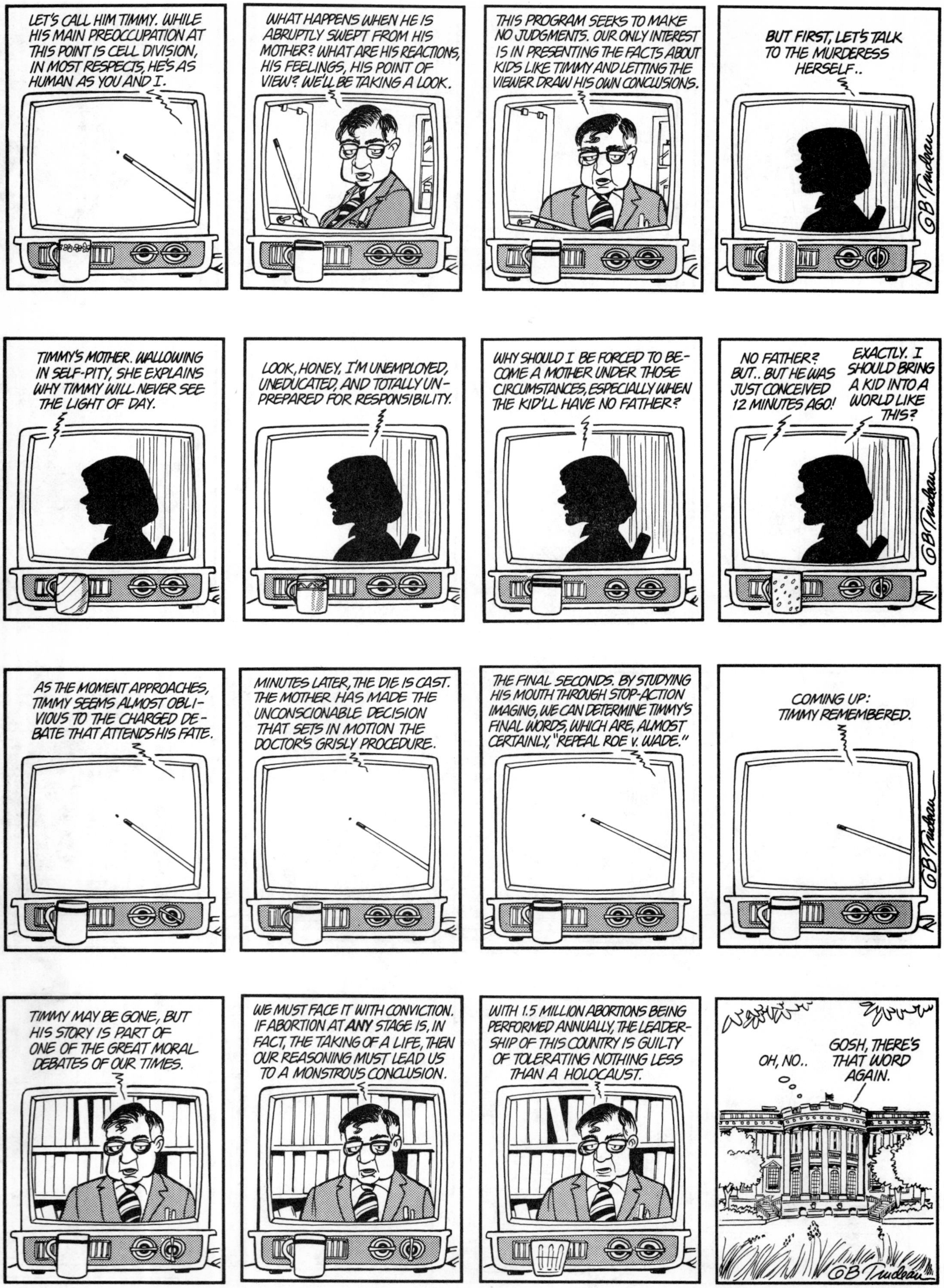
LET'S CALL HIM TIMMY. WHILE HIS MAIN PREOCCUPATION AT THIS POINT IS CELL DIVISION, IN MOST RESPECTS, HE'S AS HUMAN AS YOU AND I.
WHAT HAPPENS WHEN HE IS ABRUPTLY SWEPT FROM HIS MOTHER? WHAT ARE HIS REACTIONS, HIS FEELINGS, HIS POINT OF VIEW? WE'LL BE TAKING A LOOK.
THIS PROGRAM SEEKS TO MAKE NO JUDGMENTS. OUR ONLY INTEREST IS IN PRESENTING THE FACTS ABOUT KIDS LIKE TIMMY AND LETTING THE VIEWER DRAW HIS OWN CONCLUSIONS.
BUT FIRST, LET'S TALK TO THE MURDERESS HERSELF..
©B Trudeau
TIMMY'S MOTHER. WALLOWING IN SELF-PITY, SHE EXPLAINS WHY TIMMY WILL NEVER SEE THE LIGHT OF DAY.
LOOK, HONEY, I'M UNEMPLOYED, UNEDUCATED, AND TOTALLY UNPREPARED FOR RESPONSIBILITY.
WHY SHOULD I BE FORCED TO BECOME A MOTHER UNDER THOSE CIRCUMSTANCES, ESPECIALLY WHEN THE KID'LL HAVE NO FATHER?
NO FATHER? BUT.. BUT HE WAS JUST CONCEIVED 12 MINUTES AGO!
EXACTLY. I SHOULD BRING A KID INTO A WORLD LIKE THIS?
©B Trudeau
AS THE MOMENT APPROACHES, TIMMY SEEMS ALMOST OBLIVIOUS TO THE CHARGED DEBATE THAT ATTENDS HIS FATE.
MINUTES LATER, THE DIE IS CAST. THE MOTHER HAS MADE THE UNCONSCIONABLE DECISION THAT SETS IN MOTION THE DOCTOR'S GRISLY PROCEDURE.
THE FINAL SECONDS. BY STUDYING HIS MOUTH THROUGH STOP-ACTION IMAGING, WE CAN DETERMINE TIMMY'S FINAL WORDS, WHICH ARE, ALMOST CERTAINLY, "REPEAL ROE v. WADE."
COMING UP: TIMMY REMEMBERED.
©B Trudeau
TIMMY MAY BE GONE, BUT HIS STORY IS PART OF ONE OF THE GREAT MORAL DEBATES OF OUR TIMES.
WE MUST FACE IT WITH CONVICTION. IF ABORTION AT ANY STAGE IS, IN FACT, THE TAKING OF A LIFE, THEN OUR REASONING MUST LEAD US TO A MONSTROUS CONCLUSION.
WITH 1.5 MILLION ABORTIONS BEING PERFORMED ANNUALLY, THE LEADERSHIP OF THIS COUNTRY IS GUILTY OF TOLERATING NOTHING LESS THAN A HOLOCAUST.
OH, NO..
GOSH, THERE'S THAT WORD AGAIN.
©B Trudeau

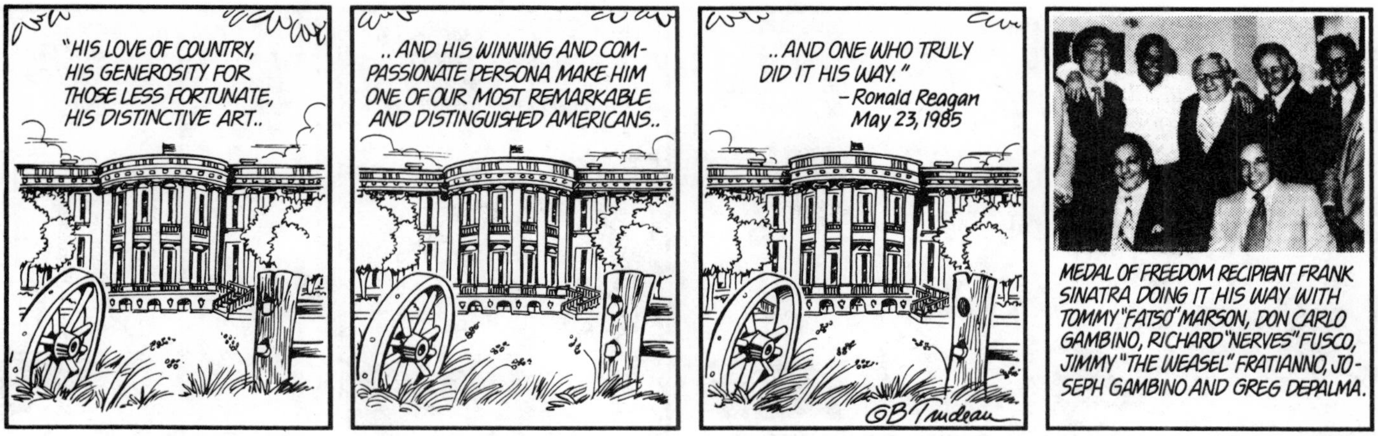
"HIS LOVE OF COUNTRY, HIS GENEROSITY FOR THOSE LESS FORTUNATE, HIS DISTINCTIVE ART..
.. AND HIS WINNING AND COMPASSIONATE PERSONA MAKE HIM ONE OF OUR MOST REMARKABLE AND DISTINGUISHED AMERICANS..
.. AND ONE WHO TRULY DID IT HIS WAY."
–Ronald Reagan
May 23, 1985
©B Trudeau
MEDAL OF FREEDOM RECIPIENT FRANK SINATRA DOING IT HIS WAY WITH TOMMY "FATSO" MARSON, DON CARLO GAMBINO, RICHARD "NERVES" FUSCO, JIMMY "THE WEASEL" FRATIANNO, JOSEPH GAMBINO AND GREG DEPALMA.

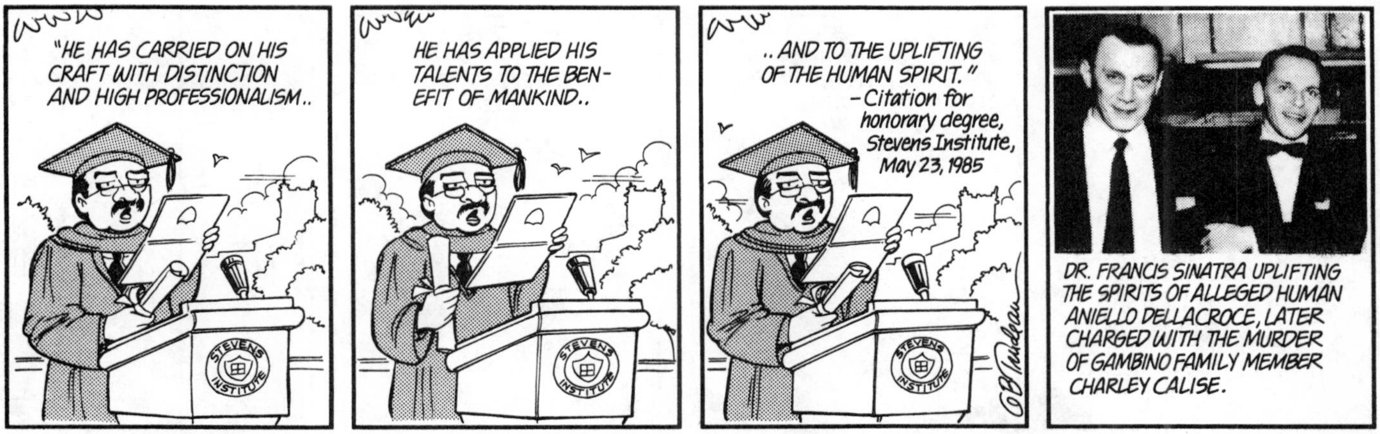
"HE HAS CARRIED ON HIS CRAFT WITH DISTINCTION AND HIGH PROFESSIONALISM..
HE HAS APPLIED HIS TALENTS TO THE BENEFIT OF MANKIND..
.. AND TO THE UPLIFTING OF THE HUMAN SPIRIT."
–Citation for honorary degree, Stevens Institute, May 23, 1985
STEVENS INSTITUTE
©B Trudeau
DR. FRANCIS SINATRA UPLIFTING THE SPIRITS OF ALLEGED HUMAN ANIELLO DELLACROCE, LATER CHARGED WITH THE MURDER OF GAMBINO FAMILY MEMBER CHARLEY CALISE.

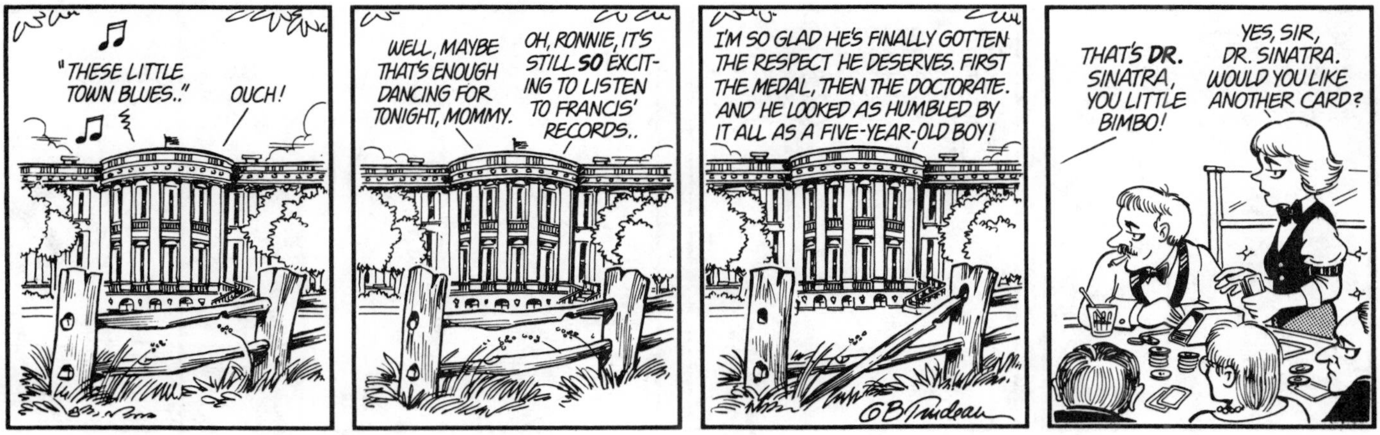
"THESE LITTLE TOWN BLUES.."
OUCH!
WELL, MAYBE THAT'S ENOUGH DANCING FOR TONIGHT, MOMMY.
OH, RONNIE, IT'S STILL **SO** EXCITING TO LISTEN TO FRANCIS' RECORDS..
I'M SO GLAD HE'S FINALLY GOTTEN THE RESPECT HE DESERVES. FIRST THE MEDAL, THEN THE DOCTORATE. AND HE LOOKED AS HUMBLED BY IT ALL AS A FIVE-YEAR-OLD BOY!
©B Trudeau
THAT'S **DR.** SINATRA, YOU LITTLE BIMBO!
YES, SIR, DR. SINATRA. WOULD YOU LIKE ANOTHER CARD?

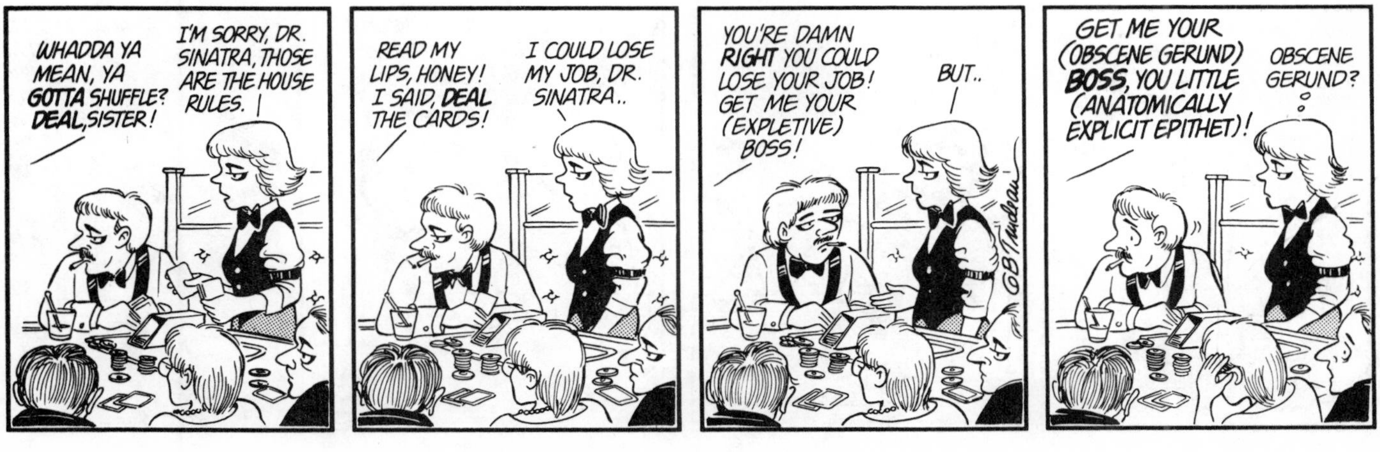
WHADDA YA MEAN, YA **GOTTA** SHUFFLE? **DEAL**, SISTER!
I'M SORRY, DR. SINATRA, THOSE ARE THE HOUSE RULES.
READ MY LIPS, HONEY! I SAID, **DEAL** THE CARDS!
I COULD LOSE MY JOB, DR. SINATRA..
YOU'RE DAMN **RIGHT** YOU COULD LOSE YOUR JOB! GET ME YOUR (EXPLETIVE) BOSS!
BUT..
©B Trudeau
GET ME YOUR (OBSCENE GERUND) **BOSS**, YOU LITTLE (ANATOMICALLY EXPLICIT EPITHET)!
OBSCENE GERUND?

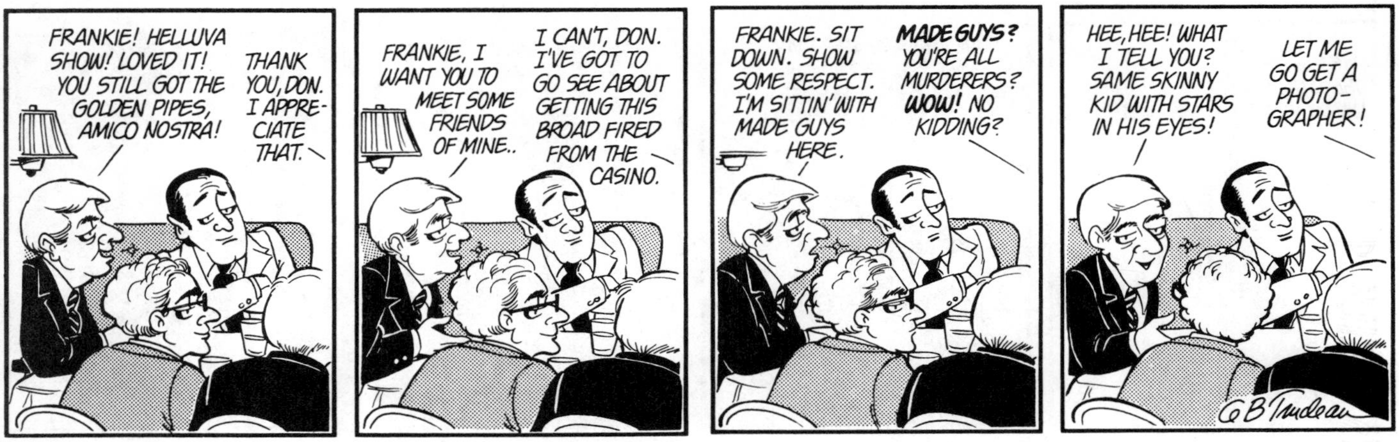
FRANKIE! HELLUVA SHOW! LOVED IT! YOU STILL GOT THE GOLDEN PIPES, AMICO NOSTRA!
THANK YOU, DON. I APPRECIATE THAT.
FRANKIE, I WANT YOU TO MEET SOME FRIENDS OF MINE..
I CAN'T, DON. I'VE GOT TO GO SEE ABOUT GETTING THIS BROAD FIRED FROM THE CASINO.
FRANKIE. SIT DOWN. SHOW SOME RESPECT. I'M SITTIN' WITH MADE GUYS HERE.
MADE GUYS? YOU'RE ALL MURDERERS? WOW! NO KIDDING?
HEE, HEE! WHAT I TELL YOU? SAME SKINNY KID WITH STARS IN HIS EYES!
LET ME GO GET A PHOTOGRAPHER!
GB Trudeau

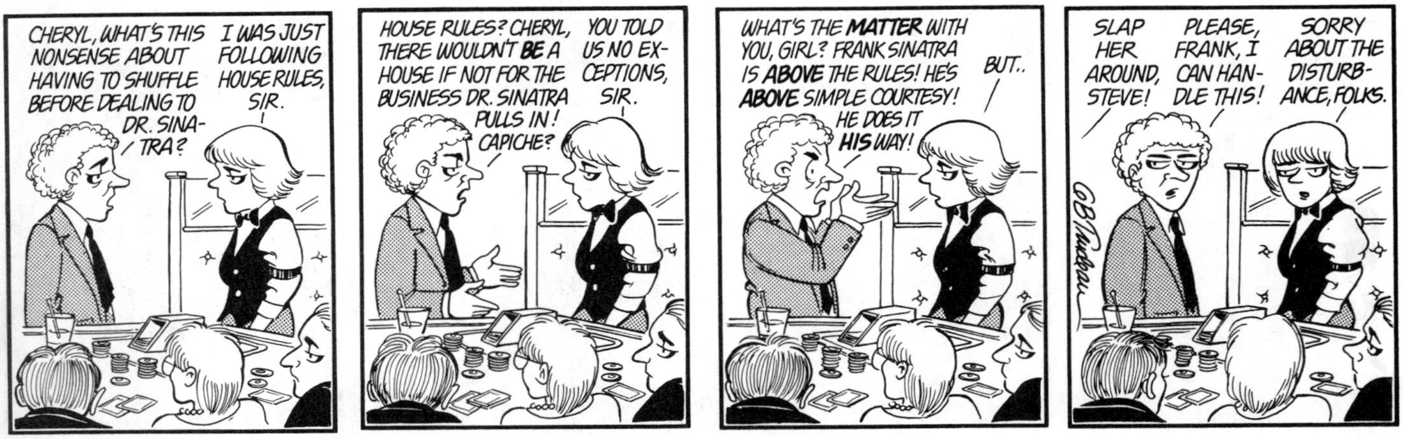
CHERYL, WHAT'S THIS NONSENSE ABOUT HAVING TO SHUFFLE BEFORE DEALING TO DR. SINATRA?
I WAS JUST FOLLOWING HOUSE RULES, SIR.
HOUSE RULES? CHERYL, THERE WOULDN'T BE A HOUSE IF NOT FOR THE BUSINESS DR. SINATRA PULLS IN! CAPICHE?
YOU TOLD US NO EXCEPTIONS, SIR.
WHAT'S THE MATTER WITH YOU, GIRL? FRANK SINATRA IS ABOVE THE RULES! HE'S ABOVE SIMPLE COURTESY! HE DOES IT HIS WAY!
BUT..
SLAP HER AROUND, STEVE!
PLEASE, FRANK, I CAN HANDLE THIS!
SORRY ABOUT THE DISTURBANCE, FOLKS.
GB Trudeau

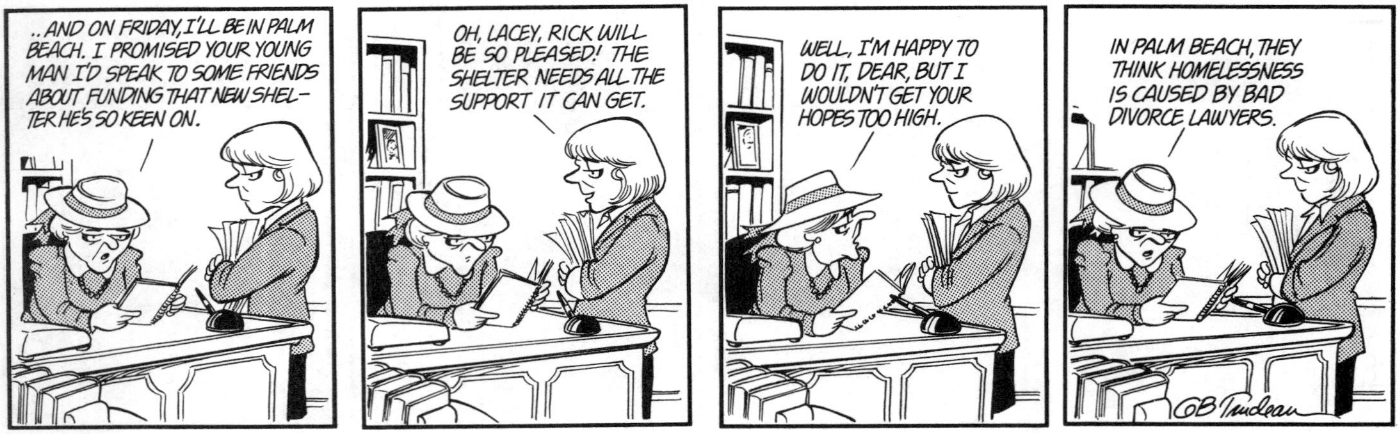
..AND ON FRIDAY, I'LL BE IN PALM BEACH. I PROMISED YOUR YOUNG MAN I'D SPEAK TO SOME FRIENDS ABOUT FUNDING THAT NEW SHELTER HE'S SO KEEN ON.
OH, LACEY, RICK WILL BE SO PLEASED! THE SHELTER NEEDS ALL THE SUPPORT IT CAN GET.
WELL, I'M HAPPY TO DO IT, DEAR, BUT I WOULDN'T GET YOUR HOPES TOO HIGH.
IN PALM BEACH, THEY THINK HOMELESSNESS IS CAUSED BY BAD DIVORCE LAWYERS.
GB Trudeau

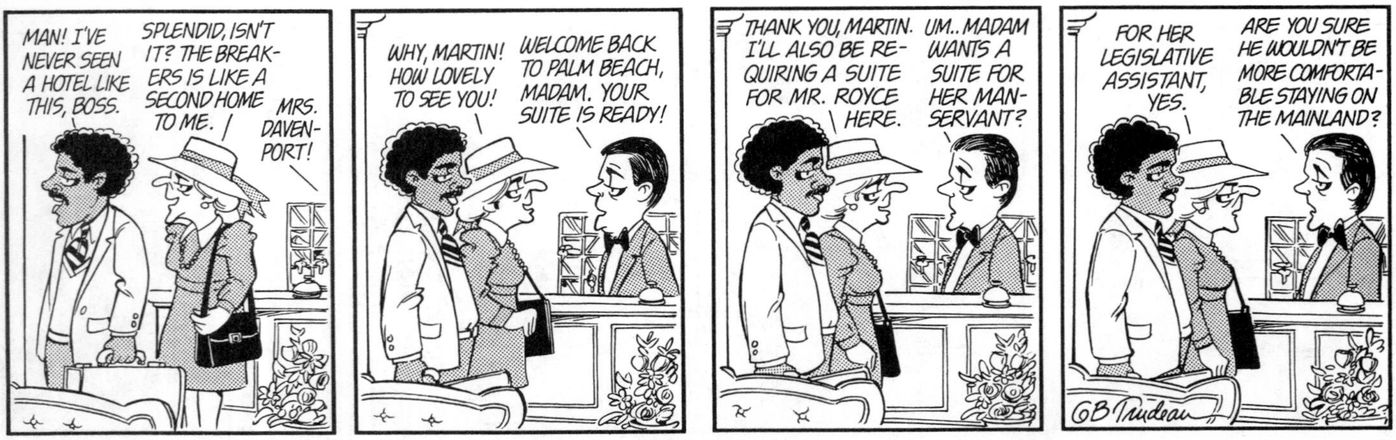
MAN! I'VE NEVER SEEN A HOTEL LIKE THIS, BOSS.
SPLENDID, ISN'T IT? THE BREAKERS IS LIKE A SECOND HOME TO ME.
MRS. DAVENPORT!
WHY, MARTIN! HOW LOVELY TO SEE YOU!
WELCOME BACK TO PALM BEACH, MADAM. YOUR SUITE IS READY!
THANK YOU, MARTIN. I'LL ALSO BE REQUIRING A SUITE FOR MR. ROYCE HERE.
UM.. MADAM WANTS A SUITE FOR HER MANSERVANT?
FOR HER LEGISLATIVE ASSISTANT, YES.
ARE YOU SURE HE WOULDN'T BE MORE COMFORTABLE STAYING ON THE MAINLAND?
GB Trudeau

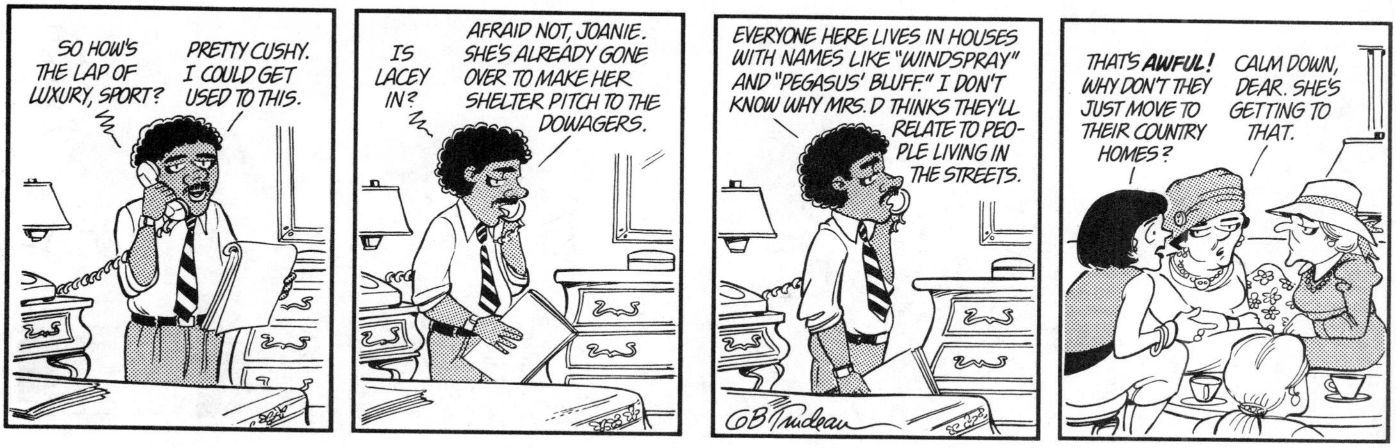
SO HOW'S THE LAP OF LUXURY, SPORT?
PRETTY CUSHY. I COULD GET USED TO THIS.
IS LACEY IN?
AFRAID NOT, JOANIE. SHE'S ALREADY GONE OVER TO MAKE HER SHELTER PITCH TO THE DOWAGERS.
EVERYONE HERE LIVES IN HOUSES WITH NAMES LIKE "WINDSPRAY" AND "PEGASUS' BLUFF." I DON'T KNOW WHY MRS. D THINKS THEY'LL RELATE TO PEOPLE LIVING IN THE STREETS.
THAT'S **AWFUL!** WHY DON'T THEY JUST MOVE TO THEIR COUNTRY HOMES?
CALM DOWN, DEAR. SHE'S GETTING TO THAT.

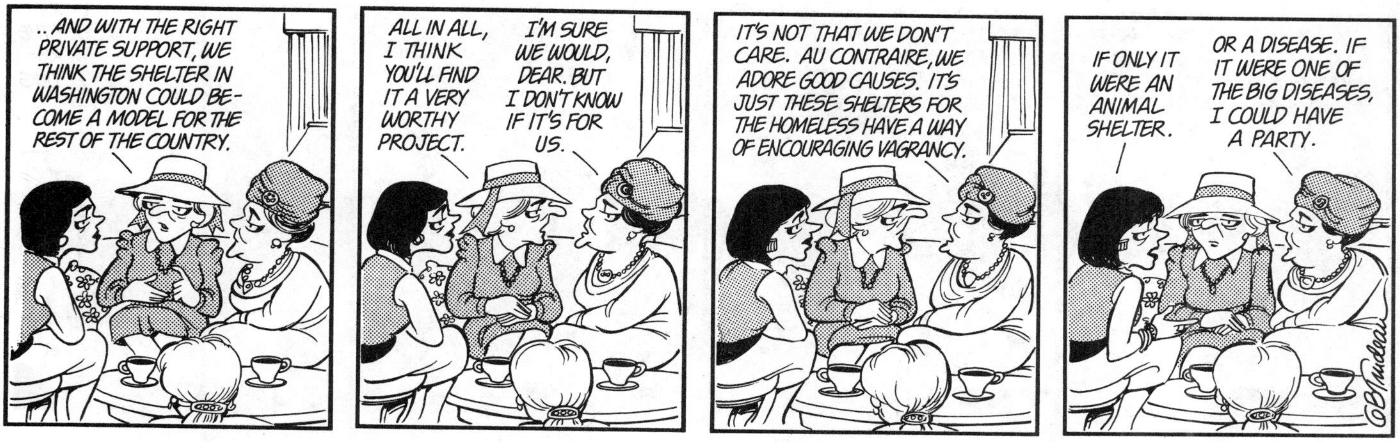
..AND WITH THE RIGHT PRIVATE SUPPORT, WE THINK THE SHELTER IN WASHINGTON COULD BECOME A MODEL FOR THE REST OF THE COUNTRY.
ALL IN ALL, I THINK YOU'LL FIND IT A VERY WORTHY PROJECT.
I'M SURE WE WOULD, DEAR. BUT I DON'T KNOW IF IT'S FOR US.
IT'S NOT THAT WE DON'T CARE. AU CONTRAIRE, WE ADORE GOOD CAUSES. IT'S JUST THESE SHELTERS FOR THE HOMELESS HAVE A WAY OF ENCOURAGING VAGRANCY.
IF ONLY IT WERE AN ANIMAL SHELTER.
OR A DISEASE. IF IT WERE ONE OF THE BIG DISEASES, I COULD HAVE A PARTY.

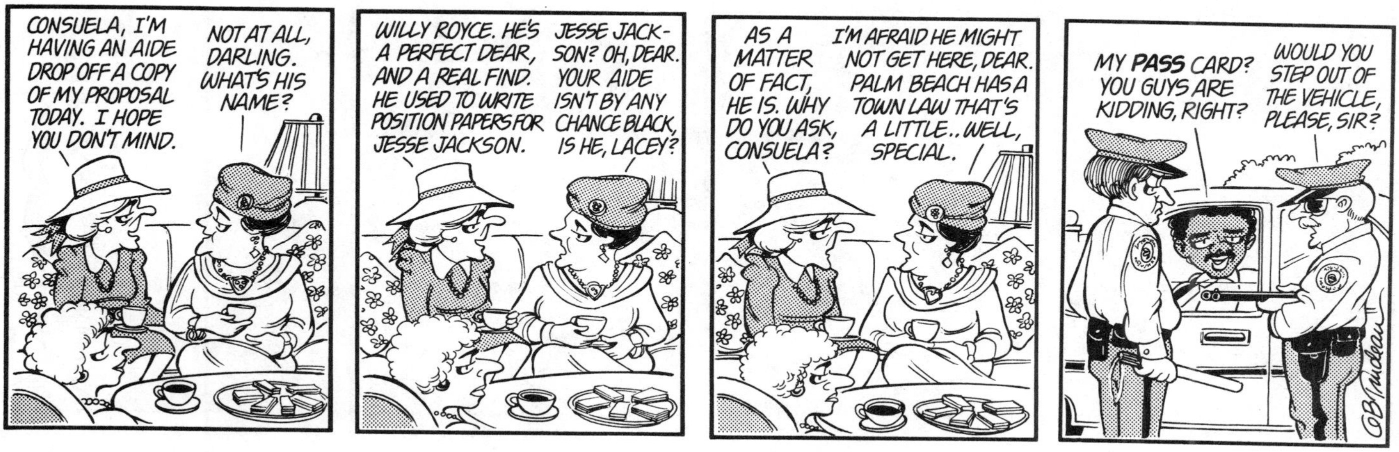
CONSUELA, I'M HAVING AN AIDE DROP OFF A COPY OF MY PROPOSAL TODAY. I HOPE YOU DON'T MIND.
NOT AT ALL, DARLING. WHAT'S HIS NAME?
WILLY ROYCE. HE'S A PERFECT DEAR, AND A REAL FIND. HE USED TO WRITE POSITION PAPERS FOR JESSE JACKSON.
JESSE JACKSON? OH, DEAR. YOUR AIDE ISN'T BY ANY CHANCE BLACK, IS HE, LACEY?
AS A MATTER OF FACT, HE IS. WHY DO YOU ASK, CONSUELA?
I'M AFRAID HE MIGHT NOT GET HERE, DEAR. PALM BEACH HAS A TOWN LAW THAT'S A LITTLE.. WELL, SPECIAL.
MY **PASS** CARD? YOU GUYS ARE KIDDING, RIGHT?
WOULD YOU STEP OUT OF THE VEHICLE, PLEASE, SIR?

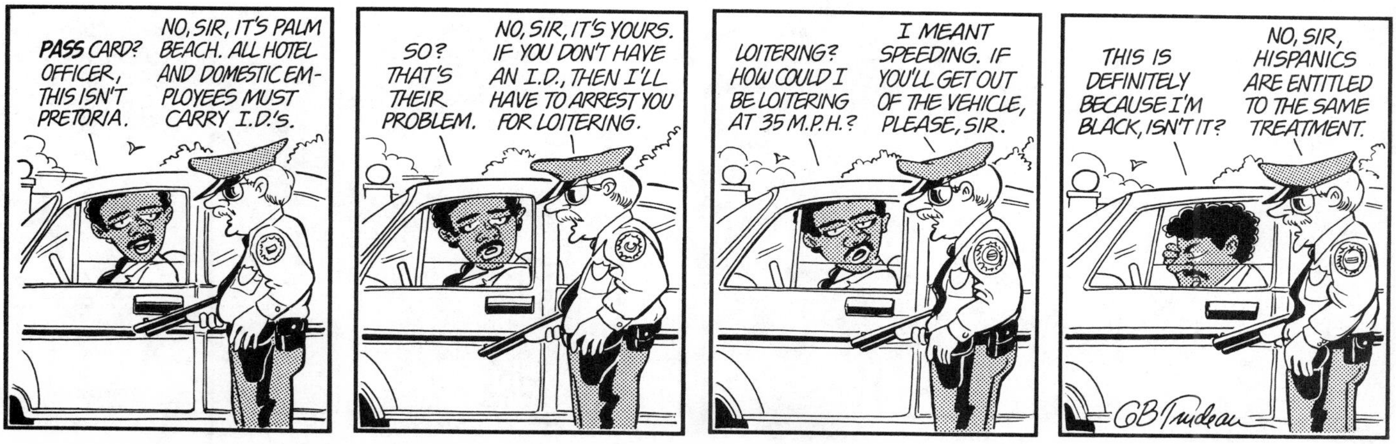
PASS CARD? OFFICER, THIS ISN'T PRETORIA.
NO, SIR, IT'S PALM BEACH. ALL HOTEL AND DOMESTIC EMPLOYEES MUST CARRY I.D.'S.
SO? THAT'S THEIR PROBLEM.
NO, SIR, IT'S YOURS. IF YOU DON'T HAVE AN I.D., THEN I'LL HAVE TO ARREST YOU FOR LOITERING.
LOITERING? HOW COULD I BE LOITERING AT 35 M.P.H.?
I MEANT SPEEDING. IF YOU'LL GET OUT OF THE VEHICLE, PLEASE, SIR.
THIS IS DEFINITELY BECAUSE I'M BLACK, ISN'T IT?
NO, SIR, HISPANICS ARE ENTITLED TO THE SAME TREATMENT.

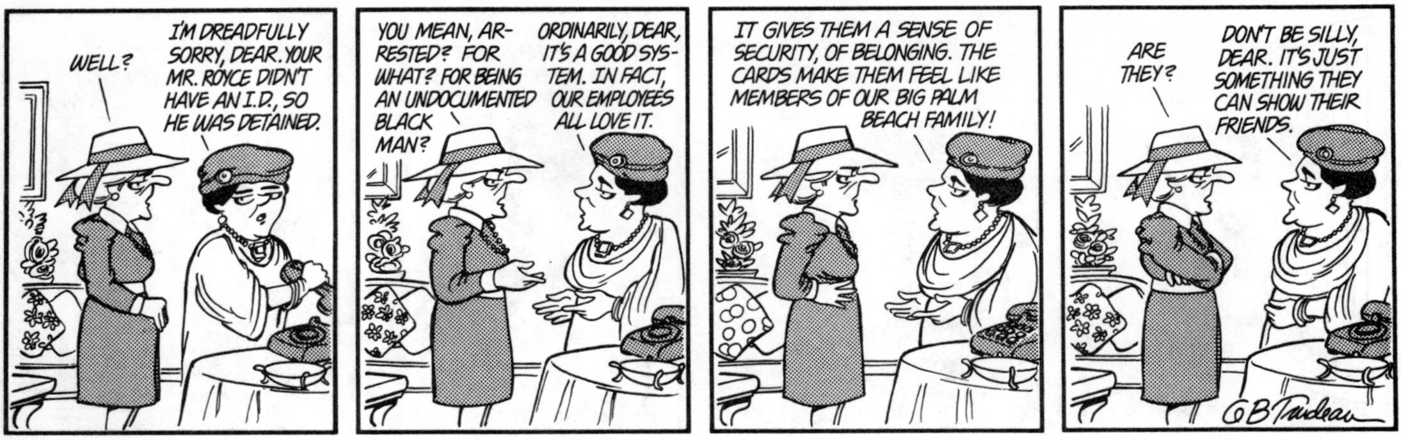
WELL?
I'M DREADFULLY SORRY, DEAR. YOUR MR. ROYCE DIDN'T HAVE AN I.D., SO HE WAS DETAINED.
YOU MEAN, ARRESTED? FOR WHAT? FOR BEING AN UNDOCUMENTED BLACK MAN?
ORDINARILY, DEAR, IT'S A GOOD SYSTEM. IN FACT, OUR EMPLOYEES ALL LOVE IT.
IT GIVES THEM A SENSE OF SECURITY, OF BELONGING. THE CARDS MAKE THEM FEEL LIKE MEMBERS OF OUR BIG PALM BEACH FAMILY!
ARE THEY?
DON'T BE SILLY, DEAR. IT'S JUST SOMETHING THEY CAN SHOW THEIR FRIENDS.
©B Trudeau

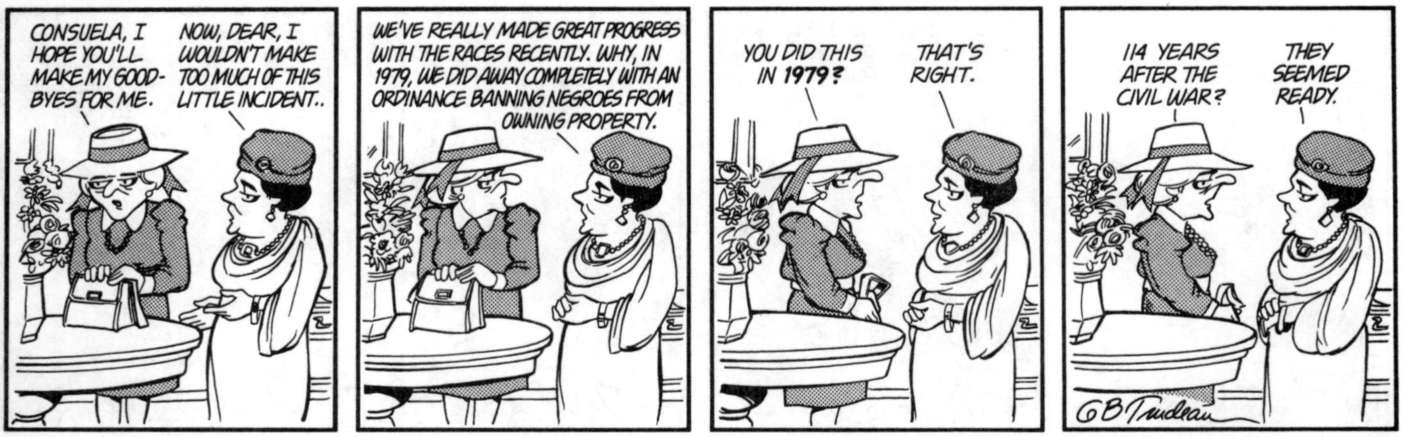
CONSUELA, I HOPE YOU'LL MAKE MY GOOD-BYES FOR ME.
NOW, DEAR, I WOULDN'T MAKE TOO MUCH OF THIS LITTLE INCIDENT..
WE'VE REALLY MADE GREAT PROGRESS WITH THE RACES RECENTLY. WHY, IN 1979, WE DID AWAY COMPLETELY WITH AN ORDINANCE BANNING NEGROES FROM OWNING PROPERTY.
YOU DID THIS IN **1979?**
THAT'S RIGHT.
114 YEARS AFTER THE CIVIL WAR?
THEY SEEMED READY.
©B Trudeau

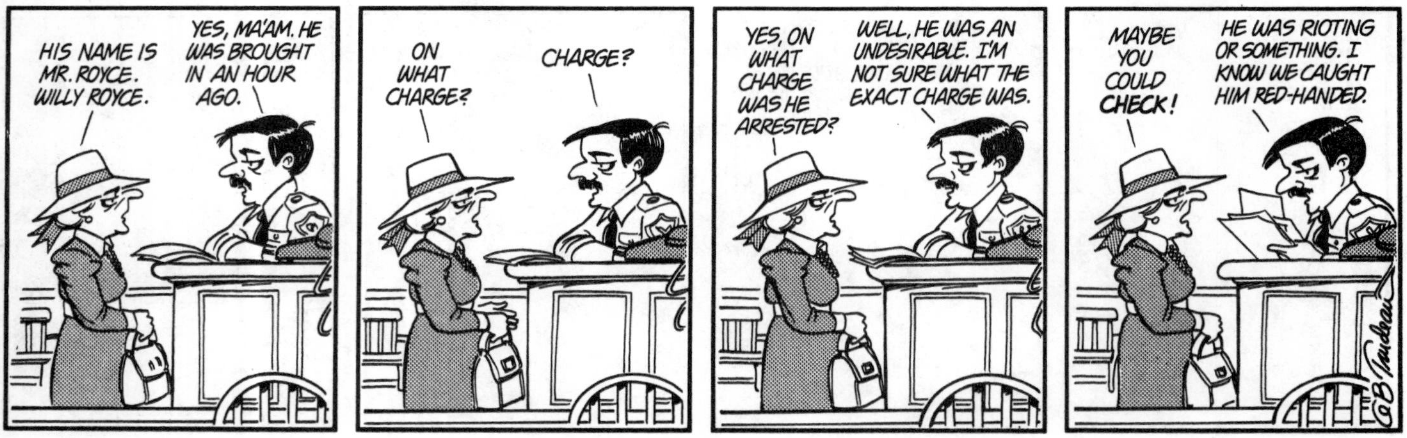
HIS NAME IS MR. ROYCE. WILLY ROYCE.
YES, MA'AM. HE WAS BROUGHT IN AN HOUR AGO.
ON WHAT CHARGE?
CHARGE?
YES, ON WHAT CHARGE WAS HE ARRESTED?
WELL, HE WAS AN UNDESIRABLE. I'M NOT SURE WHAT THE EXACT CHARGE WAS.
MAYBE YOU COULD **CHECK!**
HE WAS RIOTING OR SOMETHING. I KNOW WE CAUGHT HIM RED-HANDED.
©B Trudeau

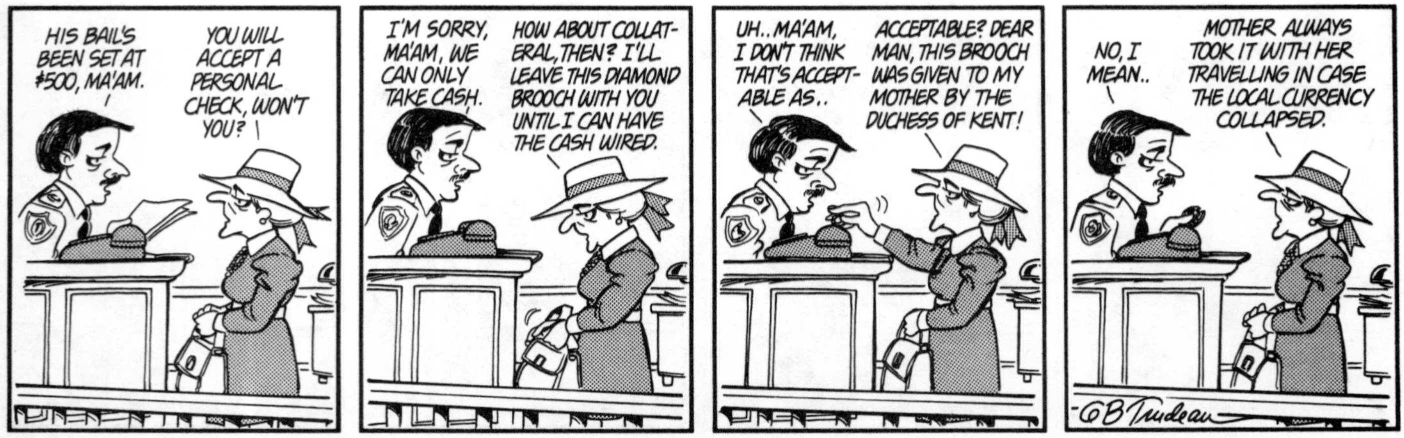
HIS BAIL'S BEEN SET AT $500, MA'AM.
YOU WILL ACCEPT A PERSONAL CHECK, WON'T YOU?
I'M SORRY, MA'AM, WE CAN ONLY TAKE CASH.
HOW ABOUT COLLATERAL, THEN? I'LL LEAVE THIS DIAMOND BROOCH WITH YOU UNTIL I CAN HAVE THE CASH WIRED.
UH.. MA'AM, I DON'T THINK THAT'S ACCEPTABLE AS..
ACCEPTABLE? DEAR MAN, THIS BROOCH WAS GIVEN TO MY MOTHER BY THE DUCHESS OF KENT!
NO, I MEAN..
MOTHER ALWAYS TOOK IT WITH HER TRAVELLING IN CASE THE LOCAL CURRENCY COLLAPSED.
©B Trudeau

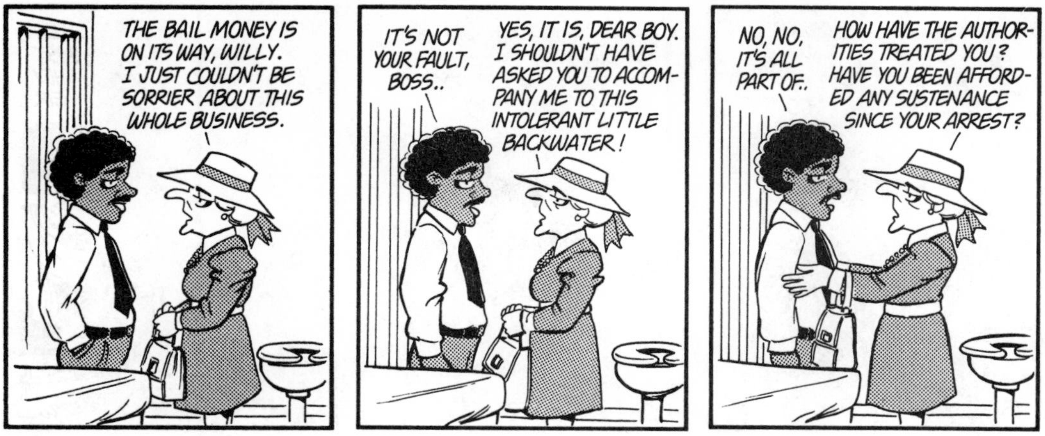
THE BAIL MONEY IS ON ITS WAY, WILLY. I JUST COULDN'T BE SORRIER ABOUT THIS WHOLE BUSINESS.
IT'S NOT YOUR FAULT, BOSS..
YES, IT IS, DEAR BOY. I SHOULDN'T HAVE ASKED YOU TO ACCOMPANY ME TO THIS INTOLERANT LITTLE BACKWATER!
NO, NO, IT'S ALL PART OF..
HOW HAVE THE AUTHORITIES TREATED YOU? HAVE YOU BEEN AFFORDED ANY SUSTENANCE SINCE YOUR ARREST?
WELL, NO, I..
GUARD! SOME COLD CUCUMBER SOUP, PLEASE!
GB Trudeau

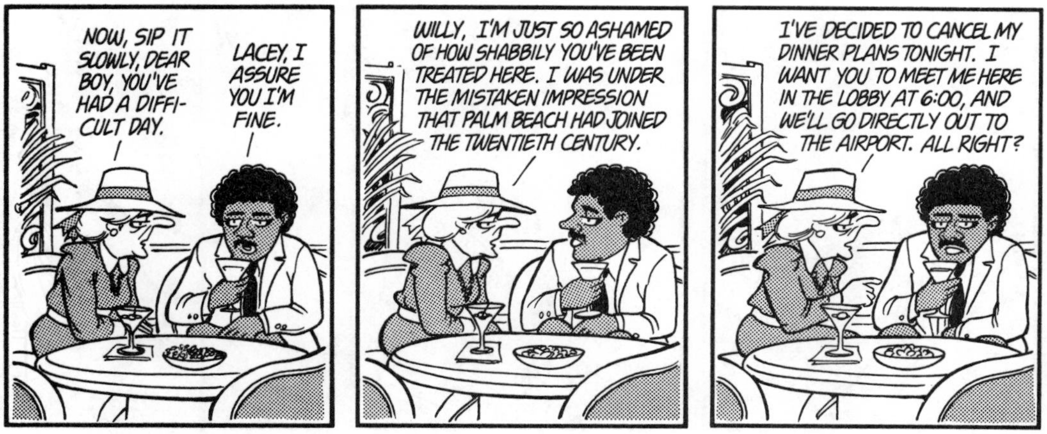
NOW, SIP IT SLOWLY, DEAR BOY, YOU'VE HAD A DIFFICULT DAY.
LACEY, I ASSURE YOU I'M FINE.
WILLY, I'M JUST SO ASHAMED OF HOW SHABBILY YOU'VE BEEN TREATED HERE. I WAS UNDER THE MISTAKEN IMPRESSION THAT PALM BEACH HAD JOINED THE TWENTIETH CENTURY.
I'VE DECIDED TO CANCEL MY DINNER PLANS TONIGHT. I WANT YOU TO MEET ME HERE IN THE LOBBY AT 6:00, AND WE'LL GO DIRECTLY OUT TO THE AIRPORT. ALL RIGHT?
EXCUSE ME, SIR. ROUTINE CHECK.
WHAT?
MAYBE I SHOULD JUST MEET YOU AT THE CITY LIMITS.
GB Trudeau

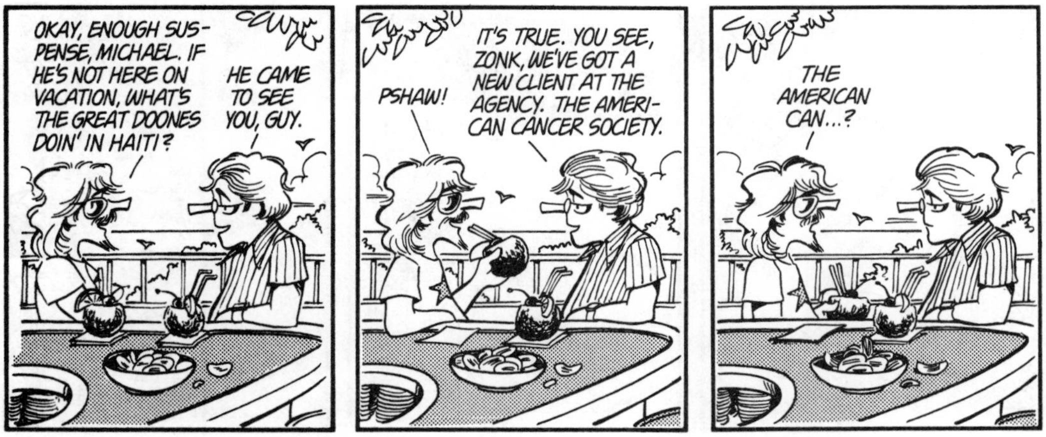
OKAY, ENOUGH SUSPENSE, MICHAEL. IF HE'S NOT HERE ON VACATION, WHAT'S THE GREAT DOONES DOIN' IN HAITI?
HE CAME TO SEE YOU, GUY.
PSHAW!
IT'S TRUE. YOU SEE, ZONK, WE'VE GOT A NEW CLIENT AT THE AGENCY. THE AMERICAN CANCER SOCIETY.
THE AMERICAN CAN...?
TANNING. THIS IS ABOUT TANNING.
YOU GOTTA HELP US, ZONK. MILLIONS OF KIDS LOOK UP TO YOU.
GB Trudeau

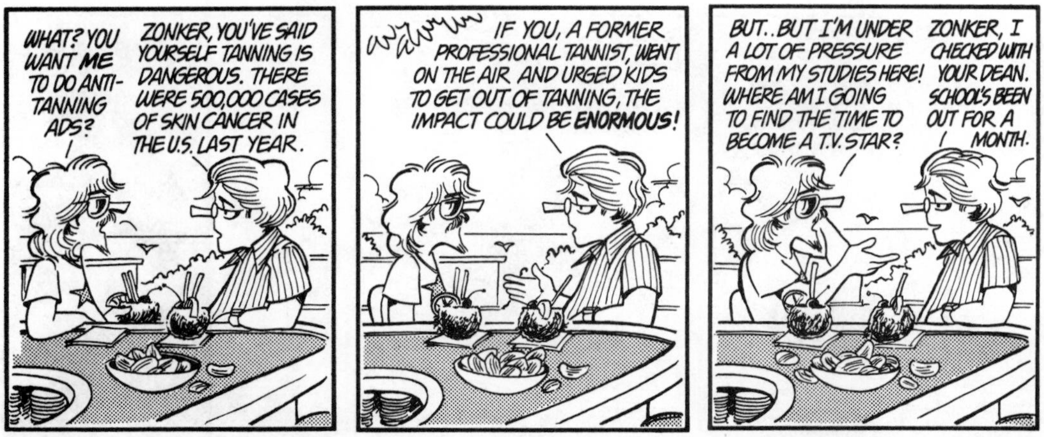
WHAT? YOU WANT ME TO DO ANTI-TANNING ADS?
ZONKER, YOU'VE SAID YOURSELF TANNING IS DANGEROUS. THERE WERE 500,000 CASES OF SKIN CANCER IN THE U.S. LAST YEAR.
IF YOU, A FORMER PROFESSIONAL TANNIST, WENT ON THE AIR AND URGED KIDS TO GET OUT OF TANNING, THE IMPACT COULD BE ENORMOUS!
BUT..BUT I'M UNDER A LOT OF PRESSURE FROM MY STUDIES HERE! WHERE AM I GOING TO FIND THE TIME TO BECOME A T.V. STAR?
ZONKER, I CHECKED WITH YOUR DEAN. SCHOOL'S BEEN OUT FOR A MONTH.
SO THAT'S WHY THE TENNIS COURTS HAVE BEEN SO FREE!
WHAT DO YOU SAY? I COULD HAVE A CREW HERE BY TOMORROW.
GB Trudeau

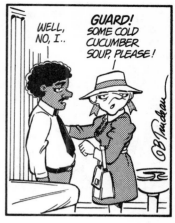

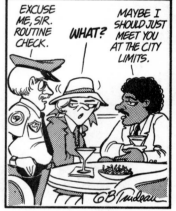

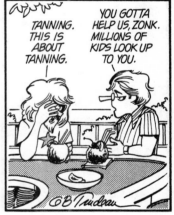

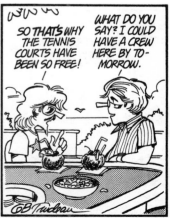

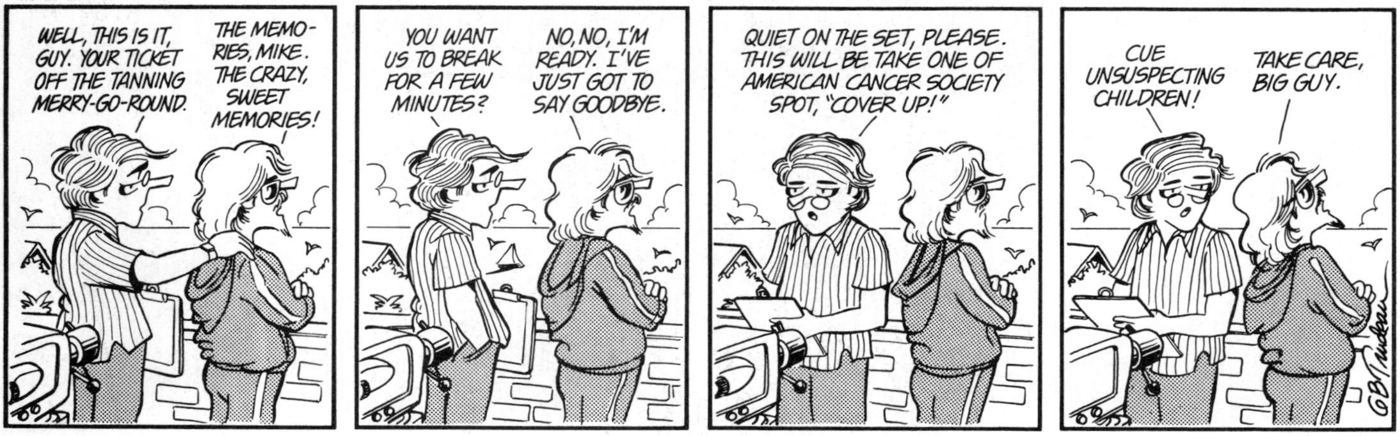
WELL, THIS IS IT, GUY. YOUR TICKET OFF THE TANNING MERRY-GO-ROUND.
THE MEMORIES, MIKE. THE CRAZY, SWEET MEMORIES!
YOU WANT US TO BREAK FOR A FEW MINUTES?
NO, NO, I'M READY. I'VE JUST GOT TO SAY GOODBYE.
QUIET ON THE SET, PLEASE. THIS WILL BE TAKE ONE OF AMERICAN CANCER SOCIETY SPOT, "COVER UP!"
CUE UNSUSPECTING CHILDREN!
TAKE CARE, BIG GUY.
GB Trudeau

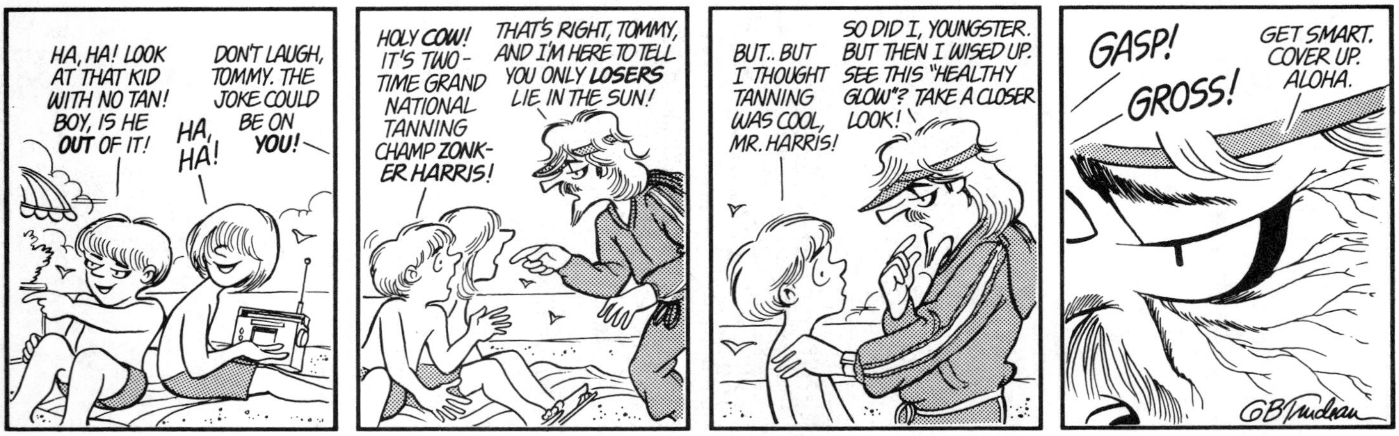
HA, HA! LOOK AT THAT KID WITH NO TAN! BOY, IS HE OUT OF IT!
HA, HA!
DON'T LAUGH, TOMMY. THE JOKE COULD BE ON YOU!
HOLY COW! IT'S TWO-TIME GRAND NATIONAL TANNING CHAMP ZONKER HARRIS!
THAT'S RIGHT, TOMMY, AND I'M HERE TO TELL YOU ONLY LOSERS LIE IN THE SUN!
BUT.. BUT I THOUGHT TANNING WAS COOL, MR. HARRIS!
SO DID I, YOUNGSTER. BUT THEN I WISED UP. SEE THIS "HEALTHY GLOW"? TAKE A CLOSER LOOK!
GASP!
GROSS!
GET SMART. COVER UP. ALOHA.
GB Trudeau

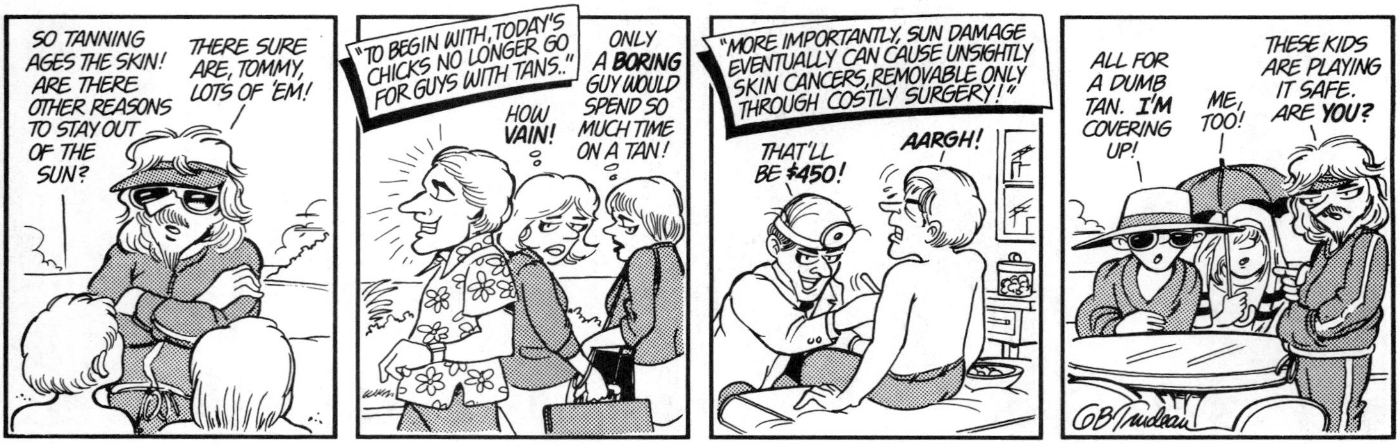
SO TANNING AGES THE SKIN! ARE THERE OTHER REASONS TO STAY OUT OF THE SUN?
THERE SURE ARE, TOMMY, LOTS OF 'EM!
"TO BEGIN WITH, TODAY'S CHICKS NO LONGER GO FOR GUYS WITH TANS.."
HOW VAIN!
ONLY A BORING GUY WOULD SPEND SO MUCH TIME ON A TAN!
"MORE IMPORTANTLY, SUN DAMAGE EVENTUALLY CAN CAUSE UNSIGHTLY SKIN CANCERS, REMOVABLE ONLY THROUGH COSTLY SURGERY!"
THAT'LL BE $450!
AARGH!
ALL FOR A DUMB TAN. I'M COVERING UP!
ME, TOO!
THESE KIDS ARE PLAYING IT SAFE. ARE YOU?
GB Trudeau

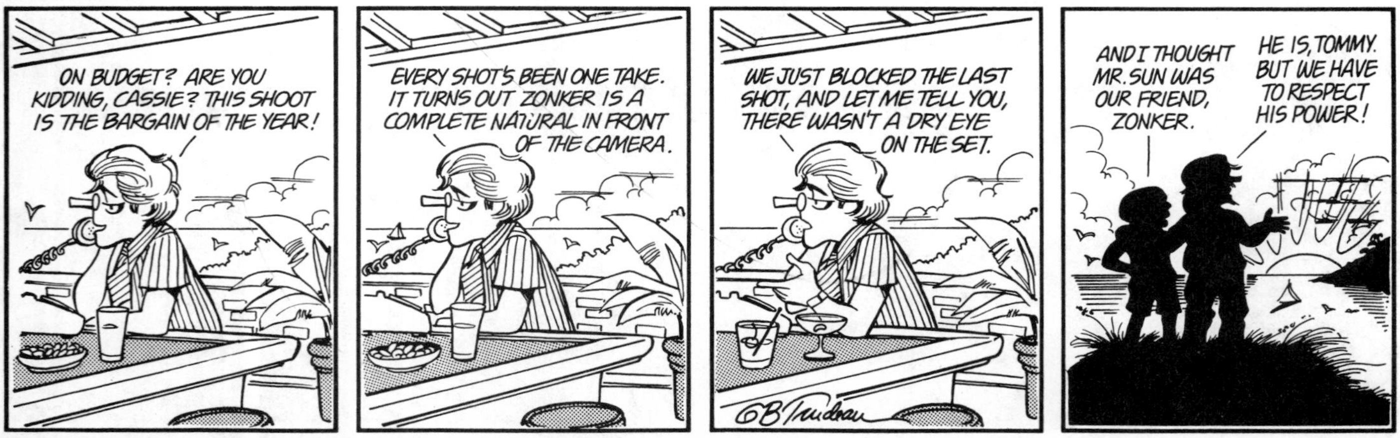
ON BUDGET? ARE YOU KIDDING, CASSIE? THIS SHOOT IS THE BARGAIN OF THE YEAR!
EVERY SHOT'S BEEN ONE TAKE. IT TURNS OUT ZONKER IS A COMPLETE NATURAL IN FRONT OF THE CAMERA.
WE JUST BLOCKED THE LAST SHOT, AND LET ME TELL YOU, THERE WASN'T A DRY EYE ON THE SET.
AND I THOUGHT MR. SUN WAS OUR FRIEND, ZONKER.
HE IS, TOMMY. BUT WE HAVE TO RESPECT HIS POWER!
GB Trudeau

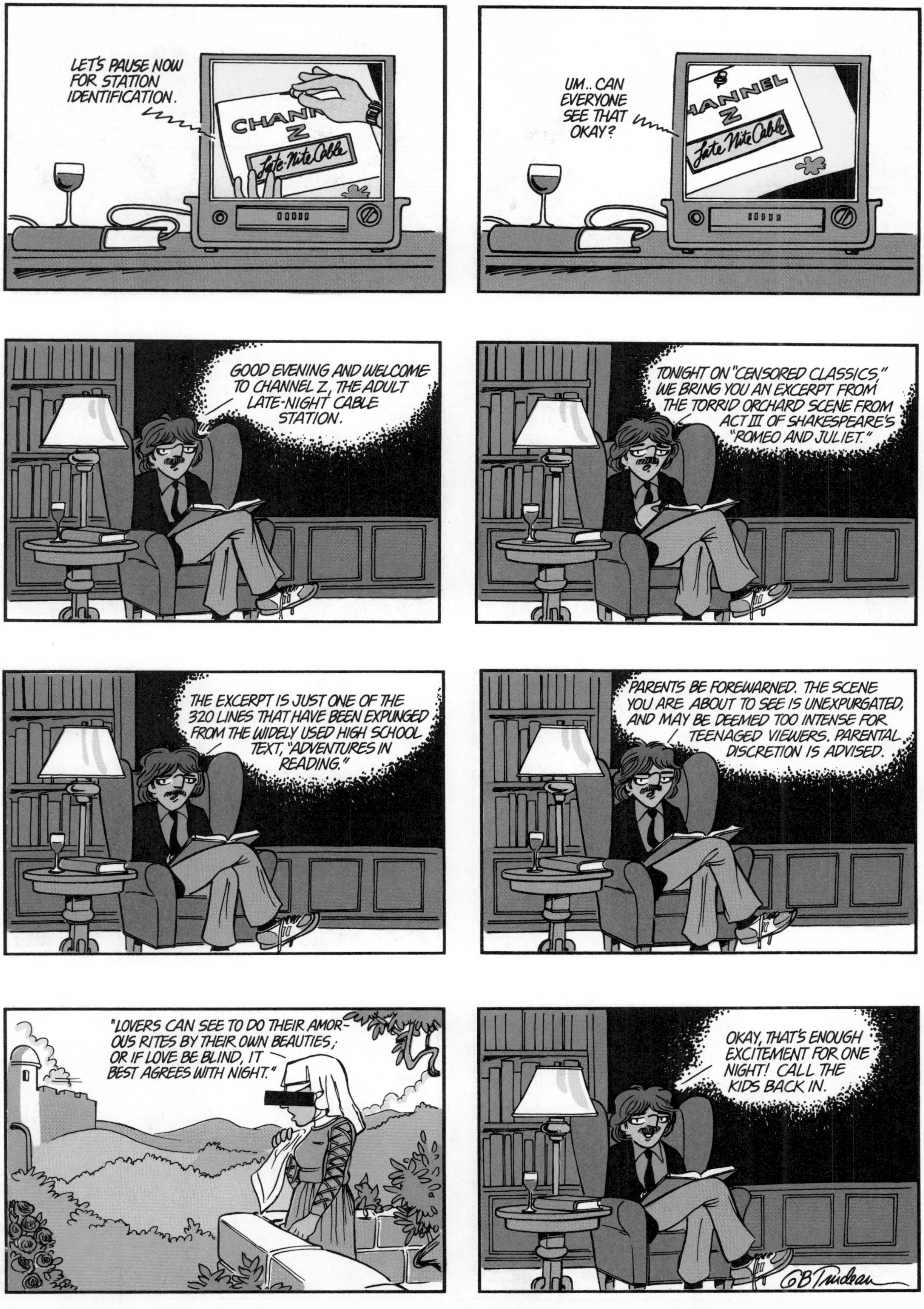

LET'S PAUSE NOW FOR STATION IDENTIFICATION.
Late-Nite Cable
UM.. CAN EVERYONE SEE THAT OKAY?
CHANNEL Z
Late-Nite Cable
GOOD EVENING AND WELCOME TO CHANNEL Z, THE ADULT LATE-NIGHT CABLE STATION.
TONIGHT ON "CENSORED CLASSICS," WE BRING YOU AN EXCERPT FROM THE TORRID ORCHARD SCENE FROM ACT III OF SHAKESPEARE'S "ROMEO AND JULIET."
THE EXCERPT IS JUST ONE OF THE 320 LINES THAT HAVE BEEN EXPUNGED FROM THE WIDELY USED HIGH SCHOOL TEXT, "ADVENTURES IN READING."
PARENTS BE FOREWARNED. THE SCENE YOU ARE ABOUT TO SEE IS UNEXPURGATED, AND MAY BE DEEMED TOO INTENSE FOR TEENAGED VIEWERS. PARENTAL DISCRETION IS ADVISED.
"LOVERS CAN SEE TO DO THEIR AMOROUS RITES BY THEIR OWN BEAUTIES; OR IF LOVE BE BLIND, IT BEST AGREES WITH NIGHT."
OKAY, THAT'S ENOUGH EXCITEMENT FOR ONE NIGHT! CALL THE KIDS BACK IN.

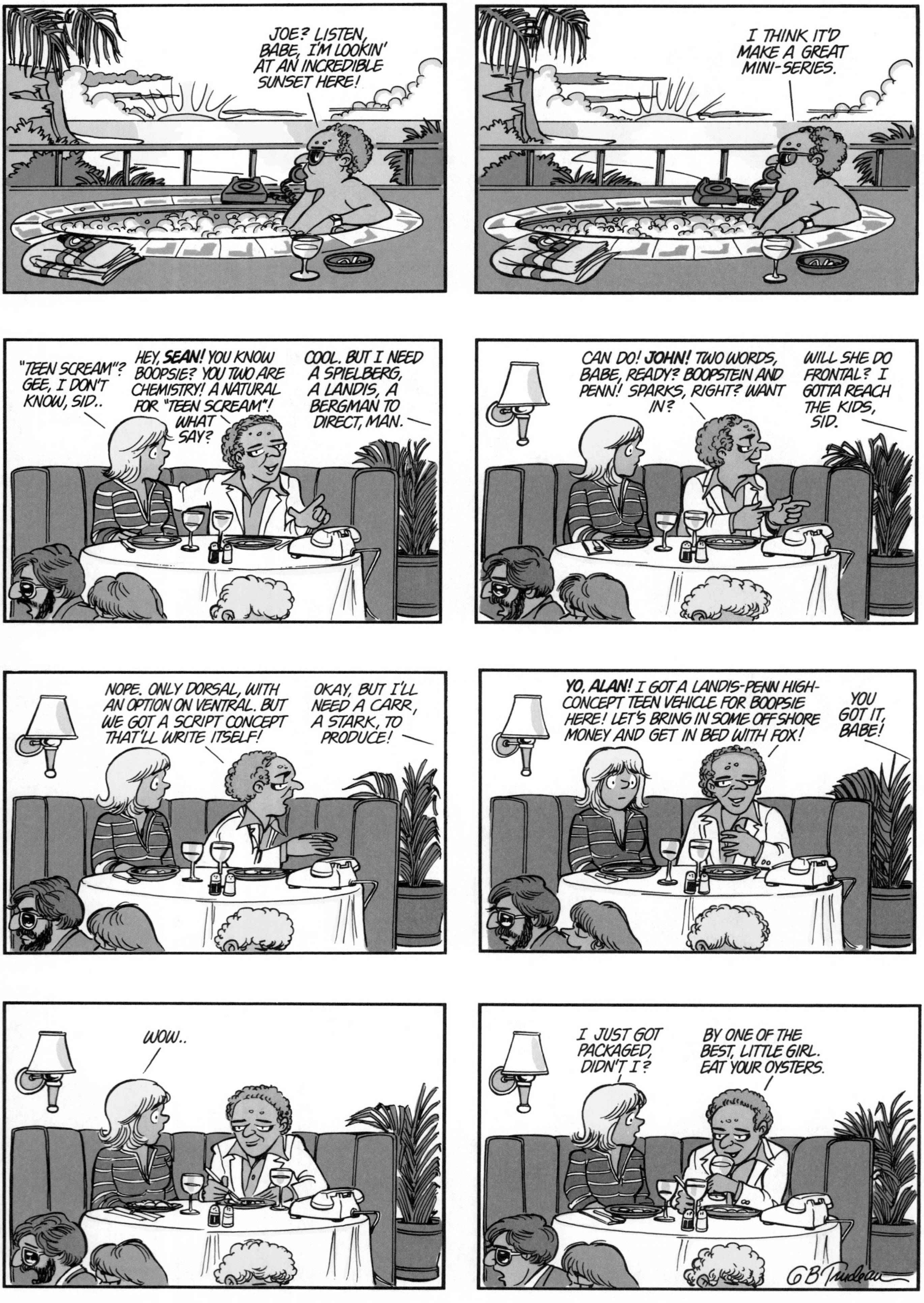
JOE? LISTEN, BABE, I'M LOOKIN' AT AN INCREDIBLE SUNSET HERE!
I THINK IT'D MAKE A GREAT MINI-SERIES.
"TEEN SCREAM"? GEE, I DON'T KNOW, SID..
HEY, **SEAN!** YOU KNOW BOOPSIE? YOU TWO ARE CHEMISTRY! A NATURAL FOR "TEEN SCREAM"! WHAT SAY?
COOL. BUT I NEED A SPIELBERG, A LANDIS, A BERGMAN TO DIRECT, MAN.
CAN DO! **JOHN!** TWO WORDS, BABE, READY? BOOPSTEIN AND PENN! SPARKS, RIGHT? WANT IN?
WILL SHE DO FRONTAL? I GOTTA REACH THE KIDS, SID.
NOPE. ONLY DORSAL, WITH AN OPTION ON VENTRAL. BUT WE GOT A SCRIPT CONCEPT THAT'LL WRITE ITSELF!
OKAY, BUT I'LL NEED A CARR, A STARK, TO PRODUCE!
YO, ALAN! I GOT A LANDIS-PENN HIGH-CONCEPT TEEN VEHICLE FOR BOOPSIE HERE! LET'S BRING IN SOME OFF SHORE MONEY AND GET IN BED WITH FOX!
YOU GOT IT, BABE!
WOW..
I JUST GOT PACKAGED, DIDN'T I?
BY ONE OF THE BEST, LITTLE GIRL. EAT YOUR OYSTERS.
GB Trudeau

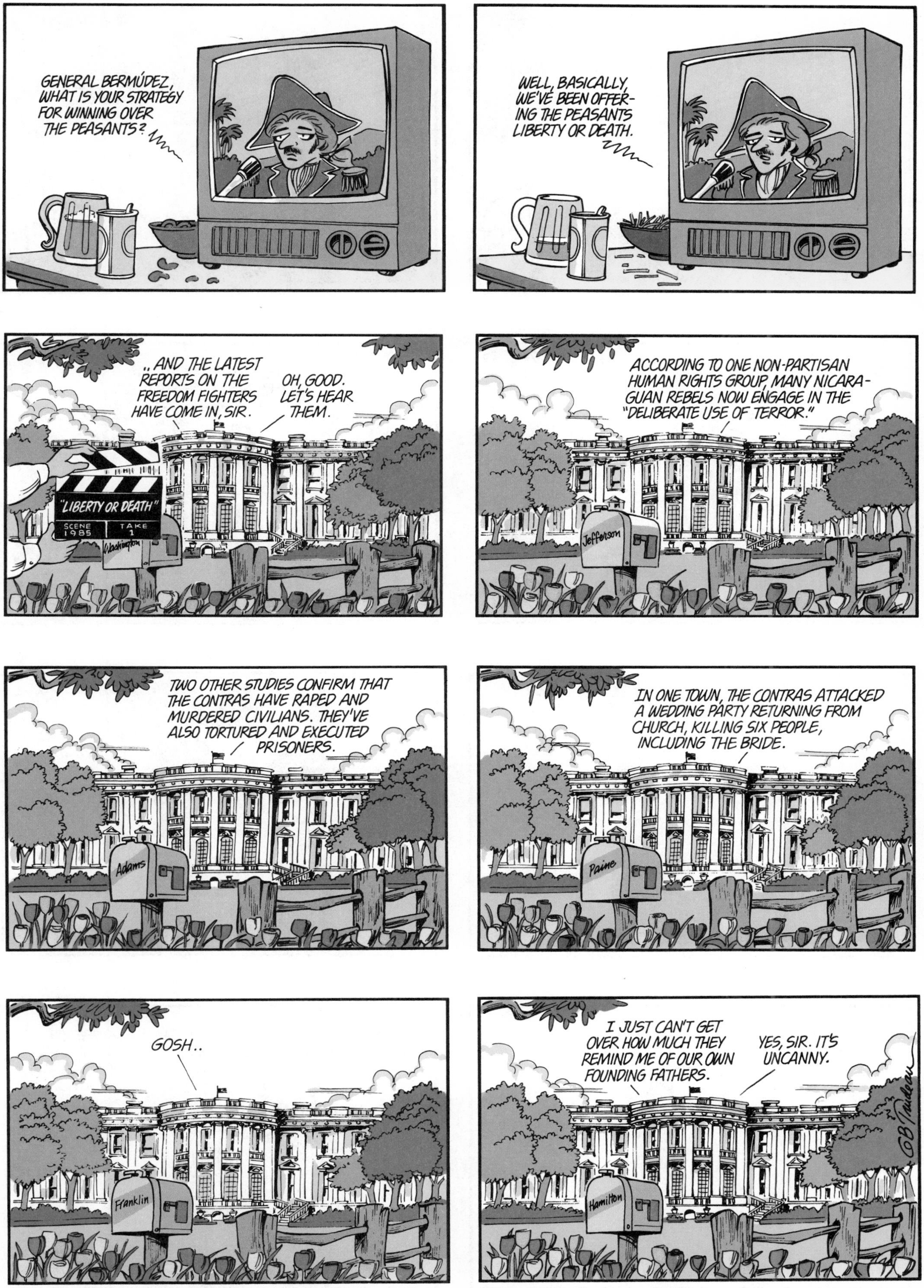
GENERAL BERMÚDEZ, WHAT IS YOUR STRATEGY FOR WINNING OVER THE PEASANTS?
WELL, BASICALLY, WE'VE BEEN OFFERING THE PEASANTS LIBERTY OR DEATH.
.. AND THE LATEST REPORTS ON THE FREEDOM FIGHTERS HAVE COME IN, SIR.
OH, GOOD. LET'S HEAR THEM.
"LIBERTY OR DEATH"
SCENE 1985
TAKE 1
Washington
ACCORDING TO ONE NON-PARTISAN HUMAN RIGHTS GROUP, MANY NICARAGUAN REBELS NOW ENGAGE IN THE "DELIBERATE USE OF TERROR."
Jefferson
TWO OTHER STUDIES CONFIRM THAT THE CONTRAS HAVE RAPED AND MURDERED CIVILIANS. THEY'VE ALSO TORTURED AND EXECUTED PRISONERS.
Adams
IN ONE TOWN, THE CONTRAS ATTACKED A WEDDING PARTY RETURNING FROM CHURCH, KILLING SIX PEOPLE, INCLUDING THE BRIDE.
Paine
GOSH..
Franklin
I JUST CAN'T GET OVER HOW MUCH THEY REMIND ME OF OUR OWN FOUNDING FATHERS.
YES, SIR. IT'S UNCANNY.
Hamilton
GBTrudeau

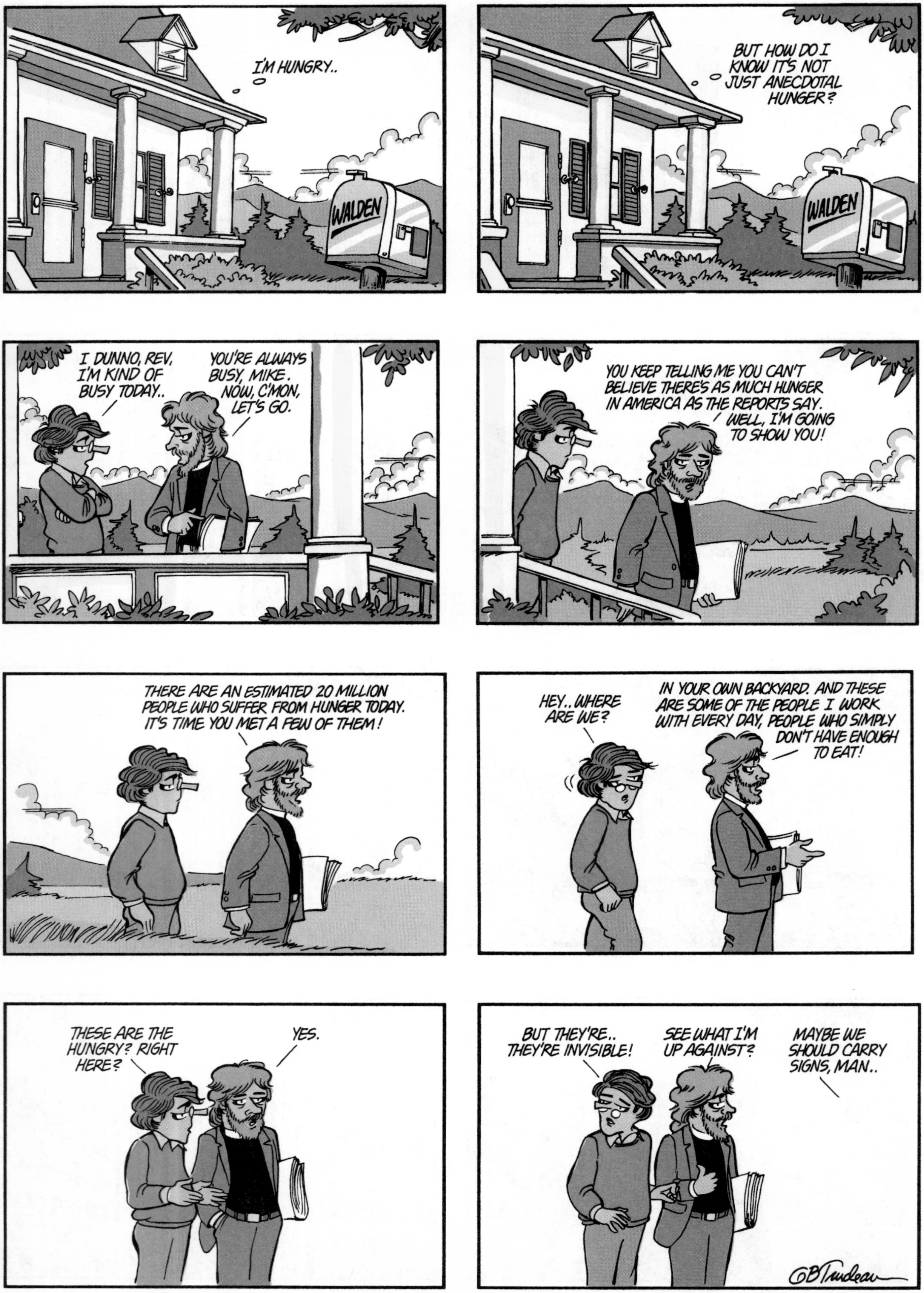

I'M HUNGRY..
WALDEN
BUT HOW DO I KNOW IT'S NOT JUST ANECDOTAL HUNGER?
WALDEN
I DUNNO, REV, I'M KIND OF BUSY TODAY..
YOU'RE ALWAYS BUSY, MIKE. NOW, C'MON, LET'S GO.
YOU KEEP TELLING ME YOU CAN'T BELIEVE THERE'S AS MUCH HUNGER IN AMERICA AS THE REPORTS SAY. WELL, I'M GOING TO SHOW YOU!
THERE ARE AN ESTIMATED 20 MILLION PEOPLE WHO SUFFER FROM HUNGER TODAY. IT'S TIME YOU MET A FEW OF THEM!
HEY.. WHERE ARE WE?
IN YOUR OWN BACKYARD. AND THESE ARE SOME OF THE PEOPLE I WORK WITH EVERY DAY, PEOPLE WHO SIMPLY DON'T HAVE ENOUGH TO EAT!
THESE ARE THE HUNGRY? RIGHT HERE?
YES.
BUT THEY'RE.. THEY'RE INVISIBLE!
SEE WHAT I'M UP AGAINST?
MAYBE WE SHOULD CARRY SIGNS, MAN..
©BTrudeau

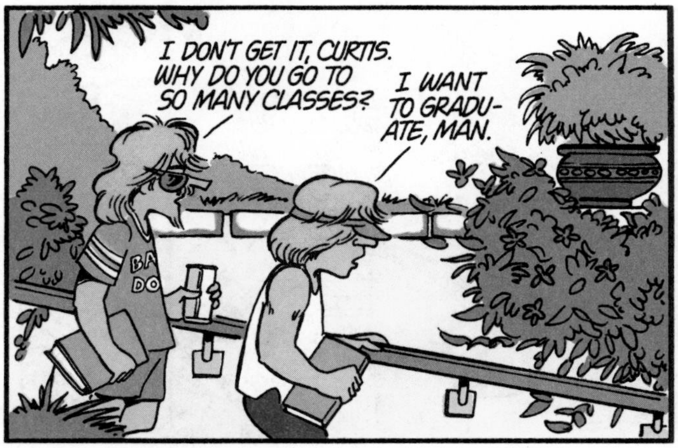
I DON'T GET IT, CURTIS. WHY DO YOU GO TO SO MANY CLASSES?
I WANT TO GRADUATE, MAN.
I'LL NEVER UNDERSTAND THAT..
BABY DOC

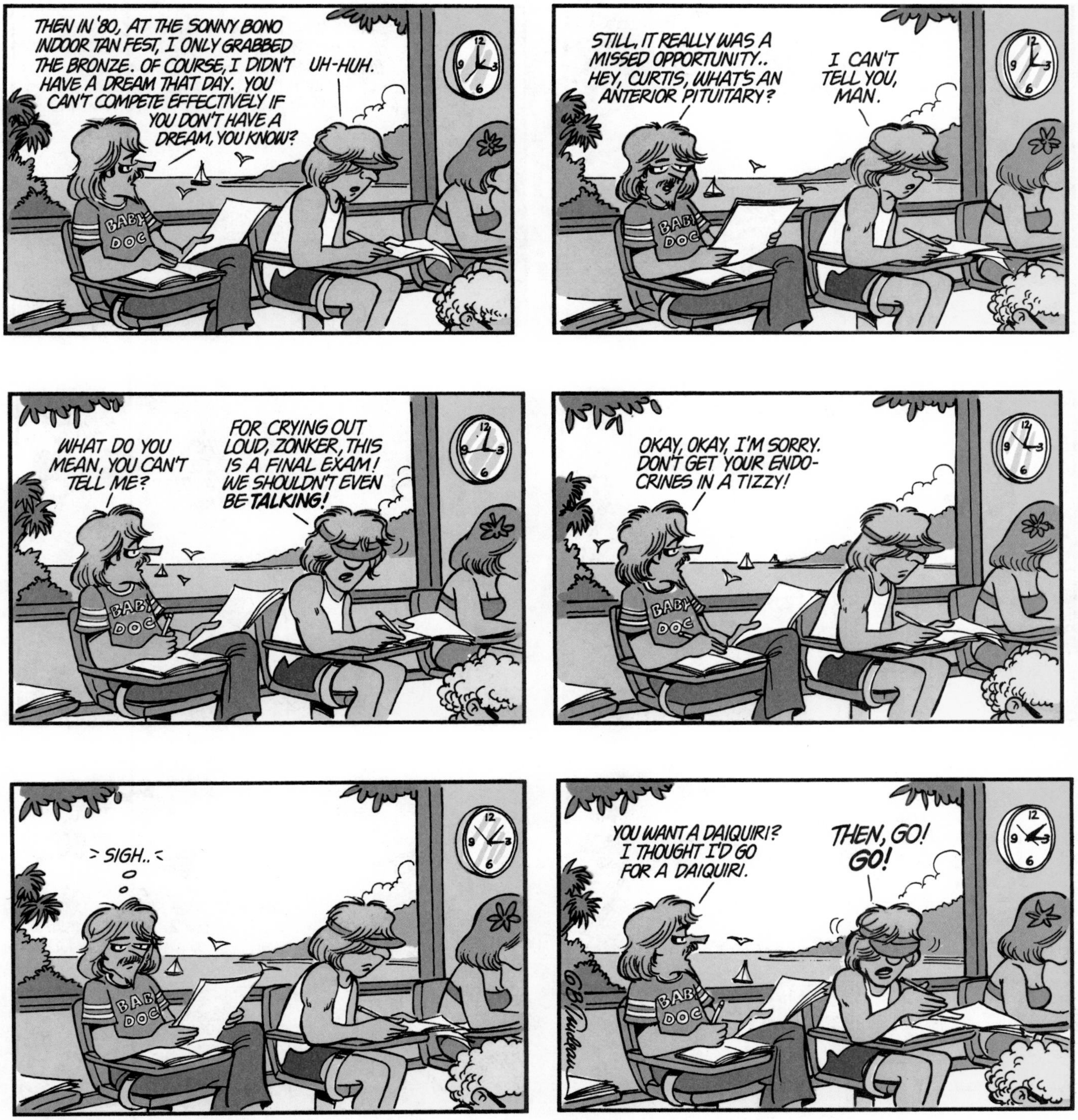
THEN IN '80, AT THE SONNY BONO INDOOR TAN FEST, I ONLY GRABBED THE BRONZE. OF COURSE, I DIDN'T HAVE A DREAM THAT DAY. YOU CAN'T COMPETE EFFECTIVELY IF YOU DON'T HAVE A DREAM, YOU KNOW?
UH-HUH.
STILL, IT REALLY WAS A MISSED OPPORTUNITY.. HEY, CURTIS, WHAT'S AN ANTERIOR PITUITARY?
I CAN'T TELL YOU, MAN.
WHAT DO YOU MEAN, YOU CAN'T TELL ME?
FOR CRYING OUT LOUD, ZONKER, THIS IS A FINAL EXAM! WE SHOULDN'T EVEN BE **TALKING!**
OKAY, OKAY, I'M SORRY. DON'T GET YOUR ENDOCRINES IN A TIZZY!
> SIGH.. <
YOU WANT A DAIQUIRI? I THOUGHT I'D GO FOR A DAIQUIRI.
THEN, GO! **GO!**

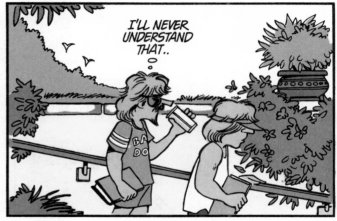

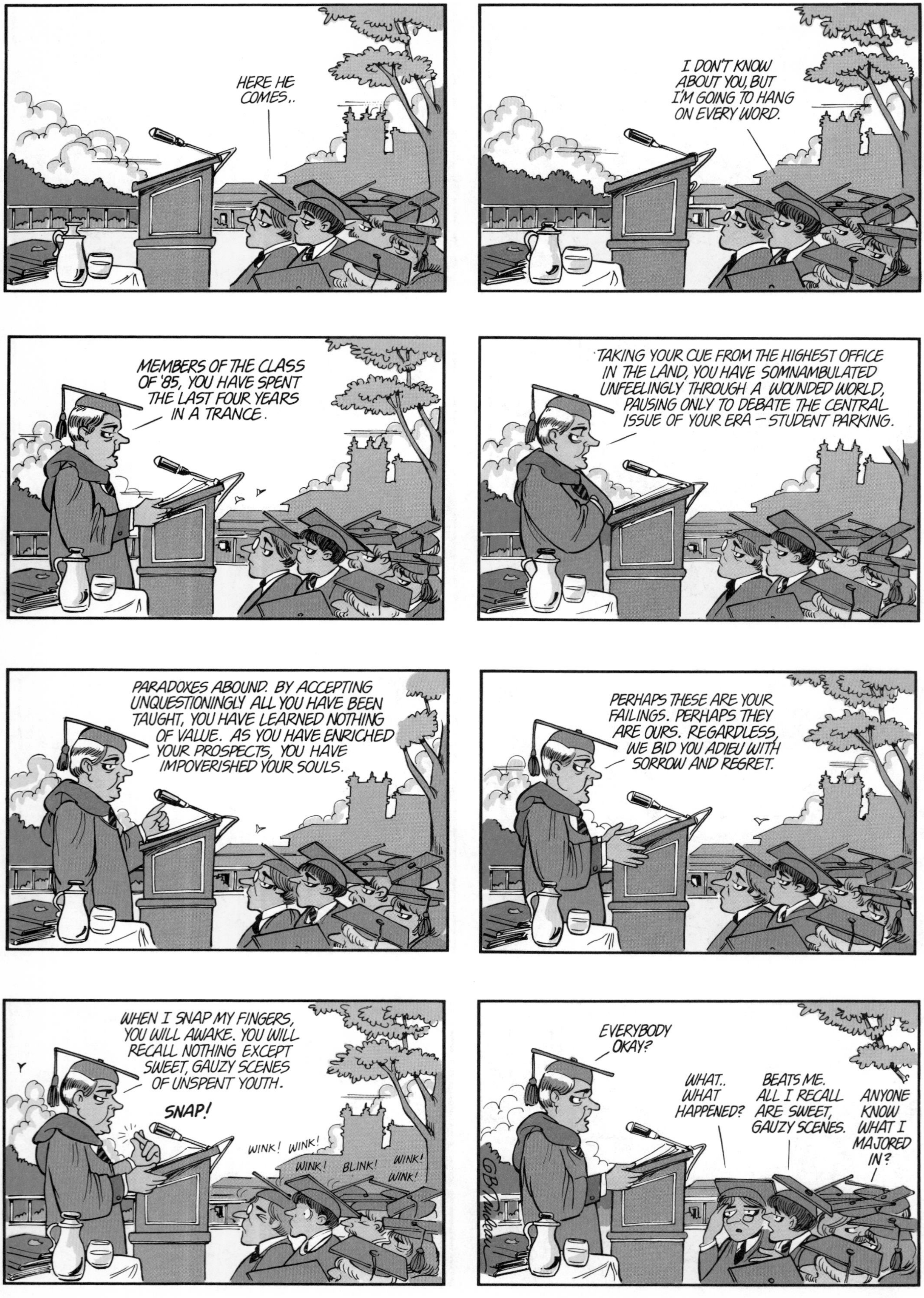
HERE HE COMES..
I DON'T KNOW ABOUT YOU, BUT I'M GOING TO HANG ON EVERY WORD.
MEMBERS OF THE CLASS OF '85, YOU HAVE SPENT THE LAST FOUR YEARS IN A TRANCE.
TAKING YOUR CUE FROM THE HIGHEST OFFICE IN THE LAND, YOU HAVE SOMNAMBULATED UNFEELINGLY THROUGH A WOUNDED WORLD, PAUSING ONLY TO DEBATE THE CENTRAL ISSUE OF YOUR ERA — STUDENT PARKING.
PARADOXES ABOUND. BY ACCEPTING UNQUESTIONINGLY ALL YOU HAVE BEEN TAUGHT, YOU HAVE LEARNED NOTHING OF VALUE. AS YOU HAVE ENRICHED YOUR PROSPECTS, YOU HAVE IMPOVERISHED YOUR SOULS.
PERHAPS THESE ARE YOUR FAILINGS. PERHAPS THEY ARE OURS. REGARDLESS, WE BID YOU ADIEU WITH SORROW AND REGRET.
WHEN I SNAP MY FINGERS, YOU WILL AWAKE. YOU WILL RECALL NOTHING EXCEPT SWEET, GAUZY SCENES OF UNSPENT YOUTH.
SNAP!
WINK! WINK!
WINK!
BLINK!
WINK!
WINK!
EVERYBODY OKAY?
WHAT.. WHAT HAPPENED?
BEATS ME. ALL I RECALL ARE SWEET, GAUZY SCENES.
ANYONE KNOW WHAT I MAJORED IN?

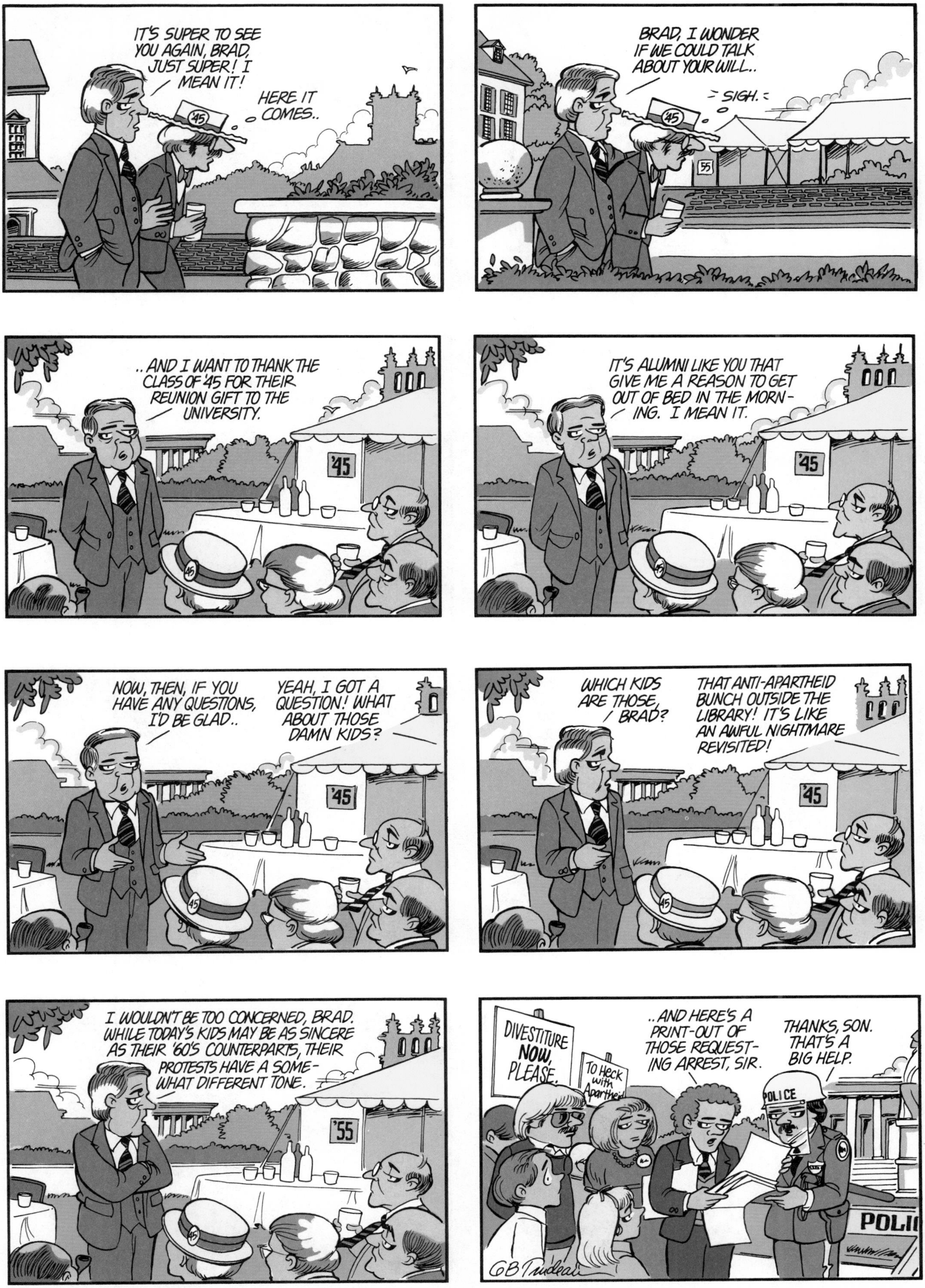
IT'S SUPER TO SEE YOU AGAIN, BRAD, JUST SUPER! I MEAN IT!
'45
HERE IT COMES..
BRAD, I WONDER IF WE COULD TALK ABOUT YOUR WILL..
SIGH.
'45
'55
..AND I WANT TO THANK THE CLASS OF '45 FOR THEIR REUNION GIFT TO THE UNIVERSITY.
'45
IT'S ALUMNI LIKE YOU THAT GIVE ME A REASON TO GET OUT OF BED IN THE MORNING. I MEAN IT.
'45
NOW, THEN, IF YOU HAVE ANY QUESTIONS, I'D BE GLAD..
YEAH, I GOT A QUESTION! WHAT ABOUT THOSE DAMN KIDS?
'45
WHICH KIDS ARE THOSE, BRAD?
THAT ANTI-APARTHEID BUNCH OUTSIDE THE LIBRARY! IT'S LIKE AN AWFUL NIGHTMARE REVISITED!
'45
I WOULDN'T BE TOO CONCERNED, BRAD. WHILE TODAY'S KIDS MAY BE AS SINCERE AS THEIR '60'S COUNTERPARTS, THEIR PROTESTS HAVE A SOMEWHAT DIFFERENT TONE.
'55
DIVESTITURE NOW, PLEASE.
To Heck with Apartheid
..AND HERE'S A PRINT-OUT OF THOSE REQUESTING ARREST, SIR.
THANKS, SON. THAT'S A BIG HELP.
POLICE
POLI
GB Trudeau

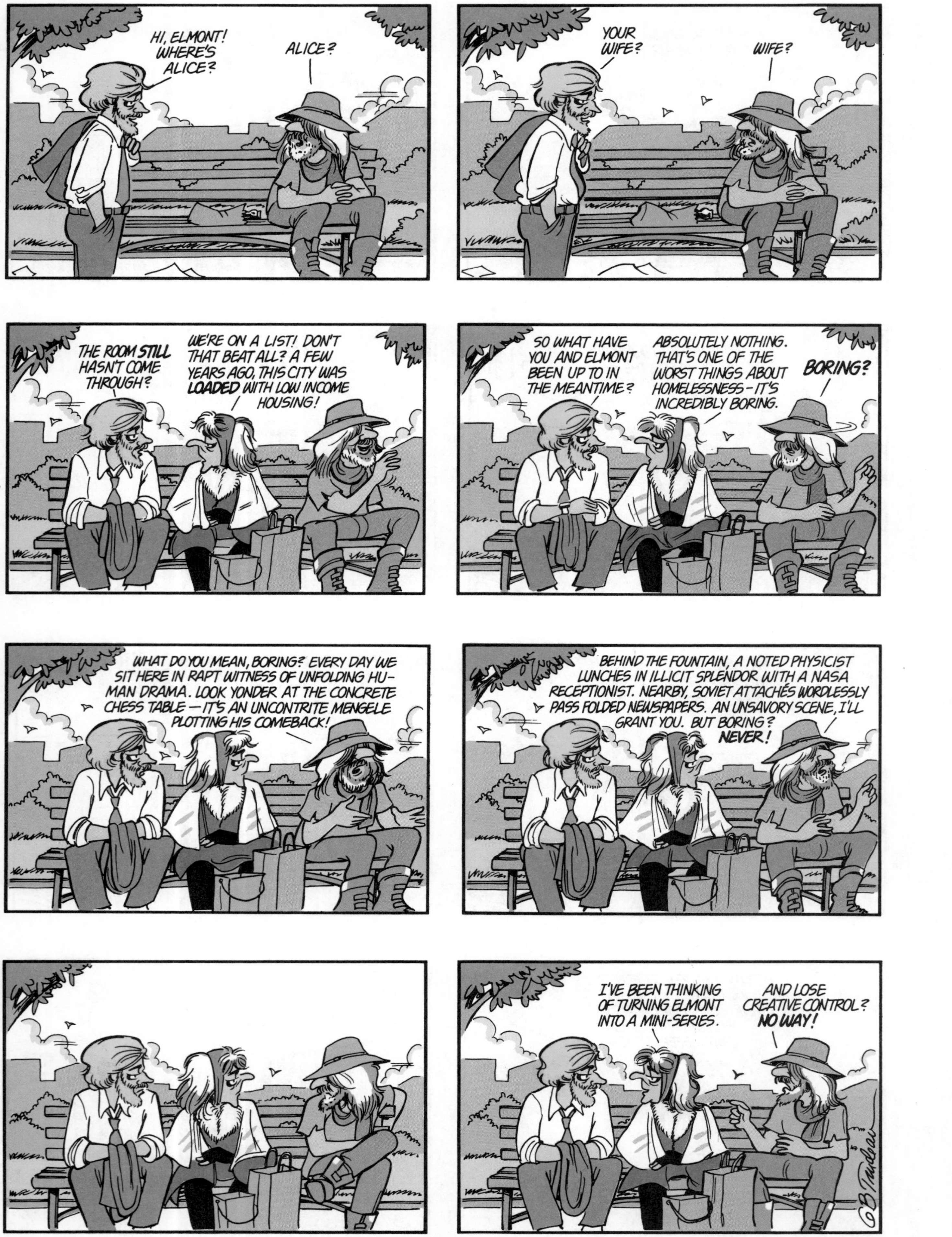
HI, ELMONT! WHERE'S ALICE?
ALICE?
YOUR WIFE?
WIFE?
THE ROOM STILL HASN'T COME THROUGH?
WE'RE ON A LIST! DON'T THAT BEAT ALL? A FEW YEARS AGO, THIS CITY WAS LOADED WITH LOW INCOME HOUSING!
SO WHAT HAVE YOU AND ELMONT BEEN UP TO IN THE MEANTIME?
ABSOLUTELY NOTHING. THAT'S ONE OF THE WORST THINGS ABOUT HOMELESSNESS – IT'S INCREDIBLY BORING.
BORING?
WHAT DO YOU MEAN, BORING? EVERY DAY WE SIT HERE IN RAPT WITNESS OF UNFOLDING HUMAN DRAMA. LOOK YONDER AT THE CONCRETE CHESS TABLE — IT'S AN UNCONTRITE MENGELE PLOTTING HIS COMEBACK!
BEHIND THE FOUNTAIN, A NOTED PHYSICIST LUNCHES IN ILLICIT SPLENDOR WITH A NASA RECEPTIONIST. NEARBY, SOVIET ATTACHÉS WORDLESSLY PASS FOLDED NEWSPAPERS. AN UNSAVORY SCENE, I'LL GRANT YOU. BUT BORING? NEVER!
I'VE BEEN THINKING OF TURNING ELMONT INTO A MINI-SERIES.
AND LOSE CREATIVE CONTROL? NO WAY!
©BTrudeau

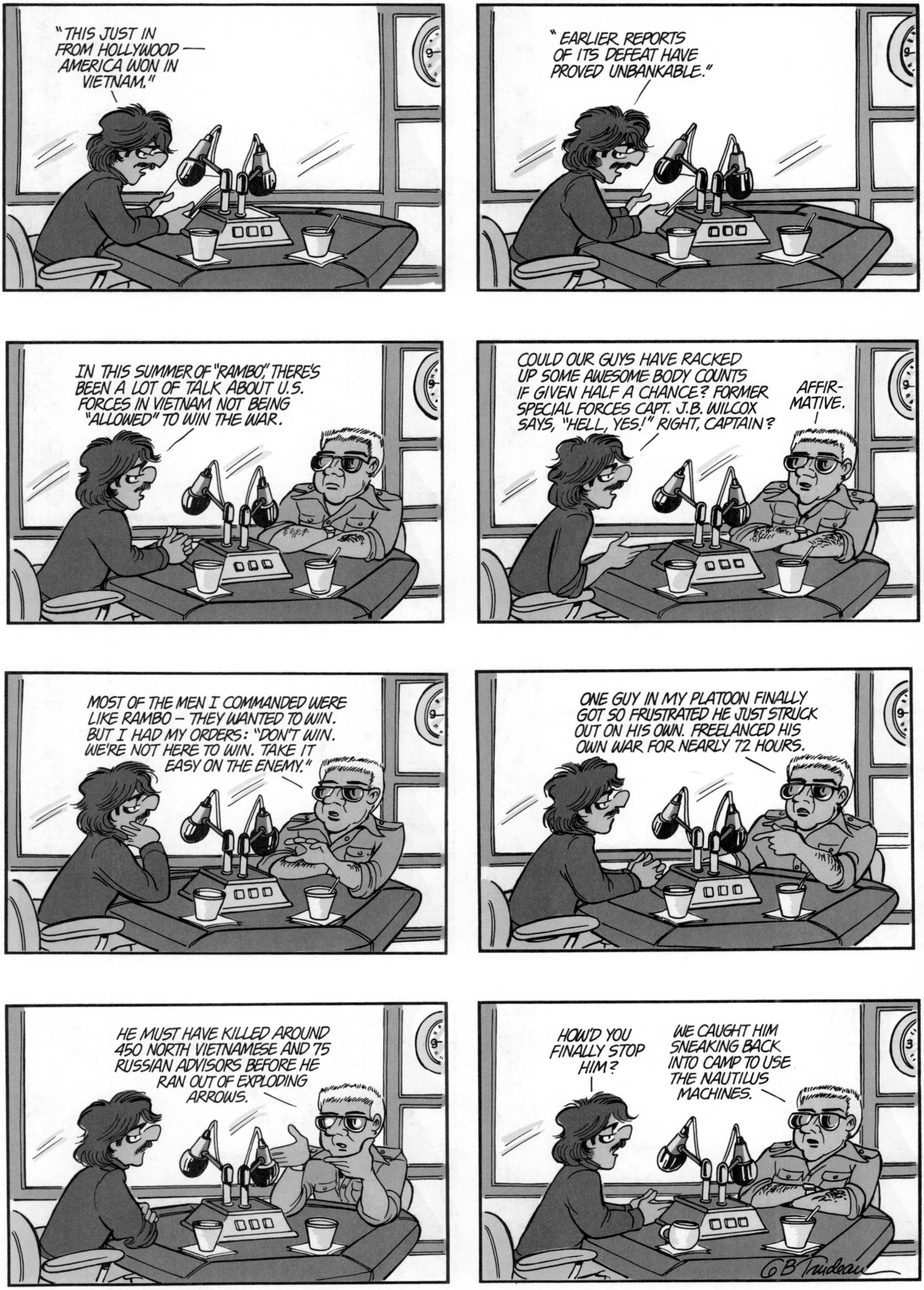
"THIS JUST IN FROM HOLLYWOOD — AMERICA WON IN VIETNAM."
"EARLIER REPORTS OF ITS DEFEAT HAVE PROVED UNBANKABLE."
IN THIS SUMMER OF "RAMBO," THERE'S BEEN A LOT OF TALK ABOUT U.S. FORCES IN VIETNAM NOT BEING "ALLOWED" TO WIN THE WAR.
COULD OUR GUYS HAVE RACKED UP SOME AWESOME BODY COUNTS IF GIVEN HALF A CHANCE? FORMER SPECIAL FORCES CAPT. J.B. WILCOX SAYS, "HELL, YES!" RIGHT, CAPTAIN?
AFFIRMATIVE.
MOST OF THE MEN I COMMANDED WERE LIKE RAMBO – THEY WANTED TO WIN. BUT I HAD MY ORDERS: "DON'T WIN. WE'RE NOT HERE TO WIN. TAKE IT EASY ON THE ENEMY."
ONE GUY IN MY PLATOON FINALLY GOT SO FRUSTRATED HE JUST STRUCK OUT ON HIS OWN. FREELANCED HIS OWN WAR FOR NEARLY 72 HOURS.
HE MUST HAVE KILLED AROUND 450 NORTH VIETNAMESE AND 75 RUSSIAN ADVISORS BEFORE HE RAN OUT OF EXPLODING ARROWS.
HOW'D YOU FINALLY STOP HIM?
WE CAUGHT HIM SNEAKING BACK INTO CAMP TO USE THE NAUTILUS MACHINES.
G.B. Trudeau

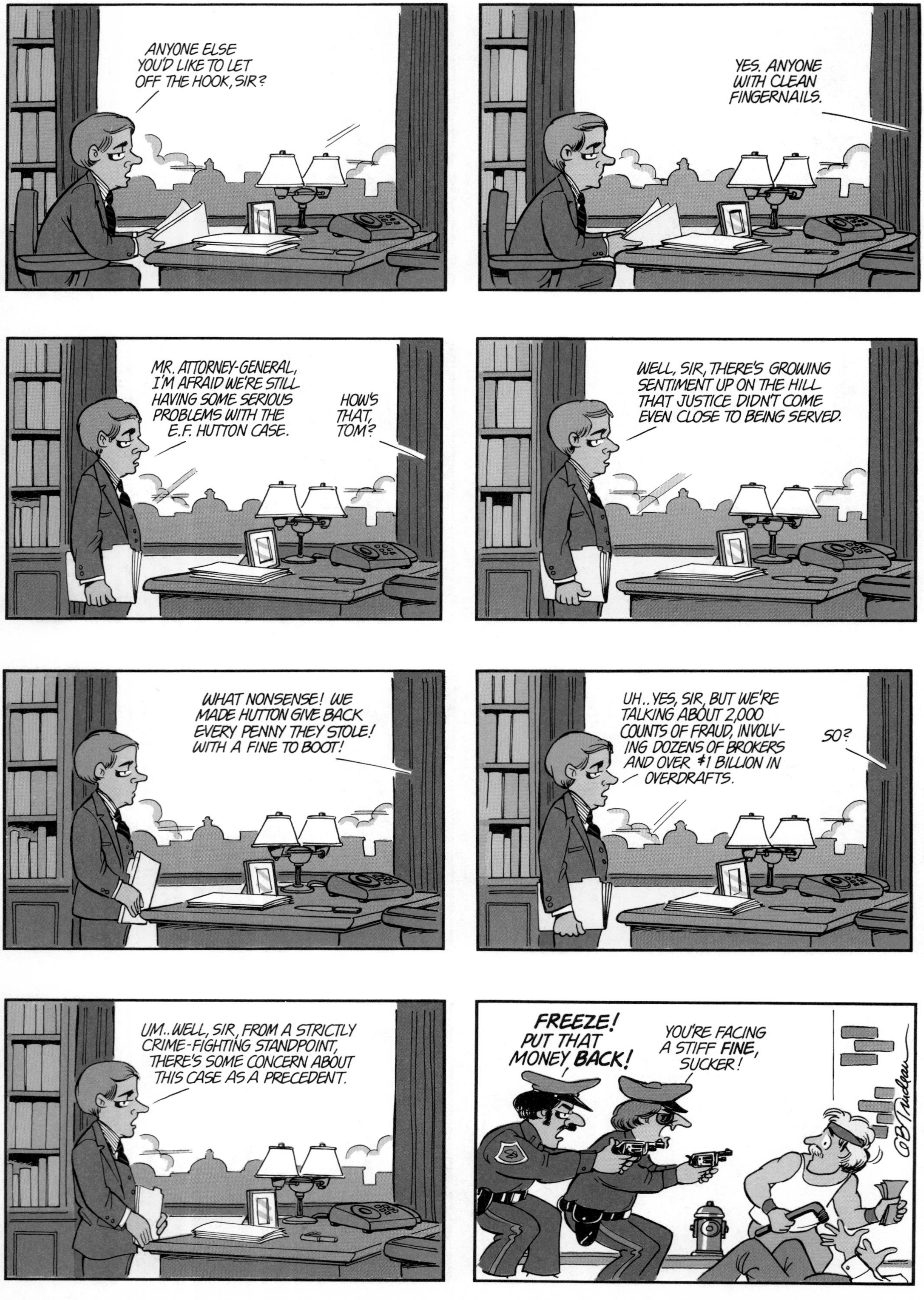
ANYONE ELSE YOU'D LIKE TO LET OFF THE HOOK, SIR?
YES. ANYONE WITH CLEAN FINGERNAILS.
MR. ATTORNEY-GENERAL, I'M AFRAID WE'RE STILL HAVING SOME SERIOUS PROBLEMS WITH THE E.F. HUTTON CASE.
HOW'S THAT, TOM?
WELL, SIR, THERE'S GROWING SENTIMENT UP ON THE HILL THAT JUSTICE DIDN'T COME EVEN CLOSE TO BEING SERVED.
WHAT NONSENSE! WE MADE HUTTON GIVE BACK EVERY PENNY THEY STOLE! WITH A FINE TO BOOT!
UH.. YES, SIR, BUT WE'RE TALKING ABOUT 2,000 COUNTS OF FRAUD, INVOLVING DOZENS OF BROKERS AND OVER $1 BILLION IN OVERDRAFTS.
SO?
UM.. WELL, SIR, FROM A STRICTLY CRIME-FIGHTING STANDPOINT, THERE'S SOME CONCERN ABOUT THIS CASE AS A PRECEDENT.
FREEZE! PUT THAT MONEY BACK!
YOU'RE FACING A STIFF FINE, SUCKER!

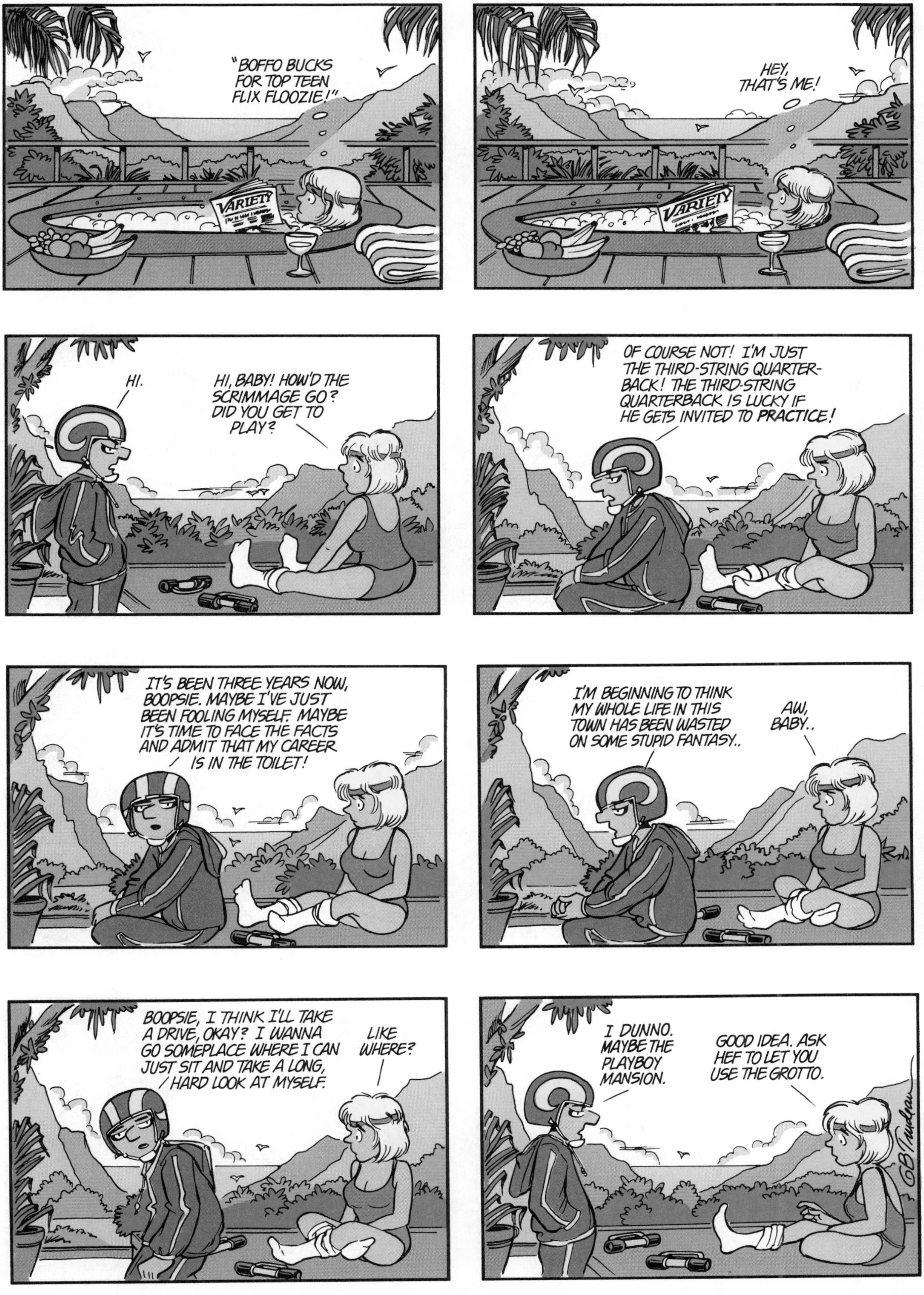
"BOFFO BUCKS FOR TOP TEEN FLIX FLOOZIE!"
VARIETY
HEY, THAT'S ME!
VARIETY
HI.
HI, BABY! HOW'D THE SCRIMMAGE GO? DID YOU GET TO PLAY?
OF COURSE NOT! I'M JUST THE THIRD-STRING QUARTER-BACK! THE THIRD-STRING QUARTERBACK IS LUCKY IF HE GETS INVITED TO PRACTICE!
IT'S BEEN THREE YEARS NOW, BOOPSIE. MAYBE I'VE JUST BEEN FOOLING MYSELF. MAYBE IT'S TIME TO FACE THE FACTS AND ADMIT THAT MY CAREER IS IN THE TOILET!
I'M BEGINNING TO THINK MY WHOLE LIFE IN THIS TOWN HAS BEEN WASTED ON SOME STUPID FANTASY..
AW, BABY..
BOOPSIE, I THINK I'LL TAKE A DRIVE, OKAY? I WANNA GO SOMEPLACE WHERE I CAN JUST SIT AND TAKE A LONG, HARD LOOK AT MYSELF.
LIKE WHERE?
I DUNNO. MAYBE THE PLAYBOY MANSION.
GOOD IDEA. ASK HEF TO LET YOU USE THE GROTTO.
GBTrudeau

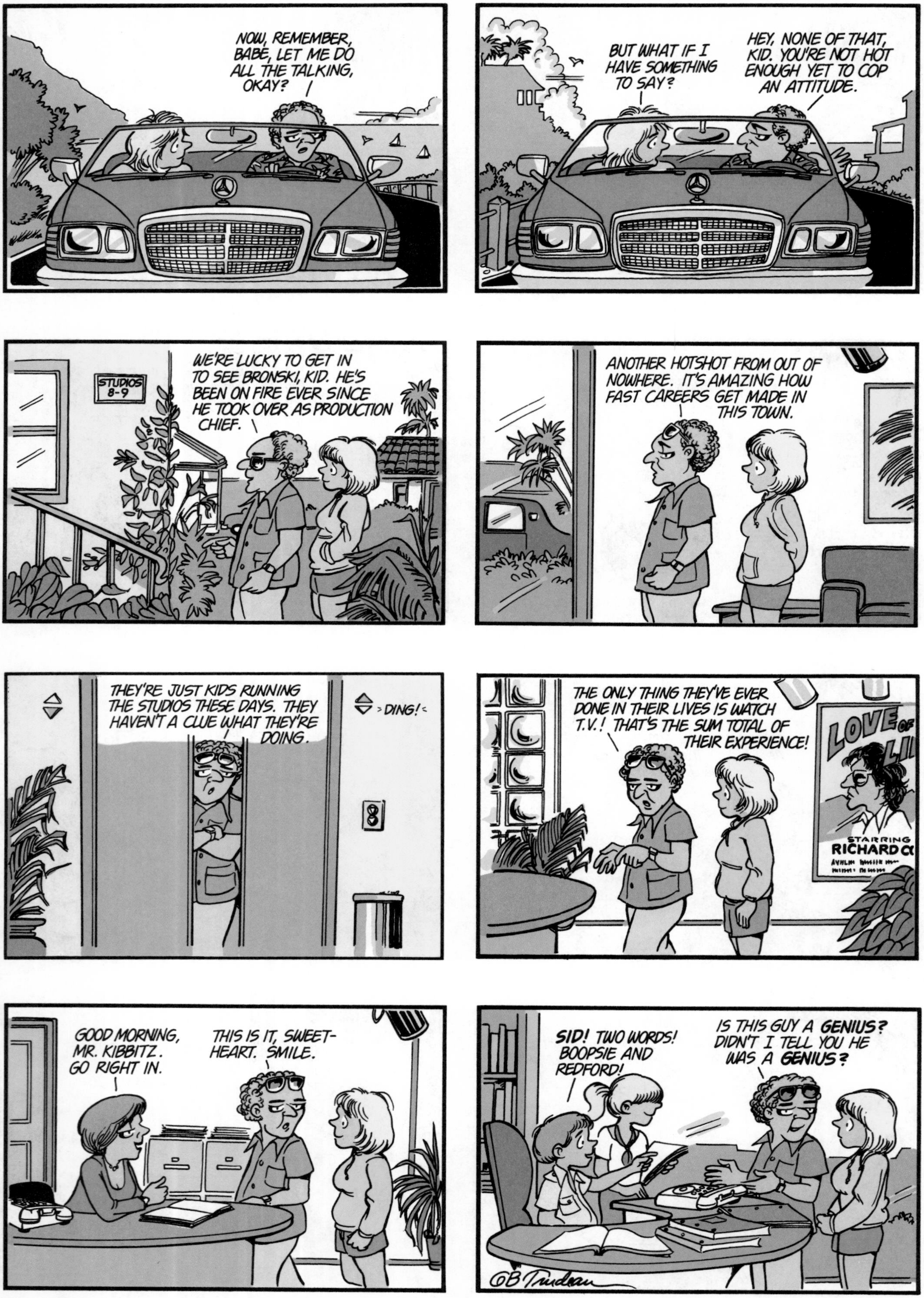

NOW, REMEMBER, BABE, LET ME DO ALL THE TALKING, OKAY?
BUT WHAT IF I HAVE SOMETHING TO SAY?
HEY, NONE OF THAT, KID. YOU'RE NOT HOT ENOUGH YET TO COP AN ATTITUDE.
STUDIOS 8-9
WE'RE LUCKY TO GET IN TO SEE BRONSKI, KID. HE'S BEEN ON FIRE EVER SINCE HE TOOK OVER AS PRODUCTION CHIEF.
ANOTHER HOTSHOT FROM OUT OF NOWHERE. IT'S AMAZING HOW FAST CAREERS GET MADE IN THIS TOWN.
THEY'RE JUST KIDS RUNNING THE STUDIOS THESE DAYS. THEY HAVEN'T A CLUE WHAT THEY'RE DOING.
DING!
THE ONLY THING THEY'VE EVER DONE IN THEIR LIVES IS WATCH T.V.! THAT'S THE SUM TOTAL OF THEIR EXPERIENCE!
STARRING
GOOD MORNING, MR. KIBBITZ. GO RIGHT IN.
THIS IS IT, SWEET-HEART. SMILE.
SID! TWO WORDS! BOOPSIE AND REDFORD!
IS THIS GUY A GENIUS? DIDN'T I TELL YOU HE WAS A GENIUS?
©B Trudeau

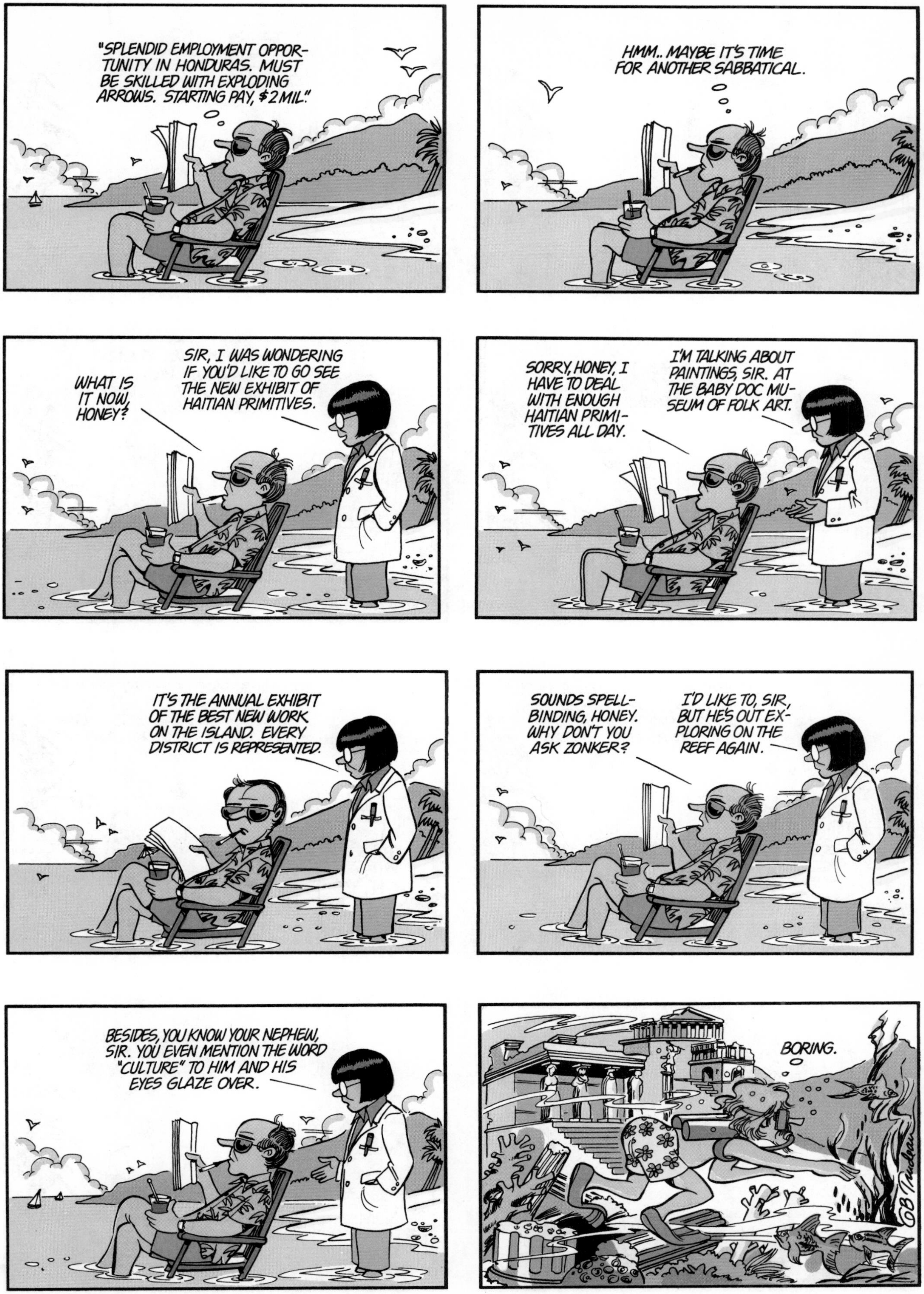
"SPLENDID EMPLOYMENT OPPORTUNITY IN HONDURAS. MUST BE SKILLED WITH EXPLODING ARROWS. STARTING PAY, $2 MIL."
HMM.. MAYBE IT'S TIME FOR ANOTHER SABBATICAL.
SIR, I WAS WONDERING IF YOU'D LIKE TO GO SEE THE NEW EXHIBIT OF HAITIAN PRIMITIVES.
WHAT IS IT NOW, HONEY?
SORRY, HONEY, I HAVE TO DEAL WITH ENOUGH HAITIAN PRIMITIVES ALL DAY.
I'M TALKING ABOUT PAINTINGS, SIR. AT THE BABY DOC MUSEUM OF FOLK ART.
IT'S THE ANNUAL EXHIBIT OF THE BEST NEW WORK ON THE ISLAND. EVERY DISTRICT IS REPRESENTED.
SOUNDS SPELLBINDING, HONEY. WHY DON'T YOU ASK ZONKER?
I'D LIKE TO, SIR, BUT HE'S OUT EXPLORING ON THE REEF AGAIN.
BESIDES, YOU KNOW YOUR NEPHEW, SIR. YOU EVEN MENTION THE WORD "CULTURE" TO HIM AND HIS EYES GLAZE OVER.
BORING.
GB Trudeau

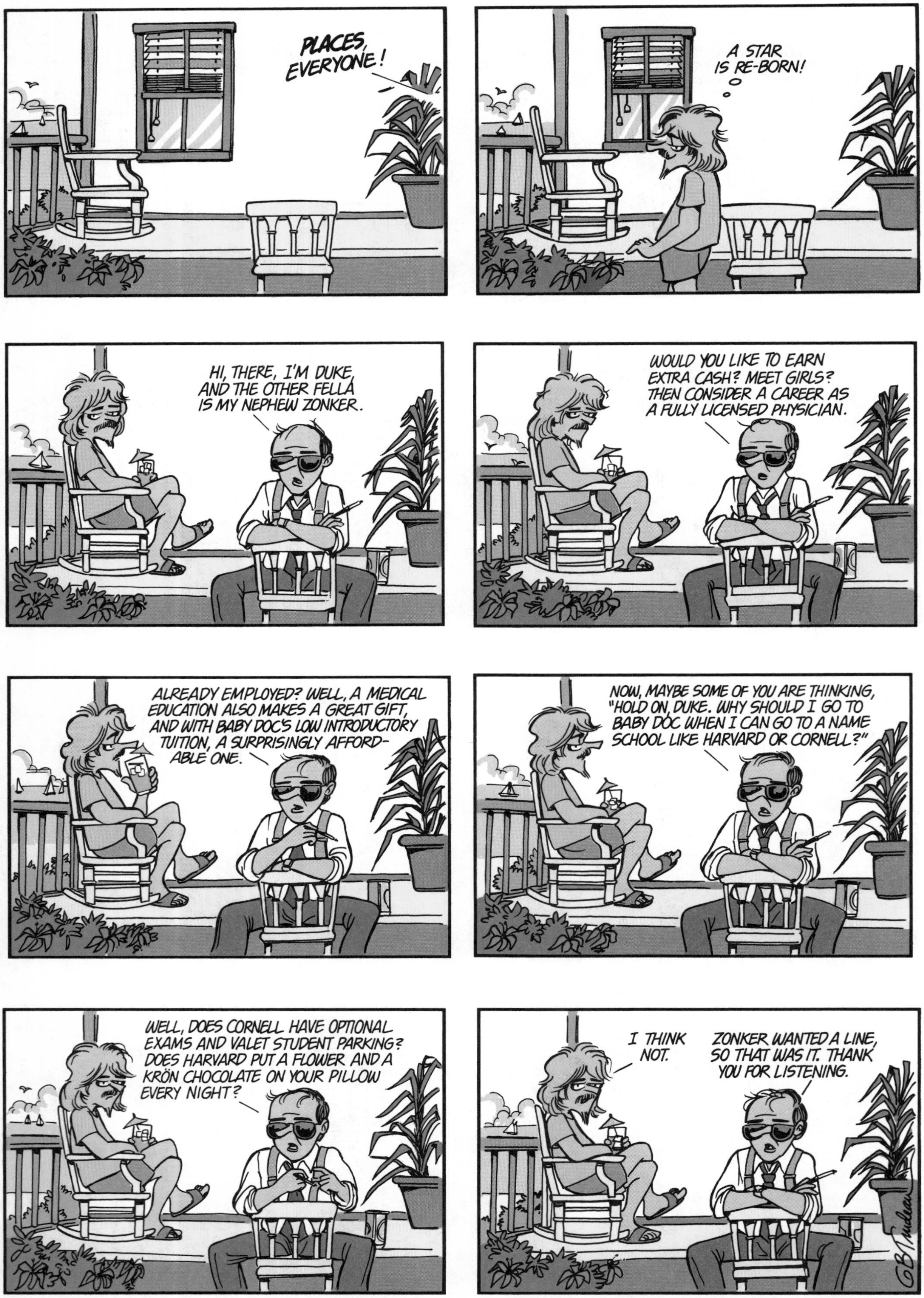
PLACES, EVERYONE!
A STAR IS RE-BORN!
HI, THERE, I'M DUKE, AND THE OTHER FELLA IS MY NEPHEW ZONKER.
WOULD YOU LIKE TO EARN EXTRA CASH? MEET GIRLS? THEN CONSIDER A CAREER AS A FULLY LICENSED PHYSICIAN.
ALREADY EMPLOYED? WELL, A MEDICAL EDUCATION ALSO MAKES A GREAT GIFT, AND WITH BABY DOC'S LOW INTRODUCTORY TUITION, A SURPRISINGLY AFFORD-ABLE ONE.
NOW, MAYBE SOME OF YOU ARE THINKING, "HOLD ON, DUKE. WHY SHOULD I GO TO BABY DOC WHEN I CAN GO TO A NAME SCHOOL LIKE HARVARD OR CORNELL?"
WELL, DOES CORNELL HAVE OPTIONAL EXAMS AND VALET STUDENT PARKING? DOES HARVARD PUT A FLOWER AND A KRÖN CHOCOLATE ON YOUR PILLOW EVERY NIGHT?
I THINK NOT.
ZONKER WANTED A LINE, SO THAT WAS IT. THANK YOU FOR LISTENING.

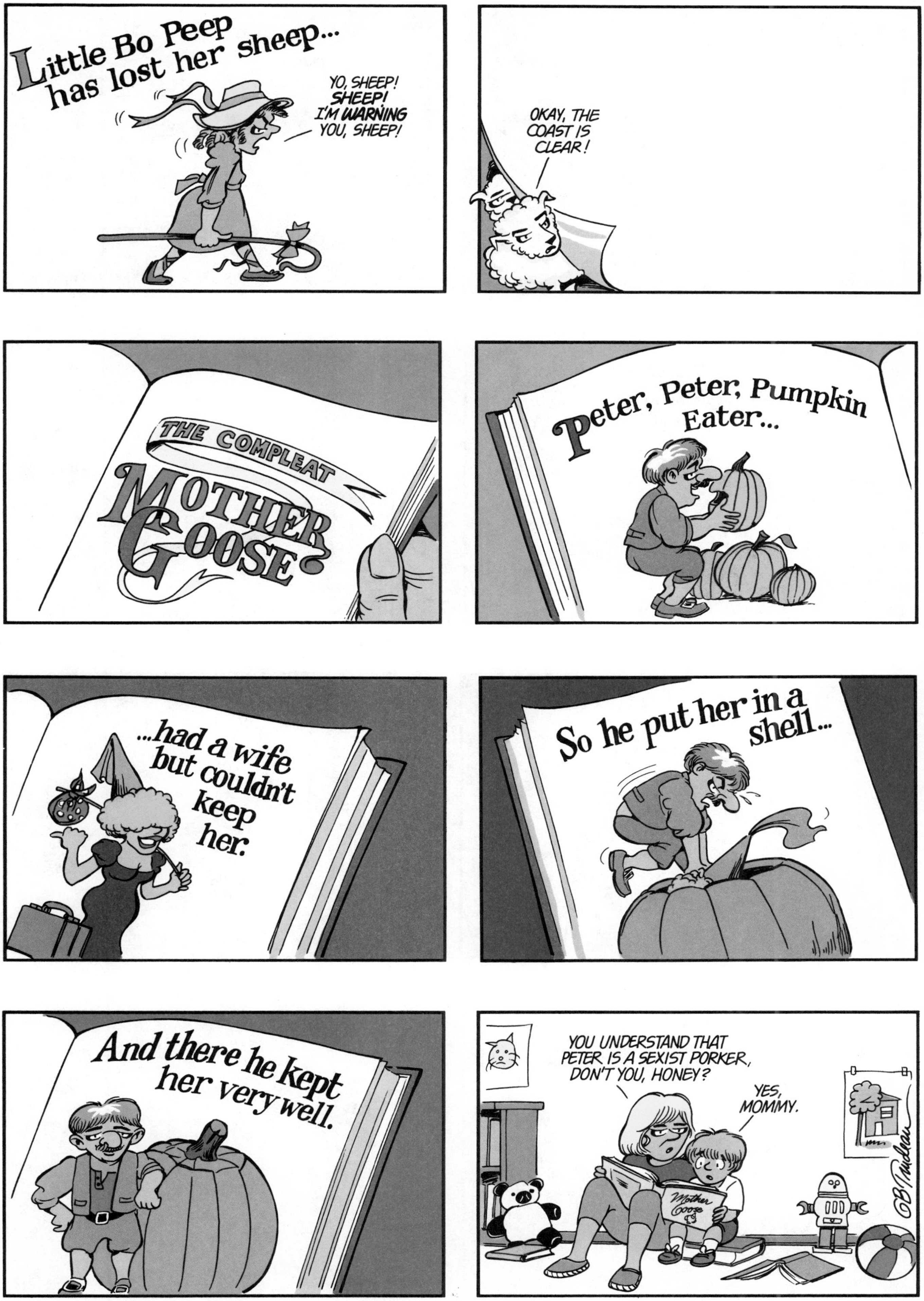
Little Bo Peep has lost her sheep...
YO, SHEEP! SHEEP! I'M WARNING YOU, SHEEP!
OKAY, THE COAST IS CLEAR!
THE COMPLEAT MOTHER GOOSE
Peter, Peter, Pumpkin Eater...
...had a wife but couldn't keep her.
So he put her in a shell...
And there he kept her very well.
YOU UNDERSTAND THAT PETER IS A SEXIST PORKER, DON'T YOU, HONEY?
YES, MOMMY.
Mother Goose
©B Trudeau

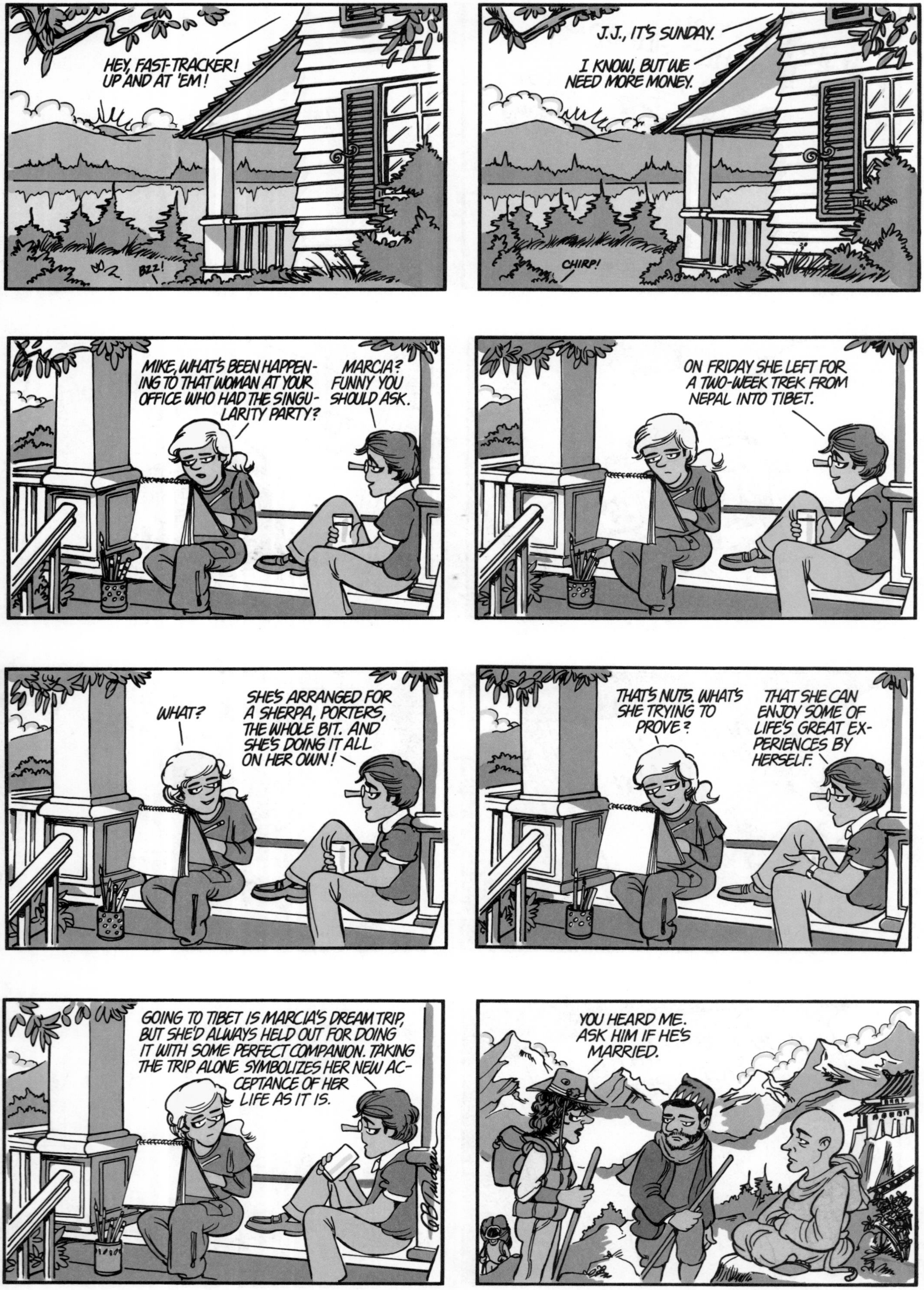
HEY, FAST-TRACKER! UP AND AT 'EM!
BZZ!
J.J., IT'S SUNDAY.
I KNOW, BUT WE NEED MORE MONEY.
CHIRP!
MIKE, WHAT'S BEEN HAPPENING TO THAT WOMAN AT YOUR OFFICE WHO HAD THE SINGULARITY PARTY?
MARCIA? FUNNY YOU SHOULD ASK.
ON FRIDAY SHE LEFT FOR A TWO-WEEK TREK FROM NEPAL INTO TIBET.
WHAT?
SHE'S ARRANGED FOR A SHERPA, PORTERS, THE WHOLE BIT. AND SHE'S DOING IT ALL ON HER OWN!
THAT'S NUTS. WHAT'S SHE TRYING TO PROVE?
THAT SHE CAN ENJOY SOME OF LIFE'S GREAT EXPERIENCES BY HERSELF.
GOING TO TIBET IS MARCIA'S DREAM TRIP, BUT SHE'D ALWAYS HELD OUT FOR DOING IT WITH SOME PERFECT COMPANION. TAKING THE TRIP ALONE SYMBOLIZES HER NEW ACCEPTANCE OF HER LIFE AS IT IS.
YOU HEARD ME. ASK HIM IF HE'S MARRIED.

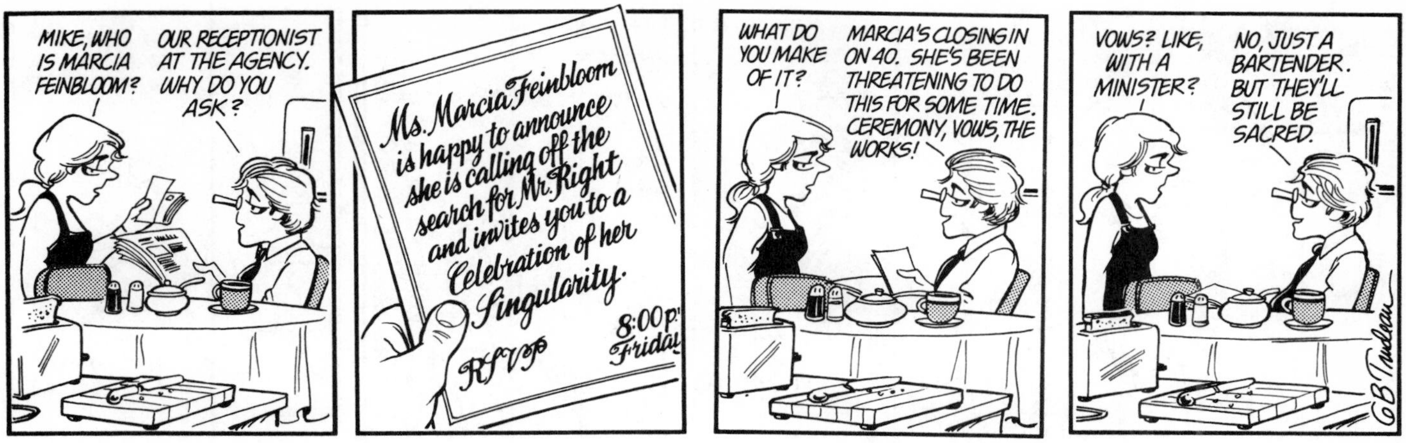
MIKE, WHO IS MARCIA FEINBLOOM?
OUR RECEPTIONIST AT THE AGENCY. WHY DO YOU ASK?
Ms. Marcia Feinbloom is happy to announce she is calling off the search for Mr. Right and invites you to a Celebration of her Singularity.
8:00p
Friday
RSVP
WHAT DO YOU MAKE OF IT?
MARCIA'S CLOSING IN ON 40. SHE'S BEEN THREATENING TO DO THIS FOR SOME TIME. CEREMONY, VOWS, THE WORKS!
VOWS? LIKE, WITH A MINISTER?
NO, JUST A BARTENDER. BUT THEY'LL STILL BE SACRED.

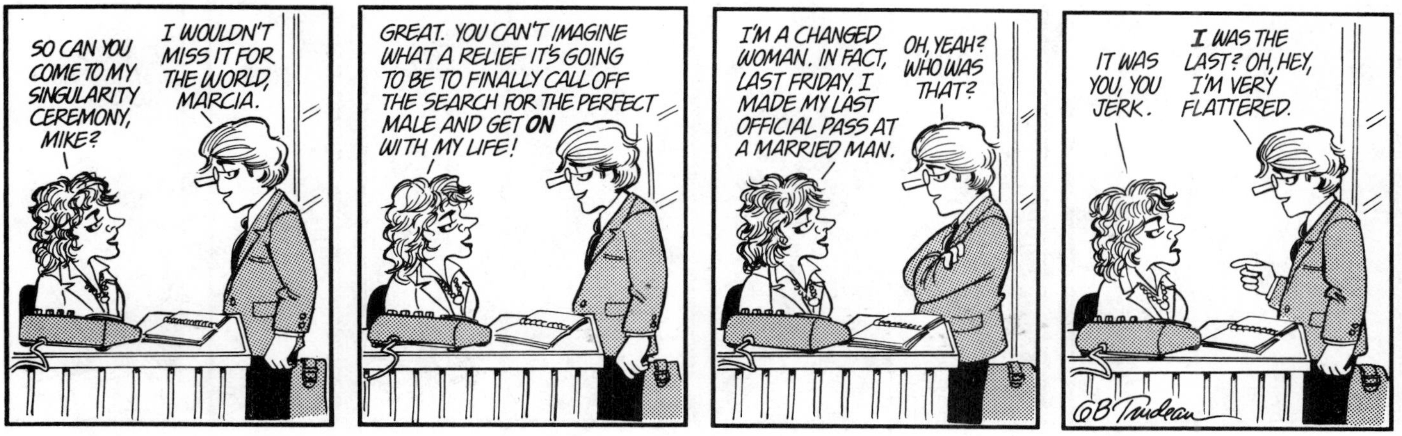
SO CAN YOU COME TO MY SINGULARITY CEREMONY, MIKE?
I WOULDN'T MISS IT FOR THE WORLD, MARCIA.
GREAT. YOU CAN'T IMAGINE WHAT A RELIEF IT'S GOING TO BE TO FINALLY CALL OFF THE SEARCH FOR THE PERFECT MALE AND GET ON WITH MY LIFE!
I'M A CHANGED WOMAN. IN FACT, LAST FRIDAY, I MADE MY LAST OFFICIAL PASS AT A MARRIED MAN.
OH, YEAH? WHO WAS THAT?
IT WAS YOU, YOU JERK.
I WAS THE LAST? OH, HEY, I'M VERY FLATTERED.

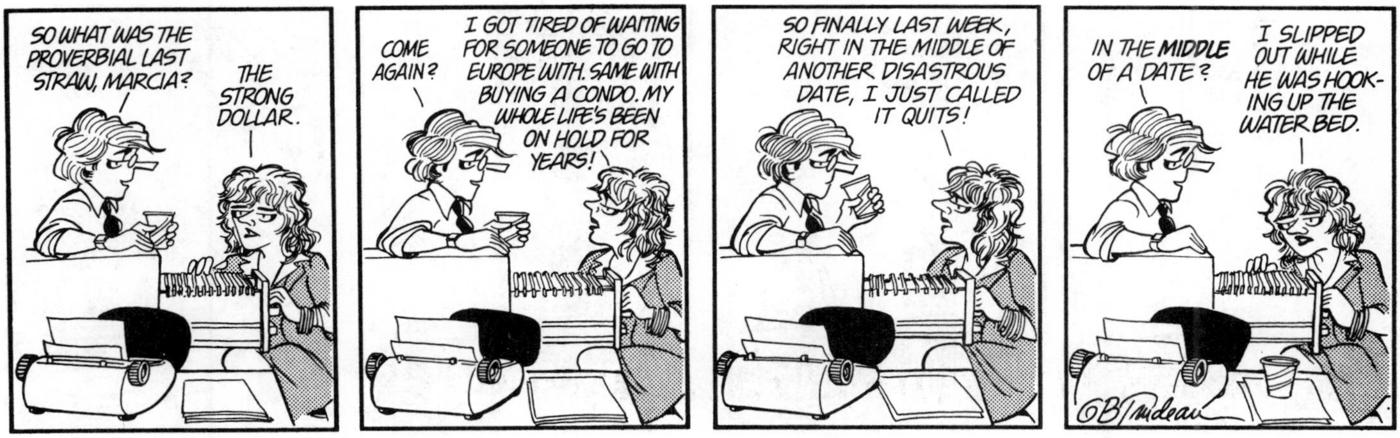
SO WHAT WAS THE PROVERBIAL LAST STRAW, MARCIA?
THE STRONG DOLLAR.
COME AGAIN?
I GOT TIRED OF WAITING FOR SOMEONE TO GO TO EUROPE WITH. SAME WITH BUYING A CONDO. MY WHOLE LIFE'S BEEN ON HOLD FOR YEARS!
SO FINALLY LAST WEEK, RIGHT IN THE MIDDLE OF ANOTHER DISASTROUS DATE, I JUST CALLED IT QUITS!
IN THE MIDDLE OF A DATE?
I SLIPPED OUT WHILE HE WAS HOOKING UP THE WATER BED.

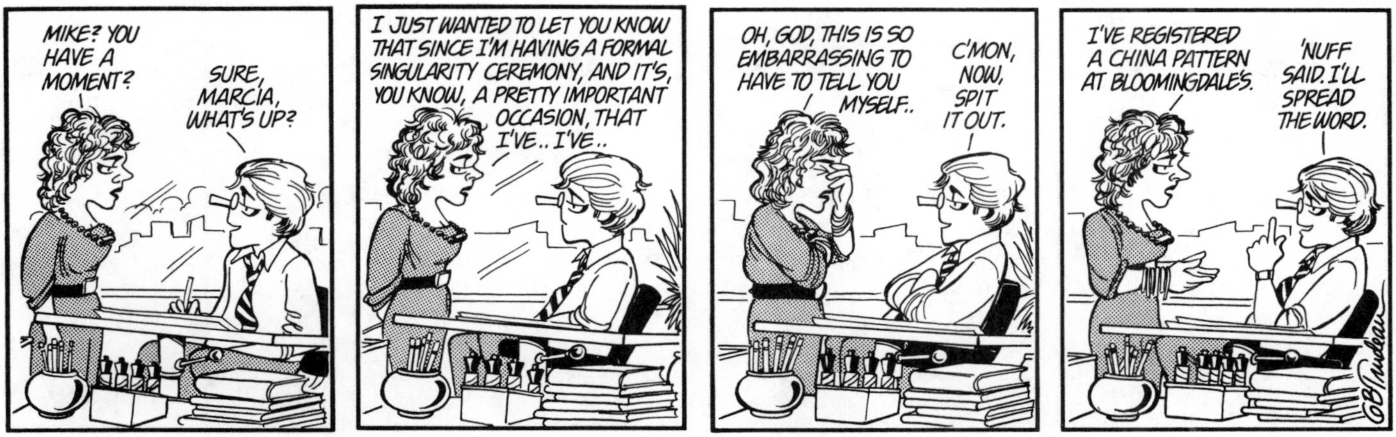
MIKE? YOU HAVE A MOMENT?
SURE, MARCIA, WHAT'S UP?
I JUST WANTED TO LET YOU KNOW THAT SINCE I'M HAVING A FORMAL SINGULARITY CEREMONY, AND IT'S, YOU KNOW, A PRETTY IMPORTANT OCCASION, THAT I'VE.. I'VE..
OH, GOD, THIS IS SO EMBARRASSING TO HAVE TO TELL YOU MYSELF..
C'MON, NOW, SPIT IT OUT.
I'VE REGISTERED A CHINA PATTERN AT BLOOMINGDALE'S.
'NUFF SAID. I'LL SPREAD THE WORD.

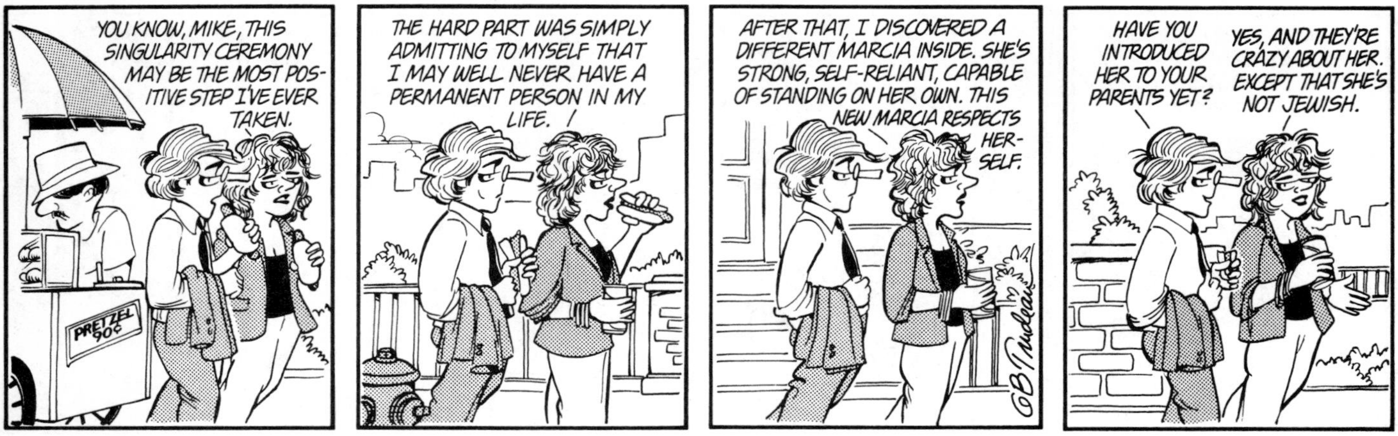
YOU KNOW, MIKE, THIS SINGULARITY CEREMONY MAY BE THE MOST POSITIVE STEP I'VE EVER TAKEN.
PRETZEL 50¢
THE HARD PART WAS SIMPLY ADMITTING TO MYSELF THAT I MAY WELL NEVER HAVE A PERMANENT PERSON IN MY LIFE.
AFTER THAT, I DISCOVERED A DIFFERENT MARCIA INSIDE. SHE'S STRONG, SELF-RELIANT, CAPABLE OF STANDING ON HER OWN. THIS NEW MARCIA RESPECTS HERSELF.
HAVE YOU INTRODUCED HER TO YOUR PARENTS YET?
YES, AND THEY'RE CRAZY ABOUT HER. EXCEPT THAT SHE'S NOT JEWISH.
GB Trudeau

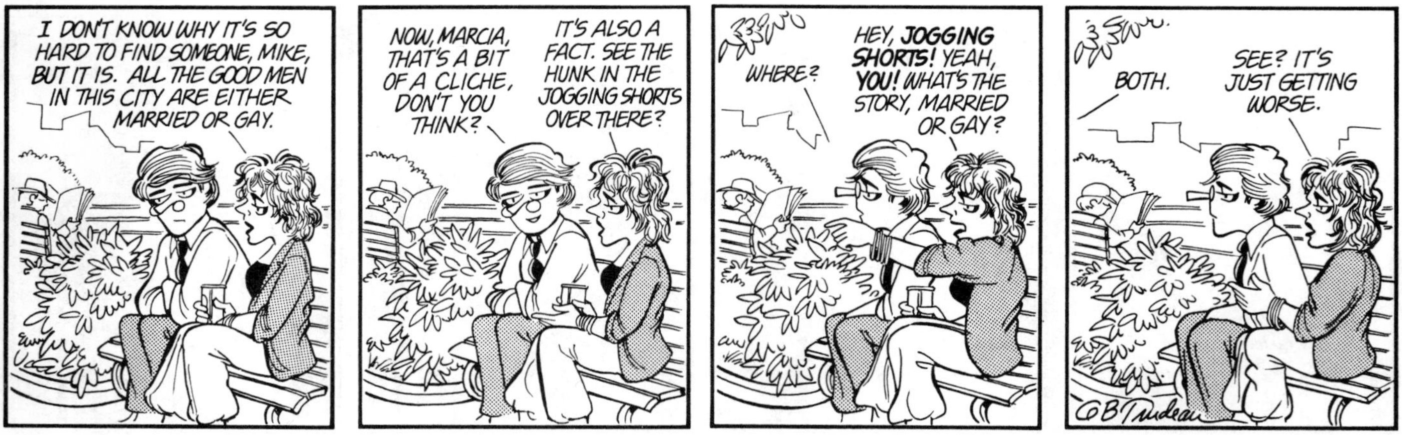
I DON'T KNOW WHY IT'S SO HARD TO FIND SOMEONE, MIKE, BUT IT IS. ALL THE GOOD MEN IN THIS CITY ARE EITHER MARRIED OR GAY.
NOW, MARCIA, THAT'S A BIT OF A CLICHE, DON'T YOU THINK?
IT'S ALSO A FACT. SEE THE HUNK IN THE JOGGING SHORTS OVER THERE?
WHERE?
HEY, JOGGING SHORTS! YEAH, YOU! WHAT'S THE STORY, MARRIED OR GAY?
BOTH.
SEE? IT'S JUST GETTING WORSE.
GB Trudeau

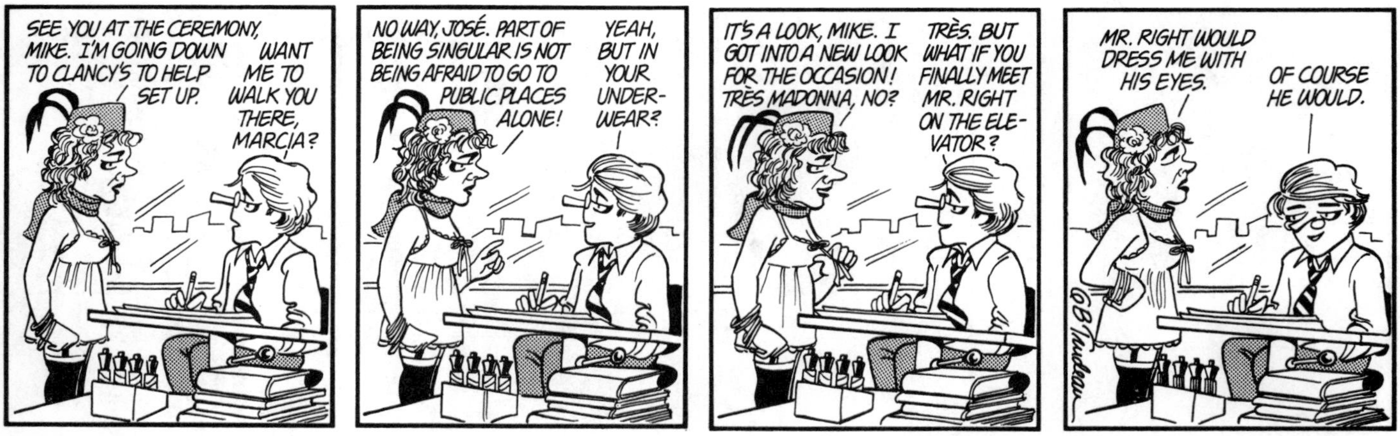
SEE YOU AT THE CEREMONY, MIKE. I'M GOING DOWN TO CLANCY'S TO HELP SET UP.
WANT ME TO WALK YOU THERE, MARCIA?
NO WAY, JOSÉ. PART OF BEING SINGULAR IS NOT BEING AFRAID TO GO TO PUBLIC PLACES ALONE!
YEAH, BUT IN YOUR UNDERWEAR?
IT'S A LOOK, MIKE. I GOT INTO A NEW LOOK FOR THE OCCASION! TRÈS MADONNA, NO?
TRÈS. BUT WHAT IF YOU FINALLY MEET MR. RIGHT ON THE ELEVATOR?
MR. RIGHT WOULD DRESS ME WITH HIS EYES.
OF COURSE HE WOULD.
GB Trudeau

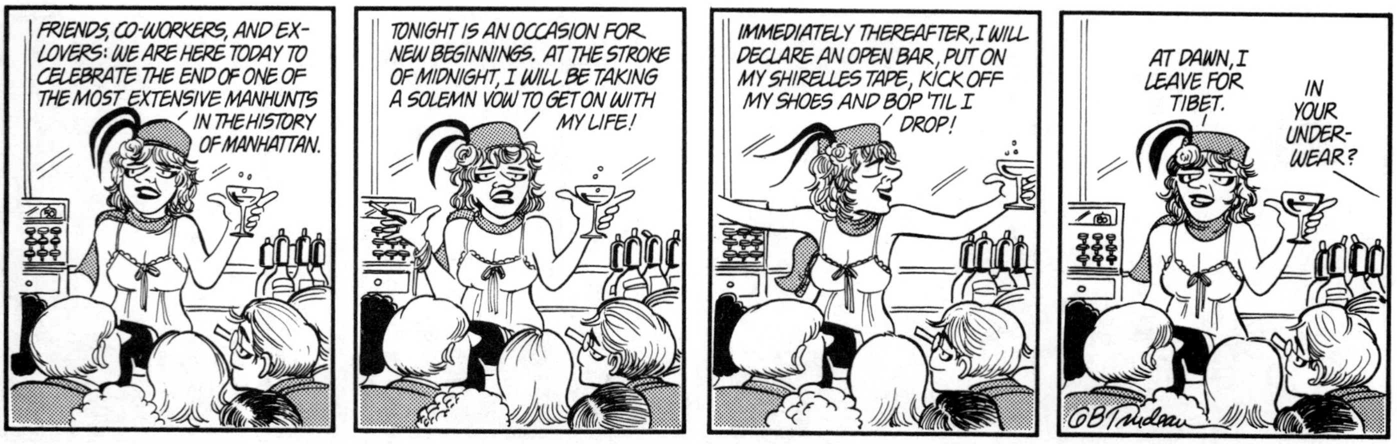
FRIENDS, CO-WORKERS, AND EX-LOVERS: WE ARE HERE TODAY TO CELEBRATE THE END OF ONE OF THE MOST EXTENSIVE MANHUNTS IN THE HISTORY OF MANHATTAN.
TONIGHT IS AN OCCASION FOR NEW BEGINNINGS. AT THE STROKE OF MIDNIGHT, I WILL BE TAKING A SOLEMN VOW TO GET ON WITH MY LIFE!
IMMEDIATELY THEREAFTER, I WILL DECLARE AN OPEN BAR, PUT ON MY SHIRELLES TAPE, KICK OFF MY SHOES AND BOP 'TIL I DROP!
AT DAWN, I LEAVE FOR TIBET.
IN YOUR UNDERWEAR?
GB Trudeau

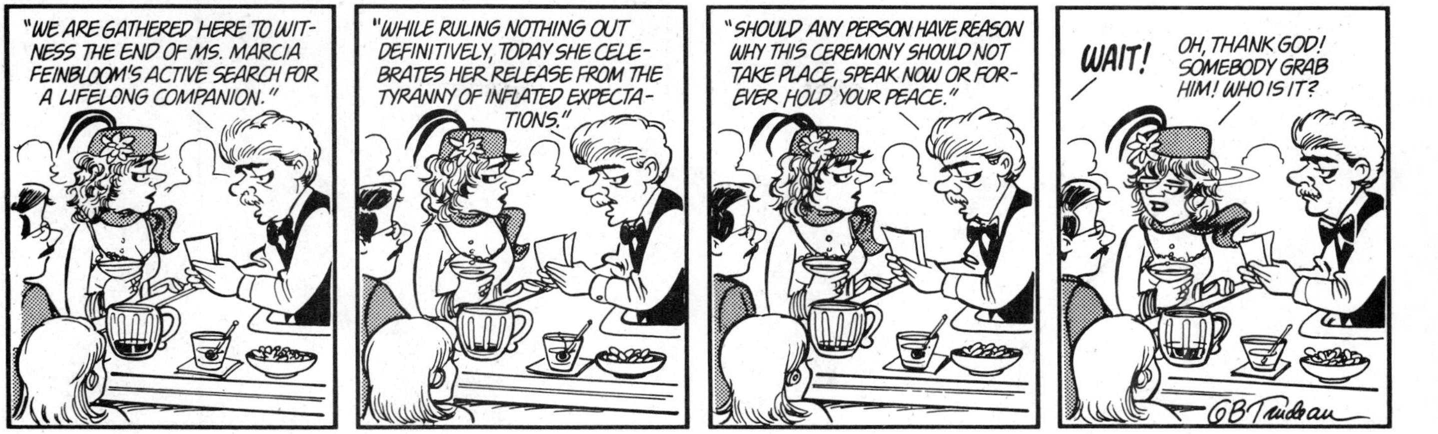
"WE ARE GATHERED HERE TO WITNESS THE END OF MS. MARCIA FEINBLOOM'S ACTIVE SEARCH FOR A LIFELONG COMPANION."
"WHILE RULING NOTHING OUT DEFINITIVELY, TODAY SHE CELEBRATES HER RELEASE FROM THE TYRANNY OF INFLATED EXPECTATIONS."
"SHOULD ANY PERSON HAVE REASON WHY THIS CEREMONY SHOULD NOT TAKE PLACE, SPEAK NOW OR FOREVER HOLD YOUR PEACE."
WAIT!
OH, THANK GOD! SOMEBODY GRAB HIM! WHO IS IT?
©B Trudeau

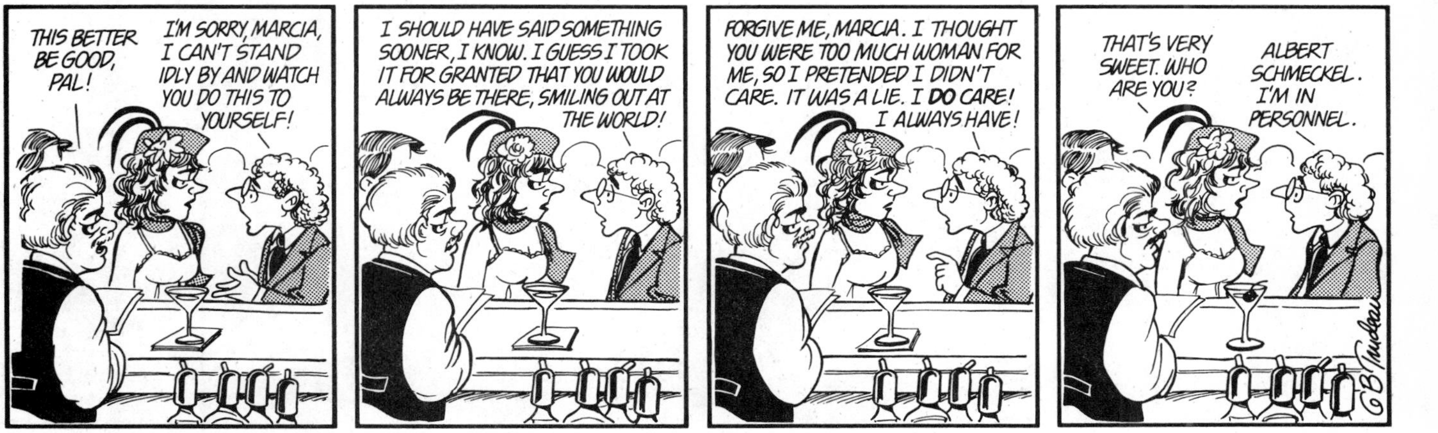
THIS BETTER BE GOOD, PAL!
I'M SORRY, MARCIA, I CAN'T STAND IDLY BY AND WATCH YOU DO THIS TO YOURSELF!
I SHOULD HAVE SAID SOMETHING SOONER, I KNOW. I GUESS I TOOK IT FOR GRANTED THAT YOU WOULD ALWAYS BE THERE, SMILING OUT AT THE WORLD!
FORGIVE ME, MARCIA. I THOUGHT YOU WERE TOO MUCH WOMAN FOR ME, SO I PRETENDED I DIDN'T CARE. IT WAS A LIE. I DO CARE! I ALWAYS HAVE!
THAT'S VERY SWEET. WHO ARE YOU?
ALBERT SCHMECKEL. I'M IN PERSONNEL.
©B Trudeau

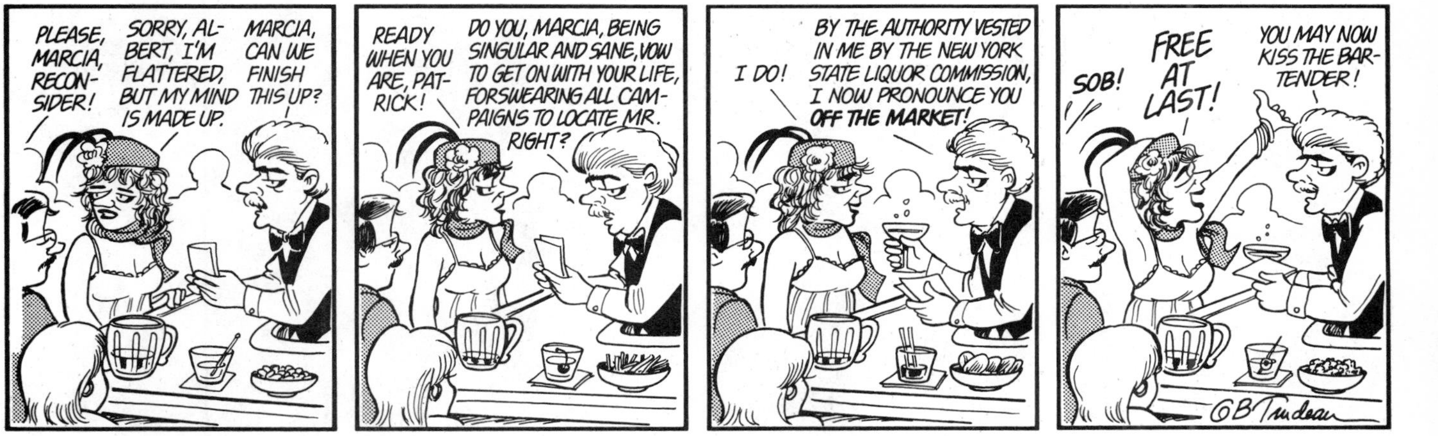
PLEASE, MARCIA, RECONSIDER!
SORRY, ALBERT, I'M FLATTERED, BUT MY MIND IS MADE UP.
MARCIA, CAN WE FINISH THIS UP?
READY WHEN YOU ARE, PATRICK!
DO YOU, MARCIA, BEING SINGULAR AND SANE, VOW TO GET ON WITH YOUR LIFE, FORSWEARING ALL CAMPAIGNS TO LOCATE MR. RIGHT?
I DO!
BY THE AUTHORITY VESTED IN ME BY THE NEW YORK STATE LIQUOR COMMISSION, I NOW PRONOUNCE YOU OFF THE MARKET!
SOB!
FREE AT LAST!
YOU MAY NOW KISS THE BARTENDER!
©B Trudeau

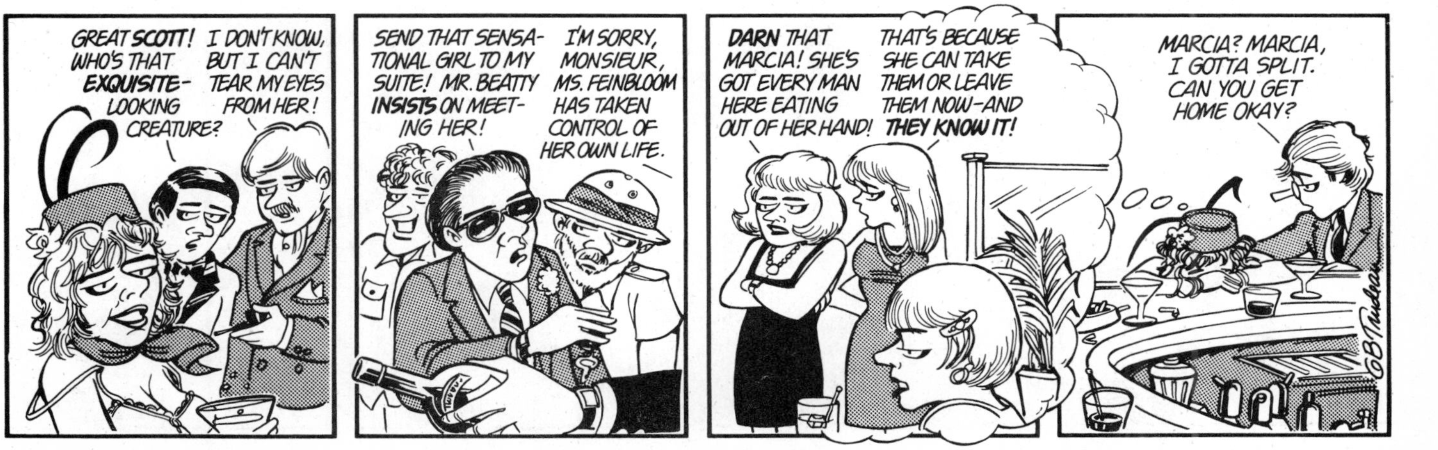
GREAT SCOTT! WHO'S THAT EXQUISITE-LOOKING CREATURE?
I DON'T KNOW, BUT I CAN'T TEAR MY EYES FROM HER!
SEND THAT SENSATIONAL GIRL TO MY SUITE! MR. BEATTY INSISTS ON MEETING HER!
I'M SORRY, MONSIEUR, MS. FEINBLOOM HAS TAKEN CONTROL OF HER OWN LIFE.
DARN THAT MARCIA! SHE'S GOT EVERY MAN HERE EATING OUT OF HER HAND!
THAT'S BECAUSE SHE CAN TAKE THEM OR LEAVE THEM NOW—AND THEY KNOW IT!
MARCIA? MARCIA, I GOTTA SPLIT. CAN YOU GET HOME OKAY?
©B Trudeau

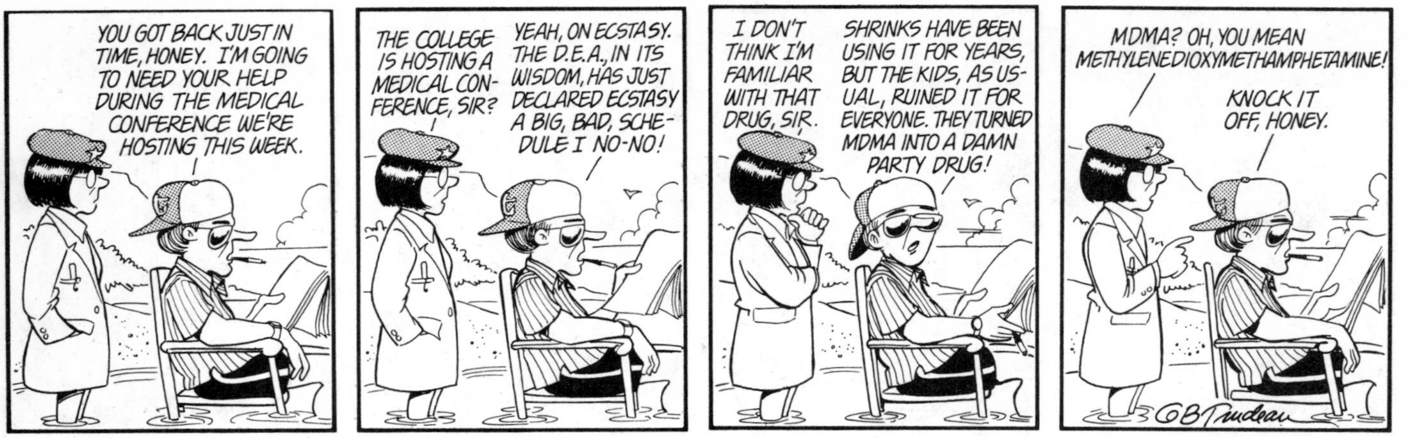
YOU GOT BACK JUST IN TIME, HONEY. I'M GOING TO NEED YOUR HELP DURING THE MEDICAL CONFERENCE WE'RE HOSTING THIS WEEK.
THE COLLEGE IS HOSTING A MEDICAL CONFERENCE, SIR?
YEAH, ON ECSTASY. THE D.E.A., IN ITS WISDOM, HAS JUST DECLARED ECSTASY A BIG, BAD, SCHEDULE I NO-NO!
I DON'T THINK I'M FAMILIAR WITH THAT DRUG, SIR.
SHRINKS HAVE BEEN USING IT FOR YEARS, BUT THE KIDS, AS USUAL, RUINED IT FOR EVERYONE. THEY TURNED MDMA INTO A DAMN PARTY DRUG!
MDMA? OH, YOU MEAN METHYLENEDIOXYMETHAMPHETAMINE!
KNOCK IT OFF, HONEY.
GB Trudeau

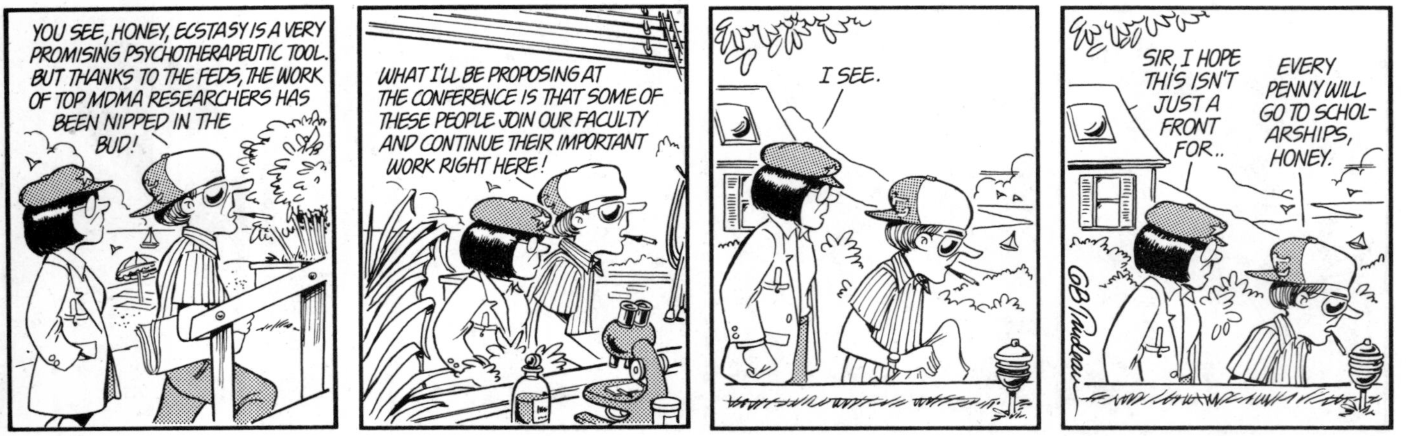
YOU SEE, HONEY, ECSTASY IS A VERY PROMISING PSYCHOTHERAPEUTIC TOOL. BUT THANKS TO THE FEDS, THE WORK OF TOP MDMA RESEARCHERS HAS BEEN NIPPED IN THE BUD!
WHAT I'LL BE PROPOSING AT THE CONFERENCE IS THAT SOME OF THESE PEOPLE JOIN OUR FACULTY AND CONTINUE THEIR IMPORTANT WORK RIGHT HERE!
I SEE.
SIR, I HOPE THIS ISN'T JUST A FRONT FOR..
EVERY PENNY WILL GO TO SCHOLARSHIPS, HONEY.
GB Trudeau

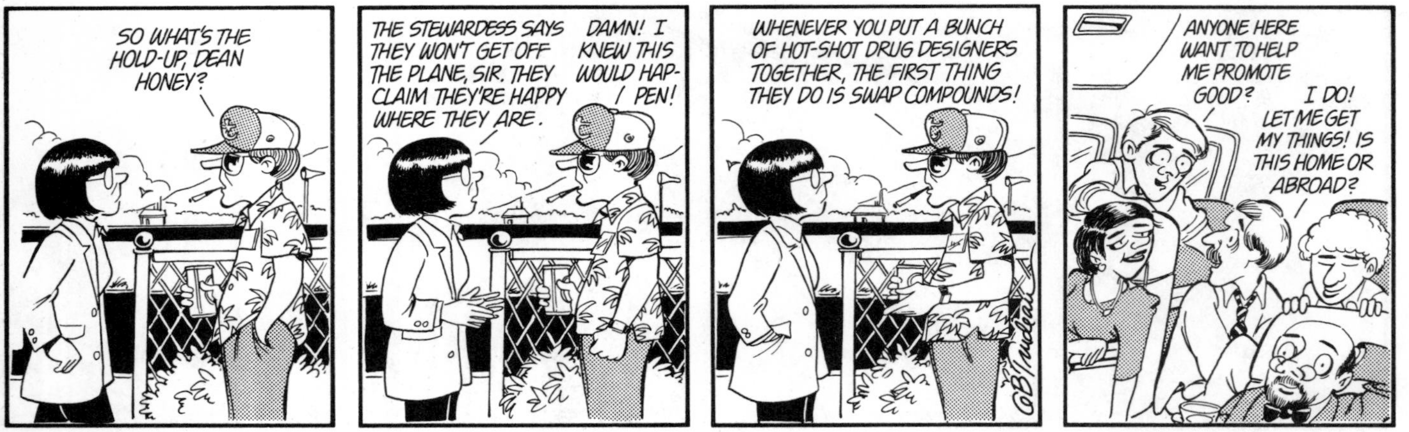
SO WHAT'S THE HOLD-UP, DEAN HONEY?
THE STEWARDESS SAYS THEY WON'T GET OFF THE PLANE, SIR. THEY CLAIM THEY'RE HAPPY WHERE THEY ARE.
DAMN! I KNEW THIS WOULD HAPPEN!
WHENEVER YOU PUT A BUNCH OF HOT-SHOT DRUG DESIGNERS TOGETHER, THE FIRST THING THEY DO IS SWAP COMPOUNDS!
GB Trudeau
ANYONE HERE WANT TO HELP ME PROMOTE GOOD?
I DO! LET ME GET MY THINGS! IS THIS HOME OR ABROAD?

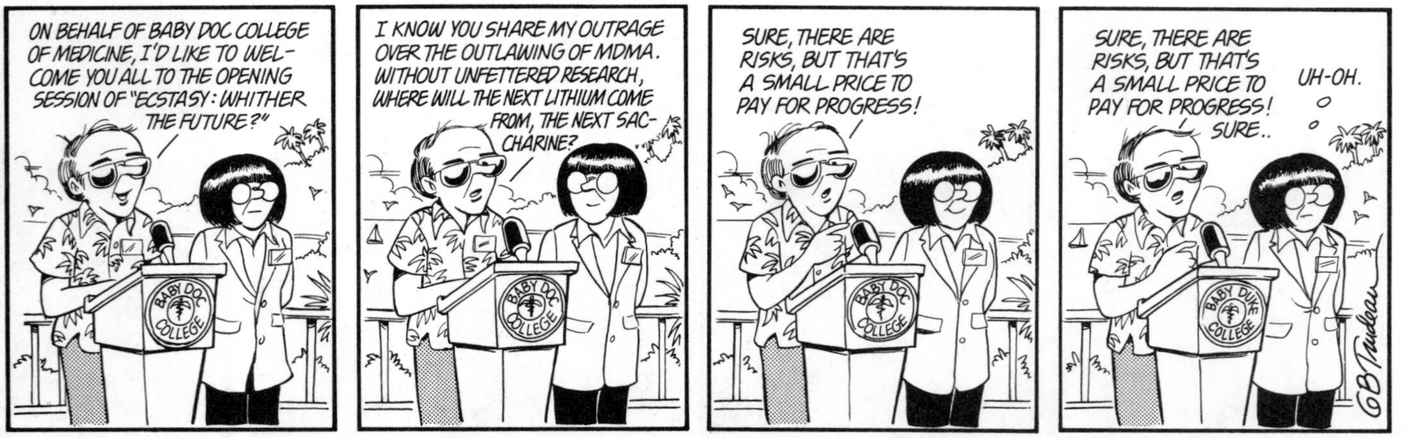
ON BEHALF OF BABY DOC COLLEGE OF MEDICINE, I'D LIKE TO WELCOME YOU ALL TO THE OPENING SESSION OF "ECSTASY: WHITHER THE FUTURE?"
BABY DOC COLLEGE
I KNOW YOU SHARE MY OUTRAGE OVER THE OUTLAWING OF MDMA. WITHOUT UNFETTERED RESEARCH, WHERE WILL THE NEXT LITHIUM COME FROM, THE NEXT SACCHARINE?
BABY DOC COLLEGE
SURE, THERE ARE RISKS, BUT THAT'S A SMALL PRICE TO PAY FOR PROGRESS!
BABY DOC COLLEGE
SURE, THERE ARE RISKS, BUT THAT'S A SMALL PRICE TO PAY FOR PROGRESS! SURE..
UH-OH.
BABY DUKE COLLEGE
GB Trudeau

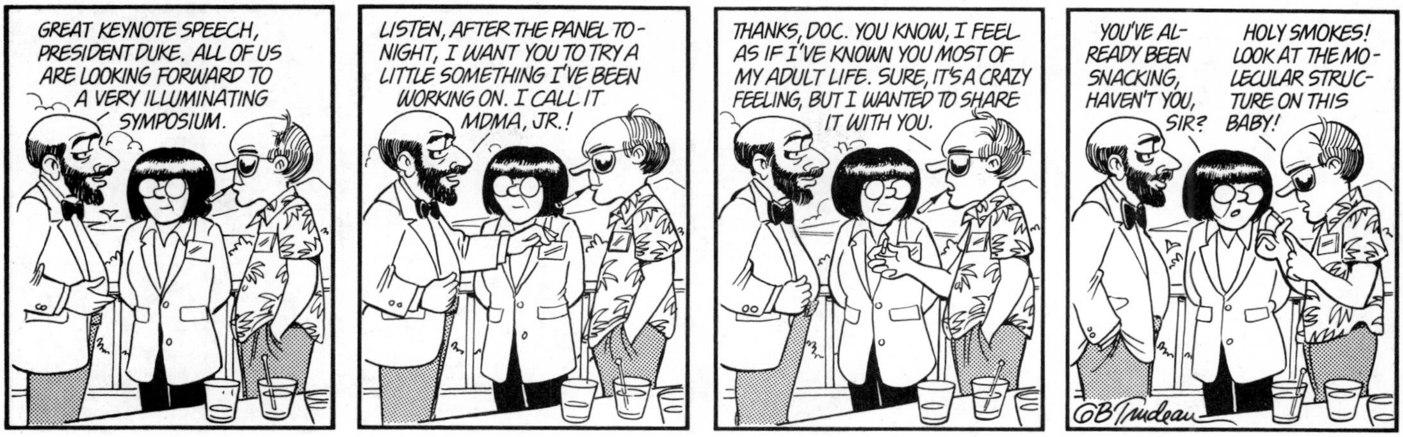
GREAT KEYNOTE SPEECH, PRESIDENT DUKE. ALL OF US ARE LOOKING FORWARD TO A VERY ILLUMINATING SYMPOSIUM.
LISTEN, AFTER THE PANEL TONIGHT, I WANT YOU TO TRY A LITTLE SOMETHING I'VE BEEN WORKING ON. I CALL IT MDMA, JR.!
THANKS, DOC. YOU KNOW, I FEEL AS IF I'VE KNOWN YOU MOST OF MY ADULT LIFE. SURE, IT'S A CRAZY FEELING, BUT I WANTED TO SHARE IT WITH YOU.
YOU'VE ALREADY BEEN SNACKING, HAVEN'T YOU, SIR?
HOLY SMOKES! LOOK AT THE MOLECULAR STRUCTURE ON THIS BABY!
GBTrudeau

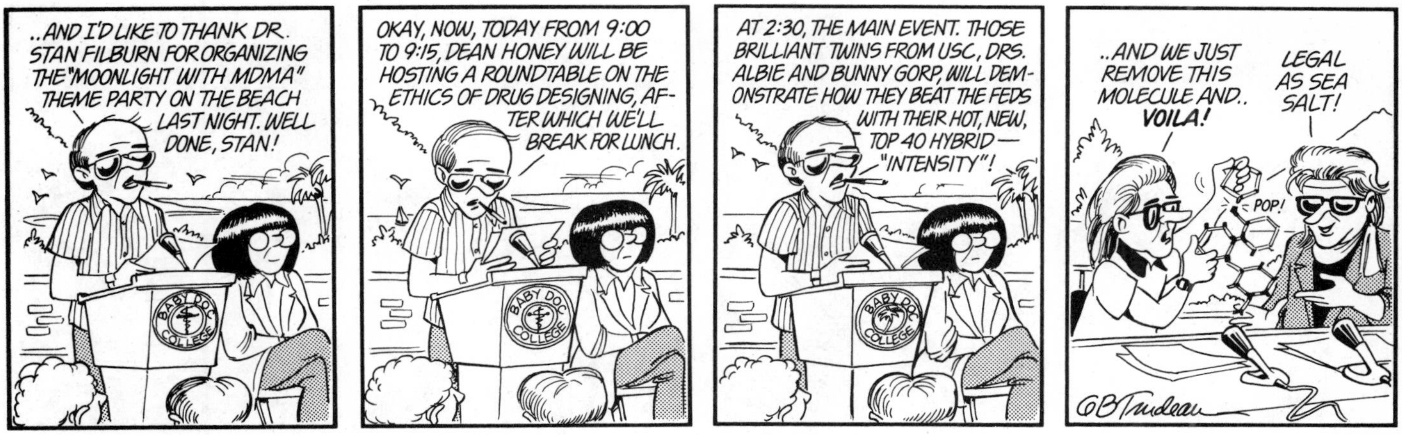
..AND I'D LIKE TO THANK DR. STAN FILBURN FOR ORGANIZING THE "MOONLIGHT WITH MDMA" THEME PARTY ON THE BEACH LAST NIGHT. WELL DONE, STAN!
BABY DOC COLLEGE
OKAY, NOW, TODAY FROM 9:00 TO 9:15, DEAN HONEY WILL BE HOSTING A ROUNDTABLE ON THE ETHICS OF DRUG DESIGNING, AFTER WHICH WE'LL BREAK FOR LUNCH.
AT 2:30, THE MAIN EVENT. THOSE BRILLIANT TWINS FROM USC, DRS. ALBIE AND BUNNY GORP, WILL DEMONSTRATE HOW THEY BEAT THE FEDS WITH THEIR HOT, NEW, TOP 40 HYBRID— "INTENSITY"!
..AND WE JUST REMOVE THIS MOLECULE AND.. **VOILA!**
POP!
LEGAL AS SEA SALT!
GBTrudeau

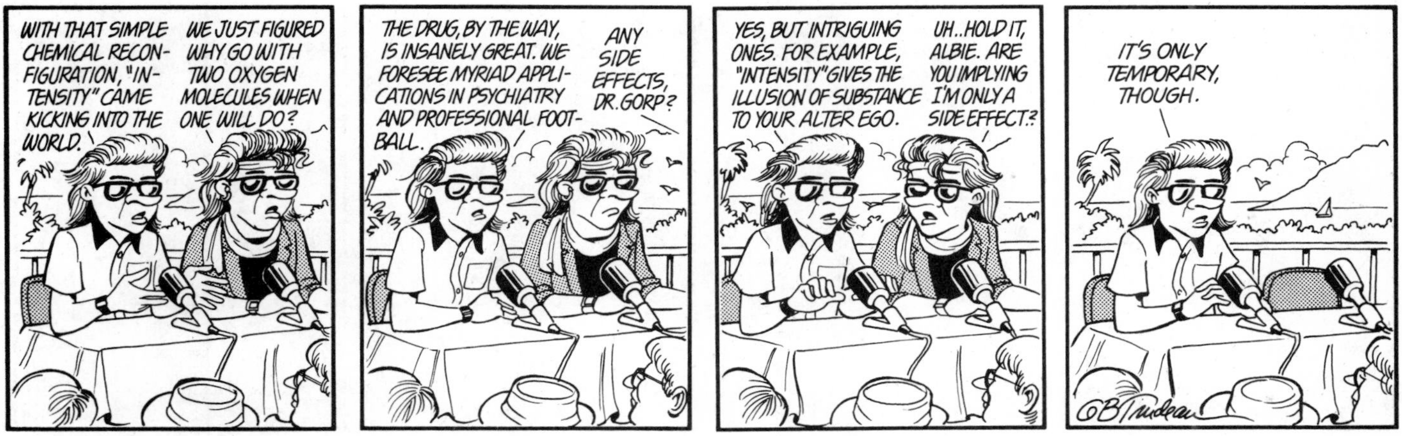
WITH THAT SIMPLE CHEMICAL RECONFIGURATION, "INTENSITY" CAME KICKING INTO THE WORLD.
WE JUST FIGURED WHY GO WITH TWO OXYGEN MOLECULES WHEN ONE WILL DO?
THE DRUG, BY THE WAY, IS INSANELY GREAT. WE FORESEE MYRIAD APPLICATIONS IN PSYCHIATRY AND PROFESSIONAL FOOTBALL.
ANY SIDE EFFECTS, DR. GORP?
YES, BUT INTRIGUING ONES. FOR EXAMPLE, "INTENSITY" GIVES THE ILLUSION OF SUBSTANCE TO YOUR ALTER EGO.
UH..HOLD IT, ALBIE. ARE YOU IMPLYING I'M ONLY A SIDE EFFECT?
IT'S ONLY TEMPORARY, THOUGH.
GBTrudeau

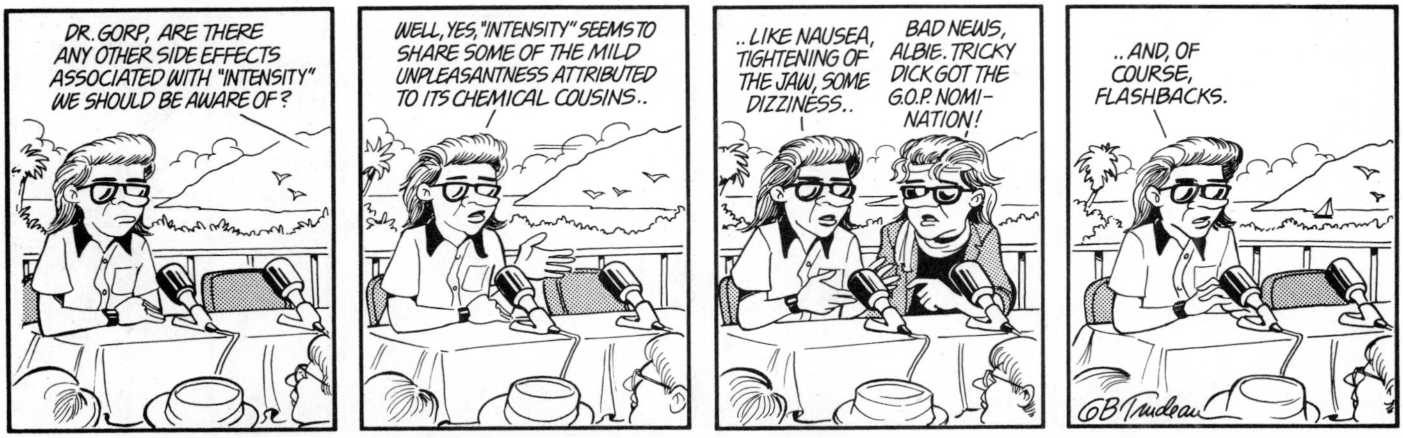
DR. GORP, ARE THERE ANY OTHER SIDE EFFECTS ASSOCIATED WITH "INTENSITY" WE SHOULD BE AWARE OF?
WELL, YES, "INTENSITY" SEEMS TO SHARE SOME OF THE MILD UNPLEASANTNESS ATTRIBUTED TO ITS CHEMICAL COUSINS..
..LIKE NAUSEA, TIGHTENING OF THE JAW, SOME DIZZINESS..
BAD NEWS, ALBIE. TRICKY DICK GOT THE G.O.P. NOMINATION!
..AND, OF COURSE, FLASHBACKS.
GBTrudeau

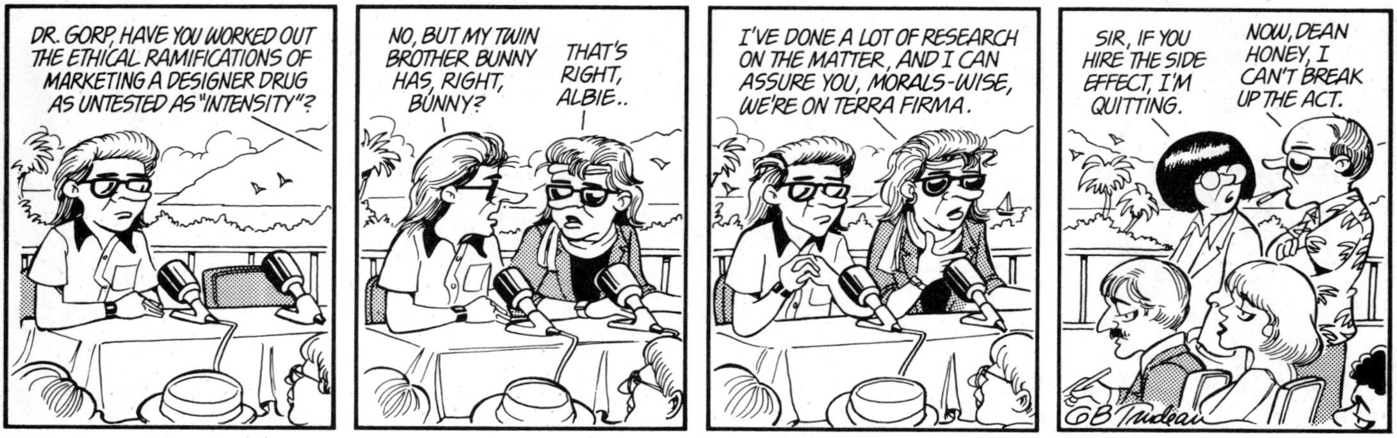
DR. GORP, HAVE YOU WORKED OUT THE ETHICAL RAMIFICATIONS OF MARKETING A DESIGNER DRUG AS UNTESTED AS "INTENSITY"?
NO, BUT MY TWIN BROTHER BUNNY HAS, RIGHT, BUNNY?
THAT'S RIGHT, ALBIE..
I'VE DONE A LOT OF RESEARCH ON THE MATTER, AND I CAN ASSURE YOU, MORALS-WISE, WE'RE ON TERRA FIRMA.
SIR, IF YOU HIRE THE SIDE EFFECT, I'M QUITTING.
NOW, DEAN HONEY, I CAN'T BREAK UP THE ACT.
GB Trudeau

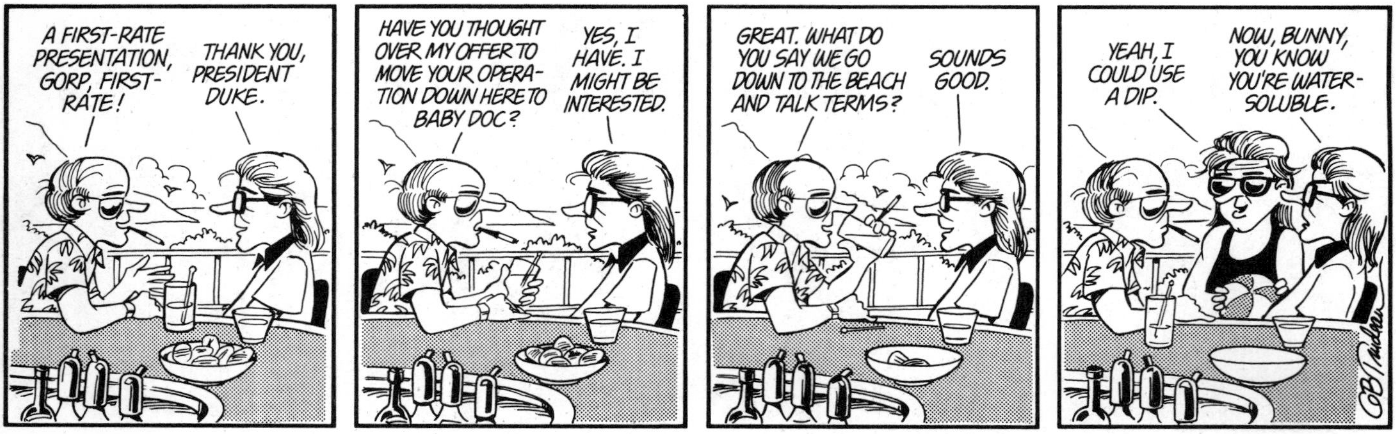
A FIRST-RATE PRESENTATION, GORP, FIRST-RATE!
THANK YOU, PRESIDENT DUKE.
HAVE YOU THOUGHT OVER MY OFFER TO MOVE YOUR OPERATION DOWN HERE TO BABY DOC?
YES, I HAVE. I MIGHT BE INTERESTED.
GREAT. WHAT DO YOU SAY WE GO DOWN TO THE BEACH AND TALK TERMS?
SOUNDS GOOD.
YEAH, I COULD USE A DIP.
NOW, BUNNY, YOU KNOW YOU'RE WATER-SOLUBLE.
GB Trudeau

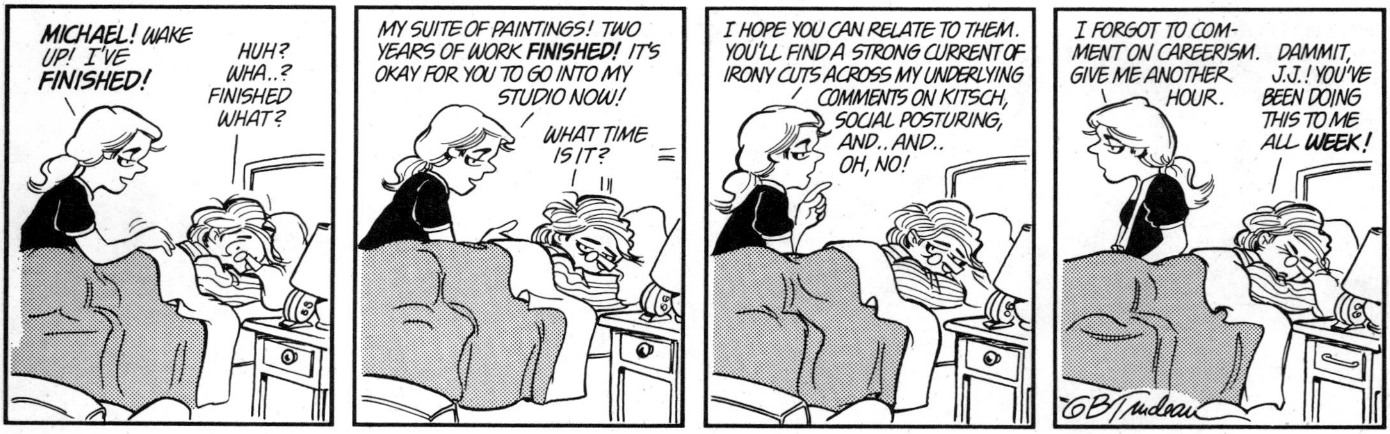
MICHAEL! WAKE UP! I'VE FINISHED!
HUH? WHA..? FINISHED WHAT?
MY SUITE OF PAINTINGS! TWO YEARS OF WORK FINISHED! IT'S OKAY FOR YOU TO GO INTO MY STUDIO NOW!
WHAT TIME IS IT?
I HOPE YOU CAN RELATE TO THEM. YOU'LL FIND A STRONG CURRENT OF IRONY CUTS ACROSS MY UNDERLYING COMMENTS ON KITSCH, SOCIAL POSTURING, AND.. AND.. OH, NO!
I FORGOT TO COMMENT ON CAREERISM. GIVE ME ANOTHER HOUR.
DAMMIT, J.J.! YOU'VE BEEN DOING THIS TO ME ALL WEEK!
GB Trudeau

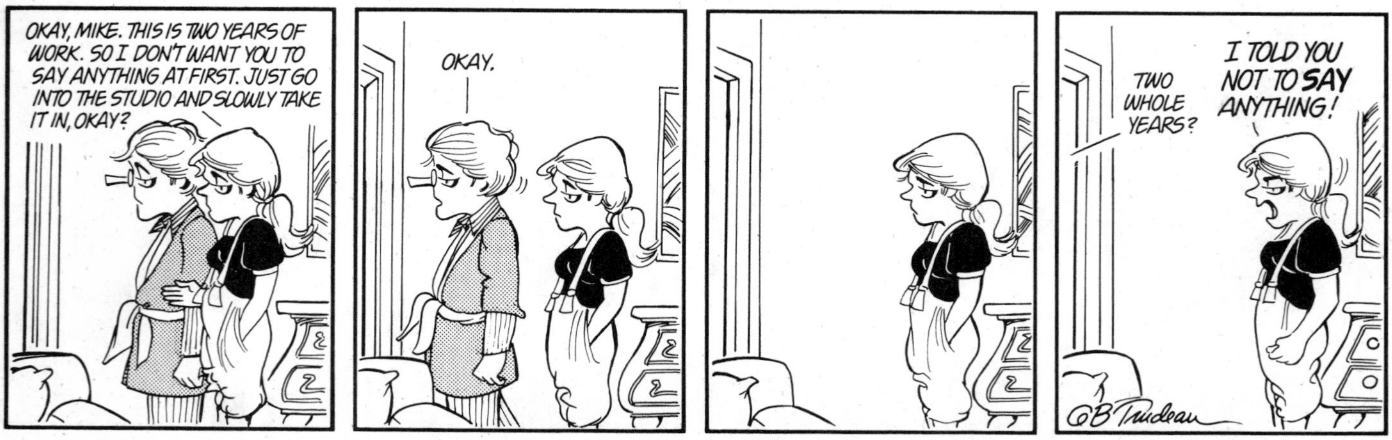
OKAY, MIKE. THIS IS TWO YEARS OF WORK. SO I DON'T WANT YOU TO SAY ANYTHING AT FIRST. JUST GO INTO THE STUDIO AND SLOWLY TAKE IT IN, OKAY?
OKAY.
TWO WHOLE YEARS?
I TOLD YOU NOT TO SAY ANYTHING!
GB Trudeau

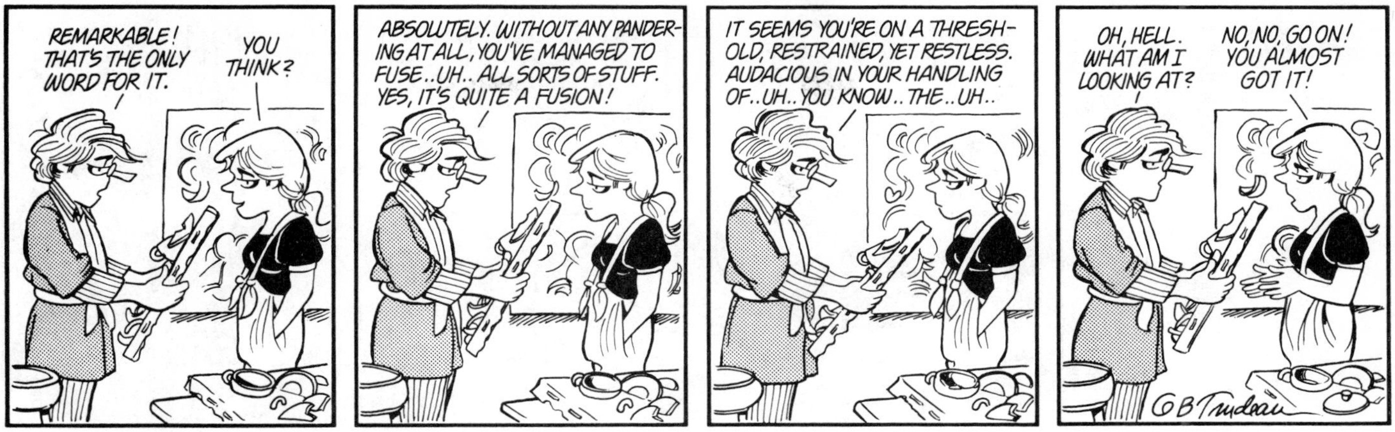
REMARKABLE! THAT'S THE ONLY WORD FOR IT.
YOU THINK?
ABSOLUTELY. WITHOUT ANY PANDERING AT ALL, YOU'VE MANAGED TO FUSE..UH.. ALL SORTS OF STUFF. YES, IT'S QUITE A FUSION!
IT SEEMS YOU'RE ON A THRESHOLD, RESTRAINED, YET RESTLESS. AUDACIOUS IN YOUR HANDLING OF..UH.. YOU KNOW.. THE..UH..
OH, HELL. WHAT AM I LOOKING AT?
NO, NO, GO ON! YOU ALMOST GOT IT!
©B Trudeau

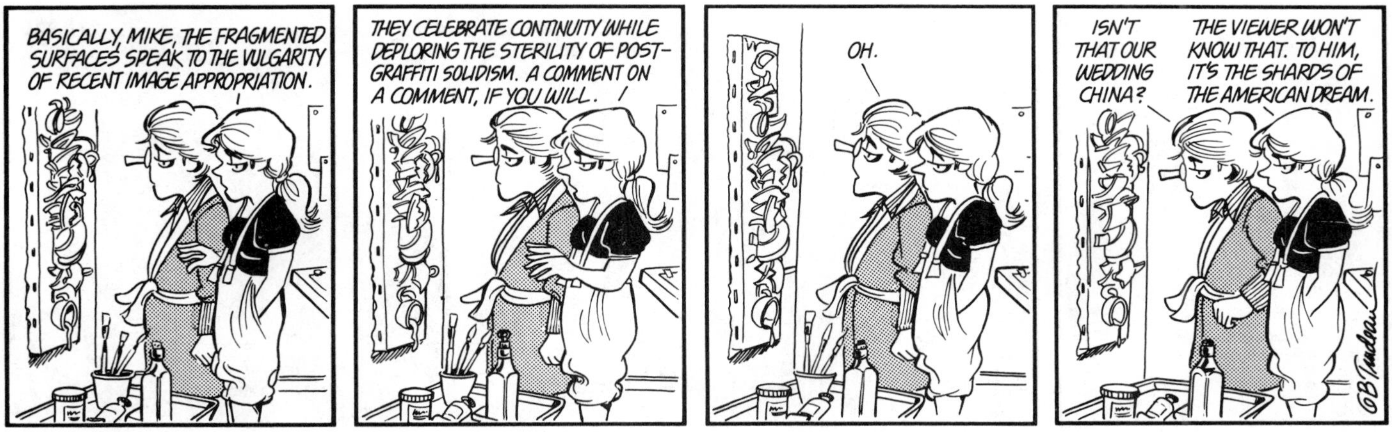
BASICALLY, MIKE, THE FRAGMENTED SURFACES SPEAK TO THE VULGARITY OF RECENT IMAGE APPROPRIATION.
THEY CELEBRATE CONTINUITY WHILE DEPLORING THE STERILITY OF POST-GRAFFITI SOLIDISM. A COMMENT ON A COMMENT, IF YOU WILL.
OH.
ISN'T THAT OUR WEDDING CHINA?
THE VIEWER WON'T KNOW THAT. TO HIM, IT'S THE SHARDS OF THE AMERICAN DREAM.
©B Trudeau

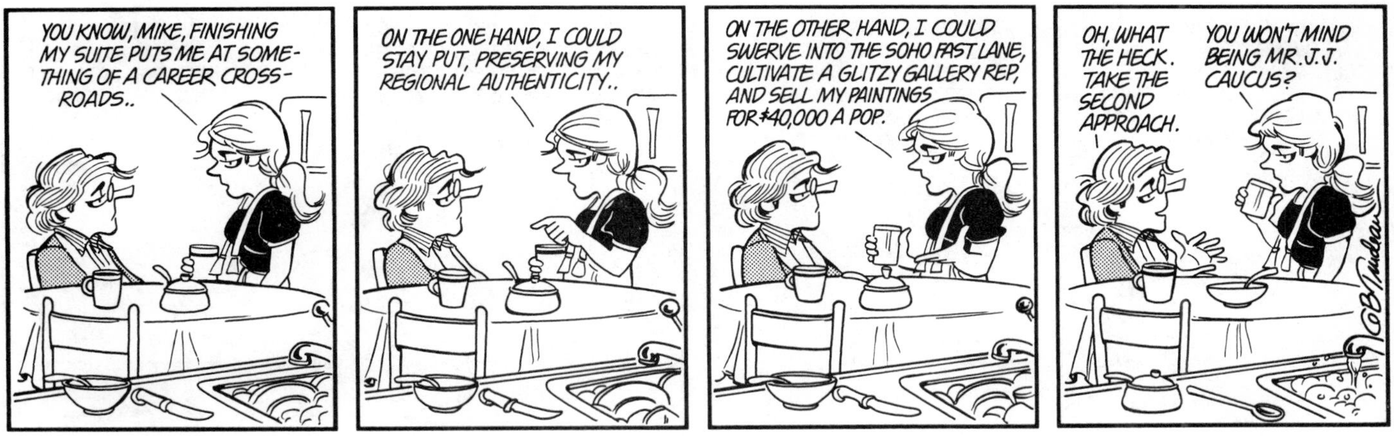
YOU KNOW, MIKE, FINISHING MY SUITE PUTS ME AT SOMETHING OF A CAREER CROSSROADS..
ON THE ONE HAND, I COULD STAY PUT, PRESERVING MY REGIONAL AUTHENTICITY..
ON THE OTHER HAND, I COULD SWERVE INTO THE SOHO FAST LANE, CULTIVATE A GLITZY GALLERY REP, AND SELL MY PAINTINGS FOR $40,000 A POP.
OH, WHAT THE HECK. TAKE THE SECOND APPROACH.
YOU WON'T MIND BEING MR. J.J. CAUCUS?
©B Trudeau

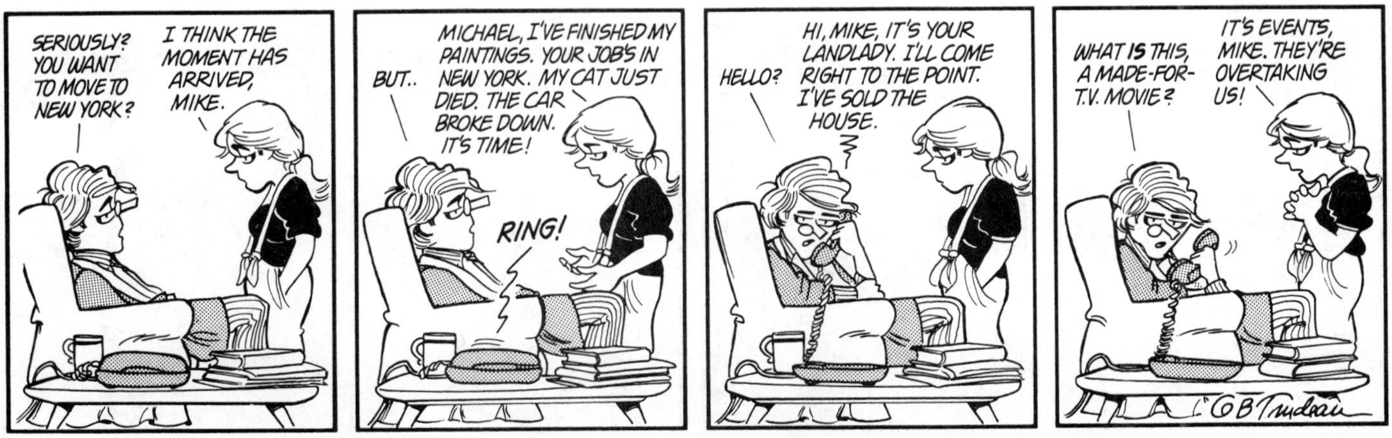
SERIOUSLY? YOU WANT TO MOVE TO NEW YORK?
I THINK THE MOMENT HAS ARRIVED, MIKE.
BUT..
MICHAEL, I'VE FINISHED MY PAINTINGS. YOUR JOB'S IN NEW YORK. MY CAT JUST DIED. THE CAR BROKE DOWN. IT'S TIME!
RING!
HELLO?
HI, MIKE, IT'S YOUR LANDLADY. I'LL COME RIGHT TO THE POINT. I'VE SOLD THE HOUSE.
WHAT IS THIS, A MADE-FOR-T.V. MOVIE?
IT'S EVENTS, MIKE. THEY'RE OVERTAKING US!
©B Trudeau

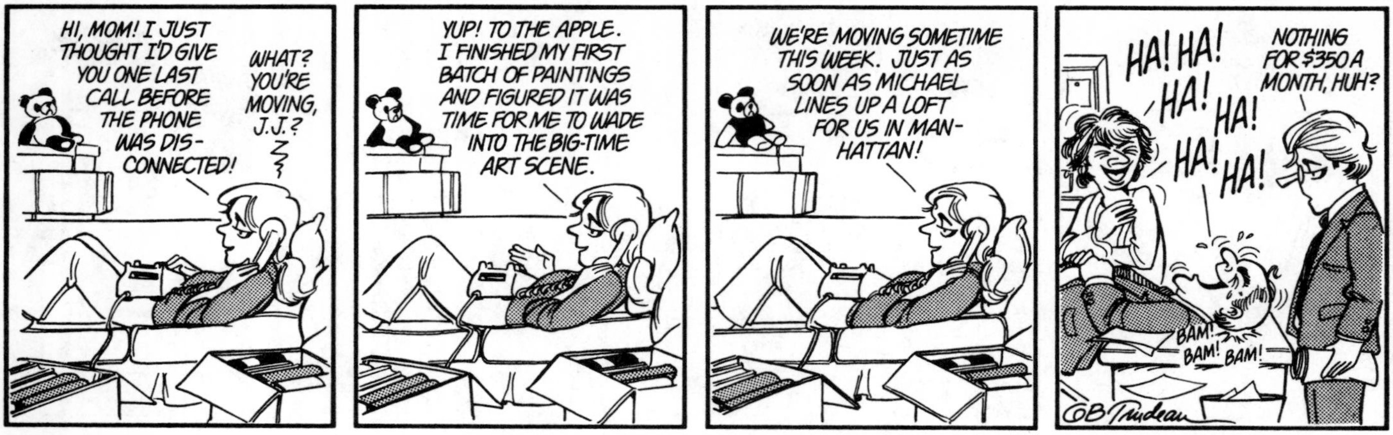
HI, MOM! I JUST THOUGHT I'D GIVE YOU ONE LAST CALL BEFORE THE PHONE WAS DIS-CONNECTED!
WHAT? YOU'RE MOVING, J.J.?
YUP! TO THE APPLE. I FINISHED MY FIRST BATCH OF PAINTINGS AND FIGURED IT WAS TIME FOR ME TO WADE INTO THE BIG-TIME ART SCENE.
WE'RE MOVING SOMETIME THIS WEEK.. JUST AS SOON AS MICHAEL LINES UP A LOFT FOR US IN MAN-HATTAN!
HA! HA! HA! HA! HA! HA!
NOTHING FOR $350 A MONTH, HUH?
BAM! BAM! BAM!
GBTrudeau

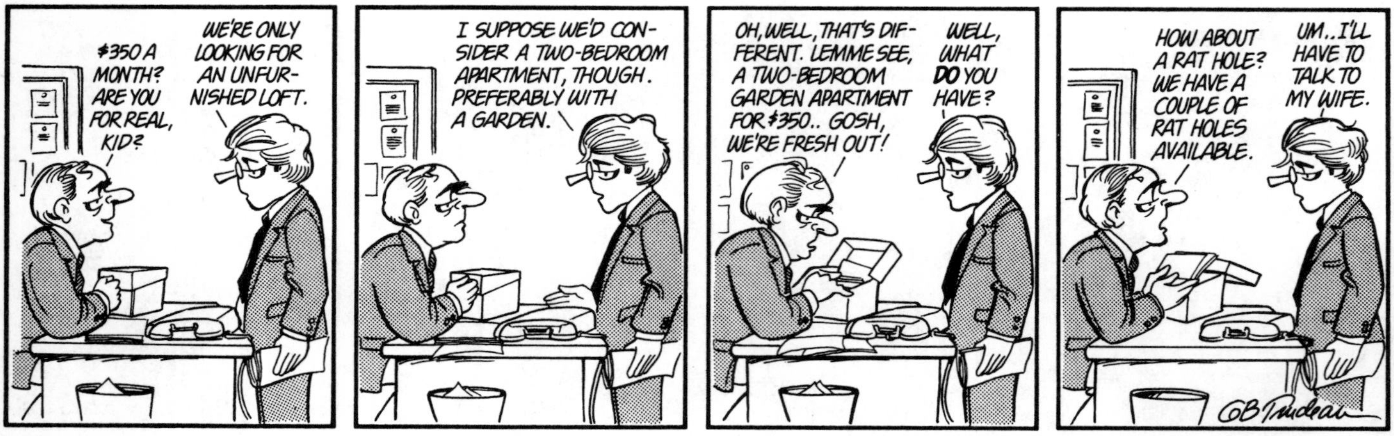
$350 A MONTH? ARE YOU FOR REAL, KID?
WE'RE ONLY LOOKING FOR AN UNFUR-NISHED LOFT.
I SUPPOSE WE'D CON-SIDER A TWO-BEDROOM APARTMENT, THOUGH. PREFERABLY WITH A GARDEN.
OH, WELL, THAT'S DIF-FERENT. LEMME SEE, A TWO-BEDROOM GARDEN APARTMENT FOR $350.. GOSH, WE'RE FRESH OUT!
WELL, WHAT DO YOU HAVE?
HOW ABOUT A RAT HOLE? WE HAVE A COUPLE OF RAT HOLES AVAILABLE.
UM.. I'LL HAVE TO TALK TO MY WIFE.
GBTrudeau

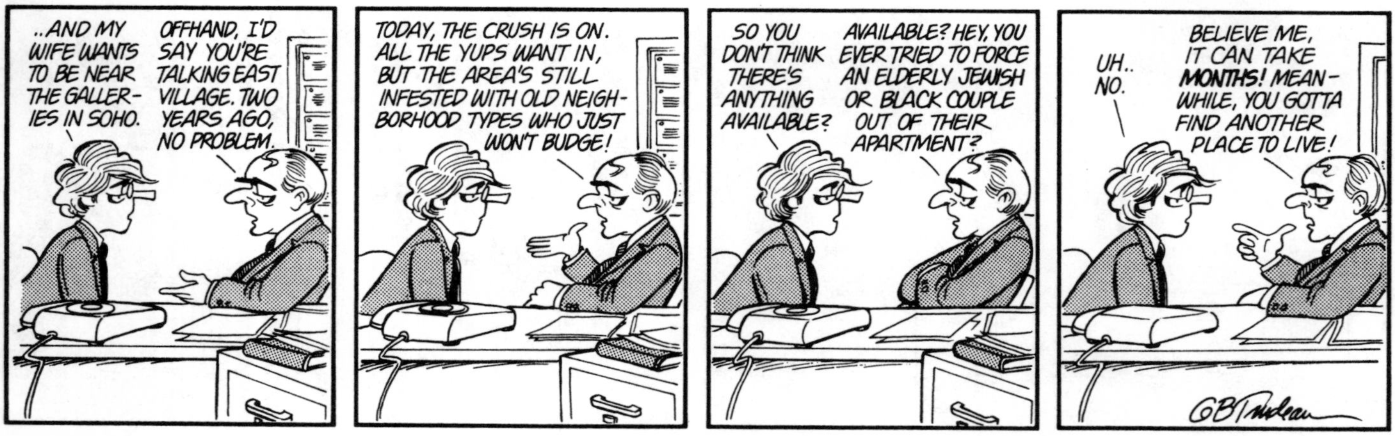
..AND MY WIFE WANTS TO BE NEAR THE GALLER-IES IN SOHO.
OFFHAND, I'D SAY YOU'RE TALKING EAST VILLAGE. TWO YEARS AGO, NO PROBLEM.
TODAY, THE CRUSH IS ON. ALL THE YUPS WANT IN, BUT THE AREA'S STILL INFESTED WITH OLD NEIGH-BORHOOD TYPES WHO JUST WON'T BUDGE!
SO YOU DON'T THINK THERE'S ANYTHING AVAILABLE?
AVAILABLE? HEY, YOU EVER TRIED TO FORCE AN ELDERLY JEWISH OR BLACK COUPLE OUT OF THEIR APARTMENT?
UH.. NO.
BELIEVE ME, IT CAN TAKE MONTHS! MEAN-WHILE, YOU GOTTA FIND ANOTHER PLACE TO LIVE!
GBTrudeau

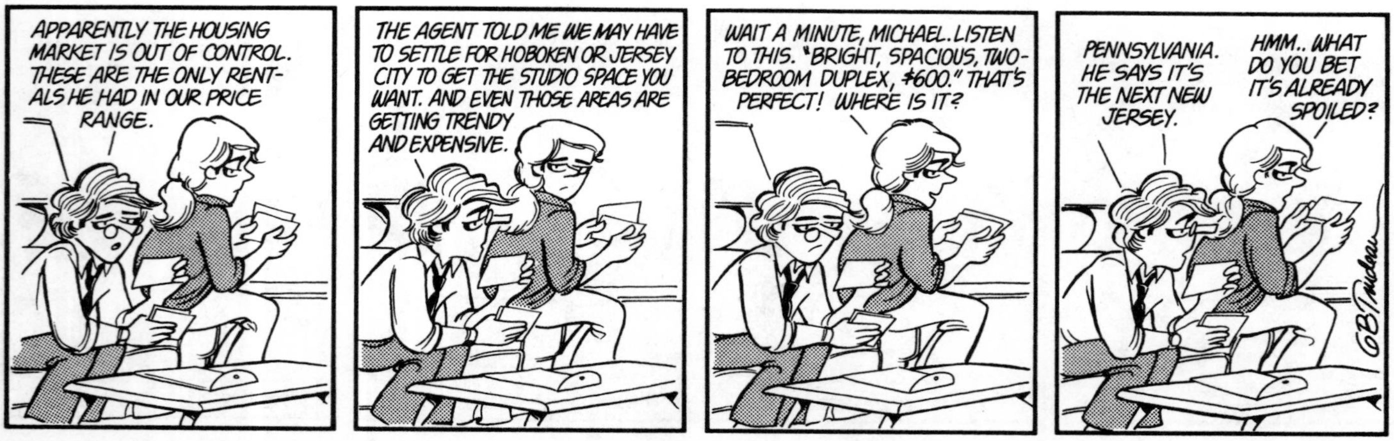
APPARENTLY THE HOUSING MARKET IS OUT OF CONTROL. THESE ARE THE ONLY RENT-ALS HE HAD IN OUR PRICE RANGE.
THE AGENT TOLD ME WE MAY HAVE TO SETTLE FOR HOBOKEN OR JERSEY CITY TO GET THE STUDIO SPACE YOU WANT. AND EVEN THOSE AREAS ARE GETTING TRENDY AND EXPENSIVE.
WAIT A MINUTE, MICHAEL. LISTEN TO THIS. "BRIGHT, SPACIOUS, TWO-BEDROOM DUPLEX, $600." THAT'S PERFECT! WHERE IS IT?
PENNSYLVANIA. HE SAYS IT'S THE NEXT NEW JERSEY.
HMM.. WHAT DO YOU BET IT'S ALREADY SPOILED?
GBTrudeau

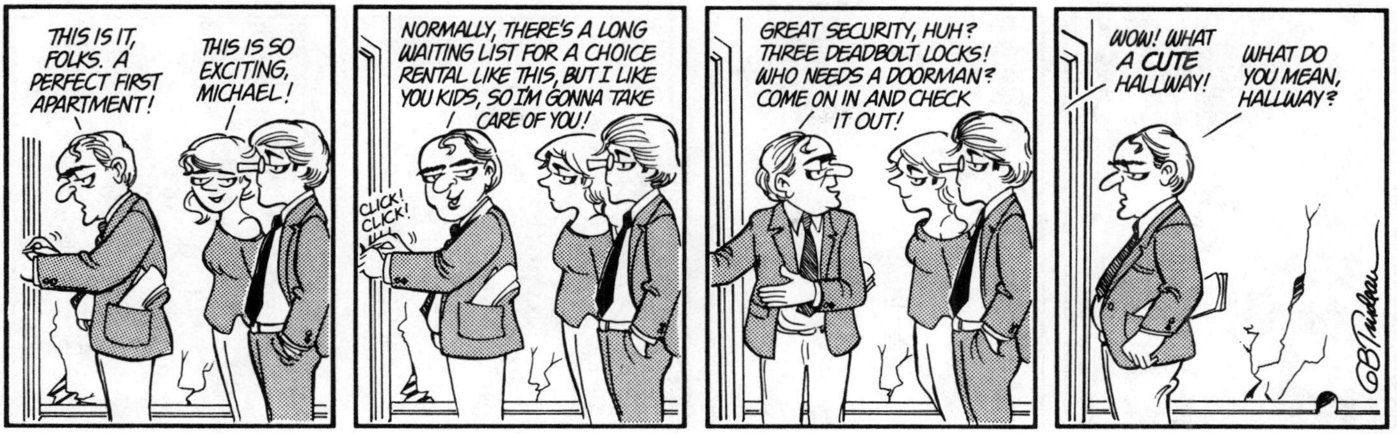
THIS IS IT, FOLKS. A PERFECT FIRST APARTMENT!
THIS IS SO EXCITING, MICHAEL!
NORMALLY, THERE'S A LONG WAITING LIST FOR A CHOICE RENTAL LIKE THIS, BUT I LIKE YOU KIDS, SO I'M GONNA TAKE CARE OF YOU!
CLICK! CLICK!
GREAT SECURITY, HUH? THREE DEADBOLT LOCKS! WHO NEEDS A DOORMAN? COME ON IN AND CHECK IT OUT!
WOW! WHAT A CUTE HALLWAY!
WHAT DO YOU MEAN, HALLWAY?

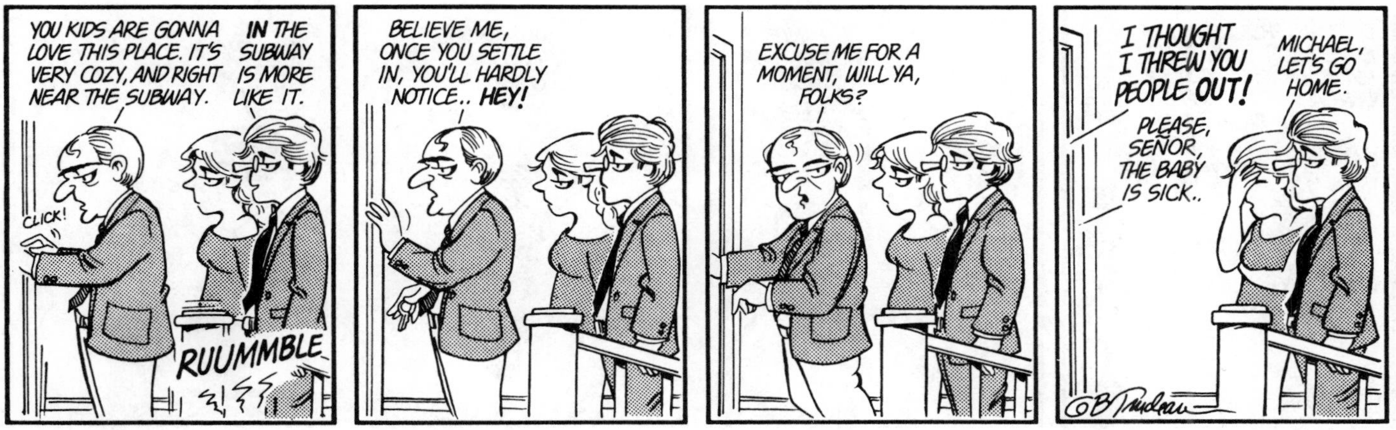
YOU KIDS ARE GONNA LOVE THIS PLACE. IT'S VERY COZY, AND RIGHT NEAR THE SUBWAY.
IN THE SUBWAY IS MORE LIKE IT.
CLICK!
RUUMMBLE
BELIEVE ME, ONCE YOU SETTLE IN, YOU'LL HARDLY NOTICE.. HEY!
EXCUSE ME FOR A MOMENT, WILL YA, FOLKS?
I THOUGHT I THREW YOU PEOPLE OUT!
PLEASE, SEÑOR, THE BABY IS SICK..
MICHAEL, LET'S GO HOME.

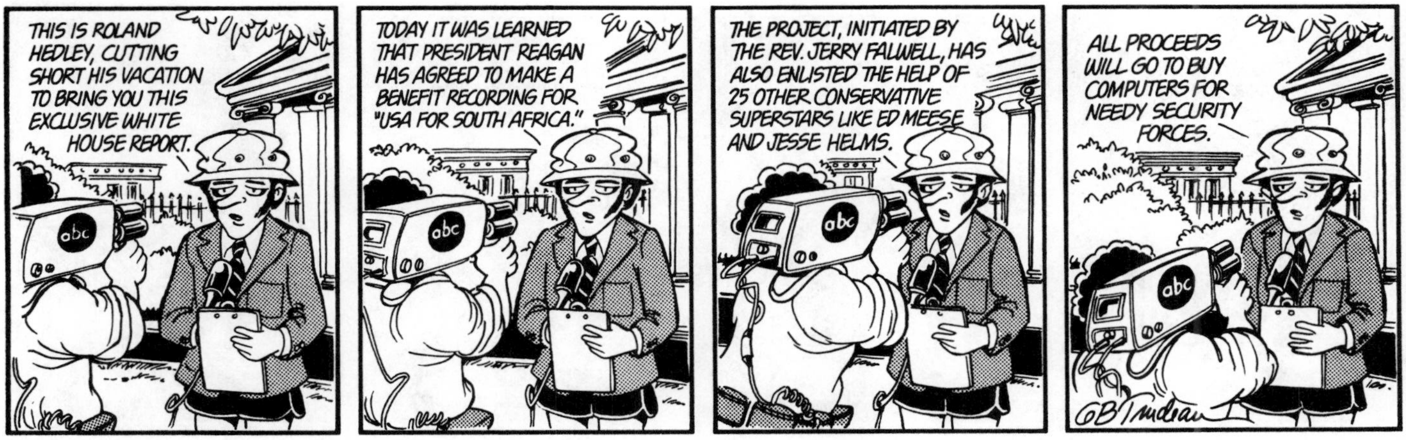
THIS IS ROLAND HEDLEY, CUTTING SHORT HIS VACATION TO BRING YOU THIS EXCLUSIVE WHITE HOUSE REPORT.
TODAY IT WAS LEARNED THAT PRESIDENT REAGAN HAS AGREED TO MAKE A BENEFIT RECORDING FOR "USA FOR SOUTH AFRICA."
THE PROJECT, INITIATED BY THE REV. JERRY FALWELL, HAS ALSO ENLISTED THE HELP OF 25 OTHER CONSERVATIVE SUPERSTARS LIKE ED MEESE AND JESSE HELMS.
ALL PROCEEDS WILL GO TO BUY COMPUTERS FOR NEEDY SECURITY FORCES.

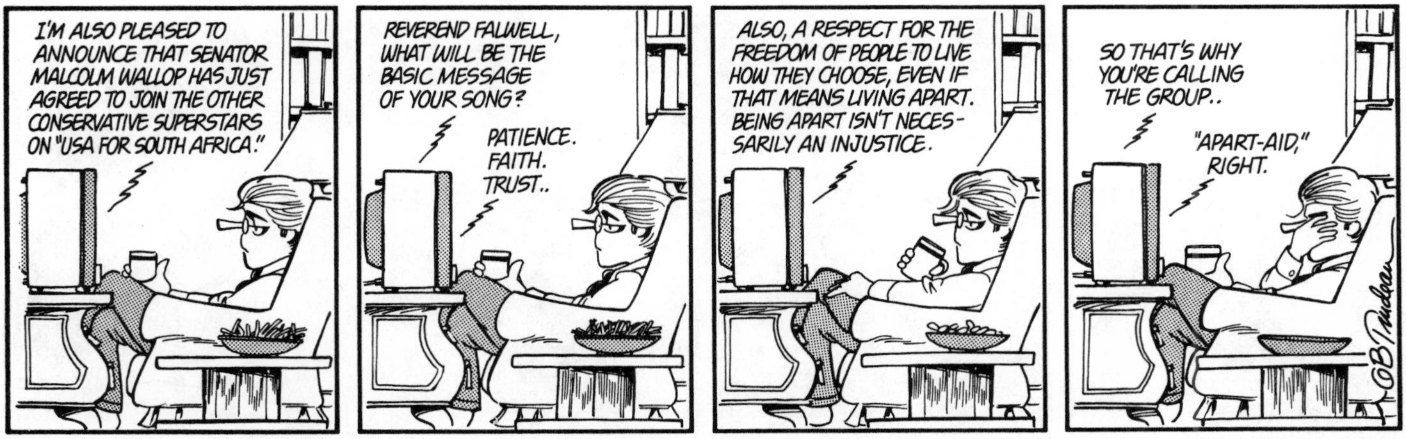
I'M ALSO PLEASED TO ANNOUNCE THAT SENATOR MALCOLM WALLOP HAS JUST AGREED TO JOIN THE OTHER CONSERVATIVE SUPERSTARS ON "USA FOR SOUTH AFRICA."
REVEREND FALWELL, WHAT WILL BE THE BASIC MESSAGE OF YOUR SONG?
PATIENCE. FAITH. TRUST..
ALSO, A RESPECT FOR THE FREEDOM OF PEOPLE TO LIVE HOW THEY CHOOSE, EVEN IF THAT MEANS LIVING APART. BEING APART ISN'T NECES-SARILY AN INJUSTICE.
SO THAT'S WHY YOU'RE CALLING THE GROUP..
"APART-AID," RIGHT.

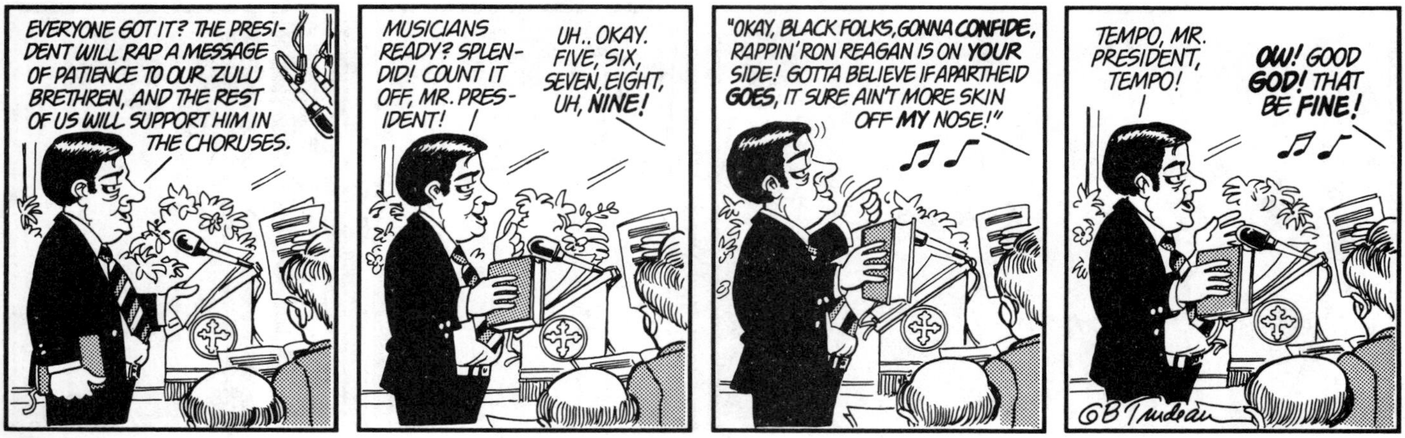
EVERYONE GOT IT? THE PRESIDENT WILL RAP A MESSAGE OF PATIENCE TO OUR ZULU BRETHREN, AND THE REST OF US WILL SUPPORT HIM IN THE CHORUSES.
MUSICIANS READY? SPLENDID! COUNT IT OFF, MR. PRESIDENT!
UH.. OKAY. FIVE, SIX, SEVEN, EIGHT, UH, NINE!
"OKAY, BLACK FOLKS, GONNA CONFIDE, RAPPIN' RON REAGAN IS ON YOUR SIDE! GOTTA BELIEVE IF APARTHEID GOES, IT SURE AIN'T MORE SKIN OFF MY NOSE!"
TEMPO, MR. PRESIDENT, TEMPO!
OW! GOOD GOD! THAT BE FINE!
©B Trudeau

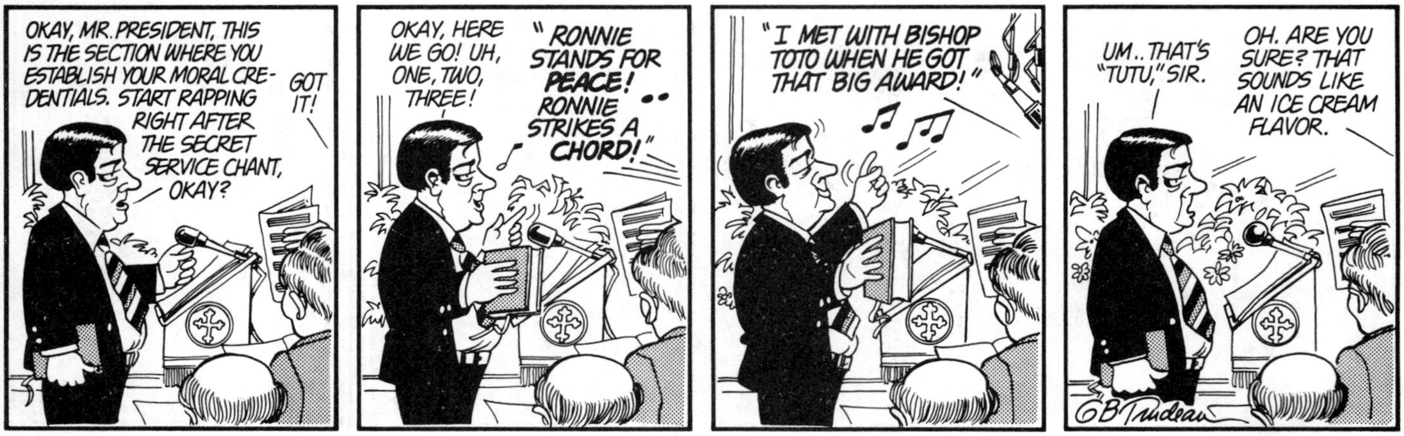
OKAY, MR. PRESIDENT, THIS IS THE SECTION WHERE YOU ESTABLISH YOUR MORAL CREDENTIALS. START RAPPING RIGHT AFTER THE SECRET SERVICE CHANT, OKAY?
GOT IT!
OKAY, HERE WE GO! UH, ONE, TWO, THREE!
"RONNIE STANDS FOR PEACE! RONNIE STRIKES A CHORD!"
"I MET WITH BISHOP TOTO WHEN HE GOT THAT BIG AWARD!"
UM.. THAT'S "TUTU," SIR.
OH. ARE YOU SURE? THAT SOUNDS LIKE AN ICE CREAM FLAVOR.
©B Trudeau

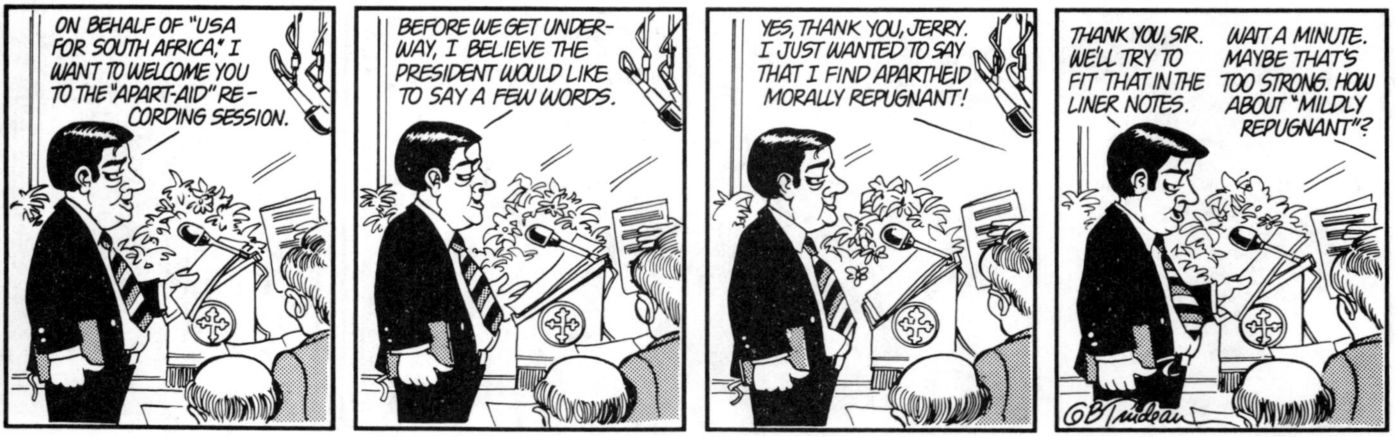
ON BEHALF OF "USA FOR SOUTH AFRICA," I WANT TO WELCOME YOU TO THE "APART-AID" RECORDING SESSION.
BEFORE WE GET UNDERWAY, I BELIEVE THE PRESIDENT WOULD LIKE TO SAY A FEW WORDS.
YES, THANK YOU, JERRY. I JUST WANTED TO SAY THAT I FIND APARTHEID MORALLY REPUGNANT!
THANK YOU, SIR. WE'LL TRY TO FIT THAT IN THE LINER NOTES.
WAIT A MINUTE. MAYBE THAT'S TOO STRONG. HOW ABOUT "MILDLY REPUGNANT"?
©B Trudeau

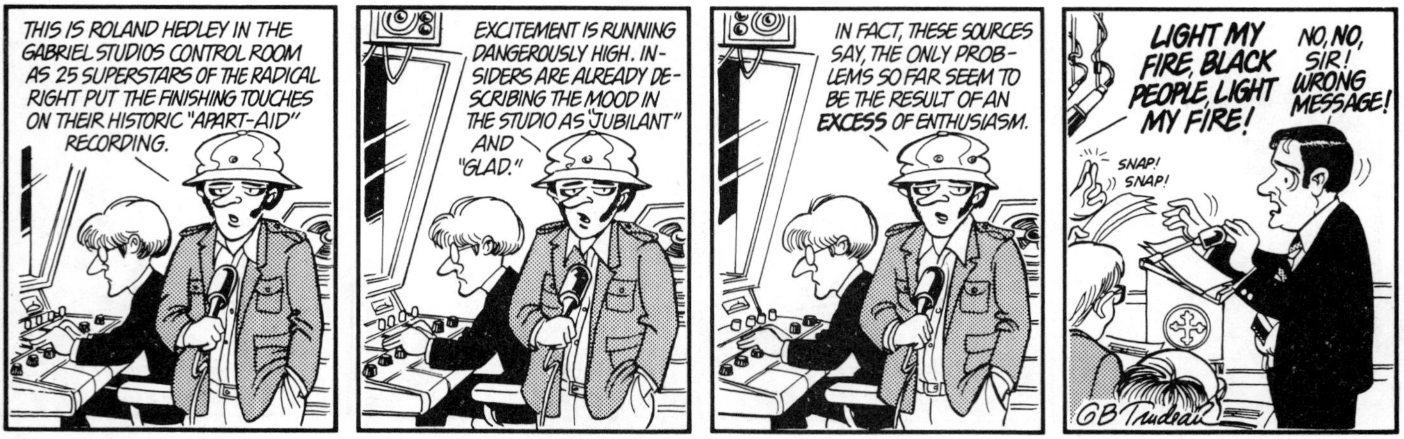
THIS IS ROLAND HEDLEY IN THE GABRIEL STUDIOS CONTROL ROOM AS 25 SUPERSTARS OF THE RADICAL RIGHT PUT THE FINISHING TOUCHES ON THEIR HISTORIC "APART-AID" RECORDING.
EXCITEMENT IS RUNNING DANGEROUSLY HIGH. INSIDERS ARE ALREADY DESCRIBING THE MOOD IN THE STUDIO AS "JUBILANT" AND "GLAD."
IN FACT, THESE SOURCES SAY, THE ONLY PROBLEMS SO FAR SEEM TO BE THE RESULT OF AN EXCESS OF ENTHUSIASM.
LIGHT MY FIRE, BLACK PEOPLE, LIGHT MY FIRE!
NO, NO, SIR! WRONG MESSAGE!
SNAP! SNAP!
©B Trudeau

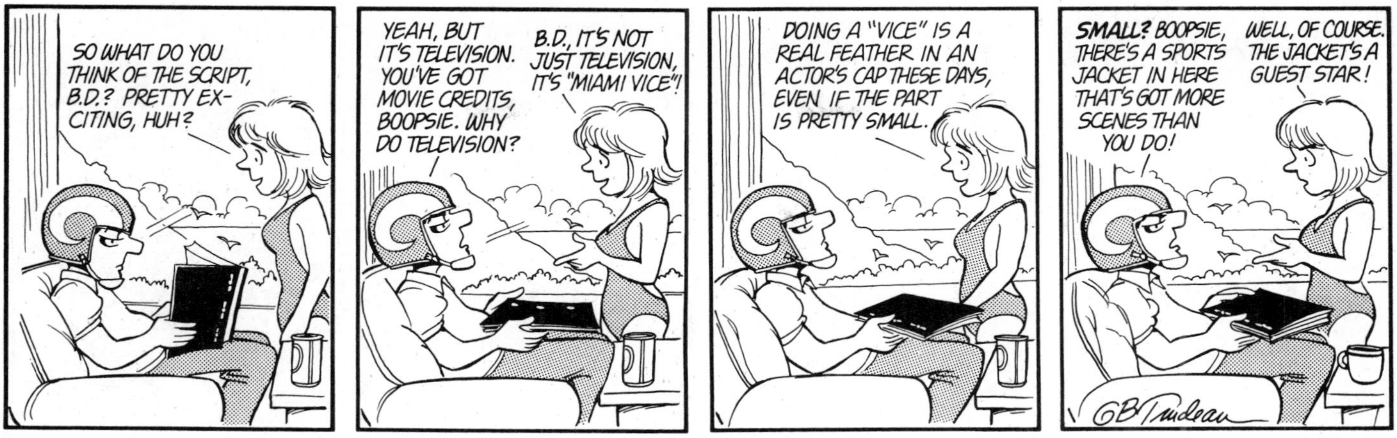
SO WHAT DO YOU THINK OF THE SCRIPT, B.D.? PRETTY EXCITING, HUH?
YEAH, BUT IT'S TELEVISION. YOU'VE GOT MOVIE CREDITS, BOOPSIE. WHY DO TELEVISION?
B.D., IT'S NOT JUST TELEVISION, IT'S "MIAMI VICE"!
DOING A "VICE" IS A REAL FEATHER IN AN ACTOR'S CAP THESE DAYS, EVEN IF THE PART IS PRETTY SMALL.
SMALL? BOOPSIE, THERE'S A SPORTS JACKET IN HERE THAT'S GOT MORE SCENES THAN YOU DO!
WELL, OF COURSE. THE JACKET'S A GUEST STAR!
GB Trudeau

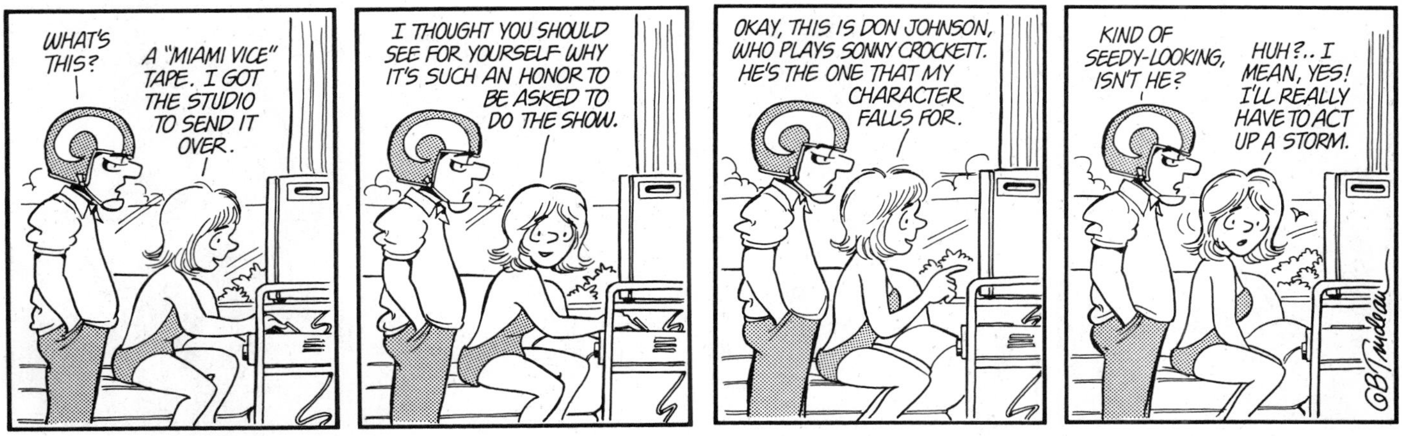
WHAT'S THIS?
A "MIAMI VICE" TAPE. I GOT THE STUDIO TO SEND IT OVER.
I THOUGHT YOU SHOULD SEE FOR YOURSELF WHY IT'S SUCH AN HONOR TO BE ASKED TO DO THE SHOW.
OKAY, THIS IS DON JOHNSON, WHO PLAYS SONNY CROCKETT. HE'S THE ONE THAT MY CHARACTER FALLS FOR.
KIND OF SEEDY-LOOKING, ISN'T HE?
HUH?.. I MEAN, YES! I'LL REALLY HAVE TO ACT UP A STORM.
GB Trudeau

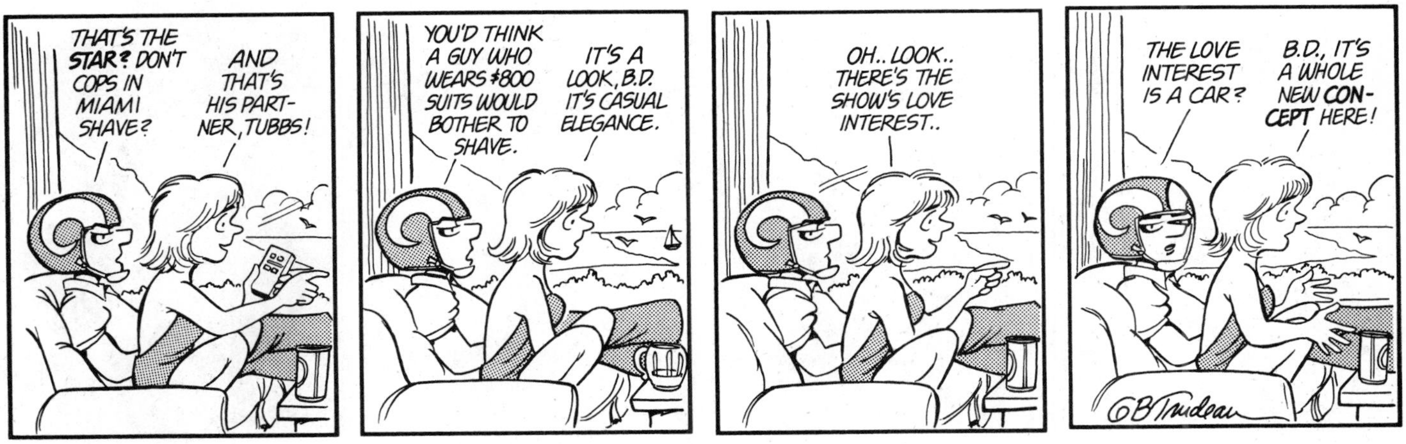
THAT'S THE **STAR?** DON'T COPS IN MIAMI SHAVE?
AND THAT'S HIS PARTNER, TUBBS!
YOU'D THINK A GUY WHO WEARS $800 SUITS WOULD BOTHER TO SHAVE.
IT'S A LOOK, B.D. IT'S CASUAL ELEGANCE.
OH.. LOOK.. THERE'S THE SHOW'S LOVE INTEREST..
THE LOVE INTEREST IS A CAR?
B.D., IT'S A WHOLE NEW **CONCEPT** HERE!
GB Trudeau

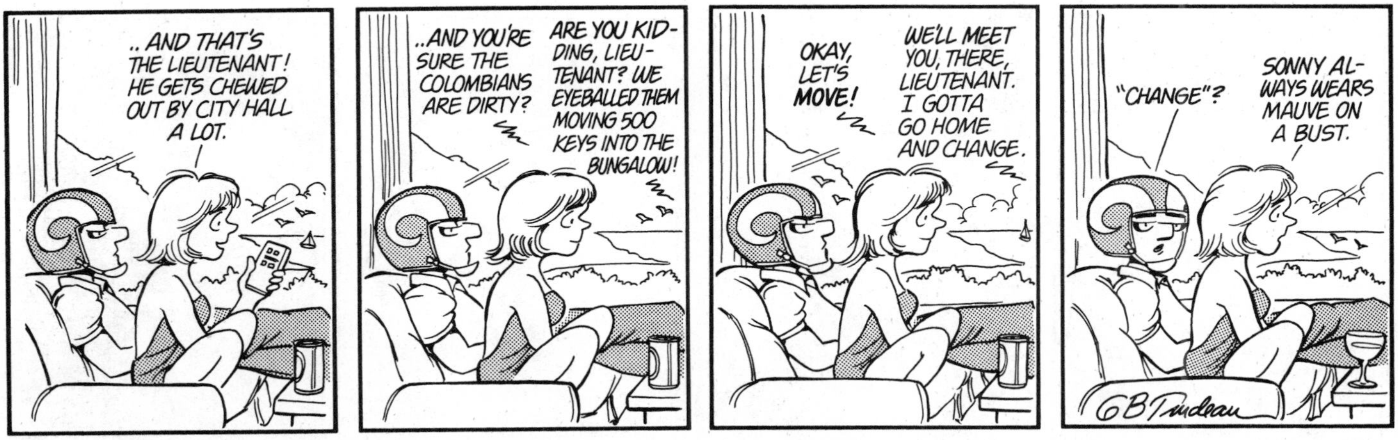
.. AND THAT'S THE LIEUTENANT! HE GETS CHEWED OUT BY CITY HALL A LOT.
..AND YOU'RE SURE THE COLOMBIANS ARE DIRTY?
ARE YOU KIDDING, LIEUTENANT? WE EYEBALLED THEM MOVING 500 KEYS INTO THE BUNGALOW!
OKAY, LET'S **MOVE!**
WE'LL MEET YOU, THERE, LIEUTENANT. I GOTTA GO HOME AND CHANGE.
"CHANGE"?
SONNY ALWAYS WEARS MAUVE ON A BUST.
GB Trudeau

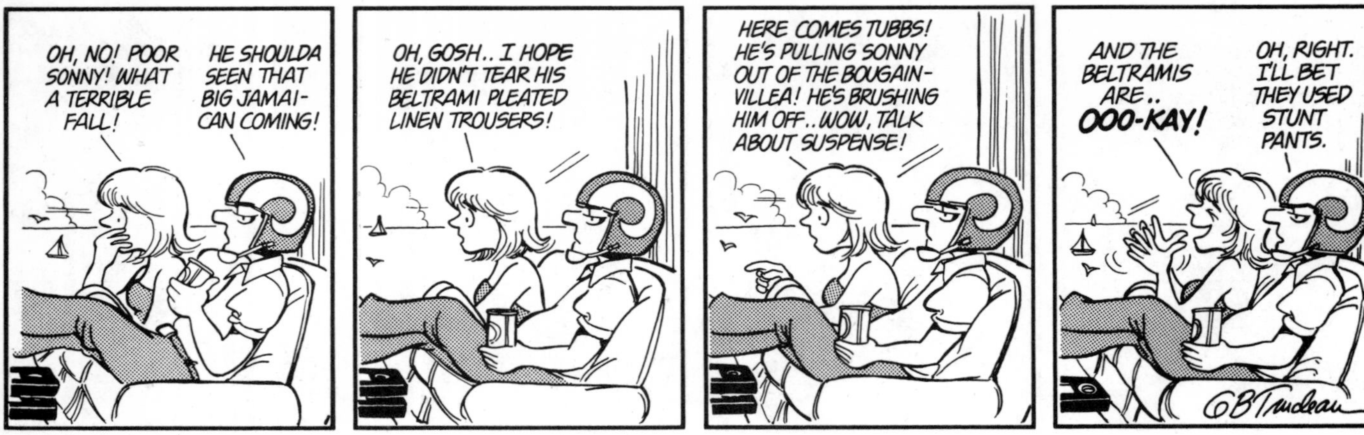
OH, NO! POOR SONNY! WHAT A TERRIBLE FALL!
HE SHOULDA SEEN THAT BIG JAMAICAN COMING!
OH, GOSH.. I HOPE HE DIDN'T TEAR HIS BELTRAMI PLEATED LINEN TROUSERS!
HERE COMES TUBBS! HE'S PULLING SONNY OUT OF THE BOUGAINVILLEA! HE'S BRUSHING HIM OFF.. WOW, TALK ABOUT SUSPENSE!
AND THE BELTRAMIS ARE.. OOO-KAY!
OH, RIGHT. I'LL BET THEY USED STUNT PANTS.
GB Trudeau

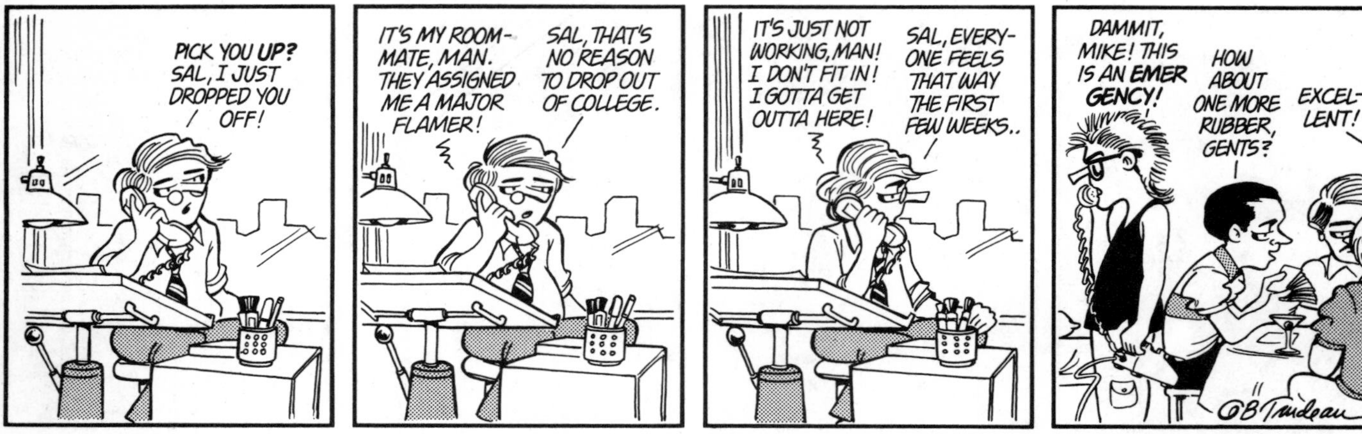
PICK YOU UP? SAL, I JUST DROPPED YOU OFF!
IT'S MY ROOMMATE, MAN. THEY ASSIGNED ME A MAJOR FLAMER!
SAL, THAT'S NO REASON TO DROP OUT OF COLLEGE.
IT'S JUST NOT WORKING, MAN! I DON'T FIT IN! I GOTTA GET OUTTA HERE!
SAL, EVERYONE FEELS THAT WAY THE FIRST FEW WEEKS..
DAMMIT, MIKE! THIS IS AN EMERGENCY!
HOW ABOUT ONE MORE RUBBER, GENTS?
EXCELLENT!
GB Trudeau

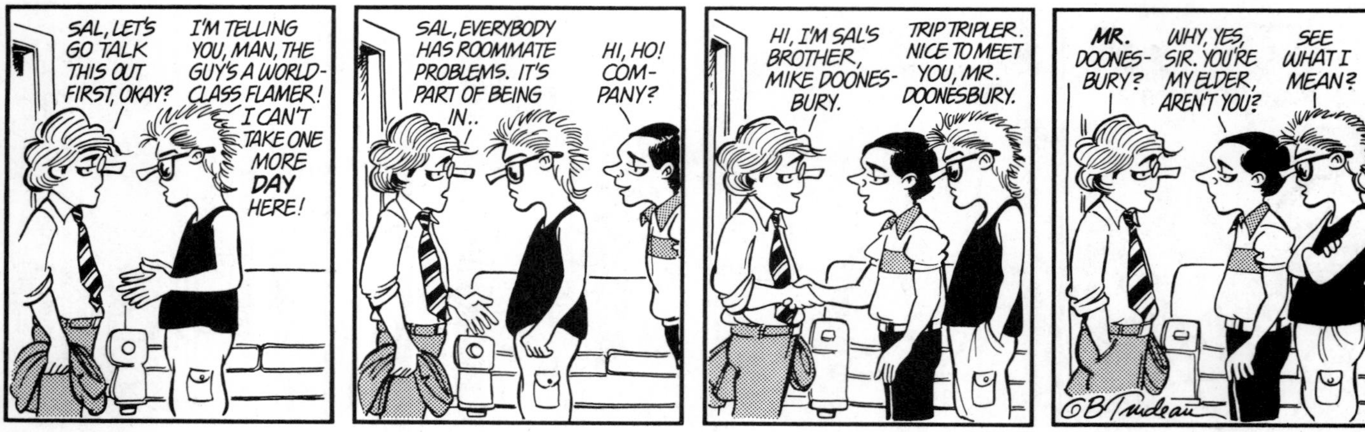
SAL, LET'S GO TALK THIS OUT FIRST, OKAY?
I'M TELLING YOU, MAN, THE GUY'S A WORLD-CLASS FLAMER! I CAN'T TAKE ONE MORE DAY HERE!
SAL, EVERYBODY HAS ROOMMATE PROBLEMS. IT'S PART OF BEING IN..
HI, HO! COMPANY?
HI, I'M SAL'S BROTHER, MIKE DOONESBURY.
TRIP TRIPLER. NICE TO MEET YOU, MR. DOONESBURY.
MR. DOONESBURY?
WHY, YES, SIR. YOU'RE MY ELDER, AREN'T YOU?
SEE WHAT I MEAN?
GB Trudeau

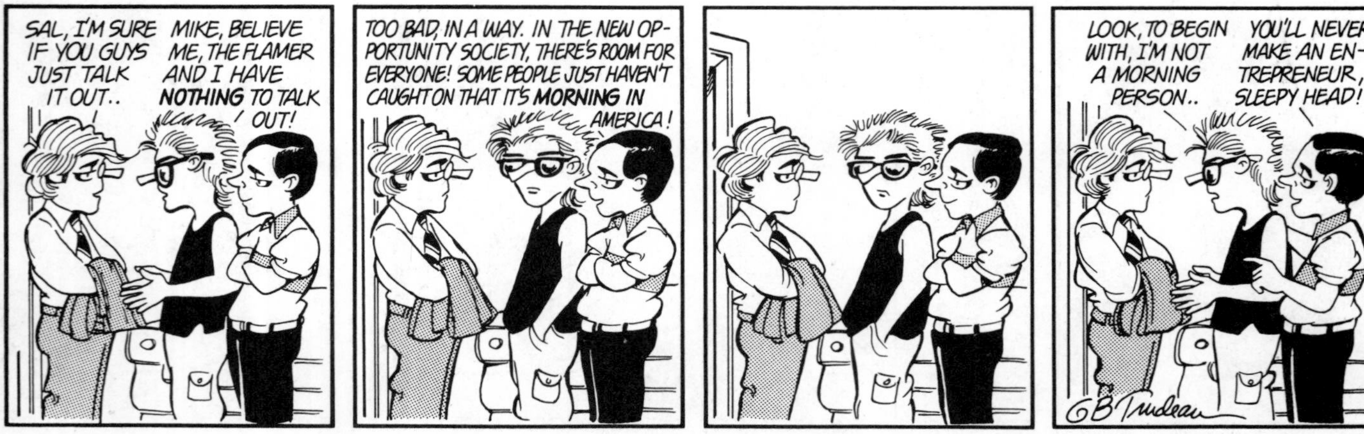
SAL, I'M SURE IF YOU GUYS JUST TALK IT OUT..
MIKE, BELIEVE ME, THE FLAMER AND I HAVE NOTHING TO TALK OUT!
TOO BAD, IN A WAY. IN THE NEW OPPORTUNITY SOCIETY, THERE'S ROOM FOR EVERYONE! SOME PEOPLE JUST HAVEN'T CAUGHT ON THAT IT'S MORNING IN AMERICA!
LOOK, TO BEGIN WITH, I'M NOT A MORNING PERSON..
YOU'LL NEVER MAKE AN ENTREPRENEUR, SLEEPY HEAD!
GB Trudeau

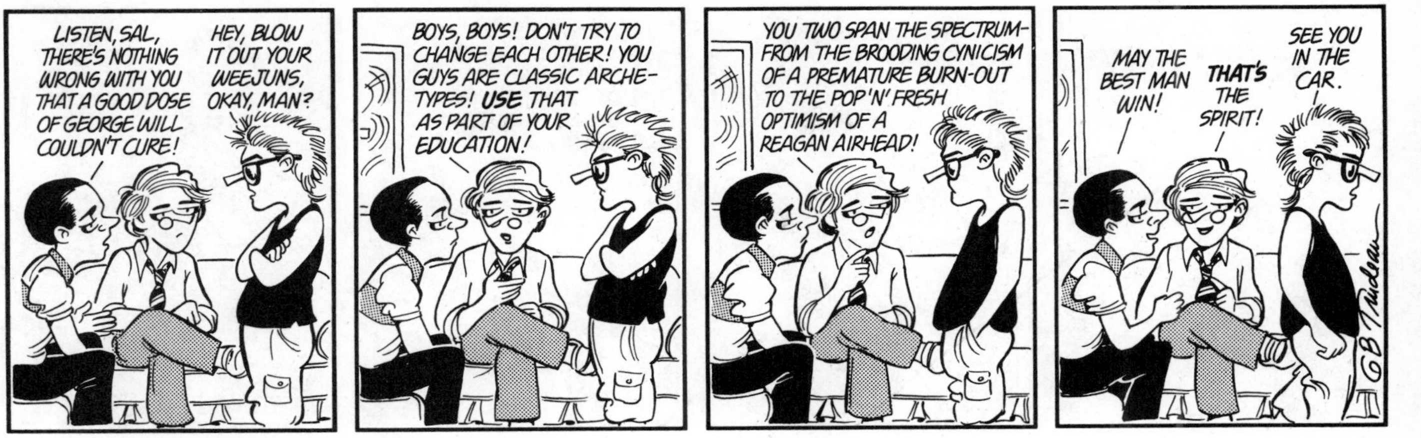
LISTEN, SAL, THERE'S NOTHING WRONG WITH YOU THAT A GOOD DOSE OF GEORGE WILL COULDN'T CURE!
HEY, BLOW IT OUT YOUR WEEJUNS, OKAY, MAN?
BOYS, BOYS! DON'T TRY TO CHANGE EACH OTHER! YOU GUYS ARE CLASSIC ARCHETYPES! USE THAT AS PART OF YOUR EDUCATION!
YOU TWO SPAN THE SPECTRUM–FROM THE BROODING CYNICISM OF A PREMATURE BURN-OUT TO THE POP 'N' FRESH OPTIMISM OF A REAGAN AIRHEAD!
MAY THE BEST MAN WIN!
THAT'S THE SPIRIT!
SEE YOU IN THE CAR.
©B Trudeau

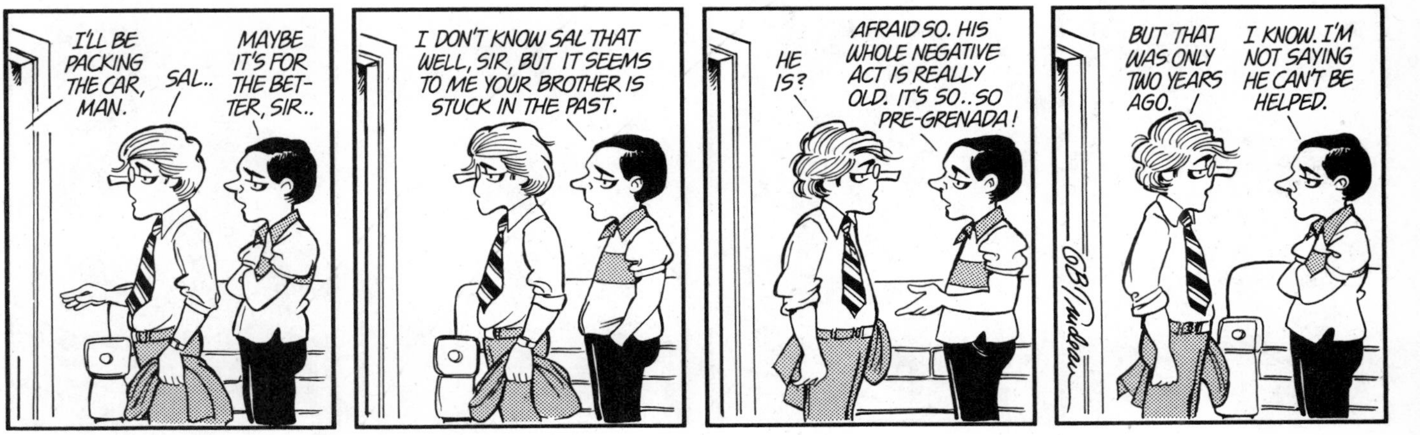
I'LL BE PACKING THE CAR, MAN.
SAL..
MAYBE IT'S FOR THE BETTER, SIR..
I DON'T KNOW SAL THAT WELL, SIR, BUT IT SEEMS TO ME YOUR BROTHER IS STUCK IN THE PAST.
HE IS?
AFRAID SO. HIS WHOLE NEGATIVE ACT IS REALLY OLD. IT'S SO..SO PRE-GRENADA!
BUT THAT WAS ONLY TWO YEARS AGO.
I KNOW. I'M NOT SAYING HE CAN'T BE HELPED.
©B Trudeau

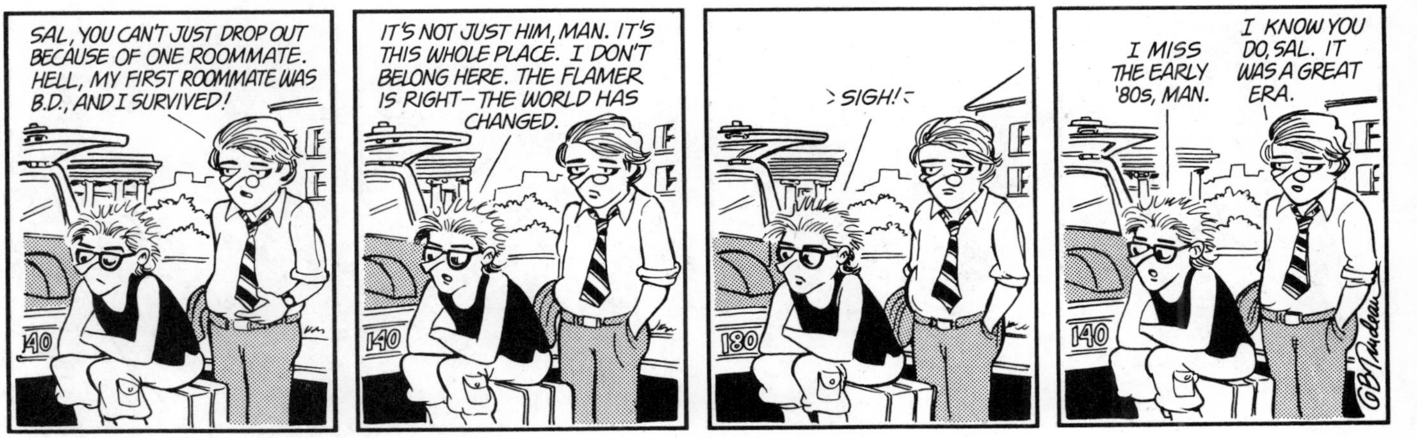
SAL, YOU CAN'T JUST DROP OUT BECAUSE OF ONE ROOMMATE. HELL, MY FIRST ROOMMATE WAS B.D., AND I SURVIVED!
IT'S NOT JUST HIM, MAN. IT'S THIS WHOLE PLACE. I DON'T BELONG HERE. THE FLAMER IS RIGHT–THE WORLD HAS CHANGED.
SIGH!
I MISS THE EARLY '80s, MAN.
I KNOW YOU DO, SAL. IT WAS A GREAT ERA.
©B Trudeau

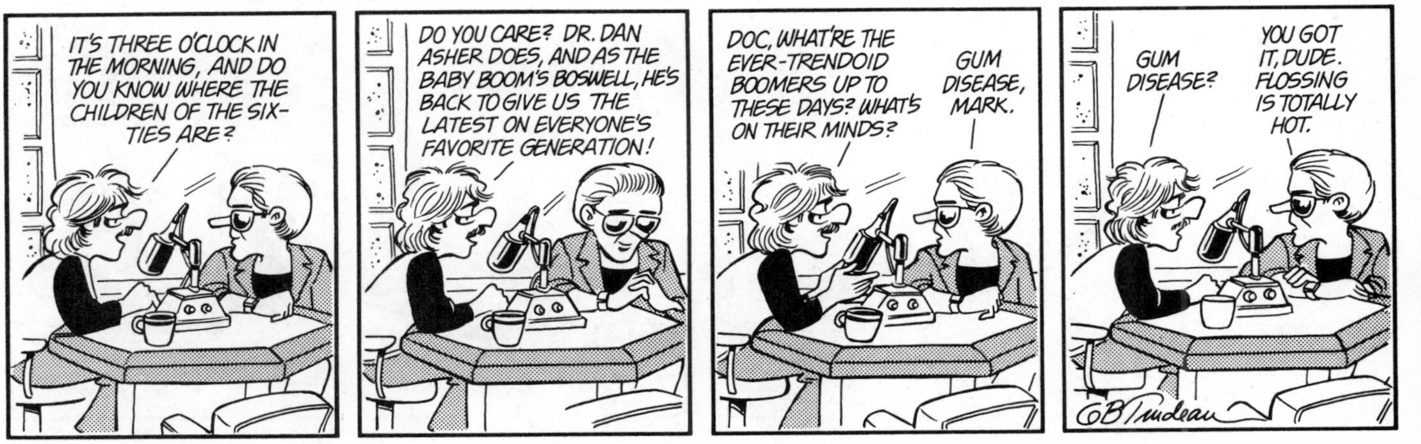
IT'S THREE O'CLOCK IN THE MORNING, AND DO YOU KNOW WHERE THE CHILDREN OF THE SIXTIES ARE?
DO YOU CARE? DR. DAN ASHER DOES, AND AS THE BABY BOOM'S BOSWELL, HE'S BACK TO GIVE US THE LATEST ON EVERYONE'S FAVORITE GENERATION!
DOC, WHAT'RE THE EVER-TRENDOID BOOMERS UP TO THESE DAYS? WHAT'S ON THEIR MINDS?
GUM DISEASE, MARK.
GUM DISEASE?
YOU GOT IT, DUDE. FLOSSING IS TOTALLY HOT.
©B Trudeau

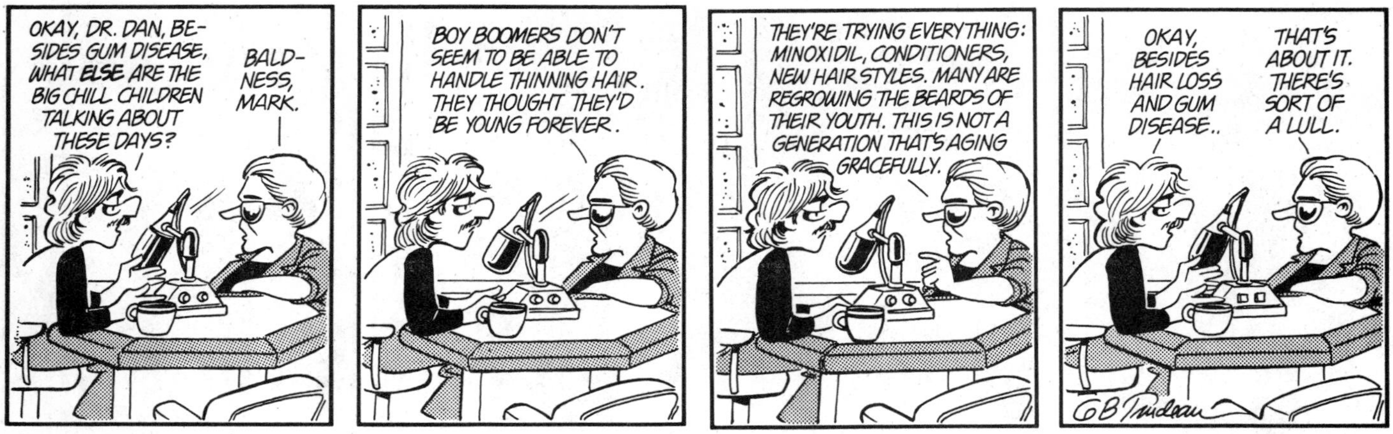
OKAY, DR. DAN, BESIDES GUM DISEASE, WHAT **ELSE** ARE THE BIG CHILL CHILDREN TALKING ABOUT THESE DAYS?
BALDNESS, MARK.
BOY BOOMERS DON'T SEEM TO BE ABLE TO HANDLE THINNING HAIR. THEY THOUGHT THEY'D BE YOUNG FOREVER.
THEY'RE TRYING EVERYTHING: MINOXIDIL, CONDITIONERS, NEW HAIR STYLES. MANY ARE REGROWING THE BEARDS OF THEIR YOUTH. THIS IS NOT A GENERATION THAT'S AGING GRACEFULLY.
OKAY, BESIDES HAIR LOSS AND GUM DISEASE..
THAT'S ABOUT IT. THERE'S SORT OF A LULL.
GB Trudeau

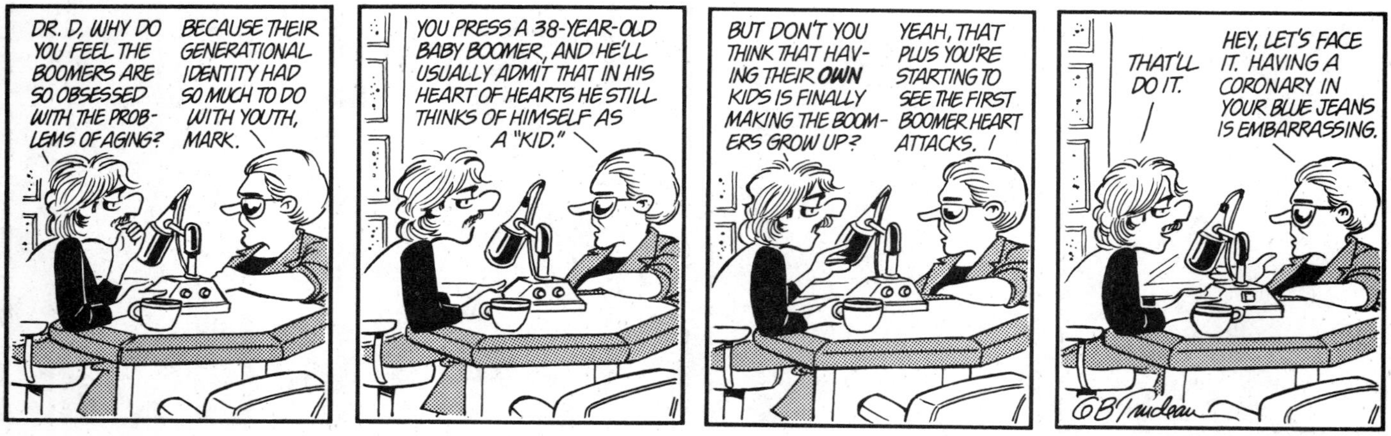
DR. D, WHY DO YOU FEEL THE BOOMERS ARE SO OBSESSED WITH THE PROBLEMS OF AGING?
BECAUSE THEIR GENERATIONAL IDENTITY HAD SO MUCH TO DO WITH YOUTH, MARK.
YOU PRESS A 38-YEAR-OLD BABY BOOMER, AND HE'LL USUALLY ADMIT THAT IN HIS HEART OF HEARTS HE STILL THINKS OF HIMSELF AS A "KID."
BUT DON'T YOU THINK THAT HAVING THEIR **OWN** KIDS IS FINALLY MAKING THE BOOMERS GROW UP?
YEAH, THAT PLUS YOU'RE STARTING TO SEE THE FIRST BOOMER HEART ATTACKS.
THAT'LL DO IT.
HEY, LET'S FACE IT. HAVING A CORONARY IN YOUR BLUE JEANS IS EMBARRASSING.
GB Trudeau

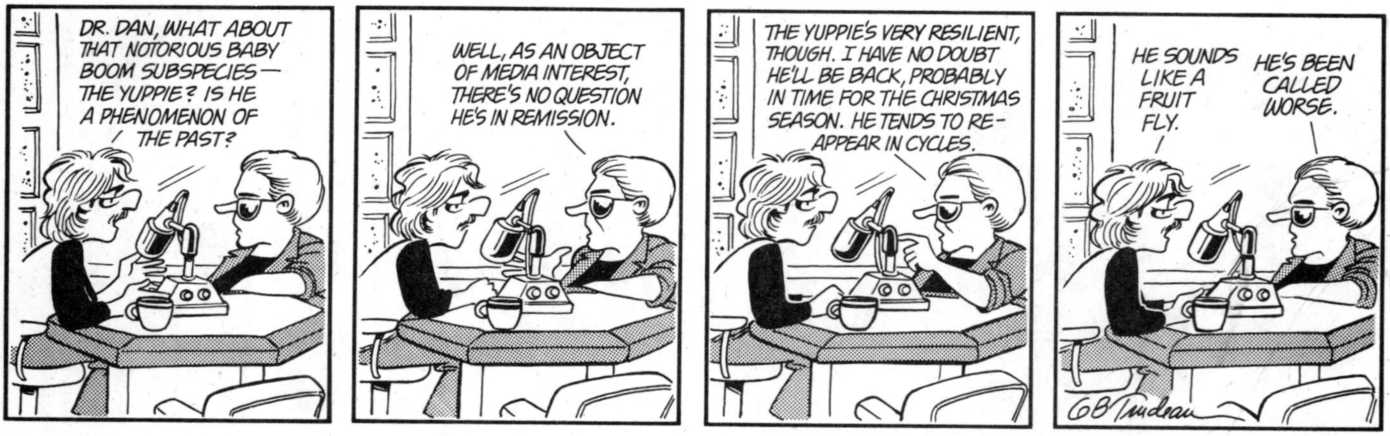
DR. DAN, WHAT ABOUT THAT NOTORIOUS BABY BOOM SUBSPECIES— THE YUPPIE? IS HE A PHENOMENON OF THE PAST?
WELL, AS AN OBJECT OF MEDIA INTEREST, THERE'S NO QUESTION HE'S IN REMISSION.
THE YUPPIE'S VERY RESILIENT, THOUGH. I HAVE NO DOUBT HE'LL BE BACK, PROBABLY IN TIME FOR THE CHRISTMAS SEASON. HE TENDS TO REAPPEAR IN CYCLES.
HE SOUNDS LIKE A FRUIT FLY.
HE'S BEEN CALLED WORSE.
GB Trudeau

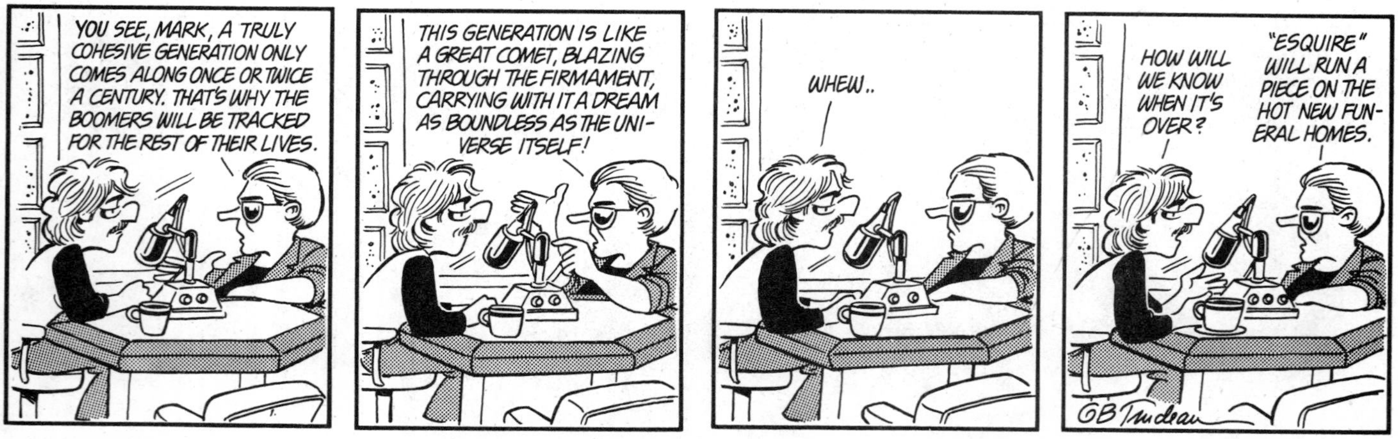
YOU SEE, MARK, A TRULY COHESIVE GENERATION ONLY COMES ALONG ONCE OR TWICE A CENTURY. THAT'S WHY THE BOOMERS WILL BE TRACKED FOR THE REST OF THEIR LIVES.
THIS GENERATION IS LIKE A GREAT COMET, BLAZING THROUGH THE FIRMAMENT, CARRYING WITH IT A DREAM AS BOUNDLESS AS THE UNIVERSE ITSELF!
WHEW..
HOW WILL WE KNOW WHEN IT'S OVER?
"ESQUIRE" WILL RUN A PIECE ON THE HOT NEW FUNERAL HOMES.
GB Trudeau

PART TWO

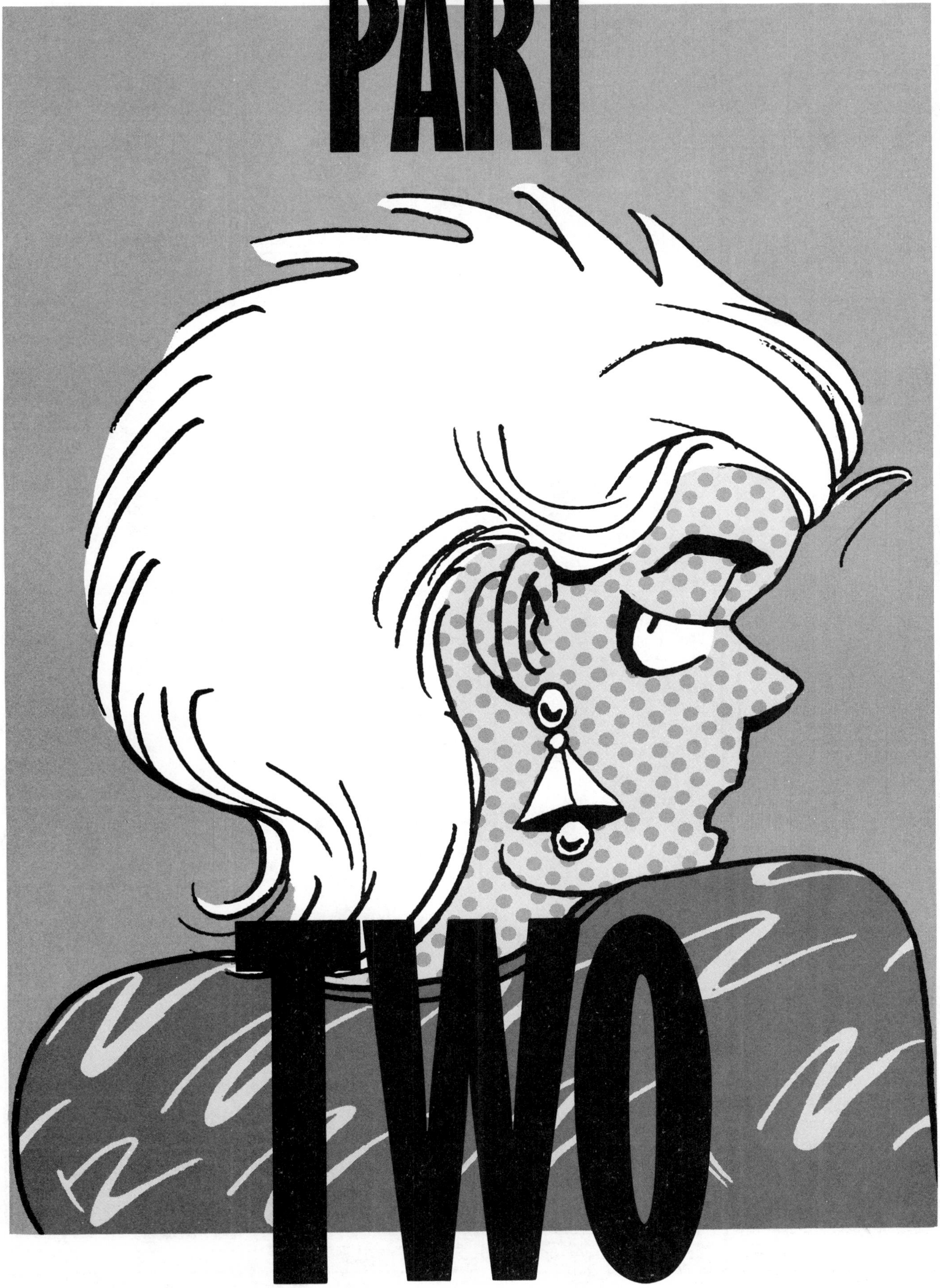

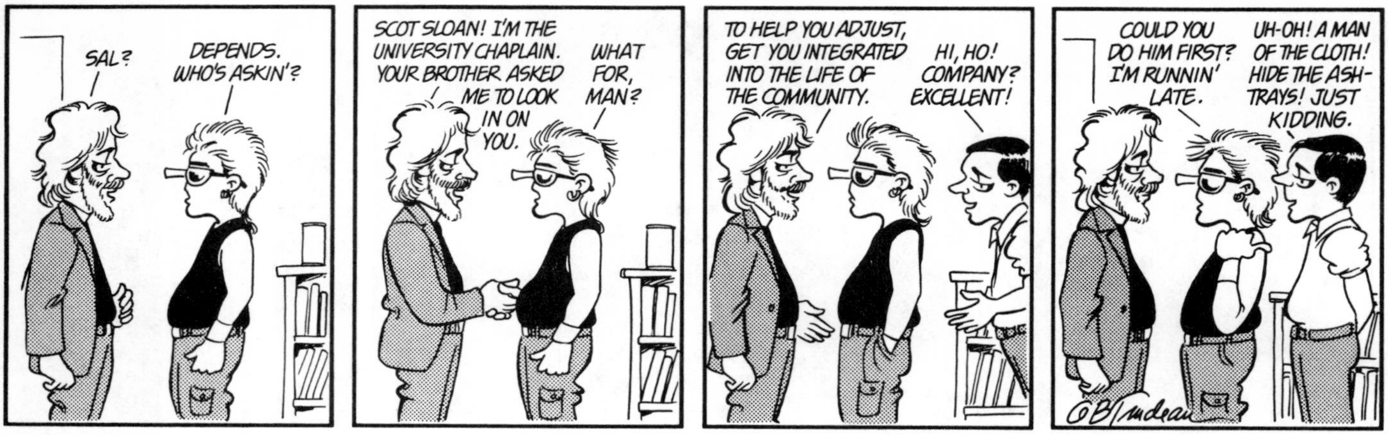
SAL?
DEPENDS. WHO'S ASKIN'?
SCOT SLOAN! I'M THE UNIVERSITY CHAPLAIN. YOUR BROTHER ASKED ME TO LOOK IN ON YOU.
WHAT FOR, MAN?
TO HELP YOU ADJUST, GET YOU INTEGRATED INTO THE LIFE OF THE COMMUNITY.
HI, HO! COMPANY? EXCELLENT!
COULD YOU DO HIM FIRST? I'M RUNNIN' LATE.
UH-OH! A MAN OF THE CLOTH! HIDE THE ASH-TRAYS! JUST KIDDING.
GBTrudeau

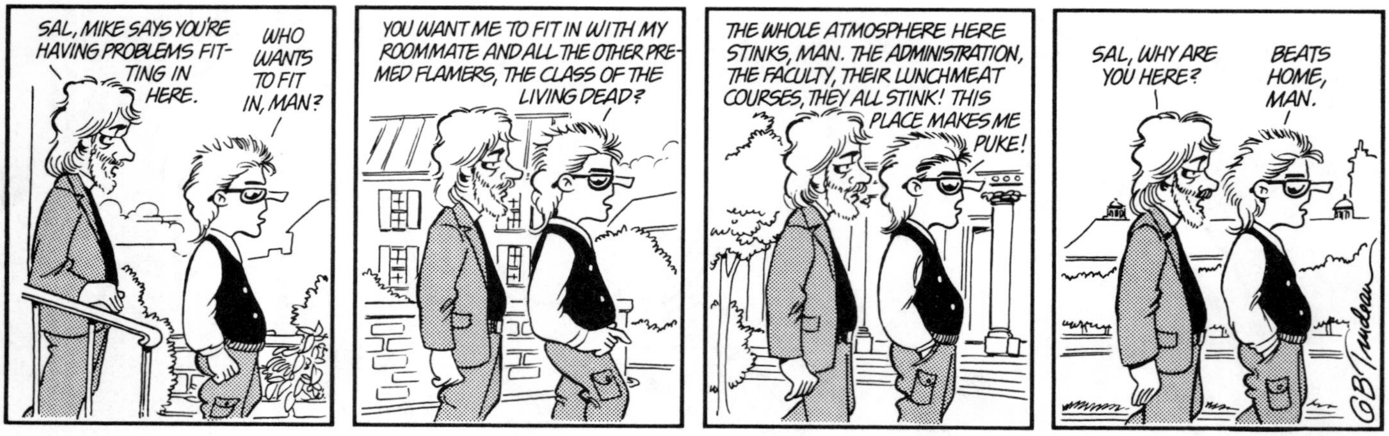
SAL, MIKE SAYS YOU'RE HAVING PROBLEMS FIT-TING IN HERE.
WHO WANTS TO FIT IN, MAN?
YOU WANT ME TO FIT IN WITH MY ROOMMATE AND ALL THE OTHER PRE-MED FLAMERS, THE CLASS OF THE LIVING DEAD?
THE WHOLE ATMOSPHERE HERE STINKS, MAN. THE ADMINISTRATION, THE FACULTY, THEIR LUNCHMEAT COURSES, THEY ALL STINK! THIS PLACE MAKES ME PUKE!
SAL, WHY ARE YOU HERE?
BEATS HOME, MAN.
GBTrudeau

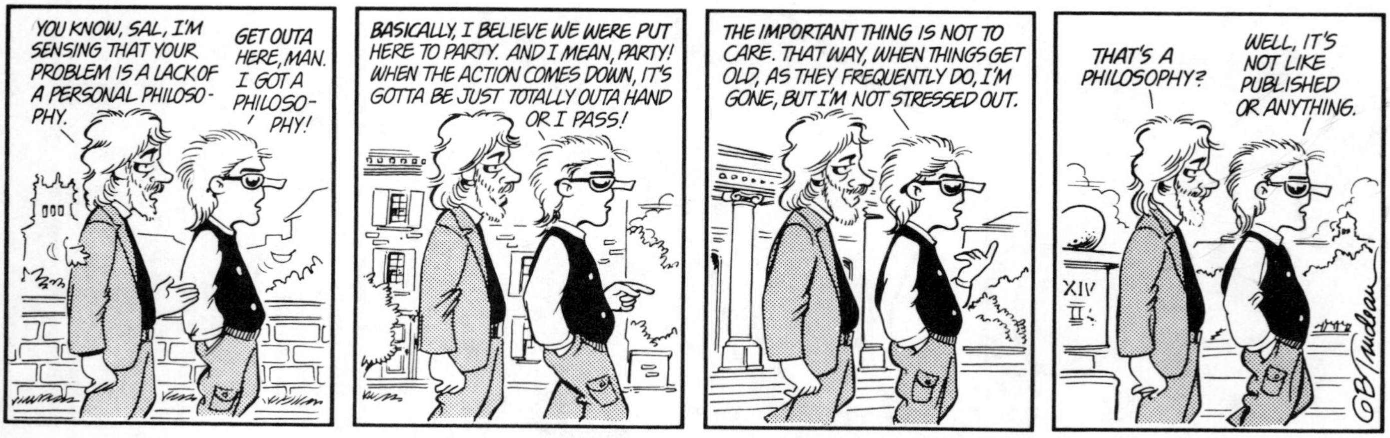
YOU KNOW, SAL, I'M SENSING THAT YOUR PROBLEM IS A LACK OF A PERSONAL PHILOSO-PHY.
GET OUTA HERE, MAN. I GOT A PHILOSO-PHY!
BASICALLY, I BELIEVE WE WERE PUT HERE TO PARTY. AND I MEAN, PARTY! WHEN THE ACTION COMES DOWN, IT'S GOTTA BE JUST TOTALLY OUTA HAND OR I PASS!
THE IMPORTANT THING IS NOT TO CARE. THAT WAY, WHEN THINGS GET OLD, AS THEY FREQUENTLY DO, I'M GONE, BUT I'M NOT STRESSED OUT.
THAT'S A PHILOSOPHY?
WELL, IT'S NOT LIKE PUBLISHED OR ANYTHING.
XIV
GBTrudeau

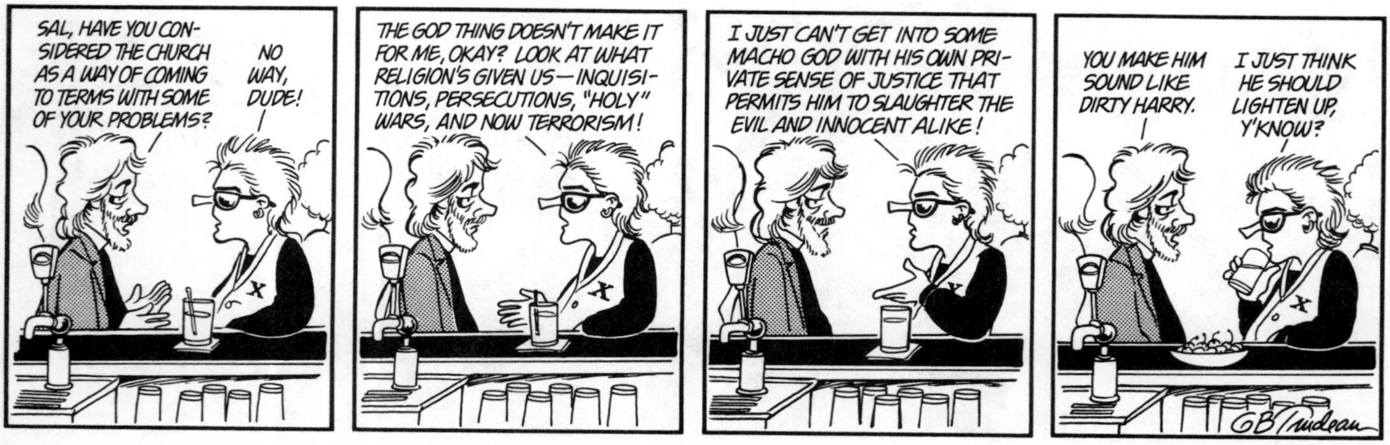
SAL, HAVE YOU CON-SIDERED THE CHURCH AS A WAY OF COMING TO TERMS WITH SOME OF YOUR PROBLEMS?
NO WAY, DUDE!
THE GOD THING DOESN'T MAKE IT FOR ME, OKAY? LOOK AT WHAT RELIGION'S GIVEN US — INQUISI-TIONS, PERSECUTIONS, "HOLY" WARS, AND NOW TERRORISM!
I JUST CAN'T GET INTO SOME MACHO GOD WITH HIS OWN PRI-VATE SENSE OF JUSTICE THAT PERMITS HIM TO SLAUGHTER THE EVIL AND INNOCENT ALIKE!
YOU MAKE HIM SOUND LIKE DIRTY HARRY.
I JUST THINK HE SHOULD LIGHTEN UP, Y'KNOW?
GBTrudeau

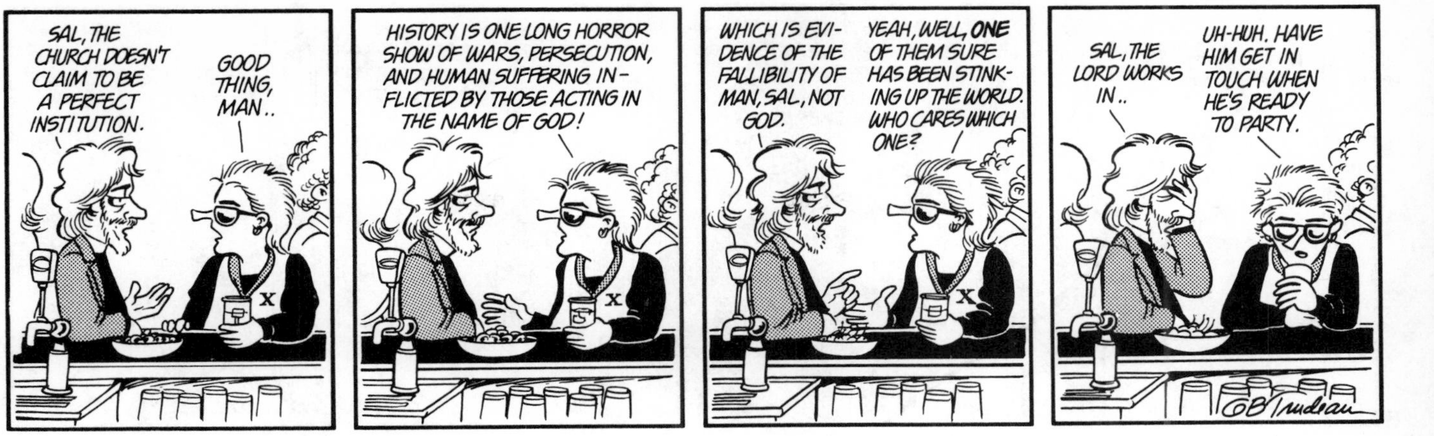
SAL, THE CHURCH DOESN'T CLAIM TO BE A PERFECT INSTITUTION.
GOOD THING, MAN..
HISTORY IS ONE LONG HORROR SHOW OF WARS, PERSECUTION, AND HUMAN SUFFERING INFLICTED BY THOSE ACTING IN THE NAME OF GOD!
WHICH IS EVIDENCE OF THE FALLIBILITY OF MAN, SAL, NOT GOD.
YEAH, WELL, ONE OF THEM SURE HAS BEEN STINKING UP THE WORLD. WHO CARES WHICH ONE?
SAL, THE LORD WORKS IN..
UH-HUH. HAVE HIM GET IN TOUCH WHEN HE'S READY TO PARTY.

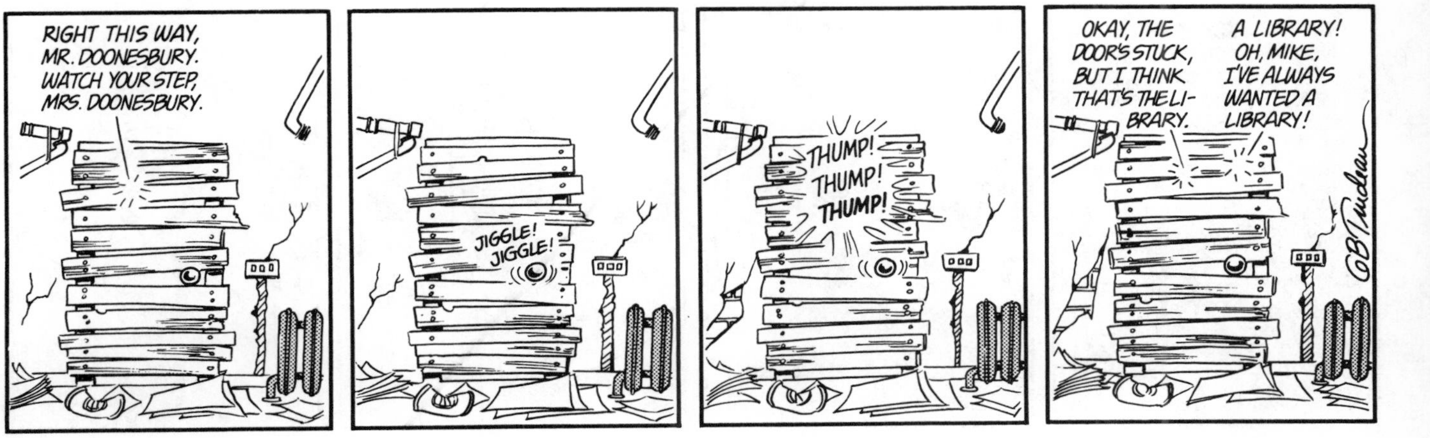
RIGHT THIS WAY, MR. DOONESBURY. WATCH YOUR STEP, MRS. DOONESBURY.
JIGGLE! JIGGLE!
THUMP! THUMP! THUMP!
OKAY, THE DOOR'S STUCK, BUT I THINK THAT'S THE LIBRARY.
A LIBRARY! OH, MIKE, I'VE ALWAYS WANTED A LIBRARY!

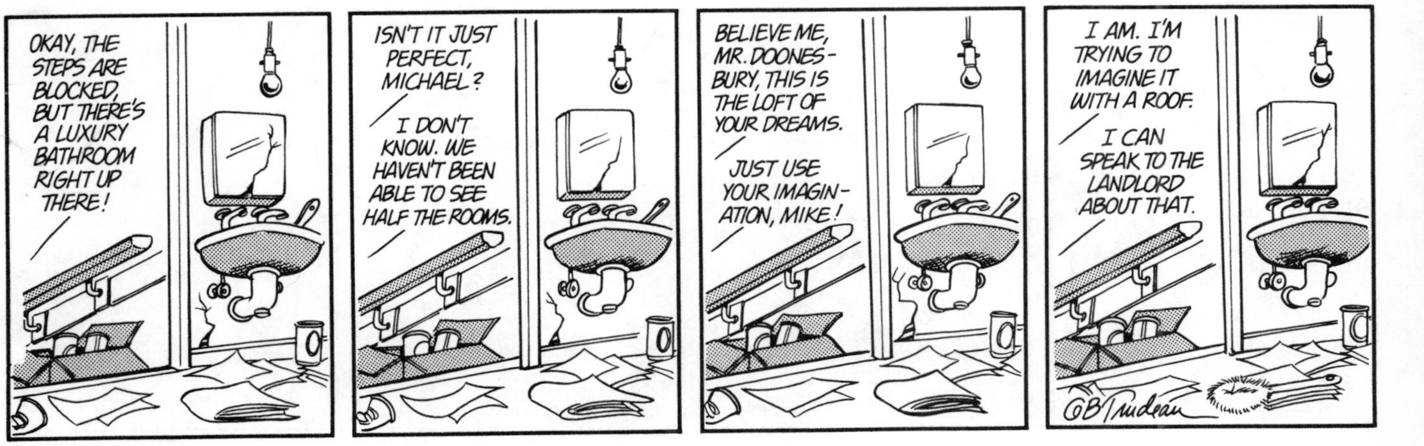
OKAY, THE STEPS ARE BLOCKED, BUT THERE'S A LUXURY BATHROOM RIGHT UP THERE!
ISN'T IT JUST PERFECT, MICHAEL?
I DON'T KNOW. WE HAVEN'T BEEN ABLE TO SEE HALF THE ROOMS.
BELIEVE ME, MR. DOONESBURY, THIS IS THE LOFT OF YOUR DREAMS.
JUST USE YOUR IMAGINATION, MIKE!
I AM. I'M TRYING TO IMAGINE IT WITH A ROOF.
I CAN SPEAK TO THE LANDLORD ABOUT THAT.

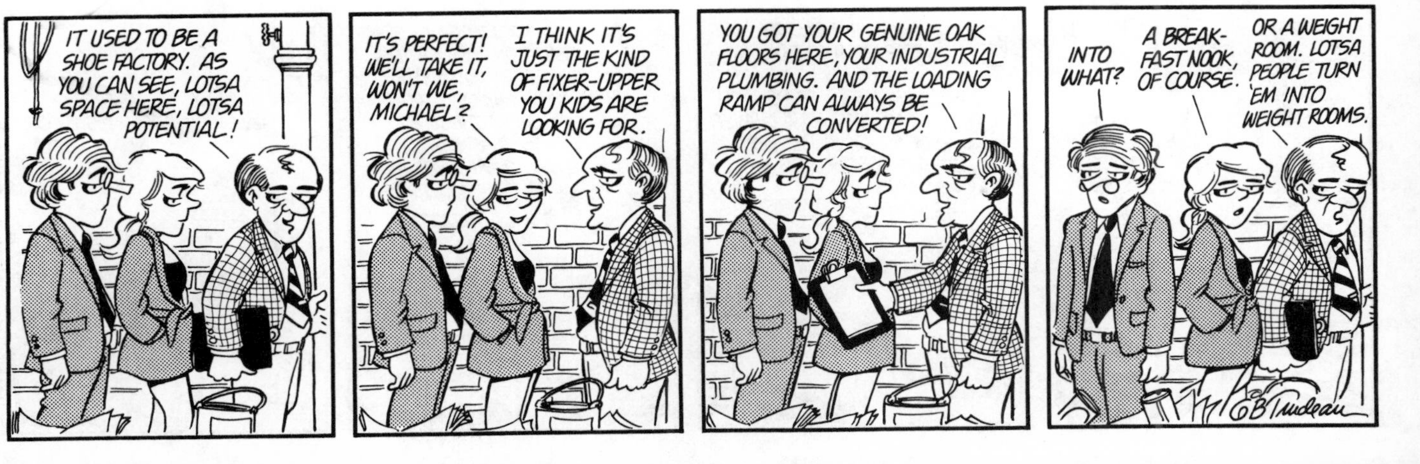
IT USED TO BE A SHOE FACTORY. AS YOU CAN SEE, LOTSA SPACE HERE, LOTSA POTENTIAL!
IT'S PERFECT! WE'LL TAKE IT, WON'T WE, MICHAEL?
I THINK IT'S JUST THE KIND OF FIXER-UPPER YOU KIDS ARE LOOKING FOR.
YOU GOT YOUR GENUINE OAK FLOORS HERE, YOUR INDUSTRIAL PLUMBING. AND THE LOADING RAMP CAN ALWAYS BE CONVERTED!
INTO WHAT?
A BREAKFAST NOOK, OF COURSE.
OR A WEIGHT ROOM. LOTSA PEOPLE TURN 'EM INTO WEIGHT ROOMS.

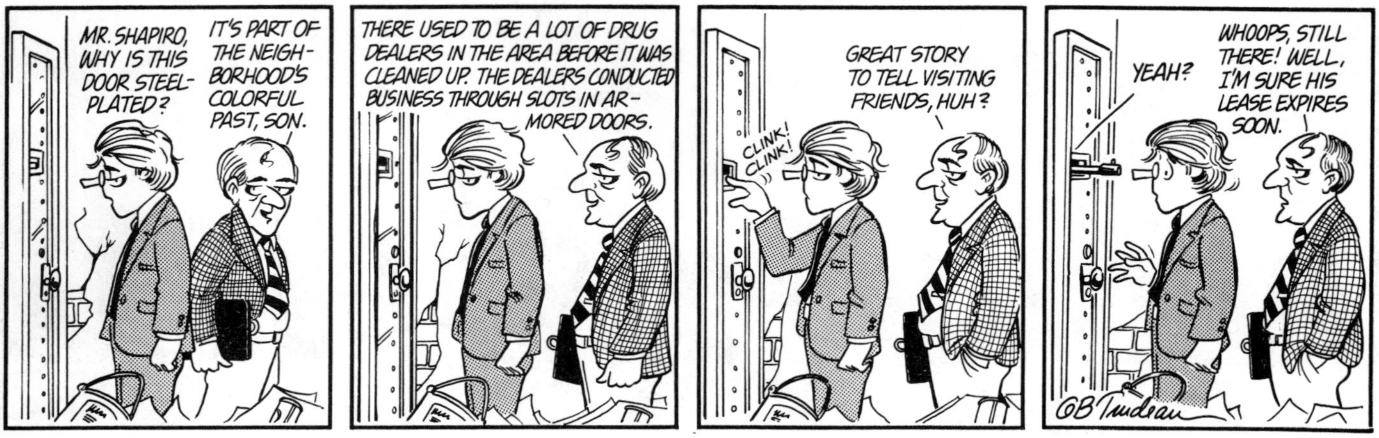
MR. SHAPIRO, WHY IS THIS DOOR STEEL-PLATED?
IT'S PART OF THE NEIGHBORHOOD'S COLORFUL PAST, SON.
THERE USED TO BE A LOT OF DRUG DEALERS IN THE AREA BEFORE IT WAS CLEANED UP. THE DEALERS CONDUCTED BUSINESS THROUGH SLOTS IN ARMORED DOORS.
CLINK! CLINK!
GREAT STORY TO TELL VISITING FRIENDS, HUH?
YEAH?
WHOOPS, STILL THERE! WELL, I'M SURE HIS LEASE EXPIRES SOON.
GB Trudeau

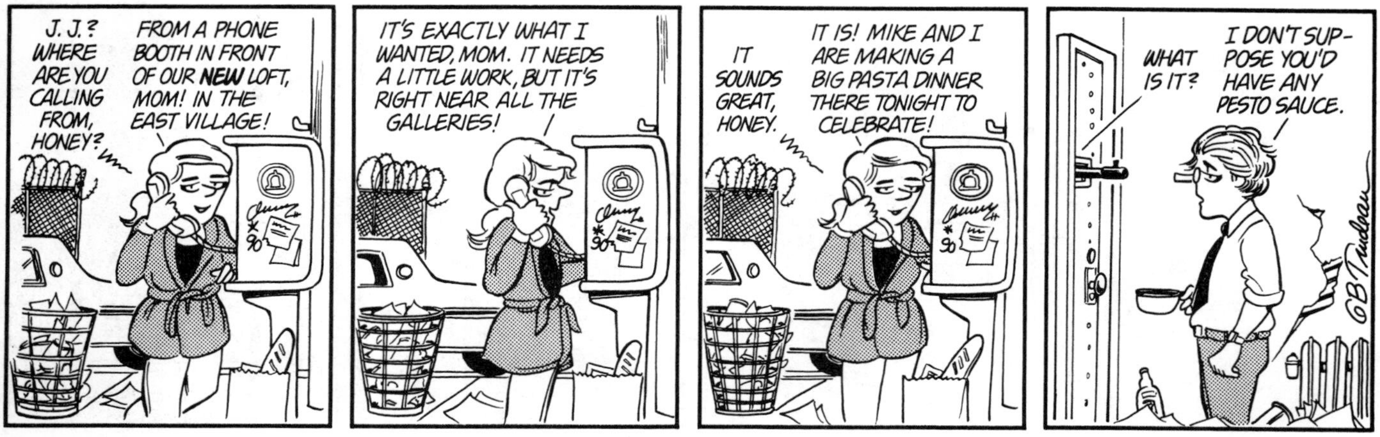
J. J.? WHERE ARE YOU CALLING FROM, HONEY?
FROM A PHONE BOOTH IN FRONT OF OUR **NEW** LOFT, MOM! IN THE EAST VILLAGE!
IT'S EXACTLY WHAT I WANTED, MOM. IT NEEDS A LITTLE WORK, BUT IT'S RIGHT NEAR ALL THE GALLERIES!
IT SOUNDS GREAT, HONEY.
IT IS! MIKE AND I ARE MAKING A BIG PASTA DINNER THERE TONIGHT TO CELEBRATE!
WHAT IS IT?
I DON'T SUPPOSE YOU'D HAVE ANY PESTO SAUCE.
GB Trudeau

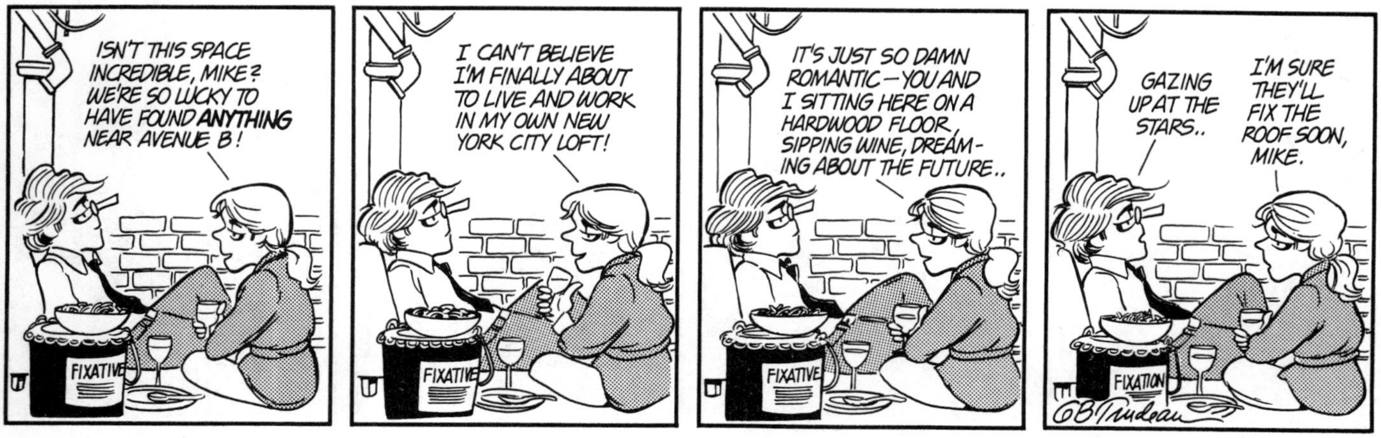
ISN'T THIS SPACE INCREDIBLE, MIKE? WE'RE SO LUCKY TO HAVE FOUND **ANYTHING** NEAR AVENUE B!
FIXATIVE
I CAN'T BELIEVE I'M FINALLY ABOUT TO LIVE AND WORK IN MY OWN NEW YORK CITY LOFT!
FIXATIVE
IT'S JUST SO DAMN ROMANTIC—YOU AND I SITTING HERE ON A HARDWOOD FLOOR, SIPPING WINE, DREAMING ABOUT THE FUTURE..
FIXATIVE
GAZING UP AT THE STARS..
I'M SURE THEY'LL FIX THE ROOF SOON, MIKE.
FIXATION
GB Trudeau

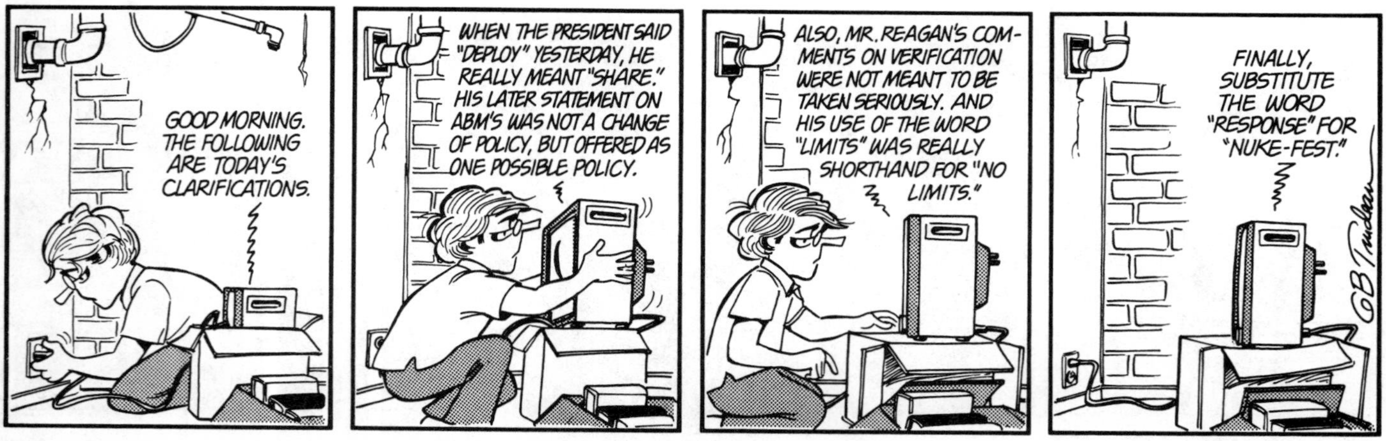
GOOD MORNING. THE FOLLOWING ARE TODAY'S CLARIFICATIONS.
WHEN THE PRESIDENT SAID "DEPLOY" YESTERDAY, HE REALLY MEANT "SHARE." HIS LATER STATEMENT ON ABM'S WAS NOT A CHANGE OF POLICY, BUT OFFERED AS ONE POSSIBLE POLICY.
ALSO, MR. REAGAN'S COMMENTS ON VERIFICATION WERE NOT MEANT TO BE TAKEN SERIOUSLY. AND HIS USE OF THE WORD "LIMITS" WAS REALLY SHORTHAND FOR "NO LIMITS."
FINALLY, SUBSTITUTE THE WORD "RESPONSE" FOR "NUKE-FEST."
GB Trudeau

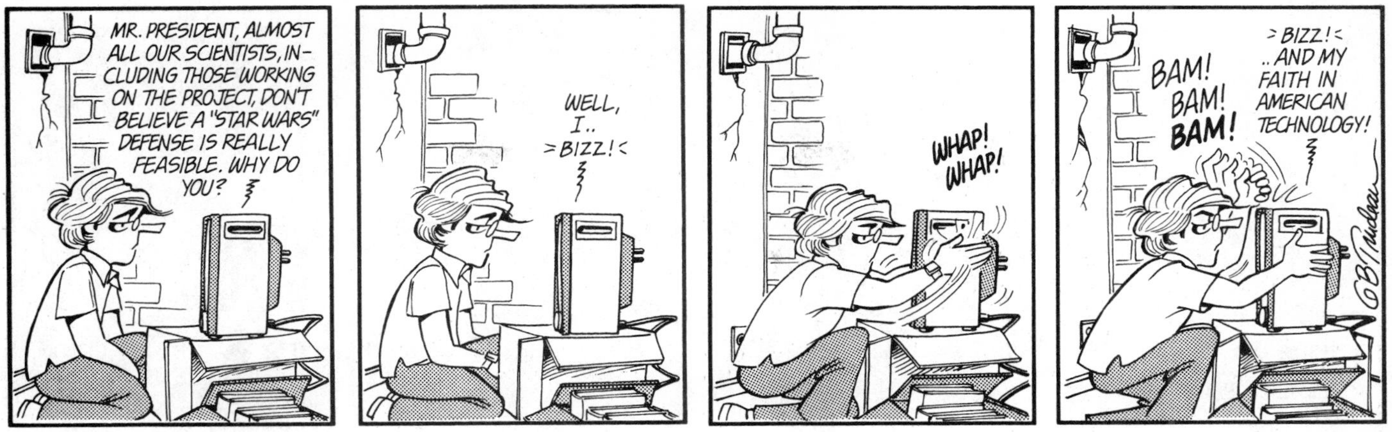
MR. PRESIDENT, ALMOST ALL OUR SCIENTISTS, INCLUDING THOSE WORKING ON THE PROJECT, DON'T BELIEVE A "STAR WARS" DEFENSE IS REALLY FEASIBLE. WHY DO YOU?
WELL, I.. >BIZZ!<
WHAP! WHAP!
BAM! BAM! BAM!
>BIZZ!< ..AND MY FAITH IN AMERICAN TECHNOLOGY!

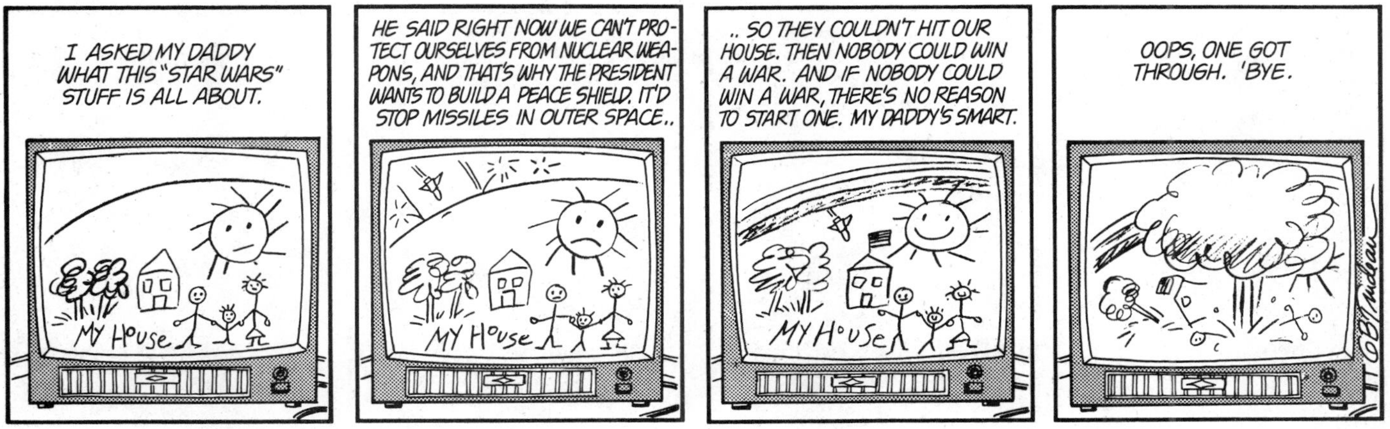
I ASKED MY DADDY WHAT THIS "STAR WARS" STUFF IS ALL ABOUT.
MY House
HE SAID RIGHT NOW WE CAN'T PROTECT OURSELVES FROM NUCLEAR WEAPONS, AND THAT'S WHY THE PRESIDENT WANTS TO BUILD A PEACE SHIELD. IT'D STOP MISSILES IN OUTER SPACE..
MY House
.. SO THEY COULDN'T HIT OUR HOUSE. THEN NOBODY COULD WIN A WAR. AND IF NOBODY COULD WIN A WAR, THERE'S NO REASON TO START ONE. MY DADDY'S SMART.
MY House
OOPS, ONE GOT THROUGH. 'BYE.

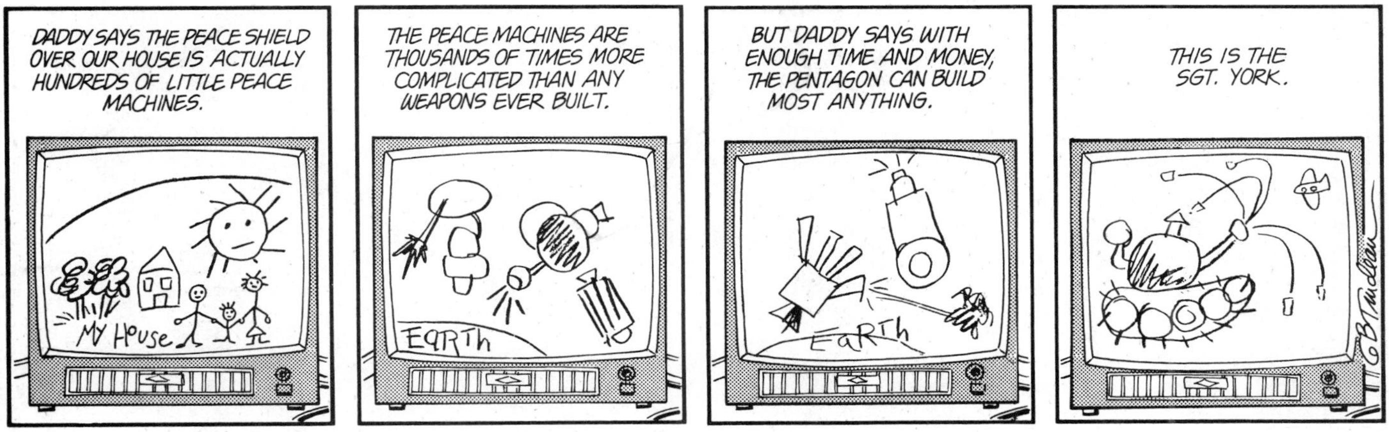
DADDY SAYS THE PEACE SHIELD OVER OUR HOUSE IS ACTUALLY HUNDREDS OF LITTLE PEACE MACHINES.
MY House
THE PEACE MACHINES ARE THOUSANDS OF TIMES MORE COMPLICATED THAN ANY WEAPONS EVER BUILT.
EarTh
BUT DADDY SAYS WITH ENOUGH TIME AND MONEY, THE PENTAGON CAN BUILD MOST ANYTHING.
EarTh
THIS IS THE SGT. YORK.

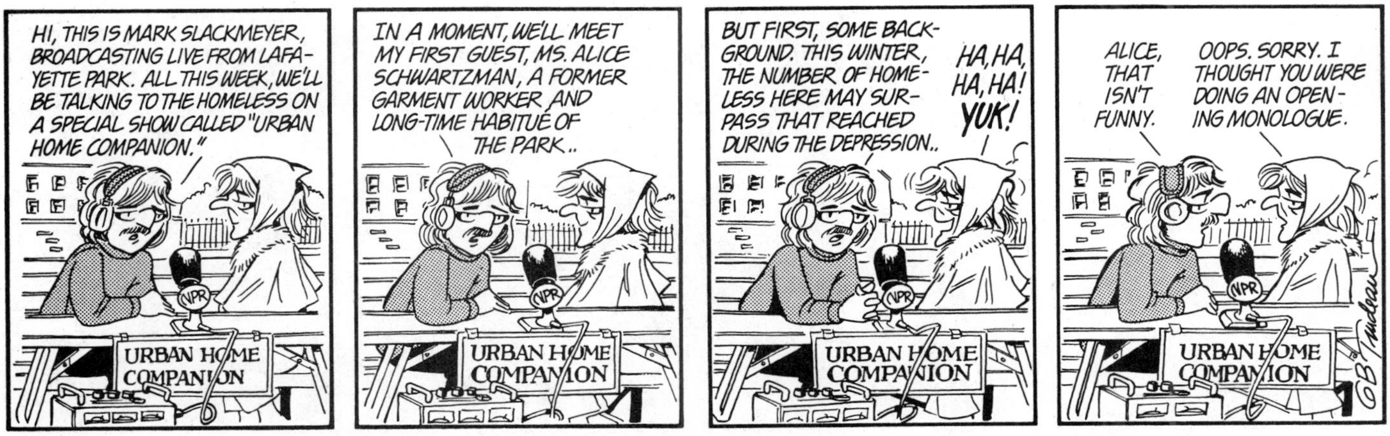
HI, THIS IS MARK SLACKMEYER, BROADCASTING LIVE FROM LAFAYETTE PARK. ALL THIS WEEK, WE'LL BE TALKING TO THE HOMELESS ON A SPECIAL SHOW CALLED "URBAN HOME COMPANION."
NPR
URBAN HOME COMPANION
IN A MOMENT, WE'LL MEET MY FIRST GUEST, MS. ALICE SCHWARTZMAN, A FORMER GARMENT WORKER AND LONG-TIME HABITUÉ OF THE PARK..
NPR
URBAN HOME COMPANION
BUT FIRST, SOME BACKGROUND. THIS WINTER, THE NUMBER OF HOMELESS HERE MAY SURPASS THAT REACHED DURING THE DEPRESSION..
HA, HA, HA, HA! YUK!
NPR
URBAN HOME COMPANION
ALICE, THAT ISN'T FUNNY.
OOPS. SORRY. I THOUGHT YOU WERE DOING AN OPENING MONOLOGUE.
NPR
URBAN HOME COMPANION

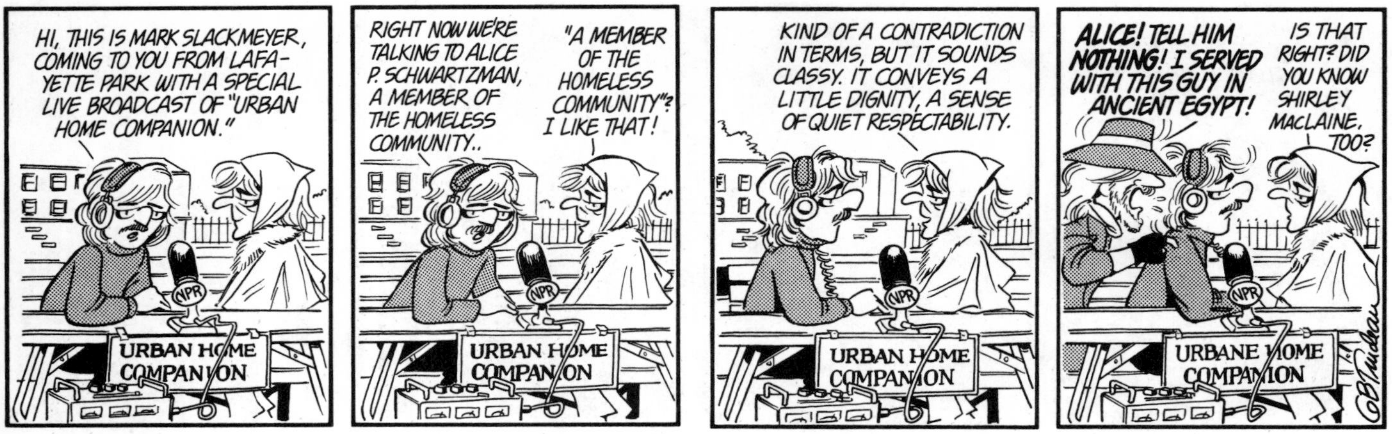
HI, THIS IS MARK SLACKMEYER, COMING TO YOU FROM LAFAYETTE PARK WITH A SPECIAL LIVE BROADCAST OF "URBAN HOME COMPANION."
NPR
URBAN HOME COMPANION
RIGHT NOW WE'RE TALKING TO ALICE P. SCHWARTZMAN, A MEMBER OF THE HOMELESS COMMUNITY..
"A MEMBER OF THE HOMELESS COMMUNITY"? I LIKE THAT!
NPR
URBAN HOME COMPANION
KIND OF A CONTRADICTION IN TERMS, BUT IT SOUNDS CLASSY. IT CONVEYS A LITTLE DIGNITY, A SENSE OF QUIET RESPECTABILITY.
NPR
URBAN HOME COMPANION
ALICE! TELL HIM NOTHING! I SERVED WITH THIS GUY IN ANCIENT EGYPT!
IS THAT RIGHT? DID YOU KNOW SHIRLEY MACLAINE, TOO?
NPR
URBANE HOME COMPANION
GBTrudeau

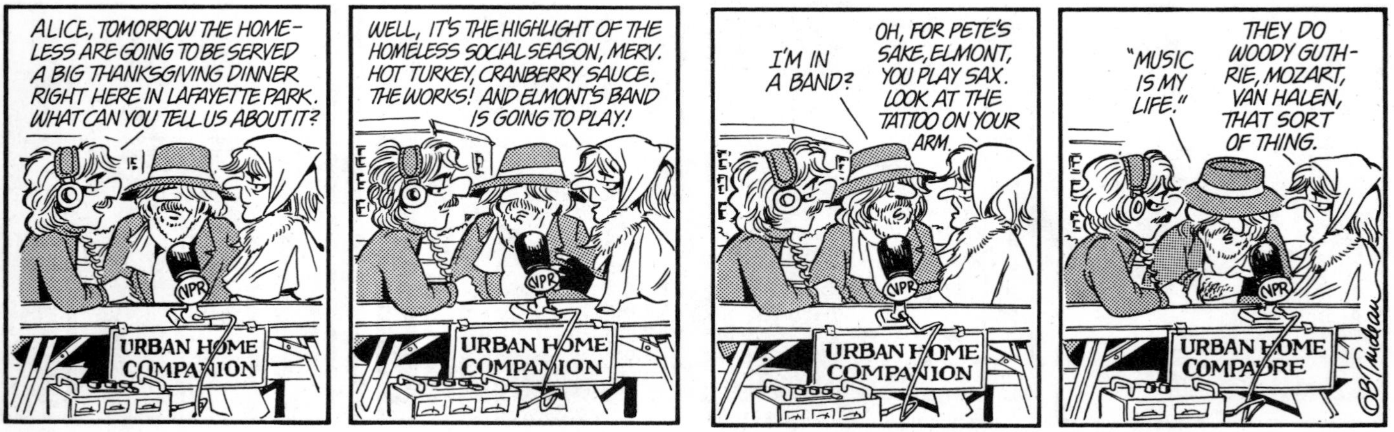
ALICE, TOMORROW THE HOMELESS ARE GOING TO BE SERVED A BIG THANKSGIVING DINNER RIGHT HERE IN LAFAYETTE PARK. WHAT CAN YOU TELL US ABOUT IT?
NPR
URBAN HOME COMPANION
WELL, IT'S THE HIGHLIGHT OF THE HOMELESS SOCIAL SEASON, MERV. HOT TURKEY, CRANBERRY SAUCE, THE WORKS! AND ELMONT'S BAND IS GOING TO PLAY!
NPR
URBAN HOME COMPANION
I'M IN A BAND?
OH, FOR PETE'S SAKE, ELMONT, YOU PLAY SAX. LOOK AT THE TATTOO ON YOUR ARM.
NPR
URBAN HOME COMPANION
"MUSIC IS MY LIFE."
THEY DO WOODY GUTHRIE, MOZART, VAN HALEN, THAT SORT OF THING.
NPR
URBAN HOME COMPADRE
GBTrudeau

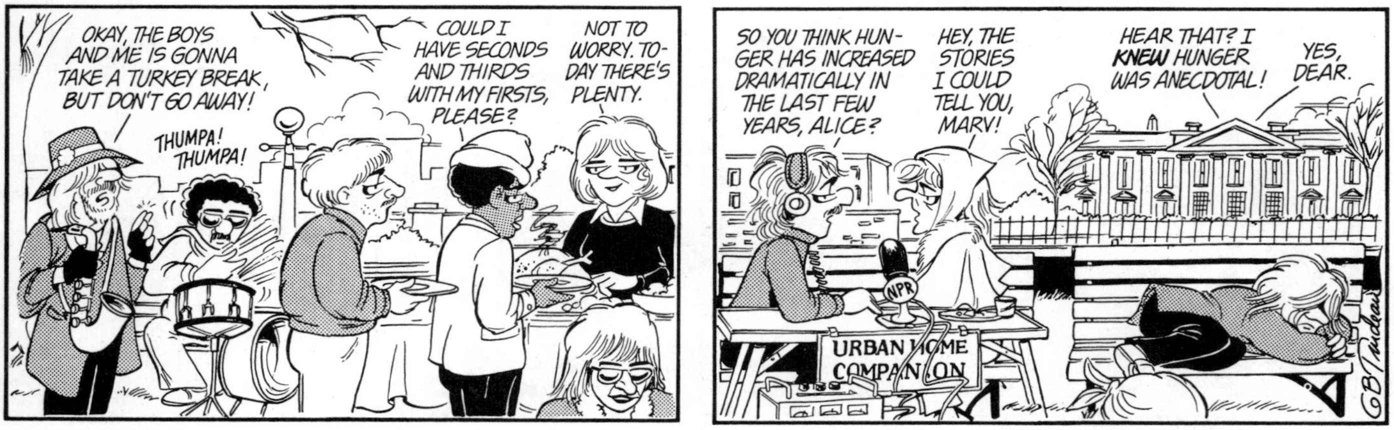
OKAY, THE BOYS AND ME IS GONNA TAKE A TURKEY BREAK, BUT DON'T GO AWAY!
THUMPA! THUMPA!
COULD I HAVE SECONDS AND THIRDS WITH MY FIRSTS, PLEASE?
NOT TO WORRY. TODAY THERE'S PLENTY.
SO YOU THINK HUNGER HAS INCREASED DRAMATICALLY IN THE LAST FEW YEARS, ALICE?
HEY, THE STORIES I COULD TELL YOU, MARV!
HEAR THAT? I KNEW HUNGER WAS ANECDOTAL!
YES, DEAR.
NPR
URBAN HOME COMPANION
GBTrudeau

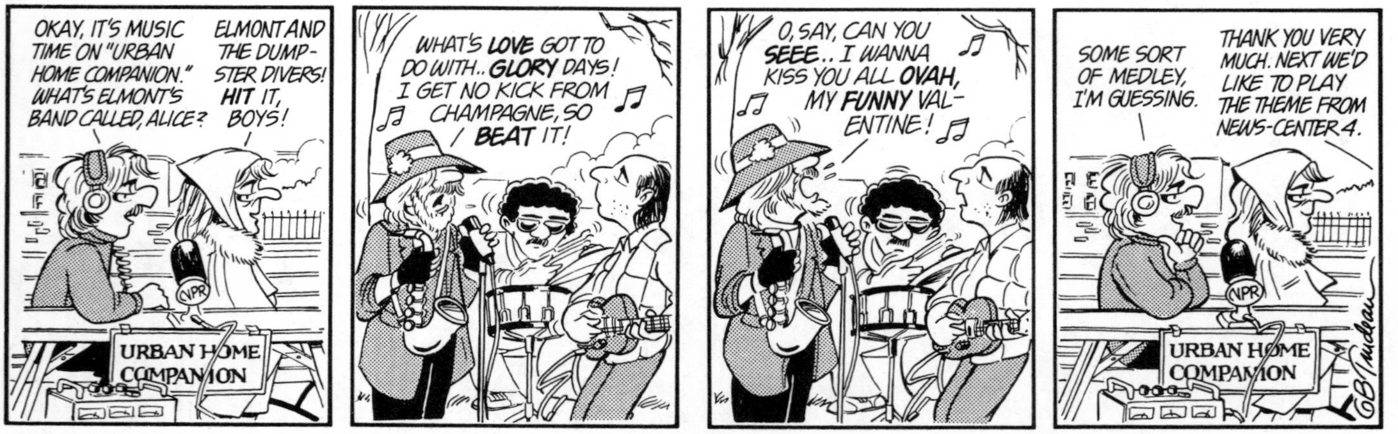
OKAY, IT'S MUSIC TIME ON "URBAN HOME COMPANION." WHAT'S ELMONT'S BAND CALLED, ALICE?
ELMONT AND THE DUMPSTER DIVERS! HIT IT, BOYS!
NPR
URBAN HOME COMPANION
WHAT'S LOVE GOT TO DO WITH.. GLORY DAYS! I GET NO KICK FROM CHAMPAGNE, SO BEAT IT!
O, SAY, CAN YOU SEEE... I WANNA KISS YOU ALL OVAH, MY FUNNY VALENTINE!
SOME SORT OF MEDLEY, I'M GUESSING.
THANK YOU VERY MUCH. NEXT WE'D LIKE TO PLAY THE THEME FROM NEWS-CENTER 4.
NPR
URBAN HOME COMPANION
GBTrudeau

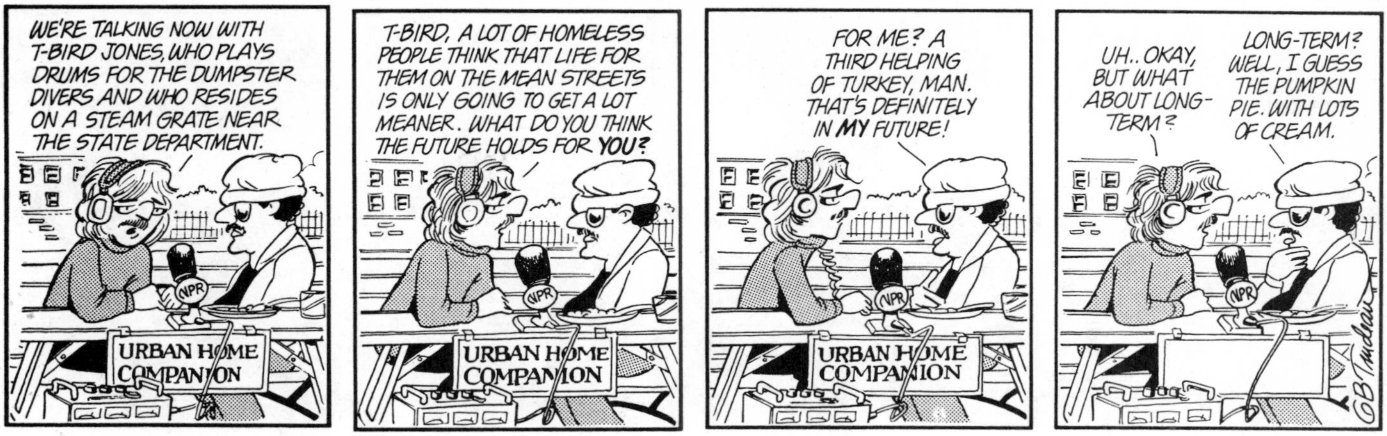
WE'RE TALKING NOW WITH T-BIRD JONES, WHO PLAYS DRUMS FOR THE DUMPSTER DIVERS AND WHO RESIDES ON A STEAM GRATE NEAR THE STATE DEPARTMENT.
URBAN HOME COMPANION
T-BIRD, A LOT OF HOMELESS PEOPLE THINK THAT LIFE FOR THEM ON THE MEAN STREETS IS ONLY GOING TO GET A LOT MEANER. WHAT DO YOU THINK THE FUTURE HOLDS FOR YOU?
URBAN HOME COMPANION
FOR ME? A THIRD HELPING OF TURKEY, MAN. THAT'S DEFINITELY IN MY FUTURE!
URBAN HOME COMPANION
UH.. OKAY, BUT WHAT ABOUT LONG-TERM?
LONG-TERM? WELL, I GUESS THE PUMPKIN PIE. WITH LOTS OF CREAM.
©B Trudeau

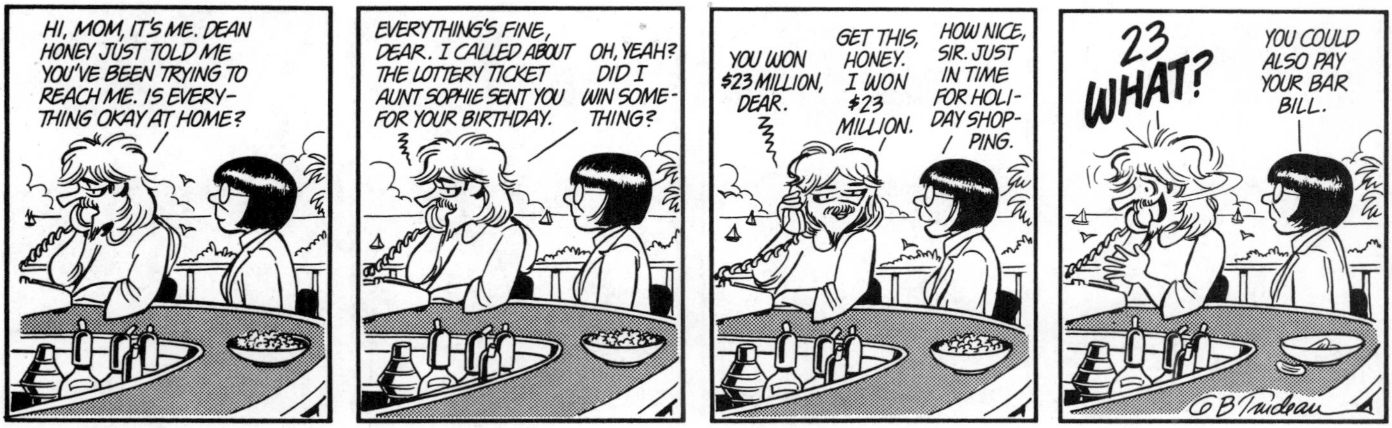
HI, MOM, IT'S ME. DEAN HONEY JUST TOLD ME YOU'VE BEEN TRYING TO REACH ME. IS EVERYTHING OKAY AT HOME?
EVERYTHING'S FINE, DEAR. I CALLED ABOUT THE LOTTERY TICKET AUNT SOPHIE SENT YOU FOR YOUR BIRTHDAY.
OH, YEAH? DID I WIN SOMETHING?
YOU WON $23 MILLION, DEAR.
GET THIS, HONEY. I WON $23 MILLION.
HOW NICE, SIR. JUST IN TIME FOR HOLIDAY SHOPPING.
23 WHAT?
YOU COULD ALSO PAY YOUR BAR BILL.
©B Trudeau

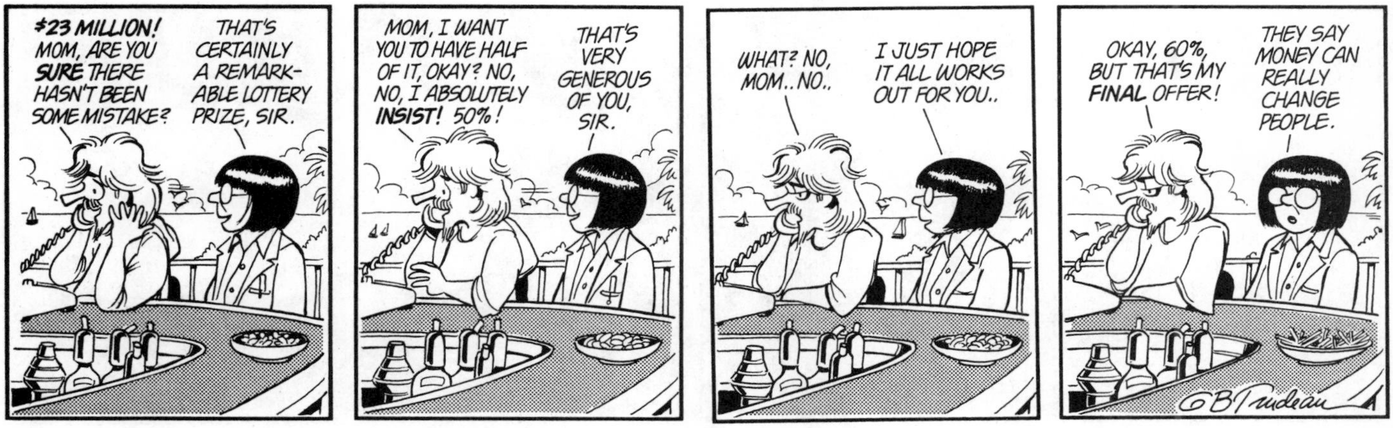
$23 MILLION! MOM, ARE YOU SURE THERE HASN'T BEEN SOME MISTAKE?
THAT'S CERTAINLY A REMARKABLE LOTTERY PRIZE, SIR.
MOM, I WANT YOU TO HAVE HALF OF IT, OKAY? NO, NO, I ABSOLUTELY INSIST! 50%!
THAT'S VERY GENEROUS OF YOU, SIR.
WHAT? NO, MOM.. NO..
I JUST HOPE IT ALL WORKS OUT FOR YOU..
OKAY, 60%, BUT THAT'S MY FINAL OFFER!
THEY SAY MONEY CAN REALLY CHANGE PEOPLE.
©B Trudeau

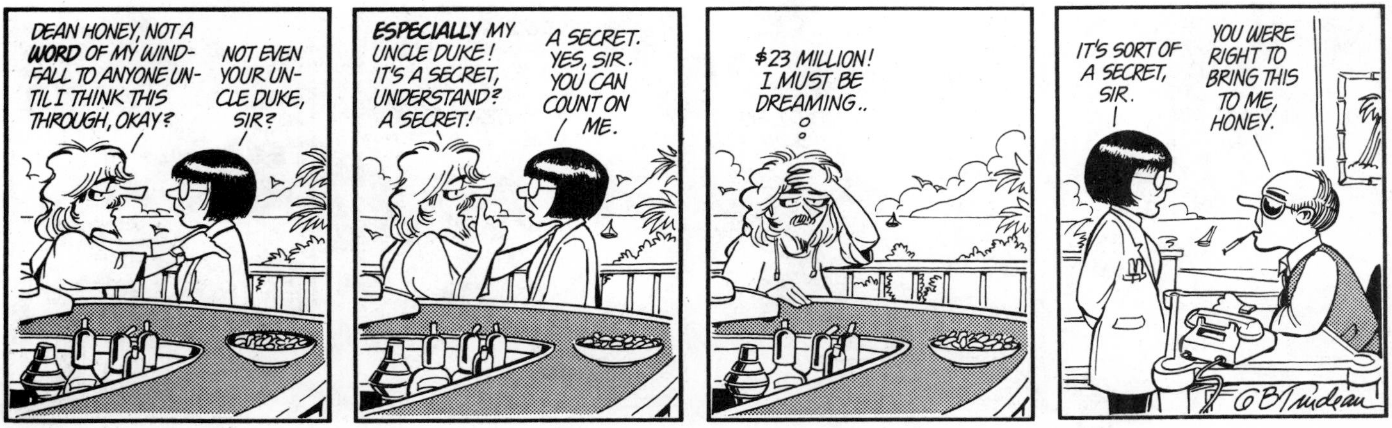
DEAN HONEY, NOT A WORD OF MY WINDFALL TO ANYONE UNTIL I THINK THIS THROUGH, OKAY?
NOT EVEN YOUR UNCLE DUKE, SIR?
ESPECIALLY MY UNCLE DUKE! IT'S A SECRET, UNDERSTAND? A SECRET!
A SECRET. YES, SIR. YOU CAN COUNT ON ME.
$23 MILLION! I MUST BE DREAMING..
IT'S SORT OF A SECRET, SIR.
YOU WERE RIGHT TO BRING THIS TO ME, HONEY.
©B Trudeau

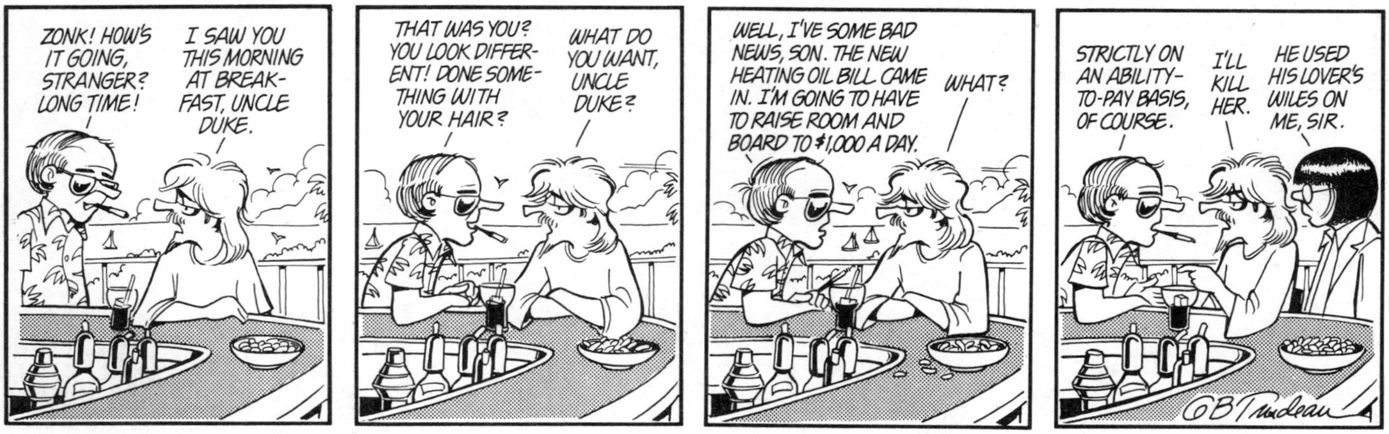
ZONK! HOW'S IT GOING, STRANGER? LONG TIME!
I SAW YOU THIS MORNING AT BREAKFAST, UNCLE DUKE.
THAT WAS YOU? YOU LOOK DIFFERENT! DONE SOMETHING WITH YOUR HAIR?
WHAT DO YOU WANT, UNCLE DUKE?
WELL, I'VE SOME BAD NEWS, SON. THE NEW HEATING OIL BILL CAME IN. I'M GOING TO HAVE TO RAISE ROOM AND BOARD TO $1,000 A DAY.
WHAT?
STRICTLY ON AN ABILITY-TO-PAY BASIS, OF COURSE.
I'LL KILL HER.
HE USED HIS LOVER'S WILES ON ME, SIR.
©B Trudeau

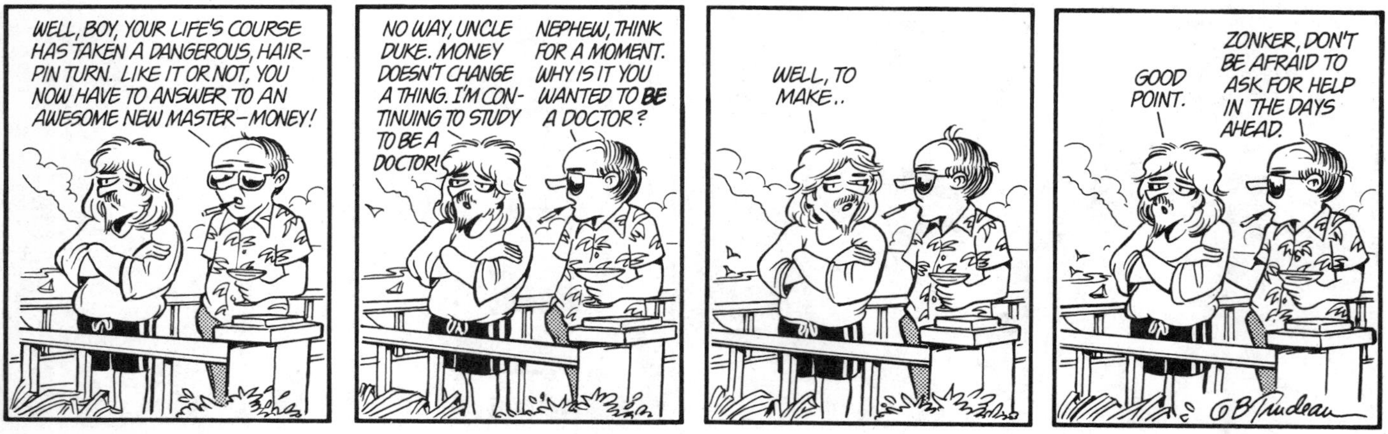
WELL, BOY, YOUR LIFE'S COURSE HAS TAKEN A DANGEROUS, HAIRPIN TURN. LIKE IT OR NOT, YOU NOW HAVE TO ANSWER TO AN AWESOME NEW MASTER—MONEY!
NO WAY, UNCLE DUKE. MONEY DOESN'T CHANGE A THING. I'M CONTINUING TO STUDY TO BE A DOCTOR!
NEPHEW, THINK FOR A MOMENT. WHY IS IT YOU WANTED TO **BE** A DOCTOR?
WELL, TO MAKE..
GOOD POINT.
ZONKER, DON'T BE AFRAID TO ASK FOR HELP IN THE DAYS AHEAD.
©B Trudeau

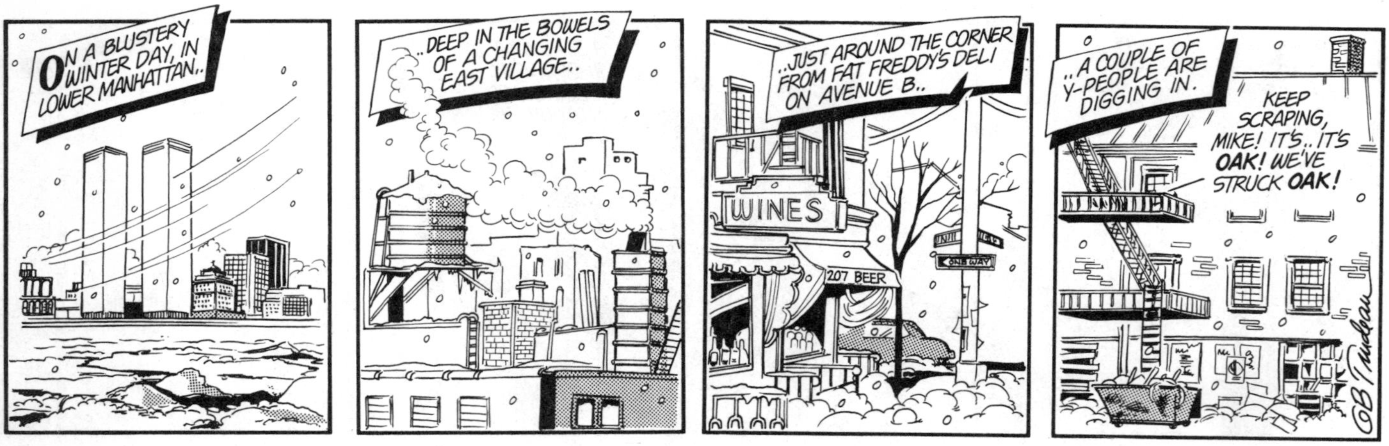
ON A BLUSTERY WINTER DAY, IN LOWER MANHATTAN..
..DEEP IN THE BOWELS OF A CHANGING EAST VILLAGE..
..JUST AROUND THE CORNER FROM FAT FREDDY'S DELI ON AVENUE B..
WINES
207 BEER
ONE WAY
..A COUPLE OF Y-PEOPLE ARE DIGGING IN.
KEEP SCRAPING, MIKE! IT'S.. IT'S **OAK**! WE'VE STRUCK **OAK**!
©B Trudeau

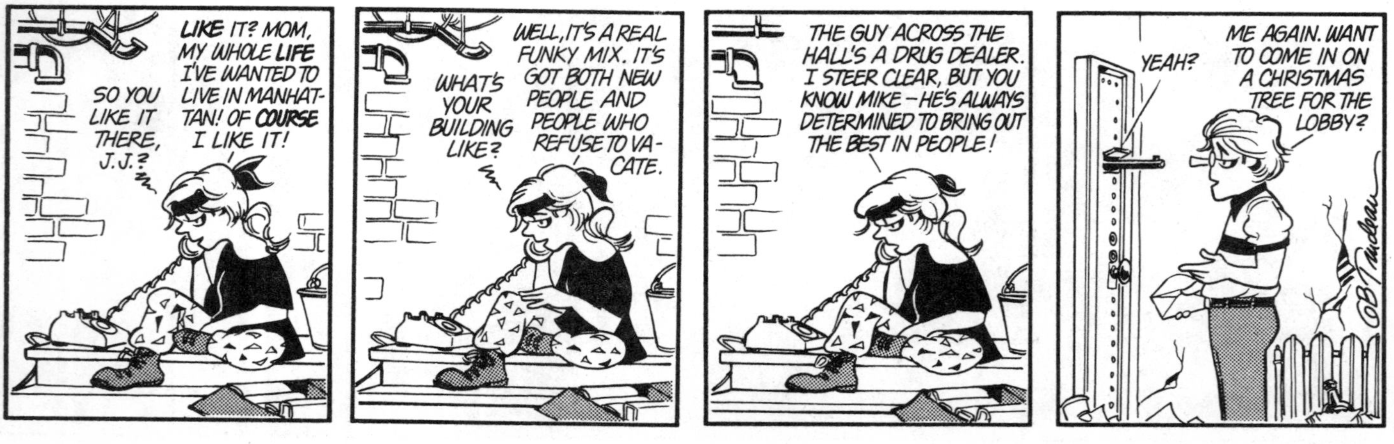
SO YOU LIKE IT THERE, J.J.?
LIKE IT? MOM, MY WHOLE **LIFE** I'VE WANTED TO LIVE IN MANHATTAN! OF **COURSE** I LIKE IT!
WHAT'S YOUR BUILDING LIKE?
WELL, IT'S A REAL FUNKY MIX. IT'S GOT BOTH NEW PEOPLE AND PEOPLE WHO REFUSE TO VACATE.
THE GUY ACROSS THE HALL'S A DRUG DEALER. I STEER CLEAR, BUT YOU KNOW MIKE—HE'S ALWAYS DETERMINED TO BRING OUT THE BEST IN PEOPLE!
YEAH?
ME AGAIN. WANT TO COME IN ON A CHRISTMAS TREE FOR THE LOBBY?
©B Trudeau

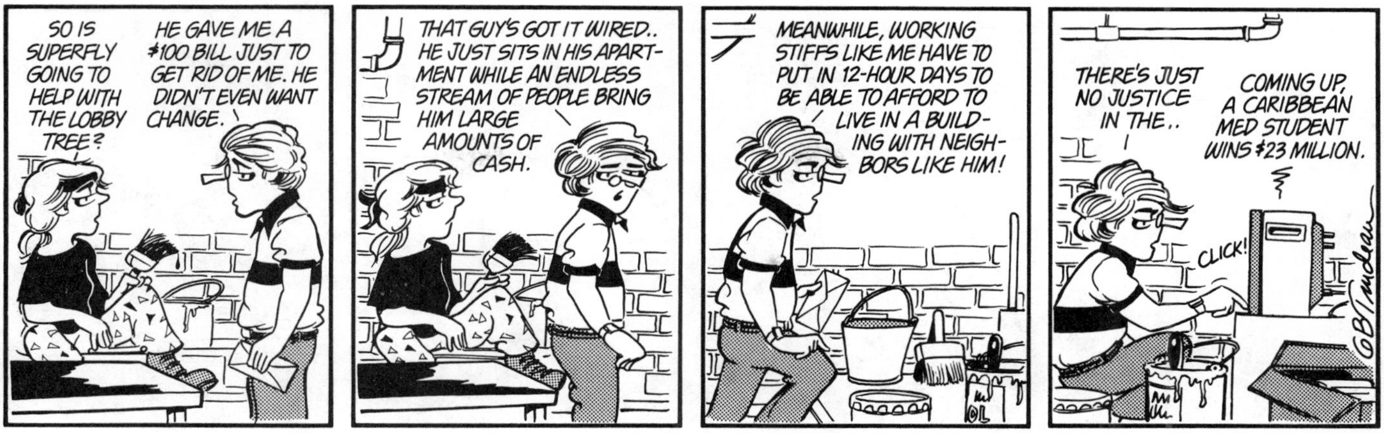
SO IS SUPERFLY GOING TO HELP WITH THE LOBBY TREE?
HE GAVE ME A $100 BILL JUST TO GET RID OF ME. HE DIDN'T EVEN WANT CHANGE.
THAT GUY'S GOT IT WIRED.. HE JUST SITS IN HIS APARTMENT WHILE AN ENDLESS STREAM OF PEOPLE BRING HIM LARGE AMOUNTS OF CASH.
MEANWHILE, WORKING STIFFS LIKE ME HAVE TO PUT IN 12-HOUR DAYS TO BE ABLE TO AFFORD TO LIVE IN A BUILDING WITH NEIGHBORS LIKE HIM!
THERE'S JUST NO JUSTICE IN THE..
COMING UP, A CARIBBEAN MED STUDENT WINS $23 MILLION.
CLICK!
G.B. Trudeau

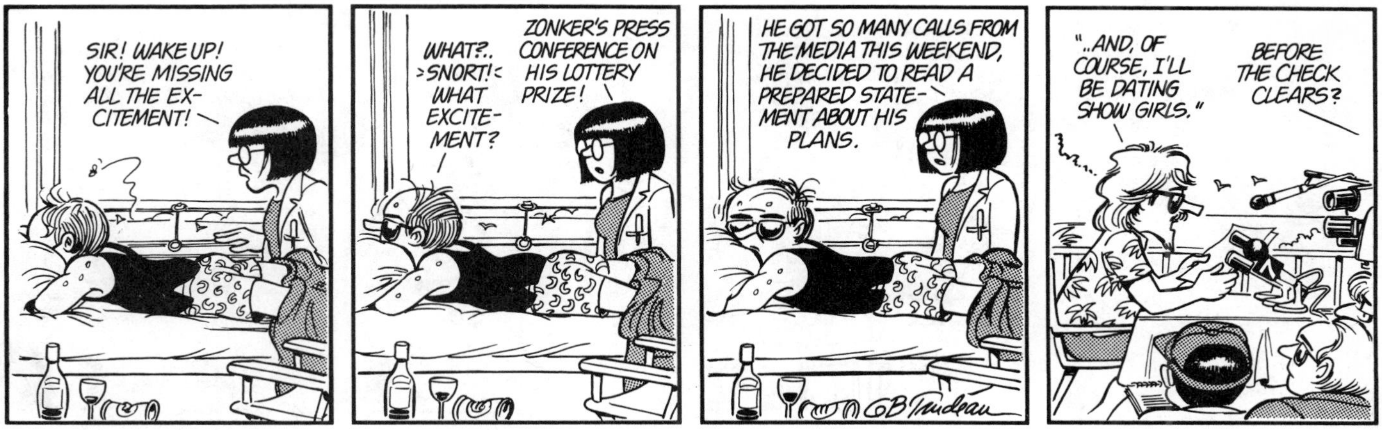
SIR! WAKE UP! YOU'RE MISSING ALL THE EXCITEMENT!
WHAT?.. >SNORT!< WHAT EXCITEMENT?
ZONKER'S PRESS CONFERENCE ON HIS LOTTERY PRIZE!
HE GOT SO MANY CALLS FROM THE MEDIA THIS WEEKEND, HE DECIDED TO READ A PREPARED STATEMENT ABOUT HIS PLANS.
G.B. Trudeau
"..AND, OF COURSE, I'LL BE DATING SHOW GIRLS."
BEFORE THE CHECK CLEARS?

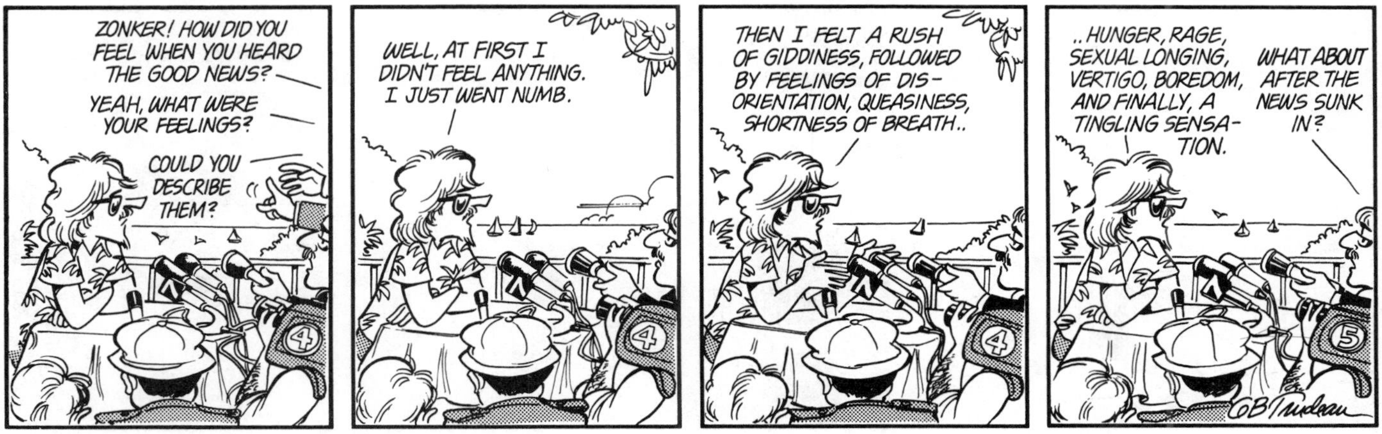
ZONKER! HOW DID YOU FEEL WHEN YOU HEARD THE GOOD NEWS?
YEAH, WHAT WERE YOUR FEELINGS?
COULD YOU DESCRIBE THEM?
WELL, AT FIRST I DIDN'T FEEL ANYTHING. I JUST WENT NUMB.
THEN I FELT A RUSH OF GIDDINESS, FOLLOWED BY FEELINGS OF DISORIENTATION, QUEASINESS, SHORTNESS OF BREATH..
..HUNGER, RAGE, SEXUAL LONGING, VERTIGO, BOREDOM, AND FINALLY, A TINGLING SENSATION.
WHAT ABOUT AFTER THE NEWS SUNK IN?
G.B. Trudeau

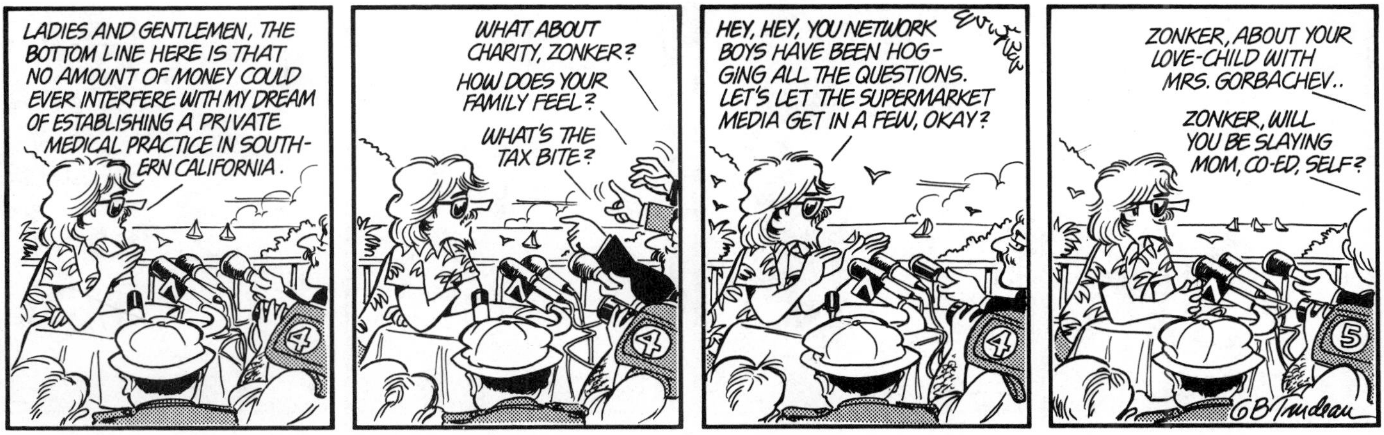
LADIES AND GENTLEMEN, THE BOTTOM LINE HERE IS THAT NO AMOUNT OF MONEY COULD EVER INTERFERE WITH MY DREAM OF ESTABLISHING A PRIVATE MEDICAL PRACTICE IN SOUTHERN CALIFORNIA.
WHAT ABOUT CHARITY, ZONKER?
HOW DOES YOUR FAMILY FEEL?
WHAT'S THE TAX BITE?
HEY, HEY, YOU NETWORK BOYS HAVE BEEN HOGGING ALL THE QUESTIONS. LET'S LET THE SUPERMARKET MEDIA GET IN A FEW, OKAY?
ZONKER, ABOUT YOUR LOVE-CHILD WITH MRS. GORBACHEV..
ZONKER, WILL YOU BE SLAYING MOM, CO-ED, SELF?
G.B. Trudeau

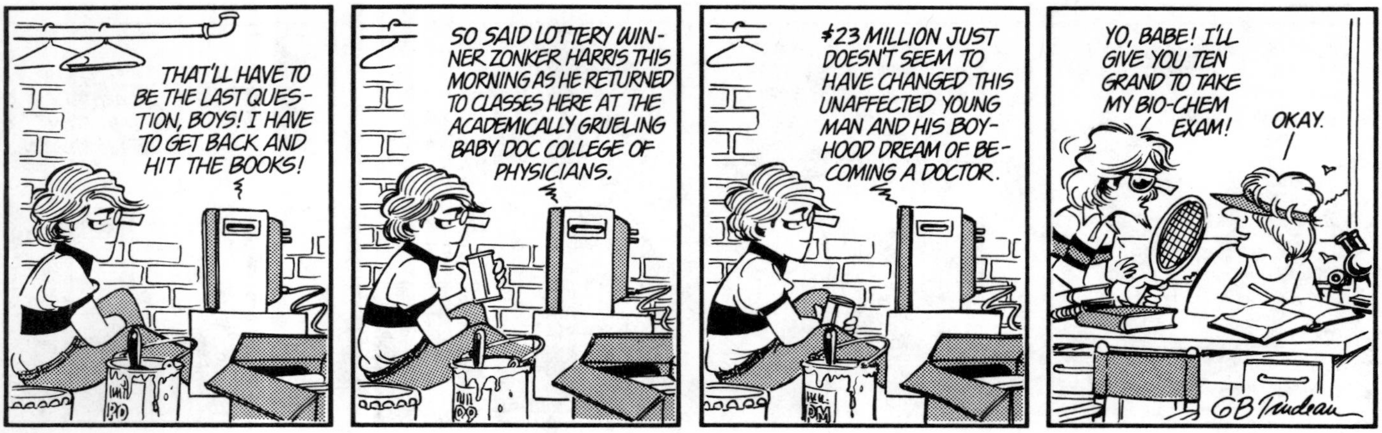
THAT'LL HAVE TO BE THE LAST QUESTION, BOYS! I HAVE TO GET BACK AND HIT THE BOOKS!
SO SAID LOTTERY WINNER ZONKER HARRIS THIS MORNING AS HE RETURNED TO CLASSES HERE AT THE ACADEMICALLY GRUELING BABY DOC COLLEGE OF PHYSICIANS.
$23 MILLION JUST DOESN'T SEEM TO HAVE CHANGED THIS UNAFFECTED YOUNG MAN AND HIS BOYHOOD DREAM OF BECOMING A DOCTOR.
YO, BABE! I'LL GIVE YOU TEN GRAND TO TAKE MY BIO-CHEM EXAM!
OKAY.
GB Trudeau

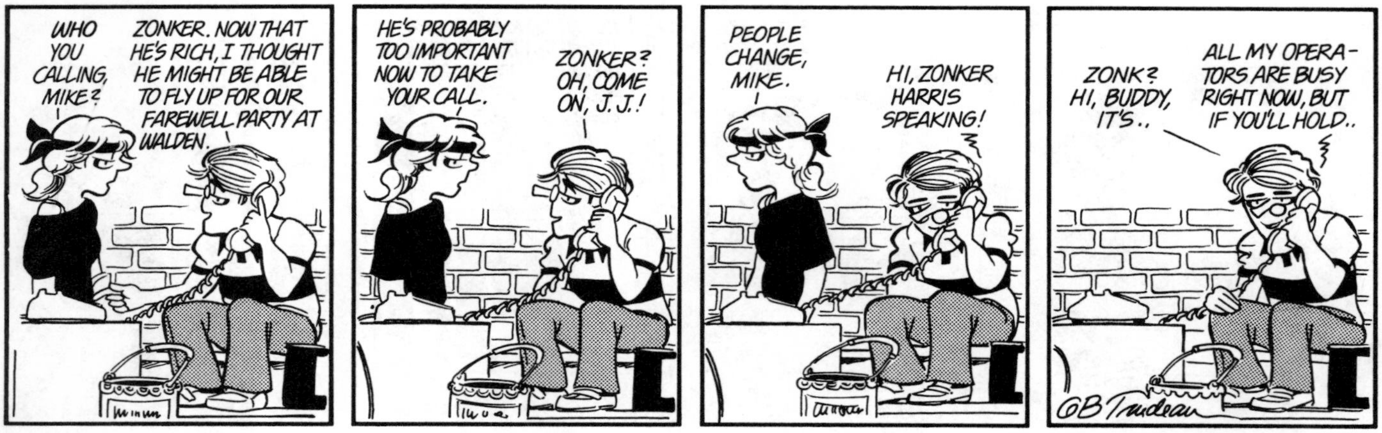
WHO YOU CALLING, MIKE?
ZONKER. NOW THAT HE'S RICH, I THOUGHT HE MIGHT BE ABLE TO FLY UP FOR OUR FAREWELL PARTY AT WALDEN.
HE'S PROBABLY TOO IMPORTANT NOW TO TAKE YOUR CALL.
ZONKER? OH, COME ON, J.J.!
PEOPLE CHANGE, MIKE.
HI, ZONKER HARRIS SPEAKING!
ZONK? HI, BUDDY, IT'S..
ALL MY OPERATORS ARE BUSY RIGHT NOW, BUT IF YOU'LL HOLD..
GB Trudeau

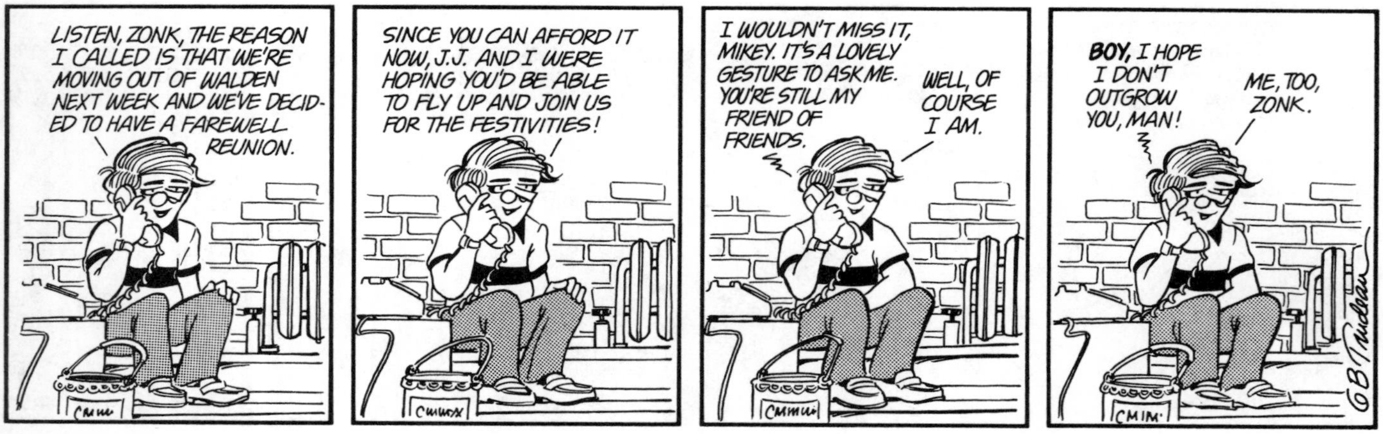
LISTEN, ZONK, THE REASON I CALLED IS THAT WE'RE MOVING OUT OF WALDEN NEXT WEEK AND WE'VE DECIDED TO HAVE A FAREWELL REUNION.
SINCE YOU CAN AFFORD IT NOW, J.J. AND I WERE HOPING YOU'D BE ABLE TO FLY UP AND JOIN US FOR THE FESTIVITIES!
I WOULDN'T MISS IT, MIKEY. IT'S A LOVELY GESTURE TO ASK ME. YOU'RE STILL MY FRIEND OF FRIENDS.
WELL, OF COURSE I AM.
BOY, I HOPE I DON'T OUTGROW YOU, MAN!
ME, TOO, ZONK.
GB Trudeau

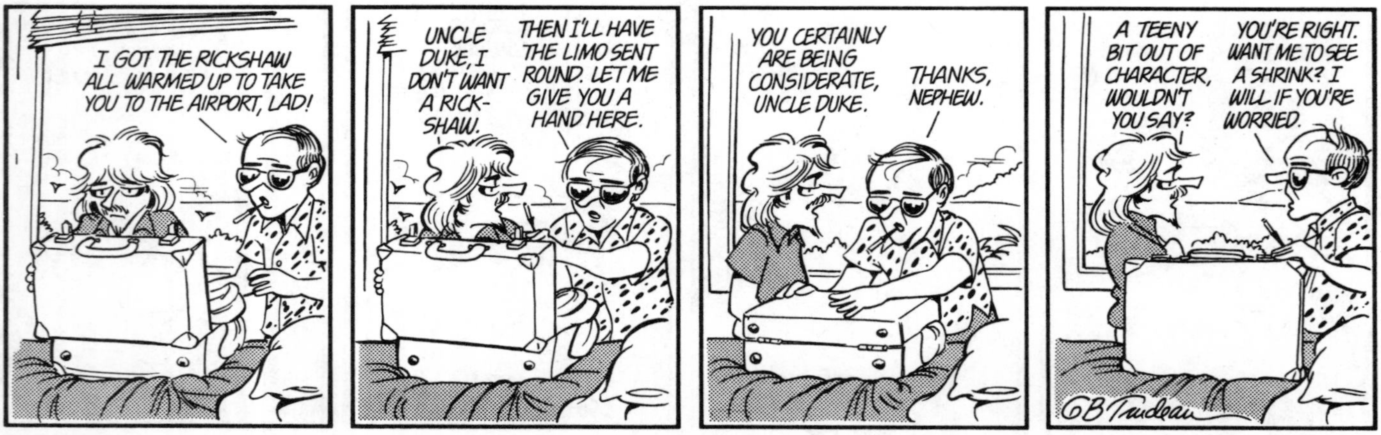
I GOT THE RICKSHAW ALL WARMED UP TO TAKE YOU TO THE AIRPORT, LAD!
UNCLE DUKE, I DON'T WANT A RICKSHAW.
THEN I'LL HAVE THE LIMO SENT ROUND. LET ME GIVE YOU A HAND HERE.
YOU CERTAINLY ARE BEING CONSIDERATE, UNCLE DUKE.
THANKS, NEPHEW.
A TEENY BIT OUT OF CHARACTER, WOULDN'T YOU SAY?
YOU'RE RIGHT. WANT ME TO SEE A SHRINK? I WILL IF YOU'RE WORRIED.
GB Trudeau

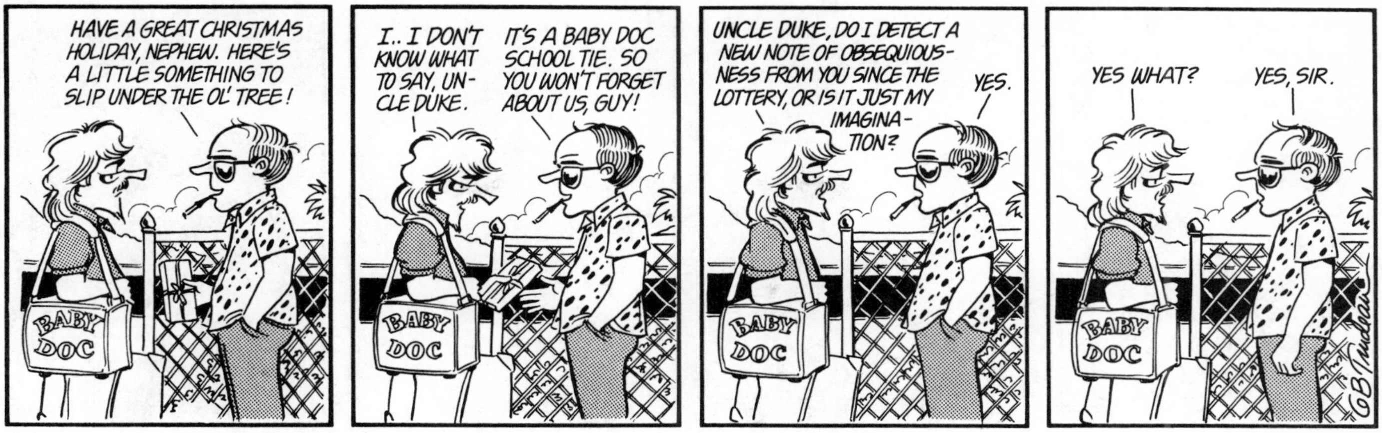
HAVE A GREAT CHRISTMAS HOLIDAY, NEPHEW. HERE'S A LITTLE SOMETHING TO SLIP UNDER THE OL' TREE!
I.. I DON'T KNOW WHAT TO SAY, UNCLE DUKE.
IT'S A BABY DOC SCHOOL TIE. SO YOU WON'T FORGET ABOUT US, GUY!
UNCLE DUKE, DO I DETECT A NEW NOTE OF OBSEQUIOUSNESS FROM YOU SINCE THE LOTTERY, OR IS IT JUST MY IMAGINATION?
YES.
YES WHAT?
YES, SIR.
BABY DOC

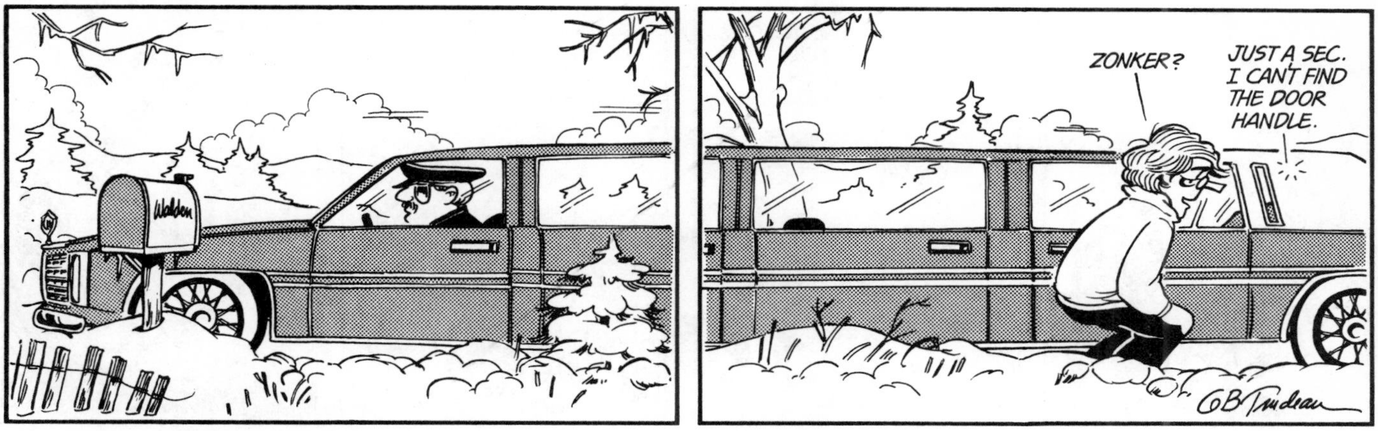
Walden
ZONKER?
JUST A SEC. I CAN'T FIND THE DOOR HANDLE.

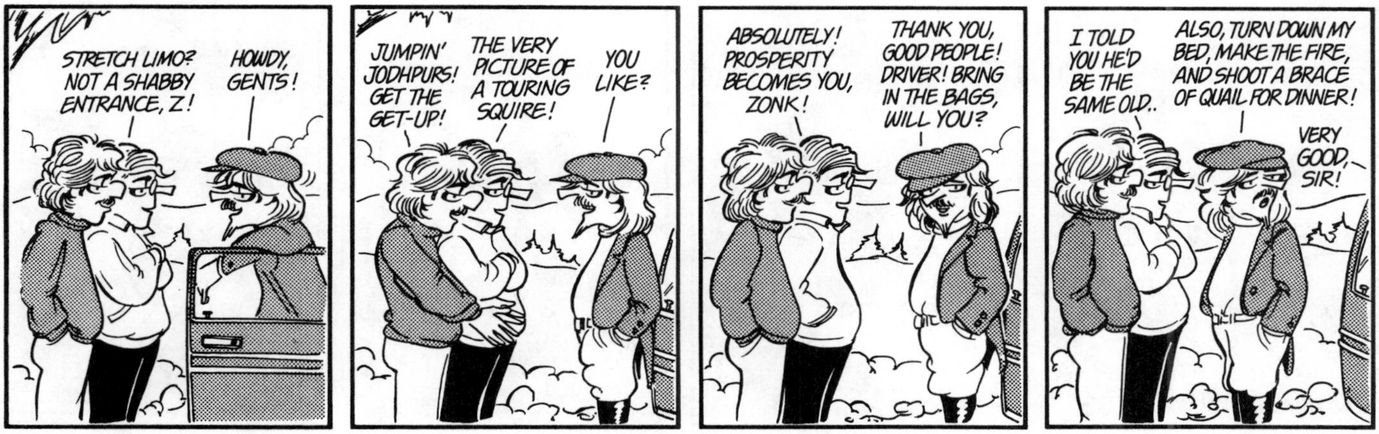
STRETCH LIMO? NOT A SHABBY ENTRANCE, Z!
HOWDY, GENTS!
JUMPIN' JODHPURS! GET THE GET-UP!
THE VERY PICTURE OF A TOURING SQUIRE!
YOU LIKE?
ABSOLUTELY! PROSPERITY BECOMES YOU, ZONK!
THANK YOU, GOOD PEOPLE! DRIVER! BRING IN THE BAGS, WILL YOU?
I TOLD YOU HE'D BE THE SAME OLD..
ALSO, TURN DOWN MY BED, MAKE THE FIRE, AND SHOOT A BRACE OF QUAIL FOR DINNER!
VERY GOOD, SIR!

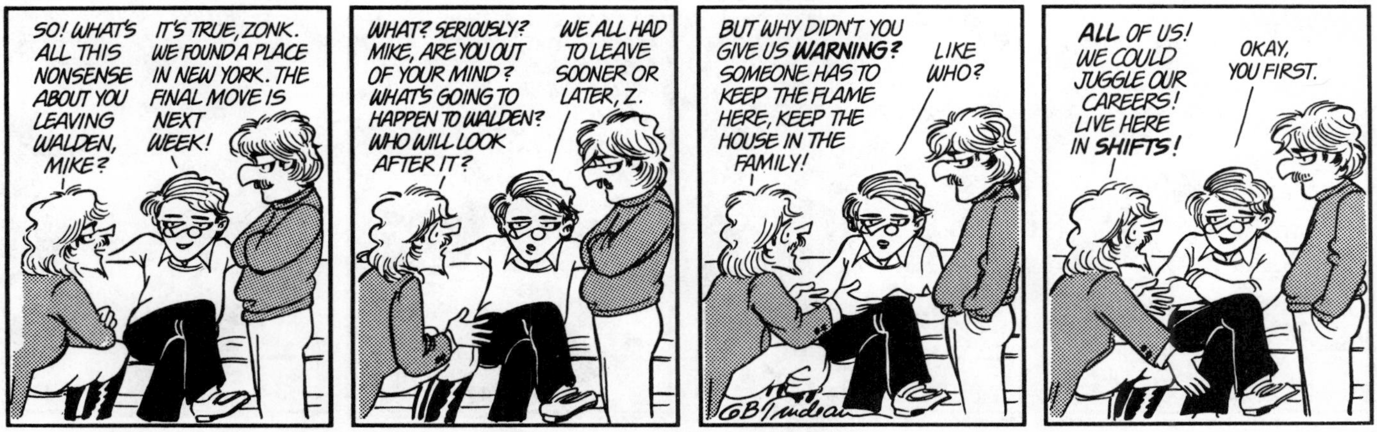
SO! WHAT'S ALL THIS NONSENSE ABOUT YOU LEAVING WALDEN, MIKE?
IT'S TRUE, ZONK. WE FOUND A PLACE IN NEW YORK. THE FINAL MOVE IS NEXT WEEK!
WHAT? SERIOUSLY? MIKE, ARE YOU OUT OF YOUR MIND? WHAT'S GOING TO HAPPEN TO WALDEN? WHO WILL LOOK AFTER IT?
WE ALL HAD TO LEAVE SOONER OR LATER, Z.
BUT WHY DIDN'T YOU GIVE US WARNING? SOMEONE HAS TO KEEP THE FLAME HERE, KEEP THE HOUSE IN THE FAMILY!
LIKE WHO?
ALL OF US! WE COULD JUGGLE OUR CAREERS! LIVE HERE IN SHIFTS!
OKAY, YOU FIRST.

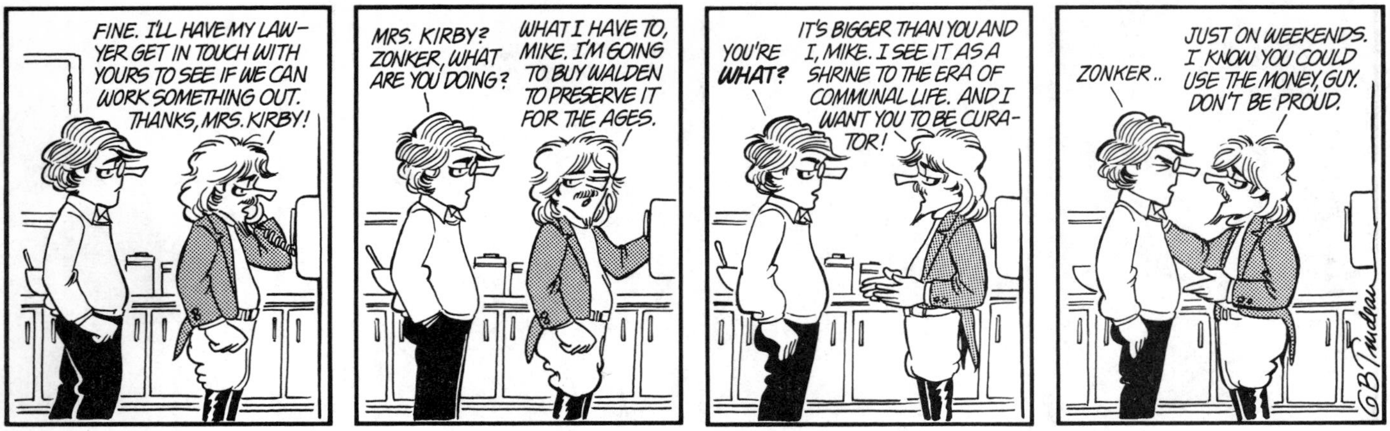
FINE. I'LL HAVE MY LAWYER GET IN TOUCH WITH YOURS TO SEE IF WE CAN WORK SOMETHING OUT. THANKS, MRS. KIRBY!
MRS. KIRBY? ZONKER, WHAT ARE YOU DOING?
WHAT I HAVE TO, MIKE. I'M GOING TO BUY WALDEN TO PRESERVE IT FOR THE AGES.
YOU'RE **WHAT?**
IT'S BIGGER THAN YOU AND I, MIKE. I SEE IT AS A SHRINE TO THE ERA OF COMMUNAL LIFE. AND I WANT YOU TO BE CURATOR!
ZONKER..
JUST ON WEEKENDS. I KNOW YOU COULD USE THE MONEY, GUY. DON'T BE PROUD.
©B Trudeau

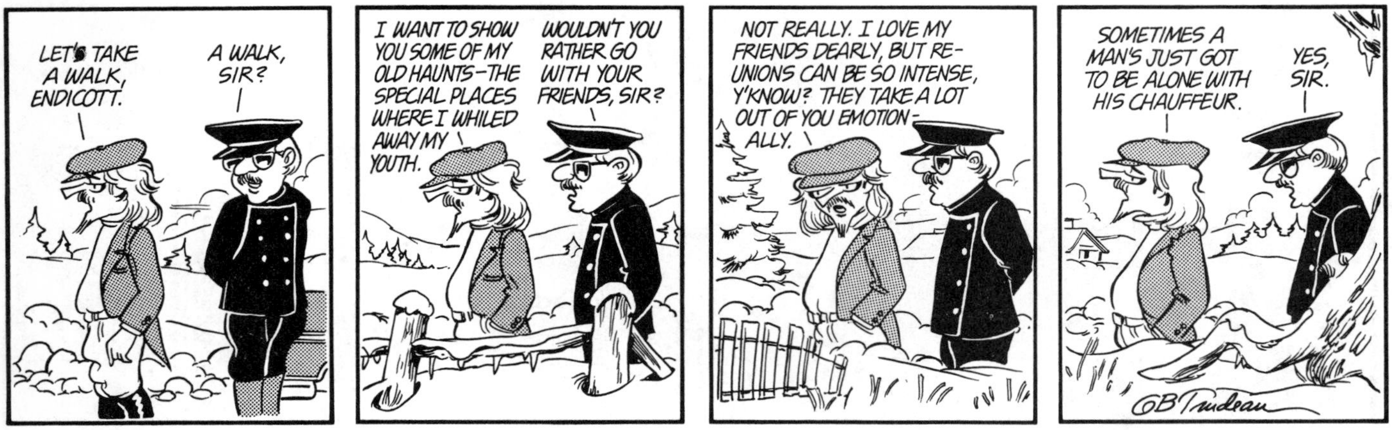
LET'S TAKE A WALK, ENDICOTT.
A WALK, SIR?
I WANT TO SHOW YOU SOME OF MY OLD HAUNTS—THE SPECIAL PLACES WHERE I WHILED AWAY MY YOUTH.
WOULDN'T YOU RATHER GO WITH YOUR FRIENDS, SIR?
NOT REALLY. I LOVE MY FRIENDS DEARLY, BUT REUNIONS CAN BE SO INTENSE, Y'KNOW? THEY TAKE A LOT OUT OF YOU EMOTIONALLY.
SOMETIMES A MAN'S JUST GOT TO BE ALONE WITH HIS CHAUFFEUR.
YES, SIR.
©B Trudeau

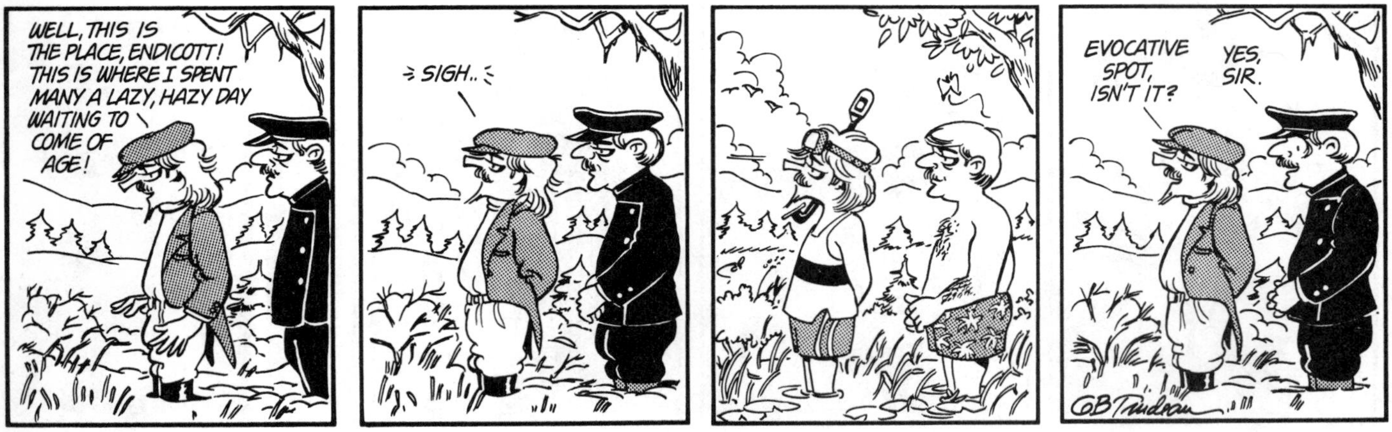
WELL, THIS IS THE PLACE, ENDICOTT! THIS IS WHERE I SPENT MANY A LAZY, HAZY DAY WAITING TO COME OF AGE!
SIGH..
EVOCATIVE SPOT, ISN'T IT?
YES, SIR.
©B Trudeau

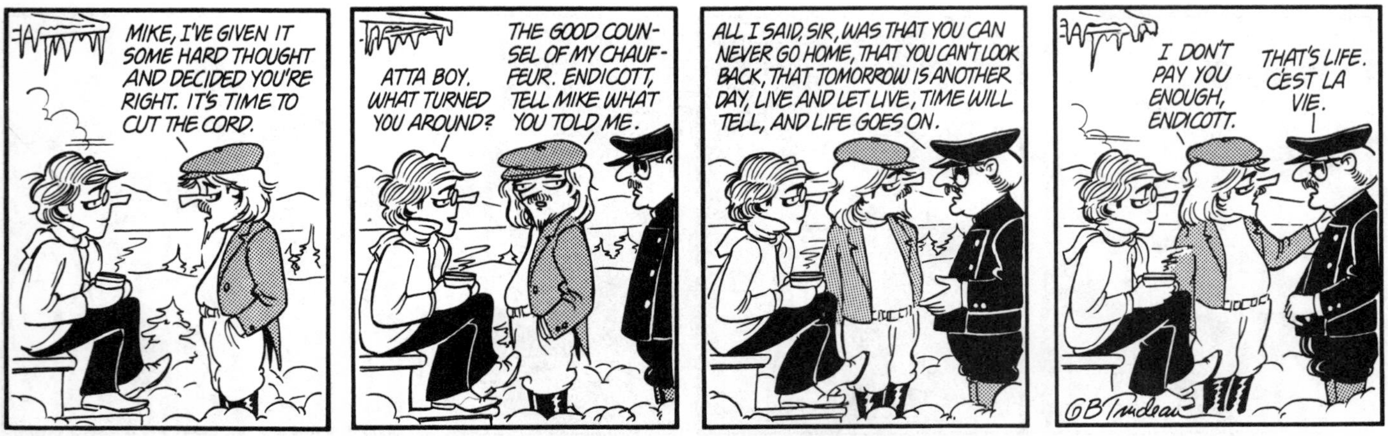
MIKE, I'VE GIVEN IT SOME HARD THOUGHT AND DECIDED YOU'RE RIGHT. IT'S TIME TO CUT THE CORD.
ATTA BOY. WHAT TURNED YOU AROUND?
THE GOOD COUNSEL OF MY CHAUFFEUR. ENDICOTT, TELL MIKE WHAT YOU TOLD ME.
ALL I SAID, SIR, WAS THAT YOU CAN NEVER GO HOME, THAT YOU CAN'T LOOK BACK, THAT TOMORROW IS ANOTHER DAY, LIVE AND LET LIVE, TIME WILL TELL, AND LIFE GOES ON.
I DON'T PAY YOU ENOUGH, ENDICOTT.
THAT'S LIFE. C'EST LA VIE.
©B Trudeau

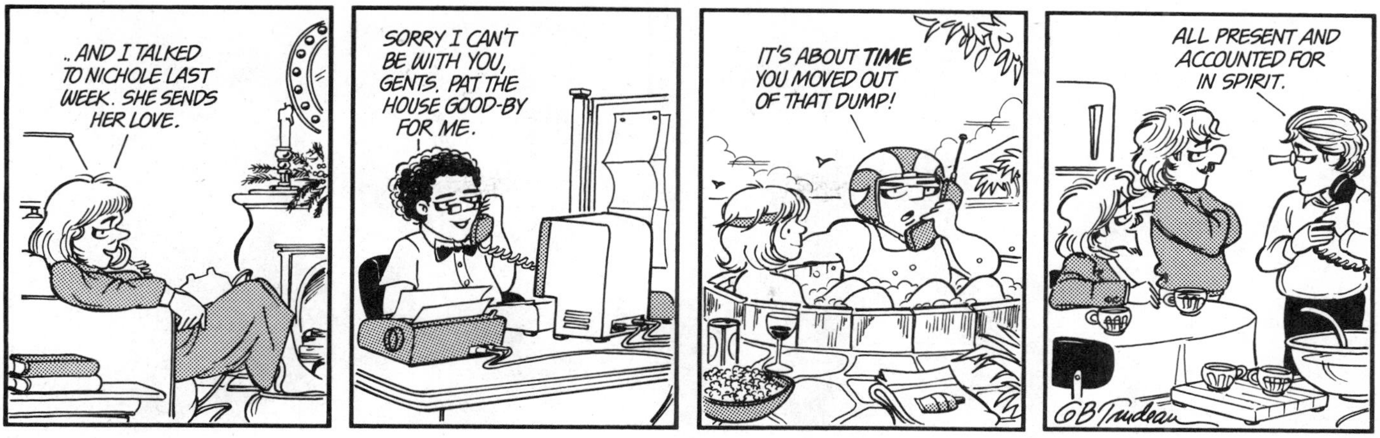
.. AND I TALKED TO NICHOLE LAST WEEK. SHE SENDS HER LOVE.
SORRY I CAN'T BE WITH YOU, GENTS. PAT THE HOUSE GOOD-BY FOR ME.
IT'S ABOUT **TIME** YOU MOVED OUT OF THAT DUMP!
ALL PRESENT AND ACCOUNTED FOR IN SPIRIT.
GB Trudeau

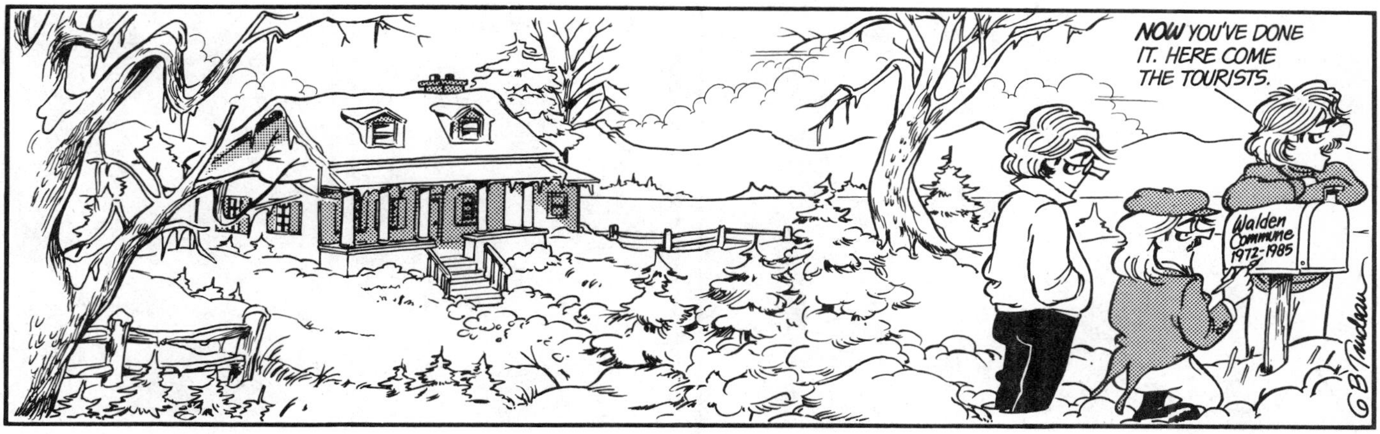
NOW YOU'VE DONE IT. HERE COME THE TOURISTS.
Walden Commune 1972-1985
GB Trudeau

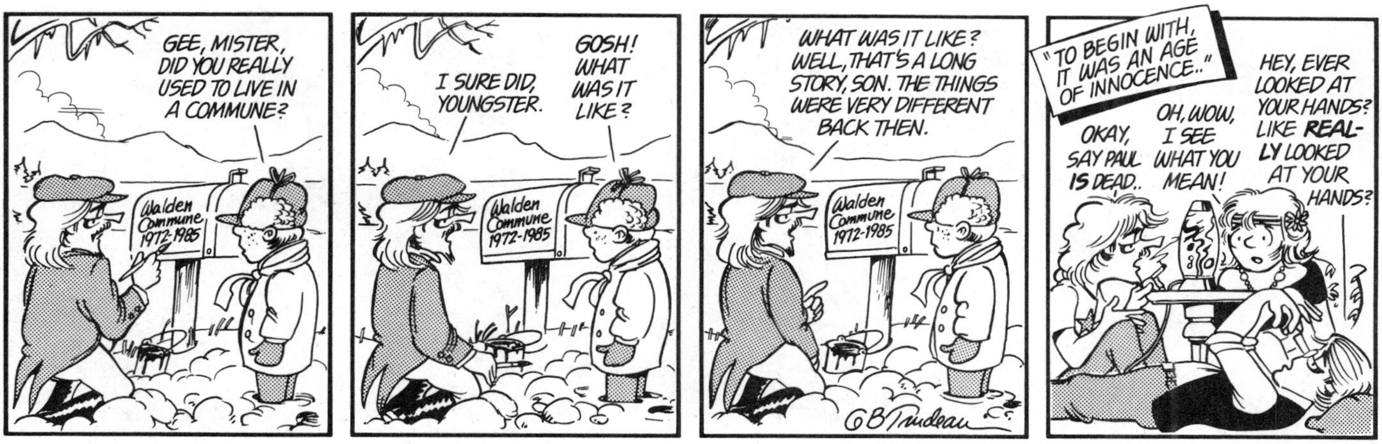
GEE, MISTER, DID YOU REALLY USED TO LIVE IN A COMMUNE?
Walden Commune 1972-1985
I SURE DID, YOUNGSTER.
GOSH! WHAT WAS IT LIKE?
WHAT WAS IT LIKE? WELL, THAT'S A LONG STORY, SON. THE THINGS WERE VERY DIFFERENT BACK THEN.
GB Trudeau
"TO BEGIN WITH, IT WAS AN AGE OF INNOCENCE.."
OKAY, SAY PAUL **IS** DEAD..
OH, WOW, I SEE WHAT YOU MEAN!
HEY, EVER LOOKED AT YOUR HANDS? LIKE **REAL-LY** LOOKED AT YOUR HANDS?

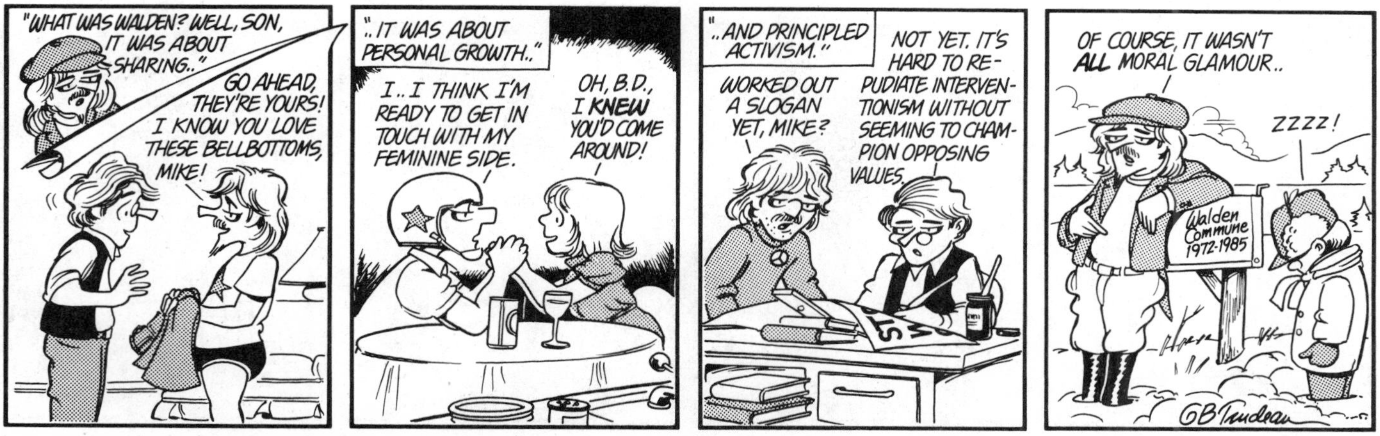
"WHAT WAS WALDEN? WELL, SON, IT WAS ABOUT SHARING.."
GO AHEAD, THEY'RE YOURS! I KNOW YOU LOVE THESE BELLBOTTOMS, MIKE!
"..IT WAS ABOUT PERSONAL GROWTH.."
I..I THINK I'M READY TO GET IN TOUCH WITH MY FEMININE SIDE.
OH, B.D., I **KNEW** YOU'D COME AROUND!
"..AND PRINCIPLED ACTIVISM."
WORKED OUT A SLOGAN YET, MIKE?
NOT YET. IT'S HARD TO RE-PUDIATE INTERVEN-TIONISM WITHOUT SEEMING TO CHAM-PION OPPOSING VALUES.
OF COURSE, IT WASN'T **ALL** MORAL GLAMOUR..
ZZZZ!
Walden Commune 1972-1985
GB Trudeau

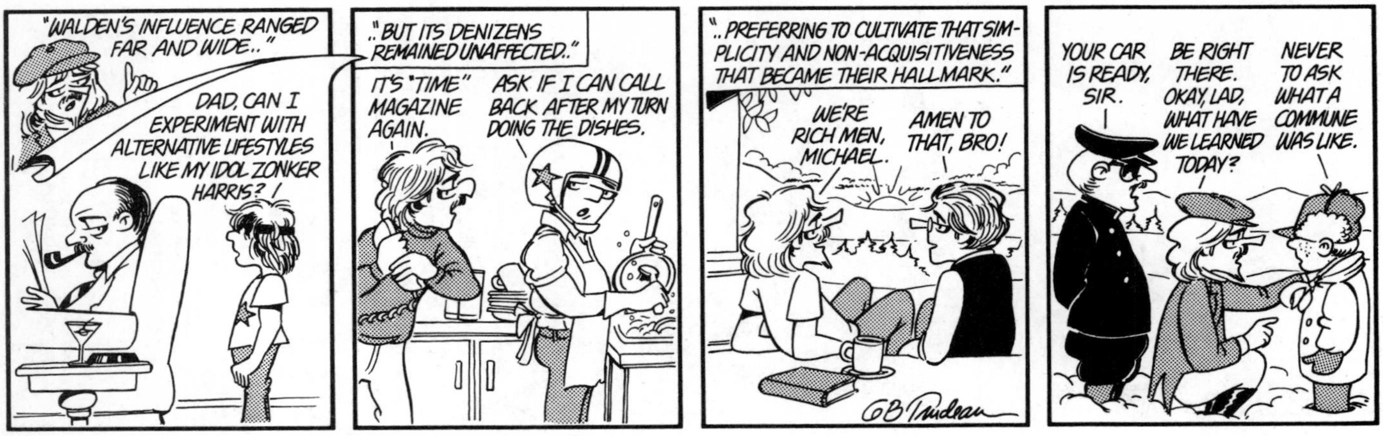
"WALDEN'S INFLUENCE RANGED FAR AND WIDE.."
DAD, CAN I EXPERIMENT WITH ALTERNATIVE LIFESTYLES LIKE MY IDOL ZONKER HARRIS? !
.." BUT ITS DENIZENS REMAINED UNAFFECTED.."
IT'S "TIME" MAGAZINE AGAIN.
ASK IF I CAN CALL BACK AFTER MY TURN DOING THE DISHES.
".. PREFERRING TO CULTIVATE THAT SIMPLICITY AND NON-ACQUISITIVENESS THAT BECAME THEIR HALLMARK."
WE'RE RICH MEN, MICHAEL.
AMEN TO THAT, BRO!
GB Trudeau
YOUR CAR IS READY, SIR.
BE RIGHT THERE. OKAY, LAD, WHAT HAVE WE LEARNED TODAY?
NEVER TO ASK WHAT A COMMUNE WAS LIKE.

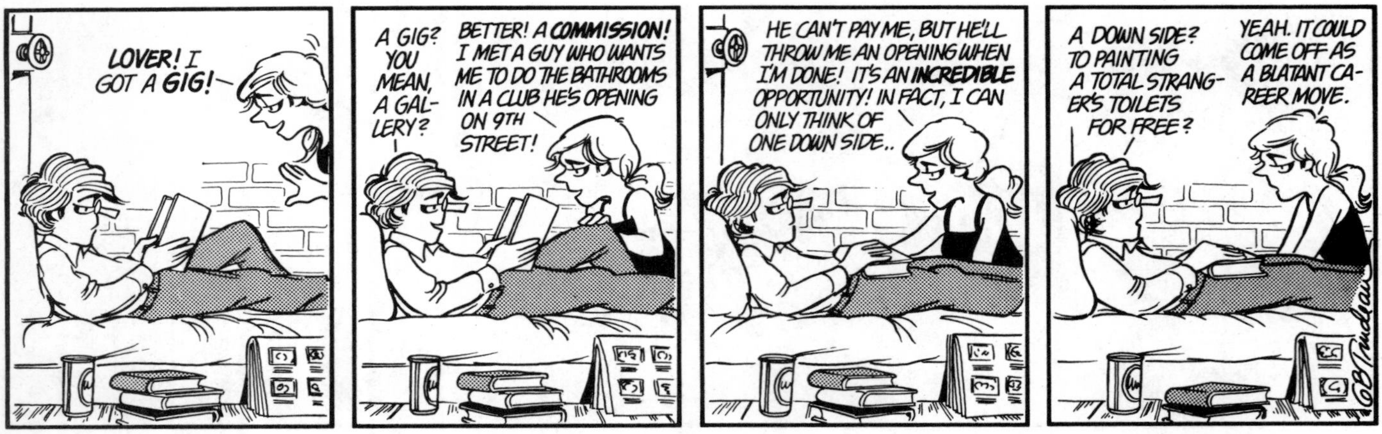
LOVER! I GOT A GIG!
A GIG? YOU MEAN, A GALLERY?
BETTER! A COMMISSION! I MET A GUY WHO WANTS ME TO DO THE BATHROOMS IN A CLUB HE'S OPENING ON 9TH STREET!
HE CAN'T PAY ME, BUT HE'LL THROW ME AN OPENING WHEN I'M DONE! IT'S AN INCREDIBLE OPPORTUNITY! IN FACT, I CAN ONLY THINK OF ONE DOWN SIDE..
A DOWN SIDE? TO PAINTING A TOTAL STRANGER'S TOILETS FOR FREE?
YEAH. IT COULD COME OFF AS A BLATANT CAREER MOVE.
GB Trudeau

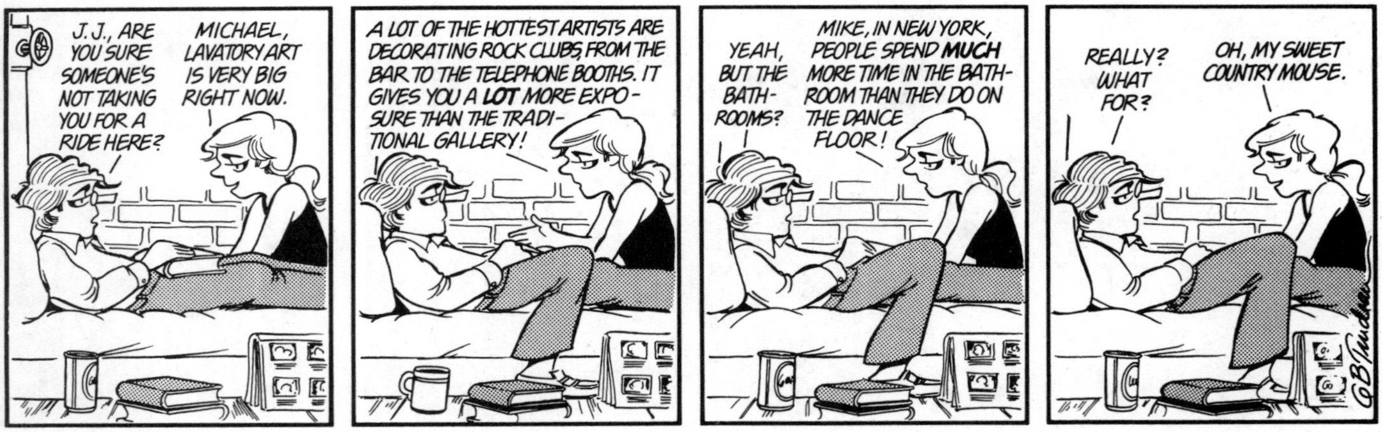
J. J., ARE YOU SURE SOMEONE'S NOT TAKING YOU FOR A RIDE HERE?
MICHAEL, LAVATORY ART IS VERY BIG RIGHT NOW.
A LOT OF THE HOTTEST ARTISTS ARE DECORATING ROCK CLUBS, FROM THE BAR TO THE TELEPHONE BOOTHS. IT GIVES YOU A LOT MORE EXPOSURE THAN THE TRADITIONAL GALLERY!
YEAH, BUT THE BATHROOMS?
MIKE, IN NEW YORK, PEOPLE SPEND MUCH MORE TIME IN THE BATHROOM THAN THEY DO ON THE DANCE FLOOR!
REALLY? WHAT FOR?
OH, MY SWEET COUNTRY MOUSE.
GB Trudeau

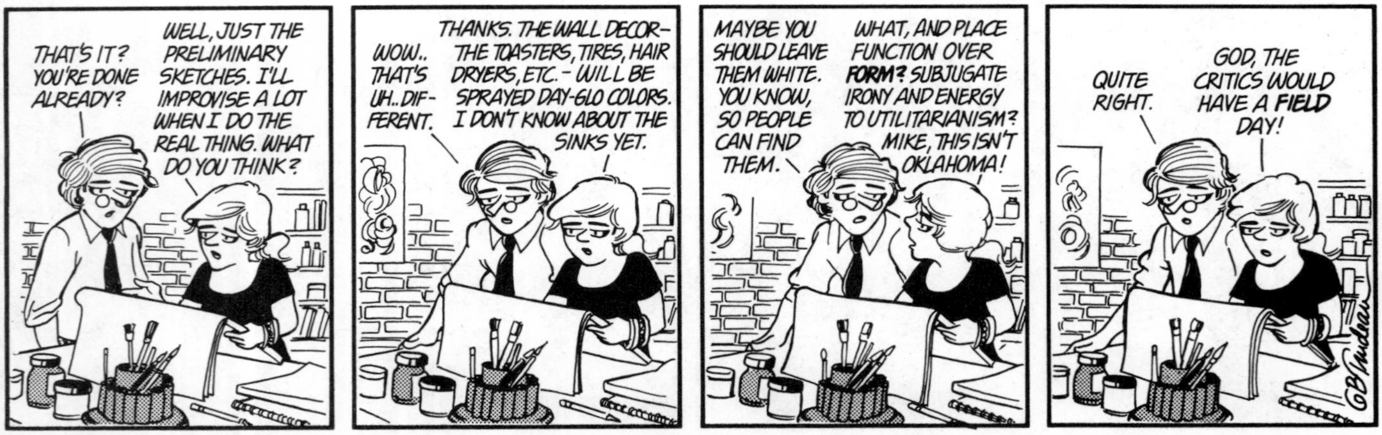
THAT'S IT? YOU'RE DONE ALREADY?
WELL, JUST THE PRELIMINARY SKETCHES. I'LL IMPROVISE A LOT WHEN I DO THE REAL THING. WHAT DO YOU THINK?
WOW.. THAT'S UH.. DIFFERENT.
THANKS. THE WALL DECOR - THE TOASTERS, TIRES, HAIR DRYERS, ETC. - WILL BE SPRAYED DAY-GLO COLORS. I DON'T KNOW ABOUT THE SINKS YET.
MAYBE YOU SHOULD LEAVE THEM WHITE. YOU KNOW, SO PEOPLE CAN FIND THEM.
WHAT, AND PLACE FUNCTION OVER FORM? SUBJUGATE IRONY AND ENERGY TO UTILITARIANISM? MIKE, THIS ISN'T OKLAHOMA!
QUITE RIGHT.
GOD, THE CRITICS WOULD HAVE A FIELD DAY!
GB Trudeau

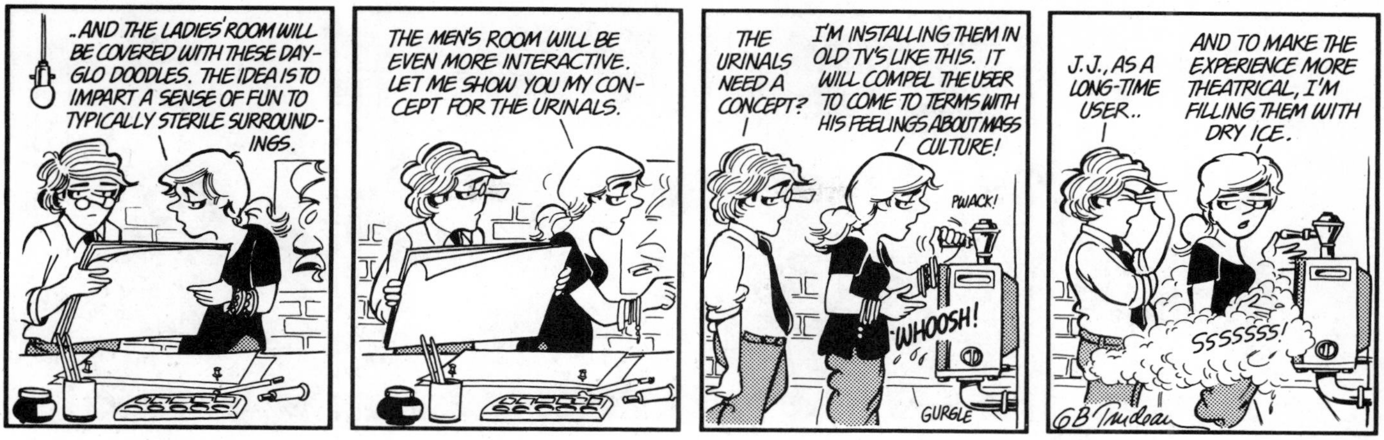
..AND THE LADIES' ROOM WILL BE COVERED WITH THESE DAY-GLO DOODLES. THE IDEA IS TO IMPART A SENSE OF FUN TO TYPICALLY STERILE SURROUNDINGS.
THE MEN'S ROOM WILL BE EVEN MORE INTERACTIVE. LET ME SHOW YOU MY CONCEPT FOR THE URINALS.
THE URINALS NEED A CONCEPT?
I'M INSTALLING THEM IN OLD TV'S LIKE THIS. IT WILL COMPEL THE USER TO COME TO TERMS WITH HIS FEELINGS ABOUT MASS CULTURE!
PWACK!
WHOOSH!
GURGLE
J.J., AS A LONG-TIME USER..
AND TO MAKE THE EXPERIENCE MORE THEATRICAL, I'M FILLING THEM WITH DRY ICE.
SSSSSSS!
GB Trudeau

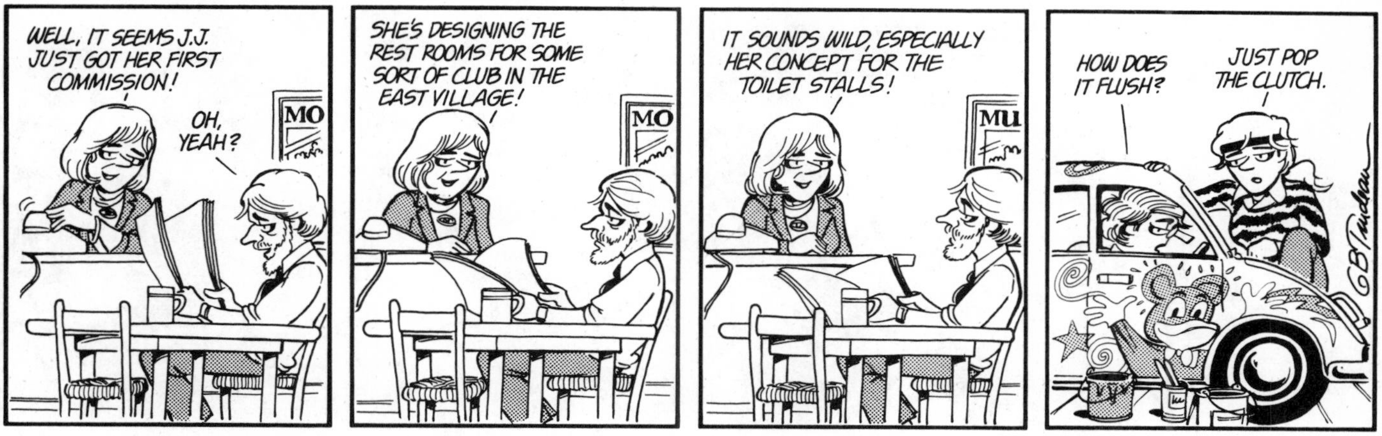
WELL, IT SEEMS J.J. JUST GOT HER FIRST COMMISSION!
OH, YEAH?
SHE'S DESIGNING THE REST ROOMS FOR SOME SORT OF CLUB IN THE EAST VILLAGE!
IT SOUNDS WILD, ESPECIALLY HER CONCEPT FOR THE TOILET STALLS!
HOW DOES IT FLUSH?
JUST POP THE CLUTCH.
GB Trudeau

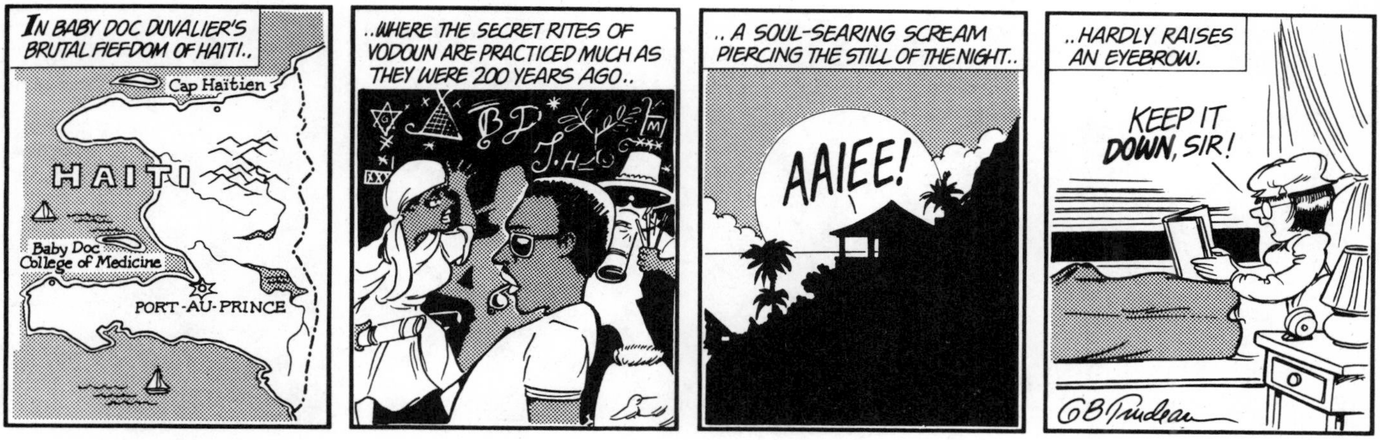
IN BABY DOC DUVALIER'S BRUTAL FIEFDOM OF HAITI..
Cap Haïtien
HAITI
Baby Doc College of Medicine
PORT-AU-PRINCE
..WHERE THE SECRET RITES OF VODOUN ARE PRACTICED MUCH AS THEY WERE 200 YEARS AGO..
.. A SOUL-SEARING SCREAM PIERCING THE STILL OF THE NIGHT..
AAIEE!
..HARDLY RAISES AN EYEBROW.
KEEP IT **DOWN**, SIR!
GB Trudeau

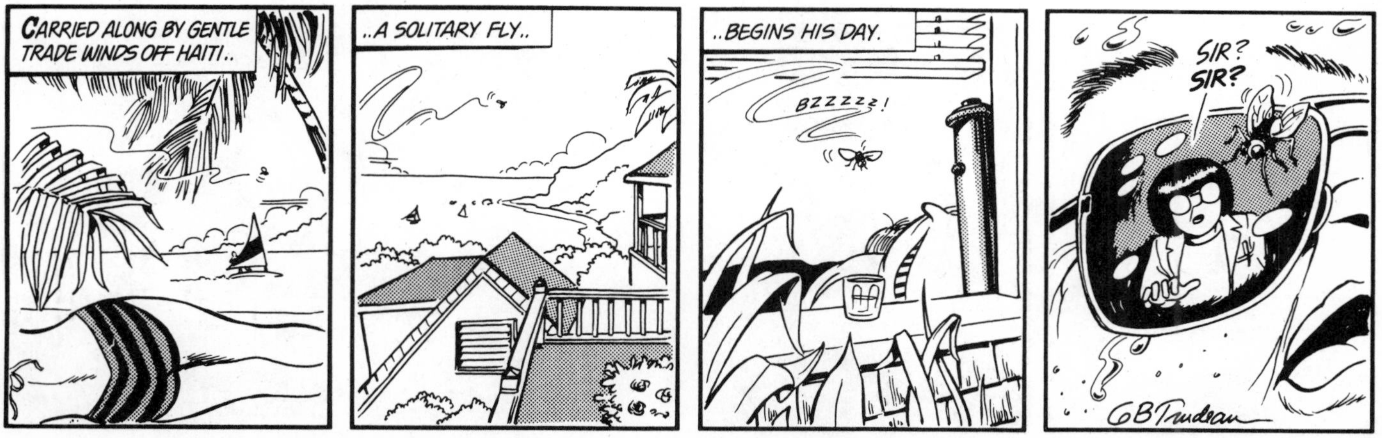
CARRIED ALONG BY GENTLE TRADE WINDS OFF HAITI..
..A SOLITARY FLY..
..BEGINS HIS DAY.
BZZZZZZ!
SIR? **SIR?**
GB Trudeau

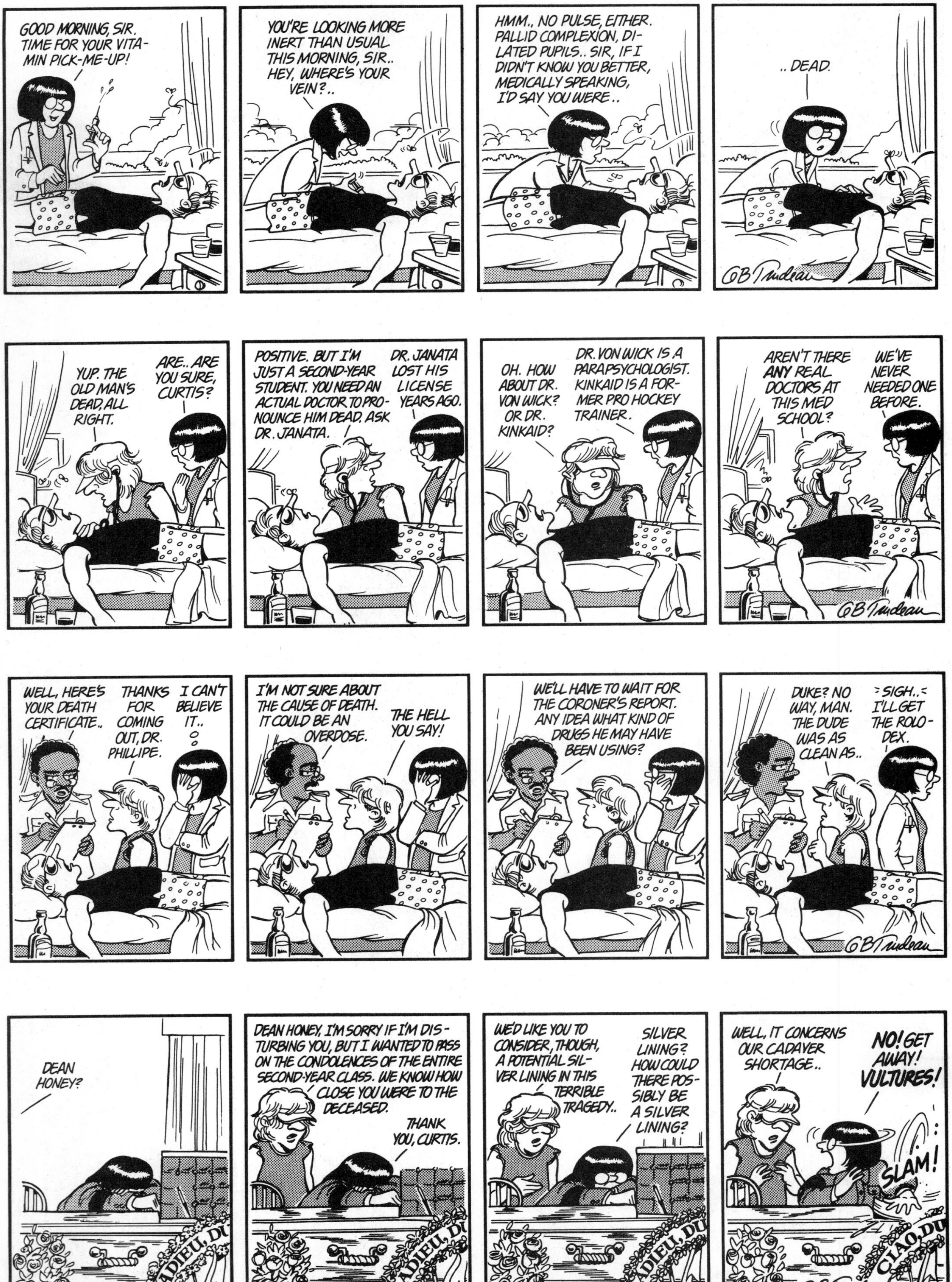
GOOD MORNING, SIR. TIME FOR YOUR VITA-MIN PICK-ME-UP!
YOU'RE LOOKING MORE INERT THAN USUAL THIS MORNING, SIR.. HEY, WHERE'S YOUR VEIN?..
HMM.. NO PULSE, EITHER. PALLID COMPLEXION, DI-LATED PUPILS.. SIR, IF I DIDN'T KNOW YOU BETTER, MEDICALLY SPEAKING, I'D SAY YOU WERE..
.. DEAD.
G.B. Trudeau
YUP. THE OLD MAN'S DEAD, ALL RIGHT.
ARE.. ARE YOU SURE, CURTIS?
POSITIVE. BUT I'M JUST A SECOND-YEAR STUDENT. YOU NEED AN ACTUAL DOCTOR TO PRO-NOUNCE HIM DEAD. ASK DR. JANATA.
DR. JANATA LOST HIS LICENSE YEARS AGO.
OH. HOW ABOUT DR. VON WICK? OR DR. KINKAID?
DR. VON WICK IS A PARAPSYCHOLOGIST. KINKAID IS A FOR-MER PRO HOCKEY TRAINER.
AREN'T THERE ANY REAL DOCTORS AT THIS MED SCHOOL?
WE'VE NEVER NEEDED ONE BEFORE.
G.B. Trudeau
WELL, HERE'S YOUR DEATH CERTIFICATE..
THANKS FOR COMING OUT, DR. PHILLIPE.
I CAN'T BELIEVE IT..
I'M NOT SURE ABOUT THE CAUSE OF DEATH. IT COULD BE AN OVERDOSE.
THE HELL YOU SAY!
WE'LL HAVE TO WAIT FOR THE CORONER'S REPORT. ANY IDEA WHAT KIND OF DRUGS HE MAY HAVE BEEN USING?
DUKE? NO WAY, MAN. THE DUDE WAS AS CLEAN AS..
SIGH..
I'LL GET THE ROLO-DEX.
G.B. Trudeau
DEAN HONEY?
ADIEU, DU
DEAN HONEY, I'M SORRY IF I'M DIS-TURBING YOU, BUT I WANTED TO PASS ON THE CONDOLENCES OF THE ENTIRE SECOND-YEAR CLASS. WE KNOW HOW CLOSE YOU WERE TO THE DECEASED.
THANK YOU, CURTIS.
ADIEU, DU
WE'D LIKE YOU TO CONSIDER, THOUGH, A POTENTIAL SIL-VER LINING IN THIS TERRIBLE TRAGEDY..
SILVER LINING? HOW COULD THERE POS-SIBLY BE A SILVER LINING?
ADIEU, DU
WELL, IT CONCERNS OUR CADAVER SHORTAGE..
NO! GET AWAY! VULTURES!
SLAM!
CIAO, DU
G.B. Trudeau

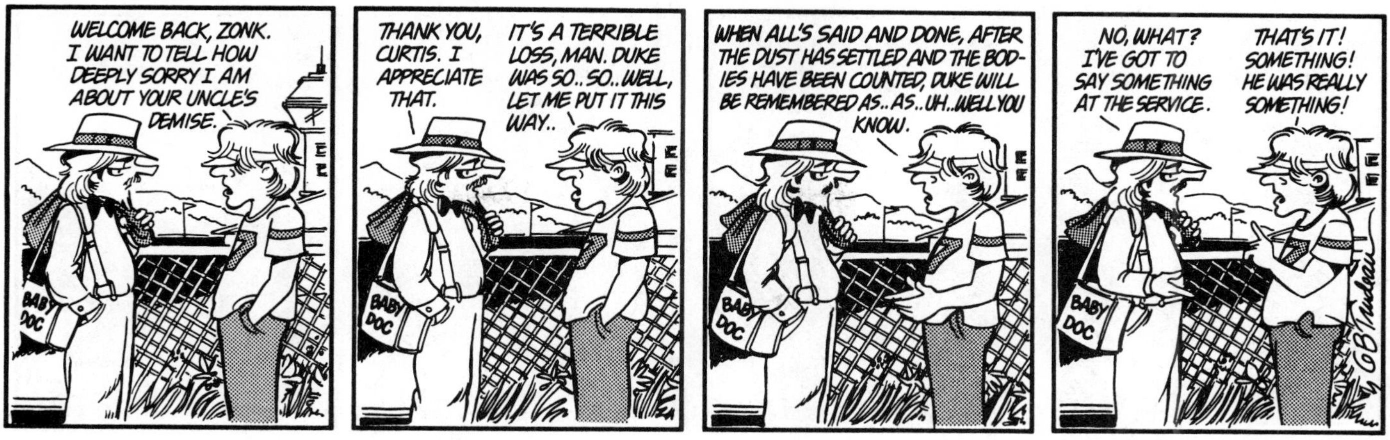
WELCOME BACK, ZONK. I WANT TO TELL HOW DEEPLY SORRY I AM ABOUT YOUR UNCLE'S DEMISE.
BABY DOC
THANK YOU, CURTIS. I APPRECIATE THAT.
IT'S A TERRIBLE LOSS, MAN. DUKE WAS SO.. SO.. WELL, LET ME PUT IT THIS WAY..
WHEN ALL'S SAID AND DONE, AFTER THE DUST HAS SETTLED AND THE BODIES HAVE BEEN COUNTED, DUKE WILL BE REMEMBERED AS.. AS.. UH.. WELL YOU KNOW.
NO, WHAT? I'VE GOT TO SAY SOMETHING AT THE SERVICE.
THAT'S IT! SOMETHING! HE WAS REALLY SOMETHING!

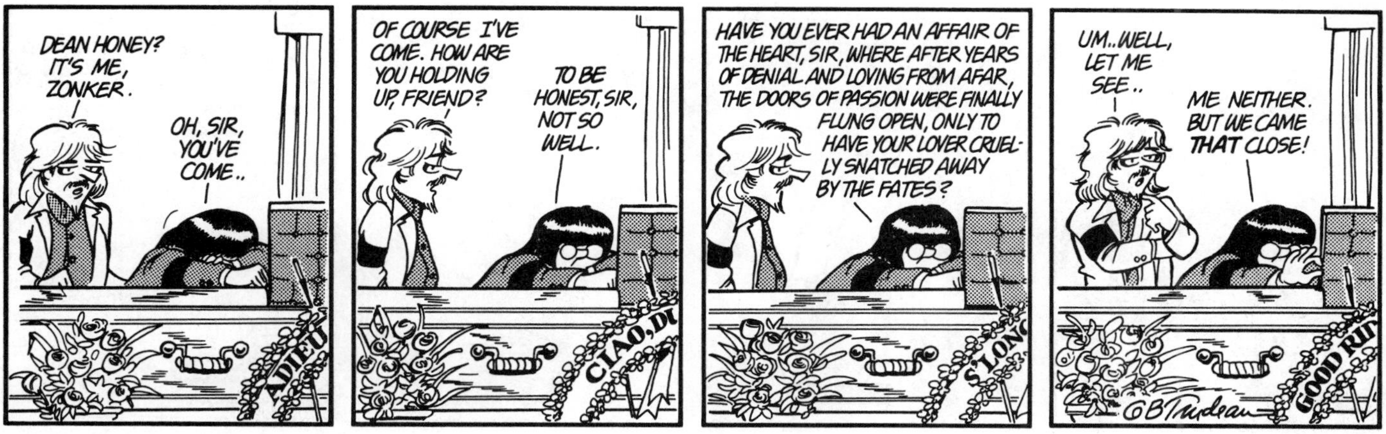
DEAN HONEY? IT'S ME, ZONKER.
OH, SIR, YOU'VE COME..
ADIEU
OF COURSE I'VE COME. HOW ARE YOU HOLDING UP, FRIEND?
TO BE HONEST, SIR, NOT SO WELL.
HAVE YOU EVER HAD AN AFFAIR OF THE HEART, SIR, WHERE AFTER YEARS OF DENIAL AND LOVING FROM AFAR, THE DOORS OF PASSION WERE FINALLY FLUNG OPEN, ONLY TO HAVE YOUR LOVER CRUELLY SNATCHED AWAY BY THE FATES?
UM.. WELL, LET ME SEE..
ME NEITHER. BUT WE CAME **THAT** CLOSE!

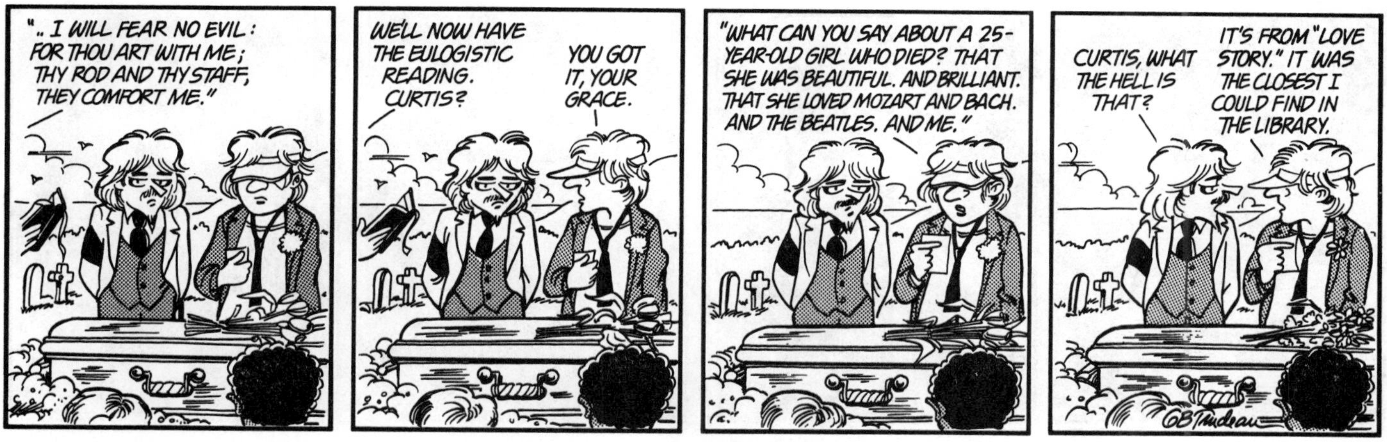
".. I WILL FEAR NO EVIL: FOR THOU ART WITH ME; THY ROD AND THY STAFF, THEY COMFORT ME."
WE'LL NOW HAVE THE EULOGISTIC READING. CURTIS?
YOU GOT IT, YOUR GRACE.
"WHAT CAN YOU SAY ABOUT A 25-YEAR-OLD GIRL WHO DIED? THAT SHE WAS BEAUTIFUL. AND BRILLIANT. THAT SHE LOVED MOZART AND BACH. AND THE BEATLES. AND ME."
CURTIS, WHAT THE HELL IS THAT?
IT'S FROM "LOVE STORY." IT WAS THE CLOSEST I COULD FIND IN THE LIBRARY.

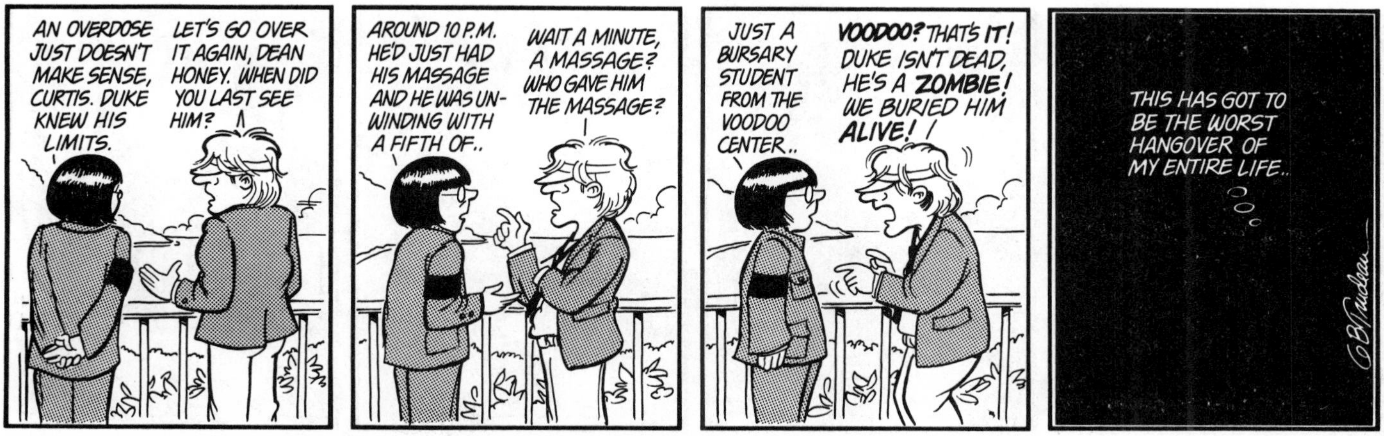
AN OVERDOSE JUST DOESN'T MAKE SENSE, CURTIS. DUKE KNEW HIS LIMITS.
LET'S GO OVER IT AGAIN, DEAN HONEY. WHEN DID YOU LAST SEE HIM?
AROUND 10 P.M. HE'D JUST HAD HIS MASSAGE AND HE WAS UNWINDING WITH A FIFTH OF..
WAIT A MINUTE, A MASSAGE? WHO GAVE HIM THE MASSAGE?
JUST A BURSARY STUDENT FROM THE VOODOO CENTER..
VOODOO? THAT'S **IT!** DUKE ISN'T DEAD, HE'S A **ZOMBIE!** WE BURIED HIM **ALIVE!**
THIS HAS GOT TO BE THE WORST HANGOVER OF MY ENTIRE LIFE..

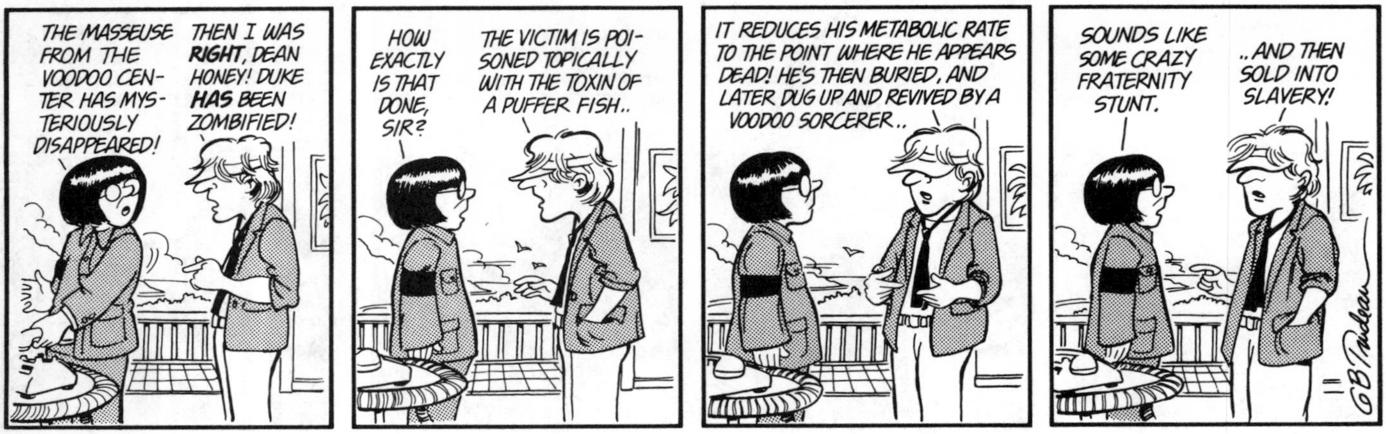
THE MASSEUSE FROM THE VOODOO CENTER HAS MYSTERIOUSLY DISAPPEARED!
THEN I WAS RIGHT, DEAN HONEY! DUKE HAS BEEN ZOMBIFIED!
HOW EXACTLY IS THAT DONE, SIR?
THE VICTIM IS POISONED TOPICALLY WITH THE TOXIN OF A PUFFER FISH..
IT REDUCES HIS METABOLIC RATE TO THE POINT WHERE HE APPEARS DEAD! HE'S THEN BURIED, AND LATER DUG UP AND REVIVED BY A VOODOO SORCERER..
SOUNDS LIKE SOME CRAZY FRATERNITY STUNT.
..AND THEN SOLD INTO SLAVERY!
GB Trudeau

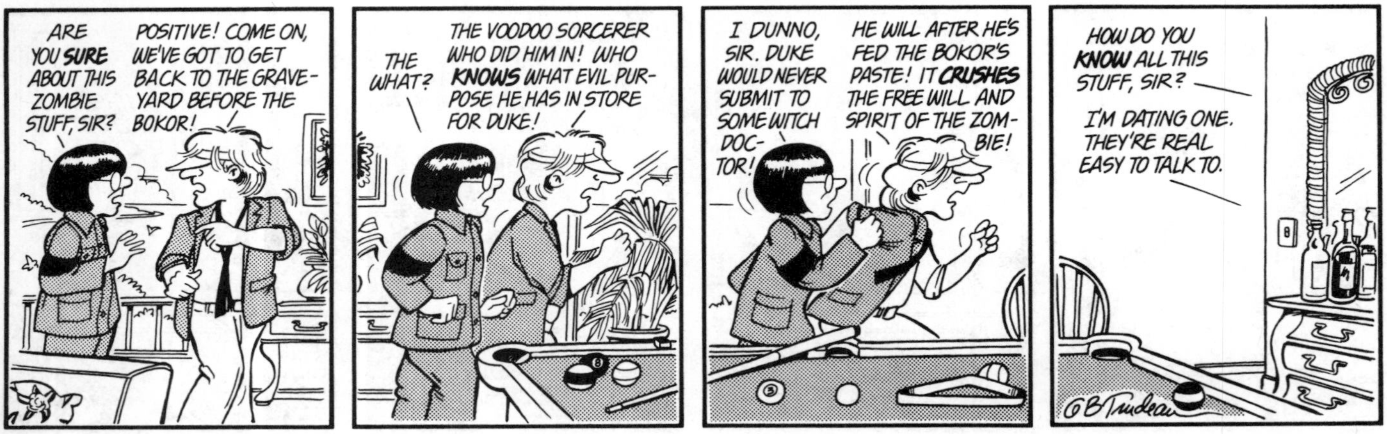
ARE YOU SURE ABOUT THIS ZOMBIE STUFF, SIR?
POSITIVE! COME ON, WE'VE GOT TO GET BACK TO THE GRAVEYARD BEFORE THE BOKOR!
THE WHAT?
THE VOODOO SORCERER WHO DID HIM IN! WHO KNOWS WHAT EVIL PURPOSE HE HAS IN STORE FOR DUKE!
I DUNNO, SIR. DUKE WOULD NEVER SUBMIT TO SOME WITCH DOCTOR!
HE WILL AFTER HE'S FED THE BOKOR'S PASTE! IT CRUSHES THE FREE WILL AND SPIRIT OF THE ZOMBIE!
HOW DO YOU KNOW ALL THIS STUFF, SIR?
I'M DATING ONE. THEY'RE REAL EASY TO TALK TO.
GB Trudeau

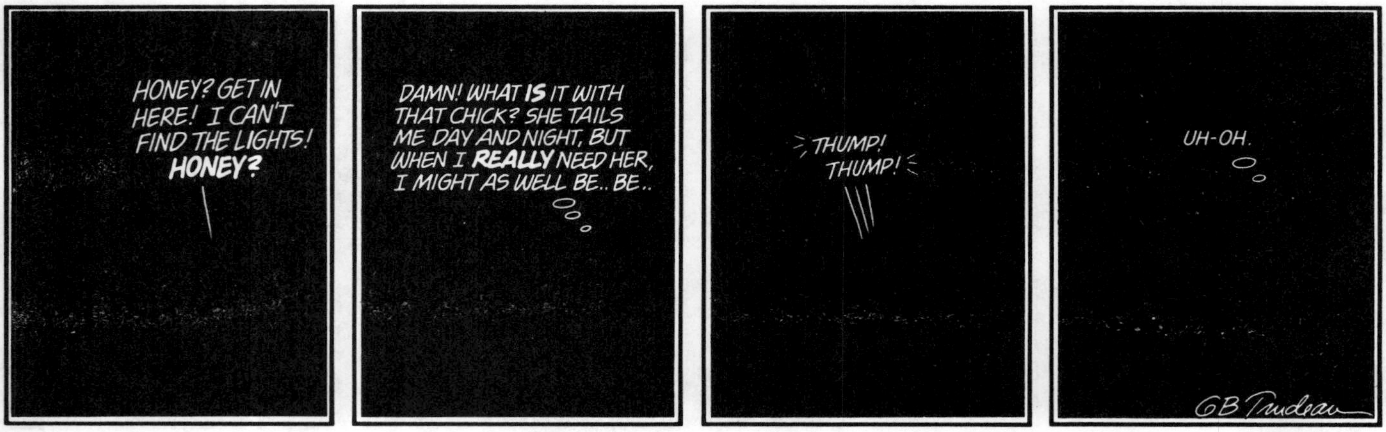
HONEY? GET IN HERE! I CAN'T FIND THE LIGHTS! HONEY?
DAMN! WHAT IS IT WITH THAT CHICK? SHE TAILS ME DAY AND NIGHT, BUT WHEN I REALLY NEED HER, I MIGHT AS WELL BE.. BE..
THUMP! THUMP!
UH-OH.
GB Trudeau

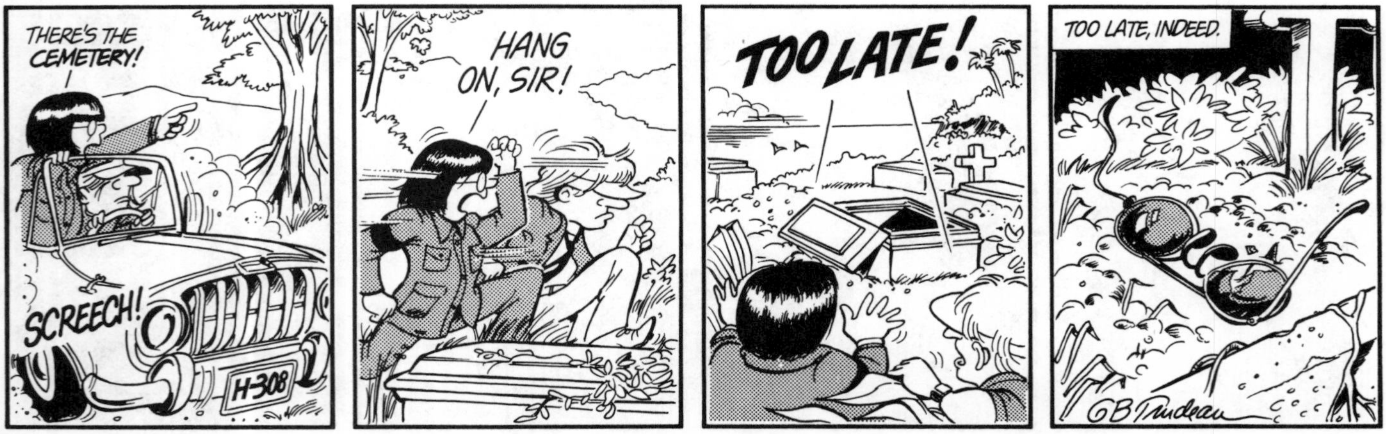
THERE'S THE CEMETERY!
SCREECH!
H-308
HANG ON, SIR!
TOO LATE!
TOO LATE, INDEED.
GB Trudeau

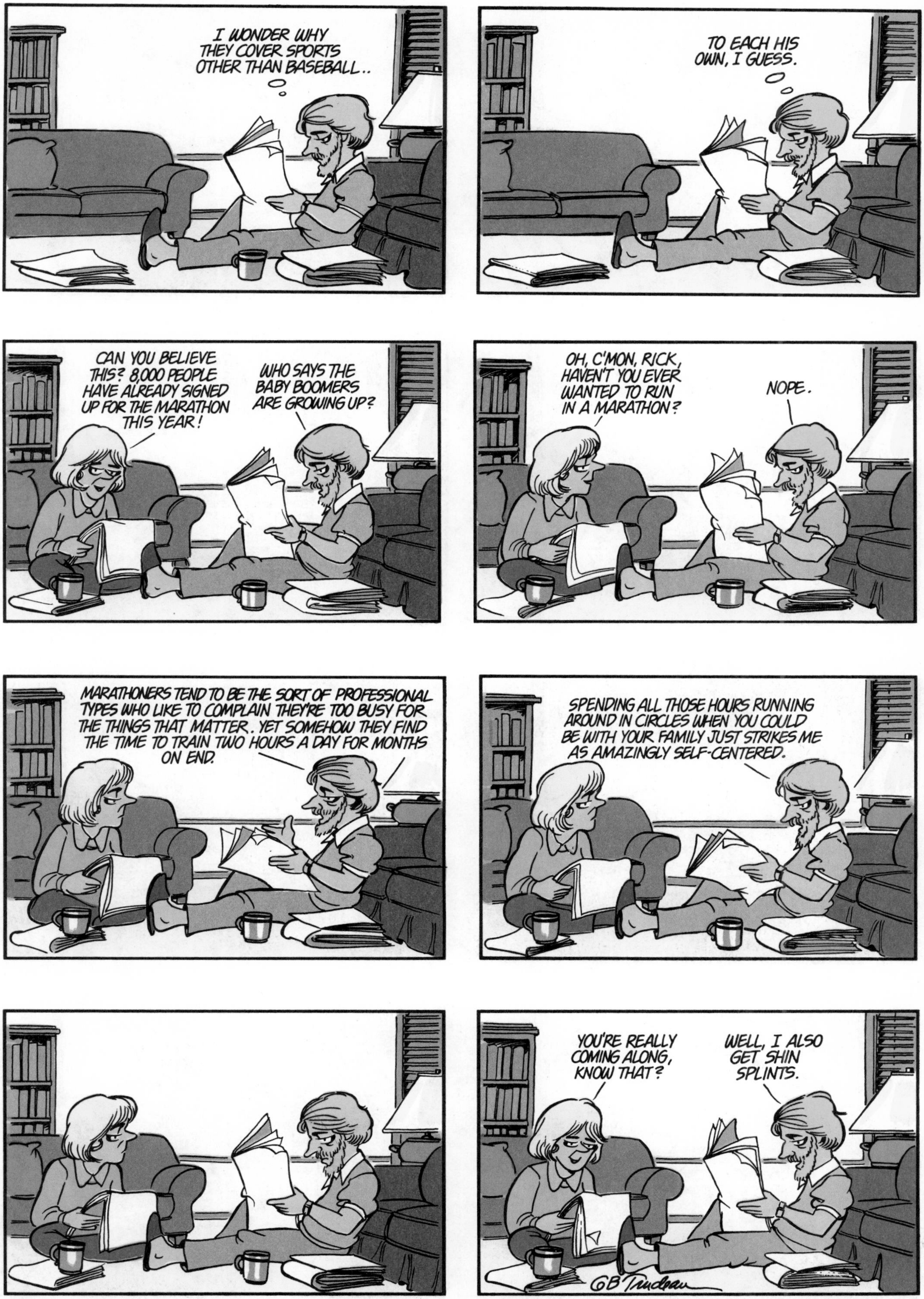
I WONDER WHY THEY COVER SPORTS OTHER THAN BASEBALL..
TO EACH HIS OWN, I GUESS.
CAN YOU BELIEVE THIS? 8,000 PEOPLE HAVE ALREADY SIGNED UP FOR THE MARATHON THIS YEAR!
WHO SAYS THE BABY BOOMERS ARE GROWING UP?
OH, C'MON, RICK, HAVEN'T YOU EVER WANTED TO RUN IN A MARATHON?
NOPE.
MARATHONERS TEND TO BE THE SORT OF PROFESSIONAL TYPES WHO LIKE TO COMPLAIN THEY'RE TOO BUSY FOR THE THINGS THAT MATTER. YET SOMEHOW THEY FIND THE TIME TO TRAIN TWO HOURS A DAY FOR MONTHS ON END.
SPENDING ALL THOSE HOURS RUNNING AROUND IN CIRCLES WHEN YOU COULD BE WITH YOUR FAMILY JUST STRIKES ME AS AMAZINGLY SELF-CENTERED.
YOU'RE REALLY COMING ALONG, KNOW THAT?
WELL, I ALSO GET SHIN SPLINTS.
GB Trudeau

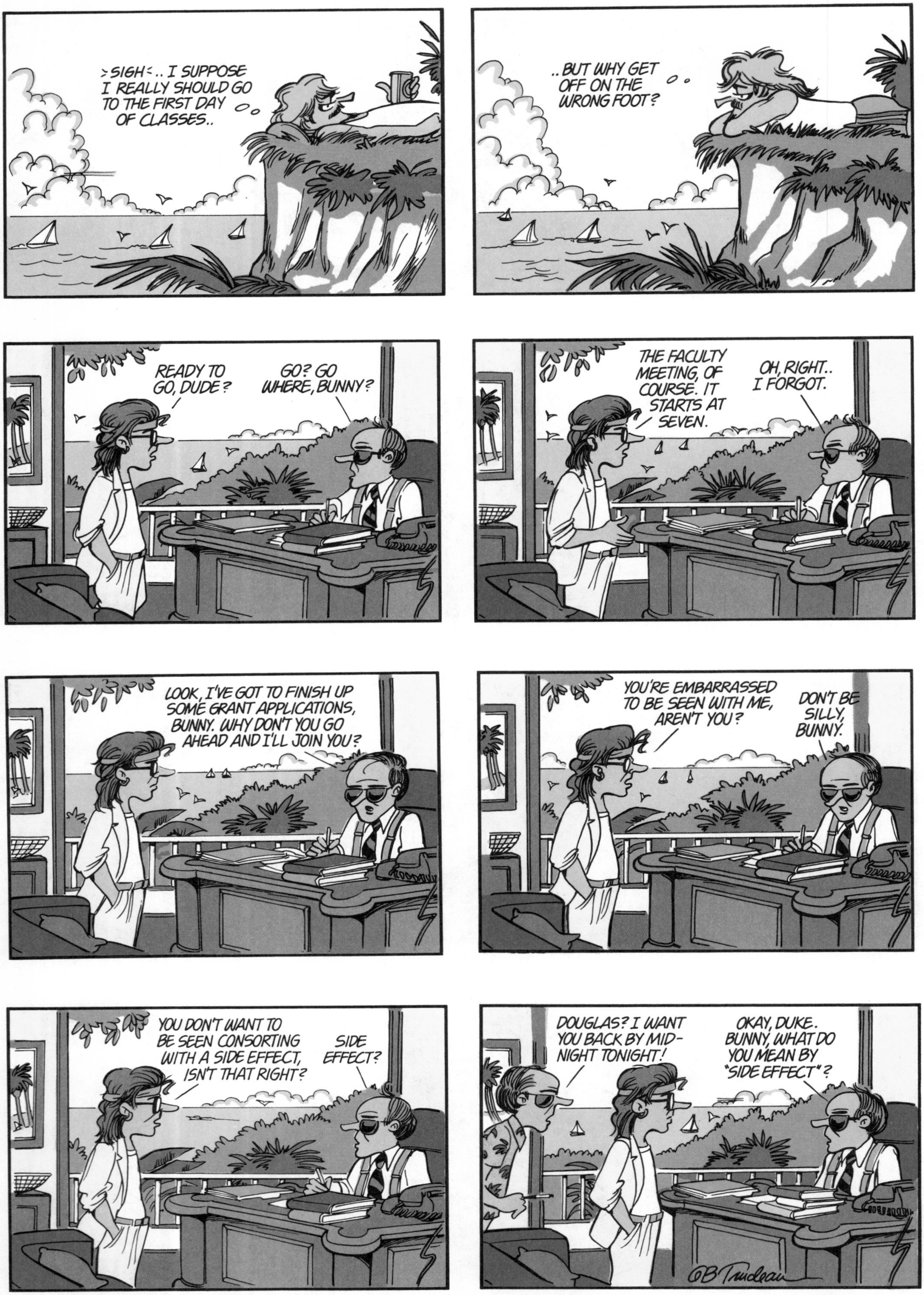
>SIGH<.. I SUPPOSE I REALLY SHOULD GO TO THE FIRST DAY OF CLASSES..
..BUT WHY GET OFF ON THE WRONG FOOT?
READY TO GO, DUDE?
GO? GO WHERE, BUNNY?
THE FACULTY MEETING, OF COURSE. IT STARTS AT SEVEN.
OH, RIGHT.. I FORGOT.
LOOK, I'VE GOT TO FINISH UP SOME GRANT APPLICATIONS, BUNNY. WHY DON'T YOU GO AHEAD AND I'LL JOIN YOU?
YOU'RE EMBARRASSED TO BE SEEN WITH ME, AREN'T YOU?
DON'T BE SILLY, BUNNY.
YOU DON'T WANT TO BE SEEN CONSORTING WITH A SIDE EFFECT, ISN'T THAT RIGHT?
SIDE EFFECT?
DOUGLAS? I WANT YOU BACK BY MIDNIGHT TONIGHT!
OKAY, DUKE. BUNNY, WHAT DO YOU MEAN BY "SIDE EFFECT"?
©B Trudeau

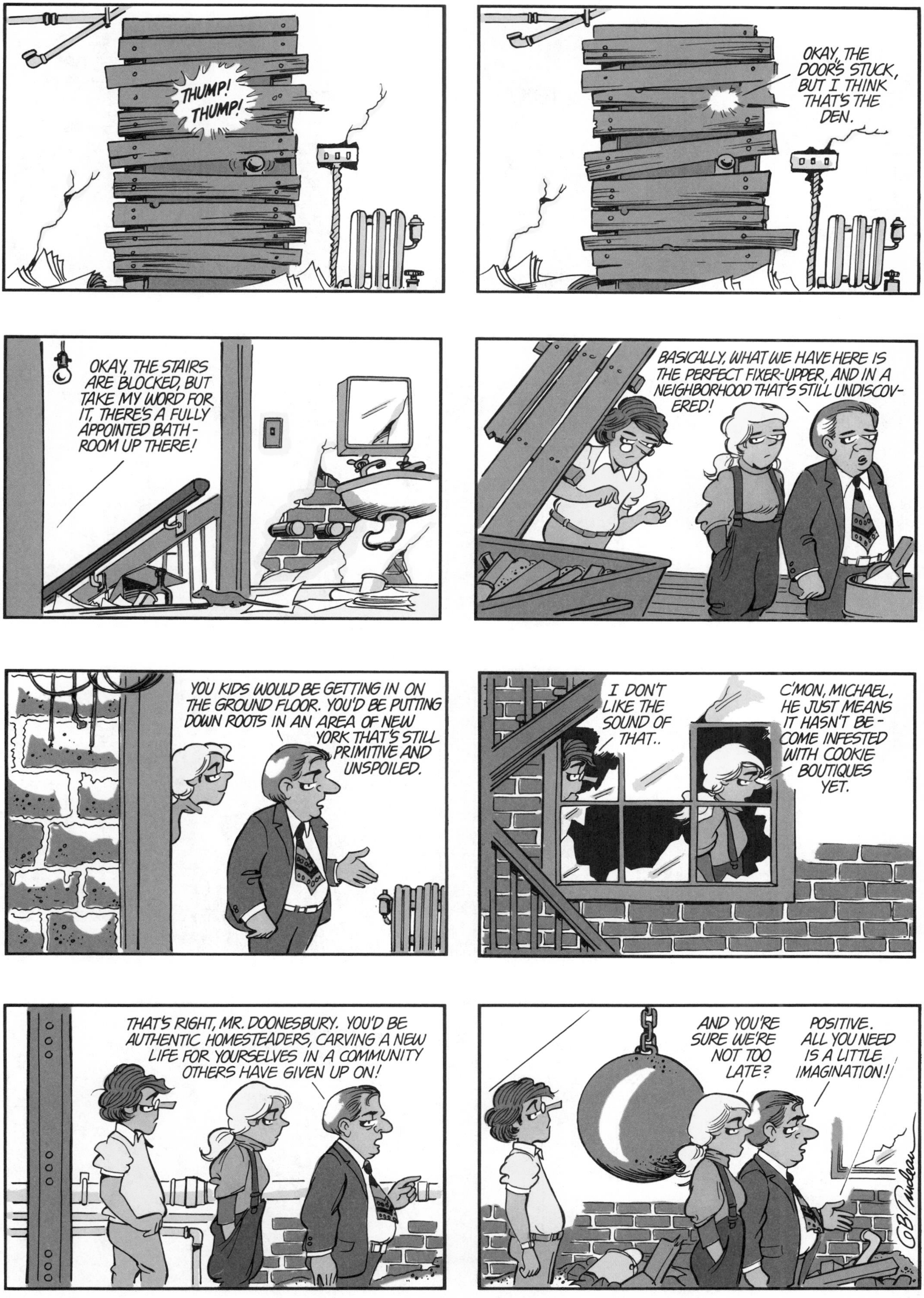
THUMP! THUMP!
OKAY, THE DOOR'S STUCK, BUT I THINK THAT'S THE DEN.
OKAY, THE STAIRS ARE BLOCKED, BUT TAKE MY WORD FOR IT, THERE'S A FULLY APPOINTED BATH-ROOM UP THERE!
BASICALLY, WHAT WE HAVE HERE IS THE PERFECT FIXER-UPPER, AND IN A NEIGHBORHOOD THAT'S STILL UNDISCOV-ERED!
YOU KIDS WOULD BE GETTING IN ON THE GROUND FLOOR. YOU'D BE PUTTING DOWN ROOTS IN AN AREA OF NEW YORK THAT'S STILL PRIMITIVE AND UNSPOILED.
I DON'T LIKE THE SOUND OF THAT..
C'MON, MICHAEL, HE JUST MEANS IT HASN'T BE-COME INFESTED WITH COOKIE BOUTIQUES YET.
THAT'S RIGHT, MR. DOONESBURY. YOU'D BE AUTHENTIC HOMESTEADERS, CARVING A NEW LIFE FOR YOURSELVES IN A COMMUNITY OTHERS HAVE GIVEN UP ON!
AND YOU'RE SURE WE'RE NOT TOO LATE?
POSITIVE. ALL YOU NEED IS A LITTLE IMAGINATION!

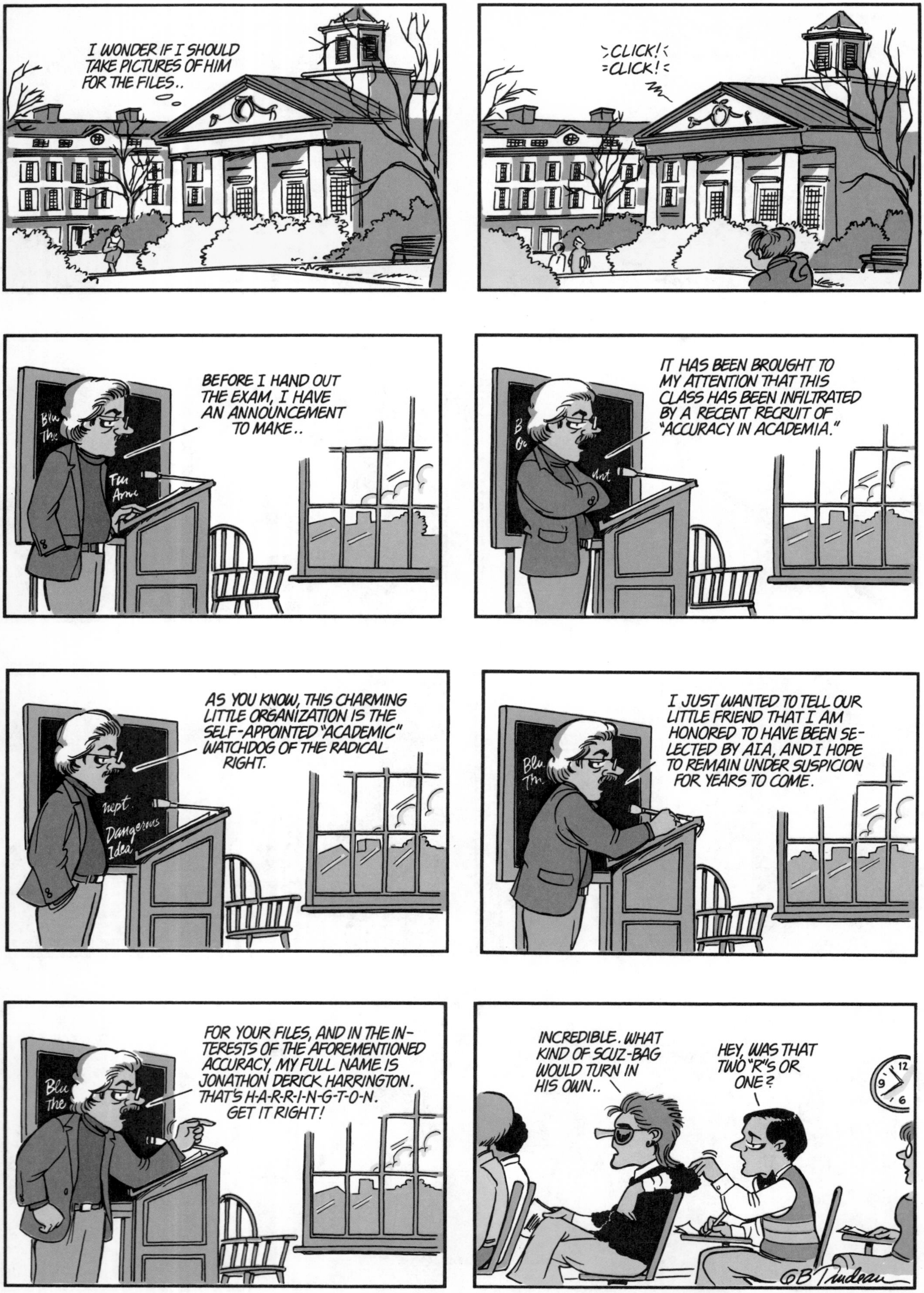
I WONDER IF I SHOULD TAKE PICTURES OF HIM FOR THE FILES..
CLICK! CLICK!
BEFORE I HAND OUT THE EXAM, I HAVE AN ANNOUNCEMENT TO MAKE..
IT HAS BEEN BROUGHT TO MY ATTENTION THAT THIS CLASS HAS BEEN INFILTRATED BY A RECENT RECRUIT OF "ACCURACY IN ACADEMIA."
AS YOU KNOW, THIS CHARMING LITTLE ORGANIZATION IS THE SELF-APPOINTED "ACADEMIC" WATCHDOG OF THE RADICAL RIGHT.
Dangerous Idea
I JUST WANTED TO TELL OUR LITTLE FRIEND THAT I AM HONORED TO HAVE BEEN SE-LECTED BY AIA, AND I HOPE TO REMAIN UNDER SUSPICION FOR YEARS TO COME.
FOR YOUR FILES, AND IN THE IN-TERESTS OF THE AFOREMENTIONED ACCURACY, MY FULL NAME IS JONATHON DERICK HARRINGTON. THAT'S H-A-R-R-I-N-G-T-O-N. GET IT RIGHT!
INCREDIBLE. WHAT KIND OF SCUZ-BAG WOULD TURN IN HIS OWN..
HEY, WAS THAT TWO "R"S OR ONE?
GB Trudeau

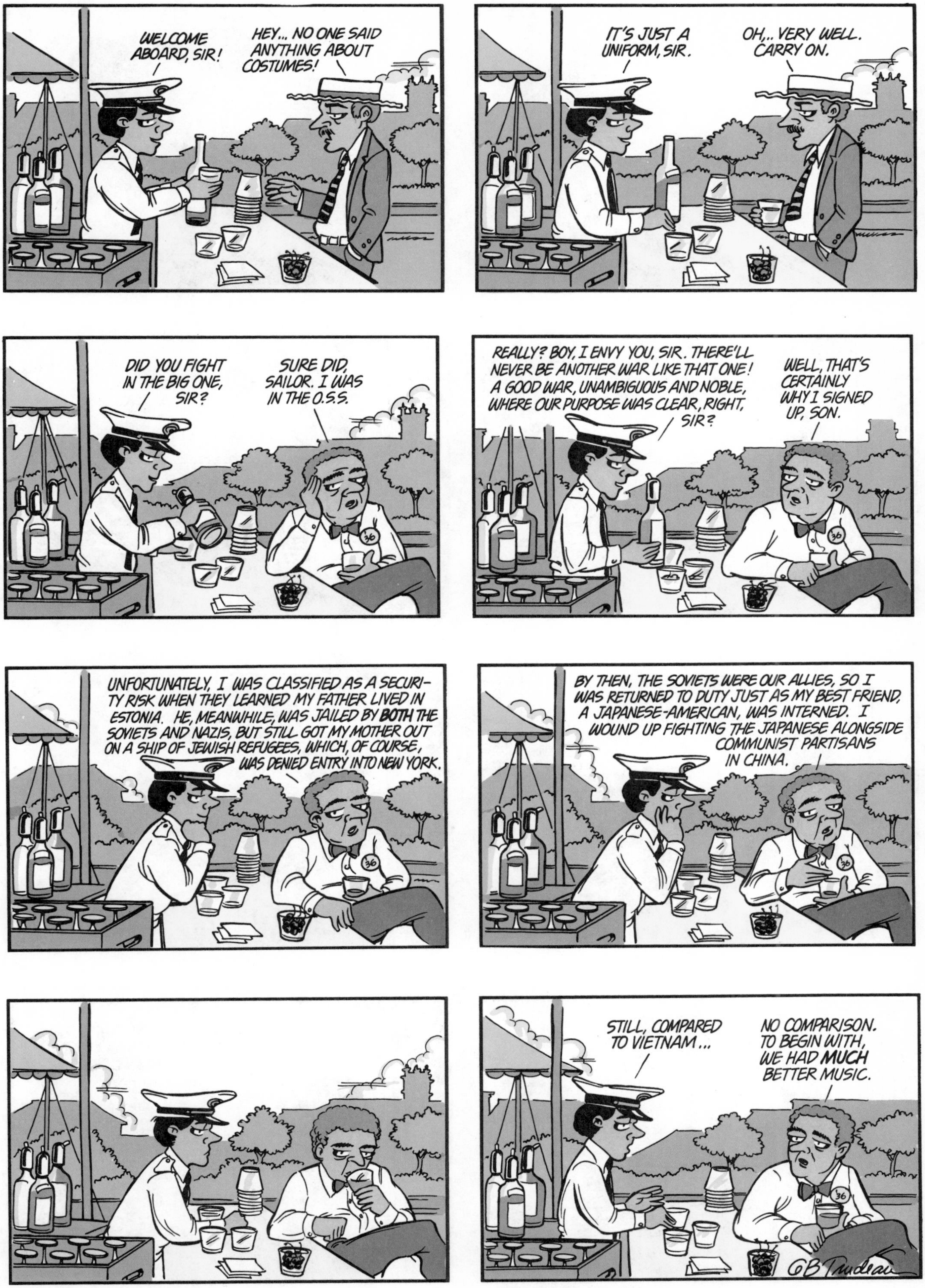
WELCOME ABOARD, SIR!
HEY... NO ONE SAID ANYTHING ABOUT COSTUMES!
IT'S JUST A UNIFORM, SIR.
OH,.. VERY WELL. CARRY ON.
DID YOU FIGHT IN THE BIG ONE, SIR?
SURE DID, SAILOR. I WAS IN THE O.S.S.
REALLY? BOY, I ENVY YOU, SIR. THERE'LL NEVER BE ANOTHER WAR LIKE THAT ONE! A GOOD WAR, UNAMBIGUOUS AND NOBLE, WHERE OUR PURPOSE WAS CLEAR, RIGHT, SIR?
WELL, THAT'S CERTAINLY WHY I SIGNED UP, SON.
UNFORTUNATELY, I WAS CLASSIFIED AS A SECURITY RISK WHEN THEY LEARNED MY FATHER LIVED IN ESTONIA. HE, MEANWHILE, WAS JAILED BY **BOTH** THE SOVIETS AND NAZIS, BUT STILL GOT MY MOTHER OUT ON A SHIP OF JEWISH REFUGEES, WHICH, OF COURSE, WAS DENIED ENTRY INTO NEW YORK.
BY THEN, THE SOVIETS WERE OUR ALLIES, SO I WAS RETURNED TO DUTY JUST AS MY BEST FRIEND, A JAPANESE-AMERICAN, WAS INTERNED. I WOUND UP FIGHTING THE JAPANESE ALONGSIDE COMMUNIST PARTISANS IN CHINA.
STILL, COMPARED TO VIETNAM...
NO COMPARISON. TO BEGIN WITH, WE HAD **MUCH** BETTER MUSIC.
GB Trudeau

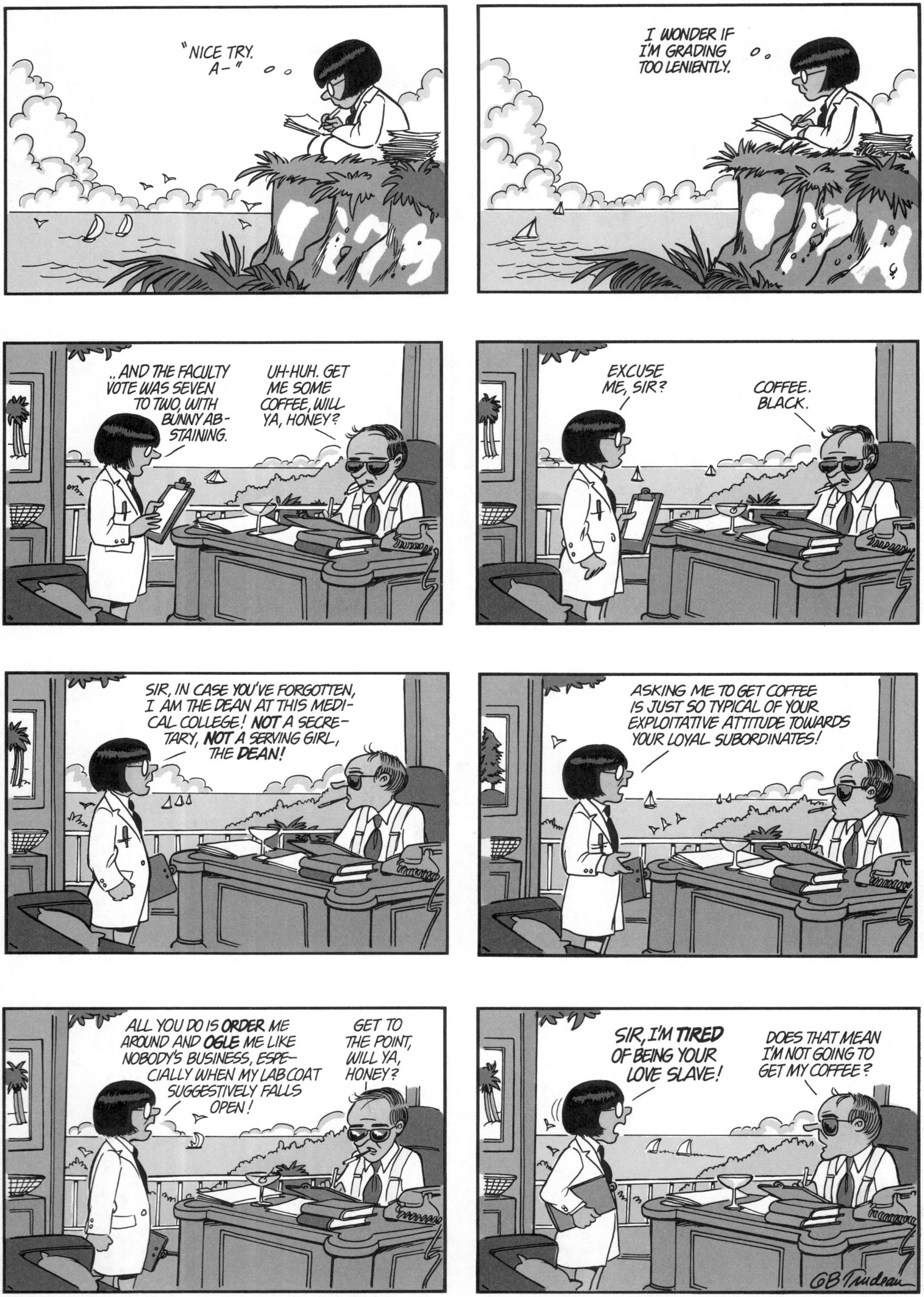

"NICE TRY. A–"
I WONDER IF I'M GRADING TOO LENIENTLY.
..AND THE FACULTY VOTE WAS SEVEN TO TWO, WITH BUNNY AB-STAINING.
UH-HUH. GET ME SOME COFFEE, WILL YA, HONEY?
EXCUSE ME, SIR?
COFFEE. BLACK.
SIR, IN CASE YOU'VE FORGOTTEN, I AM THE DEAN AT THIS MEDI-CAL COLLEGE! **NOT** A SECRE-TARY, **NOT** A SERVING GIRL, THE **DEAN!**
ASKING ME TO GET COFFEE IS JUST SO TYPICAL OF YOUR EXPLOITATIVE ATTITUDE TOWARDS YOUR LOYAL SUBORDINATES!
ALL YOU DO IS **ORDER** ME AROUND AND **OGLE** ME LIKE NOBODY'S BUSINESS, ESPE-CIALLY WHEN MY LAB COAT SUGGESTIVELY FALLS OPEN!
GET TO THE POINT, WILL YA, HONEY?
SIR, I'M **TIRED** OF BEING YOUR **LOVE SLAVE!**
DOES THAT MEAN I'M NOT GOING TO GET MY COFFEE?
GB Trudeau

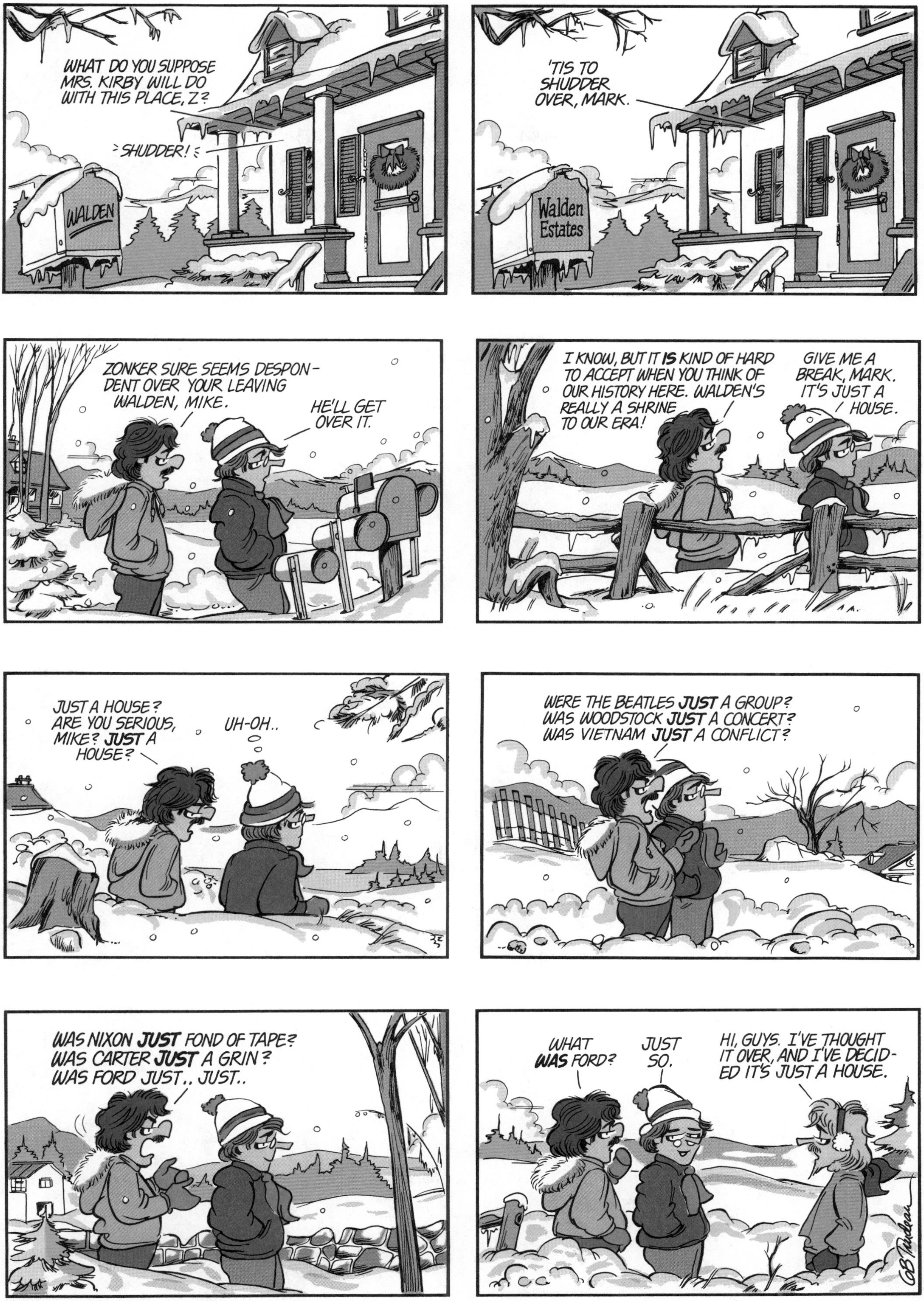

WHAT DO YOU SUPPOSE MRS. KIRBY WILL DO WITH THIS PLACE, Z?
SHUDDER!
WALDEN
'TIS TO SHUDDER OVER, MARK.
Walden Estates
ZONKER SURE SEEMS DESPONDENT OVER YOUR LEAVING WALDEN, MIKE.
HE'LL GET OVER IT.
I KNOW, BUT IT IS KIND OF HARD TO ACCEPT WHEN YOU THINK OF OUR HISTORY HERE. WALDEN'S REALLY A SHRINE TO OUR ERA!
GIVE ME A BREAK, MARK. IT'S JUST A HOUSE.
JUST A HOUSE? ARE YOU SERIOUS, MIKE? JUST A HOUSE?
UH-OH..
WERE THE BEATLES JUST A GROUP? WAS WOODSTOCK JUST A CONCERT? WAS VIETNAM JUST A CONFLICT?
WAS NIXON JUST FOND OF TAPE? WAS CARTER JUST A GRIN? WAS FORD JUST.. JUST..
WHAT WAS FORD?
JUST SO.
HI, GUYS. I'VE THOUGHT IT OVER, AND I'VE DECIDED IT'S JUST A HOUSE.
GBTrudeau

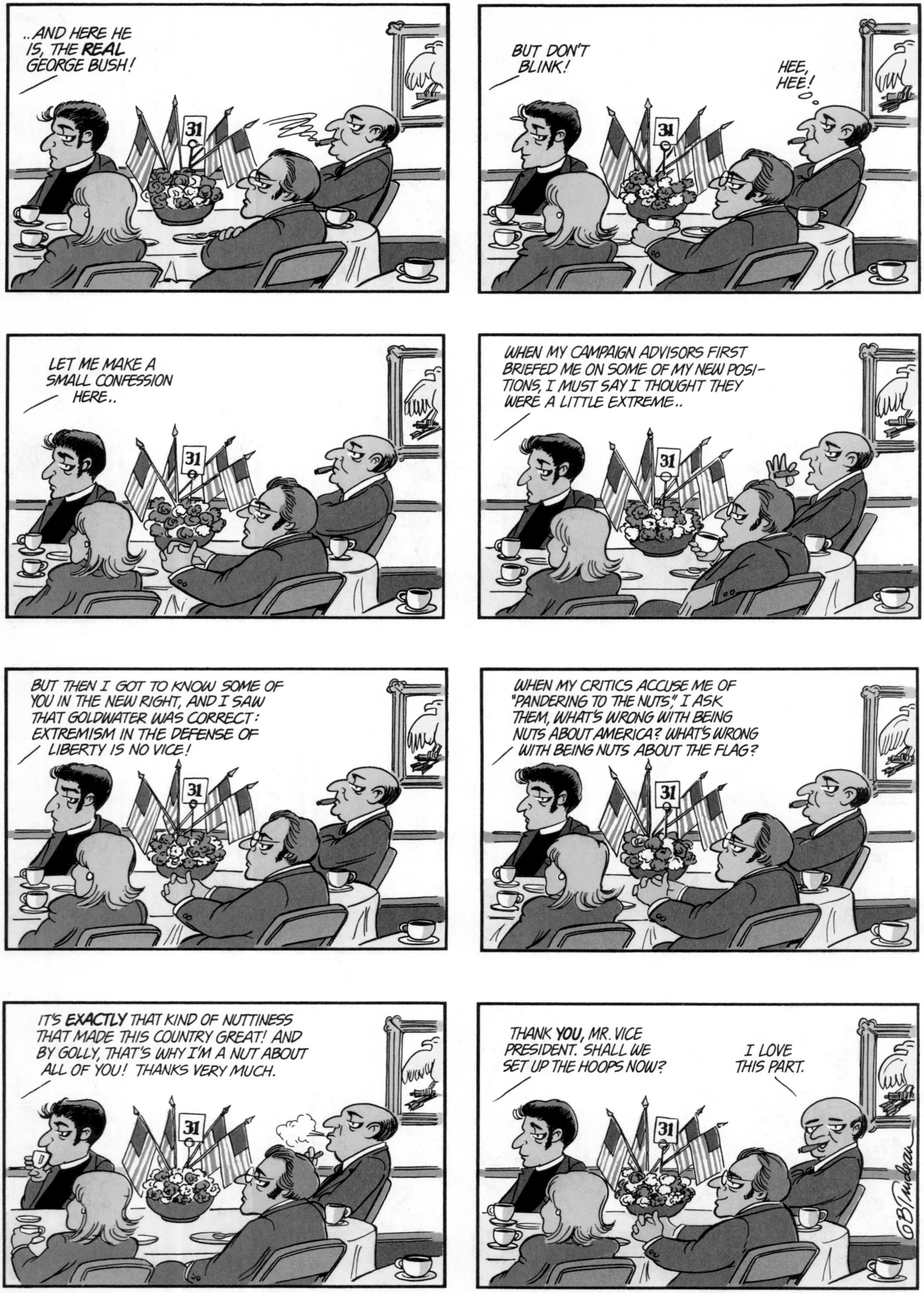
..AND HERE HE IS, THE **REAL** GEORGE BUSH!
BUT DON'T BLINK!
HEE, HEE!
LET ME MAKE A SMALL CONFESSION HERE..
WHEN MY CAMPAIGN ADVISORS FIRST BRIEFED ME ON SOME OF MY NEW POSITIONS, I MUST SAY I THOUGHT THEY WERE A LITTLE EXTREME..
BUT THEN I GOT TO KNOW SOME OF YOU IN THE NEW RIGHT, AND I SAW THAT GOLDWATER WAS CORRECT: EXTREMISM IN THE DEFENSE OF LIBERTY IS NO VICE!
WHEN MY CRITICS ACCUSE ME OF "PANDERING TO THE NUTS," I ASK THEM, WHAT'S WRONG WITH BEING NUTS ABOUT AMERICA? WHAT'S WRONG WITH BEING NUTS ABOUT THE FLAG?
IT'S **EXACTLY** THAT KIND OF NUTTINESS THAT MADE THIS COUNTRY GREAT! AND BY GOLLY, THAT'S WHY I'M A NUT ABOUT ALL OF YOU! THANKS VERY MUCH.
THANK **YOU**, MR. VICE PRESIDENT. SHALL WE SET UP THE HOOPS NOW?
I LOVE THIS PART.

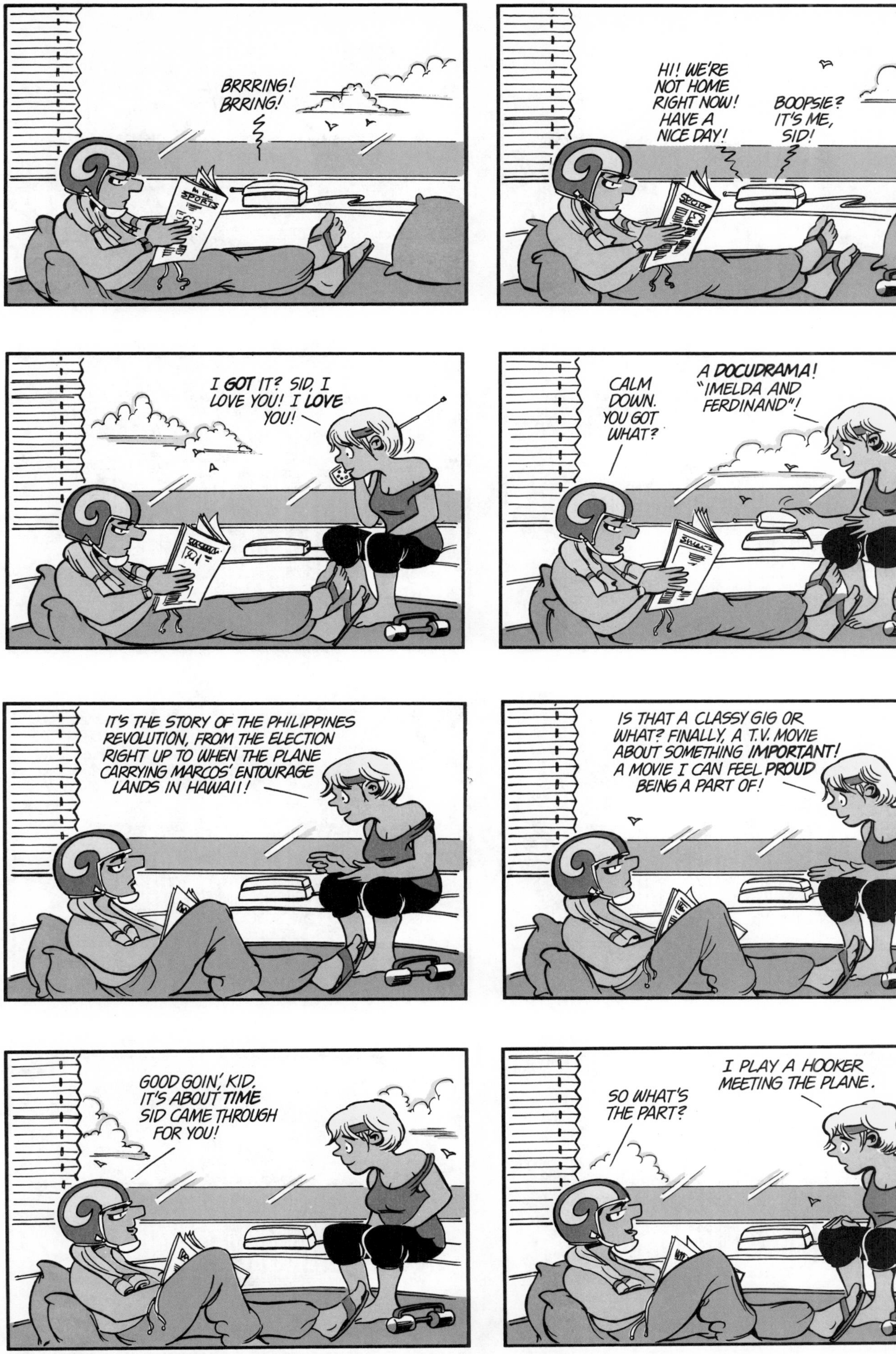
BRRRING! BRRING!
HI! WE'RE NOT HOME RIGHT NOW! HAVE A NICE DAY!
BOOPSIE? IT'S ME, SID!
I GOT IT? SID, I LOVE YOU! I LOVE YOU!
CALM DOWN. YOU GOT WHAT?
A DOCUDRAMA! "IMELDA AND FERDINAND"!
IT'S THE STORY OF THE PHILIPPINES REVOLUTION, FROM THE ELECTION RIGHT UP TO WHEN THE PLANE CARRYING MARCOS' ENTOURAGE LANDS IN HAWAII!
IS THAT A CLASSY GIG OR WHAT? FINALLY, A T.V. MOVIE ABOUT SOMETHING IMPORTANT! A MOVIE I CAN FEEL PROUD BEING A PART OF!
GOOD GOIN', KID. IT'S ABOUT TIME SID CAME THROUGH FOR YOU!
SO WHAT'S THE PART?
I PLAY A HOOKER MEETING THE PLANE.
©B Trudeau

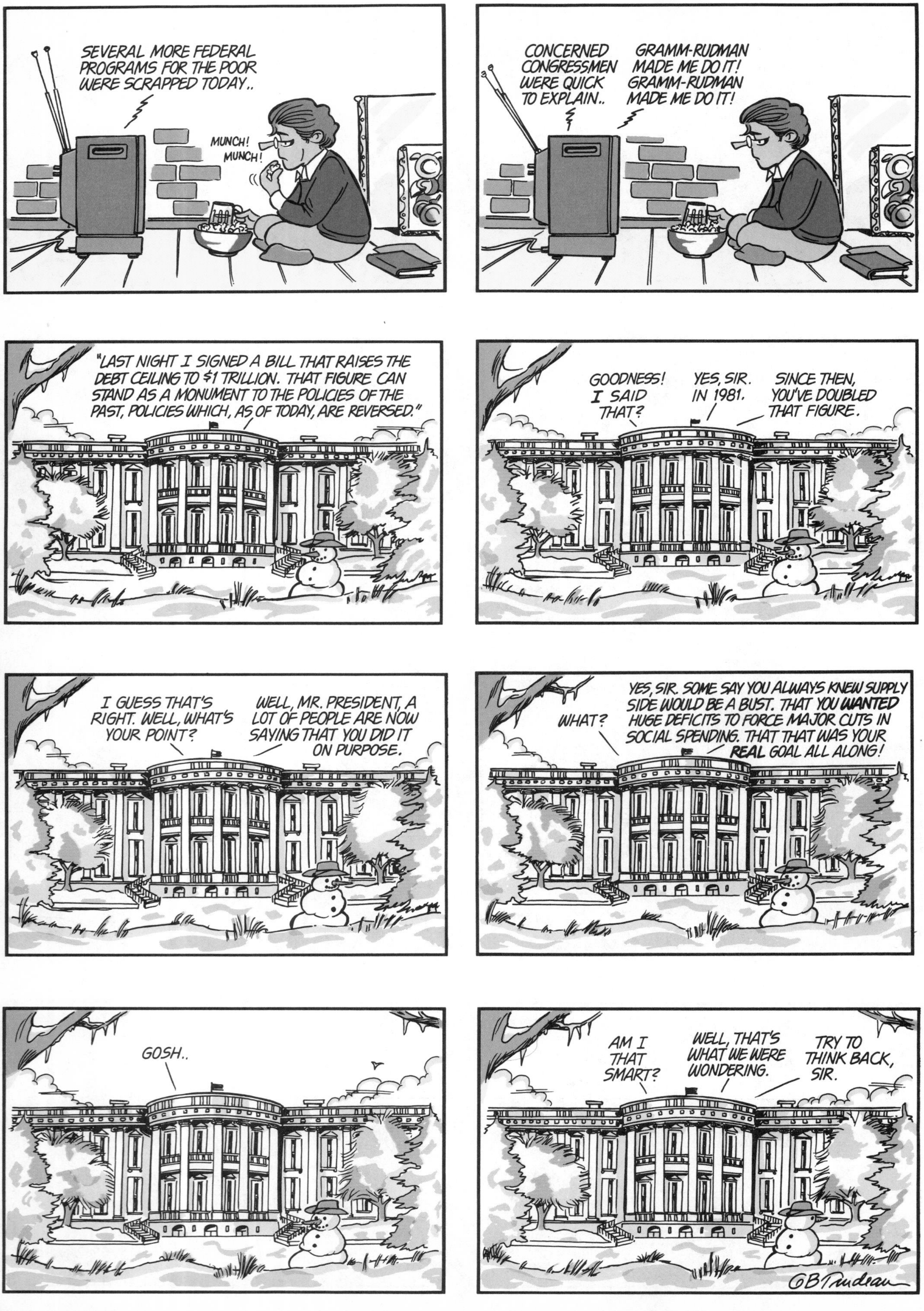
SEVERAL MORE FEDERAL PROGRAMS FOR THE POOR WERE SCRAPPED TODAY..
MUNCH! MUNCH!
CONCERNED CONGRESSMEN WERE QUICK TO EXPLAIN..
GRAMM-RUDMAN MADE ME DO IT! GRAMM-RUDMAN MADE ME DO IT!
"LAST NIGHT I SIGNED A BILL THAT RAISES THE DEBT CEILING TO $1 TRILLION. THAT FIGURE CAN STAND AS A MONUMENT TO THE POLICIES OF THE PAST, POLICIES WHICH, AS OF TODAY, ARE REVERSED."
GOODNESS! I SAID THAT?
YES, SIR. IN 1981.
SINCE THEN, YOU'VE DOUBLED THAT FIGURE.
I GUESS THAT'S RIGHT. WELL, WHAT'S YOUR POINT?
WELL, MR. PRESIDENT, A LOT OF PEOPLE ARE NOW SAYING THAT YOU DID IT ON PURPOSE.
WHAT?
YES, SIR. SOME SAY YOU ALWAYS KNEW SUPPLY SIDE WOULD BE A BUST. THAT YOU WANTED HUGE DEFICITS TO FORCE MAJOR CUTS IN SOCIAL SPENDING. THAT THAT WAS YOUR REAL GOAL ALL ALONG!
GOSH..
AM I THAT SMART?
WELL, THAT'S WHAT WE WERE WONDERING.
TRY TO THINK BACK, SIR.
GBTrudeau

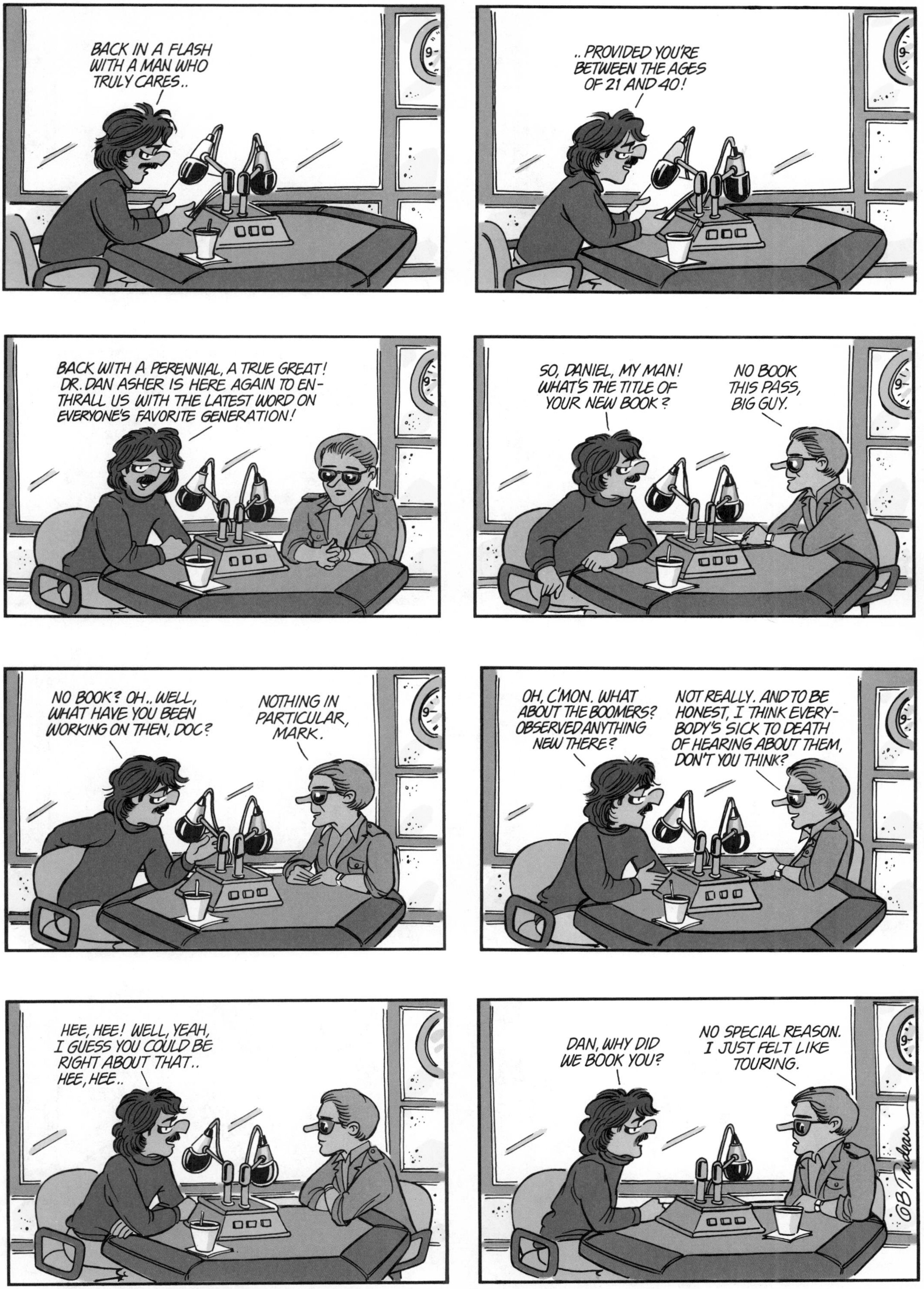
BACK IN A FLASH WITH A MAN WHO TRULY CARES..
..PROVIDED YOU'RE BETWEEN THE AGES OF 21 AND 40!
BACK WITH A PERENNIAL, A TRUE GREAT! DR. DAN ASHER IS HERE AGAIN TO ENTHRALL US WITH THE LATEST WORD ON EVERYONE'S FAVORITE GENERATION!
SO, DANIEL, MY MAN! WHAT'S THE TITLE OF YOUR NEW BOOK?
NO BOOK THIS PASS, BIG GUY.
NO BOOK? OH.. WELL, WHAT HAVE YOU BEEN WORKING ON THEN, DOC?
NOTHING IN PARTICULAR, MARK.
OH, C'MON. WHAT ABOUT THE BOOMERS? OBSERVED ANYTHING NEW THERE?
NOT REALLY. AND TO BE HONEST, I THINK EVERYBODY'S SICK TO DEATH OF HEARING ABOUT THEM, DON'T YOU THINK?
HEE, HEE! WELL, YEAH, I GUESS YOU COULD BE RIGHT ABOUT THAT.. HEE, HEE..
DAN, WHY DID WE BOOK YOU?
NO SPECIAL REASON. I JUST FELT LIKE TOURING.
©GB Trudeau

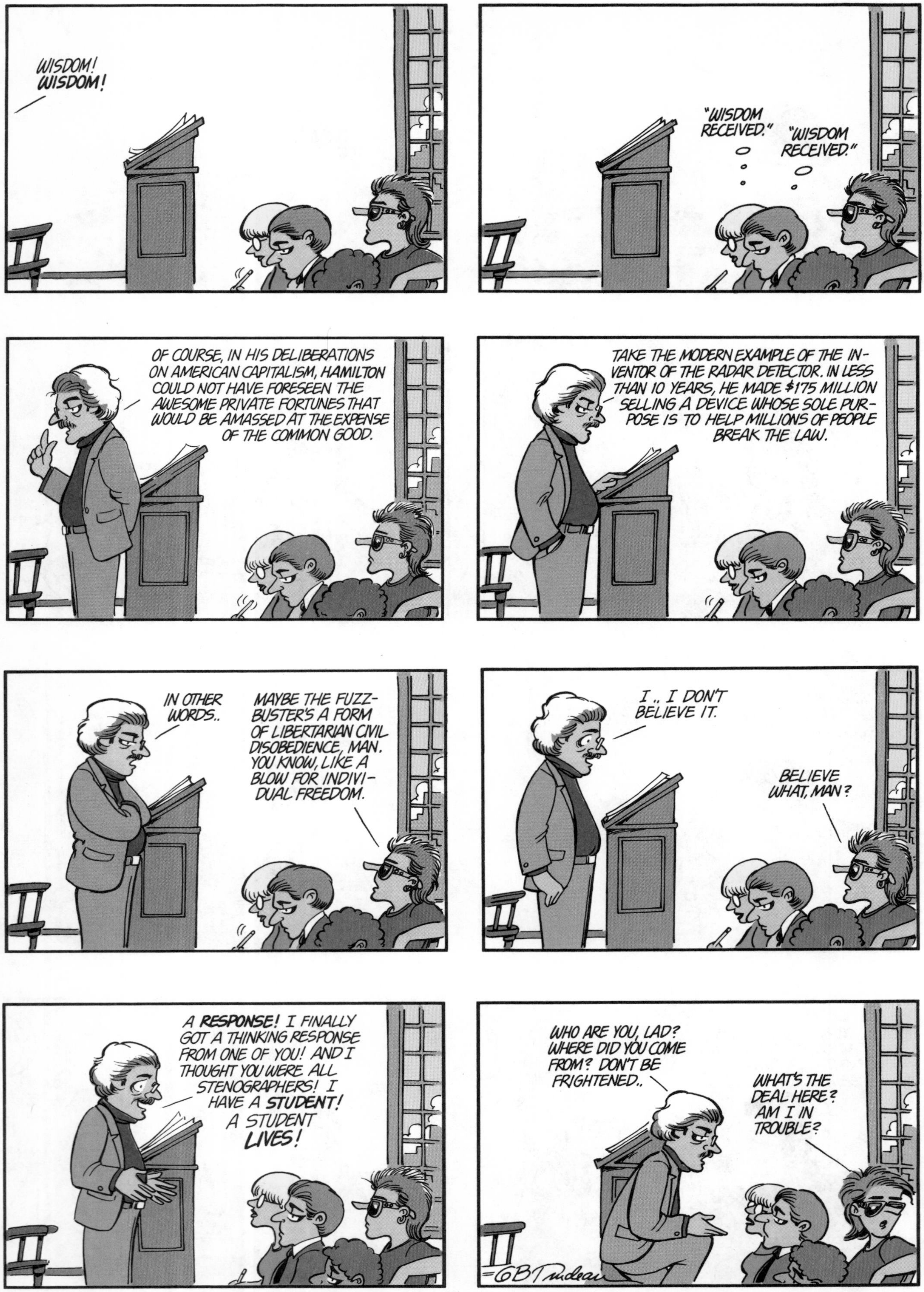
WISDOM!
WISDOM!
"WISDOM RECEIVED."
"WISDOM RECEIVED."
OF COURSE, IN HIS DELIBERATIONS ON AMERICAN CAPITALISM, HAMILTON COULD NOT HAVE FORESEEN THE AWESOME PRIVATE FORTUNES THAT WOULD BE AMASSED AT THE EXPENSE OF THE COMMON GOOD.
TAKE THE MODERN EXAMPLE OF THE INVENTOR OF THE RADAR DETECTOR. IN LESS THAN 10 YEARS, HE MADE $175 MILLION SELLING A DEVICE WHOSE SOLE PURPOSE IS TO HELP MILLIONS OF PEOPLE BREAK THE LAW.
IN OTHER WORDS..
MAYBE THE FUZZBUSTER'S A FORM OF LIBERTARIAN CIVIL DISOBEDIENCE, MAN. YOU KNOW, LIKE A BLOW FOR INDIVIDUAL FREEDOM.
I .. I DON'T BELIEVE IT.
BELIEVE WHAT, MAN?
A RESPONSE! I FINALLY GOT A THINKING RESPONSE FROM ONE OF YOU! AND I THOUGHT YOU WERE ALL STENOGRAPHERS! I HAVE A STUDENT! A STUDENT LIVES!
WHO ARE YOU, LAD? WHERE DID YOU COME FROM? DON'T BE FRIGHTENED..
WHAT'S THE DEAL HERE? AM I IN TROUBLE?
GBTrudeau

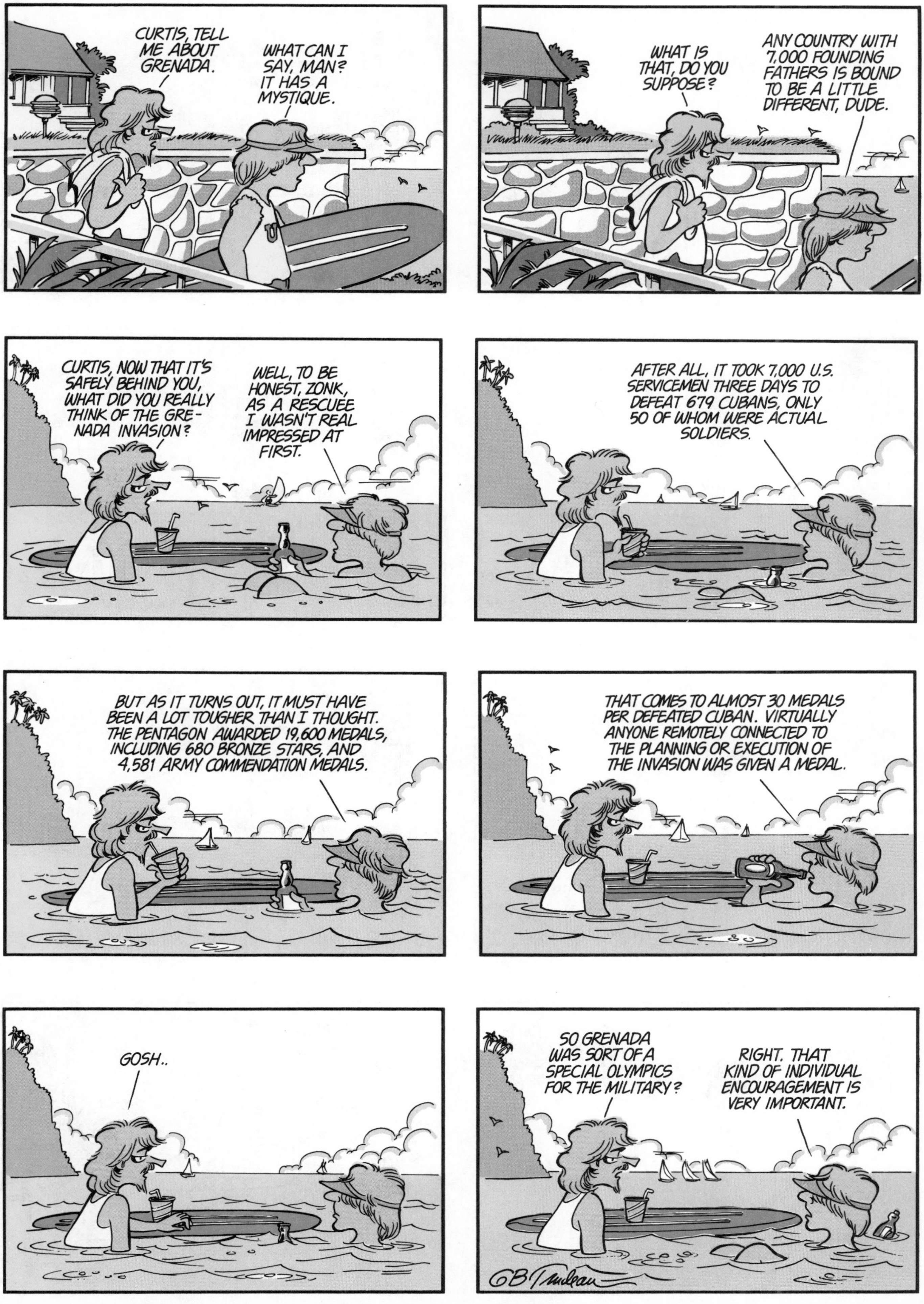
CURTIS, TELL ME ABOUT GRENADA.
WHAT CAN I SAY, MAN? IT HAS A MYSTIQUE.
WHAT IS THAT, DO YOU SUPPOSE?
ANY COUNTRY WITH 7,000 FOUNDING FATHERS IS BOUND TO BE A LITTLE DIFFERENT, DUDE.
CURTIS, NOW THAT IT'S SAFELY BEHIND YOU, WHAT DID YOU REALLY THINK OF THE GRE-NADA INVASION?
WELL, TO BE HONEST, ZONK, AS A RESCUEE I WASN'T REAL IMPRESSED AT FIRST.
AFTER ALL, IT TOOK 7,000 U.S. SERVICEMEN THREE DAYS TO DEFEAT 679 CUBANS, ONLY 50 OF WHOM WERE ACTUAL SOLDIERS.
BUT AS IT TURNS OUT, IT MUST HAVE BEEN A LOT TOUGHER THAN I THOUGHT. THE PENTAGON AWARDED 19,600 MEDALS, INCLUDING 680 BRONZE STARS, AND 4,581 ARMY COMMENDATION MEDALS.
THAT COMES TO ALMOST 30 MEDALS PER DEFEATED CUBAN. VIRTUALLY ANYONE REMOTELY CONNECTED TO THE PLANNING OR EXECUTION OF THE INVASION WAS GIVEN A MEDAL.
GOSH..
SO GRENADA WAS SORT OF A SPECIAL OLYMPICS FOR THE MILITARY?
RIGHT. THAT KIND OF INDIVIDUAL ENCOURAGEMENT IS VERY IMPORTANT.

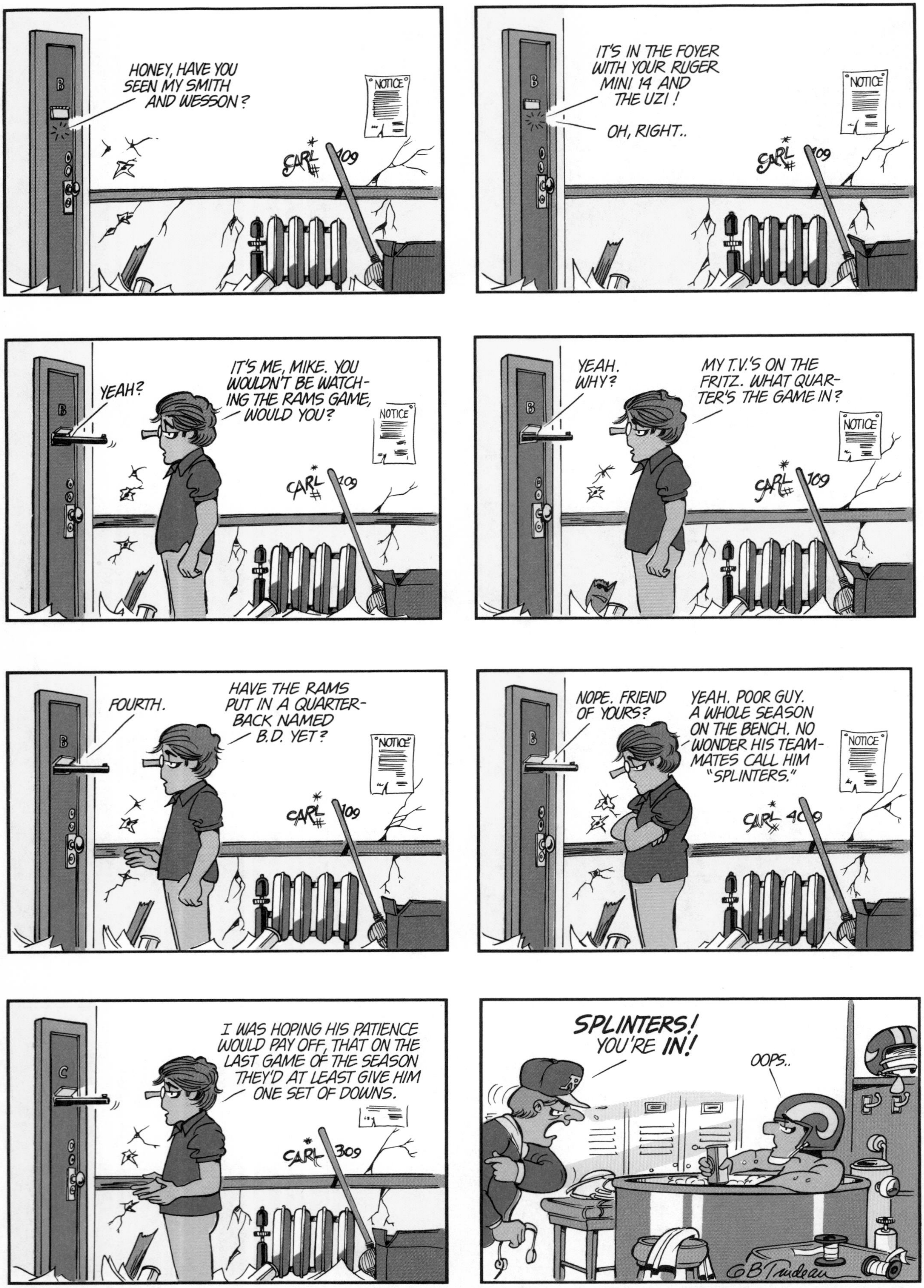
HONEY, HAVE YOU SEEN MY SMITH AND WESSON?
IT'S IN THE FOYER WITH YOUR RUGER MINI 14 AND THE UZI!
OH, RIGHT..
YEAH?
IT'S ME, MIKE. YOU WOULDN'T BE WATCHING THE RAMS GAME, WOULD YOU?
YEAH. WHY?
MY T.V.'S ON THE FRITZ. WHAT QUARTER'S THE GAME IN?
FOURTH.
HAVE THE RAMS PUT IN A QUARTERBACK NAMED B.D. YET?
NOPE. FRIEND OF YOURS?
YEAH. POOR GUY. A WHOLE SEASON ON THE BENCH. NO WONDER HIS TEAMMATES CALL HIM "SPLINTERS."
I WAS HOPING HIS PATIENCE WOULD PAY OFF, THAT ON THE LAST GAME OF THE SEASON THEY'D AT LEAST GIVE HIM ONE SET OF DOWNS.
SPLINTERS! YOU'RE IN!
OOPS..

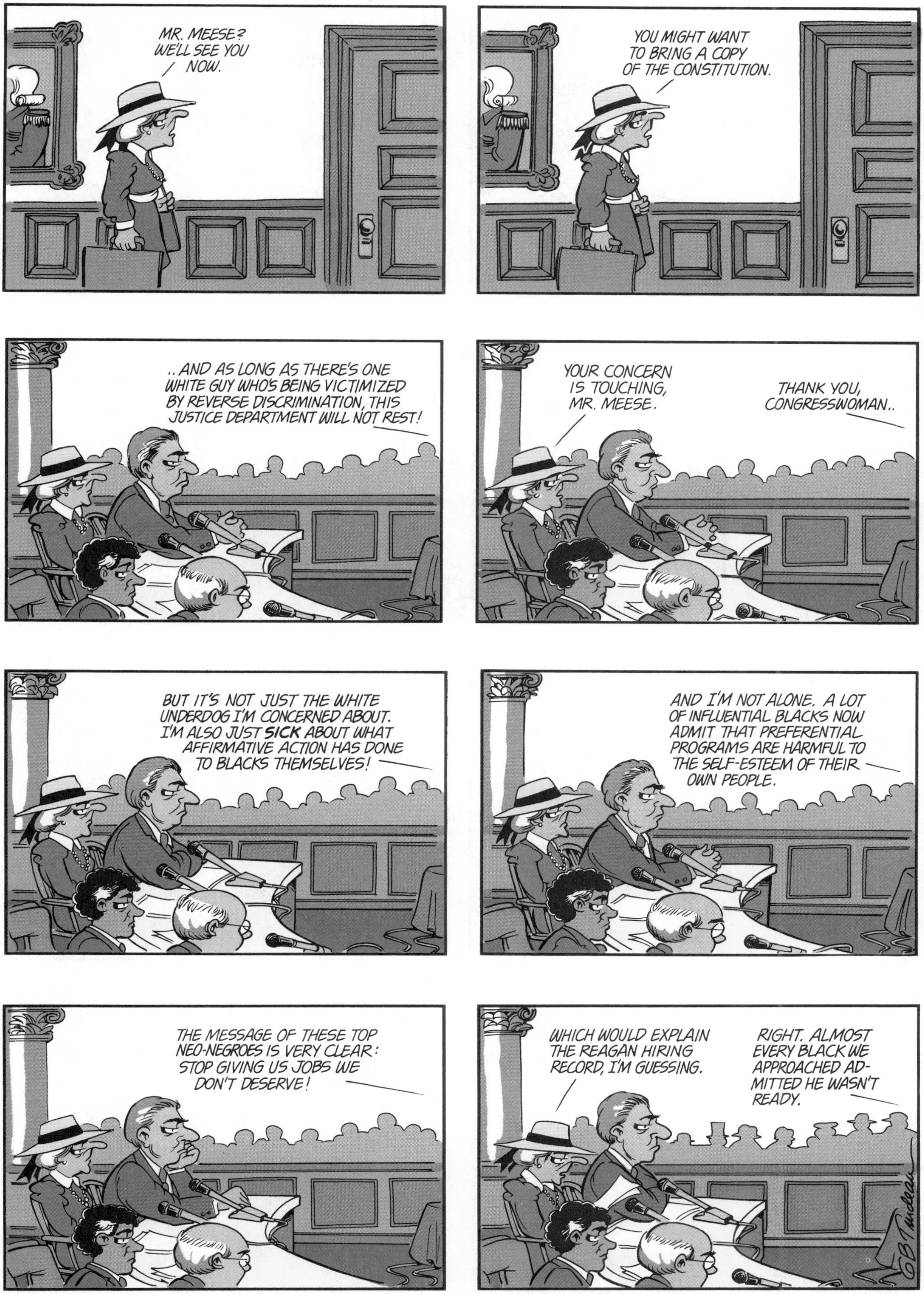
MR. MEESE? WE'LL SEE YOU NOW.
YOU MIGHT WANT TO BRING A COPY OF THE CONSTITUTION.
..AND AS LONG AS THERE'S ONE WHITE GUY WHO'S BEING VICTIMIZED BY REVERSE DISCRIMINATION, THIS JUSTICE DEPARTMENT WILL NOT REST!
YOUR CONCERN IS TOUCHING, MR. MEESE.
THANK YOU, CONGRESSWOMAN..
BUT IT'S NOT JUST THE WHITE UNDERDOG I'M CONCERNED ABOUT. I'M ALSO JUST **SICK** ABOUT WHAT AFFIRMATIVE ACTION HAS DONE TO BLACKS THEMSELVES!
AND I'M NOT ALONE. A LOT OF INFLUENTIAL BLACKS NOW ADMIT THAT PREFERENTIAL PROGRAMS ARE HARMFUL TO THE SELF-ESTEEM OF THEIR OWN PEOPLE.
THE MESSAGE OF THESE TOP NEO-NEGROES IS VERY CLEAR: STOP GIVING US JOBS WE DON'T DESERVE!
WHICH WOULD EXPLAIN THE REAGAN HIRING RECORD, I'M GUESSING.
RIGHT. ALMOST EVERY BLACK WE APPROACHED ADMITTED HE WASN'T READY.
GBTrudeau

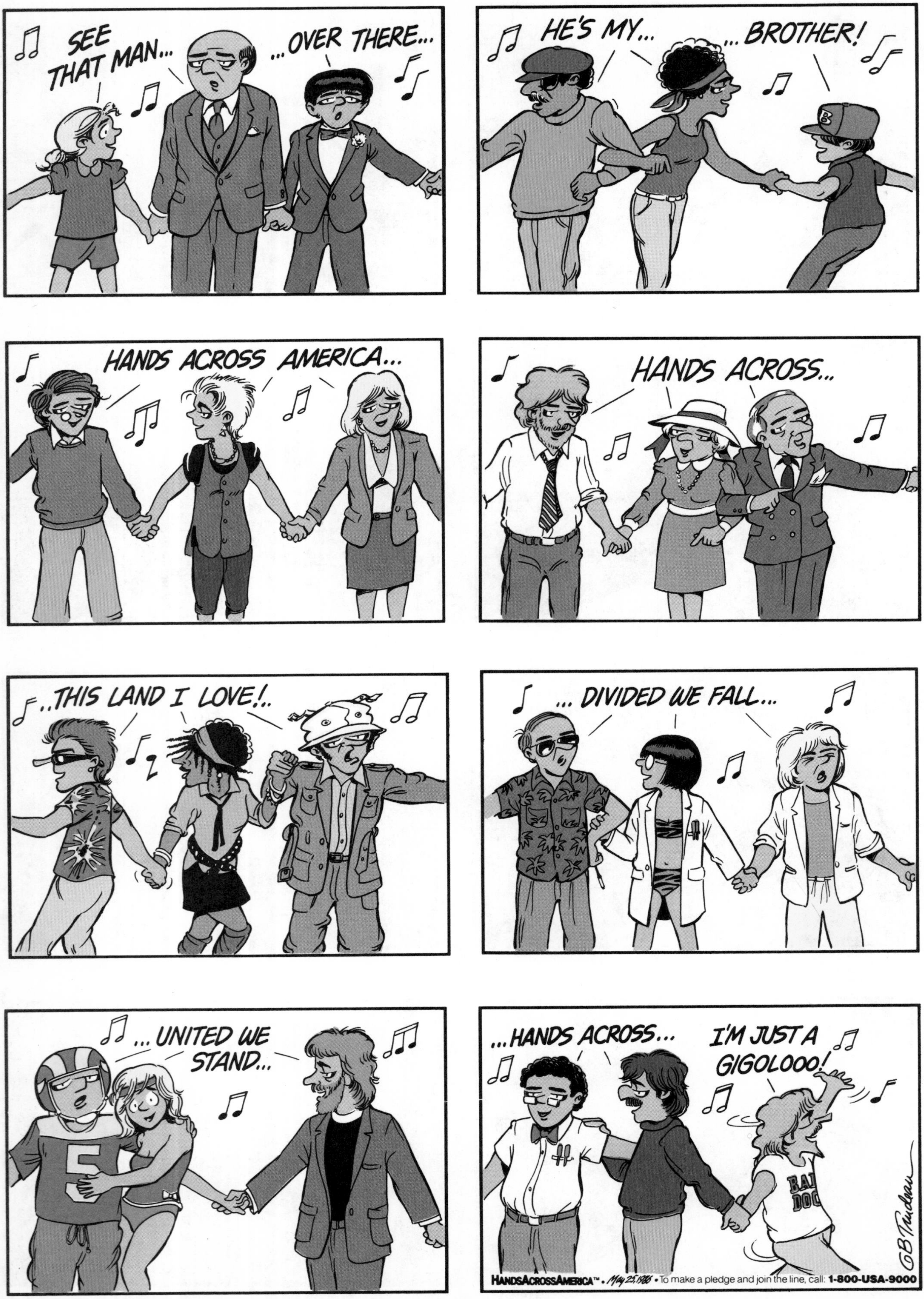
SEE THAT MAN...
...OVER THERE...
HE'S MY...
...BROTHER!
HANDS ACROSS AMERICA...
HANDS ACROSS...
..THIS LAND I LOVE!..
... DIVIDED WE FALL...
... UNITED WE STAND...
...HANDS ACROSS...
I'M JUST A GIGOLOOO!
HANDSACROSSAMERICA™ • May 25, 1986 • To make a pledge and join the line, call: 1-800-USA-9000

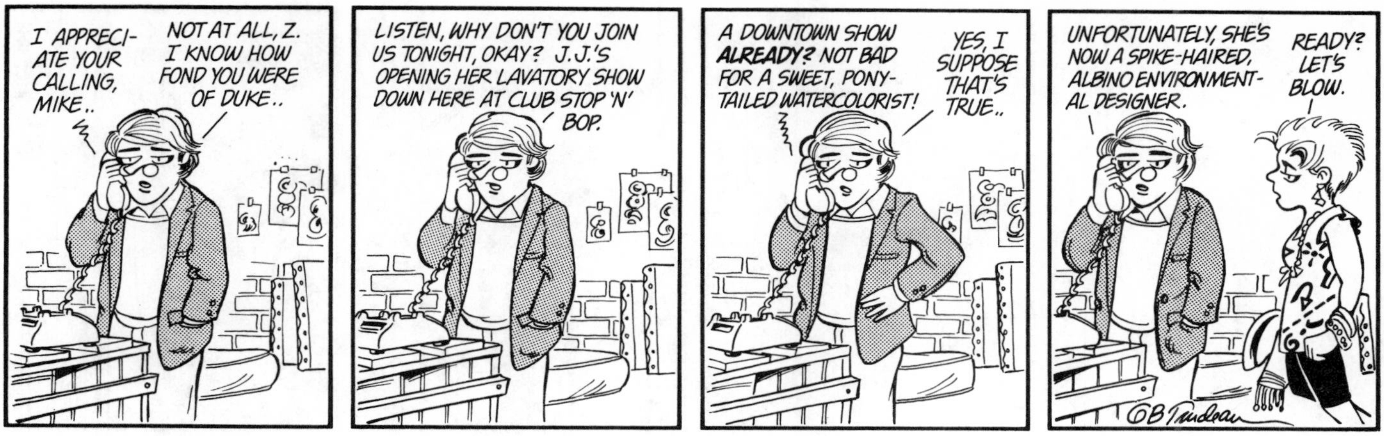
I APPRECIATE YOUR CALLING, MIKE..
NOT AT ALL, Z. I KNOW HOW FOND YOU WERE OF DUKE..
LISTEN, WHY DON'T YOU JOIN US TONIGHT, OKAY? J.J.'S OPENING HER LAVATORY SHOW DOWN HERE AT CLUB STOP 'N' BOP.
A DOWNTOWN SHOW ALREADY? NOT BAD FOR A SWEET, PONY-TAILED WATERCOLORIST!
YES, I SUPPOSE THAT'S TRUE..
UNFORTUNATELY, SHE'S NOW A SPIKE-HAIRED, ALBINO ENVIRONMENTAL DESIGNER.
READY? LET'S BLOW.
GB Trudeau

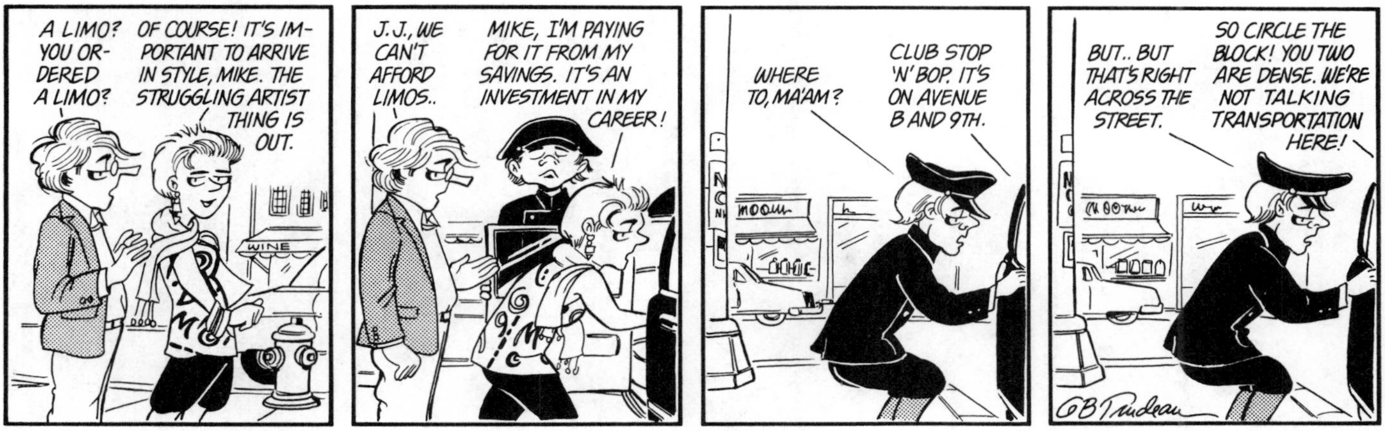
A LIMO? YOU ORDERED A LIMO?
OF COURSE! IT'S IMPORTANT TO ARRIVE IN STYLE, MIKE. THE STRUGGLING ARTIST THING IS OUT.
WINE
J.J., WE CAN'T AFFORD LIMOS..
MIKE, I'M PAYING FOR IT FROM MY SAVINGS. IT'S AN INVESTMENT IN MY CAREER!
WHERE TO, MA'AM?
CLUB STOP 'N' BOP. IT'S ON AVENUE B AND 9TH.
BUT.. BUT THAT'S RIGHT ACROSS THE STREET.
SO CIRCLE THE BLOCK! YOU TWO ARE DENSE. WE'RE NOT TALKING TRANSPORTATION HERE!
GB Trudeau

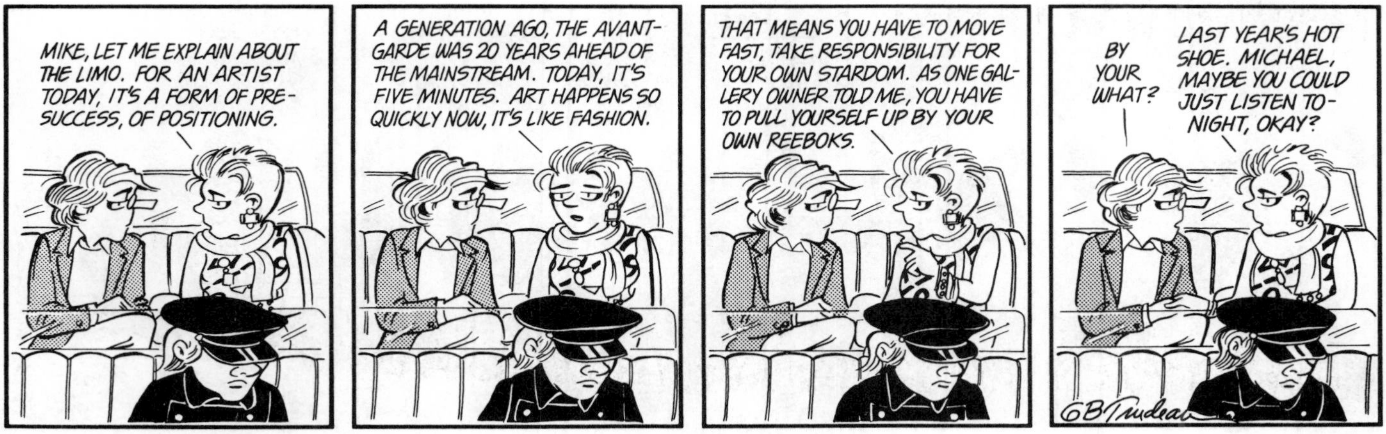
MIKE, LET ME EXPLAIN ABOUT THE LIMO. FOR AN ARTIST TODAY, IT'S A FORM OF PRE-SUCCESS, OF POSITIONING.
A GENERATION AGO, THE AVANT-GARDE WAS 20 YEARS AHEAD OF THE MAINSTREAM. TODAY, IT'S FIVE MINUTES. ART HAPPENS SO QUICKLY NOW, IT'S LIKE FASHION.
THAT MEANS YOU HAVE TO MOVE FAST, TAKE RESPONSIBILITY FOR YOUR OWN STARDOM. AS ONE GALLERY OWNER TOLD ME, YOU HAVE TO PULL YOURSELF UP BY YOUR OWN REEBOKS.
BY YOUR WHAT?
LAST YEAR'S HOT SHOE. MICHAEL, MAYBE YOU COULD JUST LISTEN TONIGHT, OKAY?
GB Trudeau

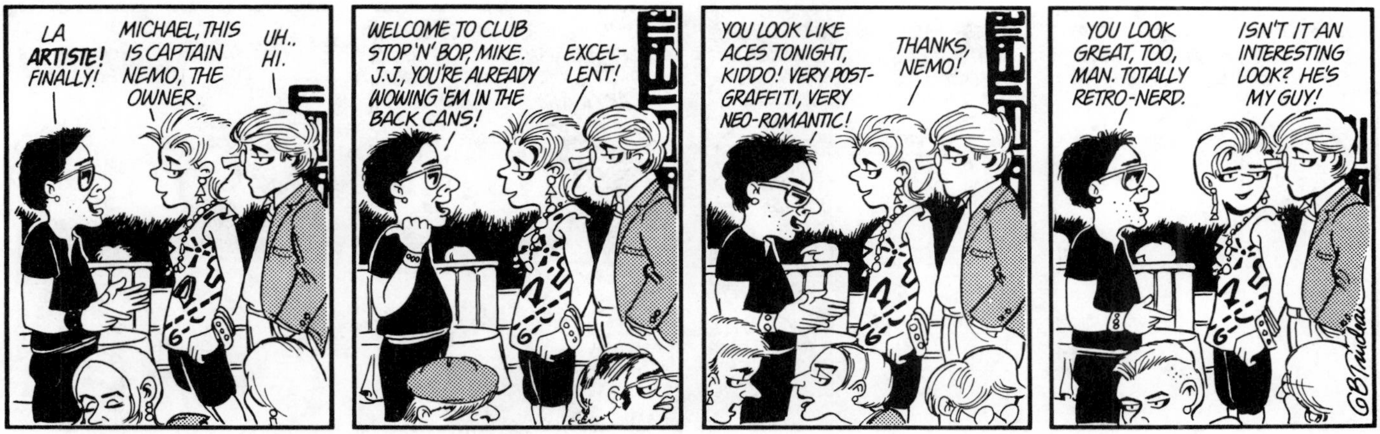
LA ARTISTE! FINALLY!
MICHAEL, THIS IS CAPTAIN NEMO, THE OWNER.
UH.. HI.
WELCOME TO CLUB STOP 'N' BOP, MIKE. J.J., YOU'RE ALREADY WOWING 'EM IN THE BACK CANS!
EXCELLENT!
YOU LOOK LIKE ACES TONIGHT, KIDDO! VERY POST-GRAFFITI, VERY NEO-ROMANTIC!
THANKS, NEMO!
YOU LOOK GREAT, TOO, MAN. TOTALLY RETRO-NERD.
ISN'T IT AN INTERESTING LOOK? HE'S MY GUY!
GB Trudeau

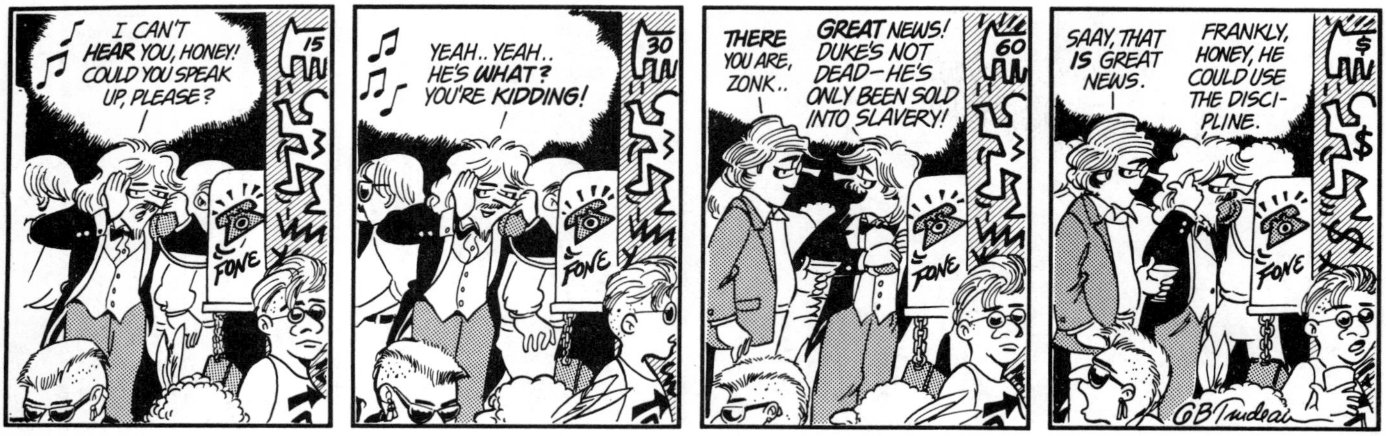
I CAN'T HEAR YOU, HONEY! COULD YOU SPEAK UP, PLEASE?
FONE
YEAH.. YEAH.. HE'S WHAT? YOU'RE KIDDING!
FONE
THERE YOU ARE, ZONK..
GREAT NEWS! DUKE'S NOT DEAD—HE'S ONLY BEEN SOLD INTO SLAVERY!
FONE
SAAY, THAT IS GREAT NEWS.
FRANKLY, HONEY, HE COULD USE THE DISCIPLINE.
FONE

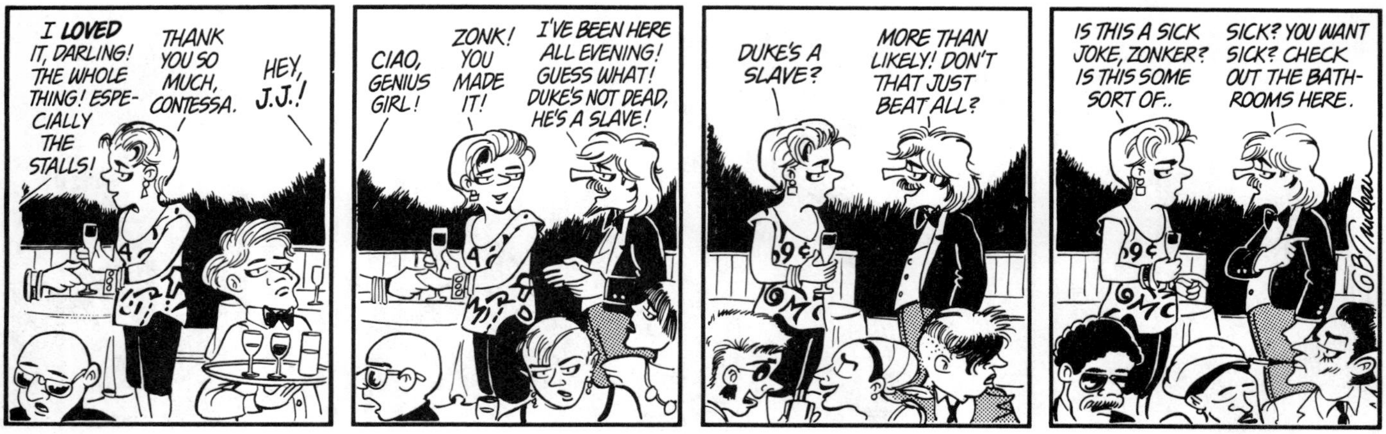
I LOVED IT, DARLING! THE WHOLE THING! ESPECIALLY THE STALLS!
THANK YOU SO MUCH, CONTESSA.
HEY, J.J.!
CIAO, GENIUS GIRL!
ZONK! YOU MADE IT!
I'VE BEEN HERE ALL EVENING! GUESS WHAT! DUKE'S NOT DEAD, HE'S A SLAVE!
DUKE'S A SLAVE?
MORE THAN LIKELY! DON'T THAT JUST BEAT ALL?
IS THIS A SICK JOKE, ZONKER? IS THIS SOME SORT OF..
SICK? YOU WANT SICK? CHECK OUT THE BATHROOMS HERE.

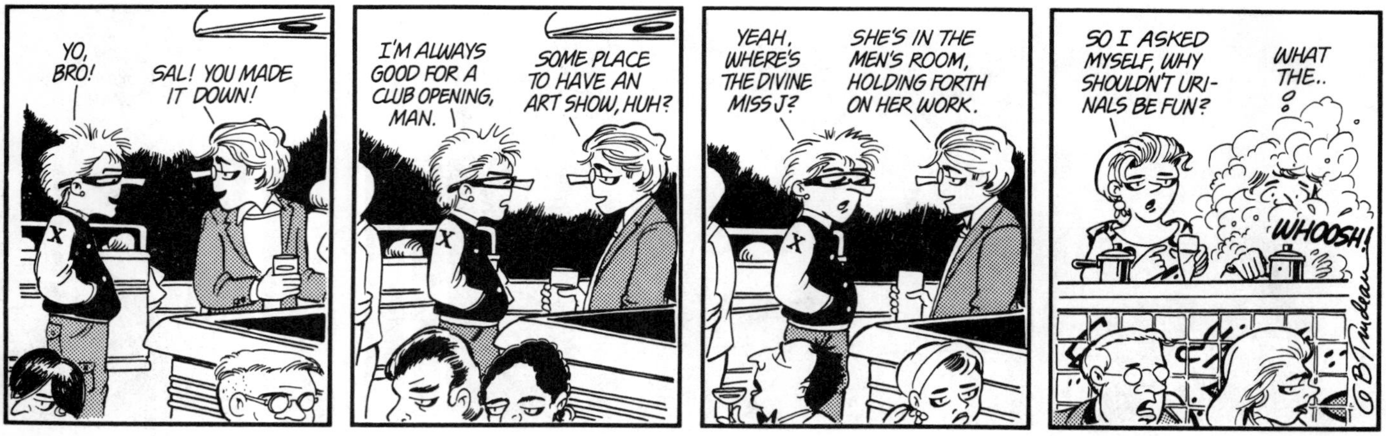
YO, BRO!
SAL! YOU MADE IT DOWN!
I'M ALWAYS GOOD FOR A CLUB OPENING, MAN.
SOME PLACE TO HAVE AN ART SHOW, HUH?
YEAH, WHERE'S THE DIVINE MISS J?
SHE'S IN THE MEN'S ROOM, HOLDING FORTH ON HER WORK.
SO I ASKED MYSELF, WHY SHOULDN'T URINALS BE FUN?
WHAT THE..
WHOOSH!

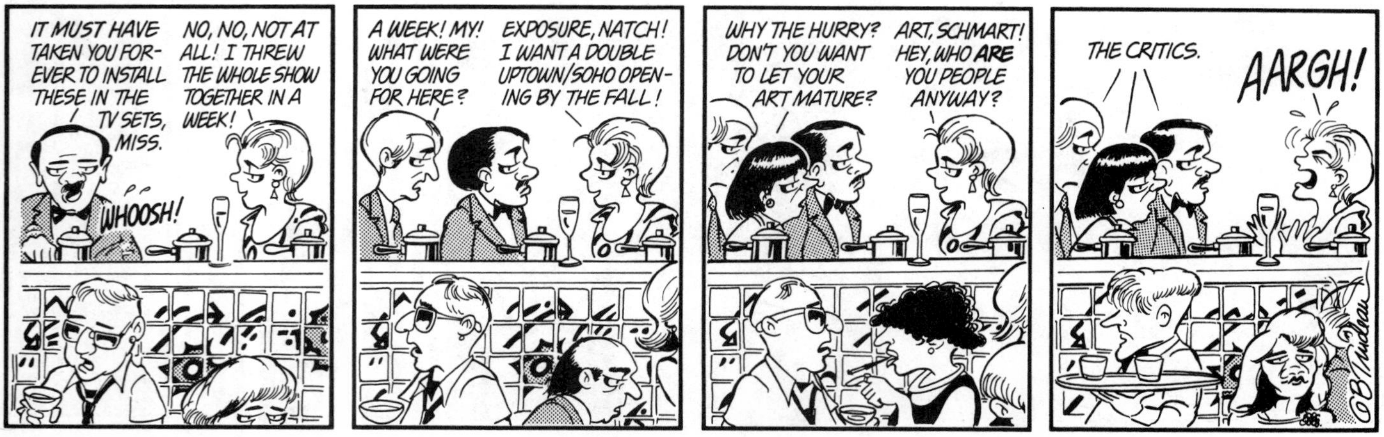
IT MUST HAVE TAKEN YOU FOREVER TO INSTALL THESE IN THE TV SETS, MISS.
NO, NO, NOT AT ALL! I THREW THE WHOLE SHOW TOGETHER IN A WEEK!
WHOOSH!
A WEEK! MY! WHAT WERE YOU GOING FOR HERE?
EXPOSURE, NATCH! I WANT A DOUBLE UPTOWN/SOHO OPENING BY THE FALL!
WHY THE HURRY? DON'T YOU WANT TO LET YOUR ART MATURE?
ART, SCHMART! HEY, WHO ARE YOU PEOPLE ANYWAY?
THE CRITICS.
AARGH!

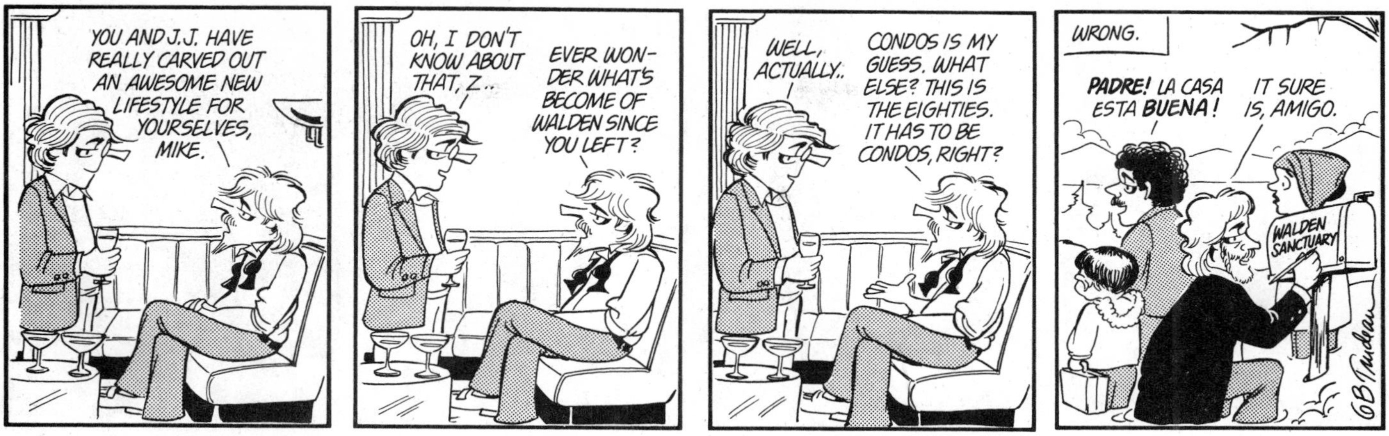

YOU AND J.J. HAVE REALLY CARVED OUT AN AWESOME NEW LIFESTYLE FOR YOURSELVES, MIKE.
OH, I DON'T KNOW ABOUT THAT, Z..
EVER WONDER WHAT'S BECOME OF WALDEN SINCE YOU LEFT?
WELL, ACTUALLY..
CONDOS IS MY GUESS. WHAT ELSE? THIS IS THE EIGHTIES. IT HAS TO BE CONDOS, RIGHT?
WRONG.
PADRE! LA CASA ESTA BUENA!
IT SURE IS, AMIGO.
WALDEN SANCTUARY
G.B. Trudeau

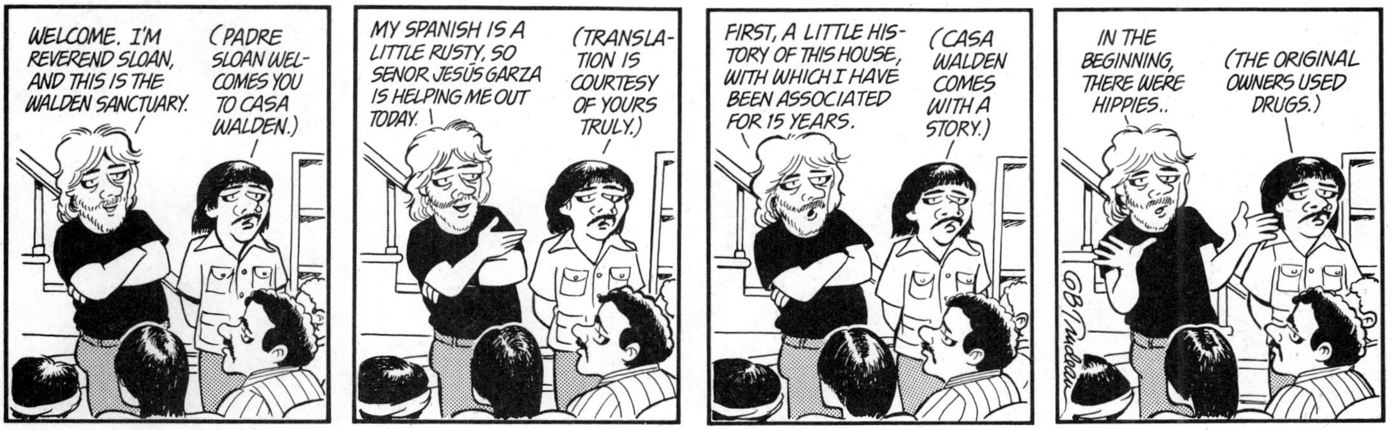

WELCOME. I'M REVEREND SLOAN, AND THIS IS THE WALDEN SANCTUARY.
(PADRE SLOAN WELCOMES YOU TO CASA WALDEN.)
MY SPANISH IS A LITTLE RUSTY, SO SENOR JESÚS GARZA IS HELPING ME OUT TODAY.
(TRANSLATION IS COURTESY OF YOURS TRULY.)
FIRST, A LITTLE HISTORY OF THIS HOUSE, WITH WHICH I HAVE BEEN ASSOCIATED FOR 15 YEARS.
(CASA WALDEN COMES WITH A STORY.)
G.B. Trudeau
IN THE BEGINNING, THERE WERE HIPPIES..
(THE ORIGINAL OWNERS USED DRUGS.)

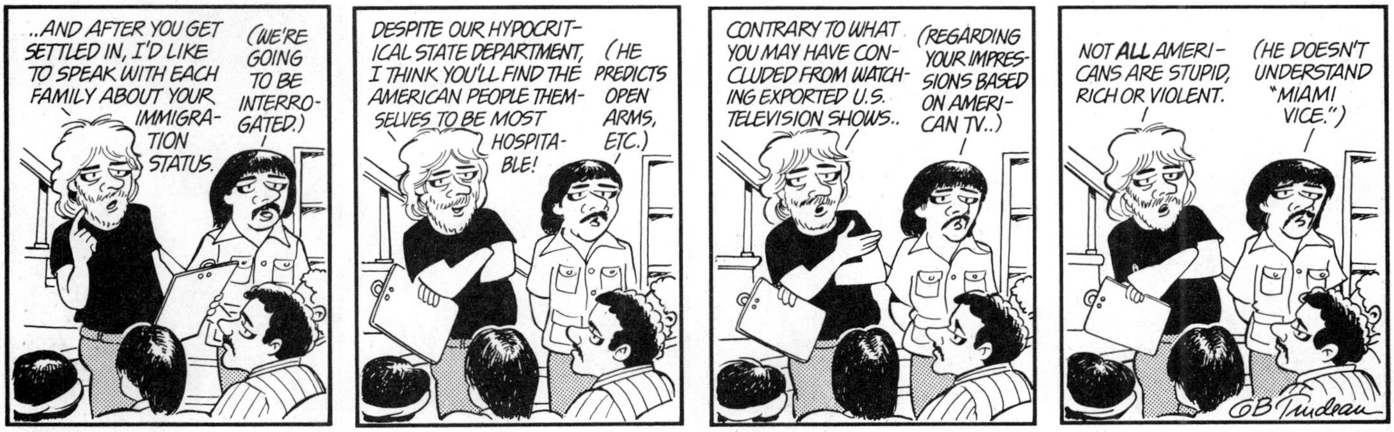

..AND AFTER YOU GET SETTLED IN, I'D LIKE TO SPEAK WITH EACH FAMILY ABOUT YOUR IMMIGRATION STATUS.
(WE'RE GOING TO BE INTERROGATED.)
DESPITE OUR HYPOCRITICAL STATE DEPARTMENT, I THINK YOU'LL FIND THE AMERICAN PEOPLE THEMSELVES TO BE MOST HOSPITABLE!
(HE PREDICTS OPEN ARMS, ETC.)
CONTRARY TO WHAT YOU MAY HAVE CONCLUDED FROM WATCHING EXPORTED U.S. TELEVISION SHOWS..
(REGARDING YOUR IMPRESSIONS BASED ON AMERICAN TV..)
NOT ALL AMERICANS ARE STUPID, RICH OR VIOLENT.
(HE DOESN'T UNDERSTAND "MIAMI VICE.")
G.B. Trudeau

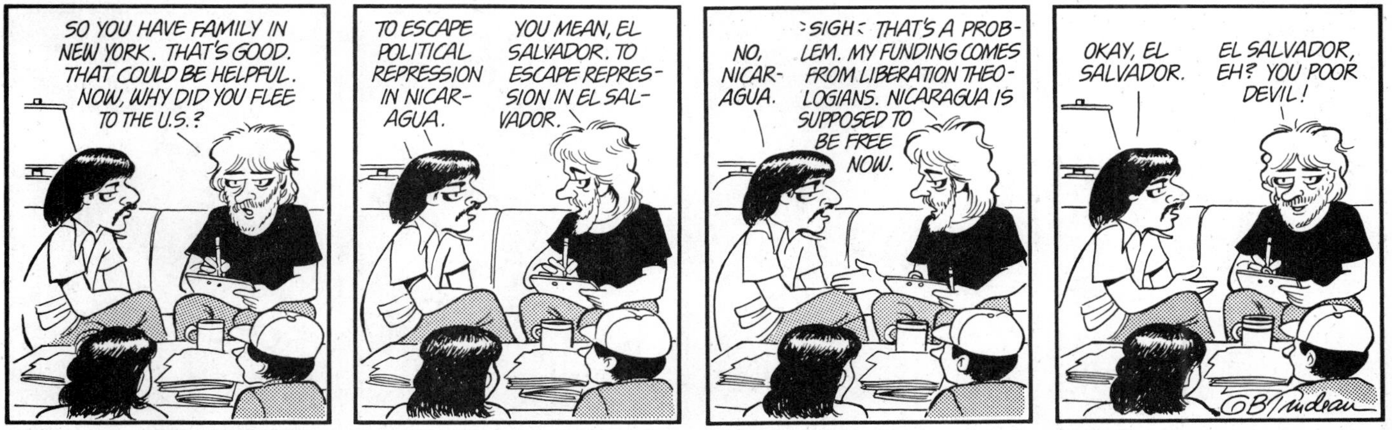

SO YOU HAVE FAMILY IN NEW YORK. THAT'S GOOD. THAT COULD BE HELPFUL. NOW, WHY DID YOU FLEE TO THE U.S.?
TO ESCAPE POLITICAL REPRESSION IN NICARAGUA.
YOU MEAN, EL SALVADOR. TO ESCAPE REPRESSION IN EL SALVADOR.
NO, NICARAGUA.
<SIGH< THAT'S A PROBLEM. MY FUNDING COMES FROM LIBERATION THEOLOGIANS. NICARAGUA IS SUPPOSED TO BE FREE NOW.
OKAY, EL SALVADOR.
EL SALVADOR, EH? YOU POOR DEVIL!
G.B. Trudeau

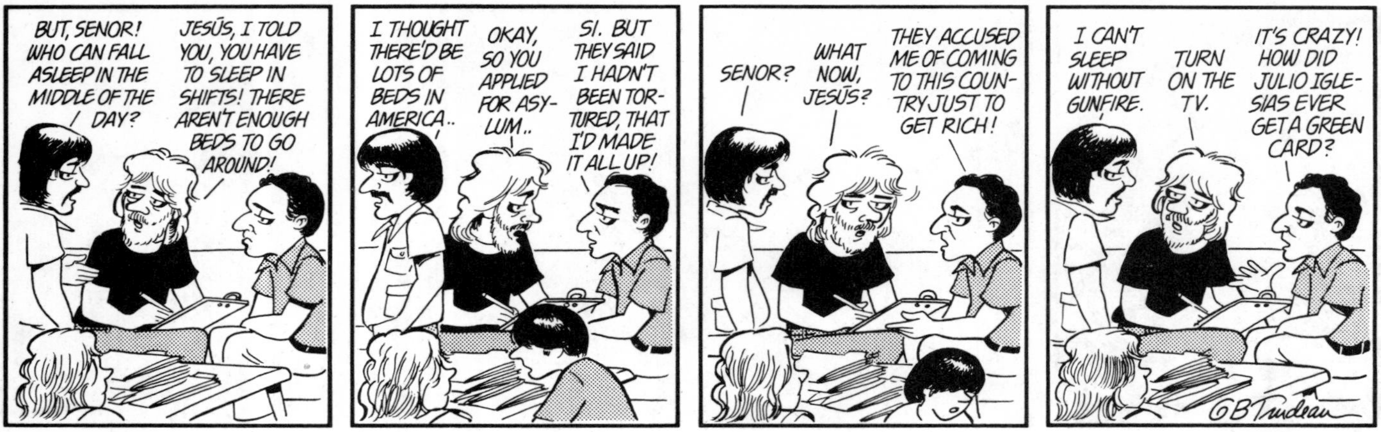
BUT, SENOR! WHO CAN FALL ASLEEP IN THE MIDDLE OF THE DAY?
JESÚS, I TOLD YOU, YOU HAVE TO SLEEP IN SHIFTS! THERE AREN'T ENOUGH BEDS TO GO AROUND!
I THOUGHT THERE'D BE LOTS OF BEDS IN AMERICA..
OKAY, SO YOU APPLIED FOR ASYLUM..
SI. BUT THEY SAID I HADN'T BEEN TORTURED, THAT I'D MADE IT ALL UP!
SENOR?
WHAT NOW, JESÚS?
THEY ACCUSED ME OF COMING TO THIS COUNTRY JUST TO GET RICH!
I CAN'T SLEEP WITHOUT GUNFIRE.
TURN ON THE TV.
IT'S CRAZY! HOW DID JULIO IGLESIAS EVER GET A GREEN CARD?
GB Trudeau

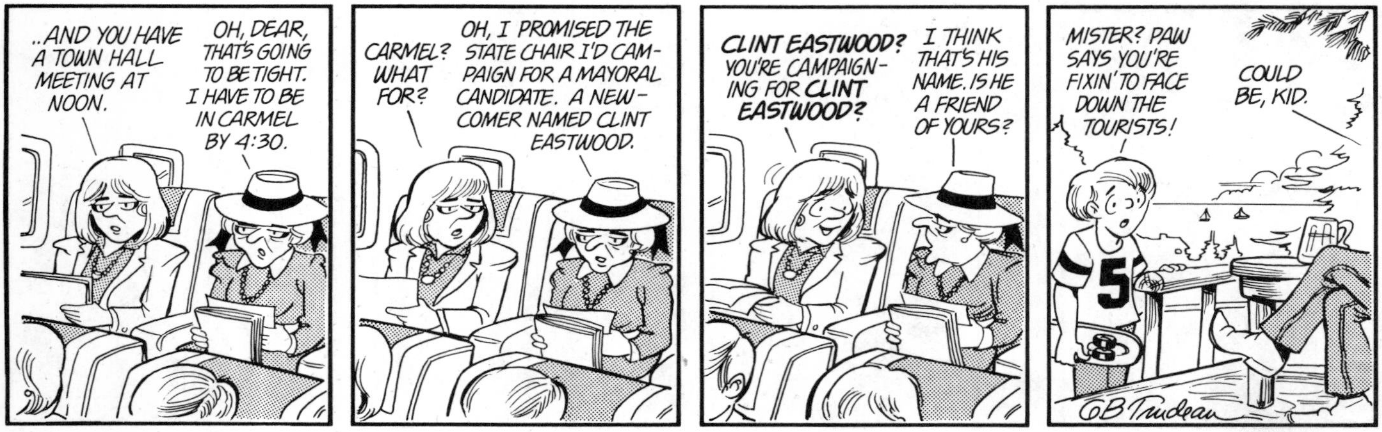
..AND YOU HAVE A TOWN HALL MEETING AT NOON.
OH, DEAR, THAT'S GOING TO BE TIGHT. I HAVE TO BE IN CARMEL BY 4:30.
CARMEL? WHAT FOR?
OH, I PROMISED THE STATE CHAIR I'D CAMPAIGN FOR A MAYORAL CANDIDATE. A NEWCOMER NAMED CLINT EASTWOOD.
CLINT EASTWOOD? YOU'RE CAMPAIGNING FOR CLINT EASTWOOD?
I THINK THAT'S HIS NAME. IS HE A FRIEND OF YOURS?
MISTER? PAW SAYS YOU'RE FIXIN' TO FACE DOWN THE TOURISTS!
COULD BE, KID.
GB Trudeau

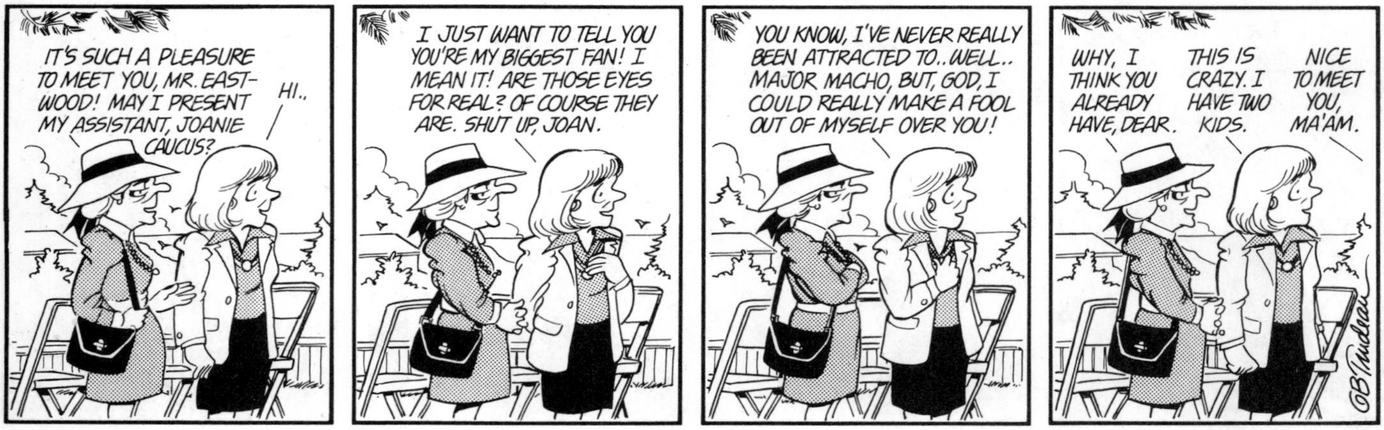
IT'S SUCH A PLEASURE TO MEET YOU, MR. EASTWOOD! MAY I PRESENT MY ASSISTANT, JOANIE CAUCUS?
HI..
I JUST WANT TO TELL YOU YOU'RE MY BIGGEST FAN! I MEAN IT! ARE THOSE EYES FOR REAL? OF COURSE THEY ARE. SHUT UP, JOAN.
YOU KNOW, I'VE NEVER REALLY BEEN ATTRACTED TO..WELL.. MAJOR MACHO, BUT, GOD, I COULD REALLY MAKE A FOOL OUT OF MYSELF OVER YOU!
WHY, I THINK YOU ALREADY HAVE, DEAR.
THIS IS CRAZY. I HAVE TWO KIDS.
NICE TO MEET YOU, MA'AM.
GB Trudeau

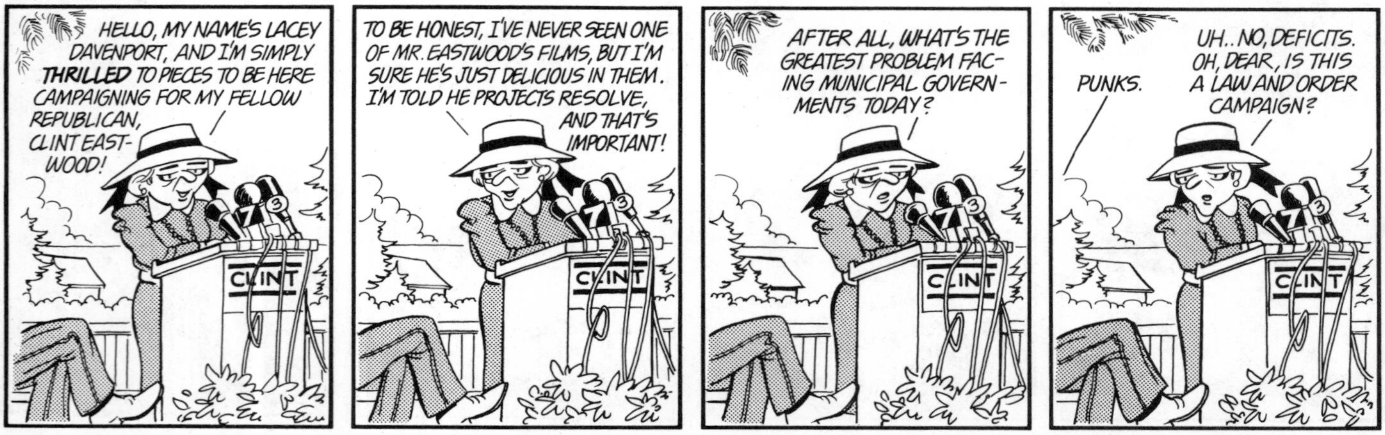
HELLO, MY NAME'S LACEY DAVENPORT, AND I'M SIMPLY THRILLED TO PIECES TO BE HERE CAMPAIGNING FOR MY FELLOW REPUBLICAN, CLINT EASTWOOD!
CLINT
TO BE HONEST, I'VE NEVER SEEN ONE OF MR. EASTWOOD'S FILMS, BUT I'M SURE HE'S JUST DELICIOUS IN THEM. I'M TOLD HE PROJECTS RESOLVE, AND THAT'S IMPORTANT!
AFTER ALL, WHAT'S THE GREATEST PROBLEM FACING MUNICIPAL GOVERNMENTS TODAY?
PUNKS.
UH.. NO, DEFICITS. OH, DEAR, IS THIS A LAW AND ORDER CAMPAIGN?

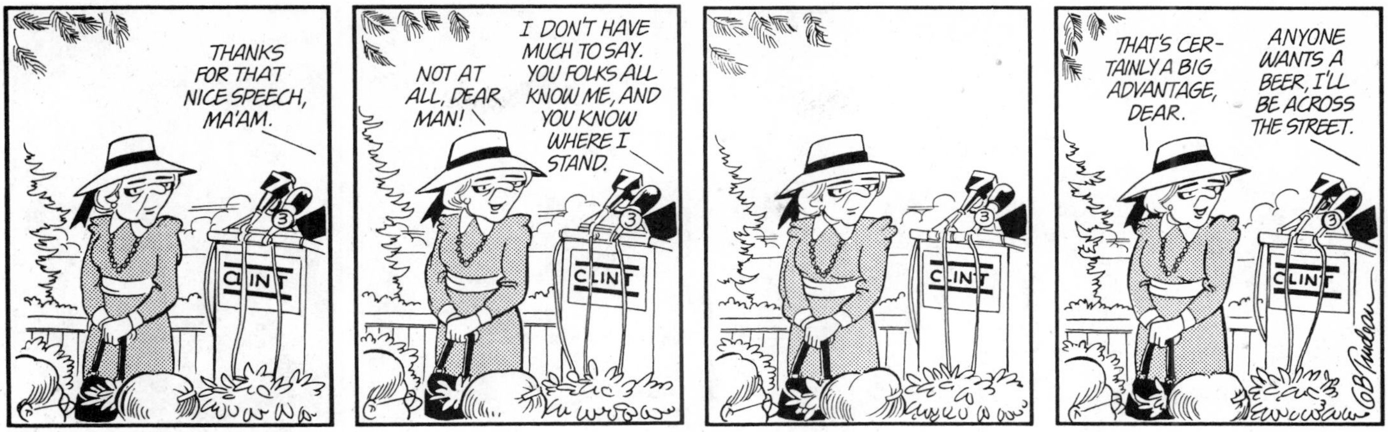
THANKS FOR THAT NICE SPEECH, MA'AM.
NOT AT ALL, DEAR MAN!
I DON'T HAVE MUCH TO SAY. YOU FOLKS ALL KNOW ME, AND YOU KNOW WHERE I STAND.
THAT'S CERTAINLY A BIG ADVANTAGE, DEAR.
ANYONE WANTS A BEER, I'LL BE ACROSS THE STREET.

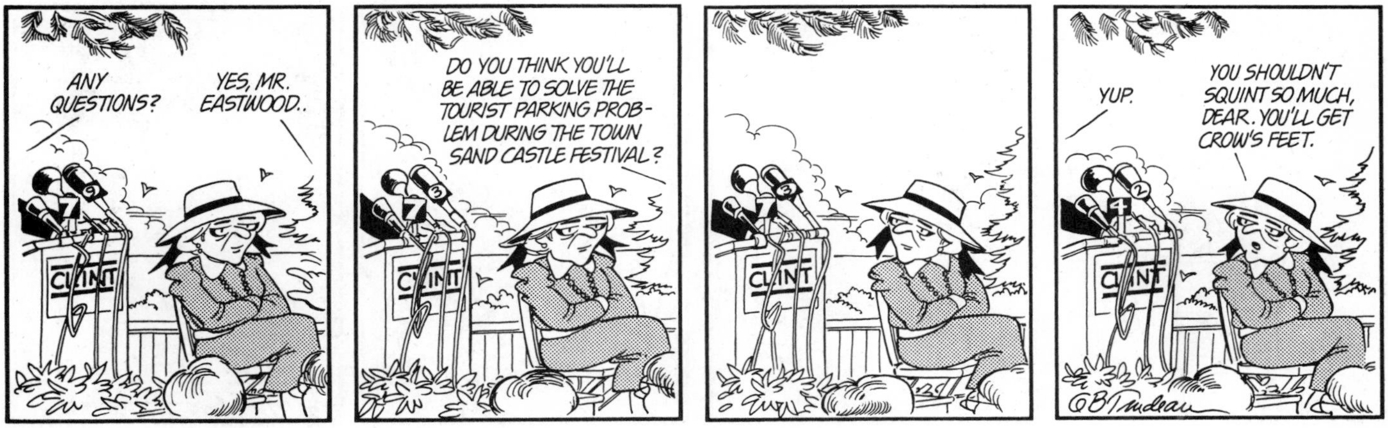
ANY QUESTIONS?
YES, MR. EASTWOOD..
DO YOU THINK YOU'LL BE ABLE TO SOLVE THE TOURIST PARKING PROBLEM DURING THE TOWN SAND CASTLE FESTIVAL?
YUP.
YOU SHOULDN'T SQUINT SO MUCH, DEAR.. YOU'LL GET CROW'S FEET.

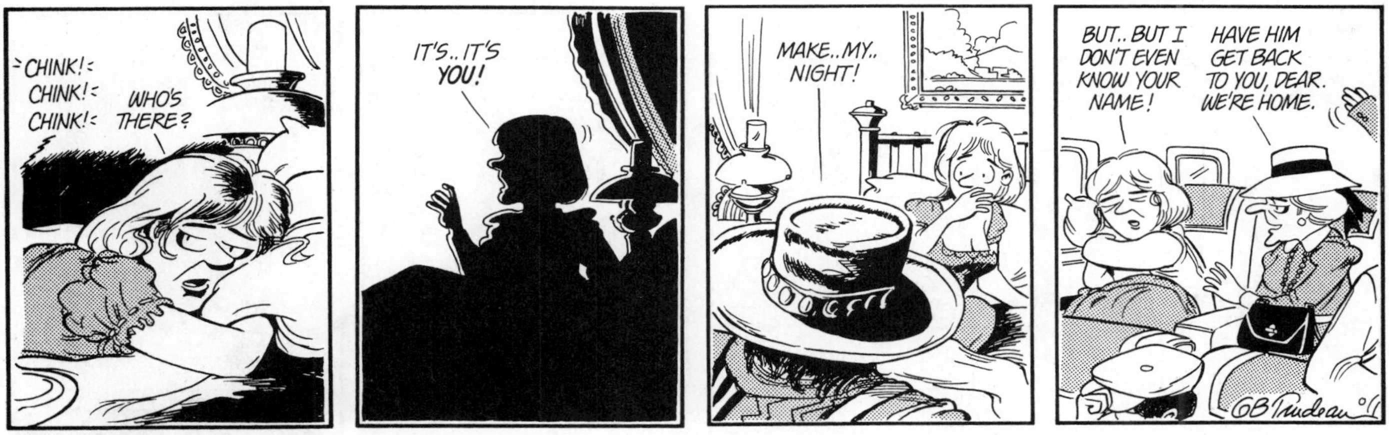
CHINK! CHINK! CHINK!
WHO'S THERE?
IT'S.. IT'S YOU!
MAKE.. MY.. NIGHT!
BUT.. BUT I DON'T EVEN KNOW YOUR NAME!
HAVE HIM GET BACK TO YOU, DEAR. WE'RE HOME.

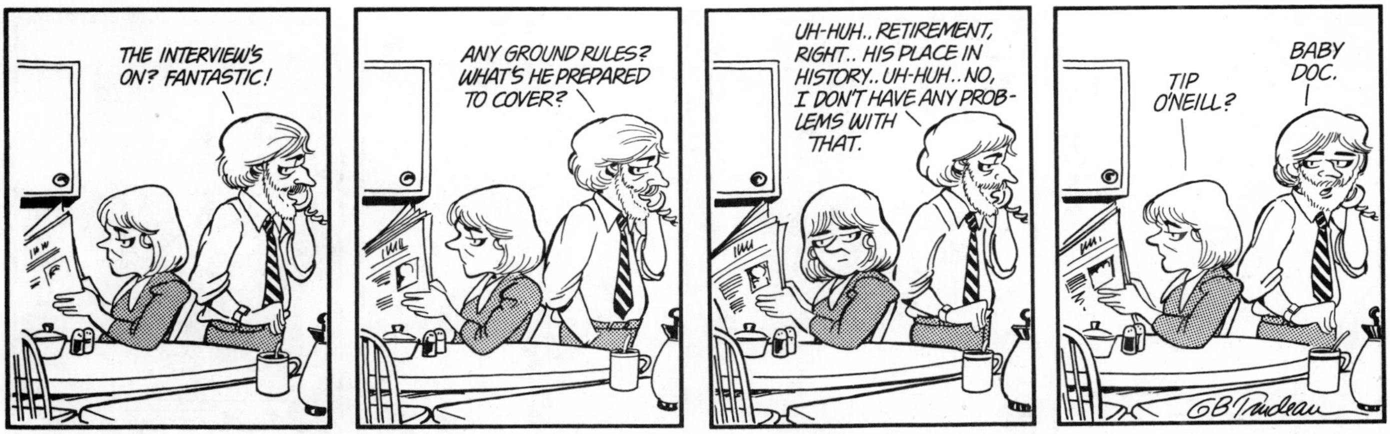
THE INTERVIEW'S ON? FANTASTIC!
ANY GROUND RULES? WHAT'S HE PREPARED TO COVER?
UH-HUH.. RETIREMENT, RIGHT.. HIS PLACE IN HISTORY.. UH-HUH.. NO, I DON'T HAVE ANY PROBLEMS WITH THAT.
TIP O'NEILL?
BABY DOC.

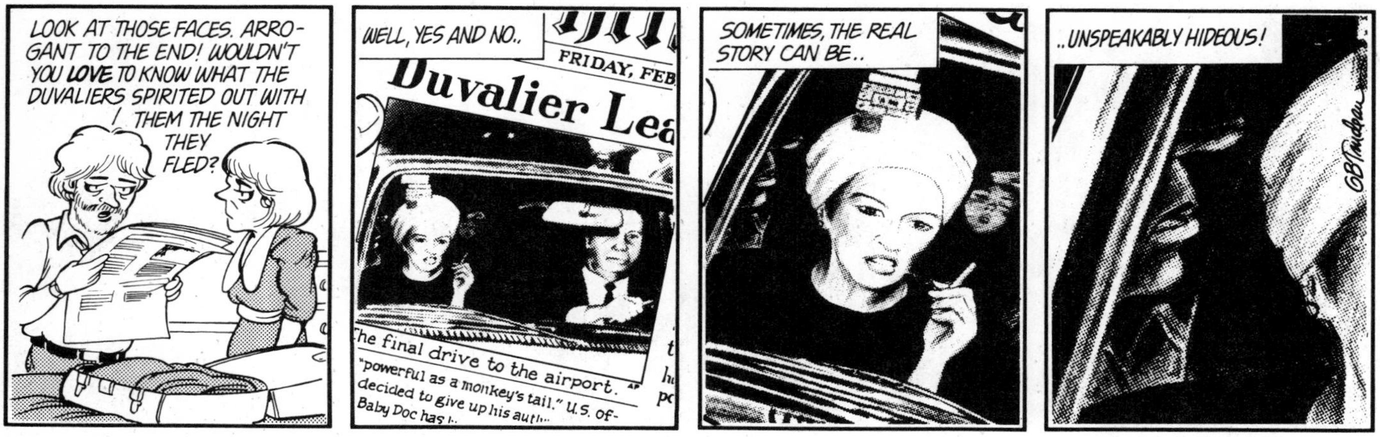
LOOK AT THOSE FACES. ARROGANT TO THE END! WOULDN'T YOU LOVE TO KNOW WHAT THE DUVALIERS SPIRITED OUT WITH THEM THE NIGHT THEY FLED?
WELL, YES AND NO..
FRIDAY, FEB
Duvalier Lea
The final drive to the airport.
"powerful as a monkey's tail." U.S. of-
decided to give up his auth
Baby Doc has
SOMETIMES, THE REAL STORY CAN BE..
..UNSPEAKABLY HIDEOUS!
GBTrudeau

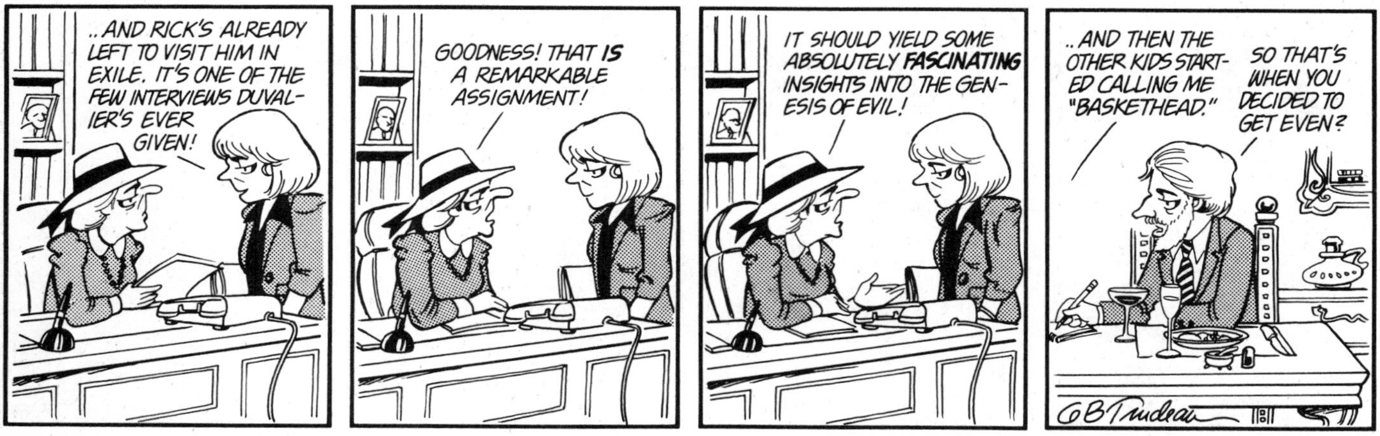
..AND RICK'S ALREADY LEFT TO VISIT HIM IN EXILE. IT'S ONE OF THE FEW INTERVIEWS DUVALIER'S EVER GIVEN!
GOODNESS! THAT IS A REMARKABLE ASSIGNMENT!
IT SHOULD YIELD SOME ABSOLUTELY FASCINATING INSIGHTS INTO THE GENESIS OF EVIL!
..AND THEN THE OTHER KIDS STARTED CALLING ME "BASKETHEAD."
SO THAT'S WHEN YOU DECIDED TO GET EVEN?
GBTrudeau

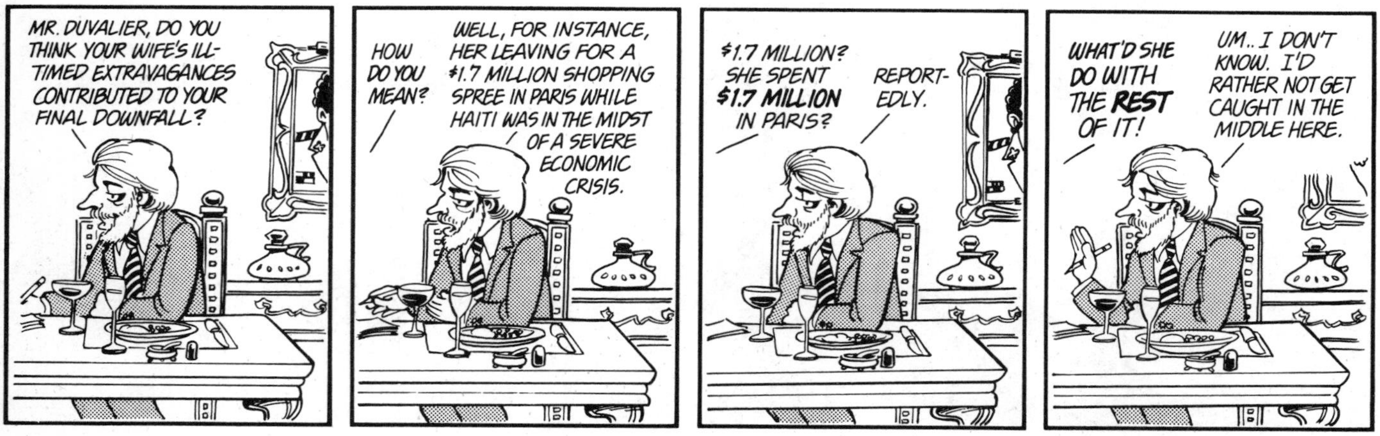
MR. DUVALIER, DO YOU THINK YOUR WIFE'S ILL-TIMED EXTRAVAGANCES CONTRIBUTED TO YOUR FINAL DOWNFALL?
HOW DO YOU MEAN?
WELL, FOR INSTANCE, HER LEAVING FOR A $1.7 MILLION SHOPPING SPREE IN PARIS WHILE HAITI WAS IN THE MIDST OF A SEVERE ECONOMIC CRISIS.
$1.7 MILLION? SHE SPENT $1.7 MILLION IN PARIS?
REPORTEDLY.
WHAT'D SHE DO WITH THE REST OF IT!
UM.. I DON'T KNOW. I'D RATHER NOT GET CAUGHT IN THE MIDDLE HERE.

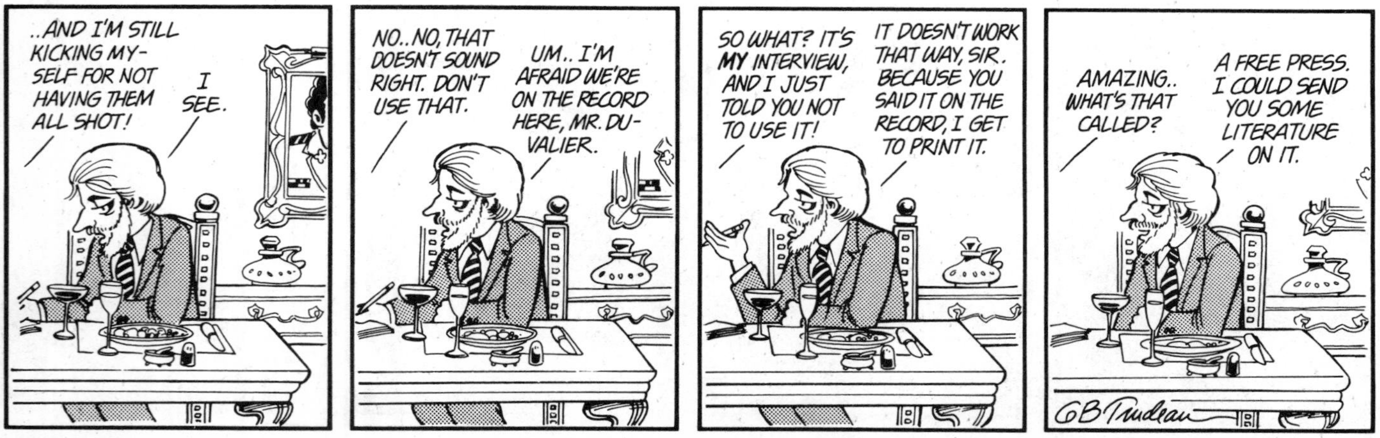
..AND I'M STILL KICKING MYSELF FOR NOT HAVING THEM ALL SHOT!
I SEE.
NO..NO, THAT DOESN'T SOUND RIGHT. DON'T USE THAT.
UM.. I'M AFRAID WE'RE ON THE RECORD HERE, MR. DUVALIER.
SO WHAT? IT'S MY INTERVIEW, AND I JUST TOLD YOU NOT TO USE IT!
IT DOESN'T WORK THAT WAY, SIR. BECAUSE YOU SAID IT ON THE RECORD, I GET TO PRINT IT.
AMAZING.. WHAT'S THAT CALLED?
A FREE PRESS. I COULD SEND YOU SOME LITERATURE ON IT.
GBTrudeau

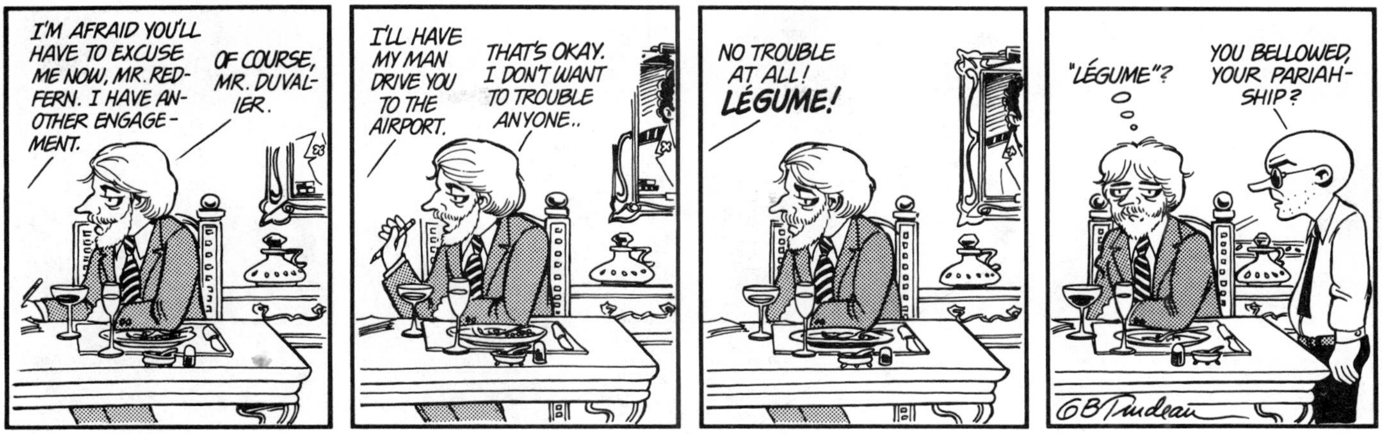
I'M AFRAID YOU'LL HAVE TO EXCUSE ME NOW, MR. REDFERN. I HAVE ANOTHER ENGAGEMENT.
OF COURSE, MR. DUVALIER.
I'LL HAVE MY MAN DRIVE YOU TO THE AIRPORT.
THAT'S OKAY. I DON'T WANT TO TROUBLE ANYONE..
NO TROUBLE AT ALL! LÉGUME!
"LÉGUME"?
YOU BELLOWED, YOUR PARIAHSHIP?

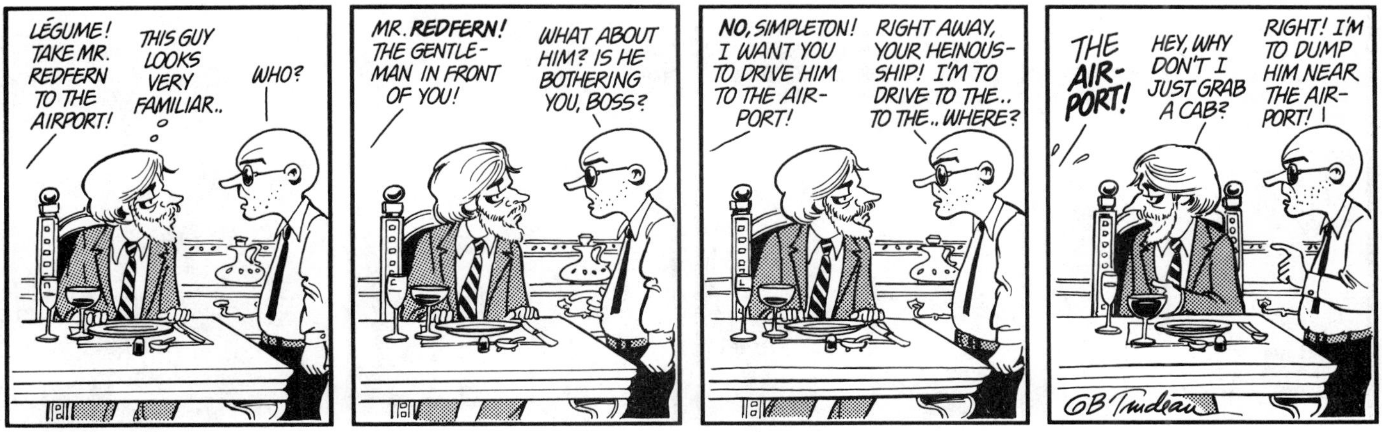
LÉGUME! TAKE MR. REDFERN TO THE AIRPORT!
THIS GUY LOOKS VERY FAMILIAR..
WHO?
MR. REDFERN! THE GENTLEMAN IN FRONT OF YOU!
WHAT ABOUT HIM? IS HE BOTHERING YOU, BOSS?
NO, SIMPLETON! I WANT YOU TO DRIVE HIM TO THE AIRPORT!
RIGHT AWAY, YOUR HEINOUSSHIP! I'M TO DRIVE TO THE.. TO THE.. WHERE?
THE AIRPORT!
HEY, WHY DON'T I JUST GRAB A CAB?
RIGHT! I'M TO DUMP HIM NEAR THE AIRPORT!

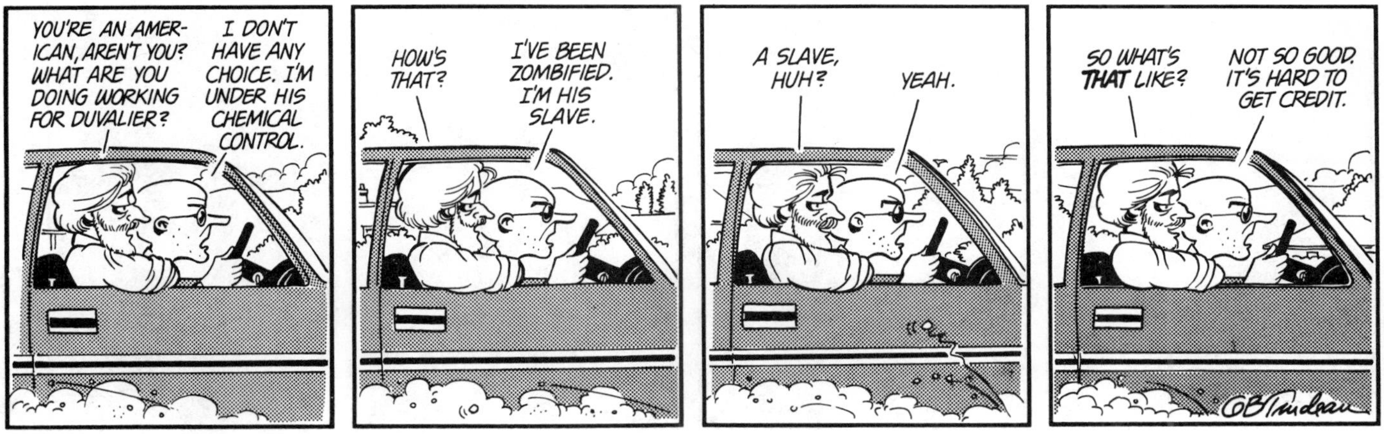
YOU'RE AN AMERICAN, AREN'T YOU? WHAT ARE YOU DOING WORKING FOR DUVALIER?
I DON'T HAVE ANY CHOICE. I'M UNDER HIS CHEMICAL CONTROL.
HOW'S THAT?
I'VE BEEN ZOMBIFIED. I'M HIS SLAVE.
A SLAVE, HUH?
YEAH.
SO WHAT'S THAT LIKE?
NOT SO GOOD. IT'S HARD TO GET CREDIT.

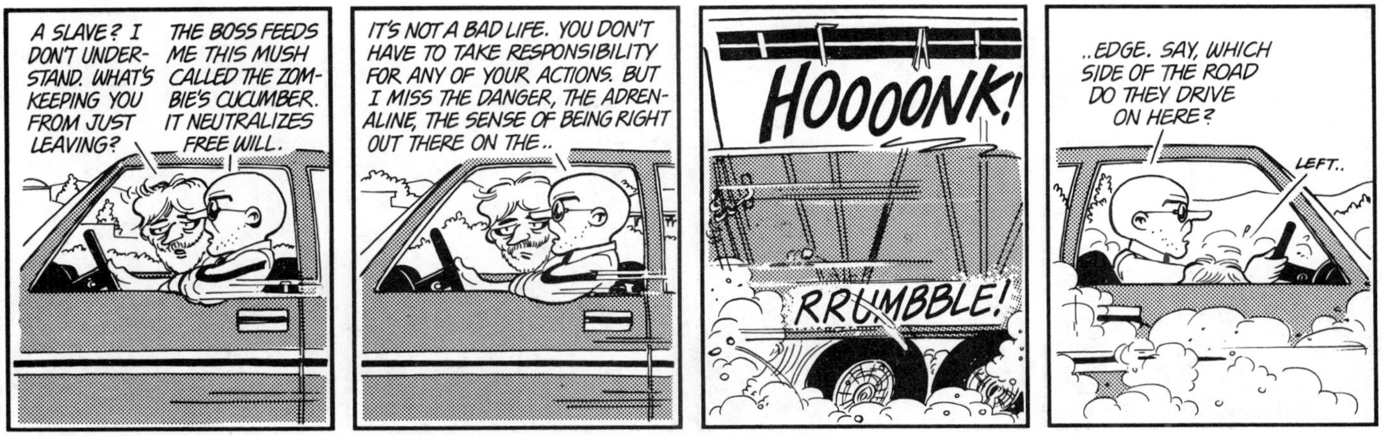
A SLAVE? I DON'T UNDERSTAND. WHAT'S KEEPING YOU FROM JUST LEAVING?
THE BOSS FEEDS ME THIS MUSH CALLED THE ZOMBIE'S CUCUMBER. IT NEUTRALIZES FREE WILL.
IT'S NOT A BAD LIFE. YOU DON'T HAVE TO TAKE RESPONSIBILITY FOR ANY OF YOUR ACTIONS. BUT I MISS THE DANGER, THE ADRENALINE, THE SENSE OF BEING RIGHT OUT THERE ON THE..
HOOOONK!
RRUMBBLE!
..EDGE. SAY, WHICH SIDE OF THE ROAD DO THEY DRIVE ON HERE?
LEFT..

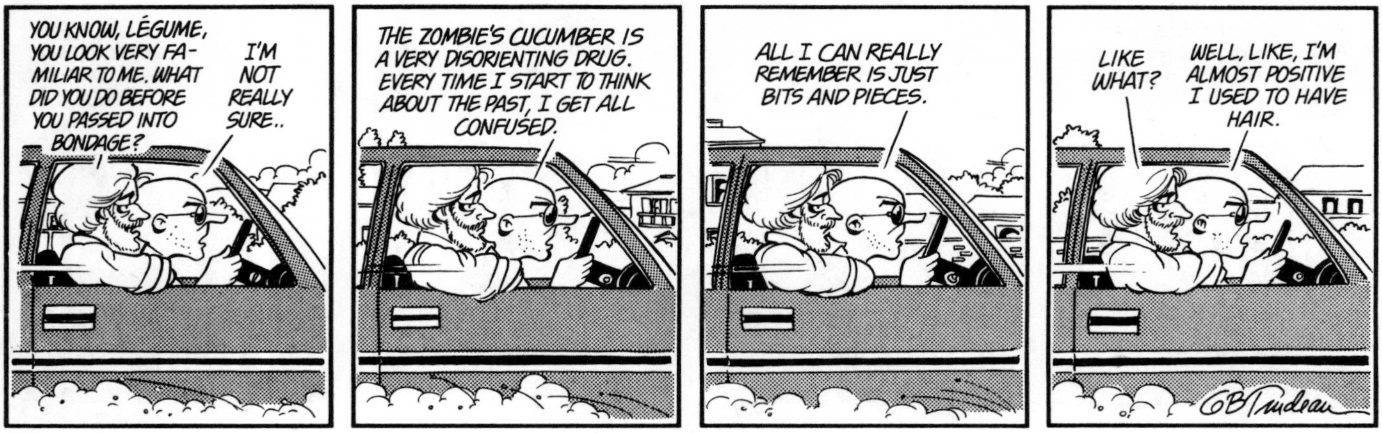
YOU KNOW, LÉGUME, YOU LOOK VERY FAMILIAR TO ME. WHAT DID YOU DO BEFORE YOU PASSED INTO BONDAGE?
I'M NOT REALLY SURE..
THE ZOMBIE'S CUCUMBER IS A VERY DISORIENTING DRUG. EVERY TIME I START TO THINK ABOUT THE PAST, I GET ALL CONFUSED.
ALL I CAN REALLY REMEMBER IS JUST BITS AND PIECES.
LIKE WHAT?
WELL, LIKE, I'M ALMOST POSITIVE I USED TO HAVE HAIR.

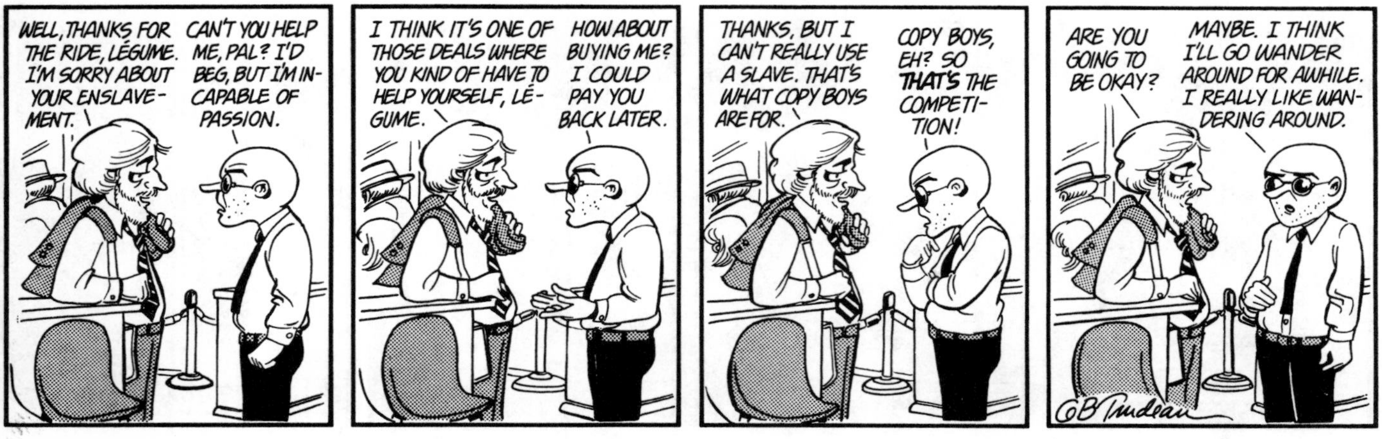
WELL, THANKS FOR THE RIDE, LÉGUME. I'M SORRY ABOUT YOUR ENSLAVEMENT.
CAN'T YOU HELP ME, PAL? I'D BEG, BUT I'M INCAPABLE OF PASSION.
I THINK IT'S ONE OF THOSE DEALS WHERE YOU KIND OF HAVE TO HELP YOURSELF, LÉGUME.
HOW ABOUT BUYING ME? I COULD PAY YOU BACK LATER.
THANKS, BUT I CAN'T REALLY USE A SLAVE. THAT'S WHAT COPY BOYS ARE FOR.
COPY BOYS, EH? SO **THAT'S** THE COMPETITION!
ARE YOU GOING TO BE OKAY?
MAYBE. I THINK I'LL GO WANDER AROUND FOR AWHILE. I REALLY LIKE WANDERING AROUND.

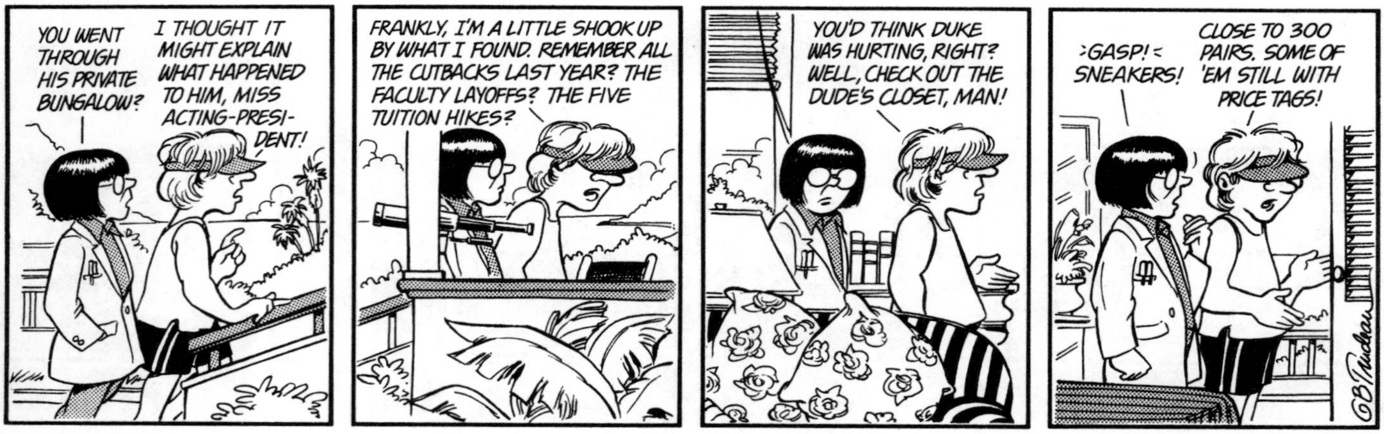
YOU WENT THROUGH HIS PRIVATE BUNGALOW?
I THOUGHT IT MIGHT EXPLAIN WHAT HAPPENED TO HIM, MISS ACTING-PRESIDENT!
FRANKLY, I'M A LITTLE SHOOK UP BY WHAT I FOUND. REMEMBER ALL THE CUTBACKS LAST YEAR? THE FACULTY LAYOFFS? THE FIVE TUITION HIKES?
YOU'D THINK DUKE WAS HURTING, RIGHT? WELL, CHECK OUT THE DUDE'S CLOSET, MAN!
>GASP!< SNEAKERS!
CLOSE TO 300 PAIRS. SOME OF 'EM STILL WITH PRICE TAGS!

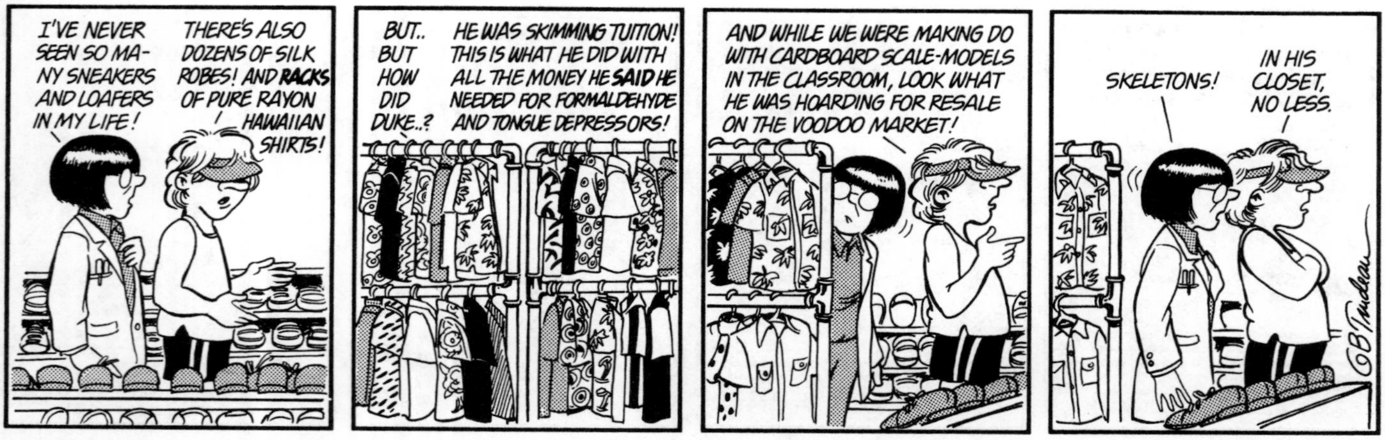
I'VE NEVER SEEN SO MANY SNEAKERS AND LOAFERS IN MY LIFE!
THERE'S ALSO DOZENS OF SILK ROBES! AND **RACKS** OF PURE RAYON HAWAIIAN SHIRTS!
BUT.. BUT HOW DID DUKE..?
HE WAS SKIMMING TUITION! THIS IS WHAT HE DID WITH ALL THE MONEY HE **SAID** HE NEEDED FOR FORMALDEHYDE AND TONGUE DEPRESSORS!
AND WHILE WE WERE MAKING DO WITH CARDBOARD SCALE-MODELS IN THE CLASSROOM, LOOK WHAT HE WAS HOARDING FOR RESALE ON THE VOODOO MARKET!
SKELETONS!
IN HIS CLOSET, NO LESS.

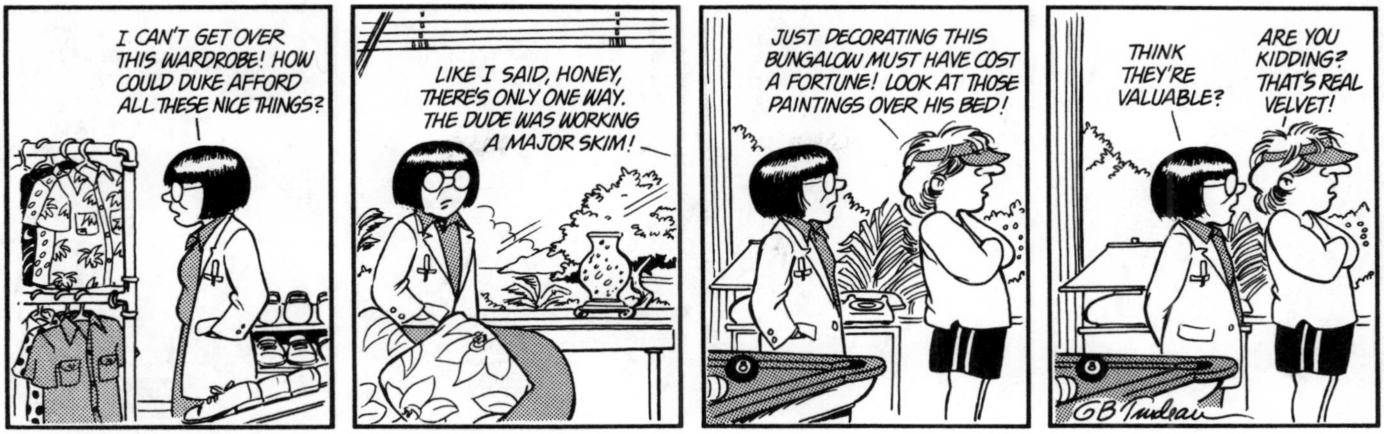
I CAN'T GET OVER THIS WARDROBE! HOW COULD DUKE AFFORD ALL THESE NICE THINGS?
LIKE I SAID, HONEY, THERE'S ONLY ONE WAY. THE DUDE WAS WORKING A MAJOR SKIM!
JUST DECORATING THIS BUNGALOW MUST HAVE COST A FORTUNE! LOOK AT THOSE PAINTINGS OVER HIS BED!
THINK THEY'RE VALUABLE?
ARE YOU KIDDING? THAT'S REAL VELVET!
©B Trudeau

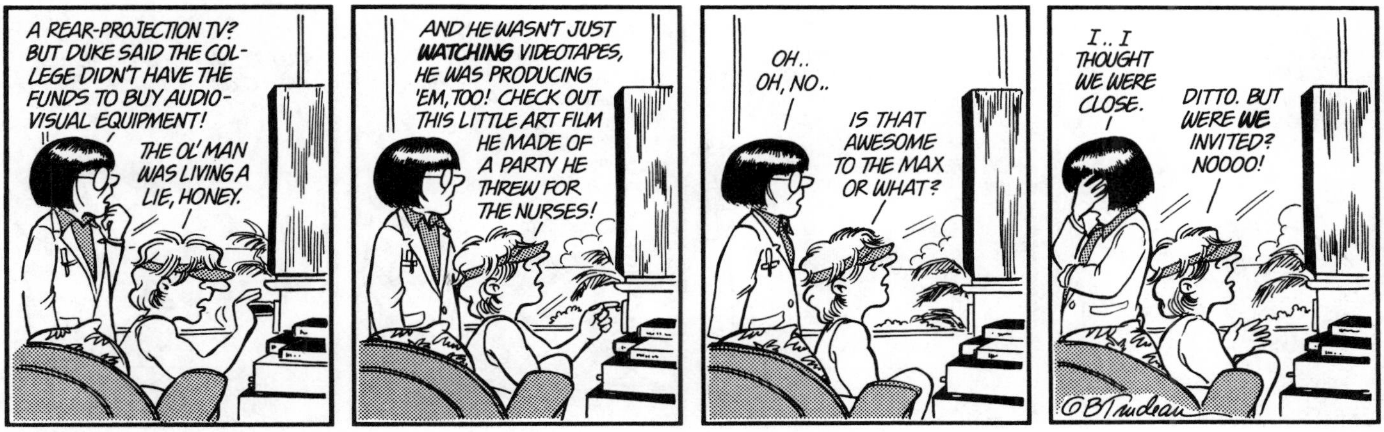
A REAR-PROJECTION TV? BUT DUKE SAID THE COL-LEGE DIDN'T HAVE THE FUNDS TO BUY AUDIO-VISUAL EQUIPMENT!
THE OL' MAN WAS LIVING A LIE, HONEY.
AND HE WASN'T JUST **WATCHING** VIDEOTAPES, HE WAS PRODUCING 'EM, TOO! CHECK OUT THIS LITTLE ART FILM HE MADE OF A PARTY HE THREW FOR THE NURSES!
OH.. OH, NO..
IS THAT AWESOME TO THE MAX OR WHAT?
I.. I THOUGHT WE WERE CLOSE.
DITTO. BUT WERE **WE** INVITED? NOOOO!
©B Trudeau

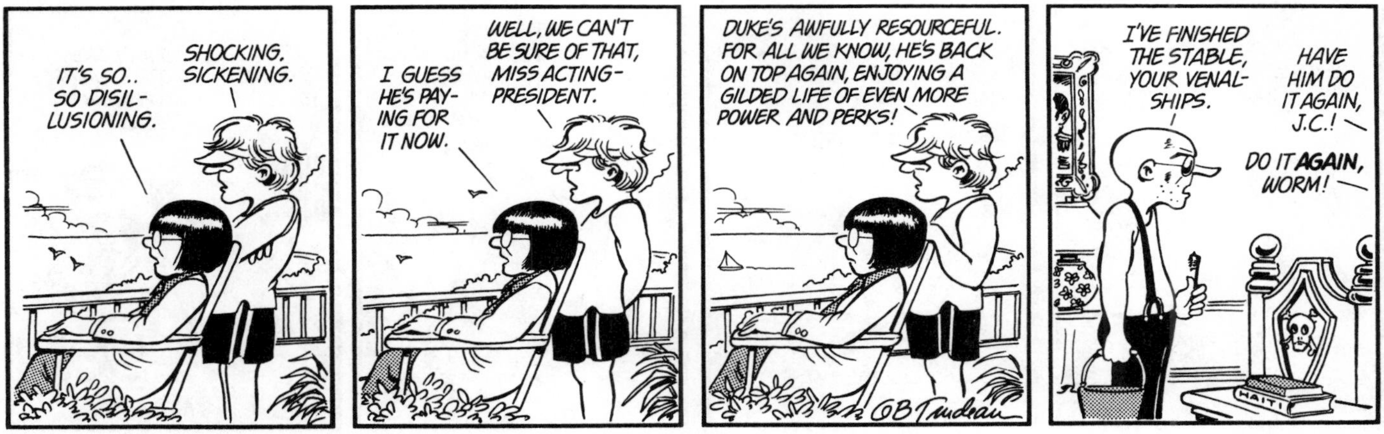
IT'S SO.. SO DISIL-LUSIONING.
SHOCKING. SICKENING.
I GUESS HE'S PAY-ING FOR IT NOW.
WELL, WE CAN'T BE SURE OF THAT, MISS ACTING-PRESIDENT.
DUKE'S AWFULLY RESOURCEFUL. FOR ALL WE KNOW, HE'S BACK ON TOP AGAIN, ENJOYING A GILDED LIFE OF EVEN MORE POWER AND PERKS!
©B Trudeau
I'VE FINISHED THE STABLE, YOUR VENAL-SHIPS.
HAVE HIM DO IT AGAIN, J.C.!
DO IT **AGAIN,** WORM!
HAITI

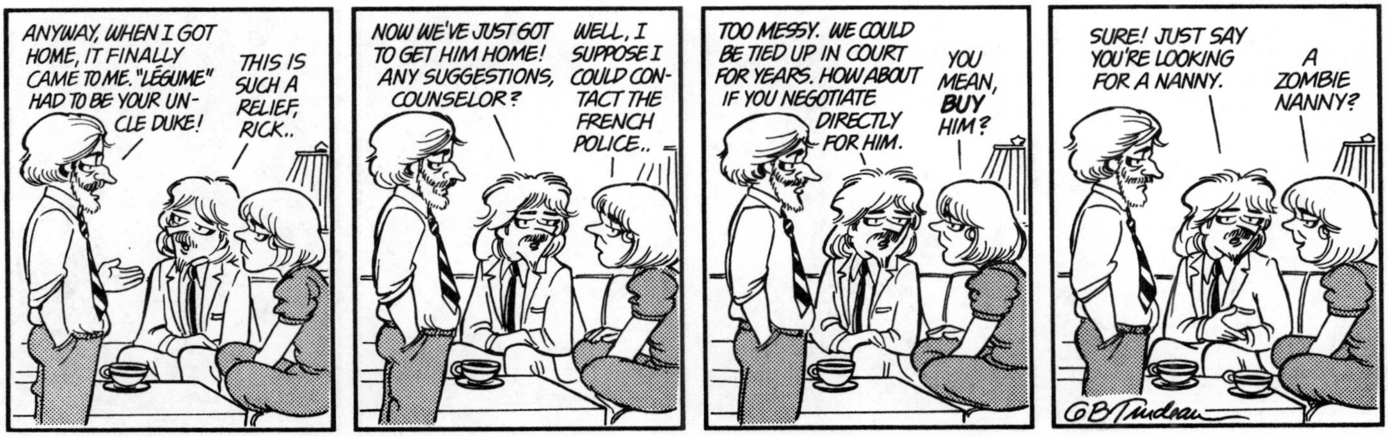
ANYWAY, WHEN I GOT HOME, IT FINALLY CAME TO ME. "LÉGUME" HAD TO BE YOUR UN-CLE DUKE!
THIS IS SUCH A RELIEF, RICK..
NOW WE'VE JUST GOT TO GET HIM HOME! ANY SUGGESTIONS, COUNSELOR?
WELL, I SUPPOSE I COULD CON-TACT THE FRENCH POLICE..
TOO MESSY. WE COULD BE TIED UP IN COURT FOR YEARS. HOW ABOUT IF YOU NEGOTIATE DIRECTLY FOR HIM.
YOU MEAN, **BUY** HIM?
SURE! JUST SAY YOU'RE LOOKING FOR A NANNY.
A ZOMBIE NANNY?
©B Trudeau

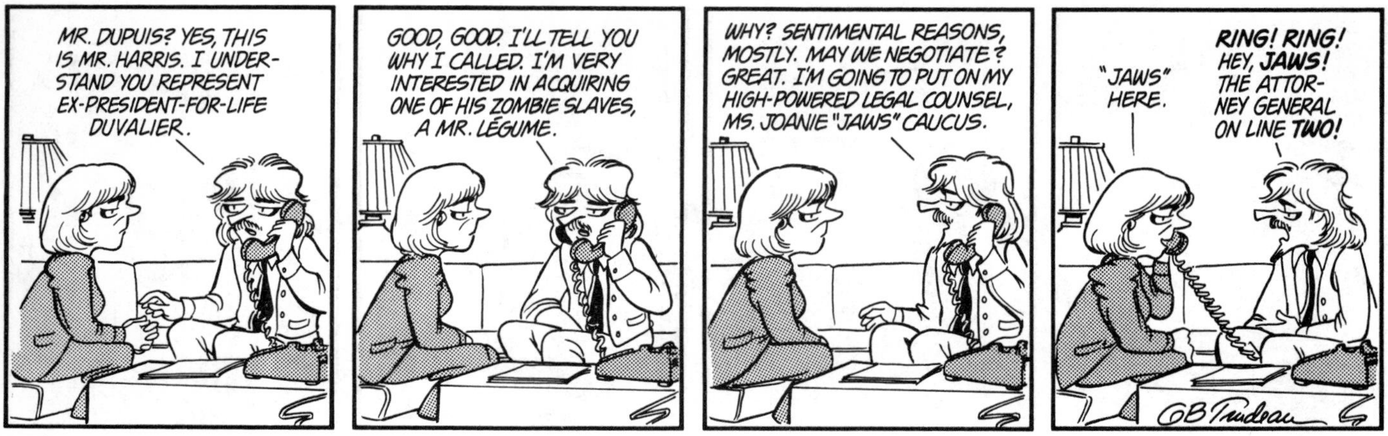
MR. DUPUIS? YES, THIS IS MR. HARRIS. I UNDERSTAND YOU REPRESENT EX-PRESIDENT-FOR-LIFE DUVALIER.
GOOD, GOOD. I'LL TELL YOU WHY I CALLED. I'M VERY INTERESTED IN ACQUIRING ONE OF HIS ZOMBIE SLAVES, A MR. LÉGUME.
WHY? SENTIMENTAL REASONS, MOSTLY. MAY WE NEGOTIATE? GREAT. I'M GOING TO PUT ON MY HIGH-POWERED LEGAL COUNSEL, MS. JOANIE "JAWS" CAUCUS.
"JAWS" HERE.
RING! RING! HEY, JAWS! THE ATTORNEY GENERAL ON LINE TWO!
GB Trudeau

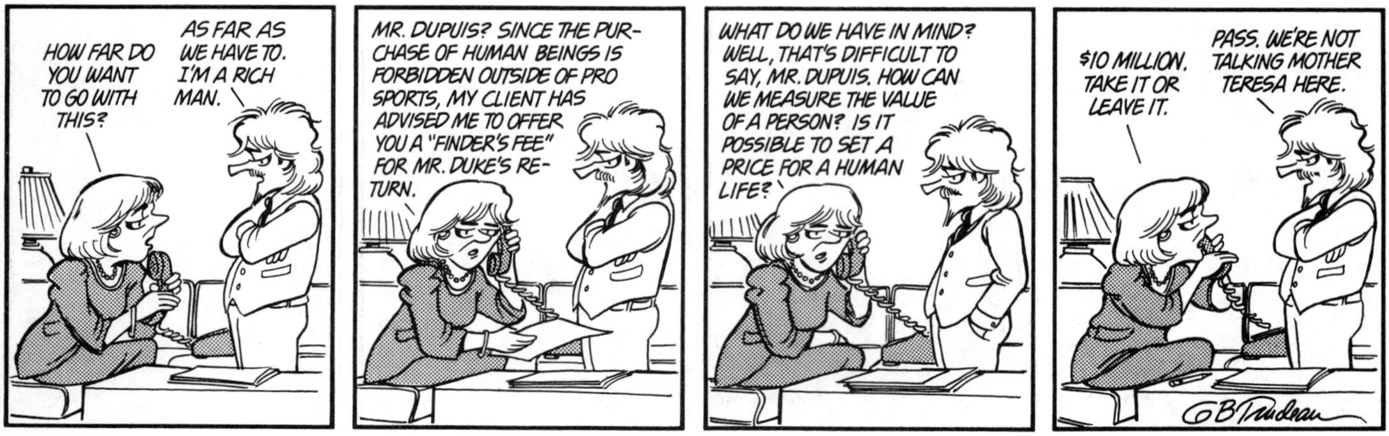
HOW FAR DO YOU WANT TO GO WITH THIS?
AS FAR AS WE HAVE TO. I'M A RICH MAN.
MR. DUPUIS? SINCE THE PURCHASE OF HUMAN BEINGS IS FORBIDDEN OUTSIDE OF PRO SPORTS, MY CLIENT HAS ADVISED ME TO OFFER YOU A "FINDER'S FEE" FOR MR. DUKE'S RETURN.
WHAT DO WE HAVE IN MIND? WELL, THAT'S DIFFICULT TO SAY, MR. DUPUIS. HOW CAN WE MEASURE THE VALUE OF A PERSON? IS IT POSSIBLE TO SET A PRICE FOR A HUMAN LIFE?
$10 MILLION. TAKE IT OR LEAVE IT.
PASS. WE'RE NOT TALKING MOTHER TERESA HERE.
GB Trudeau

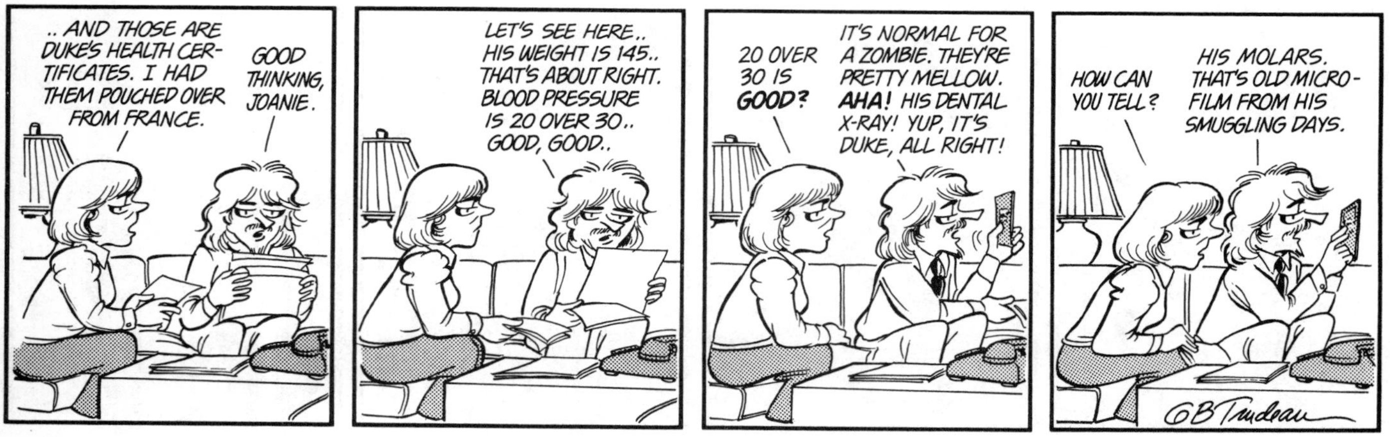
.. AND THOSE ARE DUKE'S HEALTH CERTIFICATES. I HAD THEM POUCHED OVER FROM FRANCE.
GOOD THINKING, JOANIE.
LET'S SEE HERE.. HIS WEIGHT IS 145.. THAT'S ABOUT RIGHT. BLOOD PRESSURE IS 20 OVER 30.. GOOD, GOOD..
20 OVER 30 IS GOOD?
IT'S NORMAL FOR A ZOMBIE. THEY'RE PRETTY MELLOW. AHA! HIS DENTAL X-RAY! YUP, IT'S DUKE, ALL RIGHT!
HOW CAN YOU TELL?
HIS MOLARS. THAT'S OLD MICROFILM FROM HIS SMUGGLING DAYS.
GB Trudeau

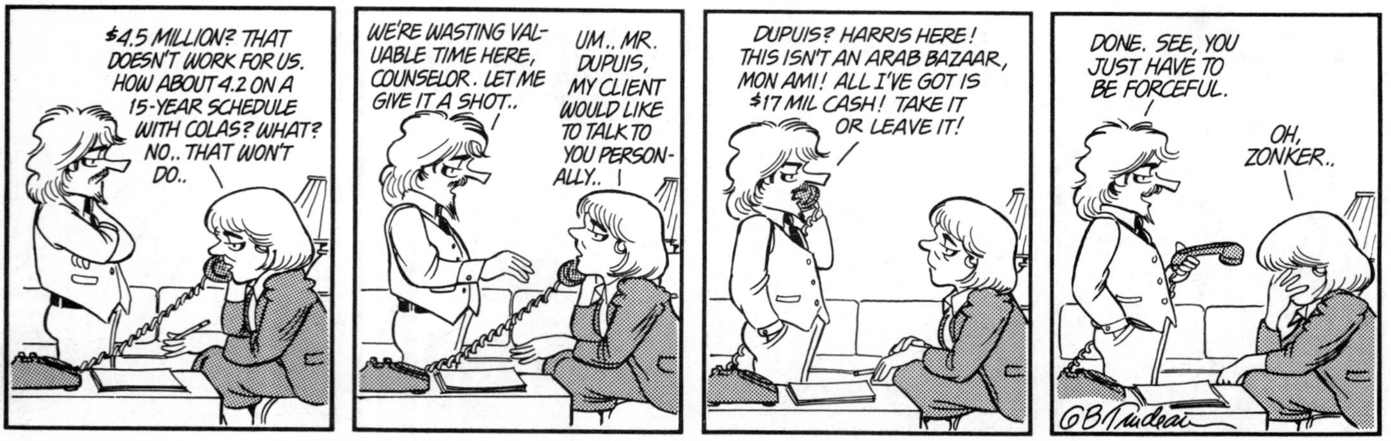
$4.5 MILLION? THAT DOESN'T WORK FOR US. HOW ABOUT 4.2 ON A 15-YEAR SCHEDULE WITH COLAS? WHAT? NO.. THAT WON'T DO..
WE'RE WASTING VALUABLE TIME HERE, COUNSELOR. LET ME GIVE IT A SHOT..
UM.. MR. DUPUIS, MY CLIENT WOULD LIKE TO TALK TO YOU PERSONALLY..
DUPUIS? HARRIS HERE! THIS ISN'T AN ARAB BAZAAR, MON AMI! ALL I'VE GOT IS $17 MIL CASH! TAKE IT OR LEAVE IT!
DONE. SEE, YOU JUST HAVE TO BE FORCEFUL.
OH, ZONKER..
GB Trudeau

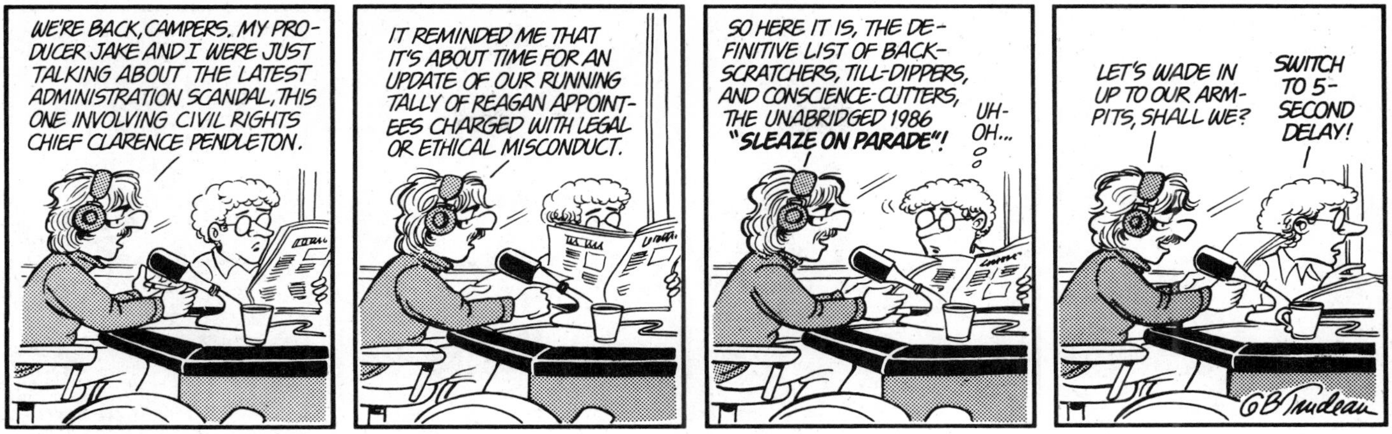
WE'RE BACK, CAMPERS. MY PRODUCER JAKE AND I WERE JUST TALKING ABOUT THE LATEST ADMINISTRATION SCANDAL, THIS ONE INVOLVING CIVIL RIGHTS CHIEF CLARENCE PENDLETON.
IT REMINDED ME THAT IT'S ABOUT TIME FOR AN UPDATE OF OUR RUNNING TALLY OF REAGAN APPOINTEES CHARGED WITH LEGAL OR ETHICAL MISCONDUCT.
SO HERE IT IS, THE DEFINITIVE LIST OF BACK-SCRATCHERS, TILL-DIPPERS, AND CONSCIENCE-CUTTERS, THE UNABRIDGED 1986 "SLEAZE ON PARADE"!
UH-OH...
LET'S WADE IN UP TO OUR ARMPITS, SHALL WE?
SWITCH TO 5-SECOND DELAY!
©B Trudeau

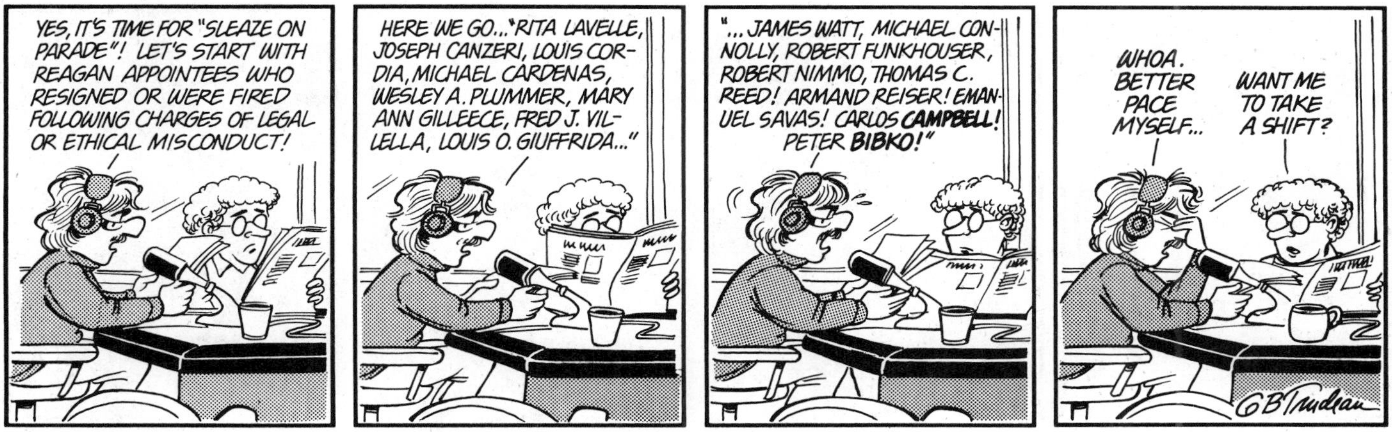
YES, IT'S TIME FOR "SLEAZE ON PARADE"! LET'S START WITH REAGAN APPOINTEES WHO RESIGNED OR WERE FIRED FOLLOWING CHARGES OF LEGAL OR ETHICAL MISCONDUCT!
HERE WE GO..."RITA LAVELLE, JOSEPH CANZERI, LOUIS CORDIA, MICHAEL CARDENAS, WESLEY A. PLUMMER, MARY ANN GILLEECE, FRED J. VILLELLA, LOUIS O. GIUFFRIDA..."
"...JAMES WATT, MICHAEL CONNOLLY, ROBERT FUNKHOUSER, ROBERT NIMMO, THOMAS C. REED! ARMAND REISER! EMANUEL SAVAS! CARLOS CAMPBELL! PETER BIBKO!"
WHOA. BETTER PACE MYSELF...
WANT ME TO TAKE A SHIFT?
©B Trudeau

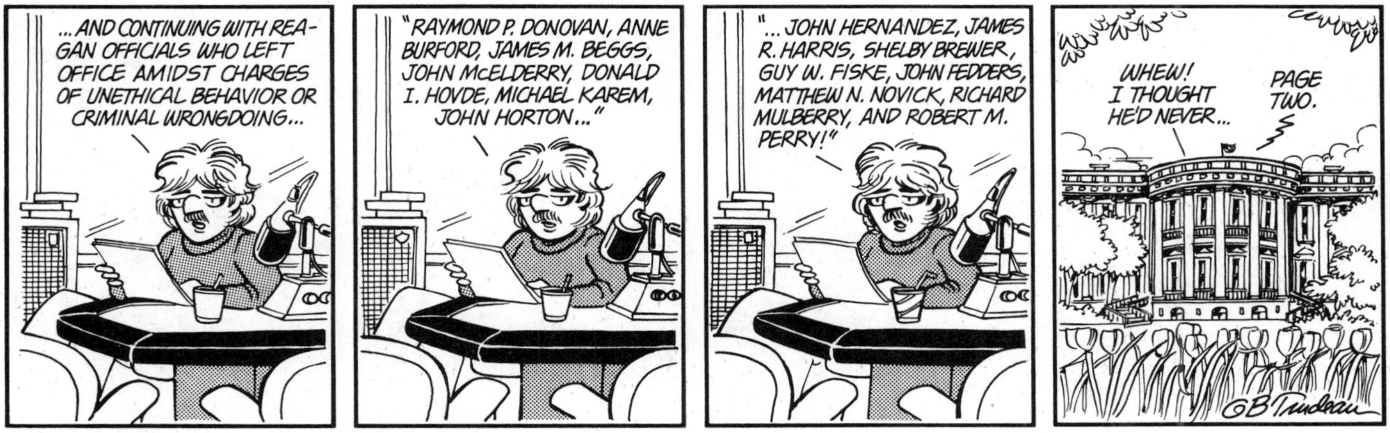
...AND CONTINUING WITH REAGAN OFFICIALS WHO LEFT OFFICE AMIDST CHARGES OF UNETHICAL BEHAVIOR OR CRIMINAL WRONGDOING...
"RAYMOND P. DONOVAN, ANNE BURFORD, JAMES M. BEGGS, JOHN McELDERRY, DONALD I. HOVDE, MICHAEL KAREM, JOHN HORTON..."
"...JOHN HERNANDEZ, JAMES R. HARRIS, SHELBY BREWER, GUY W. FISKE, JOHN FEDDERS, MATTHEW N. NOVICK, RICHARD MULBERRY, AND ROBERT M. PERRY!"
WHEW! I THOUGHT HE'D NEVER...
PAGE TWO.
©B Trudeau

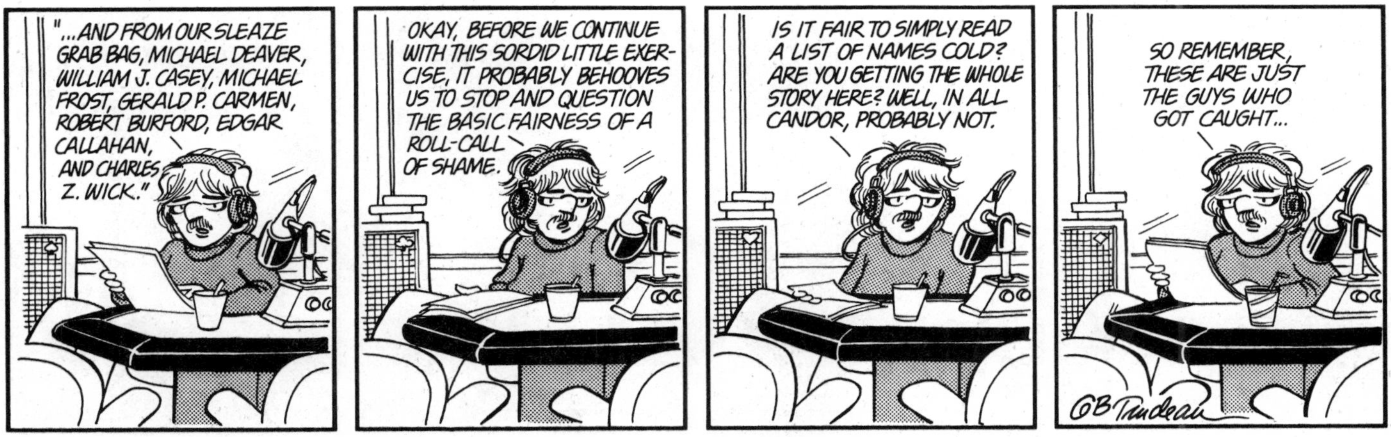
"...AND FROM OUR SLEAZE GRAB BAG, MICHAEL DEAVER, WILLIAM J. CASEY, MICHAEL FROST, GERALD P. CARMEN, ROBERT BURFORD, EDGAR CALLAHAN, AND CHARLES Z. WICK."
OKAY, BEFORE WE CONTINUE WITH THIS SORDID LITTLE EXERCISE, IT PROBABLY BEHOOVES US TO STOP AND QUESTION THE BASIC FAIRNESS OF A ROLL-CALL OF SHAME.
IS IT FAIR TO SIMPLY READ A LIST OF NAMES COLD? ARE YOU GETTING THE WHOLE STORY HERE? WELL, IN ALL CANDOR, PROBABLY NOT.
SO REMEMBER, THESE ARE JUST THE GUYS WHO GOT CAUGHT...
©B Trudeau

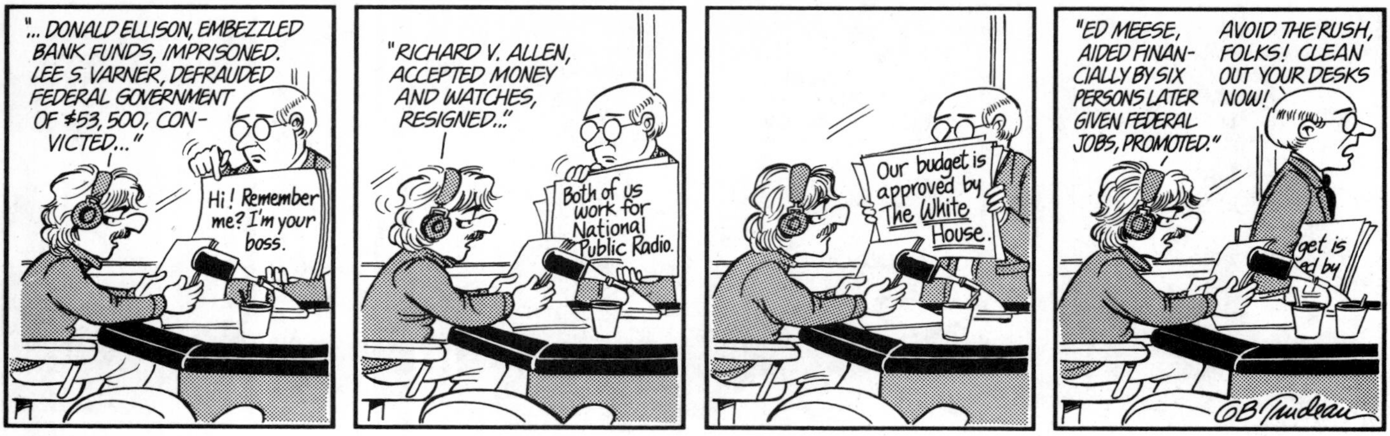
"... DONALD ELLISON, EMBEZZLED BANK FUNDS, IMPRISONED. LEE S. VARNER, DEFRAUDED FEDERAL GOVERNMENT OF $53,500, CONVICTED..."
Hi! Remember me? I'm your boss.
"RICHARD V. ALLEN, ACCEPTED MONEY AND WATCHES, RESIGNED..."
Both of us work for National Public Radio.
Our budget is approved by The White House.
"ED MEESE, AIDED FINANCIALLY BY SIX PERSONS LATER GIVEN FEDERAL JOBS, PROMOTED."
AVOID THE RUSH, FOLKS! CLEAN OUT YOUR DESKS NOW!
©B Trudeau

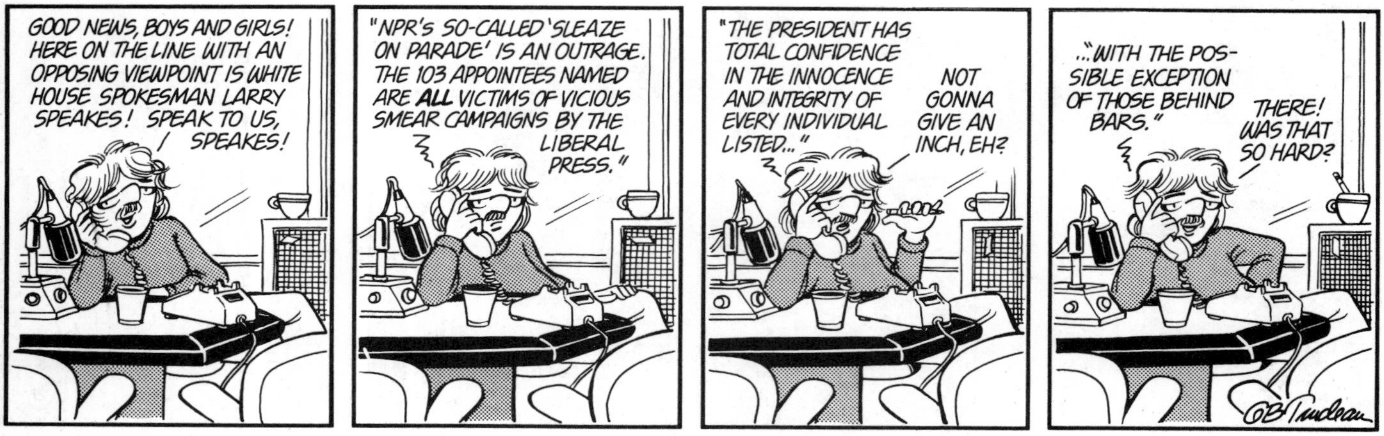
GOOD NEWS, BOYS AND GIRLS! HERE ON THE LINE WITH AN OPPOSING VIEWPOINT IS WHITE HOUSE SPOKESMAN LARRY SPEAKES! SPEAK TO US, SPEAKES!
"NPR'S SO-CALLED 'SLEAZE ON PARADE' IS AN OUTRAGE. THE 103 APPOINTEES NAMED ARE ALL VICTIMS OF VICIOUS SMEAR CAMPAIGNS BY THE LIBERAL PRESS."
"THE PRESIDENT HAS TOTAL CONFIDENCE IN THE INNOCENCE AND INTEGRITY OF EVERY INDIVIDUAL LISTED..."
NOT GONNA GIVE AN INCH, EH?
..."WITH THE POSSIBLE EXCEPTION OF THOSE BEHIND BARS."
THERE! WAS THAT SO HARD?
©B Trudeau

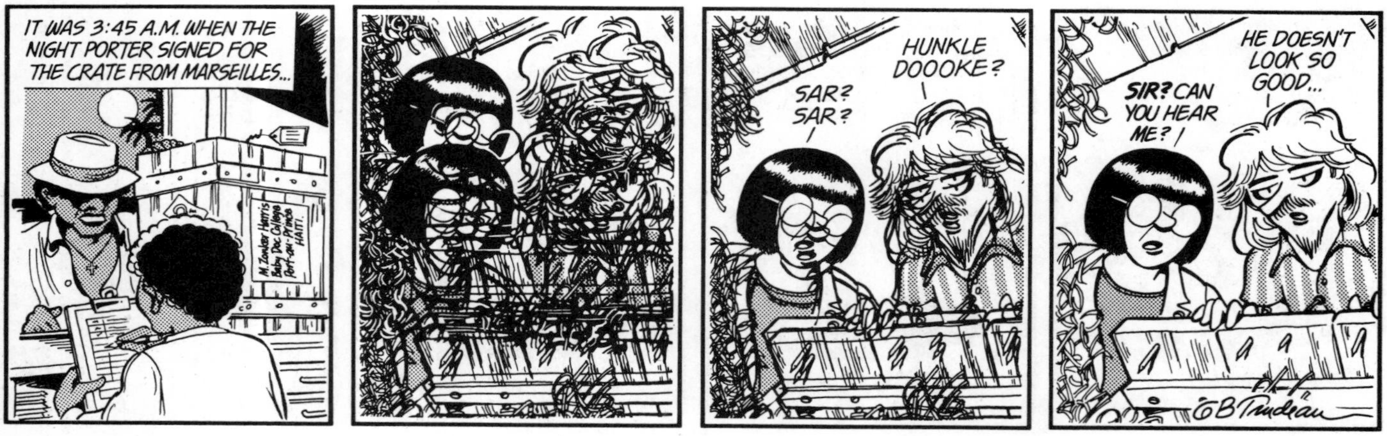
IT WAS 3:45 A.M. WHEN THE NIGHT PORTER SIGNED FOR THE CRATE FROM MARSEILLES...
SAR? SAR?
HUNKLE DOOOKE?
SIR? CAN YOU HEAR ME?
HE DOESN'T LOOK SO GOOD...
©B Trudeau

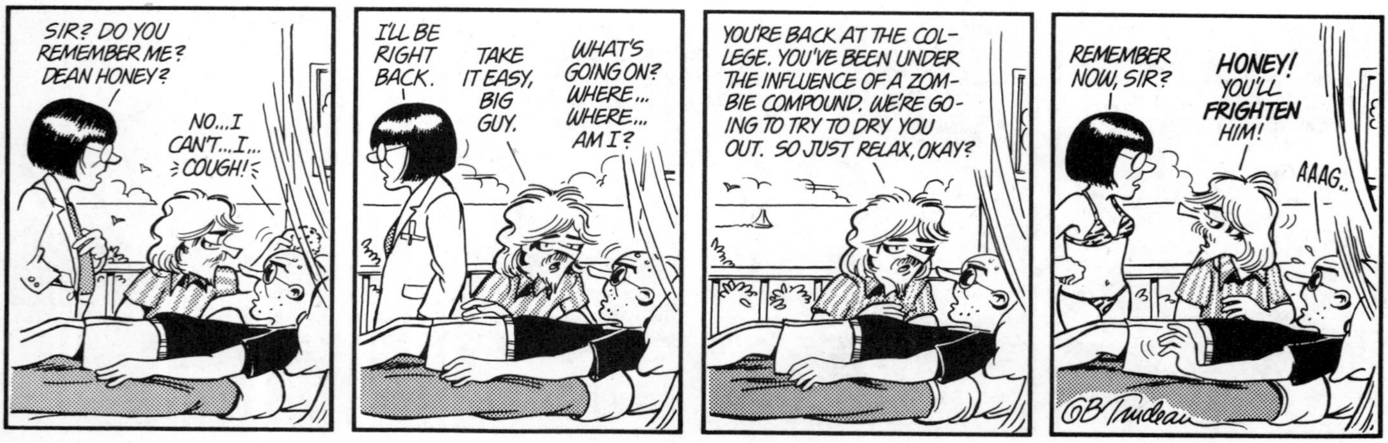
SIR? DO YOU REMEMBER ME? DEAN HONEY?
NO...I CAN'T...I... COUGH!
I'LL BE RIGHT BACK.
TAKE IT EASY, BIG GUY.
WHAT'S GOING ON? WHERE... WHERE... AM I?
YOU'RE BACK AT THE COLLEGE. YOU'VE BEEN UNDER THE INFLUENCE OF A ZOMBIE COMPOUND. WE'RE GOING TO TRY TO DRY YOU OUT. SO JUST RELAX, OKAY?
REMEMBER NOW, SIR?
HONEY! YOU'LL FRIGHTEN HIM!
AAAG..
©B Trudeau

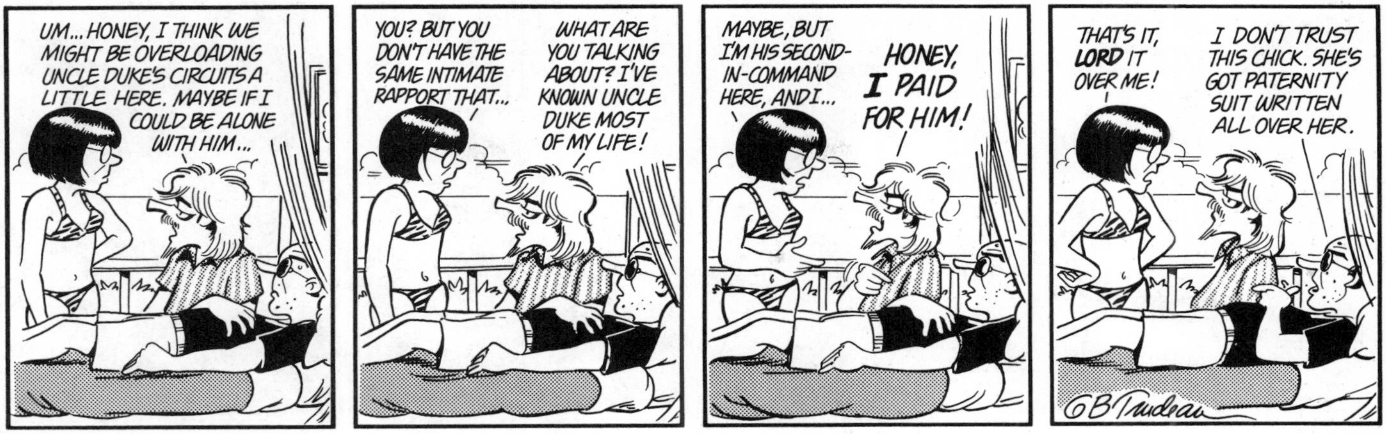
UM... HONEY, I THINK WE MIGHT BE OVERLOADING UNCLE DUKE'S CIRCUITS A LITTLE HERE. MAYBE IF I COULD BE ALONE WITH HIM...
YOU? BUT YOU DON'T HAVE THE SAME INTIMATE RAPPORT THAT...
WHAT ARE YOU TALKING ABOUT? I'VE KNOWN UNCLE DUKE MOST OF MY LIFE!
MAYBE, BUT I'M HIS SECOND-IN-COMMAND HERE, AND I...
HONEY, I PAID FOR HIM!
THAT'S IT, LORD IT OVER ME!
I DON'T TRUST THIS CHICK. SHE'S GOT PATERNITY SUIT WRITTEN ALL OVER HER.

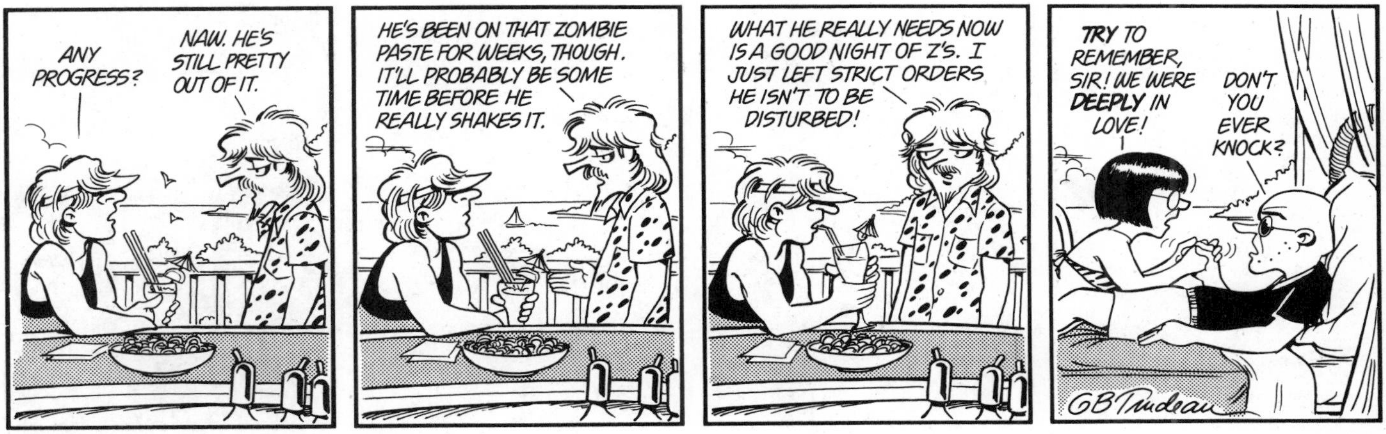
ANY PROGRESS?
NAW. HE'S STILL PRETTY OUT OF IT.
HE'S BEEN ON THAT ZOMBIE PASTE FOR WEEKS, THOUGH. IT'LL PROBABLY BE SOME TIME BEFORE HE REALLY SHAKES IT.
WHAT HE REALLY NEEDS NOW IS A GOOD NIGHT OF Z'S. I JUST LEFT STRICT ORDERS HE ISN'T TO BE DISTURBED!
TRY TO REMEMBER, SIR! WE WERE DEEPLY IN LOVE!
DON'T YOU EVER KNOCK?

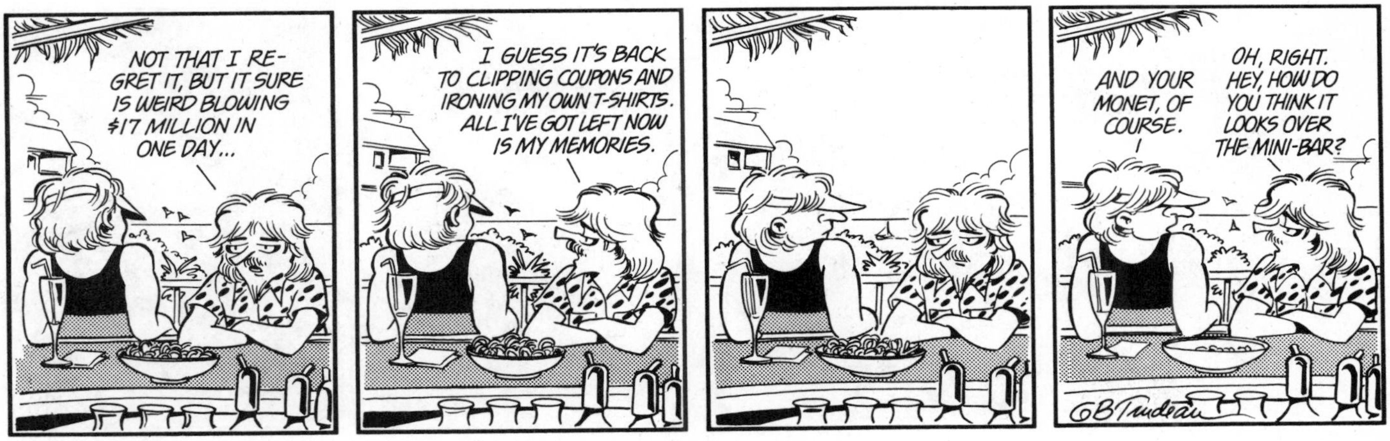
NOT THAT I REGRET IT, BUT IT SURE IS WEIRD BLOWING $17 MILLION IN ONE DAY...
I GUESS IT'S BACK TO CLIPPING COUPONS AND IRONING MY OWN T-SHIRTS. ALL I'VE GOT LEFT NOW IS MY MEMORIES.
AND YOUR MONET, OF COURSE.
OH, RIGHT. HEY, HOW DO YOU THINK IT LOOKS OVER THE MINI-BAR?

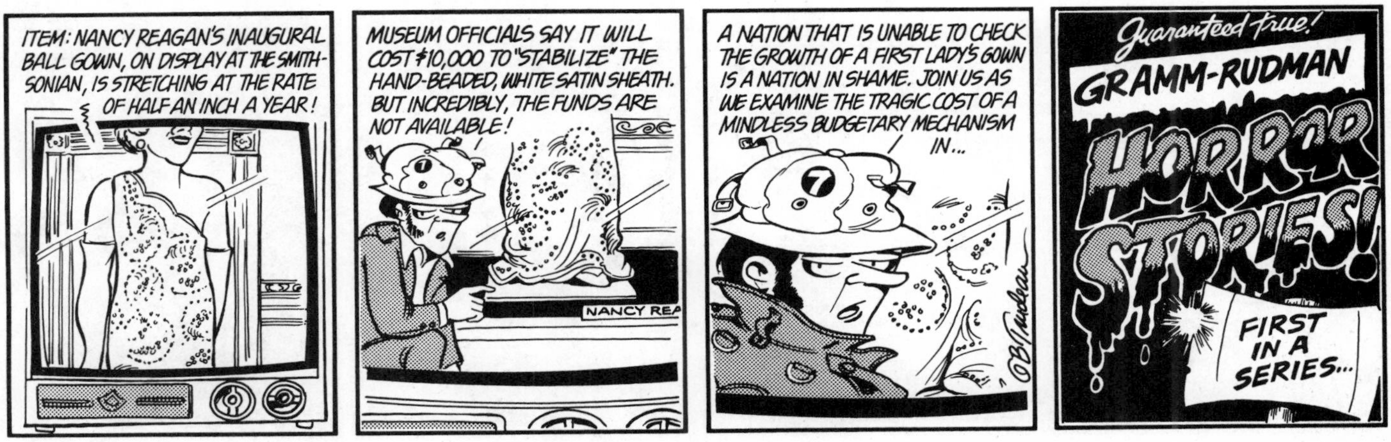
ITEM: NANCY REAGAN'S INAUGURAL BALL GOWN, ON DISPLAY AT THE SMITHSONIAN, IS STRETCHING AT THE RATE OF HALF AN INCH A YEAR!
MUSEUM OFFICIALS SAY IT WILL COST $10,000 TO "STABILIZE" THE HAND-BEADED, WHITE SATIN SHEATH. BUT INCREDIBLY, THE FUNDS ARE NOT AVAILABLE!
NANCY REA
A NATION THAT IS UNABLE TO CHECK THE GROWTH OF A FIRST LADY'S GOWN IS A NATION IN SHAME. JOIN US AS WE EXAMINE THE TRAGIC COST OF A MINDLESS BUDGETARY MECHANISM IN...
Guaranteed true!
GRAMM-RUDMAN
HORROR STORIES!
FIRST IN A SERIES...

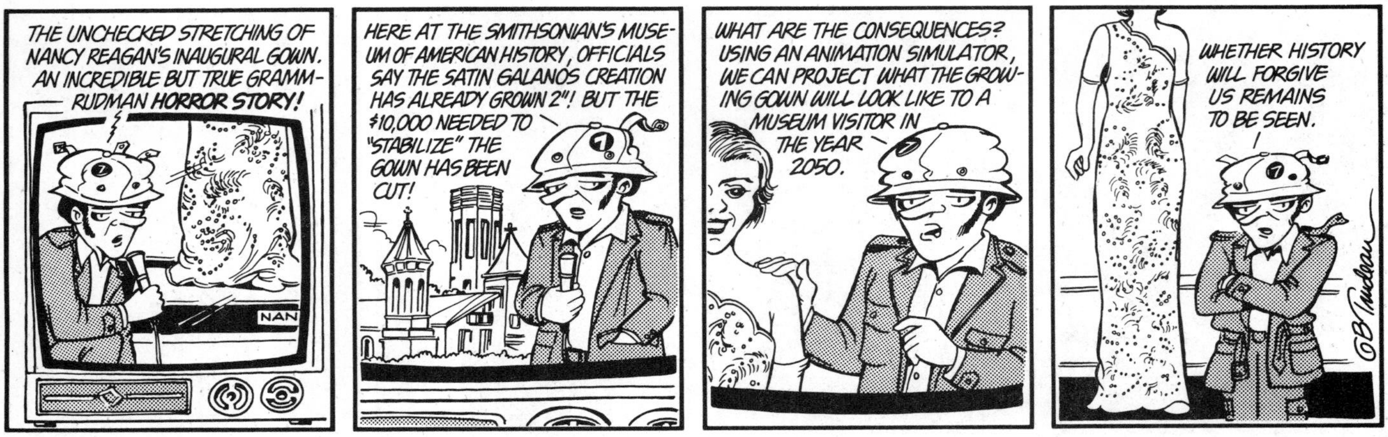
THE UNCHECKED STRETCHING OF NANCY REAGAN'S INAUGURAL GOWN. AN INCREDIBLE BUT TRUE GRAMM-RUDMAN **HORROR STORY!**
NAN
HERE AT THE SMITHSONIAN'S MUSEUM OF AMERICAN HISTORY, OFFICIALS SAY THE SATIN GALANOS CREATION HAS ALREADY GROWN 2"! BUT THE $10,000 NEEDED TO "STABILIZE" THE GOWN HAS BEEN CUT!
WHAT ARE THE CONSEQUENCES? USING AN ANIMATION SIMULATOR, WE CAN PROJECT WHAT THE GROWING GOWN WILL LOOK LIKE TO A MUSEUM VISITOR IN THE YEAR 2050.
WHETHER HISTORY WILL FORGIVE US REMAINS TO BE SEEN.
©B Trudeau

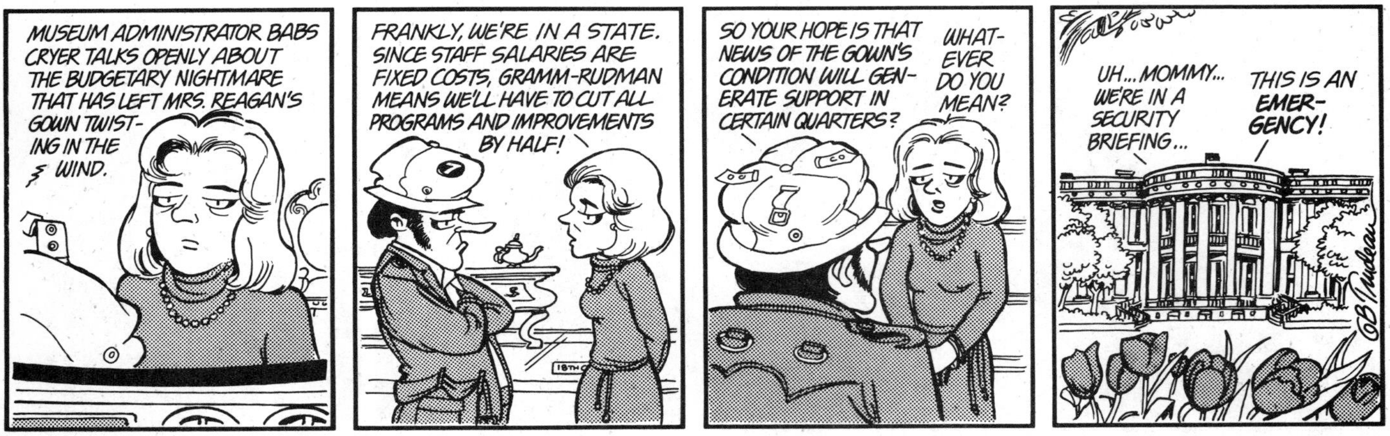
MUSEUM ADMINISTRATOR BABS CRYER TALKS OPENLY ABOUT THE BUDGETARY NIGHTMARE THAT HAS LEFT MRS. REAGAN'S GOWN TWISTING IN THE WIND.
FRANKLY, WE'RE IN A STATE. SINCE STAFF SALARIES ARE FIXED COSTS, GRAMM-RUDMAN MEANS WE'LL HAVE TO CUT ALL PROGRAMS AND IMPROVEMENTS BY HALF!
SO YOUR HOPE IS THAT NEWS OF THE GOWN'S CONDITION WILL GENERATE SUPPORT IN CERTAIN QUARTERS?
WHATEVER DO YOU MEAN?
UH... MOMMY... WE'RE IN A SECURITY BRIEFING...
THIS IS AN **EMERGENCY!**
©B Trudeau

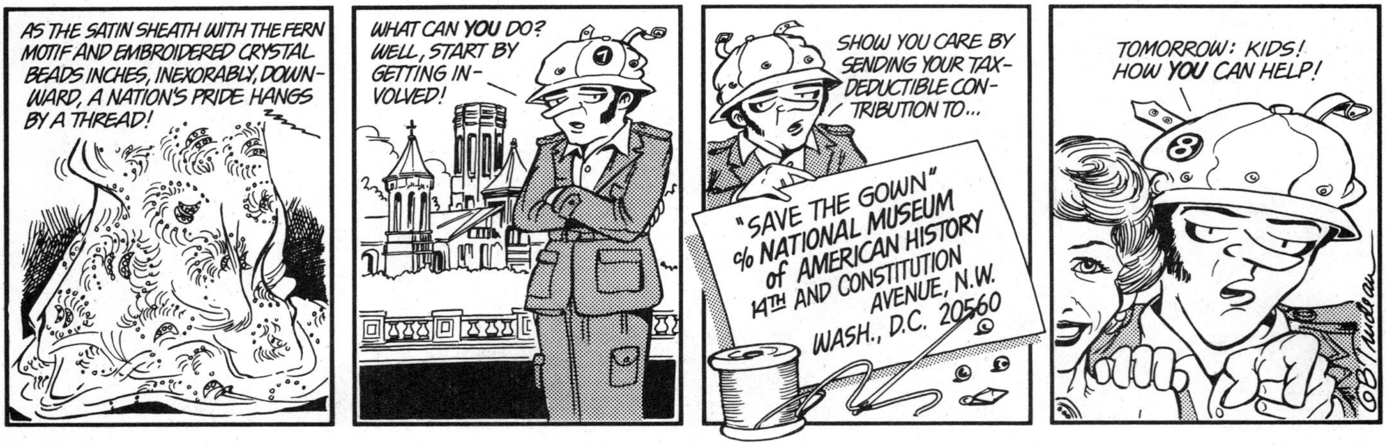
AS THE SATIN SHEATH WITH THE FERN MOTIF AND EMBROIDERED CRYSTAL BEADS INCHES, INEXORABLY, DOWNWARD, A NATION'S PRIDE HANGS BY A THREAD!
WHAT CAN **YOU** DO? WELL, START BY GETTING INVOLVED!
SHOW YOU CARE BY SENDING YOUR TAX-DEDUCTIBLE CONTRIBUTION TO...
"SAVE THE GOWN"
c/o NATIONAL MUSEUM of AMERICAN HISTORY
14TH AND CONSTITUTION AVENUE, N.W.
WASH., D.C. 20560
TOMORROW: KIDS! HOW **YOU** CAN HELP!
©B Trudeau

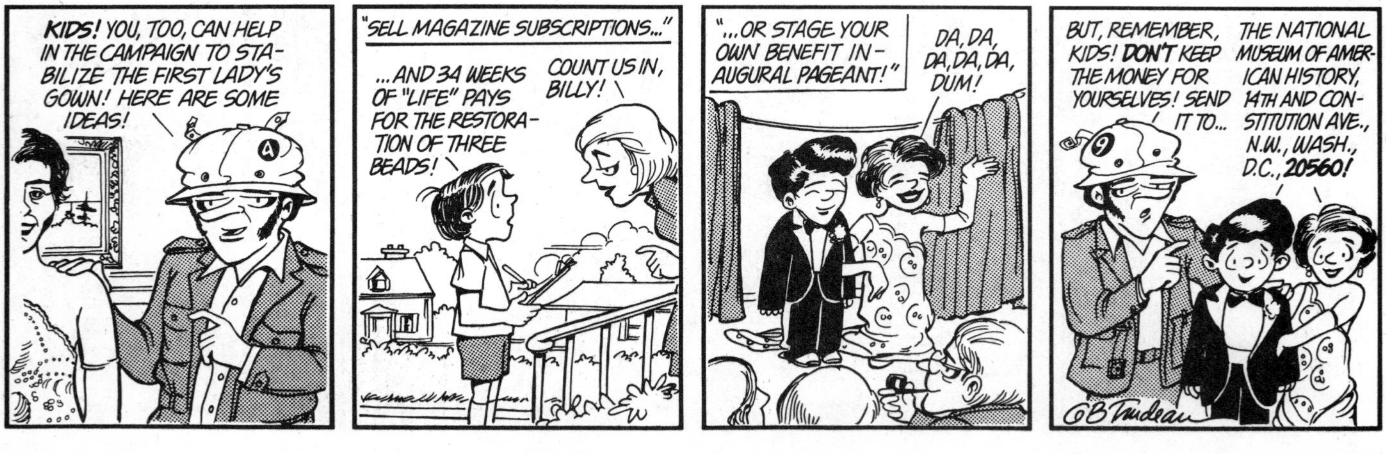
KIDS! YOU, TOO, CAN HELP IN THE CAMPAIGN TO STABILIZE THE FIRST LADY'S GOWN! HERE ARE SOME IDEAS!
"SELL MAGAZINE SUBSCRIPTIONS..."
...AND 34 WEEKS OF "LIFE" PAYS FOR THE RESTORATION OF THREE BEADS!
COUNT US IN, BILLY!
"...OR STAGE YOUR OWN BENEFIT INAUGURAL PAGEANT!"
DA, DA, DA, DA, DA, DUM!
BUT, REMEMBER, KIDS! **DON'T** KEEP THE MONEY FOR YOURSELVES! SEND IT TO...
THE NATIONAL MUSEUM OF AMERICAN HISTORY, 14TH AND CONSTITUTION AVE., N.W., WASH., D.C., **20560!**
©B Trudeau

PART THREE

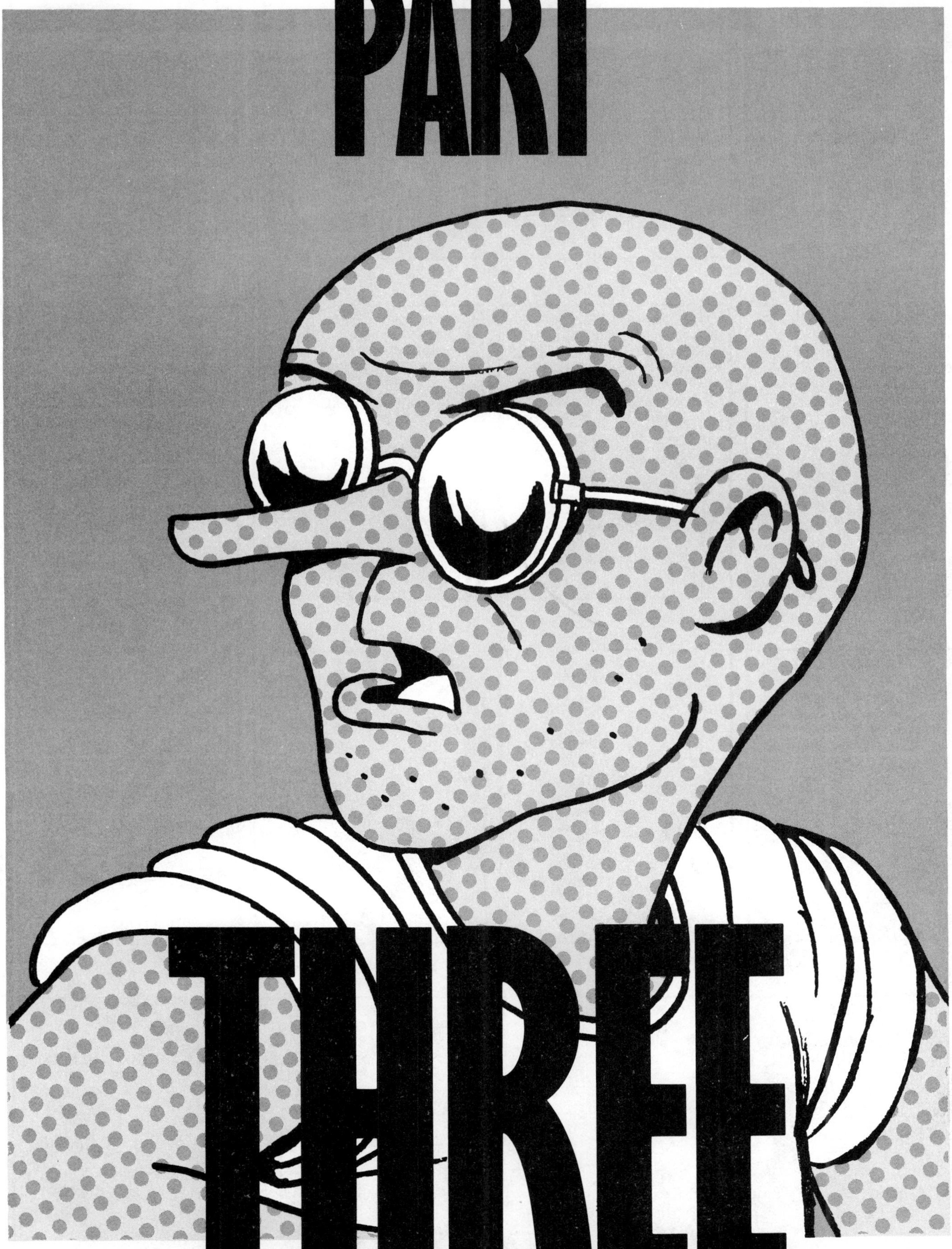

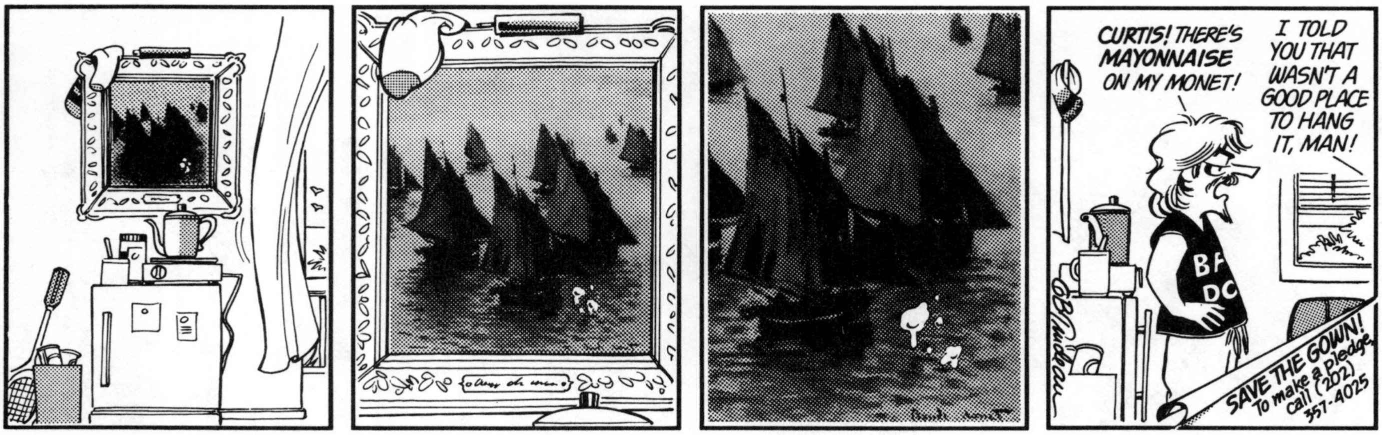
CURTIS! THERE'S MAYONNAISE ON MY MONET!
I TOLD YOU THAT WASN'T A GOOD PLACE TO HANG IT, MAN!
SAVE THE GOWN! To make a pledge call (202) 357-4025
GB Trudeau

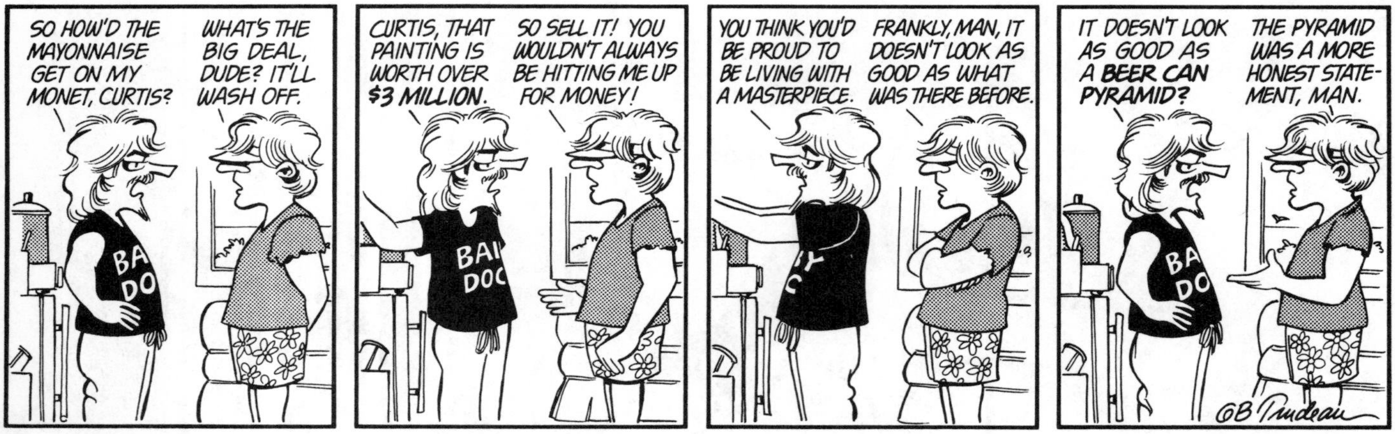
SO HOW'D THE MAYONNAISE GET ON MY MONET, CURTIS?
WHAT'S THE BIG DEAL, DUDE? IT'LL WASH OFF.
CURTIS, THAT PAINTING IS WORTH OVER $3 MILLION.
SO SELL IT! YOU WOULDN'T ALWAYS BE HITTING ME UP FOR MONEY!
YOU THINK YOU'D BE PROUD TO BE LIVING WITH A MASTERPIECE.
FRANKLY, MAN, IT DOESN'T LOOK AS GOOD AS WHAT WAS THERE BEFORE.
IT DOESN'T LOOK AS GOOD AS A BEER CAN PYRAMID?
THE PYRAMID WAS A MORE HONEST STATEMENT, MAN.
GB Trudeau

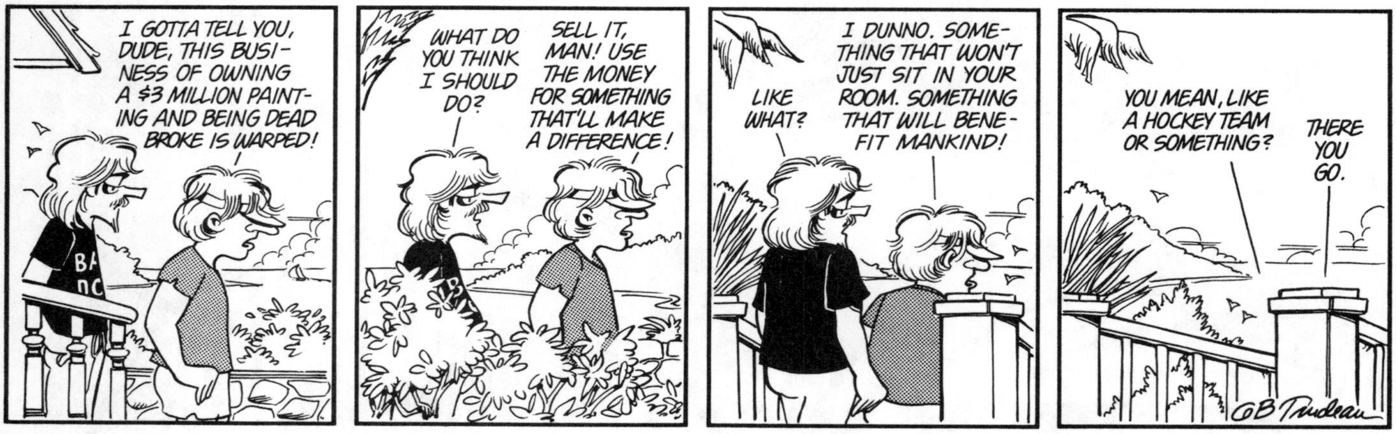
I GOTTA TELL YOU, DUDE, THIS BUSINESS OF OWNING A $3 MILLION PAINTING AND BEING DEAD BROKE IS WARPED!
WHAT DO YOU THINK I SHOULD DO?
SELL IT, MAN! USE THE MONEY FOR SOMETHING THAT'LL MAKE A DIFFERENCE!
LIKE WHAT?
I DUNNO. SOMETHING THAT WON'T JUST SIT IN YOUR ROOM. SOMETHING THAT WILL BENEFIT MANKIND!
YOU MEAN, LIKE A HOCKEY TEAM OR SOMETHING?
THERE YOU GO.
GB Trudeau

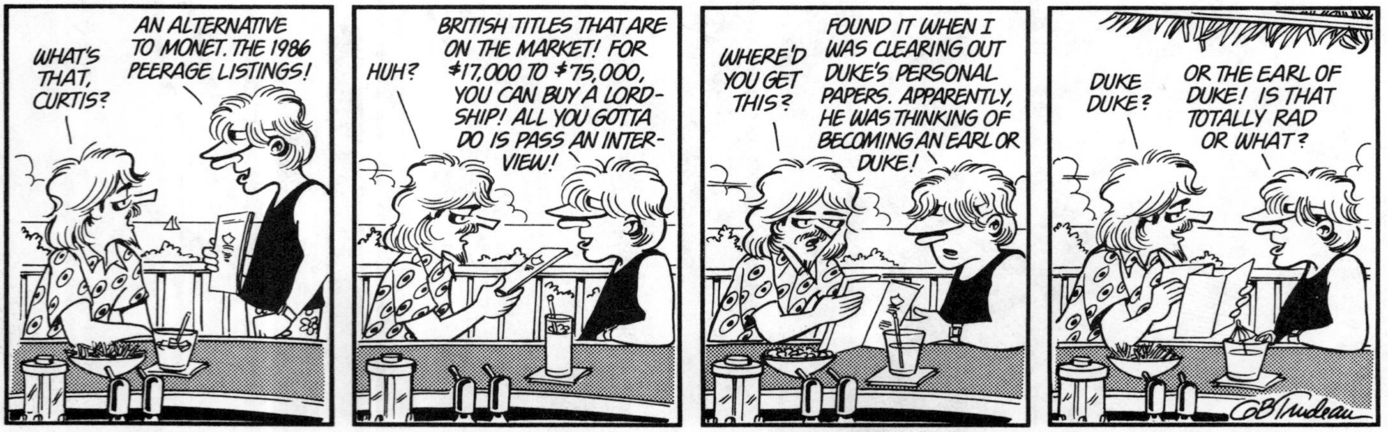
WHAT'S THAT, CURTIS?
AN ALTERNATIVE TO MONET. THE 1986 PEERAGE LISTINGS!
HUH?
BRITISH TITLES THAT ARE ON THE MARKET! FOR $17,000 TO $75,000, YOU CAN BUY A LORDSHIP! ALL YOU GOTTA DO IS PASS AN INTERVIEW!
WHERE'D YOU GET THIS?
FOUND IT WHEN I WAS CLEARING OUT DUKE'S PERSONAL PAPERS. APPARENTLY, HE WAS THINKING OF BECOMING AN EARL OR DUKE!
DUKE DUKE?
OR THE EARL OF DUKE! IS THAT TOTALLY RAD OR WHAT?
GB Trudeau

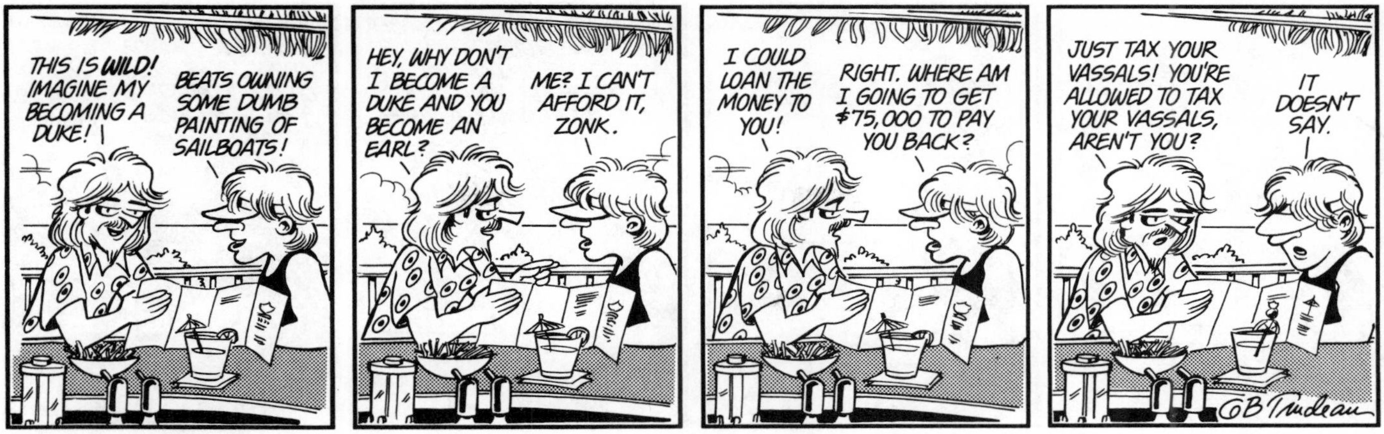
THIS IS WILD! IMAGINE MY BECOMING A DUKE!
BEATS OWNING SOME DUMB PAINTING OF SAILBOATS!
HEY, WHY DON'T I BECOME A DUKE AND YOU BECOME AN EARL?
ME? I CAN'T AFFORD IT, ZONK.
I COULD LOAN THE MONEY TO YOU!
RIGHT. WHERE AM I GOING TO GET $75,000 TO PAY YOU BACK?
JUST TAX YOUR VASSALS! YOU'RE ALLOWED TO TAX YOUR VASSALS, AREN'T YOU?
IT DOESN'T SAY.
©B Trudeau

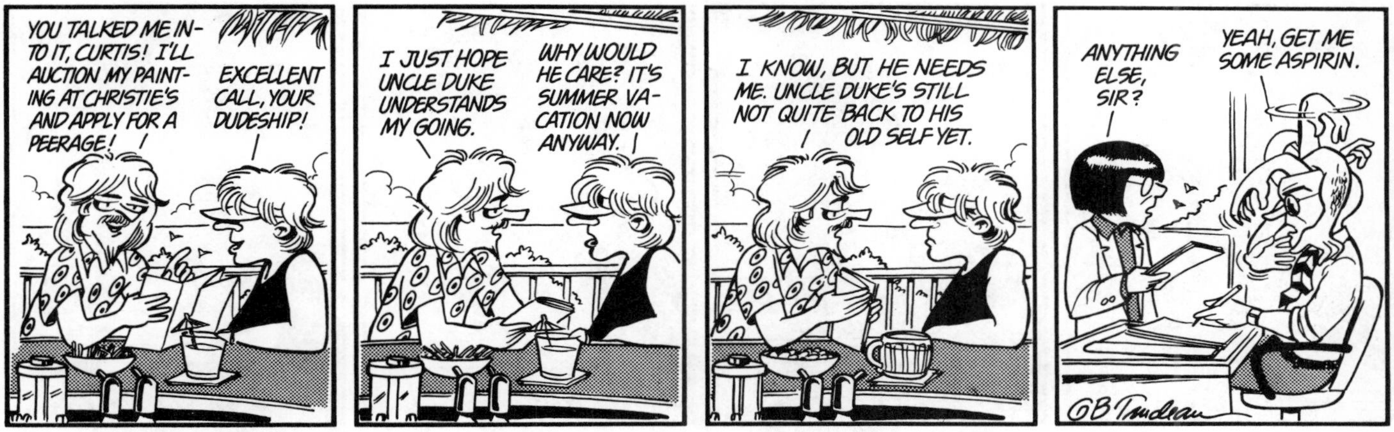
YOU TALKED ME INTO IT, CURTIS! I'LL AUCTION MY PAINTING AT CHRISTIE'S AND APPLY FOR A PEERAGE!
EXCELLENT CALL, YOUR DUDESHIP!
I JUST HOPE UNCLE DUKE UNDERSTANDS MY GOING.
WHY WOULD HE CARE? IT'S SUMMER VACATION NOW ANYWAY.
I KNOW, BUT HE NEEDS ME. UNCLE DUKE'S STILL NOT QUITE BACK TO HIS OLD SELF YET.
ANYTHING ELSE, SIR?
YEAH, GET ME SOME ASPIRIN.
©B Trudeau

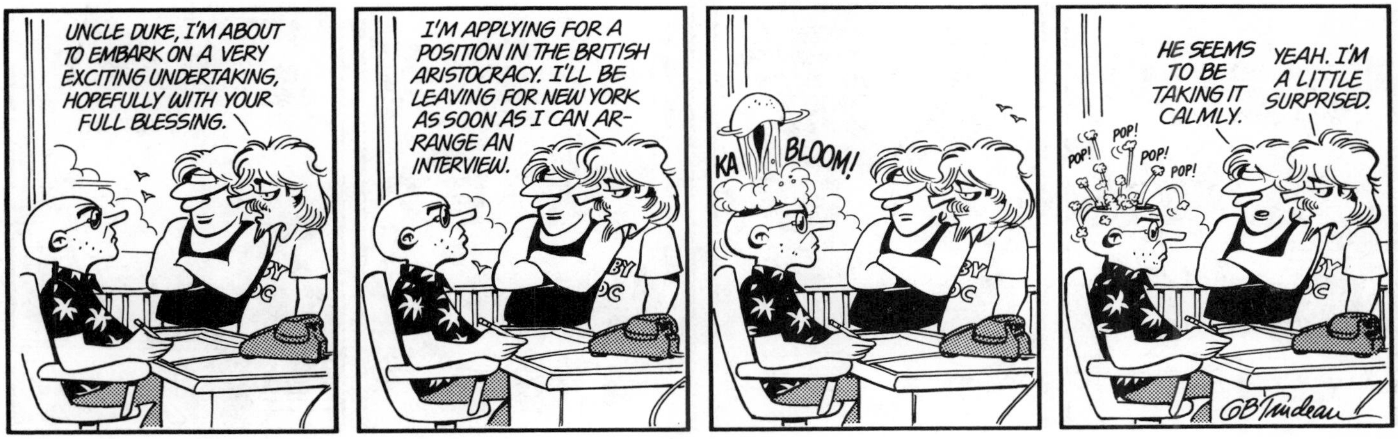
UNCLE DUKE, I'M ABOUT TO EMBARK ON A VERY EXCITING UNDERTAKING, HOPEFULLY WITH YOUR FULL BLESSING.
I'M APPLYING FOR A POSITION IN THE BRITISH ARISTOCRACY. I'LL BE LEAVING FOR NEW YORK AS SOON AS I CAN ARRANGE AN INTERVIEW.
KA BLOOM!
POP! POP! POP! POP!
HE SEEMS TO BE TAKING IT CALMLY.
YEAH. I'M A LITTLE SURPRISED.
©B Trudeau

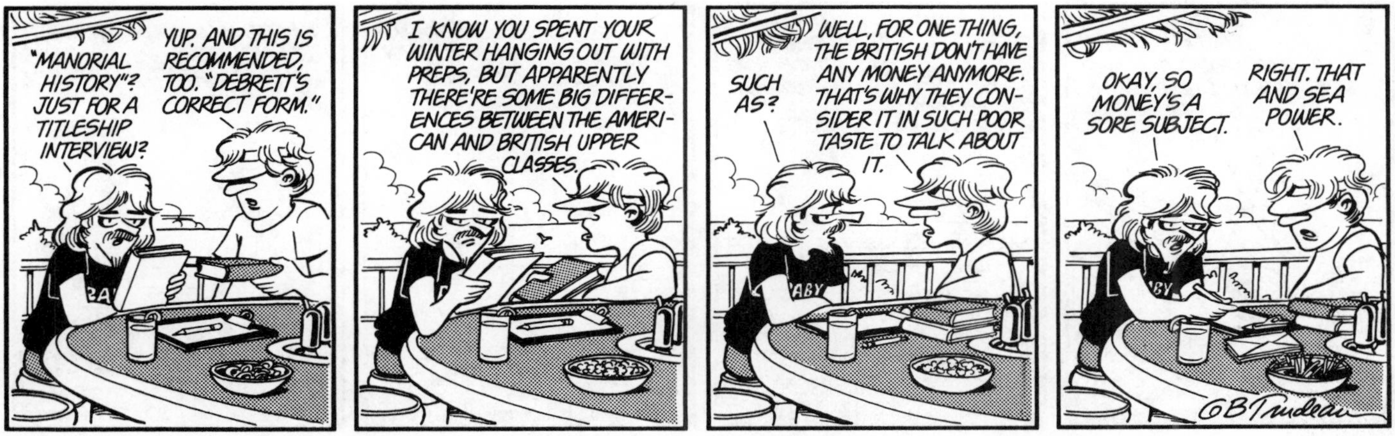
"MANORIAL HISTORY"? JUST FOR A TITLESHIP INTERVIEW?
YUP. AND THIS IS RECOMMENDED, TOO. "DEBRETT'S CORRECT FORM."
I KNOW YOU SPENT YOUR WINTER HANGING OUT WITH PREPS, BUT APPARENTLY THERE'RE SOME BIG DIFFERENCES BETWEEN THE AMERICAN AND BRITISH UPPER CLASSES.
SUCH AS?
WELL, FOR ONE THING, THE BRITISH DON'T HAVE ANY MONEY ANYMORE. THAT'S WHY THEY CONSIDER IT IN SUCH POOR TASTE TO TALK ABOUT IT.
OKAY, SO MONEY'S A SORE SUBJECT.
RIGHT. THAT AND SEA POWER.
©B Trudeau

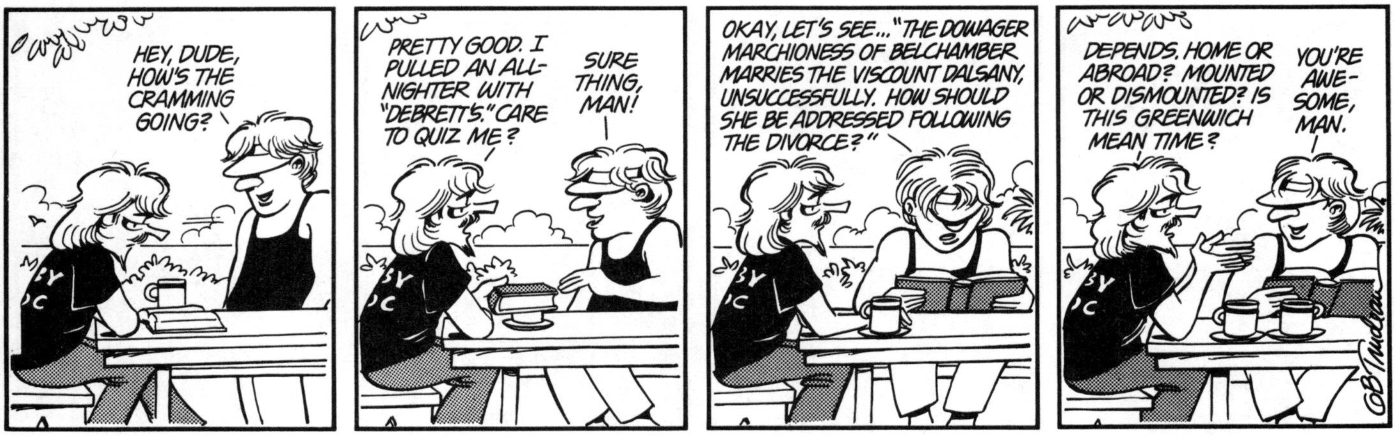
HEY, DUDE, HOW'S THE CRAMMING GOING?
PRETTY GOOD. I PULLED AN ALL-NIGHTER WITH "DEBRETT'S." CARE TO QUIZ ME?
SURE THING, MAN!
OKAY, LET'S SEE... "THE DOWAGER MARCHIONESS OF BELCHAMBER MARRIES THE VISCOUNT DALSANY, UNSUCCESSFULLY. HOW SHOULD SHE BE ADDRESSED FOLLOWING THE DIVORCE?"
DEPENDS. HOME OR ABROAD? MOUNTED OR DISMOUNTED? IS THIS GREENWICH MEAN TIME?
YOU'RE AWE-SOME, MAN.

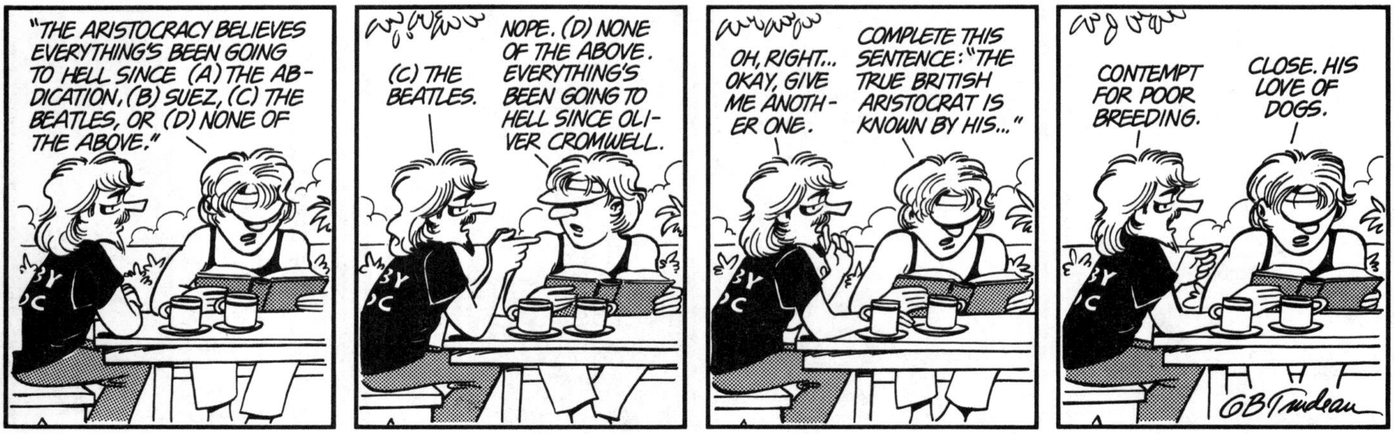
"THE ARISTOCRACY BELIEVES EVERYTHING'S BEEN GOING TO HELL SINCE (A) THE AB-DICATION, (B) SUEZ, (C) THE BEATLES, OR (D) NONE OF THE ABOVE."
(C) THE BEATLES.
NOPE. (D) NONE OF THE ABOVE. EVERYTHING'S BEEN GOING TO HELL SINCE OLI-VER CROMWELL.
OH, RIGHT... OKAY, GIVE ME ANOTH-ER ONE.
COMPLETE THIS SENTENCE: "THE TRUE BRITISH ARISTOCRAT IS KNOWN BY HIS..."
CONTEMPT FOR POOR BREEDING.
CLOSE. HIS LOVE OF DOGS.

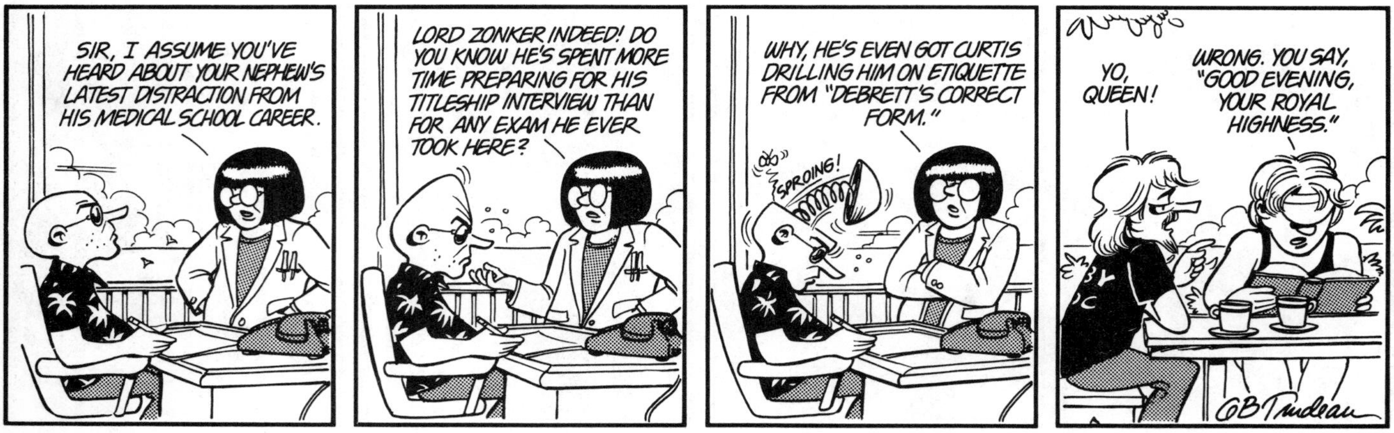
SIR, I ASSUME YOU'VE HEARD ABOUT YOUR NEPHEW'S LATEST DISTRACTION FROM HIS MEDICAL SCHOOL CAREER.
LORD ZONKER INDEED! DO YOU KNOW HE'S SPENT MORE TIME PREPARING FOR HIS TITLESHIP INTERVIEW THAN FOR ANY EXAM HE EVER TOOK HERE?
WHY, HE'S EVEN GOT CURTIS DRILLING HIM ON ETIQUETTE FROM "DEBRETT'S CORRECT FORM."
SPROING!
YO, QUEEN!
WRONG. YOU SAY, "GOOD EVENING, YOUR ROYAL HIGHNESS."

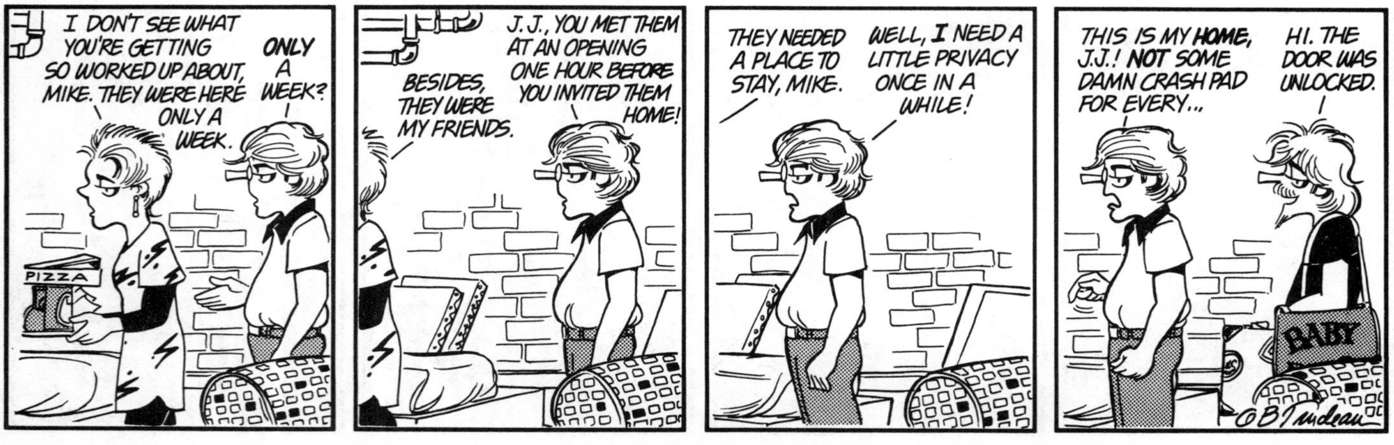
I DON'T SEE WHAT YOU'RE GETTING SO WORKED UP ABOUT, MIKE. THEY WERE HERE ONLY A WEEK.
ONLY A WEEK?
PIZZA
BESIDES, THEY WERE MY FRIENDS.
J.J., YOU MET THEM AT AN OPENING ONE HOUR BEFORE YOU INVITED THEM HOME!
THEY NEEDED A PLACE TO STAY, MIKE.
WELL, I NEED A LITTLE PRIVACY ONCE IN A WHILE!
THIS IS MY HOME, J.J.! NOT SOME DAMN CRASH PAD FOR EVERY...
HI. THE DOOR WAS UNLOCKED.
BABY

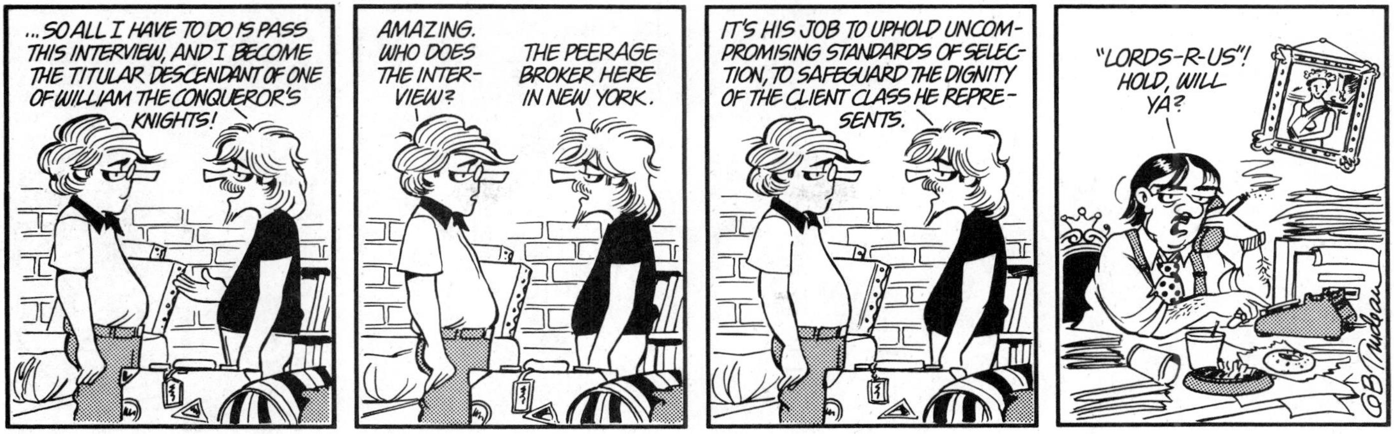
...SO ALL I HAVE TO DO IS PASS THIS INTERVIEW, AND I BECOME THE TITULAR DESCENDANT OF ONE OF WILLIAM THE CONQUEROR'S KNIGHTS!
AMAZING. WHO DOES THE INTERVIEW?
THE PEERAGE BROKER HERE IN NEW YORK.
IT'S HIS JOB TO UPHOLD UNCOMPROMISING STANDARDS OF SELECTION, TO SAFEGUARD THE DIGNITY OF THE CLIENT CLASS HE REPRESENTS.
"LORDS-R-US"! HOLD, WILL YA?
©B Trudeau

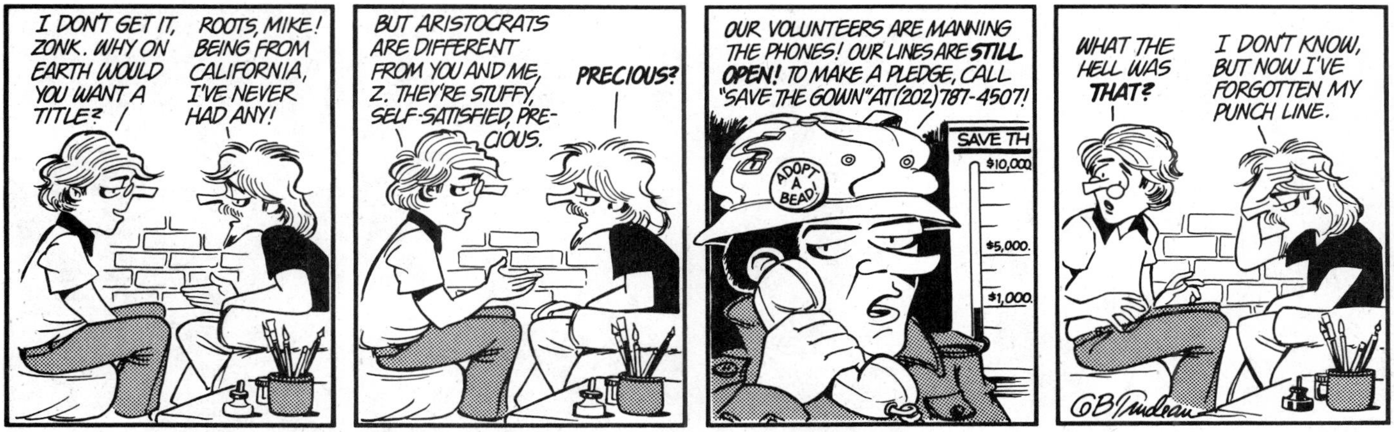
I DON'T GET IT, ZONK. WHY ON EARTH WOULD YOU WANT A TITLE?
ROOTS, MIKE! BEING FROM CALIFORNIA, I'VE NEVER HAD ANY!
BUT ARISTOCRATS ARE DIFFERENT FROM YOU AND ME, Z. THEY'RE STUFFY, SELF-SATISFIED, PRECIOUS.
PRECIOUS?
OUR VOLUNTEERS ARE MANNING THE PHONES! OUR LINES ARE **STILL OPEN!** TO MAKE A PLEDGE, CALL "SAVE THE GOWN" AT (202) 787-4507!
ADOPT A BEAD!
SAVE TH
$10,000
$5,000.
$1,000.
WHAT THE HELL WAS **THAT?**
I DON'T KNOW, BUT NOW I'VE FORGOTTEN MY PUNCH LINE.
©B Trudeau

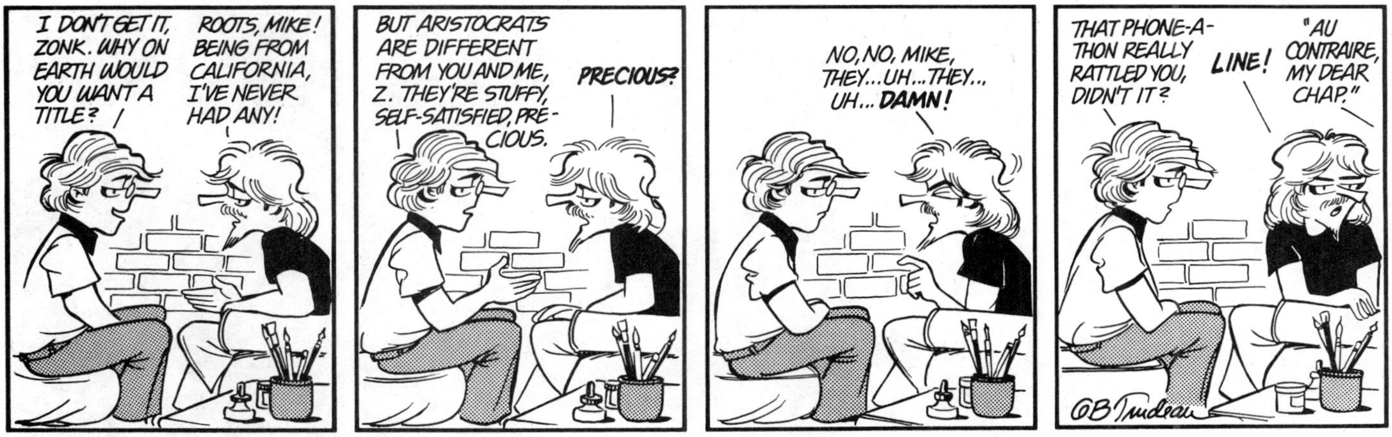
I DON'T GET IT, ZONK. WHY ON EARTH WOULD YOU WANT A TITLE?
ROOTS, MIKE! BEING FROM CALIFORNIA, I'VE NEVER HAD ANY!
BUT ARISTOCRATS ARE DIFFERENT FROM YOU AND ME, Z. THEY'RE STUFFY, SELF-SATISFIED, PRECIOUS.
PRECIOUS?
NO, NO, MIKE, THEY...UH...THEY... UH... **DAMN!**
THAT PHONE-A-THON REALLY RATTLED YOU, DIDN'T IT?
LINE!
"AU CONTRAIRE, MY DEAR CHAP."
©B Trudeau

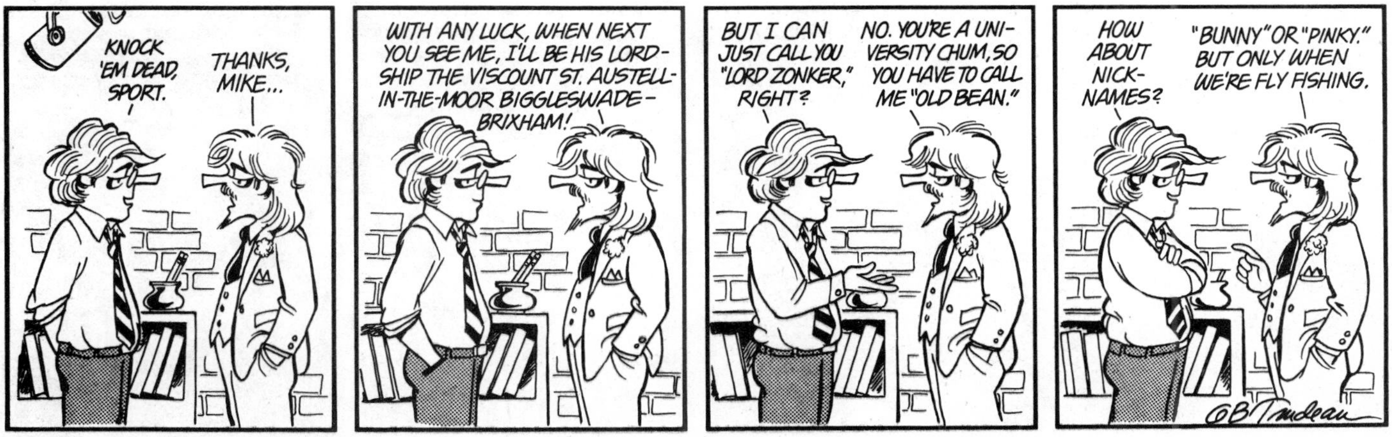
KNOCK 'EM DEAD, SPORT.
THANKS, MIKE...
WITH ANY LUCK, WHEN NEXT YOU SEE ME, I'LL BE HIS LORDSHIP THE VISCOUNT ST. AUSTELL-IN-THE-MOOR BIGGLESWADE-BRIXHAM!
BUT I CAN JUST CALL YOU "LORD ZONKER," RIGHT?
NO. YOU'RE A UNIVERSITY CHUM, SO YOU HAVE TO CALL ME "OLD BEAN."
HOW ABOUT NICKNAMES?
"BUNNY" OR "PINKY." BUT ONLY WHEN WE'RE FLY FISHING.
©B Trudeau

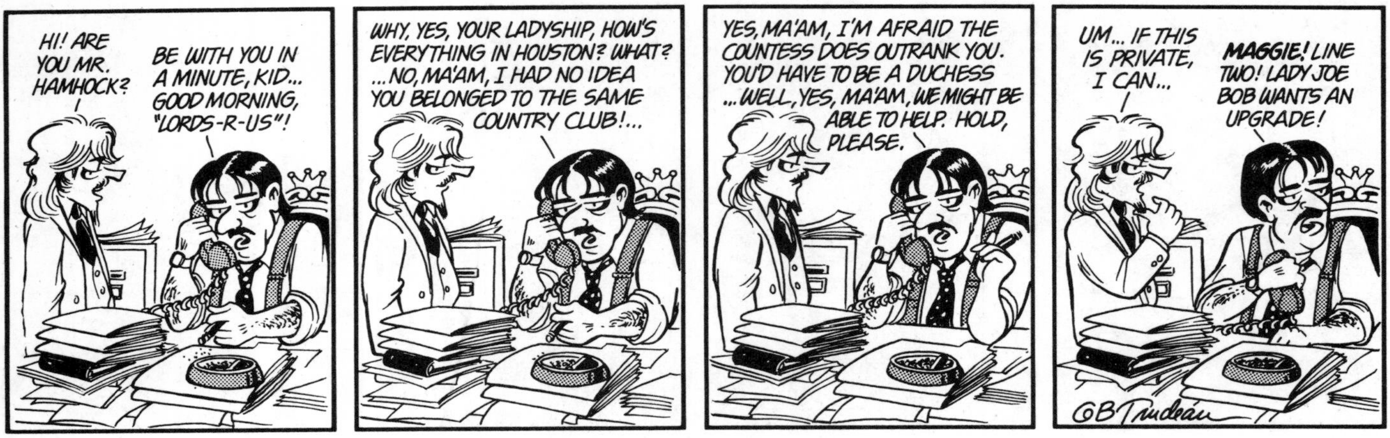
HI! ARE YOU MR. HAMHOCK?
BE WITH YOU IN A MINUTE, KID... GOOD MORNING, "LORDS-R-US"!
WHY, YES, YOUR LADYSHIP, HOW'S EVERYTHING IN HOUSTON? WHAT? ...NO, MA'AM, I HAD NO IDEA YOU BELONGED TO THE SAME COUNTRY CLUB!...
YES, MA'AM, I'M AFRAID THE COUNTESS DOES OUTRANK YOU. YOU'D HAVE TO BE A DUCHESS ...WELL, YES, MA'AM, WE MIGHT BE ABLE TO HELP. HOLD, PLEASE.
UM... IF THIS IS PRIVATE, I CAN...
MAGGIE! LINE TWO! LADY JOE BOB WANTS AN UPGRADE!
GB Trudeau

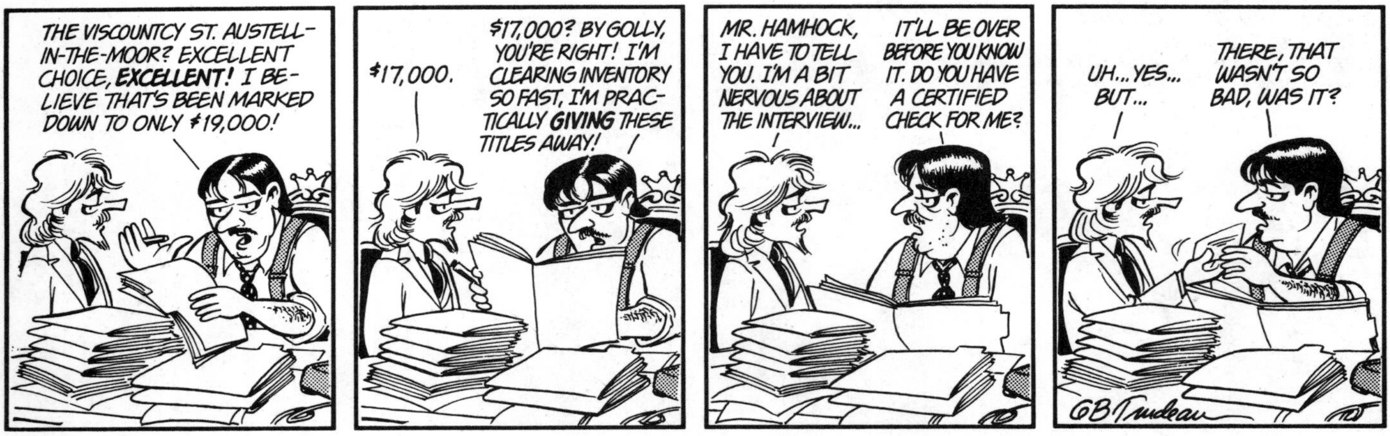
THE VISCOUNTCY ST. AUSTELL-IN-THE-MOOR? EXCELLENT CHOICE, EXCELLENT! I BELIEVE THAT'S BEEN MARKED DOWN TO ONLY $19,000!
$17,000.
$17,000? BY GOLLY, YOU'RE RIGHT! I'M CLEARING INVENTORY SO FAST, I'M PRACTICALLY GIVING THESE TITLES AWAY!
MR. HAMHOCK, I HAVE TO TELL YOU. I'M A BIT NERVOUS ABOUT THE INTERVIEW...
IT'LL BE OVER BEFORE YOU KNOW IT. DO YOU HAVE A CERTIFIED CHECK FOR ME?
UH... YES... BUT...
THERE, THAT WASN'T SO BAD, WAS IT?
GB Trudeau

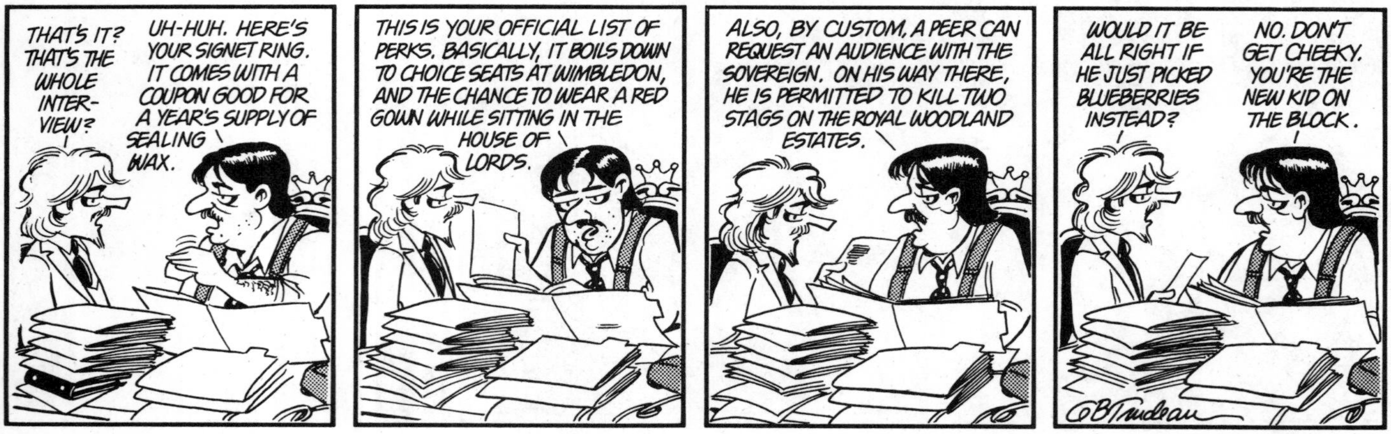
THAT'S IT? THAT'S THE WHOLE INTERVIEW?
UH-HUH. HERE'S YOUR SIGNET RING. IT COMES WITH A COUPON GOOD FOR A YEAR'S SUPPLY OF SEALING WAX.
THIS IS YOUR OFFICIAL LIST OF PERKS. BASICALLY, IT BOILS DOWN TO CHOICE SEATS AT WIMBLEDON, AND THE CHANCE TO WEAR A RED GOWN WHILE SITTING IN THE HOUSE OF LORDS.
ALSO, BY CUSTOM, A PEER CAN REQUEST AN AUDIENCE WITH THE SOVEREIGN. ON HIS WAY THERE, HE IS PERMITTED TO KILL TWO STAGS ON THE ROYAL WOODLAND ESTATES.
WOULD IT BE ALL RIGHT IF HE JUST PICKED BLUEBERRIES INSTEAD?
NO. DON'T GET CHEEKY. YOU'RE THE NEW KID ON THE BLOCK.
GB Trudeau

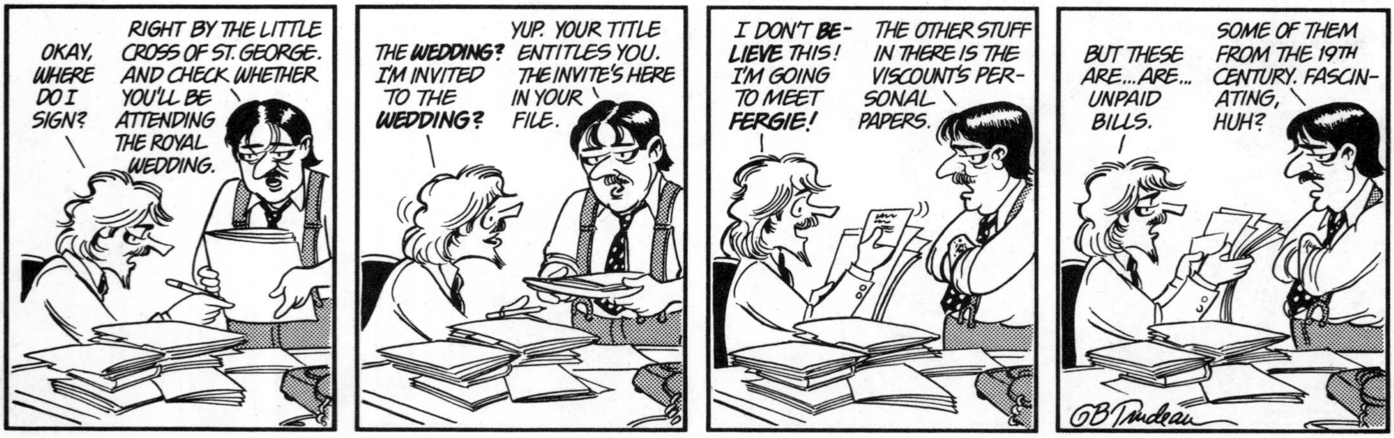
OKAY, WHERE DO I SIGN?
RIGHT BY THE LITTLE CROSS OF ST. GEORGE. AND CHECK WHETHER YOU'LL BE ATTENDING THE ROYAL WEDDING.
THE WEDDING? I'M INVITED TO THE WEDDING?
YUP. YOUR TITLE ENTITLES YOU. THE INVITE'S HERE IN YOUR FILE.
I DON'T BELIEVE THIS! I'M GOING TO MEET FERGIE!
THE OTHER STUFF IN THERE IS THE VISCOUNT'S PERSONAL PAPERS.
BUT THESE ARE... ARE... UNPAID BILLS.
SOME OF THEM FROM THE 19TH CENTURY. FASCINATING, HUH?
GB Trudeau

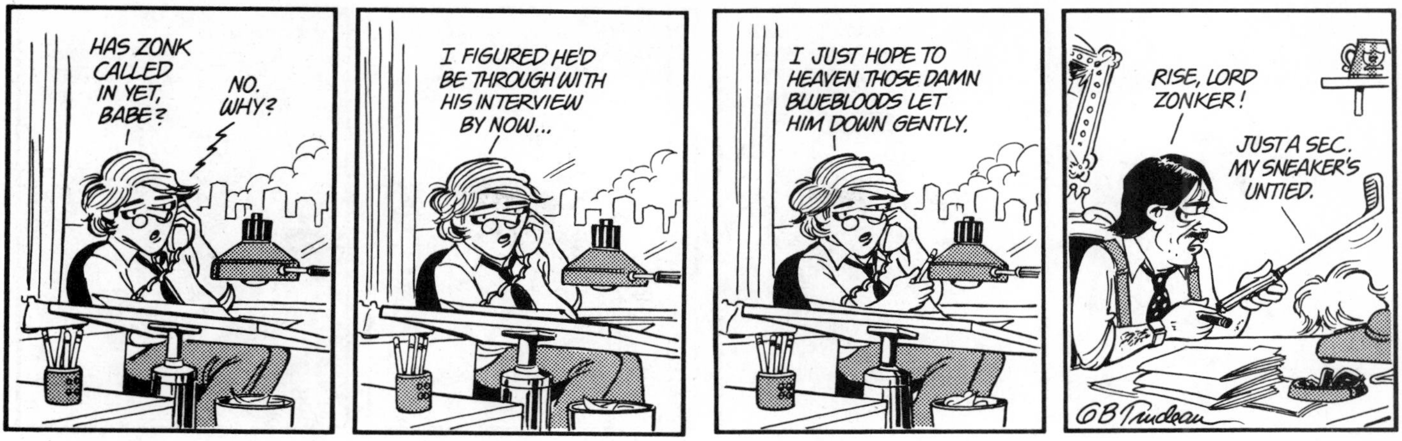
HAS ZONK CALLED IN YET, BABE?
NO. WHY?
I FIGURED HE'D BE THROUGH WITH HIS INTERVIEW BY NOW...
I JUST HOPE TO HEAVEN THOSE DAMN BLUEBLOODS LET HIM DOWN GENTLY.
RISE, LORD ZONKER!
JUST A SEC. MY SNEAKER'S UNTIED.

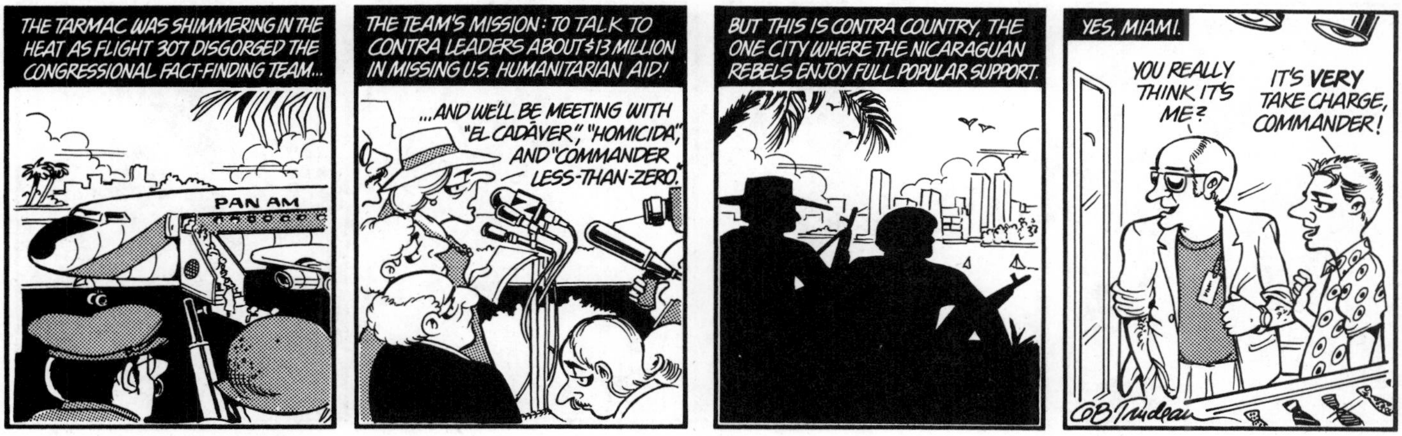
THE TARMAC WAS SHIMMERING IN THE HEAT AS FLIGHT 307 DISGORGED THE CONGRESSIONAL FACT-FINDING TEAM...
PAN AM
THE TEAM'S MISSION: TO TALK TO CONTRA LEADERS ABOUT $13 MILLION IN MISSING U.S. HUMANITARIAN AID!
...AND WE'LL BE MEETING WITH "EL CADÁVER," "HOMICIDA," AND "COMMANDER LESS-THAN-ZERO."
BUT THIS IS CONTRA COUNTRY, THE ONE CITY WHERE THE NICARAGUAN REBELS ENJOY FULL POPULAR SUPPORT.
YES, MIAMI.
YOU REALLY THINK IT'S ME?
IT'S **VERY** TAKE CHARGE, COMMANDER!

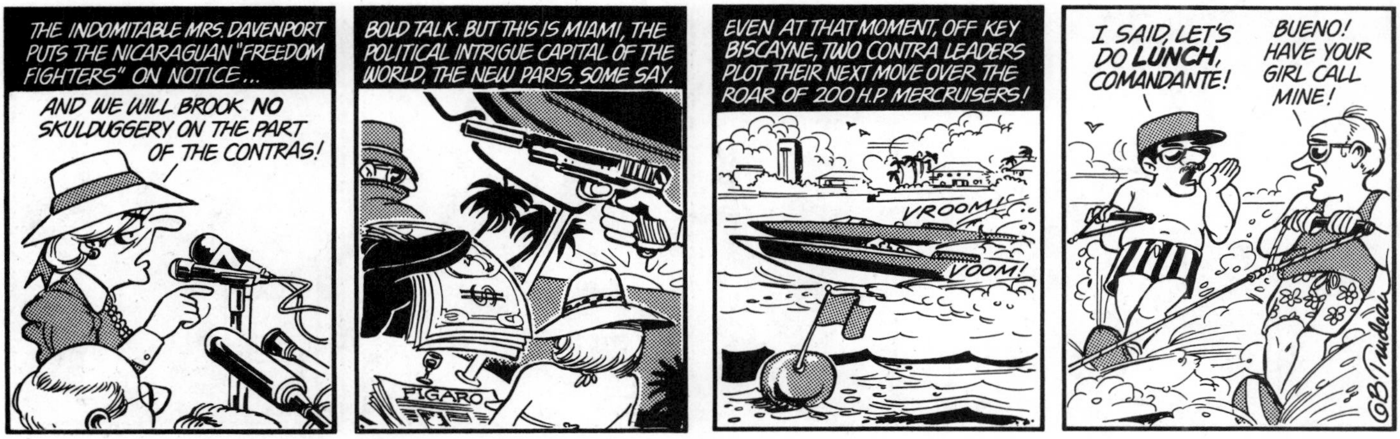
THE INDOMITABLE MRS. DAVENPORT PUTS THE NICARAGUAN "FREEDOM FIGHTERS" ON NOTICE...
AND WE WILL BROOK NO SKULDUGGERY ON THE PART OF THE CONTRAS!
BOLD TALK. BUT THIS IS MIAMI, THE POLITICAL INTRIGUE CAPITAL OF THE WORLD, THE NEW PARIS, SOME SAY.
FIGARO
EVEN AT THAT MOMENT, OFF KEY BISCAYNE, TWO CONTRA LEADERS PLOT THEIR NEXT MOVE OVER THE ROAR OF 200 H.P. MERCRUISERS!
VROOM!
VOOM!
I SAID, LET'S DO **LUNCH**, COMANDANTE!
BUENO! HAVE YOUR GIRL CALL MINE!

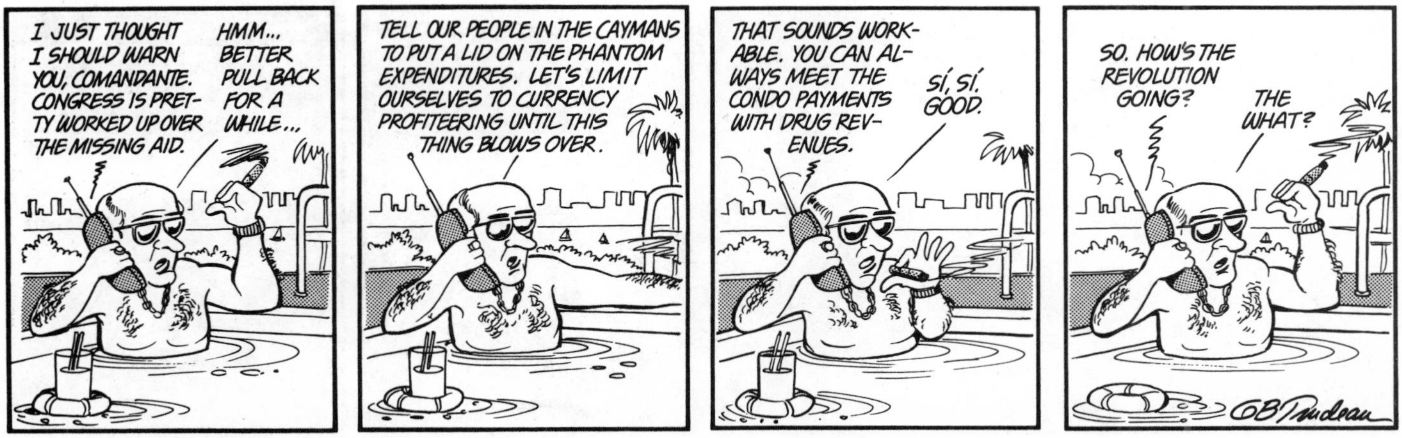
I JUST THOUGHT I SHOULD WARN YOU, COMANDANTE. CONGRESS IS PRETTY WORKED UP OVER THE MISSING AID.
HMM... BETTER PULL BACK FOR A WHILE...
TELL OUR PEOPLE IN THE CAYMANS TO PUT A LID ON THE PHANTOM EXPENDITURES. LET'S LIMIT OURSELVES TO CURRENCY PROFITEERING UNTIL THIS THING BLOWS OVER.
THAT SOUNDS WORKABLE. YOU CAN ALWAYS MEET THE CONDO PAYMENTS WITH DRUG REVENUES.
SÍ, SÍ. GOOD.
SO. HOW'S THE REVOLUTION GOING?
THE WHAT?

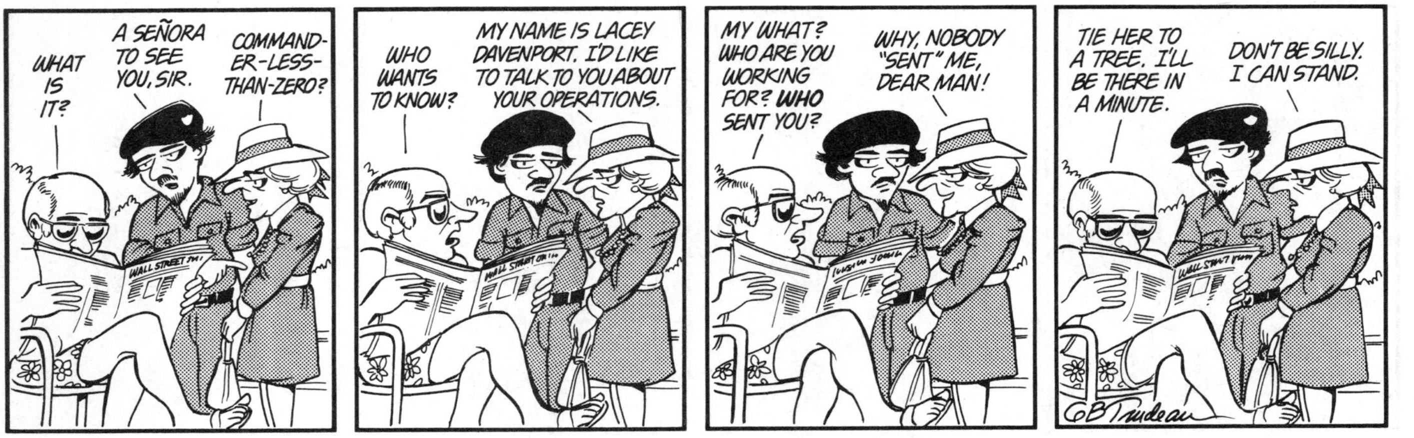
WHAT IS IT?
A SEÑORA TO SEE YOU, SIR.
COMMANDER-LESS-THAN-ZERO?
WHO WANTS TO KNOW?
MY NAME IS LACEY DAVENPORT. I'D LIKE TO TALK TO YOU ABOUT YOUR OPERATIONS.
MY WHAT? WHO ARE YOU WORKING FOR? **WHO** SENT YOU?
WHY, NOBODY "SENT" ME, DEAR MAN!
TIE HER TO A TREE. I'LL BE THERE IN A MINUTE.
DON'T BE SILLY. I CAN STAND.
GB Trudeau

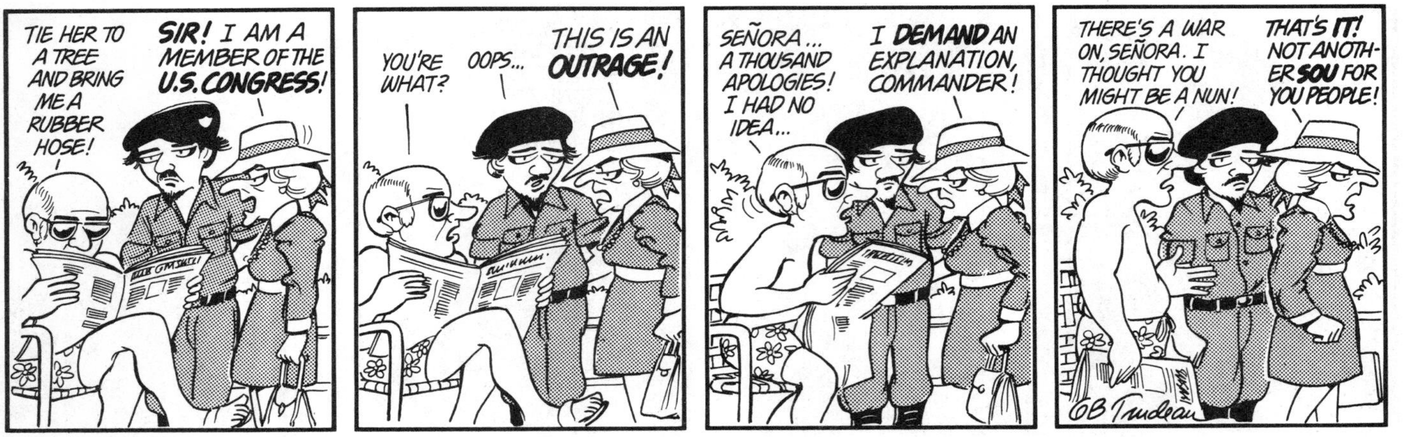
TIE HER TO A TREE AND BRING ME A RUBBER HOSE!
SIR! I AM A MEMBER OF THE **U.S. CONGRESS!**
YOU'RE WHAT?
OOPS...
THIS IS AN **OUTRAGE!**
SEÑORA... A THOUSAND APOLOGIES! I HAD NO IDEA...
I **DEMAND** AN EXPLANATION, COMMANDER!
THERE'S A WAR ON, SEÑORA. I THOUGHT YOU MIGHT BE A NUN!
THAT'S IT! NOT ANOTHER **SOU** FOR YOU PEOPLE!
GB Trudeau

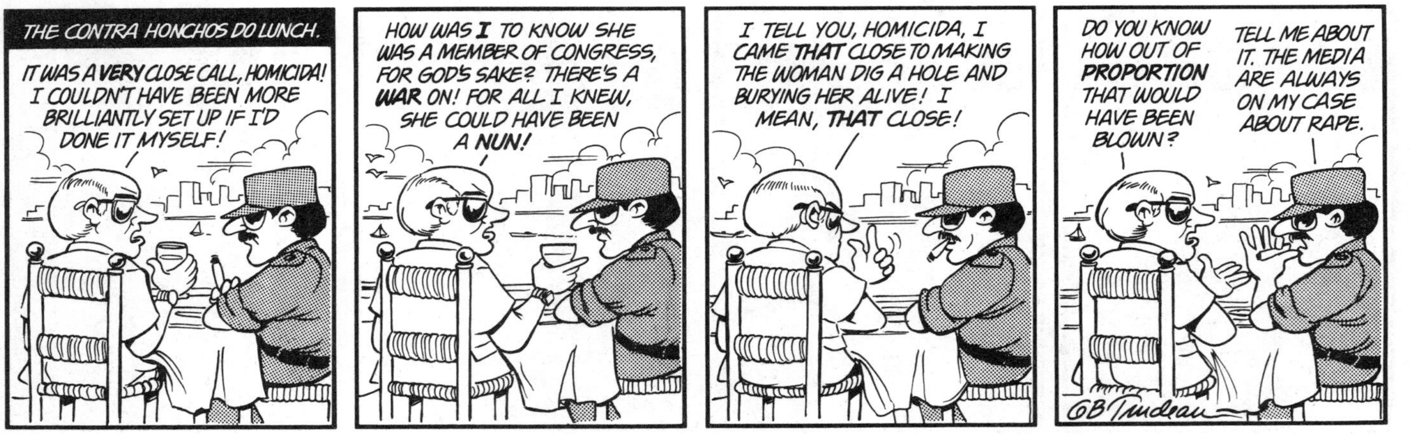
THE CONTRA HONCHOS DO LUNCH.
IT WAS A **VERY** CLOSE CALL, HOMICIDA! I COULDN'T HAVE BEEN MORE BRILLIANTLY SET UP IF I'D DONE IT MYSELF!
HOW WAS **I** TO KNOW SHE WAS A MEMBER OF CONGRESS, FOR GOD'S SAKE? THERE'S A **WAR** ON! FOR ALL I KNEW, SHE COULD HAVE BEEN A **NUN!**
I TELL YOU, HOMICIDA, I **CAME THAT** CLOSE TO MAKING THE WOMAN DIG A HOLE AND BURYING HER ALIVE! I MEAN, **THAT** CLOSE!
DO YOU KNOW HOW OUT OF **PROPORTION** THAT WOULD HAVE BEEN BLOWN?
TELL ME ABOUT IT. THE MEDIA ARE ALWAYS ON MY CASE ABOUT RAPE.
GB Trudeau

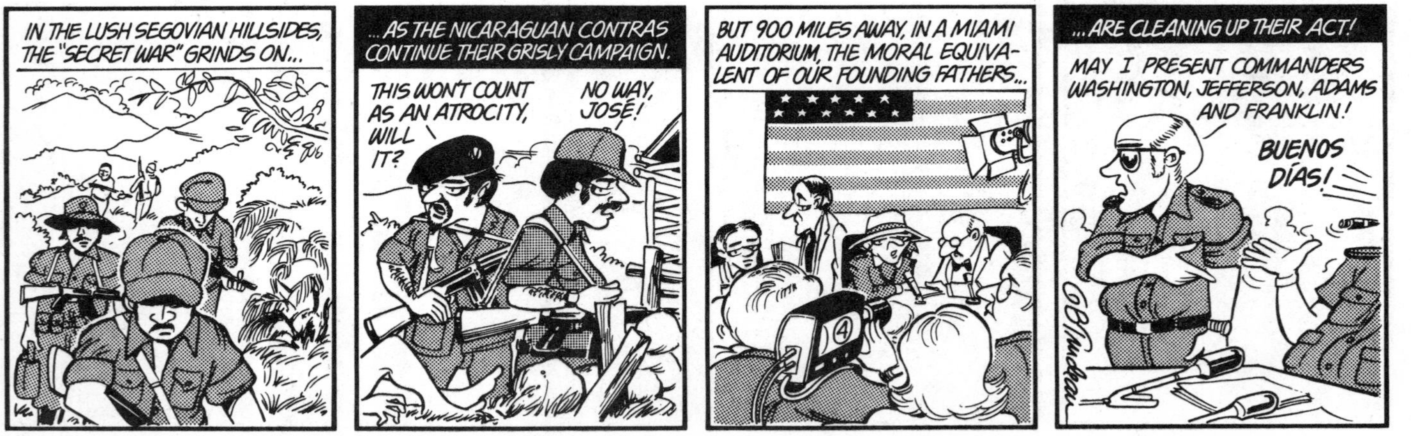
IN THE LUSH SEGOVIAN HILLSIDES, THE "SECRET WAR" GRINDS ON...
...AS THE NICARAGUAN CONTRAS CONTINUE THEIR GRISLY CAMPAIGN.
THIS WON'T COUNT AS AN ATROCITY, WILL IT?
NO WAY, JOSÉ!
BUT 900 MILES AWAY, IN A MIAMI AUDITORIUM, THE MORAL EQUIVALENT OF OUR FOUNDING FATHERS...
...ARE CLEANING UP THEIR ACT!
MAY I PRESENT COMMANDERS WASHINGTON, JEFFERSON, ADAMS AND FRANKLIN!
BUENOS DÍAS!
GB Trudeau

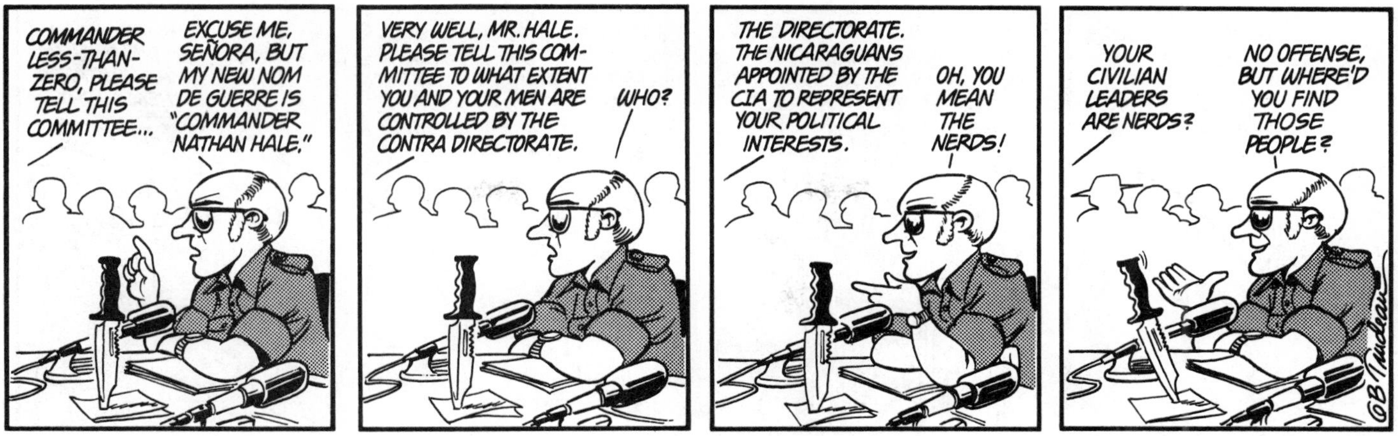
COMMANDER LESS-THAN-ZERO, PLEASE TELL THIS COMMITTEE...
EXCUSE ME, SEÑORA, BUT MY NEW NOM DE GUERRE IS "COMMANDER NATHAN HALE."
VERY WELL, MR. HALE. PLEASE TELL THIS COMMITTEE TO WHAT EXTENT YOU AND YOUR MEN ARE CONTROLLED BY THE CONTRA DIRECTORATE.
WHO?
THE DIRECTORATE. THE NICARAGUANS APPOINTED BY THE CIA TO REPRESENT YOUR POLITICAL INTERESTS.
OH, YOU MEAN THE NERDS!
YOUR CIVILIAN LEADERS ARE NERDS?
NO OFFENSE, BUT WHERE'D YOU FIND THOSE PEOPLE?
©B Trudeau

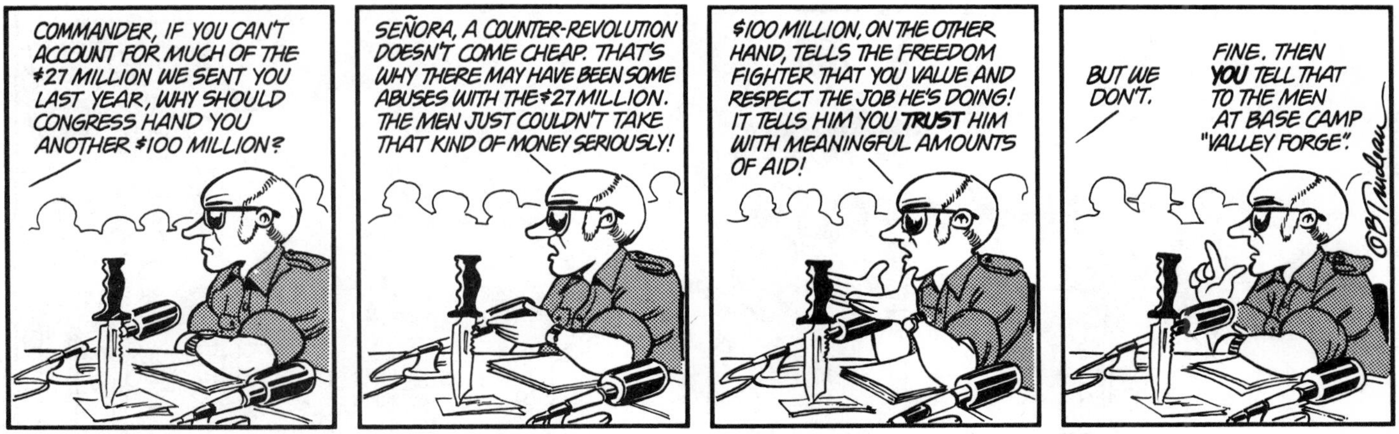
COMMANDER, IF YOU CAN'T ACCOUNT FOR MUCH OF THE $27 MILLION WE SENT YOU LAST YEAR, WHY SHOULD CONGRESS HAND YOU ANOTHER $100 MILLION?
SEÑORA, A COUNTER-REVOLUTION DOESN'T COME CHEAP. THAT'S WHY THERE MAY HAVE BEEN SOME ABUSES WITH THE $27 MILLION. THE MEN JUST COULDN'T TAKE THAT KIND OF MONEY SERIOUSLY!
$100 MILLION, ON THE OTHER HAND, TELLS THE FREEDOM FIGHTER THAT YOU VALUE AND RESPECT THE JOB HE'S DOING! IT TELLS HIM YOU TRUST HIM WITH MEANINGFUL AMOUNTS OF AID!
BUT WE DON'T.
FINE. THEN YOU TELL THAT TO THE MEN AT BASE CAMP "VALLEY FORGE."
©B Trudeau

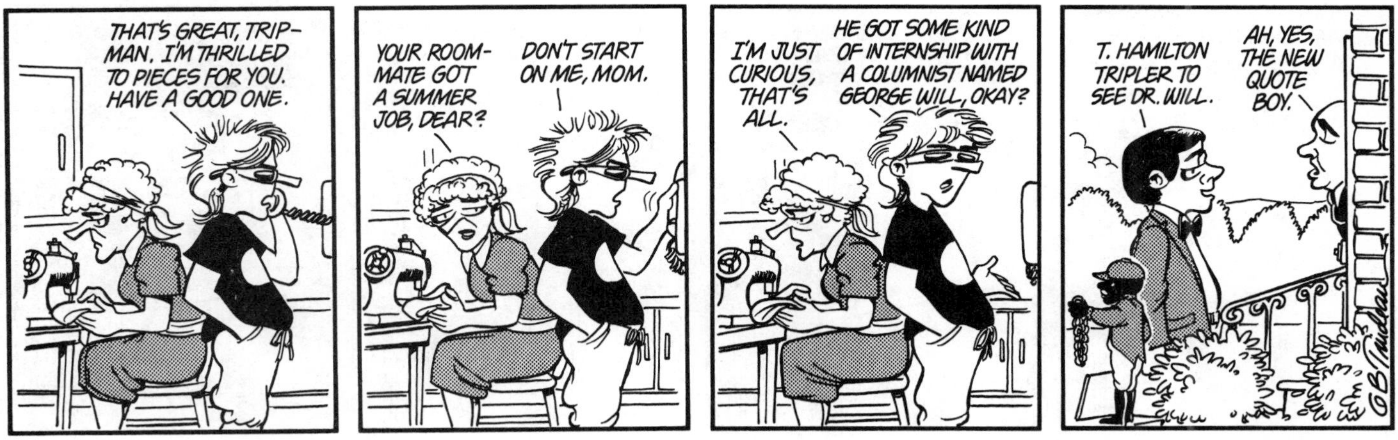
THAT'S GREAT, TRIPMAN. I'M THRILLED TO PIECES FOR YOU. HAVE A GOOD ONE.
YOUR ROOMMATE GOT A SUMMER JOB, DEAR?
DON'T START ON ME, MOM.
I'M JUST CURIOUS, THAT'S ALL.
HE GOT SOME KIND OF INTERNSHIP WITH A COLUMNIST NAMED GEORGE WILL, OKAY?
T. HAMILTON TRIPLER TO SEE DR. WILL.
AH, YES, THE NEW QUOTE BOY.
©B Trudeau

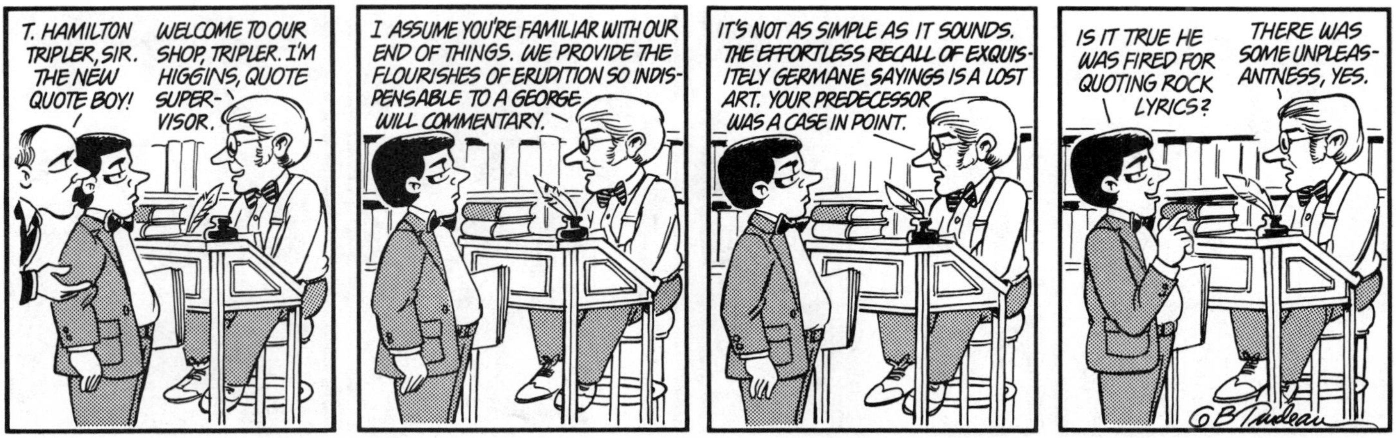
T. HAMILTON TRIPLER, SIR. THE NEW QUOTE BOY!
WELCOME TO OUR SHOP, TRIPLER. I'M HIGGINS, QUOTE SUPERVISOR.
I ASSUME YOU'RE FAMILIAR WITH OUR END OF THINGS. WE PROVIDE THE FLOURISHES OF ERUDITION SO INDISPENSABLE TO A GEORGE WILL COMMENTARY.
IT'S NOT AS SIMPLE AS IT SOUNDS. THE EFFORTLESS RECALL OF EXQUISITELY GERMANE SAYINGS IS A LOST ART. YOUR PREDECESSOR WAS A CASE IN POINT.
IS IT TRUE HE WAS FIRED FOR QUOTING ROCK LYRICS?
THERE WAS SOME UNPLEASANTNESS, YES.
©B Trudeau

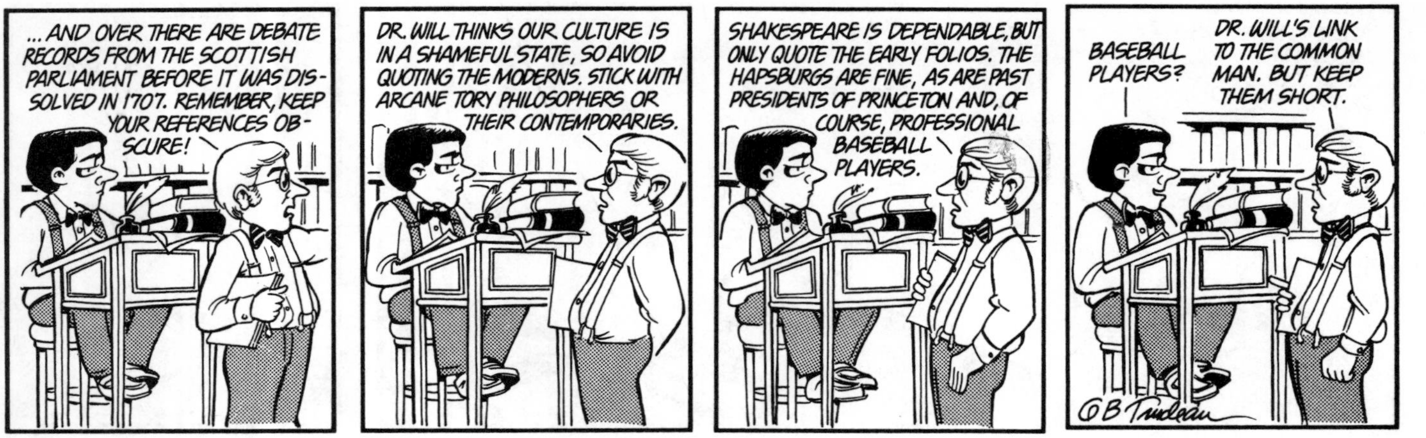
...AND OVER THERE ARE DEBATE RECORDS FROM THE SCOTTISH PARLIAMENT BEFORE IT WAS DISSOLVED IN 1707. REMEMBER, KEEP YOUR REFERENCES OBSCURE!
DR. WILL THINKS OUR CULTURE IS IN A SHAMEFUL STATE, SO AVOID QUOTING THE MODERNS. STICK WITH ARCANE TORY PHILOSOPHERS OR THEIR CONTEMPORARIES.
SHAKESPEARE IS DEPENDABLE, BUT ONLY QUOTE THE EARLY FOLIOS. THE HAPSBURGS ARE FINE, AS ARE PAST PRESIDENTS OF PRINCETON AND, OF COURSE, PROFESSIONAL BASEBALL PLAYERS.
BASEBALL PLAYERS?
DR. WILL'S LINK TO THE COMMON MAN. BUT KEEP THEM SHORT.
©B Trudeau

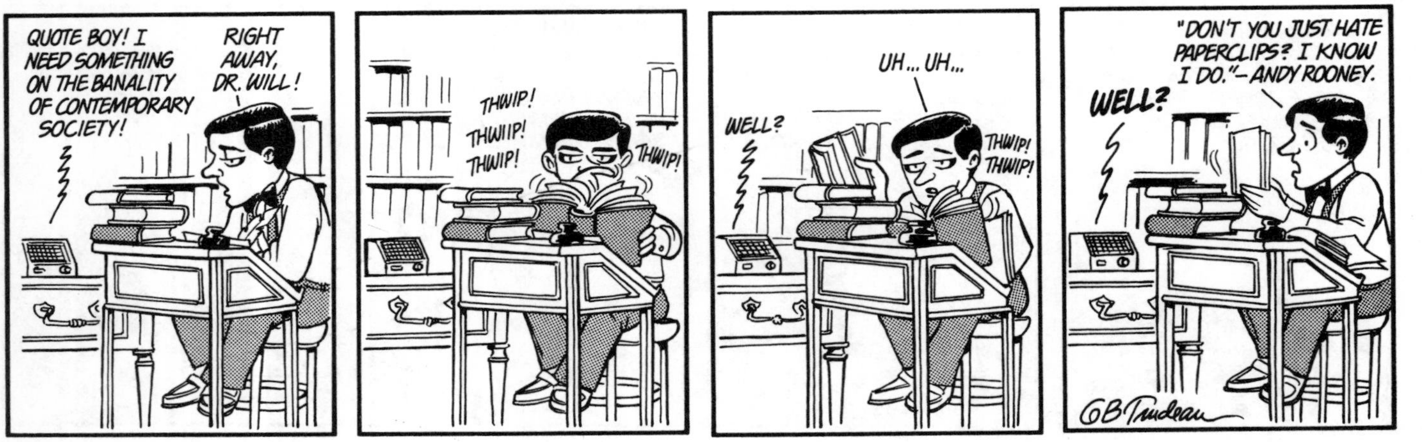
QUOTE BOY! I NEED SOMETHING ON THE BANALITY OF CONTEMPORARY SOCIETY!
RIGHT AWAY, DR. WILL!
THWIP! THWIIP! THWIP! THWIP!
UH... UH...
WELL?
THWIP! THWIP!
WELL?
"DON'T YOU JUST HATE PAPERCLIPS? I KNOW I DO." – ANDY ROONEY.
©B Trudeau

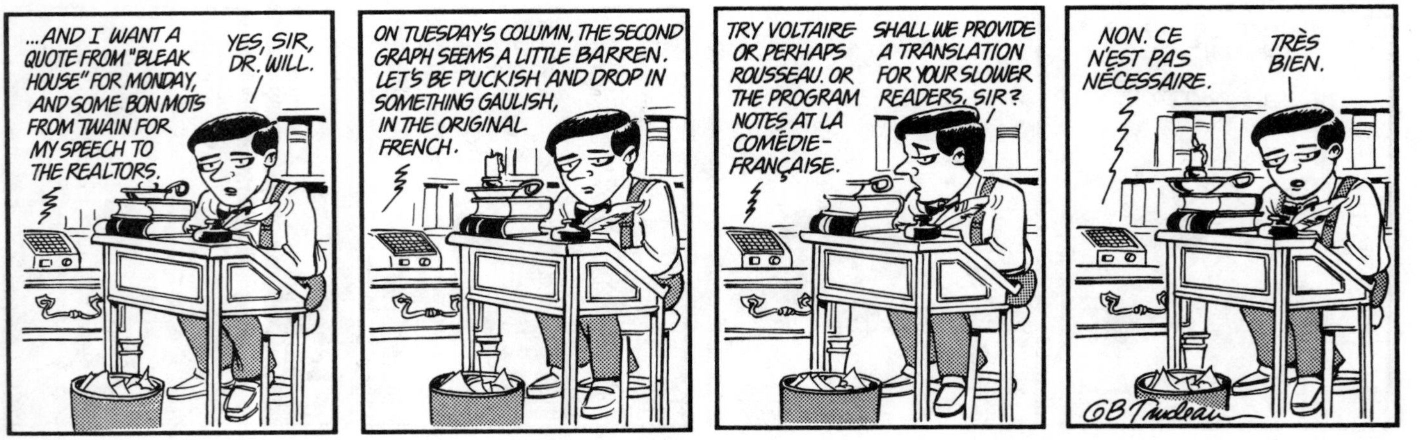
...AND I WANT A QUOTE FROM "BLEAK HOUSE" FOR MONDAY, AND SOME BON MOTS FROM TWAIN FOR MY SPEECH TO THE REALTORS.
YES, SIR, DR. WILL.
ON TUESDAY'S COLUMN, THE SECOND GRAPH SEEMS A LITTLE BARREN. LET'S BE PUCKISH AND DROP IN SOMETHING GAULISH, IN THE ORIGINAL FRENCH.
TRY VOLTAIRE OR PERHAPS ROUSSEAU. OR THE PROGRAM NOTES AT LA COMÉDIE-FRANÇAISE.
SHALL WE PROVIDE A TRANSLATION FOR YOUR SLOWER READERS, SIR?
NON. CE N'EST PAS NÉCESSAIRE.
TRÈS BIEN.
©B Trudeau

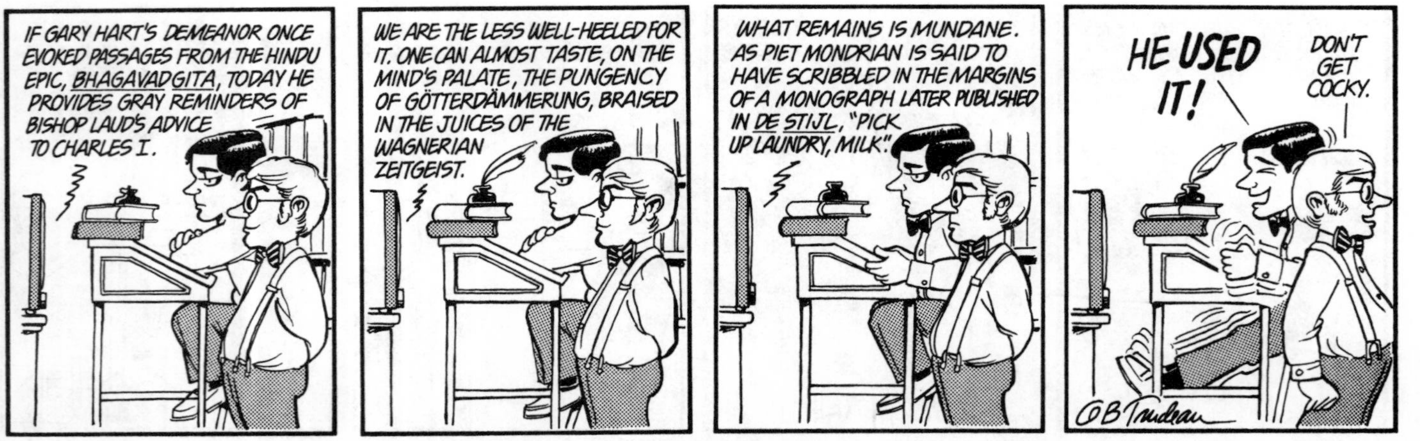
IF GARY HART'S DEMEANOR ONCE EVOKED PASSAGES FROM THE HINDU EPIC, BHAGAVADGITA, TODAY HE PROVIDES GRAY REMINDERS OF BISHOP LAUD'S ADVICE TO CHARLES I.
WE ARE THE LESS WELL-HEELED FOR IT. ONE CAN ALMOST TASTE, ON THE MIND'S PALATE, THE PUNGENCY OF GÖTTERDÄMMERUNG, BRAISED IN THE JUICES OF THE WAGNERIAN ZEITGEIST.
WHAT REMAINS IS MUNDANE. AS PIET MONDRIAN IS SAID TO HAVE SCRIBBLED IN THE MARGINS OF A MONOGRAPH LATER PUBLISHED IN DE STIJL, "PICK UP LAUNDRY, MILK."
HE USED IT!
DON'T GET COCKY.
©B Trudeau

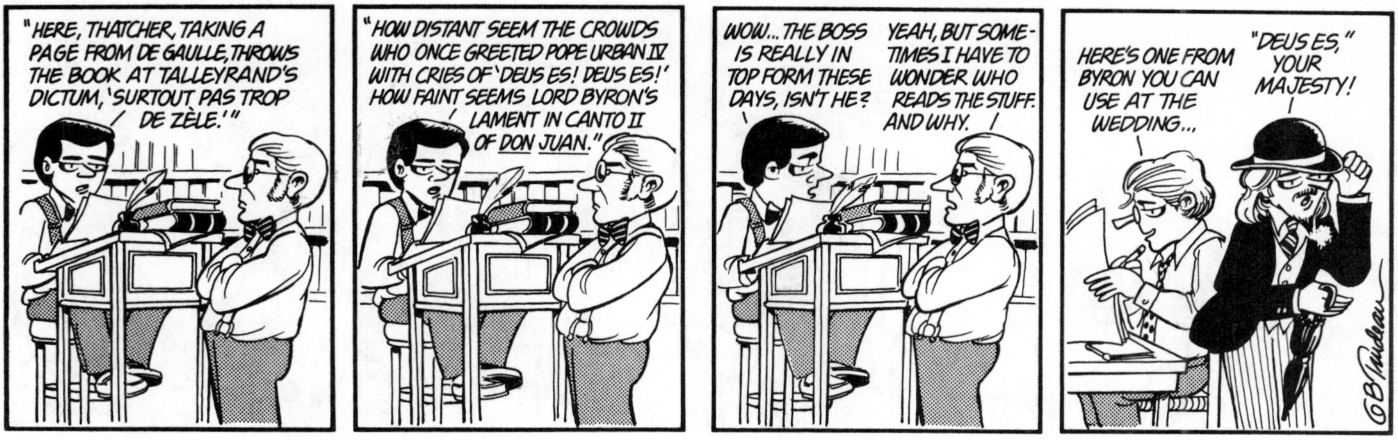
"HERE, THATCHER, TAKING A PAGE FROM DE GAULLE, THROWS THE BOOK AT TALLEYRAND'S DICTUM, 'SURTOUT PAS TROP DE ZÈLE.'"
"HOW DISTANT SEEM THE CROWDS WHO ONCE GREETED POPE URBAN IV WITH CRIES OF 'DEUS ES! DEUS ES!' HOW FAINT SEEMS LORD BYRON'S LAMENT IN CANTO II OF DON JUAN."
WOW... THE BOSS IS REALLY IN TOP FORM THESE DAYS, ISN'T HE?
YEAH, BUT SOMETIMES I HAVE TO WONDER WHO READS THE STUFF. AND WHY.
HERE'S ONE FROM BYRON YOU CAN USE AT THE WEDDING...
"DEUS ES," YOUR MAJESTY!
©B Trudeau

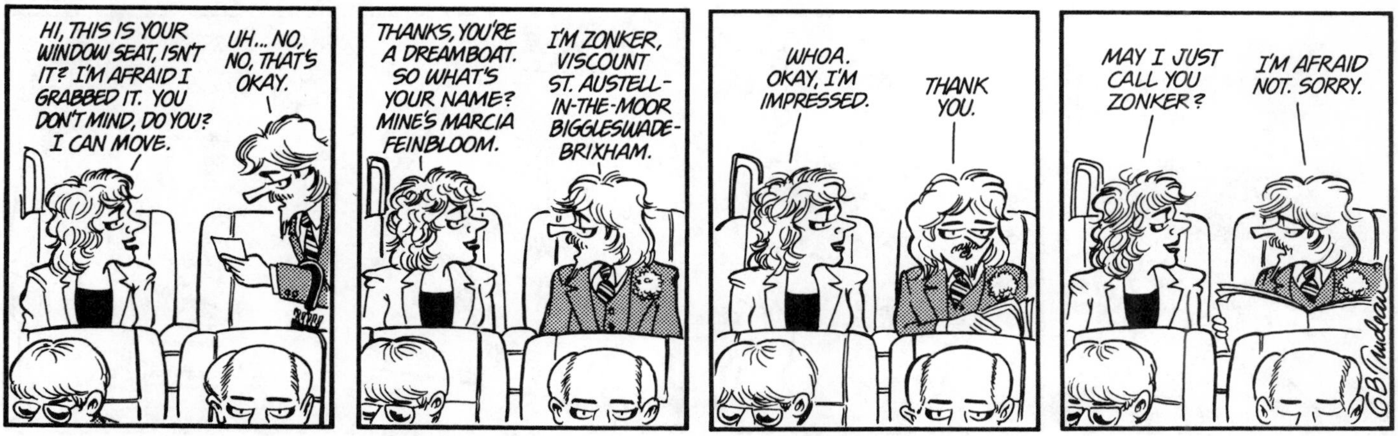
HI, THIS IS YOUR WINDOW SEAT, ISN'T IT? I'M AFRAID I GRABBED IT. YOU DON'T MIND, DO YOU? I CAN MOVE.
UH... NO, NO, THAT'S OKAY.
THANKS, YOU'RE A DREAMBOAT. SO WHAT'S YOUR NAME? MINE'S MARCIA FEINBLOOM.
I'M ZONKER, VISCOUNT ST. AUSTELL-IN-THE-MOOR BIGGLESWADE-BRIXHAM.
WHOA. OKAY, I'M IMPRESSED.
THANK YOU.
MAY I JUST CALL YOU ZONKER?
I'M AFRAID NOT. SORRY.
©B Trudeau

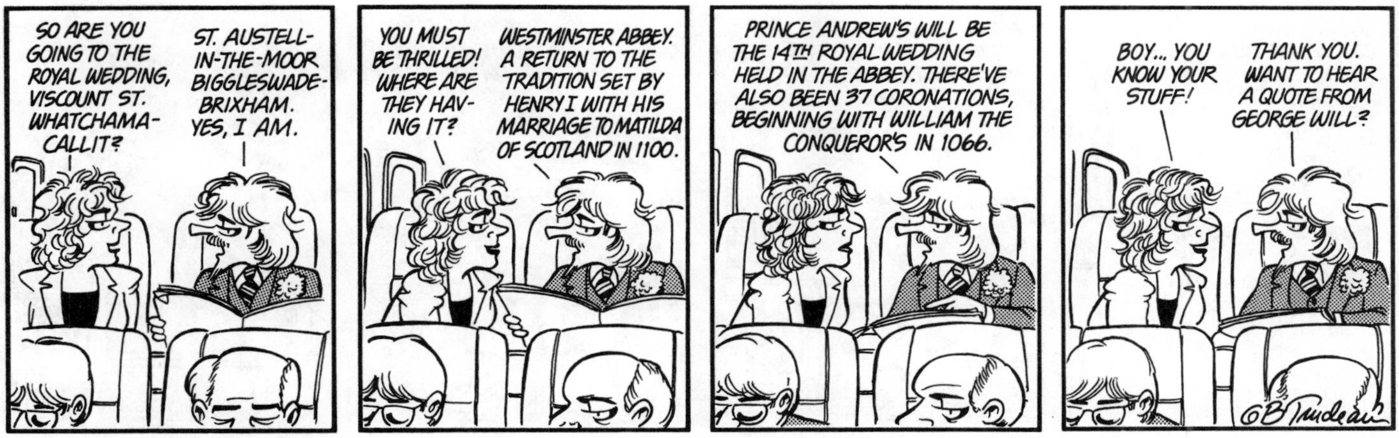
SO ARE YOU GOING TO THE ROYAL WEDDING, VISCOUNT ST. WHATCHAMACALLIT?
ST. AUSTELL-IN-THE-MOOR BIGGLESWADE-BRIXHAM. YES, I AM.
YOU MUST BE THRILLED! WHERE ARE THEY HAVING IT?
WESTMINSTER ABBEY. A RETURN TO THE TRADITION SET BY HENRY I WITH HIS MARRIAGE TO MATILDA OF SCOTLAND IN 1100.
PRINCE ANDREW'S WILL BE THE 14TH ROYAL WEDDING HELD IN THE ABBEY. THERE'VE ALSO BEEN 37 CORONATIONS, BEGINNING WITH WILLIAM THE CONQUEROR'S IN 1066.
BOY... YOU KNOW YOUR STUFF!
THANK YOU. WANT TO HEAR A QUOTE FROM GEORGE WILL?
©B Trudeau

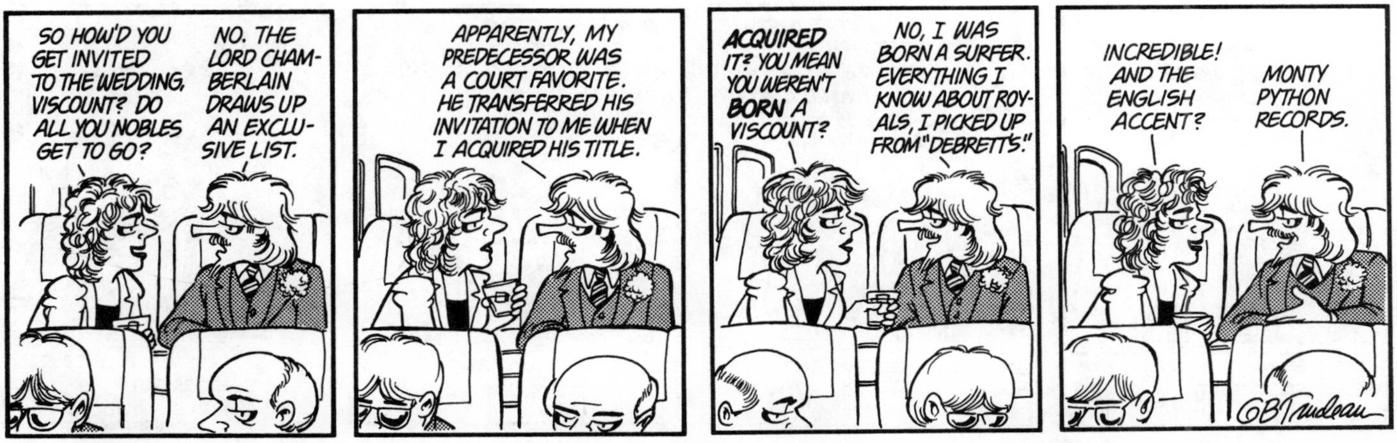
SO HOW'D YOU GET INVITED TO THE WEDDING, VISCOUNT? DO ALL YOU NOBLES GET TO GO?
NO. THE LORD CHAMBERLAIN DRAWS UP AN EXCLUSIVE LIST.
APPARENTLY, MY PREDECESSOR WAS A COURT FAVORITE. HE TRANSFERRED HIS INVITATION TO ME WHEN I ACQUIRED HIS TITLE.
ACQUIRED IT? YOU MEAN YOU WEREN'T BORN A VISCOUNT?
NO, I WAS BORN A SURFER. EVERYTHING I KNOW ABOUT ROYALS, I PICKED UP FROM "DEBRETT'S."
INCREDIBLE! AND THE ENGLISH ACCENT?
MONTY PYTHON RECORDS.
©B Trudeau

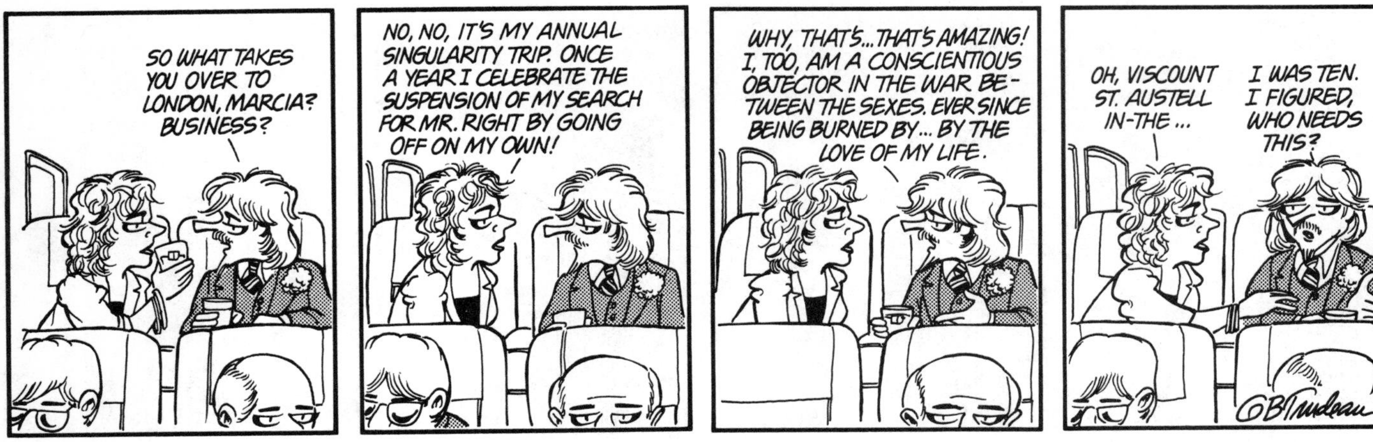

SO WHAT TAKES YOU OVER TO LONDON, MARCIA? BUSINESS?
NO, NO, IT'S MY ANNUAL SINGULARITY TRIP. ONCE A YEAR I CELEBRATE THE SUSPENSION OF MY SEARCH FOR MR. RIGHT BY GOING OFF ON MY OWN!
WHY, THAT'S... THAT'S AMAZING! I, TOO, AM A CONSCIENTIOUS OBJECTOR IN THE WAR BETWEEN THE SEXES. EVER SINCE BEING BURNED BY... BY THE LOVE OF MY LIFE.
OH, VISCOUNT ST. AUSTELL IN-THE ...
I WAS TEN. I FIGURED, WHO NEEDS THIS?
GBTrudeau

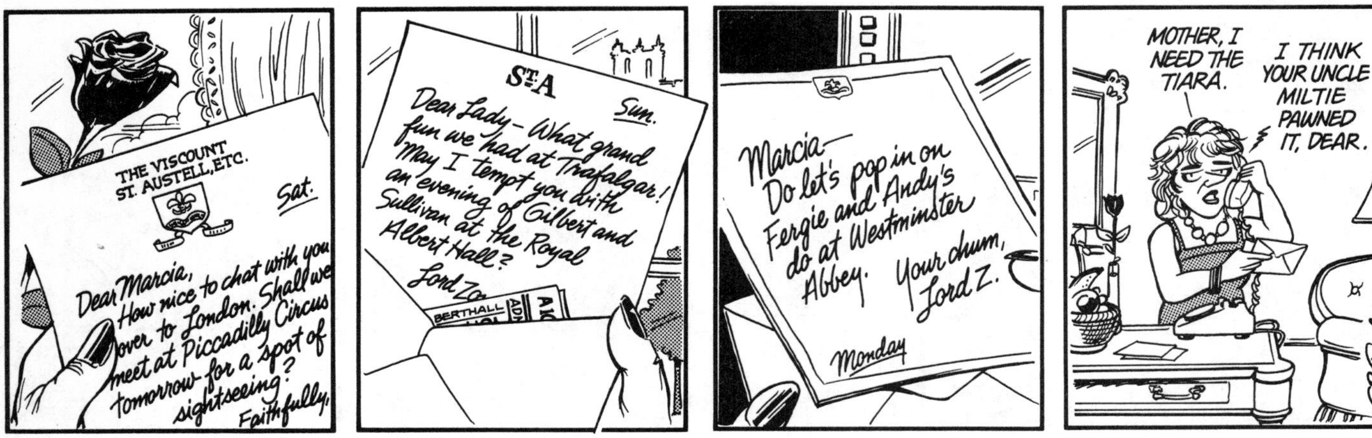

THE VISCOUNT ST. AUSTELL, ETC.
Sat.
Dear Marcia, How nice to chat with you over to London. Shall we meet at Piccadilly Circus tomorrow for a spot of sightseeing? Faithfully,
St A
Sun.
Dear Lady— What grand fun we had at Trafalgar! May I tempt you with an evening of Gilbert and Sullivan at the Royal Albert Hall?
Marcia— Do let's pop in on Fergie and Andy's do at Westminster Abbey. Your chum, Lord Z.
Monday
MOTHER, I NEED THE TIARA.
I THINK YOUR UNCLE MILTIE PAWNED IT, DEAR.
GBTrudeau

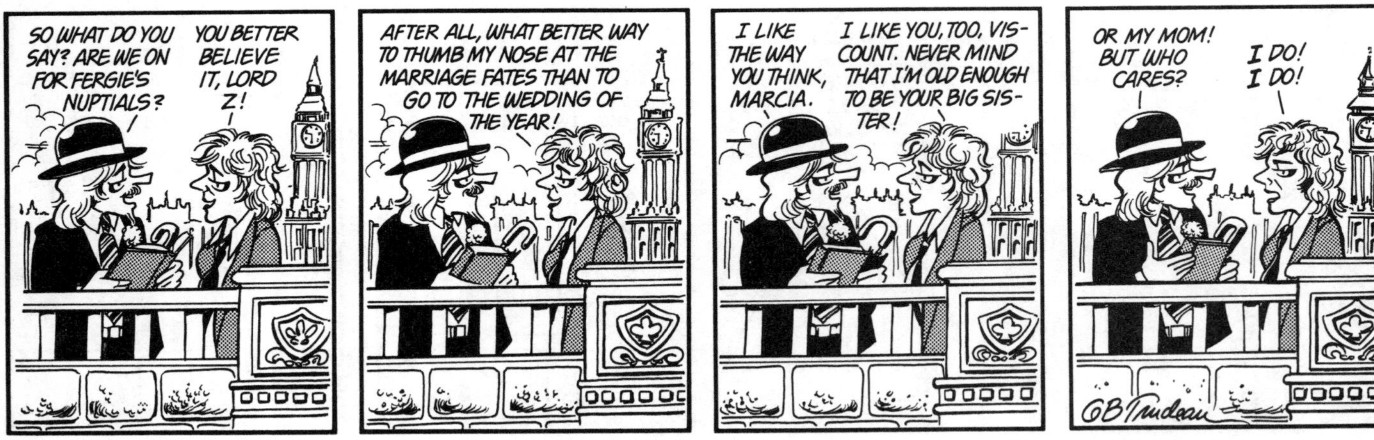

SO WHAT DO YOU SAY? ARE WE ON FOR FERGIE'S NUPTIALS?
YOU BETTER BELIEVE IT, LORD Z!
AFTER ALL, WHAT BETTER WAY TO THUMB MY NOSE AT THE MARRIAGE FATES THAN TO GO TO THE WEDDING OF THE YEAR!
I LIKE THE WAY YOU THINK, MARCIA.
I LIKE YOU, TOO, VISCOUNT. NEVER MIND THAT I'M OLD ENOUGH TO BE YOUR BIG SISTER!
OR MY MOM! BUT WHO CARES?
I DO! I DO!
GBTrudeau

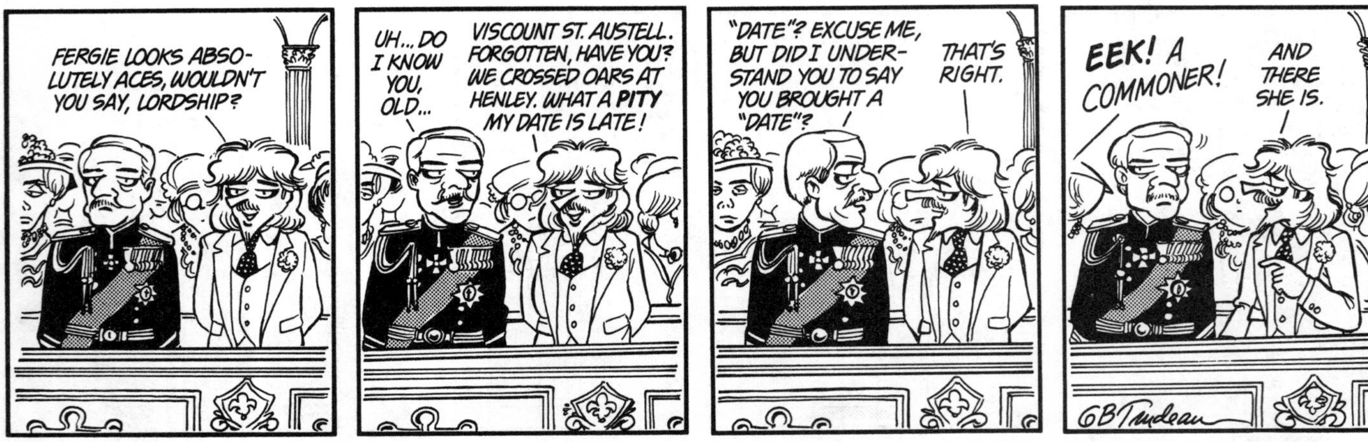

FERGIE LOOKS ABSOLUTELY ACES, WOULDN'T YOU SAY, LORDSHIP?
UH... DO I KNOW YOU, OLD...
VISCOUNT ST. AUSTELL. FORGOTTEN, HAVE YOU? WE CROSSED OARS AT HENLEY. WHAT A PITY MY DATE IS LATE!
"DATE"? EXCUSE ME, BUT DID I UNDERSTAND YOU TO SAY YOU BROUGHT A "DATE"?
THAT'S RIGHT.
EEK! A COMMONER!
AND THERE SHE IS.
GBTrudeau

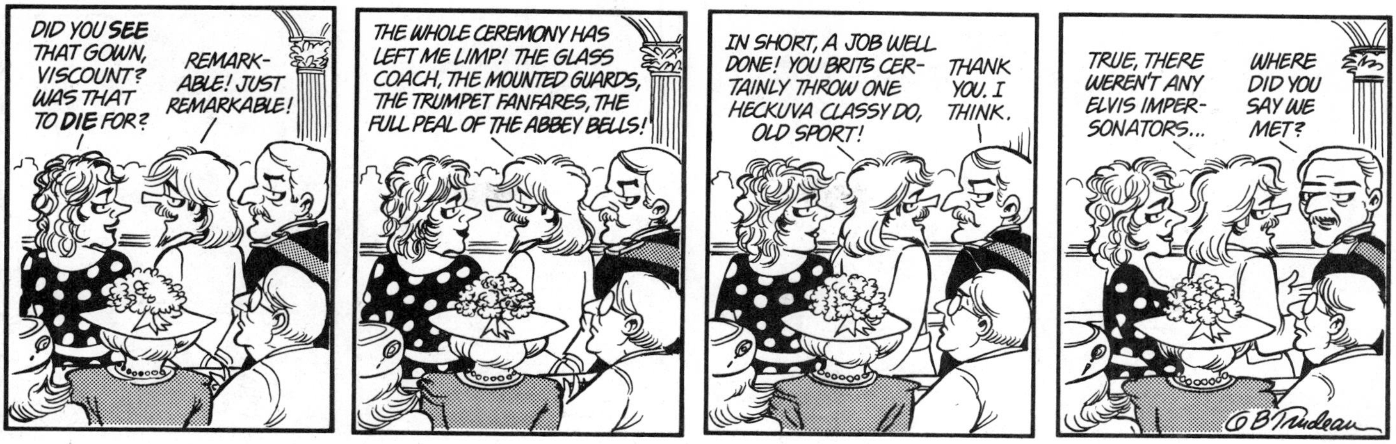
DID YOU SEE THAT GOWN, VISCOUNT? WAS THAT TO DIE FOR?
REMARK-ABLE! JUST REMARKABLE!
THE WHOLE CEREMONY HAS LEFT ME LIMP! THE GLASS COACH, THE MOUNTED GUARDS, THE TRUMPET FANFARES, THE FULL PEAL OF THE ABBEY BELLS!
IN SHORT, A JOB WELL DONE! YOU BRITS CER-TAINLY THROW ONE HECKUVA CLASSY DO, OLD SPORT!
THANK YOU. I THINK.
TRUE, THERE WEREN'T ANY ELVIS IMPER-SONATORS...
WHERE DID YOU SAY WE MET?
©B Trudeau

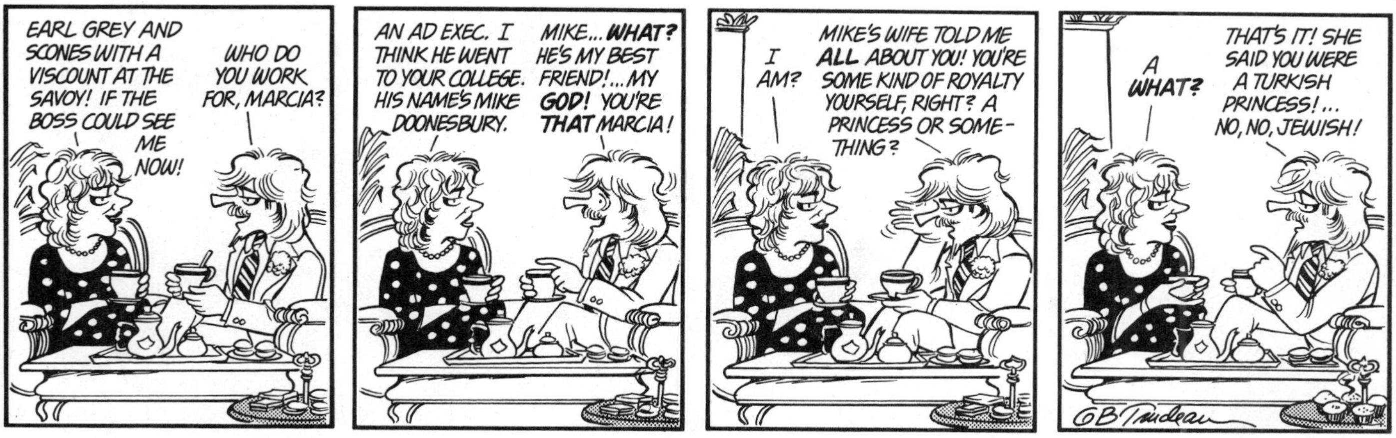
EARL GREY AND SCONES WITH A VISCOUNT AT THE SAVOY! IF THE BOSS COULD SEE ME NOW!
WHO DO YOU WORK FOR, MARCIA?
AN AD EXEC. I THINK HE WENT TO YOUR COLLEGE. HIS NAME'S MIKE DOONESBURY.
MIKE... WHAT? HE'S MY BEST FRIEND!... MY GOD! YOU'RE THAT MARCIA!
I AM?
MIKE'S WIFE TOLD ME ALL ABOUT YOU! YOU'RE SOME KIND OF ROYALTY YOURSELF, RIGHT? A PRINCESS OR SOME-THING?
A WHAT?
THAT'S IT! SHE SAID YOU WERE A TURKISH PRINCESS!... NO, NO, JEWISH!
©B Trudeau

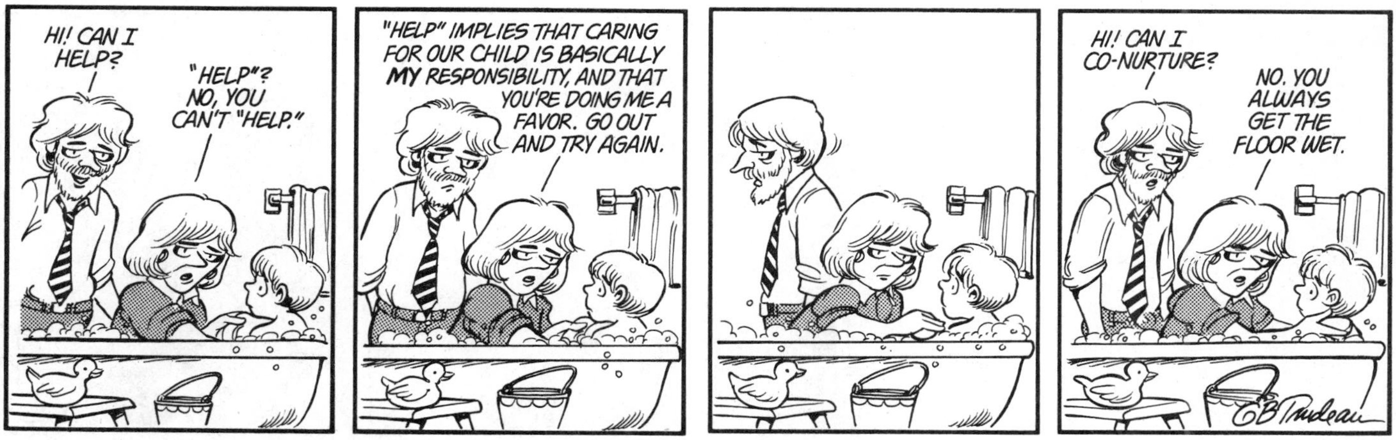
HI! CAN I HELP?
"HELP"? NO, YOU CAN'T "HELP."
"HELP" IMPLIES THAT CARING FOR OUR CHILD IS BASICALLY MY RESPONSIBILITY, AND THAT YOU'RE DOING ME A FAVOR. GO OUT AND TRY AGAIN.
HI! CAN I CO-NURTURE?
NO. YOU ALWAYS GET THE FLOOR WET.
©B Trudeau

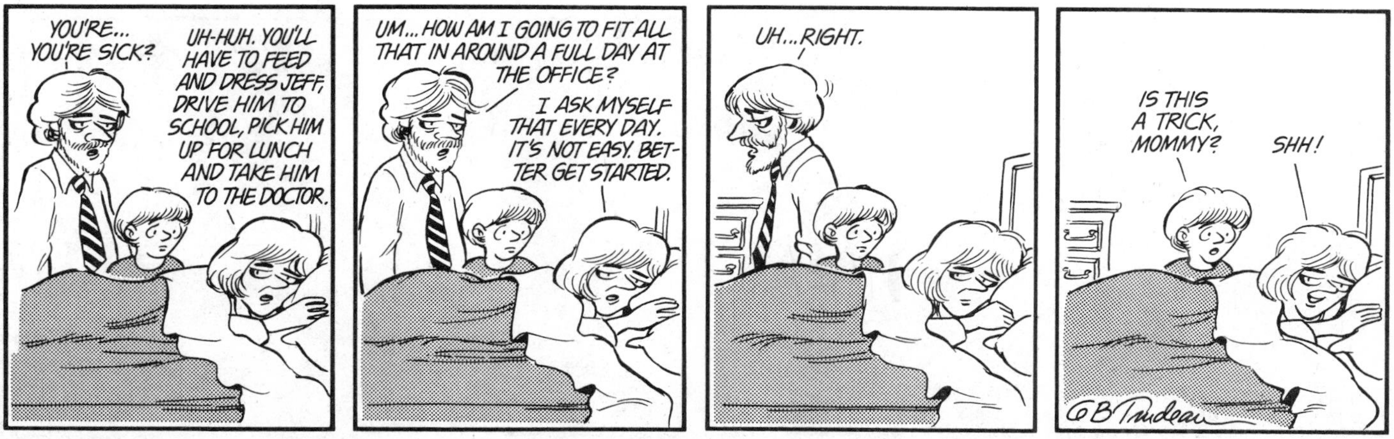
YOU'RE... YOU'RE SICK?
UH-HUH. YOU'LL HAVE TO FEED AND DRESS JEFF, DRIVE HIM TO SCHOOL, PICK HIM UP FOR LUNCH AND TAKE HIM TO THE DOCTOR.
UM... HOW AM I GOING TO FIT ALL THAT IN AROUND A FULL DAY AT THE OFFICE?
I ASK MYSELF THAT EVERY DAY. IT'S NOT EASY. BET-TER GET STARTED.
UH... RIGHT.
IS THIS A TRICK, MOMMY?
SHH!
©B Trudeau

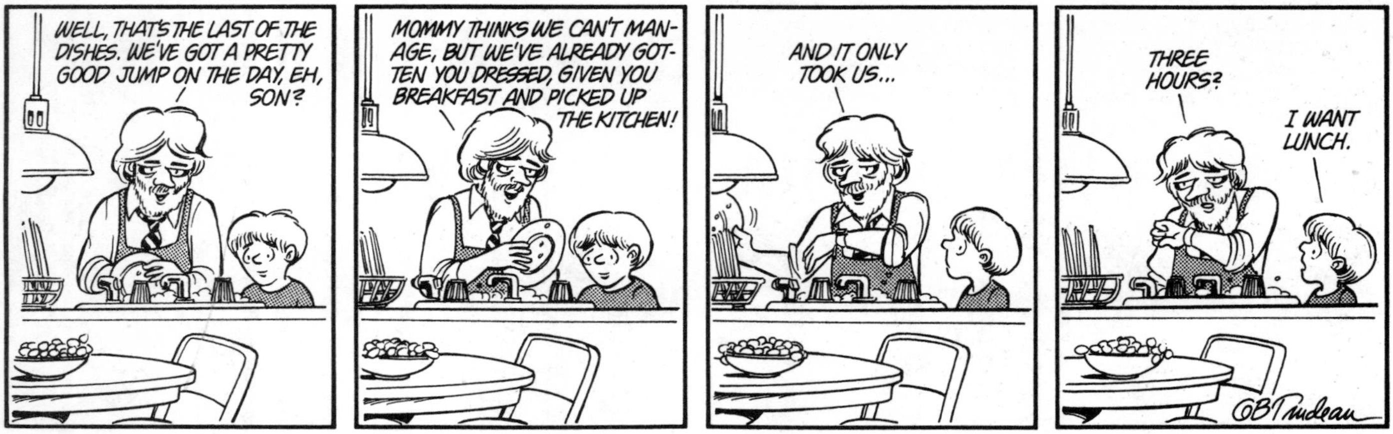
WELL, THAT'S THE LAST OF THE DISHES. WE'VE GOT A PRETTY GOOD JUMP ON THE DAY, EH, SON?
MOMMY THINKS WE CAN'T MANAGE, BUT WE'VE ALREADY GOTTEN YOU DRESSED, GIVEN YOU BREAKFAST AND PICKED UP THE KITCHEN!
AND IT ONLY TOOK US...
THREE HOURS?
I WANT LUNCH.
©BTrudeau

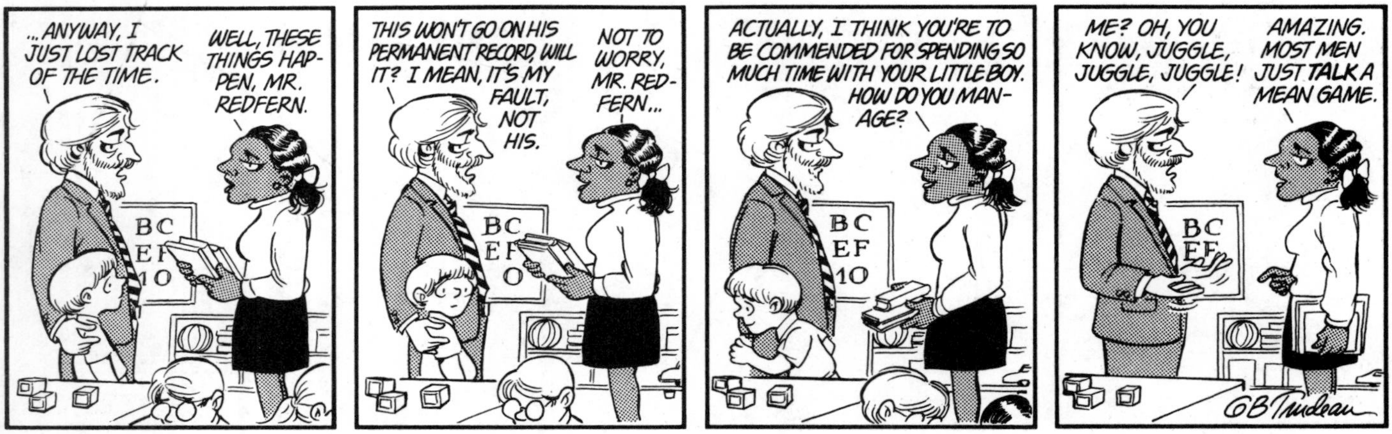
...ANYWAY, I JUST LOST TRACK OF THE TIME.
WELL, THESE THINGS HAPPEN, MR. REDFERN.
THIS WON'T GO ON HIS PERMANENT RECORD, WILL IT? I MEAN, IT'S MY FAULT, NOT HIS.
NOT TO WORRY, MR. REDFERN...
ACTUALLY, I THINK YOU'RE TO BE COMMENDED FOR SPENDING SO MUCH TIME WITH YOUR LITTLE BOY. HOW DO YOU MANAGE?
ME? OH, YOU KNOW, JUGGLE, JUGGLE, JUGGLE!
AMAZING. MOST MEN JUST TALK A MEAN GAME.
©BTrudeau

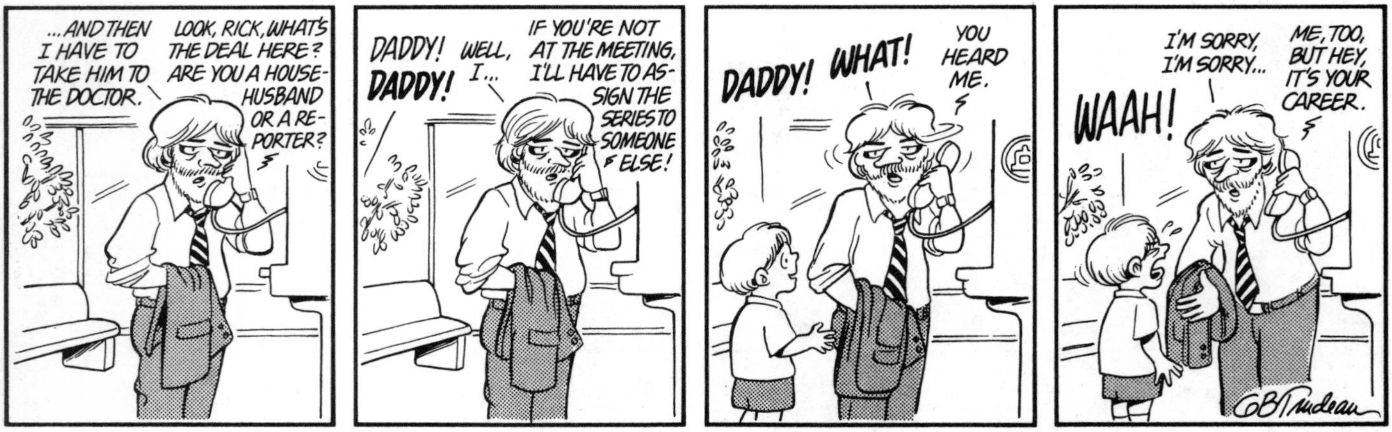
...AND THEN I HAVE TO TAKE HIM TO THE DOCTOR.
LOOK, RICK, WHAT'S THE DEAL HERE? ARE YOU A HOUSEHUSBAND OR A REPORTER?
DADDY! DADDY!
WELL, I...
IF YOU'RE NOT AT THE MEETING, I'LL HAVE TO ASSIGN THE SERIES TO SOMEONE ELSE!
DADDY!
WHAT!
YOU HEARD ME.
WAAH!
I'M SORRY, I'M SORRY...
ME, TOO, BUT HEY, IT'S YOUR CAREER.
©BTrudeau

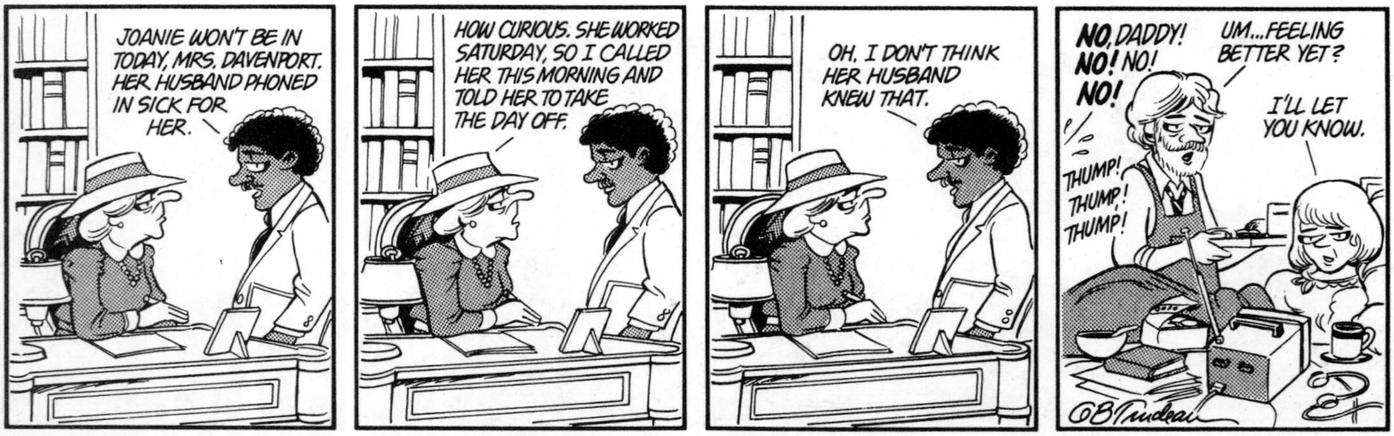
JOANIE WON'T BE IN TODAY, MRS. DAVENPORT. HER HUSBAND PHONED IN SICK FOR HER.
HOW CURIOUS. SHE WORKED SATURDAY, SO I CALLED HER THIS MORNING AND TOLD HER TO TAKE THE DAY OFF.
OH. I DON'T THINK HER HUSBAND KNEW THAT.
NO, DADDY! NO! NO! NO!
THUMP! THUMP! THUMP!
UM...FEELING BETTER YET?
I'LL LET YOU KNOW.
©BTrudeau

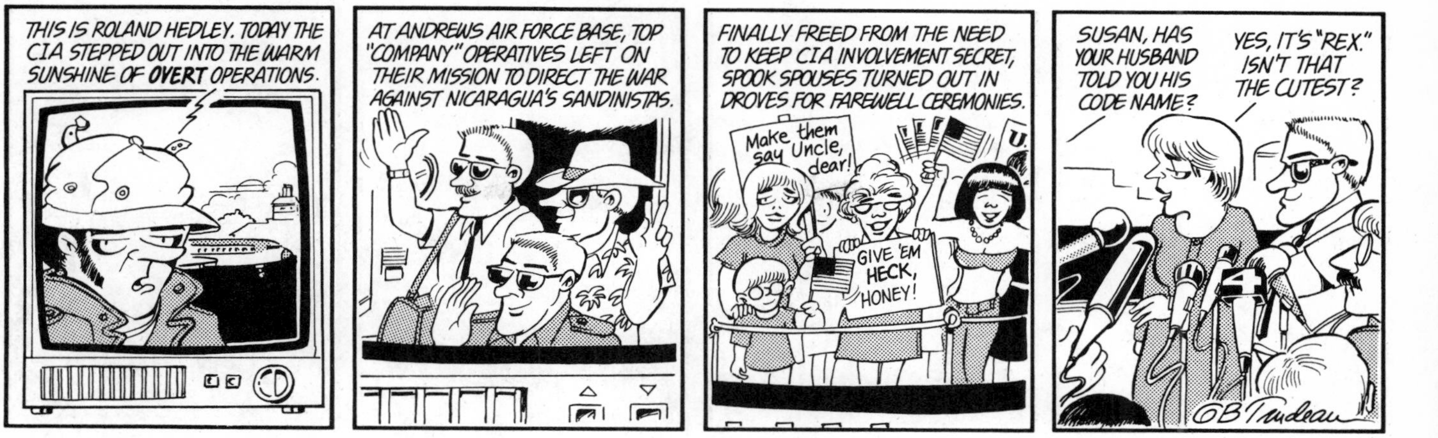
THIS IS ROLAND HEDLEY. TODAY THE CIA STEPPED OUT INTO THE WARM SUNSHINE OF **OVERT** OPERATIONS.
AT ANDREWS AIR FORCE BASE, TOP "COMPANY" OPERATIVES LEFT ON THEIR MISSION TO DIRECT THE WAR AGAINST NICARAGUA'S SANDINISTAS.
FINALLY FREED FROM THE NEED TO KEEP CIA INVOLVEMENT SECRET, SPOOK SPOUSES TURNED OUT IN DROVES FOR FAREWELL CEREMONIES.
Make them say Uncle, dear!
GIVE 'EM HECK, HONEY!
SUSAN, HAS YOUR HUSBAND TOLD YOU HIS CODE NAME?
YES, IT'S "REX." ISN'T THAT THE CUTEST?
©B Trudeau

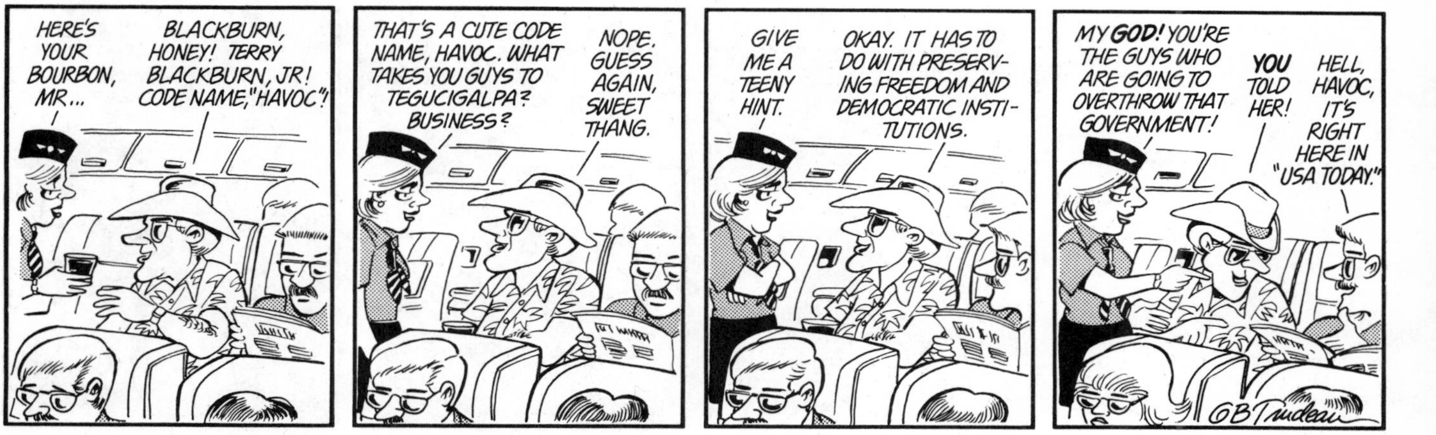
HERE'S YOUR BOURBON, MR...
BLACKBURN, HONEY! TERRY BLACKBURN, JR! CODE NAME, "HAVOC."!
THAT'S A CUTE CODE NAME, HAVOC. WHAT TAKES YOU GUYS TO TEGUCIGALPA? BUSINESS?
NOPE. GUESS AGAIN, SWEET THANG.
GIVE ME A TEENY HINT.
OKAY. IT HAS TO DO WITH PRESERVING FREEDOM AND DEMOCRATIC INSTITUTIONS.
MY **GOD!** YOU'RE THE GUYS WHO ARE GOING TO OVERTHROW THAT GOVERNMENT!
YOU TOLD HER!
HELL, HAVOC, IT'S RIGHT HERE IN "USA TODAY."
©B Trudeau

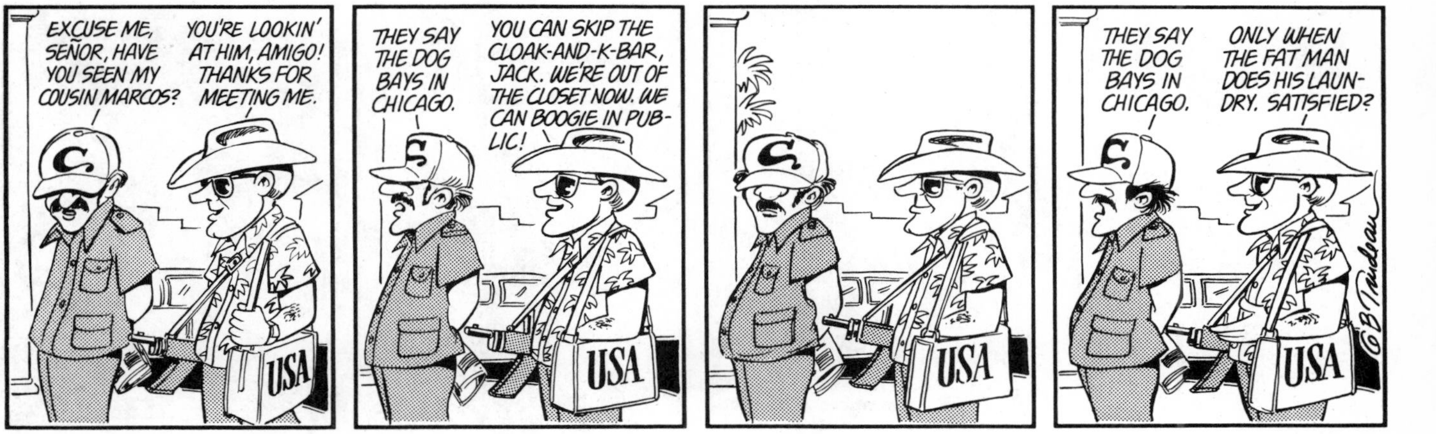
EXCUSE ME, SEÑOR, HAVE YOU SEEN MY COUSIN MARCOS?
YOU'RE LOOKIN' AT HIM, AMIGO! THANKS FOR MEETING ME.
USA
THEY SAY THE DOG BAYS IN CHICAGO.
YOU CAN SKIP THE CLOAK-AND-K-BAR, JACK. WE'RE OUT OF THE CLOSET NOW. WE CAN BOOGIE IN PUBLIC!
USA
USA
THEY SAY THE DOG BAYS IN CHICAGO.
ONLY WHEN THE FAT MAN DOES HIS LAUNDRY. SATISFIED?
USA
©B Trudeau

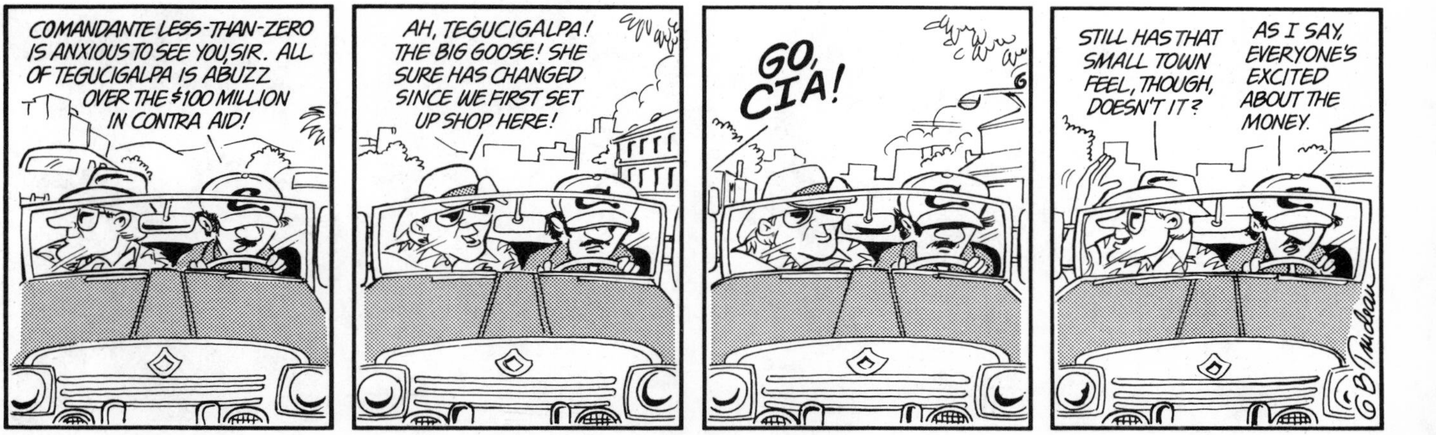
COMANDANTE LESS-THAN-ZERO IS ANXIOUS TO SEE YOU, SIR. ALL OF TEGUCIGALPA IS ABUZZ OVER THE $100 MILLION IN CONTRA AID!
AH, TEGUCIGALPA! THE BIG GOOSE! SHE SURE HAS CHANGED SINCE WE FIRST SET UP SHOP HERE!
GO, CIA!
STILL HAS THAT SMALL TOWN FEEL, THOUGH, DOESN'T IT?
AS I SAY, EVERYONE'S EXCITED ABOUT THE MONEY.
©B Trudeau

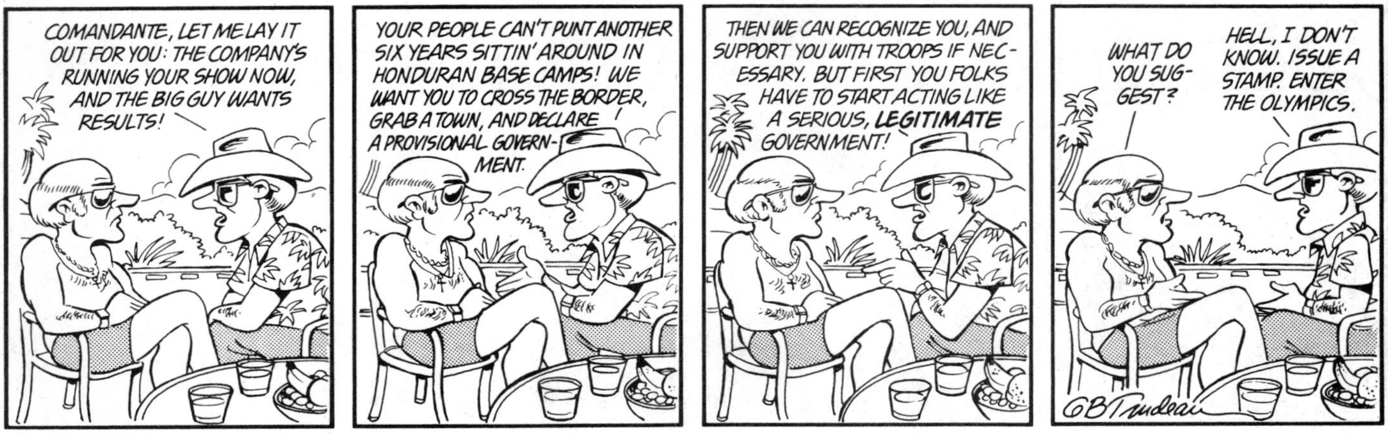
COMANDANTE, LET ME LAY IT OUT FOR YOU: THE COMPANY'S RUNNING YOUR SHOW NOW, AND THE BIG GUY WANTS RESULTS!
YOUR PEOPLE CAN'T PUNT ANOTHER SIX YEARS SITTIN' AROUND IN HONDURAN BASE CAMPS! WE WANT YOU TO CROSS THE BORDER, GRAB A TOWN, AND DECLARE A PROVISIONAL GOVERNMENT.
THEN WE CAN RECOGNIZE YOU, AND SUPPORT YOU WITH TROOPS IF NECESSARY. BUT FIRST YOU FOLKS HAVE TO START ACTING LIKE A SERIOUS, **LEGITIMATE** GOVERNMENT!
WHAT DO YOU SUGGEST?
HELL, I DON'T KNOW. ISSUE A STAMP. ENTER THE OLYMPICS.
©B Trudeau

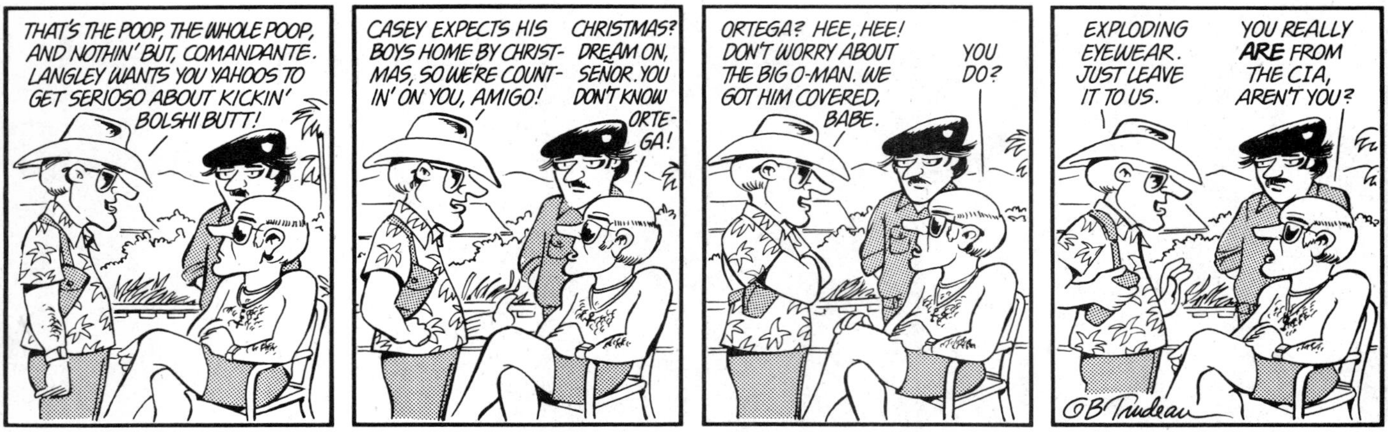
THAT'S THE POOP, THE WHOLE POOP, AND NOTHIN' BUT, COMANDANTE. LANGLEY WANTS YOU YAHOOS TO GET SERIOSO ABOUT KICKIN' BOLSHI BUTT!
CASEY EXPECTS HIS BOYS HOME BY CHRISTMAS, SO WE'RE COUNTIN' ON YOU, AMIGO!
CHRISTMAS? DREAM ON, SEÑOR. YOU DON'T KNOW ORTEGA!
ORTEGA? HEE, HEE! DON'T WORRY ABOUT THE BIG O-MAN. WE GOT HIM COVERED, BABE.
YOU DO?
EXPLODING EYEWEAR. JUST LEAVE IT TO US.
YOU REALLY **ARE** FROM THE CIA, AREN'T YOU?
©B Trudeau

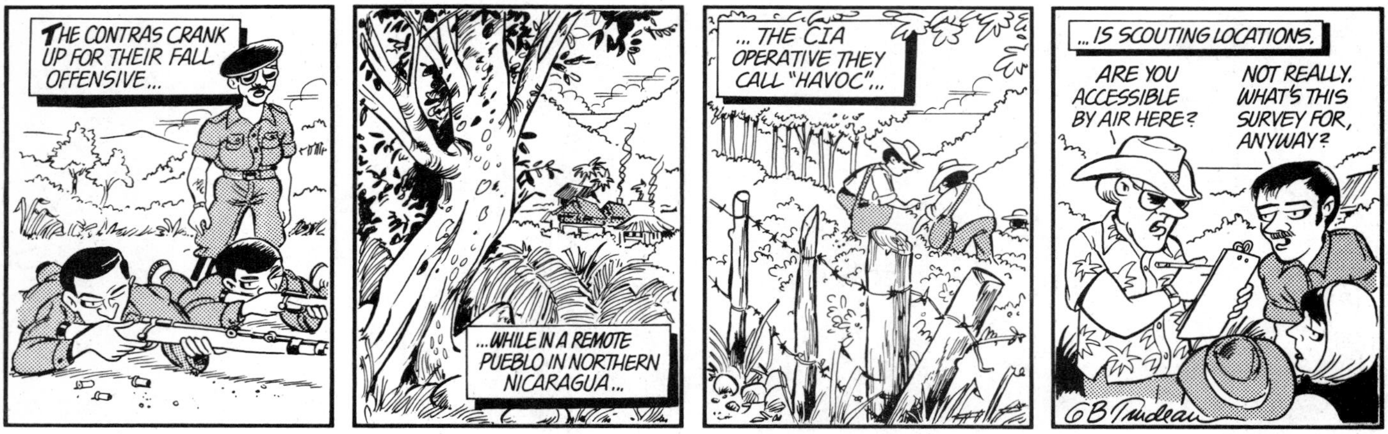
THE CONTRAS CRANK UP FOR THEIR FALL OFFENSIVE...
...WHILE IN A REMOTE PUEBLO IN NORTHERN NICARAGUA...
... THE CIA OPERATIVE THEY CALL "HAVOC"...
... IS SCOUTING LOCATIONS.
ARE YOU ACCESSIBLE BY AIR HERE?
NOT REALLY. WHAT'S THIS SURVEY FOR, ANYWAY?
©B Trudeau

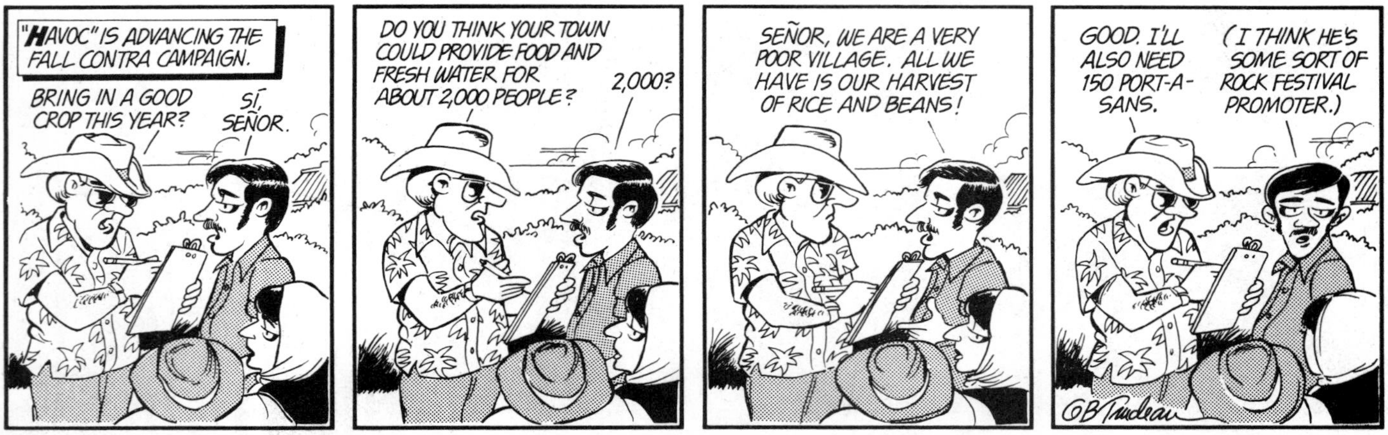
"HAVOC" IS ADVANCING THE FALL CONTRA CAMPAIGN.
BRING IN A GOOD CROP THIS YEAR?
SÍ, SEÑOR.
DO YOU THINK YOUR TOWN COULD PROVIDE FOOD AND FRESH WATER FOR ABOUT 2,000 PEOPLE?
2,000?
SEÑOR, WE ARE A VERY POOR VILLAGE. ALL WE HAVE IS OUR HARVEST OF RICE AND BEANS!
GOOD. I'LL ALSO NEED 150 PORT-A-SANS.
(I THINK HE'S SOME SORT OF ROCK FESTIVAL PROMOTER.)
©B Trudeau

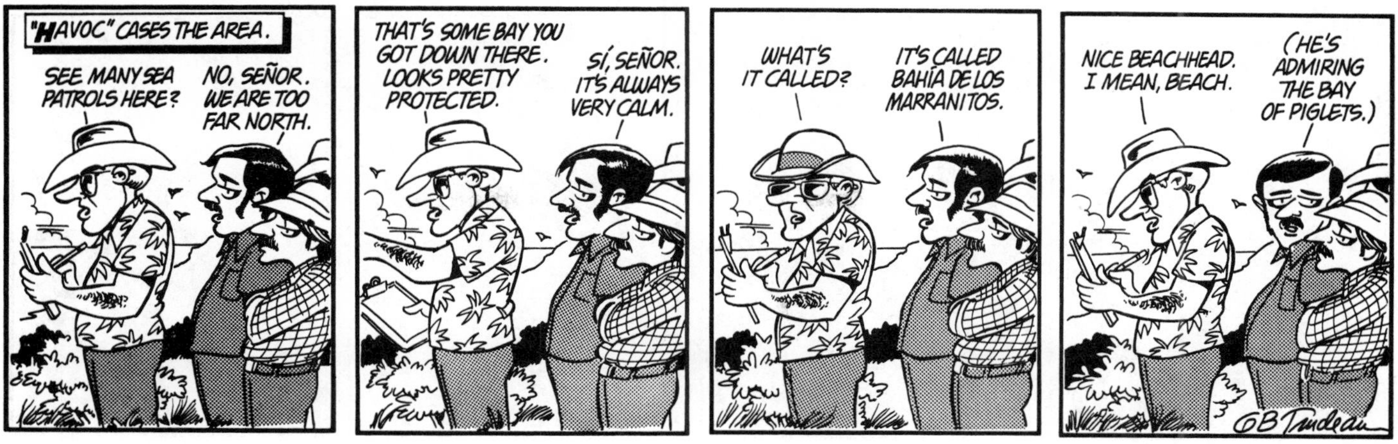
"HAVOC" CASES THE AREA.
SEE MANY SEA PATROLS HERE?
NO, SEÑOR. WE ARE TOO FAR NORTH.
THAT'S SOME BAY YOU GOT DOWN THERE. LOOKS PRETTY PROTECTED.
SÍ, SEÑOR. IT'S ALWAYS VERY CALM.
WHAT'S IT CALLED?
IT'S CALLED BAHÍA DE LOS MARRANITOS.
NICE BEACHHEAD. I MEAN, BEACH.
(HE'S ADMIRING THE BAY OF PIGLETS.)

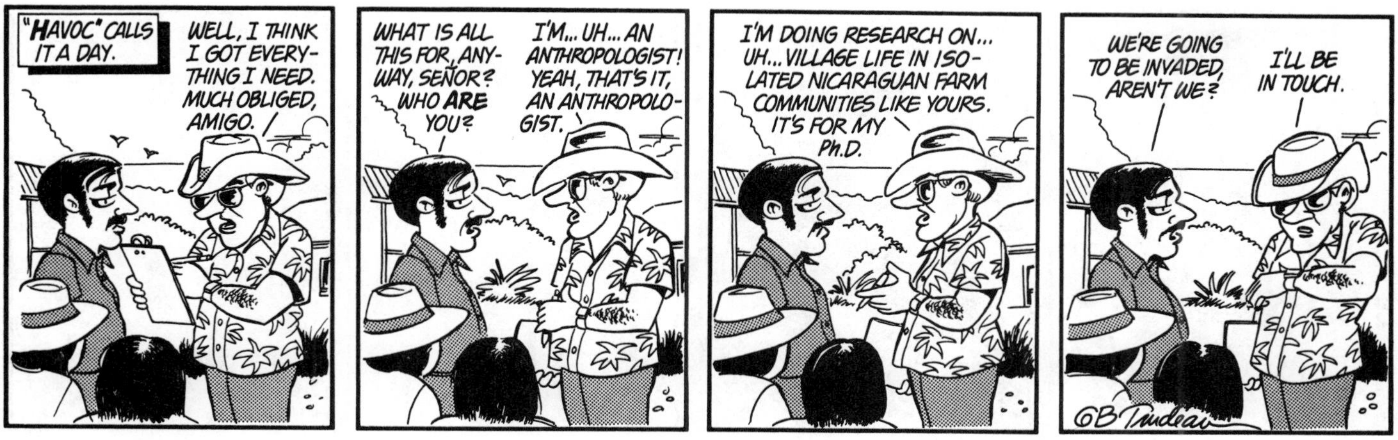
"HAVOC" CALLS IT A DAY.
WELL, I THINK I GOT EVERYTHING I NEED. MUCH OBLIGED, AMIGO.
WHAT IS ALL THIS FOR, ANYWAY, SEÑOR? WHO ARE YOU?
I'M... UH... AN ANTHROPOLOGIST! YEAH, THAT'S IT, AN ANTHROPOLOGIST.
I'M DOING RESEARCH ON... UH... VILLAGE LIFE IN ISOLATED NICARAGUAN FARM COMMUNITIES LIKE YOURS. IT'S FOR MY Ph.D.
WE'RE GOING TO BE INVADED, AREN'T WE?
I'LL BE IN TOUCH.

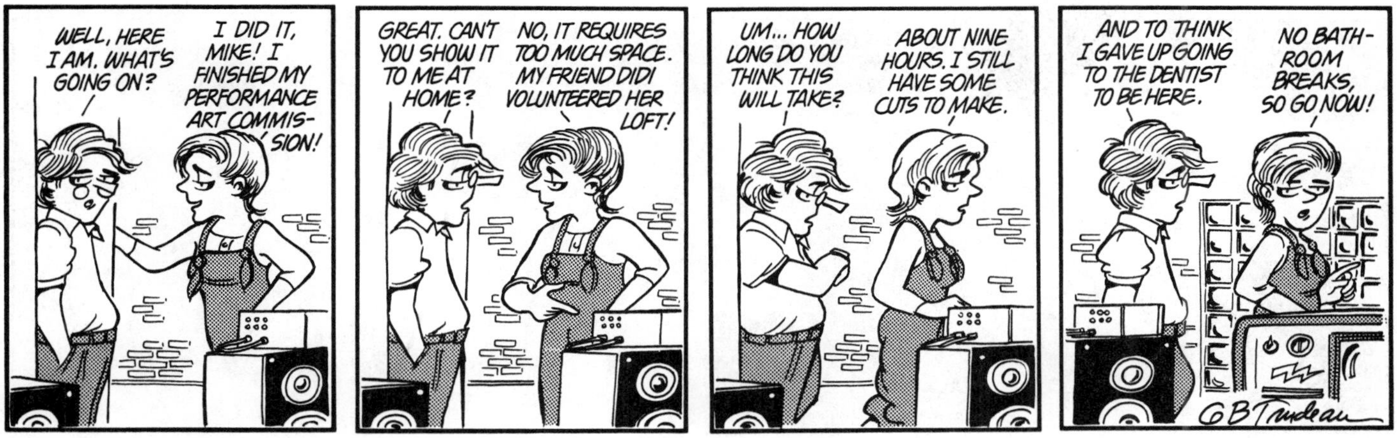
WELL, HERE I AM. WHAT'S GOING ON?
I DID IT, MIKE! I FINISHED MY PERFORMANCE ART COMMISSION!
GREAT. CAN'T YOU SHOW IT TO ME AT HOME?
NO, IT REQUIRES TOO MUCH SPACE. MY FRIEND DIDI VOLUNTEERED HER LOFT!
UM... HOW LONG DO YOU THINK THIS WILL TAKE?
ABOUT NINE HOURS. I STILL HAVE SOME CUTS TO MAKE.
AND TO THINK I GAVE UP GOING TO THE DENTIST TO BE HERE.
NO BATHROOM BREAKS, SO GO NOW!

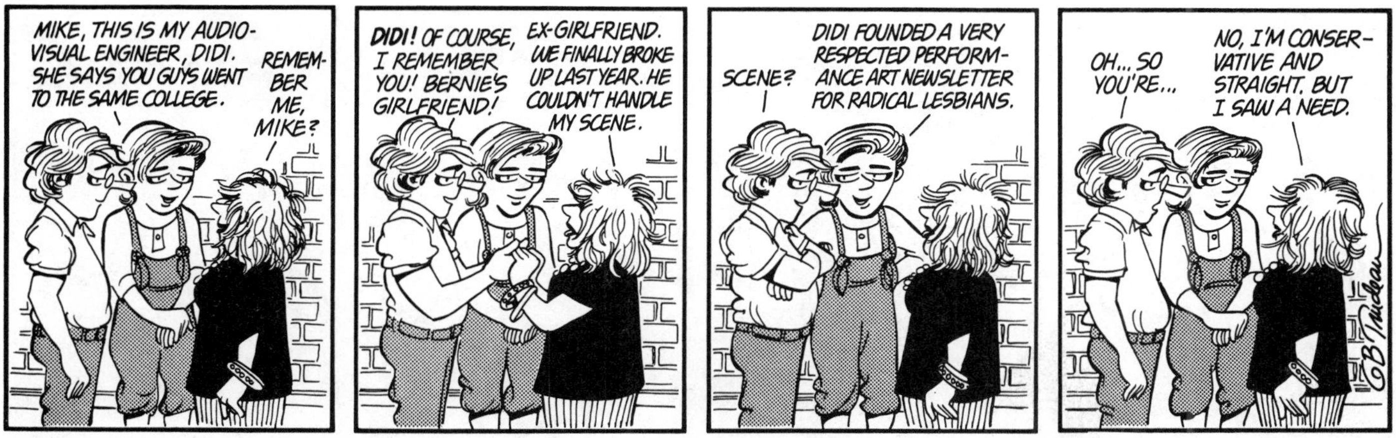
MIKE, THIS IS MY AUDIO-VISUAL ENGINEER, DIDI. SHE SAYS YOU GUYS WENT TO THE SAME COLLEGE.
REMEMBER ME, MIKE?
DIDI! OF COURSE, I REMEMBER YOU! BERNIE'S GIRLFRIEND!
EX-GIRLFRIEND. WE FINALLY BROKE UP LAST YEAR. HE COULDN'T HANDLE MY SCENE.
SCENE?
DIDI FOUNDED A VERY RESPECTED PERFORMANCE ART NEWSLETTER FOR RADICAL LESBIANS.
OH... SO YOU'RE...
NO, I'M CONSERVATIVE AND STRAIGHT. BUT I SAW A NEED.

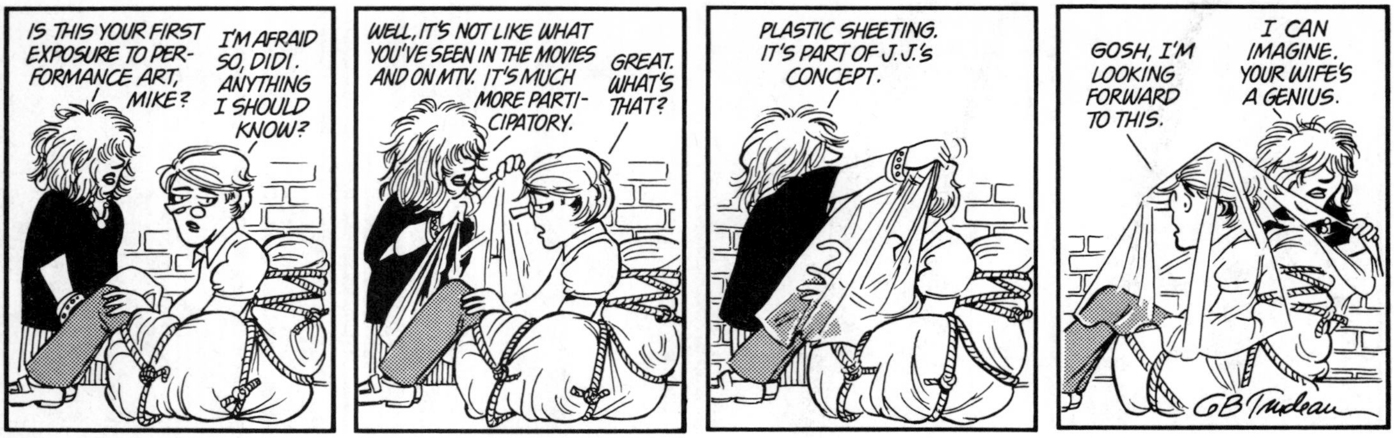
IS THIS YOUR FIRST EXPOSURE TO PERFORMANCE ART, MIKE?
I'M AFRAID SO, DIDI. ANYTHING I SHOULD KNOW?
WELL, IT'S NOT LIKE WHAT YOU'VE SEEN IN THE MOVIES AND ON MTV. IT'S MUCH MORE PARTICIPATORY.
GREAT. WHAT'S THAT?
PLASTIC SHEETING. IT'S PART OF J.J.'S CONCEPT.
GOSH, I'M LOOKING FORWARD TO THIS.
I CAN IMAGINE. YOUR WIFE'S A GENIUS.
GB Trudeau

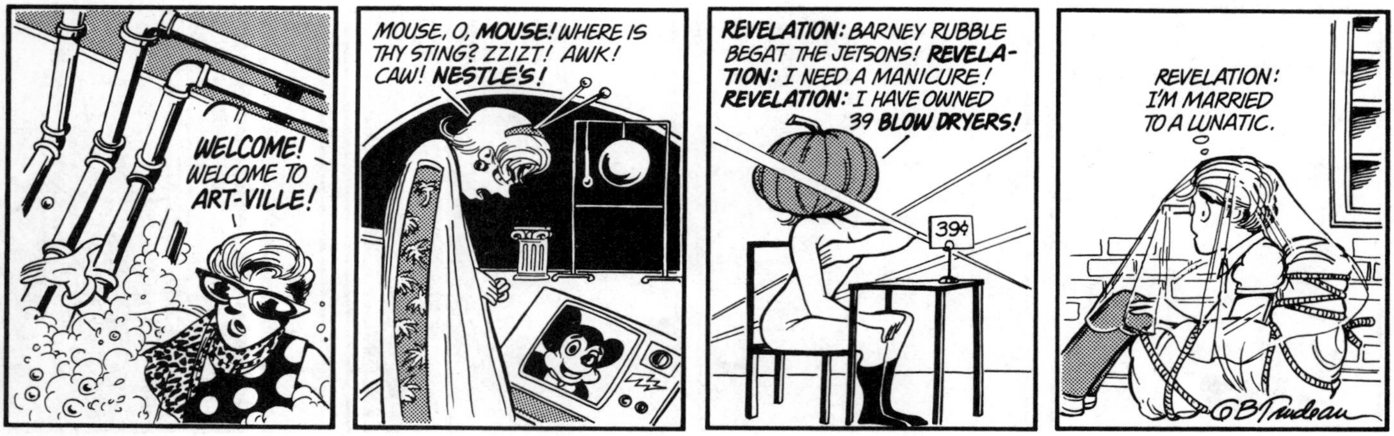
WELCOME! WELCOME TO ART-VILLE!
MOUSE, O, MOUSE! WHERE IS THY STING? ZZIZT! AWK! CAW! NESTLE'S!
REVELATION: BARNEY RUBBLE BEGAT THE JETSONS! REVELATION: I NEED A MANICURE! REVELATION: I HAVE OWNED 39 BLOW DRYERS!
39¢
REVELATION: I'M MARRIED TO A LUNATIC.
GB Trudeau

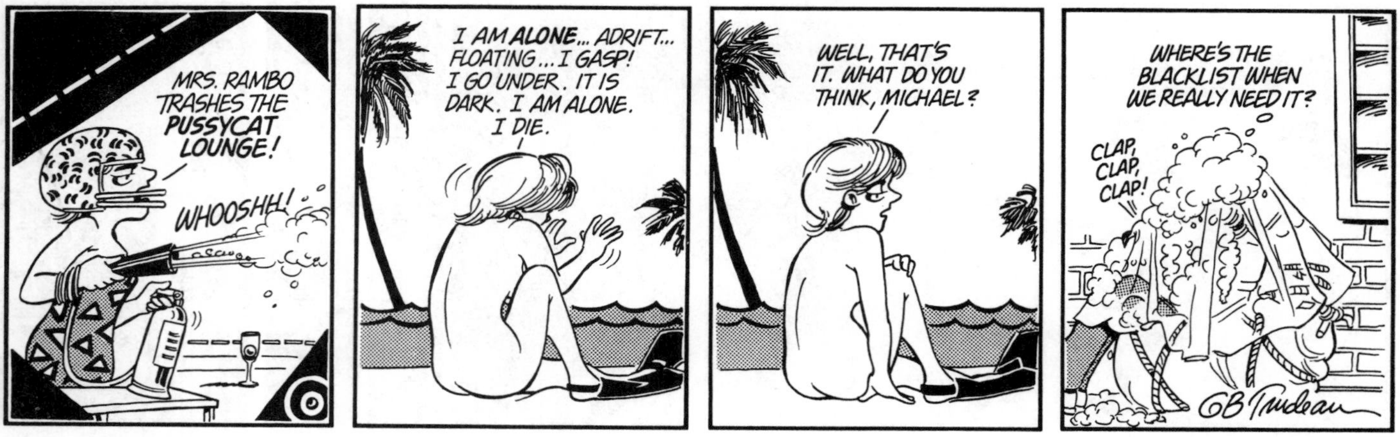
MRS. RAMBO TRASHES THE PUSSYCAT LOUNGE!
WHOOSHH!
I AM ALONE... ADRIFT... FLOATING... I GASP! I GO UNDER. IT IS DARK. I AM ALONE. I DIE.
WELL, THAT'S IT. WHAT DO YOU THINK, MICHAEL?
CLAP, CLAP, CLAP!
WHERE'S THE BLACKLIST WHEN WE REALLY NEED IT?
GB Trudeau

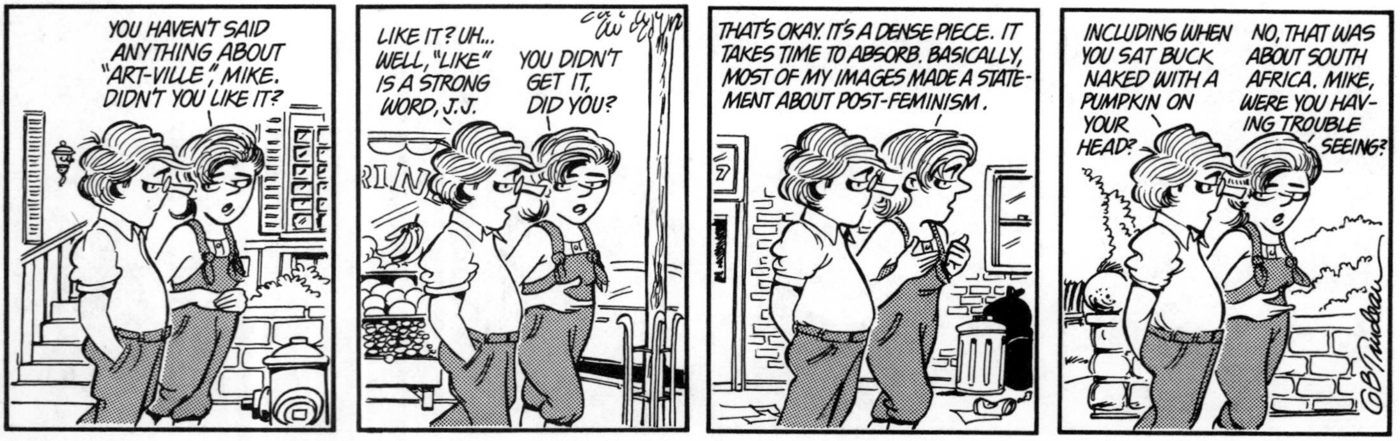
YOU HAVEN'T SAID ANYTHING ABOUT "ART-VILLE," MIKE. DIDN'T YOU LIKE IT?
LIKE IT? UH... WELL, "LIKE" IS A STRONG WORD, J.J.
YOU DIDN'T GET IT, DID YOU?
THAT'S OKAY. IT'S A DENSE PIECE. IT TAKES TIME TO ABSORB. BASICALLY, MOST OF MY IMAGES MADE A STATEMENT ABOUT POST-FEMINISM.
INCLUDING WHEN YOU SAT BUCK NAKED WITH A PUMPKIN ON YOUR HEAD?
NO, THAT WAS ABOUT SOUTH AFRICA. MIKE, WERE YOU HAVING TROUBLE SEEING?
GB Trudeau

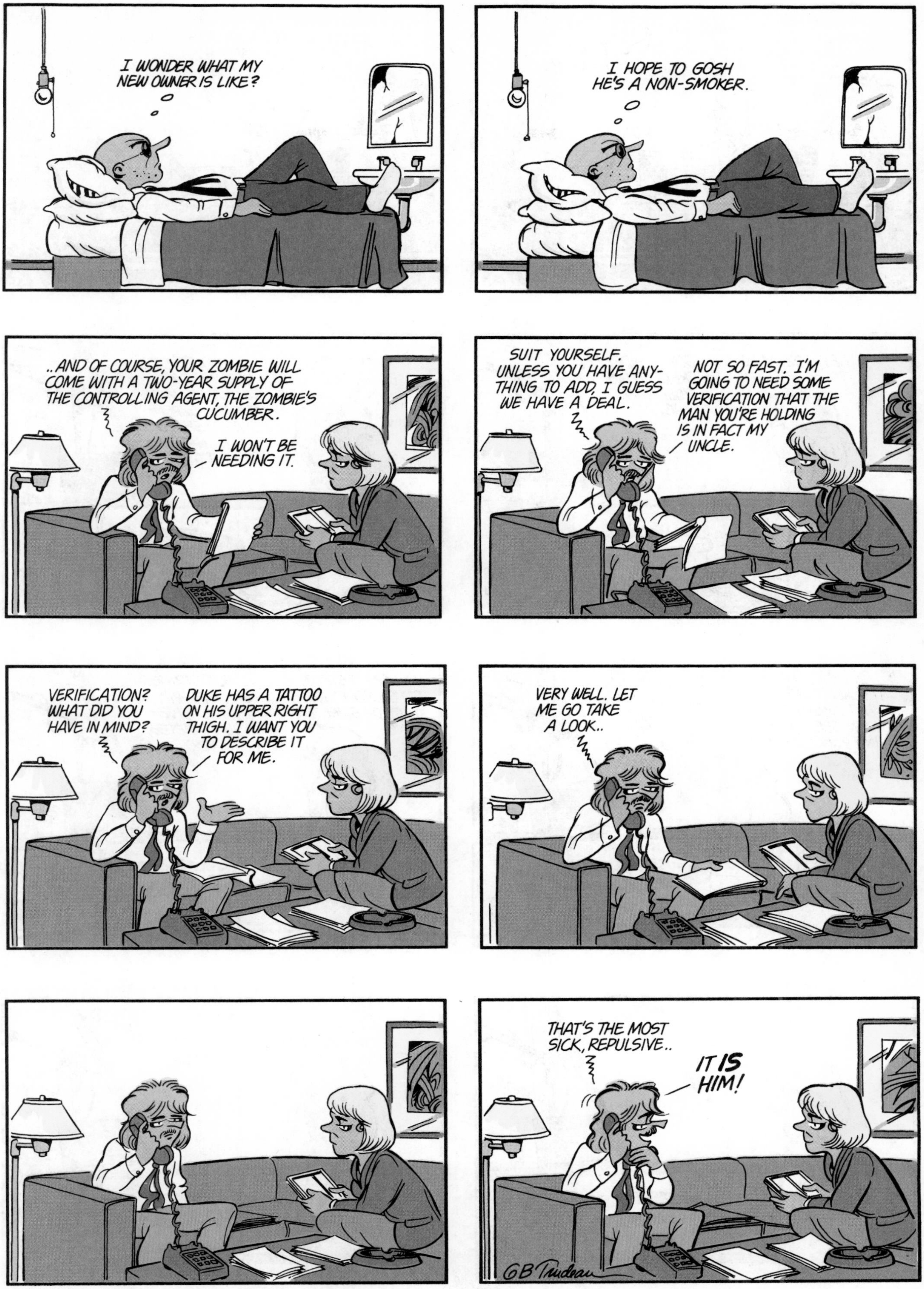
I WONDER WHAT MY NEW OWNER IS LIKE?
I HOPE TO GOSH HE'S A NON-SMOKER.
..AND OF COURSE, YOUR ZOMBIE WILL COME WITH A TWO-YEAR SUPPLY OF THE CONTROLLING AGENT, THE ZOMBIE'S CUCUMBER.
I WON'T BE NEEDING IT.
SUIT YOURSELF. UNLESS YOU HAVE ANY-THING TO ADD, I GUESS WE HAVE A DEAL.
NOT SO FAST. I'M GOING TO NEED SOME VERIFICATION THAT THE MAN YOU'RE HOLDING IS IN FACT MY UNCLE.
VERIFICATION? WHAT DID YOU HAVE IN MIND?
DUKE HAS A TATTOO ON HIS UPPER RIGHT THIGH. I WANT YOU TO DESCRIBE IT FOR ME.
VERY WELL. LET ME GO TAKE A LOOK..
THAT'S THE MOST SICK, REPULSIVE..
IT IS HIM!
GB Trudeau

COMING UP, A VERY HAPPENING KIND OF TUNE: MAHLER'S THIRD SYMPHONY!
ALL 80 PARTS PLAYED BY DAVID FOSTER.
HEY, FOZ-MAN!
BOY WONDER! GREAT TO DIG YOUR FACE AGAIN!
WHERE'S THE BAND, FOZ?
I DON'T USE SESSION CATS ANYMORE, MAN. IT'S TOO EXPENSIVE TO SHRED ON THE NATCH THESE DAYS.
IT'S ALL CANNED? WHAT ABOUT THE HORN SECTION? AND PERCUSSION?
GET REAL, JIM. DRUMMERS ARE EXTINCT. AND WITH THE EMULATOR, I GOT HORNS OUT THE KAZOO!
HOW ABOUT STRINGS? I'M GOING TO NEED A LOT OF SWEETENING.
I GOT STRINGS ON A FLOPPY THAT'LL GIVE YOU DIABETES, JIMBO.
OH.
SAY, FOZ, ABOUT MY VOCALS...
I GOT IT COVERED, DUDE.
©B Trudeau

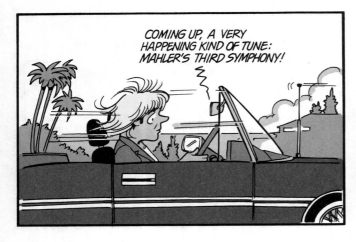

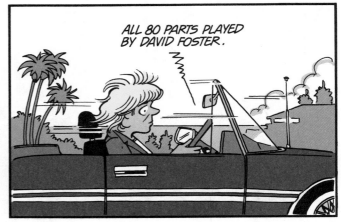

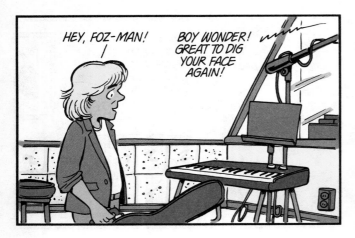

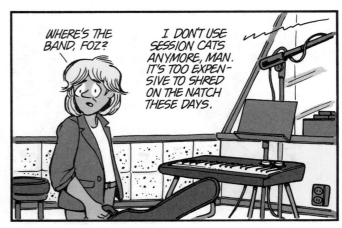

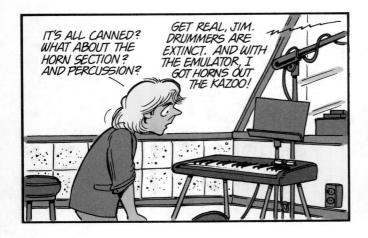

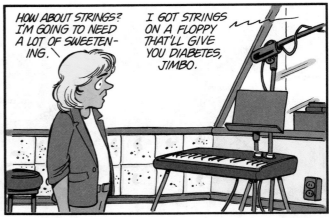

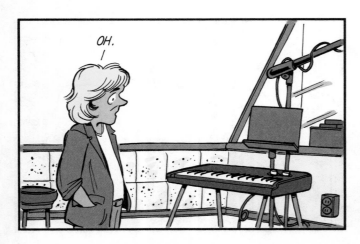

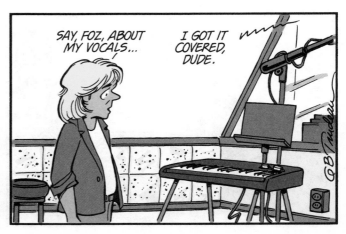

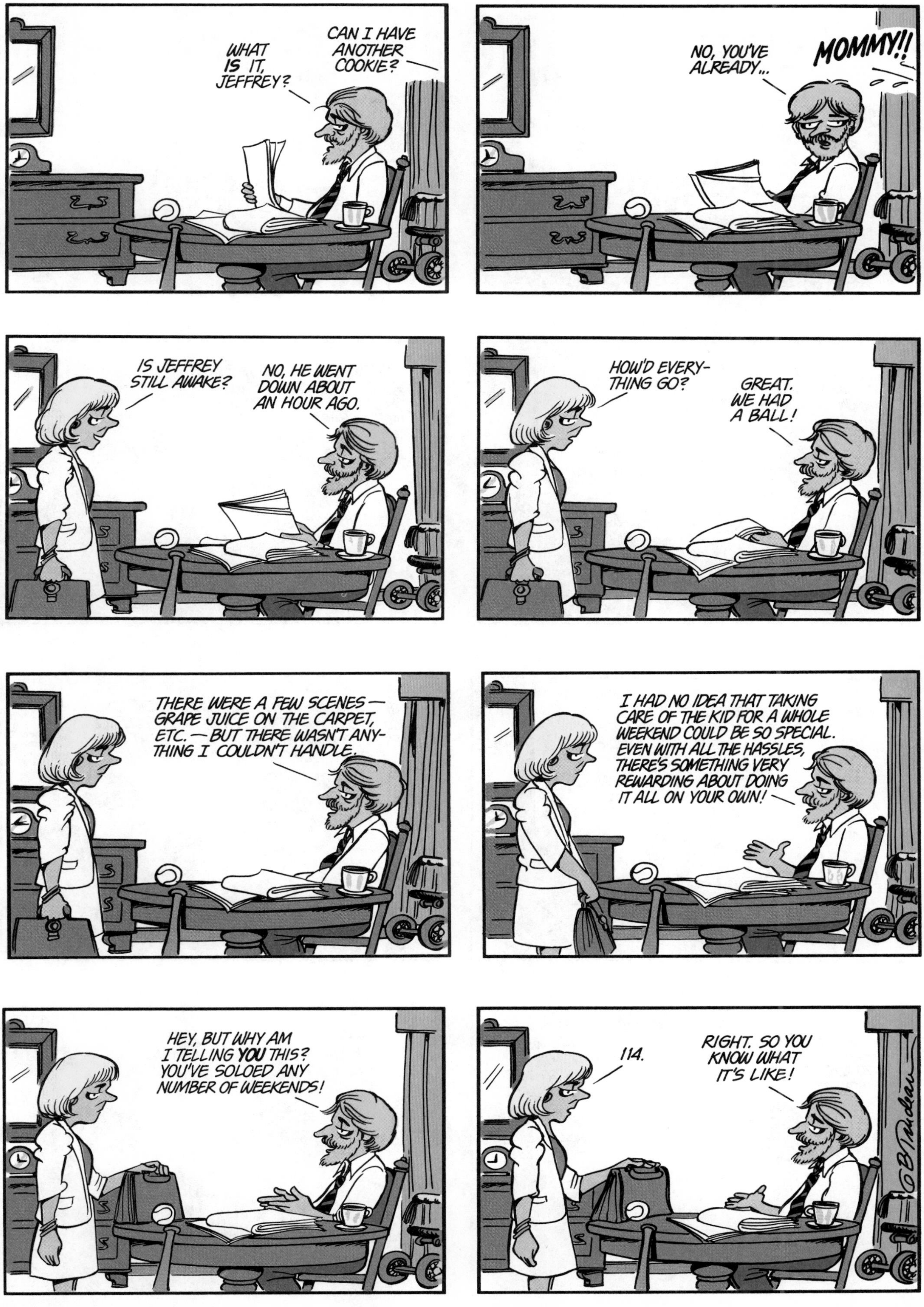

WHAT IS IT, JEFFREY?
CAN I HAVE ANOTHER COOKIE?
NO, YOU'VE ALREADY...
MOMMY!!
IS JEFFREY STILL AWAKE?
NO, HE WENT DOWN ABOUT AN HOUR AGO.
HOW'D EVERY-THING GO?
GREAT. WE HAD A BALL!
THERE WERE A FEW SCENES— GRAPE JUICE ON THE CARPET, ETC.—BUT THERE WASN'T ANY-THING I COULDN'T HANDLE.
I HAD NO IDEA THAT TAKING CARE OF THE KID FOR A WHOLE WEEKEND COULD BE SO SPECIAL. EVEN WITH ALL THE HASSLES, THERE'S SOMETHING VERY REWARDING ABOUT DOING IT ALL ON YOUR OWN!
HEY, BUT WHY AM I TELLING YOU THIS? YOU'VE SOLOED ANY NUMBER OF WEEKENDS!
114.
RIGHT. SO YOU KNOW WHAT IT'S LIKE!

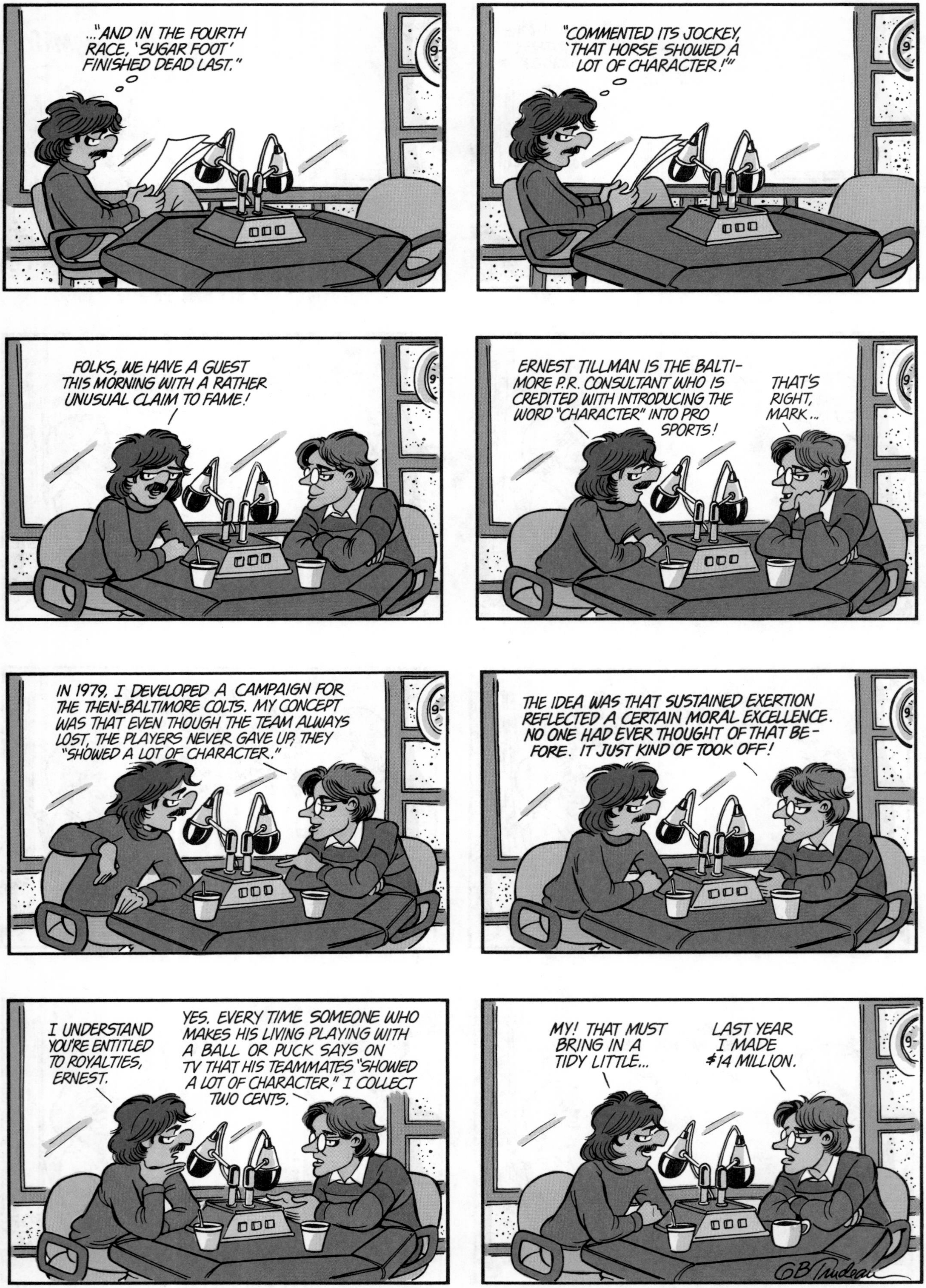
..."AND IN THE FOURTH RACE, 'SUGAR FOOT' FINISHED DEAD LAST."
"COMMENTED ITS JOCKEY, 'THAT HORSE SHOWED A LOT OF CHARACTER!'"
FOLKS, WE HAVE A GUEST THIS MORNING WITH A RATHER UNUSUAL CLAIM TO FAME!
ERNEST TILLMAN IS THE BALTIMORE P.R. CONSULTANT WHO IS CREDITED WITH INTRODUCING THE WORD "CHARACTER" INTO PRO SPORTS!
THAT'S RIGHT, MARK...
IN 1979, I DEVELOPED A CAMPAIGN FOR THE THEN-BALTIMORE COLTS. MY CONCEPT WAS THAT EVEN THOUGH THE TEAM ALWAYS LOST, THE PLAYERS NEVER GAVE UP, THEY "SHOWED A LOT OF CHARACTER."
THE IDEA WAS THAT SUSTAINED EXERTION REFLECTED A CERTAIN MORAL EXCELLENCE. NO ONE HAD EVER THOUGHT OF THAT BEFORE. IT JUST KIND OF TOOK OFF!
I UNDERSTAND YOU'RE ENTITLED TO ROYALTIES, ERNEST.
YES. EVERY TIME SOMEONE WHO MAKES HIS LIVING PLAYING WITH A BALL OR PUCK SAYS ON TV THAT HIS TEAMMATES "SHOWED A LOT OF CHARACTER," I COLLECT TWO CENTS.
MY! THAT MUST BRING IN A TIDY LITTLE...
LAST YEAR I MADE $14 MILLION.
GB Trudeau

AWESOME SIGHT, ISN'T IT?
YOU SAID IT...
WEENIES AND FLAMERS, AS FAR AS THE EYE CAN SEE!
I'D LIKE TO CONCLUDE MY REMARKS TODAY WITH AN OPEN INVITATION...
SEVERAL WEEKS AGO, EDUCATION SECRETARY WILLIAM BENNETT LASHED OUT AT THE STUDENT RADICALS WHO ARE CREATING SUCH TURMOIL ON OUR CAMPUSES.
EVER SINCE THEN, WORRIED COLLEGE PRESIDENTS EVERYWHERE HAVE BEEN ASKING THEMSELVES ONE QUESTION: "WHAT STUDENT RADICALS?" HAVE WE BEEN MISSING SOMETHING?
IF THERE'S A RADICAL IN THIS CLASS, PLEASE, THIS IS YOUR LAST CHANCE TO LET ME KNOW! GIVE ME A SIGN OF SOME SORT, A STATEMENT, A DEMAND, ANYTHING!
WELL, I THOUGHT IT WAS PRETTY WEIRD, BUT NO HARM IN...
DIVEST NOW! THANK YOU.
©B Trudeau

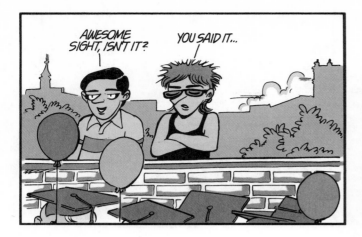

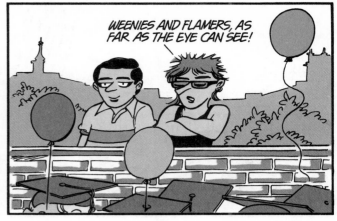

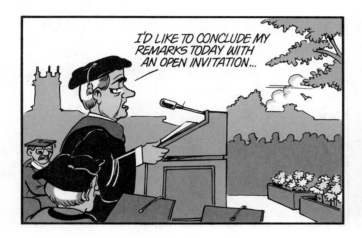

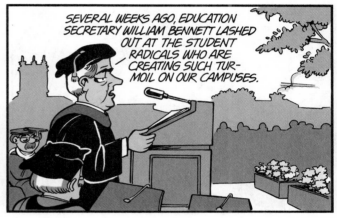

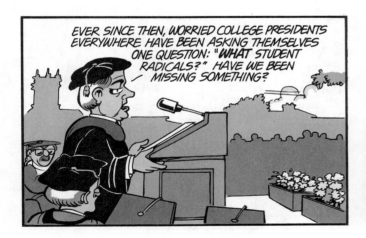

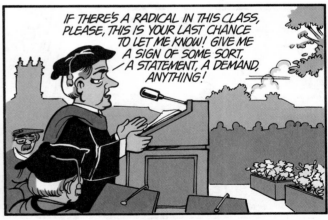

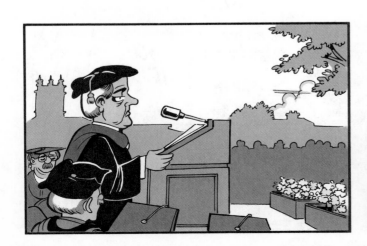

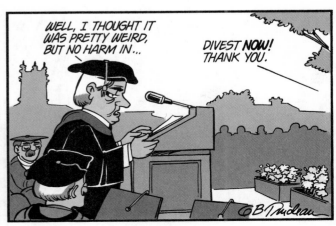

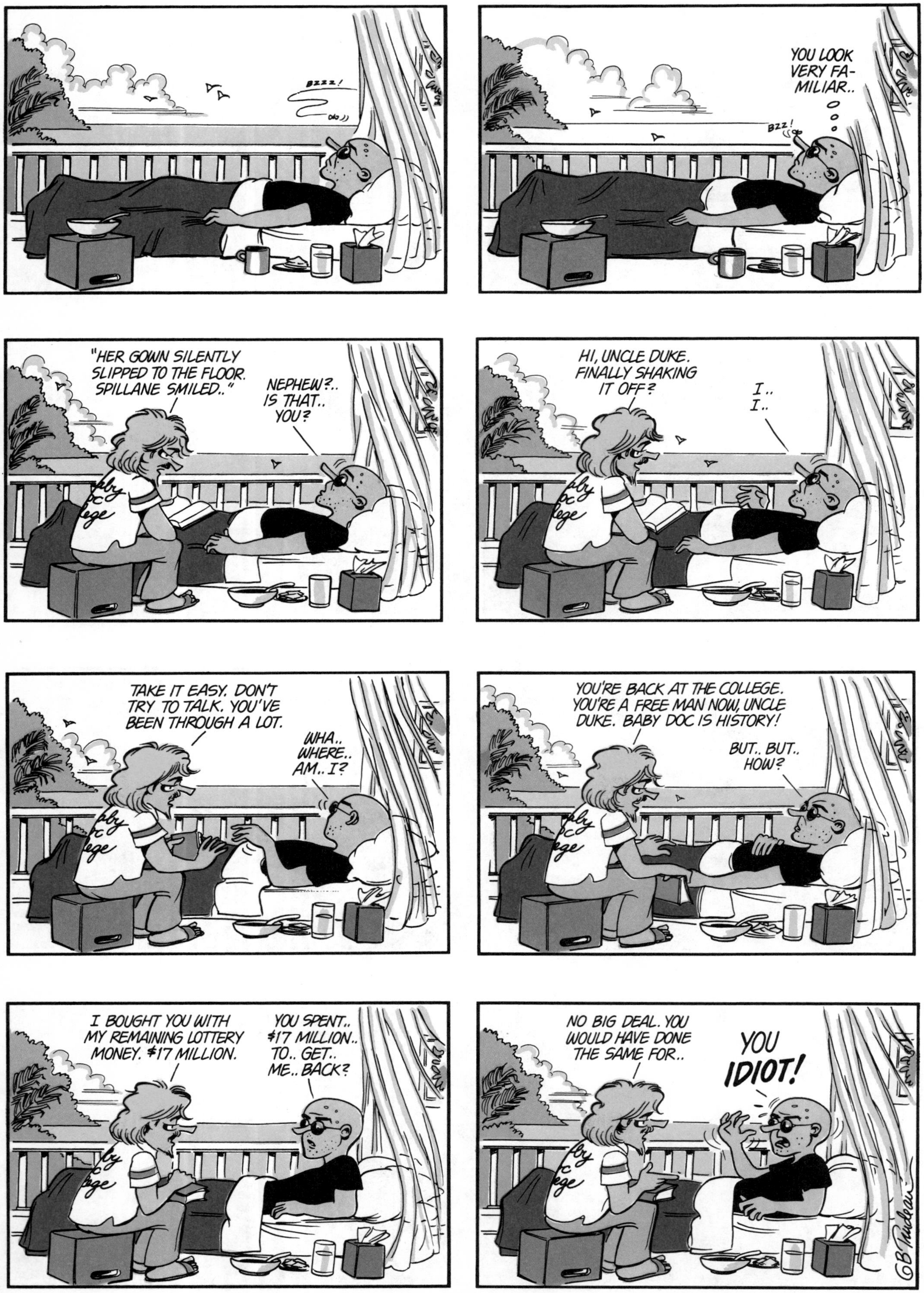
BZZZ!
YOU LOOK VERY FA-MILIAR..
BZZ!
"HER GOWN SILENTLY SLIPPED TO THE FLOOR. SPILLANE SMILED.."
NEPHEW?.. IS THAT.. YOU?
HI, UNCLE DUKE. FINALLY SHAKING IT OFF?
I.. I..
TAKE IT EASY. DON'T TRY TO TALK. YOU'VE BEEN THROUGH A LOT.
WHA.. WHERE.. AM.. I?
YOU'RE BACK AT THE COLLEGE. YOU'RE A FREE MAN NOW, UNCLE DUKE. BABY DOC IS HISTORY!
BUT.. BUT.. HOW?
I BOUGHT YOU WITH MY REMAINING LOTTERY MONEY. $17 MILLION.
YOU SPENT.. $17 MILLION.. TO.. GET.. ME.. BACK?
NO BIG DEAL. YOU WOULD HAVE DONE THE SAME FOR..
YOU IDIOT!
©GBTrudeau

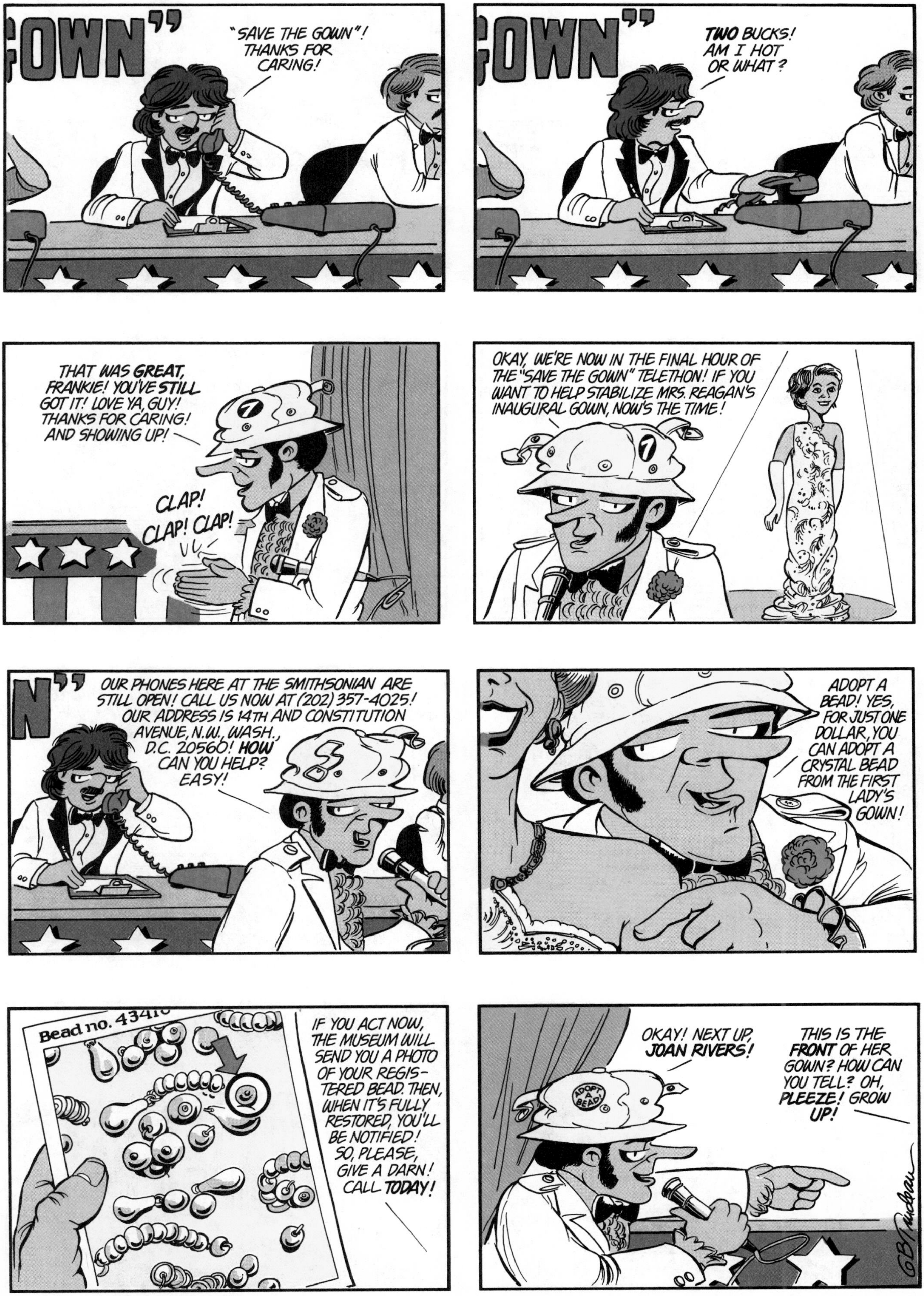
GOWN”
"SAVE THE GOWN"! THANKS FOR CARING!
GOWN”
TWO BUCKS! AM I HOT OR WHAT?
THAT WAS **GREAT**, FRANKIE! YOU'VE **STILL** GOT IT! LOVE YA, GUY! THANKS FOR CARING! AND SHOWING UP!
CLAP! CLAP! CLAP!
OKAY, WE'RE NOW IN THE FINAL HOUR OF THE "SAVE THE GOWN" TELETHON! IF YOU WANT TO HELP STABILIZE MRS. REAGAN'S INAUGURAL GOWN, NOW'S THE TIME!
N”
OUR PHONES HERE AT THE SMITHSONIAN ARE STILL OPEN! CALL US NOW AT (202) 357-4025! OUR ADDRESS IS 14TH AND CONSTITUTION AVENUE, N.W., WASH., D.C. 20560! **HOW** CAN YOU HELP? EASY!
ADOPT A BEAD! YES, FOR JUST ONE DOLLAR, YOU CAN ADOPT A CRYSTAL BEAD FROM THE FIRST LADY'S GOWN!
Bead no. 4341
IF YOU ACT NOW, THE MUSEUM WILL SEND YOU A PHOTO OF YOUR REGISTERED BEAD. THEN, WHEN IT'S FULLY RESTORED, YOU'LL BE NOTIFIED! SO, PLEASE, GIVE A DARN! CALL **TODAY**!
ADOPT A BEAD!
OKAY! NEXT UP, **JOAN RIVERS**!
THIS IS THE **FRONT** OF HER GOWN? HOW CAN YOU TELL? OH, **PLEEZE**! GROW **UP**!

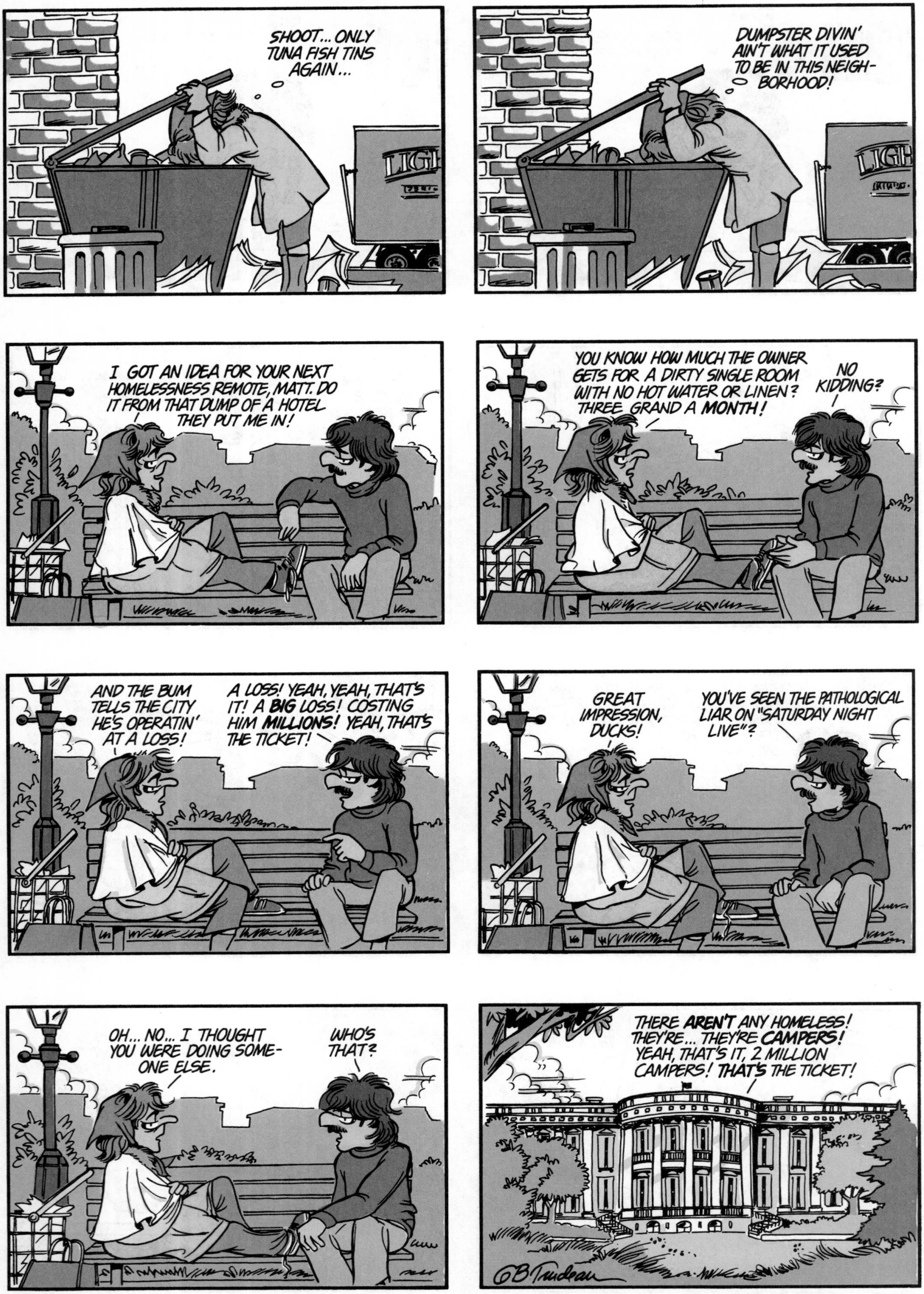
SHOOT... ONLY TUNA FISH TINS AGAIN...
LIGH
DUMPSTER DIVIN' AIN'T WHAT IT USED TO BE IN THIS NEIGH-BORHOOD!
LIGH
I GOT AN IDEA FOR YOUR NEXT HOMELESSNESS REMOTE, MATT. DO IT FROM THAT DUMP OF A HOTEL THEY PUT ME IN!
YOU KNOW HOW MUCH THE OWNER GETS FOR A DIRTY SINGLE ROOM WITH NO HOT WATER OR LINEN? THREE GRAND A MONTH!
NO KIDDING?
AND THE BUM TELLS THE CITY HE'S OPERATIN' AT A LOSS!
A LOSS! YEAH, YEAH, THAT'S IT! A BIG LOSS! COSTING HIM MILLIONS! YEAH, THAT'S THE TICKET!
GREAT IMPRESSION, DUCKS!
YOU'VE SEEN THE PATHOLOGICAL LIAR ON "SATURDAY NIGHT LIVE"?
OH... NO... I THOUGHT YOU WERE DOING SOME-ONE ELSE.
WHO'S THAT?
THERE AREN'T ANY HOMELESS! THEY'RE... THEY'RE CAMPERS! YEAH, THAT'S IT, 2 MILLION CAMPERS! THAT'S THE TICKET!
©B. Trudeau

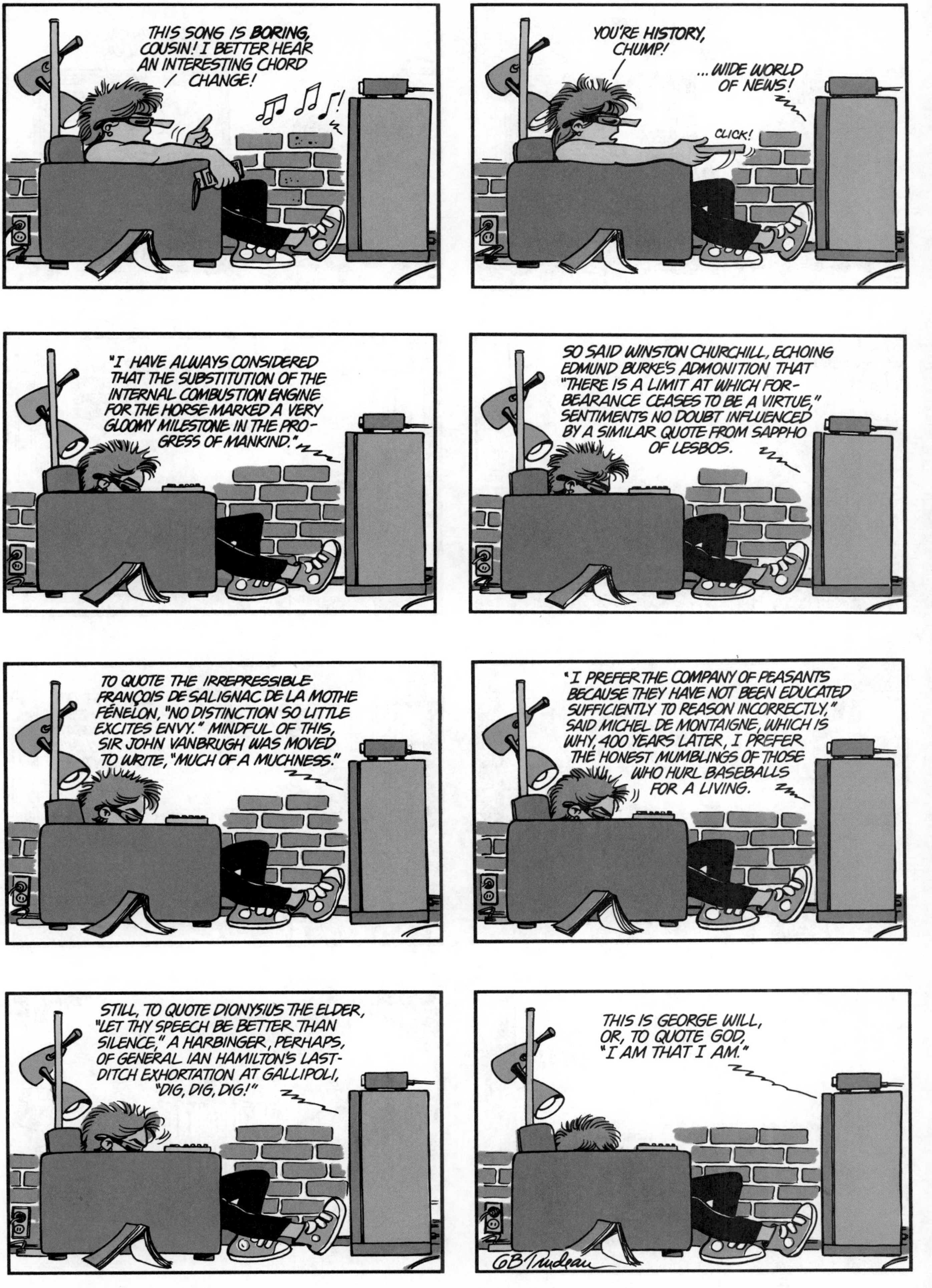
THIS SONG IS BORING, COUSIN! I BETTER HEAR AN INTERESTING CHORD CHANGE!
YOU'RE HISTORY, CHUMP!
...WIDE WORLD OF NEWS!
CLICK!
"I HAVE ALWAYS CONSIDERED THAT THE SUBSTITUTION OF THE INTERNAL COMBUSTION ENGINE FOR THE HORSE MARKED A VERY GLOOMY MILESTONE IN THE PROGRESS OF MANKIND."
SO SAID WINSTON CHURCHILL, ECHOING EDMUND BURKE'S ADMONITION THAT "THERE IS A LIMIT AT WHICH FORBEARANCE CEASES TO BE A VIRTUE," SENTIMENTS NO DOUBT INFLUENCED BY A SIMILAR QUOTE FROM SAPPHO OF LESBOS.
TO QUOTE THE IRREPRESSIBLE FRANÇOIS DE SALIGNAC DE LA MOTHE FÉNELON, "NO DISTINCTION SO LITTLE EXCITES ENVY." MINDFUL OF THIS, SIR JOHN VANBRUGH WAS MOVED TO WRITE, "MUCH OF A MUCHNESS."
"I PREFER THE COMPANY OF PEASANTS BECAUSE THEY HAVE NOT BEEN EDUCATED SUFFICIENTLY TO REASON INCORRECTLY," SAID MICHEL DE MONTAIGNE, WHICH IS WHY, 400 YEARS LATER, I PREFER THE HONEST MUMBLINGS OF THOSE WHO HURL BASEBALLS FOR A LIVING.
STILL, TO QUOTE DIONYSIUS THE ELDER, "LET THY SPEECH BE BETTER THAN SILENCE," A HARBINGER, PERHAPS, OF GENERAL IAN HAMILTON'S LAST-DITCH EXHORTATION AT GALLIPOLI, "DIG, DIG, DIG!"
THIS IS GEORGE WILL, OR, TO QUOTE GOD, "I AM THAT I AM."
GB Trudeau

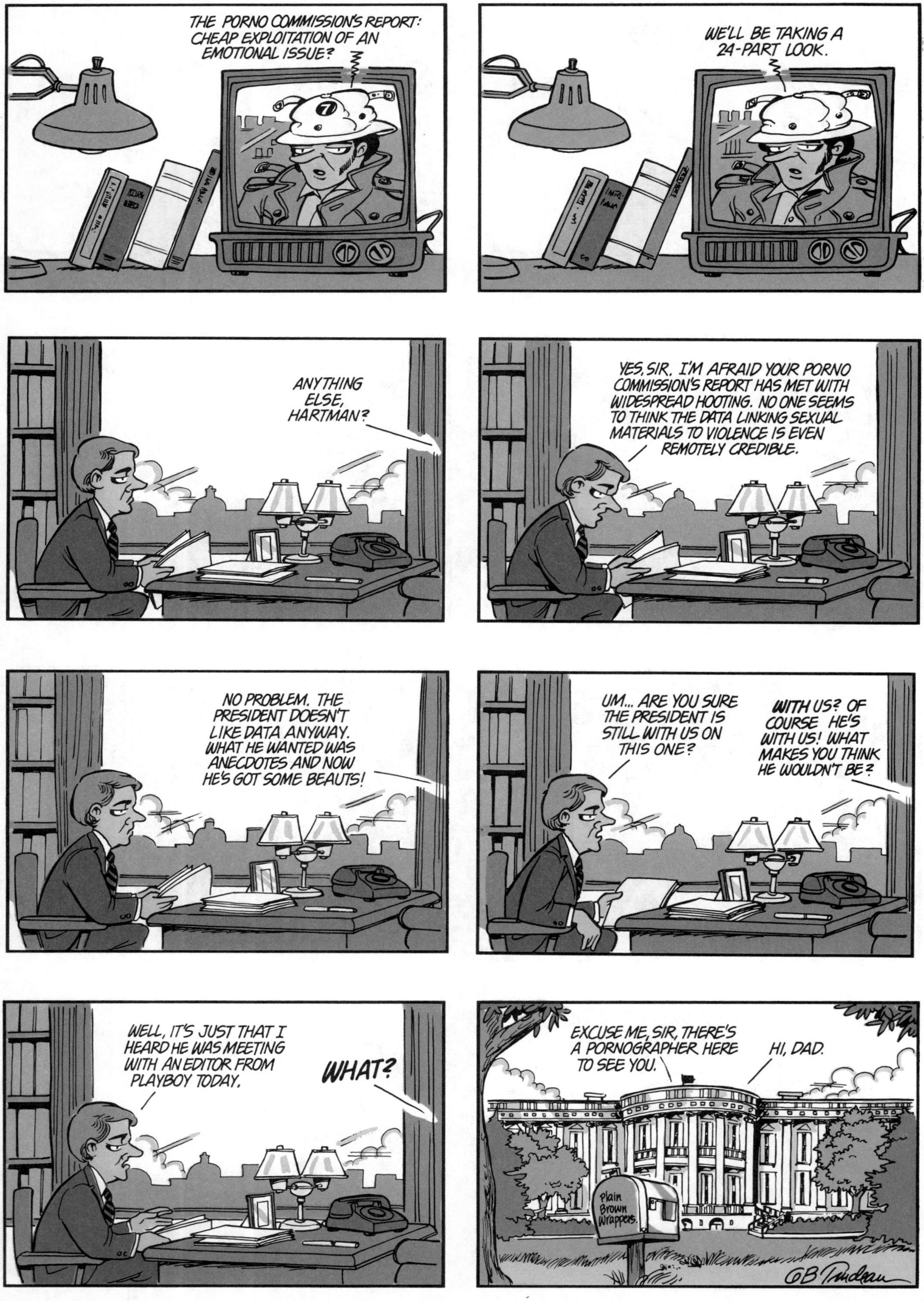
THE PORNO COMMISSION'S REPORT: CHEAP EXPLOITATION OF AN EMOTIONAL ISSUE?
WE'LL BE TAKING A 24-PART LOOK.
ANYTHING ELSE, HARTMAN?
YES, SIR. I'M AFRAID YOUR PORNO COMMISSION'S REPORT HAS MET WITH WIDESPREAD HOOTING. NO ONE SEEMS TO THINK THE DATA LINKING SEXUAL MATERIALS TO VIOLENCE IS EVEN REMOTELY CREDIBLE.
NO PROBLEM. THE PRESIDENT DOESN'T LIKE DATA ANYWAY. WHAT HE WANTED WAS ANECDOTES AND NOW HE'S GOT SOME BEAUTS!
UM... ARE YOU SURE THE PRESIDENT IS STILL WITH US ON THIS ONE?
WITH US? OF COURSE HE'S WITH US! WHAT MAKES YOU THINK HE WOULDN'T BE?
WELL, IT'S JUST THAT I HEARD HE WAS MEETING WITH AN EDITOR FROM PLAYBOY TODAY.
WHAT?
EXCUSE ME, SIR, THERE'S A PORNOGRAPHER HERE TO SEE YOU.
HI, DAD.
Plain Brown Wrappers
GB Trudeau

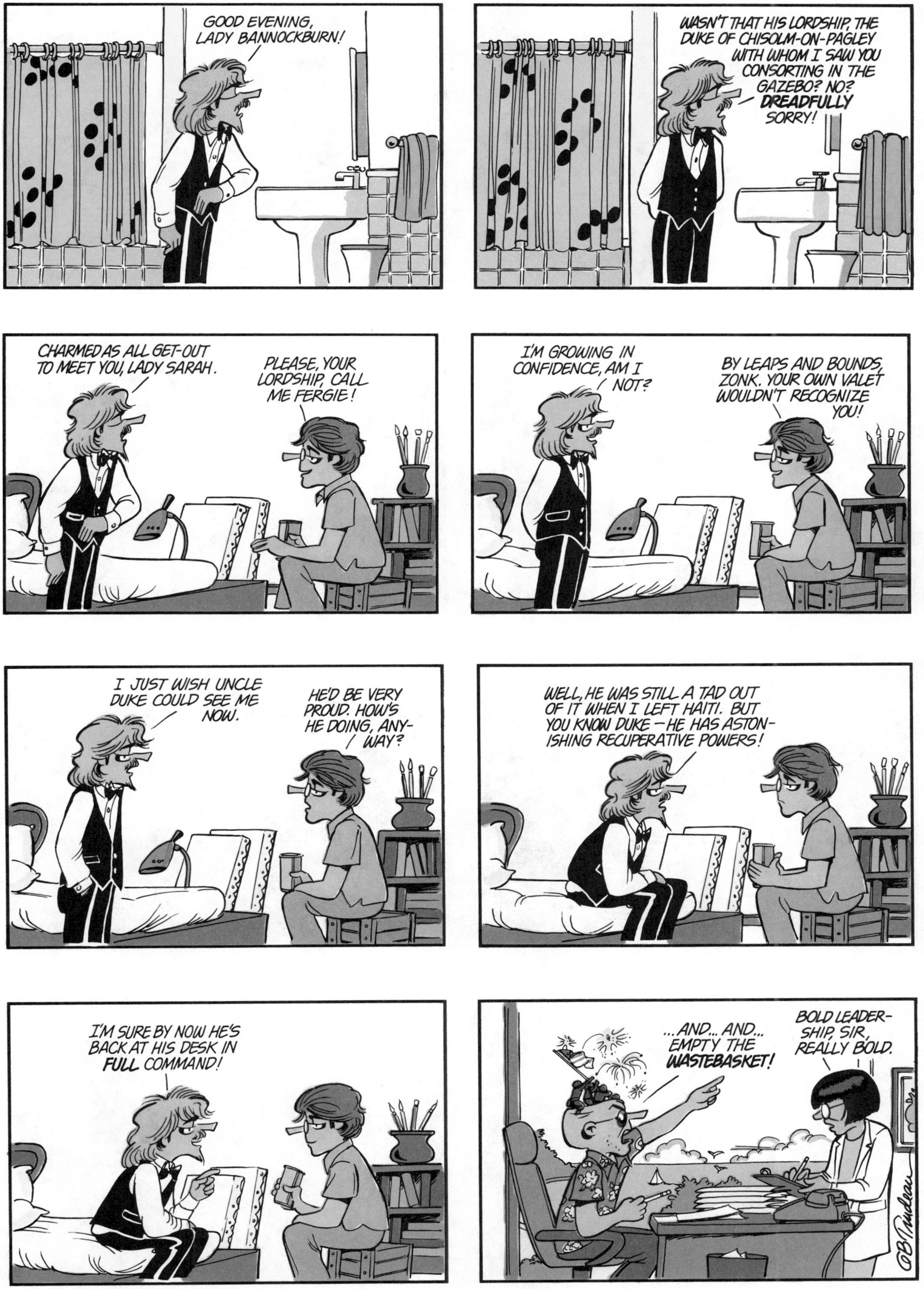
GOOD EVENING, LADY BANNOCKBURN!
WASN'T THAT HIS LORDSHIP, THE DUKE OF CHISOLM-ON-PAGLEY WITH WHOM I SAW YOU CONSORTING IN THE GAZEBO? NO? **DREADFULLY** SORRY!
CHARMED AS ALL GET-OUT TO MEET YOU, LADY SARAH.
PLEASE, YOUR LORDSHIP, CALL ME FERGIE!
I'M GROWING IN CONFIDENCE, AM I NOT?
BY LEAPS AND BOUNDS, ZONK. YOUR OWN VALET WOULDN'T RECOGNIZE YOU!
I JUST WISH UNCLE DUKE COULD SEE ME NOW.
HE'D BE VERY PROUD. HOW'S HE DOING, ANYWAY?
WELL, HE WAS STILL A TAD OUT OF IT WHEN I LEFT HAITI. BUT YOU KNOW DUKE—HE HAS ASTONISHING RECUPERATIVE POWERS!
I'M SURE BY NOW HE'S BACK AT HIS DESK IN **FULL** COMMAND!
...AND... AND... EMPTY THE **WASTEBASKET**!
BOLD LEADERSHIP, SIR, REALLY BOLD.
©B Trudeau

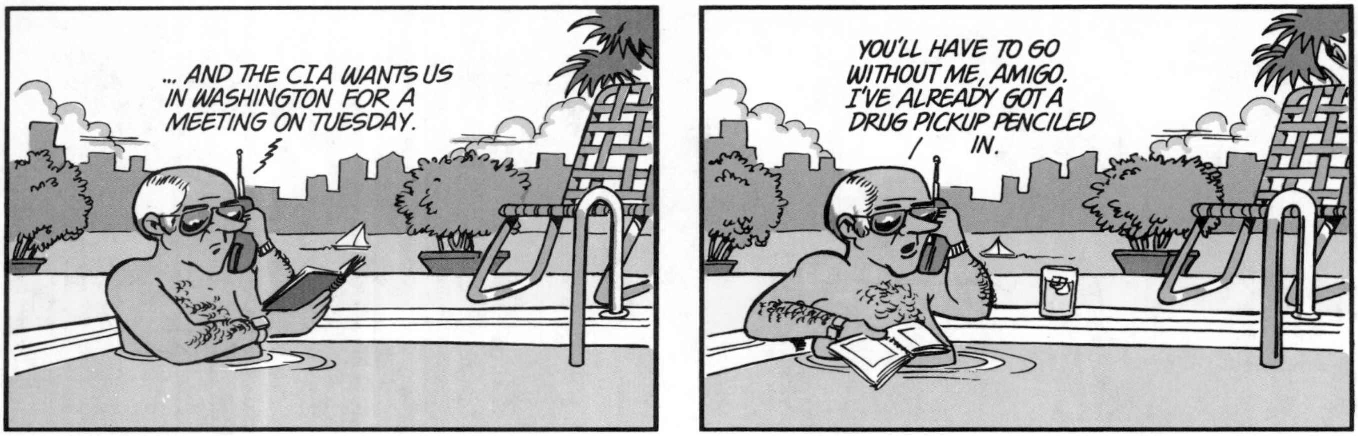
... AND THE CIA WANTS US IN WASHINGTON FOR A MEETING ON TUESDAY.
YOU'LL HAVE TO GO WITHOUT ME, AMIGO. I'VE ALREADY GOT A DRUG PICKUP PENCILED IN.

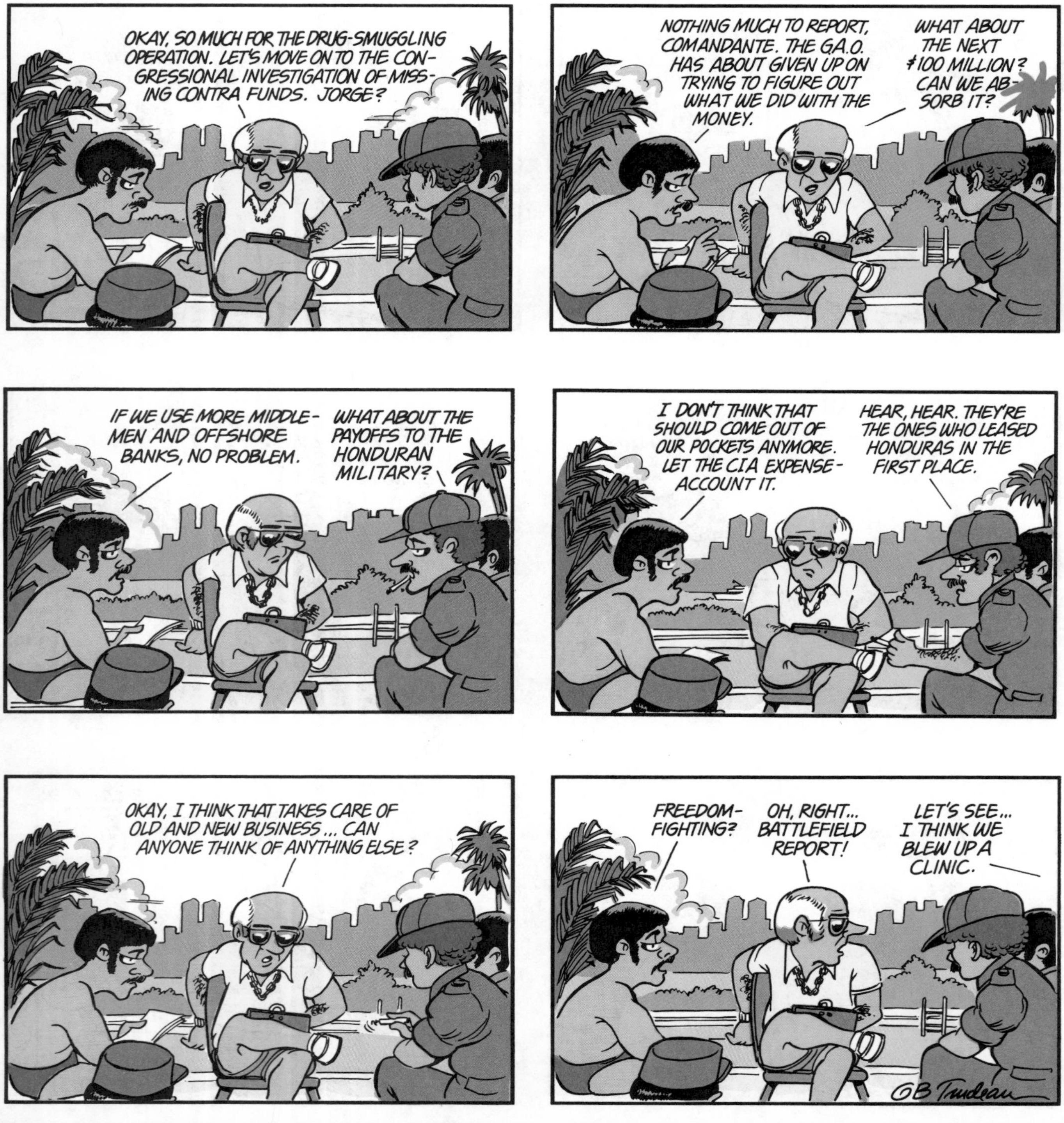
OKAY, SO MUCH FOR THE DRUG-SMUGGLING OPERATION. LET'S MOVE ON TO THE CONGRESSIONAL INVESTIGATION OF MISSING CONTRA FUNDS. JORGE?
NOTHING MUCH TO REPORT, COMANDANTE. THE G.A.O. HAS ABOUT GIVEN UP ON TRYING TO FIGURE OUT WHAT WE DID WITH THE MONEY.
WHAT ABOUT THE NEXT $100 MILLION? CAN WE ABSORB IT?
IF WE USE MORE MIDDLEMEN AND OFFSHORE BANKS, NO PROBLEM.
WHAT ABOUT THE PAYOFFS TO THE HONDURAN MILITARY?
I DON'T THINK THAT SHOULD COME OUT OF OUR POCKETS ANYMORE. LET THE CIA EXPENSE-ACCOUNT IT.
HEAR, HEAR. THEY'RE THE ONES WHO LEASED HONDURAS IN THE FIRST PLACE.
OKAY, I THINK THAT TAKES CARE OF OLD AND NEW BUSINESS ... CAN ANYONE THINK OF ANYTHING ELSE?
FREEDOM-FIGHTING?
OH, RIGHT... BATTLEFIELD REPORT!
LET'S SEE... I THINK WE BLEW UP A CLINIC.
©B Trudeau

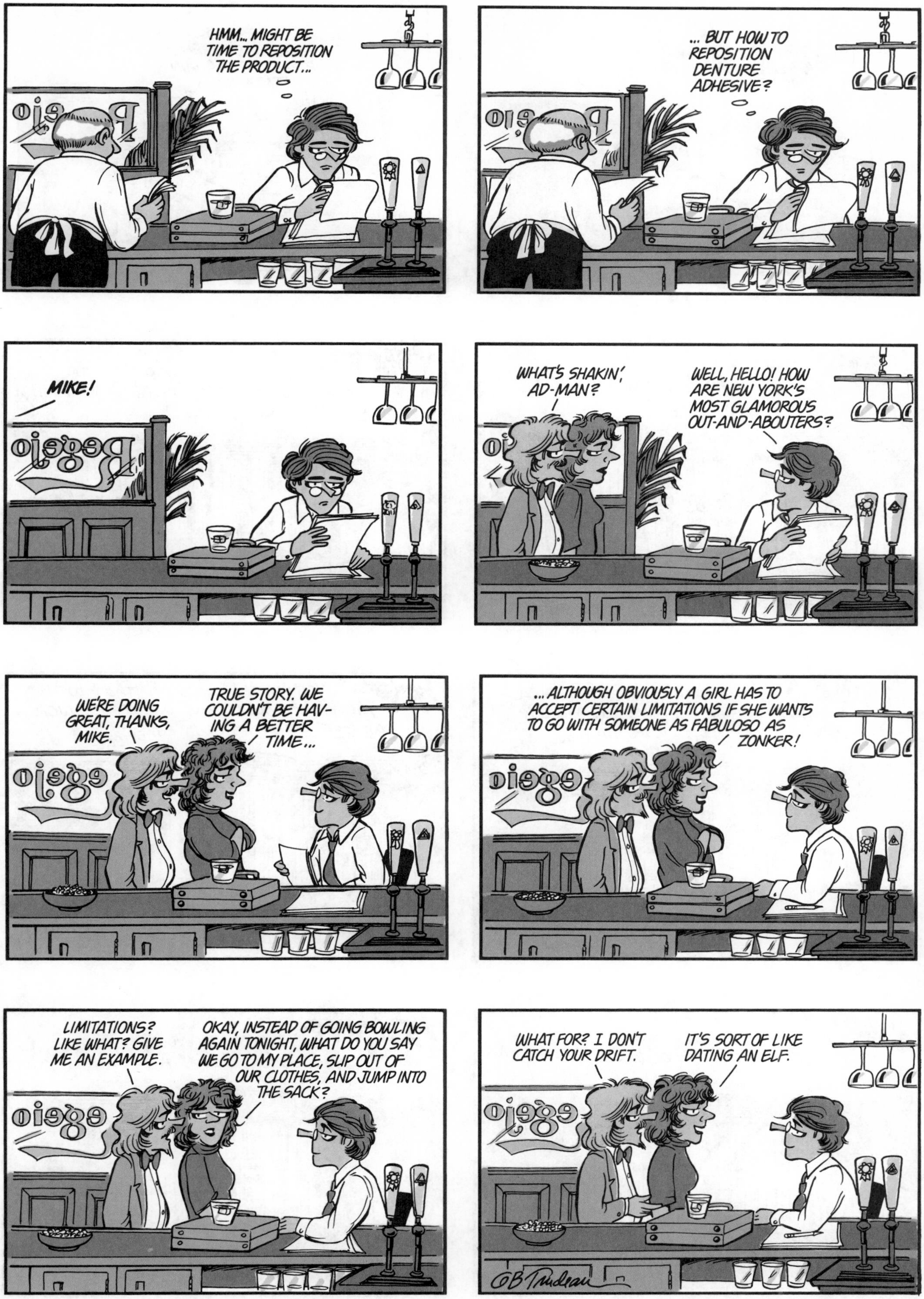
HMM... MIGHT BE TIME TO REPOSITION THE PRODUCT...
... BUT HOW TO REPOSITION DENTURE ADHESIVE?
MIKE!
WHAT'S SHAKIN', AD-MAN?
WELL, HELLO! HOW ARE NEW YORK'S MOST GLAMOROUS OUT-AND-ABOUTERS?
WE'RE DOING GREAT, THANKS, MIKE.
TRUE STORY. WE COULDN'T BE HAVING A BETTER TIME...
... ALTHOUGH OBVIOUSLY A GIRL HAS TO ACCEPT CERTAIN LIMITATIONS IF SHE WANTS TO GO WITH SOMEONE AS FABULOSO AS ZONKER!
LIMITATIONS? LIKE WHAT? GIVE ME AN EXAMPLE.
OKAY, INSTEAD OF GOING BOWLING AGAIN TONIGHT, WHAT DO YOU SAY WE GO TO MY PLACE, SLIP OUT OF OUR CLOTHES, AND JUMP INTO THE SACK?
WHAT FOR? I DON'T CATCH YOUR DRIFT.
IT'S SORT OF LIKE DATING AN ELF.
©B Trudeau

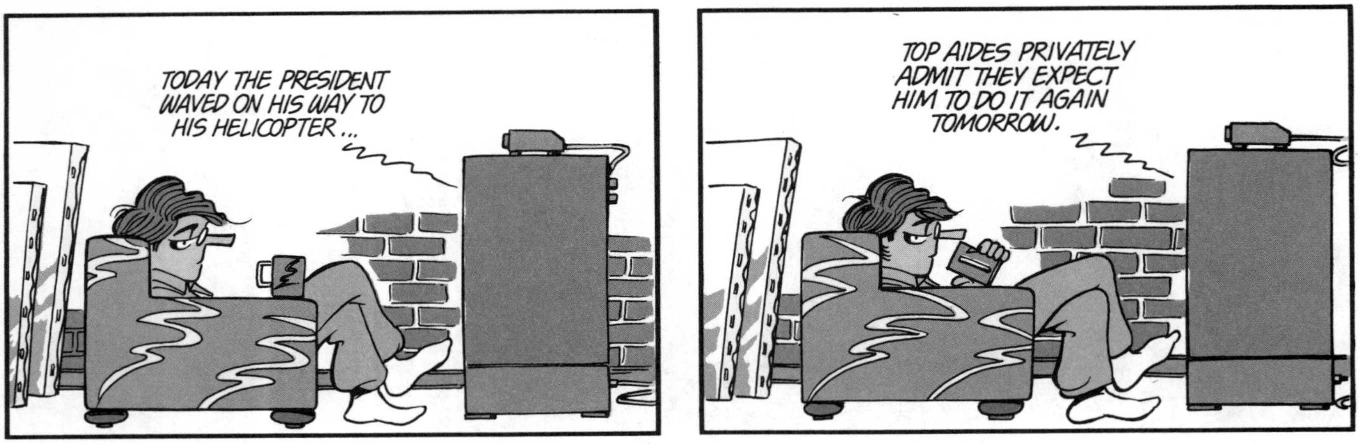
TODAY THE PRESIDENT WAVED ON HIS WAY TO HIS HELICOPTER ...
TOP AIDES PRIVATELY ADMIT THEY EXPECT HIM TO DO IT AGAIN TOMORROW.

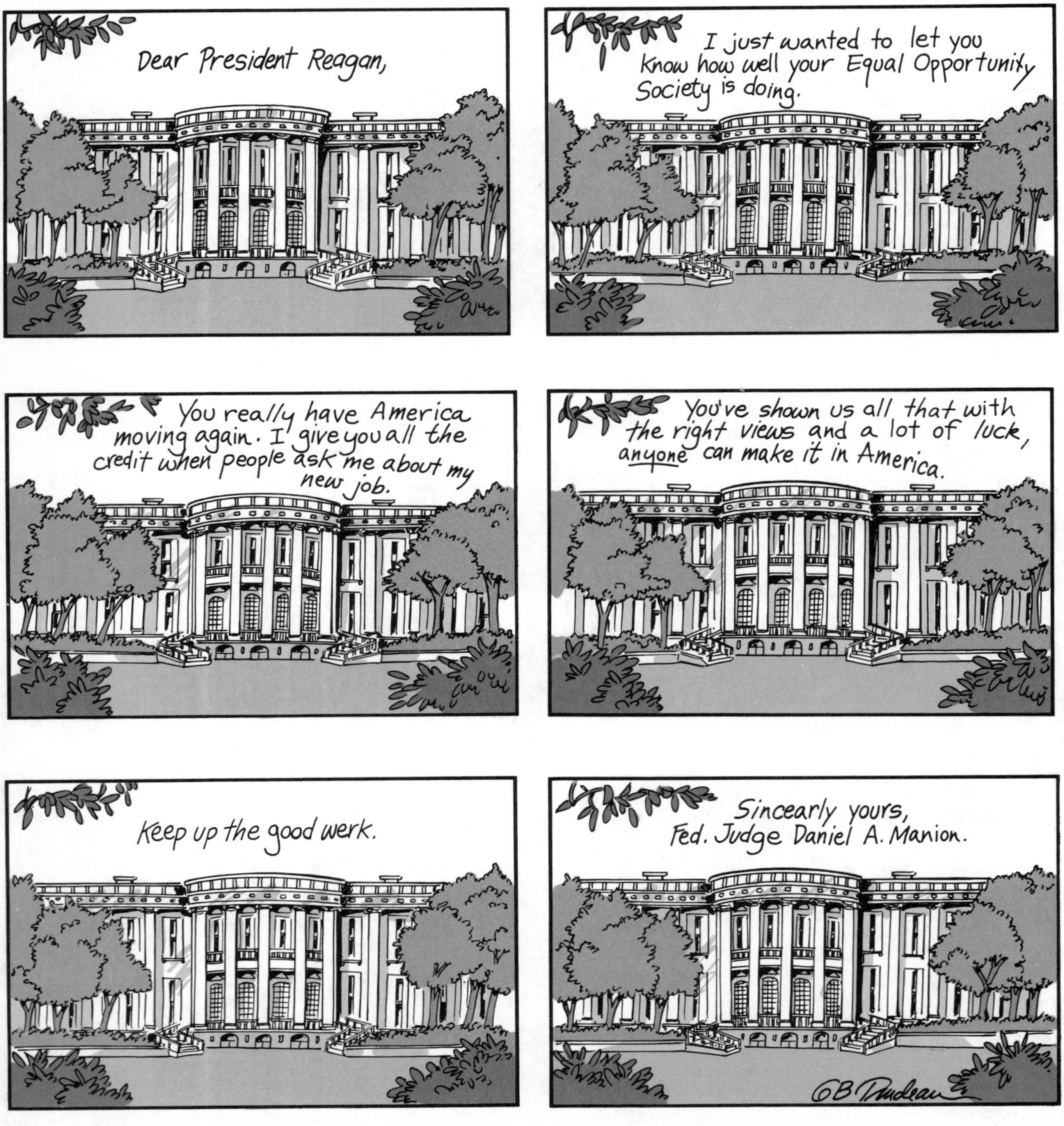
Dear President Reagan,
I just wanted to let you know how well your Equal Opportunity Society is doing.
You really have America moving again. I give you all the credit when people ask me about my new job.
You've shown us all that with the right views and a lot of luck, anyone can make it in America.
Keep up the good werk.
Sincearly yours,
Fed. Judge Daniel A. Manion.
GB Trudeau

"ERGO, PURSUANT TO THE AFOREMENTIONED, TO WIT, THE PARTIES ADDRESSED HEREIN..."
TAP! TAP! TAP!
HMM... BETTER GET TO THE POINT.
SIR, WITH SCHOOL ABOUT TO START, I DECIDED TO DRAW UP THAT MEMO I DISCUSSED WITH YOU...
IT'S JUST A TEMPORARY ARRANGEMENT BY WHICH YOU DESIGNATE ME ACTING-PRESIDENT UNTIL SUCH TIME AS YOU REGAIN YOUR FULL FACULTIES.
YOU WOULD, OF COURSE, CONTINUE ON AS SCHOOL FIGUREHEAD, PER-HAPS IN THE CAPACITY OF "BELOVED FOUNDER". SO IF YOU'LL JUST INITIAL THIS...
AWK!
AWK! AWK! AWK!
HIIIIYAK!!! WOOT! WOOT!
RRIIPP!
WHUMPA! WHUMPA!
SPROING
FRANKLY, SIR, I WAS HOPING FOR A MORE ORDERLY TRANSFER OF POWER.
MMPH...

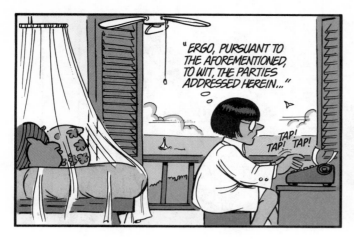

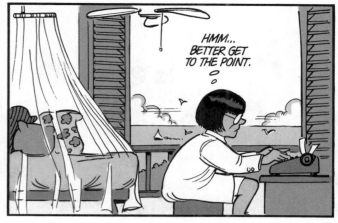

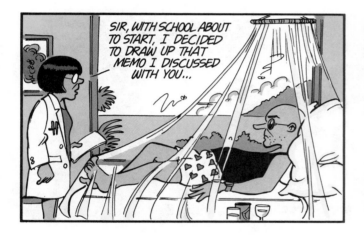

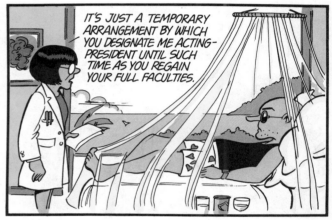

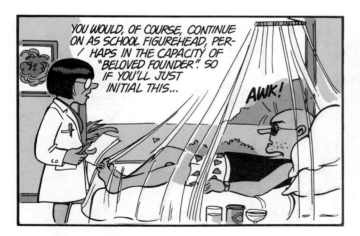

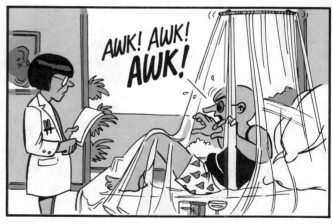

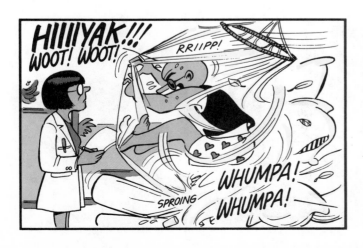

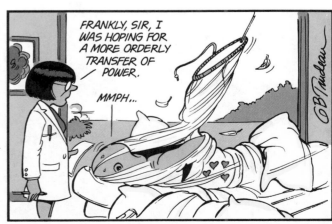

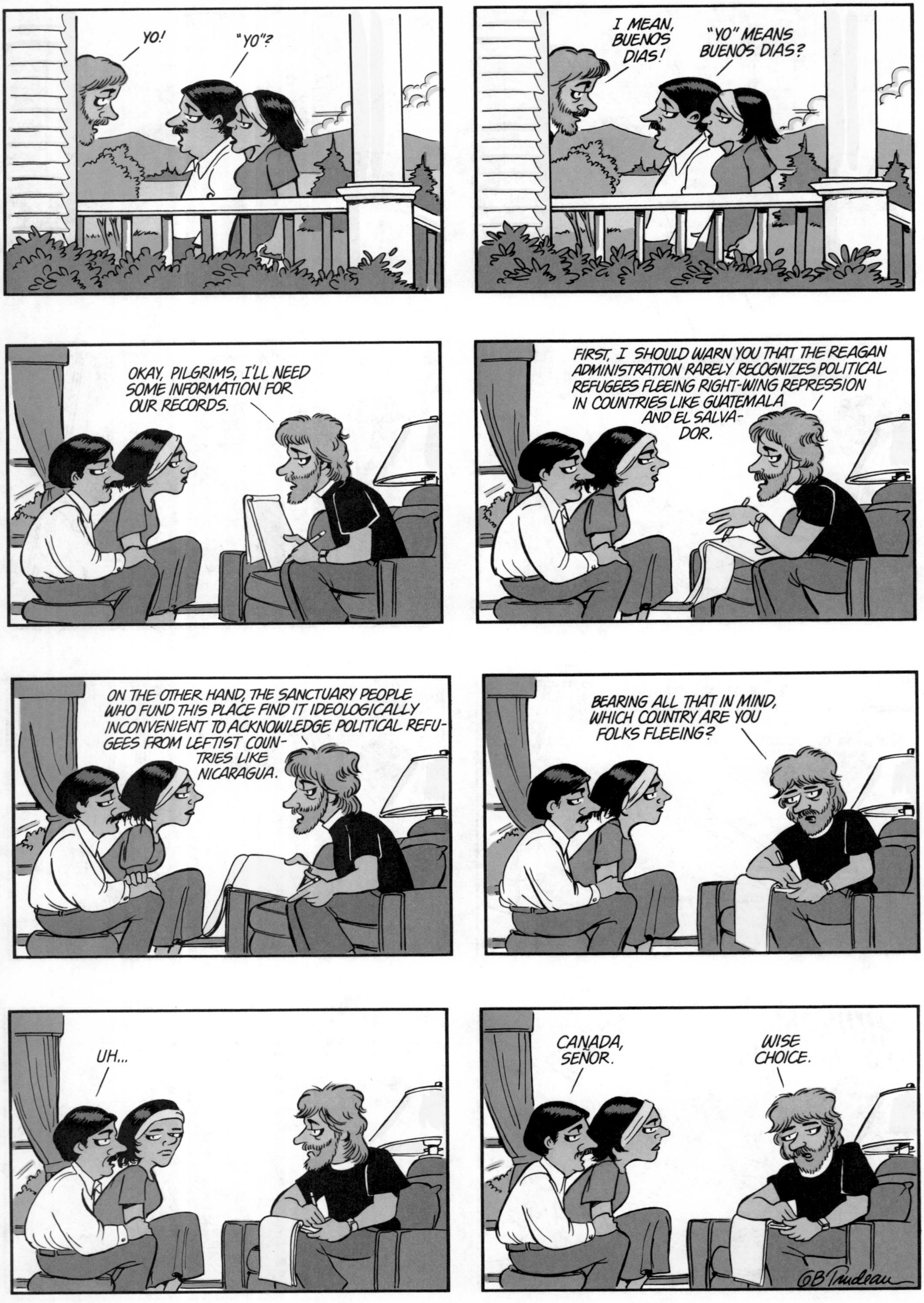
YO!
"YO"?
I MEAN, BUENOS DIAS!
"YO" MEANS BUENOS DIAS?
OKAY, PILGRIMS, I'LL NEED SOME INFORMATION FOR OUR RECORDS.
FIRST, I SHOULD WARN YOU THAT THE REAGAN ADMINISTRATION RARELY RECOGNIZES POLITICAL REFUGEES FLEEING RIGHT-WING REPRESSION IN COUNTRIES LIKE GUATEMALA AND EL SALVADOR.
ON THE OTHER HAND, THE SANCTUARY PEOPLE WHO FUND THIS PLACE FIND IT IDEOLOGICALLY INCONVENIENT TO ACKNOWLEDGE POLITICAL REFUGEES FROM LEFTIST COUNTRIES LIKE NICARAGUA.
BEARING ALL THAT IN MIND, WHICH COUNTRY ARE YOU FOLKS FLEEING?
UH...
CANADA, SEÑOR.
WISE CHOICE.
GB Trudeau

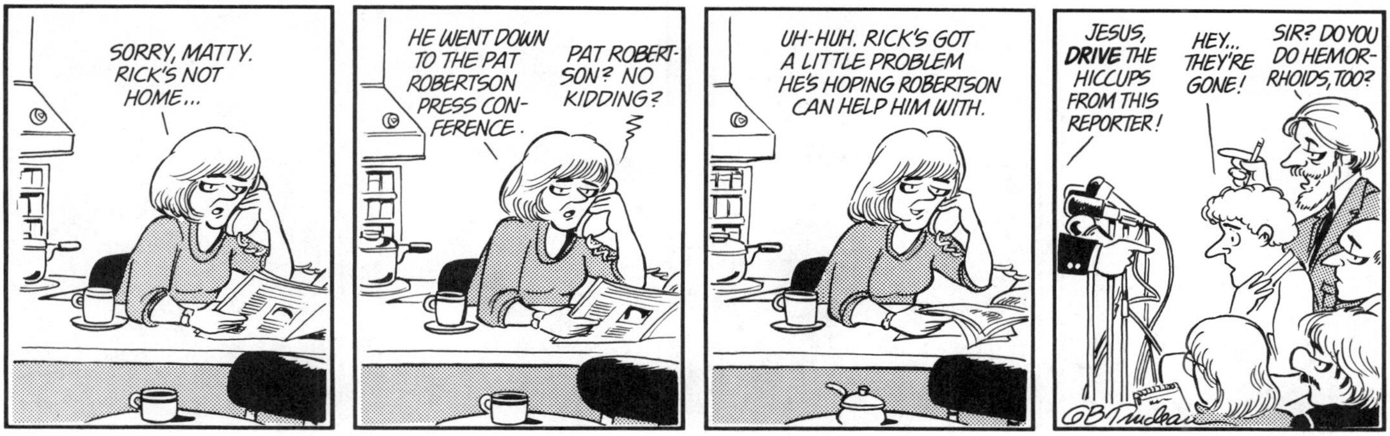
SORRY, MATTY. RICK'S NOT HOME...
HE WENT DOWN TO THE PAT ROBERTSON PRESS CONFERENCE.
PAT ROBERTSON? NO KIDDING?
UH-HUH. RICK'S GOT A LITTLE PROBLEM HE'S HOPING ROBERTSON CAN HELP HIM WITH.
JESUS, DRIVE THE HICCUPS FROM THIS REPORTER!
HEY... THEY'RE GONE!
SIR? DO YOU DO HEMORRHOIDS, TOO?

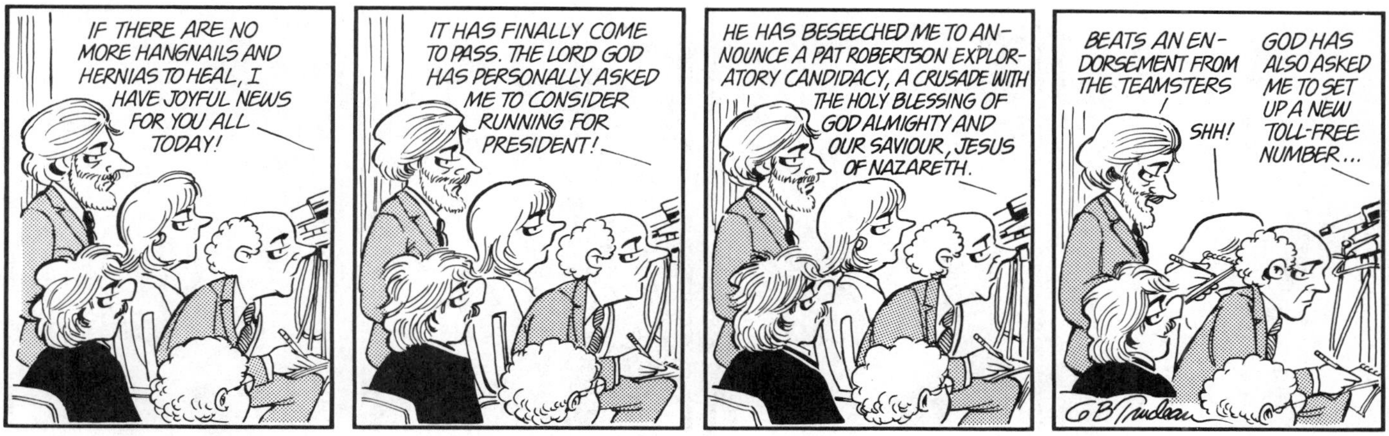
IF THERE ARE NO MORE HANGNAILS AND HERNIAS TO HEAL, I HAVE JOYFUL NEWS FOR YOU ALL TODAY!
IT HAS FINALLY COME TO PASS. THE LORD GOD HAS PERSONALLY ASKED ME TO CONSIDER RUNNING FOR PRESIDENT!
HE HAS BESEECHED ME TO ANNOUNCE A PAT ROBERTSON EXPLORATORY CANDIDACY, A CRUSADE WITH THE HOLY BLESSING OF GOD ALMIGHTY AND OUR SAVIOUR, JESUS OF NAZARETH.
BEATS AN ENDORSEMENT FROM THE TEAMSTERS
SHH!
GOD HAS ALSO ASKED ME TO SET UP A NEW TOLL-FREE NUMBER...

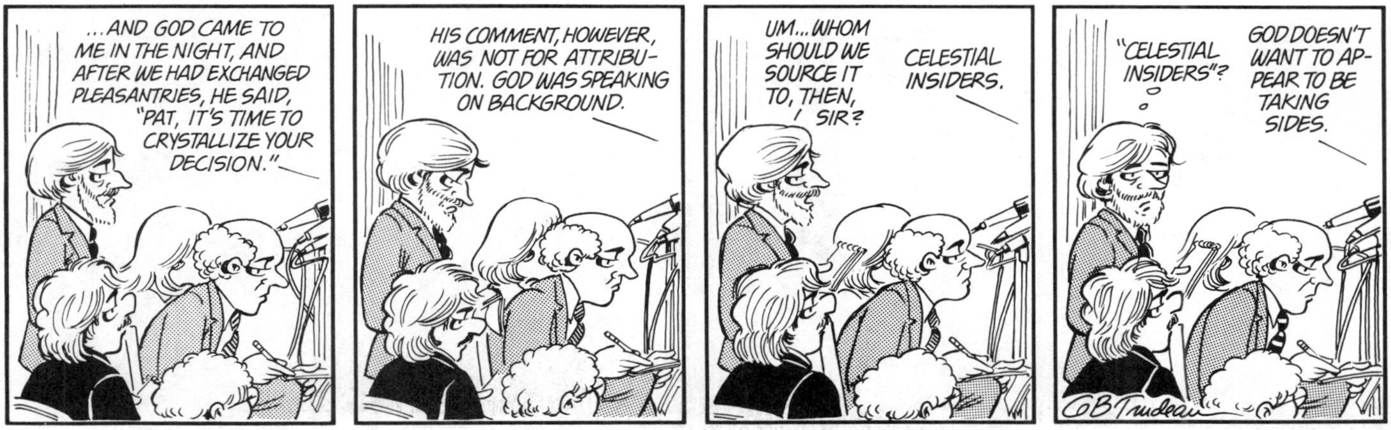
...AND GOD CAME TO ME IN THE NIGHT, AND AFTER WE HAD EXCHANGED PLEASANTRIES, HE SAID, "PAT, IT'S TIME TO CRYSTALLIZE YOUR DECISION."
HIS COMMENT, HOWEVER, WAS NOT FOR ATTRIBUTION. GOD WAS SPEAKING ON BACKGROUND.
UM... WHOM SHOULD WE SOURCE IT TO, THEN, SIR?
CELESTIAL INSIDERS.
"CELESTIAL INSIDERS"?
GOD DOESN'T WANT TO APPEAR TO BE TAKING SIDES.

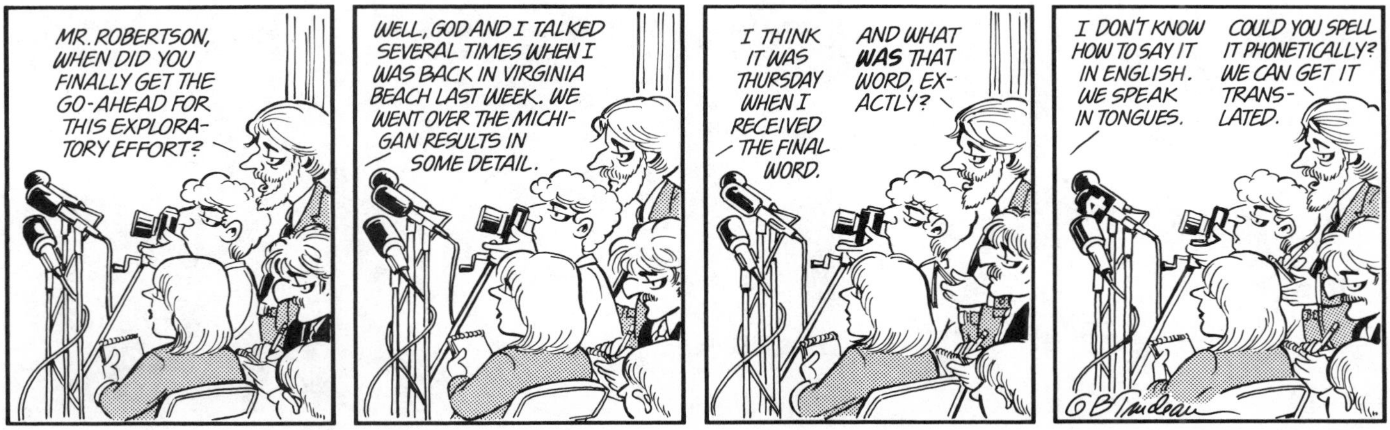
MR. ROBERTSON, WHEN DID YOU FINALLY GET THE GO-AHEAD FOR THIS EXPLORATORY EFFORT?
WELL, GOD AND I TALKED SEVERAL TIMES WHEN I WAS BACK IN VIRGINIA BEACH LAST WEEK. WE WENT OVER THE MICHIGAN RESULTS IN SOME DETAIL.
I THINK IT WAS THURSDAY WHEN I RECEIVED THE FINAL WORD.
AND WHAT WAS THAT WORD, EXACTLY?
I DON'T KNOW HOW TO SAY IT IN ENGLISH. WE SPEAK IN TONGUES.
COULD YOU SPELL IT PHONETICALLY? WE CAN GET IT TRANSLATED.

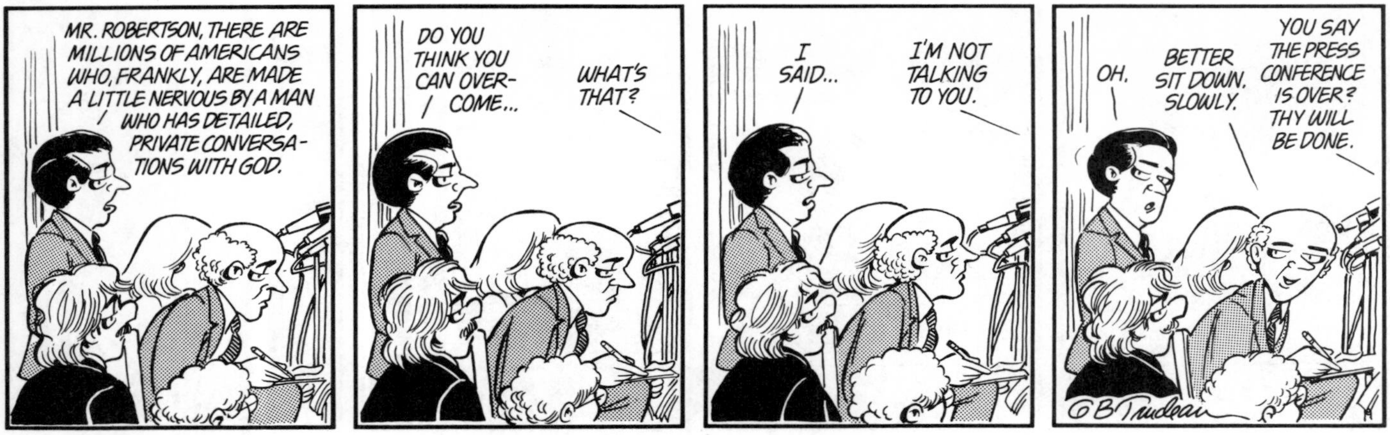
MR. ROBERTSON, THERE ARE MILLIONS OF AMERICANS WHO, FRANKLY, ARE MADE A LITTLE NERVOUS BY A MAN WHO HAS DETAILED, PRIVATE CONVERSATIONS WITH GOD.
DO YOU THINK YOU CAN OVERCOME...
WHAT'S THAT?
I SAID...
I'M NOT TALKING TO YOU.
OH.
BETTER SIT DOWN. SLOWLY.
YOU SAY THE PRESS CONFERENCE IS OVER? THY WILL BE DONE.
GBTrudeau

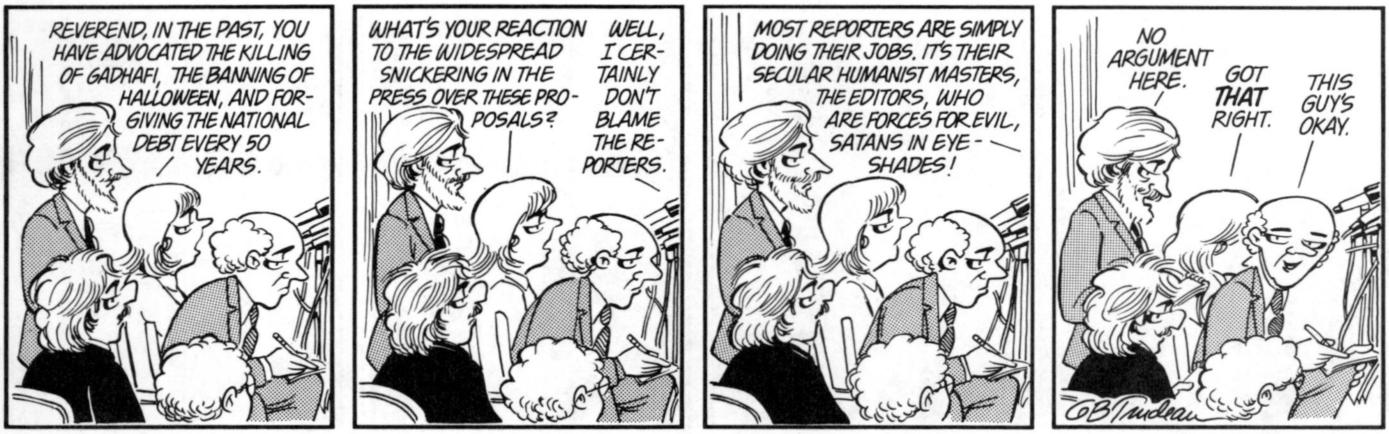
REVEREND, IN THE PAST, YOU HAVE ADVOCATED THE KILLING OF GADHAFI, THE BANNING OF HALLOWEEN, AND FORGIVING THE NATIONAL DEBT EVERY 50 YEARS.
WHAT'S YOUR REACTION TO THE WIDESPREAD SNICKERING IN THE PRESS OVER THESE PROPOSALS?
WELL, I CERTAINLY DON'T BLAME THE REPORTERS.
MOST REPORTERS ARE SIMPLY DOING THEIR JOBS. IT'S THEIR SECULAR HUMANIST MASTERS, THE EDITORS, WHO ARE FORCES FOR EVIL, SATANS IN EYESHADES!
NO ARGUMENT HERE.
GOT THAT RIGHT.
THIS GUY'S OKAY.
GBTrudeau

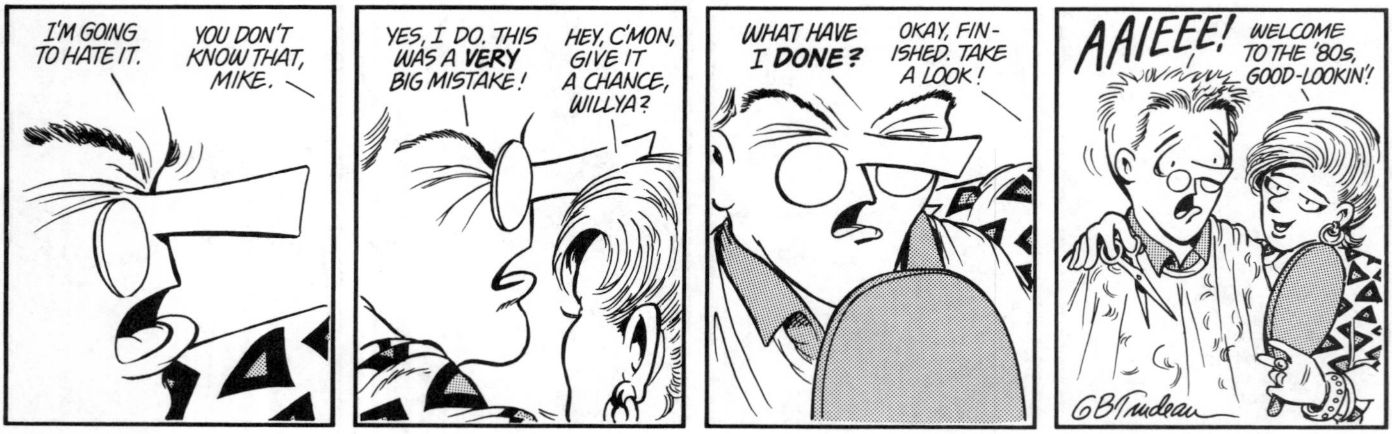
I'M GOING TO HATE IT.
YOU DON'T KNOW THAT, MIKE.
YES, I DO. THIS WAS A VERY BIG MISTAKE!
HEY, C'MON, GIVE IT A CHANCE, WILLYA?
WHAT HAVE I DONE?
OKAY, FINISHED. TAKE A LOOK!
AAIEEE!
WELCOME TO THE '80s, GOOD-LOOKIN'!
GBTrudeau

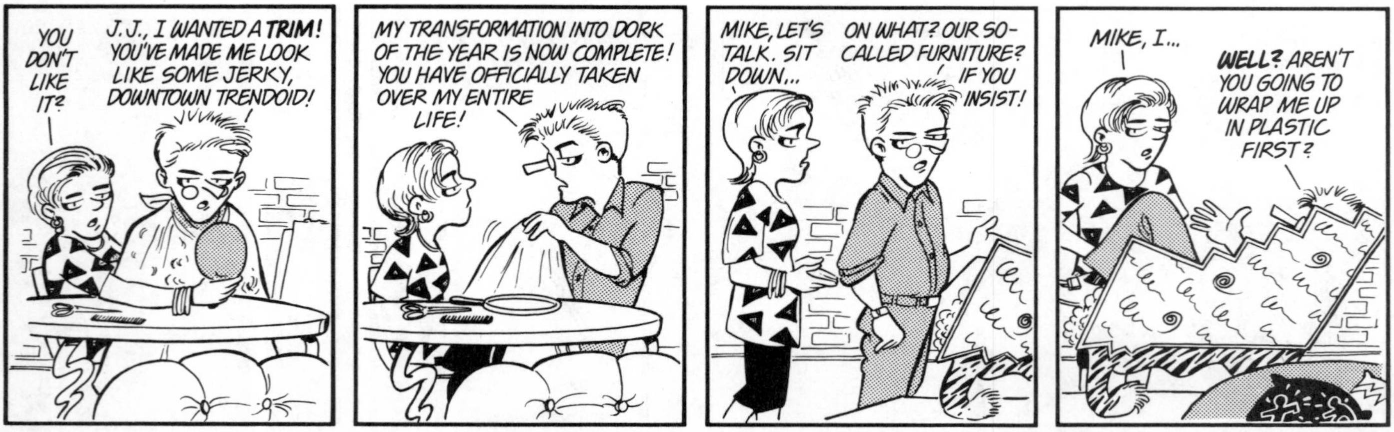
YOU DON'T LIKE IT?
J.J., I WANTED A TRIM! YOU'VE MADE ME LOOK LIKE SOME JERKY, DOWNTOWN TRENDOID!
MY TRANSFORMATION INTO DORK OF THE YEAR IS NOW COMPLETE! YOU HAVE OFFICIALLY TAKEN OVER MY ENTIRE LIFE!
MIKE, LET'S TALK. SIT DOWN...
ON WHAT? OUR SO-CALLED FURNITURE? IF YOU INSIST!
MIKE, I...
WELL? AREN'T YOU GOING TO WRAP ME UP IN PLASTIC FIRST?

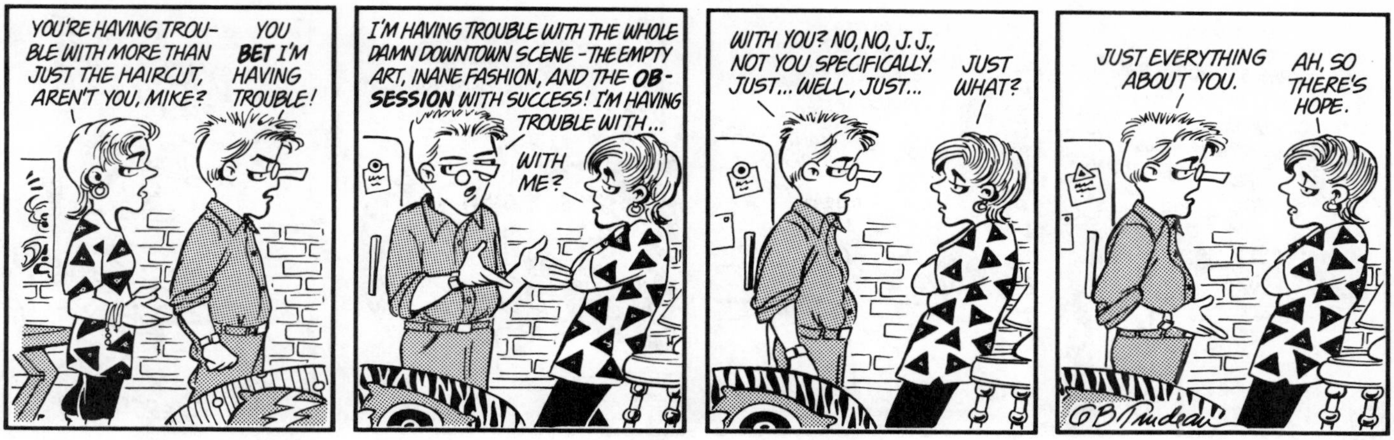
YOU'RE HAVING TROUBLE WITH MORE THAN JUST THE HAIRCUT, AREN'T YOU, MIKE?
YOU **BET** I'M HAVING TROUBLE!
I'M HAVING TROUBLE WITH THE WHOLE DAMN DOWNTOWN SCENE – THE EMPTY ART, INANE FASHION, AND THE **OBSESSION** WITH SUCCESS! I'M HAVING TROUBLE WITH...
WITH ME?
WITH YOU? NO, NO, J.J., NOT YOU SPECIFICALLY. JUST... WELL, JUST...
JUST WHAT?
JUST EVERYTHING ABOUT YOU.
AH, SO THERE'S HOPE.
GB Trudeau

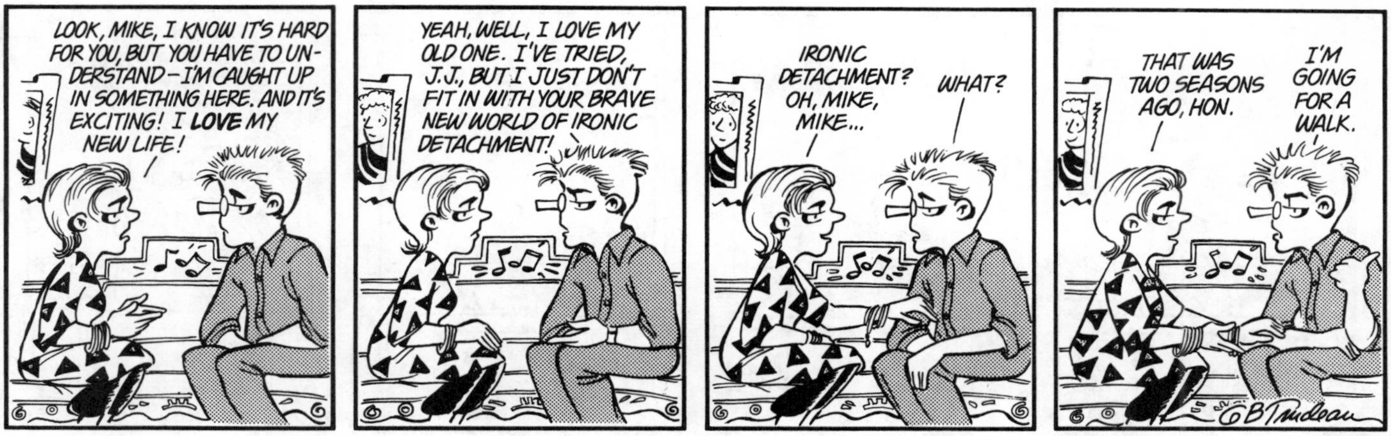
LOOK, MIKE, I KNOW IT'S HARD FOR YOU, BUT YOU HAVE TO UNDERSTAND – I'M CAUGHT UP IN SOMETHING HERE. AND IT'S EXCITING! I **LOVE** MY NEW LIFE!
YEAH, WELL, I LOVE MY OLD ONE. I'VE TRIED, J.J., BUT I JUST DON'T FIT IN WITH YOUR BRAVE NEW WORLD OF IRONIC DETACHMENT!
IRONIC DETACHMENT? OH, MIKE, MIKE...
WHAT?
THAT WAS TWO SEASONS AGO, HON.
I'M GOING FOR A WALK.
GB Trudeau

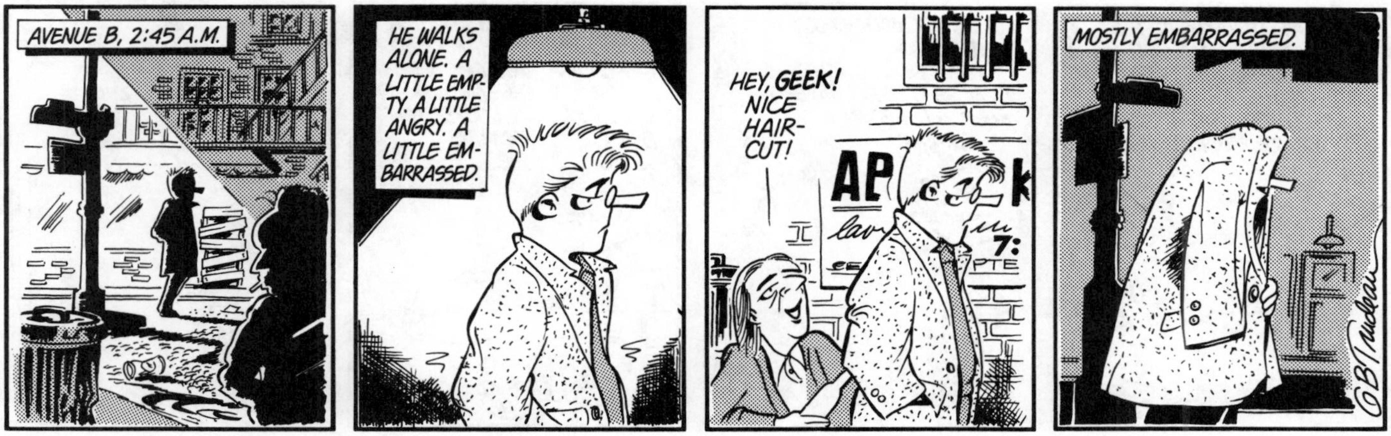
AVENUE B, 2:45 A.M.
HE WALKS ALONE. A LITTLE EMPTY. A LITTLE ANGRY. A LITTLE EMBARRASSED.
HEY, **GEEK!** NICE HAIRCUT!
MOSTLY EMBARRASSED.
GB Trudeau

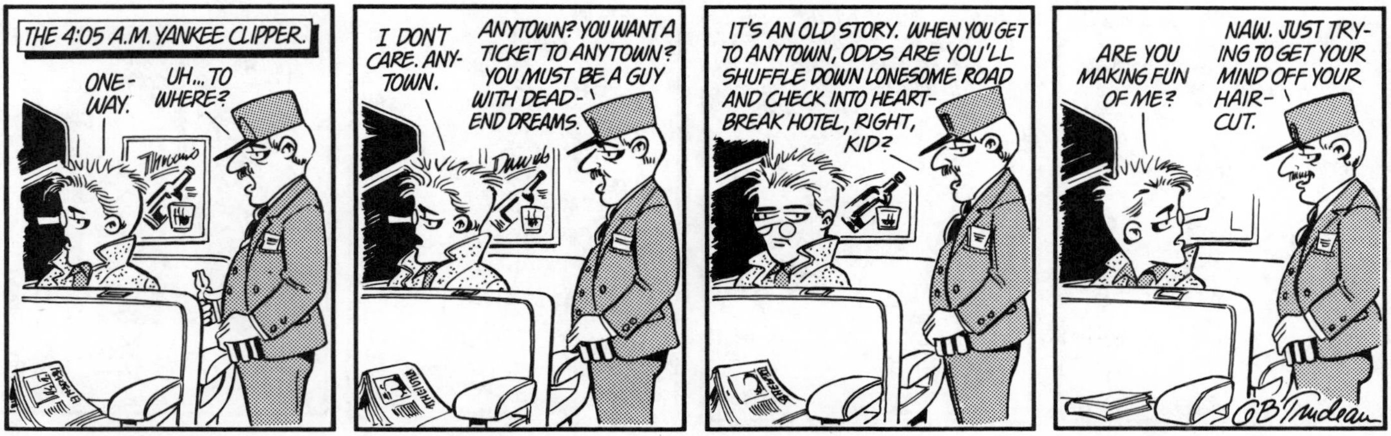
THE 4:05 A.M. YANKEE CLIPPER.
ONE-WAY.
UH... TO WHERE?
I DON'T CARE. ANYTOWN.
ANYTOWN? YOU WANT A TICKET TO ANYTOWN? YOU MUST BE A GUY WITH DEAD-END DREAMS.
IT'S AN OLD STORY. WHEN YOU GET TO ANYTOWN, ODDS ARE YOU'LL SHUFFLE DOWN LONESOME ROAD AND CHECK INTO HEARTBREAK HOTEL, RIGHT, KID?
ARE YOU MAKING FUN OF ME?
NAW. JUST TRYING TO GET YOUR MIND OFF YOUR HAIRCUT.
GB Trudeau

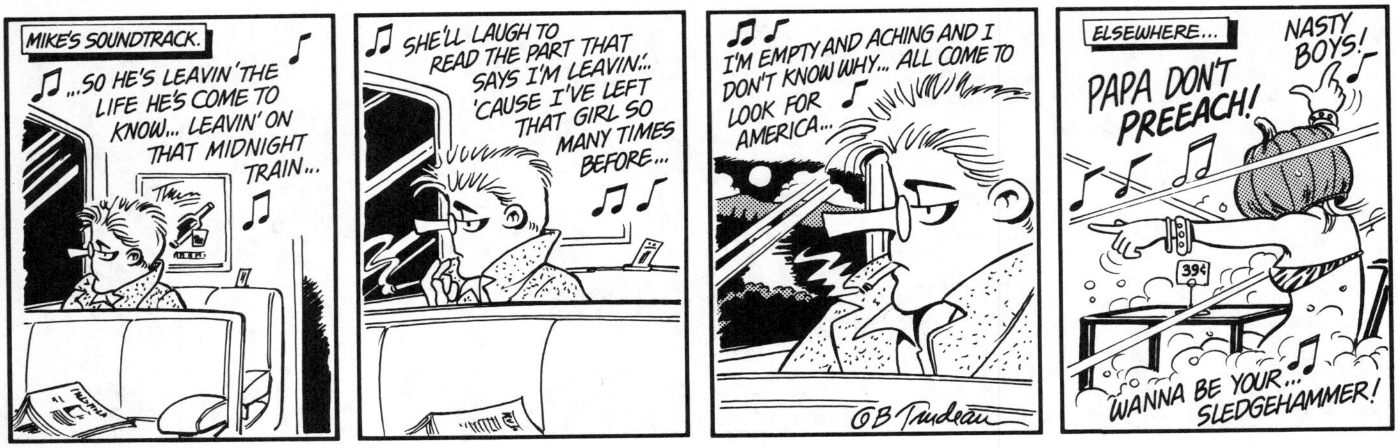
MIKE'S SOUNDTRACK.
...SO HE'S LEAVIN' THE LIFE HE'S COME TO KNOW... LEAVIN' ON THAT MIDNIGHT TRAIN...
SHE'LL LAUGH TO READ THE PART THAT SAYS I'M LEAVIN'... 'CAUSE I'VE LEFT THAT GIRL SO MANY TIMES BEFORE...
I'M EMPTY AND ACHING AND I DON'T KNOW WHY... ALL COME TO LOOK FOR AMERICA...
GB Trudeau
ELSEWHERE...
NASTY BOYS!
PAPA DON'T PREEACH!
39¢
WANNA BE YOUR... SLEDGEHAMMER!

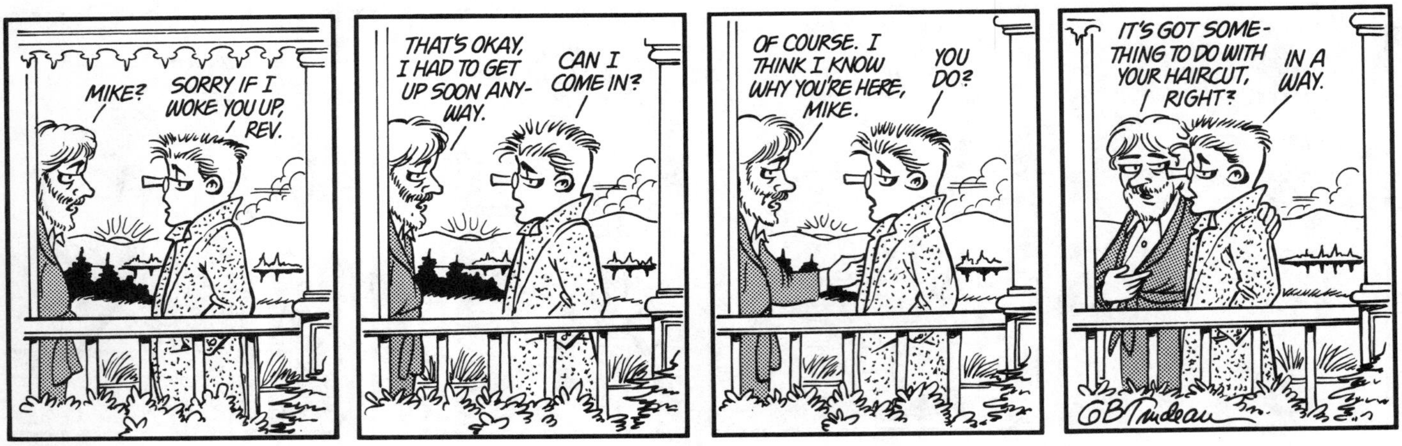
MIKE?
SORRY IF I WOKE YOU UP, REV.
THAT'S OKAY, I HAD TO GET UP SOON ANYWAY.
CAN I COME IN?
OF COURSE. I THINK I KNOW WHY YOU'RE HERE, MIKE.
YOU DO?
IT'S GOT SOMETHING TO DO WITH YOUR HAIRCUT, RIGHT?
IN A WAY.
GB Trudeau

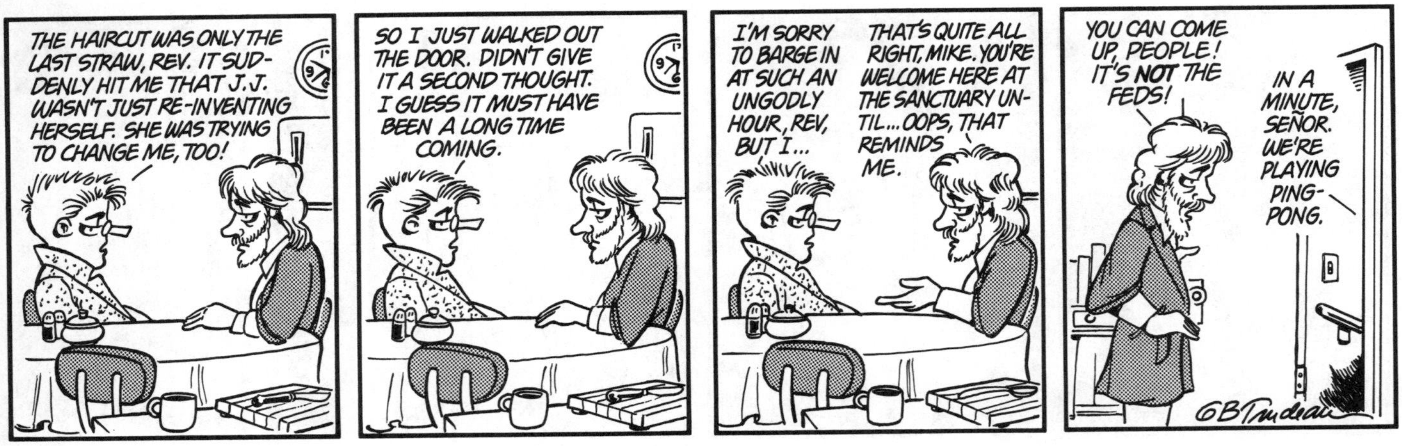
THE HAIRCUT WAS ONLY THE LAST STRAW, REV. IT SUDDENLY HIT ME THAT J.J. WASN'T JUST RE-INVENTING HERSELF. SHE WAS TRYING TO CHANGE ME, TOO!
SO I JUST WALKED OUT THE DOOR. DIDN'T GIVE IT A SECOND THOUGHT. I GUESS IT MUST HAVE BEEN A LONG TIME COMING.
I'M SORRY TO BARGE IN AT SUCH AN UNGODLY HOUR, REV, BUT I...
THAT'S QUITE ALL RIGHT, MIKE. YOU'RE WELCOME HERE AT THE SANCTUARY UNTIL... OOPS, THAT REMINDS ME.
YOU CAN COME UP, PEOPLE! IT'S NOT THE FEDS!
IN A MINUTE, SEÑOR. WE'RE PLAYING PING-PONG.
GB Trudeau

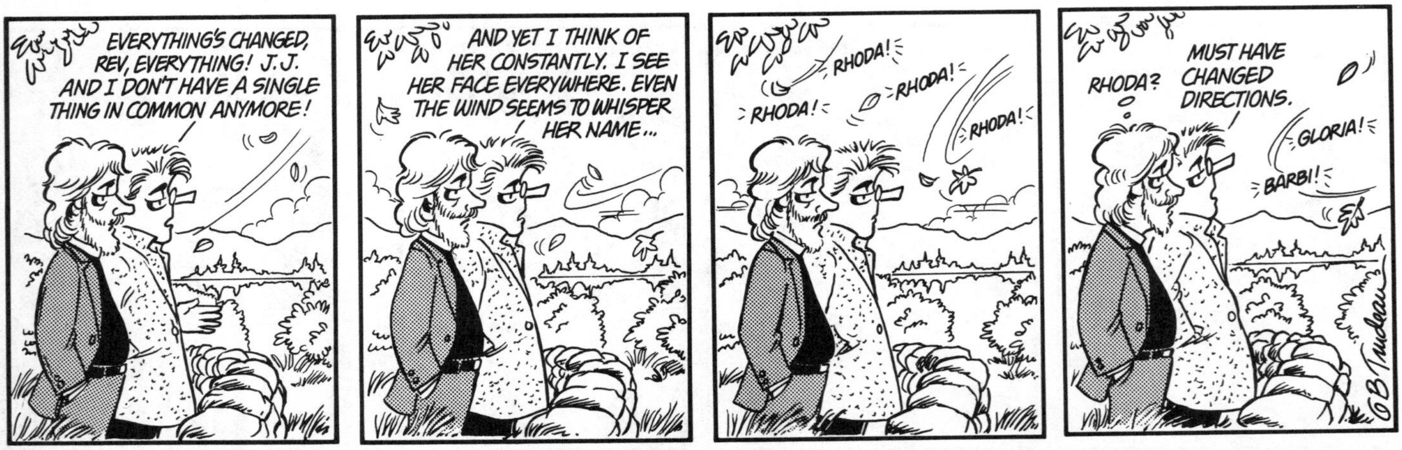
EVERYTHING'S CHANGED, REV, EVERYTHING! J.J. AND I DON'T HAVE A SINGLE THING IN COMMON ANYMORE!
AND YET I THINK OF HER CONSTANTLY. I SEE HER FACE EVERYWHERE. EVEN THE WIND SEEMS TO WHISPER HER NAME...
RHODA!
RHODA!
RHODA!
RHODA!
RHODA?
MUST HAVE CHANGED DIRECTIONS.
GLORIA!
BARBI!
GB Trudeau

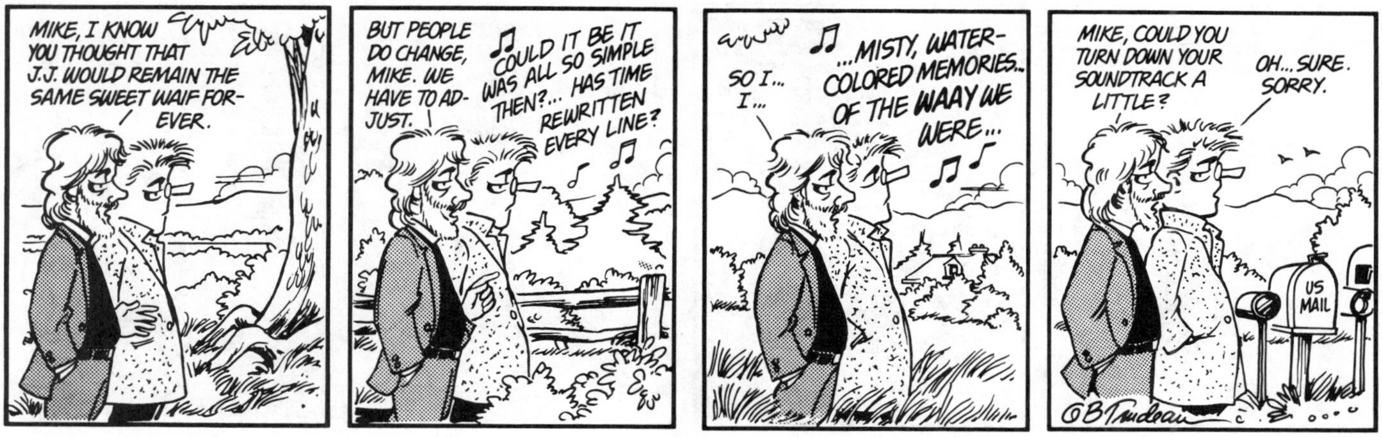
MIKE, I KNOW YOU THOUGHT THAT J.J. WOULD REMAIN THE SAME SWEET WAIF FOREVER.
BUT PEOPLE DO CHANGE, MIKE. WE HAVE TO ADJUST.
COULD IT BE IT WAS ALL SO SIMPLE THEN?... HAS TIME REWRITTEN EVERY LINE?
SO I... I...
...MISTY, WATER-COLORED MEMORIES.. OF THE WAAY WE WERE...
MIKE, COULD YOU TURN DOWN YOUR SOUNDTRACK A LITTLE?
OH... SURE. SORRY.
US MAIL
© B Trudeau

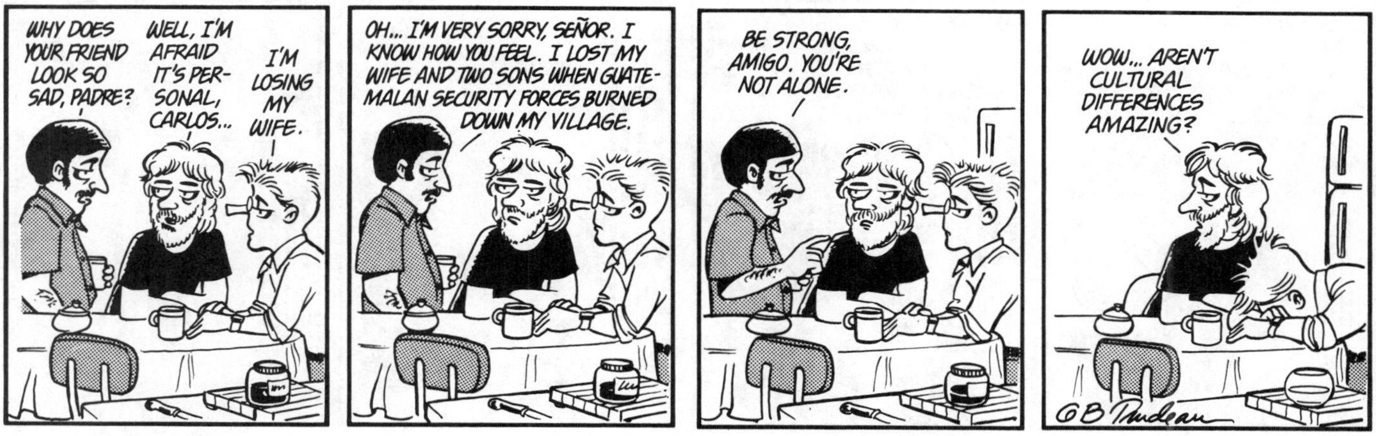
WHY DOES YOUR FRIEND LOOK SO SAD, PADRE?
WELL, I'M AFRAID IT'S PERSONAL, CARLOS...
I'M LOSING MY WIFE.
OH... I'M VERY SORRY, SEÑOR. I KNOW HOW YOU FEEL. I LOST MY WIFE AND TWO SONS WHEN GUATEMALAN SECURITY FORCES BURNED DOWN MY VILLAGE.
BE STRONG, AMIGO. YOU'RE NOT ALONE.
WOW... AREN'T CULTURAL DIFFERENCES AMAZING?
© B Trudeau

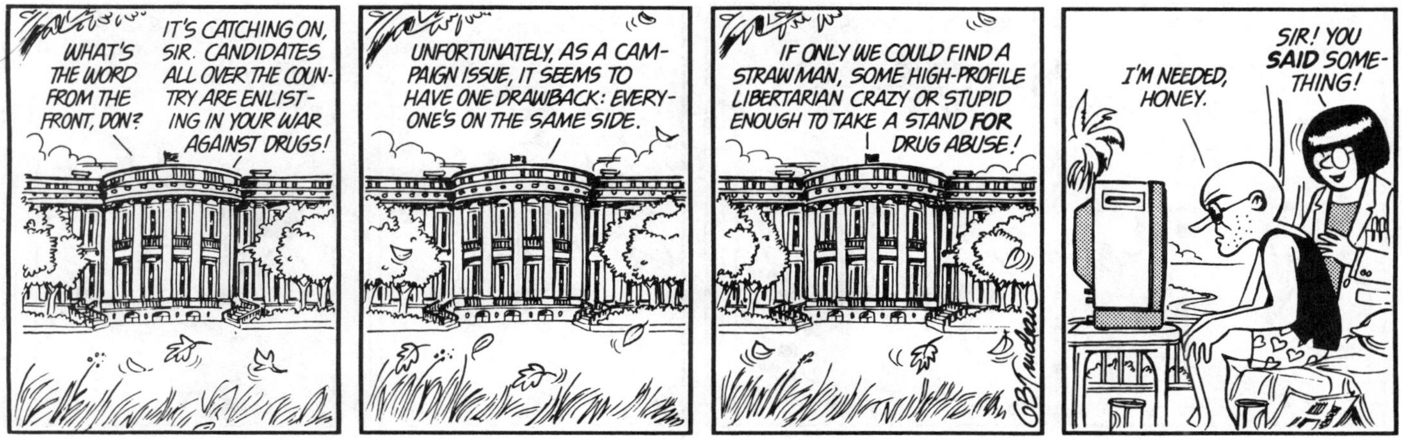
WHAT'S THE WORD FROM THE FRONT, DON?
IT'S CATCHING ON, SIR. CANDIDATES ALL OVER THE COUNTRY ARE ENLISTING IN YOUR WAR AGAINST DRUGS!
UNFORTUNATELY, AS A CAMPAIGN ISSUE, IT SEEMS TO HAVE ONE DRAWBACK: EVERYONE'S ON THE SAME SIDE.
IF ONLY WE COULD FIND A STRAW MAN, SOME HIGH-PROFILE LIBERTARIAN CRAZY OR STUPID ENOUGH TO TAKE A STAND **FOR** DRUG ABUSE!
© B Trudeau
I'M NEEDED, HONEY.
SIR! YOU **SAID** SOMETHING!

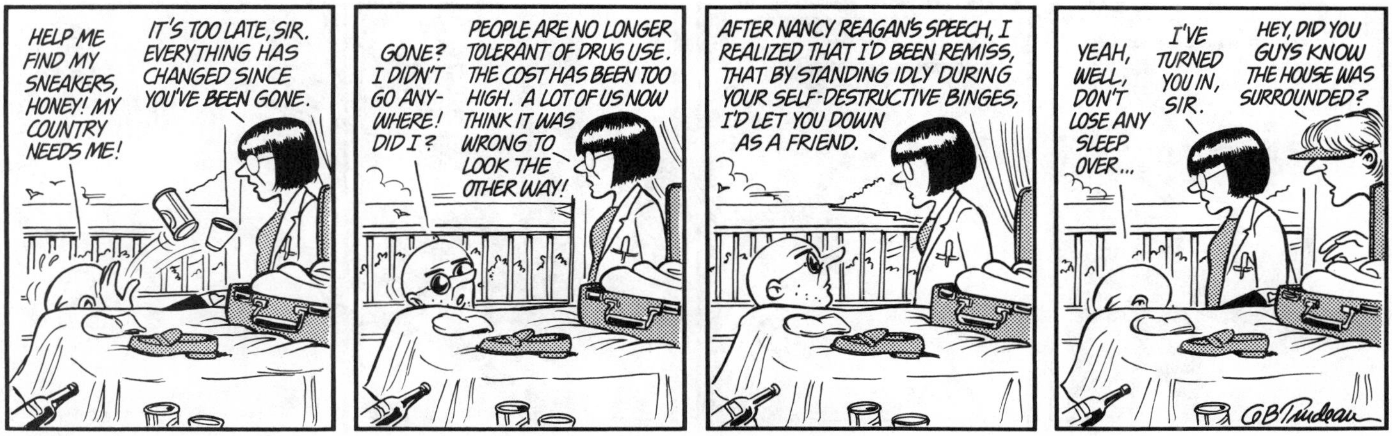
HELP ME FIND MY SNEAKERS, HONEY! MY COUNTRY NEEDS ME!
IT'S TOO LATE, SIR. EVERYTHING HAS CHANGED SINCE YOU'VE BEEN GONE.
GONE? I DIDN'T GO ANYWHERE! DID I?
PEOPLE ARE NO LONGER TOLERANT OF DRUG USE. THE COST HAS BEEN TOO HIGH. A LOT OF US NOW THINK IT WAS WRONG TO LOOK THE OTHER WAY!
AFTER NANCY REAGAN'S SPEECH, I REALIZED THAT I'D BEEN REMISS, THAT BY STANDING IDLY DURING YOUR SELF-DESTRUCTIVE BINGES, I'D LET YOU DOWN AS A FRIEND.
YEAH, WELL, DON'T LOSE ANY SLEEP OVER...
I'VE TURNED YOU IN, SIR.
HEY, DID YOU GUYS KNOW THE HOUSE WAS SURROUNDED?
© B Trudeau

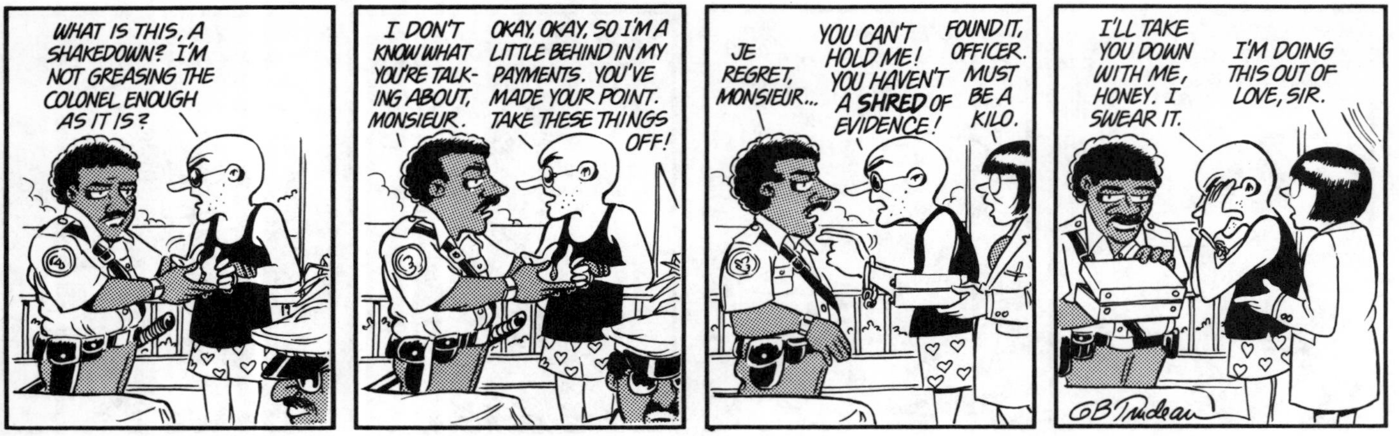
WHAT IS THIS, A SHAKEDOWN? I'M NOT GREASING THE COLONEL ENOUGH AS IT IS?
I DON'T KNOW WHAT YOU'RE TALKING ABOUT, MONSIEUR.
OKAY, OKAY, SO I'M A LITTLE BEHIND IN MY PAYMENTS. YOU'VE MADE YOUR POINT. TAKE THESE THINGS OFF!
JE REGRET, MONSIEUR...
YOU CAN'T HOLD ME! YOU HAVEN'T A **SHRED** OF EVIDENCE!
FOUND IT, OFFICER. MUST BE A KILO.
I'LL TAKE YOU DOWN WITH ME, HONEY. I SWEAR IT.
I'M DOING THIS OUT OF LOVE, SIR.
GB Trudeau

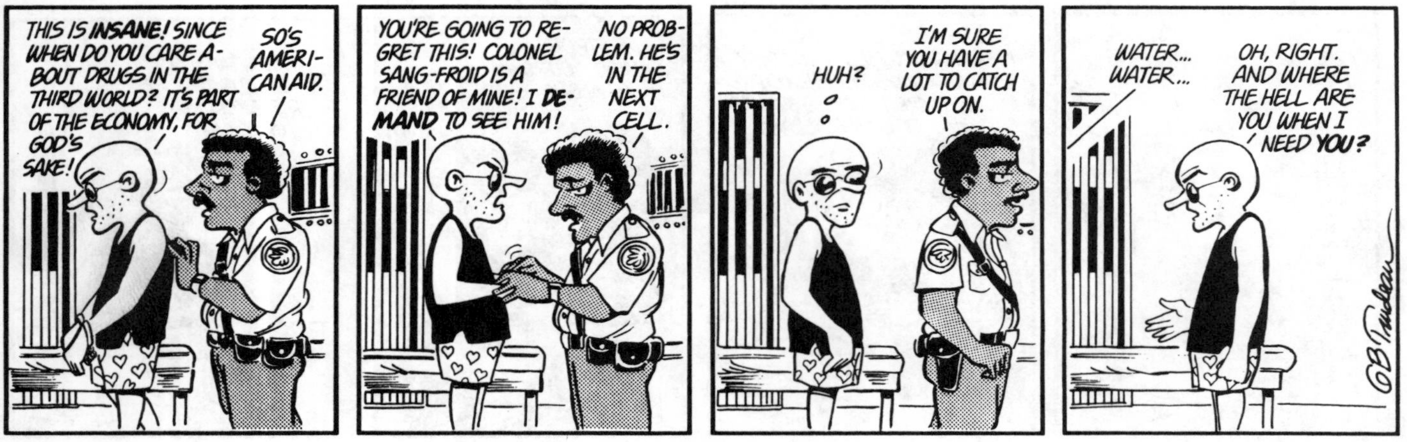
THIS IS **INSANE!** SINCE WHEN DO YOU CARE ABOUT DRUGS IN THE THIRD WORLD? IT'S PART OF THE ECONOMY, FOR GOD'S SAKE!
SO'S AMERICAN AID.
YOU'RE GOING TO REGRET THIS! COLONEL SANG-FROID IS A FRIEND OF MINE! I **DEMAND** TO SEE HIM!
NO PROBLEM. HE'S IN THE NEXT CELL.
HUH?
I'M SURE YOU HAVE A LOT TO CATCH UP ON.
WATER... WATER...
OH, RIGHT. AND WHERE THE HELL ARE YOU WHEN I NEED **YOU?**
GB Trudeau

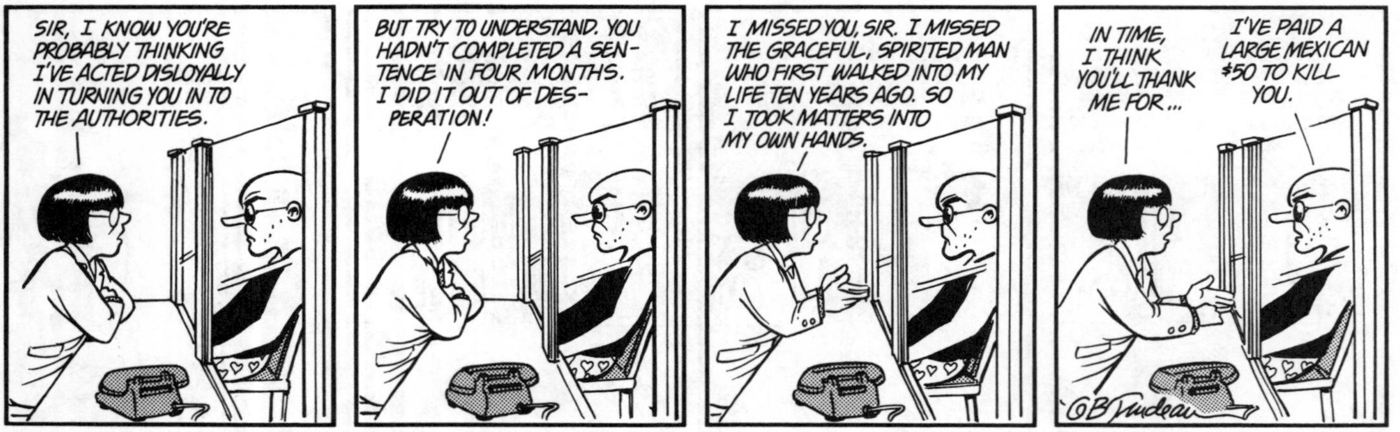
SIR, I KNOW YOU'RE PROBABLY THINKING I'VE ACTED DISLOYALLY IN TURNING YOU IN TO THE AUTHORITIES.
BUT TRY TO UNDERSTAND. YOU HADN'T COMPLETED A SENTENCE IN FOUR MONTHS. I DID IT OUT OF DESPERATION!
I MISSED YOU, SIR. I MISSED THE GRACEFUL, SPIRITED MAN WHO FIRST WALKED INTO MY LIFE TEN YEARS AGO. SO I TOOK MATTERS INTO MY OWN HANDS.
IN TIME, I THINK YOU'LL THANK ME FOR...
I'VE PAID A LARGE MEXICAN $50 TO KILL YOU.
GB Trudeau

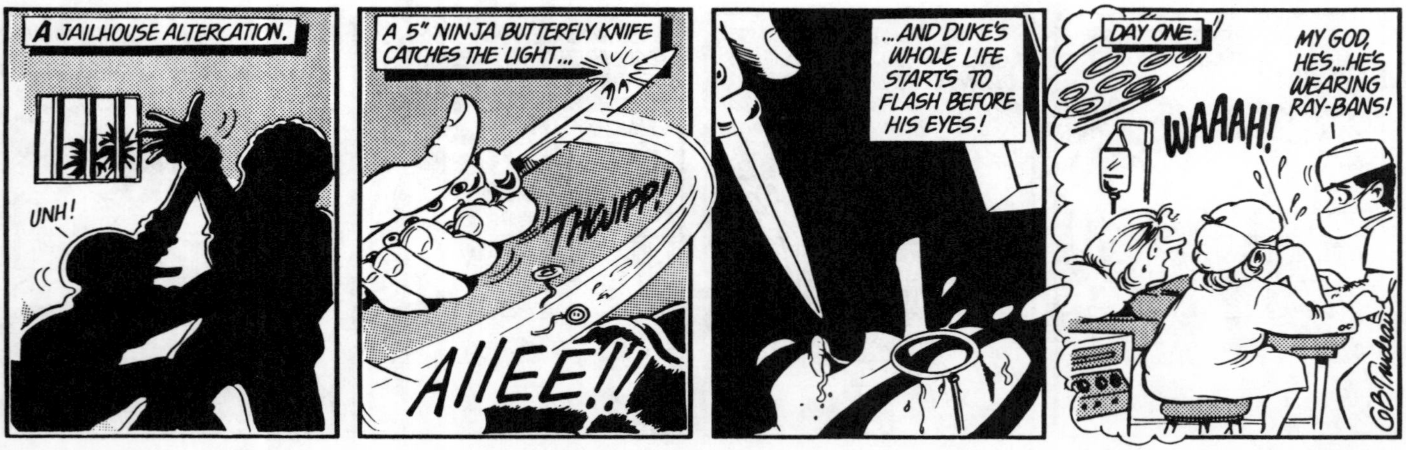
A JAILHOUSE ALTERCATION.
UNH!
A 5" NINJA BUTTERFLY KNIFE CATCHES THE LIGHT...
THWIPP!
AIIEE!!
...AND DUKE'S WHOLE LIFE STARTS TO FLASH BEFORE HIS EYES!
DAY ONE.
WAAAH!
MY GOD, HE'S...HE'S WEARING RAY-BANS!
GB Trudeau

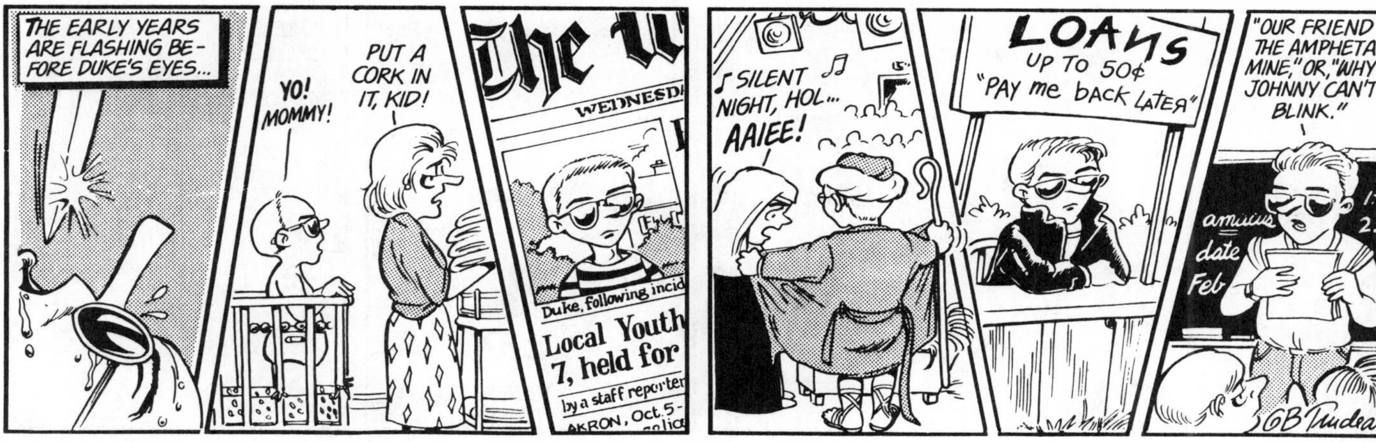
THE EARLY YEARS ARE FLASHING BEFORE DUKE'S EYES...
YO! MOMMY!
PUT A CORK IN IT, KID!
WEDNESDA
Duke, following incid
Local Youth
7, held for
by a staff reporter
AKRON, Oct.5-
♪ SILENT NIGHT, HOL... ♫
AAIEE!
LOANS
UP TO 50¢
"PAY ME BACK LATER"
"OUR FRIEND THE AMPHETAMINE," OR, "WHY JOHNNY CAN'T BLINK."
GB Trudeau

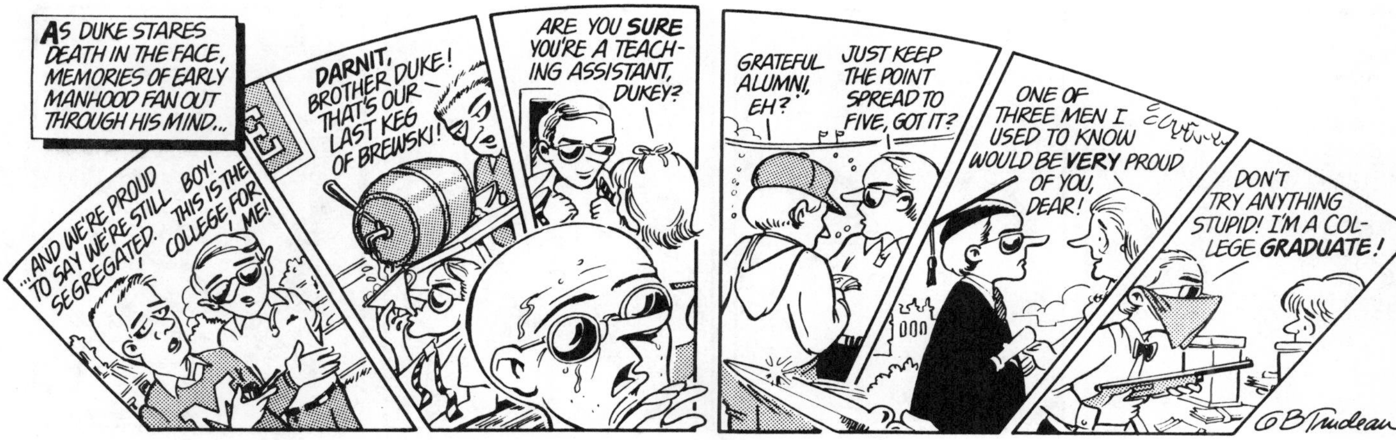
AS DUKE STARES DEATH IN THE FACE, MEMORIES OF EARLY MANHOOD FAN OUT THROUGH HIS MIND...
...AND WE'RE PROUD TO SAY WE'RE STILL SEGREGATED.
BOY! THIS IS THE COLLEGE FOR ME!
DARNIT, BROTHER DUKE! THAT'S OUR LAST KEG OF BREWSKI!
ARE YOU SURE YOU'RE A TEACHING ASSISTANT, DUKEY?
GRATEFUL ALUMNI, EH?
JUST KEEP THE POINT SPREAD TO FIVE, GOT IT?
ONE OF THREE MEN I USED TO KNOW WOULD BE VERY PROUD OF YOU, DEAR!
DON'T TRY ANYTHING STUPID! I'M A COLLEGE GRADUATE!
GB Trudeau

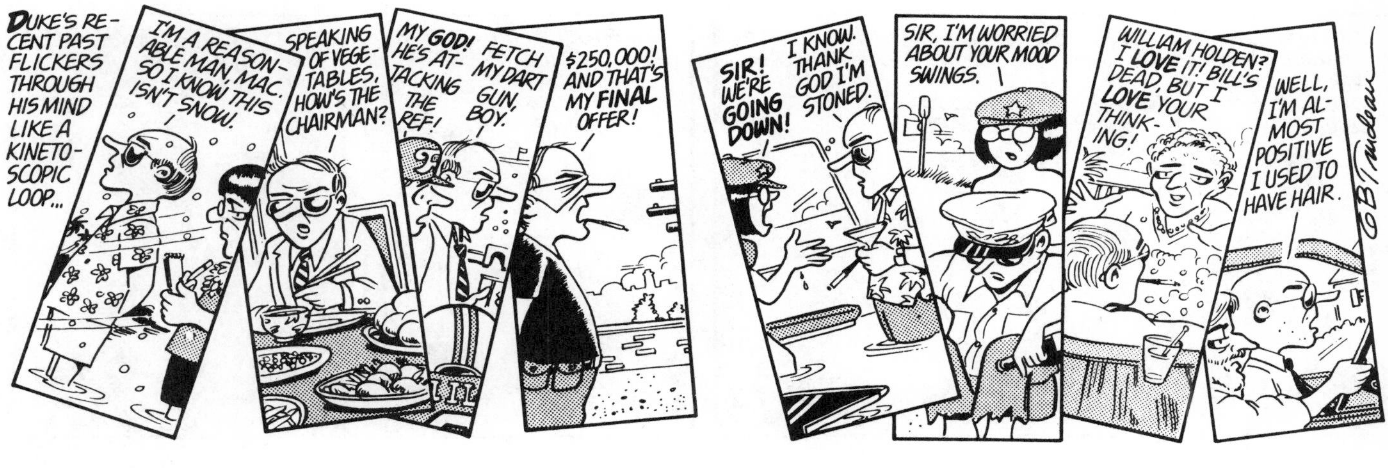
DUKE'S RECENT PAST FLICKERS THROUGH HIS MIND LIKE A KINETOSCOPIC LOOP...
I'M A REASONABLE MAN, MAC. SO I KNOW THIS ISN'T SNOW.
SPEAKING OF VEGETABLES, HOW'S THE CHAIRMAN?
MY GOD! HE'S ATTACKING THE REF!
FETCH MY DART GUN, BOY.
$250,000! AND THAT'S MY FINAL OFFER!
SIR! WE'RE GOING DOWN!
I KNOW. THANK GOD I'M STONED.
SIR, I'M WORRIED ABOUT YOUR MOOD SWINGS.
WILLIAM HOLDEN? I LOVE IT! BILL'S DEAD, BUT I LOVE YOUR THINKING!
WELL, I'M ALMOST POSITIVE I USED TO HAVE HAIR.
GB Trudeau

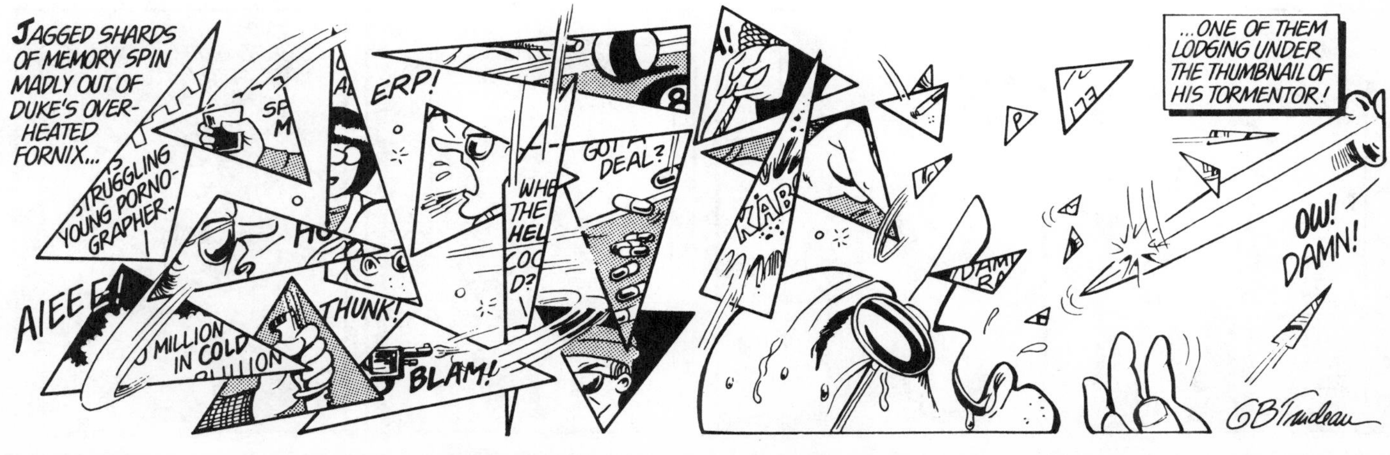
JAGGED SHARDS OF MEMORY SPIN MADLY OUT OF DUKE'S OVERHEATED FORNIX...
STRUGGLING YOUNG PORNOGRAPHER..
ERP!
DEAL?
AIEEE!
THUNK!
IN COLD
BLAM!
...ONE OF THEM LODGING UNDER THE THUMBNAIL OF HIS TORMENTOR!
OW! DAMN!
GB Trudeau

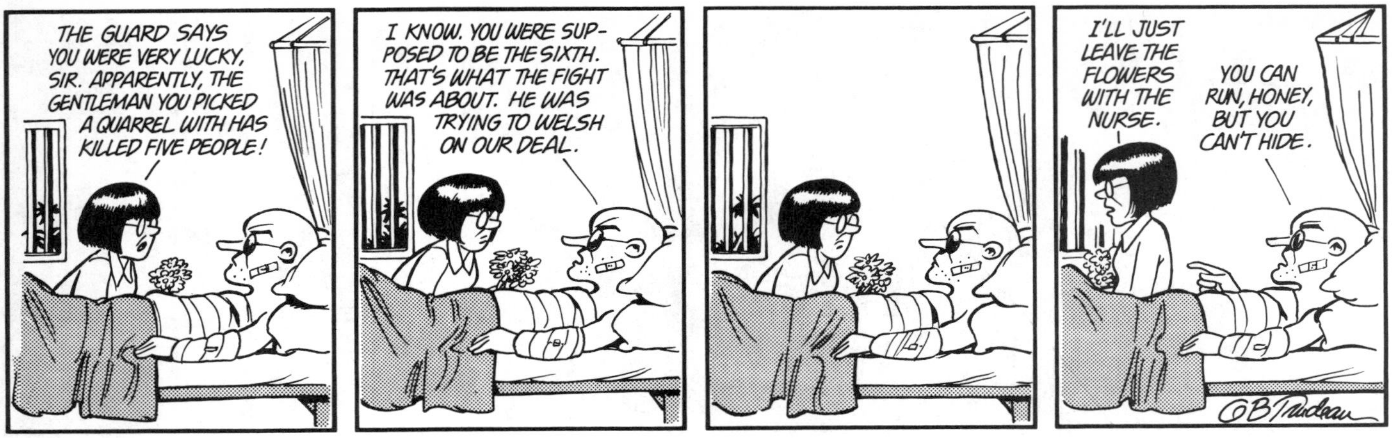
THE GUARD SAYS YOU WERE VERY LUCKY, SIR. APPARENTLY, THE GENTLEMAN YOU PICKED A QUARREL WITH HAS KILLED FIVE PEOPLE!
I KNOW. YOU WERE SUPPOSED TO BE THE SIXTH. THAT'S WHAT THE FIGHT WAS ABOUT. HE WAS TRYING TO WELSH ON OUR DEAL.
I'LL JUST LEAVE THE FLOWERS WITH THE NURSE.
YOU CAN RUN, HONEY, BUT YOU CAN'T HIDE.
GB Trudeau

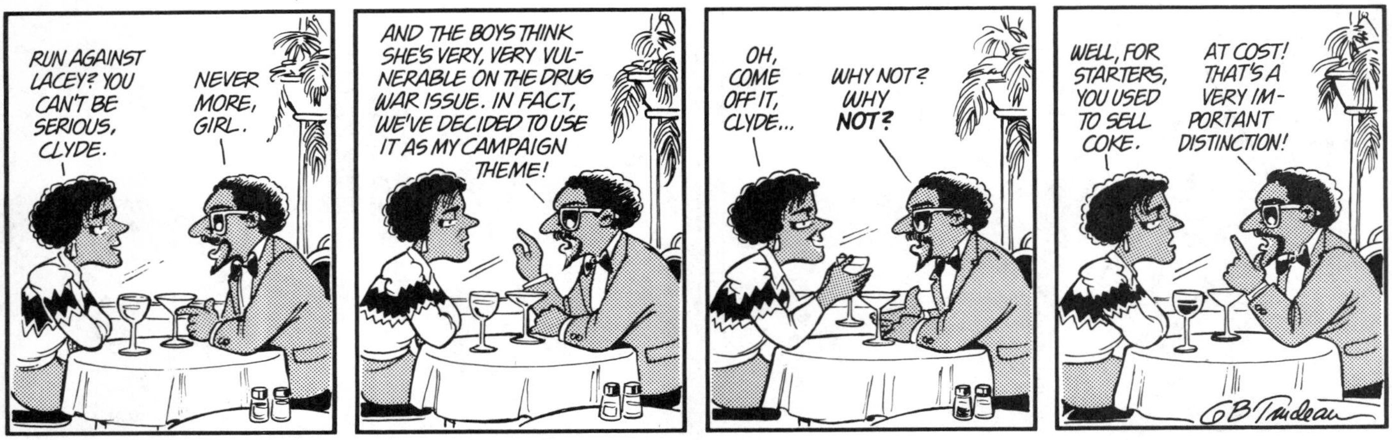
RUN AGAINST LACEY? YOU CAN'T BE SERIOUS, CLYDE.
NEVER MORE, GIRL.
AND THE BOYS THINK SHE'S VERY, VERY VULNERABLE ON THE DRUG WAR ISSUE. IN FACT, WE'VE DECIDED TO USE IT AS MY CAMPAIGN THEME!
OH, COME OFF IT, CLYDE...
WHY NOT? WHY NOT?
WELL, FOR STARTERS, YOU USED TO SELL COKE.
AT COST! THAT'S A VERY IMPORTANT DISTINCTION!
GB Trudeau

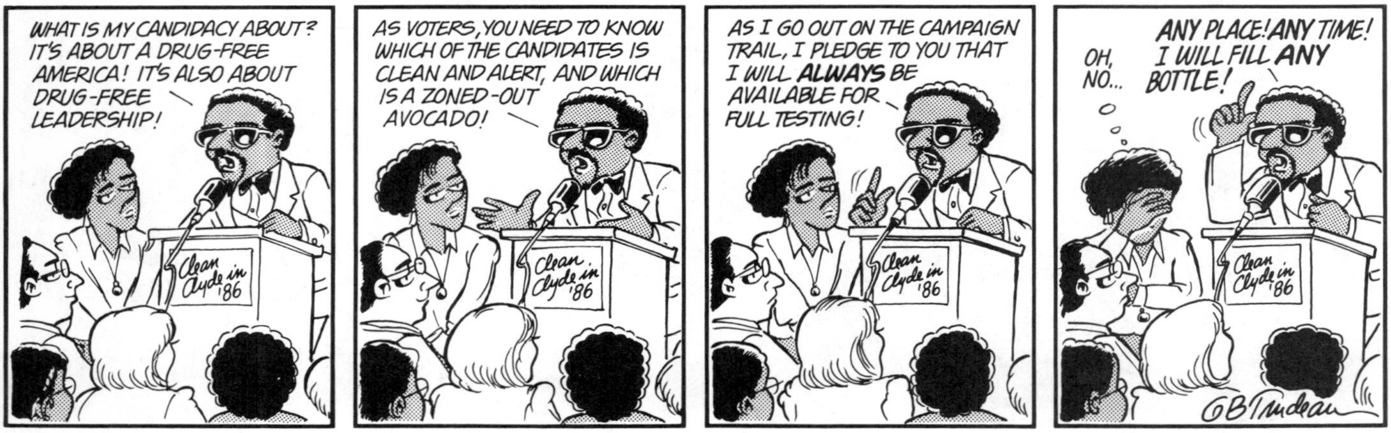
WHAT IS MY CANDIDACY ABOUT? IT'S ABOUT A DRUG-FREE AMERICA! IT'S ALSO ABOUT DRUG-FREE LEADERSHIP!
Clean Clyde in '86
AS VOTERS, YOU NEED TO KNOW WHICH OF THE CANDIDATES IS CLEAN AND ALERT, AND WHICH IS A ZONED-OUT AVOCADO!
Clean Clyde in '86
AS I GO OUT ON THE CAMPAIGN TRAIL, I PLEDGE TO YOU THAT I WILL ALWAYS BE AVAILABLE FOR FULL TESTING!
Clean Clyde in '86
OH, NO...
ANY PLACE! ANY TIME! I WILL FILL ANY BOTTLE!
Clean Clyde in '86
GB Trudeau

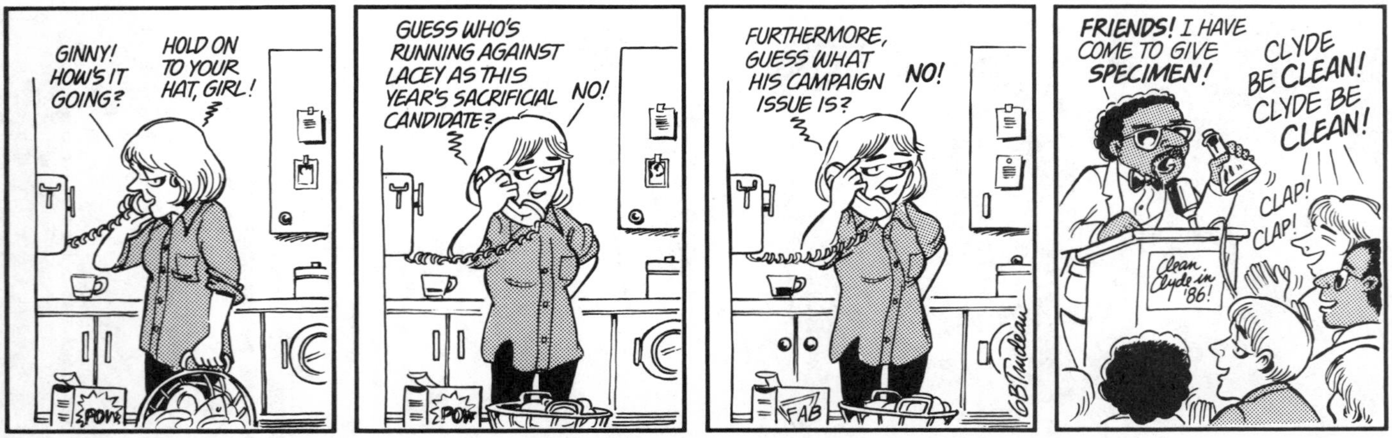
GINNY! HOW'S IT GOING?
HOLD ON TO YOUR HAT, GIRL!
POW
GUESS WHO'S RUNNING AGAINST LACEY AS THIS YEAR'S SACRIFICIAL CANDIDATE?
NO!
POW
FURTHERMORE, GUESS WHAT HIS CAMPAIGN ISSUE IS?
NO!
FAB
GB Trudeau
FRIENDS! I HAVE COME TO GIVE SPECIMEN!
CLYDE BE CLEAN! CLYDE BE CLEAN!
CLAP! CLAP!
Clean Clyde in '86!

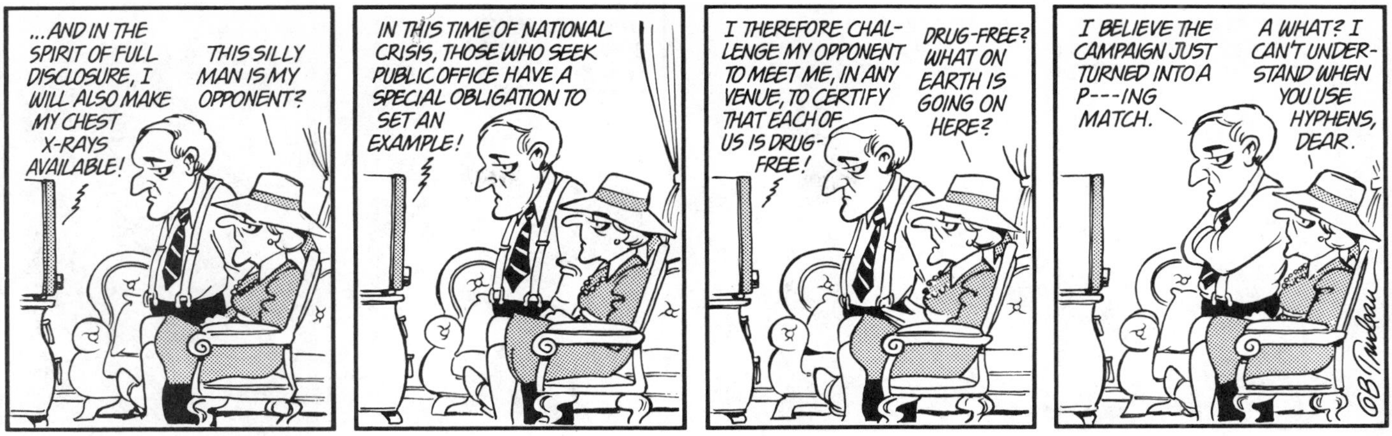
...AND IN THE SPIRIT OF FULL DISCLOSURE, I WILL ALSO MAKE MY CHEST X-RAYS AVAILABLE!
THIS SILLY MAN IS MY OPPONENT?
IN THIS TIME OF NATIONAL CRISIS, THOSE WHO SEEK PUBLIC OFFICE HAVE A SPECIAL OBLIGATION TO SET AN EXAMPLE!
I THEREFORE CHALLENGE MY OPPONENT TO MEET ME, IN ANY VENUE, TO CERTIFY THAT EACH OF US IS DRUG-FREE!
DRUG-FREE? WHAT ON EARTH IS GOING ON HERE?
I BELIEVE THE CAMPAIGN JUST TURNED INTO A P---ING MATCH.
A WHAT? I CAN'T UNDERSTAND WHEN YOU USE HYPHENS, DEAR.
GB Trudeau

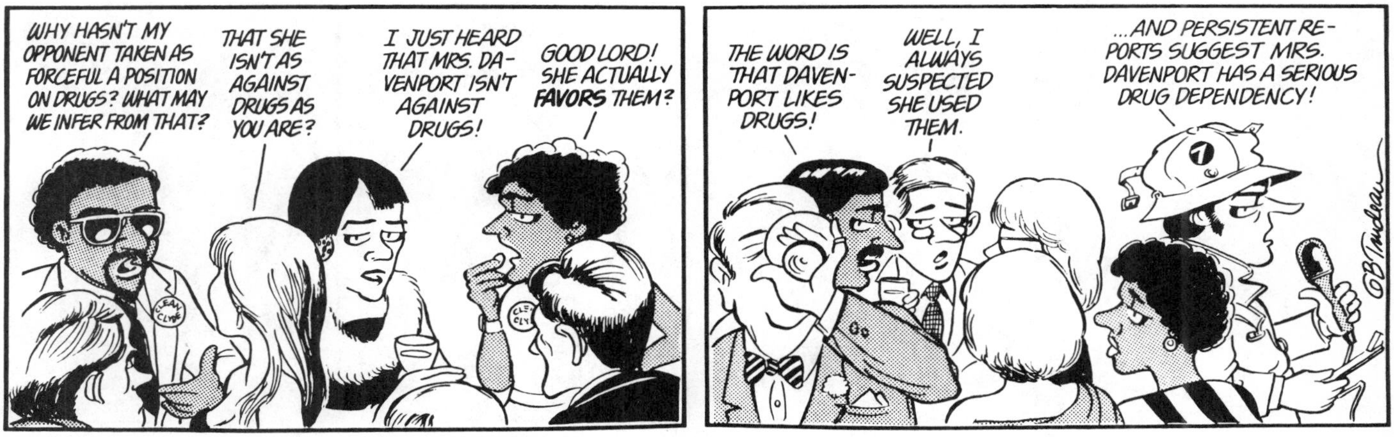
WHY HASN'T MY OPPONENT TAKEN AS FORCEFUL A POSITION ON DRUGS? WHAT MAY WE INFER FROM THAT?
THAT SHE ISN'T AS AGAINST DRUGS AS YOU ARE?
I JUST HEARD THAT MRS. DAVENPORT ISN'T AGAINST DRUGS!
GOOD LORD! SHE ACTUALLY FAVORS THEM?
THE WORD IS THAT DAVENPORT LIKES DRUGS!
WELL, I ALWAYS SUSPECTED SHE USED THEM.
...AND PERSISTENT REPORTS SUGGEST MRS. DAVENPORT HAS A SERIOUS DRUG DEPENDENCY!
GB Trudeau

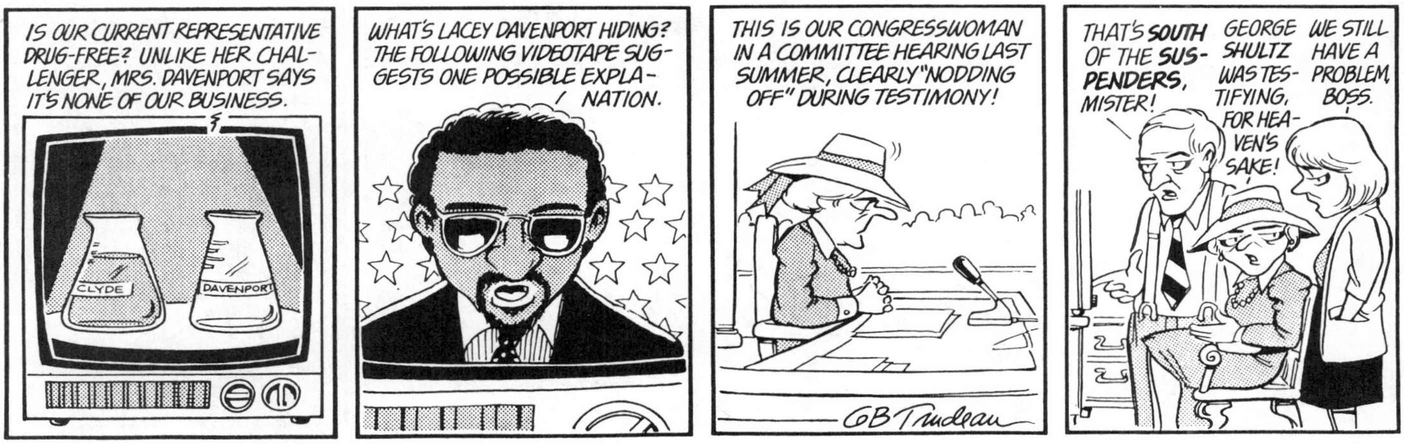
IS OUR CURRENT REPRESENTATIVE DRUG-FREE? UNLIKE HER CHALLENGER, MRS. DAVENPORT SAYS IT'S NONE OF OUR BUSINESS.
CLYDE
DAVENPORT
WHAT'S LACEY DAVENPORT HIDING? THE FOLLOWING VIDEOTAPE SUGGESTS ONE POSSIBLE EXPLANATION.
THIS IS OUR CONGRESSWOMAN IN A COMMITTEE HEARING LAST SUMMER, CLEARLY "NODDING OFF" DURING TESTIMONY!
THAT'S SOUTH OF THE SUSPENDERS, MISTER!
GEORGE SHULTZ WAS TESTIFYING, FOR HEAVEN'S SAKE!
WE STILL HAVE A PROBLEM, BOSS.
GB Trudeau

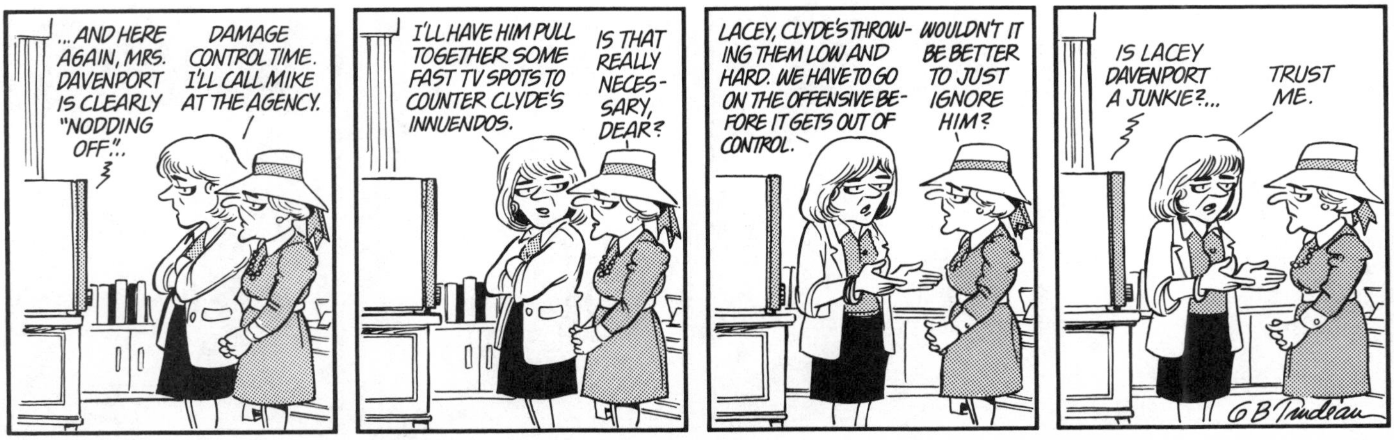
...AND HERE AGAIN, MRS. DAVENPORT IS CLEARLY "NODDING OFF"...
DAMAGE CONTROL TIME. I'LL CALL MIKE AT THE AGENCY.
I'LL HAVE HIM PULL TOGETHER SOME FAST TV SPOTS TO COUNTER CLYDE'S INNUENDOS.
IS THAT REALLY NECESSARY, DEAR?
LACEY, CLYDE'S THROWING THEM LOW AND HARD. WE HAVE TO GO ON THE OFFENSIVE BEFORE IT GETS OUT OF CONTROL.
WOULDN'T IT BE BETTER TO JUST IGNORE HIM?
IS LACEY DAVENPORT A JUNKIE?...
TRUST ME.
GB Trudeau

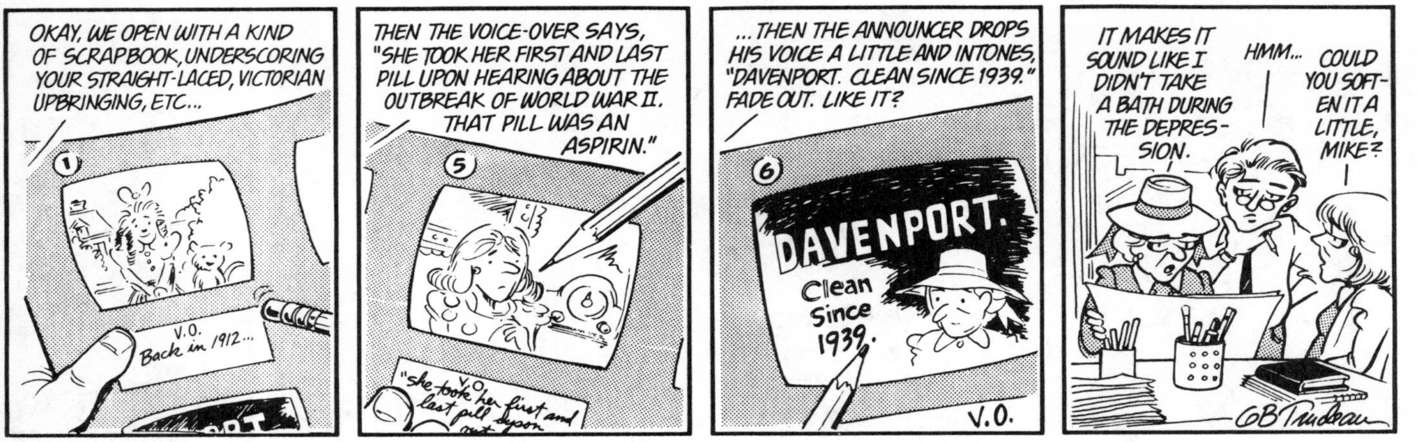
OKAY, WE OPEN WITH A KIND OF SCRAPBOOK, UNDERSCORING YOUR STRAIGHT-LACED, VICTORIAN UPBRINGING, ETC...
1
V.O. Back in 1912...
THEN THE VOICE-OVER SAYS, "SHE TOOK HER FIRST AND LAST PILL UPON HEARING ABOUT THE OUTBREAK OF WORLD WAR II. THAT PILL WAS AN ASPIRIN."
5
...THEN THE ANNOUNCER DROPS HIS VOICE A LITTLE AND INTONES, "DAVENPORT. CLEAN SINCE 1939." FADE OUT. LIKE IT?
6
DAVENPORT.
Clean Since 1939.
V.O.
IT MAKES IT SOUND LIKE I DIDN'T TAKE A BATH DURING THE DEPRESSION.
HMM...
COULD YOU SOFTEN IT A LITTLE, MIKE?
GB Trudeau

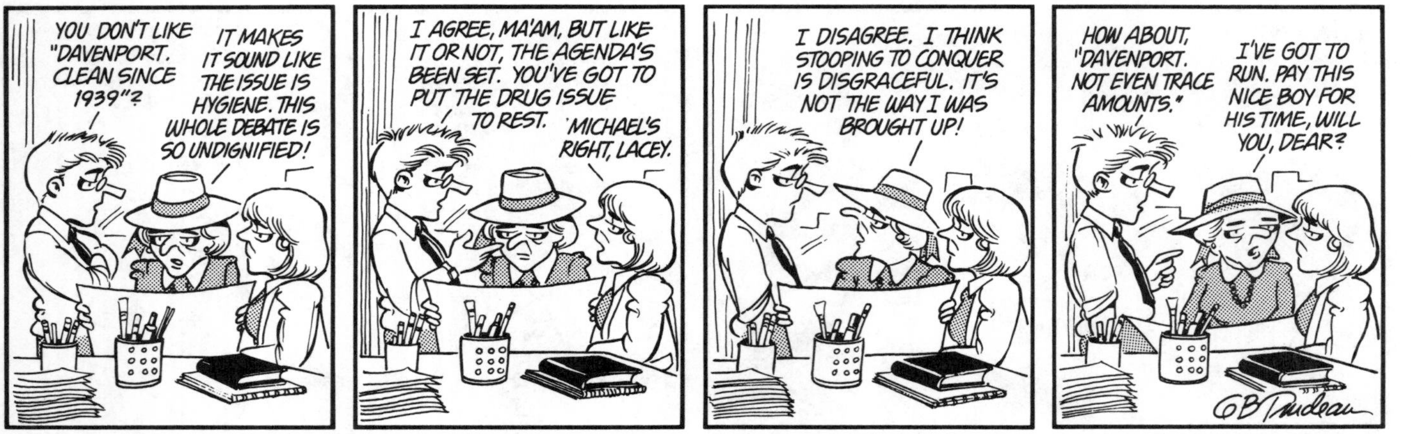
YOU DON'T LIKE "DAVENPORT. CLEAN SINCE 1939"?
IT MAKES IT SOUND LIKE THE ISSUE IS HYGIENE. THIS WHOLE DEBATE IS SO UNDIGNIFIED!
I AGREE, MA'AM, BUT LIKE IT OR NOT, THE AGENDA'S BEEN SET. YOU'VE GOT TO PUT THE DRUG ISSUE TO REST.
MICHAEL'S RIGHT, LACEY.
I DISAGREE. I THINK STOOPING TO CONQUER IS DISGRACEFUL. IT'S NOT THE WAY I WAS BROUGHT UP!
HOW ABOUT, "DAVENPORT. NOT EVEN TRACE AMOUNTS."
I'VE GOT TO RUN. PAY THIS NICE BOY FOR HIS TIME, WILL YOU, DEAR?
GB Trudeau

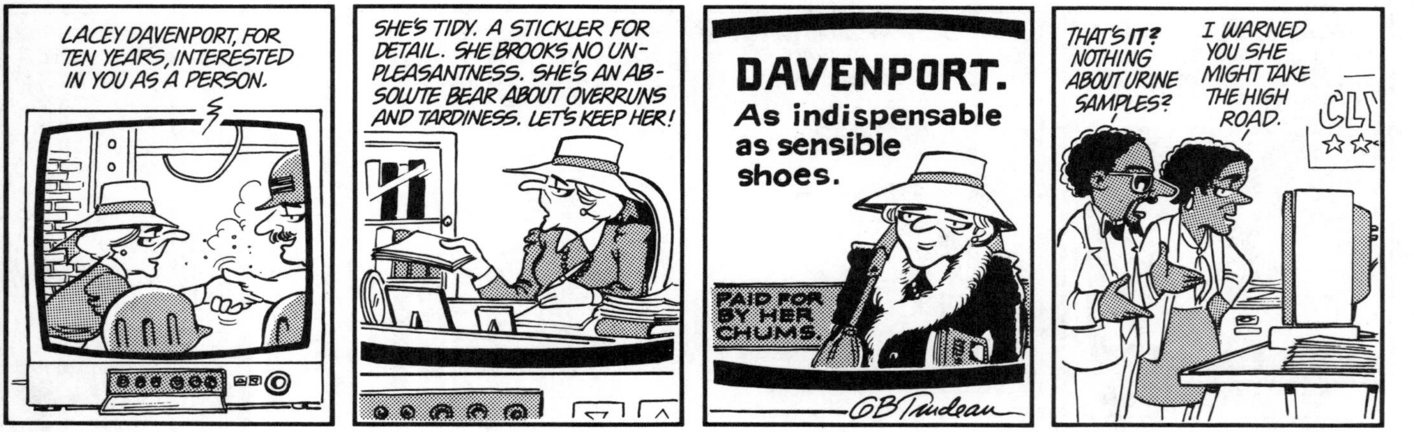
LACEY DAVENPORT, FOR TEN YEARS, INTERESTED IN YOU AS A PERSON.
SHE'S TIDY. A STICKLER FOR DETAIL. SHE BROOKS NO UNPLEASANTNESS. SHE'S AN ABSOLUTE BEAR ABOUT OVERRUNS AND TARDINESS. LET'S KEEP HER!
DAVENPORT.
As indispensable as sensible shoes.
PAID FOR BY HER CHUMS.
GB Trudeau
THAT'S IT? NOTHING ABOUT URINE SAMPLES?
I WARNED YOU SHE MIGHT TAKE THE HIGH ROAD.
CLY

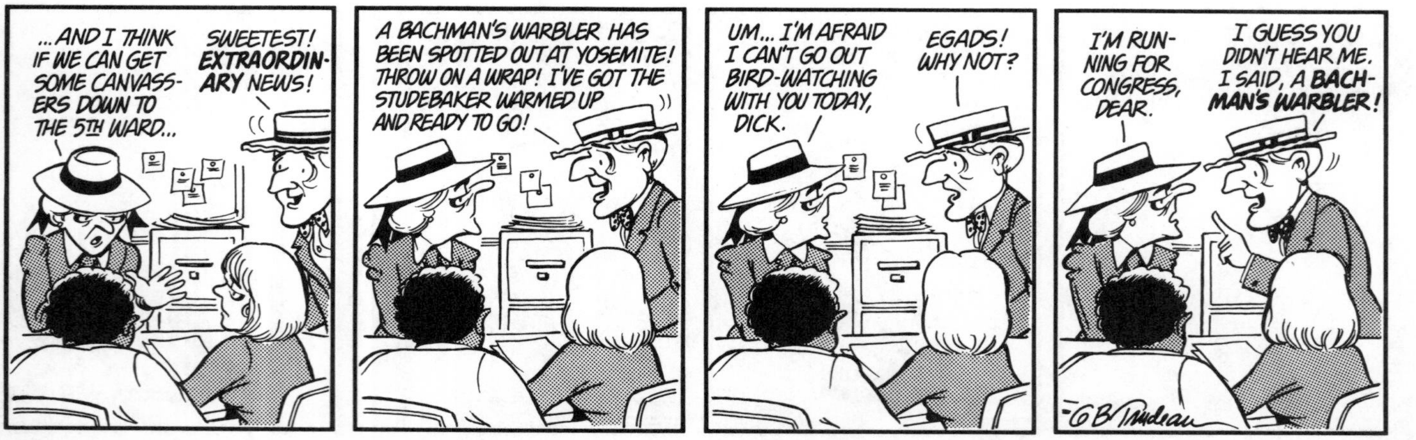
...AND I THINK IF WE CAN GET SOME CANVASSERS DOWN TO THE 5TH WARD...
SWEETEST! EXTRAORDINARY NEWS!
A BACHMAN'S WARBLER HAS BEEN SPOTTED OUT AT YOSEMITE! THROW ON A WRAP! I'VE GOT THE STUDEBAKER WARMED UP AND READY TO GO!
UM... I'M AFRAID I CAN'T GO OUT BIRD-WATCHING WITH YOU TODAY, DICK.
EGADS! WHY NOT?
I'M RUNNING FOR CONGRESS, DEAR.
I GUESS YOU DIDN'T HEAR ME. I SAID, A BACHMAN'S WARBLER!
GB Trudeau

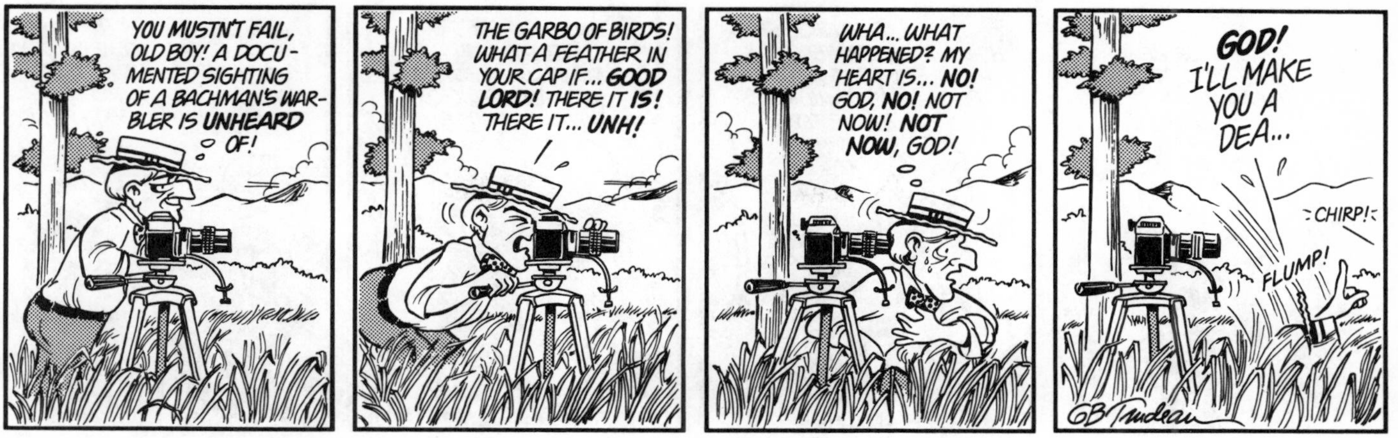
YOU MUSTN'T FAIL, OLD BOY! A DOCU-MENTED SIGHTING OF A BACHMAN'S WAR-BLER IS **UNHEARD** OF!
THE GARBO OF BIRDS! WHAT A FEATHER IN YOUR CAP IF... **GOOD LORD!** THERE IT **IS!** THERE IT... **UNH!**
WHA... WHAT HAPPENED? MY HEART IS... **NO!** GOD, **NO!** NOT NOW! **NOT NOW**, GOD!
GOD! I'LL MAKE YOU A DEA...
CHIRP!
FLUMP!

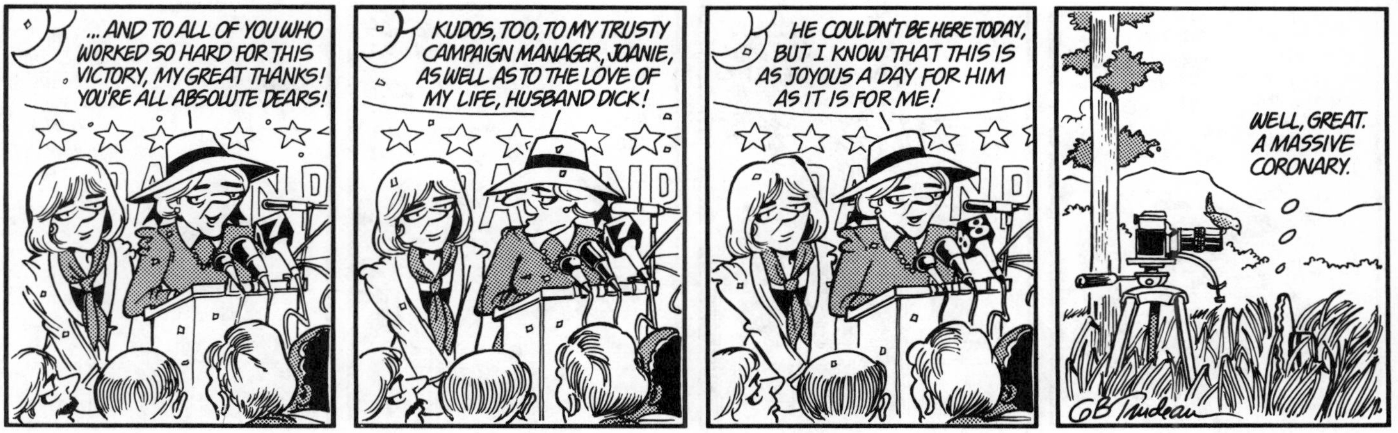
... AND TO ALL OF YOU WHO WORKED SO HARD FOR THIS VICTORY, MY GREAT THANKS! YOU'RE ALL ABSOLUTE DEARS!
KUDOS, TOO, TO MY TRUSTY CAMPAIGN MANAGER, JOANIE, AS WELL AS TO THE LOVE OF MY LIFE, HUSBAND DICK!
HE COULDN'T BE HERE TODAY, BUT I KNOW THAT THIS IS AS JOYOUS A DAY FOR HIM AS IT IS FOR ME!
WELL, GREAT. A MASSIVE CORONARY.

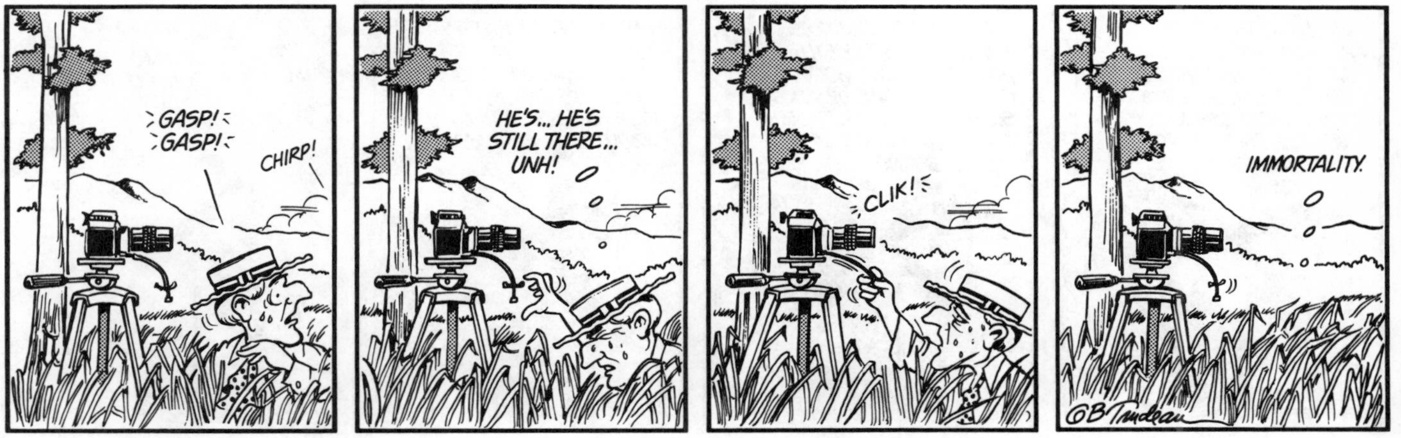
GASP! GASP!
CHIRP!
HE'S... HE'S STILL THERE... UNH!
CLIK!
IMMORTALITY.

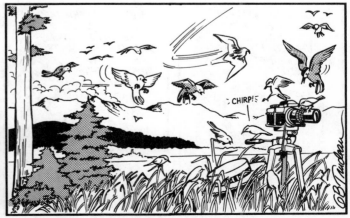

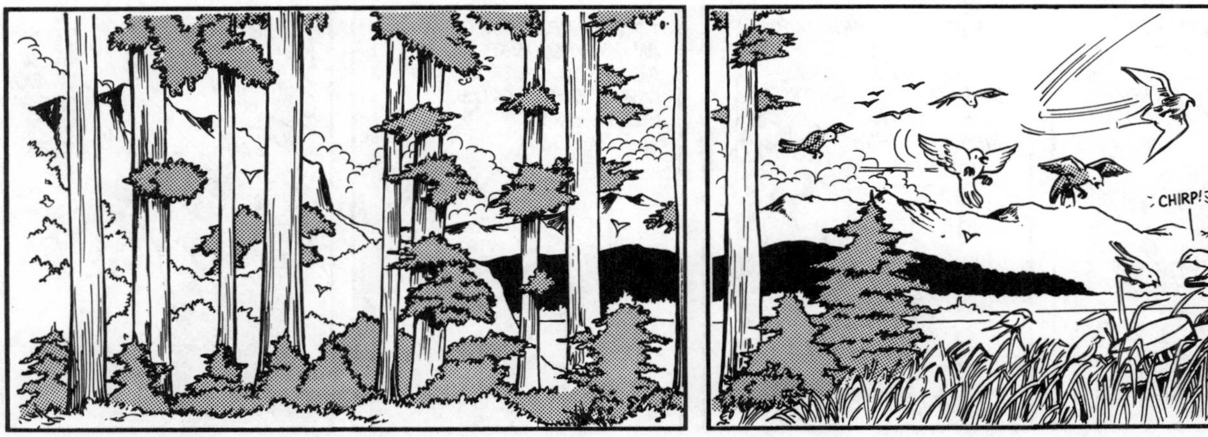
CHIRP!

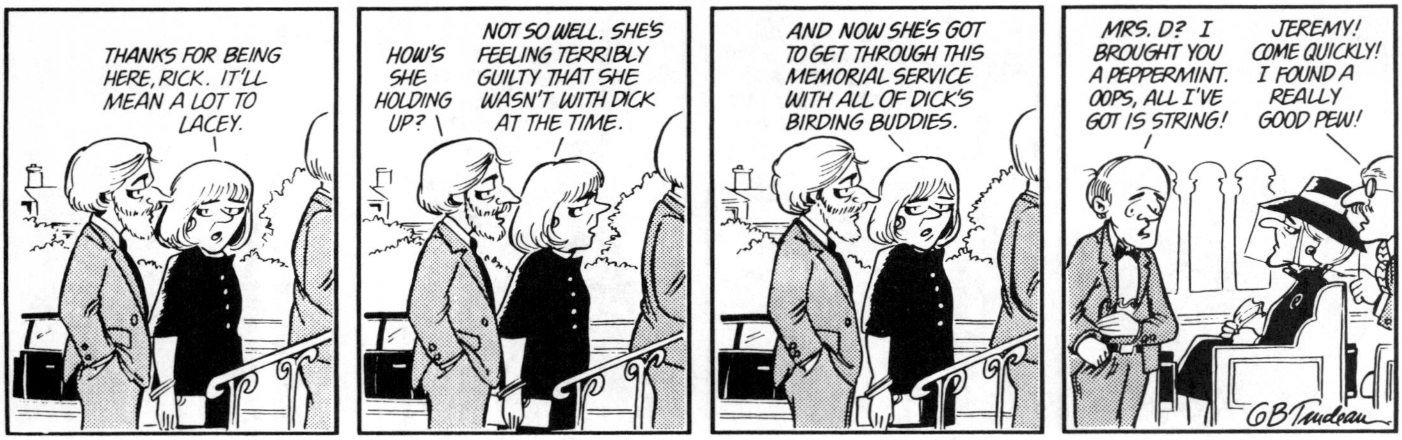
THANKS FOR BEING HERE, RICK. IT'LL MEAN A LOT TO LACEY.
HOW'S SHE HOLDING UP?
NOT SO WELL. SHE'S FEELING TERRIBLY GUILTY THAT SHE WASN'T WITH DICK AT THE TIME.
AND NOW SHE'S GOT TO GET THROUGH THIS MEMORIAL SERVICE WITH ALL OF DICK'S BIRDING BUDDIES.
MRS. D? I BROUGHT YOU A PEPPERMINT. OOPS, ALL I'VE GOT IS STRING!
JEREMY! COME QUICKLY! I FOUND A REALLY GOOD PEW!
GB Trudeau

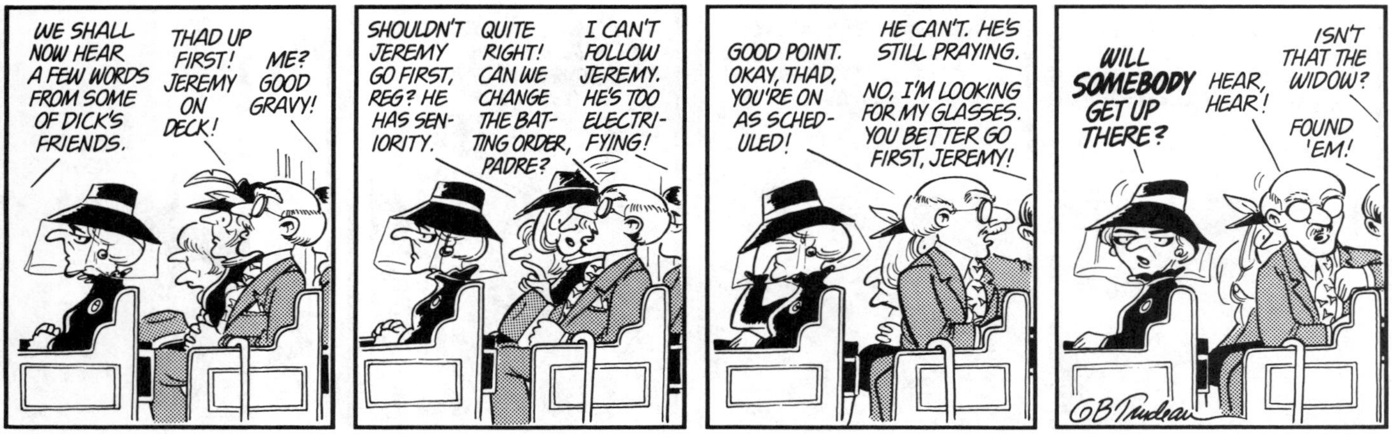
WE SHALL NOW HEAR A FEW WORDS FROM SOME OF DICK'S FRIENDS.
THAD UP FIRST! JEREMY ON DECK!
ME? GOOD GRAVY!
SHOULDN'T JEREMY GO FIRST, REG? HE HAS SENIORITY.
QUITE RIGHT! CAN WE CHANGE THE BATTING ORDER, PADRE?
I CAN'T FOLLOW JEREMY. HE'S TOO ELECTRIFYING!
GOOD POINT. OKAY, THAD, YOU'RE ON AS SCHEDULED!
HE CAN'T. HE'S STILL PRAYING.
NO, I'M LOOKING FOR MY GLASSES. YOU BETTER GO FIRST, JEREMY!
WILL SOMEBODY GET UP THERE?
HEAR, HEAR!
ISN'T THAT THE WIDOW?
FOUND 'EM!
GB Trudeau

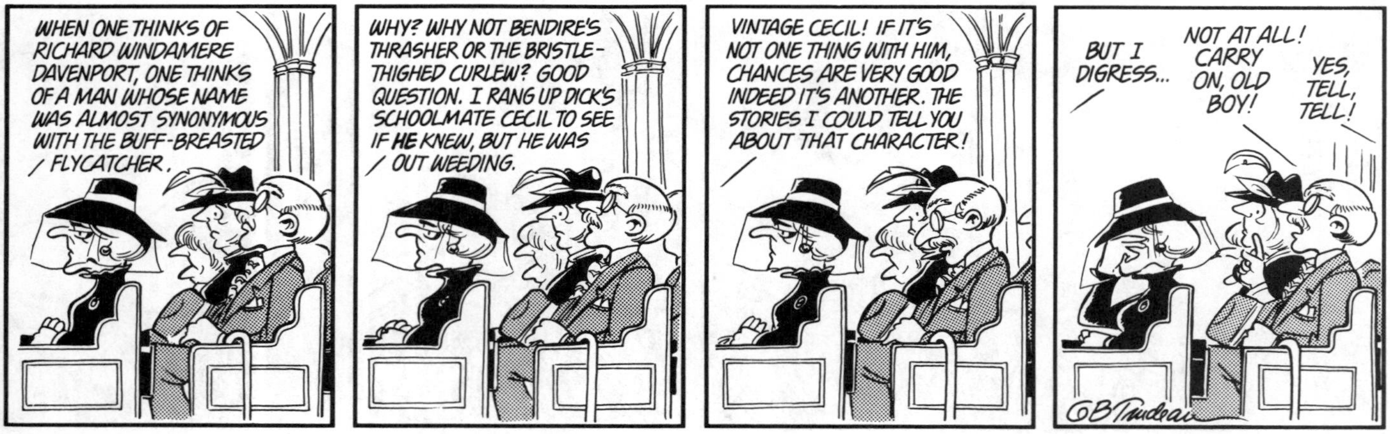
WHEN ONE THINKS OF RICHARD WINDAMERE DAVENPORT, ONE THINKS OF A MAN WHOSE NAME WAS ALMOST SYNONYMOUS WITH THE BUFF-BREASTED FLYCATCHER.
WHY? WHY NOT BENDIRE'S THRASHER OR THE BRISTLE-THIGHED CURLEW? GOOD QUESTION. I RANG UP DICK'S SCHOOLMATE CECIL TO SEE IF HE KNEW, BUT HE WAS OUT WEEDING.
VINTAGE CECIL! IF IT'S NOT ONE THING WITH HIM, CHANCES ARE VERY GOOD INDEED IT'S ANOTHER. THE STORIES I COULD TELL YOU ABOUT THAT CHARACTER!
BUT I DIGRESS...
NOT AT ALL! CARRY ON, OLD BOY!
YES, TELL, TELL!
GB Trudeau

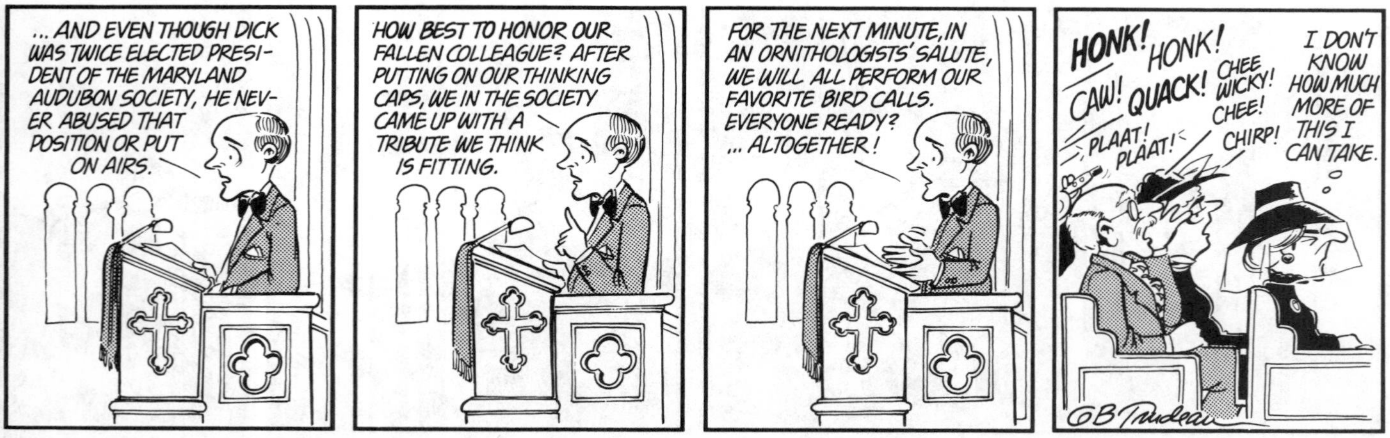
... AND EVEN THOUGH DICK WAS TWICE ELECTED PRESIDENT OF THE MARYLAND AUDUBON SOCIETY, HE NEVER ABUSED THAT POSITION OR PUT ON AIRS.
HOW BEST TO HONOR OUR FALLEN COLLEAGUE? AFTER PUTTING ON OUR THINKING CAPS, WE IN THE SOCIETY CAME UP WITH A TRIBUTE WE THINK IS FITTING.
FOR THE NEXT MINUTE, IN AN ORNITHOLOGISTS' SALUTE, WE WILL ALL PERFORM OUR FAVORITE BIRD CALLS. EVERYONE READY? ... ALTOGETHER!
HONK!
HONK!
CAW!
QUACK!
CHEE WICKY! CHEE!
PLAAT! PLAAT!
CHIRP!
I DON'T KNOW HOW MUCH MORE OF THIS I CAN TAKE.
GB Trudeau

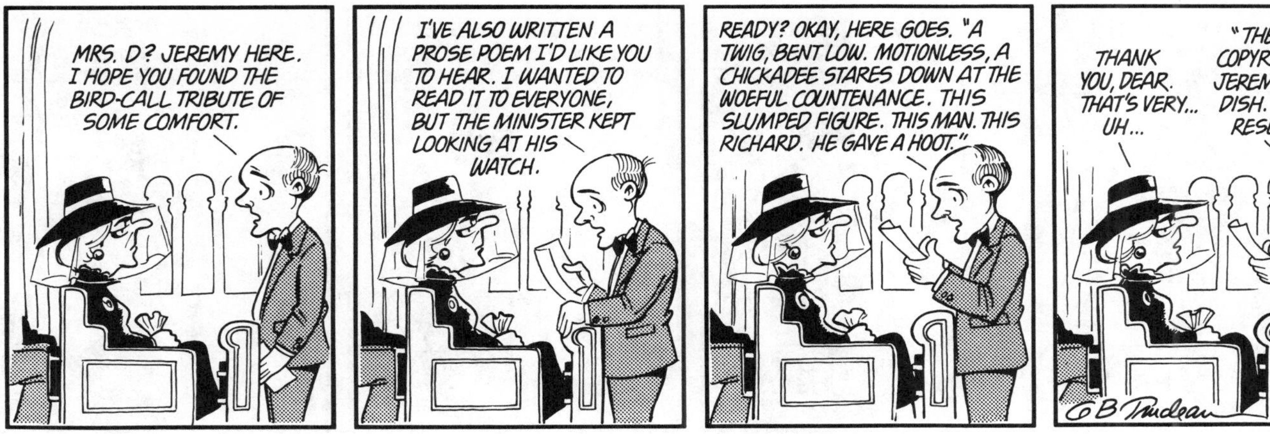
MRS. D? JEREMY HERE. I HOPE YOU FOUND THE BIRD-CALL TRIBUTE OF SOME COMFORT.
I'VE ALSO WRITTEN A PROSE POEM I'D LIKE YOU TO HEAR. I WANTED TO READ IT TO EVERYONE, BUT THE MINISTER KEPT LOOKING AT HIS WATCH.
READY? OKAY, HERE GOES. "A TWIG, BENT LOW. MOTIONLESS, A CHICKADEE STARES DOWN AT THE WOEFUL COUNTENANCE. THIS SLUMPED FIGURE. THIS MAN. THIS RICHARD. HE GAVE A HOOT."
"THE END. COPYRIGHT 1986. JEREMY CAVENDISH. ALL RIGHTS RESERVED."
THANK YOU, DEAR. THAT'S VERY... UH...

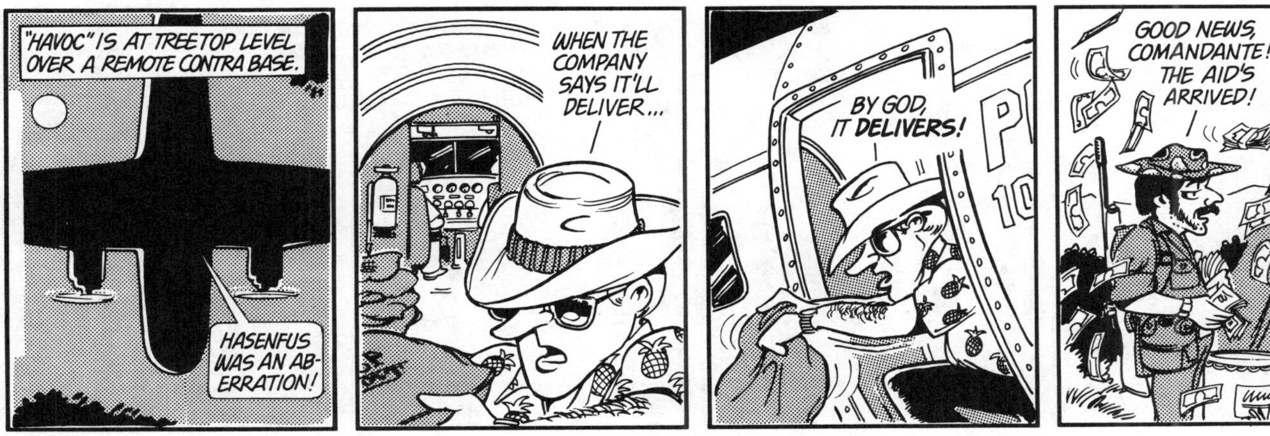
"HAVOC" IS AT TREETOP LEVEL OVER A REMOTE CONTRA BASE.
HASENFUS WAS AN ABERRATION!
WHEN THE COMPANY SAYS IT'LL DELIVER...
BY GOD, IT DELIVERS!
GOOD NEWS, COMANDANTE! THE AID'S ARRIVED!

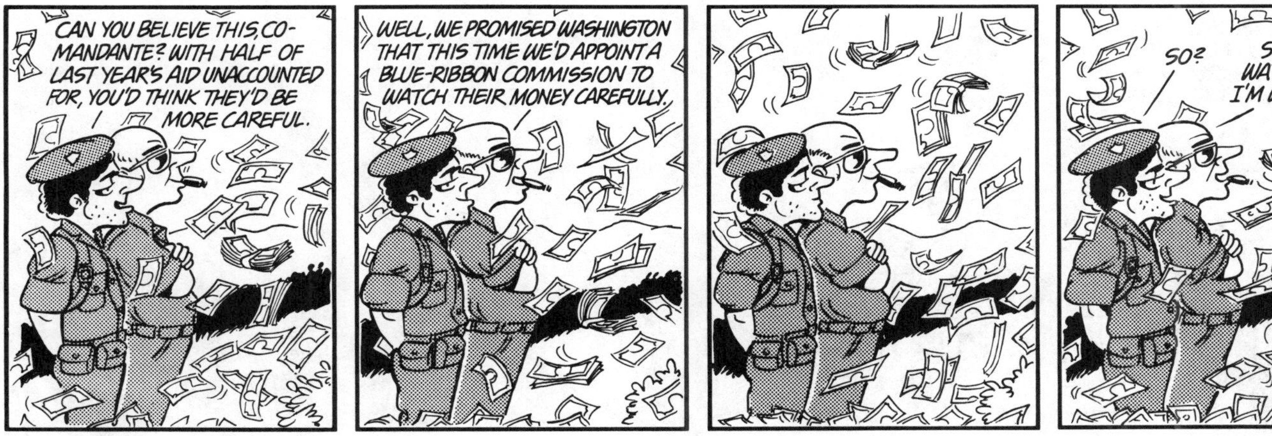
CAN YOU BELIEVE THIS, COMANDANTE? WITH HALF OF LAST YEAR'S AID UNACCOUNTED FOR, YOU'D THINK THEY'D BE MORE CAREFUL.
WELL, WE PROMISED WASHINGTON THAT THIS TIME WE'D APPOINT A BLUE-RIBBON COMMISSION TO WATCH THEIR MONEY CAREFULLY.
SO?
SO I'M WATCHING, I'M WATCHING.

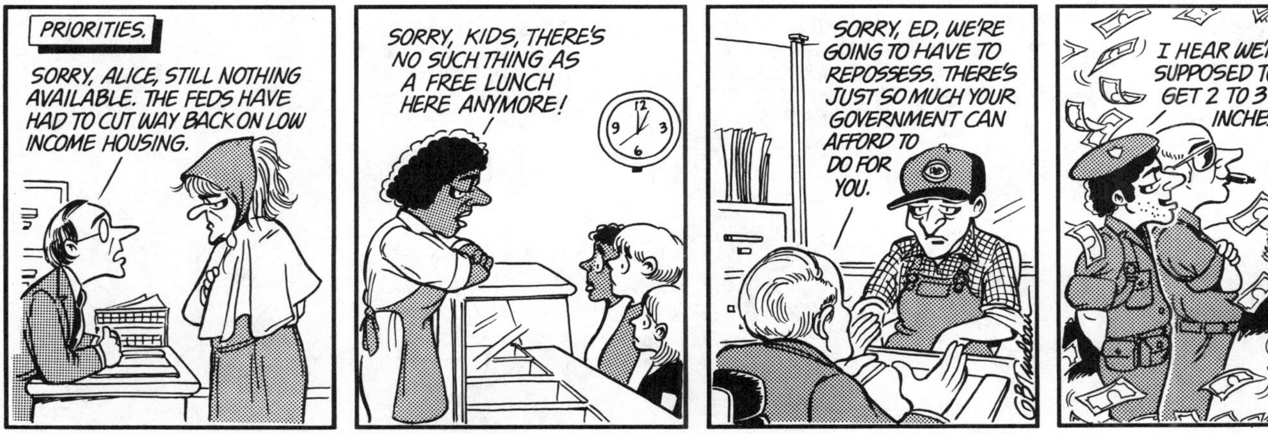
PRIORITIES.
SORRY, ALICE, STILL NOTHING AVAILABLE. THE FEDS HAVE HAD TO CUT WAY BACK ON LOW INCOME HOUSING.
SORRY, KIDS, THERE'S NO SUCH THING AS A FREE LUNCH HERE ANYMORE!
SORRY, ED, WE'RE GOING TO HAVE TO REPOSSESS. THERE'S JUST SO MUCH YOUR GOVERNMENT CAN AFFORD TO DO FOR YOU.
I HEAR WE'RE SUPPOSED TO GET 2 TO 3 INCHES.

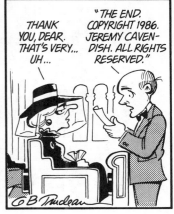

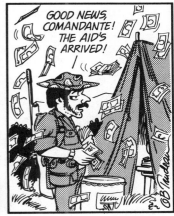

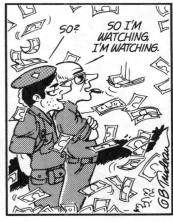

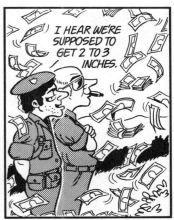

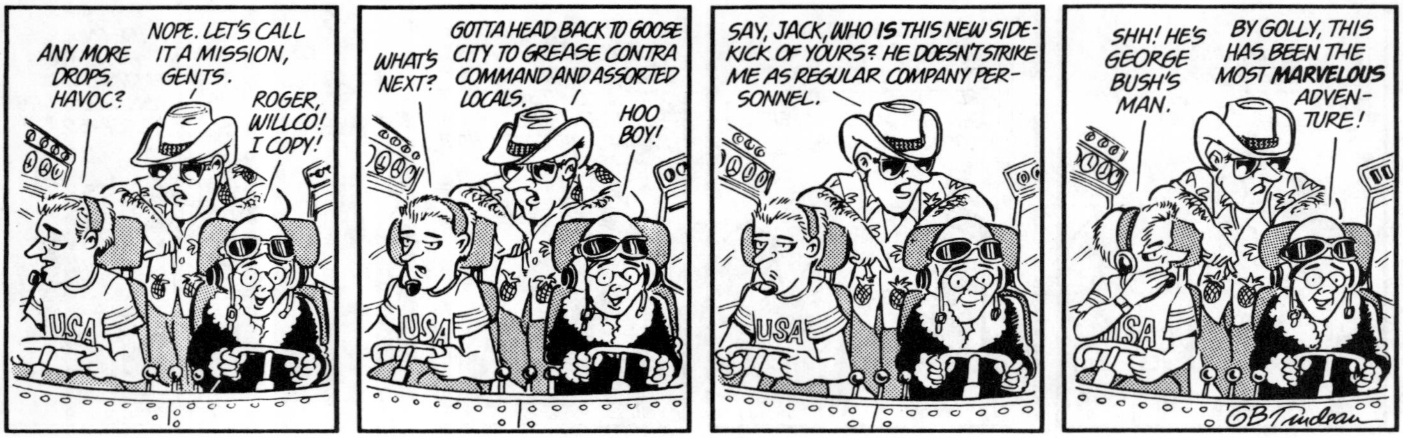
ANY MORE DROPS, HAVOC?
NOPE. LET'S CALL IT A MISSION, GENTS.
ROGER, WILLCO! I COPY!
WHAT'S NEXT?
GOTTA HEAD BACK TO GOOSE CITY TO GREASE CONTRA COMMAND AND ASSORTED LOCALS.
HOO BOY!
SAY, JACK, WHO **IS** THIS NEW SIDEKICK OF YOURS? HE DOESN'T STRIKE ME AS REGULAR COMPANY PERSONNEL.
SHH! HE'S GEORGE BUSH'S MAN.
BY GOLLY, THIS HAS BEEN THE MOST **MARVELOUS** ADVENTURE!
GBTrudeau

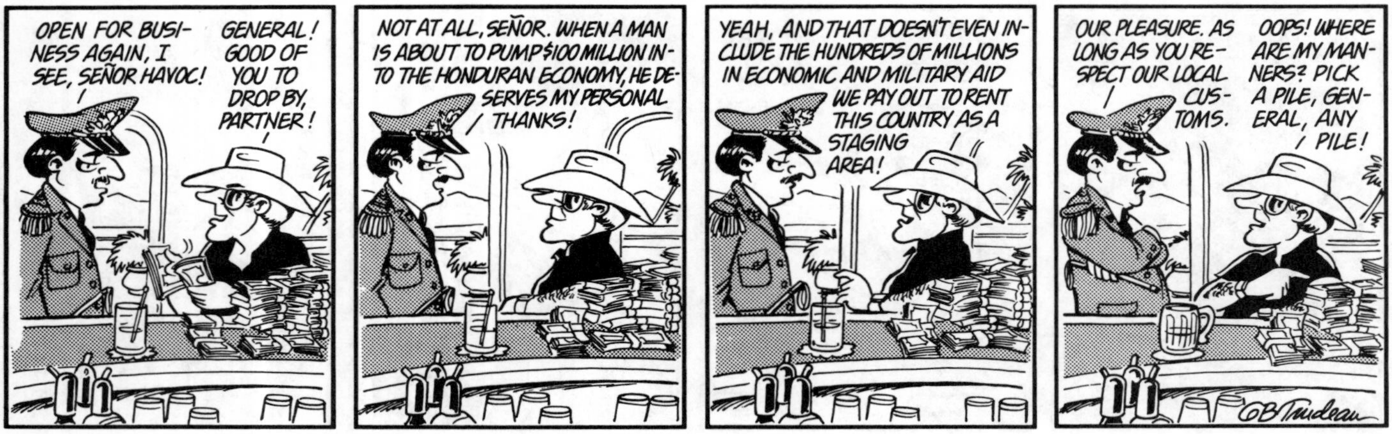
OPEN FOR BUSINESS AGAIN, I SEE, SEÑOR HAVOC!
GENERAL! GOOD OF YOU TO DROP BY, PARTNER!
NOT AT ALL, SEÑOR. WHEN A MAN IS ABOUT TO PUMP $100 MILLION INTO THE HONDURAN ECONOMY, HE DESERVES MY PERSONAL THANKS!
YEAH, AND THAT DOESN'T EVEN INCLUDE THE HUNDREDS OF MILLIONS IN ECONOMIC AND MILITARY AID WE PAY OUT TO RENT THIS COUNTRY AS A STAGING AREA!
OUR PLEASURE. AS LONG AS YOU RESPECT OUR LOCAL CUSTOMS.
OOPS! WHERE ARE MY MANNERS? PICK A PILE, GENERAL, ANY PILE!
GBTrudeau

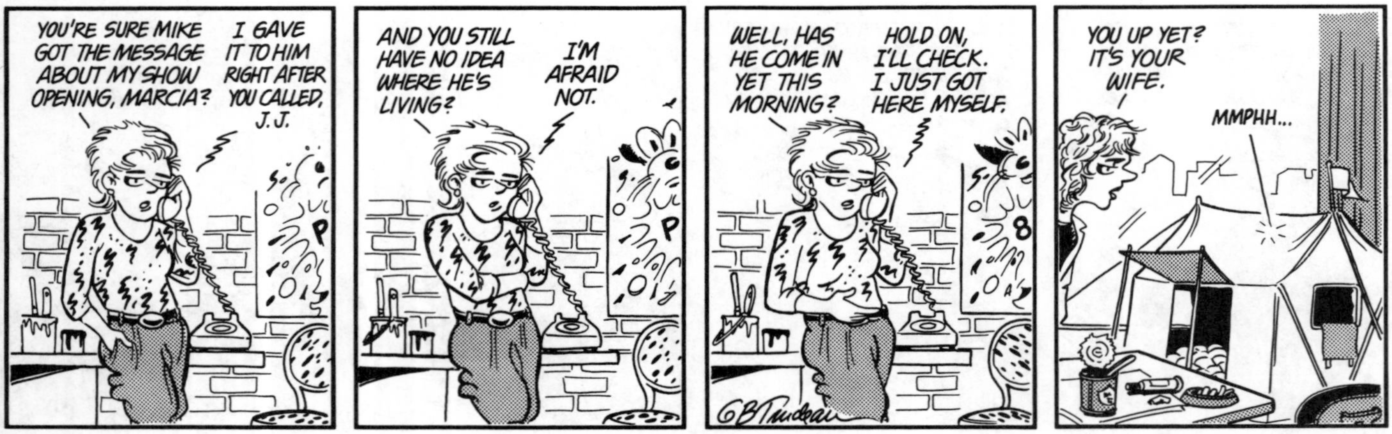
YOU'RE SURE MIKE GOT THE MESSAGE ABOUT MY SHOW OPENING, MARCIA?
I GAVE IT TO HIM RIGHT AFTER YOU CALLED, J.J.
AND YOU STILL HAVE NO IDEA WHERE HE'S LIVING?
I'M AFRAID NOT.
WELL, HAS HE COME IN YET THIS MORNING?
HOLD ON, I'LL CHECK. I JUST GOT HERE MYSELF.
GBTrudeau
YOU UP YET? IT'S YOUR WIFE.
MMPHH...

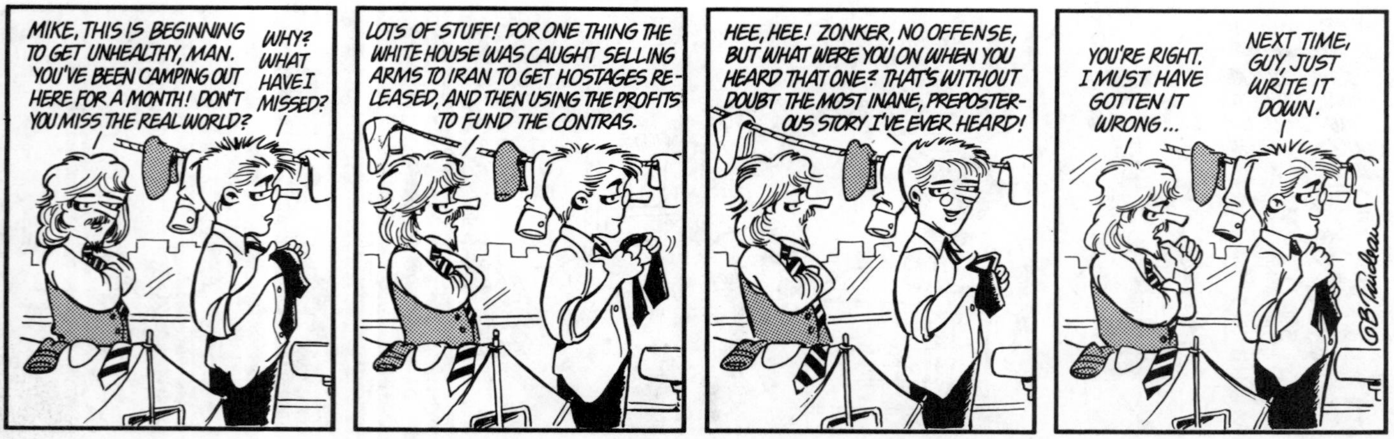
MIKE, THIS IS BEGINNING TO GET UNHEALTHY, MAN. YOU'VE BEEN CAMPING OUT HERE FOR A MONTH! DON'T YOU MISS THE REAL WORLD?
WHY? WHAT HAVE I MISSED?
LOTS OF STUFF! FOR ONE THING THE WHITE HOUSE WAS CAUGHT SELLING ARMS TO IRAN TO GET HOSTAGES RELEASED, AND THEN USING THE PROFITS TO FUND THE CONTRAS.
HEE, HEE! ZONKER, NO OFFENSE, BUT WHAT WERE YOU ON WHEN YOU HEARD THAT ONE? THAT'S WITHOUT DOUBT THE MOST INANE, PREPOSTEROUS STORY I'VE EVER HEARD!
YOU'RE RIGHT. I MUST HAVE GOTTEN IT WRONG...
NEXT TIME, GUY, JUST WRITE IT DOWN.
GBTrudeau

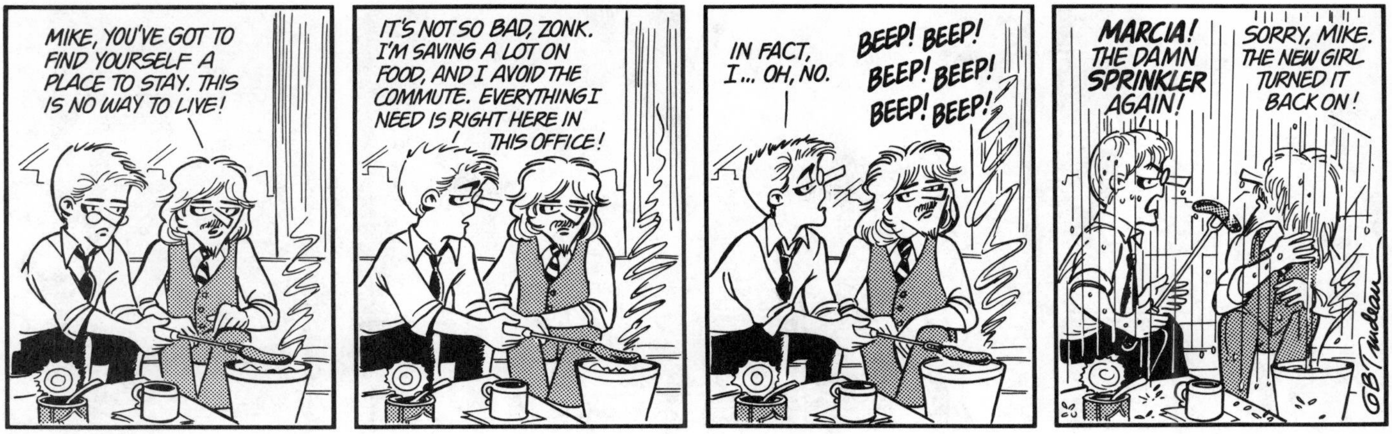
MIKE, YOU'VE GOT TO FIND YOURSELF A PLACE TO STAY. THIS IS NO WAY TO LIVE!
IT'S NOT SO BAD, ZONK. I'M SAVING A LOT ON FOOD, AND I AVOID THE COMMUTE. EVERYTHING I NEED IS RIGHT HERE IN THIS OFFICE!
IN FACT, I... OH, NO.
BEEP! BEEP! BEEP! BEEP! BEEP! BEEP!
MARCIA! THE DAMN SPRINKLER AGAIN!
SORRY, MIKE. THE NEW GIRL TURNED IT BACK ON!

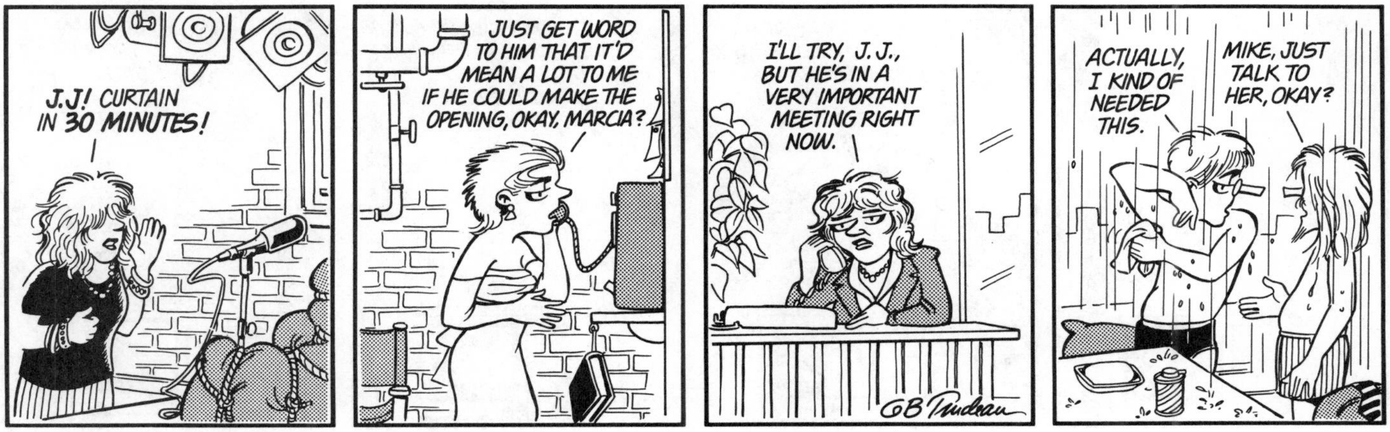
J.J! CURTAIN IN 30 MINUTES!
JUST GET WORD TO HIM THAT IT'D MEAN A LOT TO ME IF HE COULD MAKE THE OPENING, OKAY, MARCIA?
I'LL TRY, J.J., BUT HE'S IN A VERY IMPORTANT MEETING RIGHT NOW.
ACTUALLY, I KIND OF NEEDED THIS.
MIKE, JUST TALK TO HER, OKAY?

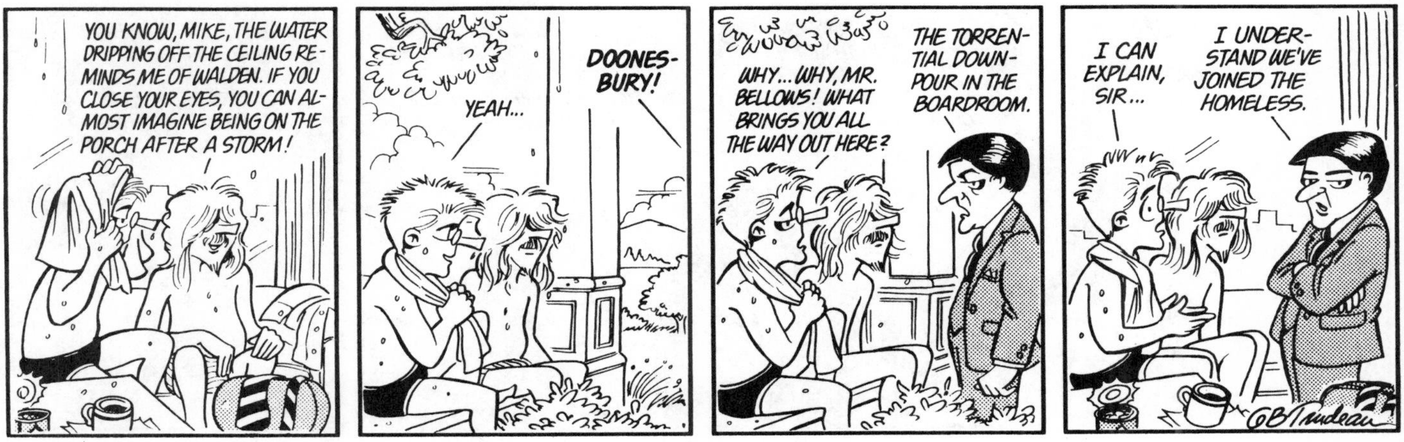
YOU KNOW, MIKE, THE WATER DRIPPING OFF THE CEILING REMINDS ME OF WALDEN. IF YOU CLOSE YOUR EYES, YOU CAN ALMOST IMAGINE BEING ON THE PORCH AFTER A STORM!
YEAH...
DOONESBURY!
WHY... WHY, MR. BELLOWS! WHAT BRINGS YOU ALL THE WAY OUT HERE?
THE TORRENTIAL DOWNPOUR IN THE BOARDROOM.
I CAN EXPLAIN, SIR...
I UNDERSTAND WE'VE JOINED THE HOMELESS.

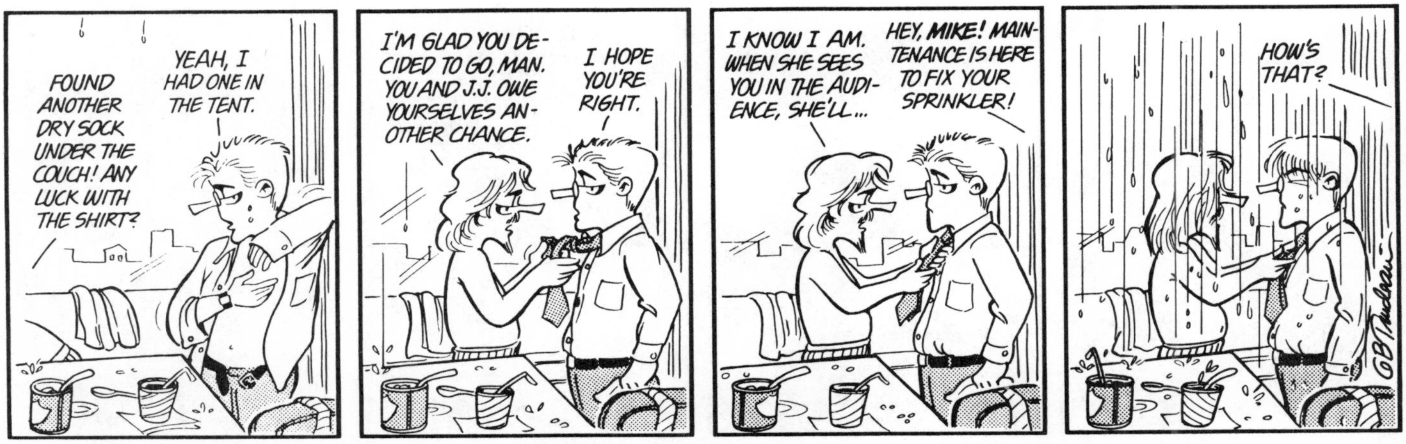
FOUND ANOTHER DRY SOCK UNDER THE COUCH! ANY LUCK WITH THE SHIRT?
YEAH, I HAD ONE IN THE TENT.
I'M GLAD YOU DECIDED TO GO, MAN. YOU AND J.J. OWE YOURSELVES ANOTHER CHANCE.
I HOPE YOU'RE RIGHT.
I KNOW I AM. WHEN SHE SEES YOU IN THE AUDIENCE, SHE'LL...
HEY, MIKE! MAINTENANCE IS HERE TO FIX YOUR SPRINKLER!
HOW'S THAT?

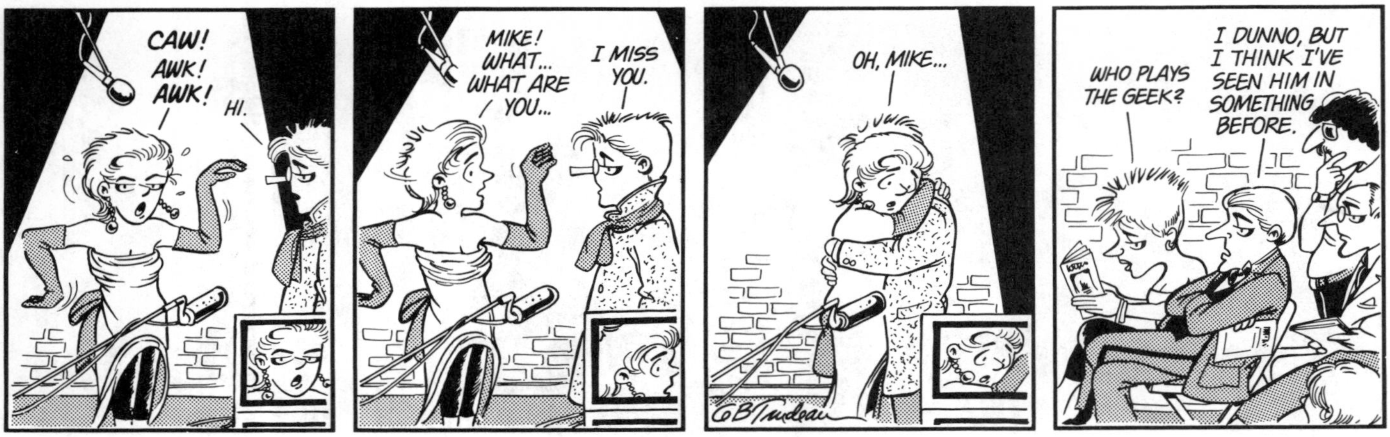
CAW! AWK! AWK!
HI.
MIKE! WHAT... WHAT ARE YOU...
I MISS YOU.
OH, MIKE...
GB Trudeau
WHO PLAYS THE GEEK?
I DUNNO, BUT I THINK I'VE SEEN HIM IN SOMETHING BEFORE.

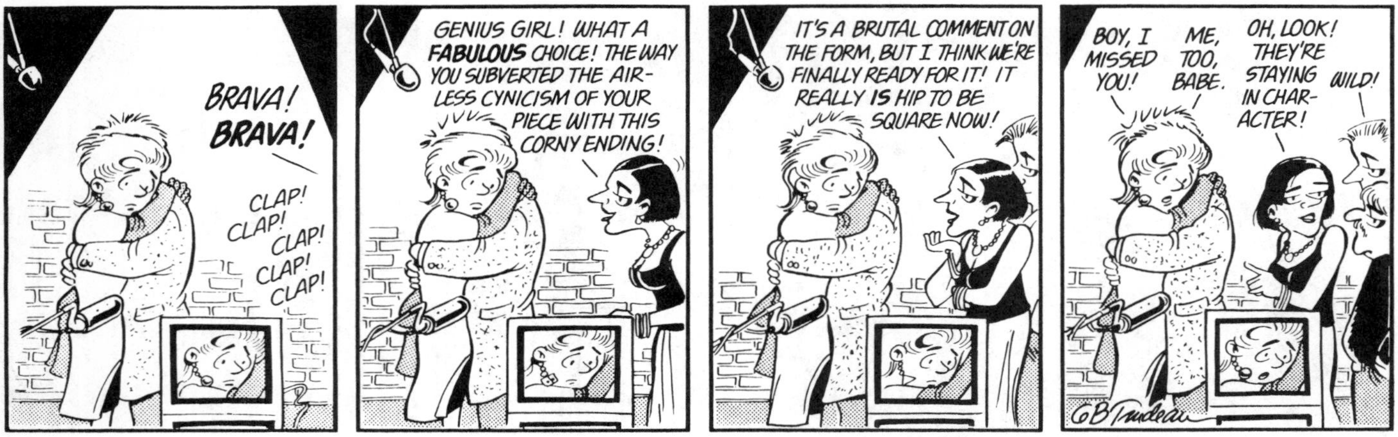
BRAVA! BRAVA!
CLAP! CLAP! CLAP! CLAP! CLAP!
GENIUS GIRL! WHAT A FABULOUS CHOICE! THE WAY YOU SUBVERTED THE AIR-LESS CYNICISM OF YOUR PIECE WITH THIS CORNY ENDING!
IT'S A BRUTAL COMMENT ON THE FORM, BUT I THINK WE'RE FINALLY READY FOR IT! IT REALLY IS HIP TO BE SQUARE NOW!
GB Trudeau
BOY, I MISSED YOU!
ME, TOO, BABE.
OH, LOOK! THEY'RE STAYING IN CHAR-ACTER!
WILD!

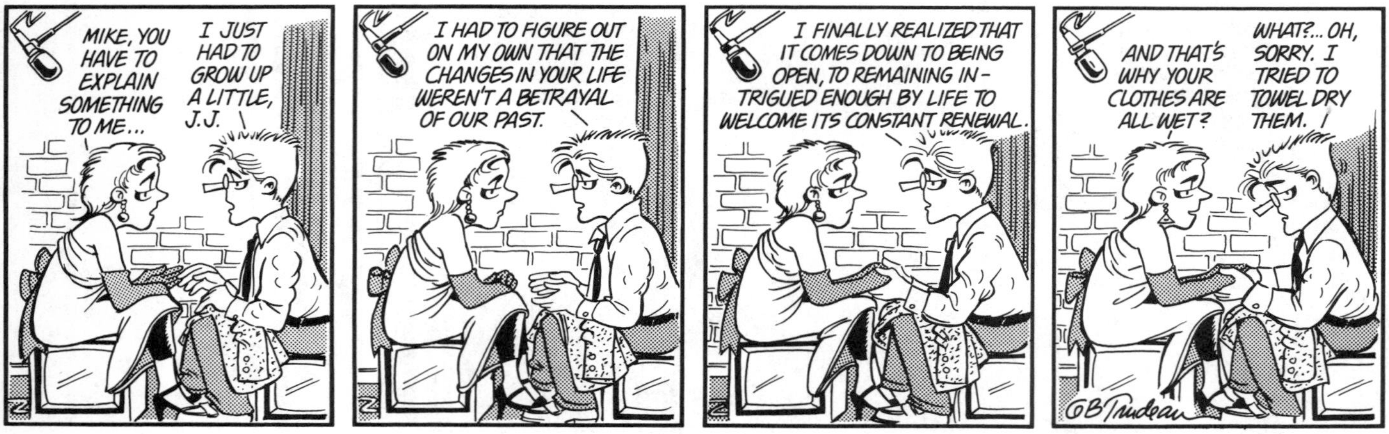
MIKE, YOU HAVE TO EXPLAIN SOMETHING TO ME...
I JUST HAD TO GROW UP A LITTLE, J.J.
I HAD TO FIGURE OUT ON MY OWN THAT THE CHANGES IN YOUR LIFE WEREN'T A BETRAYAL OF OUR PAST.
I FINALLY REALIZED THAT IT COMES DOWN TO BEING OPEN, TO REMAINING IN-TRIGUED ENOUGH BY LIFE TO WELCOME ITS CONSTANT RENEWAL.
AND THAT'S WHY YOUR CLOTHES ARE ALL WET?
WHAT?... OH, SORRY. I TRIED TO TOWEL DRY THEM.
GB Trudeau

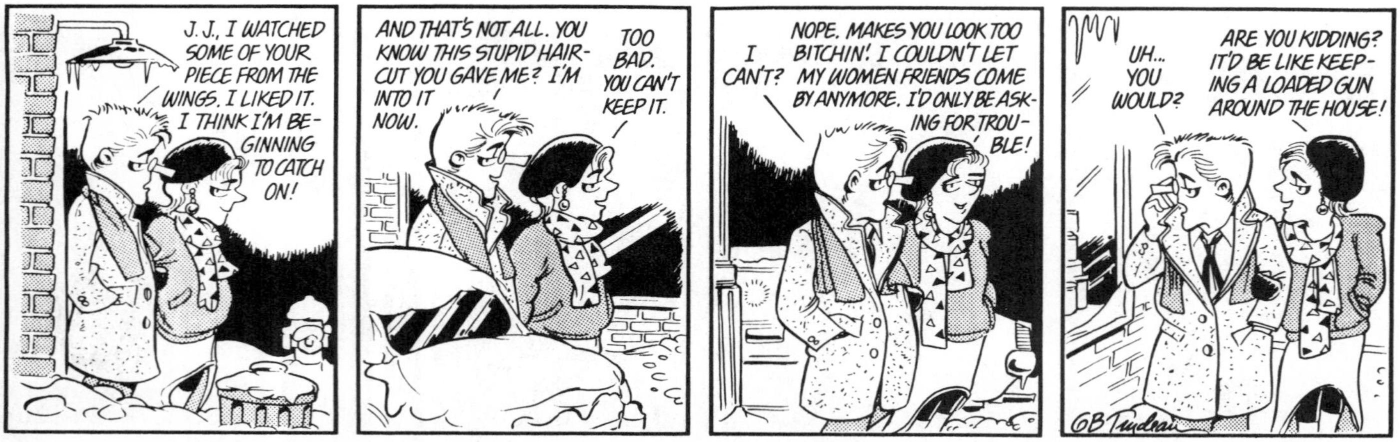
J.J., I WATCHED SOME OF YOUR PIECE FROM THE WINGS. I LIKED IT. I THINK I'M BE-GINNING TO CATCH ON!
AND THAT'S NOT ALL. YOU KNOW THIS STUPID HAIR-CUT YOU GAVE ME? I'M INTO IT NOW.
TOO BAD. YOU CAN'T KEEP IT.
I CAN'T?
NOPE. MAKES YOU LOOK TOO BITCHIN'! I COULDN'T LET MY WOMEN FRIENDS COME BY ANYMORE. I'D ONLY BE ASK-ING FOR TROU-BLE!
UH... YOU WOULD?
ARE YOU KIDDING? IT'D BE LIKE KEEP-ING A LOADED GUN AROUND THE HOUSE!
GB Trudeau

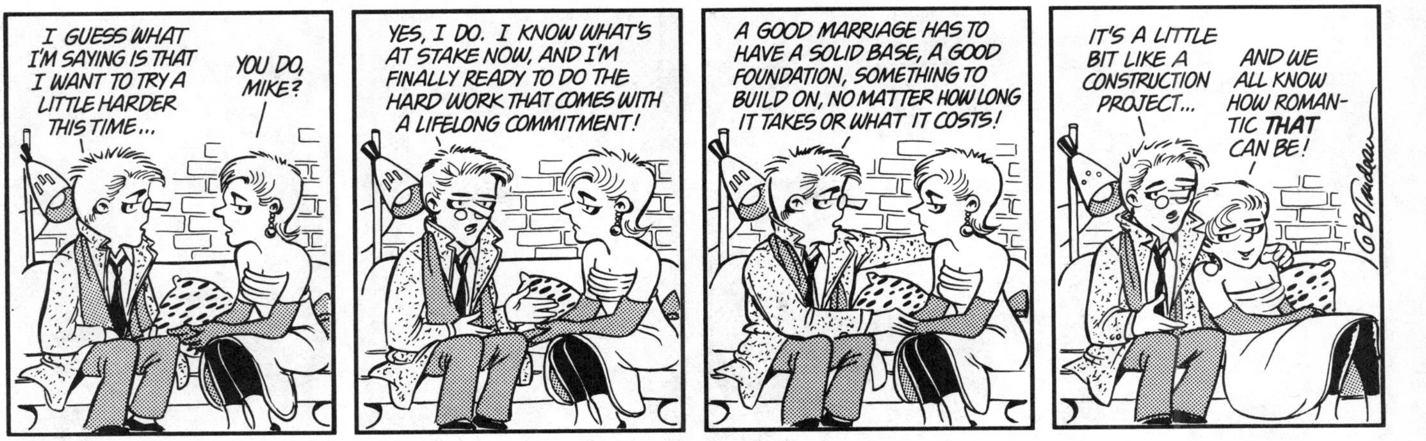
I GUESS WHAT I'M SAYING IS THAT I WANT TO TRY A LITTLE HARDER THIS TIME...
YOU DO, MIKE?
YES, I DO. I KNOW WHAT'S AT STAKE NOW, AND I'M FINALLY READY TO DO THE HARD WORK THAT COMES WITH A LIFELONG COMMITMENT!
A GOOD MARRIAGE HAS TO HAVE A SOLID BASE, A GOOD FOUNDATION, SOMETHING TO BUILD ON, NO MATTER HOW LONG IT TAKES OR WHAT IT COSTS!
IT'S A LITTLE BIT LIKE A CONSTRUCTION PROJECT...
AND WE ALL KNOW HOW ROMANTIC THAT CAN BE!
GBTrudeau

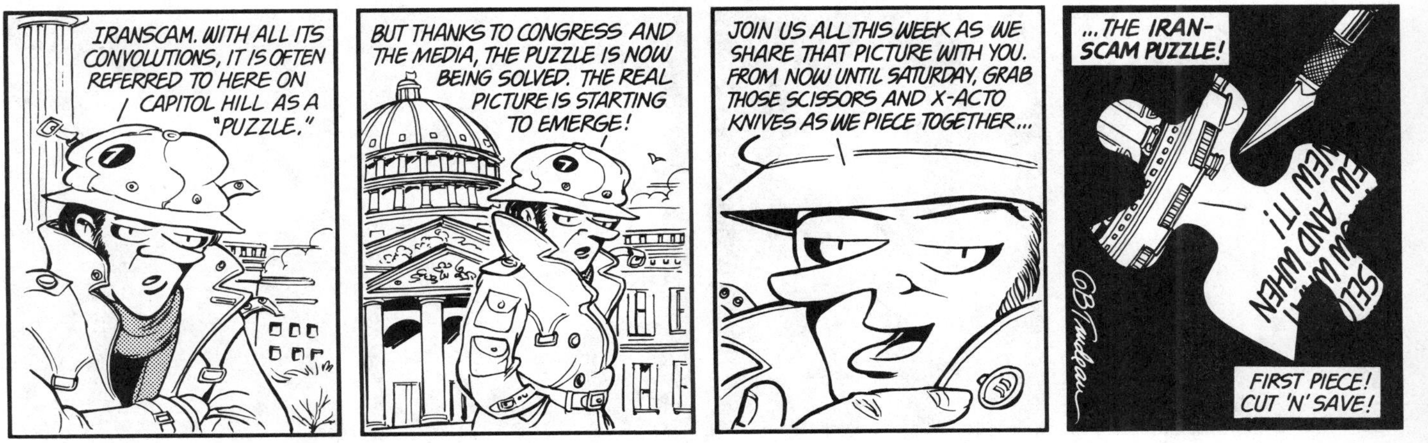
IRANSCAM. WITH ALL ITS CONVOLUTIONS, IT IS OFTEN REFERRED TO HERE ON CAPITOL HILL AS A "PUZZLE."
BUT THANKS TO CONGRESS AND THE MEDIA, THE PUZZLE IS NOW BEING SOLVED. THE REAL PICTURE IS STARTING TO EMERGE!
JOIN US ALL THIS WEEK AS WE SHARE THAT PICTURE WITH YOU. FROM NOW UNTIL SATURDAY, GRAB THOSE SCISSORS AND X-ACTO KNIVES AS WE PIECE TOGETHER...
...THE IRAN-SCAM PUZZLE!
FIRST PIECE! CUT 'N' SAVE!
GBTrudeau

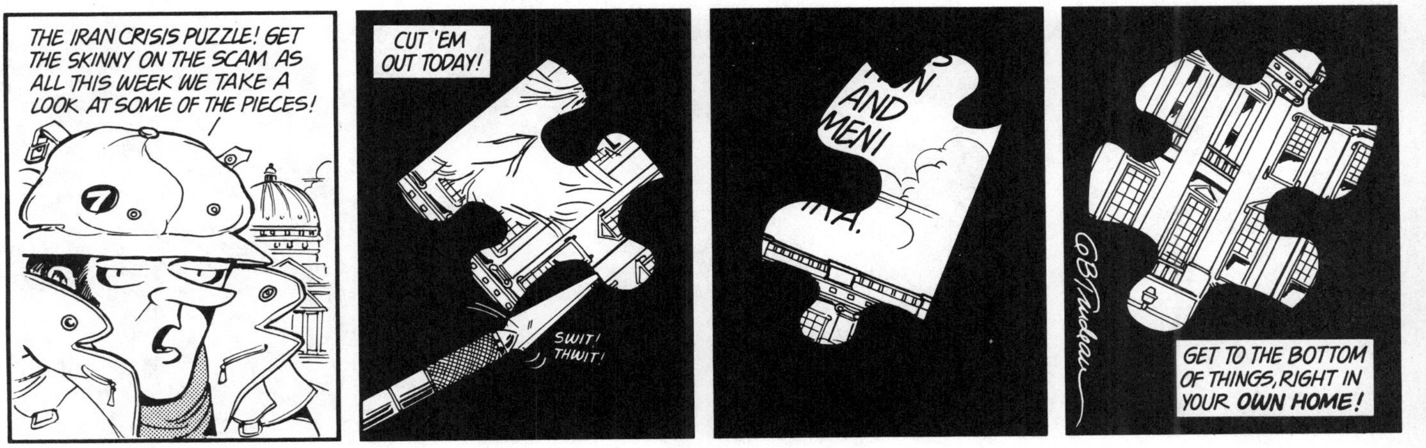
THE IRAN CRISIS PUZZLE! GET THE SKINNY ON THE SCAM AS ALL THIS WEEK WE TAKE A LOOK AT SOME OF THE PIECES!
CUT 'EM OUT TODAY!
SWIT! THWIT!
GET TO THE BOTTOM OF THINGS, RIGHT IN YOUR OWN HOME!
GBTrudeau

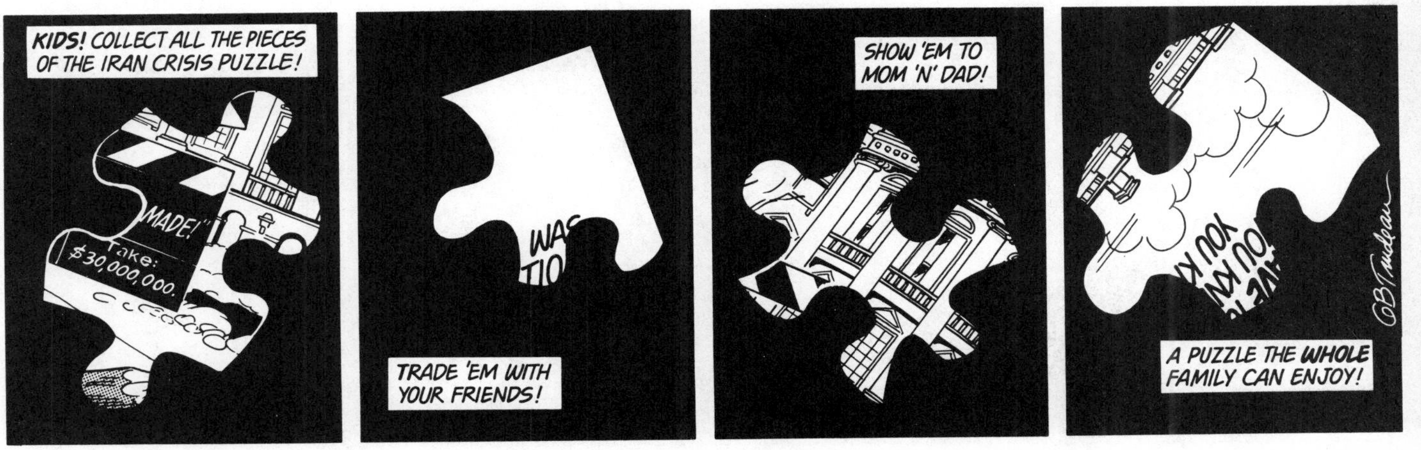
KIDS! COLLECT ALL THE PIECES OF THE IRAN CRISIS PUZZLE!
MADE!
Take: $30,000,000.
TRADE 'EM WITH YOUR FRIENDS!
SHOW 'EM TO MOM 'N' DAD!
A PUZZLE THE WHOLE FAMILY CAN ENJOY!
GBTrudeau

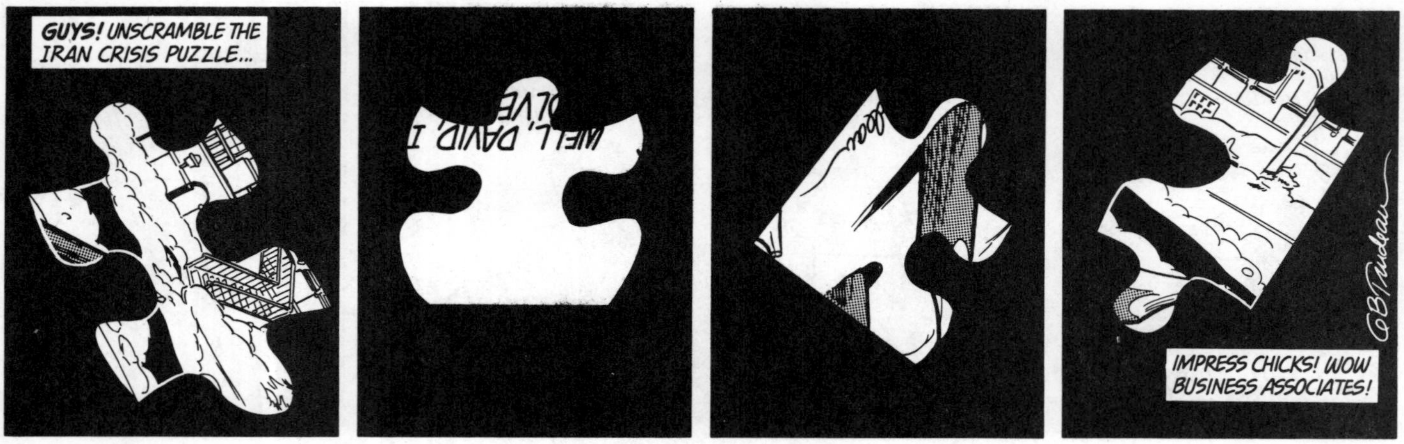
GUYS! UNSCRAMBLE THE IRAN CRISIS PUZZLE...
IMPRESS CHICKS! WOW BUSINESS ASSOCIATES!

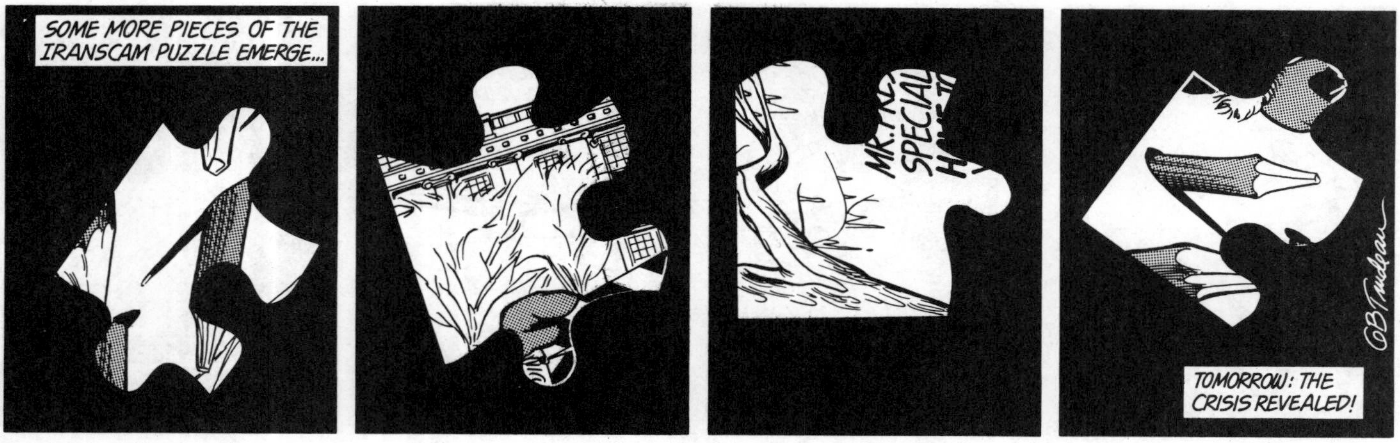
SOME MORE PIECES OF THE IRANSCAM PUZZLE EMERGE...
TOMORROW: THE CRISIS REVEALED!

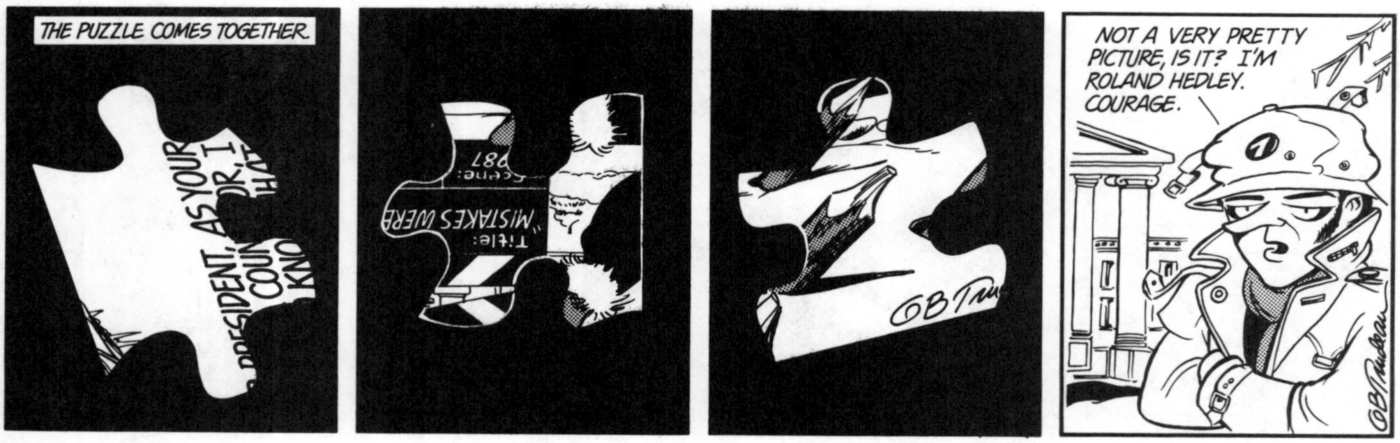
THE PUZZLE COMES TOGETHER.
NOT A VERY PRETTY PICTURE, IS IT? I'M ROLAND HEDLEY. COURAGE.

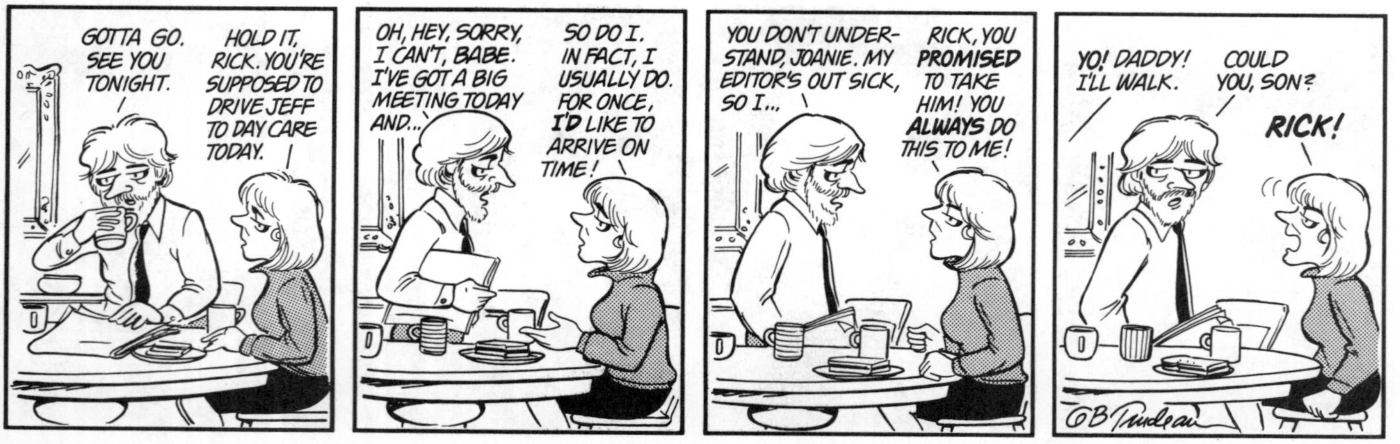
GOTTA GO. SEE YOU TONIGHT.
HOLD IT, RICK. YOU'RE SUPPOSED TO DRIVE JEFF TO DAY CARE TODAY.
OH, HEY, SORRY, I CAN'T, BABE. I'VE GOT A BIG MEETING TODAY AND...
SO DO I. IN FACT, I USUALLY DO. FOR ONCE, I'D LIKE TO ARRIVE ON TIME!
YOU DON'T UNDERSTAND, JOANIE. MY EDITOR'S OUT SICK, SO I...
RICK, YOU PROMISED TO TAKE HIM! YOU ALWAYS DO THIS TO ME!
YO! DADDY! I'LL WALK.
COULD YOU, SON?
RICK!

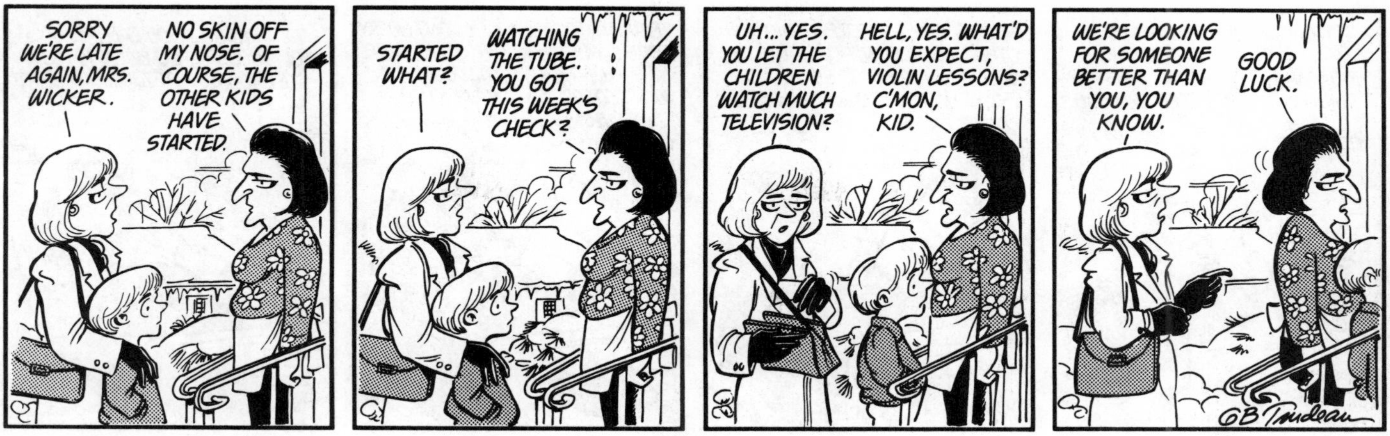
SORRY WE'RE LATE AGAIN, MRS. WICKER.
NO SKIN OFF MY NOSE. OF COURSE, THE OTHER KIDS HAVE STARTED.
STARTED WHAT?
WATCHING THE TUBE. YOU GOT THIS WEEK'S CHECK?
UH... YES. YOU LET THE CHILDREN WATCH MUCH TELEVISION?
HELL, YES. WHAT'D YOU EXPECT, VIOLIN LESSONS? C'MON, KID.
WE'RE LOOKING FOR SOMEONE BETTER THAN YOU, YOU KNOW.
GOOD LUCK.
GB Trudeau

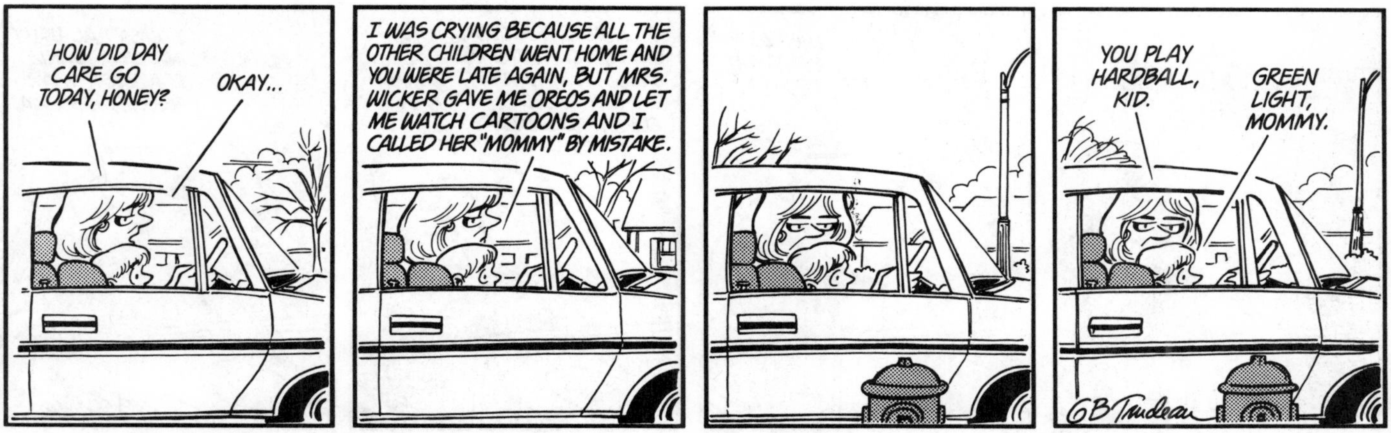
HOW DID DAY CARE GO TODAY, HONEY?
OKAY...
I WAS CRYING BECAUSE ALL THE OTHER CHILDREN WENT HOME AND YOU WERE LATE AGAIN, BUT MRS. WICKER GAVE ME OREOS AND LET ME WATCH CARTOONS AND I CALLED HER "MOMMY" BY MISTAKE.
YOU PLAY HARDBALL, KID.
GREEN LIGHT, MOMMY.
GB Trudeau

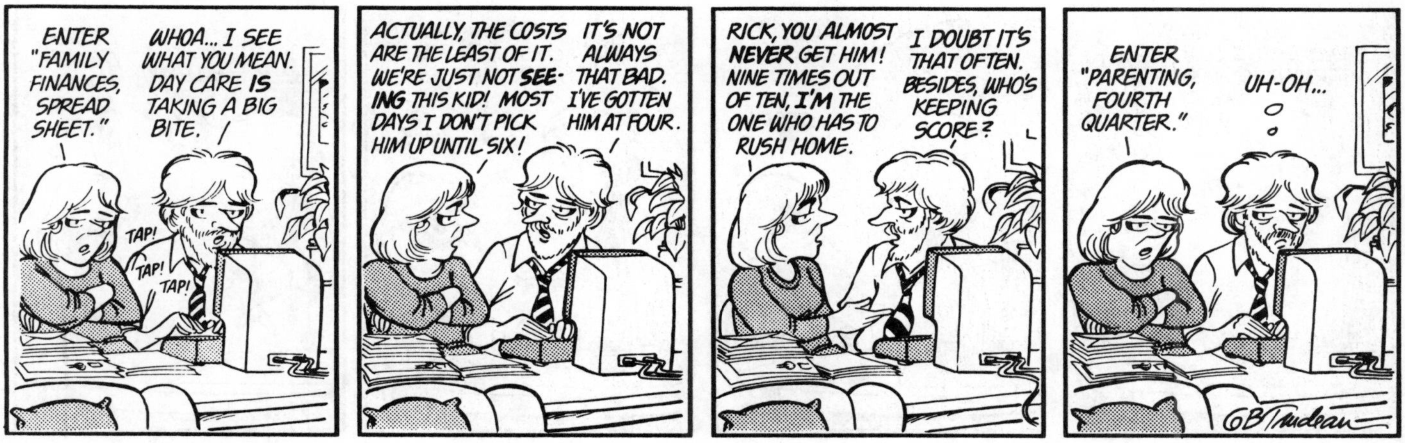
ENTER "FAMILY FINANCES, SPREAD SHEET."
WHOA... I SEE WHAT YOU MEAN. DAY CARE IS TAKING A BIG BITE.
TAP! TAP! TAP!
ACTUALLY, THE COSTS ARE THE LEAST OF IT. WE'RE JUST NOT SEEING THIS KID! MOST DAYS I DON'T PICK HIM UP UNTIL SIX!
IT'S NOT ALWAYS THAT BAD. I'VE GOTTEN HIM AT FOUR.
RICK, YOU ALMOST NEVER GET HIM! NINE TIMES OUT OF TEN, I'M THE ONE WHO HAS TO RUSH HOME.
I DOUBT IT'S THAT OFTEN. BESIDES, WHO'S KEEPING SCORE?
ENTER "PARENTING, FOURTH QUARTER."
UH-OH...
GB Trudeau

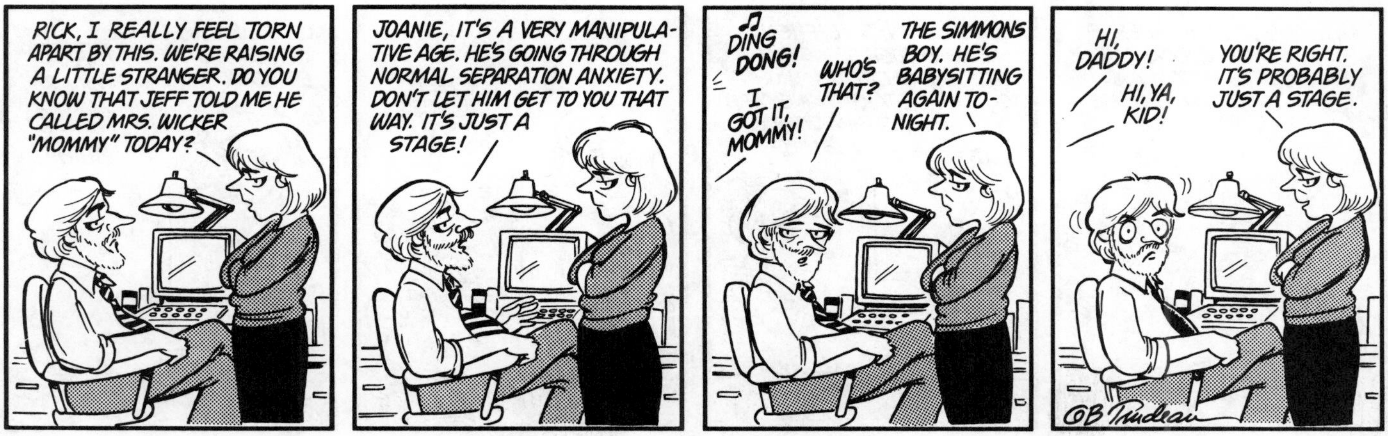
RICK, I REALLY FEEL TORN APART BY THIS. WE'RE RAISING A LITTLE STRANGER. DO YOU KNOW THAT JEFF TOLD ME HE CALLED MRS. WICKER "MOMMY" TODAY?
JOANIE, IT'S A VERY MANIPULATIVE AGE. HE'S GOING THROUGH NORMAL SEPARATION ANXIETY. DON'T LET HIM GET TO YOU THAT WAY. IT'S JUST A STAGE!
DING DONG!
I GOT IT, MOMMY!
WHO'S THAT?
THE SIMMONS BOY. HE'S BABYSITTING AGAIN TONIGHT.
HI, DADDY!
HI, YA, KID!
YOU'RE RIGHT. IT'S PROBABLY JUST A STAGE.
GB Trudeau

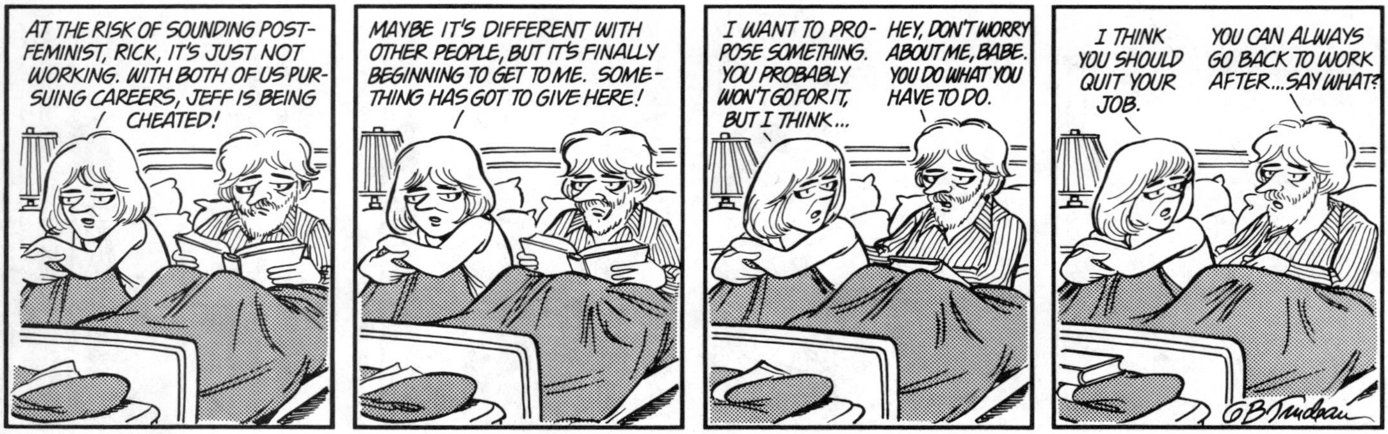
AT THE RISK OF SOUNDING POST-FEMINIST, RICK, IT'S JUST NOT WORKING. WITH BOTH OF US PURSUING CAREERS, JEFF IS BEING CHEATED!
MAYBE IT'S DIFFERENT WITH OTHER PEOPLE, BUT IT'S FINALLY BEGINNING TO GET TO ME. SOMETHING HAS GOT TO GIVE HERE!
I WANT TO PROPOSE SOMETHING. YOU PROBABLY WON'T GO FOR IT, BUT I THINK...
HEY, DON'T WORRY ABOUT ME, BABE. YOU DO WHAT YOU HAVE TO DO.
I THINK YOU SHOULD QUIT YOUR JOB.
YOU CAN ALWAYS GO BACK TO WORK AFTER... SAY WHAT?
GB Trudeau

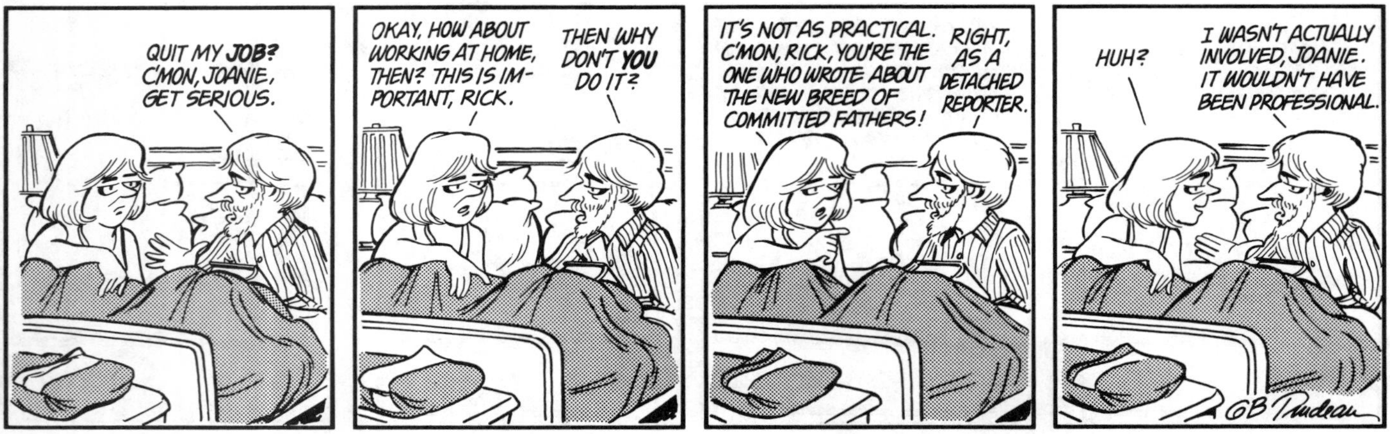
QUIT MY **JOB?** C'MON, JOANIE, GET SERIOUS.
OKAY, HOW ABOUT WORKING AT HOME, THEN? THIS IS IMPORTANT, RICK.
THEN WHY DON'T **YOU** DO IT?
IT'S NOT AS PRACTICAL. C'MON, RICK, YOU'RE THE ONE WHO WROTE ABOUT THE NEW BREED OF COMMITTED FATHERS!
RIGHT, AS A DETACHED REPORTER.
HUH?
I WASN'T ACTUALLY INVOLVED, JOANIE. IT WOULDN'T HAVE BEEN PROFESSIONAL.
GB Trudeau

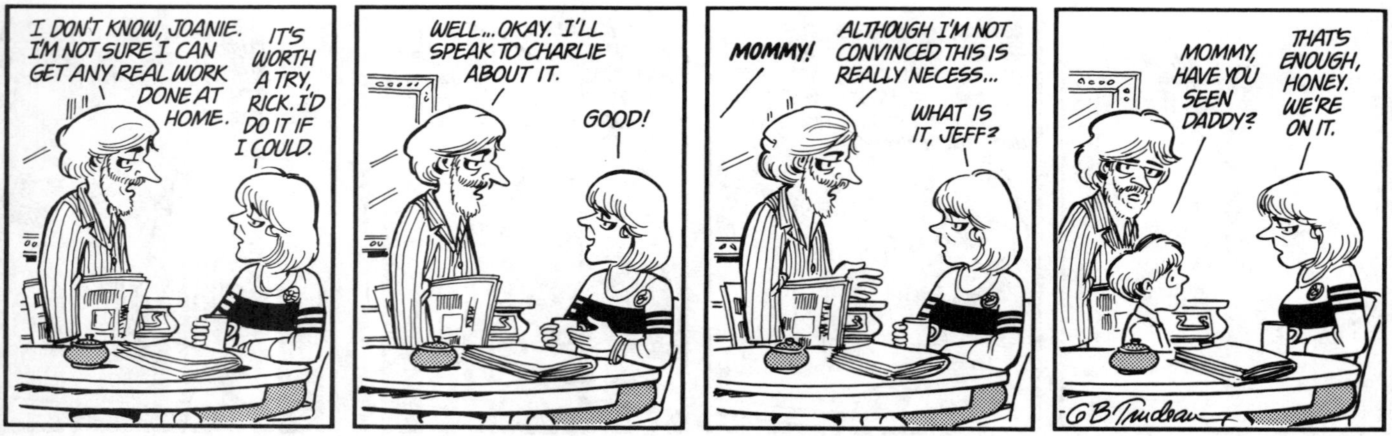
I DON'T KNOW, JOANIE. I'M NOT SURE I CAN GET ANY REAL WORK DONE AT HOME.
IT'S WORTH A TRY, RICK. I'D DO IT IF I COULD.
WELL... OKAY. I'LL SPEAK TO CHARLIE ABOUT IT.
GOOD!
MOMMY!
ALTHOUGH I'M NOT CONVINCED THIS IS REALLY NECESS...
WHAT IS IT, JEFF?
MOMMY, HAVE YOU SEEN DADDY?
THAT'S ENOUGH, HONEY. WE'RE ON IT.
GB Trudeau

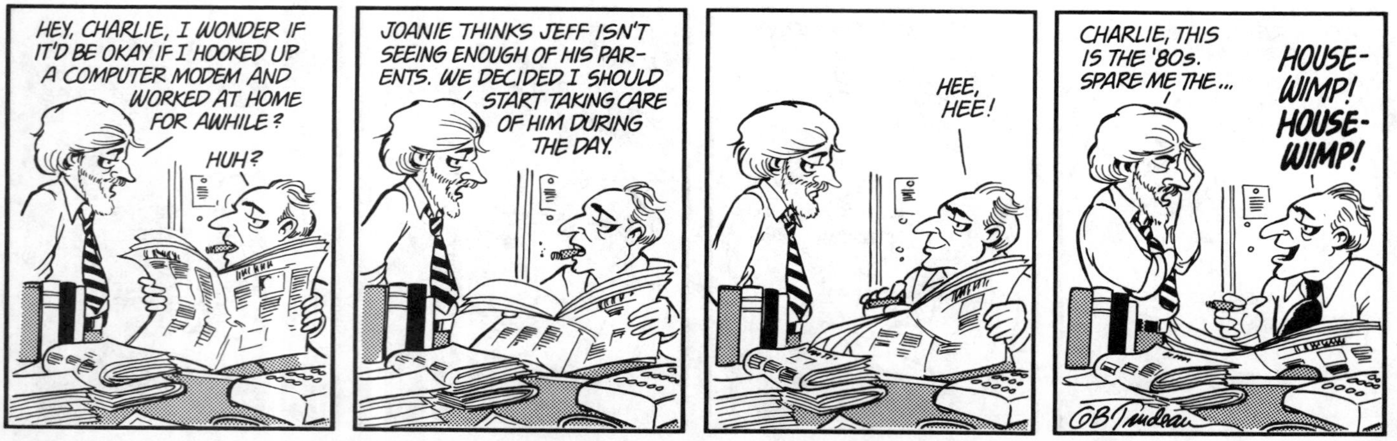
HEY, CHARLIE, I WONDER IF IT'D BE OKAY IF I HOOKED UP A COMPUTER MODEM AND WORKED AT HOME FOR AWHILE?
HUH?
JOANIE THINKS JEFF ISN'T SEEING ENOUGH OF HIS PARENTS. WE DECIDED I SHOULD START TAKING CARE OF HIM DURING THE DAY.
HEE, HEE!
CHARLIE, THIS IS THE '80s. SPARE ME THE...
HOUSE-WIMP! HOUSE-WIMP!
GB Trudeau

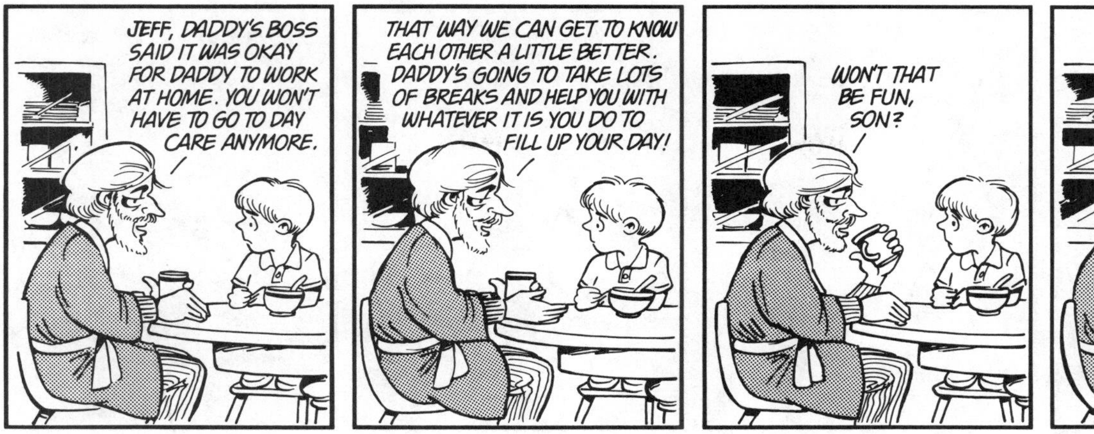
JEFF, DADDY'S BOSS SAID IT WAS OKAY FOR DADDY TO WORK AT HOME. YOU WON'T HAVE TO GO TO DAY CARE ANYMORE.
THAT WAY WE CAN GET TO KNOW EACH OTHER A LITTLE BETTER. DADDY'S GOING TO TAKE LOTS OF BREAKS AND HELP YOU WITH WHATEVER IT IS YOU DO TO FILL UP YOUR DAY!
WON'T THAT BE FUN, SON?
MOMMY! DADDY'S ACTING WEIRD!
CUT IT OUT, RICK!

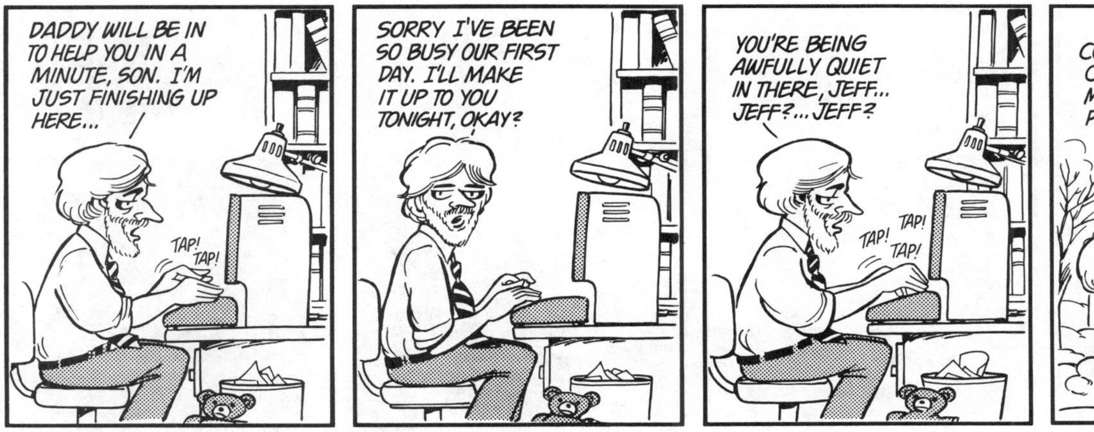
DADDY WILL BE IN TO HELP YOU IN A MINUTE, SON. I'M JUST FINISHING UP HERE...
TAP! TAP!
SORRY I'VE BEEN SO BUSY OUR FIRST DAY. I'LL MAKE IT UP TO YOU TONIGHT, OKAY?
YOU'RE BEING AWFULLY QUIET IN THERE, JEFF... JEFF?... JEFF?
TAP! TAP! TAP!
COULD YOU CALL MY MOMMY, PLEASE?
YOU POOR DEAR...

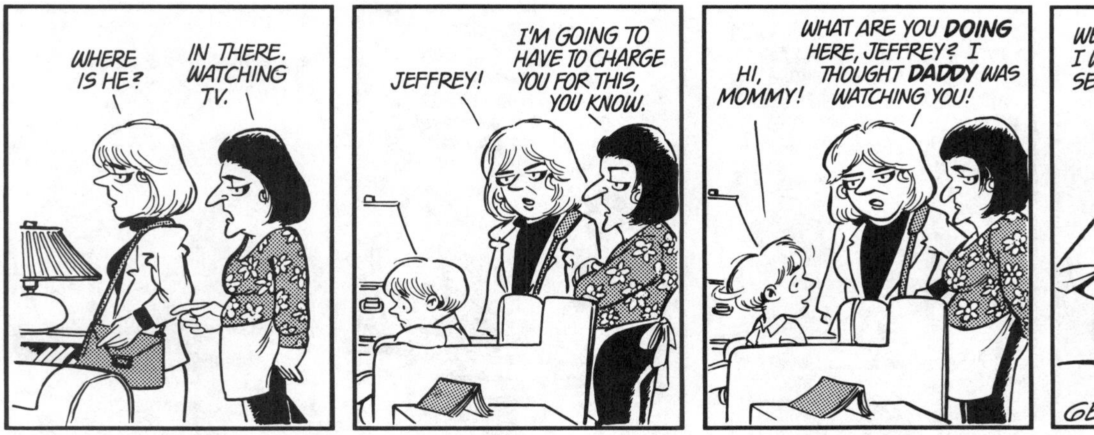
WHERE IS HE?
IN THERE. WATCHING TV.
JEFFREY!
I'M GOING TO HAVE TO CHARGE YOU FOR THIS, YOU KNOW.
HI, MOMMY!
WHAT ARE YOU DOING HERE, JEFFREY? I THOUGHT DADDY WAS WATCHING YOU!
WELL, OF COURSE I WAS HOME, SERGEANT!
EVER CONSIDERED DAY CARE, PAL?

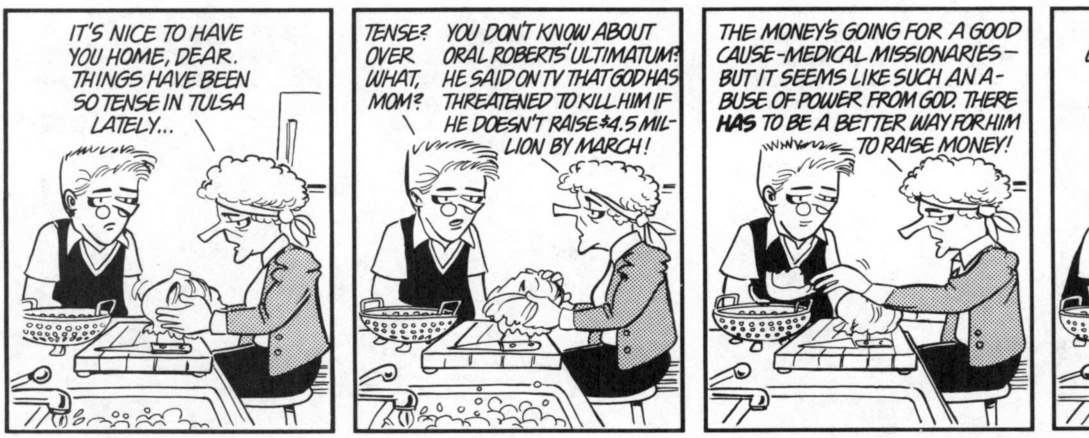
IT'S NICE TO HAVE YOU HOME, DEAR. THINGS HAVE BEEN SO TENSE IN TULSA LATELY...
TENSE? OVER WHAT, MOM?
YOU DON'T KNOW ABOUT ORAL ROBERTS' ULTIMATUM? HE SAID ON TV THAT GOD HAS THREATENED TO KILL HIM IF HE DOESN'T RAISE $4.5 MILLION BY MARCH!
THE MONEY'S GOING FOR A GOOD CAUSE-MEDICAL MISSIONARIES—BUT IT SEEMS LIKE SUCH AN ABUSE OF POWER FROM GOD. THERE HAS TO BE A BETTER WAY FOR HIM TO RAISE MONEY!
ESPECIALLY IN THIS MARKET.
WELL, YES. THINK OF HOW NICELY HE COULD DO IN FUTURES.

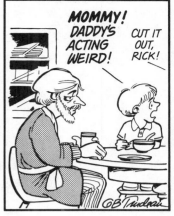

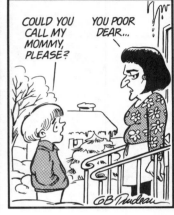

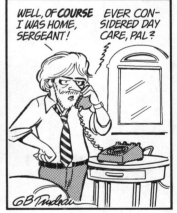

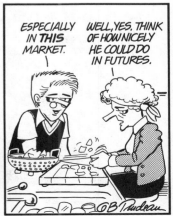

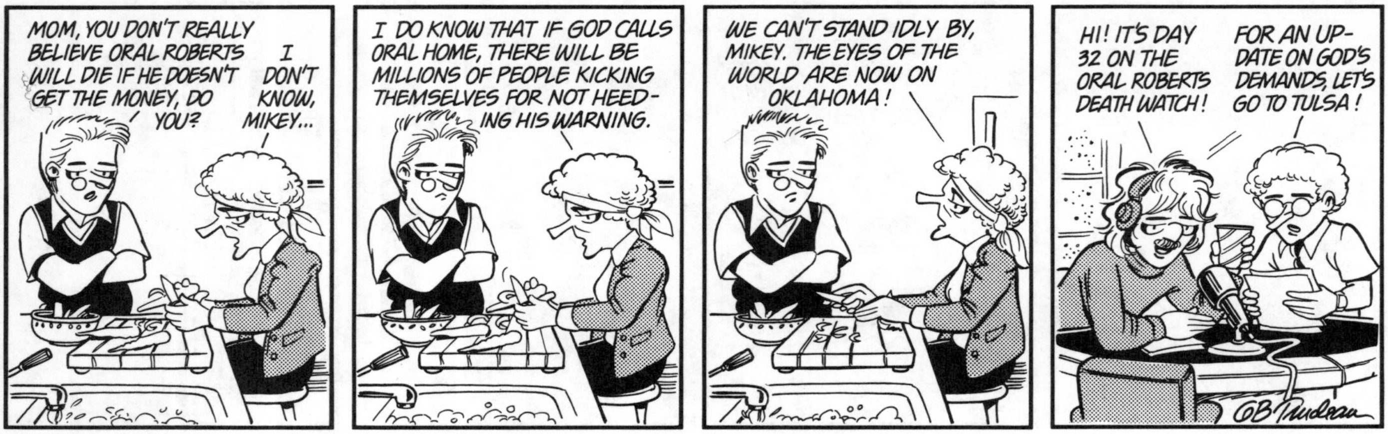
MOM, YOU DON'T REALLY BELIEVE ORAL ROBERTS WILL DIE IF HE DOESN'T GET THE MONEY, DO YOU?
I DON'T KNOW, MIKEY...
I DO KNOW THAT IF GOD CALLS ORAL HOME, THERE WILL BE MILLIONS OF PEOPLE KICKING THEMSELVES FOR NOT HEEDING HIS WARNING.
WE CAN'T STAND IDLY BY, MIKEY. THE EYES OF THE WORLD ARE NOW ON OKLAHOMA!
HI! IT'S DAY 32 ON THE ORAL ROBERTS DEATH WATCH!
FOR AN UPDATE ON GOD'S DEMANDS, LET'S GO TO TULSA!
©B Trudeau

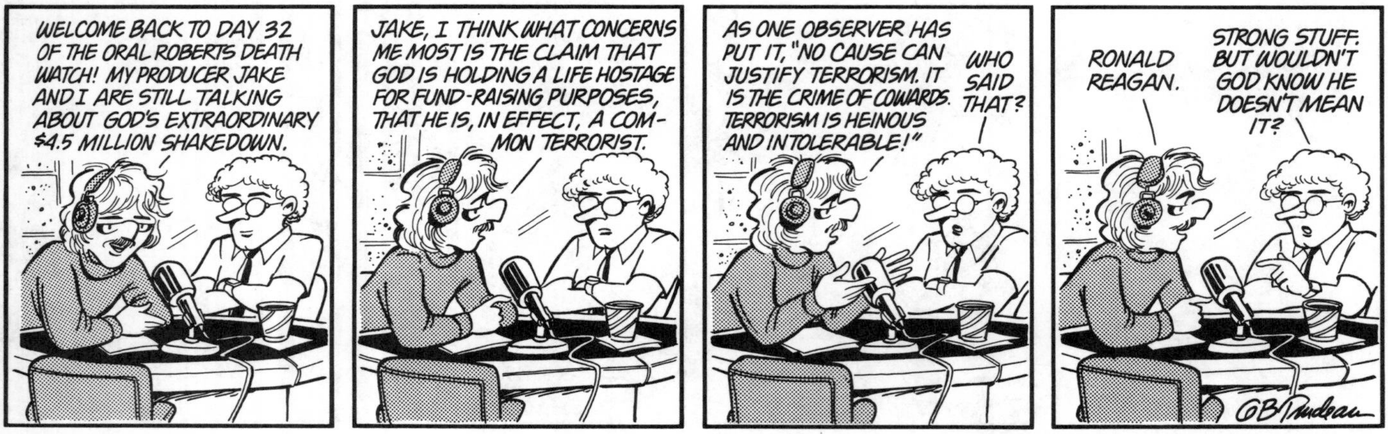
WELCOME BACK TO DAY 32 OF THE ORAL ROBERTS DEATH WATCH! MY PRODUCER JAKE AND I ARE STILL TALKING ABOUT GOD'S EXTRAORDINARY $4.5 MILLION SHAKEDOWN.
JAKE, I THINK WHAT CONCERNS ME MOST IS THE CLAIM THAT GOD IS HOLDING A LIFE HOSTAGE FOR FUND-RAISING PURPOSES, THAT HE IS, IN EFFECT, A COMMON TERRORIST.
AS ONE OBSERVER HAS PUT IT, "NO CAUSE CAN JUSTIFY TERRORISM. IT IS THE CRIME OF COWARDS. TERRORISM IS HEINOUS AND INTOLERABLE!"
WHO SAID THAT?
RONALD REAGAN.
STRONG STUFF. BUT WOULDN'T GOD KNOW HE DOESN'T MEAN IT?
©B Trudeau

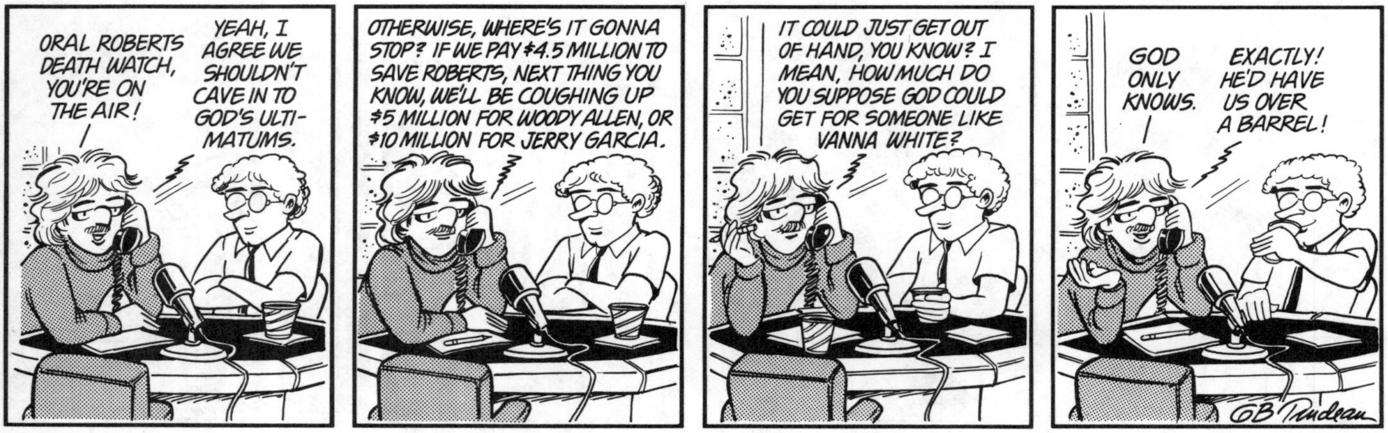
ORAL ROBERTS DEATH WATCH, YOU'RE ON THE AIR!
YEAH, I AGREE WE SHOULDN'T CAVE IN TO GOD'S ULTIMATUMS.
OTHERWISE, WHERE'S IT GONNA STOP? IF WE PAY $4.5 MILLION TO SAVE ROBERTS, NEXT THING YOU KNOW, WE'LL BE COUGHING UP $5 MILLION FOR WOODY ALLEN, OR $10 MILLION FOR JERRY GARCIA.
IT COULD JUST GET OUT OF HAND, YOU KNOW? I MEAN, HOW MUCH DO YOU SUPPOSE GOD COULD GET FOR SOMEONE LIKE VANNA WHITE?
GOD ONLY KNOWS.
EXACTLY! HE'D HAVE US OVER A BARREL!
©B Trudeau

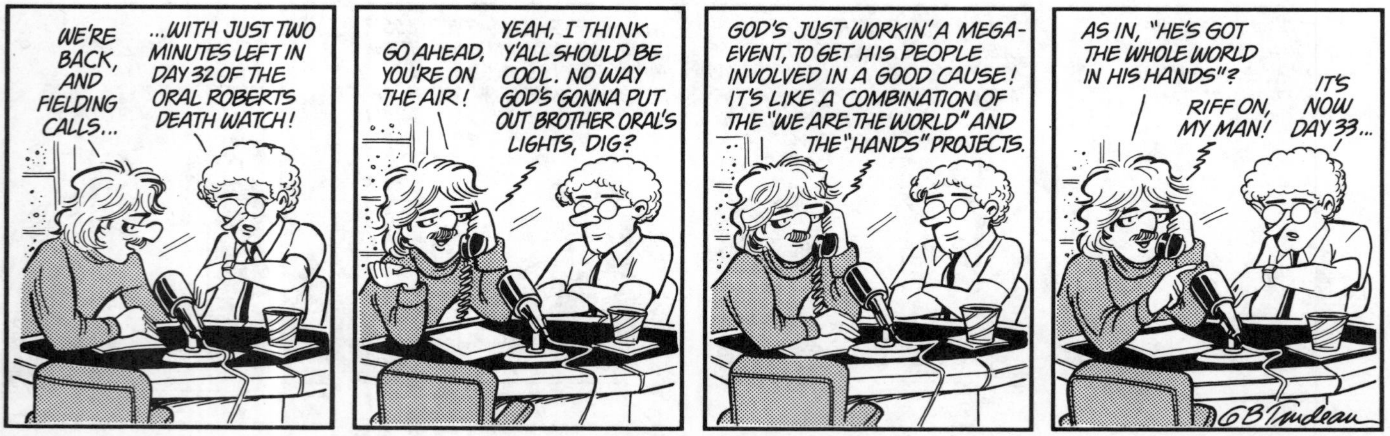
WE'RE BACK, AND FIELDING CALLS...
...WITH JUST TWO MINUTES LEFT IN DAY 32 OF THE ORAL ROBERTS DEATH WATCH!
GO AHEAD, YOU'RE ON THE AIR!
YEAH, I THINK Y'ALL SHOULD BE COOL. NO WAY GOD'S GONNA PUT OUT BROTHER ORAL'S LIGHTS, DIG?
GOD'S JUST WORKIN' A MEGA-EVENT, TO GET HIS PEOPLE INVOLVED IN A GOOD CAUSE! IT'S LIKE A COMBINATION OF THE "WE ARE THE WORLD" AND THE "HANDS" PROJECTS.
AS IN, "HE'S GOT THE WHOLE WORLD IN HIS HANDS"?
RIFF ON, MY MAN!
IT'S NOW DAY 33...
©B Trudeau

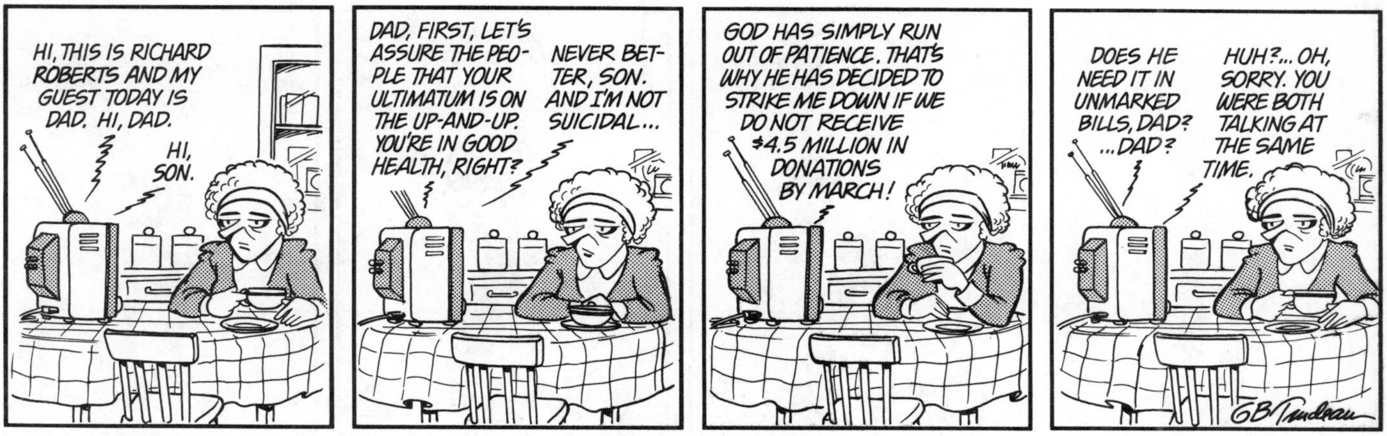
HI, THIS IS RICHARD ROBERTS AND MY GUEST TODAY IS DAD. HI, DAD.
HI, SON.
DAD, FIRST, LET'S ASSURE THE PEOPLE THAT YOUR ULTIMATUM IS ON THE UP-AND-UP. YOU'RE IN GOOD HEALTH, RIGHT?
NEVER BETTER, SON. AND I'M NOT SUICIDAL...
GOD HAS SIMPLY RUN OUT OF PATIENCE. THAT'S WHY HE HAS DECIDED TO STRIKE ME DOWN IF WE DO NOT RECEIVE $4.5 MILLION IN DONATIONS BY MARCH!
DOES HE NEED IT IN UNMARKED BILLS, DAD? ...DAD?
HUH?... OH, SORRY. YOU WERE BOTH TALKING AT THE SAME TIME.
GB Trudeau

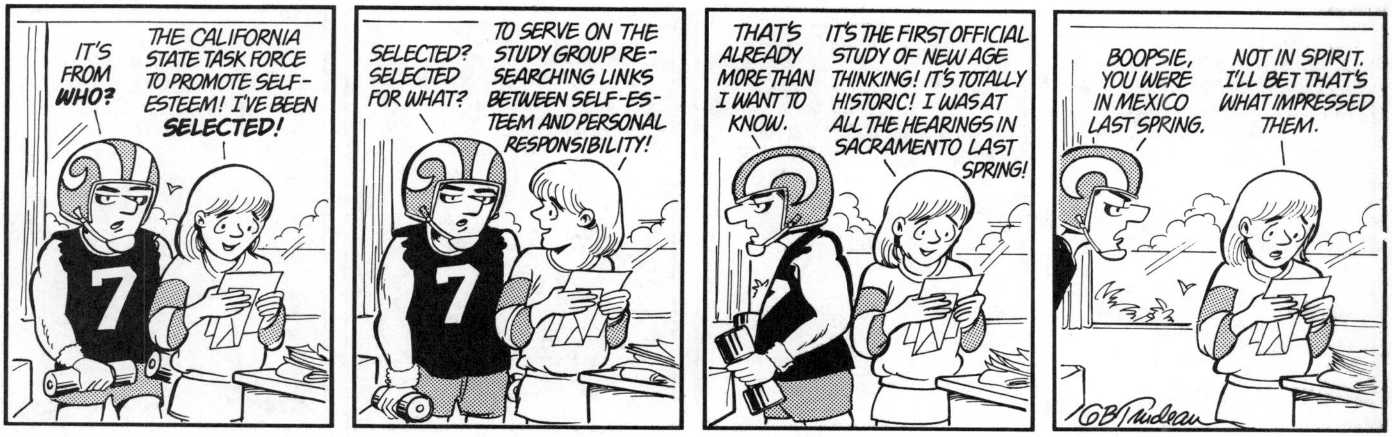
IT'S FROM WHO?
THE CALIFORNIA STATE TASK FORCE TO PROMOTE SELF-ESTEEM! I'VE BEEN SELECTED!
SELECTED? SELECTED FOR WHAT?
TO SERVE ON THE STUDY GROUP RESEARCHING LINKS BETWEEN SELF-ESTEEM AND PERSONAL RESPONSIBILITY!
THAT'S ALREADY MORE THAN I WANT TO KNOW.
IT'S THE FIRST OFFICIAL STUDY OF NEW AGE THINKING! IT'S TOTALLY HISTORIC! I WAS AT ALL THE HEARINGS IN SACRAMENTO LAST SPRING!
BOOPSIE, YOU WERE IN MEXICO LAST SPRING.
NOT IN SPIRIT. I'LL BET THAT'S WHAT IMPRESSED THEM.
GB Trudeau

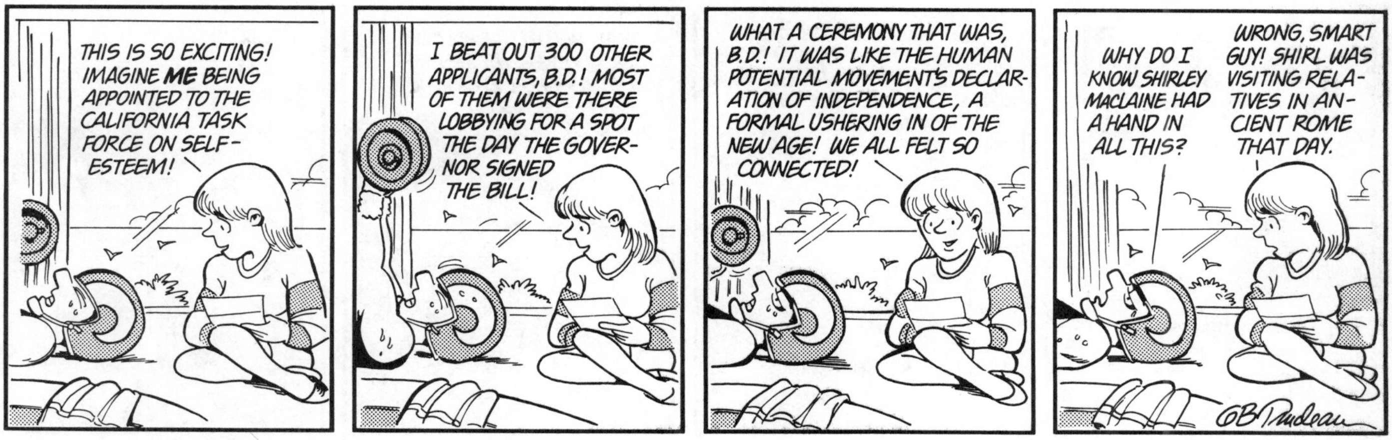
THIS IS SO EXCITING! IMAGINE ME BEING APPOINTED TO THE CALIFORNIA TASK FORCE ON SELF-ESTEEM!
I BEAT OUT 300 OTHER APPLICANTS, B.D.! MOST OF THEM WERE THERE LOBBYING FOR A SPOT THE DAY THE GOVERNOR SIGNED THE BILL!
WHAT A CEREMONY THAT WAS, B.D.! IT WAS LIKE THE HUMAN POTENTIAL MOVEMENT'S DECLARATION OF INDEPENDENCE, A FORMAL USHERING IN OF THE NEW AGE! WE ALL FELT SO CONNECTED!
WHY DO I KNOW SHIRLEY MACLAINE HAD A HAND IN ALL THIS?
WRONG, SMART GUY! SHIRL WAS VISITING RELATIVES IN ANCIENT ROME THAT DAY.
GB Trudeau

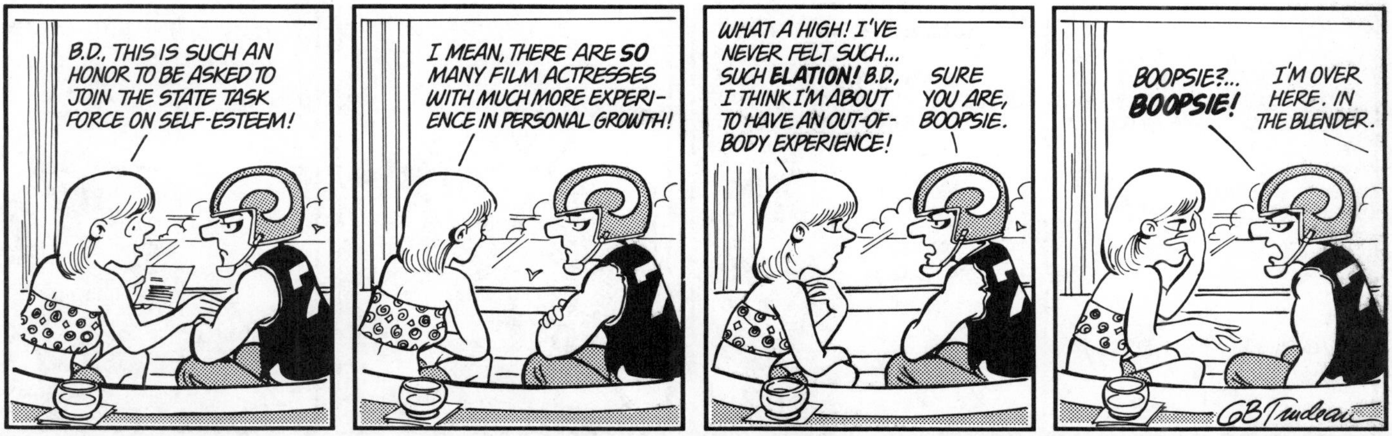
B.D., THIS IS SUCH AN HONOR TO BE ASKED TO JOIN THE STATE TASK FORCE ON SELF-ESTEEM!
I MEAN, THERE ARE SO MANY FILM ACTRESSES WITH MUCH MORE EXPERIENCE IN PERSONAL GROWTH!
WHAT A HIGH! I'VE NEVER FELT SUCH... SUCH ELATION! B.D., I THINK I'M ABOUT TO HAVE AN OUT-OF-BODY EXPERIENCE!
SURE YOU ARE, BOOPSIE.
BOOPSIE?... BOOPSIE!
I'M OVER HERE. IN THE BLENDER.
GB Trudeau

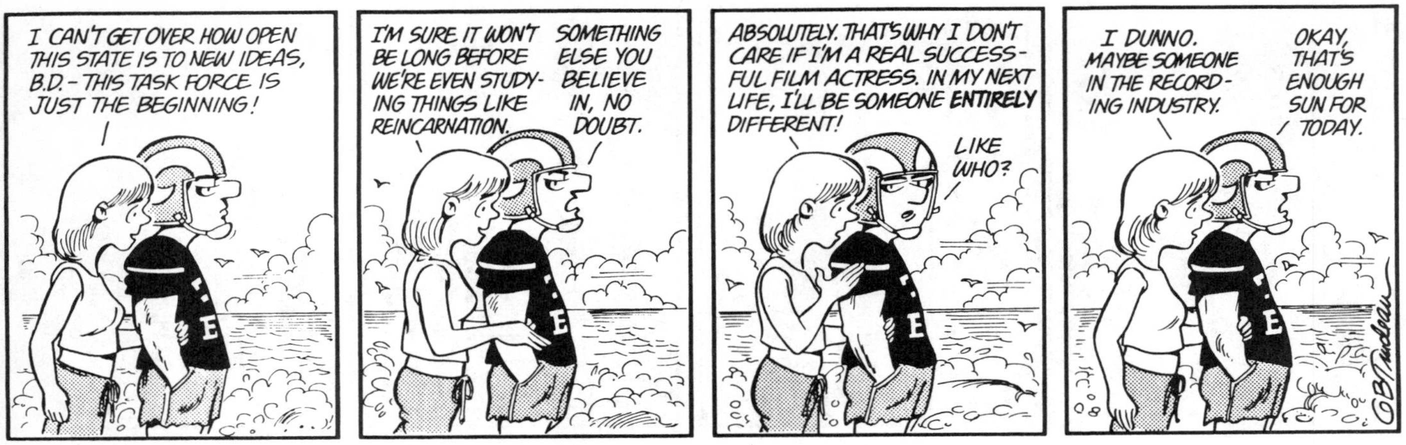
I CAN'T GET OVER HOW OPEN THIS STATE IS TO NEW IDEAS, B.D.—THIS TASK FORCE IS JUST THE BEGINNING!
I'M SURE IT WON'T BE LONG BEFORE WE'RE EVEN STUDYING THINGS LIKE REINCARNATION.
SOMETHING ELSE YOU BELIEVE IN, NO DOUBT.
ABSOLUTELY. THAT'S WHY I DON'T CARE IF I'M A REAL SUCCESSFUL FILM ACTRESS. IN MY NEXT LIFE, I'LL BE SOMEONE ENTIRELY DIFFERENT!
LIKE WHO?
I DUNNO. MAYBE SOMEONE IN THE RECORDING INDUSTRY.
OKAY, THAT'S ENOUGH SUN FOR TODAY.

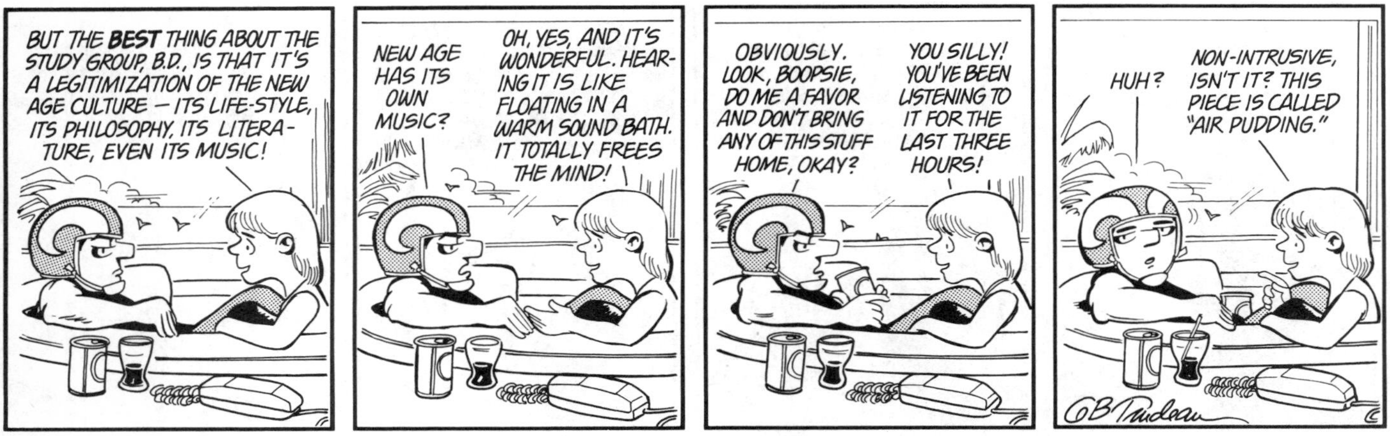
BUT THE BEST THING ABOUT THE STUDY GROUP, B.D., IS THAT IT'S A LEGITIMIZATION OF THE NEW AGE CULTURE — ITS LIFE-STYLE, ITS PHILOSOPHY, ITS LITERATURE, EVEN ITS MUSIC!
NEW AGE HAS ITS OWN MUSIC?
OH, YES, AND IT'S WONDERFUL. HEARING IT IS LIKE FLOATING IN A WARM SOUND BATH. IT TOTALLY FREES THE MIND!
OBVIOUSLY. LOOK, BOOPSIE, DO ME A FAVOR AND DON'T BRING ANY OF THIS STUFF HOME, OKAY?
YOU SILLY! YOU'VE BEEN LISTENING TO IT FOR THE LAST THREE HOURS!
HUH?
NON-INTRUSIVE, ISN'T IT? THIS PIECE IS CALLED "AIR PUDDING."

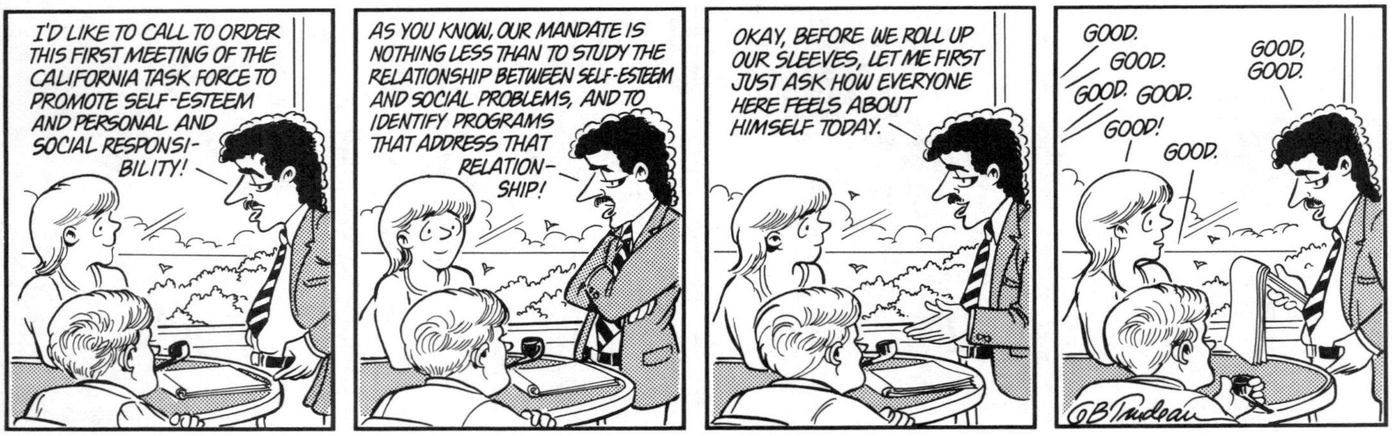
I'D LIKE TO CALL TO ORDER THIS FIRST MEETING OF THE CALIFORNIA TASK FORCE TO PROMOTE SELF-ESTEEM AND PERSONAL AND SOCIAL RESPONSIBILITY!
AS YOU KNOW, OUR MANDATE IS NOTHING LESS THAN TO STUDY THE RELATIONSHIP BETWEEN SELF-ESTEEM AND SOCIAL PROBLEMS, AND TO IDENTIFY PROGRAMS THAT ADDRESS THAT RELATIONSHIP!
OKAY, BEFORE WE ROLL UP OUR SLEEVES, LET ME FIRST JUST ASK HOW EVERYONE HERE FEELS ABOUT HIMSELF TODAY.
GOOD.
GOOD.
GOOD.
GOOD.
GOOD!
GOOD.
GOOD, GOOD.

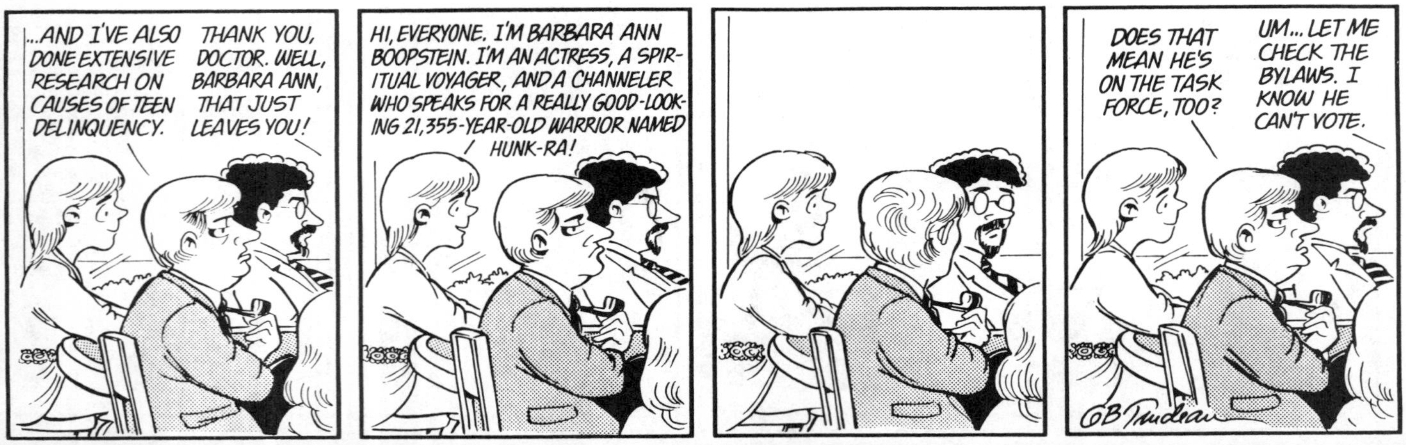
...AND I'VE ALSO DONE EXTENSIVE RESEARCH ON CAUSES OF TEEN DELINQUENCY.
THANK YOU, DOCTOR. WELL, BARBARA ANN, THAT JUST LEAVES YOU!
HI, EVERYONE. I'M BARBARA ANN BOOPSTEIN. I'M AN ACTRESS, A SPIRITUAL VOYAGER, AND A CHANNELER WHO SPEAKS FOR A REALLY GOOD-LOOKING 21,355-YEAR-OLD WARRIOR NAMED HUNK-RA!
DOES THAT MEAN HE'S ON THE TASK FORCE, TOO?
UM... LET ME CHECK THE BYLAWS. I KNOW HE CAN'T VOTE.

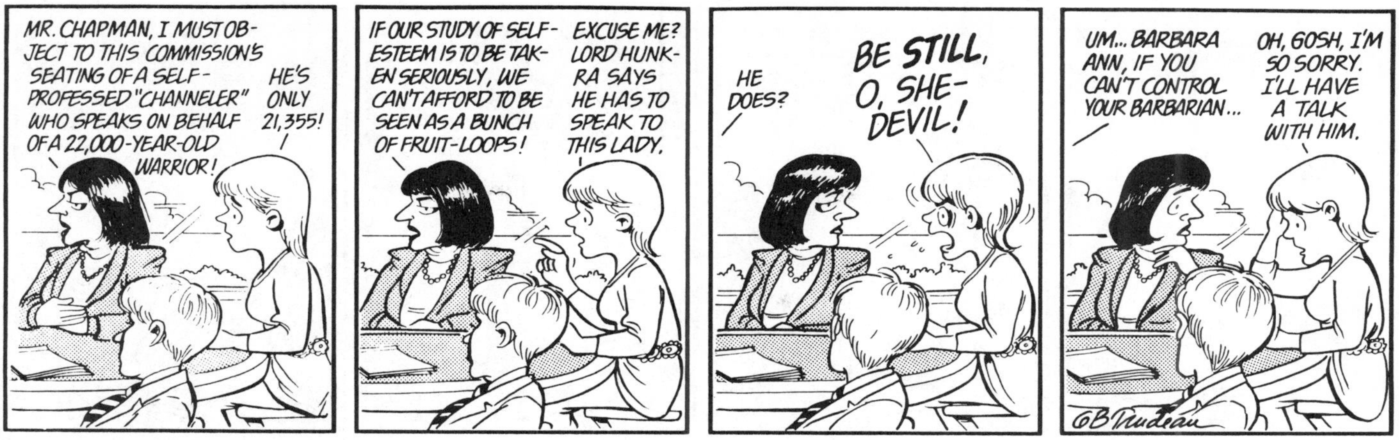
MR. CHAPMAN, I MUST OBJECT TO THIS COMMISSION'S SEATING OF A SELF-PROFESSED "CHANNELER" WHO SPEAKS ON BEHALF OF A 22,000-YEAR-OLD WARRIOR!
HE'S ONLY 21,355!
IF OUR STUDY OF SELF-ESTEEM IS TO BE TAKEN SERIOUSLY, WE CAN'T AFFORD TO BE SEEN AS A BUNCH OF FRUIT-LOOPS!
EXCUSE ME? LORD HUNK-RA SAYS HE HAS TO SPEAK TO THIS LADY.
HE DOES?
BE STILL, O, SHE-DEVIL!
UM... BARBARA ANN, IF YOU CAN'T CONTROL YOUR BARBARIAN...
OH, GOSH, I'M SO SORRY. I'LL HAVE A TALK WITH HIM.
GB Trudeau

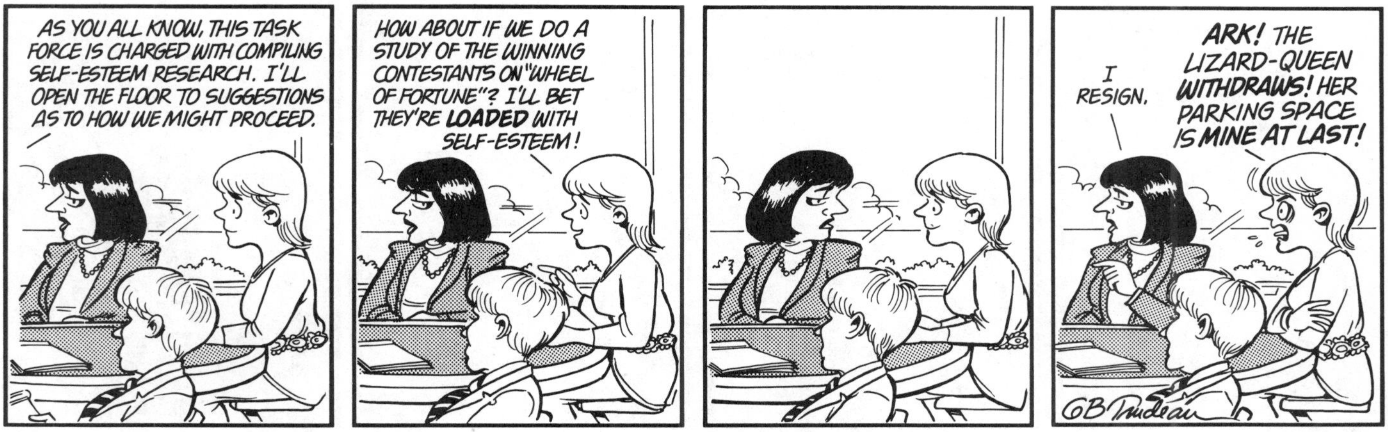
AS YOU ALL KNOW, THIS TASK FORCE IS CHARGED WITH COMPILING SELF-ESTEEM RESEARCH. I'LL OPEN THE FLOOR TO SUGGESTIONS AS TO HOW WE MIGHT PROCEED.
HOW ABOUT IF WE DO A STUDY OF THE WINNING CONTESTANTS ON "WHEEL OF FORTUNE"? I'LL BET THEY'RE LOADED WITH SELF-ESTEEM!
I RESIGN.
ARK! THE LIZARD-QUEEN WITHDRAWS! HER PARKING SPACE IS MINE AT LAST!
GB Trudeau

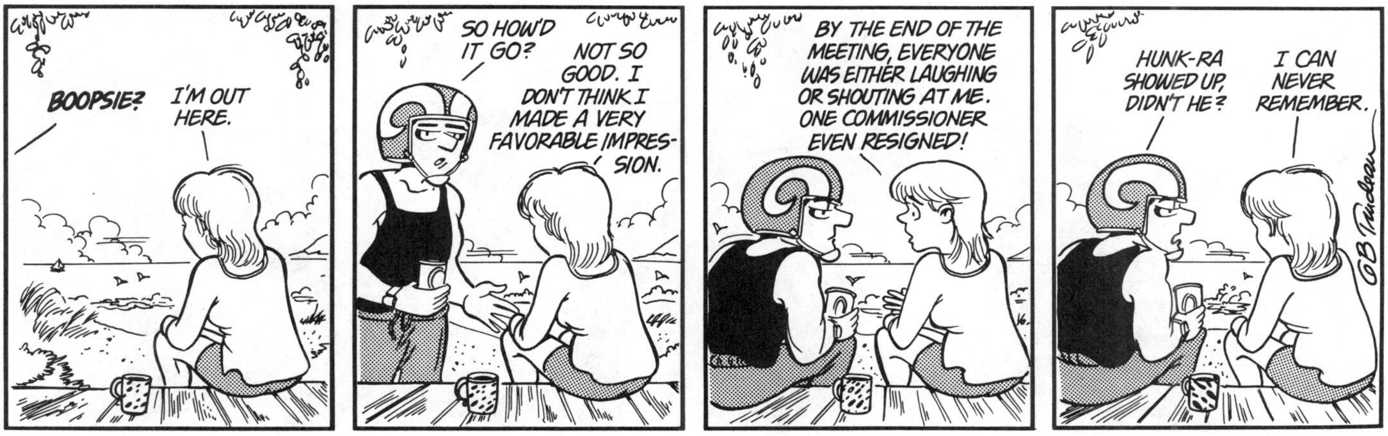
BOOPSIE?
I'M OUT HERE.
SO HOW'D IT GO?
NOT SO GOOD. I DON'T THINK I MADE A VERY FAVORABLE IMPRESSION.
BY THE END OF THE MEETING, EVERYONE WAS EITHER LAUGHING OR SHOUTING AT ME. ONE COMMISSIONER EVEN RESIGNED!
HUNK-RA SHOWED UP, DIDN'T HE?
I CAN NEVER REMEMBER.
GB Trudeau

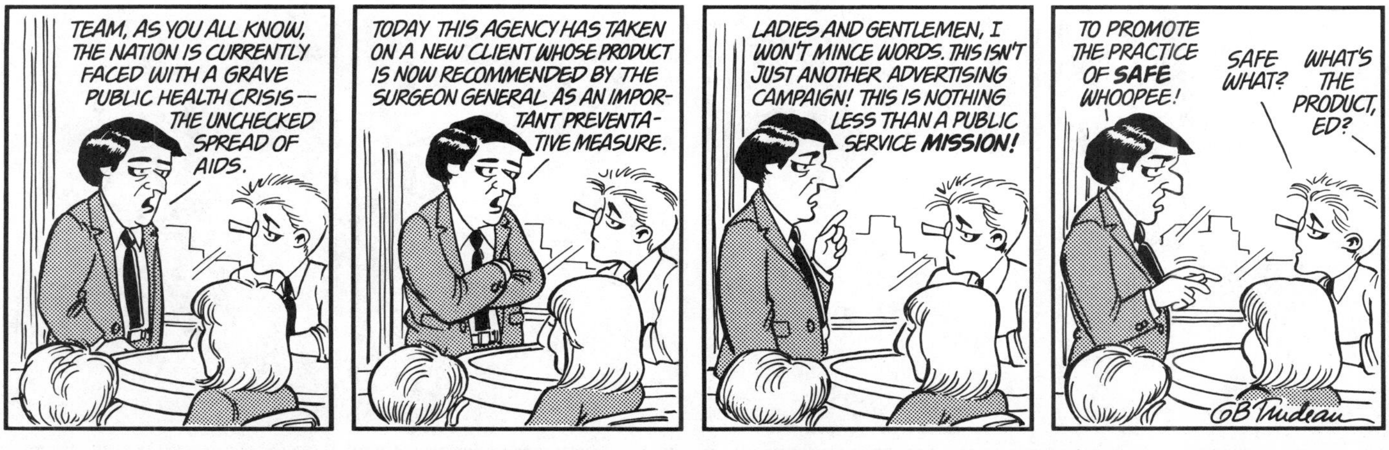
TEAM, AS YOU ALL KNOW, THE NATION IS CURRENTLY FACED WITH A GRAVE PUBLIC HEALTH CRISIS— THE UNCHECKED SPREAD OF AIDS.
TODAY THIS AGENCY HAS TAKEN ON A NEW CLIENT WHOSE PRODUCT IS NOW RECOMMENDED BY THE SURGEON GENERAL AS AN IMPORTANT PREVENTATIVE MEASURE.
LADIES AND GENTLEMEN, I WON'T MINCE WORDS. THIS ISN'T JUST ANOTHER ADVERTISING CAMPAIGN! THIS IS NOTHING LESS THAN A PUBLIC SERVICE MISSION!
TO PROMOTE THE PRACTICE OF SAFE WHOOPEE!
SAFE WHAT?
WHAT'S THE PRODUCT, ED?
GB Trudeau

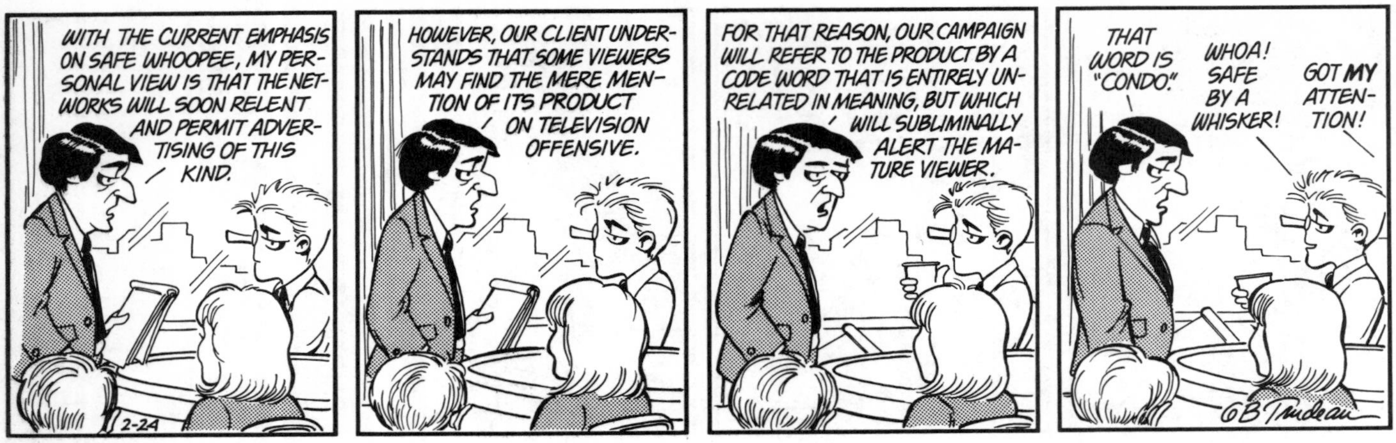
WITH THE CURRENT EMPHASIS ON SAFE WHOOPEE, MY PERSONAL VIEW IS THAT THE NETWORKS WILL SOON RELENT AND PERMIT ADVERTISING OF THIS KIND.
2-24
HOWEVER, OUR CLIENT UNDERSTANDS THAT SOME VIEWERS MAY FIND THE MERE MENTION OF ITS PRODUCT ON TELEVISION OFFENSIVE.
FOR THAT REASON, OUR CAMPAIGN WILL REFER TO THE PRODUCT BY A CODE WORD THAT IS ENTIRELY UNRELATED IN MEANING, BUT WHICH WILL SUBLIMINALLY ALERT THE MATURE VIEWER.
THAT WORD IS "CONDO."
WHOA! SAFE BY A WHISKER!
GOT MY ATTENTION!
©B Trudeau

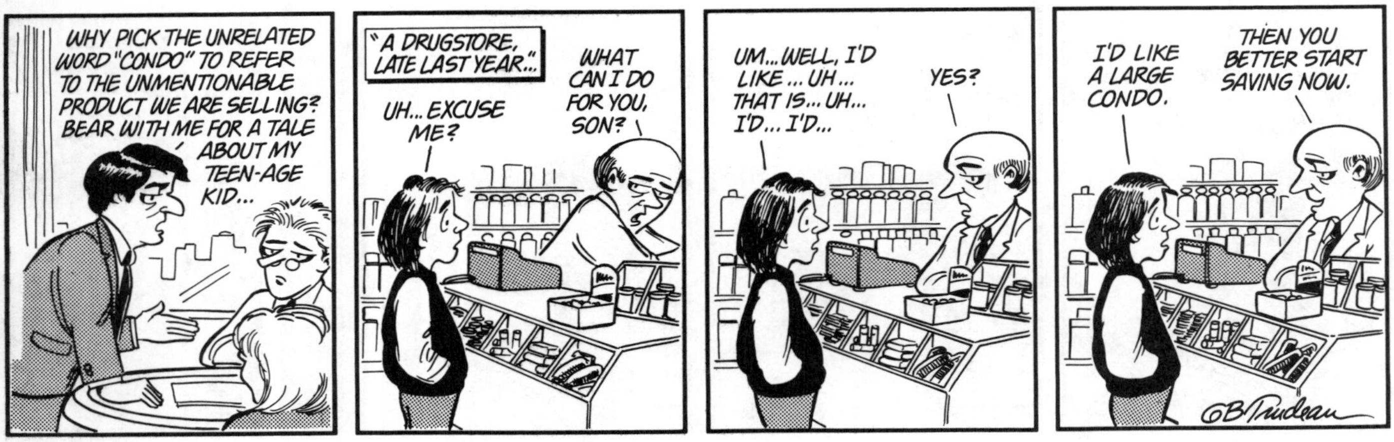
WHY PICK THE UNRELATED WORD "CONDO" TO REFER TO THE UNMENTIONABLE PRODUCT WE ARE SELLING? BEAR WITH ME FOR A TALE ABOUT MY TEEN-AGE KID...
"A DRUGSTORE, LATE LAST YEAR..."
UH... EXCUSE ME?
WHAT CAN I DO FOR YOU, SON?
UM... WELL, I'D LIKE ... UH ... THAT IS... UH... I'D... I'D...
YES?
I'D LIKE A LARGE CONDO.
THEN YOU BETTER START SAVING NOW.
©B Trudeau

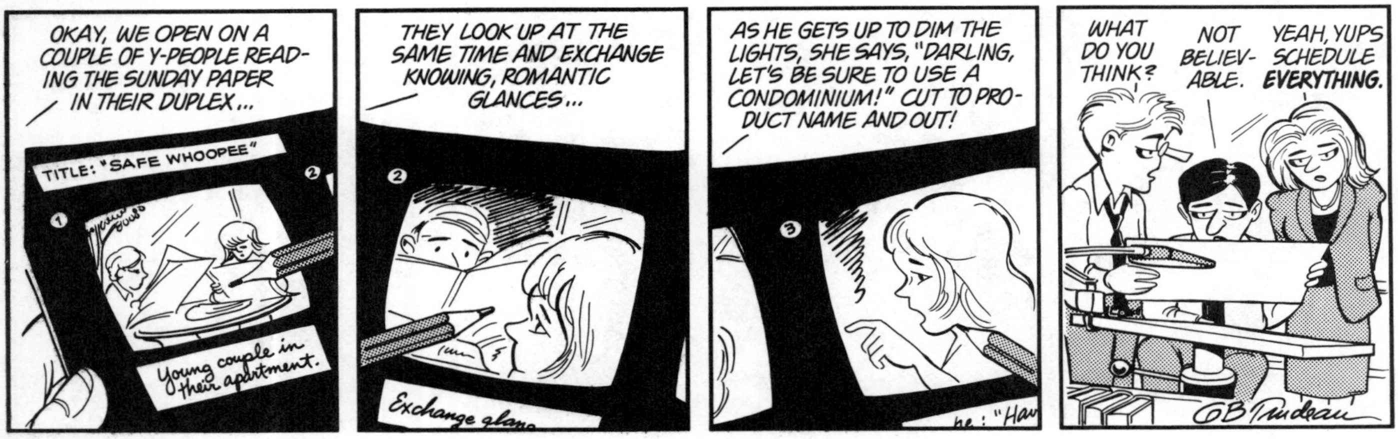
OKAY, WE OPEN ON A COUPLE OF Y-PEOPLE READING THE SUNDAY PAPER IN THEIR DUPLEX...
TITLE: "SAFE WHOOPEE"
Young couple in their apartment.
THEY LOOK UP AT THE SAME TIME AND EXCHANGE KNOWING, ROMANTIC GLANCES...
AS HE GETS UP TO DIM THE LIGHTS, SHE SAYS, "DARLING, LET'S BE SURE TO USE A CONDOMINIUM!" CUT TO PRODUCT NAME AND OUT!
WHAT DO YOU THINK?
NOT BELIEVABLE.
YEAH, YUPS SCHEDULE EVERYTHING.
©B Trudeau

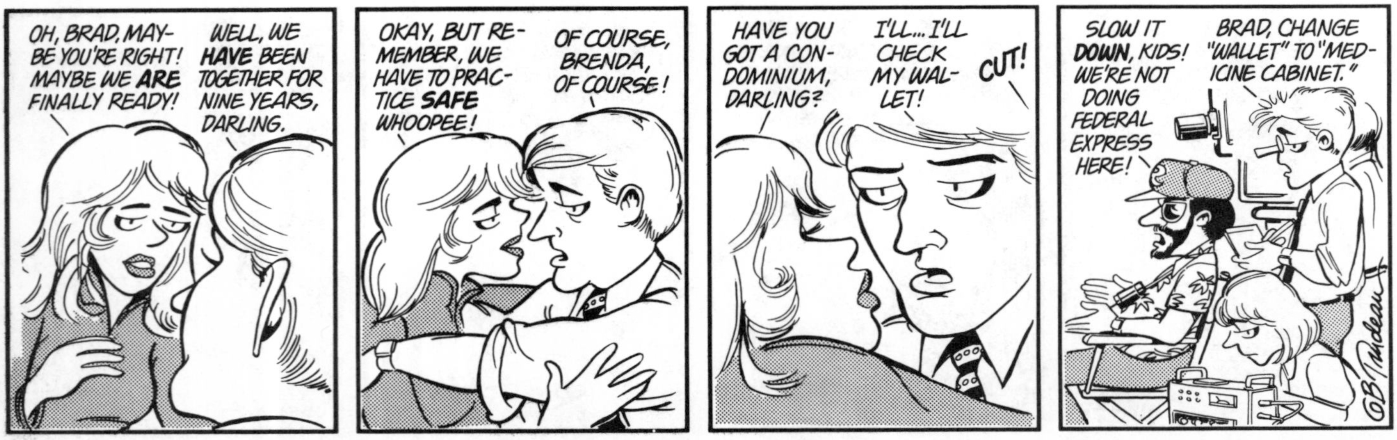
OH, BRAD, MAYBE YOU'RE RIGHT! MAYBE WE ARE FINALLY READY!
WELL, WE HAVE BEEN TOGETHER FOR NINE YEARS, DARLING.
OKAY, BUT REMEMBER, WE HAVE TO PRACTICE SAFE WHOOPEE!
OF COURSE, BRENDA, OF COURSE!
HAVE YOU GOT A CONDOMINIUM, DARLING?
I'LL... I'LL CHECK MY WALLET!
CUT!
SLOW IT DOWN, KIDS! WE'RE NOT DOING FEDERAL EXPRESS HERE!
BRAD, CHANGE "WALLET" TO "MEDICINE CABINET."
©B Trudeau

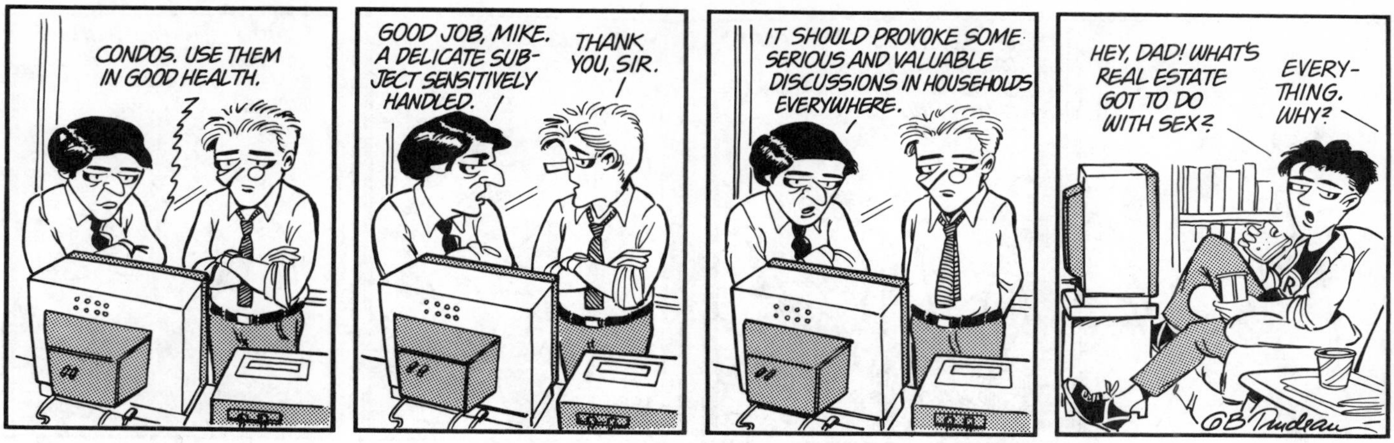
CONDOS. USE THEM IN GOOD HEALTH.
GOOD JOB, MIKE. A DELICATE SUBJECT SENSITIVELY HANDLED.
THANK YOU, SIR.
IT SHOULD PROVOKE SOME SERIOUS AND VALUABLE DISCUSSIONS IN HOUSEHOLDS EVERYWHERE.
HEY, DAD! WHAT'S REAL ESTATE GOT TO DO WITH SEX?
EVERYTHING. WHY?
©B Trudeau

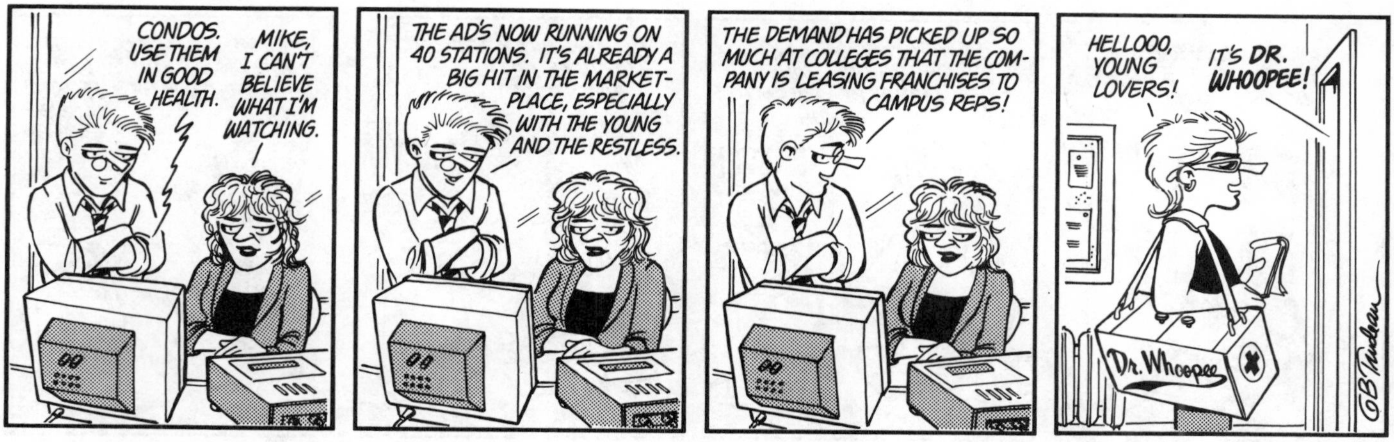
CONDOS. USE THEM IN GOOD HEALTH.
MIKE, I CAN'T BELIEVE WHAT I'M WATCHING.
THE AD'S NOW RUNNING ON 40 STATIONS. IT'S ALREADY A BIG HIT IN THE MARKETPLACE, ESPECIALLY WITH THE YOUNG AND THE RESTLESS.
THE DEMAND HAS PICKED UP SO MUCH AT COLLEGES THAT THE COMPANY IS LEASING FRANCHISES TO CAMPUS REPS!
HELLOOO, YOUNG LOVERS!
IT'S **DR. WHOOPEE!**
Dr. Whoopee
©B Trudeau

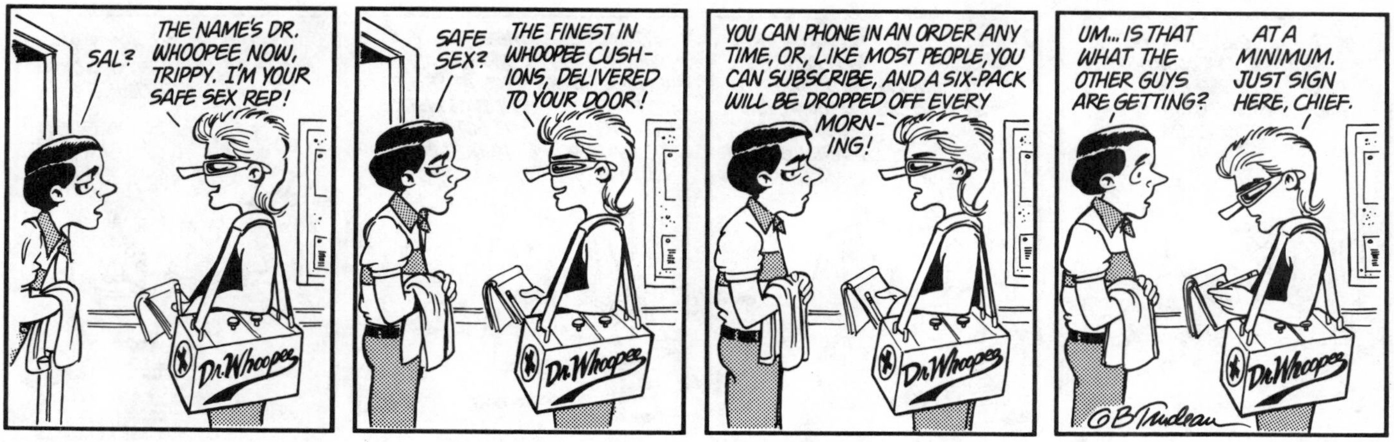
SAL?
THE NAME'S DR. WHOOPEE NOW, TRIPPY. I'M YOUR SAFE SEX REP!
Dr. Whoopee
SAFE SEX?
THE FINEST IN WHOOPEE CUSHIONS, DELIVERED TO YOUR DOOR!
Dr. Whoopee
YOU CAN PHONE IN AN ORDER ANY TIME, OR, LIKE MOST PEOPLE, YOU CAN SUBSCRIBE, AND A SIX-PACK WILL BE DROPPED OFF EVERY MORNING!
Dr. Whoopee
UM... IS THAT WHAT THE OTHER GUYS ARE GETTING?
AT A MINIMUM. JUST SIGN HERE, CHIEF.
Dr. Whoopee
©B Trudeau

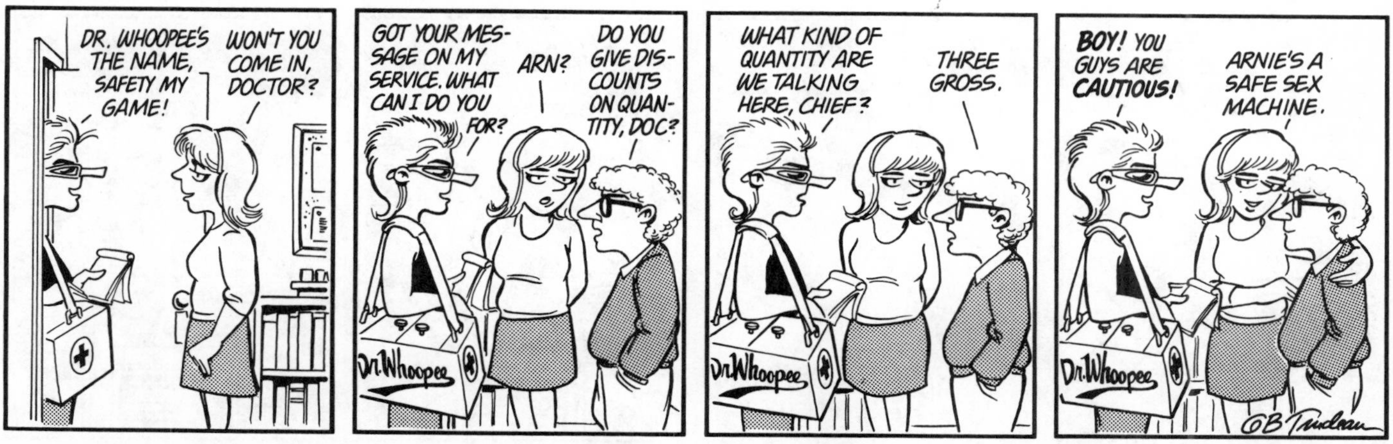
DR. WHOOPEE'S THE NAME, SAFETY MY GAME!
WON'T YOU COME IN, DOCTOR?
GOT YOUR MESSAGE ON MY SERVICE. WHAT CAN I DO YOU FOR?
ARN?
DO YOU GIVE DISCOUNTS ON QUANTITY, DOC?
Dr. Whoopee
WHAT KIND OF QUANTITY ARE WE TALKING HERE, CHIEF?
THREE GROSS.
Dr. Whoopee
BOY! YOU GUYS ARE **CAUTIOUS!**
ARNIE'S A SAFE SEX MACHINE.
Dr. Whoopee
©B Trudeau

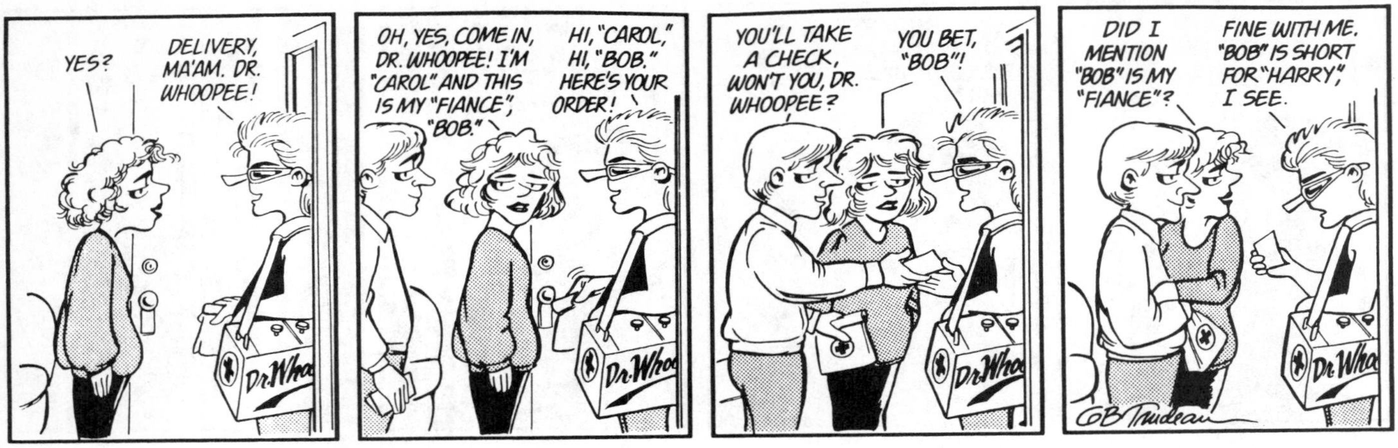
YES?
DELIVERY, MA'AM. DR. WHOOPEE!
OH, YES, COME IN, DR. WHOOPEE! I'M "CAROL" AND THIS IS MY "FIANCE", "BOB."
HI, "CAROL," HI, "BOB." HERE'S YOUR ORDER!
YOU'LL TAKE A CHECK, WON'T YOU, DR. WHOOPEE?
YOU BET, "BOB"!
DID I MENTION "BOB" IS MY "FIANCE"?
FINE WITH ME. "BOB" IS SHORT FOR "HARRY," I SEE.
GB Trudeau

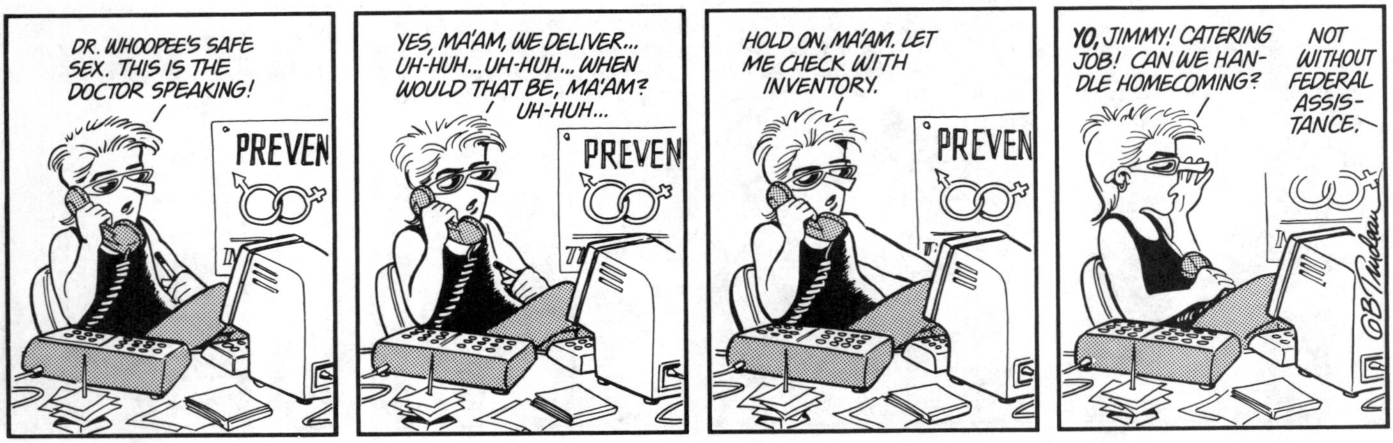
DR. WHOOPEE'S SAFE SEX. THIS IS THE DOCTOR SPEAKING!
PREVEN
YES, MA'AM, WE DELIVER... UH-HUH... UH-HUH... WHEN WOULD THAT BE, MA'AM? UH-HUH...
PREVEN
HOLD ON, MA'AM. LET ME CHECK WITH INVENTORY.
PREVEN
YO, JIMMY! CATERING JOB! CAN WE HANDLE HOMECOMING?
NOT WITHOUT FEDERAL ASSISTANCE.
GB Trudeau

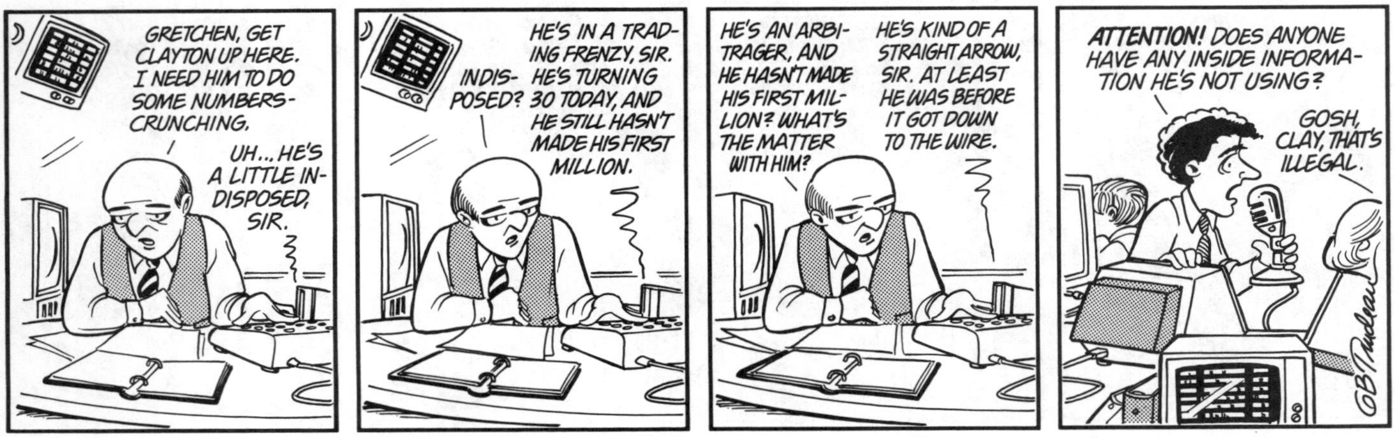
GRETCHEN, GET CLAYTON UP HERE. I NEED HIM TO DO SOME NUMBERS-CRUNCHING.
UH... HE'S A LITTLE INDISPOSED, SIR.
INDISPOSED?
HE'S IN A TRADING FRENZY, SIR. HE'S TURNING 30 TODAY, AND HE STILL HASN'T MADE HIS FIRST MILLION.
HE'S AN ARBITRAGER, AND HE HASN'T MADE HIS FIRST MILLION? WHAT'S THE MATTER WITH HIM?
HE'S KIND OF A STRAIGHT ARROW, SIR. AT LEAST HE WAS BEFORE IT GOT DOWN TO THE WIRE.
ATTENTION! DOES ANYONE HAVE ANY INSIDE INFORMATION HE'S NOT USING?
GOSH, CLAY, THAT'S ILLEGAL.
GB Trudeau

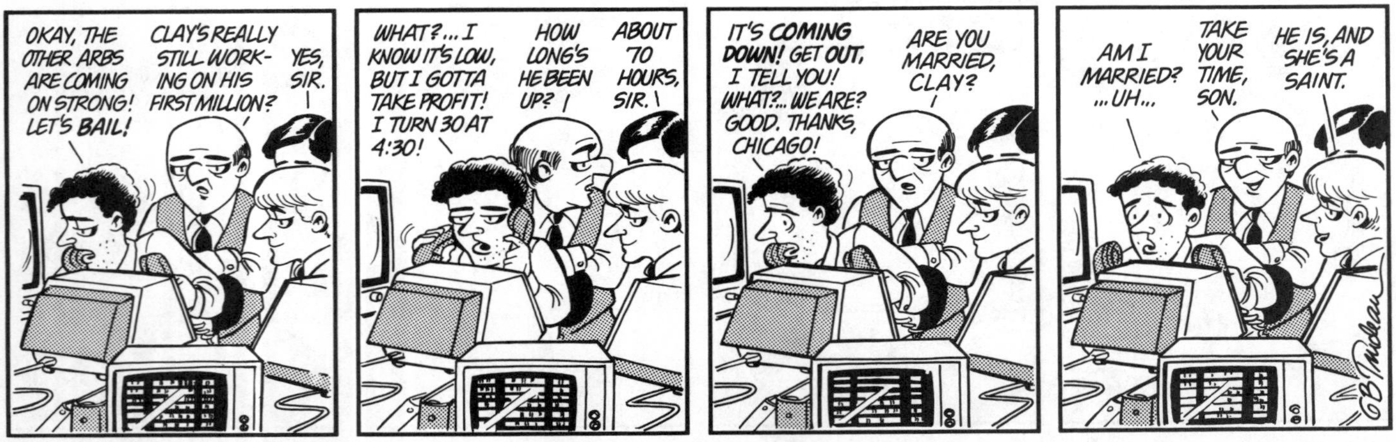
OKAY, THE OTHER ARBS ARE COMING ON STRONG! LET'S BAIL!
CLAY'S REALLY STILL WORKING ON HIS FIRST MILLION?
YES, SIR.
WHAT?... I KNOW IT'S LOW, BUT I GOTTA TAKE PROFIT! I TURN 30 AT 4:30!
HOW LONG'S HE BEEN UP?
ABOUT 70 HOURS, SIR.
IT'S COMING DOWN! GET OUT, I TELL YOU! WHAT?... WE ARE? GOOD. THANKS, CHICAGO!
ARE YOU MARRIED, CLAY?
AM I MARRIED? ...UH...
TAKE YOUR TIME, SON.
HE IS, AND SHE'S A SAINT.
GB Trudeau

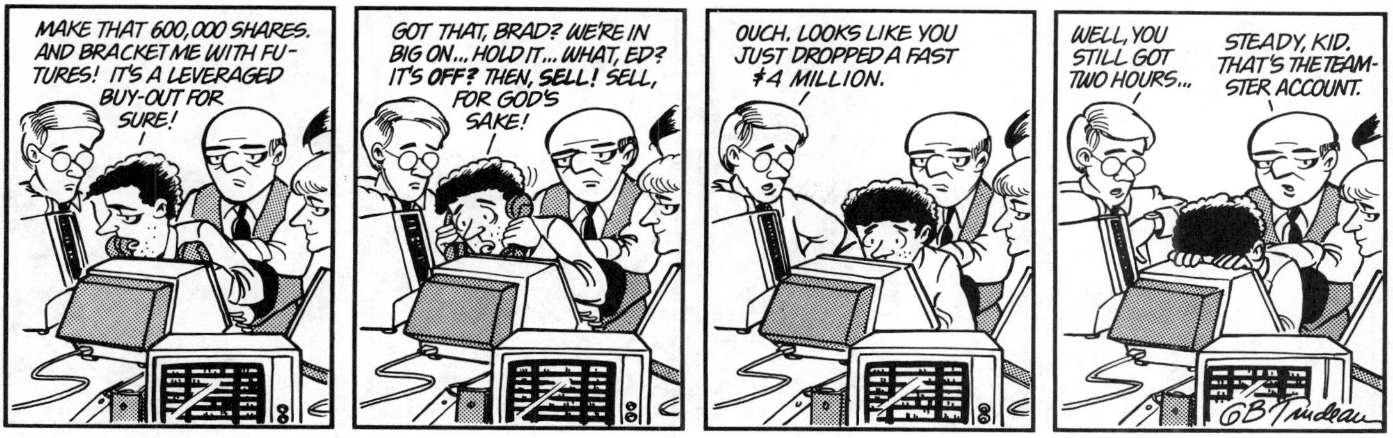
MAKE THAT 600,000 SHARES. AND BRACKET ME WITH FUTURES! IT'S A LEVERAGED BUY-OUT FOR SURE!
GOT THAT, BRAD? WE'RE IN BIG ON... HOLD IT... WHAT, ED? IT'S OFF? THEN, SELL! SELL, FOR GOD'S SAKE!
OUCH. LOOKS LIKE YOU JUST DROPPED A FAST $4 MILLION.
WELL, YOU STILL GOT TWO HOURS...
STEADY, KID. THAT'S THE TEAMSTER ACCOUNT.
©B Trudeau

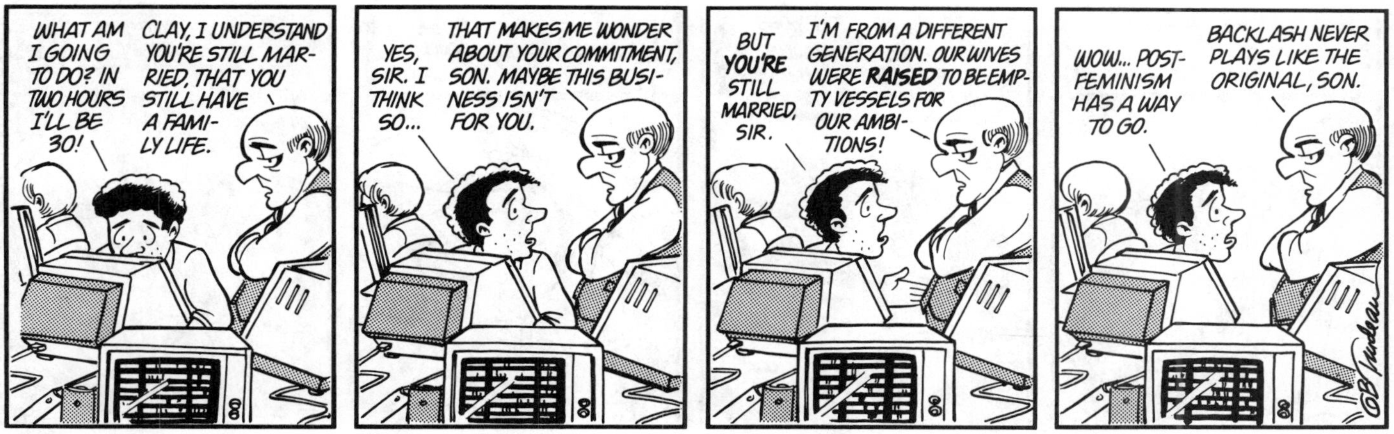
WHAT AM I GOING TO DO? IN TWO HOURS I'LL BE 30!
CLAY, I UNDERSTAND YOU'RE STILL MARRIED, THAT YOU STILL HAVE A FAMILY LIFE.
YES, SIR. I THINK SO...
THAT MAKES ME WONDER ABOUT YOUR COMMITMENT, SON. MAYBE THIS BUSINESS ISN'T FOR YOU.
BUT YOU'RE STILL MARRIED, SIR.
I'M FROM A DIFFERENT GENERATION. OUR WIVES WERE RAISED TO BE EMPTY VESSELS FOR OUR AMBITIONS!
WOW... POST-FEMINISM HAS A WAY TO GO.
BACKLASH NEVER PLAYS LIKE THE ORIGINAL, SON.
©B Trudeau

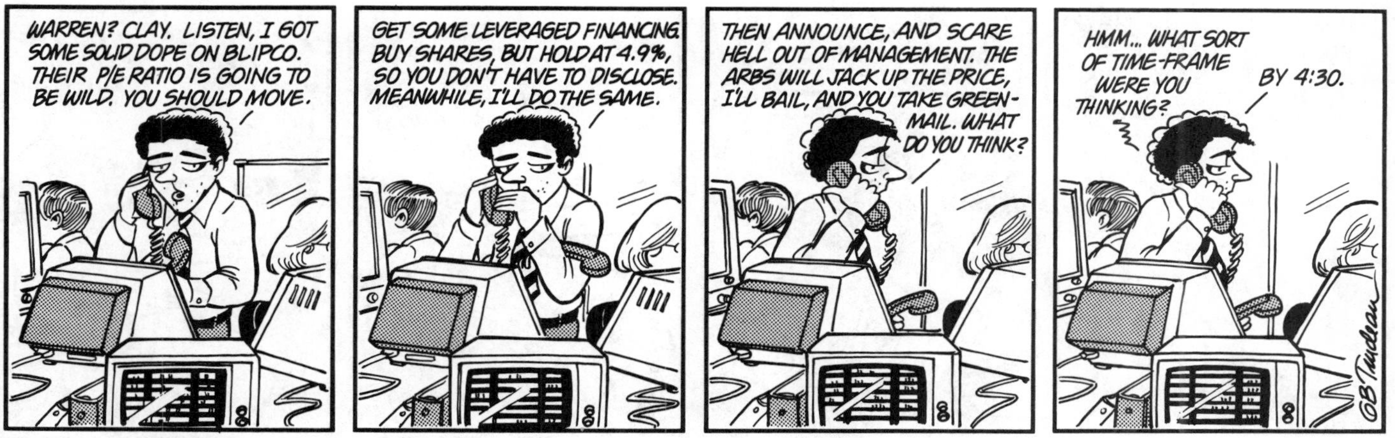
WARREN? CLAY. LISTEN, I GOT SOME SOLID DOPE ON BLIPCO. THEIR P/E RATIO IS GOING TO BE WILD. YOU SHOULD MOVE.
GET SOME LEVERAGED FINANCING. BUY SHARES, BUT HOLD AT 4.9%, SO YOU DON'T HAVE TO DISCLOSE. MEANWHILE, I'LL DO THE SAME.
THEN ANNOUNCE, AND SCARE HELL OUT OF MANAGEMENT. THE ARBS WILL JACK UP THE PRICE, I'LL BAIL, AND YOU TAKE GREENMAIL. WHAT DO YOU THINK?
HMM... WHAT SORT OF TIME-FRAME WERE YOU THINKING?
BY 4:30.
©B Trudeau

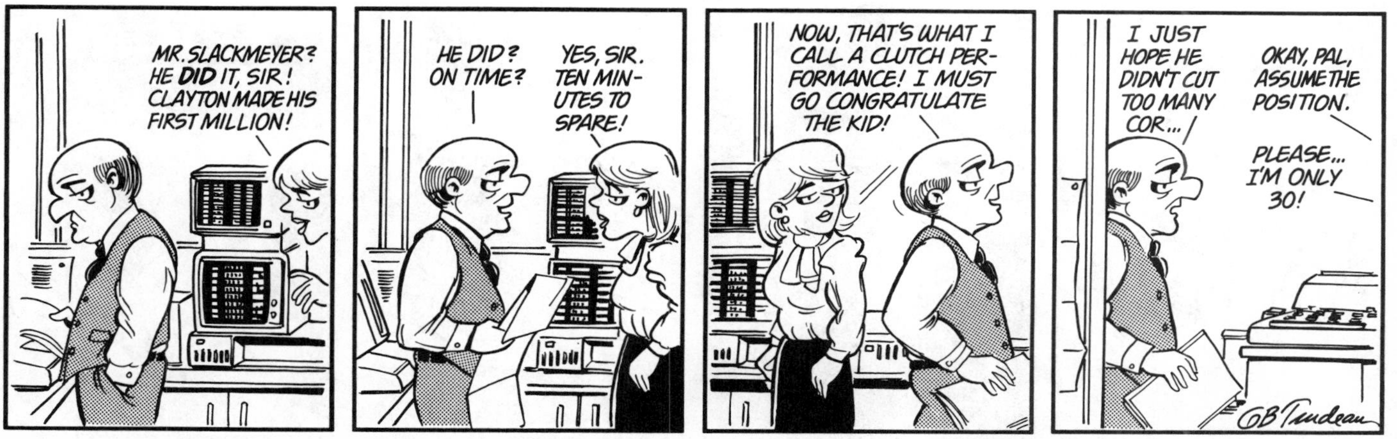
MR. SLACKMEYER? HE DID IT, SIR! CLAYTON MADE HIS FIRST MILLION!
HE DID? ON TIME?
YES, SIR. TEN MINUTES TO SPARE!
NOW, THAT'S WHAT I CALL A CLUTCH PERFORMANCE! I MUST GO CONGRATULATE THE KID!
I JUST HOPE HE DIDN'T CUT TOO MANY COR...
OKAY, PAL, ASSUME THE POSITION.
PLEASE... I'M ONLY 30!
©B Trudeau

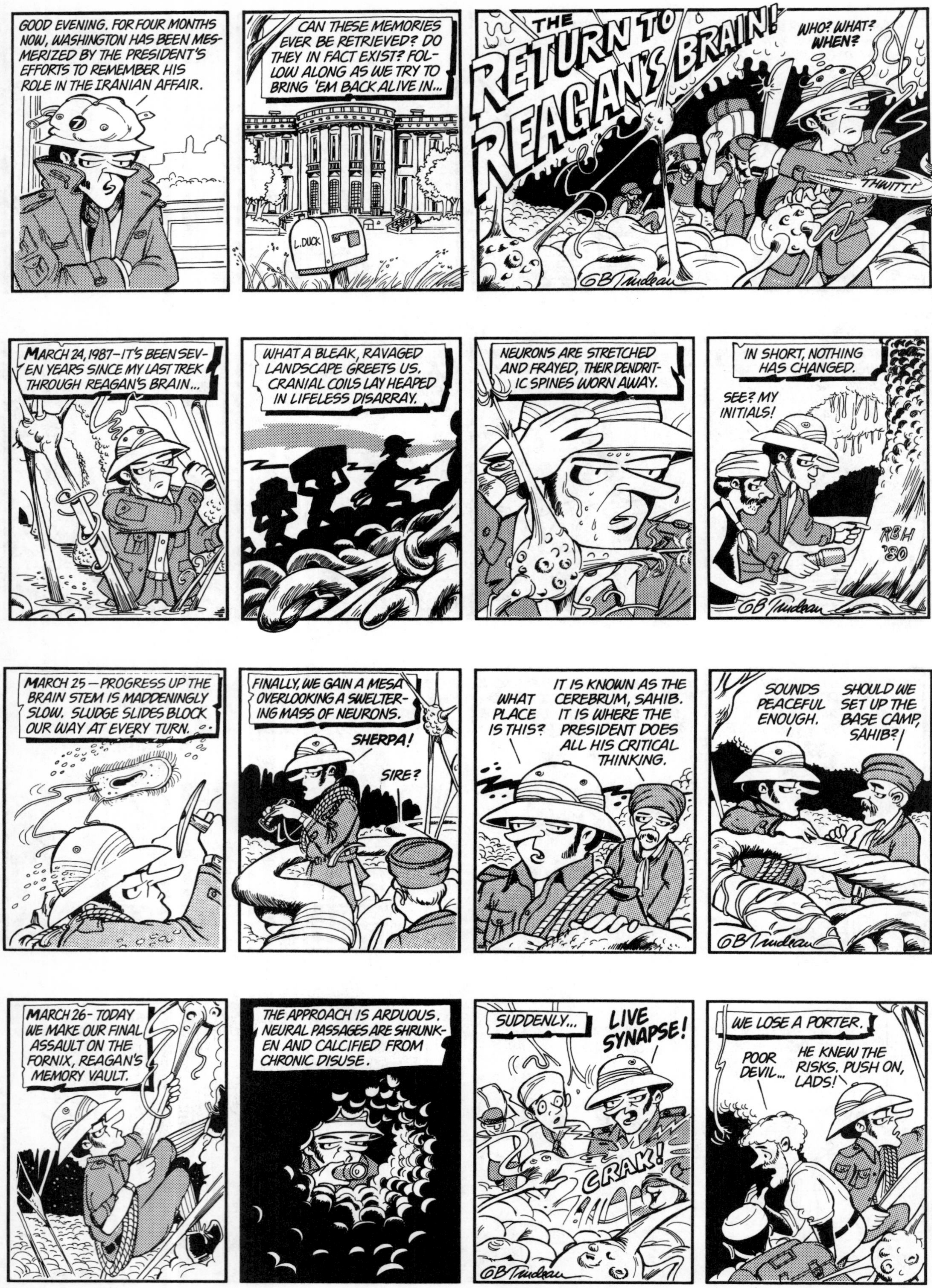
GOOD EVENING. FOR FOUR MONTHS NOW, WASHINGTON HAS BEEN MESMERIZED BY THE PRESIDENT'S EFFORTS TO REMEMBER HIS ROLE IN THE IRANIAN AFFAIR.
CAN THESE MEMORIES EVER BE RETRIEVED? DO THEY IN FACT EXIST? FOLLOW ALONG AS WE TRY TO BRING 'EM BACK ALIVE IN...
L. DUCK
THE RETURN TO REAGAN'S BRAIN!
WHO? WHAT? WHEN?
THWITT!
MARCH 24, 1987—IT'S BEEN SEVEN YEARS SINCE MY LAST TREK THROUGH REAGAN'S BRAIN...
WHAT A BLEAK, RAVAGED LANDSCAPE GREETS US. CRANIAL COILS LAY HEAPED IN LIFELESS DISARRAY.
NEURONS ARE STRETCHED AND FRAYED, THEIR DENDRITIC SPINES WORN AWAY.
IN SHORT, NOTHING HAS CHANGED.
SEE? MY INITIALS!
RBH '80
MARCH 25—PROGRESS UP THE BRAIN STEM IS MADDENINGLY SLOW. SLUDGE SLIDES BLOCK OUR WAY AT EVERY TURN.
FINALLY, WE GAIN A MESA OVERLOOKING A SWELTERING MASS OF NEURONS.
SHERPA!
SIRE?
WHAT PLACE IS THIS?
IT IS KNOWN AS THE CEREBRUM, SAHIB. IT IS WHERE THE PRESIDENT DOES ALL HIS CRITICAL THINKING.
SOUNDS PEACEFUL ENOUGH.
SHOULD WE SET UP THE BASE CAMP, SAHIB?
MARCH 26- TODAY WE MAKE OUR FINAL ASSAULT ON THE FORNIX, REAGAN'S MEMORY VAULT.
THE APPROACH IS ARDUOUS. NEURAL PASSAGES ARE SHRUNKEN AND CALCIFIED FROM CHRONIC DISUSE.
SUDDENLY...
LIVE SYNAPSE!
CRAK!
WE LOSE A PORTER.
POOR DEVIL...
HE KNEW THE RISKS. PUSH ON, LADS!
GB Trudeau

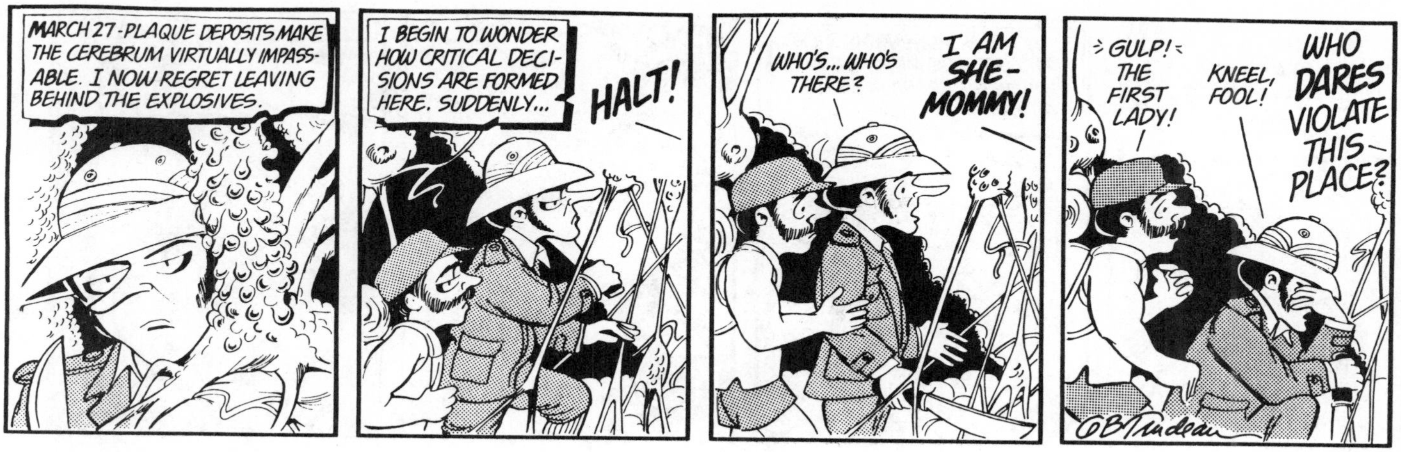
MARCH 27 - PLAQUE DEPOSITS MAKE THE CEREBRUM VIRTUALLY IMPASSABLE. I NOW REGRET LEAVING BEHIND THE EXPLOSIVES.
I BEGIN TO WONDER HOW CRITICAL DECISIONS ARE FORMED HERE. SUDDENLY...
HALT!
WHO'S... WHO'S THERE?
I AM SHE-MOMMY!
GULP! THE FIRST LADY!
KNEEL, FOOL!
WHO DARES VIOLATE THIS PLACE?
GB Trudeau

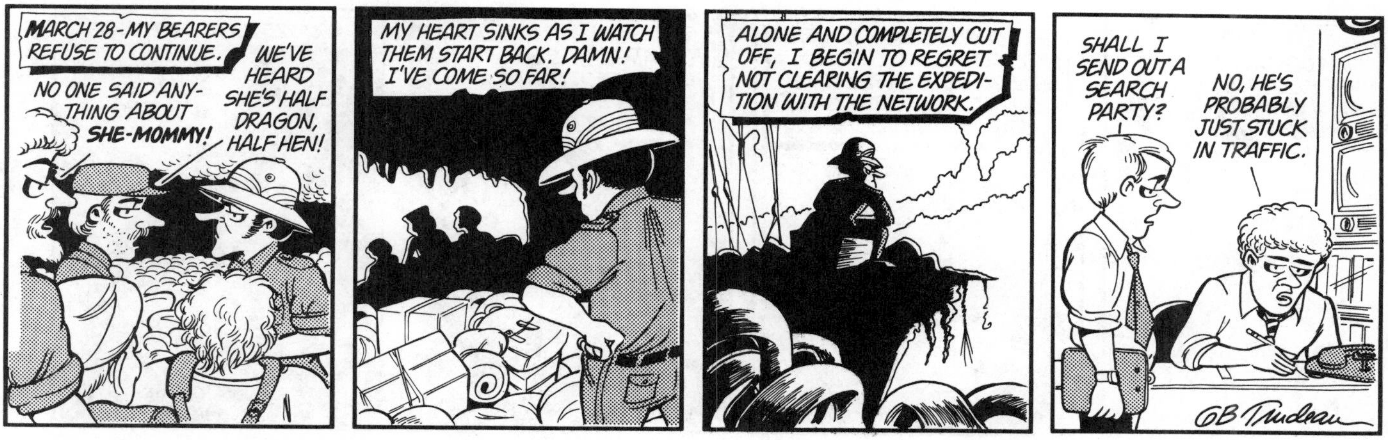
MARCH 28 - MY BEARERS REFUSE TO CONTINUE.
NO ONE SAID ANYTHING ABOUT SHE-MOMMY!
WE'VE HEARD SHE'S HALF DRAGON, HALF HEN!
MY HEART SINKS AS I WATCH THEM START BACK. DAMN! I'VE COME SO FAR!
ALONE AND COMPLETELY CUT OFF, I BEGIN TO REGRET NOT CLEARING THE EXPEDITION WITH THE NETWORK.
SHALL I SEND OUT A SEARCH PARTY?
NO, HE'S PROBABLY JUST STUCK IN TRAFFIC.
GB Trudeau

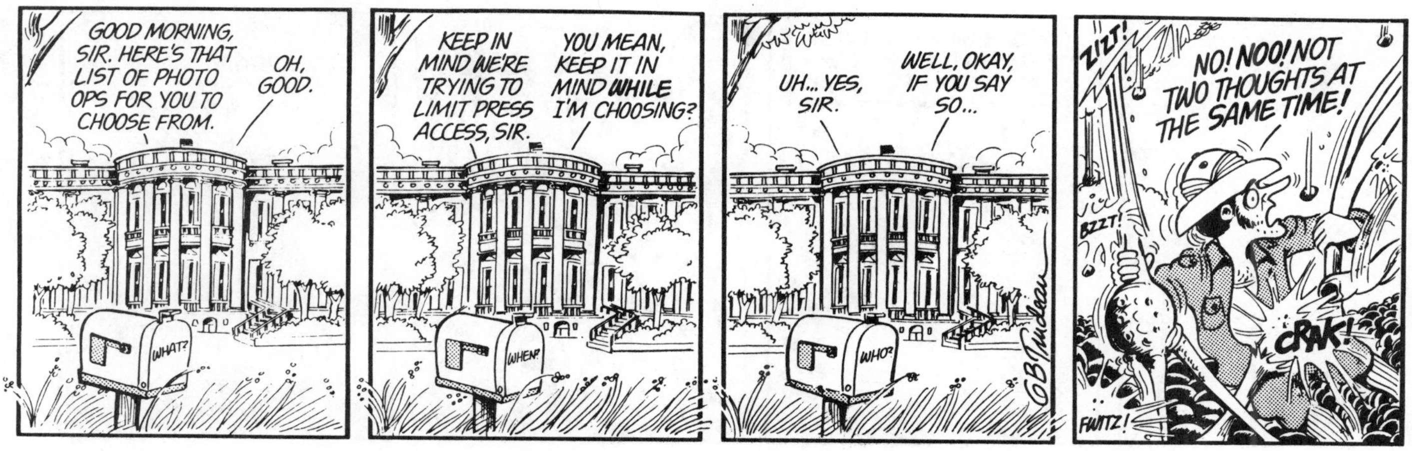
GOOD MORNING, SIR. HERE'S THAT LIST OF PHOTO OPS FOR YOU TO CHOOSE FROM.
OH, GOOD.
WHAT?
KEEP IN MIND WE'RE TRYING TO LIMIT PRESS ACCESS, SIR.
YOU MEAN, KEEP IT IN MIND WHILE I'M CHOOSING?
WHEN?
UH... YES, SIR.
WELL, OKAY, IF YOU SAY SO...
WHO?
GB Trudeau
ZIZT!
BZZT!
NO! NOO! NOT TWO THOUGHTS AT THE SAME TIME!
CRAK!
FWITZ!

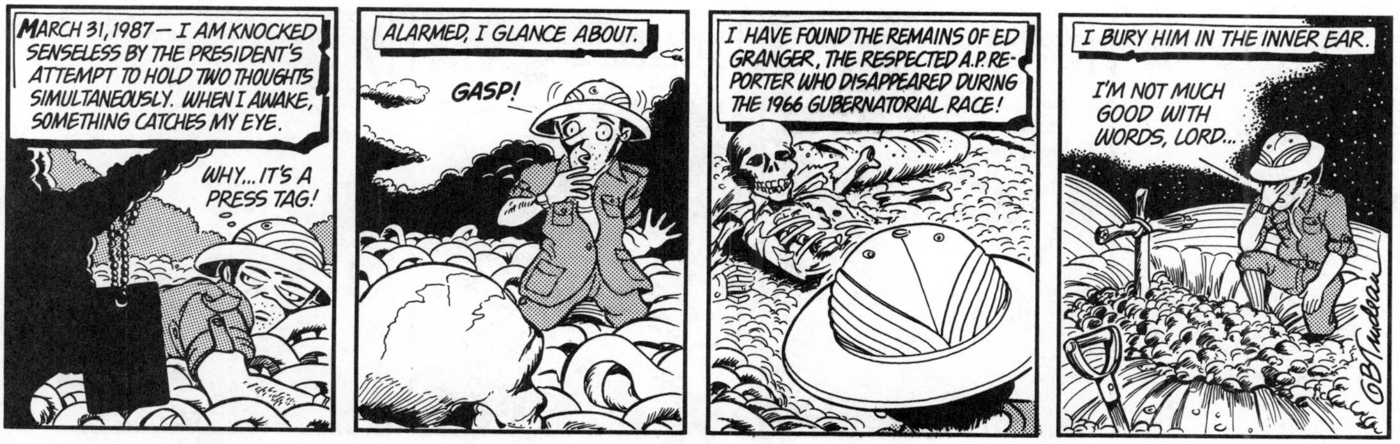
MARCH 31, 1987 — I AM KNOCKED SENSELESS BY THE PRESIDENT'S ATTEMPT TO HOLD TWO THOUGHTS SIMULTANEOUSLY. WHEN I AWAKE, SOMETHING CATCHES MY EYE.
WHY... IT'S A PRESS TAG!
ALARMED, I GLANCE ABOUT.
GASP!
I HAVE FOUND THE REMAINS OF ED GRANGER, THE RESPECTED A.P. REPORTER WHO DISAPPEARED DURING THE 1966 GUBERNATORIAL RACE!
I BURY HIM IN THE INNER EAR.
I'M NOT MUCH GOOD WITH WORDS, LORD...
GB Trudeau

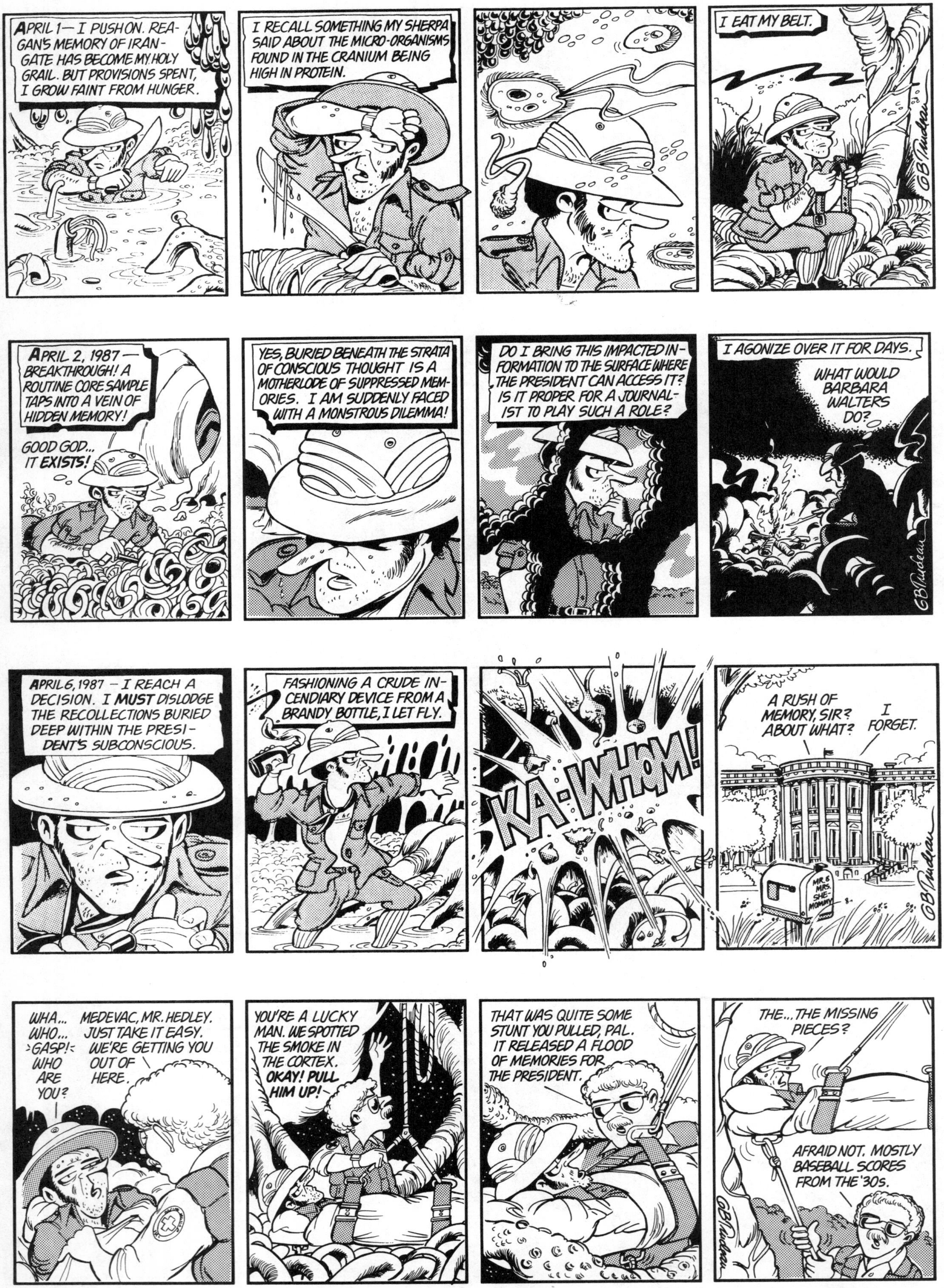
APRIL 1— I PUSH ON. REAGAN'S MEMORY OF IRAN-GATE HAS BECOME MY HOLY GRAIL. BUT PROVISIONS SPENT, I GROW FAINT FROM HUNGER.
I RECALL SOMETHING MY SHERPA SAID ABOUT THE MICRO-ORGANISMS FOUND IN THE CRANIUM BEING HIGH IN PROTEIN.
I EAT MY BELT.
APRIL 2, 1987 — BREAKTHROUGH! A ROUTINE CORE SAMPLE TAPS INTO A VEIN OF HIDDEN MEMORY!
GOOD GOD... IT EXISTS!
YES, BURIED BENEATH THE STRATA OF CONSCIOUS THOUGHT IS A MOTHERLODE OF SUPPRESSED MEMORIES. I AM SUDDENLY FACED WITH A MONSTROUS DILEMMA!
DO I BRING THIS IMPACTED INFORMATION TO THE SURFACE WHERE THE PRESIDENT CAN ACCESS IT? IS IT PROPER FOR A JOURNALIST TO PLAY SUCH A ROLE?
I AGONIZE OVER IT FOR DAYS.
WHAT WOULD BARBARA WALTERS DO?
APRIL 6, 1987 — I REACH A DECISION. I MUST DISLODGE THE RECOLLECTIONS BURIED DEEP WITHIN THE PRESIDENT'S SUBCONSCIOUS.
FASHIONING A CRUDE INCENDIARY DEVICE FROM A BRANDY BOTTLE, I LET FLY.
KA-WHOM!
A RUSH OF MEMORY, SIR? ABOUT WHAT?
I FORGET.
MR. & MRS. SHE-MOMMY
WHA... WHO... GASP! WHO ARE YOU?
MEDEVAC, MR. HEDLEY. JUST TAKE IT EASY. WE'RE GETTING YOU OUT OF HERE.
YOU'RE A LUCKY MAN. WE SPOTTED THE SMOKE IN THE CORTEX. OKAY! PULL HIM UP!
THAT WAS QUITE SOME STUNT YOU PULLED, PAL. IT RELEASED A FLOOD OF MEMORIES FOR THE PRESIDENT.
THE... THE MISSING PIECES?
AFRAID NOT. MOSTLY BASEBALL SCORES FROM THE '30S.
GBTrudeau

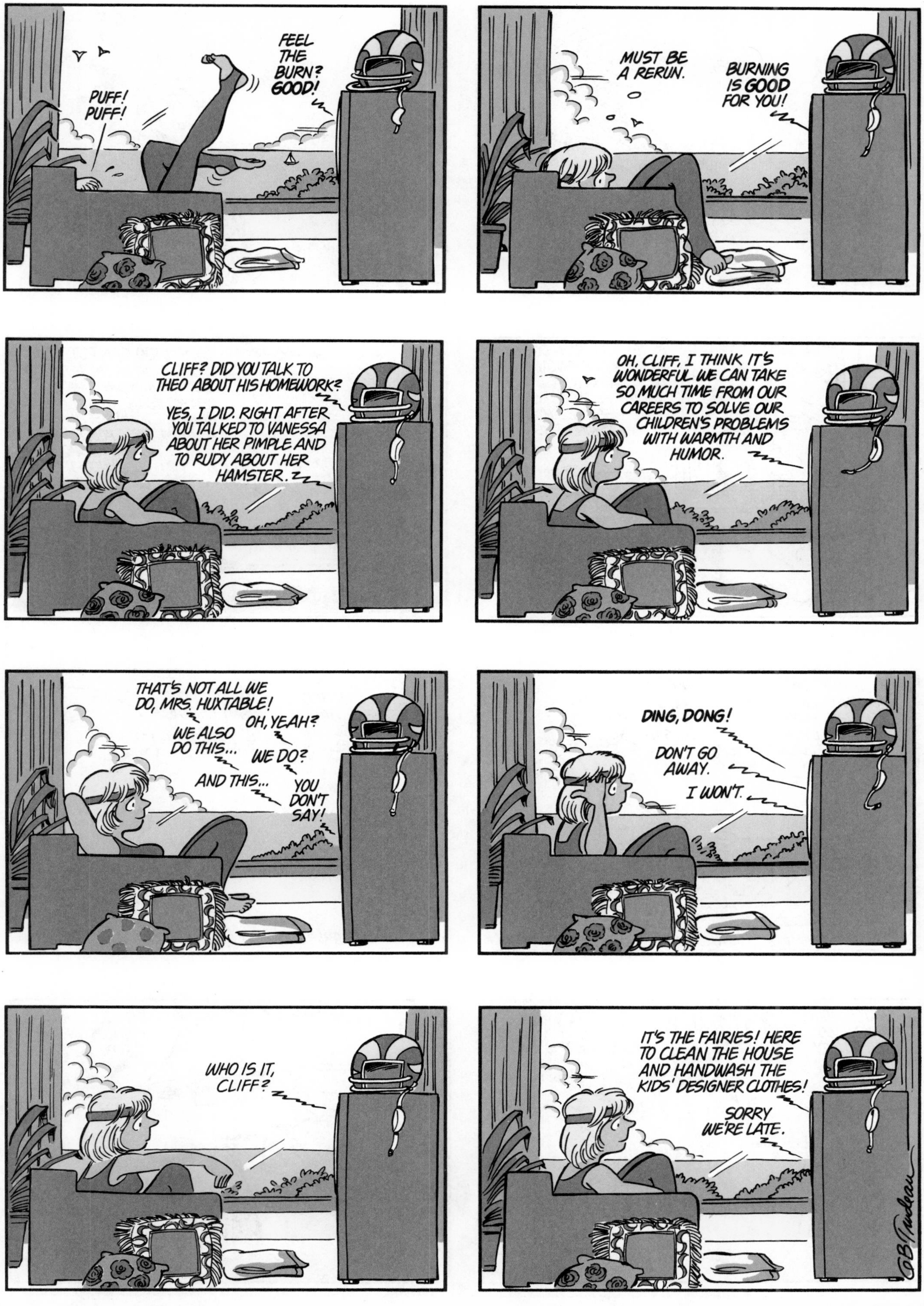
PUFF! PUFF!
FEEL THE BURN? GOOD!
MUST BE A RERUN.
BURNING IS GOOD FOR YOU!
CLIFF? DID YOU TALK TO THEO ABOUT HIS HOMEWORK?
YES, I DID. RIGHT AFTER YOU TALKED TO VANESSA ABOUT HER PIMPLE AND TO RUDY ABOUT HER HAMSTER.
OH, CLIFF, I THINK IT'S WONDERFUL WE CAN TAKE SO MUCH TIME FROM OUR CAREERS TO SOLVE OUR CHILDREN'S PROBLEMS WITH WARMTH AND HUMOR.
THAT'S NOT ALL WE DO, MRS. HUXTABLE!
OH, YEAH?
WE ALSO DO THIS...
WE DO?
AND THIS...
YOU DON'T SAY!
DING, DONG!
DON'T GO AWAY.
I WON'T.
WHO IS IT, CLIFF?
IT'S THE FAIRIES! HERE TO CLEAN THE HOUSE AND HANDWASH THE KIDS' DESIGNER CLOTHES!
SORRY WE'RE LATE.
GBTrudeau

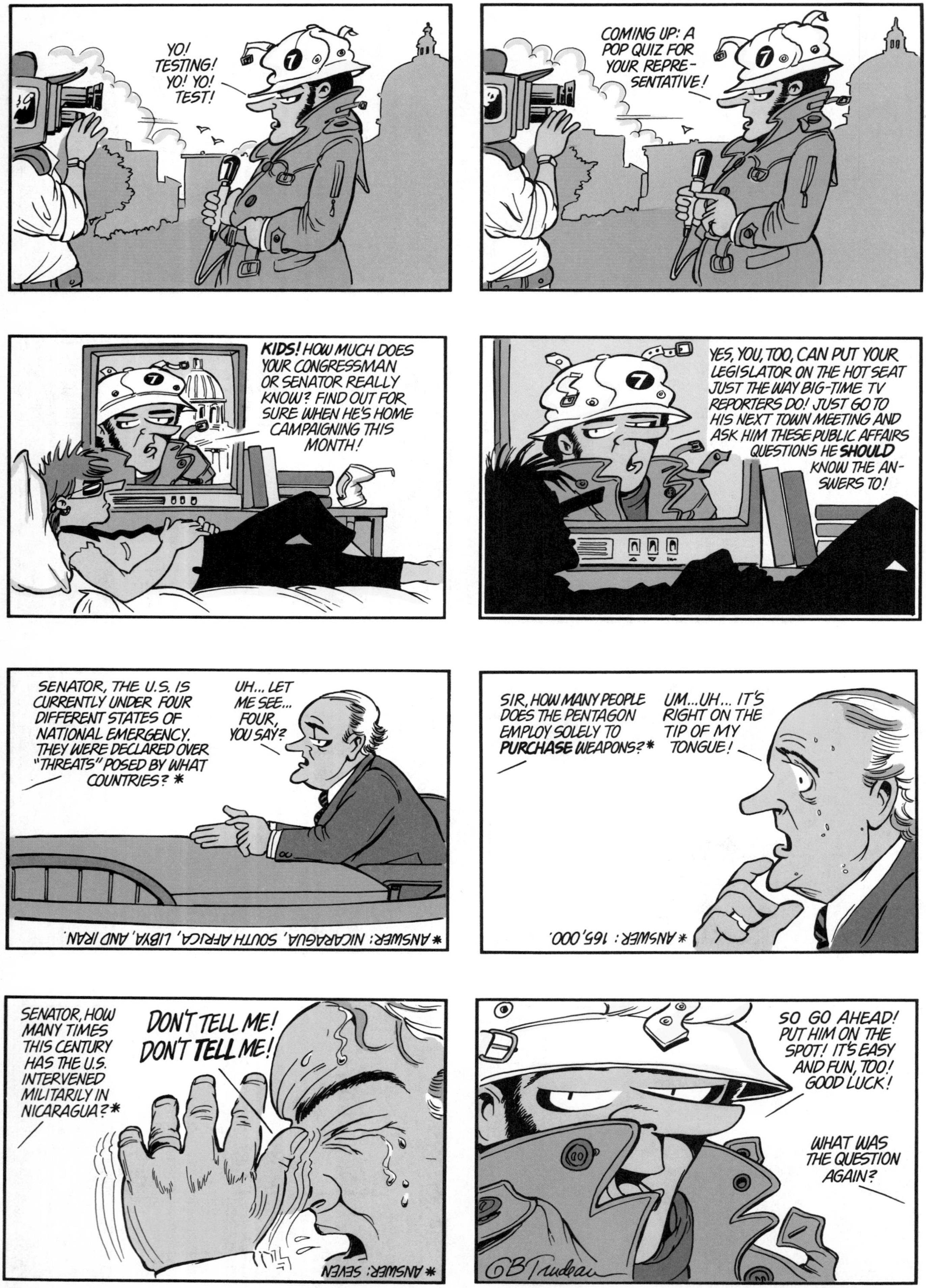
YO! TESTING! YO! YO! TEST!
COMING UP: A POP QUIZ FOR YOUR REPRE-SENTATIVE!
KIDS! HOW MUCH DOES YOUR CONGRESSMAN OR SENATOR REALLY KNOW? FIND OUT FOR SURE WHEN HE'S HOME CAMPAIGNING THIS MONTH!
YES, YOU, TOO, CAN PUT YOUR LEGISLATOR ON THE HOT SEAT JUST THE WAY BIG-TIME TV REPORTERS DO! JUST GO TO HIS NEXT TOWN MEETING AND ASK HIM THESE PUBLIC AFFAIRS QUESTIONS HE SHOULD KNOW THE AN-SWERS TO!
SENATOR, THE U.S. IS CURRENTLY UNDER FOUR DIFFERENT STATES OF NATIONAL EMERGENCY. THEY WERE DECLARED OVER "THREATS" POSED BY WHAT COUNTRIES? *
UH... LET ME SEE... FOUR, YOU SAY?
* ANSWER: NICARAGUA, SOUTH AFRICA, LIBYA, AND IRAN.
SIR, HOW MANY PEOPLE DOES THE PENTAGON EMPLOY SOLELY TO PURCHASE WEAPONS? *
UM... UH... IT'S RIGHT ON THE TIP OF MY TONGUE!
* ANSWER: 165,000.
SENATOR, HOW MANY TIMES THIS CENTURY HAS THE U.S. INTERVENED MILITARILY IN NICARAGUA? *
DON'T TELL ME! DON'T TELL ME!
* ANSWER: SEVEN
SO GO AHEAD! PUT HIM ON THE SPOT! IT'S EASY AND FUN, TOO! GOOD LUCK!
WHAT WAS THE QUESTION AGAIN?
GB Trudeau

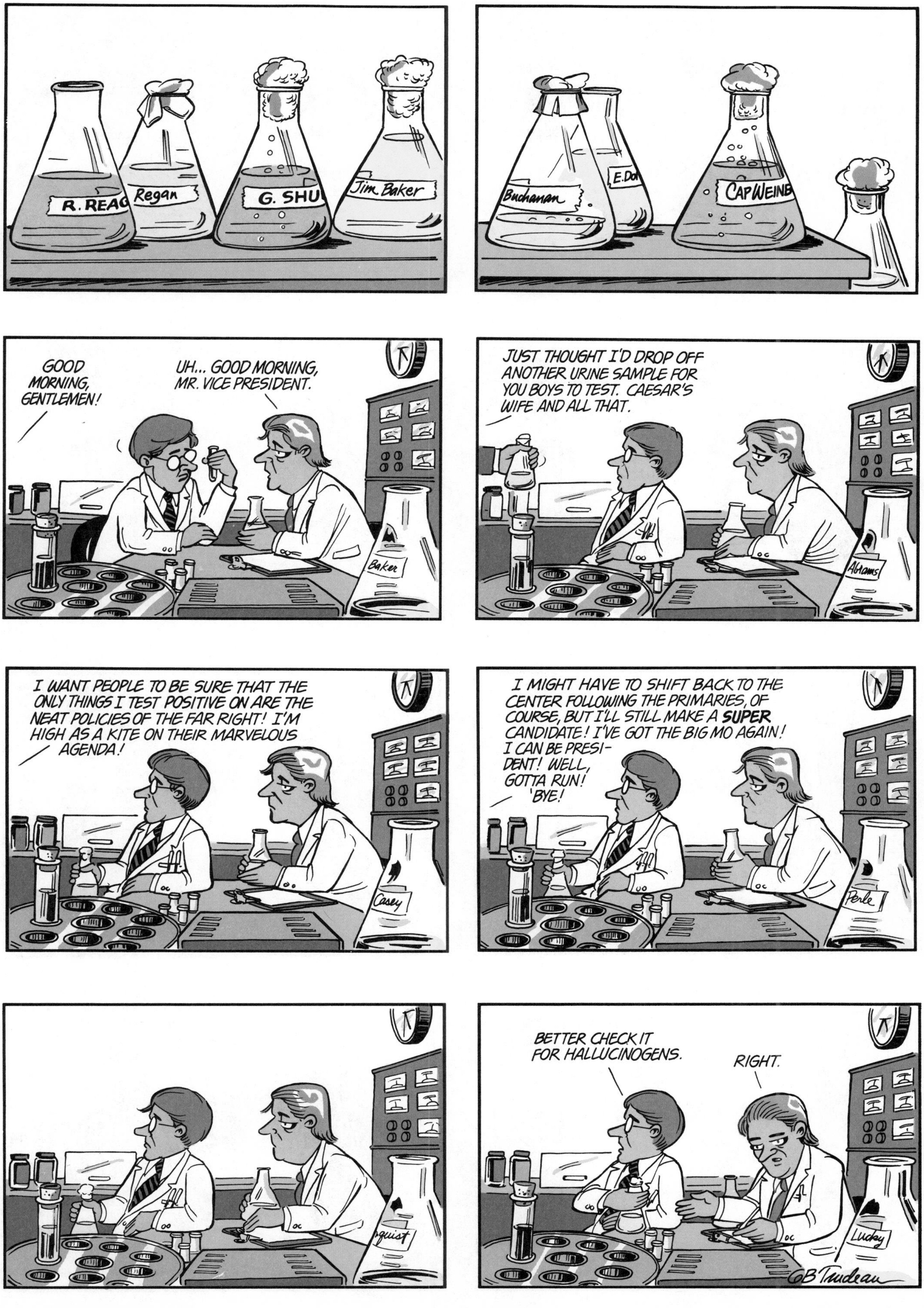
R. REAG
Regan
G. SHU
Jim Baker
Buchanan
CAPWEINB
GOOD MORNING, GENTLEMEN!
UH... GOOD MORNING, MR. VICE PRESIDENT.
Baker
JUST THOUGHT I'D DROP OFF ANOTHER URINE SAMPLE FOR YOU BOYS TO TEST. CAESAR'S WIFE AND ALL THAT.
Abrams
I WANT PEOPLE TO BE SURE THAT THE ONLY THINGS I TEST POSITIVE ON ARE THE NEAT POLICIES OF THE FAR RIGHT! I'M HIGH AS A KITE ON THEIR MARVELOUS AGENDA!
Casey
I MIGHT HAVE TO SHIFT BACK TO THE CENTER FOLLOWING THE PRIMARIES, OF COURSE, BUT I'LL STILL MAKE A **SUPER** CANDIDATE! I'VE GOT THE BIG MO AGAIN! I CAN BE PRESIDENT! WELL, GOTTA RUN! 'BYE!
Perle
BETTER CHECK IT FOR HALLUCINOGENS.
RIGHT.
Lucky
GB Trudeau

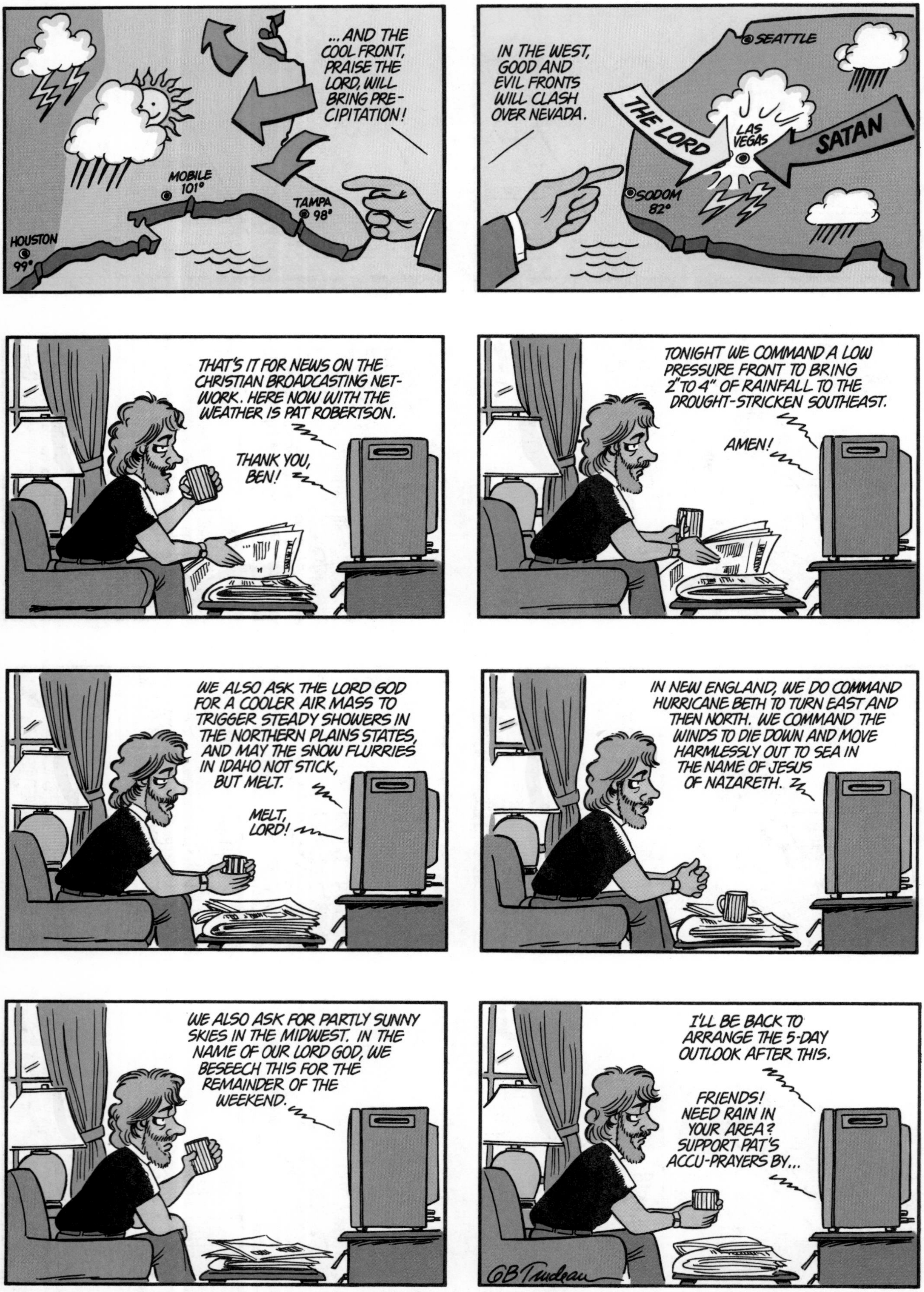
...AND THE COOL FRONT, PRAISE THE LORD, WILL BRING PRE-CIPITATION!
MOBILE 101°
TAMPA 98°
HOUSTON 99°
IN THE WEST, GOOD AND EVIL FRONTS WILL CLASH OVER NEVADA.
SEATTLE
THE LORD
LAS VEGAS
SATAN
SODOM 82°
THAT'S IT FOR NEWS ON THE CHRISTIAN BROADCASTING NET-WORK. HERE NOW WITH THE WEATHER IS PAT ROBERTSON.
THANK YOU, BEN!
TONIGHT WE COMMAND A LOW PRESSURE FRONT TO BRING 2" TO 4" OF RAINFALL TO THE DROUGHT-STRICKEN SOUTHEAST.
AMEN!
WE ALSO ASK THE LORD GOD FOR A COOLER AIR MASS TO TRIGGER STEADY SHOWERS IN THE NORTHERN PLAINS STATES, AND MAY THE SNOW FLURRIES IN IDAHO NOT STICK, BUT MELT.
MELT, LORD!
IN NEW ENGLAND, WE DO COMMAND HURRICANE BETH TO TURN EAST AND THEN NORTH. WE COMMAND THE WINDS TO DIE DOWN AND MOVE HARMLESSLY OUT TO SEA IN THE NAME OF JESUS OF NAZARETH.
WE ALSO ASK FOR PARTLY SUNNY SKIES IN THE MIDWEST. IN THE NAME OF OUR LORD GOD, WE BESEECH THIS FOR THE REMAINDER OF THE WEEKEND.
I'LL BE BACK TO ARRANGE THE 5-DAY OUTLOOK AFTER THIS.
FRIENDS! NEED RAIN IN YOUR AREA? SUPPORT PAT'S ACCU-PRAYERS BY...
©B Trudeau

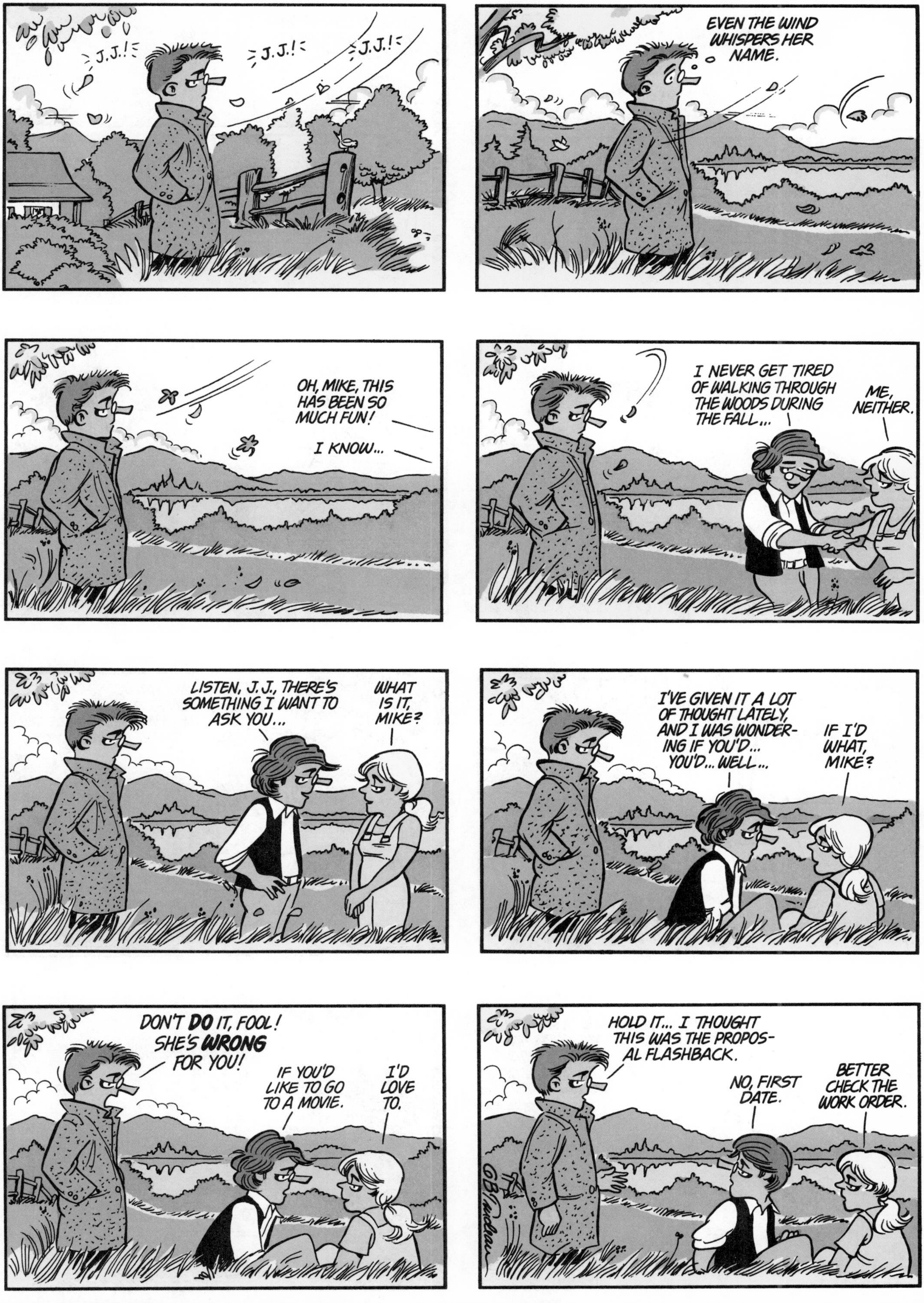

J.J.!
J.J.!
J.J.!
EVEN THE WIND WHISPERS HER NAME.
OH, MIKE, THIS HAS BEEN SO MUCH FUN!
I KNOW...
I NEVER GET TIRED OF WALKING THROUGH THE WOODS DURING THE FALL...
ME, NEITHER.
LISTEN, J.J., THERE'S SOMETHING I WANT TO ASK YOU...
WHAT IS IT, MIKE?
I'VE GIVEN IT A LOT OF THOUGHT LATELY, AND I WAS WONDERING IF YOU'D... YOU'D... WELL...
IF I'D WHAT, MIKE?
DON'T DO IT, FOOL! SHE'S WRONG FOR YOU!
IF YOU'D LIKE TO GO TO A MOVIE.
I'D LOVE TO.
HOLD IT... I THOUGHT THIS WAS THE PROPOSAL FLASHBACK.
NO, FIRST DATE.
BETTER CHECK THE WORK ORDER.

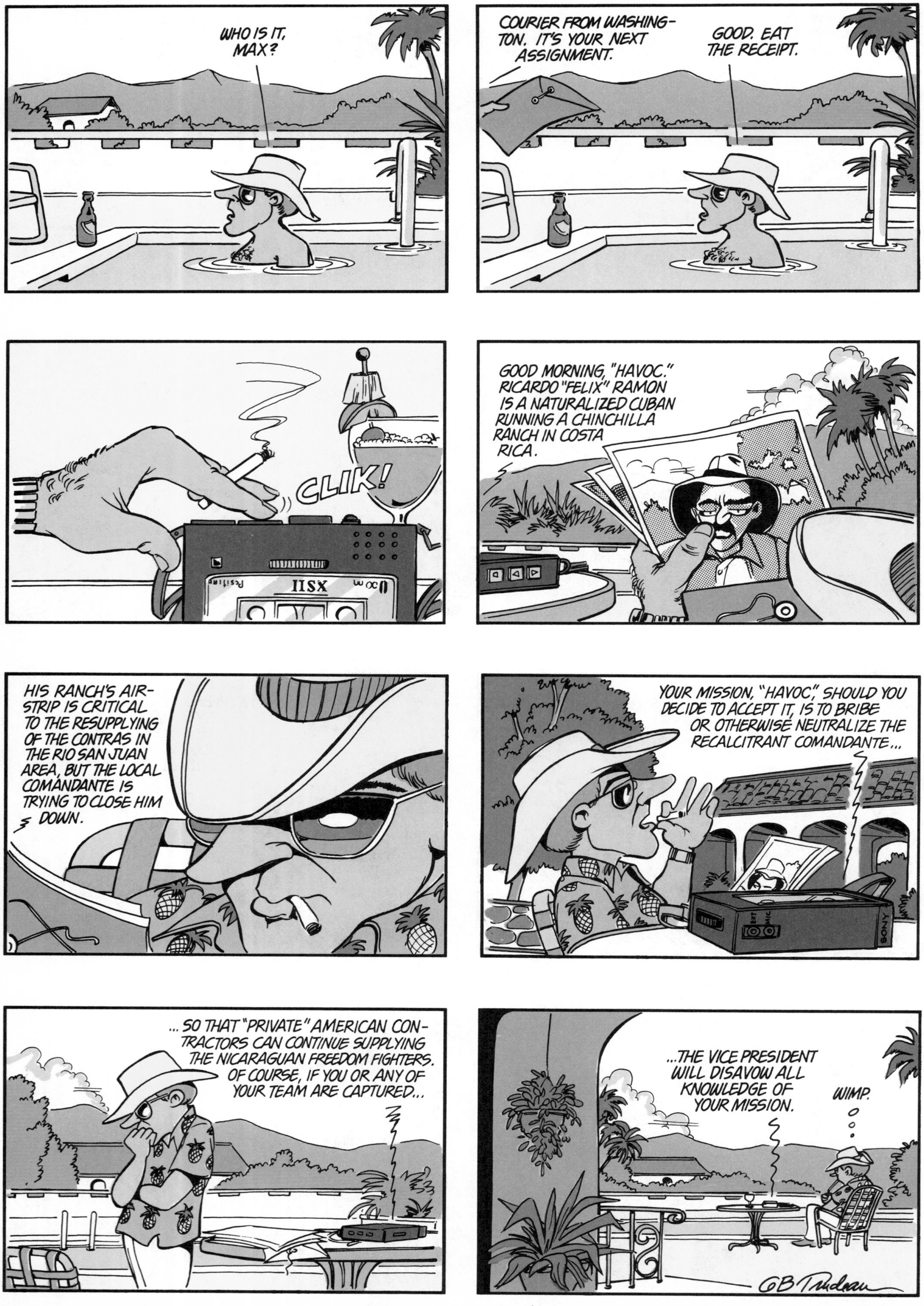
WHO IS IT, MAX?
COURIER FROM WASHINGTON. IT'S YOUR NEXT ASSIGNMENT.
GOOD. EAT THE RECEIPT.
CLIK!
GOOD MORNING, "HAVOC." RICARDO "FELIX" RAMON IS A NATURALIZED CUBAN RUNNING A CHINCHILLA RANCH IN COSTA RICA.
HIS RANCH'S AIRSTRIP IS CRITICAL TO THE RESUPPLYING OF THE CONTRAS IN THE RIO SAN JUAN AREA, BUT THE LOCAL COMANDANTE IS TRYING TO CLOSE HIM DOWN.
YOUR MISSION, "HAVOC," SHOULD YOU DECIDE TO ACCEPT IT, IS TO BRIBE OR OTHERWISE NEUTRALIZE THE RECALCITRANT COMANDANTE...
SONY
...SO THAT "PRIVATE" AMERICAN CONTRACTORS CAN CONTINUE SUPPLYING THE NICARAGUAN FREEDOM FIGHTERS. OF COURSE, IF YOU OR ANY OF YOUR TEAM ARE CAPTURED...
...THE VICE PRESIDENT WILL DISAVOW ALL KNOWLEDGE OF YOUR MISSION.
WIMP.
GB Trudeau

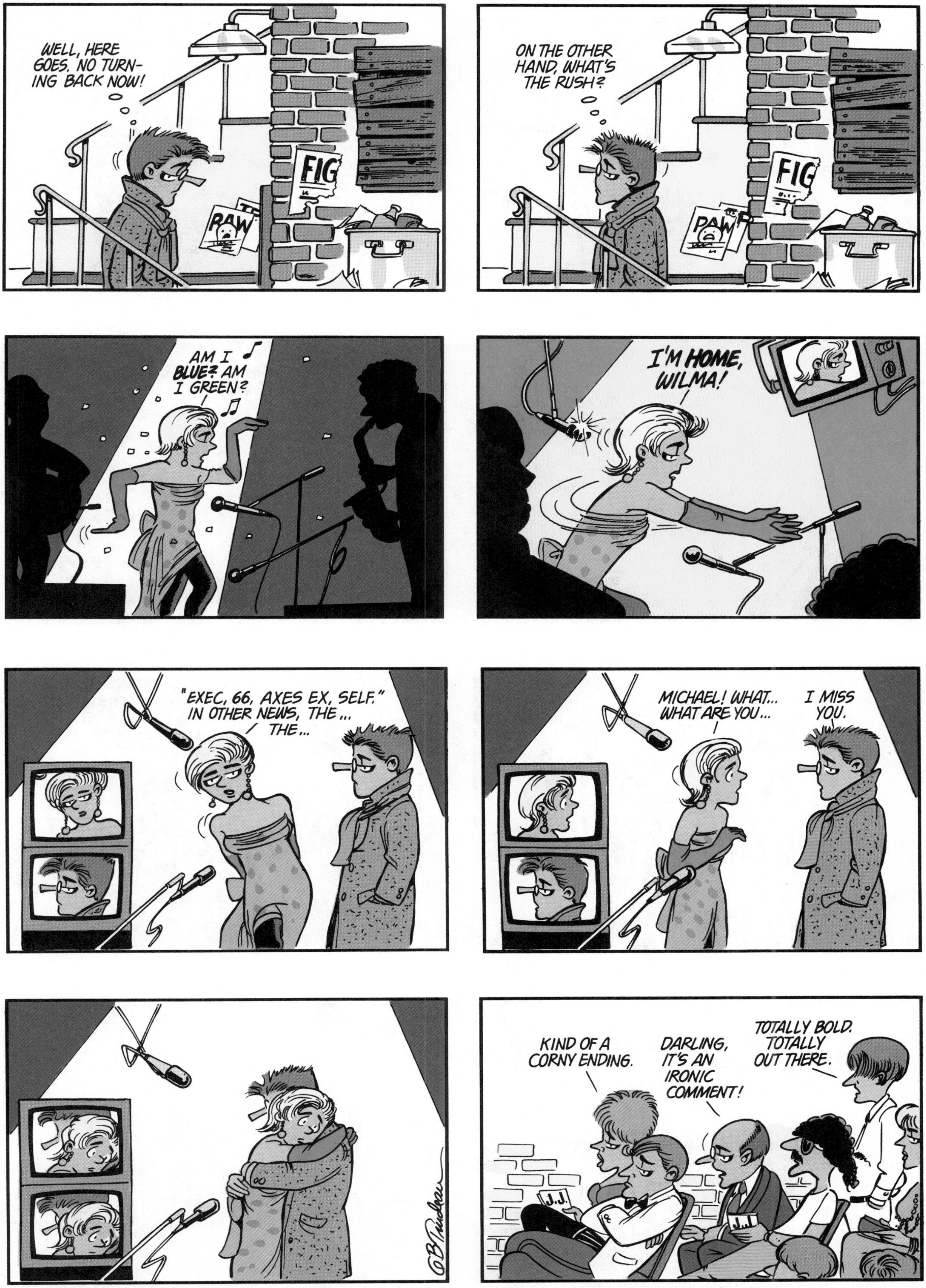

WELL, HERE GOES. NO TURNING BACK NOW!
FIG
PAW
ON THE OTHER HAND, WHAT'S THE RUSH?
FIG
PAW
AM I BLUE? AM I GREEN?
I'M HOME, WILMA!
"EXEC, 66, AXES EX, SELF." IN OTHER NEWS, THE ... THE ...
MICHAEL! WHAT... WHAT ARE YOU...
I MISS YOU.
KIND OF A CORNY ENDING.
DARLING, IT'S AN IRONIC COMMENT!
TOTALLY BOLD. TOTALLY OUT THERE.
J.J.
J.J.

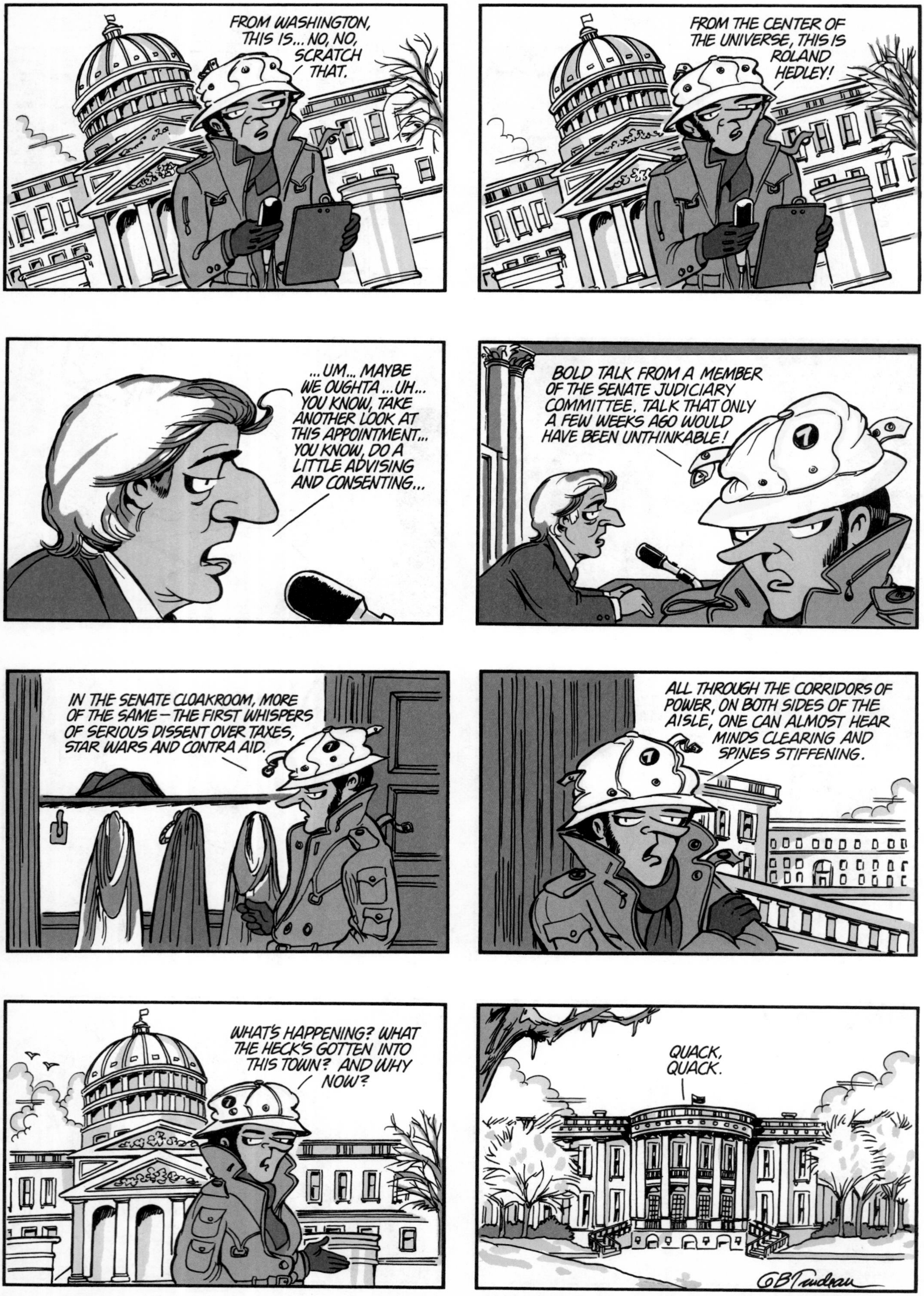
FROM WASHINGTON, THIS IS... NO, NO, SCRATCH THAT.
FROM THE CENTER OF THE UNIVERSE, THIS IS ROLAND HEDLEY!
...UM... MAYBE WE OUGHTA ...UH... YOU KNOW, TAKE ANOTHER LOOK AT THIS APPOINTMENT... YOU KNOW, DO A LITTLE ADVISING AND CONSENTING...
BOLD TALK FROM A MEMBER OF THE SENATE JUDICIARY COMMITTEE. TALK THAT ONLY A FEW WEEKS AGO WOULD HAVE BEEN UNTHINKABLE!
IN THE SENATE CLOAKROOM, MORE OF THE SAME — THE FIRST WHISPERS OF SERIOUS DISSENT OVER TAXES, STAR WARS AND CONTRA AID.
ALL THROUGH THE CORRIDORS OF POWER, ON BOTH SIDES OF THE AISLE, ONE CAN ALMOST HEAR MINDS CLEARING AND SPINES STIFFENING.
WHAT'S HAPPENING? WHAT THE HECK'S GOTTEN INTO THIS TOWN? AND WHY NOW?
QUACK, QUACK.
GBTrudeau

YOU'RE KIND OF STEAMED, AREN'T YOU, MIKE?
YOU BET I AM!
IF YOU ASK ME, IT'S A KIND OF VANDALISM.
IT'S JUST NOT RIGHT!
MUCH OF THE VISUAL APPEAL OF CLASSIC FILMS LIES IN THE MASTERY OF THE MONOCHROMATIC SCALE.
> SIGH... <
COLORIZING BLACK-AND-WHITE FILMS IS A SIN AGAINST THE CULTURE, ZONKER. IT CHEAPENS THE ICO-NOGRAPHY OF A GREAT ERA!
WE'RE TALKING ABOUT ART, DAMMIT!
OH. I THOUGHT WE WERE DISCUSSING MOVIES.
© B Trudeau

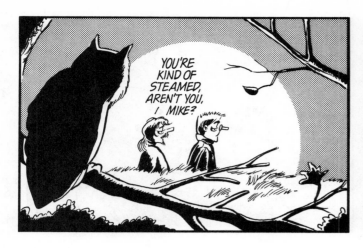

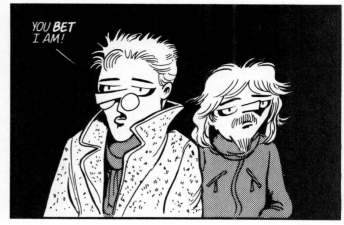

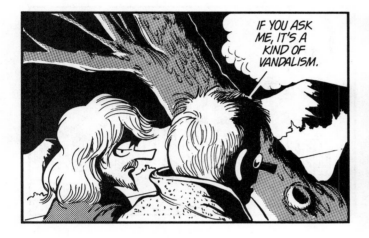

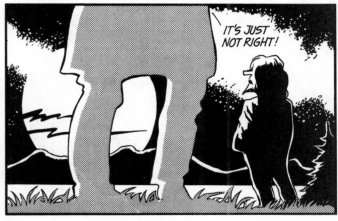

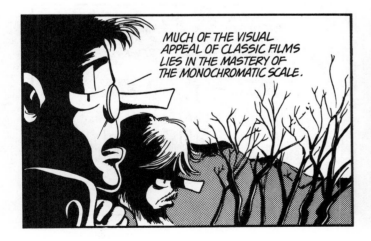

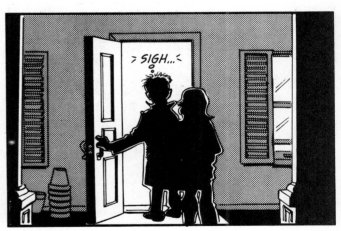

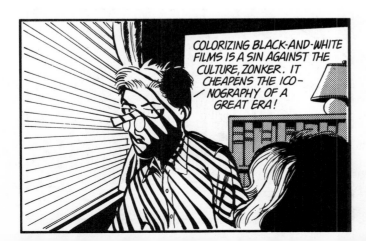

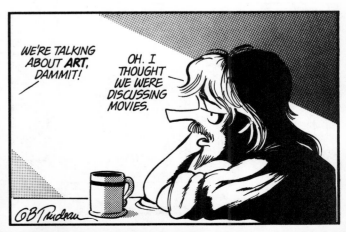

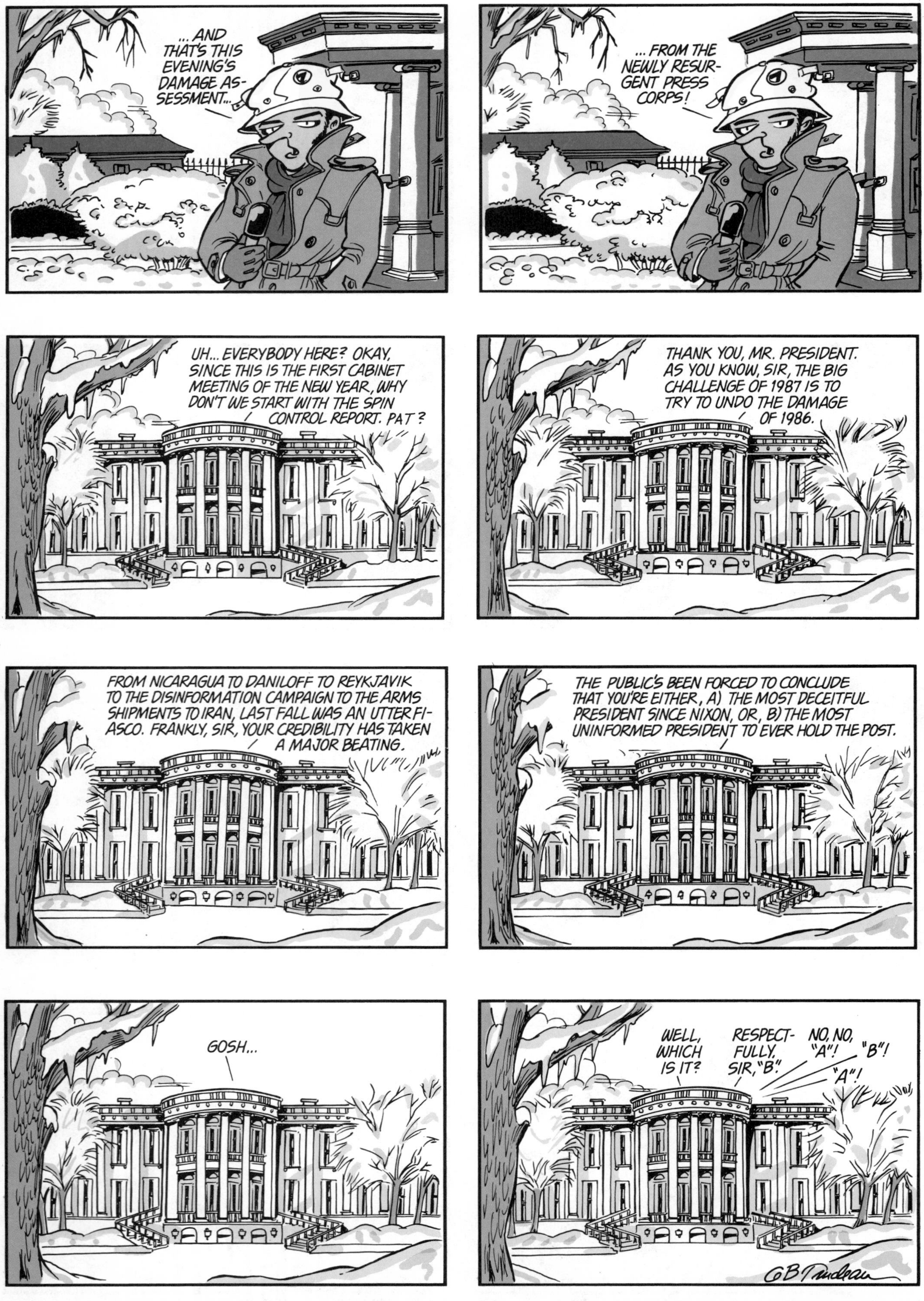
... AND THAT'S THIS EVENING'S DAMAGE ASSESSMENT...
... FROM THE NEWLY RESURGENT PRESS CORPS!
UH... EVERYBODY HERE? OKAY, SINCE THIS IS THE FIRST CABINET MEETING OF THE NEW YEAR, WHY DON'T WE START WITH THE SPIN CONTROL REPORT. PAT?
THANK YOU, MR. PRESIDENT. AS YOU KNOW, SIR, THE BIG CHALLENGE OF 1987 IS TO TRY TO UNDO THE DAMAGE OF 1986.
FROM NICARAGUA TO DANILOFF TO REYKJAVIK TO THE DISINFORMATION CAMPAIGN TO THE ARMS SHIPMENTS TO IRAN, LAST FALL WAS AN UTTER FIASCO. FRANKLY, SIR, YOUR CREDIBILITY HAS TAKEN A MAJOR BEATING.
THE PUBLIC'S BEEN FORCED TO CONCLUDE THAT YOU'RE EITHER, A) THE MOST DECEITFUL PRESIDENT SINCE NIXON, OR, B) THE MOST UNINFORMED PRESIDENT TO EVER HOLD THE POST.
GOSH...
WELL, WHICH IS IT?
RESPECTFULLY, SIR, "B."
NO, NO, "A"!
"B"!
"A"!
GB Trudeau

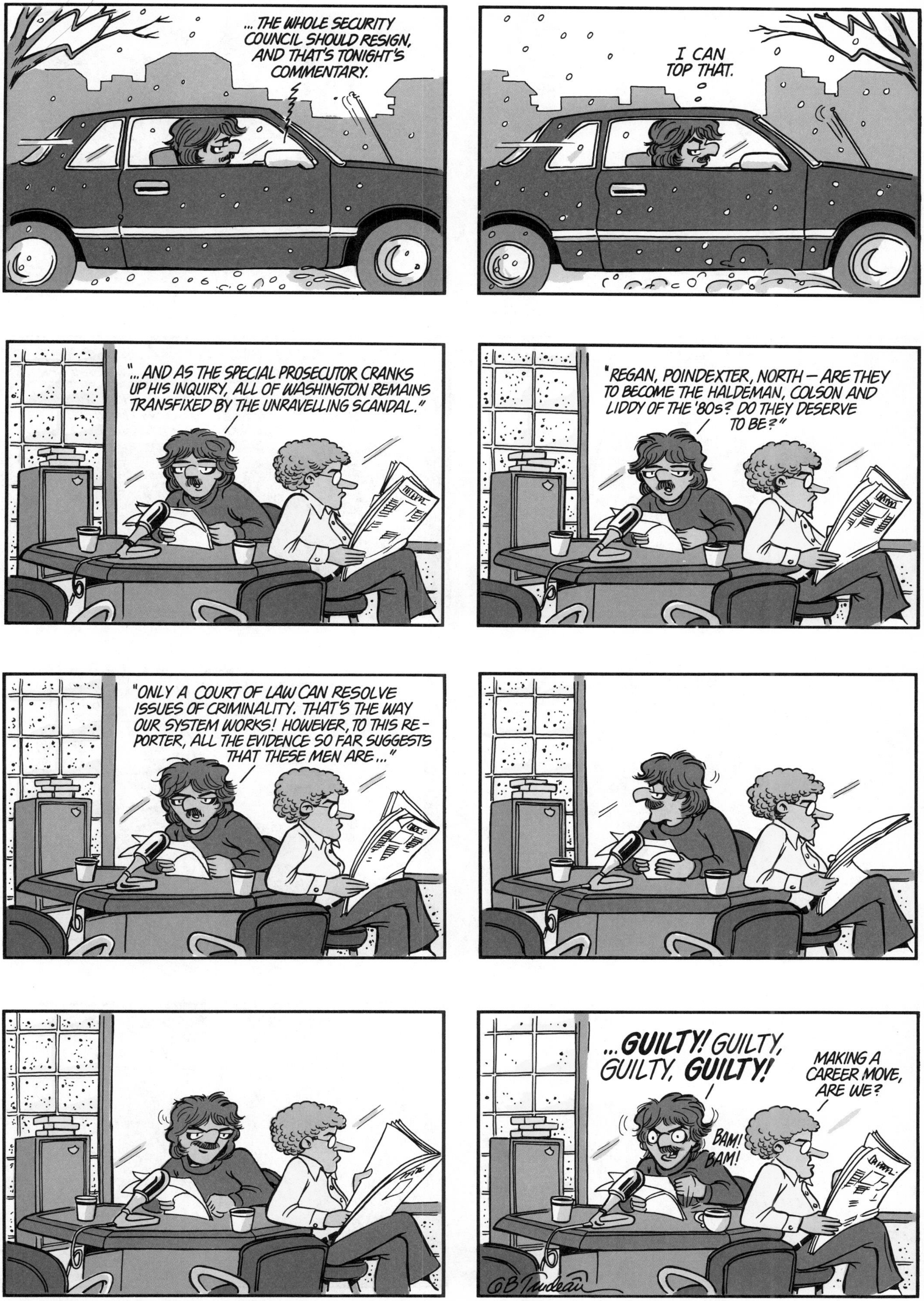

... THE WHOLE SECURITY COUNCIL SHOULD RESIGN, AND THAT'S TONIGHT'S COMMENTARY.
I CAN TOP THAT.
"... AND AS THE SPECIAL PROSECUTOR CRANKS UP HIS INQUIRY, ALL OF WASHINGTON REMAINS TRANSFIXED BY THE UNRAVELLING SCANDAL."
"REGAN, POINDEXTER, NORTH — ARE THEY TO BECOME THE HALDEMAN, COLSON AND LIDDY OF THE '80s? DO THEY DESERVE TO BE?"
"ONLY A COURT OF LAW CAN RESOLVE ISSUES OF CRIMINALITY. THAT'S THE WAY OUR SYSTEM WORKS! HOWEVER, TO THIS REPORTER, ALL THE EVIDENCE SO FAR SUGGESTS THAT THESE MEN ARE ..."
... GUILTY! GUILTY, GUILTY, GUILTY!
BAM! BAM!
MAKING A CAREER MOVE, ARE WE?
© B Trudeau

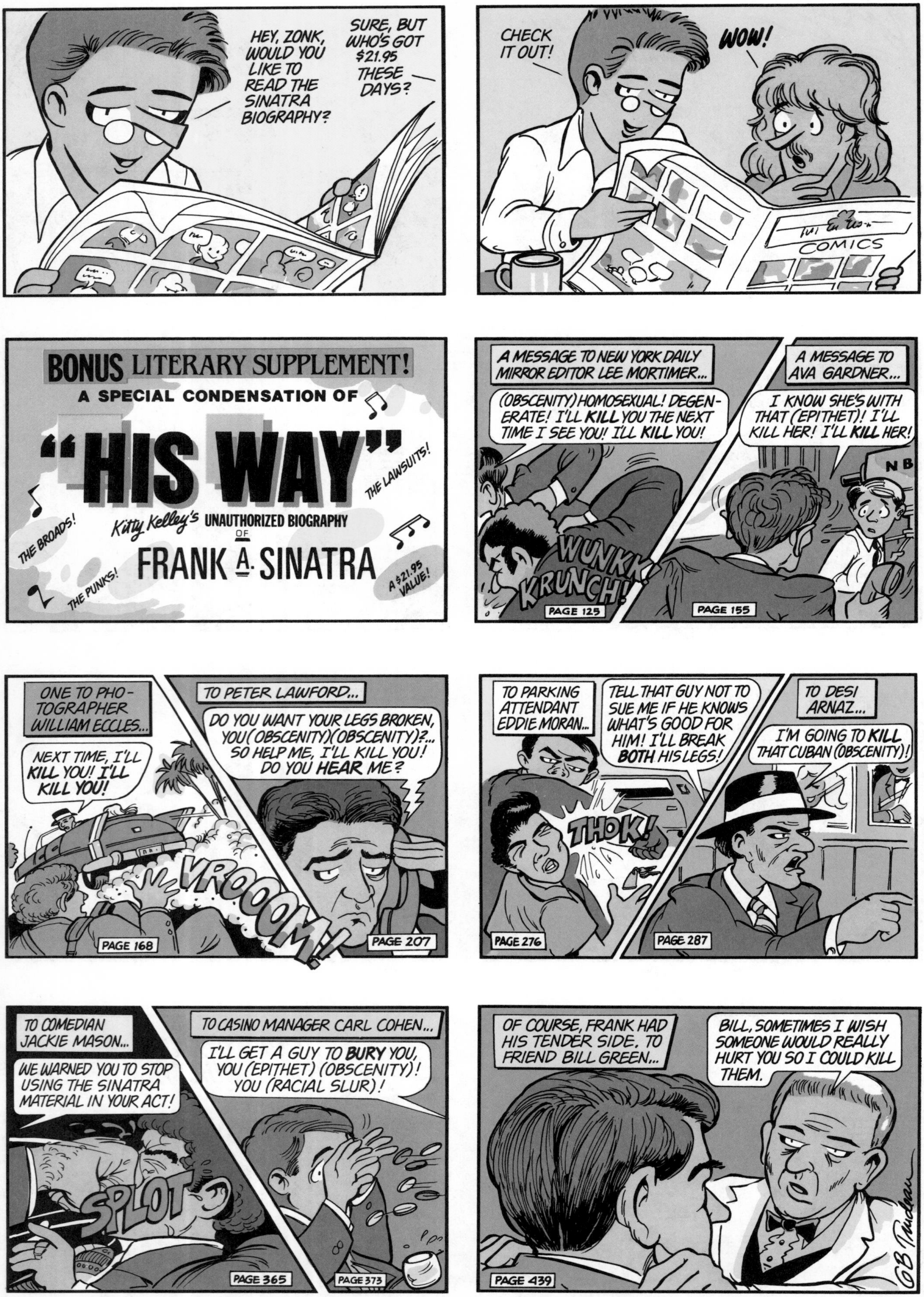
HEY, ZONK, WOULD YOU LIKE TO READ THE SINATRA BIOGRAPHY?
SURE, BUT WHO'S GOT $21.95 THESE DAYS?
CHECK IT OUT!
WOW!
COMICS
BONUS LITERARY SUPPLEMENT!
A SPECIAL CONDENSATION OF
"HIS WAY"
Kitty Kelley's UNAUTHORIZED BIOGRAPHY OF FRANK A. SINATRA
THE BROADS!
THE PUNKS!
THE LAWSUITS!
A $21.95 VALUE!
A MESSAGE TO NEW YORK DAILY MIRROR EDITOR LEE MORTIMER...
(OBSCENITY) HOMOSEXUAL! DEGENERATE! I'LL KILL YOU THE NEXT TIME I SEE YOU! I'LL KILL YOU!
WUNKK KRUNCH!
PAGE 125
A MESSAGE TO AVA GARDNER...
I KNOW SHE'S WITH THAT (EPITHET)! I'LL KILL HER! I'LL KILL HER!
NB
PAGE 155
ONE TO PHOTOGRAPHER WILLIAM ECCLES...
NEXT TIME, I'LL KILL YOU! I'LL KILL YOU!
VROOOOM!
PAGE 168
TO PETER LAWFORD...
DO YOU WANT YOUR LEGS BROKEN, YOU (OBSCENITY) (OBSCENITY)?... SO HELP ME, I'LL KILL YOU! DO YOU HEAR ME?
PAGE 207
TO PARKING ATTENDANT EDDIE MORAN...
TELL THAT GUY NOT TO SUE ME IF HE KNOWS WHAT'S GOOD FOR HIM! I'LL BREAK BOTH HIS LEGS!
THOK!
PAGE 276
TO DESI ARNAZ...
I'M GOING TO KILL THAT CUBAN (OBSCENITY)!
PAGE 287
TO COMEDIAN JACKIE MASON...
WE WARNED YOU TO STOP USING THE SINATRA MATERIAL IN YOUR ACT!
SPLOT
PAGE 365
TO CASINO MANAGER CARL COHEN...
I'LL GET A GUY TO BURY YOU, YOU (EPITHET) (OBSCENITY)! YOU (RACIAL SLUR)!
PAGE 373
OF COURSE, FRANK HAD HIS TENDER SIDE. TO FRIEND BILL GREEN...
BILL, SOMETIMES I WISH SOMEONE WOULD REALLY HURT YOU SO I COULD KILL THEM.
PAGE 439
GB Trudeau

SO WHAT IS IT, HASSIM?
A BIBLE!
WHO'S IT FROM?
I CAN'T MAKE IT OUT. RONALD SOMEBODY.
BIBLES INSCRIBED BY RONALD REAGAN, 1980-86.
"And the scripture, foreseeing that God would justify the Gentiles by faith, preached the gospel beforehand to Abraham, saying, 'All the nations shall be blessed in you.'" Galatians 3:8
Ronald Reagan Oct. 3, 1986
The Open Bible
Presented t
Moderate Element
on this 3
TO THE MULLAHS.
TO MIKHAIL GORBACHEV...
"Or what king, going to make war against another king, sitteth not down first and consulteth whether he be able with ten thousand to meet him that cometh against him with twenty thousand?"
Luke 14:31
Ronald Reagan Oct 11, 1986
The Open Bible
Presented to
The Evil Emperor
on this 11th day
TO A U.S. FARMER...
"To every thing there is a season, and a time to every purpose under the heaven. A time to be born, and a time to die; a time to plant, and a time to pluck up that which is planted."
The Byrds, 1965
Ronald Reagan
1984
The Open Bible
Presented
Farmer Bob
on this 7th
TO A WELFARE MOTHER...
"Yip, yip, yip, yip, yip, yip, yip, boom, boom, boom, boom, Get a job, Sha na na na, Sha na na na na na."
The Silhouettes, 1958
Ronald Reagan Nov. 4, 1980
The Open Bible
Presented to
A Welfare Queen
on this 4th day
TO NAZI S.S. VETERANS...
"They were victims, just as surely as the victims in the concentration camps."
— Me, April 18, 1985
Ronald Reagan April 19, 1985
The Open Bible
Presented t
Bitburg Memorial Soc
on this 19th d
TO LT. COLONEL OLIVER NORTH...
Ollie —
[redacted]
Good luck,
Ronald Reagan
[redacted]
The Open Bible
Presented to
An American Hero
on this [redacted] day of [redacted]
©GBTrudeau

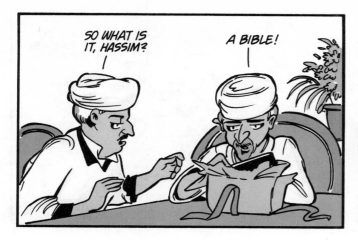

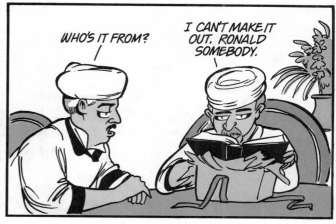

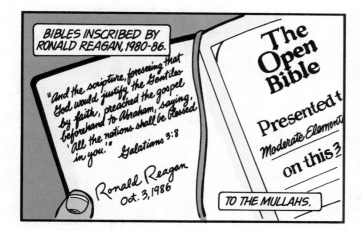

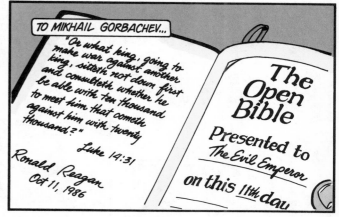

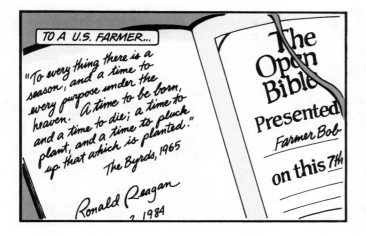

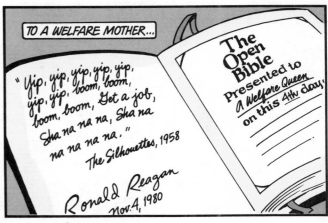

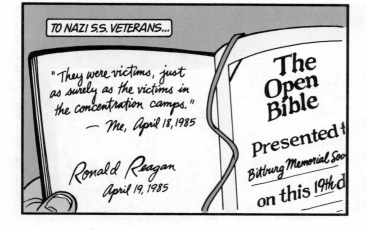

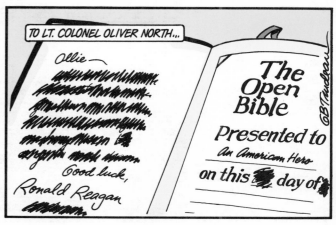

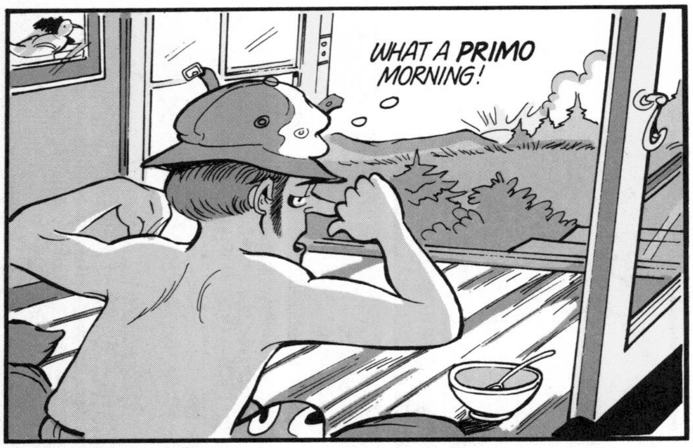
WHAT A PRIMO MORNING!

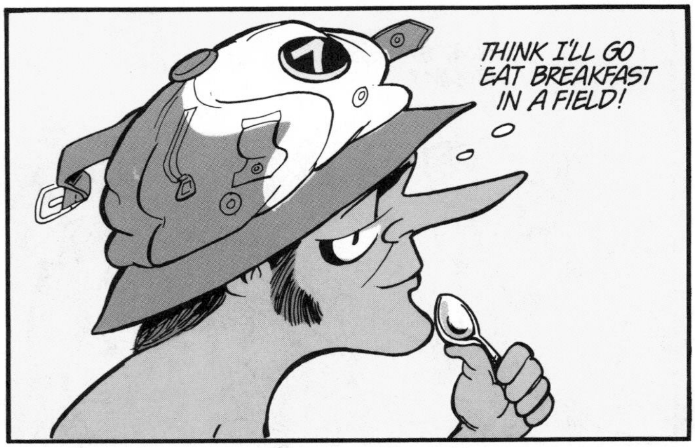
THINK I'LL GO EAT BREAKFAST IN A FIELD!

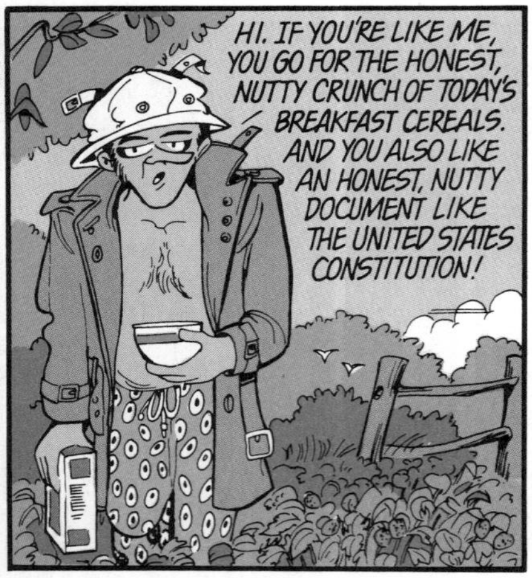
HI. IF YOU'RE LIKE ME, YOU GO FOR THE HONEST, NUTTY CRUNCH OF TODAY'S BREAKFAST CEREALS. AND YOU ALSO LIKE AN HONEST, NUTTY DOCUMENT LIKE THE UNITED STATES CONSTITUTION!

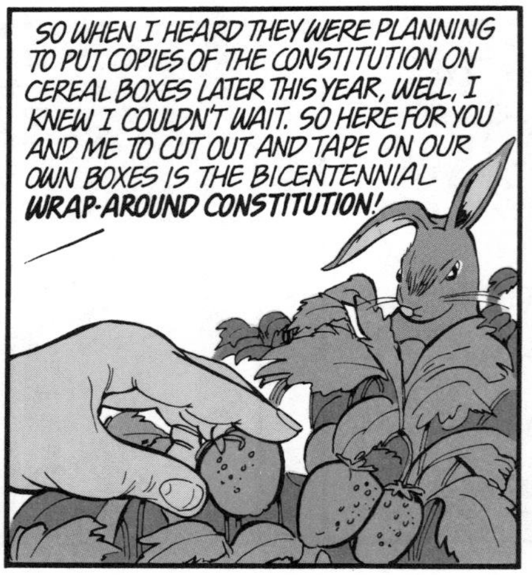
SO WHEN I HEARD THEY WERE PLANNING TO PUT COPIES OF THE CONSTITUTION ON CEREAL BOXES LATER THIS YEAR, WELL, I KNEW I COULDN'T WAIT. SO HERE FOR YOU AND ME TO CUT OUT AND TAPE ON OUR OWN BOXES IS THE BICENTENNIAL WRAP-AROUND CONSTITUTION!

Constitution of the United States
The Original 7 Articles

PREAMBLE

We, the people of the United States, in order to form a more perfect Union, establish justice, insure domestic tranquility, provide for the common defense, promote the general welfare, and secure the blessings of liberty to ourselves and our posterity do ordain and establish this Constitution for the United States of America.

ARTICLE I.

Section 1—Legislative powers; in whom vested:

All legislative powers herein granted shall be vested in a Congress of the United States, which shall consist of a Senate and House of Representatives.

Section 2—House of Representatives, how and by whom chosen. Qualifications of a Representative. Representatives and direct taxes, how apportioned. Enumeration. Vacancies to be filled. Power of choosing officers, and of impeachment.

1. The House of Representatives shall be composed of members chosen every second year by the people of the several States, and the electors in each State shall have the qualifications requisite for electors of the most numerous branch of the State Legislature.

2. No person shall be a Representative who shall not have attained to the age of twenty-five years, and been seven years a citizen of the United States, and who shall not, when elected, be an inhabitant of that State in which he shall be chosen.

3. *(Representatives and direct taxes shall be apportioned among the several States which may be included within this Union, according to their respective numbers, which shall be determined by adding to the whole number of free persons, including those bound to service for a term of years, and excluding Indians not taxed, three-fifths of all other persons.) (The previous sentence was superseded by Amendment XIV, section 2.)* The actual enumeration shall be made within three years after the first meeting of the Congress of the United States, and within every subsequent term of ten years, in such manner as they shall by law direct. The number of Representatives shall not exceed one for every thirty thousand, but each State shall have at least one Representative; and until such enumeration shall be made, the State of New Hampshire shall be entitled to choose three, Massachusetts eight, Rhode Island and Providence Plantations one, Connecticut five, New York six, New Jersey four, Pennsylvania eight, Delaware one, Maryland six, Virginia ten, North Carolina five, South Carolina five, and Georgia three.

4. When vacancies happen in the representation from any State, the Executive Authority thereof shall issue writs of election to fill such vacancies.

5. The House of Representatives shall choose their Speaker and other officers; and shall have the sole power of impeachment.

Section 3—Senators, how and by whom chosen. How classified. Qualifications of a Senator. President of the Senate, his right to vote. President pro tem., and other officers of the Senate, how chosen. Power to try impeachments. When President is tried, Chief Justice to preside. Sentence.

1. The Senate of the United States shall be composed of two Senators from each State, *(chosen by the Legislature thereof), (The preceding five words were superseded by Amendment XVII, section 1.)* for six years; and each Senator shall have one vote.

2. Immediately after they shall be assembled in consequence of the first election, they shall be divided as equally as may be into three classes. The seats of the Senators of the first class shall be vacated at the expiration of the second year, of the second class at the expiration of the fourth year, and of the third class at the expiration of the sixth year, so that one-third may be chosen every second year; *(and if vacancies happen by resignation, or otherwise, during the recess of the Legislature of any State, the Executive thereof may make temporary appointments until the next meeting of the Legislature, which shall then fill such vacancies.) (The words in parentheses were superseded by Amendment XVII, section 2.)*

3. No person shall be a Senator who shall not have attained to the age of thirty years, and been nine years a citizen of the United States, and who shall not, when elected, be an inhabitant of that State for which he shall be chosen.

4. The Vice President of the United States shall be President of the Senate, but shall have no vote, unless they be equally divided.

5. The Senate shall choose their other officers, and also a President pro tempore, in the absence of the Vice President, or when he shall exercise the office of President of the United States.

6. The Senate shall have the sole power to try all impeachments. When sitting for that purpose, they shall be on oath or affirmation. When the President of the United States is tried, the Chief Justice shall preside: and no person shall be convicted without the concurrence of two-thirds of the members present.

7. Judgment in cases of impeachment shall not extend further than to removal from office, and disqualification to hold and enjoy any office of honor, trust or profit under the United States: but the party convicted shall nevertheless be liable and subject to indictment, trial, judgment and punishment, according to law.

Section 4—Times, etc., of holding elections, how prescribed. One session each year.

1. The times, places and manner of holding elections for Senators and Representatives, shall be prescribed in each State by the Legislature thereof; but the Congress may at any time by law make or alter such regulations, except as to the places of choosing Senators.

2. The Congress shall assemble at least once in every year, and such meeting shall *(be on the first Monday in December,) (The words in parentheses were superseded by Amendment XX, section 2),* unless they shall by law appoint a different day.

Section 5—Membership, quorum, adjournments, rules. Power to punish or expel. Journal. Time of adjournments, how limited, etc.

1. Each House shall be the judge of the elections, returns and qualifications of its own members, and a majority of each shall constitute a quorum to do business; but a smaller number may adjourn from day to day, and may be authorized to compel the attendance of absent members, in such manner, and under such penalties as each House may provide.

2. Each House may determine the rules of its proceedings, punish its members for disorderly behavior, and, with the concurrence of two-thirds, expel a member.

3. Each House shall keep a journal of its proceedings, and from time to time publish the same, excepting such parts as may in their judgment require secrecy; and the yeas and nays of the members of either House on any question shall, at the desire of one-fifth of those present, be entered on the journal.

4 Neither House, during the session of Congress, shall, without the consent of the other, adjourn for more than three days, nor to any other place than that in which the two Houses shall be sitting.

Section 6—Compensation, privileges, disqualifications in certain cases.

1. The Senators and Representatives shall receive a compensation for their services, to be ascertained by law, and paid out of the Treasury of the United States. They shall in all cases, except treason, felony and breach of the peace, be privileged from arrest during their attendance at the session of their respective Houses, and in going to and returning from the same; and for any speech or debate in either House, they shall not be questioned in any other place.

2. No Senator or Representative shall, during the time for which he was elected, be appointed to any civil office under the authority of the United States, which shall have been created, or the emoluments whereof shall have been increased during such time; and no person holding any office under the United States, shall be a member of either House during his continuance in office.

Section 7—House to originate all revenue bills. Veto. Bill may be passed by two-thirds of each House, notwithstanding, etc. Bill, not returned in ten days, to become a law. Provisions as to orders, concurrent resolutions, etc.

1. All bills for raising revenue shall originate in the House of Representatives; but the Senate may propose or concur with amendments as on other bills.

2. Every bill which shall have passed the House of Representatives and the Senate, shall, before it becomes a law, be presented to the President of the United States; if he approves he shall sign it, but if not he shall return it, with his objections to that House in which it shall have originated, who shall enter the objections at large on their journal, and proceed to reconsider it. If after such reconsideration two-thirds of that House shall agree to pass the bill, it shall be sent, together with the objections, to the other House, by which it shall likewise be reconsidered, and if approved by two-thirds of that House, it shall become a law. But in all such cases the votes of both Houses shall be determined by yeas and nays, and the names of the persons voting for and against the bill shall be entered on the journal of each House respectively. If any bill shall not be returned by the President within ten days (Sundays excepted) after it shall have been presented to him, the same shall be a law, in like manner as if he had signed it, unless the Congress by their adjournment prevent its return, in which case it shall not be a law.

3. Every order, resolution, or vote to which the concurrence of the Senate and House of Representatives may be necessary (except on a question of adjournment) shall be presented to the President of the United States; and before the same shall take effect, shall be approved by him, or being disapproved by him, shall be repassed by two-thirds of the Senate and House of Representatives, according to the rules and limitations prescribed in the case of a bill.

Section 8—Powers of Congress.

The Congress shall have power

1. To lay and collect taxes, duties, imposts and excises, to pay the debts and provide for the common defense and general welfare of the United States; but all duties, imposts and excises shall be uniform throughout the United States;

2. To borrow money on the credit of the United States;

3. To regulate commerce with foreign nations, and among the several States, and with the Indian tribes;

4. To establish a uniform rule of naturalization, and uniform laws on the subject of bankruptcies throughout the United States;

5. To coin money, regulate the value thereof, and of foreign coin, and fix the standard of weights and measures;

6. To provide for the punishment of counterfeiting the securities and current coin of the United States;

7. To establish post-offices and post-roads;

8. To promote the progress of science and useful arts, by securing for limited times to authors and inventors the exclusive right to their respective writings and discoveries;

9. To constitute tribunals inferior to the Supreme Court;

10. To define and punish piracies and felonies committed on the high seas, and offenses against the law of nations;

11. To declare war, grant letters of marque and reprisal, and make rules concerning captures on land and water;

12. To raise and support armies, but no appropriation of money to that use shall be for a longer term than two years;

13. To provide and maintain a navy;

14. To make rules for the government and regulation of the land and naval forces;

15. To provide for calling forth the militia to execute the laws of the Union, suppress insurrections and repel invasions;

16. To provide for organizing, arming, and disciplining the militia, and for governing such part of them as may be employed in the service of the United States, reserving to the States respectively, the appointment of the officers, and the authority of training and militia according to the discipline prescribed by Congress;

17. To exercise exclusive legislation in all cases whatsoever, over such district (not exceeding ten miles square) as may, by cession of particular States, and the acceptance of Congress, become the seat of the Government of the United States, and to exercise like authority over all places purchased by the consent of the Legislature of the State in which the same shall be, for the erection of forts, magazines, arsenals, dockyards, and other needful buildings;—And

18. To make all laws which shall be necessary and proper for carrying into execution the foregoing powers, and all other powers vested by this Constitution in the Government of the United States, or in any department or officer therof.

Section 9—Provision as to migration or importation of certain persons. Habeas corpus, bills of attainder, etc. Taxes, how apportioned. No export duty. No commercial preference. Money, how drawn from Treasury, etc. No titular nobility. Officers not to receive presents, etc.

1. The migration or importation of such persons as any of the States now existing shall think proper to admit, shall not be prohibited by the Congress prior to the year one thousand eight hundred and eight, but a tax or duty may be imposed on such importation, not exceeding ten dollars for each person.

2. The privilege of the writ of habeas corpus shall not be suspended, unless when in cases of rebellion or invasion the public safety may require it.

3. No bill of attainder or ex post facto law shall be passed.

4. No capitation, or other direct, tax shall be laid, unless in proportion to the census or enumeration herein before directed to be taken. *(Modified by Amendment XVI.)*

5. No tax or duty shall be laid on articles exported from any State.

6. No preference shall be given by any regulation of commerce or revenue to the ports of one State over those of another: nor shall vessels bound to, or from, one State, be obliged to enter, clear, or pay duties in another.

7. No money shall be drawn from the Treasury, but in consequence of appropriations made by law; and a regular statement and account of the receipts and expenditures of all public money shall be published from time to time.

8. No title of nobility shall be granted by the United States: and no person holding any office of profit or trust under them, shall, without the consent of the Congress, accept of any present, emolument, office, or title, of any kind whatever, from any king, prince, or foreign state.

Section 10—States prohibited from the exercise of certain powers.

1. No State shall enter into any treaty, alliance, or confederation; grant letters of marque and reprisal; coin money; emit bills of credit; make anything but gold and silver coin a tender in payment of debts; pass any bill of attainder, ex post facto law, or law impairing the obligation of contracts, or grant any title of nobility.

2. No State shall, without the consent of the Congress, lay any imposts or duties on imports or exports, except what may be absolutely necessary for executing its inspection laws: and the net produce of all duties and imposts, laid by any State on imports or exports, shall be for the use of the Treasury of the United States; and all such laws shall be subject to the revision and control of the Congress.

3. No State shall, without the consent of Congress, lay any duty of tonnage, keep troops, or ships of war in time of peace, enter into any agreement or compact with another State, or with a foreign power, or engage in war, unless actually invaded, or in such imminent danger as will not admit of delay.

ARTICLE II.

Section 1—President: his term of office. Electors of President; number and how appointed. Electors to vote on same day. Qualification of President. On whom his duties devolve in case of his removal, death, etc. President's compensation. His oath of office.

1. The Executive power shall be vested in a President of the United States of America. He shall hold his office during the term of four years, and together with the Vice President, chosen for the same term, be elected as follows

2. Each State shall appoint, in such manner as the Legislature thereof may direct, a number of electors, equal to the whole number of Senators and Representatives to which the State may be entitled in the Congress: but no Senator or Representative, or person holding an office of trust or profit under the United States, shall be appointed an elector.

(The electors shall meet in their respective States, and vote by ballot for two persons, of whom one at least shall not be an inhabitant of the same State with themselves. And they shall make a list of all the persons voted for, and of the number of votes for each; which list they shall sign and certify, and transmit sealed to the seat of the Government of the United States, directed to the President of the Senate. The President of the Senate shall, in the presence of the Senate and House of Representatives, open all the certificates, and the votes shall then be counted. The person having the greatest number of votes shall be the President, if such number be a majority of the whole number of electors appointed; and if there be more than one who have such majority, and have an equal number of votes, then the House of Representatives shall immediately choose by ballot one of them for President; and if no person have a majority, then from the five highest on the list the said House shall in like manner choose the President. But in choosing the President, the votes shall be taken by States, the representation from each State having one vote; a quorum for this purpose shall consist of a member or members from two-thirds of the States, and a majority of all the States shall be necessary to a choice. In every case, after the choice of the President, the person having the greatest number of votes of the electors shall be the Vice President. But if there should remain two or more who have equal votes, the Senate shall choose from them by ballot the Vice President.)

(This clause was superseded by Amendment XII.)

3. The Congress may determine the time of choosing the electors, and the day on which they shall give their votes; which day shall be the same throughout the United States.

4. No person except a natural born citizen, or a citizen of the United States, at the time of the adoption of this Constitution, shall be eligible to the office of President; neither shall any person be eligible to that office who shall not have attained to the age of thirty-five years, and been fourteen years a resident within the United States.

(For qualification of the Vice President, see Amendment XII.)

5. In case of the removal of the President from office, or of his death, resignation, or inability to discharge the powers and duties of the said office, the same shall devolve on the Vice President, and the Congress may by law provide for the case of removal, death, resignation or inability, both of the President and Vice President, declaring what officer shall then act as President, and such officer shall act accordingly, until the disability be removed, or a President shall be elected.

(This clause has been modified by Amendments XX and XXV.)

6. The President shall, at stated times, receive for his services, a compensation, which shall neither be increased nor diminished during the period for which he shall have been elected, and he shall not receive within that period any other emolument from the United States, or any of them.

7. Before he enter on the execution of his office, he shall take the following oath or affirmation:

"I do solemnly swear (or affirm) that I will faithfully execute the office of President of the United States, and will to the best of my ability, preserve, protect and defend the Constitution of the United States."

Section 2—President to be Commander-in-Chief. He may require opinions of cabinet officers, etc., may pardon. Treaty-making power. Nomination of certain officers. When President may fill vacancies.

1. The President shall be Commander-in-Chief of the Army and Navy of the United States, and of the militia of the several States, when called into the actual service of the United States; he may require the opinion, in writing, of the principal officer in each of the executive departments, upon any subject relating to the duties of their respective offices, and he shall have power to grant reprieves and pardons for offenses against the United States, except in cases of impeachment.

2. He shall have power, by and with the advice and consent of the Senate, to make treaties, provided two-thirds of the Senators present concur; and he shall nominate, and by and with the advice and consent of the Senate, shall appoint ambassadors, other public ministers and consuls, judges of the Supreme Court, and all other officers of the United States, whose appointments are not herein otherwise provided for, and which shall be established by law: but the Congress may by law vest the appointment of such inferior officers, as they think proper, in the President alone, in the courts of law, or in the heads of departments.

3. The President shall have power to fill up all vacancies that may happen during the recess of the Senate, by granting commissions, which shall expire at the end of their next session.

Section 3—President shall communicate to Congress. He may convene and adjourn Congress, in case of disagreement, etc. Shall receive ambassadors, execute laws, and commission officers.

He shall from time to time give to the Congress information of the state of the Union, and recommend to their consideration such measures as he shall judge necessary and expedient; he may, on extraordinary occasions, convene both Houses, or either of them, and in case of disagreement between them, with respect to the time of adjournment, he may adjourn them to such time as he shall think proper; he shall receive ambassadors and other public ministers; he shall take care that the laws be faithfully executed, and shall commission all the officers of the United States.

Section 4—All civil offices forfeited for certain crimes.

The President, Vice President, and all civil officers of the United States, shall be removed from office on impeachment for, and conviction of, treason, bribery, or other high crimes and misdemeanors.

ARTICLE III.

Section 1—Judicial powers, Tenure. Compensation.

The judicial power of the United States, shall be vested in one Supreme Court, and in such inferior courts as the Congress may from time to time ordain and establish. The judges, both of the Supreme and inferior courts, shall hold their offices during good behavior, and shall at stated times, receive for their services, a compensation, which shall not be diminished during their continuance in office.

Section 2—Judicial power; to what cases it extends. Original jurisdiction of Supreme Court; appellate jurisdiction. Trial by jury, etc. Trial, where.

1. The judicial power shall extend to all cases, in law and equity, arising under this Constitution, the laws of the United States, and treaties made, or which shall be made, under their authority, to all cases affecting ambassadors, other public ministers and consuls; to all cases of admiralty and maritime jurisdiction; to controversies to which the United States shall be a party; to controversies between two or more States; between a State and citizens of another State; between citizens of different States, between citizens of the same State claiming lands under grants of different States, and between a State, or the citizens thereof, and foreign states, citizens or subjects.

(This section is modified by Amendment XI.)

2. In all cases affecting ambassadors, other public ministers and consuls, and those in which a State shall be party, the Supreme Court shall have original jurisdiction. In all the other cases before mentioned, the Supreme Court shall have appellate jurisdiction, both as to law and fact, with such exceptions, and under such regulations as the Congress shall make.

3. The trial of all crimes, except in cases of impeachment, shall be by jury; and such trial shall be held in the State where the said crimes shall have been committed; but when not committed within any State, the trial shall be at such place or places as the Congress may by law have directed.

Section 3—Treason Defined, Proof of, Punishment of.

1. Treason against the United States, shall consist only in levying war against them, or in adhering to their enemies, giving them aid and comfort. No person shall be convicted of treason unless on the testimony of two witnesses to the same overt act, or on confession in open court.

2. The Congress shall have power to declare the punishment of treason, but no attainder of treason shall work corruption of blood, or forfeiture except during the life of the person attainted.

ARTICLE IV.

Section 1—Each State to give credit to the public acts, etc., of every other State.

Full faith and credit shall be given in each State to the public acts, records, and judicial proceedings of every other State. And the Congress may by general laws prescribe the manner in which such acts, records and proceedings shall be proved, and the effect thereof.

Section 2—Privileges of citizens of each State. Fugitives from justice to be delivered up. Persons held to service having escaped, to be delivered up.

1. The citizens of each State shall be entitled to all privileges and immunities of citizens in the several States.

2. A person charged in any State with treason, felony, or other crime, who shall flee from justice, and be found in another State, shall on demand of the Executive authority of the State from which he fled, be delivered up, to be removed to the State having jurisdiction of the crime.

(3. No person held to service or labor in one State, under the laws thereof, escaping into another, shall in consequence of any law or regulation therein, be discharged from such service or labor, but shall be delivered up on claim of the party to whom such service or labor may be due.) (This clause was superseded by Amendment XIII.)

Section 3—Admission of new States. Power of Congress over territory and other property.

1. New States may be admitted by the Congress into this Union; but no new State shall be formed or erected within the jurisdiction of any other State; nor any State be formed by the junction of two or more States, or parts of States, without the consent of the Legislatures of the States concerned as well as of the Congress.

2. The Congress shall have power to dispose of and make all needful rules and regulations respecting the territory or other property belonging to the United States; and nothing in this Constitution shall be so construed as to prejudice any claims of the United States, or of any particular State.

Section 4—Republican form of government guaranteed. Each state to be protected.

The United States shall guarantee to every State in this Union a Republican form of government, and shall protect each of them against invasion; and on application of the Legislature, or of the Executive (when the Legislature cannot be convened) against domestic violence.

ARTICLE V.

Constitution: how amended; proviso.

The Congress, whenever two-thirds of both Houses shall deem it necessary, shall propose amendments to this Constitution, or, on the application of the Legislatures of two-thirds of the several States, shall call a convention for proposing amendments, which, in either case, shall be valid to all intents and purposes, as part of this Constitution, when ratified by the Legislatures of three-fourths of the several States, or by conventions in three-fourths thereof, as the one or the other mode of ratification may be proposed by the Congress; provided that no amendment which may be made prior to the year one thousand eight hundred and eight shall in any manner affect the first and fourth clauses in the Ninth Section of the First Article; and that no State, without its consent, shall be deprived of its equal suffrage in the Senate.

ARTICLE VI.

Certain debts, etc., declared valid. Supremacy of Constitution, treaties, and laws of the United States. Oath to support Constitution, by whom taken. No religious test.

1. All debts contracted and engagements entered into, before the adoption of this Constitution, shall be as valid against the United States under this Constitution, as under the Confederation.

2. This Constitution, and the laws of the United States which shall be made in pursuance thereof; and all treaties made, or which shall be made, under the authority of the United States, shall be the supreme law of the land; and the judges in every State shall be bound thereby, any thing in the Constitution or laws of any State to the contrary notwithstanding.

3. The Senators and Representatives before mentioned, and the members of the several State Legislatures, and all executive and judicial officers, both of the United States and of the several States, shall be bound by oath or affirmation, to support this Constitution; but no religious test shall ever be required as a qualification to any office or public trust under the United States.

ARTICLE VII.

What ratification shall establish Constitution.

The ratification of the Conventions of nine States, shall be sufficient for the establishment of this Constitution between the States so ratifying the same.

Done in convention by the unanimous consent of the States present the Seventeenth day of September in the year of our Lord one thousand seven hundred and eighty seven, and of the independence of the United States of America the Twelfth. In witness whereof we have hereunto subscribed our names.

George Washington, John Langdon, Nicholas Gilman, Nathaniel Gorham, Rufus King, Wm. Saml. Johnson, Roger Sherman, Alexander Hamilton, Wil: Livingston, David Brearley, Wm. Paterson, Jona: Dayton, B. Franklin, Thomas Mifflin, Robt. Morris, Geo. Clymer, Thos. FitzSimons, Jared Ingersoll, James Wilson, Gouv. Morris, Geo: Read, Gunning Bedford Jun., John Dickinson, Richard Bassett, Jaco: Broom, James McHenry, Daniel of Saint Thomas' Jenifer, Danl. Carroll, John Blair, James Madison Jr, Wm. Blount, Rich'd. Dobbs Spaight, Hugh Williamson, J. Rutledge, Charles Cotesworth Pinckney, Charles Pinckney, Pierce Butler, William Few, Abr. Baldwin. Attest: William Jackson, Secretary.

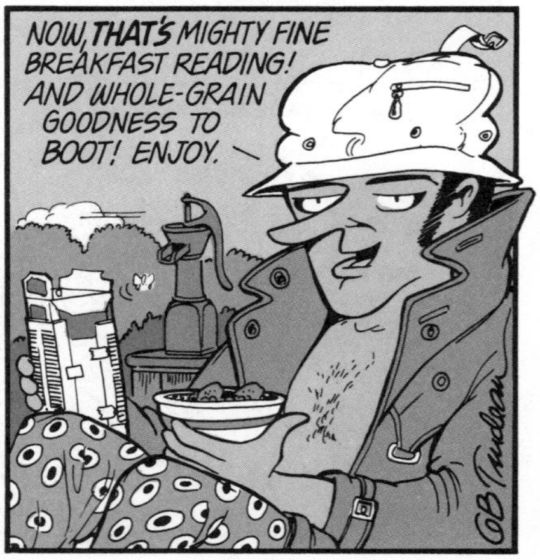
NOW, THAT'S MIGHTY FINE BREAKFAST READING! AND WHOLE-GRAIN GOODNESS TO BOOT! ENJOY.
GBTrudeau

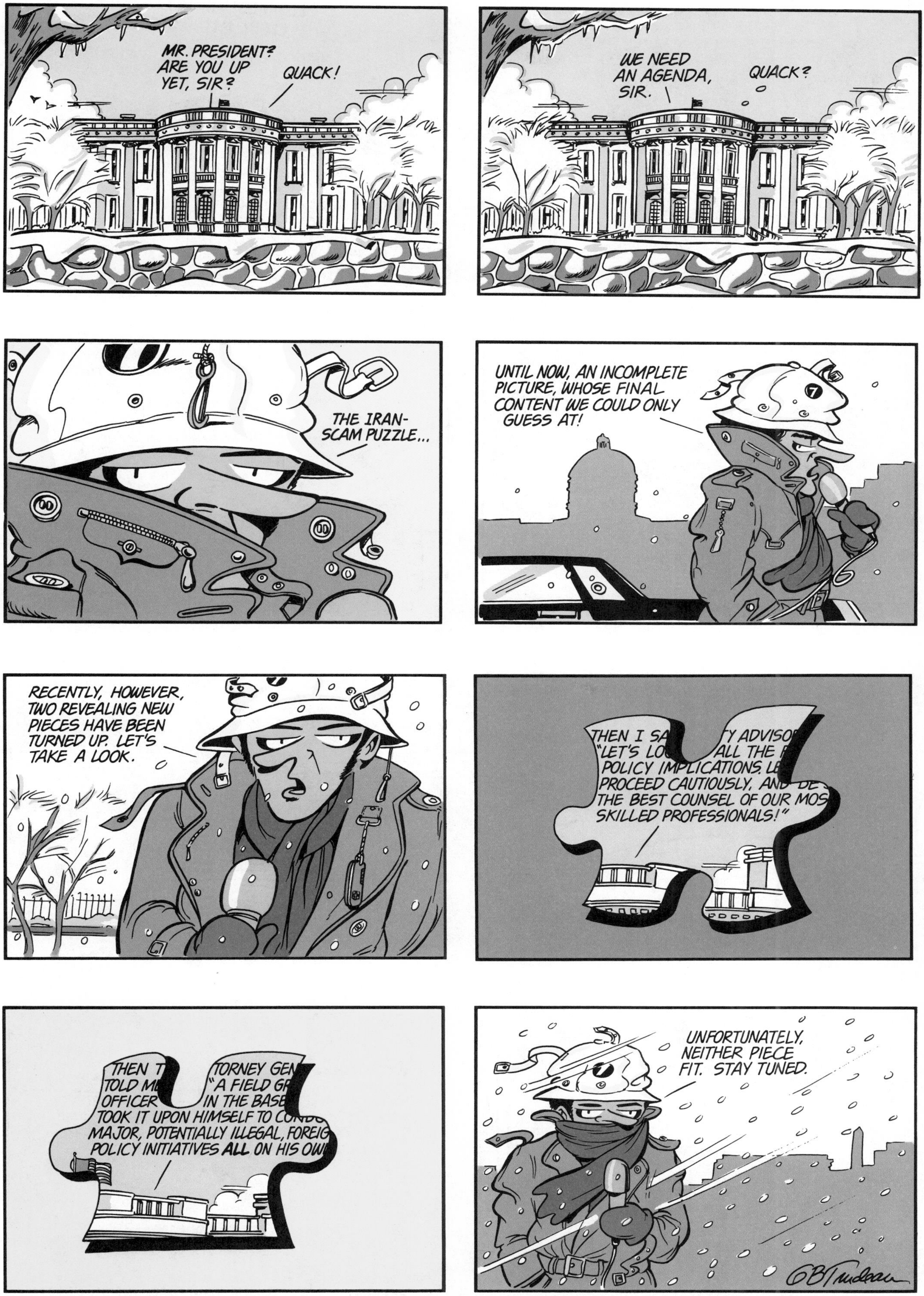
MR. PRESIDENT? ARE YOU UP YET, SIR?
QUACK!
WE NEED AN AGENDA, SIR.
QUACK?
THE IRAN-SCAM PUZZLE...
UNTIL NOW, AN INCOMPLETE PICTURE, WHOSE FINAL CONTENT WE COULD ONLY GUESS AT!
RECENTLY, HOWEVER, TWO REVEALING NEW PIECES HAVE BEEN TURNED UP. LET'S TAKE A LOOK.
THEN I SA TY ADVISO "LET'S LO ALL THE POLICY IMPLICATIONS. LE PROCEED CAUTIOUSLY, AND THE BEST COUNSEL OF OUR MOS SKILLED PROFESSIONALS!"
THEN T TORNEY GEN TOLD M "A FIELD GR OFFICER IN THE BASE TOOK IT UPON HIMSELF TO CONDU MAJOR, POTENTIALLY ILLEGAL, FOREIG POLICY INITIATIVES ALL ON HIS OW
UNFORTUNATELY, NEITHER PIECE FIT. STAY TUNED.
GBTrudeau

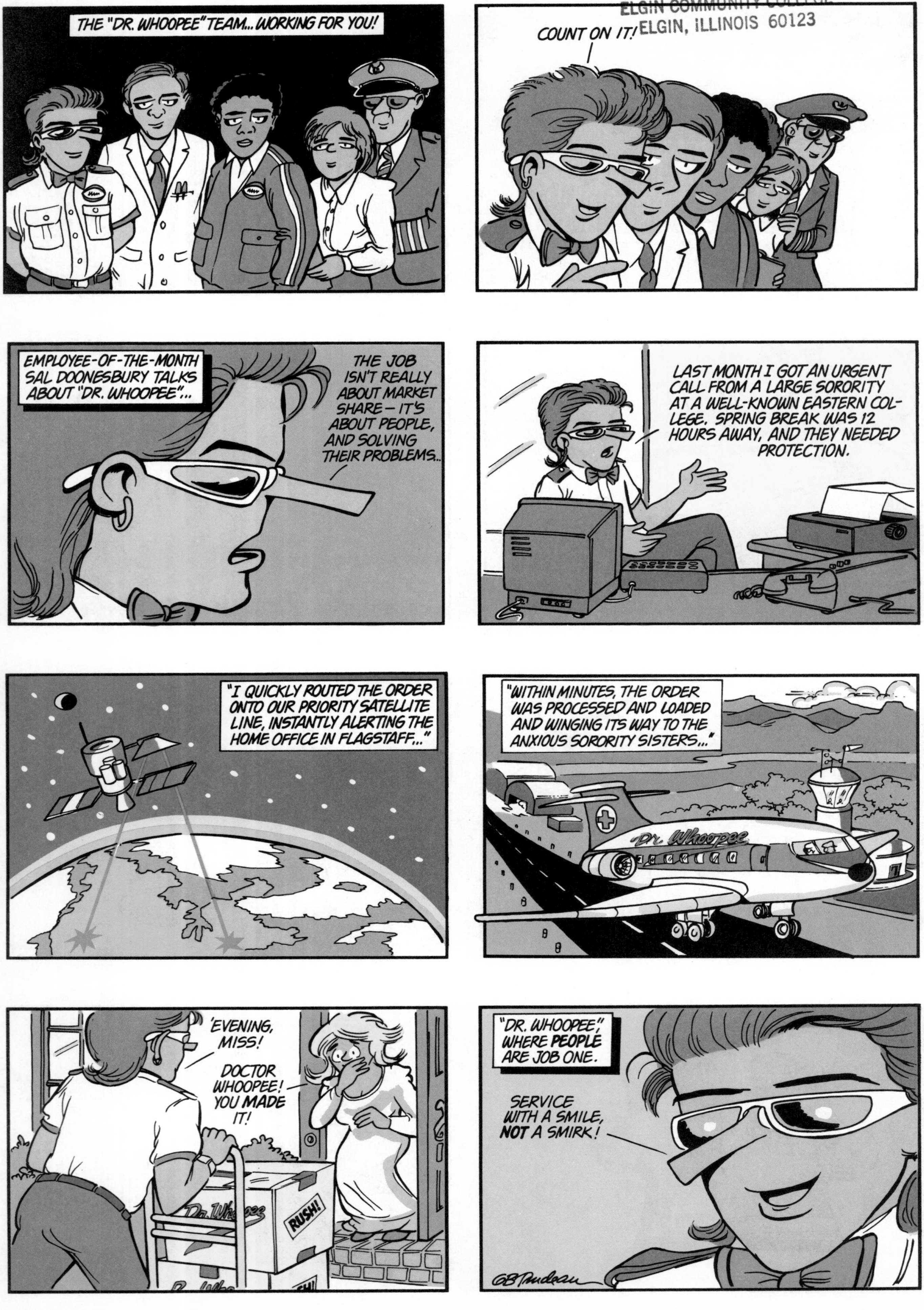
THE "DR. WHOOPEE" TEAM... WORKING FOR YOU!
COUNT ON IT!
EMPLOYEE-OF-THE-MONTH SAL DOONESBURY TALKS ABOUT "DR. WHOOPEE"...
THE JOB ISN'T REALLY ABOUT MARKET SHARE – IT'S ABOUT PEOPLE, AND SOLVING THEIR PROBLEMS...
LAST MONTH I GOT AN URGENT CALL FROM A LARGE SORORITY AT A WELL-KNOWN EASTERN COLLEGE. SPRING BREAK WAS 12 HOURS AWAY, AND THEY NEEDED PROTECTION.
"I QUICKLY ROUTED THE ORDER ONTO OUR PRIORITY SATELLITE LINE, INSTANTLY ALERTING THE HOME OFFICE IN FLAGSTAFF..."
"WITHIN MINUTES, THE ORDER WAS PROCESSED AND LOADED AND WINGING ITS WAY TO THE ANXIOUS SORORITY SISTERS..."
Dr. Whoopee
'EVENING, MISS!
DOCTOR WHOOPEE! YOU MADE IT!
Dr. Whoopee
RUSH!
"DR. WHOOPEE," WHERE PEOPLE ARE JOB ONE.
SERVICE WITH A SMILE, NOT A SMIRK!